D0362641

An Anthology of
Colonial and Postcolonial
Short Fiction

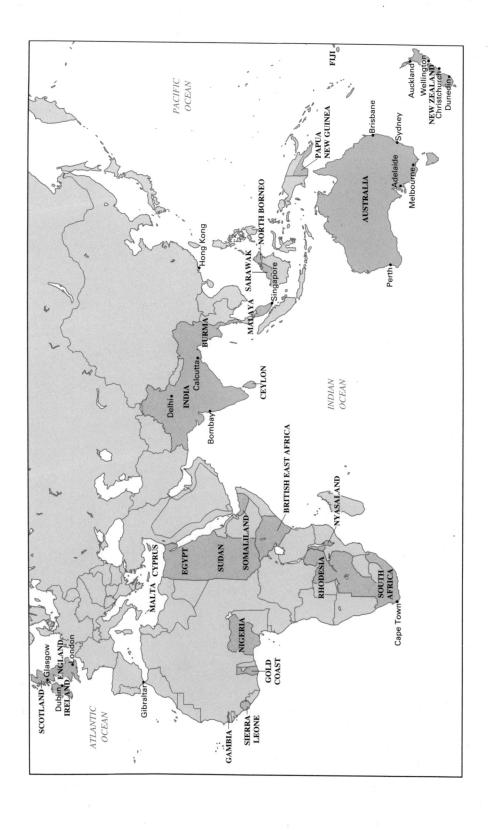

PACIFIC
OCEAN

FIJI

Auckland
Wellington
NEW ZEALAND
Christchurch
Dunedin

Brisbane

Sydney

PAPUA
NEW GUINEA

Adelaide
Melbourne

AUSTRALIA

NORTH BORNEO

Perth

Hong Kong

SARAWAK

MALAYA

Singapore

BURMA

CEYLON

INDIAN
OCEAN

Calcutta

INDIA

Delhi

Bombay

BRITISH EAST AFRICA

CYPRUS

NYASALAND

MALTA

EGYPT

SUDAN

SOMALILAND

RHODESIA

SOUTH
AFRICA

SCOTLAND

Glasgow

NIGERIA

Cape Town

Dublin ENGLAND
IRELAND London

GOLD
COAST

Gibraltar

ATLANTIC
OCEAN

GAMBIA

SIERRA
LEONE

An Anthology of Colonial and Postcolonial Short Fiction

Dean Baldwin
Penn State Erie, The Behrend College

Patrick J. Quinn
University of Mississippi

WADSWORTH
CENGAGE Learning™

Australia • Brazil • Japan • Korea • Mexico • Singapore • Spain • United Kingdom • United States

An Anthology of Colonial and Postcolonial Short Fiction
Dean Baldwin and
Patrick J. Quinn

Publisher: Patricia Coryell

Senior Sponsoring Editor:
Lisa Kimball

Associate Editor: Bruce Cantley

Editorial Assistant:
Katilyn Crowley

Senior Project Editor:
Christina Horn

Editorial Assistant: Carrie Parker

Design Manager: Gary Crespo

Composition Buyer:
Chuck Dutton

Manufacturing Coordinator:
Brian Pieragostini

Executive Marketing Manager:
Annamarie Rice

Cover image: "Untitled,"
Mick Namarari Tjapaltjarri, 1972.
Synthetic Polymer Powder Paint on
Composition Board, 64 x 40.5 cm.
Private Collection, New York City.
Copyright © Aboriginal Artists
Agency Limited, Cammeray, NSA
20062, Australia.

Text credits begin on page 909,
which constitutes an extension of
the copyright page.

© 2007 Wadsworth, Cengage Learning

ALL RIGHTS RESERVED. No part of this work covered by the copyright herein may be reproduced, transmitted, stored, or used in any form or by any means graphic, electronic, or mechanical, including but not limited to photocopying, recording, scanning, digitizing, taping, Web distribution, information networks, or information storage and retrieval systems, except as permitted under Section 107 or 108 of the 1976 United States Copyright Act, without the prior written permission of the publisher.

For product information and
technology assistance, contact us at **Cengage Learning
Customer & Sales Support, 1-800-354-9706**

For permission to use material from this text or product,
submit all requests online at **www.cengage.com/permissions**
Further permissions questions can be e-mailed to
permissionrequest@cengage.com

Library of Congress Control Number: 2003109881

ISBN-13: 978-0-618-31881-0

ISBN-10: 0-618-31881-X

Wadsworth Cengage Learning
20 Davis Drive
Belmont, CA 94002-3098
USA

Cengage Learning is a leading provider of customized learning solutions with office locations around the globe, including Singapore, the United Kingdom, Australia, Mexico, Brazil, and Japan. Locate your local office at **www.cengage.com/global**

Cengage Learning products are represented in Canada by Nelson Education, Ltd.

To learn more about Wadsworth, visit
www.cengage.com/wadsworth

Purchase any of our products at your local college store or at our preferred online store **www.cengagebrain.com**

Dean Baldwin dedicates the book to Thomas, William, James, and Jay Ananda. Patrick Quinn dedicates the book to Angela, who inspires the passion.

Printed in the United States of America
3 4 5 14 13 12

Contents

The Caribbean   433

Preface

During the past forty years, postcolonial studies have emerged as one of the fastest growing and most lively areas of literary study, yet very few textbooks have been developed to suit the needs of instructors looking for a convenient and relatively inexpensive way to introduce students to this fascinating field. *An Anthology of Colonial and Postcolonial Short Fiction* is designed to meet the requirements of instructors and students who need a handy, one-volume textbook on which to base their investigation into this comparatively new field. Obviously, no volume of whatever size could contain the multiplicity of literary materials that could be included in such a study, but this collection of short fiction by British writers and by writers from the former British colonies of Ireland, India, Pakistan, Africa, Canada, the Caribbean, Australia, and New Zealand provides a convenient starting point.

Taken together, the stories in this collection provide valuable insights into the experiences of those involved in Britain's colonial enterprise and those who were directly or indirectly affected by colonialism. Readers witness the literary response to the colonial enterprise from the British perspective. They will also come to appreciate not only the support this imperial impetus received through fiction but also fiction's ability to question both the basis and the results of colonialism. Far from being unanimously in favor or against, the British authors included in this collection frequently register ambivalent reactions to Britain's conquest and administration.

On the receiving end of British colonial practices were the conquered peoples of the Empire on whose territory, as Sir George Macartney said, "the sun never set." Their voices are heard in this anthology in their adopted language of English, which they used effectively to protest against British rule and its attendant injuries. They, too, tell complex tales registering a wide variety of reactions and emotions, from anger and despair to puzzlement and resignation, from the desire for liberation to the anguish of independence granted without sufficient preparation or support.

Between these groups are the British settlers who carried out the work of empire and then chafed under or exulted in the conditions they found, the laws under which they were ruled, and the opportunities their adventure provided or denied. Their stories are here, recording not only the hardships and triumphs of the colonial experience, but also registering the personal costs their accomplishments exacted.

The stories collected here provide, then, a rich tapestry of thematic ideas and points of view. But literature is more than its ideas, however important these may be to the postcolonial enterprise. Stories are about people and their experiences, their strengths and weaknesses, insights and blind spots; and they are aesthetic achievements, not simply political statements or records of social struggle. We have selected the stories in this collection to reflect the art of the short story as practiced on a nearly global scale, a Western art form adopted by these writers for their own thematic and aesthetic ends. Like the British institutions and practices they sometimes adopted, sometimes rejected, and sometimes altered, the short story takes new shapes and directions in their hands, permanently altering the genre's form and character.

SELECTION RATIONALE FOR THE ANTHOLOGY

The anthologist's lot, as Gilbert and Sullivan said of the policeman's, is "not a happy one." However diligently the editors survey the field, however conscientious they are in selecting materials, they are bound to leave out stories some readers regard as essential and include stories some readers regard as unnecessary.

Having said this, it seems only proper that we should explain the bases on which we have made our selections. First, we decided at the outset to limit ourselves to stories written in English or translated into English by or under the auspices of the author. This was both a practical choice, since it limited the number of stories from which to choose, and a theoretical choice, based on our belief that literature is best studied in its original language. Moreover, choosing stories in English eliminates the impossible task of deciding whether stories have been well or poorly translated. We have allowed only one or two exceptions to this rule, when a translated story seemed to us so compelling that we could not exclude it.

Second, we thought it proper to include stories both by British writers connected in some way with the colonial enterprise, as well as stories by writers from decolonized countries. We believe that juxtaposing these two broad categories provides the most comprehensive view of the phenomenon we now call postcolonial literature in English. Once this decision was made, the choice of stories by certain authors—Conrad and Kipling, for example—seemed inevitable.

Third, having made this broad choice, we were confronted with the question as to whether Ireland should be represented. Many scholars of postcolonial literature do not study Ireland, as its conquest predates the usual period of colonization and its proximity to England makes its situation somewhat different from other, more distant colonies. Nevertheless, a growing body of scholarship treats Ireland as a postcolonial entity. Indeed, for many scholars, Ireland is the prototypical colony, exhibiting all the characteristics and traits of England's other conquests.

Fourth, in the remaining regional selections—Canada, the Caribbean, Africa, India/Pakistan, Australia, and New Zealand—we have tried to be as inclusive as space and availability would allow; that is, we have selected stories by both genders, and by as many racial, religious, and ethnic groups as possible. However, mere "political correctness" has not been our intent; rather, we have tried to provide broad chronological coverage and to represent as many different "types" of the story as we could. Moreover, some stories lend themselves to postcolonial analysis more readily than others, and this criterion, too, has been influential. Finally, and perhaps most important, we have tried in all cases to include stories that are of high quality. Thus, within each section, we have endeavored to present a selection of excellent stories illustrating the development of the short story in that country or continent by representative writers whose stories reflect some aspect of the colonial/postcolonial experience. If there is one type of story that we have perhaps slighted, it is the "experimental" variety. In truth, it seems that literary experiments in these areas are relatively rare and that the "realistic" story predominates because that is the style most writers have found conducive to their needs.

Fifth, we must acknowledge that we could have filled twice the space Houghton Mifflin has so generously made available to us, for there were painful choices to make. To keep the cost of this textbook down, and to keep the stories to a number that could reasonably be read and discussed in an academic term, we had to keep the book's length from becoming unwieldy. Thus, some longer stories we would like to have included, such as James Joyce's "The Dead," were replaced with equally appropriate but shorter works by the same authors. With one exception, we did not include multiple stories by the same author (several works by writers such as Kipling, Achebe, Gordimer, Rushdie, and many others could have been included). And we had to omit some authors in the interest of keeping some regional sections (particularly Africa and the Caribbean) from overshadowing others. Also, because the rights-holders for many of the stories we originally planned to anthologize proved impossible to locate, we were regretfully unable to include such writers as Jan Carew (the Caribbean), Ahmed Essop (Africa), Krushwant Singh (India), Robert Finlayson (New Zealand), and Elizabeth Harrower (Australia).

Finally, we must address the issue of what might be called the "provenance" of many writers. In this era of international mobility, assigning writers to a single country is often arbitrary at best. Doris Lessing was born in Persia, grew up in Rhodesia, and since 1949 has lived in England. Where does she "belong"? Salman Rushdie was born in Bombay, lived some years with his family in Pakistan, and finally, like Lessing, moved to Britain. Chitra Banerjee Divakaruni was born in India but now lives in California. Frequently, we have placed such authors in their adopted countries as a way of emphasizing the various diasporas; at other times it seemed more logical to place an author in his or her country of birth. Anyone so inclined is welcome to challenge our choices and place the author (at least mentally) elsewhere in the book.

Playing policeman, even in the literary sense, is frustrating and seldom satisfactory to more than a few. Fortunately, we cannot be arrested for our errors and oversights, though we ask for clemency from those who find us in error. We can only hope that the virtues of the book outweigh its limitations. In any event, the authors represented need no apology: They can stand on their own merits.

ORGANIZATION AND KEY FEATURES

Part One, "Contexts"

- **"Defining Imperialism and Colonialism."** Since the terms "imperialism" and "colonialism" are an inevitable part of postcolonial studies, an introductory essay discusses these two terms and attempts to provide at least one way to distinguish between them. This essay also introduces students to the contentious issue of the United States's own imperialist tendencies, as seen in its military, diplomatic, and cultural activities.

- **"The Colonial and Postcolonial Short Story."** We believe that the short story is the ideal classroom genre for a study of postcolonial literature because it combines the best features of fiction and poetry. With the advantages of fiction's immediacy—plot, characters, setting, atmosphere, and so on—the short story is both compelling in itself and accessible to students whose primary "reading" is from television and film. At the same time, the short story's compression requires careful attention to nuance and detail—the qualities required to read poetry. Introductions to the short story as it developed in various locations call attention to the particular qualities of the stories from these countries and regions as well as help students to develop critical reading habits and literary appreciation.

- **"Postcolonial Theory: A Primer."** Postcolonial literary study emerged from a complicated history of critical methodologies, cultural practices, and academic interdisciplinary work. Few undergraduates can have a sufficient grasp of this field of study to enter it without guidance. This primer on postcolonial theory provides a concise and readable introduction to this complicated field.

Part Two, "Stories"

- **Regional introductions.** Recognizing that students often lack the historical information they need to appreciate fully the stories of a country or region, we have prefaced each section with a brief historical overview of the country or region's colonial experience. Obviously, no brief introduction can do full justice to the complexities of such a history, but we have endeavored to provide a reliable outline of the major events and developments in each country so that students can more fully understand the institutions, events, and people who shaped the colonial history in each case.

- **Biographical headnotes.** Most of the authors included in this collection will be new to students, even to those well-read in British literature. Therefore, each author's story is prefaced by a brief biographical headnote to help the student place the writer in his or her historical, geographical, political, and aesthetic context.

- **Questions for study and discussion.** After each story, students are invited to reflect upon what they have read through questions designed to stimulate critical thinking about the story. Some of these questions call attention to political and social ideas; others focus on the aesthetic and technical aspects of the story. Some questions also compare features of one story with other stories in the collection.

- **Explanatory footnotes.** Obviously, stories derived from a variety of countries and regions will contain words, ideas, references, and allusions unfamiliar to most students. The footnotes are intended to help students overcome the distance between their world and the worlds of these stories—and of course to help them better comprehend the stories themselves.

- **Maps.** The maps included on the inside front and back covers help students to understand the reach and extent of the British Empire at its height and also the present names and locations of these former colonies.

THE INSTRUCTOR'S MANUAL

An online instructor's manual (available at **www.cengage.com/literature**) is available to help instructors prepare effective courses based on this anthology. It includes sample syllabi, discussions of each story, and an extensive bibliography of materials relating to Britain's colonial history, each country represented in the anthology, and each author. The purpose of the manual is to provide teaching ideas and strategies that have been found useful in our experience, as well as information on resources beyond those that can be provided in a single volume.

ACKNOWLEDGMENTS

It is a pleasure to acknowledge here those without whose help this book would not have been possible. This list must begin with our editors at Houghton Mifflin, whose foresight and encouragement recognized the need for this book and who worked so hard to see it through to conclusion: Bruce Cantley, Michael Gillespie, Lisa Kimball, and Christina Horn. Special thanks must go to the indefatigable and resourceful Maria Leon Maimone, who worked so hard to track down elusive authors and other rightsholders, and to our keen-eyed copyeditor, Lisa Wehrle.

We are grateful also to our editorial board members. Their assistance, suggestions, and corrections saved us from many an embarrassment and contributed significantly to whatever virtues this book may enjoy, though of course only we are responsible for whatever failings it may have. Each board member assisted not only with the general introductions and the England and Ireland sections but also took on the role of expert in one or more regional sections. The editorial board members are as follows:

Neil Besner, The University of Winnipeg (Canada section)
Saros Cowasjee, The University of Regina (India/Pakistan section)
Douglas Killam, The University of Guelph (Africa section)
Sarah Lawson-Welch, The University of Northampton (Caribbean section)
Janet Wilson, The University of Northampton (Australia and New Zealand sections).

In addition, we extend our gratitude to those scholars and teachers who reviewed our proposal/first draft and made invaluable suggestions: Paul Brians, Washington State University; Joseph N. Clarke, The University of Pennsylvania; Samir

Dayal, Bentley College; Gillian Gane, Hamilton College; Indira Karamcheti, Wesleyan University; Brian Kiteley, University of Denver; Cynthia A. Leenerts, The George Washington University; Patrick D. Morrow, Auburn University; Romanus Muoneke, University of St. Thomas; Cynthia Anne vanden Driesen, Edith Cowan University; Mark Wollaeger, Vanderbilt University; and Al Zolynas, Alliant International University.

Dean Baldwin would like to thank all his students in English 182, Literature and Empire, for their participation in the classes that made so many valuable contributions to the aim, scope, and emphasis of this anthology, and who thereby assisted in their professor's struggle to create a book their successors would use. He especially thanks his undergraduate assistant, Erica Zilleruelo, who did so much valuable research for the footnotes.

Patrick Quinn would like to thank his students at the University of Northampton and Worcester Polytechnic Institute for the fascinating dialogues and class discussions that reminded him of the joys of the short story genre in its multiform variations.

Above all, we thank our wives, Vicki and Angela, for their unfailing support, even as we neglected them to work on this project.

D. B., P. J. Q.

Part One

Contexts

Defining Imperialism and Colonialism

In his seminal study, *Culture and Imperialism,* Edward W. Said points out the unprecedented extent of European domination during the nineteenth and early twentieth centuries:

> Consider that in 1800 Western powers claimed 55 percent but actually held approximately 35 percent of the earth's surface, and that by 1878 the proportion was 67 percent. . . . By 1914 . . . Europe held a grand total of roughly 85 percent of the earth as colonies, protectorates, dependencies, dominions, and commonwealths. No other associated set of colonies in history was as large, none so totally dominated, none so unequal in power to the Western metropolis. As a result, says William McNeill in *The Pursuit of Power,* "the world was united into a single interacting whole as never before." (8)

Although Said uses the word *imperialism* in his title, he offers a number of different terms, including *colonies,* to describe Britain's means of control over the lands it governed. Many people use the words *imperialism* and *colonialism* synonymously, especially since in both cases the territories controlled are called *empires.* It is useful, however, to distinguish between these two terms.

Some theorists regard imperialism as territorial expansion from a center outwards, driven by ideology, and resulting in a coherent geographical entity. The Roman and Ottoman Empires are typical examples. The criterion of coherent geography as an essential aspect of the definition disappeared when European countries (Spain, for example) were able to conquer and communicate with distant territories via sailing ships. The primary distinguishing factors in imperialism, then, are its practice as a policy of state and its ideological motivation (Young 25–29).

Colonialism, in contrast, is a less homogeneous practice than imperialism and tends to develop without a coherent plan or driving ideology; rather, it comes about for commercial motives and therefore frequently presents problems of centralized control for the government of the colonizing power. Furthermore, it is helpful to distinguish between two types of colonies: settler colonies, consisting of emigrants from the home country who take most of the land and dominate economically and politically (for example, Australia and Canada); and administered colonies, whose main goal is economic exploitation (for example, India and the Congo). In administered colonies, Europeans dominate politically and economically but do not settle a large portion of the land (Young 15–16).

Using the above definitions, England was a colonial, not an imperial, power from the seventeenth to about the last quarter of the nineteenth century. The year 1876 serves as an arbitrary but highly indicative date for this transformation, for in this year Queen Victoria was proclaimed "Empress of India." As noted in the next chapter, "The Colonial and Postcolonial Short Story," there was also an interesting coincidence in literary and political history during this time period: The height of British consciousness about its colonies and their political, economic, and military value coincided with the emergence of the British short story and one of its first great practitioners, Rudyard Kipling. His stories of India, three collections of which were published in 1888, made the Empire—and the sacrifices and dangers of those who kept it—an everyday reality to ordinary Britons. Moreover, Kipling and many authors who followed him kept the question of Empire before the British public, sometimes extolling it, sometimes questioning it, but almost always romanticizing it as a locus of exotic adventure.

The intersection of culture and conquest is thus one subject of this book. To an extent unmatched by any of its nineteenth-century competitors, Great Britain's colonial enterprise involved cultural as well as military conquests. All empires bring the conquering nation's culture with them, of course, but Britain made cultural domination an integral part of its colonial policy. As Marlow says in Joseph Conrad's "Heart of Darkness":

> The conquest of the earth, which mostly means the taking it away from those who have a different complexion or slightly flatter noses than ourselves, is not a pretty thing when you look into it too much. What redeems it is the idea only. An idea at the back of it; not a sentimental pretense but an idea; and an unselfish belief in the idea—something you can set up, and bow down before, and offer a sacrifice to. . . . [Ellipses in original.]

By the late nineteenth century, then, Britain's colonizing impulse (based on trade and economic exploitation) had transformed into an imperial (ideologically motivated) one. In addition to its goal of conquering and exploiting other peoples, Britain added an attempt to "civilize" them, using education, Christian missionary work, technical and infrastructure improvements (like railroads, bridges, and telegraph systems), and even political and social reforms to do so. The idea, as Marlow and many others saw it, was to bring to conquered peoples the advantages of "progress."

The British Empire's redefined sense of colonialism was eventually adopted by the United States. Americans are often shocked and even hurt to have their country's policies labeled as "imperialist" by other countries. Americans see themselves, as did the British before them, as bringing the light of civilization and the benefits of democracy and liberty to those within their sphere of influence. Admittedly, the United States has engaged in relatively little direct military conquest, but its political, economic, and cultural domination—as well as its overt and covert support for "friendly nations" and client states—has had much the same effect as outright conquest. U.S. (and by extension, Western) consumer goods and culture are inescapable, and they are reshaping the world. To cite Said once again:

> American attitudes to American "greatness," to hierarchies of race, to the perils of *other* revolutions . . . have remained constant, have dictated, have obscured, the realities of empire, while apologists for overseas American interests have insisted on American innocence, doing good, fighting for freedom. (*Culture and Imperialism* 8)

Since World War II, and especially since the collapse of the Soviet Union in 1991, the United States has only strengthened its leadership role in the world. At the same time, the English language has extended its international reach, pushed by both U.S. influence and the influence of other English-speaking countries. For these reasons, and for a host of related ones, the term *imperialism* as used in this book includes cultural and economic forces that impinge on the lives of those who believe their own languages, cultural institutions, and values are threatened or already controlled by Western (that is, European and American) culture. In many of the stories collected here, the postcolonial legacy entails not only the remnants of British control but also the very real pressure of the United States in particular and the Western powers in general, as a de facto imperialist presence. Many of these influences, of course, are willingly adopted by other countries: One need think only of the enormous influence of U.S. popular music, styles of dress, and ideas about self-determination and liberty to see this aspect of the phenomenon. But from the point of view of those trying to preserve their indigenous cultures, to find alternatives to capitalism, or to base their political and social structures on traditional, local ways, such influences (however gladly embraced by parts of the population) can be seen as an unwarranted imposition—that is, as imperialism.

Whether colonial and imperial practices are ultimately beneficial or harmful is open to debate. But one point the stories in this book constantly bring to the fore is how those who have experienced colonialism and imperialism react. Learning to see these issues from their point of view is crucial to understanding the phenomenon of postcolonial studies and benefiting from reading postcolonial texts.

The Colonial and Postcolonial Short Story

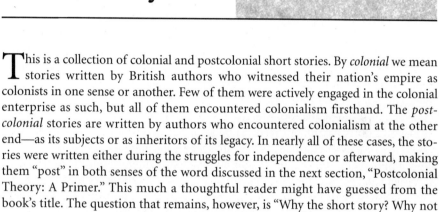

This is a collection of colonial and postcolonial short stories. By *colonial* we mean stories written by British authors who witnessed their nation's empire as colonists in one sense or another. Few of them were actively engaged in the colonial enterprise as such, but all of them encountered colonialism firsthand. The *postcolonial* stories are written by authors who encountered colonialism at the other end—as its subjects or as inheritors of its legacy. In nearly all of these cases, the stories were written either during the struggles for independence or afterward, making them "post" in both senses of the word discussed in the next section, "Postcolonial Theory: A Primer." This much a thoughtful reader might have guessed from the book's title. The question that remains, however, is "Why the short story? Why not novels, poems, plays, essays?"

One answer to this question lies in the history of the short story itself. The short story is often called both the oldest and the newest literary genre. It is perhaps the oldest because brief narratives must be among the most ancient (oral) literary forms. We have no contemporaneous written records of the earliest short fictions because they were created long before writing in any language. But among the earliest literary works that were written down are short tales—legends, folktales, fairy stories, myths, fables—that survive in such ancient texts as the Indian *Mahabharata* and the Hebrew Bible, and in such recently collected material as Australian aboriginal and African legends.

But the short story is also called the newest literary genre because what we now call the modern short story developed first in the early years of the nineteenth century in Russia, France, and the United States, largely in response to the rise of magazines. Several authors can claim to have "invented" the short story: Prosper Merimee in France, E. T. A. Hoffman in Germany, Walter Scott in Scotland, and Washington Irving or Edgar Allan Poe in the United States. Whoever deserves the title as the genre's originator, the form itself has always been an international one. Not only do its precursors trace themselves to many languages and cultures, but also the history of the short story, more so even than that of the novel, is vigorously international. In addition to the authors named above, many nineteenth-century authors made important contributions: Guy de Maupassant in France; Aleksandr Pushkin, Nikolai Gogol, Ivan Turgenev, and Anton Chekhov in Russia; Bret Harte, Mark Twain, and Henry James in the United States; and, near the end of the century, Robert Louis

Stevenson, Arthur Conan Doyle, and Rudyard Kipling in Great Britain. Twentieth-century contributors from all over the globe brought their own original flourishes to the genre: Gabriel García Márquez (Colombia), Jorge Luis Borges (Argentina), James Joyce (Ireland), Raymond Carver (the United States), Franz Kafka (Czechoslovakia), Yukio Mishima (Japan), Isaac Bashevis Singer (Poland), and Naguib Mahfouz (Egypt), not to mention all the writers collected in this anthology.

In Britain, however, the short story was quite late to develop; in fact, Kipling and Stevenson were among its first masters, and they began writing stories only in the 1880s. Even then, their idea of a "short story" differed from that of their U.S. and continental counterparts, for many British short stories were quite long by comparison. "Heart of Darkness," "The Beach at Falesá," and "The Man Who Would Be King" are sometimes classed as novellas or even as novels, but they fit the Victorian idea of a short story and are often treated today as such and hence will be here. In any event, the short story includes some of Britain's first and most important fictional accounts of colonialism. Moreover, this happened at a time when the British Empire was at its height. (It needs to be said that many British novels, like Jane Austen's *Mansfield Park*, Charlotte Brontë's *Jane Eyre*, and Charles Dickens's *Great Expectations*, mention colonialism, but no major British novel until E. M. Forster's *Passage to India* made colonialism its primary subject.) So the short story occupies a unique place in British fiction, especially British colonial fiction, and for this reason a collection of colonial short stories is particularly appropriate.

A second reason for compiling an anthology of short stories is a practical one. Unlike novels, stories can be collected into a reasonably sized volume. Hence, the fictions of many countries and regions can be put between the covers of a single book and the stories themselves can thereby be easily compared, contrasted, juxtaposed, analyzed. Recurring themes and ideas—such as resistance to racism, political oppression, personal identity, gender issues, linguistic imperialism, economic exploitation, environmental ravages, and human rights—can be identified and analyzed across cultures. Styles, narrative techniques, characters, and literary experiments also can be compared and contrasted. It would be difficult to perform such thematic and technical analyses on more than a few novels in a typical academic term.

Yet another reason might be called pedagogical. Many instructors regard the short story as the ideal classroom form. Short stories, unlike novels, can be seen "whole." A reader can, in a sense, perceive and hold a short story in mind far better than a novel, which tends to be read over many sittings and to cover many characters, incidents, and ideas. The size of the novel is in one sense an advantage because it can encompass so much, but whereas it can be relatively difficult to analyze a novel in less than a couple of weeks' classes, stories can often be quite satisfactorily covered in a single class period or less. Literary discussions of short stories, therefore, can be very satisfying for both students and instructors.

If brevity is the issue, then why not poems? Indeed, poems have much to recommend them as material for classroom use, but most poems lack the narrative drive, dramatic conflict, and characters that are almost mandatory in the short story. And narrative is, after all, the literary device that most of us are familiar with—from television and films, especially. Furthermore, the short story is often called the most poetic of fictional forms because, like the poem, the short story is concentrated and focused in ways that few novels can match. In a well-written short story, every detail counts. Seldom do readers find any incidental descriptions or irrelevant episodes in a well-crafted short story. Time does not allow for digression; interesting but unessential material must be ruthlessly excised.

Many commentators on the short story (including the editors of this volume) argue, therefore, that the short story combines the best features of fiction and poetry. It employs all the fictional techniques—narrative line (plot), characterization, point of view, setting, atmosphere, and so on. But it also employs the concentration and stylistic devices of poetry—imagery, metaphor, symbolism, tone. To be fair, the novel (or the drama, for that matter) combines all these elements as well, but the focus and concentration of the short story compel us as readers to pay attention to all of these. We *must* read the short story with the attention to detail that we would bring to poetry, but we must also pay attention to its narrative devices. The short story, therefore, is uniquely qualified to bring out the best in us as readers: It demands that we focus and concentrate, that we see the story whole; it also asks us to read linearly, to note beginning, middle, and end; to pay attention to character and incident; to note progressions and changes.

Lest all this sound too high-minded, even pretentious, let us put it another way: The short story is, quite simply, a lot of fun to read. It can be amusing, challenging, shocking, eye-opening, exciting, even life changing. We believe it is the ideal form to introduce students to the wide world of fiction in English, fiction that goes beyond national borders even as it crosses decades in time. It allows us to sample the literature and culture of a wide variety of countries and authors so that, having sampled various delights, as at a buffet table, we can go back for more. We hope that you will enjoy each and every one of the stories collected here and, having sampled the stories of many authors, will go on to pursue fictions both long and short by those writers who most engage and stimulate your imagination.

Postcolonial Theory: A Primer

Nearly everyone who picks up this book has studied English literature in some form, and most of us know—or think we know—what it is. English literature is the material collected in big anthologies that include works from "*Beowulf* to Virginia Woolf," as the saying goes. It's the poems, novels, plays, essays, and stories written in England by English men and women. It's sometimes equated with British literature to include works by Scottish, Welsh, and Irish authors, but to exclude, say, U.S. or Canadian literature.

As commonsensical as the above seems to be, the term *English literature* or even the more inclusive term *British literature* is not without ambiguity. *Beowulf*, for example, is written in Old English, a Germanic dialect so unlike Modern English that it requires specialized study to comprehend. Geoffrey Chaucer's *Canterbury Tales* is more or less readable by today's students, but the works of his contemporaries—the Gawain-poet and William Langland, for example—are almost as impenetrable as *Beowulf* because they are written in English dialects that did not become, like Chaucer's, "standard English." Beyond the question of language is that of nationality. Are the Irish and Scottish ballads "English"? Are writers such as Jonathan Swift, W. B. Yeats, James Joyce, and George Bernard Shaw English or Irish? Robert Louis Stevenson was born in Scotland, Joseph Conrad was born in Poland, and Doris Lessing was born in Persia and grew up in Southern Rhodesia (present-day Zimbabwe). But all of these authors are considered "English," or at least "British."

The problem of what constitutes English literature has been complicated even further by the spread of English through the expansion of the British Empire, which at its height governed about one-fifth of the world's population. The rise of the United States and Canada as world powers in the twentieth century also contributed to the spread of English as the language of commerce, education, and diplomacy. As a result, by the end of World War II there was a growing body of "world literature in English," or what many at the time called *Commonwealth literature*. The term arose in part because a growing body of literature was being written in English by inhabitants of the former British Empire, some of whom remained loosely tied with the "mother country" through the British Commonwealth (which included Canada, Australia, and New Zealand, among other countries).

The ambiguities and complications outlined above pale in comparison, however, to the difficulties, controversies, and continuing problems associated with the relatively new term *postcolonial*. In fact, debate arises over its very spelling: Should the term appear as *postcolonial* or *post-colonial*? One widely used text is titled *The Post-Colonial Studies Reader* (Ashcroft, Griffiths, and Tiffin), whereas Elleke Boehmer does without the hyphen in *Colonial and Postcolonial Literature.* Some argue that the hyphenated spelling refers to the historical period, "after colonialism," while the un-hyphenated word denotes the body of literary theory and practice used to describe this quite new area of study. This is the usage we will follow, employing synonyms such as "after the colonial period" for the historical era and using the unhyphenated *postcolonial* to refer to the literature and theory relating to the contemporary discipline of postcolonial studies.

But spelling the term is only one tiny part of the contentious arena called "postcolonial studies."

> Post-colonial theory involves discussion about experience of various kinds: migration, slavery, suppression, resistance, representation, difference, race, gender, place, and responses to the influential master discourses of imperial Europe such as history, philosophy and linguistics, and the fundamental experiences of speaking and writing by which all these come into being. None of these is "essentially" post-colonial, but together they form the complex fabric of the field. (Ashcroft, Griffiths, and Tiffin, *Post-Colonial Studies* 2)

How does all this differ from the theory and practice of studying Commonwealth literature? In part, the differences between the two reflect the general movement of literary and cultural studies since the mid-1960s. Much of the theory and practice of Commonwealth literary study reflected the humanistic and New Critical ideas of the 1930s and 1940s. Most of the energy of these critics was directed at showing that literatures from the former colonies demonstrated the same "lasting and universal" qualities as the canonical works of English literature, for example, the works of John Milton, Thomas Hardy, or T. S. Eliot. Critics under this dispensation argued for the appreciation and understanding of Commonwealth literature on the grounds that it was in the "great tradition" (to use F. R. Leavis's term) and that it merited study for these reasons.

Postcolonial critics and theorists, by contrast, focus much more directly, sometimes even exclusively, on the regional historical, literary, aesthetic, and political conditions that produce a given work of literature. Postcolonial criticism is thus a more explicitly political endeavor than New Criticism, which attempts to identify and discuss "objective" aesthetic and thematic aspects of literature. The most important influence or determining factor of concern to postcolonial critics is colonialism itself, particularly the ways by which colonial practices imposed European culture and appropriated indigenous rights, authority, and culture. A lasting effect of colonialism was to undermine the ways in which Indians, Africans, Caribbeans, and others viewed themselves and understood their cultures—replacing indigenous ideas of identity and value with those derived from European models and practices. A blatant form of this is the inferiority colonized peoples were made to feel as a result of political and cultural subjugation. The implicit and often explicit message of European missionaries, for example, was that indigenous religions were "heathen," "barbaric," "unenlightened," and hence inferior to Christianity.

One aim of postcolonial study, then, is to "decolonize" the minds of colonized peoples, to question the political, psychological, linguistic, and cultural effects of colonialism. To read the literature of previously colonized people (that written after the mid-nineteenth century) is to look for ways in which colonialism is consciously or unconsciously reflected in the literary work. Postcolonial criticism also emphasizes the racist and culturally imperialist aspects of how English literature portrays the colonial experience; for example, Conrad's "Heart of Darkness" and Stevenson's "The Beach at Falesá" are often analyzed from this point of view.

We may say, therefore, that postcolonial theory offers at least two broad approaches to the various literatures in English. One of these is to examine works by authors from decolonized countries for evidence of their response to the colonial experience and its aftereffects. The other is to read or reread the literature of the colonial period to ask whether it challenges or supports colonialism, or whether it contains subtle or obvious reflections of imperialist attitudes and values. In either case, we are looking at the literature for its social and political discourse, the conditions under which it was written and published, and the underlying assumptions, biases, values, and ideas of the cultures from which it arises.

EDWARD SAID AND THE BEGINNINGS OF POSTCOLONIAL THEORY

It will help to clarify these points by turning briefly to the critic often considered the founder of postcolonial discourse analysis, Edward Said, the late Palestinian scholar and professor at Columbia University. Said's *Orientalism* argues that Western societies constructed their "knowledge" of "the Orient" in a way that justified colonial domination. In fact, he argues, Western scholars, explorers, missionaries, and travelers did not investigate Eastern cultures so much as they imposed on them previously held assumptions, using what they observed to reinforce and verify these assumptions. Thus, according to Said, not only the whole idea of "the Orient" but also virtually everything that was claimed to be true about it was in whole or in part an imaginative construct, a fantasy, by which the West defined itself in opposition to the East, legitimized its power, and justified its superiority (4–24). In a subsequent book, *Culture and Imperialism*, Said extended the ideas put forth in *Orientalism* to countries outside the Middle East and also focused on Western fictional depictions of these countries. His analyses of Conrad's "Heart of Darkness," Jane Austen's *Mansfield Park*, and Verdi's opera *Aida*, among many others, demonstrated the ways in which even the most elevated cultural products may be complicit in the colonial enterprise, in treating one set of people, ideas, values, or institutions as superior to another. Said is a subtle, thoughtful, and perceptive critic who values the aesthetic achievement of the works he analyzes while also insisting that they perpetuate and reinforce racist and imperialist ideas.

Even sympathetic critics of Said's work point out that, for all its brilliance and influence, it overlooks certain phenomena. For one thing, his critics argue that a literary text (or any text for that matter) seldom conveys only one message. Often a work embeds ambiguities and contradictions that undermine its dominant idea, so that even apparently pro-imperialist works like those by Kipling may contain ideas and passages that show the dark side of empire. In addition, some claim that Said ignores the fact that even within imperialist countries there were writers, politicians, and commentators who opposed colonialism. English Prime Minister William Gladstone (1809–1898) is an example of one such opponent. Moreover, critics argue, Said overlooks the way in which colonized people reacted against their conquerors. An early and very influential book that emphasizes the resistance of colonized people is *The Empire Writes Back: Theory and Practice in Post-Colonial Literatures* (Ashcroft, Griffiths, and Tiffin). This book focuses on the ways in which writers from previously colonized countries are reshaping the English language to express new cultural realities and identities. The stories in this anthology that incorporate non-English words and expressions, experiment with syntax and style, and "creolized" English can be analyzed using the tools of *The Empire Writes Back.* Of course, authors can "write back" in other ways as well, by advocating resistance to colonial power, using folk and other native sources as the basis for their work, emphasizing the value of indigenous traditions and cultural practices, opposing Eurocentric ideas, and so on. Many of the stories in this anthology express some form of "writing back."

New Forms of Colonialism

But of course writers from previously colonized countries are not concerned exclusively with issues of European colonialism and its aftermath. A blind spot in early postcolonial theories was that they focused almost entirely on literature that dealt directly with colonialism and its legacies. The years after World War II (1939–1945), however, brought independence to most previous colonies (India in 1947; Kenya in 1963, for example). Sadly, independence did not always produce good government or economic prosperity for those newly liberated. One possible cause of the problems that have plagued newly created countries, particularly in Africa, is that the colonial powers drew national boundaries arbitrarily, with little or no concern for geographical features, ethnic populations, or religious differences. A basic idea behind the European notion of "the nation" is that those within national boundaries share certain commonalities of language, culture, values, religion, and ideals. The new nations created out of former colonies were often arbitrary groupings of peoples, some of whom had long histories of opposition or hostility to one another. Worse, colonizers had sometimes exploited these differences in a strategy of "divide and conquer," but then left the newly independent countries to deal with the consequences of this divisive tactic. One continuing debate, therefore, is whether such lingering conflicts as the border dispute between India and Pakistan or the periodic outbreaks of civil war in new African countries are the direct results of colonial legacies or the results of forces not connected to colonialism.

These issues are complicated by continuing pressures for Westernization. The relentless dissemination of Western culture, primarily from the United States, Europe, and others like Australia and Canada, is sometimes called *cultural imperialism.* It has poured new ideas, values, products, lifestyles, and practices into non-Western countries. Unfamiliar ideas and cultural practices have always accompanied colonists and settlers, of course, and some were adopted voluntarily or developed indigenously. But the aggressive export of secularism, feminism, and science, not to mention the music, films, clothing, products (such as McDonald's and Coca-Cola), and many other Western cultural practices and ideas were like new wine in old wine skins—with all too predicable results. Indigenous medicine, family structures, clothing styles, food, literature, religion, folk ways, languages, living patterns, and social organizations have often been altered or obliterated. This approach has been extended by some postcolonial critics (for example, Spivak and Chatterjee) to include Western skepticism, rationality, and science. According to them, these habits of mind amount to "epistemic violence" on Third World countries, replacing indigenous ways of knowing with Western ones. Only by rejecting such Western practices, the argument goes, can former colonies fully regain their cultural heritages.

A related but different phenomenon is *globalization*. Often defined simply as the impact of giant, multinational corporations, globalization as a concept involves more than simply the pervasive influence of companies like General Motors, Shell Oil, or Microsoft. The term refers also to the general blurring of national boundaries, whether that means the ability of social activists, news organizations, nongovernmental organizations, and scholars to work nearly everywhere in the world, or the cultural integration that results when travel and communication barriers are erased by air travel, the telephone, and the Internet. The outsourcing of U.S. jobs to Latin America, India, and Indochina is one manifestation of globalization, as is the rise of India and China as economic "superpowers." Postcolonial theory forces us to assess the impact of Western culture and globalization on traditional peoples and cultures and to ask if the result is loss or gain—and for whom.

But direct and indirect colonial influences and current cultural effects are not the only or perhaps even the most important factors affecting previously colonized countries. Since the end of World War II, newly independent states have been the focal point of global power struggles. Until 1989, the so-called Cold War between the Soviet Union and the United States dominated politics and economics in emerging nations. Governments were supported or toppled, popular movements encouraged or discouraged, economic and social reforms supported or not depending on whether an emerging nation was in the U.S. or Soviet camp. Since the fall of the Soviet Union, the emphasis has shifted to "the war on drugs," "the war on poverty," and "the war on terrorism," but the stakes and tactics have remained much the same. Acting both overtly and covertly, the United States and other Western countries have intervened directly and indirectly in the domestic policies and economies of former European colonies, using such instruments as military aid, trade agreements, subsidies, and loans to earn the support, loyalty, or cooperation of these countries. The result is often called *neocolonialism* because the combined effects of these efforts (some of them well meaning) are to reinstate many of the features of old-style colonialism. The term can also refer to the fact that in some previously colonized countries, particularly in Africa and Southeast Asia, native elites have stepped into the power vacuum left by colonizing Europeans and effectively run these countries and shaped their cultures in ways that are little different from those of the colonial past.

LITERATURE AS "MEDIATION"

Many of the stories in this anthology reflect the immediate and lingering issues of national unity, civil war, and economic and cultural tensions. Stories dealing with the horrible outbreaks of violence following the partition of India and Pakistan and those growing out of civil strife in Africa are obvious ways in which literature can reflect, comment on, and critique such situations. The postcolonial term for literature's participating in such issues and commenting on them or advocating a particular point of view is *mediation*. For example, the continuing tensions between settler colonists and First Nation peoples in North America, Australia, New Zealand, and the Caribbean are part of the cultural legacy of colonialism. *Mediation* means that literature does not simply reflect these issues but participates directly in them by advocating a point of view, opposing other points of view, or critiquing the situation. Postcolonial literary theory makes us aware of these mediations and also provides tools for analyzing literature. Critics like Frantz Fanon, Partha Chaterjee, and Homi K. Bhabha theorize about what literature *should* do under such circumstances. All of them observe that after independence, educated elites (for example, in Africa, India, and the Caribbean) could use their political and economic leverage to impose their will and ideas on those who lack such power: neocolonialism. Having themselves absorbed Western ideas and values, these elites may be no more sensitive to the culture of ordinary people than were the Europeans. Moreover, they may use the symbols of nationalism (the flag, money, national anthems, clothing styles, and so on) and cultural products like literary works to further their own political and social goals. Postcolonial theory, therefore, urges readers to be alert to the ways by which cultural divisions and power relations are mediated by literature.

One such issue facing previously colonized countries involves the place of women in society. Traditional societies in India, the Middle East, Africa, and the Caribbean assigned specific roles to women, roles that by Western standards are sometimes considered unequal or even degrading. Early in the colonial period, Christian missionaries attempted to change some practices—for example, the custom among Brahmins in India of expecting widows to throw themselves on their husbands' funeral pyres (a practice known as *suttee*). Missionaries also opposed (unsuccessfully) the practice of polygamy, which was widespread in Africa (for example, in Basutoland and among the Turkana of Kenya). But even without pressure from missionaries, colonialism, industrialization, and urbanization significantly altered male-female relations, whether intentionally or not. For instance, a particularly egregious practice by South African mine owners was the requirement that men move from their rural villages to the mines without their wives and children, thus separating families and concentrating young men in camps where infidelity and prostitution became serious temptations. Similarly, cities needing workers became magnets for single men and women seeking employment, and new styles of living that undermined traditional village life, separated extended members, and upset traditional patterns of courtship and marriage altered society and created new roles for women.

Gender issues have become especially acute since the mid-1960s with the emergence of worldwide feminism. Some postcolonial critics argue that nationalism itself is a source of female oppression: In harking back to the pre-colonial past for tradi-tional ideas and social structures, nationalism can reinforce or even reinstate policies and practices that relegate women to second-class citizenship, or, conversely, manip-ulate traditional ideas of womanhood into bogus symbols of national identity. The promises of education, hopes for upward mobility, and desires for increased roles for women in business, government, and the professions often bring women into direct conflict with men, who are reluctant to give up their traditional privileges. Postcolo-nial feminist critics—Partha Chaterjee, Chandra Mohanty, and Gayatri Spivak among them—point out that women can be twice oppressed: by neocolonialist po-litical structures and by traditions of patriarchy. But to what extent can the ideals and goals of Western feminisms (note the plural) be applied in non-Western soci-eties? Can the imposition of feminist ideas on Third World countries upset tradi-tional gender and family relations in ways that themselves constitute a new form of colonialism? The dilemma expresses itself in a myriad ways, but one controversial and especially visible flashpoint is the issue of female circumcision, which in the West is often called "female genital mutilation." Women in societies where female circumcision is traditionally practiced argue that it is an important rite of passage marking the end of girlhood and the entrance to womanhood. Opponents claim that it constitutes a serious health hazard, reinforces patriarchy, and robs women of sexual pleasure. This issue is both a vexing political topic and one sometimes medi-ated in literature. It is mentioned here as representative of the dilemmas faced by First World critics and theorists—and Western aid agencies and medical authori-ties—when they attempt to respond to Third World practices. The unease felt by some women writers in Africa over the importing of Western feminism has led to their adopting the term *womanist* to define their position—a position that attempts to assert women's equal rights and value without necessarily adopting the rhetoric and goals of Western feminism(s).

This leads to yet another aspect of feminism as a part of postcolonial theory, one raised in particular by the influential theorist Gayatri Spivak. She points out that postcolonial theorists and critics tend to treat Third World people as a single entity, as if all are alike and share the same concerns. She warns that we risk reducing Third World "subalterns" to a homogenous "construct," much as early Western commenta-tors did in creating "the Oriental mind." Spivak's argument is dense and complex, based in turn on other complicated arguments about consciousness and selfhood, so it cannot be summarized here. However, it can be said that Spivak raises questions about the representation of oppressed groups and about who, if anyone, can speak on their behalf. (After all, most published writers in whatever country come from the middle class, not from the peasantry or the urban poor.) Representations of op-pressed people in literature may not be accurate, and our attempts to understand these representations may induce additional distortions and misunderstandings. This is particularly true of women, Spivak asserts, because of the disproportionate emphasis given to men and their writings. Can we, she asks, ever hear the voices of women in the literature we read? Have women's voices been drowned out by those who attempt to speak for them? At the very least, the reader and interpreter of literature must be fully aware of the assumptions, prejudices, preconceived ideas, and limited perspectives that he or she brings to reading any work of literature.

POSTCOLONIALISM AND LANGUAGE

Language is a key issue in postcolonial theory and literary practice. Many writers and theorists argue that the colonizing country—in this case, Great Britain—imposed not only its institutions, values, modes of dress, and ideas on its colonies, but also the very essence of its communication system: language. Under colonial rule, facility with English became essential to get ahead or lead a successful life, and hence many colonized people were forced (or chose) to learn English for the same reasons one needed Latin under the Romans. Along with the English language came the British system of education and British literary modes, standards, and tastes. For writers in formerly colonized countries, an important question is whether to write in English—the language of the oppressor—or to write in a native tongue.

From the point of view of writers in previously colonized countries, the choice of the language in which to write presents both literary and nonliterary problems. As a "world" language, English is an attractive choice since it potentially reaches a much wider audience than, say, Urdu, Farsi, or Yoruba. In India, which has some fifteen "official" languages, not to mention numerous other languages and dialects, or across the African continent with its great multiplicity of tongues, English can bridge linguistic divides; it can serve as a kind of pan-Indian or pan-African medium. English is a tempting choice, then, for many native writers because it can be read not only within the author's geographic area but also throughout the world. Writers such as R. K. Narayan, Ezekiel Mphahele, and Chinua Achebe have embraced it willingly. But what is lost by choosing English? Many literate people in the author's country or continent may not know English, especially since English fluency tends to be a middle-class accomplishment. Moreover, is English capable of expressing the author's ideas, of reflecting the author's culture and experience, or of accurately conveying the dialogue of the story's characters? However fluent the author may be in English, the language itself may lack the capacity to convey accurately the writer's vision, to communicate the texture and nuances of the culture, to express the rhythms, tones of voice, and subtle connotations of words and expressions that are essential to literary effects.

But language is not just a practical or literary issue; it is also political. Even at the local level, it involves choices. Should children be educated in English, their native language, or both? Clearly there are advantages to learning English, but what will happen to indigenous languages and to the oral and written traditions of these languages if English is the exclusive or dominant language in the schools? Ngugi wa Thiong'o speaks eloquently of growing up in Kenya speaking Gikuyu and absorbing the culture of his people and the expressiveness of their language through the stories told by adults. But at a colonial school, Gikuyu was forbidden as the language of "stupid people." He concludes by saying:

> In other words writers in African languages should reconnect themselves
> to the revolutionary traditions of an organized peasantry and working
> class in Africa and their struggle to defeat imperialism and create a higher
> system of democracy and socialism in alliance with all other peoples of
> the world.

Ngugi—and many others who share his opinion—see the imposition of English as
another aspect of imperialism or neocolonialism, and therefore something that
should be resisted, not only in the name of culture but also in the cause of genuine
democracy. He has ceased writing in English and has returned to his native Gikuyu.

Yet another reason for resistance to English lies in the assumptions, ideals, and
prejudices buried in the language itself. Hierarchies of light-dark, black-white, male-
female have often been pointed to as endemic to English and hence inherently demeaning to people of darker skin color and to women generally. Nor is this feature
always subtle: Hate words, racial smears, cultural insults, and such seemingly neutral
terms as *primitive, pagan,* and *uncivilized* carry overtones that place European values
and practices above those of other people. One form of postcolonial analysis, therefore, is to ferret out such linguistically loaded terms and to assess their place and impact in a given work of literature. Alternatively, critics can suggest ways of avoiding
words with such negative connotations and substitute more subtle, less loaded expressions.

The relation of spoken dialects to "received standard English" (that is, the so-
called proper English of educated English men and women) raises yet another issue
sometimes addressed by postcolonial theorists: the relation between oral and written
literature. Strictly speaking, literature is something written down, so that oral tales,
legends, stories, myths, riddles, poems, and even epics are not literature at all. But all
cultures have their own oral traditions and folklore, and for centuries the stories
passed by one generation to another constituted the only "literature" some languages
and cultures possessed. Nor should it be assumed that oral traditions are short or
simple forms, for some of the most sophisticated products of the human imagination existed solely in oral form for centuries before finally being written down. The
Hebrew Bible and the Hindu epics *Ramayana* and *Mahabharata* are obvious examples. Indeed, it was not until Christian missionaries developed scripts for many
African, Indian, and Caribbean languages that the oral materials could be written
down in their original languages. But should the products of oral culture be put in
the same category with works written on paper and published? Are they legitimate
subjects of literary inquiry? The issue is complicated by the fact that oral forms often
lie behind written ones, just as the folktale, the parable, and the short narrative
poem lie behind the modern short story. Among emerging nations, where illiteracy
is still common and written forms are unavailable to large portions of the population, oral forms may well be more culturally important than written ones. Moreover,
written forms may well incorporate oral genres or features: The Indian short story,
for example, often exhibits the digressions, exaggerations, miraculous events, and
mythical characters that characterize popular materials. For reasons of space, this

anthology deals only with stories that began life in written form, but those who wish to explore the rich oral traditions of any or all of the countries included here will find many collections and translations to assist in their search.

LITERATURE AND DIASPORA

One issue remains—the phenomenon known as the *literatures of diasporas. Diaspora* is the term originally applied to the scattering of the Jews after the Babylonian captivity in the sixth century B.C.E. Recently the term has been applied to any racial or ethnic group that has experienced a dispersion of its peoples to various parts of the globe. Thus, it is possible to speak of the black diaspora (largely due to the slave trade), the Indian diaspora, and even the Irish diaspora. The phenomenon is not new by any means; people have always migrated and emigrated. But the decades since World War II have seen an extraordinary increase in this movement of peoples: North Africans into France and Spain; Turks into Germany; Indians, Pakistanis, and West Indians into Britain, Canada, and the United States; Asians into Europe and North America, and so on. An important aspect of this movement is that peoples have moved in such numbers that they form tightly knit communities in their adopted countries and hence retain a sense of being part of the old country as well as participants in the new. They experience not only culture shock but also a sense of belonging to a previous community. Such divided loyalties are often felt strongest among adults who migrate, but the children born of these immigrants are also torn in their loyalties, being pulled on the one hand toward the language, customs, dress, religion, and mores of their parents' culture and on the other hand propelled toward assimilation into the new country's ways.

Postcolonial writers and theorists ponder the effects of such displacement—on the individuals concerned and on the writings they produce. Concepts such as *home, belonging, personal identity, marginalization,* and *hybridity* are debated as theories of postcolonial identity. For example, some experience a life that seems constantly to exist on the borders of different nations, but these borders may not sharply divide so much as they blur and mingle. Old ideas of identity no longer fit; the self is not single but multiple. For the writer, as for any individual, such an ambivalent and shifting position can be frightening or liberating; it can bring confusion or new ways of seeing and expressing. (Indeed, it can be both frightening and liberating, debilitating and creative.) One response is to attempt to define some essential qualities that are particular to the black, Indian, or Asian experience; on the other hand, writers may emphasize the variety of individualities within a given community. Postcolonial theory attempts to understand and explain these complex phenomena and the writings they produce. An obvious problem created by diasporas and their literature involves the very issue we encountered at the beginning of this chapter: that of a writer's national identity or a nation's literary identity. To what country do we assign diasporic writers such as V. S. Naipaul, Ruth Prawer Jhabvala, Salman Rushdie, and Doris Lessing? To what country (if any) do they themselves believe they belong? And what happens to the concept of British, U.S., Canadian, or Jamaican literature under the pressures of the restless movements of people from place to place? Is it even possible to speak any longer about U.S., Australian, or British literature? Or should we follow Rushdie's advice and just speak of literatures in English, without regard for national identities?

There are no obvious or easy answers to these or to the host of new and exciting questions raised by postcolonial literature and the theories devised to analyze and (one hopes) to illuminate it. Postcolonial theory does not provide a set of tools for analysis so much as it raises a host of questions that can help us dig into the literature (and into our own preconceived ideas about it). Postcolonial theory challenges us as readers to see the world differently, to look at history, literature, language, and culture in new ways. The theories are not a substitute for the literature but a way of entering into it. Reading the literature itself and thereby entering vicariously the lives and cultures out of which it springs must remain primary. And, of course, short stories are only one small part of this total literature. Like this introduction, this book is only a primer, a starting point; but like any good primer, it can open whole worlds of exciting ideas and new experiences.

Works Cited

Ashcroft, Bill, Gareth Griffiths, and Helen Tiffin. *The Empire Writes Back: Theory and Practice in Post-Colonial Literatures.* 2nd ed. London: Routledge, 2002.

———, eds. *The Post-Colonial Studies Reader.* London: Routledge, 1995.

Bhahba, Homi K. *The Location of Culture.* London: Routledge, 1994.

Boehmer, Elleke. *Colonial and Postcolonial Literature: Migrant Metaphors.* New York: Oxford UP, 1995.

Chaterjee, Partha. *Nationalist Thought and the Colonial World: A Derivative Discourse.* London: Zed, 1996.

Fanon, Frantz. *The Wretched of the Earth.* Trans. Constance Farrington. New York: Grove, 1968.

Leavis, F. R. *The Great Tradition: George Eliot, James, and Conrad.* London: Chatto & Windus, 1948.

Mohanty, Chandra. "Under Western Eyes: Feminist Scholarship and Colonial Discourses." *Dangerous Liaisons: Gender, Nation, and Postcolonial Perspectives.* Ed. Anne McClintock, Aamir Muftin, and Ella Shohat. Minneapolis: U of Minnesota P, 1997. 255–277.

Ngugi, wa Thiong'o. *Decolonising the Mind: The Politics of Language in African Literature.* London: Currey, 1986.

Rushdie, Salman. *Imaginary Homelands: Essays and Criticism, 1981–1991.* London: Granta, 1991.

Said, Edward W. *Culture and Imperialism.* New York: Knopf, 1993.

———. *Orientalism.* 1978. Rpt. Harmondsworth, UK: Penguin, 1991.

Spivak, Gayatri Chakravorty. "Can the Subaltern Speak?" *Marxism and the Interpretation of Culture.* Ed. Cary Nelson and Lawrence Grossberg. Urbana: U of Illinois P, 1988. 271–323.

Young, Robert J. C. *Postcolonialism: An Historical Introduction.* Oxford: Blackwell, 2001.

Part Two

Stories

England

Exploration and Colonialism

When Christopher Columbus "discovered the New World" (new, of course, only from a European perspective), he could hardly have imagined the extent of exploration and conquest that would ensue. Following Columbus, the explorers John Cabot, Vasco Núñez de Balboa, Ferdinand Magellan, and Hernando Cortés led the way for colonial expansion, mainly by the Spanish and Portuguese in Central and South America and the West Indies. England's entry into colonialism was at first confined to Elizabeth I's (r. 1558–1603) clever and effective use of English sea-dogs (essentially pirates, unofficially supported by the English crown) to raid Spanish shipping, culminating in the defeat of the Spanish Armada in 1588. Sir Walter Raleigh attempted to settle a colony in Virginia in 1585, but it failed. Meanwhile, Elizabeth consolidated her hold on Ireland and in 1600 chartered the East India Company, a private trading company she authorized to trade in India. A successful North American colony had to wait until the reign of James I (r. 1603–1625), during which Jamestown was founded in 1607. James I of England (he was also James VI of Scotland) hoped to link Scotland with England and Wales, but Parliament demurred, and union did not officially occur with Scotland until 1707 and Ireland until 1801.

Successful colonies in North America quickly followed Jamestown, the most famous being that of the Pilgrims at Plymouth in 1620. Less often noted is that slaves had been brought to Virginia the year previous to harvest tobacco, the colonists' first important export to England. Meanwhile, rivalry between the French and English was underway in Canada. The first European settlement there was a French undertaking at Port Royal, Nova Scotia, in 1605, which the English attacked in 1614. The French, being primarily interested in exploration and the fur trade, sent relatively few settlers, while the English established populated settlements. By 1750, English settlers outnumbered the French by 20 to 1. Conflicts between the two countries intensified on both sides of the Atlantic, culminating in the French and Indian Wars (as the war was called in the New World) or the Seven Years' War (as the war was called in Europe). The Peace of Utrecht (1713) ceded Nova Scotia, Hudson's Bay, and Newfoundland to England, but this did not end hostilities: In 1759, British General James Wolfe defeated General Louis-Joseph de Montcalm on the Plains of Abraham, and the following year Montreal fell. The French abandoned all claims in

North America, except the Louisiana Territory, in the Treaty of Paris (1763). Just thirteen years later, America would proclaim its independence from England and secure it after victory at Yorktown (1781). The loss of America initiated a debate within England over the value of colonies, with some arguing that the cost of maintaining overseas possessions outweighed any advantages. On the other hand, Britain's victories in the Napoleonic Wars (1803–1815) resulted in the acquisition of Cape Colony (South Africa), Mauritius, Ceylon (present-day Sri Lanka), Trinidad and Tobago, St. Lucia, British Guiana (in Central America), and Malta.

Rivalry among European powers in the Caribbean during this period was equally fierce, with Spain, Holland, France, and England claiming and holding various islands, mainly for their tea, their spices, and especially their sugar. Imported African slaves supplied the necessary labor for the islands' plantations. The British controlled a significant share of these islands, the most important being the Bahamas, Barbados, Antigua, and the British Virgin Islands.

Britain's imperial expansion into the southern Pacific occurred at about the same time as America was cutting itself loose from British control. Australia, New Zealand, Tahiti, Hawaii, and other islands in the South Pacific had been "discovered" long ago, but the voyages of Captain James Cook between 1768 and 1779 revived interest in these territories. In 1787, the first penal colony was established at Botany Bay, just south of present-day Sydney, Australia, as an alternative to the southern United States, which were no longer in British control. Thousands of British criminals were transported to eastern Australia until 1840 and until 1868 to western Australia, by which time the more lawless elements of the population had been tamed and respectable citizens no longer welcomed England's surplus criminals. Sheep raising was the backbone of the Australian economy, but in 1851 gold was discovered in southeastern provinces, and a mad rush was on. Within twenty years, most of Australia was self-governing, though nominally still under the British crown. New Zealand was first invaded by lawless traders, whalers, and ex-convicts, then by missionaries hoping to convert the native tribes—the Maoris. Britain assumed control in 1840 and annexed it to the Empire in 1841.

Trade with Asia under the auspices of the East India Company had been going on for many years (see the chapter on India), but access to China was strictly limited by the country's suspicion of Westerners. Much of this trade was fueled by opium, which the East India Company brought from India. In 1800, China officially outlawed the importation of opium, but little was done to actually prevent its entering the country until 1839, when millions of pounds' worth was seized from British merchants and destroyed. The British quickly retaliated to save this lucrative trade. Badly outgunned, the Chinese were forced to surrender in 1842. The resulting treaty opened several ports to European settlement and ceded Hong Kong to Britain. A second war in 1856 led to further concessions to Britain, France, Russia, and the United States.

Historians of the British Empire note that a significant change in the tone of British rhetoric regarding the Empire occurred about 1870. By this time, the extent of the modern Empire was in place, except for Africa. (See the maps inside the front cover.) The Indian Mutiny of 1857 and its aftermath had shattered the fiction that

the East India Company was in control in India, and the British government officially assumed power in that country in 1858. Another pivotal event, according to
some historians, was the Franco-Prussian War of 1870–1871 because from this conflict there emerged a united and powerful Germany and a weakened, defeated
France. Germany now felt itself in a position to challenge Britain's imperial and
commercial supremacy, altering the balance of power in Europe. According to this
theory, the rise of German power, together with King Leopold's ambitions in the
Congo, touched off the "scramble for Africa" in the 1880s.

But domestic forces also contributed. The Victorian era was a period of enormous political and social reform in England. The Reform Bill of 1832 enlarged the
pool of eligible voters and reorganized Parliamentary districts, but these reforms
were merely the beginning. Agitation by William Wilberforce and others succeeded
in outlawing slavery from all British colonies in 1833. Reformist zeal was especially
strong among humanitarian groups and missionary societies hoping to abolish slavery throughout the world. Inspired by William Carey, a Baptist preacher and author
of *Enquiry into the Obligations of Christians to Use Means for the Conversion of the
Heathens* (1792), Protestant denominations sent thousands of young men and
women into every part of the globe. Although these groups have subsequently been
severely criticized for indirectly or even directly contributing to colonial conquest,
their motives and aims seemed to most Westerners at the time to be entirely altruistic and laudable. They were generally regarded as purveyors of education, Christianity, and modern medicine to the "ignorant, heathen masses." It did not occur to
most Europeans that Africans did not consider themselves as ignorant, heathen, or
in need of medical care. Simultaneously, the activities of European explorers, most
notably David Livingstone and Henry Morton Stanley, fueled a wide and passionate
interest in "the dark continent" and other remote areas of the globe.

Nevertheless, counterimperialist forces were active too. Critics of Parliament's
lax oversight of colonial affairs caused the establishment of a permanent undersecre-
tary in 1837, but even with theoretically tighter reins on its overseas possessions,
Britain could not stop the expansion of white settlements in Canada, Australia,
South Africa, and New Zealand, in part because some 7 million people emigrated
from England and Ireland between 1815 and 1870. In 1867, the British North American Act loosened control of Canada and unified its provinces into a single country
having dominion (that is, semi-independent) status. Four years later, Britain withdrew her troops from Canada and the other white-majority settlements, with the result that Australia and New Zealand gradually followed Canada's example—
Australia becoming a united dominion in 1901, New Zealand in 1907. Thus, in the
same year that Germany's victory over France encouraged Britain to think about
guarding its interests against German expansion, "little Englanders" had succeeded
in pressuring the crown to withdraw militarily from some of its largest possessions.
By 1871, therefore, a two-tiered system had evolved: White-dominated colonies had
achieved considerable self-determination, whereas white-minority colonies remained firmly under British control. In general, this meant a British-appointed governor or viceroy at the top, served by deliberative councils appointed by him, which
in turn delegated some authority for everyday affairs to local rulers. Flexibility was a

key factor in Britain's colonial success, as variations on this general plan allowed for local differences and conditions.

What, then, tipped the balance between pro-imperialist forces and those opposed to England's further colonial expansion? Two answers have already been suggested—the rise of Germany and the subsequent need felt by England to check German, French, and Belgian expansionist tendencies, together with the internal pressures exerted by evangelicals and reformers to use Britain's international power for humanitarian purposes. Another possibility is that the British began to feel an almost divine calling to exert their influence over and rule those they regarded as benighted darker races, who in their ignorance (as the British conceived it) did not even know that they needed such assistance. Literature played a particularly important role in this theory since writers like Rudyard Kipling promoted the idea of "the white man's burden" to "raise" the plight of the uncivilized. And, of course, there were economic incentives, the classic explanation being that European powers, especially Great Britain, needed new colonies as sources for raw materials and as markets for surplus manufactured goods. Of course, various combinations of these and other causes may be invoked to explain what many historians regard as the "new imperialism" of the late nineteenth century.

One point cannot be debated: From the 1870s onward, there was a sharp rise in competition for new colonial territories among the major European powers that resulted in the carving up of Africa and the energetic westward push of North Americans at the expense of native populations.

There is no way to calculate the human cost of this phase of European colonialism. Defenders of the system point to the material benefits conveyed by European technological progress—schools, hospitals, railroads, communication systems, and economic development. Critics point to the destruction of indigenous civilizations and cultures and the deaths of millions of people from military battles, or overwork, disease, or starvation. By some estimates, 10 million Africans died in the Congo alone under King Leopold's despotism. Loss of life in other colonies was proportionate.

Considering the lasting and far-reaching effects of colonialism, it is easy to forget that colonialism began to collapse within a relatively short period. When the smoke cleared from the carnage of World War I (1914–1918), an estimated 10 million men were dead, nearly a million of them from Britain and its colonies and dominions. Superficially, Britain emerged as one of the victors, and in 1920 its empire increased in size when the League of Nations awarded it mandates over Germany's colonies in Africa and Turkey's holdings in the Middle East and North Africa. But the war left Britain in disastrous economic shape, with astronomical debts, high unemployment, and shrinking overseas markets. Colonies that had supported Britain in the war demanded or fought for increased autonomy, beginning with Ireland and the Easter uprising of 1916. Mahatma Gandhi's "Quit India" campaign quickly followed after the India Act of 1919 failed to deliver on Britain's promise of significant self-determination. Canada, Australia, and South Africa further loosened the ties of dominion; in 1926, all three were declared partners, not possessions, of the crown.

The worldwide depression that followed the stock market crash of October 1929 in the United States exacerbated England's problems. Ten years later, World War II erupted.

Once again, Britain's colonies and dominions rallied to the country's defense, although with far less enthusiasm in India and some reluctance in Canada and South Africa. Ireland remained neutral. With the end of war in 1945, England was once again broke and exhausted, and the postwar Liberal government of Clement Atlee acknowledged that independence movements in the colonies could no longer be resisted. In the Middle East, Iraq and Egypt had already left the Empire before World War II; Jordan did so in 1946, and Palestine two years later. India was next to go in 1947; Ceylon (Sri Lanka) followed by a few months, as did Burma early in 1948. Most African colonies were less anxious for independence, although Ghana became self-governing in 1948 and an independent member of the Commonwealth in 1957. To its credit, Britain increased its educational and technical assistance in the 1950s to help prepare Africans for self-rule. In Kenya, however, open rebellion erupted in 1952 with the so-called Mau-Mau uprising against white farmers that was brutally repressed and yet not put down until 1960. Nigeria became the twelfth member of the Commonwealth in 1960. In the same year, South Africa voted to become a republic, though it remained a member of the Commonwealth. Among other examples, Gambia and Kenya became free in 1963; Zanzibar and Tanganyika formed independent Tanzania in 1964. Also in 1964, the northern part of Rhodesia became Zambia, leaving Southern Rhodesia as a white-ruled state that declared its independence in 1965 and remained under white minority rule until 1980, when it became Zimbabwe.

By the end of the 1960s, then, nearly all of Europe's former colonies had become independent, although white minority rule persisted in Southern Rhodesia until 1980 and in South Africa until 1994. The end of colonialism, however, did not spell the end of European and U.S. interference in the former colonies' affairs. Since the end of World War II, nations throughout the world have complained of U.S. imperialism, wielded not through direct political rule but through various forms of economic control—the International Monetary Fund, the World Bank, foreign aid schemes, and multinational corporations. The legacy of colonialism is also evident in the political instability of former colonies, many of which have been ravaged by civil war, economic collapse, and environmental degradation.

LITERARY RESPONSES TO EXPLORATION AND COLONIAL EXPANSION

English literature naturally reflected exploration and expansion, directly or indirectly. From the time of Geoffrey Chaucer (1342?–1400), English writers had satisfied their audiences' desires for the exotic and marvelous through travel literature such as Sir John Mandeville's *The Voyage and Travels of Sir John Mandeville, Knight* (ca. 1357), which purported to describe such faraway lands as Turkey and India. Christopher Marlowe whetted a similar appetite, with *Tamburlaine the Great* (ca. 1587), a bloody and sensational dramatization of the life of Timur, a Scythian who usurped the throne of Persia and subsequently conquered Egypt and Turkey. Post-colonial critics interpret William Shakespeare's *The Tempest* (ca. 1611) as one of English literature's first justifications for colonialism. In a postcolonial reading, the play's hero, Prospero, usurps a Mediterranean island from its only inhabitant, Caliban, a half-human, half-devil figure said to represent the typical "savage." Prospero makes Caliban his slave until Prospero's magic powers can be used to liberate himself and his daughter Miranda from the island and restore Prospero to the Dukedom of Milan. *Tamburlaine, The Tempest*, and other works, like Shakespeare's *Othello*, are often interpreted as expressing Elizabethan racism. Conversely, Aphra Behn's novel, *Oroonoko; or, The Royal Slave* (1688), exploited the myth of the noble savage to depict European slave traders as the degenerate perpetrators of barbaric practices against innocent and virtuous Africans. Another significant and relatively early work in colonial literature is Daniel Defoe's *Robinson Crusoe* (1719). In postcolonial theory, Crusoe, who is shipwrecked on a deserted island, is a prototypical colonist, surviving by his ingenuity and bourgeois values; "civilizing" the island and one of its natives, whom he names Friday; and surviving the attacks of indigenous cannibals. Here, in miniature, is the colonial enterprise and myth: The superior intellect, fortitude, technology, and Protestant work ethic of the European outwits and overcomes the savage and uncivilized "native." Defoe's *Moll Flanders* (1722) capitalizes on another aspect of colonialism—the colony as a place of exile for British criminals. In this case, the criminal is Moll herself, a prostitute and thief, who is transported to the American colonies and there prospers and repents.

Traditional literary critics maintained that imperialist attitudes were seldom expressed in English literature written before 1870, although the existence of the colonies and the fortunes that could be made there sometimes formed the backgrounds of major novels by, for example, Jane Austen, Charles Dickens, and Charlotte Brontë. In these critics' view, Sir Thomas Bertram's sojourn in Antiqua in *Mansfield Park* (1814), or the fact that Pip's benefactor in *Great Expectations* (1861) is a returned convict from Australia, or that Rochester's first wife in *Jane Eyre* (1847) is a Creole from the West Indies are all more or less incidental to the novels in which they appear. Postcolonial theorists, however, have looked more closely at these and other works, and broadened the field of research to include political treatises, travel literature, adventure stories, and patriotic poetry to argue that pro-colonial, racist, and "civilizing" ideas were commonplace in British thought throughout the eighteenth and nineteenth centuries. Relatively few literary voices were raised against imperialism itself, although antislavery groups campaigned vigorously for the elimination of this practice; ironically, this campaign became an excuse for British domination in Africa. In other words, the prevailing ideology of the period accepted Britain's domination of India and other countries as right and just. Indeed, the supposed benefits of Christianity, science, industry, British law, and even European clothes and manners were accepted as justifications for the British Empire by most

British people. A corollary was that white colonies like Canada, Australia, and New Zealand were in a different category—inferior to Britain itself, but worthy of limited self-government. The rights of indigenous peoples in such colonies, on the other hand, were seldom considered.

While admitting that canonical imaginative literature directly or indirectly reinforced prevailing notions of white supremacy and the superiority of European institutions, it is nevertheless true that much of the direct support for imperialism came not from literary writers but from journalists, historians, travel writers, political thinkers, and economists. Thomas Babington Macaulay (1800–1859), for example, was a historian and newspaper columnist before he entered politics. In 1834 Macaulay joined the Supreme Council of India, from which position he shaped the legal and educational foundations of the Raj. The reformist zeal that led to greater economic and political democracy in Great Britain itself contributed to imperial ambitions by championing Jeremy Bentham's utilitarian ideas, which, among other attitudes, scorned as superstition the religious systems of Hinduism and African animism. John Stuart Mill, the champion of individual liberty, lamented that Europeans tended to regard the people of India as beneath contempt, but he paradoxically argued that the East India Company was India's most likely champion of progress. Scientists' work too was used to support imperialism. Charles Darwin's *On the Origin of Species* (1859), for example, was misused to justify the rule of "more highly evolved" white races over "primitive" darker ones, a theory that became known as scientific racism.

Moreover, pro-imperialist ideas were promulgated directly and effectively in the popular literature of the period. The adventure yarns of Captain Frederick Marryat (1792–1848) fueled the imaginations of young men for overseas adventure in exotic colonial countries. Marryat's influence is found in the stories of Robert Louis Stevenson, Joseph Conrad, and H. Rider Haggard, to name just three. Haggard was the most popular and effective pro-imperialist propagandist through such wildly popular romances as *King Solomon's Mines* (1886), *She* (1887), and *Allan Quatermain* (1887). Haggard's heroes were idealized as manly, sporting, chaste, brave, and ethical—the very qualities needed in young empire builders, according to the prevailing ethos of the day. Lesser imitators such as G. A. Henty and John Buchan picked up Haggard's themes and conventions in their own stories and novels. Many of Haggard's followers published in periodicals such as *Boy's Own*, which was aimed at young readers. Indeed, the influence of Haggard is difficult to overstate and yet is seldom acknowledged. Major writers such as Graham Greene and Somerset Maugham confess to having been deeply influenced by Haggard's adventure stories.

Since this is an anthology of short stories, it is important to point out that the British short story did not blossom until the late nineteenth century, even though the short story genre had been flourishing in the United States, France, and Russia since the 1820s. Victorian literature was dominated by the novel, and the short fiction that writers such as Dickens did produce tended to be longer, more diffuse, and less consciously artistic than short stories elsewhere. Marryat's "The Last Voyage of Huckaback" is typical. Although it stands alone as an independent story, it is part of a sequence of linked tales, somewhat in the manner of *The Thousand and One Arabian Nights*. The story follows the conventions of that collection in being narrated on a succession of evenings to a Middle Eastern potentate who frequently interrupts Huckaback's marvelous adventures with questions and comments. The stories are loosely constructed, remarkable mainly for their adventurous and exotic qualities, and offer little, if anything, by way of comment or thematic ideas.

Robert Louis Stevenson and Rudyard Kipling are among Britain's early practitioners of what we recognize today as the short story. Comparisons with Marryat's yarn will help make the distinction clear. Although both "The Beach of Falesá" and "The Man Who Would Be King" are, like "Huckaback," narrated in the first person to a listener, Stevenson's and Kipling's stories are tightly constructed and economically told. The characters are far beyond Marryat's stereotypes, and the stories are told not simply to fill an idle hour but to evoke the reader's thoughtful responses to their attitudes and ideas.

Through these and other writers, the development of the short story in England coincided with the new imperialism of 1870 onward, and Kipling was a major figure in both movements. The content and tone of Kipling's stories are often labeled chauvinistic and racist. Some critics, however, believe that Kipling has been unfairly labeled and simplistically read. These critics maintain that there is a consistent questioning or ironic undercurrent in Kipling's stories that undercuts or at least questions their apparently pro-colonialist stance.

No writer in this anthology has come in for more critical scrutiny than Joseph Conrad. Hundreds of critics have examined "Heart of Darkness" from every possible point of view, and no critical consensus seems likely soon. Most readings until relatively recently stressed the story's psychological and moral dimensions, with the journey into Africa's interior being seen as parallel to the journey into Marlow's and Kurtz's inner beings. More recent readings have stressed the story's contribution to the colonial debate. Many postcolonial critics see the story as at best a mild criticism of some of King Leopold's excesses in the Congo, while others regard the story as racist and rampantly pro-imperialist. Superficially, too, Conrad's fictional techniques resemble those of his predecessors, for Marlow resembles the other first-person narrators by spinning an adventure yarn of exploration and conquest. But such are Conrad's stylistic and narrative resources that he takes us more deeply into the experience than do any of his predecessors. For this and other reasons, Conrad's story is at the heart of postcolonial debates about the function and meaning of literature and its significance in the imperialism of the 1870–1914 period.

Alice Perrin was another contemporary of Kipling's and shared the Anglo-Indian experience. She too attempted in her fiction to communicate something of that experience to readers, some of whom were Anglo-Indians and others of whom were in England, far from the heat and dust of India. Like Kipling, she generally supported the Raj, but she too understood at least some of its limitations. A generation later, George Orwell would join the thousands of public school graduates who worked in the colonial administration—the only British writer of note to do so. Orwell's "A Hanging" is usually classified as an essay, although from its beginnings the short story shares features with the informal essay, such as frequent use of narrative and character development. Like Stevenson, Kipling, and Perrin, Orwell was ambivalent about imperialism, and the climactic moment in this story brings a crucial insight into the cruel side of Britain's administration in Burma.

The remaining stories illustrate growing disillusion with imperialism. Like Orwell, William Plomer left school and went directly to a colonial territory, though not as a government official but as an aspiring entrepreneur. His "A Child of Queen Victoria" is a coming-of-age story, an innocence-to-experience journey leading, as so many such stories do, to a moment of disillusionment and heartache. It is also a challenge to prevailing racial attitudes and thus a questioning of some of the assumptions and stereotypes that underlay the imperialist creed. Leonard Woolf's "Pearls and Swine" is even more direct in its criticism of colonialism.

The short stories included in this section cannot hope to capture all the complexities and issues raised by Great Britain's domination of one of the world's largest empires. Nevertheless, they are a rich repository of the attitudes and values held by some of those who observed the imperial venture at very close range, and they serve to put a human face on what otherwise could be impersonal historical events. If we claim to be able to see more clearly than the characters in these stories, or even their authors, perhaps we would do well to remind ourselves that the imperial impulse has not died, but only taken somewhat different forms.

Robert Louis Stevenson

(1850–1894)

The reputation of Robert Louis Stevenson provides something of a barometer of changing literary fashions over the twentieth century. At his death, Stevenson was hailed as one of the great writers of his age, but detractors regard him as primarily a writer for children and young readers for his *Child's Garden of Verses* (1885) and *Treasure Island* (1883), or as the lightweight author of Gothic thrillers like *The Strange Case of Dr. Jekyll and Mr. Hyde* (1886).

He was born in Edinburgh, Scotland, into a family of lighthouse architects and engineers, and was expected to follow in the family's business. However, ill health (he suffered much of his life from tuberculosis) dictated a less strenuous profession, and at his father's insistence he studied law, though he never practiced. Over his father's objections, he insisted on becoming a writer and, in spite of his health, traveled widely—first on the continent, then in the United States, and finally in the South Seas. While in France in 1876, Stevenson fell in love with Mrs. Fanny Osbourne, who was still married at the time. Two years later, at the peril of his health, Stevenson followed her to California, where she divorced her husband and married Stevenson in 1880. They spent the rest of their married life searching for a climate compatible with Stevenson's physical ailments, finally settling in Samoa in 1889. Samoa at the time was used as a coaling station by U.S., British, and German ships, and these countries essentially took over the islands as "protectorates," usurping the powers of King Mataafa. Stevenson vigorously defended the deposed king and attacked the Western powers who had taken control of the territory.

"The Beach of Falesá" is regarded by some as the first true short story by a British writer, but whatever the validity of that claim, it is remarkable for its daring moral stance—tolerance for a "mixed" marriage. (Reference to the marriage certificate was dropped in early printed editions, and the issue was hotly debated by Stevenson's publishers.) It is also unsparing in its depiction of the economic exploitation of Samoans. Unlike many of his Victorian contemporaries who believed optimistically in man's moral progress and who used literature as an instrument of moral uplift, Stevenson probed the dark side of the psyche and often created morally ambiguous protagonists.

Stevenson's support for Samoan independence won him the affection of the islands' people, and "The Beach of Falesá" is among the earliest stories to deal directly with the moral and practical issues of interracial marriage and colonial exploitation.

The Beach of Falesá   1882

Chapter I   A South-Sea Bridal

I saw that island first when it was neither night nor morning. The moon was to the west, setting, but still broad and bright. To the east, and right amidships of the dawn, which was all pink, the day-star sparkled like a diamond. The land breeze blew in our faces, and smelt strong of wild lime and vanilla; other things besides, but these were the most plain; and the chill of it set me sneezing. I should say I had been for years on a low island near the line,[1] living for the most part solitary among natives. Here was a fresh experience; even the tongue would be quite strange to me; and the look of these woods and mountains, and the rare smell of them, renewed my blood.

The captain blew out the binnacle-lamp.

"There!" said he, "there goes a bit of smoke, Mr. Wiltshire, behind the break of the reef. That's Falesá, where your station is, the last village to the east; nobody lives to windward—I don't know why. Take my glass, and you can make the houses out."

I took the glass; and the shores leaped nearer, and I saw the tangle of the woods and the breach of the surf, and the brown roofs and the black insides of houses peeped among the trees.

---

1 **the line:** The equator.

"Do you catch a bit of white there to the east'ard?" the captain continued. "That's your house. Coral built, stands high, veranda you could walk on three abreast; best station in the South Pacific. When old Adams saw it, he took and shook me by the hand. 'I've dropped into a soft thing here,' says he. 'So you have,' says I, 'and time too!' Poor Johnny! I never saw him again but the once, and then he had changed his tune—couldn't get on with the natives, or the whites, or something; and the next time we came round there, he was dead and buried. I took and put up a bit of a stick to him: 'John Adams, *obit* eighteen and sixty-eight. Go thou and do likewise.' I missed that man. I never could see much harm in Johnny."

"What did he die of?" I inquired.

"Some kind of sickness," says the captain. "It appears it took him sudden. Seems he got up in the night, and filled up on Pain Killer and Kennedy's Discovery.[2] No go—he was booked beyond Kennedy. Then he had tried to open a case of gin. No go again—not strong enough. Then he must have turned to and run out on the veranda, and capsized over the rail. When they found him, the next day, he was clean crazy—carried on all the time about somebody watering his copra.[3] Poor John!"

"Was it thought to be the island?" I asked.

"Well, it was thought to be the island, or the trouble, or something," he replied. "I never could hear but what it was a healthy place. Our last man, Vigours, never turned a hair. He left because of the beach—said he was afraid of Black Jack and Case and Whistling Jimmie, who was still alive at the time, but got drowned soon afterward when drunk. As for old Captain Randall, he's been here any time since eighteen-forty, forty-five. I never could see much harm in Billy, nor much change. Seems as if he might live to be Old Kafoozleum.[4] No, I guess it's healthy."

"There's a boat coming now," said I. "She's right in the pass; looks to be a sixteen-foot whale; two white men in the stern-sheets."

"That's the boat that drowned Whistling Jimmie!" cried the captain; "let's see the glass. Yes, that's Case, sure enough, and the darkie. They've got a gallows bad reputation, but you know what a place the beach[5] is for talking. My belief, that Whistling Jimmie was the worst of the trouble; and he's gone to glory, you see. What'll you bet they ain't after gin? Lay you five to two they take six cases."

When these two traders came aboard I was pleased with the looks of them at once, or, rather, with the looks of both, and the speech of one. I was sick for white neighbours after my four years at the line, which I always counted years of prison; getting tabooed, and going down to the Speak House to see and get it taken off; buying gin and going on a break, and then repenting; sitting in the house at night with the lamp for company; or walking on the beach and wondering what kind of a fool to call myself for being where I was. There were no other whites upon my island, and when I sailed to the next, rough customers made the most of the society. Now to see

---

2 **Pain Killer and Kennedy's Discovery:** Patent medicines.
3 **copra:** Dried cocoanut meat, usually used as a source of oil.
4 **Old Kafoozleum:** A mistake for Methuselah, who, according to Genesis 5:27, lived 969 years.
5 **the beach:** Because most whites lived on the coast, the term refers to the white community.

these two when they came aboard was a pleasure. One was a negro, to be sure; but they were both rigged out smart in striped pajamas and straw hats, and Case would have passed muster in a city. He was yellow and smallish, had a hawk's nose to his face, pale eyes, and his beard trimmed with scissors. No man knew his country, beyond he was of English speech; and it was clear he came of a good family and was splendidly educated. He was accomplished too; played the accordion first rate; and give him a piece of a string or a cork or a pack of cards, and he could show you tricks equal to any professional. He could speak, when he chose, fit for a drawing-room; and when he chose he could blaspheme worse than a Yankee boatswain, and talk smart to sicken a Kanaka.[6] The way he thought would pay best at the moment, that was Case's way, and it always seemed to come natural, and like as if he was born to it. He had the courage of a lion and the cunning of a rat; and if he's not in hell to-day, there's no such place. I know but one good point to the man—that he was fond of his wife, and kind to her. She was a Samoa woman, and dyed her hair red—Samoa style; and when he came to die (as I have to tell of) they found one strange thing— that he had made a will, like a Christian, and the widow got the lot; all his, they said, and all Black Jack's, and the most of Billy Randall's in the bargain, for it was Case that kept the books. So she went off home in the schooner Manu'a, and does the lady to this day in her own place.

But of all this on that first morning I knew no more than a fly. Case used me like a gentleman and like a friend, made me welcome to Falesá, and put his services at my disposal, which was the more helpful from my ignorance of the natives. All the better part of the day we sat drinking better acquaintance in the cabin, and I never heard a man talk more to the point. There was no smarter trader, and none dodgier, in the islands. I thought Falesá seemed to be the right kind of a place; and the more I drank the lighter my heart. Our last trader had fled the place at half an hour's notice, taking a chance passage in a labor ship from up west. The captain, when he came, had found the station closed, the keys left with the native pastor, and a letter from the runaway, confessing he was fairly frightened of his life. Since then the firm had not been represented, and of course there was no cargo. The wind, besides, was fair, the captain hoped he could make his next island by dawn, with a good tide, and the business of landing my trade was gone about lively. There was no call for me to fool with it, Case said; nobody would touch my things, everyone was honest in Falesá, only about chickens or an odd knife or an odd stick of tobacco; and the best I could do was to sit quiet till the vessel left, then come straight to his house, see old Captain Randall, the father of the beach, take pot-luck, and go home to sleep when it got dark. So it was high noon, and the schooner was under way before I set my foot on shore at Falesá.

I had a glass or two on board; I was just off a long cruise, and the ground heaved under me like a ship's deck. The world was like all new painted; my foot went along to music; Falesá might have been Fiddler's Green,[7] if there is such a place, and more's

6 **Kanaka:** A derogatory term used by whites to refer to South Sea natives.
7 **Fiddler's Green:** A sailors' legendary heaven, characterized by wine, women, and song.

the pity if there isn't! It was good to foot the grass, to look aloft at the green mountains, to see the men with their green wreaths and the women in their bright dresses, red and blue. On we went, in the strong sun and the cool shadow, liking both; and all the children in the town came trotting after with their shaven heads and their brown bodies, and raising a thin kind of a cheer in our wake, like crowing poultry.

"By the bye," says Case, "we must get you a wife."

"That's so," said I; "I had forgotten."

There was a crowd of girls about us, and I pulled myself up and looked among them like a bashaw.[8] They were all dressed out for the sake of the ship being in; and the women of Falesá are a handsome lot to see. If they have a fault, they are a trifle broad in the beam; and I was just thinking so when Case touched me.

"That's pretty," says he.

I saw one coming on the other side alone. She had been fishing; all she wore was a chemise, and it was wetted through. She was young and very slender for an island maid, with a long face, a high forehead, and a shy, strange, blindish look, between a cat's and a baby's.

"Who's she?" said I. "She'll do."

"That's Uma," said Case, and he called her up and spoke to her in the native. I didn't know what he said; but when he was in the midst she looked up at me quick and timid, like a child dodging a blow, then down again, and presently smiled. She had a wide mouth, the lips and the chin cut like any statue's; and the smile came out for a moment and was gone. Then she stood with her head bent, and heard Case to an end, spoke back in the pretty Polynesian voice, looking him full in the face, heard him again in answer, and then with an obeisance started off. I had just a share of the bow, but never another shot of her eye, and there was no more word of smiling.

"I guess it's all right," said Case. "I guess you can have her. I'll make it square with the old lady. You can have your pick of the lot for a plug of tobacco," he added, sneering.

I suppose it was the smile that stuck in my memory, for I spoke back sharp. "She doesn't look that sort," I cried.

"I don't know that she is," said Case. "I believe she's as right as the mail. Keeps to herself, don't go round with the gang, and that. Oh, no, don't you misunderstand me—Uma's on the square." He spoke eager, I thought, and that surprised and pleased me. "Indeed," he went on, "I shouldn't make so sure of getting her, only she cottoned to the cut of your jib. All you have to do is to keep dark and let me work the mother my own way; and I'll bring the girl round to the captain's for the marriage."

I didn't care for the word marriage, and I said so.

"Oh, there's nothing to hurt in the marriage," says he. "Black Jack's the chaplain."

By this time we had come in view of the house of these three white men; for a negro is counted a white man, and so is a Chinese! A strange idea, but common in

---

8 **bashaw:** An early form of the Turkish title, *Pasha*—a high official.

the islands. It was a board house with a strip of rickety veranda. The store was to the front, with a counter, scales, and the finest possible display of trade: a case or two of tinned meats; a barrel of hard bread, a few bolts of cotton stuff, not to be compared with mine; the only thing well represented being the contraband firearms and liquor. "If these are my only rivals," thinks I, "I should do well in Falesá." Indeed, there was only the one way they could touch me, and that was with the guns and drink.

In the back room was old Captain Randall, squatting on the floor native fashion, fat and pale, naked to the waist, grey as a badger, and his eyes set with drink. His body was covered with gray hair and crawled over by flies; one was in the corner of his eye—he never heeded; and the mosquitoes hummed about the man like bees. Any clean-minded man would have had the creature out at once and buried him; and to see him, and think he was seventy, and remember he had once commanded a ship, and come ashore in his smart togs, and talked big in bars and consulates, and sat in club verandas, turned me sick and sober.

He tried to get up when I came in, but that was hopeless; so he reached me a hand instead, and stumbled out some salutation.

"Papa's pretty full this morning," observed Case. "We've had an epidemic here; and Captain Randall takes gin for a prophylactic⁹—don't you, papa?"

"Never took such a thing in my life!" cried the captain, indignantly. "Take gin for my health's sake, Mr. Wha's-ever-your-name— 's a precautionary measure."

"That's all right, papa," said Case. "But you'll have to brace up. There's going to be a marriage—Mr. Wiltshire here is going to get spliced."

The old man asked to whom.

"To Uma," said Case.

"Uma!" cried the captain. "Wha's he want Uma for? 's he come here for his health, anyway? Wha' 'n hell's he want Uma for?"

"Dry up, papa," said Case. " 'Tain't you that's to marry her. I guess you're not her godfather and godmother. I guess Mr. Wiltshire's going to please himself."

With that he made an excuse to me that he must move about the marriage, and left me alone with the poor wretch that was his partner and (to speak truth) his gull.¹⁰ Trade and station belonged both to Randall; Case and the negro were parasites; they crawled and fed upon him like the flies, he none the wiser. Indeed, I have no harm to say of Billy Randall beyond the fact that my gorge rose at him, and the time I now passed in his company was like a nightmare.

The room was stifling hot and full of flies; for the house was dirty and low and small, and stood in a bad place, behind the village, in the borders of the bush, and sheltered from the trade. The three men's beds were on the floor, and a litter of pans and dishes. There was no standing furniture; Randall, when he was violent, tearing it to laths. There I sat and had a meal which was served us by Case's wife; and there I was entertained all day by that remains of man, his tongue stumbling among low old

9 **prophylactic:** Any preventative against disease.
10 **gull:** Fool; dupe.

jokes and long old stories, and his own wheezy laughter always ready, so that he had no sense of my depression. He was nipping gin all the while. Sometimes he fell asleep, and awoke again, whimpering and shivering, and every now and again he would ask me why I wanted to marry Uma. "My friend," I was telling myself all day, "you must not come to be an old gentleman like this."

It might be four in the afternoon, perhaps, when the back door was thrust slowly open, and a strange old native woman crawled into the house almost on her belly. She was swathed in black stuff to her heels; her hair was gray in swatches; her face was tattooed, which was not the practice in that island; her eyes big and bright and crazy. These she fixed upon me with a rapt expression that I saw to be part acting. She said no plain word, but smacked and mumbled with her lips, and hummed aloud, like a child over its Christmas pudding. She came straight across the house, heading for me, and, as soon as she was alongside, caught up my hand and purred and crooned over it like a great cat. From this she slipped into a kind of song.

"Who the devil's this?" cried I, for the thing startled me.

"It's Faavao," says Randall; and I saw he had hitched along the floor into the farthest corner.

"You ain't afraid of her?" I cried.

"Me 'fraid!" cried the captain. "My dear friend, I defy her! I don't let her put her foot in here, only I suppose 's different to-day for the marriage. 's Uma's mother."

"Well, suppose it is; what's she carrying on about?" I asked, more irritated, perhaps more frightened, than I cared to show; and the captain told me she was making up a quantity of poetry in my praise because I was to marry Uma. "All right, old lady," says I, with rather a failure of a laugh, "anything to oblige. But when you're done with my hand, you might let me know."

She did as though she understood; the song rose into a cry, and stopped; the woman crouched out of the house the same way that she came in, and must have plunged straight into the bush, for when I followed her to the door she had already vanished.

"These are rum manners," said I.

" 'S a rum crowd," said the captain, and, to my surprise, he made the sign of the cross on his bare bosom.

"Hillo!" says I, "are you a Papist?"

He repudiated the idea with contempt. "Hard-shell Baptis' " said he. "But, my dear friend, the Papists got some good ideas too; and th' 's one of 'em. You take my advice, and whenever you come across Uma or Faavao or Vigours, or any of that crowd, you take a leaf out o' the priests, and do what I do. Savvy?" says he, repeated the sign, and winked his dim eye at me. "No, *sir!*" he broke out again, "no Papists here!" and for a long time entertained me with his religious opinions.

I must have been taken with Uma from the first, or I should certainly have fled from that house, and got into the clean air, and the clean sea, or some convenient river—though, it's true, I was committed to Case; and, besides, I could never have held my head up in that island if I had run from a girl upon my wedding-night.

The sun was down, the sky all on fire, and the lamp had been some time lighted, when Case came back with Uma and the negro. She was dressed and scented; her kilt was of fine tapa, looking richer in the folds than any silk; her bust, which was of the color of dark honey, she wore bare, only for some half a dozen necklaces of seeds and flowers; and behind her ears and in her hair she had the scarlet flowers of the hibiscus. She showed the best bearing for a bride conceivable, serious and still; and I thought shame to stand up with her in that mean house and before that grinning negro. I thought shame, I say; for the mountebank[11] was dressed with a big paper collar, the book he made believe to read from was an odd volume of a novel, and the words of his service not fit to be set down. My conscience smote me when we joined hands; and when she got her certificate I was tempted to throw up the bargain and confess. Here is the document. It was Case that wrote it, signatures and all, in a leaf out of the ledger:

> This is to certify that Uma, daughter of Faavao of Falesá, Island of —, is illegally married to Mr. John Wiltshire, and Mr. John Wiltshire is at liberty to send her packing when he pleases.
>
> JOHN BLACKAMOAR,
> Chaplain to the Hulks.
>
> Extracted from the Register
> by William T. Randall,
> Master Mariner.

A nice paper to put in a girl's hand and see her hide away like gold. A man might easily feel cheap for less. But it was the practice in these parts, and (as I told myself) not the least the fault of us white men, but of the missionaries. If they had let the natives be, I had never needed this deception, but taken all the wives I wished, and left them when I pleased, with a clear conscience.

The more ashamed I was, the more hurry I was in to be gone; and our desires thus jumping together, I made the less remark of a change in the traders. Case had been all eagerness to keep me; now, as though he had attained a purpose, he seemed all eagerness to have me go. Uma, he said, could show me to my house, and the three bade us farewell indoors.

The night was nearly come; the village smelt of trees and flowers and the sea and bread-fruit-cooking; there came a fine roll of sea from the reef, and from a distance, among the woods and houses, many pretty sounds of men and children. It did me good to breathe free air; it did me good to be done with the captain, and see, instead, the creature at my side. I felt for all the world as though she were some girl at home in the Old Country, and forgetting myself for the minute, took her hand to walk with. Her fingers nestled into mine, I heard her breathe deep and quick, and all at once she caught my hand to her face and pressed it there. "You good!" she cried, and ran ahead of me, and stopped and looked back and smiled, and ran ahead of me

---

11 **mountebank:** Imposter.

again, thus guiding me through the edge of the bush, and by a quiet way to my own house.

The truth is, Case had done the courting for me in style—told her I was mad to have her, and cared nothing for the consequences; and the poor soul, knowing that which I was still ignorant of, believed it, every word, and had her head nigh turned with vanity and gratitude. Now, of all this I had no guess; I was one of those most opposed to any nonsense about native women, having seen so many whites eaten up by their wives' relatives, and made fools of into the bargain; and I told myself I must make a stand at once, and bring her to her bearings. But she looked so quaint and pretty as she ran away and then awaited me, and the thing was done so like a child or a kind dog, that the best I could do was just to follow her whenever she went on, to listen for the fall of her bare feet, and to watch in the dusk for the shining of her body. And there was another thought came in my head. She played kitten with me now when we were alone; but in the house she had carried it the way a countess might, so proud and humble. And what with her dress—for all there was so little of it, and that native enough—what with her fine tapa[12] and fine scents, and her red flowers and seeds, that were quite as bright as jewels, only larger—it came over me she was a kind of countess really, dressed to hear great singers at a concert, and no even mate for a poor trader like myself.

She was the first in the house; and while I was still without I saw a match flash and the lamplight kindle in the windows. The station was a wonderful fine place, coral built, with quite a wide veranda, and the main room high and wide. My chests and cases had been piled in, and made rather of a mess; and there, in the thick of the confusion, stood Uma by the table, awaiting me. Her shadow went all the way up behind her into the hollow of the iron roof; she stood against it bright, the lamplight shining on her skin. I stopped in the door, and she looked at me, not speaking, with eyes that were eager and yet daunted; then she touched herself on the bosom.

"Me—your wifie," she said. It had never taken me like that before; but the want of her took and shook all through me, like the wind in the luff of a sail.

I could not speak if I had wanted; and if I could, I would not. I was ashamed to be so much moved about a native, ashamed of the marriage too, and the certificate she had treasured in her kilt; and I turned aside and made believe to rummage among my cases. The first thing I lighted on was a case of gin, the only one that I had brought; and partly for the girl's sake, and partly for horror of the recollections of old Randall, took a sudden resolve. I pried the lid off. One by one I drew the bottles with a pocket corkscrew, and sent Uma out to pour the stuff from the veranda.

She came back after the last, and looked at me puzzled like.

"No good," said I, for I was now a little better master of my tongue. "Man he drink, he no good."

She agreed with this, but kept considering. "Why you bring him?" she asked, presently. "Suppose you no want drink, you no bring him, I think."

---

12 **tapa:** A coarse cloth of pounded bark, common in the South Seas.

"That's all right," said I. "One time I want drink too much; now no want. You see, I no savvy, I get one little wifie. Suppose I drink gin, my little wifie be 'fraid."

To speak to her kindly was about more than I was fit for; I had made my vow I would never let on to weakness with a native, and I had nothing for it but to stop.

She stood looking gravely down at me where I sat by the open case. "I think you good man," she said. And suddenly she had fallen before me on the floor. "I belong you all-e-same pig!" she cried.

Chapter II   The Ban

I came on the veranda just before the sun rose on the morrow. My house was the last on the east; there was a cape of woods and cliffs behind that hid the sunrise. To the west, a swift, cold river ran down, and beyond was the green of the village, dotted with cocoa-palms and bread-fruits and houses. The shutters were some of them down and some open; I saw the mosquito bars still stretched, with shadows of people new-awakened sitting up inside; and all over the green others were stalking silent, wrapped in their many-coloured sleeping clothes, like Bedouins in Bible pictures. It was mortal still and solemn and chilly, and the light of the dawn on the lagoon was like the shining of a fire.

But the thing that troubled me was nearer hand. Some dozen young men and children made a piece of a half-circle, flanking my house: the river divided them, some were on the near side, some on the far, and one on a boulder in the midst; and they all sat silent, wrapped in their sheets, and stared at me and my house as straight as pointer dogs. I thought it strange as I went out. When I had bathed and come back again, and found them all there, and two or three more along with them, I thought it stranger still. What could they see to gaze at in my house I wondered, and went in.

But the thought of these starers stuck in my mind, and presently I came out again. The sun was now up, but it was still behind the cape of woods. Say a quarter of an hour had come and gone. The crowd was greatly increased, the far bank of the river was lined for quite a way—perhaps thirty grown folk, and of children twice as many, some standing, some squatted on the ground, and all staring at my house. I have seen a house in a South-Sea village thus surrounded, but then a trader was thrashing his wife inside, and she singing out. Here was nothing—the stove was alight, the smoke going up in a Christian manner; all was shipshape and Bristol fashion. To be sure, there was a stranger come, but they had a chance to see that stranger yesterday, and took it quiet enough. What ailed them now? I leaned my arms on the rail and stared back. Devil a wink they had in them! Now and then I could see the children chatter, but they spoke so low not even the hum of their speaking came my length. The rest were like graven images: they stared at me, dumb and sorrowful, with their bright eyes; and it came upon me things would look not much different if I were on the platform of the gallows, and these good folk had come to see me hanged.

I felt I was getting daunted, and began to be afraid I looked it, which would never do. Up I stood, made believe to stretch myself, came down the veranda stair, and strolled toward the river. There went a short buzz from one to the other, like what you hear in theatres when the curtain goes up; and some of the nearest gave back the matter of a pace. I saw a girl lay one hand on a young man and make a gesture upward with the other; at the same time she said something in the native with a gasping voice. Three little boys sat beside my path, where I must pass within three feet of them. Wrapped in their sheets, with their shaved heads and bits of topknots, and queer faces, they looked like figures on a chimney-piece. Awhile they sat their ground, solemn as judges. I came up hand over fist, doing my five knots, like a man that meant business; and I thought I saw a sort of a wink and gulp in the three faces. Then one jumped up (he was the farthest off) and ran for his mammy. The other two, trying to follow suit, got foul, came to the ground together bawling, wriggled right out of their sheets, and in a moment there were all three of them scampering for their lives, and singing out like pigs. The natives, who would never let a joke slip, even at a burial, laughed and let up, as short as a dog's bark.

They say it scares a man to be alone. No such thing. What scares him in the dark or the high bush is that he can't make sure, and there might be an army at his elbow. What scares him worst is to be right in the midst of a crowd, and have no guess of what they're driving at. When that laugh stopped, I stopped too. The boys had not yet made their offing; they were still on the full stretch going the one way, when I had already gone about ship and was sheering off the other. Like a fool I had come out, doing my five knots; like a fool I went back again. It must have been the funniest thing to see, and what knocked me silly, this time no one laughed; only one old woman gave a kind of pious moan, the way you have heard Dissenters in their chapels at the sermon.

"I never saw such fools of Kanakas as your people here," I said once to Uma, glancing out of the window at the starers.

"Savvy nothing," says Uma, with a kind of disgusted air that she was good at.

And that was all the talk we had upon the matter, for I was put out, and Uma took the thing so much as a matter of course that I was fairly ashamed.

All day, off and on, now fewer and now more, the fools sat about the west end of my house and across the river, waiting for the show, whatever that was—fire to come down from heaven, I suppose, and consume me, bones and baggage. But by evening, like real islanders, they had wearied of the business, and got away, and had a dance instead in the big house of the village, where I heard them singing and clapping hands till, maybe, ten at night, and the next day it seemed they had forgotten I existed. If fire had come down from heaven or the earth opened and swallowed me, there would have been nobody to see the sport or take the lesson, or whatever you like to call it. But I was to find they hadn't forgot either, and kept an eye lifting for phenomena over my way.

I was hard at it both these days getting my trade in order and taking stock of what Vigours had left. This was a job that made me pretty sick, and kept me from thinking on much else. Ben had taken stock the trip before—I knew I could trust Ben—but it was plain somebody had been making free in the meantime. I found I was out by what might easily cover six months' salary and profit, and I could have kicked myself all round the village to have been such a blamed ass, sitting boozing with that Case instead of attending to my own affairs and taking stock.

However, there's no use crying over spilt milk. It was done now, and couldn't be undone. All I could do was to get what was left of it, and my new stuff (my own choice) in order, to go round and get after the rats and cockroaches, and to fix up that store regular Sydney style. A fine show I made of it; and the third morning, when I had lit my pipe and stood in the doorway and looked in, and turned and looked far up the mountain and saw the cocoa-nuts waving and posted up the tons of copra, and over the village green and saw the island dandies and reckoned up the yards of print they wanted for their kilts and dresses, I felt as if I was in the right place to make a fortune, and go home again and start a public-house.[13] There was I, sitting in that veranda, in as handsome a piece of scenery as you could find, a splendid sun, and a fine, fresh, healthy trade that stirred up a man's blood like sea-bathing; and the whole thing was clean gone from me, and I was dreaming England, which is, after all, a nasty, cold, muddy hole, with not enough light to see to read by; and dreaming the looks of my public, by a cant of a broad high-road like an avenue and with the sign on a green tree.

So much for the morning, but the day passed and the devil anyone looked near me, and from all I knew of natives in other islands I thought this strange. People laughed a little at our firm and their fine stations, and at this station of Falesá in particular; all the copra in the district wouldn't pay for it (I heard them say) in fifty years, which I supposed was an exaggeration. But when the day went, and no business came at all, I began to get downhearted; and, about three in the afternoon, I went out for a stroll to cheer me up. On the green I saw a white man coming with a cassook on, by which and by the face of him I knew he was a priest. He was a good-natured old soul to look at, gone a little grizzled, and so dirty you could have written with him on a piece of paper.

"Good-day, sir," said I.

He answered me eagerly in native.

"Don't you speak any English?" said I.

"French," says he.

"Well," said I, "I'm sorry, but I can't do anything there."

He tried me a while in the French, and then again in native, which he seemed to think was the best chance. I made out he was after more than passing the time of day with me, but had something to communicate, and I listened the harder. I heard the names of Adams and Case and of Randall—Randall the oftenest—and the word "poison," or something like it, and a native word that he said very often. I went home, repeating it to myself.

"What does fussy-ocky mean?" I asked of Uma, for that was as near as I could come to it.

"Make dead," said she.

13 **public-house:** A pub or tavern.

"The devil it does!" says I. "Did ever you hear that Case had poisoned Johnny Adams?"

"Every man he savvy that," says Uma, scornful-like. "Give him white sand—bad sand. He got the bottle still. Suppose he give you gin, you no take him."

Now I had heard much the same sort of story in other islands, and the same white powder always to the front, which made me think the less of it. For all that, I went over to Randall's place to see what I could pick up, and found Case on the doorstep, cleaning a gun.

"Good shooting here?" says I.

"A 1," says he. "The bush is full of all kinds of birds. I wish copra was as plenty," says he—I thought, slyly—"but there don't seem anything doing."

I could see Black Jack in the store, serving a customer.

"That looks like business, though," said I.

"That's the first sale we've made in three weeks," said he.

"You don't tell me?" says I. "Three weeks? Well, well."

"If you don't believe me," he cries, a little hot, "you can go and look at the copra-house. It's half empty to this blessed hour."

"I shouldn't be much the better for that, you see," says I. "For all I can tell, it might have been whole empty yesterday."

"That's so," says he, with a bit of a laugh.

"By the by," I said, "what sort of a party is that priest? Seems rather a friendly sort."

At this Case laughed right out loud. "Ah!" says he, "I see what ails you now. Galuchet's been at you." *Father Galoshes* was the name he went by most, but Case always gave it the French quirk, which was another reason we had for thinking him above the common.

"Yes, I have seen him," I says. "I made out he didn't think much of your Captain Randall."

"That he don't!" says Case. "It was the trouble about poor Adams. The last day, when he lay dying, there was young Buncombe round. Ever met Buncombe?"

I told him no.

"He's a cure, is Buncombe!" laughs Case. "Well, Buncombe took it in his head that, as there was no other clergyman about, bar Kanaka pastors, we ought to call in Father Galuchet, and have the old man administered and take the sacrament. It was all the same to me, you may suppose; but I said I thought Adams was the fellow to consult. He was jawing away about watered copra and a sight of foolery. 'Look here,' I said, 'you're pretty sick. Would you like to see Galoshes?' He sat right up on his elbow. 'Get the priest,' says he, 'get the priest; don't let me die here like a dog!' He spoke kind of fierce and eager, but sensible enough. There was nothing to say against that, so we sent and asked Galuchet if he would come. You bet he would. He jumped in his dirty linen at the thought of it. But we had reckoned without Papa. He's a hard-shelled Baptist, is Papa; no Papists need apply. And he took and locked the door. Buncombe told him he was bigoted, and I thought he would have had a fit. 'Bigoted!' he says. 'Me bigoted? Have I lived to hear it from a jackanapes like you?'

And he made for Buncombe, and I had to hold them apart; and there was Adams in the middle, gone luny again, and carrying on about copra like a born fool. It was good as the play, and I was about knocked out of time with laughing, when all of a sudden Adams sat up, clapped his hands to his chest, and went into the horrors. He died hard, did John Adams," says Case, with a kind of a sudden sternness.

"And what became of the priest?" I asked.

"The priest?" says Case. "Oh! he was hammering on the door outside, and crying on the natives to come and beat it in, and singing out it was a soul he wished to save, and that. He was in a rare taking, was the priest. But what would you have? Johnny had slipped his cable; no more Johnny in the market; and the administration racket clean played out. Next thing, word came to Randall that the priest was praying upon Johnny's grave. Papa was pretty full, and got a club, and lit out straight for the place, and there was Galoshes on his knees, and a lot of natives looking on. You wouldn't think Papa cared that much about anything, unless it was liquor; but he and the priest stuck to it two hours, slanging each other in native, and every time Galoshes tried to kneel down Papa went for him with the club. There never were such larks in Falesá. The end of it was that Captain Randall knocked over with some kind of a fit or stroke, and the priest got in his goods after all. But he was the angriest priest you ever heard of, and complained to the chiefs about the outrage, as he called it. That was no account, for our chiefs are Protestant here; and, anyway, he had been making trouble about the drum for morning school, and they were glad to give him a wipe. Now he swears old Randall gave Adams poison or something, and when the two meet they grin at each other like baboons."

He told this story as natural as could be, and like a man that enjoyed the fun; though now I come to think of it after so long, it seems rather a sickening yarn. However, Case never set up to be soft, only to be square and hearty, and a man all round; and, to tell the truth, he puzzled me entirely.

I went home and asked Uma if she were a Popey, which I had made out to be the native word for Catholics.

"*E le ai!*" says she. She always used the native when she meant "no" more than usually strong, and, indeed, there's more of it. "No good Popey," she added.

Then I asked her about Adams and the priest, and she told me much the same yarn in her own way. So that I was left not much farther on, but inclined, upon the whole, to think the bottom of the matter was the row about the sacrament, and the poisoning only talk.

The next day was a Sunday, when there was no business to be looked for. Uma asked me in the morning if I was going to "pray;" I told her she bet not, and she stopped home herself, with no more words. I thought this seemed unlike a native, and a native woman, and a woman that had new clothes to show off; however, it suited me to the ground, and I made the less of it. The queer thing was that I came next door to going to church after all, a thing I'm little likely to forget. I had turned out for a stroll, and heard the hymn tune up. You know how it is. If you hear folk singing, it seems to draw you; and pretty soon I found myself alongside the church. It was a little, long, low place, coral built, rounded off at both ends like a whaleboat, a big native roof on the top of it, windows without sashes and doorways without doors. I stuck my head into one of the windows, and the sight was so new to me—for things went quite different in the islands I was acquainted with—that I stayed and looked on. The congregation sat on the floor on mats, the women on one side, the men on the other, all rigged out to kill—the women with dresses and trade hats, the men in white jackets and shirts. The hymn was over; the pastor, a big buck Kanaka, was in the pulpit, preaching for his life; and by the way he wagged his hand, and worked his voice, and made his points, and seemed to argue with the folk, I made out he was a gun at the business. Well, he looked up suddenly and caught my eye, and I give you my word he staggered in the pulpit; his eyes bulged out of his head, his hand rose and pointed at me like as if against his will, and the sermon stopped right there.

It isn't a fine thing to say for yourself, but I ran away; and, if the same kind of a shock was given me, I should run away again to-morrow. To see that palavering Kanaka struck all of a heap at the mere sight of me gave me a feeling as if the bottom had dropped out of the world. I went right home, and stayed there, and said nothing. You might think I would tell Uma, but that was against my system. You might have thought I would have gone over and consulted Case; but the truth was I was ashamed to speak of such a thing, I thought everyone would blurt out laughing in my face. So I held my tongue, and thought all the more; and the more I thought, the less I liked the business.

By Monday night I got it clearly in my head I must be tabooed. A new store to stand open two days in a village and not a man or woman come to see the trade, was past believing.

"Uma," said I, "I think I'm tabooed."

"I think so," said she.

I thought a while whether I should ask her more, but it's a bad idea to set natives up with any notion of consulting them, so I went to Case. It was dark, and he was sitting alone, as he did mostly, smoking on the stairs.

"Case," said I, "here's a queer thing. I'm tabooed."

"Oh, fudge!" says he; "'tain't the practice in these islands."

"That maybe, or it mayn't," said I. "It's the practice where I was before. You can bet I know what it's like; and I tell it you for a fact, I'm tabooed."

"Well," said he, "what have you been doing?"

"That's what I want to find out," said I.

"Oh, you can't be," said he; "it ain't possible. However, I'll tell you what I'll do. Just to put your mind at rest, I'll go round and find out for sure. Just you waltz in and talk to Papa."

"Thank you," I said, "I'd rather stay right out here on the veranda. Your house is so close."

"I'll call Papa out here, then," says he.

"My dear fellow," I says, "I wish you wouldn't. The fact is, I don't take to Mr. Randall."

Case laughed, took a lantern from the store, and set out into the village. He was gone perhaps a quarter of an hour, and he looked mighty serious when he came back.

"Well," said he, clapping down the lantern on the veranda steps, "I would never have believed it. I don't know where the impudence of these Kanakas'll go next; they seem to have lost all idea of respect for whites. What we want is a man-of-war—a German, if we could—they know how to manage Kanakas."

"I *am* tabooed, then?" I cried.

"Something of the sort," said he. "It's the worst thing of the kind I've heard of yet. But I'll stand by you, Wiltshire, man to man. You come round here tomorrow about nine, and we'll have it out with the chiefs. They're afraid of me, or they used to be; but their heads are so big by now, I don't know what to think. Understand me, Wiltshire; I don't count this your quarrel," he went on, with a great deal of resolution, "I count it all of our quarrel, I count it the White Man's Quarrel, and I'll stand to it through thick and thin, and there's my hand on it,"

"Have you found out what's the reason?" I asked.

"Not yet," said Case. "But we'll fire them down to-morrow."

Altogether I was pretty well pleased with his attitude, and almost more the next day, when we met to go before the chiefs, to see him so stern and resolved. The chiefs awaited us in one of their big oval houses, which was marked out to us from a long way off by the crowd about the eaves, a hundred strong if there was one—men, women, and children. Many of the men were on their way to work and wore green wreaths, and it put me in thoughts of the first of May[14] at home. This crowd opened and buzzed about the pair of us as we went in, with a sudden angry animation. Five chiefs were there; four mighty, stately men, the fifth old and puckered. They sat on mats in their white kilts and jackets; they had fans in their hands, like fine ladies; and two of the younger ones wore Catholic medals, which gave me matter of reflection. Our place was set, and the mats laid for us over against these grandees, on the near side of the house; the midst was empty; the crowd, close at our backs, murmured and craned and jostled to look on, and the shadows of them tossed in front of us on the clean pebbles of the floor. I was just a hair put out by the excitement of the commons, but the quiet, civil appearance of the chiefs reassured me, all the more when their spokesman began and made a long speech in a low tone of voice, sometimes waving his hand toward Case, sometimes toward me, and sometimes knocking with his knuckles on the mat. One thing was clear: there was no sign of anger in the chiefs.

"What's he been saying?" I asked, when he had done.

"Oh, just that they're glad to see you, and they understand by me you wish to make some kind of complaint, and you're to fire away, and they'll do the square thing."

"It took a precious long time to say that," said I.

"Oh, the rest was sawder and *bonjour* and that," said Case. "You know what Kanakas are."

14 **first of May:** May Day celebrations, when garlands of flowers were worn to celebrate spring and fertility.

"Well, they don't get much *bonjour* out of me," said I. "You tell them who I am. I'm a white man, and a British subject, and no end of a big chief at home; and I've come here to do them good, and bring them civilisation; and no sooner have I got my trade sorted out than they go and taboo me, and no one dare come near my place! Tell them I don't mean to fly in the face of anything legal; and if what they want's a present, I'll do what's fair. I don't blame any man looking out for himself, tell them, for that's human nature; but if they think they're going to come any of their native ideas over me, they'll find themselves mistaken. And tell them plain that I demand the reason of this treatment as a white man and a British subject."

That was my speech. I knew how to deal with Kanakas: give them plain sense and fair dealing, and—I'll do them that much justice—they knuckle under every time. They haven't any real government or any real law, that's what you've got to knock into their heads; and even if they had, it would be a good joke if it was to apply to a white man. It would be a strange thing if we came all this way and couldn't do what we pleased. The mere idea has always put my monkey up, and I rapped my speech out pretty big. Then Case translated it—or made believe to, rather—and the first chief replied, and then a second, and a third, all in the same style—easy and genteel, but solemn underneath. Once a question was put to Case, and he answered it, and all hands (both chiefs and commons) laughed out aloud, and looked at me. Last of all, the puckered old fellow and the big young chief that spoke first started in to put Case through a kind of catechism. Sometimes I made out that Case was trying to fence, and they stuck to him like hounds, and the sweat ran down his face, which was no very pleasant sight to me, and at some of his answers the crowd moaned and murmured, which was a worse hearing. It's a cruel shame I knew no native, for (as I now believe) they were asking Case about my marriage, and he must have had a tough job of it to clear his feet. But leave Case alone; he had the brains to run a parliament.

"Well, is that all?" I asked, when a pause came.

"Come along," says he, mopping his face; "I'll tell you outside."

"Do you mean they won't take the taboo off?" I cried.

"It's something queer," said he. "I'll tell you outside. Better come away."

"I won't take it at their hands," cried I. "I ain't that kind of a man. You don't find me turn my back on a parcel of Kanakas."

"You'd better," said Case.

He looked at me with a signal in his eye; and the five chiefs looked at me civilly enough, but kind of pointed; and the people looked at me and craned and jostled. I remembered the folks that watched my house, and how the pastor had jumped in his pulpit at the bare sight of me; and the whole business seemed so out of the way that I rose and followed Case. The crowd opened again to let us through, but wider than before, the children on the skirts running and singing out, and as we two white men walked away they all stood and watched us.

"And now," said I, "what is all this about?"

"The truth is I can't rightly make it out myself. They have a down on you," says Case.

"Taboo a man because they have a down on him!" I cried. "I never heard the like."

"It's worse than that, you see," said Case. "You ain't tabooed—I told you that couldn't be. The people won't go near you, Wiltshire, and there's where it is."

"They won't go near me? What do you mean by that? Why won't they go near me?" I cried.

Case hesitated. "Seems they're frightened," says he, in a low voice.

I stopped dead short. "Frightened?" I repeated. "Are you gone crazy, Case? What are they frightened of?"

"I wish I could make out," Case answered, shaking his head. "Appears like one of their tomfool superstitions. That's what I don't cotton to," he said. "It's like the business about Vigours."

"I'd like to know what you mean by that, and I'll trouble you to tell me," says I.

"Well, you know, Vigours lit out and left all standing," said he. "It was some superstition business—I never got the hang of it; but it began to look bad before the end."

"I've heard a different story about that," said I, "and I had better tell you so. I heard he ran away because of you."

"Oh! well, I suppose he was ashamed to tell the truth," says Case; "I guess he thought it silly. And it's a fact that I packed him off. 'What would you do, old man?' says he. 'Get,' says I, 'and not think twice about it.' I was the gladdest kind of man to see him clear away. It ain't my notion to turn my back on a mate when he's in a tight place, but there was that much trouble in the village that I couldn't see where it might likely end. I was a fool to be so much about with Vigours. They cast it up to me to-day. Didn't you hear Maea—that's the young chief, the big one—ripping out about 'Vika?' That was him they were after. They don't seem to forget it, somehow."

"This is all very well," said I, "but it don't tell me what's wrong; it don't tell me what they're afraid of—what their idea is."

"Well, I wish I knew," said Case. "I can't say fairer than that."

"You might have asked, I think," says I.

"And so I did," says he. "But you must have seen for yourself, unless you're blind, that the asking got the other way. I'll go as far as I dare for another white man; but when I find I'm in the scrape myself, I think first of my own bacon. The loss of me is I'm too good-natured. And I'll take the freedom of telling you you show a queer kind of gratitude to a man who's got into all this mess along of your affairs."

"There's a thing I'm thinking of," said I. "You were a fool to be so much about with Vigours. One comfort, you haven't been much about with me. I notice you've never been inside my house. Own up now; you had word of this before?"

"It's a fact I haven't been," said he. "It was an oversight, and I am sorry for it, Wiltshire. But about coming now, I'll be quite plain."

"You mean you won't?" I asked.

"Awfully sorry, old man, but that's the size of it," says Case.

"In short, you're afraid?" says I.

"In short, I'm afraid," says he.

"And I'm still to be tabooed for nothing?" I asked.

"I tell you you're not tabooed," said he. "The Kanakas won't go near you, that's all. And who's to make 'em. We traders have a lot of gall, I must say; we make these poor Kanakas take back their laws, and take up their taboos, and that, whenever it happens to suit us. But you don't mean to say you expect a law obliging people to deal in your store whether they want to or not? You don't mean to tell me you've got the gall for that? And if you had, it would be a queer thing to propose to me. I would just like to point out to you, Wiltshire, that I'm a trader myself."

"I don't think I would talk of gall if I was you," said I. "Here's about what it comes to, as well as I can make out: None of the people are to trade with me, and they're all to trade with you. You're to have the copra, and I'm to go to the devil and shake myself. And I don't know any native, and you're the only man here worth mention that speaks English, and you have the gall to up and hint to me my life's in danger, and all you've got to tell me is you don't know why!"

"Well, it *is* all I have to tell you," said he. "I don't know—I wish I did."

"And so you turn your back and leave me to myself! Is that the position?" says I.

"If you like to put it nasty," says he. "I don't put it so. I say merely, 'I'm going to keep clear of you; or, if I don't I'll get in danger for myself.'"

"Well," says I, "you're a nice kind of a white man!"

"Oh, I understand; you're riled," said he. "I would be myself. I can make excuses."

"All right," I said, "go and make excuses somewhere else. Here's my way, there's yours!"

With that we parted, and I went straight home, in a hot temper, and found Uma trying on a lot of trade goods like a baby.

"Here," I said, "you quit that foolery! Here's pretty mess to have made, as if I wasn't bothered enough anyway! And I thought I told you to get dinner!"

And then I believe I gave her a bit of the rough side of my tongue, as she deserved. She stood up at once, like a sentry to his officer; for I must say she was always well brought up, and had a great respect for whites.

"And now," says I, "you belong round here, you're bound to understand this. What am I tabooed for, anyway? Or, if I ain't tabooed, what makes the folks afraid of me?"

She stood and looked at me with eyes like saucers.

"You no savvy?" she gasps at last.

"No," said I. "How would you expect me to? We don't have any such craziness where I come from."

"Ese no tell you?" she asked again.

(*Ese* was the name the natives had for Case; it may mean foreign, or extraordinary; or it might mean a mummy apple; but most like it was only his own name misheard and put in a Kanaka spelling.)

"Not much," said I.

"D—n Ese!" she cried.

You might think it funny to hear this Kanaka girl come out with a big swear. No such thing. There was no swearing in her—no, nor anger; she was beyond anger, and meant the word simple and serious. She stood there straight as she said it. I cannot justly say that I ever saw a woman look like that before or after, and it struck me mum. Then she made a kind of an obeisance, but it was the proudest kind, and threw her hands out open.

"I 'shamed," she said. "I think you savvy. Ese he tell me you savvy, he tell me you no mind, tell me you love me too much. Taboo belong me," she said, touching herself on the bosom, as she had done upon our wedding-night. "Now I go 'way, taboo he go 'way too. Then you get too much copra. You like more better, I think. Tofá, alii," says she in the native—"Farewell chief!"

"Hold on!" I cried. "Don't be in such a hurry."

She looked at me sidelong with a smile. "You see, you get copra," she said, the same as you might offer candies to a child.

"Uma," said I, "hear reason. I didn't know, and that's a fact; and Case seems to have played it pretty mean upon the pair of us. But I do know now, and I don't mind; I love you too much. You no go 'way, you no leave me, I too much sorry."

"You no love me," she cried, "you talk me bad words!" And she threw herself in a corner of the floor, and began to cry.

Well, I'm no scholar, but I wasn't born yesterday, and I thought the worst of that trouble was over. However, there she lay—her back turned, her face to the wall—and shook with sobbing like a little child, so that her feet jumped with it. It's strange how it hits a man when he's in love; for there's no use mincing things; Kanaka and all, I was in love with her, or just as good. I tried to take her hand, but she would none of that. "Uma," I said, "there's no sense in carrying on like this. I want you stop here, I want my little wifie, I tell you true."

"No tell me true," she sobbed.

"All right," says I, "I'll wait till you're through with this." And I sat right down beside her on the floor, and set to smooth her hair with my hand. At first she wriggled away when I touched her; then she seemed to notice me no more; then her sobs grew gradually less; and presently stopped; and the next thing I knew, she raised her face to mine.

"You tell me true? You like me stop?" she asked.

"Uma," I said, "I would rather have you than all the copra in the South Seas," which was a very big expression, and the strangest thing was that I meant it.

She threw her arms about me, sprang close up, and pressed her face to mine, in the island way of kissing, so that I was all wetted with her tears, and my heart went out to her wholly. I never had anything so near me as this little brown bit of a girl. Many things went together, and all helped to turn my head. She was pretty enough to eat; it seemed she was my only friend in that queer place; I was ashamed that I had spoken rough to her: and she was a woman, and my wife, and a kind of a baby besides that I was sorry for; and the salt of her tears was in my mouth. And I forgot Case and the natives; and I forgot that I knew nothing of the story, or only remembered it to banish the remembrance; and I forgot that I was to get no copra, and so could make no livelihood; and I forgot my employers, and the strange kind of service I was doing them, when I preferred my fancy to their business; and I forgot even that Uma was no true wife of mine, but just a maid beguiled, and that in a pretty shabby style. But that is to look too far on. I will come to that part of it next.

It was late before we thought of getting dinner. The stove was out, and gone stone cold; but we fired up after a while, and cooked each a dish, helping and hindering each other, and making a play of it like children. I was so greedy of her nearness that I sat down to dinner with my lass upon my knee, made sure of her with one hand, and ate with the other. Ay, and more than that. She was the worst cook I suppose God made; the things she set her hand to it would have sickened an honest horse to eat of; yet I made my meal that day on Uma's cookery, and can never call to mind to have been better pleased.

I didn't pretend to myself, and I didn't pretend to her. I saw I was clean gone; and if she was to make a fool of me, she must. And I suppose it was this that set her talking, for now she made sure that we were friends. A lot she told me, sitting in my lap and eating my dish, as I ate hers, from foolery—a lot about herself and her mother and Case, all which would be very tedious, and fill sheets if I set it down in Beach de Mar,[15] but which I must give a hint of in plain English, and one thing about myself, which had a very big effect on my concerns, as you are soon to hear.

It seems she was born in one of the Line Islands; had been only two or three years in these parts, where she had come with a white man, who was married to her mother and then died; and only the one year in Falesá. Before that they had been a good deal on the move, trekking about after the white man, who was one of those rolling stones that keep going round after a soft job. They talk about looking for gold at the end of a rainbow; but if a man wants an employment that'll last him till he dies, let him start out on the soft-job hunt. There's meat and drink in it too, and beer and skittles, for you never hear of them starving, and rarely see them sober; and as for steady sport, cock-fighting isn't in the same county with it. Anyway, this beachcomber carried the woman and her daughter all over the shop, but mostly to out-of-the-way islands, where there were no police, and he thought, perhaps, the soft job hung out. I've my own view of this old party; but I was just as glad he had kept Uma clear of Apia and Papeete and these flash towns. At last he struck Falealii on this island, got some trade—the Lord knows how!—muddled it all away in the usual style, and died worth next to nothing, bar a bit of land at Falesá that he had got for a bad debt, which was what put it in the minds of the mother and daughter to come there and live. It seems Case encouraged them all he could, and helped to get their house built. He was very kind those days, and gave Uma trade, and there is no doubt he had his eye on her from the beginning. However, they had scarce settled, when up turned a young man, a native, and wanted to marry her. He was a small chief, and had some fine mats and old songs in his family, and was "very pretty," Uma said; and, altogether, it was an extraordinary match for a penniless girl and an out-islander.

At the first word of this I got downright sick with jealousy.

"And you mean to say you would have married him?" I cried.

"Ioe, yes," said she. "I like too much!"

15 **Beach de Mar:** The pidgin English of the South Sea islanders.

"Well!" I said. "And suppose I had come round after?"

"I like you more better now," said she. "But suppose I marry Ioane, I one good wife. I no common Kanaka. Good girl!" says she.

Well, I had to be pleased with that; but I promise you I didn't care about the business one little bit. And I liked the end of that yarn no better than the beginning. For it seems this proposal of marriage was the start of all the trouble. It seems, before that, Uma and her mother had been looked down upon, of course, for kinless folk and out-islanders, but nothing to hurt; and, even when Ioane came forward, there was less trouble at first than might have been looked for. And then, all of a sudden, about six months before my coming, Ioane backed out and left that part of the island, and from that day to this Uma and her mother had found themselves alone. None called at their house—none spoke to them on the roads. If they went to church, the other women drew their mats away and left them in a clear place by themselves. It was a regular excommunication, like what you read of in the Middle Ages; and the cause or sense of it beyond guessing. It was some *talo pepelo*, Uma said, some lie, some calumny; and all she knew of it was that the girls who had been jealous of her luck with Ioane used to twit her with his desertion, and cry out, when they met her alone in the woods, that she would never be married. "They tell me no man he marry me. He too much 'fraid," she said.

The only soul that came about them after this desertion was Master Case. Even he was chary of showing himself, and turned up mostly by night; and pretty soon he began to table his cards and make up to Uma. I was still sore about Ioane, and when Case turned up in the same line of business I cut up downright rough.

"Well," I said, sneering, "and I suppose you thought Case 'very pretty' and 'liked too much'?"

"Now you talk silly," said she. "White man, he come here, I marry him all-a-same Kanaka; very well then, he marry me all-e-same white woman, Suppose he no marry, he go 'way, woman he stop. All-e-same thief, empty hand, Tonga-heart—no can love! Now you come marry me. You big heart—you no 'shamed island-girl. That thing I love you far too much. I proud."

I don't know that ever I felt sicker all the days of my life. I laid down my fork, and I put away the "island-girl;" I didn't seem somehow to have any use for either, and I went and walked up and down in the house, and Uma followed me with her eyes, for she was troubled, and small wonder! But troubled was no word for it with me. I so wanted, and so feared, to make a clean breast of the sweep[16] that I had been.

And just then there came a sound of singing out of the sea; it sprang up suddenly clear and near, as the boat turned the headland, and Uma, running to the window, cried out it was "Misi" come upon his rounds.

I thought it was a strange thing I should be glad to have a missionary; but, if it was strange, it was still true.

"Uma," said I, "you stop here in this room, and don't budge a foot out of it till I come back."

---

16 **sweep:** A disreputable person; a rascal.

Chapter III The Missionary

As I came out on the veranda, the mission-boat was shooting for the mouth of the river. She was a long whale-boat painted white; a bit of an awning astern; a native pastor crouched on the wedge of poop, steering; some four-and-twenty paddles flashing and dipping, true to the boat-song; and the missionary under the awning, in his white clothes, reading in a book; and set him up! It was pretty to see and hear; there's no smarter sight in the islands than a missionary boat with a good crew and a good pipe to them; and I considered it for half a minute with a bit of envy perhaps, and then strolled down toward the river.

From the opposite side there was another man aiming for the same place, but he ran and got there first. It was Case; doubtless his idea was to keep me apart from the missionary, who might serve me as interpreter; but my mind was upon other things. I was thinking how he had jockeyed us about the marriage, and tried his hand on Uma before; and at the sight of him rage flew into my nostrils.

"Get out of that, you low, swindling thief!" I cried.

"What's that you say?" says he.

I gave him the word again, and rammed it down with a good oath. "And if ever I catch you within six fathoms of my house," I cried, "I'll clap a bullet in your measly carcass."

"You must do as you like about your house," said he, "where I told you I have no thought of going; but this is a public place."

"It's a place where I have private business," said I. "I have no idea of a hound like you eavesdropping, and I give you notice to clear out."

"I don't take it, though," says Case.

"I'll show you then," said I.

"We'll have to see about that," said he.

He was quick with his hands, but he had neither the height nor the weight, being a flimsy creature alongside a man like me, and, besides, I was blazing to that height of wrath that I could have bit into a chisel. I gave him first the one and then the other, so that I could hear his head rattle and crack, and he went down straight.

"Have you had enough?" cries I. But he only looked up white and blank, and the blood spread upon his face like wine upon a napkin. "Have you had enough?" I cried again. "Speak up, and don't lie malingering there, or I'll take my feet to you."

He sat up at that, and held his head—by the look of him you could see it was spinning—and the blood poured on his pajamas.

"I've had enough for this time," says he, and he got up staggering, and went off by the way that he had come.

The boat was close in; I saw the missionary had laid his book to one side, and I smiled to myself. "He'll know I'm a man, anyway," thinks I.

This was the first time, in all my years in the Pacific, I had ever exchanged two words with any missionary, let alone asked one for a favour. I didn't like the lot, no trader does; they look down upon us, and make no concealment; and, besides, they're partly Kanakaized, and suck up with natives instead of with other white men like themselves. I had on a rig of clean, striped pajamas—for, of course, I had dressed decent to go before the chiefs; but when I saw the missionary step out of this boat in the regular uniform, white duck clothes, pith helmet, white shirt and tie, and yellow boots to his feet, I could have bunged stones at him. As he came nearer, queering me pretty curious (because of the fight, I suppose), I saw he looked mortal sick, for the truth was he had a fever on, and had just had a chill in the boat.

"Mr. Tarleton, I believe?" says I, for I had got his name.

"And you, I suppose, are the new trader?" says he.

"I want to tell you first that I don't hold with missions," I went on, "and that I think you and the likes of you do a sight of harm, filling up the natives with old wives' tales and bumptiousness."

"You are perfectly entitled to your opinions," says he, looking a bit ugly, "but I have no call to hear them."

"It so happens that you've got to hear them," I said. "I'm no missionary, nor missionary lover; I'm no Kanaka, nor favourer of Kanakas—I'm just a trader; I'm just a common low God-damned white man and British subject, the sort you would like to wipe your boots on. I hope that's plain!"

"Yes, my man," said he. "It's more plain than creditable. When you are sober, you'll be sorry for this."

He tried to pass on, but I stopped him with my hand. The Kanakas were beginning to growl. Guess they didn't like my tone, for I spoke to that man as free as I would to you.

"Now, you can't say I've deceived you," said I, "and I can go on. I want a service—I want two services, in fact; and, if you care to give me them, I'll perhaps take more stock in what you call your Christianity."

He was silent for a moment. Then he smiled. "You are rather a strange sort of man," says he.

"I'm the sort of man God made me," says I. "I don't set up to be a gentleman," I said.

"I am not quite so sure," said he. "And what can I do for you, Mr. ——?"

"Wiltshire," I says, "though I'm mostly called Welsher; but Wiltshire is the way it's spelt, if the people on the beach could only get their tongues about it. And what do I want? Well, I'll tell you the first thing. I'm what you call a sinner—what I call a sweep—and I want you to help me make it up to a person I've deceived."

He turned and spoke to his crew in the native. "And now I am at your service," said he, "but only for the time my crew are dining. I must be much farther down the coast before right. I was delayed at Papa-Malulu till this morning, and I have an engagement in Falealii to-morrow night."

I led the way to my house in silence, and rather pleased with myself for the way I had managed the talk, for I like a man to keep his self-respect.

"I was sorry to see you fighting," says he.

"Oh, that's part of the yarn I want to tell you," I said. "That's service number two. After you've heard it you'll let me know whether you're sorry or not."

We walked right in through the store, and I was surprised to find Uma had cleared away the dinner things. This was so unlike her ways that I saw she had done it out of gratitude, and liked her the better. She and Mr. Tarleton called each other by name, and he was very civil to her seemingly. But I thought little of that; they can always find civility for a Kanaka, it's us white men they lord it over. Besides, I didn't want much Tarleton just then. I was going to do my pitch.

"Uma," said I, "give us your marriage certificate." She looked put out. "Come," said I, "you can trust me. Hand it up."

She had it about her person, as usual; I believe she thought it was a pass to heaven, and if she died without having it handy she would go to hell. I couldn't see where she put it the first time, I couldn't see now where she took it from; it seemed to jump into her hand like that Blavatsky[17] business in the papers. But it's the same way with all island women, and I guess they're taught it when young.

"Now," said I, with the certificate in my hand, "I was married to this girl by Black Jack, the negro. The certificate was wrote by Case, and it's a dandy piece of literature, I promise you. Since then I've found that there's a kind of cry in the place against this wife of mine, and so long as I keep her I cannot trade. Now, what would any man do in my place, if he was a man?" I said. "The first thing he would do is this, I guess." And I took and tore up the certificate and bunged the pieces on the floor.

"Aue!"[18] cried Uma, and began to clap her hands; but I caught one of them in mine.

"And the second thing that he would do," said I, "if he was what I would call a man and you would call a man, Mr. Tarleton, is to bring the girl right before you or any other missionary, and to up and say: 'I was wrong married to this wife of mine, but I think a heap of her, and now I want to be married to her right.' Fire away, Mr. Tarleton. And I guess you'd better do it in native; it'll please the old lady," I said, giving her the proper name of a man's wife upon the spot.

So we had in two of the crew for to witness, and were spliced in our own house; and the parson prayed a good bit, I must say—but not so long as some—and shook hands with the pair of us.

"Mr. Wiltshire," he says, when he had made out the lines and packed off the witnesses, "I have to thank you for a very lively pleasure. I have rarely performed the marriage ceremony with more grateful emotions."

That was what you would call talking. He was going on, besides, with more of it, and I was ready for as much taffy as he had in stock, for I felt good. But Uma had been taken up with something half through the marriage, and cut straight in.

"How your hand he get hurt?" she asked.

"You ask Case's head, old lady," says I.

She jumped with joy, and sang out.

"You haven't made much of a Christian of this one," says I to Mr. Tarleton.

"We didn't think her one of our worst," says he, "when she was at Fale-alii; and if Uma bears malice I shall be tempted to fancy she has good cause."

---

17 **Blavatsky:** Helena Blavatsky (1831–1891), Theosophist and psychic.
18 **"Aue!":** Alas! [Stevenson's note.]

"Well, there we are at service number two," said I. "I want to tell you our yarn, and see if you can let a little daylight in."

"Is it long?" he asked.

"Yes," I cried; "it's a goodish bit of a yarn!"

"Well, I'll give you all the time I can spare," says he, looking at his watch. "But I must tell you fairly, I haven't eaten since five this morning, and, unless you can let me have something, I am not likely to eat again before seven or eight to-night."

"By God, we'll give you dinner!" I cried.

I was a little caught up at my swearing, just when all was going straight; and so was the missionary, I suppose, but he made believe to look out of the window, and thanked us.

So we ran him up a bit of a meal. I was bound to let the old lady have a hand in it, to show off, so I deputized her to brew the tea. I don't think I ever met such tea as she turned out. But that was not the worst, for she got round with the salt-box, which she considered an extra European touch, and turned my stew into sea-water. Altogether, Mr. Tarleton had a devil of a dinner of it; but he had plenty of entertainment by the way, for all the while that we were cooking, and afterward, when he was making believe to eat, I kept posting him up on Master Case and the beach of Falesá, and he putting questions that showed he was following close.

"Well," said he at last, "I am afraid you have a dangerous enemy. This man Case is very clever and seems really wicked. I must tell you I have had my eye on him for nearly a year, and have rather had the worst of our encounters. About the time when the last representative of your firm ran so suddenly away, I had a letter from Namu, the native pastor, begging me to come to Falesá at my earliest convenience, as his flock were all 'adopting Catholic practices.' I had great confidence in Namu; I fear it only shows how easily we are deceived. No one could hear him preach and not be persuaded he was a man of extraordinary parts. All our islanders easily acquire a kind of eloquence, and can roll out and illustrate, with a great deal of vigor and fancy, second-hand sermons; but Namu's sermons are his own, and I cannot deny that I have found them means of grace. Moreover, he has a keen curiosity in secular things, does not fear work, is clever at carpentering, and has made himself so much respected among the neighboring pastors that we call him, in a jest which is half serious, the Bishop of the East. In short, I was proud of the man; all the more puzzled by his letter, and took an occasion to come this way. The morning before my arrival, Vigours had been sent on board the Lion, and Namu was perfectly at his ease, apparently ashamed of his letter, and quite unwilling to explain it. This, of course, I could not allow, and he ended by confessing that he had been much concerned to find his people using the sign of the cross, but since he had learned the explanation his mind was satisfied. For Vigours had the Evil Eye, a common thing in a country of Europe called Italy, where men were often struck dead by that kind of devil, and it appeared the sign of the cross was a charm against its power.

"'And I explain it, Misi,' said Namu, 'in this way: the country in Europe is a Popey country, and the devil of the Evil Eye may be a Catholic devil, or, at least, used to Catholic ways. So then I reasoned thus: if this sign of the cross were used in a Popey manner it would be sinful, but when it is used only to protect men from a devil, which is a thing harmless in itself, the sign too must be harmless. For the sign is neither good nor bad. But if the bottle be full of gin, the gin is bad; and if the sign made in idolatry be bad, so is the idolatry.' And, very like a native pastor, he had a text apposite about the casting out of devils.

"'And who has been telling you about the Evil Eye?' I asked.

"He admitted it was Case. Now, I am afraid you will think me very narrow, Mr. Wiltshire, but I must tell you I was displeased, and cannot think a trader at all a good man to advise or have an influence upon my pastors. And, besides, there had been some flying talk in the country of old Adams and his being poisoned, to which I had paid no great heed; but it came back to me at the moment.

"'And is this Case a man of a sanctified life?' I asked.

"He admitted he was not; for, though he did not drink, he was profligate with women, and had no religion.

"'Then,' said I, 'I think the less you have to do with him the better.'

"But it is not easy to have the last word with a man like Namu. He was ready in a moment with an illustration. 'Misi,' said he, 'you have told me there were wise men, not pastors, not even holy, who knew many things useful to be taught—about trees, for instance, and beasts, and to print books, and about the stones that are burned to make knives of. Such men teach you in your college, and you learn from them, but take care not to learn to be unholy. Misi, Case is my college.'

"I knew not what to say. Mr. Vigours had evidently been driven out of Falesá by the machinations of Case and with something not very unlike the collusion of my pastor. I called to mind it was Namu who had reassured me about Adams and traced the rumour to the ill-will of the priest. And I saw I must inform myself more thoroughly from an impartial source. There is an old rascal of a chief here, Faiaso, whom I dare say you saw to-day at the council; he has been all his life turbulent and shy, a great fomenter of rebellions, and a thorn in the side of the mission and the island. For all that he is very shrewd, and, except in politics or about his own misdemeanours, a teller of the truth. I went to his house, told him what I had heard, and besought him to be frank. I do not think I had ever a more painful interview. Perhaps you will understand me, Mr. Wiltshire, if I tell you that I am perfectly serious in these old wives' tales with which you reproached me, and as anxious to do well for these islands as you can be to please and to protect your pretty wife. And you are to remember that I thought Namu a paragon, and was proud of the man as one of the first ripe fruits of the mission. And now I was informed that he had fallen in a sort of dependence upon Case. The beginning of it was not corrupt; it began, doubtless, in fear and respect, produced by trickery and pretence; but I was shocked to find that another element had been lately added, that Namu helped himself in the store, and was believed to be deep in Case's debt. Whatever the trader said, that Namu believed with trembling. He was not alone in this; many in the village lived in a similar subjection; but Namu's case was the most influential, it was through Namu that Case had wrought most evil; and with a certain following among the chiefs, and the pastor in his pocket, the man was as good as master of the village. You know something of Vigours and Adams, but perhaps you have never heard of old Underhill, Adams's predecessor. He was a quiet, mild old fellow, I remember, and we were told he had died suddenly: white men die very suddenly in Falesá. The truth, as I now heard it, made my blood run cold. It seems he was struck with a general palsy, all of him dead but one eye, which he continually winked. Word was started that the helpless old man was now a devil, and this vile fellow Case worked upon the natives' fears, which he professed to share, and pretended he durst not go into the house alone. At last a grave was dug, and the living body buried at the far end of the village. Namu, my pastor, whom I had helped to educate, offered up a prayer at the hateful scene.

"I felt myself in a very difficult position. Perhaps it was my duty to have denounced Namu and had him deposed. Perhaps I think so now, but at the time it seemed less clear. He had a great influence, it might prove greater than mine. The natives are prone to superstition; perhaps by stirring them up I might but ingrain and spread these dangerous fancies. And Namu besides, apart from this novel and accursed influence, was a good pastor, an able man, and spiritually minded. Where should I look for a better? How was I to find as good? At that moment, with Namu's failure fresh in my view, the work of my life appeared a mockery; hope was dead in me. I would rather repair such tools as I had than go abroad in quest of others that must certainly prove worse; and a scandal is, at the best, a thing to be avoided when humanly possible. Right or wrong, then, I determined on a quiet course. All that night I denounced and reasoned with the erring pastor, twitted him with his ignorance and want of faith, twitted him with his wretched attitude, making clean the outside of the cup and platter, callously helping at a murder, childishly flying in excitement about a few childish, unnecessary, and inconvenient gestures; and long before day I had him on his knees and bathed in the tears of what seemed a genuine repentance. On Sunday I took the pulpit in the morning, and preached from First Kings, nineteenth, on the fire, the earthquake, and the voice, distinguishing the true spiritual power, and referring with such plainness as I dared to recent events in Falesá. The effect produced was great, and it was much increased when Namu rose in his turn and confessed that he had been wanting in faith and conduct, and was convinced of sin. So far, then, all was well; but there was one unfortunate circumstance. It was nearing the time of our 'May' in the island, when the native contributions to the missions are received; it fell in my duty to make a notification on the subject, and this gave my enemy his chance, by which he was not slow to profit.

"News of the whole proceedings must have been carried to Case as soon as church was over, and the same afternoon he made an occasion to meet me in the midst of the village. He came up with so much intentness and animosity that I felt it would be damaging to avoid him.

"'So,' says he, in native, 'here is the holy man. He has been preaching against me, but that was not in his heart. He has been preaching upon the love of God; but that was not in his heart, it was between his teeth. Will you know what was in his heart?' cries he. 'I will show it to you!' And, making a snatch at my head, he made believe to pluck out a dollar, and held it in the air.

"There went that rumour through the crowd with which Polynesians receive a prodigy. As for myself, I stood amazed. The thing was a common conjuring trick which I have seen performed at home a score of times; but how was I to convince the villagers of that? I wished I had learned legerdemain instead of Hebrew, that I might have paid the fellow out with his own coin. But there I was; I could not stand there silent, and the best I could find to say was weak.

"'I will trouble you not to lay hands on me again,' said I.

"'I have no such thought,' said he, 'nor will I deprive you of your dollar. Here it is,' he said, and flung it at my feet. I am told it lay where it fell three days."

"I must say it was well played," said I.

"Oh! he is clever," said Mr. Tarleton, "and you can now see for yourself how dangerous. He was a party to the horrid death of the paralytic; he is accused of poisoning Adams; he drove Vigours out of the place by lies that might have led to murder; and there is no question but he has now made up his mind to rid himself of you. How he means to try we have no guess; only be sure, it's something new. There is no end to his readiness and invention."

"He gives himself a sight of trouble," says I. "And after all, what for?"

"Why, how many tons of copra may they make in this district?" asked the missionary.

"I dare say as much as sixty tons," says I.

"And what is the profit to the local trader?" he asked.

"You may call it three pounds," said I.

"Then you can reckon for yourself how much he does it for," said Mr. Tarleton. "But the more important thing is to defeat him. It is clear he spread some report against Uma, in order to isolate and have his wicked will of her. Failing of that, and seeing a new rival come upon the scene, he used her in a different way. Now, the first point to find out is about Namu. Uma, when people began to leave you and your mother alone, what did Namu do?"

"Stop away all-a-same," says Uma.

"I fear the dog has returned to his vomit," said Mr. Tarleton. "And now what am I to do for you? I will speak to Namu, I will warn him he is observed; it will be strange if he allow anything to go on amiss when he is put upon his guard. At the same time, this precaution may fail, and then you must turn elsewhere. You have two people at hand to whom you might apply. There is, first of all, the priest, who might protect you by the Catholic interest; they are a wretchedly small body, but they count two chiefs. And then there is old Faiaso. Ah! if it had been some years ago you would have needed no one else; but his influence is much reduced, it has gone into Maea's hands, and Maea, I fear, is one of Case's jackals. In fine, if the worst comes to the worst, you must send up or come yourself to Falealii, and, though I am not due at this end of the island for a month, I will just see what can be done."

So Mr. Tarleton said farewell; and half an hour later the crew were singing and the paddles flashing in the missionary-boat.

Chapter IV Devil-Work

Near a month went by without much doing. The same night of our marriage Galoshes called round, and made himself mighty civil, and got into a habit of dropping in about dark and smoking his pipe with the family. He could talk to Uma, of course, and started to teach me native and French at the same time. He was a kind old buffer, though the dirtiest you would wish to see, and he muddled me up with foreign languages worse than the Tower of Babel.

That was one employment we had, and it made me feel less lonesome; but there was no profit in the thing, for though the priest came and sat and yarned, none of his folks could be enticed into my store, and if it hadn't been for the other occupation I struck out, there wouldn't have been a pound of copra in the house. This was the idea: Fa'avao (Uma's mother) had a score of bearing-trees. Of course we could get no labour, being all as good as tabooed, and the two women and I turned to and made copra with our own hands. It was copra to make your mouth water when it was done—I never understood how much the natives cheated me till I had made that four hundred pounds of my own hand—and it weighed so light I felt inclined to take and water it myself.

When we were at the job a good many Kanakas used to put in the best of the day looking on, and once that nigger turned up. He stood back with the natives and laughed and did the big don and the funny dog, till I began to get riled.

"Here, you nigger!" says I.

"I don't address myself to you, Sah," says the nigger. "Only speak to gen'le'um."

"I know," says I, "but it happens I was addressing myself to you, Mr. Black Jack. And all I want to know is just this: did you see Case's figure-head about a week ago?"

"No, Sah," says he.

"That's all right, then," says I; "for I'll show you the own brother to it, only black, in the inside of about two minutes."

And I began to walk toward him, quite slow, and my hands down; only there was trouble in my eye, if anybody took the pains to look.

"You're a low, obstropulous fellow, Sah," says he.

"You bet!" says I.

By that time he thought I was about as near as convenient, and lit out so it would have done your heart good to see him travel. And that was all I saw of that precious gang until what I am about to tell you.

It was one of my chief employments these days to go pot-hunting in the woods, which I found (as Case had told me) very rich in game. I have spoken of the cape which shut up the village and my station from the east. A path went about the end of it, and led into the next bay. A strong wind blew here daily, and as the line of the barrier reef stopped at the end of the cape, a heavy surf ran on the shores of the bay. A little cliffy hill cut the valley in two parts, and stood close on the beach; and at high water the sea broke right on the face of it, so that all passage was stopped. Woody mountains hemmed the place all round; the barrier to the east was particularly steep and leafy, the lower parts of it, along the sea, falling in sheer black cliffs streaked with cinnabar; the upper part lumpy with the tops of the great trees. Some of the trees were bright green, and some red, and the sand of the beach as black as your shoes. Many birds hovered round the bay, some of them snow-white; and the flying-fox (or vampire) flew there in broad daylight, gnashing its teeth.

For a long while I came as far as this shooting, and went no farther. There was no sign of any path beyond, and the cocoa-palms in the front of the foot of the valley were the last this way. For the whole "eye" of the island, as natives call the wind-ward end, lay desert. From Falesá round about to Papa-malulu, there was neither house, nor man, nor planted fruit-tree; and the reef being mostly absent, and the shores bluff, the sea beat direct among crags, and there was scarce a landing-place.

I should tell you that after I began to go in the woods, although no one appeared to come near my store, I found people willing enough to pass the time of day with me where nobody could see them; and as I had begun to pick up native, and most of them had a word or two of English, I began to hold little odds and ends of conversation, not to much purpose, to be sure, but they took off the worst of the feeling, for it's a miserable thing to be made a leper of.

It chanced one day, toward the end of the month, that I was sitting in this bay in the edge of the bush, looking east, with a Kanaka. I had given him a fill of tobacco, and we were making out to talk as best we could; indeed, he had more English than most.

I asked him if there was no road going eastward.

"One time one road," said he. "Now he dead."

"Nobody he go there?" I asked.

"No good," said he. "Too much devil he stop there."

"Oho!" says I, "got-um plenty devil, that bush?"

"Man devil, woman devil; too much devil," said my friend. "Stop there all-e-time. Man he go there, no come back."

I thought if this fellow was so well posted on devils and spoke of them so free, which is not common, I had better fish for a little information about myself and Uma.

"You think me one devil?" I asked.

"No think devil," said he, soothingly. "Think all-e-same fool."

"Uma, she devil?" I asked again.

"No, no; no devil. Devil stop bush," said the young man.

I was looking in front of me across the bay, and I saw the hanging front of the woods pushed suddenly open, and Case, with a gun in his hand, step forth into the sunshine on the black beach. He was got up in light pyjamas, near white, his gun sparkled, he looked mighty conspicuous; and the land-crabs scuttled from all around him to their holes.

"Hullo, my friend!" says I, "you no talk all-e-same true. Ese he go, he come back."

"Ese no all-e-same; Ese *Tiapolo*," says my friend; and, with a "Good-by," slunk off among the trees.

I watched Case all around the beach, where the tide was low; and let him pass me on the homeward way to Falesá. He was in deep thought, and the birds seemed to know it, trotting quite near him on the sand, or wheeling and calling in his ears. When he passed me I could see by the working of his lips that he was talking to himself, and what pleased me mightily, he had still my trade-mark on his brow. I tell you the plain truth: I had a mind to give him a gunful in his ugly mug, but I thought better of it.

All this time, and all the time I was following home, I kept repeating that native word, which I remembered by "Polly, put the kettle on and make us all some tea," tea-a-pollo.

"Uma," says I, when I got back, "what does *Tiapolo* mean?"

"Devil," says she.

"I thought *aitu* was the word for that," I said.

"*Aitu* 'nother kind of devil," said she; "stop bush, eat Kanaka. Tiapolo big chief devil, stop home; all-e-same Christian devil."

"Well, then," said I, "I'm no farther forward. How can Case be Tiapolo?"

"No all-e-same," said she. "Ese belong Tiapolo. Tiapolo too much like; Ese all-e-same his son. Suppose Ese he wish something, Tiapolo he make him."

"That's mighty convenient for Ese," says I. "And what kind of things does he make for him?"

Well, out came a rigmarole of all sorts of stories, many of which (like the dollar he took from Mr. Tarleton's head) were plain enough to me, but others I could make nothing of; and the thing that most surprised the Kanakas was what surprised me least—namely, that he would go in the desert among all the *aitus*. Some of the boldest, however, had accompanied him, and had heard him speak with the dead and give them orders, and, safe in his protection, had returned unscathed. Some said he had a church there, where he worshipped Tiapolo, and Tiapolo appeared to him; others swore that there was no sorcery at all, that he performed his miracles by the power of prayer, and the church was no church, but a prison, in which he had confined a dangerous *aitu*. Namu had been in the bush with him once, and returned glorifying God for these wonders. Altogether, I began to have a glimmer of the man's position, and the means by which he had acquired it, and, though I saw he was a tough nut to crack, I was noways cast down.

"Very well," said I, "I'll have a look at Master Case's place of worship myself, and we'll see about the glorifying."

At this Uma fell in a terrible taking; if I went in the high bush I should never return; none could go there but by the protection of Tiapolo.

"I'll chance it on God's," said I. "I'm a good sort of a fellow, Uma, as fellows go, and I guess God'll con me through."

She was silent for a while. "I think," said she, mighty solemn—and then, presently—"Victoreea, he big chief?"

"You bet!" said I.

"He like you too much?" she asked again. I told her, with a grin, I believed the old lady was rather partial to me.

"All right," said she. "Victoreea he big chief, like you too much. No can help you here in Falesá; no can do—too far off. Maea he be small chief—stop here. Suppose he like you—make you all right. All-e-same God and Tiapolo. God he big chief—got too much work. Tiapolo he small chief—he like too much make-see, work very hard."

"I'll have to hand you over to Mr. Tarleton," said I. "Your theology's out of its bearings, Uma."

However, we stuck to this business all the evening, and, with the stories she told me of the desert and its dangers, she came near frightening herself into a fit. I don't remember half a quarter of them, of course, for I paid little heed; but two come back to me kind of clear.

About six miles up the coast there is a sheltered cove they call *Fanga-anaana*— "the haven full of caves." I've seen it from the sea myself, as near as I could get my boys to venture in; and it's a little strip of yellow sand, black cliffs overhang it, full of the black mouths of caves; great trees overhang the cliffs, and dangle-down lianas; and in one place, about the middle, a big brook pours over in a cascade. Well, there was a boat going by here, with six young men of Falesá, "all very pretty," Uma said, which was the loss of them. It blew strong, there was a heavy head sea, and by the time they opened Fanga-anaana, and saw the white cascade and the shady beach, they were all tired and thirsty, and their water had run out. One proposed to land and get a drink, and, being reckless fellows, they were all of the same mind except the youngest. Lotu was his name; he was a very good young gentleman, and very wise; and he held out that they were crazy, telling them the place was given over to spirits and devils and the dead, and there were no living folk nearer than six miles the one way, and maybe twelve the other. But they laughed at his words, and, being five to one, pulled in, beached the boat, and landed. It was a wonderful pleasant place, Lotu said, and the water excellent. They walked round the beach, but could see nowhere any way to mount the cliffs, which made them easier in their mind; and at last they sat down to make a meal on the food they had brought with them. They were scarce set, when there came out of the mouth of one of the black caves six of the most beautiful ladies ever seen; they had flowers in their hair, and the most beautiful breasts, and necklaces of scarlet seeds; and began to jest with these young gentlemen, and the young gentlemen to jest back with them, all but Lotu. As for Lotu, he saw there could be no living woman in such a place, and ran, and flung himself in the bottom of the boat, and covered his face, and prayed. All the time the business lasted Lotu made one clean break of prayer, and that was all he knew of it, until his friends came back, and made him sit up, and they put to sea again out of the bay, which was now quite desert, and no word of the six ladies. But, what frightened Lotu most, not one of the five remembered anything of what had passed, but they were all like drunken men, and sang and laughed in the boat, and skylarked. The wind freshened and came squally, and the sea rose extraordinary high; it was such weather as any man in the islands would have turned his back to and fled home to Falesá; but these five were like crazy folk, and cracked on all sail and drove their boat into the seas. Lotu went to the bailing; none of the others thought to help him, but sang and skylarked and carried on, and spoke singular things beyond a man's comprehension, and laughed out loud when they said them. So the rest of the day Lotu bailed for his life in the bottom of the boat, and was all drenched with sweat and cold sea-water; and none heeded him. Against all expectation, they came safe in a dreadful tempest to Papa-malulu, where the palms were singing out, and the cocoa-nuts flying like cannon-balls about the village green; and the same night the five young gentlemen sickened, and spoke never a reasonable word until they died.

"And do you mean to tell me you can swallow a yarn like that," I asked.

She told me the thing was well known, and with handsome young men alone it was even common; but this was the only case where five had been slain the same day and in a company by the love of the women-devils; and it had made a great stir in the island, and she would be crazy if she doubted.

"Well, anyway," says I, "you needn't be frightened about me. I've no use for the women-devils. You're all the women I want, and all the devil too, old lady."

To this she answered there were other sorts, and she had seen one with her own eyes. She had gone one day alone to the next bay, and, perhaps, got too near the margin of the bad place. The boughs of the high bush overshadowed her from the cant of the hill, but she herself was outside on a flat place, very stony and growing full of young mummy-apples four and five feet high. It was a dark day in the rainy season, and now there came squalls that tore off the leaves and sent them flying, and now it was all still as in a house. It was in one of these still times that a whole gang of birds and flying-foxes came pegging out of the bush like creatures frightened. Presently after she heard a rustle nearer hand, and saw, coming out of the margin of the trees, among the mummy-apples, the appearance of a lean gray old boar. It seemed to think as it came, like a person; and all of a sudden, as she looked at it coming, she was aware it was no boar, but a thing that was a man with a man's thoughts. At that she ran, and the pig after her, and as the pig ran it holla'd aloud, so that the place rang with it.

"I wish I had been there with my gun," said I. "I guess that pig would have holla'd so as to surprise himself."

But she told me a gun was of no use with the like of these, which were the spirits of the dead.

Well, this kind of talk put in the evening, which was the best of it; but of course it didn't change my notion, and the next day, with my gun and a good knife, I set off upon a voyage of discovery. I made, as near as I could, for the place where I had seen Case come out; for if it was true he had some kind of establishment in the bush I reckoned I should find a path. The beginning of the desert was marked off by a wall, to call it so, for it was more of a long mound of stones. They say it reaches right across the island, but how they know it is another question, for I doubt if any one has made the journey in a hundred years, the natives sticking chiefly to the sea and their little colonies along the coast, and that part being mortal high and steep and full of cliffs. Up to the west side of the wall the ground has been cleared, and there are cocoa-palms and mummy-apples and guavas, and lots of sensitive. Just across, the bush begins outright; high bush at that, trees going up like the masts of ships, and ropes of liana hanging down like a ship's rigging, and nasty orchids growing in the forks like funguses. The ground where there was no underwood looked to be a heap of boulders. I saw many green pigeons which I might have shot, only I was there with a different idea. A number of butterflies flopped up and down along the ground like dead leaves; sometimes I would hear a bird calling, sometimes the wind overhead, and always the sea along the coast.

But the queerness of the place it's more difficult to tell of, unless to one who has been alone in the high bush himself. The brightest kind of a day it is always dim down there. A man can see to the end of nothing; whichever way he looks the wood shuts up, one bough folding with another like the fingers of your hand; and whenever he listens he hears always something new—men talking, children laughing, the strokes of an axe a far way ahead of him, and sometimes a sort of a quick, stealthy scurry near at hand that makes him jump and look to his weapons. It's all very well for him to tell himself that he's alone, bar trees and birds; he can't make out to believe it; whichever way he turns the whole place seems to be alive and looking on. Don't think it was Uma's yarns that put me out; I don't value native talk a fourpenny-piece; it's a thing that's natural in the bush, and that's the end of it.

As I got near the top of the hill, for the ground of the wood goes up in this place steep as a ladder, the wind began to sound straight on, and the leaves to toss and switch open and let in the sun. This suited me better; it was the same noise all the time, and nothing to startle. Well, I had got to a place where there was an underwood of what they call wild cocoanut—mighty pretty with its scarlet fruit—when there came a sound of singing in the wind that I thought I had never heard the like of. It was all very fine to tell myself it was the branches; I knew better. It was all very fine to tell myself it was a bird; I knew never a bird that sang like that. It rose and swelled, and died away and swelled again; and now I thought it was like someone weeping, only prettier; and now I thought it was like harps; and there was one thing I made sure of, it was a sight too sweet to be wholesome in a place like that. You may laugh if you like; but I declare I called to mind the six young ladies that came, with their scarlet necklaces, out of the cave at Fanga-anaana, and wondered if they sang like that. We laugh at the natives and their superstitions; but see how many traders take them up, splendidly educated white men, that have been bookkeepers (some of them) and clerks in the old country. It's my belief a superstition grows up in a place like the different kind of weeds; and as I stood there and listened to that wailing I twittered in my shoes.

You may call me a coward to be frightened; I thought myself brave enough to go on ahead. But I went mighty carefully, with my gun cocked, spying all about me like a hunter, fully expecting to see a handsome young woman sitting somewhere in the bush, and fully determined (if I did) to try her with a charge of duck-shot. And sure enough, I had not gone far when I met with a queer thing. The wind came on the top of the wood in a strong puff, the leaves in front of me burst open, and I saw for a second something hanging in a tree. It was gone in a wink, the puff blowing by and the leaves closing. I tell you the truth: I had made up my mind to see an *aitu;* and if the thing had looked like a pig or a woman, it wouldn't have given me the same turn. The trouble was that it seemed kind of square, and the idea of a square thing that was alive and sang knocked me sick and silly. I must have stood quite a while; and I made pretty certain it was right out of the same tree that the singing came. Then I began to come to myself a bit.

"Well," says I, "if this is really so, if this is a place where there are square things that sing, I'm gone up anyway. Let's have my fun for my money."

But I thought I might as well take the off-chance of a prayer being any good; so I plumped on my knees and prayed out loud; and all the time I was praying the strange sounds came out of the tree, and went up and down, and changed, for all the world like music, only you could see it wasn't human—there was nothing there that you could whistle.

As soon as I had made an end in proper style, I laid down my gun, stuck my knife between my teeth, walked right up to that tree and began to climb. I tell you my heart was like ice. But presently, as I went up, I caught another glimpse of the thing, and that relieved me, for I thought it seemed like a box; and when I had got right up to it I near fell out of the tree with laughing.

A box it was, sure enough, and a candle-box at that, with the brand upon the side of it; and it had banjo-strings stretched so as to sound when the wind blew. I believe they call the thing a Tyrolean harp[19] whatever that may mean.

"Well, Mr. Case," said I, "you frightened me once, but I defy you to frighten me again," I says, and slipped down the tree, and set out again to find my enemy's head office, which I guessed would not be far away.

The undergrowth was thick in this part; I couldn't see before my nose, and must burst my way through by main force and ply the knife as I went, slicing the cords of the lianas and slashing down whole trees at a blow. I call them trees for the bigness, but in truth they were just big weeds, and sappy to cut through like carrot. From all this crowd and kind of vegetation, I was just thinking to myself, the place might have once been cleared, when I came on my nose over a pile of stones, and saw in a moment it was some kind of a work of man. The Lord knows when it was made or when deserted, for this part of the island has lain undisturbed since long before the whites came. A few steps beyond I hit into the path I had been always looking for. It was narrow, but well beaten, and I saw that Case had plenty of disciples. It seems, indeed it was, a piece of fashionable boldness to venture up here with the trader, and a young man scarce reckoned himself grown till he had got his breech tatooed, for one thing, and seen Case's devils for another. This is mighty like Kanakas: but, if you look at it another way, it's mighty like white folks too.

A bit along the path I was brought to a clear stand, and had to rub my eyes. There was a wall in front of me, the path passing it by a gap; it was tumbledown and plainly very old, but built of big stones very well laid; and there is no native alive to-day upon that island that could dream of such a piece of building! Along all the top of it was a line of queer figures, idols or scarecrows, or what not. They had carved and painted faces ugly to view, their eyes and teeth were of shell, their hair and their bright clothes blew in the wind, and some of them worked with the tugging. There are islands up west where they make these kind of figures till to-day; but if ever they were made in this island, the practice and the very recollection of it are now long forgotten. And the singular thing was that all these bogies were as fresh as toys out of a shop.

Then it came in my mind that Case had let out to me the first day that he was a good forger of island curiosities—a thing by which so many traders turn an honest

19 **Tyrolean harp:** Wiltshire's mistake for Aeolian harp, a stringed instrument hung so as to resonate in the wind. [Stevenson's note.]

penny. And with that I saw the whole business, and how this display served the man a double purpose: first of all, to season his curiosities, and then to frighten those that came to visit him.

But I should tell you (what made the thing more curious) that all the time the Tyrolean harps were harping round me in the trees, and even while I looked, a green-and-yellow bird (that, I suppose, was building) began to tear the hair off the head of one of the figures.

A little farther on I found the best curiosity of the museum. The first I saw of it was a longish mound of earth with a twist to it. Digging off the earth with my hands, I found underneath tarpaulin stretched on boards, so that this was plainly the roof of a cellar. It stood right on the top of the hill, and the entrance was on the far side, between two rocks, like the entrance to a cave, I went as far in as the bend, and, looking round the corner, saw a shining face. It was big and ugly, like a pantomime mask, and the brightness of it waxed and dwindled, and at times it smoked.

"Oho!" says I, "luminous paint!"

And I must say I rather admired the man's ingenuity. With a box of tools and a few mighty simple contrivances he had made out to have a devil of a temple. Any poor Kanaka brought up here in the dark, with the harps whining all round him, and shown that smoking face in the bottom of a hole, would make no kind of doubt but he had seen and heard enough devils for a lifetime. It's easy to find out what Kanakas think. Just go back to yourself anyway around from ten to fifteen years old, and there's an average Kanaka. There are some pious, just as there are pious boys; and the most of them, like the boys again, are middling honest and yet think it rather larks to steal, and are easy scared, and rather like to be so. I remember a boy I was at school with at home who played the Case business. He didn't know anything, that boy; he couldn't do anything; he had no luminous paint and no Tyrolean harps; he just boldly said he was a sorcerer, and frightened us out of our boots, and we loved it. And then it came in my mind how the master had once flogged that boy, and the surprise we were all in to see the sorcerer catch it and hum like anybody else. Thinks I to myself: "I must find some way of fixing it so for Master Case." And the next moment I had my idea.

I went back by the path, which, when once you had found it, was quite plain and easy walking; and when I stepped out on the black sands; who should I see but Master Case himself. I cocked my gun and held it handy, and we marched up and passed without a word, each keeping the tail of his eye on the other; and no sooner had we passed than we each wheeled round like fellows drilling, and stood face to face. We had each taken the same notion in his head, you see, that the other fellow might give him the load of his gun in the stern.

"You've shot nothing," says Case.

"I'm not on the shoot to-day," said I.

"Well, the devil go with you for me," says he.

"The same to you," says I.

But we stuck just the way we were; no fear of either of us moving.

Case laughed. "We can't stop here all day, though," said he.

"Don't let me detain you," says I.

He laughed again. "Look here, Wiltshire, do you think me a fool?" he asked.

"More of a knave, if you want to know," says I.

"Well, do you think it would better me to shoot you here, on this open beach?" said he. "Because I don't. Folks come fishing every day. There may be a score of them up the valley now, making copra; there might be half a dozen on the hill behind you, after pigeons; they might be watching us this minute, and I shouldn't wonder. I give you my word I don't want to shoot you. Why should I? You don't hinder me any. You haven't got one pound of copra but what you made with your own hands, like a negro slave. You're vegetating—that's what I call it—and I don't care where you vegetate, nor yet how long. Give me your word you don't mean to shoot me, and I'll give you a lead and walk away."

"Well," said I, "you're frank and pleasant, ain't you? And I'll be the same. I don't mean to shoot you today. Why should I? This business is beginning; it ain't done yet, Mr. Case. I've given you one turn already. I can see the marks of my knuckles on your head to this blooming hour, and I've more cooking for you. I'm not a paralee, like Underhill. My name ain't Adams, and it ain't Vigours; and I mean to show you that you've met your match."

"This is a silly way to talk," said he. "This is not the talk to make me move on with."

"All right," said I, "stay where you are. I ain't in any hurry, and you know it. I can put in a day on this beach and never mind. I ain't got any copra to bother with. I ain't got any luminous paint to see to."

I was sorry I said that last, but it whipped out before I knew. I could see it took the wind out of his sails, and he stood and stared at me with his brow drawn up. Then I suppose he made up his mind he must get to the bottom of this.

"I take you at your word," says he, and turned his back, and walked right into the devil's bush.

I let him go, of course, for I had passed my word. But I watched him as long as he was in sight, and after he was gone lit out for cover as lively as you would want to see, and went the rest of the way home under the bush, for I didn't trust him sixpence worth. One thing I saw, I had been ass enough to give him warning, and that which I meant to do I must do at once.

You would think I had had about enough excitement for one morning, but there was another turn waiting me. As soon as I got far enough round the cape to see my house I made out there were strangers there; a little farther, and no doubt about it. There was a couple of armed sentinels squatting at my door. I could only suppose the trouble about Uma must have come to a head, and the station been seized. For aught I could think, Uma was taken up already, and these armed men were waiting to do the like with me.

However, as I came nearer, which I did at top speed, I saw there was a third native sitting on the veranda like a guest, and Uma was talking with him like a hostess. Nearer still I made out it was the big young chief, Maea, and that he was smiling away and smoking. And what was he smoking? None of your European cigarettes fit for a cat, not even the genuine big, knock-me-down native article that a fellow can really put in the time with if his pipe is broke—but a cigar, and one of my Mexicans at that, that I could swear to. At sight of this my heart started beating, and I took a wild hope in my head that the trouble was over, and Maea had come round.

Uma pointed me out to him as I came up, and he met me at the head of my own stairs like a thorough gentleman.

"Vilivili," said he, which was the best they could make of my name, "I pleased."

There is no doubt when an island chief wants to be civil he can do it. I saw the way things were from the word go. There was no call for Uma to say to me:

"He no 'fraid Ese now, come bring copra." I tell you I shook hands with that Kanaka like as if he was the best white man in Europe.

The fact was, Case and he had got after the same girl, or Maea suspected it, and concluded to make hay of the trader on the chance. He had dressed himself up, got a couple of his retainers cleaned and armed to kind of make the thing more public, and, just waiting till Case was clear of the village, came round to put the whole of his business my way. He was rich as well as powerful. I suppose that man was worth fifty thousand nuts per annum. I gave him the price of the beach and a quarter cent better, and as for credit, I would have advanced him the inside of the store and the fittings besides, I was so pleased to see him. I must say he bought like a gentleman: rice and tins and biscuits enough for a week's feast, and stuffs by the bolt. He was agreeable besides; he had plenty fun to him; and we cracked jests together, mostly through the interpreter, because he had mighty little English, and my native was still off colour. One thing I made out: he could never really have thought much harm of Uma; he could never have been really frightened, and must just have made believe from dodginess, and because he thought Case had a strong pull in the village and could help him on.

This set me thinking that both he and I were in a tightish place. What he had done was to fly in the face of the whole village, and the thing might cost him his authority. More than that, after my talk with Case on the beach, I thought it might very well cost me my life. Case had as good as said he would pot me if ever I got any copra; he would come home to find the best business in the village had changed hands, and the best thing I thought I could do was to get in first with the potting.

"See here, Uma," says I, "tell him I'm sorry I made him wait, but I was up looking at Case's Tiapolo store in the bush."

"He want savvy if you no 'fraid?" translated Uma.

I laughed out. "Not much!" says I. "Tell him the place is a blooming toy-shop! Tell him in England we give these things to the kid to play with."

"He want savvy if you hear devil sing?" she asked next.

"Look here," I said, "I can't do it now, because I've got no banjo-strings in stock; but the next time the ship comes round I'll have one of these same contraptions right here in my veranda, and he can see for himself how much devil there is to it. Tell him, as soon as I can get the strings I'll make one for his pickaninnies. The name of the concern is a Tyrolean harp; and you can tell him the name means in English that nobody but dam-fools give a cent for it."

This time he was so pleased he had to try his English again. "You talk true?" says he.

"Rather!" said I. "Talk all-a-same Bible. Bring out a Bible here, Uma, if you've got such a thing, and I'll kiss it. Or, I'll tell you what's better still," says I, taking a header,[20] "ask him if he's afraid to go up there himself by day."

It appeared he wasn't; he could venture as far as that by day and in company.

"That's the ticket, then!" said I. "Tell him the man's a fraud and the place foolishness, and if he'll go up there to-morrow he'll see all that's left of it. But tell him this, Uma, and mind he understands it: If he gets talking it's bound to come to Case, and I'm a dead man! I'm playing his game, tell him, and if he says one word my blood will be at his door and be the damnation of him here and after."

She told him, and he shook hands with me up to the hilt, and, says he: "No talk. Go up to-mollow. You my friend?"

"No, sir," says I, "no such foolishness. I've come here to trade, tell him, and not to make friends. But, as to Case, I'll send that man to glory!"

So off Maea went, pretty well pleased, as I could see.

Chapter V Night in the Bush

Well, I was committed now; Tiapolo had to be smashed up before next day, and my hands were pretty full, not only with preparations, but with argument. My house was like a mechanics' debating society. Uma was so made up that I shouldn't go into the bush by night, or that, if I did, I was never to come back again. You know her style of arguing: you've had a specimen about Queen Victoria and the devil; and I leave you to fancy if I was tired of it before dark.

At last I had a good idea. "What was the use of casting my pearls before her?" I thought; some of her own chopped hay would be likelier to do the business.

"I'll tell you what, then," said I. "You fish out your Bible, and I'll take that up along with me. That'll make me right."

She swore a Bible was no use.

"That's just your Kanaka ignorance," said I. "Bring the Bible out."

She brought it, and I turned to the title-page, where I thought there would likely be some English, and so there was. "There!" said I, "Look at that! *London: Printed for the British and Foreign Bible Society, Blackfriars,*' and the date, which I can't read, owing to it's being in these X's. There's no devil in hell can look near the Bible Society, Blackfriars. Why, you silly," I said, "how do you suppose we get along with our own *aitus* at home! All Bible Society!"

"I think you no got any," said she. "White man, he tell me you no got."

"Sounds likely, don't it?" I asked. "Why would these islands all be chock full of them and none in Europe?"

"Well, you no got bread-fruit," said she.

---

20 **header:** A head-first dive; a gamble.

I could have torn my hair. "Now, look here, old lady," said I, "you dry up, for I'm tired of you. I'll take the Bible, which'll put me as straight as the mail, and that's the last word I've got to say."

The night fell extraordinary dark, clouds coming up with sundown and over-spreading all; not a star showed; there was only an end of a moon, and that not due before the small hours. Round the village, what with the lights and the fires in the open houses, and the torches of many fishers moving on the reef, it kept as gay as an illumination; but the sea and the mountains and woods were all clean gone. I suppose it might be eight o'clock when I took the road, laden like a donkey. First there was that Bible, a book as big as your head, which I had let myself in for by my own tomfoolery. Then there was my gun, and knife, and lantern, and patent matches, all necessary. And then there was the real plant of the affair in hand, a mortal weight of gunpowder, a pair of dynamite fishing-bombs, and two or three pieces of slowmatch that I had hauled out of the tin cases and spliced together the best way I could; for the match was only trade stuff, and a man would be crazy that trusted it. Altogether, you see, I had the materials of a pretty good blow up! Expense was nothing to me; I wanted that thing done right.

As long as I was in the open, and had the lamp in my house to steer by, I did well. But when I got to the path, it fell so dark I could make no headway, walking into trees and swearing there, like a man looking for the matches in his bed-room. I knew it was risky to light up, for my lantern would be visible all the way to the point of the cape, and as no one went there after dark, it would be talked about, and come to Case's ears. But what was I to do? I had either to give the business over and lose caste with Maea, or light up, take my chance, and get through the thing the smartest I was able.

As long as I was on the path I walked hard, but when I came to the black beach I had to run. For the tide was now nearly flowed; and to get through with my powder dry between the surf and the steep hill, took all the quickness I possessed. As it was, even the wash caught me to the knees, and I came near falling on a stone. All this time the hurry I was in, and the free air and smell of the sea, kept my spirits lively; but when I was once in the bush and began to climb the path I took it easier. The fearsomeness of the wood had been a good bit rubbed off for me by Master Case's banjo-strings and graven images, yet I thought it was a dreary walk, and guessed, when the disciples went up there, they must be badly scared. The light of the lantern, striking among all these trunks and forked branches and twisted rope-ends of lianas, made the whole place, or all that you could see of it, a kind of a puzzle of turning shadows. They came to meet you, solid and quick like giants, and then spun off and vanished; they hove up over your head like clubs, and flew away into the night like birds. The floor of the bush glimmered with dead wood, the way the match-box used to shine after you had struck a lucifer.[21] Big, cold drops fell on me from the

---

21 **lucifer:** A match. Dead wood glows faintly as it rots.

branches overhead like sweat. There was no wind to mention; only a little icy breath of a land breeze that stirred nothing; and the harps were silent.

The first landfall I made was when I got through the bush of wild cocoanuts, and came in view of the bogies on the wall. Mighty queer they looked by the shining of the lantern, with their painted faces and shell eyes, and their clothes, and their hair hanging. One after another I pulled them all up and piled them in a bundle on the cellar roof, so as they might go to glory with the rest. Then I chose a place behind one of the big stones at the entrance, buried my powder and the two shells, and arranged my match along the passage. And then I had a look at the smoking head, just for good-by. It was doing fine.

"Cheer up," says I. "You're booked."

It was my first idea to light up and be getting homeward; for the darkness and the glimmer of the dead wood and the shadows of the lantern made me lonely. But I knew where one of the harps hung; it seemed a pity it shouldn't go with the rest; and at the same time I couldn't help letting on to myself that I was mortal tired of my employment, and would like best to be at home and have the door shut. I stepped out of the cellar and argued it fore and back. There was a sound of the sea far down below me on the coast; nearer hand not a leaf stirred; I might have been the only living creature this side of Cape Horn. Well, as I stood there thinking, it seemed the bush woke and became full of little noises. Little noises they were, and nothing to hurt; a bit of a crackle, a bit of a rush; but the breath jumped right out of me and my throat went as dry as a biscuit. It wasn't Case I was afraid of, which would have been common-sense; I never thought of Case; what took me, as sharp as the colic, was the old wives' tales—the devil-women and the man-pigs. It was the toss of a penny whether I should run; but I got a purchase on myself, and stepped out, and held up the lantern (like a fool) and looked all round.

In the direction of the village and the path there was nothing to be seen; but when I turned inland it's a wonder to me I didn't drop. There, coming right up out of the desert and the bad bush—there, sure enough, was a devil-woman, just as the way I had figured she would look. I saw the light shine on her bare arms and her bright eyes, and there went out of me a yell so big that I thought it was my death.

"Ah! No sing out!" says the devil-woman, in a kind of a high whisper. "Why you talk big voice? Put out light! Ese he come."

"My God Almighty, Uma, is that you?" says I.

"*Ioe,*"[22] says she. "I come quick. Ese here soon."

"You come along?" I asked. "You no 'fraid?"

"Ah, too much 'fraid!" she whispered, clutching me. "I think die."

"Well," says I, with a kind of a weak grin. "I'm not the one to laugh at you, Mrs. Wiltshire, for I'm about the worst scared man in the South Pacific myself."

She told me in two words what brought her. I was scarce gone, it seems, when Faavao came in, and the old woman had met Black Jack running as hard as he was fit from our house to Case's. Uma neither spoke nor stopped, but lit right out to come

---

22 *"Ioe":* Yes. [Stevenson's note.]

and warn me. She was so close at my heels that the lantern was her guide across the beach, and afterward, by the glimmer of it in the trees, she got her line up hill. It was only when I had got to the top or was in the cellar that she wandered—Lord knows where!—and lost a sight of precious time, afraid to call out lest Case was at the heels of her, and falling in the bush, so that she was all knocked and bruised. That must have been when she got too far to the southward, and how she came to take me in the flank at last and frighten me beyond what I've got the words to tell of.

Well, anything was better than a devil-woman, but I thought her yarn serious enough. Black Jack had no call to be about my house, unless he was set there to watch; and it looked to me as if my tomfool word about the paint, and perhaps some chatter of Maea's, had got us all in a clove hitch.[23] One thing was clear: Uma and I were here for the night; we daren't try to go home before day, and even then it would be safer to strike round up the mountain and come in by the back of the village, or we might walk into an ambuscade. It was plain, too, that the mine should be sprung immediately, or Case might be in time to stop it.

I marched into the tunnel, Uma keeping tight hold of me, opened my lantern and lit the match. The first length of it burned like a spill of paper, and I stood stupid, watching it burn, and thinking we were going aloft with Tiapolo, which was none of my views. The second took to a better rate, though faster than I cared about; and at that I got my wits again, hauled Uma clear of the passage, blew out and dropped the lantern, and the pair of us groped our way into the bush until I thought it might be safe, and lay down together by a tree.

"Old lady," I said, "I wont forget this night. You're a trump, and that's what's wrong with you."

She bumped herself close up to me. She had run out the way she was, with nothing on her but her kilt; and she was all wet with the dews and the sea on the black beach, and shook straight on with cold and the terror of the dark and the devils.

"Too much 'fraid," was all she said.

The far side of Case's hill goes down near as steep as a precipice into the next valley. We were on the very edge of it, and I could see the dead wood shine and hear the sea sound far below. I didn't care about the position, which left me no retreat, but I was afraid to change. Then I saw I had made a worse mistake about the lantern, which I should have left lighted, so that I could have had a crack at Case when he stepped into the shine of it. And since I hadn't had the wit to do that, it seemed a senseless thing to leave the good lantern to blow up with the graven images. The thing belonged to me, after all, and was worth money, and might come in handy. If I could have trusted the match, I might have run in still and rescued it. But who was going to trust to the match? You know what trade is. The stuff was good enough for Kanakas to go fishing with, where they've got to look lively anyway, and the most they risk is only to have their hand blown off. But for anyone that wanted to fool around a blow-up like mine that match was rubbish.

---

23 **clove hitch:** A sailor's knot.

Altogether the best I could do was to lie still, see my shot-gun handy, and wait for the explosion. But it was a solemn kind of a business. The blackness of the night was like solid; the only thing you could see was the nasty bogy glimmer of the dead wood, and that showed you nothing but itself; and as for sounds, I stretched my ears till I thought I could have heard the match burn in the tunnel, and that bush was as silent as a coffin. Now and then there was a bit of a crack; but whether it was near or far, whether it was Case stubbing his toes within a few yards of me, or a tree breaking miles away, I knew no more than the babe unborn.

And then, all of a sudden, Vesuvius went off. It was a long time coming; but when it came (though I say it that shouldn't) no man could ask to see a better. At first it was just a son of a gun of a row, and a spout of fire, and the wood lighted up so that you could see to read. And then the trouble began. Uma and I were half buried under a wagonful of earth, and glad it was no worse, for one of the rocks at the entrance of the tunnel was fired clean into the air, fell within a couple of fathoms of where we lay, and bounded over the edge of the hill, and went pounding down into the next valley. I saw I had rather under-calculated our distance, or overdone the dynamite and powder, which you please.

And presently I saw I had made another slip. The noise of the thing began to die off, shaking the island; the dazzle was over; and yet the night didn't come back the way I expected. For the whole wood was scattered with red coals and brands from the explosion; they were all round me on the flat, some had fallen below in the valley, and some stuck and flared in the tree-tops. I had no fear of fire, for these forests are too wet to kindle. But the trouble was that the place was all lit up—not very bright, but good enough to get a shot by; and the way the coals were scattered, it was just as likely Case might have the advantage as myself. I looked all round for his white face, you may be sure; but there was not a sign of him. As for Uma, the life seemed to have been knocked right out of her by the bang and blaze of it.

There was one bad point in my game. One of the blessed graven images had come down all afire, hair and clothes and body, not four yards away from me. I cast a mighty noticing glance all round; there was still no Case, and I made up my mind I must get rid of that burning stick before he came, or I should be shot there like a dog.

It was my first idea to have crawled, and then I thought speed was the main thing, and stood half up to make a rush. The same moment, from somewhere between me and the sea, there came a flash and a report, and a rifle-bullet screeched in my ear. I swung straight round and up with my gun, but the brute had a Winchester, and before I could as much as see him his second shot knocked me over like a ninepin. I seemed to fly in the air, then came down by the run and lay half a minute, silly; and then I found my hands empty, and my gun had flown over my head as I fell. It makes a man mighty wide awake to be in the kind of box that I was in. I scarcely knew where I was hurt, or whether I was hurt or not, but turned right over on my face to crawl after my weapon. Unless you have tried to get about with a smashed leg you don't know what pain is, and I let out a howl like a bullock's.

This was the unluckiest noise that ever I made in my life. Up to then Uma had stuck to her tree like a sensible woman, knowing she would be only in the way; but as soon as she heard me sing out she ran forward. The Winchester cracked again, and down she went.

I had sat up, leg and all, to stop her; but when I saw her tumble I clapped down again where I was, lay still, and felt the handle of my knife. I had been scurried and put out before. No more of that for me. He had knocked over my girl, I had got to fix him for it; and I lay there and gritted my teeth, and footed up the chances. My leg was broke, my gun was gone. Case had still ten shots in his Winchester. It looked a kind of hopeless business. But I never despaired nor thought upon despairing: that man had got to go.

For a goodish bit not one of us let on. Then I heard Case begin to move nearer in the bush, but mighty careful. The image had burned out, there were only a few coals left here and there, and the wood was main dark, but had a kind of a low glow in it like a fire on its last legs. It was by this that I made out Case's head looking at me over a big tuft of ferns, and at the same time the brute saw me and shouldered his Winchester. I lay quite still, and as good as looked into the barrel: it was my last chance, but I thought my heart would have come right out of its bearings. Then he fired. Lucky for me it was no shot-gun, for the bullet struck within an inch of me and knocked the dirt in my eyes.

Just you try and see if you can lie quiet, and let a man take a sitting shot at you and miss you by a hair. But I did, and lucky, too. A while Case stood with the Winchester at the port-arms; then he gave a little laugh to himself and stepped round the ferns.

"Laugh!" thought I. "If you had the wit of a louse you would be praying!"

I was all as taut as a ship's hawser or the spring of a watch, and as soon as he came within reach of me I had him by the ankle, plucked the feet right out from under him, laid him out, and was upon the top of him, broken leg and all, before he breathed. His Winchester had gone the same road as my shot-gun; it was nothing to me—I defied him now. I'm a pretty strong man anyway, but I never knew what strength was till I got hold of Case. He was knocked out of time by the rattle he came down with, and threw up his hands together, more like a frightened woman, so that I caught both of them with my left. This wakened him up, and he fastened his teeth in my forearm like a weasel. Much I cared. My leg gave me all the pain I had any use for, and I drew my knife and got it in the place.

"Now," said I, "I've got you; and you're gone up, and a good job too! Do you feel the point of that? That's for Underhill! And there's for Adams! And now here's for Uma, and that's going to knock your blooming soul right out of you!"

With that I gave him the cold steel for all I was worth. His body kicked under me like a spring sofa; he gave a dreadful kind of a long moan, and lay still.

"I wonder if you're dead? I hope so!" I thought, for my head was swimming. But I wasn't going to take chances; I had his own example too close before me for that; and I tried to draw the knife out to give it him again. The blood came over my hands, I remember, hot as tea; and with that I fainted clean away, and fell with my head on the man's mouth.

When I came to myself it was pitch dark; the cinders had burned out; there was nothing to be seen but the shine of the dead wood, and I couldn't remember where I was nor why I was in such pain, nor what I was all wetted with. Then it came back, and the first thing I attended to was to give him the knife again a half a dozen times up to the handle. I believe he was dead already, but it did him no harm and did me good.

"I bet you're dead now," I said, and then I called to Uma.

Nothing answered, and I made a move to go and grope for her, fouled my broken leg, and fainted again.

When I came to myself the second time the clouds had all cleared away, except a few that sailed there, white as cotton. The moon was up—a tropic moon. The moon at home turns a wood black, but even this old butt-end of a one showed up that forest as green as by day. The night birds—or, rather, they're a kind of early morning bird—sang out with their long, falling notes like nightingales. And I could see the dead man, that I was still half resting on, looking right up into the sky with his open eyes, no paler than when he was alive; and a little way off Uma tumbled on her side. I got over to her the best way I was able, and when I got there she was broad awake and crying, and sobbing to herself with no more noise than an insect. It appears she was afraid to cry out loud, because of the *aitus*. Altogether she was not much hurt, but scared beyond belief; she had come to her senses a long while ago, cried out to me, heard nothing in reply, made out we were both dead, and had lain there ever since, afraid to budge a finger. The ball had ploughed up her shoulder, and she had lost a main quantity of blood; but I soon had that tied up the way it ought to be with the tail of my shirt and a scarf I had on, got her head on my sound knee and my back against a trunk, and settled down to wait for morning. Uma was for neither use nor ornament, and could only clutch hold of me and shake and cry. I don't suppose there was ever anybody worse scared, and, to do her justice, she had had a lively night of it. As for me, I was in a good bit of pain and fever, but not so bad when I sat still; and every time I looked over to Case I could have sung and whistled. Talk about meat and drink! To see that man lying there dead as a herring filled me full.

The night birds stopped after a while; and then the light began to change, the east came orange, the whole wood began to whirr with singing like a musical box, and there was the broad day.

I didn't expect Maea for a long while yet; and, indeed, I thought there was an off-chance he might go back on the whole idea and not come at all. I was the better pleased when, about an hour after daylight, I heard sticks smashing and a lot of Kanakas laughing and singing out to keep their courage up. Uma sat up quite brisk at the first word of it; and presently we saw a party come stringing out of the path, Maea in front, and behind him a white man in a pith helmet. It was Mr. Tarleton, who had turned up late last night in Falesá, having left his boat and walked the last stage with a lantern.

They buried Case upon the field of glory, right in the hole where he had kept the smoking head. I waited till the thing was done; and Mr. Tarleton prayed, which I thought tom-foolery, but I'm bound to say he gave a pretty sick view of the dear departed's prospects, and seemed to have his own ideas of hell. I had it out with him afterward, told him he had scamped his duty; and what he had ought to have done was to up like a man and tell the Kanakas plainly Case was damned, and a good riddance; but I never could get him to see it my way. Then they made me a litter of poles and carried me down to the station. Mr. Tarleton set my leg, and made a regular missionary splice of it, so that I limp to this day. That done, he took down my evidence, and Uma's, and Maea's, wrote it all out fine, and had us sign it; and then he got the chiefs and marched over to Papa Randall's to seize Case's papers.

All they found was a bit of a diary, kept for a good many years, and all about the price of copra, and chickens being stolen, and that; and the books of the business and the will I told you of in the beginning, by both of which the whole thing (stock, lock, and barrel) appeared to belong to the Samoa woman. It was I that bought her out at a mighty reasonable figure, for she was in a hurry to get home. As for Randall and the black, they had to tramp; got into some kind of a station on the Papamalulu side; did very bad business, for the truth is neither of the pair was fit for it, and lived mostly on fish, which was the means of Randall's death. It seems there was a nice shoal in one day, and papa went after them with the dynamite; either the match burned too fast, or papa was full, or both, but the shell went off (in the usual way) before he threw it, and where was papa's hand? Well, there's nothing to hurt in that; the islands up north are all full of one-handed men like the parties in the "Arabian Nights;" but either Randall was too old, or he drank too much, and the short and the long of it was that he died. Pretty soon after, the nigger was turned out of the island for stealing from white men, and went off to the west, where he found men of his own colour, in case he liked that, and the men of his own colour took and ate him at some kind of a corroborree, and I'm sure I hope he was to their fancy!

So there was I, left alone in my glory at Falesá; and when the schooner came round I filled her up, and gave her a deck cargo halt as high as the house. I must say Mr. Tarleton did the right thing by us; but he took a meanish kind of a revenge.

"Now, Mr. Wiltshire," said he, "I've put you all square with everybody here. It wasn't difficult to do, Case being gone; but I have done it, and given my pledge besides that you will deal fairly with the natives. I must ask you to keep my word."

Well, so I did. I used to be bothered about my balances, but I reasoned it out this way. We all have queerish balances, and the natives all know it and water their copra in a proportion so that it's fair all round; but the truth is, it did use to bother me, and, though I did well in Falesá, I was half glad when the firm moved me on to another station where I was under no kind of a pledge and could look my balances in the face.

As for the old lady, you know her as well as I do. She's only the one fault. If you don't keep your eye lifting she would give away the roof off the station. Well, it seems it's natural in Kanakas. She's turned a powerful big woman now, and could throw a London bobby over her shoulder. But that's natural in Kanakas too, and there's no manner of doubt that she's an A 1 wife.

Mr. Tarleton's gone home, his trick being over. He was the best missionary I ever struck, and now, it seems, he's parsonising down Somerset way. Well, that's best for him; he'll have no Kanakas there to get luny over.

My public-house? Not a bit of it, nor ever likely. I'm stuck here, I fancy. I don't like to leave the kids, you see: and—there's no use talking—they're better here than what they would be in a white man's country, though Ben took the eldest up to Auckland, where he's being schooled with the best. But what bothers me is the girls. They're only half-castes, of course; I know that as well as you do, and there's nobody thinks less of half-castes than I do; but they're mine, and about all I've got. I can't reconcile my mind to their taking up with Kanakas, and I'd like to know where I'm to find the whites?

QUESTIONS

1. As in any story told in first person, the character and reliability of the narrator are of great importance. Analyze Wiltshire as a narrator.

2. Describe the attitude of whites toward those of other races—the Polynesians in particular. What is Wiltshire's attitude? Does Wiltshire's attitude remain constant through the story, or does it change?

3. How do the Polynesians regard Christianity? How do they regard Europeans? Give details from the story to support your answers.

4. Sexuality plays an important role in this story. How do the whites tend to regard Polynesian women? What is Wiltshire's attitude? Is Uma portrayed as a stereotype of the "oriental" woman—submissive, dependent, humble?

5. How do you interpret the last paragraph of the story? In particular, what does Wiltshire imply when he says, "I can't reconcile my mind to their taking up with Kanakas, and I'd like to know where I'm to find the whites?"

6. What does the story reveal about Victorian attitudes toward interracial marriage?

Rudyard Kipling

(1865–1936)

Rudyard Kipling's name is permanently linked with British colonialist literature, and his place in that literature (indeed his place in the British literary canon) is one of the most hotly debated subjects in literary history and criticism. Born in Bombay, India, where his father, an artist, was curator of the Lahore museum from 1875 to 1893, he was sent to England at age six with his younger sister to live with an aunt. He was miserable until 1878, when he entered the United Services Military school, whose discipline and male camaraderie he loved. Upon graduation, he returned to India and worked as a journalist, contributing poems and stories in his spare time to the Lahore *Civil and Military Gazette*. His work as a journalist brought him into intimate contact with the whole of

British society in India, as well as with Indians of every rank and caste. At twenty-one, Kipling became famous in India almost overnight for *Departmental Ditties* (1886), a series of light poems written about and often from the point of view of ordinary soldiers stationed in India. Two years later he published *Plain Tales from the Hills*, short stories that had appeared previously in his newspaper. Six little volumes of stories followed in the next two years.

When Kipling's travels took him back to England in 1889, he found himself a celebrity. Britons thrilled to his stories of life in exotic India, told in an swift and energetic style with flashes of authentic insight into the lives of British colonials and their Indian subjects. Hasty production ensured that the stories were of uneven quality, but as their author was only twenty-four, his potential seemed boundless. And that potential seemed confirmed with the publication of *Barrack-Room Ballads* (1892), poems told about and from the point of view of ordinary British soldiers. He followed this with the children's classic, *The Jungle Book* (1894), his only novel, *Kim* (1901), plus many more stories, poems, and juvenile works. He was awarded the Nobel Prize in 1907. Kipling's energetic and optimistic strain was severely tested by the death in World War I of his only son. Much of his work after this date is sour or pessimistic in outlook.

Kipling is often labeled as a jingoist who supported the Empire and believed in "the white man's burden," the title of a poem he published in 1899 to encourage U.S. President Theodore Roosevelt to annex the Philippines. But while Kipling's work certainly contains hearty pro-colonialist themes, it also includes cross-currents and complexities of doubt. If Kipling overtly admires men and women of action who actually do the work of empire, often at great cost to themselves, he also acknowledges their limitations. While some describe Kipling's tone as one-dimensional in its realism, many of his stories recognize that much about India and human existence is beyond our ken. There is in Kipling a strong streak of anti-establishment rebellion.

All of these qualities are exhibited by the story included here, "The Man Who Would Be King." To read this story simplistically, as one only illustrating the superiority of European civilization and race, is to miss much of what Kipling is doing to complicate and even question such easy responses.

The Man Who Would Be King   1888

Brother to a Prince and fellow to a beggar if he be found worthy

The law, as quoted, lays down a fair conduct of life, and one not easy to follow. I have been fellow to a beggar again and again under circumstances which prevented either of us finding out whether the other was worthy. I have still to be brother to a Prince, though I once came near to kinship with what might have been a veritable King and was promised the reversion of a Kingdom—army, law-courts, revenue and policy all complete. But, to-day, I greatly fear that my King is dead, and if I want a crown I must go hunt it for myself.

The beginning of everything was in a railway train upon the road to Mhow from Ajmir. There had been a Deficit in the Budget which necessitated travelling, not Second-class, which is only half as dear[1] as First-class, but by Intermediate, which is very awful indeed. There are no cushions in the Intermediate class, and the population are either Intermediate, which is Eurasian, or native, which for a long night journey is nasty, or Loafer, which is amusing though intoxicated. Intermediates do not buy from refreshment-rooms. They carry their food in bundles and pots, and buy sweets from the native sweetmeat-sellers, and drink the roadside water. That is why in hot weather Intermediates are taken out of the carriages dead, and in all weathers are most properly looked down upon.

My particular Intermediate happened to be empty till I reached Nasirabad, when a big black-browed gentleman in shirt-sleeves entered, and, following the custom of Intermediates, passed the time of day. He was a wanderer and a vagabond like myself, but with an educated taste for whiskey. He told tales of things he had seen and done, of out-of-the-way corners of the Empire into which he had penetrated, and of adventures in which he risked his life for a few days' food.

"If India was filled with men like you and me, not knowing more than the crows where they'd get their next day's rations, it isn't seventy millions of revenue the land would be paying—it's seven hundred millions," said he; and as I looked at his mouth and chin I was disposed to agree with him.

We talked politics—the politics of Loaferdom that sees things from the underside where the lath and plaster is not smoothed off—and we talked postal arrangements because my friend wanted to send a telegram back from the next station to Ajmir, the turning-off place from the Bombay to the Mhow line as you travel westward. My friend had no money beyond eight annas[2] which he wanted for dinner, and I had no money at all, owing to the hitch in the Budget before mentioned. Further, I was going into a wilderness where, though I should resume touch with the Treasury, there were no telegraph offices. I was, therefore, unable to help him in any way.

"We might threaten a Station-master, and make him send a wire on tick,[3] said my friend, "but that'd mean enquiries for you and for me, and I've got my hands full these days. Did you say you were travelling back along this line within any days?"

"Within ten," I said.

"Can't you make it eight?" said he. "Mine is rather urgent business."

"I can send your telegram within ten days if that will serve you," I said.

"I couldn't trust the wire to fetch him now I think of it. It's this way. He leaves Delhi on the 23rd for Bombay. That means he'll be running through Ajmir about the night of the 23rd."

---

1 **dear:** Expensive.
2 **annas:** Coins worth one-sixteenth of a rupee; eight annas is a paltry sum.
3 **tick:** Credit.

"But I'm going into the Indian Desert," I explained.

"Well *and* good," said he. "You'll be changing at Marwar Junction to get into Jodhpore territory—you must do that—and he'll be coming through Marwar Junction in the early morning of the 24th by the Bombay Mail. Can you be at Marwar Junction on that time? 'Twon't be inconveniencing you because I know that there's precious few pickings to be got out of these Central India States—even though you pretend to be correspondent of the *Backwoodsman*."

"Have you ever tried that trick?" I asked.

"Again and again, but the Residents find you out, and then you get escorted to the Border before you've time to get your knife into them.[4] But about my friend here. I *must* give him a word o' mouth to tell him what's come to me or else he won't know where to go. I would take it more than kind of you if you was to come out of Central India in time to catch him at Marwar Junction, and say to him: 'He has gone South for the week.' He'll know what that means. He's a big man with a red beard, and a great swell[5] he is. You'll find him sleeping like a gentleman with all his luggage round him in a Second-class apartment. But don't you be afraid. Slip down the window and say: 'He has gone South for the week,' and he'll tumble. It's only cutting your time of stay in those parts by two days. I ask you as a stranger—going to the West," he said with emphasis.

"Where have *you* come from?" said I.

"From the East," said he, "and I am hoping that you will give him the message on the Square—for the sake of my Mother as well as your own."

Englishmen are not usually softened by appeals to the memory of their mothers; but for certain reasons, which will be fully apparent, I saw fit to agree.

"It's more than a little matter," said he, "and that's why I asked you to do it—and now I know that I can depend on you doing it. A Second-class carriage at Marwar Junction, and a red-haired man asleep in it. You'll be sure to remember. I get out at the next station, and I must hold on there till he comes or sends me what I want."

"I'll give the message if I catch him," I said, "and for the sake of your Mother as well as mine I'll give you a word of advice. Don't try to run the Central India States just now as the correspondent of the *Backwoodsman*. There's real one knocking about here, and it might lead to trouble."

"Thank you," said he simply, "and when will the swine be gone? I can't starve because he's ruining my work. I wanted to get hold of the Degumber Rajah down here about his father's widow, and give him a jump."

"What did he do to his father's widow, then?"

"Filled her up with red pepper and slippered her to death as she hung from a beam. I found that out myself and I'm the only man that would dare going into the State to get hush-money for it. They'll try to poison me, same as they did in Chortumna when I went on the loot there. But you'll give the man at Marwar Junction my message?"

---

4 **get your knife into them:** Make money from them.
5 **swell:** Pompous; self-important.

He got out at a little roadside station, and I reflected. I had heard, more than once, of men personating correspondents of newspapers and bleeding small Native States with threats of exposure, but I had never met any of the caste before. They lead a hard life, and generally die with great suddenness. The Native States have a wholesome horror of English newspapers, which may throw light on their peculiar methods of government, and do their best to choke correspondents with champagne, or drive them out of their mind with four-in-hand barouches.[6] They do not understand that nobody cares a straw for the internal administration of Native States so long as oppression and crime are kept within decent limits, and the ruler is not drugged, drunk, or diseased from one end of the year to the other. They are the dark places of the earth, full of unimaginable cruelty, touching the Railway and the Telegraph on one side, and, on the other, the days of Harun-al-Raschid.[7] When I left the train I did business with divers Kings, and in eight days passed through many changes of life. Sometimes I wore dress-clothes and consorted with Princes and Politicals, drinking from crystal and eating from silver. Sometimes I lay out upon the ground and devoured what I could get, from a plate made of leaves, and drank the running water, and slept under the same rug as my servant. It was all in the day's work.

Then I headed for the Great Indian Desert upon the proper date, as I had promised, and the night Mail set me down at Marwar Junction, where a funny little, happy-go-lucky, native-managed railway runs to Jodhpore. The Bombay Mail from Delhi makes a short halt at Marwar. She arrived as I got in, and I had just time to hurry to her platform and go down the carriages. There was only one Second-class on the train. I slipped the window and looked down upon a flaming red beard, half covered by a railway rug. That was my man, fast asleep, and I dug him gently in the ribs. He woke with a grunt and I saw his face in the light of the lamps. It was a great and shining face.

"Tickets again?" said he.

"No," said I. "I am to tell you that he is gone South for the week. He has gone South for the week!"

The train had begun to move out. The red man rubbed his eyes. He has gone South for the week," he repeated. "Now that's just like his impidence. Did he say that I was to give you anything? 'Cause I won't."

"He didn't," I said and dropped away, and watched the red lights die out in the dark. It was horribly cold because the wind was blowing off the sands. I climbed into my own train—not an Intermediate carriage this time—and went to sleep.

If the man with the beard had given me a rupee I should have kept it as a memento of a rather curious affair. But the consciousness of having done my duty was my only reward.

Later on I reflected that two gentlemen like my friends could not do any good if they foregathered and personated correspondents of newspapers, and might, if they

---

6 **four-in-hand barouches:** Large, four-wheeled carriages pulled by four horses.
7 **Harun-al-Raschid:** In *The Thousand and One Nights,* the caliph of Baghdad.

black-mailed one of the little rat-trap states of Central India or Southern Rajputana, get themselves into serious difficulties. I therefore took some trouble to describe them as accurately as I could remember to people who would be interested in de-porting them: and succeeded, so I was later informed, in having them headed back from the Degumber borders.

Then I became respectable, and returned to an Office where there were no Kings and no incidents outside the daily manufacture of a newspaper. A newspaper office seems to attract every conceivable sort of person, to the prejudice of disci-pline. Zenana-mission[8] ladies arrive, and beg that the Editor will instantly abandon all his duties to describe a Christian prize-giving in a back-slum of a perfectly inac-cessible village; Colonels who have been over-passed for command sit down and sketch the outline of a series of ten, twelve, or twenty-four leading articles on Senior-ity *versus* Selection; missionaries wish to know why they have not been permitted to escape from their regular vehicles of abuse and swear at a brother-missionary under special patronage of the editorial We; stranded theatrical companies troop up to ex-plain that they cannot pay for their advertisements, but on their return from New Zealand or Tahiti will do so with interest; inventors of patent punkah-pulling ma-chines,[9] carriage couplings and unbreakable swords and axle-trees call with specifi-cations in their pockets and hours at their disposal; tea-companies enter and elaborate their prospectuses with the office pens; secretaries of ball-committees clamour to have the glories of their last dance more fully described; strange ladies rustle in and say: "I want a hundred lady's cards printed *at once,* please," which is manifestly part of an Editor's duty; and every dissolute ruffian that ever tramped the Grand Trunk Road makes it his business to ask for employment as a proof-reader. And, all the time, the telephone-bell is ringing madly, and Kings are being killed on the Continent, and Empires are saying—"You're another," and Mister Gladstone[10] is calling down brimstone upon the British Dominions, and the little black copy-boys are whining, "*kaa-pi chay-ha-yeh*" (copy wanted) like tired bees, and most of the paper is as blank as Modred's shield.

But that is the amusing part of the year. There are six other months when none ever come to call, and the thermometer walks inch by inch up to the top of the glass, and the office is darkened to just above reading-light, and the press-machines are red-hot of touch, and nobody writes anything but accounts of amusements in the Hill-stations or obituary notices. Then the telephone becomes a tinkling terror, be-cause it tells you of the sudden deaths of men and women that you knew intimately, and the prickly-heat covers you with a garment, and you sit down and write: "A slight increase of sickness is reported from the Khuda Janta Khan District. The out-break is purely sporadic in its nature, and, thanks to the energetic efforts of the

---

8 **Zenana-mission:** A Christian mission to help women of the zenana, or harem.
9 **punkah-pulling machines:** Machines operated by punkahs, or large ceiling fans that use pull cords.
10 **Mister Gladstone:** W. E. Gladstone, Liberal Prime Minister of England and opponent of the British Empire.

District authorities, is now almost at an end. It is, however, with deep regret we record the death," etc.

Then the sickness really breaks out, and the less recording and reporting the better for the peace of the subscribers. But the Empires and the Kings continue to divert themselves as selfishly as before, and the Foreman thinks that a daily paper really ought to come out once in twenty-four hours, and all the people at the Hill-stations in the middle of their amusements say: "Good gracious! Why can't the paper be sparkling? I'm sure there's plenty going on up here."

That is the dark half of the moon, and, as the advertisements say, "must be experienced to be appreciated."

It was in that season, and a remarkably evil season, that the paper began running the last issue of the week on Saturday night, which is to say Sunday morning, after the custom of a London paper. This was a great convenience, for immediately after the paper was put to bed, the dawn would lower the thermometer from 96° to almost 84° for half an hour, and in that chill—you have no idea how cold is 84° on the grass until you begin to pray for it—a very tired man could get off to sleep ere the heat roused him.

One Saturday night it was my pleasant duty to put the paper to bed alone. A King or courtier or a courtesan or a Community was going to die or get a new Constitution, or do something that was important on the other side of the world, and the paper was to be held open till the latest possible minute in order to catch the telegram.

It was a pitchy black night, as stifling as a June night can be, and the *loo,* the red-hot wind from the westward, was booming among the tinder-dry trees and pretending that the rain was on its heels. Now and again a spot of almost boiling water would fall on the dust with the flop of a frog, but all our weary world knew that was only pretence. It was a shade cooler in the press-room than the office, so I sat there, while the type ticked and clicked, and the night-jars[11] hooted at the windows, and the all but naked compositors wiped the sweat from their foreheads, and called for water. The thing that was keeping us back, whatever it was, would not come off, though the *loo* dropped and the last type was set, and the whole round earth stood still in the choking heat, with its finger on its lip, to wait the event. I drowsed, and wondered whether the telegraph was a blessing, and whether this dying man, or struggling people, might be aware of the inconvenience the delay was causing. There was no special reason beyond the heat and worry to make tension, but, as the clock-hands crept up to three o'clock and the machines spun their fly-wheels two and three times to see that all was in order, before I said the word that would set them off, I could have shrieked aloud.

Then the roar and rattle of the wheels shivered the quiet into little bits. I rose to go away, but two men in white clothes stood in front of me. The first one said: "It's him!" The second said: "So it is!" And they both laughed almost as loudly as the machinery roared, and mopped their foreheads. "We seed there was a light burning across the road and we were sleeping in that ditch there for coolness, and I said to

11 **night-jars:** Nocturnal, insect-eating birds.

my friend here, The office is open. Let's come along and speak to him as turned us back from the Degumber State," said the smaller of the two. He was the man I had met in the Mhow train, and his fellow was the red-bearded man of Marwar Junction. There was no mistaking the eyebrows of the one or the beard of the other.

I was not pleased, because I wished to go to sleep, not to squabble with loafers. "What do you want?" I asked.

"Half an hour's talk with you, cool and comfortable, in the office," said the red-bearded man. "We'd *like* some drink—the Contrack doesn't begin yet, Peachey, so you needn't look—but what we really want is advice. We don't want money. We ask you as a favour, because we found out you did us a bad turn about Degumber State."

I led from the press-room to the stifling office with the maps on the walls, and the red-haired man rubbed his hands. "That's something like," said he. "This was the proper shop to come to. Now, Sir, let me introduce to you Brother Peachey Carnehan, that's him, and Brother Daniel Dravot, that is *me*, and the less said about our professions the better, for we have been most things in our time. Soldier, sailor, compositor, photographer, proof-reader, street-preacher, and correspondents of the *Backwoodsman* when we thought the paper wanted one. Carnehan is sober, and so am I. Look at us first, and see that's sure. It will save you cutting into my talk. We'll take one of your cigars apiece, and you shall see us light up."

I watched the test. The men were absolutely sober, so I gave them each a tepid whiskey and soda.

"Well *and* good," said Carnehan of the eyebrows, wiping the froth from his moustache. "Let me talk now, Dan. We have been all over India, mostly on foot. We have been boiler-fitters, engine-drivers, petty contractors, and all that, and we have decided that India isn't big enough for such as us."

They certainly were too big for the office. Dravot's beard seemed to fill half the room and Carnehan's shoulders the other half, as they sat on the big table. Carnehan continued: "The country isn't half worked out because they that governs it won't let you touch it. They spend all their blessed time in governing it, and you can't lift a spade, nor chip a rock, nor look for oil, nor anything like that without all the Government saying—'Leave it alone, and let us govern.' Therefore, such *as* it is, we will let it alone, and go away to some other place where a man isn't crowded and can come to his own. We are not little men, and there is nothing we are afraid of except Drink, and we have signed a Contrack on that. *Therefore,* we are going away to be Kings."

"Kings in our own right," muttered Dravot.

"Yes, of course," I said. "You've been tramping in the sun, and it's a very warm night, and hadn't you better sleep over the notion? Come tomorrow."

"Neither drunk nor sunstruck," said Dravot. "We have slept over the notion half a year, and require to see Books and Atlases, and we have decided that there is only one place now in the world that two strong men can Sar-a-*whack*. They call it Kafiristan.[12] By my reckoning it's the top right hand corner of Afghanistan, not more

12 **Kafiristan:** A mountainous region north of India, covering parts of present-day Afghanistan and Pakistan.

than three hundred miles from Peshawar. They have two-and-thirty heathen idols there, and we'll be the thirty-third and fourth. It's a mountaineous country, and the women of those parts are very beautiful."

"But that is provided against in the Contrack," said Garnehan. "Neither Woman nor Liqu-or, Daniel."

"And that's all we know, except that no one has gone there, and they fight, and in any place where they fight a man who knows how to drill men can always be a King. We shall go to those parts and say to any King we find—'D'you want to vanquish your foes?' and we will show him how to drill men; for that we know better than anything else. Then we will subvert that King and seize his Throne and establish a Dy-nasty."

"You'll be cut to pieces before you're fifty miles across the Border," I said. "You have to travel through Afghanistan to get to that country. It's one mass of mountains and peaks and glaciers, and no Englishman has been through it. The people are utter brutes, and even if you reached them you couldn't do anything."

"That's more like," said Carnehan. "If you could think us a little more mad we would be more pleased. We have come to you to know about this country, to read a book about it, and to be shown maps. We want you to tell us that we are fools and to show us your books." He turned to the book-cases.

"Are you at all in earnest?" I said.

"A little," said Dravot sweetly. "As big a map as you have got, even if it's all blank where Kafiristan is, and any books you've got. We can read, though we aren't very educated."

I uncased the big thirty-two-miles-to-the-inch map of India, and two smaller Frontier maps, hauled down volume INF-KAN of the *Encyclopædia Britannica,* and the men consulted them.

"See here!" said Dravot, his thumb on the map. "Up to Jagdallak, Peachey and me know the road. We was there with Roberts' Army. We'll have to turn off to the right at Jagdallak through Laghmann territory. Then we get among the hills—fourteen thousand feet—fifteen thousand—it will be cold work there, but it don't look very far on the map."

I handed him Wood on the *Sources of the Oxus.* Carnehan was deep in the *Encyclopædia.*

"They're a mixed lot," said Dravot reflectively; "and it won't help us to know the names of their tribes. The more tribes the more they'll fight, and the better for us. From Jagdallak to Ashang. H'mm!"

"But all the information about the country is as sketchy and inaccurate as can be," I protested. "No one knows anything about it really. Here's the file of the *United Services' Institute.* Read what Bellew says."

"Blow Bellew!" said Carnehan. "Dan, they're a stinkin' lot of heathens, but this book here says they think they're related to us English."

I smoked while the men pored over *Raverty, Wood,* the maps, and the *Encyclopædia.*

"There is no use your waiting," said Dravot politely. "It's about four o'clock now. We'll go before six o'clock if you want to sleep, and we won't steal any of the papers. Don't you sit up. We're two harmless lunatics, and if you come to-morrow evening down to the Serai we'll say good-bye to you."

"You *are* two fools," I answered. "You'll be turned back at the Frontier or cut up the minute you set foot in Afghanistan. Do you want any money or a recommendation down-country? I can help you to the chance of work next week."

"Next week we shall be hard at work ourselves, thank you," said Dravot. "It isn't so easy being a King as it looks. When we've got our Kingdom in going order we'll let you know, and you can come up and help us to govern it."

"Would two lunatics make a Contrack like that?" said Carnehan, with subdued pride, showing me a greasy half-sheet of notepaper on which was written the following. I copied it, then and there, as a curiosity—

> This Contract between me and you persuing witnesseth in the name of God—Amen and so forth.
>
> (One) That me and you will settle this matter together; i.e., to be Kings of Kafiristan.
>
> (Two) That you and me will not, while this matter is being settled, look at any Liquor, nor any Woman black, white, or brown, so as to get mixed up with one or the other harmful.
>
> (Three) That we conduct ourselves with Dignity and Discretion, and if one of us gets into trouble the other will stay by him.
>
> Signed by you and me this day.
>
> Peachey Taliaferro Carnehan.
>
> Daniel Dravot.
>
> Both Gentlemen at Large.

"There was no need for the last article," said Carnehan, blushing modestly; "but it looks regular. Now you know the sort of men that loafers are—we *are* loafers, Dan, until we get out of India—and *do* you think that we would sign a Contrack like that unless we was in earnest? We have kept away from the two things that make life worth having."

"You won't enjoy your lives much longer if you are going to try this idiotic adventure. Don't set the office on fire," I said, "and go away before nine o'clock."

I left them still poring over the maps and making notes on the back of the "Contrack." "Be sure to come down to the Serai to-morrow," were their parting words.

The Kumharsen Serai is the great four-square sink of humanity where the strings of camels and horses from the North load and unload. All the nationalities of Central Asia may be found there, and most of the folk of India proper. Balkh and Bokhara there meet Bengal and Bombay, and try to draw eye-teeth. You can buy ponies, turquoises, Persian pussy-cats, saddlebags, fat-tailed sheep and musk in the Kumharsen Serai, and get many strange things for nothing. In the afternoon I went down to see whether my friends intended to keep their word or were lying there drunk.

A priest attired in fragments of ribbons and rags stalked up to me, gravely twisting a child's paper whirligig. Behind him was his servant bending under the load of a crate of mud toys. The two were loading up two camels, and the inhabitants of the Serai watched them with shrieks of laughter.

"The priest is mad," said a horse-dealer to me. "He is going up to Kabul to sell toys to the Amir. He will either be raised to honour or have his head cut off. He came in here this morning and has been behaving madly ever since."

"The witless are under the protection of God," stammered a flat-cheeked Usbeg in broken Hindi. "They foretell future events."

"Would they could have foretold that my caravan would have been cut up by the Shinwaris almost within shadow of the Pass!" grunted the Eusufzai agent of a Rajputana trading-house whose goods had been diverted into the hands of other robbers just across the Border, and whose misfortunes were the laughing-stock of the bazar. "Ohé, priest, whence come you and whither do you go?"

"From Roum have I come," shouted the priest, waving his whirligig; "from Roum, blown by the breath of a hundred devils across the sea! O thieves, robbers, liars, the blessing of Pir Khan on pigs, dogs, and perjurers! Who will take the protected of God to the North to sell charms that are never still to the Amir? The camels shall not gall, the sons shall not fall sick, and the wives shall remain faithful while they are away, of the men who give me place in their caravan. Who will assist me to slipper the King of the Roos with a golden slipper with a silver heel? The protection of Pir Khan be upon his labours!" He spread out the skirts of his gaberdine and pirouetted between the lines of tethered horses.

"There starts a caravan from Peshawar to Kabul in twenty days, *Huzrut*," said the Eusufzai trader. "My camels go therewith. Do thou also go and bring us good-luck."

"I will go even now!" shouted the priest. "I will depart upon my winged camels, and be at Peshawar in a day! Ho! Hazar Mir Khan," he yelled to his servant, "drive out the camels, but let me first mount my own."

He leaped on the back of his beast as it knelt, and, turning round to me, cried: "Come thou also, Sahib, a little along the road, and I will sell thee a charm—an amulet that shall make thee King of Kafiristan."

Then the light broke upon me, and I followed the two camels out of the Serai till we reached open road and the priest halted.

"What d'you think o' that?" said he in English. "Carnehan can't talk their patter, so I've made him my servant. He makes a handsome servant. 'Tisn't for nothing that I've been knocking about the country for fourteen years. Didn't I do that talk neat? We'll hitch on to a caravan at Peshawar till we get to Jagdallak, and then we'll see if we can get donkeys for our camels, and strike into Kafiristan. Whirligigs for the Amir, O Lor! Put your hand under the camel-bags and tell me what you feel."

I felt the butt of a Martini,[13] and another and another.

13 **Martini:** Martini-Henry military rifle.

"Twenty of 'em," said Dravot placidly. "Twenty of 'em and ammunition to correspond, under the whirligigs and the mud dolls."

"Heaven help you if you are caught with those things!" I said. "A Martini is worth her weight in silver among the Pathans."

"Fifteen hundred rupees of capital—every rupee we could beg, borrow, or steal—are invested on these two camels," said Dravot. "We won't get caught. We're going through the Khaiber with a regular caravan. Who'd touch a poor mad priest?"

"Have you got everything you want?" I asked, overcome with astonishment.

"Not yet, but we shall soon. Give us a memento of your kindness, *Brother*. You did me a service, yesterday, and that time in Marwar. Half my Kingdom shall you have, as the saying is." I slipped a small charm compass from my watch chain and handed it up to the priest.

"Good-bye," said Dravot, giving me hand cautiously. "It's the last time we'll shake hands with an Englishman these many days. Shake hands with him, Carnehan," he cried, as the second camel passed me.

Carnehan leaned down and shook hands. Then the camels passed away along the dusty road, and I was left alone to wonder. My eye could detect no failure in the disguises. The scene in the Serai proved that they were complete to the native mind. There was just the chance, therefore, that Carnehan and Dravot would be able to wander through Afghanistan without detection. But, beyond, they would find death—certain and awful death.

Ten days later a native correspondent giving me the news of the day from Peshawar, wound up his letter with: "There has been much laughter here on account of a certain mad priest who is going in his estimation to sell petty gauds and insignificant trinkets which he ascribes as great charms to H.H. the Amir of Bokhara.[14] He passed through Peshawar and associated himself to the Second Summer caravan that goes to Kabul. The merchants are pleased because through superstition they imagine that such mad fellows bring good-fortune."

The two, then, were beyond the Border. I would have prayed for them, but, that night, a real King died in Europe, and demanded an obituary notice.

The wheel of the world swings through the same phases again and again. Summer passed and winter thereafter, and came and passed again. The daily paper continued and I with it, and upon the third summer there fell a hot night, a night-issue, and a strained waiting for something to be telegraphed from the other side of the world, exactly as had happened before. A few great men had died in the past two years, the machines worked with more clatter, and some of the trees in the Office garden were a few feet taller. But that was all the difference.

I passed over to the press-room, and went through just such a scene as I have already described. The nervous tension was stronger than it had been two years before, and I felt the heat more acutely. At three o'clock I cried, "Print off," and turned

14 **H.H. the Amir of Bokhara:** His Highness the Emir (native ruler) of Bukhara, in western Asia.

to go, when there crept to my chair what was left of a man. He was bent into a circle, his head was sunk between his shoulders, and he moved his feet one over the other like a bear. I could hardly see whether he walked or crawled—this rag-wrapped, whining cripple who addressed me by name, crying that he was come back. "Can you give me a drink?" he whimpered. "For the Lord's sake, give me a drink!"

I went back to the office, the man following with groans of pain, and I turned up the lamp.

"Don't you know me?" he gasped, dropping into a chair and he turned his drawn face, surmounted by a shock of gray hair, to the light.

I looked at him intently. Once before had I seen eyebrows that met over the nose in an inch-broad black band, but for the life of me I could not tell where.

"I don't know you," I said, handing him the whiskey. "What can I do for you?"

He took a gulp of the spirit raw, and shivered in spite of the suffocating heat.

"I've come back," he repeated; "and I was the King of Kafiristan—me and Dravot—crowned Kings we was! In this office we settled it—you setting there and giving us the books. I am Peachey—Peachey Taliaferro Carnehan, and you've been setting here ever since—O Lord!"

I was more than a little astonished, and expressed my feelings accordingly.

"It's true," said Carnehan, with a dry cackle, nursing his feet, which were wrapped in rags. "True as gospel. Kings we were, with crowns upon our heads—me and Dravot—poor Dan—oh, poor, poor Dan, that would never take advice, not though I begged of him!"

"Take the whiskey," I said, "and take your own time. Tell me all you can recollect of everything from beginning to end. You got across the border on your camels, Dravot dressed as a mad priest and you his servant. Do you remember that?"

"I ain't mad—yet, but I shall be that way soon. Of course I remember. Keep looking at me, or maybe my words will go all to pieces. Keep looking at me in my eyes and don't say anything."

I leaned forward and looked into his face as steadily as I could. He dropped one hand upon the table and I grasped it by the wrist. It was twisted like a bird's claw, and upon the back was a ragged, red, diamond-shaped scar.

"No, don't look there. Look at *me*," said Carnehan. "That comes afterwards, but for the Lord's sake don't distrack me. We left with that caravan, me and Dravot playing all sorts of antics to amuse the people we were with. Dravot used to make us laugh in the evenings when all the people was cooking their dinners—cooking their dinners, and . . . what did they do then? They lit little fires with sparks that went into Dravot's beard, and we all laughed—fit to die. Little red fires they was, going into Dravot's big red beard—so funny." His eyes left mine and he smiled foolishly.

"You went as far as Jagdallak with that caravan," I said at a venture, "after you had lit those fires. To Jagdallak, where you turned off to try to get into Kafiristan."

"No, we didn't neither. What are you talking about? We turned off before Jagdallak, because we heard the roads was good. But they wasn't good enough for our two camels—mine and Dravot's. When we left the caravan, Dravot took off all his clothes and mine too, and said we would be heathen, because the Kafirs didn't allow

Mohammedans to talk to them. So we dressed betwixt and between, and such a sight as Daniel Dravot I never saw yet nor expect to see again. He burned half his beard, and slung a sheep-skin over his shoulder, and shaved his head into patterns. He shaved mine, too, and made me wear outrageous things to look like a heathen. That was in a most mountaineous country, and our camels couldn't go along any more because of the mountains. They were tall and black, and coming home I saw them fight like wild goats—there are lots of goats in Kafiristan. And these mountains, they never keep still, no more than the goats. Always fighting they are, and don't let you sleep at night."

"Take some more whiskey," I said very slowly. "What did you and Daniel Dravot do when the camels could go no further because of the rough roads that led into Kafiristan?"

"What did which do? There was a party called Peachey Taliaferro Carnehan that was with Dravot. Shall I tell you about him? He died out there in the cold. Slap from the bridge fell old Peachey, turning and twisting in the air like a penny whirligig that you can sell to the Amir.—No; they was two for three ha'pence, those whirligigs, or I am much mistaken and woeful sore. . . . And then these camels were no use, and Peachey said to Dravot—'For the Lord's sake let's get out of this before our heads are chopped off,' and with that they killed the camels all among the mountains, not having anything in particular to eat, but first they took off the boxes with the guns and the ammunition, till two men came along driving four mules. Dravot up and dances in front of them, singing—'Sell me four mules.' Says the first man—'If you are rich enough to buy, you are rich enough to rob'; but before ever he could put his hand to his knife, Dravot breaks his neck over his knee, and the other party runs away. So Carnehan loaded the mules with the rifles that was taken off the camels, and together we starts forward into those bitter cold mountaineous parts, and never a road broader than the back of your hand."

He paused for a moment, while I asked him if he could remember the nature of the country through which he had journeyed.

"I am telling you as straight as I can, but my head isn't as good as it might be. They drove nails through it to make me hear better how Dravot died. The country was mountaineous and the mules were most contrary, and the inhabitants was dispersed and solitary. They went up and up, and down and down, and that other party, Carnehan, was imploring of Dravot not to sing and whistle so loud, for fear of bringing down the tremenjus avalanches. But Dravot says that if a King couldn't sing it wasn't worth being King, and whacked the mules over the rump, and never took no heed for ten cold days. We came to a big level valley all among the mountains, and the mules were near dead, so we killed them, not having anything in special for them or us to eat. We sat upon the boxes, and played odd and even with the cartridges that was jolted out.

"Then ten men with bows and arrows ran down that valley, chasing twenty men with bows and arrows, and the row was tremenjus. They was fair men—fairer than you or me—with yellow hair and remarkable well built. Says Dravot, unpacking the guns—'This is the beginning of the business. We'll fight for the ten men,' and with that he fires two rifles at the twenty men, and drops one of them at two hundred yards from the rock where he was sitting. The other men began to run, but Carnehan and Dravot sits on the boxes picking them off at all ranges, up and down the valley. Then we goes up to the ten men that had run across the snow too, and they fires a footy little arrow at us. Dravot he shoots above their heads and they all falls down flat. Then he walks over them and kicks them, and then he lifts them up and shakes hands all round to make them friendly like. He calls them and gives them the boxes to carry, and waves his hand for all the world as though he was King already. They takes the boxes and him across the valley and up the hill into a pine wood on the top, where there was half a dozen big stone idols. Dravot he goes to the biggest—a fellow they call Imbra—and lays a rifle and a cartridge at his feet, rubbing his nose respectful with his own nose, patting him on the head, and saluting in front of it. He turns round to the men and nods his head, and says—'That's all right. I'm in the know too, and all these old jim-jams are my friends.' Then he opens his mouth and points down it, and when the first man brings him food, he says—'No'; and when the second man brings him food he says—'No'; but when one of the old priests and the boss of the village brings him food, he says—'Yes'; very haughty, and eats it slow. That was how he came to our first village, without any trouble, just as though we had tumbled from the skies. But we tumbled from one of those damned rope-bridges, you see and—you couldn't expect a man to laugh much after that?"

"Take some more whiskey and go on," I said. "That was the first village you came into. How did you get to be King?"

"I wasn't King," said Carnehan. "Dravot he was the King, and a handsome man he looked with the gold crown on his head and all. Him and the other party stayed in that village, and every morning Dravot sat by the side of old Imbra, and the people came and worshipped. That was Dravot's order. Then a lot of men came into the valley, and Carnehan and Dravot picks them off with the rifles before they knew where they was, and runs down into the valley and up again the other side and finds another village, same as the first one, and the people all falls down flat on their faces, and Dravot says—'Now what is the trouble between you two villages?' and the people points to a woman, as fair[15] as you or me, that was carried off, and Dravot takes her back to the first village and counts up the dead—eight there was. For each dead man Dravot pours a little milk on the ground and waves his arms like a whirligig and 'That's all right,' says he. Then he and Carnehan takes the big boss of each village by the arm and walks them down into the valley, and shows them how to scratch a line with a spear right down the valley, and gives each a sod of turf from both sides of the line. Then all the people comes down and shouts like the devil and all, and Dravot says—'Go and dig the land, and be fruitful and multiply,' which they did, though they didn't understand. Then we asks the names of things in their lingo—bread and water and fire and idols and such, and Dravot leads the priest of each village up to the idol, and says he must sit there and judge the people, and if anything goes wrong he is to be shot.

---

15 **fair:** Light-skinned.

"Next week they was all turning up the land in the valley as quiet as bees and much prettier, and the priests heard all the complaints and told Dravot in dumb show what it was about. 'That's just the beginning,' says Dravot. 'They think we're Gods.' He and Carnehan picks out twenty good men and shows them how to click off a rifle, and form fours, and advance in line, and they was very pleased to do so, and clever to see the hang of it. Then he takes out his pipe and his baccy-pouch and leaves one at one village, and one at the other, and off we two goes to see what was to be done in the next valley. That was all rock, and there was a little village there, and Carnehan says—'Send 'em to the old valley to plant,' and takes 'em there and gives 'em some land that wasn't took before. They were a poor lot, and we blooded 'em with a kid before letting 'em into the new Kingdom. That was to impress the people, and then they settled down quiet, and Carnehan went back to Dravot who had got into another valley, all snow and ice and most mountaineous. There was no people there and the Army got afraid, so Dravot shoots one of them, and goes on till he finds some people in a village, and the Army explains that unless the people wants to be killed they had better not shoot their little matchlocks;[16] for they had matchlocks. We makes friends with the priest and I stays there alone with two of the Army, teaching the men how to drill, and a thundering big Chief comes across the snow with kettle-drums and horns twanging, because he heard there was a new God kicking about. Carnehan sights for the brown of the men half a mile across the snow and wings one of them. Then he sends a message to the Chief that, unless he wished to be killed, he must come and shake hands with me and leave his arms behind. The Chief comes alone first, and Carnehan shakes hands with him and whirls his arms about, same as Dravot used, and very much surprised that Chief was, and strokes my eyebrows. Then Carnehan goes alone to the Chief, and asks him in dumb show if he had an enemy he hated. 'I have,' says the Chief. So Carnehan weeds out the pick of his men, and sets the two of the Army to show them drill and at the end of two weeks the men can manœuvre about as well as Volunteers. So he marches with the Chief to a great big plain on the top of a mountain, and the Chief's men rushes into a village and takes it; we three Martinis firing into the brown[17] of the enemy. So we took that village too, and I gives the Chief a rag from my coat and says, 'Occupy till I come'; which was scriptural. By way of a reminder, when me and the Army was eighteen hundred yards away, I drops a bullet near him standing on the snow, and all the people falls flat on their faces. Then I sends a letter to Dravot wherever he be by land or by sea."

At the risk of throwing the creature out of train I interrupted—"How could you write a letter up yonder?"

"The letter?—Oh!—The letter! Keep looking at me between the eyes, please. It was a string-talk letter, that we'd learned the way of it from a blind beggar in the Punjab."

---

16 **matchlocks:** Old-fashioned, muzzle-loading muskets.
17 **brown:** Midst or heart.

I remember that there had once come to the office a blind man with a knotted twig and a piece of string which he wound round the twig according to some cipher of his own. He could, after the lapse of days or hours, repeat the sentence which he had reeled up. He had reduced the alphabet to eleven primitive sounds; and tried to teach me his method, but I could not understand.

"I sent that letter to Dravot," said Carnehan; "and told him to come back because this Kingdom was growing too big for me to handle, and then I struck for the first valley, to see how the priests were working. They called the village we took along with the Chief, Bashkai, and the first village we took, Er-Heb. The priests at Er-Heb was doing all right, but they had a lot of pending cases about land to show me, and some men from another village had been firing arrows at night. I went out and looked for that village, and fired four rounds at it from a thousand yards. That used all the cartridges I cared to spend, and I waited for Dravot, who had been away two or three months, and I kept my people quiet.

"One morning I heard the devil's own noise of drums and horns, and Dan Dravot marches down the hill with his Army and a tail of hundreds of men, and, which was the most amazing, a great gold crown on his head. 'My Gord, Carnehan,' says Daniel, this is a tremenjus business, and we've got the whole country as far as it's worth having. I am the son of Alexander by Queen Semiramis,[18] and you're my younger brother and a God too! It's the biggest thing we've ever seen. I've been marching and fighting for six weeks with the Army, and every footy little village for fifty miles has come in rejoiceful; and more than that, I've got the key of the whole show, as you'll see, and I've got a crown for you! I told 'em to make two of 'em at a place called Shu, where the gold lies in the rock like suet in mutton. Gold I've seen, and turquoise I've kicked out of the cliffs, and there's garnets in the sands of the river, and here's a chunk of amber that a man brought me. Call up all the priests, and, here, take your crown.'

"One of the men opens a black hair bag, and I slips the crown on. It was too small and too heavy, but I wore it for the glory. Hammered gold it was—five pound weight, like a hoop of a barrel.

"'Peachey,' says Dravot, 'we don't want to fight no more. The Craft's[19] the trick so help me!' and he brings forward that same Chief that I left at Bashkai—Billy Fish we called him afterwards, because he was so like Billy Fish that drove the big tank-engine at Mach on the Bolan in the old days. 'Shake hands with him,' says Dravot, and I shook hands and nearly dropped, for Billy Fish gave me the Grip. I said nothing, but tried him with the Fellow Craft Grip. He answers, all right, and I tried the Master's Grip, but that was a slip. 'A Fellow Craft he is!' I says to Dan. 'Does he know the word?'—'He does,' says Dan, 'and all the priests know. It's a miracle! The Chiefs

18 **Queen Semiramis:** A queen of ancient Assyria. Alexander the Great's empire stretched as far east as parts of northern India; hence, it was believed, Alexander was the source of the fair-skinned inhabitants of those regions, whom Dravot later refers to as "Sons of Alexander."
19 **The Craft:** Slang term for Freemasonry. The rituals Peachy and Dravot used are derived from the Masons, as are many of the signs exchanged between the narrator and the two "kings."

and the priests can work a Fellow Craft Lodge in a way that's very like ours, and they've cut the marks on the rocks, but they don't know the Third Degree,[20] and they've come to find out. It's Gord's Truth. I've known these long years that the Afghans knew up to the Fellow Craft Degree, but this is a miracle. A God and a Grand-Master of the Craft am I, and a Lodge in the Third Degree I will open, and we'll raise the head priests and the Chiefs of the villages.'

" 'It's against all the law,' I says, 'holding a Lodge without warrant from any one; and you know we never held office in any Lodge.'

" 'It's a master-stroke o' policy,' says Dravot. 'It means running the country as easy as a four-wheeled bogie on a down grade. We can't stop to enquire now, or they'll turn against us. I've forty Chiefs at my heel, and passed and raised according to their merit they shall be. Billet these men on the villages, and see that we run up a Lodge of some kind. The temple of Imbra will do for the Lodge-room. The women must make aprons[21] as you show them. I'll hold a levee of Chief's to-night and Lodge to-morrow.'

"I was fair run off my legs, but I wasn't such a fool as not to see what a pull this Craft business gave us. I showed the priests' families how to make aprons of the degrees, but for Dravot's apron the blue border and marks was made of turquoise lumps on white hide, not cloth. We took a great square stone in the temple for the Master's chair, and little stones for the officers' chairs, and painted the black pavement with white squares, and did what we could to make things regular.

"At the levee which was held that night on the hillside with big bonfires, Dravot gives out that him and me were Gods and sons of Alexander, and Past Grand-Masters in the Craft, and was come to make Kafiristan a country where every man should eat in peace and drink in quiet, and specially obey us. Then the Chiefs come round to shake hands, and they were so hairy and white and fair it was just shaking hands with old friends. We gave them names according as they was like men we had known in India—Billy Fish, Holly Dilworth, Pikky Kergan, that was Bazar-master when I was at Mhow, and so on, and so on.

"*The* most amazing miracles was at Lodge next night. One of the old priests was watching us continuous, and I felt uneasy, for I knew we'd have to fudge the Ritual, and I didn't know what the men knew. The old priest was a stranger come in from beyond the village of Bashkai. The minute Dravot puts on the Master's apron that the girls had made for him, the priest fetches a whoop and a howl, and tries to overturn the stone that Dravot was sitting on. 'It's all up now,' I says. 'That comes of meddling with the Craft without warrant!' Dravot never winked an eye, not when ten priests took and tilted over the Grand-Master's chair—which was to say the stone of Imbra. The priest begins rubbing the bottom end of it to clear away the black dirt, and presently he shows all the other priests the Master's Mark,[22] same as was on

---

20 **Third Degree:** The highest rank in Masonry. Dravot is pretending to know the proper rituals for promotion to that rank.
21 **aprons:** In Masonry, aprons indicate a person's rank within the society.
22 **Master's Mark:** Symbol of a Masonic Grand Master.

Dravot's apron, cut into the stone. Not even the priests of the temple of Imbra knew it was there. The old chap falls flat on his face at Dravot's feet and kisses 'em. 'Luck again,' said Dravot, across the Lodge to me, 'they say it's the missing Mark that no one could understand the why of. We're more than safe now.' Then he bangs the butt of his gun for a gavel and says: 'By virtue of the authority vested in me by my own right hand and the help of Peachey, I declare myself Grand-Master of all Freemasonry in Kafiristan in this the Mother Lodge o' the country, and King of Kafiristan equally with Peachey!' At that he puts on his crown and I puts on mine—I was doing Senior Warden—and we opens the Lodge in most ample form. It was a amazing miracle! The priests moved in Lodge through the first two degrees almost without telling, as if the memory was coming back to them. After that, Peachey and Dravot raised such as was worthy—high priests and Chiefs of far-off villages. Billy Fish was the first, and I can tell you we scared the soul out of him. It was not in any way according to Ritual, but it served our turn. We didn't raise more than ten of the biggest men, because we didn't want to make the Degree common. And they was clamouring to be raised.

" 'In another six months,' said Dravot, 'we'll hold another Communication, and see how you are working.' Then he asks them about their villages, and learns that they was fighting one against the other, and were sick and tired of it. And when they wasn't doing that they was fighting with the Mohammedans. 'You can fight those when they come into our country,' says Dravot. 'Tell off every tenth man of your tribes for a Frontier guard, and send two hundred at a time to this valley to be drilled. Nobody is going to be shot or speared any more so long as he does well, and I know that you won't cheat me, because you're white people—sons of Alexander— and not like common, black Mohammedans. You are *my* people, and by God,' says he, running off into English at the end—'I'll make a damned fine Nation of you, or I'll die in the making!'

"I can't tell all we did for the next six months, because Dravot did a lot I couldn't see the hang of, and he learned their lingo in a way I never could. My work was to help the people plough, and now and again go out with some of the Army and see what the other villages were doing, and make 'em throw rope-bridges across the ravines which cut up the country horrid. Dravot was very kind to me, but when he walked up and down in the pine wood pulling that bloody red beard of his with both fists I knew he was thinking plans I could not advise about, and I just waited for orders.

"But Dravot never showed me disrepect before the people. They were afraid of me and the Army, but they loved Dan. He was the best of friends with the priests and the Chiefs; but any one could come across the hills with a complaint, and Dravot would hear him out fair, and call four priests together and say what was to be done. He used to call in Billy Fish from Bashkai, and Pikky Kergan from Shu, and an old Chief we called Kafuzelum—it was like enough to his real name—and hold councils with 'em when there was any fighting to be done in small villages. That was his Council of War, and the four priests of Bashkai, Shu, Khawak, and Madora was his Privy Council. Between the lot of 'em they sent me, with forty men and twenty rifles, and sixty men carrying turquoises, into the Ghorband country to buy those hand-made Martini rifles, that come out of the Amir's workshops at Kabul, from one of the Amir's Herati regiments that would have sold the very teeth out of their mouths for turquoises.

"I stayed in Ghorband a month, and gave the Governor there the pick of my baskets for hush-money, and bribed the Colonel of the regiment some more, and, between the two and the tribes-people, we got more than a hundred hand-made Martinis, a hundred good Kohat Jezails that'll throw to six hundred yards, and forty man-loads of very bad ammunition for the rifles. I came back with what I had, and distributed 'em among the men that the Chiefs sent into me to drill. Dravot was too busy to attend to those things, but the old Army that we first made helped me, and we turned out five hundred men that could drill, and two hundred that knew how to hold arms pretty straight. Even those cork-screwed, hand-made guns was a miracle to them. Dravot talked big about powder-shops and factories, walking up and down in the pine wood when the winter was coming on.

" 'I won't make a Nation,' says he. 'I'll make an Empire! These men aren't niggers; they're English! Look at their eyes—look at their mouths. Look at the way they stand up. They sit on chairs in their own houses. They're the Lost Tribes,[23] or something like it, and they've grown to be English. I'll take a census in the spring if the priests don't get frightened. There must be a fair two million of 'em in these hills. The villages are full o' little children. Two million people—two hundred and fifty thousand fighting men—and all English! They only want the rifles and a little drilling. Two hundred and fifty thousand men, ready to cut in on Russia's[24] right flank when she tries for India! Peachey, man,' he says, chewing his beard in great hunks, 'we shall be Emperors—Emperors of the Earth! Rajah Brooke will be a suckling to us. I'll treat with the Viceroy on equal terms. I'll ask him to send me twelve picked English—twelve that I know of—to help us govern a bit. There's Mackray, Sergeant-pensioner at Segowli—many's the good dinner he's given me, and his wife a pair of trousers. There's Donkin, the Warder of Tounghoo Jail; there's hundreds that I could lay my hand on if I was in India. The Viceroy shall do it for me, I'll send a man through in the spring for those men, and I'll write for a dispensation from the Grand Lodge for what I've done as Grand-Master. That—and all the Sniders that'll be thrown out when the native troops in India take up the Martini. They'll be worn smooth, but they'll do for fighting in these hills. Twelve English, a hundred thousands Sniders run through the Amir's country in driblets—I'd be content with twenty thousand in one year—and we'd be an Empire. When everything was ship-shape, I'd hand over the crown—this crown I'm wearing now—to Queen Victoria on my knees, and she'd say: "Rise up, Sir Daniel Dravot." Oh, it's big! It's big, I tell you! But there's so much to be done in every place—Bashkai Khawak, Shu, and everywhere else.'

---

23 **Lost Tribes:** The lost tribes of Israel.
24 **Russia:** At the time of the story, Russia was a rival with Britain for control of the areas north of India.

"'What is it?' I says. 'There are no more men coming in to be drilled this autumn. Look at those, fat, black clouds. They're bringing the snow.'

"'It isn't that,' says Daniel, putting his hand very hard on my shoulder; 'and I don't wish to say anything that's against you, for no other living man would have followed me and made me what I am as you have done. You're a first-class Commander-in-Chief, and the people know you; but—it's a big country, and somehow you can't help me, Peachey, in the way I want to be helped.'

"'Go to your blasted priests, then!' I said, and I was sorry when I made that remark, but it did hurt me sore to find Daniel talking so superior when I'd drilled all the men, and done all he told me.

"'Don't let's quarrel, Peachey,' says Daniel without cursing. 'You're a King too, and the half of this Kingdom is yours; but can't you see, Peachey, we want cleverer men than us now—three or four of 'em, that we can scatter about for our Deputies. It's a hugeous great State, and I can't always tell the right thing to do, and I haven't time for all I want to do, and here's the winter coming on and all.' He put half his beard into his mouth, all red like the gold of his crown.

"'I'm sorry, Daniel,' says I. 'I've done all I could. I've drilled the men and shown the people how to stack their oats better; and I've brought in those tinware rifles from Ghorband—but I know what you're driving at. I take it Kings always feel oppressed that way.'

"'There's another thing too,' says Dravot, walking up and down. 'The winter's coming and these people won't be giving much trouble, and if they do we can't move about. I want a wife.'

"'For Gord's sake leave the women alone!' I says. 'We've both got all the work we can, though I *am* a fool. Remember the Contrack, and keep clear o' women.'

"'The Contrack only lasted till such time as we was Kings; and Kings we have been these months past,' says Dravot, weighing his crown in his hand. 'You go get a wife too, Peachey—a nice, strappin', plump girl that'll keep you warm in the winter. They're prettier than English girls, and we can take the pick of 'em. Boil 'em once or twice in hot water, and they'll come out like chicken and ham.'

"'Don't tempt me!' I says. 'I will not have any dealings with a woman not till we are a dam' sight more settled than we are now. I've been doing the work o' two men, and you've been doing the work o' three. Let's lie off a bit, and see if we can get some better tobacco from Afghan country and run in some good liquor; but no women.'

"'Who's talking o' *women?*' says Dravot. 'I said *wife*—a Queen to breed a King's son for the King. A Queen out of the strongest tribe, that'll make them your blood-brothers, and that'll lie by your side and tell you all the people thinks about you and their own affairs. That's what I want.'

"'Do you remember that Bengali woman I kept at Mogul Serai when I was a plate-layer?' says I. 'A fat lot o' good she was to me. She taught me the lingo and one or two other things; but what happened? She ran away with the Station Master's servant and half my month's pay. Then she turned up at Dadur Junction in tow of a half-caste, and had the impidence to say I was her husband—all among the drivers in the running-shed too!'

"'We've done with that,' says Dravot, 'these women are whiter than you or me, and a Queen I will have for the winter months.'

"'For the last time o' asking, Dan, do *not*,' I says. 'It'll only bring us harm. The Bible says that Kings ain't to waste their strength on women, 'specially when they've got a new raw Kingdom to work over.'

"'For the last time of answering I will,' said Dravot, and he went away through the pine-trees looking like a big red devil, the sun being on his crown and beard and all.

"But getting a wife was not as easy as Dan thought. He put it before the Council, and there was no answer till Billy Fish said that he'd better ask the girls. Dravot damned them all round. 'What's wrong with me?' he shouts, standing by the idol Imbra. 'Am I a dog or am I not enough of a man for your wenches? Haven't I put the shadow of my hand over this country? Who stopped the last Afghan raid?' It was me really, but Dravot was too angry to remember. 'Who bought your guns? Who repaired the bridges? Who's the Grand-Master of the sign cut in the stone?' says he, and he thumped his hand on the block that he used to sit on in Lodge, and at Council, which opened like Lodge always. Billy Fish said nothing and no more did the others. 'Keep your hair on, Dan,' said I; 'and ask the girls. That's how it's done at Home, and these people are quite English.'

"'The marriage of the King is a matter of State,' says Dan, in a white-hot rage, for he could feel, I hope, that he was going against his better mind. He walked out of the Council-room, and the others sat still, looking at the ground.

"'Billy Fish,' says I to the Chief of Bashkai, 'what's the difficulty here? A straight answer to a true friend.'

"'You know,' says Billy Fish. 'How should a man tell you who knows everything? How can daughters of men marry Gods or Devils? It's not proper.'

"I remembered something like that in the Bible; but if, after seeing us as long as they had, they still believed we were Gods, it wasn't for me to undeceive them.

"'A God can do anything,' says I. 'If the King is fond of a girl he'll not let her die.'—'She'll have to,' said Billy Fish. 'There are all sorts of Gods and Devils in these mountains, and now and again a girl marries one of them and isn't seen any more. Besides, you two know the Mark cut in the stone. Only the Gods knows that. We thought you were men till you showed the sign of the Master.'

"I wished then that we had explained about the loss of the genuine secrets of a Master-Mason at the first go-off; but I said nothing. All that night there was a blowing of horns in a little dark temple half-way down the hill, and I heard a girl crying fit to die. One of the priests told us that she was being prepared to marry the King.

"'I'll have no nonsense of that kind,' says Dan. 'I don't want to interfere with your customs, but I'll take my own wife.'—'The girl's a little bit afraid,' says the priest. 'She thinks she's going to die, and they are a-heartening of her up down in the temple.'

"'Hearten her very tender, then,' says Dravot, 'or I'll hearten you with the butt of a gun so you'll never want to be heartened again.' He licked his lips, did Dan, and stayed up walking about more than half the night, thinking of the wife that he was going to get in the morning. I wasn't any means comfortable, for I knew that dealings with a woman in foreign parts, though you was a crowned King twenty times over, could not but be risky. I got up very early in the morning while Dravot was asleep, and I saw the priests talking together in whispers, and the Chiefs talking together too, and they looked at me out of the corners of their eyes.

"'What is up, Fish?' I say to the Bashkai man, who was wrapped up in his furs and looking splendid to behold.

"'I can't rightly say,' says he; 'but if you can make the King drop all this nonsense about marriage, you'll be doing him and me and yourself a great service.'

"'That I do believe,' says I. 'But sure, you know, Billy, as well as me, having fought against and for us, that the King and me are nothing more than two of the finest men that God Almighty ever made. Nothing more, I do assure you.'

"'That may be,' says Billy Fish, 'and yet I should be sorry if it was.' He sinks his head upon his great fur cloak for a minute and thinks. 'King,' says he, 'be you man or God or Devil, I'll stick by you to-day. I have twenty of my men with me, and they will follow me. We'll go to Bashkai until the storm blows over.'

"A little snow had fallen in the night, and everything was white except the greasy fat clouds that blew down and down from the north. Dravot came out with his crown on his head, swinging his arms and stamping his feet, and looking more pleased than Punch.

"'For the last time, drop it, Dan,' says I in a whisper, 'Billy Fish here says that there will be a row.'

"'A row among my people!' says Dravot. 'Not much. Peachey, you're a fool not to get a wife too. Where's the girl?' says he with a voice as loud as the braying of a jackass. 'Call up all the Chiefs and priests, and let the Emperor see if his wife suits him.'

"There was no need to call any one. They were all there leaning on their guns and spears round the clearing in the centre of the pine wood. A lot of priests went down to the little temple to bring up the girl, and the horns blew fit to wake the dead. Billy Fish saunters round and gets as close to Daniel as he could, and behind him stood his twenty men with matchlocks. Not a man of them under six feet. I was next to Dravot, and behind me was twenty men of the regular Army. Up comes the girl, and a strapping wench she was, covered with silver and turquoises but white as death, and looking back every minute at the priests.

"'She'll do,' said Dan, looking her over. 'What's to be afraid of, lass? Come and kiss me.' He puts his arm round her. She shuts her eyes, gives a bit of a squeak, and down goes her face in the side of Dan's flaming red beard.

"'The slut's bitten me!' says he, clapping his hand to his neck, and, sure enough, his hand was red with blood. Billy Fish and two of his matchlock-men catches hold of Dan by the shoulders and drags him into the Bashkai lot, while the priests howls in their lingo,—'Neither God nor Devil but a man!' I was all taken aback, for a priest cut at me in front, and the Army behind began firing into the Bashkai men.

"'God A'mighty!' says Dan. 'What is the meaning o' this?'

"'Come back! Come away!' says Billy Fish. 'Ruin and Mutiny is the matter. We'll break for Bashkai if we can.'

"I tried to give some sort of orders to my men—the men o' the regular Army—but it was no use, so I fired into the brown of 'em with an English Martini and drilled three beggars in a line. The valley was full of shouting, howling creatures, and every soul was shrieking, 'Not a God nor a Devil but only a man!' The Bashkai troops stuck to Billy Fish all they were worth, but their matchlocks wasn't half as good as the Kabul breech-loaders, and four of them dropped. Dan was bellowing like a bull, for he was very wrathy; and Billy Fish had a hard job to prevent him running out at the crowd.

"'We can't stand,' says Billy Fish. 'Make a run for it down the valley! The whole place is against us.' The matchlock-men ran, and we went down the valley in spite of Dravot. He was swearing horrible and crying out he was a King. The priests rolled great stones on us, and the regular Army fired hard, and there wasn't more than six men, not counting Dan, Billy Fish, and Me, that came down to the bottom of the valley alive.

"Then they stopped firing and the horns in the temple blew again. 'Come away—for Gord's sake come away!' says Billy Fish. 'They'll send runners out to all the villages before ever we get to Bashkai. I can protect you there, but I can't do anything now.'

"My own notion is that Dan began to go mad in his head from that hour. He stared up and down like a stuck pig. Then he was all for walking back alone and killing the priests with his bare hands; which he could have done. 'An Emperor am I,' says Daniel, 'and next year I shall be a Knight of the Queen.'

"'All right, Dan,' says I; 'but come along now while there's time.'

"'It's your fault,' says he, 'for not looking after your Army better. There was mutiny in the midst, and you didn't know—you damned engine-driving, plate-laying, missionary's-pass-hunting hound!' He sat upon a rock and called me every foul name he could lay tongue to. I was too heart-sick to care, though it was all his foolishness that brought the smash.

"'I'm sorry, Dan,' says I, 'but there's no accounting for natives. This business is our Fifty-Seven.[25] Maybe we'll make something out of it yet, when we've got to Bashkai.'

"'Let's get to Bashkai, then,' says Dan, 'and, by God, when I come back here again I'll sweep the valley so there isn't a bug in a blanket left!'

"We walked all that day, and all that night Dan was stumping up and down on the snow, chewing his beard and muttering to himself.

"'There's no hope o' getting clear,' said Billy Fish. 'The priests will have sent runners to the villages to say that you are only men. Why didn't you stick on as Gods till things was more settled? I'm a dead man,' says Billy Fish, and he throws himself down on the snow and begins to pray to his Gods.

"Next morning we was in a cruel bad country—all up and down, no level ground at all, and no food either. The six Bashkai men looked at Billy Fish hungry-way as if they wanted to ask something, but they said never a word. At noon we came

---

25 **Fifty-Seven:** An allusion to the Indian Mutiny (or First War of Independence) of 1857.

to the top of a flat mountain all covered with snow, and when we climbed up into it, behold, there was an Army in position waiting in the middle!

"'The runners have been very quick,' says Billy Fish, with a little bit of a laugh. 'They are waiting for us.'

"Three or four men began to fire from the enemy's side, and a chance shot took Daniel in the calf of the leg. That brought him to his senses. He looks across the snow at the Army, and sees the rifles that we had brought into the country.

"'We're done for,' says he. 'They are Englishmen, these people,—and it's my blasted nonsense that has brought you to this. Get back, Billy Fish, and take your men away; you've done what you could, and now cut for it. Carnehan,' says he, 'shake hands with me and go along with Billy. Maybe they won't kill you. I'll go and meet 'em alone. It's me that did it. Me, the King!'

"'Go!' says I. 'Go to Hell, Dan. I'm with you here. Billy Fish, you clear out, and we two will meet those folk.'

"'I'm a Chief,' says Billy Fish, quite quiet. 'I stay with you. My men can go.'

"The Bashkai fellows didn't wait for a second word but ran off, and Dan and Me and Billy Fish walked across to where the drums were drumming and the horns were horning. It was cold—awful cold. I've got that cold in the back of my head now. There's a lump of it there."

The punkah-coolies had gone to sleep. Two kerosene lamps were blazing in the office, and the perspiration poured down my face and splashed on the blotter as I leaned forward. Carnehan was shivering, and I feared that his mind might go. I wiped my face, took a fresh grip of the piteously mangled hands, and said: "What happened after that?"

The momentary shift of my eyes had broken the clear current.

"What was you pleased to say?" whined Carnehan. "They took them without any sound. Not a little whisper all along the snow, not though the King knocked down the first man that set hand on him—not though old Peachey fired his last cartridge into the brown of 'em. Not a single solitary sound did those swines make. They just closed up tight, and I tell you their furs stunk. There was a man called Billy Fish, a good friend of us all, and they cut his throat, Sir, then and there, like a pig; and the King kicks up the bloody snow and says: 'We've had a dashed fine run for our money. What's coming next?' But Peachey, Peachey Taliaferro, I tell you, Sir, in confidence as betwixt two friends, he lost his head, Sir. No, he didn't neither. The King lost his head, so he did, all along o' one of those cunning rope-bridges. Kindly let me have the paper-cutter, Sir. It tilted this way. They marched him a mile across that snow to a rope-bridge over a ravine with a river at the bottom. You may have seen such. They prodded him behind like an ox. 'Damn your eyes!' says the King. 'D'you suppose I can't die like a gentleman?' He turns to Peachey—Peachey that was crying like a child. 'I've brought you to this, Peachey,' says he. 'Brought you out of your happy life to be killed in Kafiristan, where you was late Commander-in-Chief of the Emperor's forces. Say you forgive me, Peachey.' —'I do,' says Peachey. 'Fully and freely do I forgive you, Dan.'—'Shake hands, Peachey,' says he. 'I'm going now.'

Out he goes, looking neither right nor left, and when he was plumb in the middle of those dizzy dancing ropes,—'Cut, you beggars,' he shouts; and they cut, and old Dan fell, turning round and round and round, twenty thousand miles, for he took half an hour to fall till he struck the water, and I could see his body caught on a rock with the gold crown close beside.

"But do you know what they did to Peachey between two pine-trees? They crucified him, Sir, as Peachey's hand will show. They used wooden pegs for his hands and his feet; and he didn't die. He hung there and screamed, and they took him down next day, and said it was a miracle that he wasn't dead. They took him down— poor old Peachey that hadn't done them any harm—that hadn't done them any——."

He rocked to and fro and wept bitterly, wiping his eyes with the back of his scarred hands and moaning like a child for some ten minutes.

"They was cruel enough to feed him up in the temple, because they said he was more of a God than old Daniel that was a man. Then they turned him out on the snow, and told him to go home, and Peachey came home in about a year, begging along the roads quite safe; for Daniel Dravot he walked before and said: 'Come along, Peachey. It's a big thing we're doing.' The mountains they danced at night, and the mountains they tried to fall on Peachey's head, but Dan he held up his hand, and Peachey came along bent double. He never let go of Dan's hand, and he never let go of Dan's head. They gave it to him as a present in the temple, to remind him not to come again, and though the crown was pure gold, and Peachey was starving, never would Peachey sell the same. You knew Dravot, Sir! You knew Right Worshipful Brother Dravot! Look at him now!"

He fumbled in the mass of rags round his bent waist; brought out a black horse-hair bag embroidered with silver thread; and shook therefrom on to my table—the dried, withered head of Daniel Dravot! The morning sun that had long been paling the lamps struck the red beard and blind sunken eyes; struck, too, a heavy circlet of gold studded with raw turquoises, that Carnehan placed tenderly on the battered temples.

"You be'old now," said Carnehan, "the Emperor in his 'abit as he lived—the King of Kafiristan with his crown upon his head. Poor old Daniel that was a monarch once!"

I shuddered, for, in spite of defacements manifold, I recognised the head of the man of Marwar Junction. Carnehan rose to go. I attempted to stop him. He was not fit to walk abroad. "Let me take away the whiskey, and give me a little money," he gasped. "I was a King once. I'll go to the Deputy Commissioner and ask to set in the Poorhouse till I get my health. No, thank you, I can't wait till you get a carriage for me. I've urgent private affairs—in the south—at Marwar."

He shambled out of the office and departed in the direction of the Deputy Commissioner's house. That day at noon I had occasion to go down the blinding hot Mall, and I saw a crooked man crawling along the white dust of the roadside, his hat in his hand, quavering dolorously after the fashion of street-singers at Home. There was not a soul in sight, and he was out of all possible earshot of the houses. And he sang through his nose, turning his head from right to left:—

"The Son of Man goes forth to war,
    A golden crown to gain;
His blood-red banner streams afar—
    Who follows in his train?"[26]

I waited to hear no more, but put the poor wretch into my carriage and drove him off to the nearest missionary for eventual transfer to the Asylum. He repeated the hymn twice while he was with me whom he did not in the least recognise, and I left him singing it to the missionary.

Two days later I enquired after his welfare of the Superintendent of the Asylum.

"He was admitted suffering from sun-stroke. He died early yesterday morning," said the Superintendent. "Is it true that he was half an hour bare-headed in the sun at midday?"

"Yes," said I, "but do you happen to know if he had anything upon him by any chance when he died?"

"Not to my knowledge," said the Superintendent.

And there the matter rests.

QUESTIONS

1. Many critics see Kipling's stories, especially this one, as supporting the British Empire and glamorizing the men who ruled and worked within it. Others see him as often critical of the Empire and its practices. Which reading do you support? Point to specific passages to support your answer.

2. How are Dravot and Carnehan able to conquer and control the inhabitants of Kafiristan? What part does technology play in their conquest? What part does "religion" play?

3. Does the reign of Dravot and Carnehan bring any benefits to the inhabitants of Kafiristan? If so, how do these benefits relate to arguments defending the British Empire?

4. What role does the frame narrator (the newspaper man) play in shaping our impressions of Dravot and Carnehan?

5. What devices does Kipling use in this story to convince his readers that he (or his narrator) knows India intimately and can see beneath the surface of things?

6. The hymn that Carnehan sings at the end of the story, like "Onward Christian Soldiers," is often seen as a justification for the imposition of Christianity on the people of the Empire. Is Kipling's purpose in using the hymn serious or ironical? Defend your interpretation.

7. Some critics see the protagonists of Kipling's stories as men defeated by the irrationality of the universe. Comment on this reading.

---

26 **The Son of Man . . . :** The first verse of a popular Evangelical hymn.

Joseph Conrad

(1857–1924)

The life of Joseph Conrad is in many ways as romantic and improbable as the lives of some of his fictional characters. He was born Josef Teodor Konrad Korzeniowski , son of a Polish gentleman and fanatical nationalist at a time when Poland was occupied by Russia. When Josef was only six, his father was arrested and exiled to Vologda, a village about one hundred miles north of Moscow, where his mother died in 1865. His mother's uncle, Tadeusz Bobrowski, adopted the boy and sent him to school in Krakow, Poland, and then in Geneva, Switzerland, but Josef disliked school and begged his uncle let him join the French merchant marine at age seventeen. For the next four years, Josef sailed to the West Indies and South America and even became involved in gun smuggling. In debt from gambling and the failed gun smuggling enterprise, Josef attempted suicide in 1878. Upon recovery, he joined the British merchant fleet, where he remained for the next sixteen years, working his way up from third mate to master and becoming a British citizen in 1886.

In 1889, Conrad left his British employ and, as he said later, followed a boyhood dream of exploring the interior of Africa by seeking employment with a Belgian company to pilot a steamboat up the Congo River from Stanley Pool to Stanley Falls. During the journey downriver, Conrad fell ill with dysentery, gout, and fever, and nearly died. He returned to England and merchant sailing but retired in 1894 to write, publishing his first novel, *Almayer's Folly,* the following year under the name Joseph Conrad. He married in 1896 and until his death continued to publish novels and stories, the greatest of these being *Lord Jim* (1900), *Nostromo* (1904), and *Victory* (1915).

Conrad struggled as a writer, in part because English was his third language, which he always spoke with a strong accent. But if his financial progress was slow and his production always behind schedule, he nevertheless became one of the great fiction writers of his time, an early figure in modernism because of his highly suggestive and symbolic style and his probing of the dark side of human psychology. "Heart of Darkness," like many of his novels and stories, is based largely and directly on his personal experience. But while it is tempting to read his work biographically, Conrad transforms direct experience into something very different—often something dreamlike, even nightmarish. Indeed, "Heart of Darkness" has been compared to Dante's *Inferno* for the depravities it reveals about human actions and the human soul, but as a depiction of colonial atrocities, it barely suggests the full reality. Nevertheless, "Heart of Darkness" is a pivotal work in British literature, in part because of its treatment of colonialism and its use of the conventions of the adventure story to reveal deep insights into what Kurtz, with his final breath, calls "the horror." However one interprets this complex and compelling story, Kurtz's final words echo down the twentieth century and into the twenty-first.

sea is always the same. In the immutability of their surroundings the foreign shores, the foreign faces, the changing immensity of life, glide past, veiled not by a sense of mystery but by a slightly disdainful ignorance; for there is nothing mysterious to a seaman unless it be the sea itself, which is the mistress of his existence and as inscrutable as Destiny. For the rest, after his hours of work, a casual stroll or a casual spree on shore suffices to unfold for him the secret of a whole continent, and generally he finds the secret not worth knowing. The yarns of seamen have a direct simplicity, the whole meaning of which lies within the shell of a cracked nut. But Marlow was not typical (if his propensity to spin yarns be excepted), and to him the meaning of an episode was not inside like a kernel but outside, enveloping the tale which brought it out only as a glow brings out a haze, in the likeness of one of these misty halos that sometimes are made visible by the spectral illumination of moonshine.

His remark did not seem at all surprising. It was just like Marlow. It was accepted in silence. No one took the trouble to grunt even; and presently he said, very slow—

"I was thinking of very old times, when the Romans first came here, nineteen hundred years ago—the other day. . . . Light came out of this river since—you say Knights? Yes; but it is like a running blaze on a plain, like a flash of lightning in the clouds. We live in the flicker—may it last as long as the old earth keeps rolling! But darkness was here yesterday. Imagine the feelings of a commander of a fine—what d'ye call 'em?—trireme in the Mediterranean, ordered suddenly to the north; run overland across the Gauls in a hurry; put in charge of one of these craft the legionaries,—a wonderful lot of handy men they must have been too—used to build, apparently by the hundred, in a month or two, if we may believe what we read. Imagine him here—the very end of the world, a sea the color of lead, a sky the color of smoke, a kind of ship about as rigid as a concertina—and going up this river with stores, or orders, or what you like. Sandbanks, marshes, forests, savages,—precious little to eat fit for a civilized man, nothing but Thames water to drink. No Falernian wine here, no going ashore. Here and there a military camp lost in a wilderness, like a needle in a bundle of hay—cold, fog, tempests, disease, exile, and death,—death skulking in the air, in the water, in the bush. They must have been dying like flies here. Oh yes—he did it. Did it very well, too, no doubt, and without thinking much about it either, except afterwards to brag of what he had gone through in his time, perhaps. They were men enough to face the darkness. And perhaps he was cheered by keeping his eye on a chance of promotion to the fleet at Ravenna by-and-by, if he had good friends in Rome and survived the awful climate. Or think of a decent young citizen in a toga—perhaps too much dice, you know—coming out here in the train of some prefect, or tax-gatherer or trader even, to mend his fortunes. Land in a swamp, march through the woods, and in some inland post feel the savagery, the utter savagery, had closed round him,—all that mysterious life of the wilderness that stirs in the forest, in the jungles, in the hearts of wild men. There's no initiation either into such mysteries. He has to live in the midst of the incomprehensible, which is also detestable. And it has a fascination, too, that goes to work upon him. The fascination of the abomination—you know. Imagine the growing regrets, the longing to escape, the powerless disgust, the surrender, the hate."

He paused.

"Mind," he began again, lifting one arm from the elbow, the palm of the hand outwards, so that, with his legs folded before him, he had the pose of a Buddha preaching in European clothes and without a lotus-flower—"Mind, none of us would feel exactly like this. What saves us is efficiency—the devotion to efficiency. But these chaps were not much account, really. They were no colonists; their administration was merely a squeeze, and nothing more, I suspect. They were conquerors, and for that you want only brute force—nothing to boast of, when you have it, since your strength is just an accident arising from the weakness of others. They grabbed what they could get for the sake of what was to be got. It was just robbery with violence, aggravated murder on a great scale, and men going at it blind—as is very proper for those who tackle a darkness. The conquest of the earth, which mostly means the taking it away from those who have a different complexion or slightly flatter noses than ourselves, is not a pretty thing when you look into it too much. What redeems it is the idea only. An idea at the back of it; not a sentimental pretense but an idea; and an unselfish belief in the idea—something you can set up, and bow down before, and offer a sacrifice to. . . ."

He broke off. Flames glided in the river, small green flames, red flames, white flames,[4] pursuing, overtaking, joining, crossing each other—then separating slowly or hastily. The traffic of the great city went on in the deepening night upon the sleepless river. We looked on, waiting patiently—there was nothing else to do till the end of the flood; but it was only after a long silence, when he said, in a hesitating voice, "I suppose you fellows remember I did once turn fresh-water sailor for a bit," that we knew we were fated, before the ebb began to run, to hear about one of Marlow's inconclusive experiences.

"I don't want to bother you much with what happened to me personally," he began, showing in this remark the weakness of many tellers of tales who seem so often unaware of what their audience would best like to hear: "yet to understand the effect of it on me you ought to know how I got out there, what I saw, how I went up that river to the place where I first met the poor chap. It was the farthest point of navigation and the culminating point of my experience. It seemed somehow to throw a kind of light on everything about me—and into my thoughts. It was somber enough too—and pitiful—not extraordinary in any way—not very clear either. No, not very clear. And yet it seemed to throw a kind of light.

"I had then, as you remember, just returned to London after a lot of Indian Ocean, Pacific, China Seas—a regular dose of the East—six years or so, and I was loafing about, hindering you fellows in your work and invading your homes, just as though I had got a heavenly mission to civilize you. It was very fine for a time, but after a bit I did get tired of resting. Then I began to look for a ship—I should think

---

4 **white flames:** Each color of light designated a particular kind of boat.

the hardest work on earth. But the ships wouldn't even look at me. And I got tired of that game too.

"Now when I was a little chap I had a passion for maps. I would look for hours at South America, or Africa, or Australia, and lose myself in all the glories of exploration. At that time there were many blank spaces on the earth, and when I saw one that looked particularly inviting on a map (but they all look that) I would put my finger on it and say, When I grow up I will go there. The North Pole was one of these places, I remember. Well, I haven't been there yet, and shall not try now. The glamour's off. Other places were scattered about the Equator, and in every sort of latitude all over the two hemispheres. I have been in some of them, . . . well, we won't talk about that. But there was one yet—the biggest, the most blank, so to speak—that I had a hankering after.

"True, by this time it was not a blank space any more. It had got filled since my boyhood with rivers and lakes and names. It had ceased to be a blank space of delightful mystery—a white patch for a boy to dream gloriously over. It had become a place of darkness. But there was in it one river especially, a mighty big river, that you could see on the map, resembling an immense snake uncoiled, with its head in the sea, its body at rest curving afar over a vast country, and its tail lost in the depths of the land. And as I looked at the map of it in a shop-window, it fascinated me as a snake would a bird—a silly little bird. Then I remembered there was a big concern, a Company for trade on that river. Dash it all! I thought to myself, they can't trade without using some kind of craft on that lot of fresh water—steamboats! Why shouldn't I try to get charge of one. I went on along Fleet Street, but could not shake off the idea. The snake had charmed me.

"You understand it was a Continental concern, that Trading society; but I have a lot of relations living on the Continent, because it's cheap and not so nasty as it looks, they say.

"I am sorry to own I began to worry[5] them. This was already a fresh departure for me. I was not used to get things that way, you know. I always went my own road and on my own legs where I had a mind to go. I wouldn't have believed it of myself; but, then—you see—I felt somehow I must get there by hook or by crook. So I worried them. The men said 'My dear fellow,' and did nothing. Then—would you believe it?—I tried the women. I, Charlie Marlow, set the women to work—to get a job. Heavens! Well, you see, the notion drove me. I had an aunt, a dear enthusiastic soul. She wrote: 'It will be delightful. I am ready to do anything, anything for you. It is a glorious idea. I know the wife of a very high personage in the Administration, and also a man who has lots of influence with,' &c., &c. She was determined to make no end of fuss to get me appointed skipper of a river steamboat, if such was my fancy.

"I got my appointment—of course; and I got it very quick. It appears the Company had received news that one of their captains had been killed in a scuffle with the natives. This was my chance, and it made me the more anxious to go. It was only

---

5 **worry**: Pester.

months and months afterwards, when I made the attempt to recover what was left of the body, that I heard the original quarrel arose from a misunderstanding about some hens. Yes, two black hens. Fresleven—that was the fellow's name, a Dane—thought himself wronged somehow in the bargain, so he went ashore and started to hammer the chief of the village with a stick. Oh, it didn't surprise me in the least to hear this, and at the same time to be told that Fresleven was the gentlest, quietest creature that ever walked on two legs. No doubt he was; but he had been a couple of years already out there engaged in the noble cause, you know, and he probably felt the need at last of asserting his self-respect in some way. Therefore he whacked the old nigger mercilessly, while a big crowd of his people watched him, thunderstruck, till some man,—I was told the chief's son,—in desperation at hearing the old chap yell, made a tentative jab with a spear at the white man—and of course it went quite easy between the shoulder-blades. Then the whole population cleared into the forest, expecting all kinds of calamities to happen, while, on the other hand, the steamer Fresleven commanded left also in a bad panic, in charge of the engineer, I believe. Afterwards nobody seemed to trouble much about Fresleven's remains, till I got out and stepped into his shoes. I couldn't let it rest, though; but when an opportunity offered at last to meet my predecessor, the grass growing through his ribs was tall enough to hide his bones. They were all there. The supernatural being had not been touched after he fell. And the village was deserted, the huts gaped black, rotting, all askew within the fallen enclosures. A calamity had come to it, sure enough. The people had vanished. Mad terror had scattered them, men, women, and children, through the bush, and they had never returned. What became of the hens I don't know either. I should think the cause of progress got them, anyhow. However, through this glorious affair I got my appointment, before I had fairly begun to hope for it.

"I flew around like mad to get ready, and before forty-eight hours I was crossing the Channel to show myself to my employers, and sign the contract. In a very few hours I arrived in a city that always makes me think of a whited sepulcher.[6] Prejudice no doubt. I had no difficulty in finding the Company's offices. It was the biggest thing in the town, and everybody I met was full of it. They were going to run an over-sea empire, and make no end of coin by trade.

"A narrow and deserted street in deep shadow, high houses, innumerable windows with venetian blinds, a dead silence, grass sprouting between the stones, imposing carriage archways right and left, immense double doors standing ponderously ajar. I slipped through one of these cracks, went up a swept and ungarnished staircase, as arid as a desert, and opened the first door I came to. Two women, one fat and the other slim, sat on straw-bottomed chairs, knitting black wool. The slim one got up and walked straight at me—still knitting with downcast eyes—and only just as I began to think of getting out of her way, as you would for a somnambulist, stood still, and looked up. Her dress was as plain as an umbrella-cover, and

---

6 **whited sepulcher:** Matthew 23: 27–28: Jesus used the term to describe hypocrites who appear beautiful on the outside but are rotten inside.

she turned round without a word and preceded me into a waiting-room. I gave my name, and looked about. Deal table in the middle, plain chairs all round the walls, on one end a large shining map, marked with all the colors of a rainbow. There was a vast amount of red—good to see at any time, because one knows that some real work is done in there, a deuce of a lot of blue, a little green, smears of orange, and, on the East Coast, a purple patch, to show where the jolly pioneers of progress drink the jolly lager-beer.[7] However, I wasn't going into any of these. I was going into the yellow. Dead in the center. And the river was there—fascinating—deadly—like a snake. Ough! A door opened, a white-haired secretarial head, but wearing a compassionate expression, appeared, and a skinny forefinger beckoned me into the sanctuary. Its light was dim, and a heavy writing-desk squatted in the middle. From behind that structure came out an impression of pale plumpness in a frock-coat. The great man himself. He was five feet six, I should judge, and had his grip on the handle-end of ever so many millions. He shook hands, I fancy, murmured vaguely, was satisfied with my French. *Bon voyage.*

"In about forty-five seconds I found myself again in the waiting-room with the compassionate secretary, who, full of desolation and sympathy, made me sign some document. I believe I undertook amongst other things not to disclose any trade secrets. Well, I am not going to.

"I began to feel slightly uneasy. You know I am not used to such ceremonies, and there was something ominous in the atmosphere. It was just as though I had been let into some conspiracy—I don't know—something not quite right; and I was glad to get out. In the other room the two women knitted black wool feverishly. People were arriving, and the younger one was walking back and forth introducing them. The old one sat on her chair. Her flat cloth slippers were propped up on a foot-warmer, and a cat reposed on her lap. She wore a starched white affair on her head, had a wart on one cheek, and silver-rimmed spectacles hung on the tip of her nose. She glanced at me above the glasses. The swift and indifferent placidity of that look troubled me. Two youths with foolish and cheery countenances were being piloted over, and she threw at them the same quick glance of unconcerned wisdom. She seemed to know all about them and about me too. An eerie feeling came over me. She seemed uncanny and fateful. Often far away there I thought of these two, guarding the door of Darkness, knitting black wool as for a warm pall, one introducing, introducing continuously to the unknown, the other scrutinizing the cheery and foolish faces with unconcerned old eyes. *Ave!* Old knitter of black wool. *Morituri te salutant.*[8] Not many of those she looked at ever saw her again—not half, by a long way.

---

7 **There was . . . lager-beer:** Victorian maps were color-coded to show which countries controlled which colonies: red, blue, green, orange, purple, yellow were for British, French, Portuguese, Italian, German, and Belgian possessions respectively. Marlow was sailing to the Belgian Congo, present-day Democratic Republic of the Congo.

8 *Morituri te salutant:* The full Phrase is "Ave Caesar, morituri te salutamus": "Hail, Caesar, they who are about to die salute you"—the gladiators' salute to the emperor before the games.

"There was yet a visit to the doctor. 'A simple formality,' assured me the secretary, with an air of taking an immense part in all my sorrows. Accordingly a young chap wearing his hat over the left eyebrow, some clerk I suppose,—there must have been clerks in the business, though the house was as still as a house in a city of the dead,—came from somewhere up-stairs, and led me forth. He was shabby and careless, with ink-stains on the sleeves of his jacket, and his cravat was large and billowy, under a chin shaped like the toe of an old boot. It was a little too early for the doctor, so I proposed a drink, and thereupon he developed a vein of joviality. As we sat over our vermouths he glorified the Company's business, and by-and-by I expressed casually my surprise at him not going out there. He became very cool and collected all at once. 'I am not such a fool as I look, quoth Plato to his disciples,' he said sententiously, emptied his glass with great resolution, and we rose.

"The old doctor felt my pulse, evidently thinking of something else the while. 'Good, good for there,' he mumbled, and then with a certain eagerness asked me whether I would let him measure my head. Rather surprised, I said Yes, when he produced a thing like calipers and got the dimensions back and front and every way, taking notes carefully. He was an unshaven little man in a threadbare coat like a gabardine, with his feet in slippers, and I thought him a harmless fool. 'I always ask leave, in the interests of science, to measure the crania of those going out there,' he said. 'And when they come back too?' I asked. 'Oh, I never see them,' he remarked; 'and, moreover, the changes take place inside, you know.' He smiled, as if at some quiet joke. 'So you are going out there. Famous. Interesting too.' He gave me a searching glance, and made another note. 'Ever any madness in your family?' he asked, in a matter-of-fact tone. I felt very annoyed. 'Is that question in the interests of science too?' 'It would be,' he said, without taking notice of my irritation, 'interesting for science to watch the mental changes of individuals, on the spot, but. . .' 'Are you an alienist?'[9] I interrupted. 'Every doctor should be—a little,' answered that original, imperturbably. 'I have a little theory which you Messieurs who go out there must help me to prove. This is my share in the advantages my country shall reap from the possession of such a magnificent dependency. The mere wealth I leave to others. Pardon my questions, but you are the first Englishman coming under my observation. . . .' I hastened to assure him I was not in the least typical. 'If I were,' said I, 'I wouldn't be talking like this with you.' 'What you say is rather profound, and probably erroneous,' he said, with a laugh. 'Avoid irritation more than exposure to the sun. Adieu. How do you English say, eh? Good-by. Ah! Good-by. Adieu. In the tropics one must before everything keep calm.' . . . He lifted a warning forefinger. . . . '*Du calme, du calme. Adieu.*'[10]

"One thing more remained to do—say good-by to my excellent aunt. I found her triumphant. I had a cup of tea—the last decent cup of tea for many days—and in a room that most soothingly looked just as you would expect a lady's drawing-room to

9 **alienist:** One who treats mental illness.
10 *Du calme, . . . Adieu:* "Keep calm, keep calm. Good-bye."

look, we had a long quiet chat by the fireside. In the course of these confidences it became quite plain to me I had been represented to the wife of the high dignitary, and goodness knows to how many more people besides, as an exceptional and gifted creature—a piece of good fortune for the Company—a man you don't get hold of every day. Good heavens! and I was going to take charge of a two-penny-halfpenny river-steamboat with a penny whistle attached! It appeared, however, I was also one of the Workers, with a capital—you know. Something like an emissary of light, something like a lower sort of apostle. There had been a lot of such rot let loose in print and talk just about that time, and the excellent woman, living right in the rush of all that humbug, got carried off her feet. She talked about 'weaning those ignorant millions from their horrid ways,' till, upon my word, she made me quite uncomfortable.[11] I ventured to hint that the Company was run for profit.

"'You forget, dear Charlie, that the laborer is worthy of his hire,' she said, brightly. It's queer how out of touch with truth women are. They live in a world of their own, and there had never been anything like it, and never can be. It is too beautiful altogether, and if they were to set it up it would go to pieces before the first sunset. Some confounded fact we men have been living contentedly with ever since the day of creation would start up and knock the whole thing over.

"After this I got embraced, told to wear flannel, be sure to write often, and so on—and I left. In the street—I don't know why—a queer feeling came to me that I was an imposter. Odd thing that I, who used to clear out for any part of the world at twenty-four hours' notice, with less thought than most men give to the crossing of a street, had a moment—I won't say of hesitation, but of startled pause, before this commonplace affair. The best way I can explain it to you is by saying that, for a second or two, I felt as though, instead of going to the center of a continent, I were about to set off for the center of the earth.

"I left in a French steamer, and she called in every blamed port they have out there, for, as far as I could see, the sole purpose of landing soldiers and customhouse officers. I watched the coast. Watching a coast as it slips by the ship is like thinking about an enigma. There it is before you—smiling, frowning, inviting, grand, mean, insipid, or savage, and always mute with an air of whispering, Come and find out. This one was almost featureless, as if still in the making, with an aspect of monotonous grimness. The edge of a colossal jungle, so dark-green as to be almost black, fringed with white surf, ran straight, like a ruled line, far, far away along a blue sea whose glitter was blurred by a creeping mist. The sun was fierce, the land seemed to glisten and drip with steam. Here and there grayish-whitish specks showed up, clustered inside the white surf, with a flag flying above them perhaps. Settlements some centuries old, and still no bigger than pin-heads on the untouched expanse of their background. We pounded along, stopped, landed soldiers; went on, landed custom-

11 **She talked . . . uncomfortable:** Marlow refers here to what Rudyard Kipling called "The white man's burden," the idea that "civilized" Europeans were morally obliged to "raise" the "savages" of Africa and other "uncivilized" countries. The extent to which Marlow (and Conrad) believed in this idea is hotly debated by critics.

house clerks to levy toll in what looked like a God-forsaken wilderness, with a tin shed and a flag-pole lost in it; landed more soldiers—to take care of the custom-house clerks, presumably. Some, I heard, got drowned in the surf; but whether they did or not, nobody seemed particularly to care. They were just flung out there, and on we went. Every day the coast looked the same, as though we had not moved; but we passed various places—trading places—with names like Gran' Bassam Little Popo; names that seemed to belong to some sordid farce acted in front of a sinister backcloth. The idleness of a passenger, my isolation amongst all these men with whom I had no point of contact, the oily and languid sea, the uniform somberness of the coast, seemed to keep me away from the truth of things, within the toil of a mournful and senseless delusion. The voice of the surf heard now and then was a positive pleasure, like the speech of a brother. It was something natural, that had its reason, that had a meaning. Now and then a boat from the shore gave one a momentary contact with reality. It was paddled by black fellows. You could see from afar the white of their eyeballs glistening. They shouted, sang; their bodies streamed with perspiration; they had faces like grotesque masks—these chaps; but they had bone, muscle, a wild vitality, an intense energy of movement, that was as natural and true as the surf along their coast. They wanted no excuse for being there. They were a great comfort to look at. For a time I would feel I belonged still to a world of straightforward facts; but the feeling would not last long. Something would turn up to scare it away. Once, I remember, we came upon a man-of-war anchored off the coast. There wasn't even a shed there, and she was shelling the bush. It appears the French had one of their wars going on thereabouts. Her ensign dropped limp like a rag; the muzzles of the long six-inch guns stuck out all over the low hull; the greasy, slimy swell swung her up lazily and let her down, swaying her thin masts. In the empty immensity of earth, sky, and water, there she was, incomprehensible, firing into a continent. Pop, would go one of the six-inch guns; a small flame would dart and vanish, a little white smoke would disappear, a tiny projectile would give a feeble screech—and nothing happened. Nothing could happen. There was a touch of insanity in the proceeding, a sense of lugubrious drollery in the sight; and it was not dissipated by somebody on board assuring me earnestly there was a camp of natives—he called them enemies!—hidden out of sight somewhere.

"We gave her her letters (I heard the men in that lonely ship were dying of fever at the rate of three a day) and went on. We called at some more places with farcical names, where the merry dance of death and trade goes on in a still and earthy atmosphere as of an overheated catacomb; all along the formless coast bordered by dangerous surf, as if Nature herself had tried to ward off intruders; in and out of rivers, streams of death in life, whose banks were rotting into mud, whose waters, thickened into slime, invaded the contorted mangroves, that seemed to writhe at us in the extremity of an impotent despair. Nowhere did we stop long enough to get a particularized impression, but the general sense of vague and oppressive wonder grew upon me. It was like a weary pilgrimage amongst hints for nightmares.

"It was upward of thirty days before I saw the mouth of the big river. We anchored off the seat of the government. But my work would not begin till some two hundred miles farther on. So as soon as I could I made a start for a place thirty miles higher up.

"I had my passage on a little sea-going steamer. Her captain was a Swede, and knowing me for a seaman, invited me on the bridge. He was a young man, lean, fair, and morose, with lanky hair and a shuffling gait. As we left the miserable little wharf, he tossed his head contemptuously at the shore. 'Been living there?' he asked. I said, 'Yes.' 'Fine lot these government chaps—are they not?' he went on, speaking English with great precision and considerable bitterness. 'It is funny what some people will do for a few francs a month. I wonder what becomes of that kind when it goes up country?' I said to him I expected to see that soon. 'So-o-o!' he exclaimed. He shuffled athwart, keeping one eye ahead vigilantly. 'Don't be too sure,' he continued. 'The other day I took up a man who hanged himself on the road. He was a Swede, too.' 'Hanged himself! Why, in God's name?' I cried. He kept on looking out watchfully. 'Who knows? The sun too much for him, or the country perhaps.'

"At last we opened a reach. A rocky cliff appeared, mounds of turned-up earth by the shore, houses on a hill, others, with iron roofs, amongst a waste of excavations, or hanging to the declivity. A continuous noise of the rapids above hovered over this scene of inhabited devastation. A lot of people, mostly black and naked, moved about like ants. A jetty projected into the river. A blinding sunlight drowned all this at times in a sudden recrudescence of glare. 'There's your Company's station,' said the Swede, pointing to three wooden barrack-like structures on the rocky slope. 'I will send your things up. Four boxes did you say? So. Farewell.'

"I came upon a boiler wallowing in the grass, then found a path leading up the hill. It turned aside for the bowlders, and also for an undersized railway-truck lying there on its back with its wheels in the air. One was off. The thing looked as dead as the carcass of some animal. I came upon more pieces of decaying machinery, a stack of rusty nails. To the left a clump of trees made a shady spot, where dark things seemed to stir feebly. I blinked, the path was steep. A horn tooted to the right, and I saw the black people run. A heavy and dull detonation shook the ground, a puff of smoke came out of the cliff, and that was all. No change appeared on the face of the rock. They were building a railway. The cliff was not in the way or anything; but this objectless blasting was all the work going on.

"A slight clinking behind me made me turn my head. Six black men advanced in a file, toiling up the path. They walked erect and slow, balancing small baskets full of earth on their heads, and the clink kept time with their footsteps. Black rags were wound round their loins, and the short ends behind waggled to and fro like tails. I could see every rib, the joints of their limbs were like knots in a rope; each had an iron collar on his neck, and all were connected together with a chain whose bights[12] swung between them, rhythmically clinking. Another report from the cliff made me think suddenly of that ship of war I had seen firing into a continent. It was the same kind of ominous voice; but these men could by no stretch of imagination be called

12 **bights:** Bends (of chain).

enemies. They were called criminals, and the outraged law, like the bursting shells, had come to them, an insoluble mystery from the sea. All their meager breasts panted together, the violently dilated nostrils quivered, the eyes stared stonily uphill. They passed me within six inches, without a glance, with that complete, deathlike indifference of unhappy savages. Behind this raw matter one of the reclaimed, the product of the new forces at work, strolled despondently, carrying a rifle by its middle. He had a uniform jacket with one button off, and seeing a white man on the path, hoisted his weapon to his shoulder with alacrity. This was simple prudence, white men being so much alike at a distance that he could not tell who I might be. He was speedily reassured, and with a large, white, rascally grin, and a glance at his charge, seemed to take me into partnership in his exalted trust. After all, I also was a part of the great cause of these high and just proceedings.

"Instead of going up, I turned and descended to the left. My idea was to let that chain-gang get out of sight before I climbed the hill. You know I am not particularly tender; I've had to strike and to fend off. I've had to resist and to attack sometimes—that's only one way of resisting—without counting the exact cost, according to the demands of such sort of life as I had blundered into. I've seen the devil of violence, and the devil of greed, and the devil of hot desire; but, by all the stars! these were strong, lusty, red-eyed devils, that swayed and drove men—men, I tell you. But as I stood on this hillside, I foresaw that in the blinding sunshine of that land I would become acquainted with a flabby, pretending, weak-eyed devil of a rapacious and pitiless folly. How insidious he could be, too, I was only to find out several months later and a thousand miles farther. For a moment I stood appalled, as though by a warning. Finally I descended the hill, obliquely, towards the trees I had seen.

"I avoided a vast artificial hole somebody had been digging on the slope, the purpose of which I found it impossible to divine. It wasn't a quarry or a sandpit, anyhow. It was just a hole. It might have been connected with the philanthropic desire of giving the criminals something to do. I don't know. Then I nearly fell into a very narrow ravine, almost no more than a scar in the hillside. I discovered that a lot of imported drainage-pipes for the settlement had been tumbled in there. There wasn't one that was not broken. It was a wanton smash-up. At last I got under the trees. My purpose was to stroll into the shade for a moment; but no sooner within than it seemed to me I had stepped into a gloomy circle of some Inferno. The rapids were near, and an uninterrupted, uniform, headlong, rushing noise filled the mournful stillness of the grove, where not a breath stirred, not a leaf moved, with a mysterious sound—as though the tearing pace of the launched earth had suddenly become audible.

"Black shapes crouched, lay, sat between the trees, leaning against the trunks, clinging to the earth, half coming out, half effaced within the dim light, in all the attitudes of pain, abandonment, and despair. Another mine on the cliff went off, followed by a slight shudder of the soil under my feet. The work was going on. The work! And this was the place where some of the helpers had withdrawn to die.

"They were dying slowly—it was very clear. They were not enemies, they were not criminals, they were nothing earthly now,—nothing but black shadows of disease and starvation, lying confusedly in the greenish gloom. Brought from all the recesses of the coast in all the legality of time contracts, lost in uncongenial surroundings, fed on unfamiliar food, they sickened, became inefficient, and were then allowed to crawl away and rest. These moribund shapes were free as air—and nearly as thin. I began to distinguish the gleam of the eyes under the trees. Then, glancing down, I saw a face near my hand. The black bones reclined at full length with one shoulder against the tree, and slowly the eyelids rose and the sunken eyes looked up at me, enormous and vacant, a kind of blind, white flicker in the depths of the orbs, which died out slowly. The man seemed young—almost a boy—but you know with them it's hard to tell. I found nothing else to do but to offer him one of my good Swede's ship's biscuits I had in my pocket. The fingers closed slowly on it and held—there was no other movement and no other glance. He had tied a bit of white worsted round his neck—Why? Where did he get it? Was it a badge—an ornament—a charm—a propitiatory act? Was there any idea at all connected with it? It looked startling round his black neck, this bit of white thread from beyond the seas.

"Near the same tree two more bundles of acute angles sat with their legs drawn up. One, with his chin propped on his knees, stared at nothing, in an intolerable and appalling manner: his brother phantom rested its forehead, as if overcome with a great weariness; and all about others scattered in every pose of contorted collapse, as in some picture of a massacre or a pestilence. While I stood horror-struck, one of these creatures rose to his hands and knees, and went off on all-fours towards the river to drink. He lapped out of his hand, then sat up in the sunlight, crossing his shins in front of him, and after a time let his woolly head fall on his breastbone.

"I didn't want any more loitering in the shade, and I made haste towards the station. When near the buildings I met a white man, in such an unexpected elegance of get-up that in the first moment I took him for a sort of vision. I saw a high starched collar, white cuffs, a light alpaca jacket, snowy trousers, a clean necktie, and varnished boots. No hat. Hair parted, brushed, oiled, under a green-lined parasol held in a big white hand. He was amazing, and had a penholder behind his ear.

"I shook hands with this miracle, and I learned he was the Company's chief accountant, and that all the bookkeeping was done at this station. He had come out for a moment, he said, 'to get a breath of fresh air.' The expression sounded wonderfully odd, with its suggestion of sedentary desk-life. I wouldn't have mentioned the fellow to you at all, only it was from his lips that I first heard the name of the man who is so indissolubly connected with the memories of that time. Moreover, I respected the fellow. Yes; I respected his collars, his vast cuffs, his brushed hair. His appearance was certainly that of a hairdresser's dummy; but in the great demoralization of the land he kept up his appearance. That's backbone. His starched collars and got-up shirt-fronts were achievements of character. He had been out nearly three years; and, later on, I could not help asking him how he managed to sport such linen. He had just the faintest blush, and said modestly, 'I've been teaching one of the native women about the station. It was difficult. She had a distaste for the work.' Thus this man had verily accomplished something. And he was devoted to his books, which were in apple-pie order.

"Everything else in the station was in a muddle,—heads, things, buildings. Strings of dusty niggers with splay feet arrived and departed; a stream of manufactured goods, rubbishy cottons, beads, and brass-wire sent into the depths of darkness, and in the return came a precious trickle of ivory.

"I had to wait in the station for ten days—an eternity. I lived in a hut in the yard, but to be out of the chaos I would sometimes get into the accountant's office. It was built of horizontal planks, and so badly put together that, as he bent over his desk, he was barred from neck to heels with narrow strips of sunlight. There was no need to open the big shutter to see. It was hot there too; big flies buzzed fiendishly, and did not sting, but stabbed. I sat generally on the floor, while, of faultless appearance (and even slightly scented), perching on a high stool, he wrote, he wrote. Sometimes he stood up for exercise. When a truckle-bed with a sick man (some invalided agent from up-country) was put in there, he exhibited a gentle annoyance. 'The groans of this sick person,' he said, 'distract my attention. And without that it is extremely difficult to guard against clerical errors in this climate.'

"One day he remarked, without lifting his head, 'In the interior you will no doubt meet Mr. Kurtz.' On my asking who Mr. Kurtz was, he said he was a first-class agent; and seeing my disappointment at this information, he added slowly, laying down his pen, 'He is a very remarkable person.' Further questions elicited from him that Mr. Kurtz was at present in charge of a trading post, a very important one, in the true ivory-country, at 'the very bottom of there. Sends in as much ivory as all the others put together. . . .' He began to write again. The sick man was too ill to groan. The flies buzzed in a great peace.

"Suddenly there was a growing murmur of voices and a great tramping of feet. A caravan had come in. A violent babble of uncouth sounds burst out on the other side of the planks. All the carriers were speaking together, and in the midst of the uproar the lamentable voice of the chief agent was heard 'giving it up' tearfully for the twentieth time that day. . . . He rose slowly. 'What a frightful row,' he said. He crossed the room gently to look at the sick man, and returning, said to me, 'He does not hear.' 'What! Dead?' I asked, startled. 'No, not yet,' he answered, with great composure. Then, alluding with a toss of the head to the tumult in the station-yard, 'When one has got to make correct entries, one comes to hate those savages—hate them to the death.' He remained thoughtful for a moment. 'When you see Mr. Kurtz,' he went on, 'tell him from me that everything here'—he glanced at the desk—'is very satisfactory. I don't like to write to him—with those messengers of ours you never know who may get hold of your letter—at that Central Station.' He stared at me for a moment with his mild, bulging eyes. 'Oh, he will go far, very far,' he began again. 'He will be a somebody in the Administration before long. They, above—the Council in Europe, you know—mean him to be.'

"He turned to his work. The noise outside had ceased, and presently in going out I stopped at the door. In the steady buzz of flies the homeward-bound agent was lying flushed and insensible; the other, bent over his books, was making correct entries of perfectly correct transactions; and fifty feet below the doorstep I could see the still tree-tops of the grove of death.

"Next day I left that station at last, with a caravan of sixty men, for a two-hundred-mile tramp.

"No use telling you much about that. Paths, paths, everywhere; a stamped-in network of paths spreading over the empty land, through long grass, through burnt grass, through thickets, down and up chilly ravines, up and down stony hills ablaze with heat; and a solitude, nobody, not a hut. The population had cleared out a long time ago. Well, if a lot of mysterious niggers armed with all kinds of fearful weapons suddenly took to traveling on the road between Deal and Gravesend, catching the yokels right and left to carry heavy loads for them, I fancy every farm and cottage thereabouts would get empty very soon. Only here the dwellings were gone too. Still I passed through several abandoned villages. There's something pathetically childish in the ruins of grass walls. Day after day, with the stamp and shuffle of sixty pair of bare feet behind me, each pair under a 60-lb load. Camp, cook, sleep, strike camp, march. Now and then a carrier dead in harness, at rest in the long grass near the path, with an empty water-gourd and his long staff lying by his side. A great silence around and above. Perhaps on some quiet night the tremor of far-off drums, sinking, swelling, a tremor vast, faint; a sound weird, appealing, suggestive, and wild—and perhaps with as profound a meaning as the sound of bells in a Christian country. Once a white man in an unbuttoned uniform, camping on the path with an armed escort of lank Zanzibaris, very hospitable and festive—not to say drunk. Was looking after the upkeep of the road, he declared. Can't say I saw any road or any upkeep, unless the body of a middle-aged negro, with a bullet-hole in the forehead, upon which I absolutely stumbled three miles farther on, may be considered as a permanent improvement. I had a white companion too, not a bad chap, but rather too fleshy and with the exasperating habit of fainting on the hot hillsides, miles away from the least bit of shade and water. Annoying, you know, to hold your own coat like a parasol over a man's head while he is coming-to. I couldn't help asking him once what he meant by coming there at all. 'To make money, of course. What do you think?' he said, scornfully. Then he got fever, and had to be carried in a hammock slung under a pole. As he weighed sixteen stone[13] I had no end of rows with the carriers. They jibbed, ran away, sneaked off with their loads in the night—quite a mutiny. So, one evening, I made a speech in English with gestures, not one of which was lost to the sixty pairs of eyes before me, and the next morning I started the hammock off in front all right. An hour afterwards I came upon the whole concern wrecked in a bush—man, hammock, groans, blankets, horrors. The heavy pole had skinned his poor nose. He was very anxious for me to kill somebody, but there wasn't the shadow of a carrier near. I remembered the old doctor,—'It would be interesting for science to watch the mental changes of individuals, on the spot.' I felt I was becoming scientifically interesting. However, all that is to no purpose. On the fifteenth day I came in sight of the big river again, and hobbled into the Central Station. It was on a back water surrounded by scrub and forest, with a pretty border of

---

13 **sixteen stone:** A stone is 14 pounds; hence 224 pounds.

smelly mud on one side, and on the three others inclosed by a crazy fence of rushes. A neglected gap was all the gate it had, and the first glance at the place was enough to let you see the flabby devil was running that show. White men with long staves in their hands appeared languidly from amongst the buildings, strolling up to take a look at me, and then retired out of sight somewhere. One of them, a stout, excitable chap with black mustaches, informed me with great volubility and many digressions, as soon as I told him who I was, that my steamer was at the bottom of the river. I was thunderstruck. What, how, why? Oh, it was 'all right.' The 'manager himself' was there. All quite correct. 'Everybody had behaved splendidly! splendidly!'— 'you must,' he said in agitation, 'go and see the general manager at once. He is waiting!'

"I did not see the real significance of that wreck at once. I fancy I see it now, but I am not sure—not at all. Certainly the affair was too stupid—when I think of it—to be altogether natural. Still. . . . But at the moment it presented itself simply as a confounded nuisance. The steamer was sunk. They had started two days before in a sudden hurry up the river with the manager on board, in charge of some volunteer skipper, and before they had been out three hours they tore the bottom out of her on stones, and she sank near the south bank. I asked myself what I was to do there, now my boat was lost. As a matter of fact, I had plenty to do in fishing my command out of the river. I had to set about it the very next day. That, and the repairs when I brought the pieces to the station, took some months.

"My first interview with the manager was curious. He did not ask me to sit down after my twenty-mile walk that morning. He was commonplace in complexion, in feature, in manners, and in voice. He was of middle size and of ordinary build. His eyes, of the usual blue, were perhaps remarkably cold, and he certainly could make his glance fall on one as trenchant and heavy as an ax. But even at these times the rest of his person seemed to disclaim the intention. Otherwise there was only an indefinable, faint expression of his lips, something stealthy—a smile—not a smile—I remember it, but I can't explain. It was unconscious, this smile was, though just after he had said something it got intensified for an instant. It came at the end of his speeches like a seal applied on the words to make the meaning of the commonest phrase appear absolutely inscrutable. He was a common trader, from his youth up employed in these parts—nothing more. He was obeyed, yet he inspired neither love nor fear, nor even respect. He inspired uneasiness. That was it! Uneasiness. Not a definite mistrust—just uneasiness—nothing more. You have no idea how effective such a . . . a . . . faculty can be. He had no genius for organizing, for initiative, or for order even. That was evident in such things as the deplorable state of the station. He had no learning, and no intelligence. His position had come to him—why? Perhaps because he was never ill . . . He had served three terms of three years out there . . . Because triumphant health in the general rout of constitutions is a kind of power in itself. When he went home on leave he rioted on a large scale—pompously. Jack ashore—with a difference—in externals only. This one could gather from his casual talk. He originated nothing, he could keep the routine going—that's all. But he was great. He was great by this little thing that it was impossible to tell what could control such a man. He never gave that secret away. Perhaps there was nothing within him. Such a suspicion made one pause—for out there there were no external checks. Once when various tropical diseases had laid low almost every 'agent' in the station, he was heard to say, 'Men who come out here should have no entrails.' He sealed the utterance with that smile of his, as though it had been a door opening into a darkness he had in his keeping. You fancied you had seen things—but the seal was on. When annoyed at meal-times by the constant quarrels of the white men about precedence, he ordered an immense round table to be made, for which a special house had to be built. This was the station's mess-room. Where he sat was the first place—the rest were nowhere. One felt this to be his unalterable conviction. He was neither civil nor uncivil. He was quiet. He allowed his 'boy'—an overfed young negro from the coast—to treat the white men, under his very eyes, with provoking insolence.

"He began to speak as soon as he saw me. I had been very long on the road. He could not wait. Had to start without me. The up-river stations had to be relieved. There had been so many delays already that he did not know who was dead and who was alive, and how they got on—and so on, and so on. He paid no attention to my explanations, and, playing with a stick of sealing-wax, repeated several times that the situation was 'very grave, very grave.' There were rumors that a very important station was in jeopardy, and its chief, Mr. Kurtz, was ill. Hoped it was not true. Mr. Kurtz was . . . I felt weary and irritable. Hang Kurtz, I thought. I interrupted him by saying I had heard of Mr. Kurtz on the coast. 'Ah! So they talk of him down there,' he murmured to himself. Then he began again, assuring me Mr. Kurtz was the best agent he had, an exceptional man, of the greatest importance to the Company; therefore I could understand his anxiety. He was, he said, 'very, very uneasy.' Certainly he fidgeted on his chair a good deal, exclaimed, 'Ah, Mr. Kurtz!' broke the stick of sealing-wax and seemed dumbfounded by the accident. Next thing he wanted to know 'how long it would take to' . . . I interrupted him again. Being hungry, you know, and kept on my feet too, I was getting savage. 'How could I tell,' I said. 'I hadn't even seen the wreck yet—some months, no doubt!' All this talk seemed to me so futile. 'Some months,' he said. 'Well, let us say three months before we can make a start. Yes. That ought to do the affair.' I flung out of his hut (he lived all alone in a clay hut with a sort of veranda) muttering to myself my opinion of him. He was a chattering idiot. Afterwards I took it back when it was borne in upon me startlingly with what extreme nicety he had estimated the time requisite for the 'affair.'

"I went to work the next day, turning, so to speak, my back on that station. In that way only it seemed to me I could keep my hold on the redeeming facts of life. Still, one must look about sometimes; and then I saw this station, these men strolling aimlessly about in the sunshine of the yard. I asked myself sometimes what it all meant. They wandered here and there with their absurd long staves in their hands, like a lot of faithless pilgrims bewitched inside a rotten fence. The word 'ivory' rang in the air, was whispered, was sighed. You would think they were praying to it. A taint of imbecile rapacity blew through it all, like a whiff from some corpse. By Jove! I've never seen anything so unreal in my life. And outside, the silent wilderness surrounding this cleared speck on the earth struck me as something great and invincible, like evil or truth, waiting patiently for the passing away of this fantastic invasion.

"Oh, these months! well, never mind. Various things happened. One evening a grass shed full of calico, cotton prints, beads, and I don't know what else, burst into a blaze so suddenly that you would have thought the earth had opened to let an avenging fire consume all that trash. I was smoking my pipe quietly by my dismantled steamer, and saw them all cutting capers in the light, with their arms lifted high, when the stout man with mustaches came tearing down to the river, a tin pail in his hand, assured me that everybody was 'behaving splendidly, splendidly,' dipped about a quart of water and tore back again. I noticed there was a hole in the bottom of his pail.

"I strolled up. There was no hurry. You see the thing had gone off like a box of matches. It had been hopeless from the very first. The flame had leaped high, driven everybody back, lighted up everything—and collapsed. The shed was already a heap of embers glowing fiercely. A nigger was being beaten near by. They said he had caused the fire in some way; be that as it may, he was screeching most horribly. I saw him, later on, for several days, sitting in a bit of shade looking very sick and trying to recover himself: afterwards he arose and went out—and the wilderness without a sound took him into its bosom again. As I approached the glow from the dark I found myself at the back of two men, talking. I heard the name of Kurtz pronounced, then the words, 'take advantage of this unfortunate accident.' One of the men was the manager. I wished him a good evening. 'Did you ever see anything like it—eh? it is incredible,' he said and walked off. The other man remained. He was a first-class agent, young, gentlemanly, a bit reserved, with a forked little beard and a hooked nose. He was standoffish with the other agents, and they on their side said he was the manager's spy upon them. As to me, I had hardly ever spoken to him before. We got into talk, and by-and-by we strolled away from the hissing ruins. Then he asked me to his room, which was in the main building of the station. He struck a match, and I perceived that this young aristocrat had only a silver-mounted dressing-case but also a whole candle all to himself. Just at that time the manager was the only man supposed to have any right to candles. Native mats covered the clay walls; a collection of spears, assegais, shields, knives was hung up in trophies. The business intrusted to this fellow was the making of bricks—so I had been informed; but there wasn't a fragment of a brick anywhere in the station, and he had been there more than a year—waiting. It seems he could not make bricks without something, I don't know what—straw maybe. Anyways, it could not be found there, and as it was not likely to be sent from Europe, it did not appear clear to me what he was waiting for. An act of special creation perhaps. However, they were all waiting—all the sixteen or twenty pilgrims of them—for something; and upon my word it did not seem an uncongenial occupation, from they way they took it, though the only thing that ever came to them was disease—as far as I could see. They beguiled the time by backbiting and intriguing against each other in a foolish kind of way. There was an air of plotting about that station, but nothing came of it, of course. It was as unreal as everything else—as the philanthropic pretense of the whole concern, as their talk, as their government, as their show of work. The only real feeling was a desire to get appointed to a trading-post where ivory was to be had, so that they could earn percentages. They intrigued and slandered and hated each other only on that account,—but as to effectually lifting a little finger—oh, no. By heavens! there is something after all in the world allowing one man to steal a horse while another must not look at a halter. Steal a horse straight out. Very well. He has done it. Perhaps he can ride. But there is a way of looking at a halter that would provoke the most charitable of saints into a kick.

"I had no idea why he wanted to be sociable, but as we chatted in there it suddenly occurred to me the fellow was trying to get at something—in fact, pumping me. He alluded constantly to Europe, to the people I was supposed to know there— putting leading questions as to my acquaintances in the sepulchral city, and so on. His little eyes glittered like mica discs—with curiosity,—though he tried to keep up a bit of superciliousness. At first I was astonished, but very soon I became awfully curious to see what he would find out from me. I couldn't possibly imagine what I had in me to make it worth his while. It was very pretty to see how he baffled himself, for in truth my body was full of chills, and my head had nothing in it but that wretched steamboat business. It was evident he took me for a perfectly shameless prevaricator. At last he got angry, and, to conceal a movement of furious annoyance, he yawned. I rose. Then I noticed a small sketch in oils, on a panel, representing a woman, draped and blindfolded, carrying a lighted torch. The background was somber—almost black. The movement of the woman was stately, and the effect of the torchlight on the face was sinister.

"It arrested me, and he stood by civilly, holding an empty half-pint champagne bottle (medical comforts) with the candle stuck in it. To my question he said Mr. Kurtz had painted this—in this very station more than a year ago—while waiting for means to go to his trading-post. 'Tell me, pray,' said I, 'who is this Mr. Kurtz?'

" 'The chief of the Inner Station,' he answered in a short tone, looking away. 'Much obliged,' I said, laughing. 'And you are the brickmaker of the Central Station. Everyone knows that.' He was silent for a while. 'He is a prodigy,' he said at last. 'He is an emissary of pity, and science, and progress, and devil knows what else. We want,' he began to declaim suddenly, 'for the guidance of the cause intrusted to us by Europe, so to speak, higher intelligence, wide sympathies, a singleness of purpose.' 'Who says that?' I asked. 'Lots of them,' he replied. 'Some even write that; and so *he* comes here, a special being, as you ought to know.' 'Why ought I to know?' I interrupted, really surprised. He paid no attention. 'Yes. To-day he is chief of the best station, next year he will be assistant-manager, two years more and . . . but I dare say you know what he will be in two years' time. You are the new gang—the gang of virtue. The same people who sent him specially also recommended you. Oh, don't say no. I've my own eyes to trust.' Light dawned upon me. My dear aunt's influential acquaintances were producing an unexpected effect upon that young man. I nearly burst into a laugh. 'Do you read the Company's confidential correspondence?' I asked. He hadn't a word to say. It was great fun. 'When Mr. Kurtz,' I continued severely, 'is General Manager, you won't have the opportunity.'

"He blew the candle out suddenly, and we went outside. The moon had risen. Black figures strolled about listlessly, pouring water on the glow, whence proceeded a sound of hissing; steam ascended in the moonlight, the beaten nigger groaned somewhere. 'What a row the brute makes!' said the indefatigable man with the mustaches, appearing near us. 'Serve him right. Transgression—punishment—bang! Pitiless, pitiless. That's the only way. This will prevent all conflagration for the future. I was just telling the manager . . .' He noticed my companion, and became crestfallen all at once. 'Not in bed yet,' he said, with a kind of servile heartiness; 'it's so natural. Ha! Danger-agitation.' He vanished. I went on to the river-side, and the other followed me. I heard a scathing murmur at my ear. 'Heap of muffs—go to.' The pilgrims could be seen in knots gesticulating, discussing. Several had still their staves in their hands. I verily believe they took these sticks to bed with them. Beyond the fence the forest stood up spectrally in the moonlight, and through the dim stir, through the faint sounds of that lamentable courtyard, the silence of the land when home to one's very heart,—its mystery, its greatness, the amazing reality of its concealed life. The hurt nigger moaned feebly somewhere near by, and then fetched a deep sigh that made me mend my pace away from there. I felt a hand introducing itself under my arm. 'My dear sir,' said the fellow, 'I don't want to be misunderstood, and especially by you, who will see Mr. Kurtz long before I can have that pleasure. I wouldn't like him to get a false idea of my disposition. . . .'

"I let him run on, this papier-maché Mephistopheles, and it seemed to me that if I tried I could poke my forefinger through him, and would find nothing inside but a little loose dirt, maybe. He, don't you see, had been planning to be assistant-manager by-and-by under the present man, and I could see that the coming of that Kurtz had upset them both not a little. He talked precipitately, and I did not try to stop him. I had my shoulders against the wreck of my steamer, hauled up on the slope like a carcass of some big river animal. The smell of mud, of primeval mud, by Jove! was in my nostrils, the high stillness of primeval forest was before my eyes; there were shiny patches on the black creek. The moon had spread over everything a thin layer of silver—over the rank grass, over the mud, upon the wall of matted vegetation standing higher than the wall of a temple, over the great river I could see through a somber gap glittering, glittering, as it flowed broadly by without a murmur. All this was great, expectant, mute, while the man jabbered about himself. I wondered whether the stillness on the face of the immensity looking at us two were meant as an appeal or as a menace. What were we who had strayed in here? Could we handle that dumb thing, or would it handle us? I felt how big, how confoundedly big, was that thing that couldn't talk, and perhaps was deaf as well. What was in there? I could see a little ivory coming out from there, and I had heard Mr. Kurtz was in there. I had heard enough about it too—God knows! Yet somehow it didn't bring any image with it—no more than if I had been told an angel or a fiend was in there. I believed it in the same way one of you might believe there are inhabitants in the planet Mars. I knew once a Scotch sailmaker who was certain, dead sure, there were people in Mars. If you asked him for some idea how they looked and behaved, he would get shy and mutter something about 'walking on all-fours.' If you as much as smiled, he would—though a man of sixty—offer to fight you. I would not have gone so far as to fight for Kurtz, but I went for him near enough to a lie. You know I hate, detest, and can't bear a lie, not because I am straighter than the rest of us, but simply because it appalls me. There is a taint of death, a flavor of mortality in lies,—which is exactly what I hate and detest in the world—what I want to forget. It makes me miserable and sick, like biting something rotten would do. Temperament, I suppose. Well, I went near enough to it by letting the young fool there believe anything he liked to imagine as to my influence in Europe. I became in an instant as much of a pretense as the rest of the bewitched pilgrims. This simply because I had a notion it somehow would be of help to that Kurtz whom at the time I did not see—you understand. He was just a word for me. I did not see the man in the name any more than you do. Do you see him? Do you see the story? Do you see anything? It seems to me I am trying to tell you a dream—making a vain attempt, because no relation of a dream can convey the dream-sensation, that commingling of absurdity, surprise, and bewilderment in a tremor of struggling revolt, that notion of being captured by the incredible which is of the very essence of dreams. . . ."

He was silent for a while.

". . . No, it is impossible; it is impossible to convey the life-sensation of any given epoch of one's existence,—that which makes its truth, its meaning—its subtle and penetrating essence. It is impossible. We live, as we dream—alone. . . ."

He paused again as if reflecting, then added—

"Of course in this you fellows see more than I could then. You see me, whom you know. . . ."

It had become so pitch dark that we listeners could hardly see one another. For a long time already he, sitting apart, had been no more to us than a voice. There was not a word from anybody. The others might have been asleep, but I was awake. I listened, I listened on the watch for the sentence, for the word, that would give me the clew to the faint uneasiness inspired by this narrative that seemed to shape itself without human lips in the heavy night-air of the river.

". . . Yes—I let him run on," Marlow began again, "and think what he pleased about the powers that were behind me. I did! And there was nothing behind me! There was nothing but that wretched, old, mangled steamboat I was leaning against, while he talked fluently about 'the necessity for every man to get on.' 'And when one comes out here, you conceive, it is not to gaze at the moon.' Mr. Kurtz was a 'universal genius,' but even a genius would find it easier to work with 'adequate tools—intelligent men.' He did not make bricks—why, there was a physical impossibility in the way—as I was well aware; and if he did secretarial work for the manager, it was because 'no sensible man rejects wantonly the confidence of his superiors.' Did I see it? I saw it. What more did I want? What I really wanted was rivets, by heaven! Rivets. To get on with the work—to stop the hole. Rivets I wanted. There were cases of them down at the coast—cases—piled up—burst—split! You kicked a loose rivet at every second step in that station yard on the hillside. Rivets had rolled into the grove of death. You could fill your pockets with rivets for the trouble of stooping down—and there wasn't one rivet to be found where it was wanted. We had plates that would do, but nothing to fasten them with. And every week the messenger, a lone negro, letter-bag on shoulder and staff in hand, left our station for the coast. And several times a week a coast caravan came in with trade goods,—ghastly glazed calico that made you shudder only to look at it, glass beads value about a penny a quart, confounded spotted cotton handkerchiefs. And no rivets. Three carriers could have brought all that was wanted to set that steamboat afloat.

"He was becoming confidential now, but I fancy my unresponsive attitude must have exasperated him at last, for he judged it necessary to inform me he feared neither God nor devil, let alone any mere man. I said I could see that very well, but what I wanted was a certain quantity of rivets—and rivets were what really Mr. Kurtz wanted, if he had only known it. Now letters went to the coast every week. . . .'My dear sir,' he cried, 'I write from dictation.' I demanded rivets. There was a way—for an intelligent man. He changed his manner; became very cold, and suddenly began to talk about a hippopotamus; wondered whether sleeping on board the steamer (I stuck to my salvage night and day) I wasn't disturbed. There was an old hippo that had the bad habit of getting out on the bank and roaming at night over the station grounds. The pilgrims use to turn out in a body and empty every rifle they could lay hands on at him. Some even had sat up o' nights for him. All this energy was wasted, though. 'That animal has a charmed life,' he said; 'but you can say this only of brutes in this country. No man—you apprehend me?—no man here bears a charmed life.' He stood there for a moment in the moonlight with his delicate hooked nose set a little askew, and his mica eyes glittering without a wink, then, with a curt Good night, he strode off. I could see he was disturbed and considerably puzzled, which made me feel more hopeful than I had been for days. It was a great comfort to turn from that chap to my influential friend, the battered, twisted, ruined, tin-pot steamboat. I clambered on board. She rang under my feet like an empty Huntley & Palmer biscuit-tin kicked along a gutter; she was nothing so solid in make, and rather less pretty in shape, but I had expended enough hard work on her to make me love her. No influential friend would have served me better. She had given me a chance to come out a bit—to find out what I could do. No, I don't like work. I had rather laze about and think of all the fine things that can be done. I don't like work—no man does—but I like what is in the work,—the chance to find yourself. Your own reality—for yourself, not for others—what no other man can ever know. They can only see the mere show, and never can tell what it really means.

"I was not surprised to see somebody sitting aft, on the deck, with his legs dangling over the mud. You see I rather chummed with the few mechanics there were in that station, whom the other pilgrims naturally despised—on account of their imperfect manners, I suppose. This was the foreman—a boiler-maker by trade—a good worker. He was a lank, bony, yellow-faced man, with big intense eyes. His aspect was worried, and his head was as bald as the palm of my hand; but his hair in falling seemed to have stuck to his chin, and had prospered in the new locality, for his beard hung down to his waist. He was a widower with six young children (he had left them in charge of a sister of his to come out there), and the passion of his life was pigeon-flying. He was an enthusiast and a connoisseur. He would rave about pigeons. After work hours he used sometimes to come over from his hut for a talk about his children and his pigeons; at work, when he had to crawl in the mud under the bottom of the steamboat, he would tie up that beard of his in a kind of white serviette he brought for the purpose. It had loops to go over his ears. In the evening he could be seen squatted on the bank rinsing that wrapper in the creek with great care, then spreading it solemnly on a bush to dry.

"I slapped him on the back and shouted 'We shall have rivets!' He scrambled to his feet exclaiming 'No! Rivets!' as though he couldn't believe his ears. Then in a low voice, 'You . . . eh?' I don't know why we behaved like lunatics. I put my finger to the side of my nose and nodded mysteriously. 'Good for you!' he cried, snapped his fingers above his head, lifting one foot. I tried a jig. We capered on the iron deck. A frightful clatter came out of that hulk, and the virgin forest on the other bank of the creek sent it back in a thundering roll upon the sleeping station. It must have made some of the pilgrims sit up in their hovels. A dark figure obscured the lighted doorway of the manager's hut, vanished, then, a second or so after, the doorway itself vanished too. We stopped, and the silence driven away by the stamping of our feet flowed back again from the recesses of the land. The great wall of vegetation, an exuberant and entangled mass of trunks branches, leaves, boughs, festoons, motionless in the moonlight, was like a rioting invasion of soundless life, a rolling wave of plants piled up, crested, ready to topple over the creek, to sweep every little man of us out of his little existence. And it moved not. A deadened burst of mighty splashes and snorts reached us from afar, as though an ichthyosaurus had been taking a bath of glitter in that great river. 'After all,' said the boiler-maker in a reasonable tone, 'why shouldn't we get the rivets?' Why not, indeed! I did not know of any reason why we shouldn't. 'They'll come in three weeks,' I said, confidently.

"But they didn't. Instead of rivets there came an invasion, an infliction, a visitation. It came in sections during the next three weeks, each section headed by a donkey carrying a white man in new clothes and tan shoes, bowing from that elevation right and left to the impressed pilgrims. A quarrelsome band of footsore sulky niggers trod on the heels of the donkey; a lot of tents, camp-stools, tin boxes, white cases, brown bales would be shot down in the courtyard, and the air of mystery would deepen a little over the muddle of the station. Five such installments came, with their absurd air of disorderly flight with the loot of innumerable outfit shops and provision stores, that, one would think, they were lugging, after a raid, into the wilderness for equitable division. It was an inextricable mess of things decent in themselves but that human folly made look like the spoils of thieving.

"This devoted band called itself the Eldorado Exploring Expedition, and I believe they were sworn to secrecy. Their talk, however, was the talk of sordid buccaneers; it was reckless without hardihood, greedy without audacity, and cruel without courage; there was not an atom of foresight or of serious intention in the whole batch of them, and they did not seem aware these things are wanted for the work of the world. To tear treasure out of the bowels of the land was their desire, with no more moral purpose at the back of it than there is in burglars breaking into a safe. Who paid the expenses of the noble enterprise I don't know; but the uncle of our manager was leader of that lot.

"In exterior he resembled a butcher in a poor neighborhood, and his eyes had a look of sleepy cunning. He carried his fat paunch with ostentation on his short legs, and during the time his gang infested the station spoke to no one but his nephew. You could see these two roaming about all day long with their heads close together in an everlasting confab.

"I had given up worrying myself about the rivets. One's capacity for that kind of folly is more limited than you would suppose. I said Hang!—and let things slide. I had plenty of time for meditation, and now and then I would give some thought to Kurtz. I wasn't very interested in him. No. Still, I was curious to see whether this man, who had come out equipped with moral ideas of some sort, would climb to the top after all, and how he would set about his work when there."

II

"One evening as I was lying flat on the deck of my steamboat, I heard voices approaching—and there were the nephew and the uncle strolling along the bank. I laid my head on my arm again, and had nearly lost myself in a doze, when somebody said in my ear, as it were: 'I am as harmless as a little child, but I don't like to be dictated to. Am I the manager—or am I not? I was ordered to send him there. It's incredible.' . . . I became aware that the two were standing on the shore alongside the forepart of the steamboat, just below my head. I did not move; it did not occur to me to move: I was sleepy. 'It is unpleasant,' grunted the uncle. 'He asked the Administration to be sent there,' said the other, 'with the idea of showing what he could do; and I was instructed accordingly. Look at the influence that man must have. Is it not frightful?' They both agreed it was frightful, then made several bizarre remarks: 'Make rain and fine weather—one man—the Council—by the nose'—bits of absurd sentences that got the better of my drowsiness, so that I had pretty near the whole of my wits about me when the uncle said, 'The climate may do away with this difficulty for you. Is he alone there?' 'Yes,' answered the manager; 'he sent his assistant down the river with a note to me in these terms: "Clear this poor devil out of the country, and don't bother sending more of that sort. I had rather be alone than have the kind of men you can dispose of with me." It was more than a year ago. Can you imagine such impudence!' 'Anything since then?' asked the other, hoarsely. 'Ivory,' jerked the nephew; "lots of it—prime sort—lots—most annoying, from him. 'And with that?' questioned the heavy rumble. 'Invoice,' was the reply fired out, so to speak. Then silence. They had been talking about Kurtz.

"I was broad awake by this time, but, lying perfectly at ease, remained still, having no inducement to change my position. 'How did that ivory come all this way?' growled the elder man, who seemed very vexed. The other explained that it had come with a fleet of canoes in charge of an English half-caste clerk Kurtz had with him; that Kurtz had apparently intended to return himself, the station being by that time bare of goods and stores, but after coming three hundred miles, had suddenly decided to go back, which he started to do alone in a small dug-out with four paddlers, leaving the half-caste to continue down the river with the ivory. The two fellows there seemed astounded at anybody attempting such a thing. They were at a loss for an adequate motive. As to me, I seemed to see Kurtz for the first time. It was a distinct glimpse: the dug-out, four paddling savages, and the lone white man turning his back suddenly on the headquarters, on relief, on thoughts of home—perhaps; setting his face towards the depths of the wilderness, towards his empty and desolate station. I did not know the motive. Perhaps he was just simply a fine fellow who stuck to his work for its own sake. His name, you understand, had not been pronounced once. He was 'that man.' The half-caste, who, as far as I could see, had conducted a difficult trip with great prudence and pluck, was invariably alluded to as 'that scoundrel.' The 'scoundrel' had reported that the 'man' had been very ill—had recovered imperfectly. . . . The two below me moved away then a few paces, and strolled back and forth at some little distance. I heard: 'Military post—doctor—two hundred miles—quite alone now—unavoidable delays—nine months—no news—strange rumors.' They approached again, just as the manager was saying, 'No one, as far as I know, unless a species of wandering trader—a pestilential fellow, snapping ivory from the natives.' Who was it they were talking about now? I gathered in snatches that this was some man supposed to be in Kurtz's district, and of whom the manager did not approve. 'We will not be free from unfair competition till one of these fellows is hanged for an example,' he said. 'Certainly,' grunted the other, 'get him hanged! Why not? Anything—anything can be done in this country. That's what I say; nobody here, you understand, *here*, can endanger your position. And why? You stand the climate—you outlast them all. The danger is in Europe; but there before I left I took care to—' They moved off and whispered, then their voices rose again. 'The extraordinary series of delays is not my fault. I did my possible.' The fat man sighed, 'Very sad.' 'And the pestiferous absurdity of his talk,' continued the other; 'he bothered me enough when he was here. "Each station should be like a beacon on the road towards better things, a center for trade of course, but also for humanizing, improving, instructing." Conceive you—that ass! And he wants to be manager! No, it's—' Here he got choked by excessive indignation, and I lifted my head the least bit. I was surprised to see how near they were—right under me. I could have spat upon their hats. They were looking on the ground, absorbed in thought. The manager was switching his leg with a slender twig: his sagacious relative lifted his head. 'You have been well since you came out this time?' he asked. The other gave a start. 'Who? I? Oh! Like a charm—like a charm. But the rest—oh, my goodness! All sick. They die so quick, too, that I haven't the time to send them out of the country—it's incredible!' 'H'm. Just so,' grunted the uncle. 'Ah! my boy, trust to this—I say, trust to this.' I saw him extend his short flipper of an arm for a gesture that took in the forest, the creek, the mud, the river,—seemed to beckon with a dishonoring flourish before the sunlit face of the land a treacherous appeal to the lurking death, to the hidden evil, to the profound darkness of its heart. It was so startling that I leaped to my feet and looked back at the edge of the forest, as though I had expected an answer of some sort to that black display of confidence. You know the foolish notions that come to one sometimes. The high stillness confronted these two figures with its ominous patience, waiting for the passing away of a fantastic invasion.

"They swore aloud together—out of sheer fright, I believe—then pretending not to know anything of my existence, turned back to the station. The sun was low; and leaning forward side by side, they seemed to be tugging painfully uphill their two ridiculous shadows of unequal length, that trailed behind them slowly over the tall grass without bending a single blade.

"In a few days the Eldorado Expedition went into the patient wilderness, that closed upon it as the sea closes over a diver. Long afterwards the news came that all the donkeys were dead. I know nothing as to the fate of the less valuable animals. They, no doubt, like the rest of us, found what they deserved. I did not inquire. I was then rather excited at the prospect of meeting Kurtz very soon. When I say very soon I mean it comparatively. It was just two months from the day we left the creek when we came to the bank below Kurtz's station.

"Going up that river was like traveling back to the earliest beginnings of the world, when vegetation rioted on the earth and the big trees were kings. An empty stream, a great silence, and impenetrable forest. The air was warm, thick, heavy, sluggish. There was no joy in the brilliance of sunshine. The long stretches of the waterway ran on, deserted, into the gloom of over-shadowed distances. On silvery sandbanks hippos and alligators sunned themselves side by side. The broadening waters flowed through a mob of wooded islands; you lost your way on that river as you would in a desert, and butted all day long against shoals, trying to find the channel, till you thought yourself bewitched and cut off for ever from everything you had known once—somewhere—far away—in another existence perhaps. There were moments when one's past came back to one, as it will sometimes when you have not a moment to spare to yourself; but it came in the shape of an unrestful and noisy dream, remembered with wonder amongst the overwhelming realities of this strange world of plants, and water, and silence. And this stillness of life did not in the least resemble a peace. It was the stillness of an implacable force brooding over an inscrutable intention. It looked at you with a vengeful aspect. I got used to it afterwards; I did not see it any more; I had no time; I had to keep guessing at the channel; I had to discern, mostly by inspiration, the signs of hidden banks; I watched for sunken stones; I was learning to clap my teeth smartly before my heart flew out, when I shaved by a fluke some infernal sly old snag that would have ripped the life out of the tin-pot steamboat and drowned all the pilgrims; I had to keep a look-out for the signs of dead wood we could cut up in the night for next days steaming. When you have to attend to things of that sort, to the mere incidents of the surface, the reality—the reality, I tell you—fades. The inner truth is hidden—luckily, luckily. But I felt it all the same; I felt often its mysterious stillness watching me at my monkey tricks, just as it watches you fellows performing on your respective tight-ropes for—what is it? half-a-crown a tumble—"

"Try to be civil, Marlow," growled a voice, and I knew there was at least one listener awake besides myself.

"I beg your pardon. I forgot the heartache which makes up the rest of the price. And indeed what does the price matter, if the trick be well done? You do your tricks very well. And I didn't do badly either, since I managed not to sink that steamboat on my first trip. It's a wonder to me yet. Imagine a blindfolded man set to drive a van over a bad road. I sweated and shivered over that business considerably, I can tell you. After all, for a seaman, to scrape the bottom of the thing that's supposed to float all the time under his care is the unpardonable sin. No one may know of it, but you never forget the thump—eh? A blow on the very heart. You remember it, you dream of it, you wake up at night and think of it—years after—and go hot and cold all over. I don't pretend to say that steamboat floated all the time. More than once she had to wade for a bit, with twenty cannibals splashing around and pushing. We had enlisted some of these chaps on the way for a crew. Fine fellows—cannibals—in their place. They were men one could work with, and I am grateful to them. And, after all, they did not eat each other before my face: they had brought along a provision of hippo-meat which went rotten, and made the mystery of the wilderness stink in my nostrils. Phoo! I can sniff it now. I had the manager on board and three or four pilgrims with their staves—all complete. Sometimes we came upon a station close by the bank, clinging to the skirts of the unknown, and the white men rushing out of a tumble-down hovel, with great gestures of joy and surprise and welcome, seemed very strange,—had the appearance of being held there captive by a spell. The word ivory would ring in the air for a while—and on we went again into the silence, along empty reaches, round the still bends, between the high walls of our winding way, reverberating in hollow claps the ponderous beat of the stern-wheel. Trees, trees, millions of trees, massive, immense, running up high; and at their foot, hugging the bank against the stream, crept the little begrimed steamboat, like a sluggish beetle crawling on the floor of a lofty portico. It made you feel very small, very lost, and yet it was not altogether depressing that feeling. After all, if you were small, the grimy beetle crawled on—which was just what you wanted it to do. Where the pilgrims imagined it crawled to I don't know. To some place where they expected to get something, I bet! For me it crawled toward Kurtz—exclusively; but when the steam-pipes started leaking we crawled very slow. The reaches opened before us and closed behind, as if the forest had stepped leisurely across the water to bar the way for our return. We penetrated deeper and deeper into the heart of darkness. It was very quiet there. At night sometimes the roll of drums behind the curtain of trees would run up the river and remain sustained faintly, as if hovering in the air high over our heads, till the first break of day. Whether it meant war, peace, or prayer we could not tell. The dawns were heralded by the descent of a chill stillness; the woodcutters slept, their fires burned low; the snapping of a twig would make you start. We were wanderers in a prehistoric earth, on an earth that wore the aspect of an unknown planet. We could have fancied ourselves the first of men taking possession of an accursed inheritance, to be subdued at the cost of profound anguish and of excessive toil. But suddenly, as we struggled round a bend, there would be a glimpse of rush walls, of peaked grass-roofs, a burst of yells, a whirl of black limbs, a mass of hands clapping, of feet stamping, of bodies swaying, of eyes rolling, under the droop of heavy and motionless foliage. The steamer toiled along slowly on the edge of a black and incomprehensible frenzy. The prehistoric man was cursing us, praying to us, welcoming us—who could tell? We were cut off from the comprehension of our surroundings; we glided past like phantoms, wondering and secretly appalled, as sane men would be before an enthusiastic outbreak in a madhouse. We could not understand, because we were too far and could not remember, because we were traveling in the night of first ages, of those ages that are gone, leaving hardly a sign—and no memories.

"The earth seemed unearthly. We are accustomed to look upon the shackled form of a conquered monster, but there—there you could look at a thing monstrous and free. It was unearthly, and the men were—No, they were not inhuman. Well, you know, that was the worst of it—this suspicion of their not being inhuman. It would come slowly to one. They howled, and leaped, and spun, and made horrid faces; but what thrilled you was just the thought of their humanity—like yours—the thought of your remote kinship with this wild and passionate uproar. Ugly. Yes, it was ugly enough; but if you were man enough you would admit to yourself that there was in you just the faintest trace of a response to the terrible frankness of that noise, a dim suspicion of there being a meaning in which you—you so remote from the night of first ages—could comprehend. And why not? The mind of a man is capable of anything—because everything is in it, all the past as well as all the future. What was there after all? Joy, fear, sorrow, devotion, valor, rage—who can tell?—but truth—truth stripped of its cloak of time. Let the fool gape and shudder—the man knows, and can look on without a wink. But he must at least be as much of a man as these on the shore. He must meet that truth with his own true stuff—with his own inborn strength. Principles? Principles won't do. Acquisitions, clothes, pretty rags—rags that would fly off at the first good shake. No; you want a deliberate belief. An appeal to me in this fiendish row—is there? Very well; I hear; I admit, but I have a voice, too, and for good or evil mine is the speech that cannot be silenced. Of course, a fool, what with sheer fright and fine sentiments, is always safe. Who's that grunting? You wonder I didn't go ashore for a howl and a dance? Well, no—I didn't. Fine sentiments, you say? Fine sentiments, be hanged! I had no time. I had to mess about with white-lead and strips of woolen blanket helping to put bandages on those leaky steam-pipes—I tell you. I had to watch the steering, and circumvent those snags, and get the tin-pot along by hook or by crook. There was surface-truth enough in these things to save a wiser man. And between whiles I had to look after the savage who was fireman. He was an improved specimen; he could fire up a vertical boiler. He was there below me, and, upon my word, to look at him was as edifying as seeing a dog in a parody of breeches and a feather hat, walking on his hindlegs. A few months of training had done for that really fine chap. He squinted at the steam-gauge and at the water-gauge with an evident effort of intrepidity—and he had filed teeth too, the poor devil, and the wool of his pate shaved into queer patterns, and three ornamental scars on each of his cheeks. He ought to have been clapping his hands and stamping

a gun had been fired. When the sun rose there was a white fog, very warm and clammy, and more blinding than the night. It did not shift or drive; it was just there, standing all round you like something solid. At eight or nine, perhaps, it lifted as a shutter lifts. We had a glimpse of the towering multitude of trees, of the immense matted jungle, with the blazing little ball of the sun hanging over it—all perfectly still—and then the white shutter came down again, smoothly, as if sliding in greased grooves. I ordered the chain, which we had begun to heave in, to be paid out again. Before it stopped running with a muffled rattle, a cry, a very loud cry, as of infinite desolation, soared slowly in the opaque air. It ceased. A complaining clamor, modulated in savage discords, filled our ears. The sheer unexpectedness of it made my hair stir under my cap. I don't know how it struck the others: to me it seemed as though the mist itself had screamed, so suddenly, and apparently from all sides at once, did this tumultuous and mournful uproar arise. It culminated in a hurried outbreak of almost intolerably excessive shrieking, which stopped short, leaving us stiffened in a variety of silly attitudes, and obstinately listening to the nearly as appalling and excessive silence. 'Good God! What is the meaning—?' stammered at my elbow one of the pilgrims,—a little fat man, with sandy hair and red whiskers, who wore side-spring boots, and pink pyjamas tucked into his socks. Two others remained open-mouthed a whole minute, then dashed into the little cabin, to rush out incontinently and stand darting scared glances, with Winchesters at 'ready' in their hands. What we could see was just the steamer we were on, her outlines blurred as though she had been on the point of dissolving, and a misty strip of water, perhaps two feet broad, around her—and that was all. The rest of the world was nowhere, as far as our eyes and ears were concerned. Just nowhere. Gone, disappeared; swept off without leaving a whisper or a shadow behind.

"I went forward, and ordering the chain to be hauled in short, so as to be ready to trip the anchor and move the steamboat at once if necessary. 'Will they attack?' whispered an awed voice. 'We will be butchered in this fog,' murmured another. The faces twitched with the strain, the hands trembled slightly, the eyes forgot to wink. It was very curious to see the contrast of expressions of the white men and of the black fellows of our crew, who were as much strangers to that part of the river as we, though their homes were only eight hundred miles away. The whites, of course greatly discomposed, had besides a curious look of being painfully shocked by such an outrageous row. The others had an alert, naturally interested expression; but their faces were essentially quiet, even those of the one or two who grinned as they hauled at the chain. Several exchanged short, grunting phrases, which seemed to settle the matter to their satisfaction. Their headman, a young, broad-chested black, severely draped in dark-blue fringed cloths, with fierce nostrils and his hair all done up artfully in oily ringlets, stood near me. 'Aha!' I said, just for good fellowship's sake. 'Catch 'im,' he snapped, with a blood-shot widening of his eyes and a flash of sharp teeth—'catch 'im. Give 'im to us.' 'To you, eh?' I asked; 'what would you do with them?' 'Eat 'im!' he said curtly, and, leaning his elbow on the rail, looked out into the fog in a dignified and profoundly pensive attitude. I would no doubt have been properly horrified, had it not occurred to me that he and his chaps must be very hungry: that they must have been growing increasingly hungry for at least this month past. They had been engaged for six months (I don't think a single one of them had any clear idea of time, as we at the end of countless ages have. They still belonged to the beginnings of time—had no inherited experience to teach them as it were), and of course, as long as there was a piece of paper written over in accordance with some farcical law or other made down the river, it didn't enter anybody's head to trouble how they would live. Certainly they had brought with them some rotten hippo-meat, which couldn't have lasted very long, anyway, even if the pilgrims hadn't, in the midst of a shocking hullabaloo, thrown a considerable quantity of it over-board. It looked like a high-handed proceeding; but it was really a case of legitimate self-defense. You can't breathe dead hippo waking, sleeping, and eating, and at the same time keep your precarious grip on existence. Besides that, they had given them every week three pieces of brass wire, each about nine inches long; and the theory was they were to buy their provisions with that currency in river-side villages. You can see how *that* worked. There were either no villages, or the people were hostile, or the director, who like the rest of us fed out of tins, with an occasional old he-goat thrown in, didn't want to stop the steamer for some more or less recondite reason. So, unless they swallowed the wire itself, or made loops of it to snare the fishes with, I don't see what good their extravagant salary could be to them. I must say it was paid with a regularity worthy of a large and honorable trading company. For the rest, the only thing to eat—though it didn't look eatable in the least—I saw in their possession was a few lumps of some stuff like half-cooked dough, of a dirty *lavender* color,[14] they kept wrapped in leaves, and now and then swallowed a piece of, but so small that it seemed done for more for the looks of the thing than for any serious purpose of sustenance. Why in the name of all the gnawing devils of hunger they didn't go for us—they were thirty to five—and have a good tuck in for once, amazes me now when I think of it. They were big powerful men, with not much capacity to weigh the consequences, with courage, with strength, even yet, though their skins were no longer glossy and their muscles no longer hard. And I saw that something restraining, one of those human secrets that baffle probability, had come into play there. I looked at them with a swift quickening of interest—not because it occurred to me I might be eaten by them before very long, though I own to you that just then I perceived—in a new light, as it were—how unwholesome the pilgrims looked, and I hoped, yes, I positively hoped, that my aspect was not so—what shall I say?—so—unappetizing: a touch of fantastic vanity which fitted well with the dream-sensation that pervaded all my days at that time. Perhaps I had a little fever too. One can't live with one's finger everlastingly on one's pulse. I had often 'a little fever,' or a little touch of other things—the playful paw-strokes of the wilderness, the preliminary trifling before the more serious onslaught which came in due course. Yes; I looked at them as you would on any human being, with a curiosity of their impulses, motives, capacities, weaknesses, when brought to the test of an inexorable physical necessity.

---

14 **a few lumps . . . color:** An accurate description of cassava dough, which is nutritious and keeps a long time.

Restraint! What possible restraint? Was it superstition, disgust, patience, fear—or some kind of primitive honor? No fear can stand up to hunger, no patience can wear it out, disgust simply does not exist where hunger is; and as to superstition, beliefs, and what you may call principles, they are less than chaff in a breeze. Don't you know the devilry of lingering starvation, its exasperating torment, its black thoughts, its somber and brooding ferocity? Well, I do. It takes a man all his inborn strength to fight hunger properly. It's really easier to face bereavement, dishonor, and the perdition of one's soul—than this kind of prolonged hunger. Sad, but true. And these chaps too had no earthly reason for any kind of scruple. Restraint! I would just as soon have expected restraint from a hyena prowling amongst the corpses of a battle-field. But there was the fact facing me—the fact dazzling, to be seen, like the foam on the depths of the sea, like a ripple on a unfathomable enigma, a mystery greater—when I thought of it—than the curious, inexplicable note of desperate grief in this savage clamor that had swept by us on the river-bank, behind the blind whiteness of the fog.

"Two pilgrims were quarreling in hurried whispers as to which bank. 'Left.' 'No, no; how can you? Right, right, of course.' 'It is very serious,' said the manager's voice behind me; 'I would be desolated if anything should happen to Mr. Kurtz before we came up.' I looked at him, and had not the slightest doubt he was sincere. He was just the kind of man who would wish to preserve appearances. That was his restraint. But when he muttered something about going on at once, I did not even take the trouble to answer him. I knew, and he knew, that it was impossible. Were we to let go our hold of the bottom, we would be absolutely in the air—in space. We wouldn't be able to tell where we were going to—whether up or down stream, or across—till we fetched against one bank or the other,—and then we wouldn't know at first which it was. Of course I made no move. I had no mind for a smash-up. You couldn't imagine a more deadly place for a shipwreck. Whether drowned at once or not, we were sure to perish speedily in one way or another. 'I authorize you to take all the risks,' he said, after a short silence. 'I refuse to take any,' I said shortly; which was just the answer he expected, though its tone might have surprised him. 'Well, I must defer to your judgment. You are captain,' he said, with marked civility. I turned my shoulder to him in sign of my appreciation, and looked into the fog. How long would it last? It was the most hopeless look-out. The approach to this Kurtz grubbing for ivory in the wretched bush was beset by as many dangers as though he had been an enchanted princess sleeping in a fabulous castle. 'Will they attack, do you think?' asked the manager, in a confidential tone.

"I did not think they would attack, for several obvious reasons. The thick fog was one. If they left the bank in their canoes they would get lost in it, as we would be if we attempted to move. Still, I had also judged the jungle of both banks quite impenetrable—and yet eyes were in it, eyes that had seen us. The river-side bushes were certainly thick; but the undergrowth behind was evidently penetrable. However, during the short lift I had seen no canoes anywhere in the reach—certainly not abreast of the steamer. But what made the idea of attack inconceivable to me was the nature of the noise—of the cries we had heard. They had not the fierce character boding of immediate hostile intention. Unexpected, wild, and violent as they had been, they had given me an irresistible impression of sorrow. The glimpse of the steamboat had for some reason filled those savages with unrestrained grief. The danger, if any, I expounded, was from our proximity to a great human passion let loose. Even extreme grief may ultimately vent itself in violence—but more generally takes the form of apathy. . . .

"You should have seen the pilgrims stare! They had no heart to grin, or even to revile me; but I believe they thought me gone mad—with fright, maybe. I delivered a regular lecture. My dear boys, it was no good bothering. Keep a look-out? Well, you may guess I watched the fog for the signs of lifting as a cat watches a mouse; but for anything else our eyes were of no more use to us than if we had been buried miles deep in a heap of cotton-wool. It felt like it too—choking, warm, stifling. Besides, all I said, though it sounded extravagant, was absolutely true to fact. What we afterwards alluded to as an attack was really an attempt at repulse. The action was very far from being aggressive—it was not even defensive, in the usual sense: it was undertaken under the stress of desperation, and in its essence was purely protective.

"It developed itself, I should say, two hours after the fog lifted, and its commencement was at a spot, roughly speaking, about a mile and a half below Kurtz's station. We had just floundered and flopped round a bend, when I saw an islet, a mere grassy hummock of bright green, in the middle of the stream. It was the only thing of the kind; but as we opened the reach more, I perceived it was the head of a long sandbank, or rather a chain of shallow patches stretching down the middle of the river. They were discolored, just awash, and the whole lot was seen just under the water, exactly as a man's backbone is seen running down the middle of his back under the skin. Now, as far as I did see, I could go to the right or to the left of this. I didn't know either channel, of course. The banks looked pretty well alike, the depth appeared the same; but as I had been informed the station was on the west side, I naturally headed for the western passage.

"No sooner had we fairly entered it than I became aware it was much narrower than I had supposed. To the left of us there was the long uninterrupted shoal, and to the right a high, steep bank heavily overgrown with bushes. Above the bush the trees stood in serried ranks. The twigs overhung the current thickly, and from distance to distance a large limb of some tree projected rigidly over the stream. It was then well on in the afternoon, the face of the forest was gloomy, and a broad strip of shadow had already fallen on the water. In this shadow we steamed up—very slowly, as you may imagine. I sheered her well inshore—the water being deepest near the bank, as the sounding-pole informed me.

"One of my hungry and forbearing friends was sounding in the bows just below me. This steamboat was exactly like a decked scow. On the deck there were two little teak-wood houses, with doors and windows. The boiler was in the fore-end, and the machinery right astern. Over the whole there was a light roof, supported on stanchions. The funnel projected through that roof, and in front of the funnel a small cabin built of light planks served for a pilot-house. It contained a couch, two campstools, a loaded Martini-Henry leaning in one corner, a tiny table, and the steering-wheel.

It had a wide door in front and a broad shutter at each side. All these were always thrown open, of course. I spent my days perched up there on the extreme fore-end of that roof, before the door. At night I slept, or tried to, on the couch. An athletic black belonging to some coast tribe, and educated by my poor predecessor, was the helmsman. He sported a pair of brass earrings, wore a blue cloth wrapper from the waist to the ankles, and thought all the world of himself. He was the most unstable kind of fool I had ever seen. He steered with no end of a swagger while you were by; but if he lost sight of you, he became instantly the prey of an abject funk, and would let that cripple of a steamboat get the upper hand of him in a minute.

"I was looking down at the sounding-pole, and feeling much annoyed to see at each try a little more of it stick out of that river, when I saw my poleman give up the business suddenly, and stretch himself flat on the deck, without even taking the trouble to haul his pole in. He kept hold on it though, and it trailed in the water. At the same time the fireman, whom I could also see below me, sat down abruptly before his furnace and ducked his head. I was amazed. Then I had to look at the river mighty quick, because there was a snag in the fairway. Sticks, little sticks, were flying about—thick: they were whizzing before my nose, dropping below me, striking behind me against my pilot-house. All this time the river, the shore, the woods, were very quiet—perfectly quiet. I could only hear the heavy splashing thump of the stern-wheel and the patter of these things. We cleared the snag clumsily. Arrows, by Jove! We were being shot at! I stepped in quickly to close the shutter on the land side. That fool-helmsman, his hands on the spokes, was lifting his knees high, stamping his feet, champing his mouth, like a reined-in horse. Confound him! And we were staggering within ten feet of the bank. I had to lean right out to swing the heavy shutter, and I saw a face amongst the leaves on the level with my own, looking at me very fierce and steady; and then suddenly, as though a veil had been removed from my eyes, I made out, deep in the tangled gloom, naked breasts, arms, legs, glaring eyes,—the bush was swarming with human limbs in movement, glistening, of bronze color. The twigs shook, swayed, and rustled, the arrows flew out of them, and then the shutter came to. 'Steer her straight,' I said to the helmsman. He held his head rigid, face forward; but his eyes rolled, he kept lifting and setting down his feet gently, his mouth foamed a little. 'Keep quiet!' I said in a fury. I might just as well have ordered a tree not to sway in the wind. I darted out. Below me there was a great scuffle of feet on the iron deck; confused exclamations; a voice screamed, 'Can you turn back?' I caught sight of a V-shaped ripple on the water ahead. What? Another snag! A fusillade burst out under my feet. The pilgrims had opened their little Winchesters, and were simply squirting lead into that bush. A deuce of a lot of smoke came up and drove slowly forward. I swore at it. Now I couldn't see the ripple or the snag either. I stood in the doorway, peering, and the arrows came in swarms. They might have been poisoned, but they looked as though they wouldn't kill a cat. The bush began to howl. Our wood-cutters raised a warlike whoop; the report of a rifle just at my back deafened me. I glanced over my shoulder, and the pilot-house was yet full of noise and smoke when I made a dash at the wheel. The fool-nigger had dropped everything, to throw the shutter open and let off that Martini-Henry. He stood before the wide opening, glaring, and I yelled at him to come back, while I straightened the sudden twist out of that steamboat. There was no room to turn even if I had wanted to, the snag was somewhere very near ahead in that confounded smoke, there was no time to lose, so I just crowded her into the bank—right into the bank, where I knew the water was deep.

"We tore slowly along the overhanging bushes in a whirl of broken twigs and flying leaves. The fusillade below stopped short, as I had foreseen it would when the squirts got empty. I threw my head back to a glinting whizz that traversed the pilot-house, in at one shutter-hole and out at the other. Looking past that mad helmsman, who was shaking the empty rifle and yelling at the shore, I saw vague forms of men running bent double, leaping, gliding, distinct, incomplete, evanescent. Something big appeared in the air before the shutter, the rifle went overboard, and the man stepped back swiftly, looked at me over his shoulder in an extraordinary, profound, familiar manner, and fell upon my feet. The side of his head hit the wheel twice, and the end of what appeared a long cane clattered round and knocked over a little camp-stool. It looked as though after wrenching that thing from somebody ashore he had lost his balance in the effort. The thin smoke had blown away, we were clear of the snag, and looking ahead I could see that in another hundred yards or so I would be free to sheer off, away from the bank; but my feet felt so very warm and wet that I had to look down. The man had rolled on his back and stared straight up at me; both his hands clutched that cane. It was the shaft of a spear that, either thrown or lunged through the opening, had caught him in the side just below the ribs; the blade had gone in out of sight, after making a frightful gash; my shoes were full; a pool of blood lay very still, gleaming dark-red under the wheel; his eyes shone with an amazing luster. The fusillade burst out again. He looked at me anxiously, gripping the spear like something precious, with an air of being afraid I would try to take it away from him. I had to make an effort to free my eyes from his gaze and attend to the steering. With one hand I felt above my head for the line of the steam-whistle, and jerked out screech after screech hurriedly. The tumult of angry and warlike yells was checked instantly, and then from the depths of the woods went out such a tremulous and prolonged wail of mournful fear and utter despair as may be imagined to follow the flight of the last hope from the earth. There was a great commotion in the bush; the shower of arrows stopped, a few dropping shots rang out sharply—then silence, in which the languid beat of the stern-wheel came plainly to my ears. I put the helm hard a-starboard at the moment when the pilgrim in pink pyjamas, very hot and agitated, appeared in the doorway. 'The manager sends me—' he began in an official tone, and stopped short. 'Good God!' he said, glaring at the wounded man.

"We two whites stood over him, and his lustrous and inquiring glance enveloped us both. I declare it looked as though he would presently put to us some question in an understandable language; but he died without uttering a sound, without moving a limb, without twitching a muscle. Only in the very last moment, as though in response to some sign we could not see, to some whisper we could not hear, he frowned heavily, and that frown gave to his black death-mask an inconceivably somber, brooding, and menacing expression. The luster of inquiring glance faded swiftly into vacant glassiness. 'Can you steer?' I asked the agent eagerly. He looked very dubious; but I made a grab at his arm, and he understood at once I meant him to steer whether or no. To tell you the truth, I was morbidly anxious to change my shoes and socks. 'He is dead,' murmured the fellow, immensely impressed. 'No doubt about it,' said I, tugging like mad at the shoe-laces. 'And, by the way, I suppose Mr. Kurtz is dead as well by this time.'

"For the moment that was the dominant thought. There was a sense of extreme disappointment, as though I had found out I had been striving after something altogether without a substance. I couldn't have been more disgusted if I had traveled all this way for the sole purpose of talking with Mr. Kurtz. Talking with . . . I flung one shoe overboard, and became aware that was exactly what I had been looking forward to—a talk with Kurtz. I made the strange discovery that I had never imagined him as doing, you know, but as discoursing. I didn't say to myself, 'Now I will never see him,' or 'Now I will never shake him by the hand,' but, 'Now I will never hear him.' The man presented himself as a voice. Not of course that I did not connect him with some sort of action. Hadn't I been told in all the tones of jealousy and admiration that he had collected, bartered, swindled, or stolen more ivory than all the other agents together? That was not the point. The point was in his being a gifted creature, and that of all his gifts the one that stood out preeminently, that carried with it a sense of real presence, was his ability to talk, his words—the gift of expression, the bewildering, the illuminating, the most exalted and the most contemptible, the pulsating stream of light, or the deceitful flow from the heart of an impenetrable darkness.

"The other shoe went flying unto the devil-god of that river. I thought, By Jove! it's all over. We are too late; he has vanished—the gift has vanished, by means of some spear, arrow, or club. I will never hear that chap speak after all,—and my sorrow had a startling extravagance of emotion, even such as I had noticed in the howling sorrow of these savages in the bush. I couldn't have felt more of lonely desolation somehow, had I been robbed of a belief or had missed my destiny in life. . . . Why do you sigh in this beastly way, somebody? Absurd? Well, absurd. Good Lord! mustn't a man ever—Here, give me some tobacco."

There was a pause of profound stillness, then a match flared, and Marlow's lean face appeared, worn, hollow, with downward folds and dropped eyelids, with an aspect of concentrated attention; and as he took vigorous draws at his pipe, it seemed to retreat and advance out of the night in the regular flicker of the tiny flame. The match went out.

"Absurd!" he cried. "This is the worst of trying to tell. . . . Here you all are, each moored with two good addresses, like a hulk with two anchors, a butcher round one corner, a policeman round another, excellent appetites, and temperature normal— you hear—normal from year's end to year's end. And you say, Absurd! Absurd be— exploded! Absurd! My dear boys, what can you expect from a man who out of sheer nervousness had just flung overboard a pair of new shoes. Now I think of it, it is amazing I did not shed tears. I am, upon the whole, proud of my fortitude. I was cut to the quick at the idea of having lost the inestimable privilege of listening to the gifted Kurtz. Of course I was wrong. The privilege was waiting for me. Oh yes, I heard more than enough. And I was right, too. A voice. He was very little more than a voice. And I heard—him—it—this voice—other voices—all of them were so little more than voices—and the memory of that time itself lingers around me, impalpable, like a dying vibration of one immense jabber, silly, atrocious, sordid, savage, or simply mean, without any kind of sense. Voices, voices—even the girl herself—now—"

He was silent for a long time.

"I laid the ghost of his gifts at last with a lie," he began suddenly. "Girl! What? Did I mention a girl? Oh, she is out of it—completely. They—the women I mean—are out of it—should be out of it. We must help them to stay in that beautiful world of their own, lest ours gets worse. Oh, she had to be out of it. You should have heard the disinterred body of Mr. Kurtz saying, 'My Intended.' You would have perceived directly then how completely she was out of it. And the lofty frontal bone of Mr. Kurtz! They say the hair goes on growing sometimes,[15] but this—ah—specimen, was impressively bald. The wilderness had patted him on the head, and, behold, it was like a ball—an ivory ball; it had caressed him, and—lo!—he had withered; it had taken him, loved him, embraced him, got into his veins, consumed his flesh, and sealed his soul to its own by the inconceivable ceremonies of some devilish initiation. He was its spoiled and pampered favorite. Ivory? I should think so. Heaps of it, stacks of it. The old mud shanty was bursting with it. You would think there was not a single tusk left either above or below the ground in the whole country. 'Mostly fossil,' the manager had remarked disparagingly. It was no more fossil than I am; but they call it fossil when it is dug up. It appears these niggers do bury the tusks sometimes—but evidently they couldn't bury this parcel deep enough to save the gifted Mr. Kurtz from his fate. We filled the steamboat with it, and had to pile a lot on the deck. Thus he could see and enjoy as long as he could see, because the appreciation of this favor had remained with him to the last. You should have heard him say, 'My ivory.' Oh yes, I heard him. 'My Intended, my ivory, my station, my river, my—' everything belonged to him. It made me hold my breath in expectation of hearing the wilderness burst in to a prodigious peal of laughter that would shake the fixed stars in their places. Everything belonged to him—but that was a trifle. The thing was to know what he belonged to, how many powers of darkness claimed him for their own. That was the reflection that made you creepy all over. It was impossible—it was not good for one either—trying to imagine. He had taken a high seat amongst the devils of the land—I mean literally. You can't understand. How could you?—with solid pavement under your feet, surrounded by kind neighbors ready to cheer you or to fall on you, stepping delicately between the butcher and the policeman, in the holy terror of scandal and gallows and lunatic asylums—how can you imagine what particular region of the first ages a man's untrammeled feet may take him into

---

15 **They say . . . sometimes:** A reference to the idea that hair continues to grow after death.

by the way of solitude—utter solitude without a policeman—by the way of silence—
utter silence, where no warning voice of a kind neighbor can be heard whispering of
public opinion? These little things make all the great difference. When they are gone
you must fall back upon your own innate strength, upon your own capacity for
faithfulness. Of course you may be too much of a fool to go wrong—too dull even to
know you are being assaulted by the powers of darkness. I take it, no fool ever made
a bargain for this soul with the devil: the fool is too much of a fool, or the devil too
much of a devil—I don't know which. Or you may be such a thunderingly exalted
creature as to be altogether deaf and blind to anything but heavenly sights and
sounds. Then the earth for you is only a standing place—and whether to be like this
is your loss or your gain I won't pretend to say. But most of us are neither one nor
the other. The earth for us is a place to live in, where we must put up with sights,
with sounds, with smells too by Jove!—breathe dead hippo, so to speak, and not be
contaminated. And there, don't you see? your strength comes in, the faith in your
ability for the digging of unostentatious holes to bury the stuff in—your power of
devotion, not to yourself, but to an obscure, back-breaking business. And that's difficult enough. Mind, I am not trying to excuse or even explain—I am trying to account to myself for—for—Mr. Kurtz—for the shade of Mr. Kurtz. This initiated
wraith from the back of Nowhere honored me with its amazing confidence before it
vanished altogether. This was because it could speak English to me. The original
Kurtz had been educated partly in England, and—as he was good enough to say
himself—his sympathies were in the right place. His mother was half-English, his father was half-French. All Europe contributed to the making of Kurtz; and by-and-by
I learned that, most appropriately, the International Society for the Suppression of
Savage Customs[16] had entrusted him with the making of a report, for its future guidance. And he had written it too. I've seen it. I've read it. It was eloquent, vibrating
with eloquence, but too high-strung, I think. Seventeen pages of close writing he had
found time for! But this must have been before his—let us say—nerves, went wrong,
and caused him to preside at certain midnight dances ending with unspeakable rites,
which—as far as I reluctantly gathered from what I heard at various times—were offered up to him—do you understand?—to Mr. Kurtz himself. But it was a beautiful
piece of writing. The opening paragraph, however, in the light of later information,
strikes me now as ominous. He began with the argument that we whites, from the
point of development we had arrived at, 'must necessarily appear to them [savages]
in the nature of supernatural beings—we approach them with the might as of a
deity,' and so on, and so on. 'By the simple exercise of our will we can exert a power
for good practically unbounded,' &c., &c. From that point he soared and took me
with him. The peroration was magnificent, though difficult to remember, you know.
It gave me the notion of an exotic Immensity ruled by an august Benevolence. It
made me tingle with enthusiasm. This was the unbounded power of eloquence—of

16 **International Society . . . Customs:** Perhaps a reference to the International Society for the Suppression of Savage Customs, headed by King Leopold of Belgium.

words—of burning noble words. There were no practical hints to interrupt the magic current of phrases, unless a kind of note at the foot of the last page, scrawled evidently much later, in an unsteady hand, may be regarded as the exposition of a method. It was very simple, and at the end of that moving appeal to every altruistic sentiment it blazed at you, luminous and terrifying, like a flash of lightning in a serene sky: 'Exterminate all the brutes!' The curious part was that he had apparently forgotten all about that valuable postscriptum, because, later on, when he in a sense came to himself, he repeatedly entreated me to take good care of 'my pamphlet' (he called it), as it was sure to have in the future a good influence upon his career. I had full information about all these things, and, besides, as it turned out, I was to have the care of his memory. I've done enough for it to give me the indisputable right to lay it, if I choose, for an everlasting rest in the dust-bin of progress, amongst all the sweepings and, figuratively speaking, all the dead cats of civilization. But then, you see, I can't choose. He wouldn't be forgotten. Whatever he was, he was not common. He had the power to charm or frighten rudimentary souls into an aggravated witch-dance in his honor; he could also fill the small souls of the pilgrims with bitter mis-givings: he had one devoted friend at least, and he had conquered one soul in the world that was neither rudimentary nor tainted with self-seeking. No; I can't forget him, though I am not prepared to affirm the fellow was exactly worth the life we lost in getting to him. I missed my late helmsman awfully,—I missed him even while his body was still lying in the pilot-house. Perhaps you will think it passing strange this regret for a savage who was no more account than a grain of sand in a black Sahara. Well, don't you see, he had done something, he had steered; for months I had him at my back—a help—an instrument. It was a kind of partnership. He steered for me—I had to look after him, I worried about his deficiencies, and thus a subtle bond had been created, of which I only became aware when it was suddenly broken. And the intimate profundity of that look he gave me when he received his hurt remains to this day in my memory—like a claim of distant kinship affirmed in a supreme moment.

"Poor fool! If he had only left that shutter alone. He had no restraint, no re-straint—just like Kurtz—a tree swayed in the wind. As soon as I had put on a dry pair of slippers, I dragged him out, after first jerking the spear out of his side, which operation I confess I performed with my eyes shut tight. His heels leaped together over the little door-step; his shoulders were pressed to my breast; I hugged him from behind desperately. Oh! he was heavy, heavy; heavier than any man on earth, I should imagine. Then without more ado I tipped him overboard. The current snatched him as though he had been a wisp of grass, and I saw the body roll over twice before I lost sight of it for ever. All the pilgrims and the manager were then congregated on the awning-deck about the pilot-house, chattering at each other like a flock of excited magpies, and there was a scandalized murmur at my heartless promptitude. What they wanted to keep that body hanging about for I can't guess. Embalm it, maybe. But I had also heard another, and a very ominous, murmur on the deck below. My friends the wood-cutters were likewise scandalized, and with a better show of reason—though I admit that the reason itself was quite inadmissible.

Oh, quite! I had made up my mind that if my late helmsman was to be eaten, the fishes alone should have him. He had been a very second-rate helmsman while alive, but now he was dead he might have become a first-class temptation, and possibly cause some startling trouble. Besides, I was anxious to take the wheel, the man in pink pyjamas showing himself a hopeless duffer at the business.

"This I did directly the simple funeral was over. We were going half-speed, keeping right in the middle of the stream, and I listened to the talk about me. They had given up Kurtz, they had given up the station; Kurtz was dead, and the station had been burnt—and so on—and so on. The red-haired pilgrim was beside himself with the thought that at least this poor Kurtz had been properly revenged. 'Say! We must have made a glorious slaughter of them in the bush. Eh? What do you think? Say?' He positively danced, the bloodthirsty little gingery beggar. And he had nearly fainted when he saw the wounded man! I could not help saying, 'You made a glorious lot of smoke, anyhow.' I had seen, from the way the tops of the bushes rustled and flew, that almost all the shots had gone too high. You can't hit anything unless you take aim and fire from the shoulder; but these chaps fired from the hip with their eyes shut. The retreat, I maintained—and I was right—was caused by the screeching of the steam-whistle. Upon this they forgot Kurtz, and began to howl at me with indignant protests.

"The manager stood by the wheel murmuring confidentially about the necessity of getting well away down the river before dark at all events, when I saw in the distance a clearing on the river-side and the outlines of some sort of building. 'What's this?' I asked. He clapped his hands in wonder. 'The station!' he cried. I edged in at once, still going half-speed.

"Through my glasses I saw the slope of a hill interspersed with rare trees and perfectly free from undergrowth. A long decaying building on the summit was half buried in the high grass; the large holes in the peaked roof gaped back from afar; the jungle and the woods made a background. There was no inclosure or fence of any kind; but there had been one apparently, for near the house half-a-dozen slim posts remained in a row, roughly trimmed, and with their upper ends ornamented with round curved balls. The rails, or whatever there had been between, had disappeared. Of course the forest surrounded all that. The river-bank was clear, and on the water-side I saw a white man under a hat like a cart-wheel beckoning persistently with his whole arm. Examining the edge of the forest above and below, I was almost certain I could see movements—human forms gliding here and there. I steamed past prudently, then stopped the engines and let her drift down. The man on the shore began to shout, urging us to land. 'We have been attacked,' screamed the manager. 'I know—I know. It's all right,' yelled back the other, as cheerful as you please. 'Come along. It's all right. I am glad.'

"His aspect reminded me of something I had seen—something funny I had seen somewhere. As I maneuvered to get alongside, I was asking myself, 'What does this fellow look like?' Suddenly I got it. He looked like a harlequin. His clothes had been made of some stuff that was brown holland probably, but it was covered with patches all over, with bright patches, blue, red, and yellow,—patches on the back, patches on front, patches on elbows, on knees; colored binding round his jacket, scarlet edging at the bottom of his trousers; and the sunshine made him look extremely gay and wonderfully neat withal, because you could see how beautifully all this patching had been done. A beardless, boyish face, very fair, no features to speak of, nose peeling, little blue eyes, smiles and frowns chasing each other over that open countenance like sunshine and shadow on a windswept plain. 'Look out, captain!' he cried; 'there's a snag lodged in here last night.' What! Another snag? I confess I swore shamefully. I had nearly holed my cripple, to finish off that charming trip. The harlequin on the bank turned his little pug nose up to me. 'You English?' he asked, all smiles. 'Are you?' I shouted from the wheel. The smiles vanished, and he shook his head as if sorry for my disappointment. Then he brightened up. 'Never mind!' he cried encouragingly. 'Are we in time?' I asked. 'He is up there,' he replied, with a toss of the head up the hill, and becoming gloomy all of a sudden. His face was like the autumn sky, overcast one moment and bright the next.

'When the manager, escorted by the pilgrims, all of them armed to the teeth, had gone to the house, this chap came on board. 'I say, I don't like this. These natives are in the bush,' I said. He assured me earnestly it was all right. 'They are simple people,' he added; 'well, I am glad you came. It took me all my time to keep them off.' 'But you said it was all right,' I cried. 'Oh, they meant no harm,' he said; and as I stared he corrected himself, 'Not exactly.' Then vivaciously, 'My faith, your pilot-house wants a clean up!' In the next breath he advised me to keep enough steam on the boiler to blow the whistle in case of any trouble. 'One good screech will do more for you than all your rifles. They are simple people,' he repeated. He rattled away at such a rate he quite overwhelmed me. He seemed to be trying to make up for lots of silence, and actually hinted, laughing, that such was the case. 'Don't you talk with Mr. Kurtz?' I said. 'You don't talk with that man—you listen to him,' he exclaimed with severe exaltation. 'But now—' He waved his arm, and in the twinkling of an eye was in the uttermost depths of despondency. In a moment he came up again with a jump, possessed himself of both my hands, shook them continuously, while he gabbed: 'Brother sailor . . . honor . . . pleasure . . . delight . . . introduce myself . . . Russian . . . son of an arch-priest . . . Government of Tambov . . . What? Tobacco! English tobacco; the excellent English tobacco! Now, that's brotherly. Smoke? Where's a sailor that does not smoke?"

"The pipe soothed him, and gradually I made out he had run away from school, had gone to sea in a Russian ship; ran away again; served some time in English ships; was now reconciled with the arch-priest. He made a point of that. 'But when one is young one must see things, gather experience, ideas; enlarge the mind.' 'Here!' I interrupted. 'You can never tell! Here I have met Mr. Kurtz,' he said, youthfully solemn and reproachful. I held my tongue after that. It appears he had persuaded a Dutch trading-house on the coast to fit him out with stores and goods, and had started for the interior with a light heart, and no more idea of what would happen to him than a baby. He had been wandering about that river for nearly two years alone, cut off from everybody and everything. 'I am not so young as I look. I am twenty-five,' he said. 'At first old Van Shuyten would tell me to go to the devil,' he narrated with keen enjoyment; 'but I stuck to him, and talked and talked, till at last he got afraid I would talk the hind-leg off his favorite dog, so he gave me some cheap things and a few guns, and told me he hoped he would never see my face again. Good old Dutchman, Van Shuyten. I've sent him one small lot of ivory a year ago, so that he can't call me a little thief when I get back. I hope he got it. And for the rest I don't care. I had some wood stacked for you. That was my old house. Did you see?

"I gave him Towson's book. He made as though he would kiss me, but restrained himself. 'The only book I had left, and I thought I had lost it,' he said, looking at it ecstatically. 'So many accidents happen to a man going about alone, you know. Canoes get upset sometimes—and sometimes you've got to clear out so quick when the people get angry.' He thumbed the pages. 'You made notes in Russian?' I asked. He nodded. 'I thought they were written in cipher,' I said. He laughed, then became serious. 'I had lots of trouble to keep these people off,' he said. 'Did they want to kill you?' I asked. 'Oh no!' he cried, and checked himself. 'Why did they attack us?' I pursued. He hesitated, then said shamefacedly, 'They don't want him to go.' 'Don't they?' I said, curiously. He nodded a nod full of mystery and wisdom. 'I tell you,' he cried, 'this man has enlarged my mind.' He opened his arms wide, staring at me with his little blue eyes that were perfectly round."

III

"I looked at him, lost in astonishment. There he was before me, in motley,[17] as though he had absconded from a troupe of mimes, enthusiastic, fabulous. His very existence was improbable, inexplicable, and altogether bewildering. He was an insoluble problem. It was inconceivable how he had existed, how he had succeeded in getting so far, how he had managed to remain—why he did not instantly disappear. 'I went a little farther,' he said, 'then still a little farther—till I had gone so far that I don't know how I'll ever get back. Never mind. Plenty time. I can manage. You take Kurtz away quick—quick—I tell you.' The glamour of youth enveloped his particolored rags, his destitution, his loneliness, the essential desolation of his futile wanderings. For months—for years—his life hadn't been worth a day's purchase; and there he was gallantly, thoughtlessly alive, to all appearance indestructible solely by the virtue of his few years and of his unreflecting audacity. I was seduced into something like admiration—like envy. Glamour urged him on, glamour kept him unscathed. He surely wanted nothing from the wilderness but space to breathe in and to push on through. His need was to exist, and to move onwards at the greatest possible risk, and with a maximum of privation. If the absolutely pure, uncalculating, unpractical spirit of adventure had ever ruled a human being, it ruled this be-patched youth. I almost envied him the possession of this modest and clear flame. It seemed to have consumed all thought of self so completely, that, even while he was talking to you,

17 **motley:** The many-colored clothes of a harlequin or jester.

you forgot that it was he—the man before your eyes—who had gone through these things. I did not envy him his devotion to Kurtz, though. He had not meditated over it. It came to him, and he accepted it with a sort of eager fatalism. I must say that to me it appeared about the most dangerous thing in every way he had come upon so far.

"They had come together unavoidably, like two ships becalmed near each other, and lay rubbing sides at last. I suppose Kurtz wanted an audience, because on a certain occasion, when encamped in the forest, they had talked all night, or more probably Kurtz had talked. 'We talked of everything,' he said, quite transported at the recollection. 'I forgot there was such a thing as sleep. The night did not seem to last an hour. Everything! Everything! . . . Of love too.' 'Ah, he talked to you of love!' I said, much amused, 'It isn't what you think,' he cried, almost passionately. 'It was in general. He made me see things—things.'

"He threw his arms up. We were on deck at the time, and the headman of my wood-cutters, lounging near by, turned upon him his heavy and glittering eyes. I looked around, and I don't know why, but I assure you that never, never before, did this land, this river, this jungle, the very arch of this blazing sky, appear to me so hopeless and so dark, so impenetrable to human thought, so pitiless to human weakness. 'And, ever since, you have been with him, of course?' I said.

"On the contrary. It appears their intercourse had been very much broken by various causes. He had, as he informed me proudly, managed to nurse Kurtz through two illnesses (he alluded to it as you would to some risky feat), but as a rule Kurtz wandered alone, far in the depths of the forest. 'Very often coming to this station, I had to wait days and days before he would turn up,' he said. 'Ah, it was worth waiting for!—sometimes.' 'What was he doing? exploring or what?' I asked. 'Oh yes, of course'; he had discovered lots of villages, a lake too—he did not know exactly in what direction, it was dangerous to inquire too much—but mostly his expeditions had been for ivory. 'But he had no goods to trade with by that time,' I objected. 'There's a good lot of cartridges left even yet,' he answered, looking away. 'To speak plainly, he raided the country,' I said. He nodded. 'Not alone, surely!' He muttered something about the villages round that lake. 'Kurtz got the tribe to follow him, did he?' I suggested. He fidgeted a little. 'They adored him,' he said. The tone of these words was so extraordinary that I looked at him searchingly. It was curious to see his mingled eagerness and reluctance to speak of Kurtz. The man filled his life, occupied his thoughts, swayed his emotions. 'What can you expect?' he burst out; 'he came to them with thunder and lightning, you know—and they had never seen anything like it—and very terrible. He could be very terrible. You can't judge Mr. Kurtz as you would an ordinary man. No, no, no! Now—just to give you an idea—I don't mind telling you, he wanted to shoot me too one day—but I don't judge him.' 'Shoot you!' I cried. 'What for?' 'Well, I had a small lot of ivory the chief of that village near my house gave me. You see I used to shoot game for them. Well, he wanted it, and wouldn't hear reason. He declared he would shoot me unless I gave him the ivory and then cleared out of the country, because he could do so, and had a fancy for it, and there was nothing on earth to prevent him killing whom he jolly well pleased.

And it was true too. I gave him the ivory. What did I care! But I didn't clear out. No, no. I couldn't leave him. I had to be careful, of course, till we got friendly again for a time. He had his second illness then. Afterwards I had to keep out of the way; but I don't mind. He was living for the most part in those villages on the lake. When he came down to the river, sometimes he would take me, and sometimes it was better for me to be careful. This man suffered too much. He hated all this, and somehow he couldn't get away. When I had a chance I begged him to try and leave while there was time; I offered to go back with him. And he would say yes, and then he would remain; go off on another ivory hunt; disappear for weeks; forget himself amongst these people—forget himself—you know.' 'Why! he's mad,' I said. He protested indignantly. Mr. Kurtz couldn't be mad. If I had heard him talk, only two days ago, I wouldn't dare hint at such a thing. . . . I had taken up my binoculars while we talked and was looking at the shore, sweeping the limit of the forest at each side and at the back of the house. The consciousness of there being people in that bush, so silent, so quiet—as silent and quiet as the ruined house on the hill—made me uneasy. There was no sign on the face of nature of this amazing tale that was not so much told as suggested to me in desolate exclamations, completed by shrugs, in interrupted phrases, in hints ending in deep sighs. The woods were unmoved, like a mask—heavy, like the closed door of a prison—they looked with their air of hidden knowledge, of patient expectation, of unapproachable silence. The Russian was explaining to me that it was only lately that Mr. Kurtz had come down to the river, bringing along with him all the fighting men of that lake tribe. He had been absent for several months—getting himself adored, I suppose—and had come down unexpectedly, with the intention to all appearance of making a raid either across the river or down stream. Evidently the appetite for more ivory had got the better of the—what shall I say?—less material aspirations. However he had got much worse suddenly. 'I heard he was lying helpless, and so I came up—took my chance,' said the Russian. 'Oh, he is bad, very bad.' I directed my glass to the house. There were no signs of life, but there was the ruined roof, the long mud wall peeping above the grass, with three little square window-holes, no two of the same size; all this brought within reach of my hand, as it were. And then I made a brusque movement, and one of the remaining posts of that vanished fence leaped up in the field of my glass. You remember I told you I had been struck at the distance by certain attempts at ornamentation, rather remarkable in the ruinous aspect of the place. Now I had suddenly a nearer view, and its first result was to make me throw my head back as if before a blow. Then I went carefully from post to post with my glass, and I saw my mistake. These round knobs were not ornamental but symbolic; they were expressive and puzzling, striking and disturbing—food for thought and also for the vultures if there had been any looking down from the sky; but at all events for such ants as were industrious enough to ascend the pole. They would have been even more impressive, those heads on the stakes, if their faces had not been turned to the house. Only one, the first I had made out, was facing my way. I was not so shocked as you may think. The start back I had given was really nothing but a movement of surprise. I had expected to see a knob of wood there, you know. I returned deliberately to the first I had seen—

and there it was, black, dried, sunken, with closed eyelids—a head that seemed to sleep at the top of that pole, and, with the shrunken dry lips showing a narrow white line of the teeth, was smiling too, smiling continuously at some endless and jocose dream of that eternal slumber.

"I am not disclosing any trade secrets. In fact the manager said afterwards that Mr. Kurtz's methods had ruined the district. I have no opinion on that point, but I want you clearly to understand that there was nothing exactly profitable in these heads being there. They only showed that Mr. Kurtz lacked restraint in the gratification of his various lusts, that there was something wanting in him—some small matter which, when the pressing need arose, could not be found under his magnificent eloquence. Whether he knew of this deficiency himself I can't say. I think the knowledge came to him at last—only at the very last. But the wilderness had found him out early, and had taken on him a terrible vengeance for the fantastic invasion. I think it had whispered to him things about himself which he did not know, things of which he had no conception till he took counsel with this great solitude—and the whisper had proved irresistibly fascinating. It echoed loudly within him because he was hollow at the core. . . . I put down the glass, and the head that had appeared near enough to be spoken to seemed at once to have leaped away from me into inaccessible distance.

"The admirer of Mr. Kurtz was a bit crestfallen. In a hurried, indistinct voice he began to assure me he had not dared to take these—say, symbols—down. He was not afraid of the natives; they would not stir till Mr. Kurtz gave the word. His ascendancy was extraordinary. The camps of these people surrounded the place, and the chiefs came every day to see him. They would crawl. . . . 'I don't want to know anything of the ceremonies used when approaching Mr. Kurtz,' I shouted. Curious, this feeling that came over me that such details would be more intolerable than those heads drying on the stakes under Mr. Kurtz's windows. After all, that was only a savage sight, while I seemed at one bound to have been transported into some lightless region of subtle horrors, where pure, uncomplicated savagery was a positive relief, being something that had a right to exist—obviously—in the sunshine. The young man looked at me with surprise. I suppose it did not occur to him that Mr. Kurtz was no idol of mine. He forgot I hadn't heard any of these splendid monologues on, what was it? on love, justice, conduct of life—or what not. If it had come to crawling before Mr. Kurtz, he crawled as much as the veriest savage of them all. I had no idea of the conditions, he said: these heads were the heads of rebels. I shocked him excessively by laughing. Rebels! What would be the next definition I was to hear? There had been enemies, criminals, workers—and these were rebels. Those rebellious heads looked very subdued to me on their sticks. 'You don't know how such a life tries a man like Kurtz,' cried Kurtz's last disciple. 'Well, and you?' I said. 'I! I! I am a simple man. I have no great thoughts. I want nothing from anybody. How can you compare me to . . . ?' His feelings were too much for speech, and suddenly he broke down. 'I don't understand,' he groaned. 'I've been doing my best to keep him alive, and that's enough I had no hand in all this. I have no abilities. There hasn't been a drop of medicine or a mouthful of invalid food for months here. He was shamefully abandoned. A man like this, with such ideas. Shamefully! Shamefully! I—I—haven't slept for the last ten nights. . . .'

"His voice lost itself in the calm of the evening. The long shadows of the forest had slipped down hill while we talked, had gone far beyond the ruined hovel, beyond the symbolic row of stakes. All this was in the gloom, while we down there were yet in the sunshine, and the stretch of the river abreast of the clearing glittered in a still and dazzling splendor, with a murky and over-shadowed bend above and below. Not a living soul was seen on the shore. The bushes did not rustle.

"Suddenly round the corner of the house a group of men appeared, as though they had come up from the ground. They waded waist-deep in the grass, in a compact body, bearing an improvised stretcher in their midst. Instantly, in the emptiness of the landscape, a cry arose whose shrillness pierced the still air like a sharp arrow flying straight to the very heart of the land; and, as if by enchantment, streams of human beings—of naked human beings—with spears in their hands, with bows, with shields, with wild glances and savage movements, were poured into the clearing by the dark-faced and pensive forest. The bushes shook, the grass swayed for a time, and then everything stood still in attentive immobility.

" 'Now, if he does not say the right thing to them we are all done for,' said the Russian at my elbow. The knot of men with the stretcher had stopped too, half-way to the steamer, as if petrified. I saw the man on the stretcher sit up, lank and with an uplifted arm, above the shoulders of the bearers. 'Let us hope that the man who can talk so well of love in general will find some particular reason to spare us this time,' I said. I resented bitterly the absurd danger of our situation, as if to be at the mercy of that atrocious phantom had been a dishonoring necessity. I could not hear a sound, but through my glasses I saw the thin arm extended commandingly, the lower jaw moving, the eyes of that apparition shining darkly far in its bony head that nodded with grotesque jerks. Kurtz—Kurtz—that means short in German—don't it? Well, the name was as true as everything else in his life—and death. He looked at least seven feet long. His covering had fallen off, and his body emerged from it pitiful and appalling as from a winding-sheet. I would see the cage of his ribs all astir, the bones of his arm waving. It was as though an animated image of death carved out of old ivory had been shaking its hand with menaces at a motionless crowd of men made of dark and glittering bronze. I saw him open his mouth wide—it gave him a weirdly voracious aspect, as though he had wanted to swallow all the air, all the earth, all the men before him. A deep voice reached me faintly. He must have been shouting. He fell back suddenly. The stretcher shook as the bearers staggered forward again, and almost at the same time I noticed that the crowd of savages was vanishing without any perceptible movement of retreat, as if the forest that had ejected these beings so suddenly had drawn them in again as the breath is drawn in a long aspiration.

"Some of the pilgrims behind the stretcher carried his arms—two shot-guns, a heavy rifle, and a light revolver-carbine —the thunderbolts of that pitiful Jupiter.[18]

18 **Jupiter:** Chief god of the Romans.

The manager bent over him murmuring as he walked beside his head. They laid him down in one of the little cabins—just a room for a bed-place and a camp-stool or two, you know. We had brought his belated correspondence, and a lot of torn envelopes and open letters littered his bed. His hand roamed feebly amongst these papers. I was struck by the fire of his eyes and the composed languor of his expression. It was not so much the exhaustion of disease. He did not seem in pain. This shadow looked satiated and calm, as though for the moment it had had its fill of all the emotions.

"He rustled one of the letters, and looking straight in my face said, 'I am glad.' Somebody had been writing to him about me. These special recommendations were turning up again. The volume of tone he emitted without effort, almost without the trouble of moving his lips, amazed me. A voice! a voice! It was grave, profound, vibrating, while the man did not seem capable of a whisper. However, he had enough strength in him—factitious no doubt—to very nearly make an end of us, as you shall hear directly.

"The manager appeared silently in the doorway; I stepped out at once and he drew the curtain after me. The Russian, eyed curiously by the pilgrims, was staring at the shore. I followed the direction of his glance.

"Dark human shapes could be made out in the distance, flitting indistinctly against the gloomy border of the forest, and near the river two bronze figures, leaning on tall spears, stood in the sunlight under fantastic head-dresses of spotted skins, warlike and still in statuesque repose. And from right to left along the lighted shore moved a wild and gorgeous apparition of a woman.

"She walked with measured steps, draped in striped and fringed cloths, treading the earth proudly, with a slight jingle and flash of barbarous ornaments. She carried her head high; her hair was done in the shape of a helmet; she had brass leggings to the knee, brass wire gauntlets to the elbow, a crimson spot on her tawny cheek, innumerable necklaces of glass beads on her neck; bizarre things, charms, gifts of witchmen, that hung about her, glittered and trembled at every step. She must have had the value of several elephant tusks upon her. She was savage and superb, wild-eyed and magnificent; there was something ominous and stately in her deliberate progress. And in the hush that had fallen suddenly upon the whole sorrowful land, the immense wilderness, the colossal body of the fecund and mysterious life seemed to look at her, pensive, as though it had been looking at the image of its own tenebrous and passionate soul.

"She came abreast of the steamer, stood still, and faced us. Her long shadow fell to the water's edge. Her face had a tragic and fierce aspect of wild sorrow and of dumb pain mingled with the fear of some struggling, half-shaped resolve. She stood looking at us without a stir and like the wilderness itself, with an air of brooding over an inscrutable purpose. A whole minute passed, and then she made a step forward. There was a low jingle, a glint of yellow metal, a sway of fringed draperies, and she stopped as if her heart had failed her. The young fellow by my side growled. The pilgrims murmured at my back. She looked at us all as if her life had depended upon the unswerving steadiness of her glance. Suddenly she opened her bared arms and threw them up rigid above her head, as though in an uncontrollable desire to touch the sky, and at the same time the swift shadows darted out on the earth, swept around on the river, gathering the steamer into a shadowy embrace. A formidable silence hung over the scene.

"She turned away slowly, walked on, following the bank, and passed into the bushes to the left. Once only her eyes gleamed back at us in the dusk of the thickets before she disappeared.

" 'If she had offered to come aboard I really think I would have tried to shoot her,' said the man of patches, nervously. 'I had been risking my life every day for the last fortnight to keep her out of the house. She got in one day and kicked up a row about those miserable rags I picked up in the storeroom to mend my clothes with. I wasn't decent. At least it must have been that, for she talked like a fury to Kurtz for an hour, pointing at me now and then. I don't understand the dialect of this tribe. Luckily for me, I fancy Kurtz felt too ill that day to care, or there would have been mischief. I don't understand. . . . No —it's too much for me. Ah, well, it's all over now.'

"At this moment I heard Kurtz's deep voice behind the curtain, 'Save me!—save the ivory, you mean. Don't tell me. Save *me*! Why, I've had to save you. You are interrupting my plans now. Sick! Sick! Not so sick as you would like to believe. Never mind. I'll carry my ideas out yet—I will return. I'll show you what can be done. You with your little peddling notions—you are interfering with me. I will return. I . . .'

"The manager came out. He did me the honor to take me under the arm and lead me aside. 'He is very low, very low,' he said. He considered it necessary to sigh, but neglected to be consistently sorrowful. 'We have done all we could for him— haven't we? But there is no disguising the fact, Mr. Kurtz has done more harm than good to the Company. He did not see the time was not ripe for vigorous action. Cautiously, cautiously—that's my principle. We must be cautious yet. The district is closed to us for a time. Deplorable! Upon the whole, the trade will suffer. I don't deny there is a remarkable quantity of ivory—mostly fossil. We must save it, at all events—but look how precarious the position is—and why? Because the method is unsound.' 'Do you,' said I, looking at the shore, 'call it "unsound method"?' 'Without doubt,' he exclaimed, hotly. 'Don't you?' . . . 'No method at all,' I murmured after a while. 'Exactly,' he exulted. 'I anticipated this. Shows a complete want of judgment. It is my duty to point it out in the proper quarter.' 'Oh,' said I, 'that fellow—what's his name?—the brickmaker, will make a readable report for you.' He appeared confounded for a moment. It seemed to me I had never breathed an atmosphere so vile, and I turned mentally to Kurtz for relief—positively for relief. 'Nevertheless I think Mr. Kurtz is a remarkable man,' I said with emphasis. He started, dropped on me a cold heavy glance, said very quietly, 'He *was*,' and turned his back on me. My hour of favor was over, I found myself lumped along with Kurtz as a partisan of methods for which the time was not ripe: I was unsound! Ah! but it was something to have at least a choice of nightmares.

"I had turned to the wilderness really, not to Mr. Kurtz, who, I was ready to admit, was as good as buried. And for a moment it seemed to me as if I also were buried in a vast grave full of unspeakable secrets. I felt an intolerable weight oppressing my breast, the smell of the damp earth, the unseen presence of victorious corruption, the darkness of an impenetrable night. . . . The Russian tapped me on the shoulder. I heard him mumbling and stammering something about 'brother seaman—couldn't conceal—knowledge of matters that would affect Mr. Kurtz's reputation.' I waited. For him evidently Mr. Kurtz was not in his grave; I suspect that for him Mr. Kurtz was one of the immortals. 'Well!' said I at last, 'speak out. As it happens, I am Mr. Kurtz's friend—in a way.'

"He stated with a good deal of formality that had we not been 'of the same profession,' he would have kept the matter to himself without regard to consequences. 'He suspected there was an active ill-will towards him on the part of these white men that—' 'You are right,' I said, remembering a certain conversation I had overheard. 'The manager thinks you ought to be hanged.' He showed a concern at this intelligence which amused me at first. 'I had better get out of the way quietly,' he said, earnestly. 'I can do no more for Kurtz now, and they would soon find some excuse. What's to stop them? There's a military post three hundred miles from here.' 'Well, upon my word,' said I, 'perhaps you had better go if you have any friends amongst the savages near by.' 'Plenty,' he said. 'They are simple people—and I want nothing, you know.' He stood biting his lip, then: 'I don't want any harm to happen to these whites here, but of course I was thinking of Mr. Kurtz's reputation—but you are a brother seaman and—' 'All right,' said I, after a time. 'Mr. Kurtz's reputation is safe with me.' I did not know how truly I spoke.

"He informed me, lowering his voice, that it was Kurtz who had ordered the attack to be made on the steamer. 'He hated sometimes the idea of being taken away—and then again. . . . But I don't understand these matters. I am a simple man. He thought it would scare you away—that you would give it up, thinking him dead. I could not stop him. Oh, I had an awful time of it this last month.' 'Very well,' I said. 'He is all right now.' 'Ye-e-es,' he muttered, not very convinced apparently. 'Thanks,' said I; 'I shall keep my eyes open.' 'But quiet—eh?' he urged, anxiously. 'It would be awful for his reputation if anybody here—.' I promised a complete discretion with great gravity. 'I have a canoe and three black fellows waiting not very far. I am off. Could you give me a few Martini-Henry cartridges?' I could, and did, with proper secrecy. He helped himself, with a wink at me, to a handful of my tobacco. 'Between sailors—you know—good English tobacco.' At the door of the pilot-house he turned round—'I say, haven't you a pair of shoes you could spare?' He raised one leg. 'Look,' The soles were tied with knotted strings sandal-wise under his bare feet. I rooted out an old pair, at which he looked with admiration before tucking it under his left arm. One of his pockets (bright red) was bulging with cartridges, from the other (dark blue) peeped 'Towson's Inquiry,' &c., &c. He seemed to think himself excellently well equipped for a renewed encounter with the wilderness. 'Ah! I'll never, never meet such a man again. You ought to have heard him recite poetry—his own too it was, he told me. Poetry!' He rolled his eyes at the recollection of these delights. 'Oh, he enlarged my mind!' 'Good-by,' said I. He shook hands and vanished in the night. Sometimes I ask myself whether I had every really seen him—whether it was possible to meet such a phenomenon! . . .

"When I woke up shortly after midnight his warning came to mind with its hint of danger that seemed, in the starred darkness, real enough to make me get up for the purpose of having a look round. On the hill a big fire burned, illuminating fitfully a crooked corner of the station-house. One of the agents with a picket of a few of our blacks, armed for the purpose, was keeping guard over the ivory; but deep within the forest, red gleams that wavered, that seemed to sink and rise from the ground amongst confused columnar shapes of intense blackness, showed the exact position of the camp where Mr. Kurtz's adorers were keeping their uneasy vigil. The monotonous beating of a big drum filled the air with muffled shocks and a lingering vibration. A steady droning sound of many men chanting each to himself some weird incantation came out from the black, flat wall of the woods as the humming of bees comes out of a hive, and had a strange narcotic effect upon my half-awake senses. I believe I dozed off leaning over the rail, till an abrupt burst of yells, an overwhelming outbreak of a pent-up and mysterious frenzy, woke me up in a bewildered wonder. It was cut short all at once, and the low droning went on with an effect of audible and soothing silence. I glanced casually into the little cabin. A light was burning within, but Mr. Kurtz was not there.

"I think I would have raised an outcry if I had believed my eyes. But I didn't believe them at first—the thing seemed so impossible. The fact is I was completely unnerved by a sheer blank fright, pure abstract terror, unconnected with any distinct shape of physical danger. What made this emotion so overpowering was—how shall I define it?—the moral shock I received, as if something altogether monstrous, intolerable to thought and odious to the soul, had been thrust upon me unexpectedly. This lasted of course the merest fraction of a second, and then the usual sense of commonplace, deadly danger, the possibility of a sudden on-slaught and massacre, or something of the kind, which I saw impending, was positively welcome and composing. It pacified me, in fact, so much, that I did not raise an alarm.

"There was an agent buttoned up inside an ulster and sleeping on a chair on deck within three feet of me. The yells had not awakened him; he snored very slightly; I left him to his slumbers and leaped shore. I did not betray Mr. Kurtz—it was ordered I should never betray him—it was written I should be loyal to the nightmare of my choice. I was anxious to deal with this shadow by myself alone,— and to this day I don't know why I was so jealous of sharing with anyone the peculiar blackness of that experience.

"As soon as I got on the bank I saw a trail—a broad trail through the grass. I remember the exultation with which I said to myself, 'He can't walk—he is crawling on all-fours—I've got him.' The grass was wet with dew. I strode rapidly with clenched fists. I fancy I had some vague notion of falling upon him and giving him a drubbing. I don't know. I had some imbecile thoughts. The knitting old woman with the cat obtruded herself upon my memory as a most improper person to be sitting at the other end of such an affair. I saw a row of pilgrims squirting lead in the air out of Winchesters held to the hip. I thought I would never get back to the steamer, and imagined myself living alone and unarmed in the woods to an advanced age. Such silly things—you know. And I remember I confounded the beat of the drum with the beating of my heart, and was pleased at its calm regularity.

"I kept to the track though—then stopped to listen. The night was very clear: a dark blue space, sparkling with dew and starlight, in which black things stood very still. I thought I could see a kind of motion ahead of me. I was strangely cocksure of everything that night. I actually left the track and ran in a wide semicircle (I verily believe chuckling to myself) so as to get in front of that stir, of that motion I had seen—if indeed I had seen anything. I was circumventing Kurtz as though it had been a boyish game.

"I came upon him, and, if he had not heard me coming, I would have fallen over him too, but he got up in time. He rose, unsteady, long, pale, indistinct, like a vapor exhaled by the earth, and swayed slightly, misty and silent before me; while at my back the fires loomed between the trees, and the murmur of many voices issued from the forest. I had cut him off cleverly; but when actually confronting him I seemed to come to my senses, I saw the danger in its right proportion. It was by no means over yet. Suppose he began to shout? Though he could hardly stand, there was still plenty of vigor in his voice. 'Go away—hide yourself,' he said, in that profound tone. It was very awful. I glanced back. We were within thirty yards from the nearest fire. A black figure stood up, strode on long black legs, waving long black arms, across the glow. It had horns—antelope horns, I think—on its head. Some sorcerer, some witch-man, no doubt; it looked fiend-like enough. 'Do you know what you are doing?' I whispered. 'Perfectly,' he answered, raising his voice for that single word: it sounded to me far off and yet loud, like a hail through a speaking-trumpet. If he makes a row we are lost, I thought to myself. This clearly was not a case for fisticuffs, even apart from the very natural aversion I had to beat that Shadow—this wandering and tormented thing. 'You will be lost,' I said—'utterly lost.' One gets sometimes such a flash of inspiration, you know. I did say the right thing, though indeed he could not have been more irretrievably lost than he was at this very moment, when the foundations of our intimacy were being laid—to endure—to endure—even to the end—even beyond.

" 'I had immense plans,' he muttered irresolutely. 'Yes,' said I; 'but if you try to shout I'll smash your head with—' there was not a stick or a stone near. 'I will throttle you for good,' I corrected myself. 'I was on the threshold of great things,' he pleaded, in a voice of longing, with a wistfulness of tone that made my blood run cold. 'And now for this stupid scoundrel—' 'Your success in Europe is assured in any case,' I affirmed, steadily. I did not want to have the throttling of him, you understand—and indeed it would have been very little use for any practical purpose. I tried to break the spell—the heavy, mute spell of the wilderness—that seemed to draw him to its pitiless breast by the awakening of forgotten and brutal instincts, by the memory of gratified and monstrous passions. This alone, I was convinced, had driven him out to the edge of the forest, to the bush, towards the gleam of fires, the throb of drums, the drone of weird incantations; this alone had beguiled his unlawful soul beyond the bounds of permitted aspirations. And, don't you see, the terror of the position was not in being knocked on the head—though I had a very lively sense of that danger too—but in this, that I had to deal with a being to whom I could not appeal in the name of anything high or low. I had, even like the niggers, to invoke him—himself—his own exalted and incredible degradation. There was nothing either above or below him, and I knew it. He had kicked himself loose of the earth. Confound the man! he had kicked the very earth to pieces. He was alone, and I before him did not know whether I stood on the ground or floated in the air. I've been telling you what we said—repeating the phrases we pronounced,—but what's the good? They were common everyday words,—the familiar, vague sounds exchanged on every waking day of life. But what of that? They had behind them, to my mind, the terrific suggestiveness of words heard in dreams, of phrases spoken in nightmares. Soul! If anybody had ever struggled with a soul, I am the man. And I wasn't arguing with a lunatic either. Believe me or not, his intelligence was perfectly clear—concentrated, it is true, upon himself with horrible intensity, yet clear; and therein was my only chance—barring, of course, the killing him there and then, which wasn't so good, on account of unavoidable noise. But his soul was mad. Being alone in the wilderness, it had looked within itself, and, by heavens! I tell you, it had gone mad. I had—for my sins, I suppose—to go through the ordeal of looking into it myself. No eloquence could have been so withering to one's belief in mankind as his final burst of sincerity. He struggled with himself, too. I saw it,—I heard it. I saw the inconceivable mystery of a soul that knew no restraint, no faith, and no fear, yet struggling blindly with itself. I kept my head pretty well; but when I had him at last stretched on the couch, I wiped my forehead, while my legs shook under me as though I had carried half a ton on my back down that hill. And yet I had only supported him, his bony arm clasped around my neck—and he was not much heavier than a child.

"When next day we left at noon, the crowd, of whose presence behind the curtain of trees I had been acutely conscious all the time, flowed out of the woods again, filled the clearing, covered the slope with a mass of naked, breathing, quivering, bronze bodies. I steamed up a bit, then swung down-stream, and two thousand eyes followed the evolutions of the splashing, thumping, fierce river-demon beating the water with its terrible tail and breathing black smoke into the air. In front of the first rank, along the river, three men, plastered with bright red earth from head to foot, strutted to and fro restlessly. When we came abreast again, they faced the river, stamped their feet, nodded their horned heads, swayed their scarlet bodies; they shook towards the fierce river-demon a bunch of black feathers, a mangy skin with a pendent tail—something that looked like a dried gourd; they shouted periodically together strings of amazing words that resembled no sounds of human language; and the deep murmurs of the crowd, interrupted suddenly, were like the response of some satanic litany.

"We had carried Kurtz into the pilot-house: there was more air there. Lying on the couch, he stared through the open shutter. There was an eddy in the mass of human bodies, and the woman with helmeted head and tawny cheeks rushed out to the very brink of the stream. She put out her hands, shouted something, and all that wild mob took up the shout in a roaring chorus of articulated, rapid, breathless utterance.

" 'Do you understand this?' I asked.

"He kept on looking out past me with fiery, longing eyes, with a mingled expression of wistfulness and hate. He made no answer, but I saw a smile, a smile of indefinable meaning, appear on his colorless lips that a moment after twitched convulsively. 'Do I not?' he said slowly, gasping, as if the words had been torn out of him by a supernatural power.

"I pulled the string of the whistle, and I did this because I saw the pilgrims on deck getting out their rifles with an air of anticipating a jolly lark. At the sudden screech there was a movement of abject terror through that wedged mass of bodies. 'Don't! don't! you frighten them away,' cried someone on deck disconsolately. I pulled the string time after time. They broke and ran, they leaped, they crouched, they swerved, they dodged the flying terror of the sound. The three red chaps had fallen flat, face down on the shore, as though they had been shot dead. Only the barbarous and superb woman did not so much as flinch, and stretched tragically her bare arms after us over the somber and glittering river.

"And then that imbecile crowd down on the deck started their little fun, and I could see nothing more for smoke.

"The brown current ran swiftly out of the heart of darkness, bearing us down towards the sea with twice the speed of our upward progress; and Kurtz's life was running swiftly too, ebbing, ebbing out of his heart into the sea of inexorable time. The manager was very placid, he had no vital anxieties now, he took us both in with a comprehensive and satisfied glance: the 'affair' had come off as well as could be wished. I saw the time approaching when I would be left alone of the party of 'unsound method.' The pilgrims looked upon me with disfavor. I was, so to speak, numbered with the dead. It is strange how I accepted this unforeseen partnership, this choice of nightmares forced upon me in the tenebrous land invaded by these mean and greedy phantoms.

"Kurtz discoursed. A voice! a voice! It rang deep to the very last. It survived his strength to hide in the magnificent folds of eloquence the barren darkness of his heart. Oh, he struggled! he struggled! The wastes of his weary brain were haunted by shadowy images now—images of wealth and fame revolving obsequiously round his unextinguishable gift of noble and lofty expression. My Intended, my station, my career, my ideas—these were the subjects for the occasional utterances of elevated sentiments. The shade of the original Kurtz frequented the bedside of the hollow sham, whose fate it was to be buried presently in the mold of primeval earth. But both the diabolic love and the unearthly hate of the mysteries it had penetrated fought for the possession of that soul satiated with primitive emotions, avid of lying fame, of sham distinction, of all the appearances of success and power.

"Sometimes he was contemptibly childish. He desired to have kings meet him at railway-stations on his return from some ghastly Nowhere, where he intended to accomplish great things. 'You show them you have in you something that is really profitable, and then there will be no limits to the recognition of your ability,' he would say. 'Of course you must take care of the motives—right motives—always.' The long reaches that were like one and the same reach, monotonous bends that were exactly alike, slipped past the steamer with their multitude of secular trees looking patiently after this grimy fragment of another world, the forerunner of change, of conquest, of trade, of massacres, of blessings. I looked ahead—piloting. 'Close the shutter,' said Kurtz suddenly one day; 'I can't bear to look at this.' I did so. There was a silence. 'Oh, but I will wring your heart yet!' he cried at the invisible wilderness.

"We broke down—as I had expected—and had to lie up for repairs at the head of an island. This delay was the first thing that shook Kurtz's confidence. One morning he gave me a packet of papers and a photograph,—the lot tied together with a shoestring. 'Keep this for me,' he said. 'This noxious fool' (meaning the manager) 'is capable of prying into my boxes when I am not looking.' In the afternoon I saw him. He was lying on his back with closed eyes, and I withdrew quietly, but I heard him mutter, 'Live rightly, die, die . . .' I listened. There was nothing more. Was he rehearsing some speech in his sleep, or was it a fragment of a phrase from some newspaper article? He had been writing for the papers and meant to do so again, 'for the furthering of my ideas. It's a duty.'

"His was an impenetrable darkness. I looked at him as you peer down at a man who is lying at the bottom of a precipice where the sun never shines. But I had not much time to give him, because I was helping the engine-driver to take to pieces the leaky cylinders, to straighten a bent connecting-rod, and in other such matters. I lived in an infernal mess of rust, filings, nuts, bolts, spanners, hammers, ratchet-drills—things I abominate, because I don't get on with them. I tended the little forge we fortunately had aboard; I toiled wearily in a wretched scrap-heap—unless I had the shakes too bad to stand.

"One evening coming in with a candle I was startled to hear him say a little tremulously, 'I am lying here in the dark waiting for death.' The light was within a foot of his eyes. I forced myself to murmur. 'Oh, nonsense!' and stood over him as if transfixed.

"Anything approaching the change that came over his features I have never seen before, and hope never to see again. Oh, I wasn't touched. I was fascinated. It was as though a veil had been rent. I saw on that ivory face the expression of somber pride, of ruthless power, of craven terror—of an intense and hopeless despair. Did he live his life again in every detail of desire, temptation, and surrender during that supreme moment of complete knowledge? He cried in a whisper at some image, at some vision,—he cried out twice, a cry that was no more than a breath—

"'The horror! The horror!'

"I blew the candle out and left the cabin. The pilgrims were dining in the mess-room, and I took my place opposite the manager, who lifted his eyes to give me a questioning glance, which I successfully ignored. He leaned back, serene, with that peculiar smile of his sealing the unexpressed depths of his meanness. A continuous shower of small flies streamed upon the lamp, upon the cloth, upon our hands and faces. Suddenly the manager's boy put his insolent black head in the doorway, and said in a tone of scathing contempt—

"'Mistah Kurtz—he dead.'

"All the pilgrims rushed out to see. I remained, and went on with my dinner. I believe I was considered brutally callous. However, I did not eat much. There was a lamp in there—light, don't you know—and outside it was so beastly, beastly dark. I went no more near the remarkable man who had pronounced a judgment upon the adventures of his soul on this earth. The voice was gone. What else had been there? But I am of course aware that next day the pilgrims buried something in a muddy hole.

"And then they very nearly buried me.

"However, as you see, I did not go to join Kurtz there and then. I did not. I remained to dream the nightmare out to the end, and to show my loyalty to Kurtz once more. Destiny. My destiny! Droll thing life is—that mysterious arrangement of merciless logic for a futile purpose. The most you can hope from it is some knowledge of yourself—that comes too late—a crop of unextinguishable regrets. I have wrestled with death. It is the most unexciting contest you can imagine. It takes place in an impalpable grayness, with nothing underfoot, with nothing around, without spectators, without clamor, without glory, without the great desire of victory, without the great fear of defeat, in a sickly atmosphere of tepid skepticism, without much belief in your own right, and still less in that of your adversary. If such is the form of ultimate wisdom, then life is a greater riddle than some of us think it to be. I was within a hair's-breadth of the last opportunity for pronouncement, and I found with humiliation that probably I would have nothing to say. This is the reason why I affirm that Kurtz was a remarkable man. He had something to say. He said it. Since I had peeped over the edge myself, I understand better the meaning of his stare, that could not see the flame of the candle, but was wide enough to embrace the whole universe, piercing enough to penetrate all the hearts that beat in the darkness. He had summed up—he had judged. 'The horror!' He was a remarkable man. After all, this was the expression of some sort of belief; it had candor, it had conviction, it had a vibrating note of revolt in its whisper, it had the appalling face of a glimpsed truth—the strange commingling of desire and hate. And it is not my own extremity I remember best—a vision of grayness without form filled with physical pain, and a careless contempt for the evanescence of all things—even of this pain itself. No! It is his extremity that I seem to have lived through. True, he had made that last stride, he had stepped over the edge, while I had been permitted to draw back my hesitating foot. And perhaps in this is the whole difference; perhaps all the wisdom, and all truth, and all sincerity, are just compressed into the inappreciable moment of time in which we step over the threshold of the invisible. Perhaps! I like to think my summing-up would not have been a world of careless contempt. Better his cry—much better. It was an affirmation, a moral victory paid for by innumerable defeats, by abominable terrors, by abominable satisfactions. But it was a victory! That is why I have remained loyal to Kurtz to the last, and even beyond, when a long time after I heard once more, not his own voice, but the echo of his magnificent eloquence thrown to me from a soul as translucently pure as a cliff of crystal.

"No, they did not bury me, though there is a period of time which I remember mistily, with a shuddering wonder, like a passage through some inconceivable world

that had no hope in it and no desire. I found myself back in the sepulchral city re-
senting the sight of people hurrying through the streets to filch a little money from
each other, to devour their infamous cookery, to gulp their unwholesome beer, to
dream their insignificant and silly dreams. They trespassed upon my thoughts. They
were intruders whose knowledge of life was to me an irritating pretense, because I
felt so sure they could not possibly know the things I knew. Their bearing, which was
simply the bearing of commonplace individuals going about their business in the assurance of perfect safety, was offensive to me like the outrageous flauntings of folly
in the face of a danger it is unable to comprehend. I had no particular desire to en-
lighten them, but I had some difficulty in restraining myself from laughing in their
faces, so full of stupid importance. I dare say I was not very well at that time. I tot-
tered about the streets—there were various affairs to settle—grinning bitterly at perfectly respectable persons. I admit my behavior was inexcusable, but then my
temperature was seldom normal in these days. My dear aunt's endeavors to 'nurse up
my strength' seemed altogether beside the mark. It was not my strength that wanted
nursing, it was my imagination that wanted soothing. I kept the bundle of papers
given me by Kurtz, not knowing exactly what to do with it. His mother had died
lately, watched over, as I was told, by his Intended. A clean-shaved man, with an official manner and wearing gold-rimmed spectacles, called on me one day and made
inquiries, at first circuitous, afterwards suavely pressing, about what he was pleased
to denominate certain 'documents.' I was not surprised, because I had had two rows
with the manager on the subject out there. I had refused to give up the smallest scrap
out of that package, and I took the same attitude with the spectacled man. He became darkly menacing at last, and with much heat argued that the Company had the
right to every bit of information about its 'territories.' And, said he, 'Mr. Kurtz's
knowledge of unexplored regions must have been necessarily extensive and peculiar—owing to his great abilities and to the deplorable circumstances in which he
had been placed: therefore'—I assured him Mr. Kurtz's knowledge, however extensive, did not bear upon the problems of commerce or administration. He invoked
then the name of science. 'It would be an incalculable loss if,' &c., &c. I offered him
the report on the 'Suppression of Savage Customs,' with the postscriptum torn off.
He took it up eagerly, but ended by sniffing at it with an air of contempt. 'This is not
what we had a right to expect,' he remarked. 'Expect nothing else,' I said. There are
only private letters.' He withdrew upon some threat of legal proceedings, and I saw
him no more; but another fellow, calling himself Kurtz's cousin, appeared two days
later, and was anxious to hear all the details about his dear relative's last moments.
Incidentally he gave me to understand that Kurtz had been essentially a great musician. 'There was the making of an immense success,' said the man, who was an or-
ganist, I believe, with lank gray hair flowing over a greasy coat-collar. I had no reason
to doubt his statement; and to this day I am unable to say what was Kurtz's profession, whether he ever had any—which was the greatest of his talents. I had taken
him for a painter who wrote for the papers, or else for a journalist who could
print—but even the cousin (who took snuff during the interview) could not tell me
what he had been—exactly. He was a universal genius—on that point I agreed with

the old chap, who thereupon blew his nose noisily into a large cotton handkerchief and withdrew in senile agitation, bearing off some family letters and memoranda without importance. Ultimately a journalist anxious to know something of the fate of his 'dear colleague' turned up. This visitor informed me Kurtz's proper sphere ought to have been politics 'on the popular side.' He had furry straight eyebrows, bristly hair cropped short, an eye-glass on a broad ribbon, and, becoming expansive, confessed his opinion that Kurtz really couldn't write a bit—'but heavens! how that man could talk! He electrified large meetings. He had faith—don't you see?—he had the faith. He could get himself to believe anything—anything. He would have been a splendid leader of an extreme party.' 'What party?' I asked. 'Any party,' answered the other. 'He was an—an—extremist.' Did I not think so? I assented. Did I know, he asked, with a sudden flash of curiosity, 'what it was that had induced him to go out there?' 'Yes,' said I, and forthwith handed him the famous Report for publication, if he thought fit. He glanced through it hurriedly, mumbling all the time, judged 'it would do,' and took himself off with this plunder.

"Thus I was left at last with a slim packet of letters and the girl's portrait. She struck me as beautiful—I mean she had a beautiful expression. I know that the sunlight can be made to lie too, yet one felt that no manipulation of light and pose could have conveyed the delicate shade of truthfulness upon those features. She seemed ready to listen without mental reservation, without suspicion, without a thought for herself. I concluded I would go and give her back her portrait and those letters myself. Curiosity? Yes; and also some other feeling perhaps. All that had been Kurtz's had passed out of my hands: his soul, his body, his station, his plans, his ivory, his career. There remained only his memory and his Intended—and I wanted to give that up too to the past, in a way,—to surrender personally all that remained of him with me to that oblivion which is the last word of our common fate. I don't defend myself. I had no clear perception of what it was I really wanted. Perhaps it was an impulse of unconscious loyalty, or the fulfillment of one of these ironic necessities that lurk in the facts of human existence. I don't know. I can't tell. But I went.

"I thought his memory was like the other memories of the dead that accumulate in every man's life—a vague impress on the brain of shadows that had fallen on it in their swift and final passage; but before the high and ponderous door, between the tall houses of a street as still and decorous as a well-kept alley in a cemetery, I had a vision of him on the stretcher, opening his mouth voraciously, as if to devour all the earth with all its mankind. He lived then before me; he lived as much as he had ever lived—a shadow insatiable of splendid appearances, of frightful realities; a shadow darker than the shadow of the night, and draped nobly in the folds of a gorgeous eloquence. The vision seemed to enter the house with me—the stretcher, the phantom-bearers, the wild crowd of obedient worshipers, the gloom of the forests, the glitter of the reach between the murky bends, the beat of the drum, regular and muffled like the beating of a heart—the heart of a conquering darkness. It was a moment of triumph for the wilderness, an invading and vengeful rush which, it seemed to me, I would have to keep back alone for the salvation of another soul. And the memory of what I had heard him say afar there, with the horned shapes stirring at my back, in the glow of fires, within the patient woods, those broken phrases came back to me, were heard again in their ominous and terrifying simplicity. I remembered his abject pleading, his abject threats, the colossal scale of his vile desires, the meanness, the torment, the tempestuous anguish of his soul. And later on I seemed to see his collected languid manner, when he said one day, 'This lot of ivory now is really mine. The Company did not pay for it. I collected it myself at a very great personal risk. I am afraid they will try to claim it as theirs though. H'm. It is a difficult case. What do you think I ought to do—resist? Eh? I want no more than justice.' . . . He wanted no more than justice—no more than justice. I rang the bell before a mahogany door on the first floor, and while I waited he seemed to stare at me out of the glassy panel— stare with that wide and immense stare embracing, condemning, loathing all the universe. I seemed to hear the whispered cry, 'The horror! The horror!'

"The dusk was falling. I had to wait in a lofty drawing-room with three long windows from floor to ceiling that were like three luminous and bedraped columns. The bent gilt legs and backs of the furniture shone in indistinct curves. The tall marble fireplace had a cold and monumental whiteness. A grand piano stood massively in a corner, with dark gleams on the flat surfaces like a somber and polished sarcophagus. A high door opened—closed. I rose.

"She came forward, all in black, with a pale head, floating towards me in the dusk. She was in mourning. It was more than a year since his death, more than a year since the news came; she seemed as though she would remember and mourn for ever. She took both my hands in hers and murmured, 'I had heard you were coming.' I noticed she was not very young—I mean not girlish. She had a mature capacity for fidelity, for belief, for suffering. The room seemed to have grown darker, as if all the sad light of the cloudy evening had taken refuge on her forehead. This fair hair, this pale visage, this pure brow, seemed surrounded by an ashy halo from which the dark eyes looked out at me. Their glance was guileless, profound, confident, and trustful. She carried her sorrowful head as though she were proud of that sorrow, as though she would say, I—I alone know how to mourn for him as he deserves. But while we were shaking hands, such a look of awful desolation came upon her face that I perceived she was one of those creatures that are not the playthings of Time. For her he had died only yesterday. And, by Jove! The impression was so powerful that for me too he seemed to have died only yesterday—nay, this very minute. I saw her and him in the same instant of time—his death and her sorrow—I saw her sorrow in the very moment of his death. Do you understand? I saw them together—I heard them together. She had said, with a deep catch of the breath, 'I have survived;' while my strained ears seemed to hear distinctly, mingled with her tone of despairing regret, the summing-up whisper of his eternal condemnation. I asked myself what I was doing there, with a sensation of panic in my heart as though I had blundered into a place of cruel and absurd mysteries not fit for a human being to behold. She motioned me to a chair. We sat down, I laid the packet gently on the little table, and she put her hand over it . . . 'You knew him well,' she murmured, after a moment of mourning silence.

" 'Intimacy grows quick out there,' I said. 'I knew him as well as it is possible for one man to know another.'

" 'And you admired him,' she said. 'It was impossible to know him and not to admire him. Was it?'

" 'He was a remarkable man,' I said, unsteadily. Then before the appealing fixity of her gaze, that seemed to watch for more words on my lips, I went on, 'It was impossible not to—'

" 'Love him,' she finished eagerly, silencing me into an appalled dumbness. 'How true! how true! But when you think that no one knew him so well as I! I had all his noble confidence. I knew him best.'

" 'You knew him best,' I repeated. And perhaps she did. But with every word spoken the room was growing darker, and only her forehead, smooth and white, remained illumined by the unextinguishable light of belief and love.

" 'You were his friend,' she went on. 'His friend,' she repeated, a little louder. 'You must have been, if he had given you this, and sent you to me. I feel I can speak to you—and oh! I must speak. I want you—you who have heard his last words—to know I have been worthy of him. . . . It is not pride. . . . Yes! I am proud to know I understood him better than anyone on earth—he told me so himself. And since his mother died I have had no one—no one—to—to—'

"I listened. The darkness deepened. I was not even sure whether he had given me the right bundle. I rather suspect he wanted me to take care of another batch of his papers which, after his death, I saw the manager examining under the lamp. And the girl talked, easing her pain in the certitude of my sympathy; she talked as thirsty men drink. I had heard that her engagement with Kurtz had been disapproved by her people. He wasn't rich enough or something. And indeed I don't know whether he had not been a pauper all his life. He had given me some reason to infer that it was his impatience of comparative poverty that drove him out there.

" '. . . Who was not his friend who had heard him speak once?' she was saying. 'He drew men towards him by what was best in them.' She looked at me with intensity. 'It is the gift of the great,' she went on, and the sound of her low voice seemed to have the accompaniment of all the other sounds, full of mystery, desolation, and sorrow, I had ever heard—the ripple of the river, the soughing of the trees swayed by the wind, the murmurs of wild crows, the faint ring of incomprehensible words cried from afar, the whisper of a voice speaking from beyond the threshold of an eternal darkness. 'But you have heard him! You know!' she cried.

" 'Yes, I know,' I said with something like despair in my heart, but bowing my head before the faith that was in her, before that great and saving illusion that shone with an unearthly glow in the darkness, in the triumphant darkness from which I could not have defended her—from which I could not even defend myself.

" 'What a loss to me—to us!'—she corrected herself with beautiful generosity; then added in a murmur, 'To the world.' By the last gleams of twilight I could see the glitter of her eyes, full of tears—of tears that would not fall.

" 'I have been very happy—very fortunate—very proud,' she went on. 'Too fortunate. Too happy for a little while. And now I am unhappy—for life.'

"She stood up; her fair hair seemed to catch all the remaining light in a glimmer of gold. I rose too.

"'And of all this,' she went on, mournfully, 'of all his promise, and of all his greatness, of his generous mind, of his noble heart, nothing remains—nothing but a memory. You and I—'

"'We shall always remember him,' I said, hastily.

"'No!' she cried. 'It is impossible that all this should be lost—that such a life should be sacrificed to leave nothing—but sorrow. You know what vast plans he had. I knew of them too—I could not perhaps understand,—but others knew of them. Something must remain. His words, at least, have not died.'

"'His words will remain,' I said.

"'And his example,' she whispered to herself. 'Men looked up to him,—his goodness shone in every act. His example—'

"'True,' I said; 'his example too. Yes, his example. I forgot that.'

"'But I do not. I cannot—I cannot believe—not yet. I cannot believe that I shall never see him again, that nobody will see him again, never, never, never.'

"She put out her arms as if after a retreating figure, stretching them back and with clasped pale hands across the fading and narrow sheen of the window. Never see him! I saw him clearly enough then. I shall see this eloquent phantom as long as I live, and I shall see her too, a tragic and familiar Shade, resembling in this gesture another one, tragic also, and bedecked with powerless charms, stretching bare brown arms over the glitter of the infernal stream, the stream of darkness. She said suddenly very low, 'He died as he lived.'

"'His end,' said I, with dull anger stirring in me, 'was in every way worthy of his life.'

"'And I was not with him,' she murmured. My anger subsided before a feeling of infinite pity.

"'Everything that could be done—' I mumbled.

"'Ah, but I believed in him more than anyone on earth—more than his own mother, more than—himself. He needed me! Me! I would have treasured every sigh, every word, every sign, every glance.'

"I felt like a chill grip on my chest. 'Don't,' I said, in a muffled voice.

"'Forgive me. I—I—have mourned so long in silence—in silence. . . . You were with him—to the last? I think of his loneliness. Nobody near to understand him as I would have understood. Perhaps no one to hear. . . .'

"'To the very end,' I said, shakily. 'I heard his very last words. . . .' I stopped in a fright.

"'Repeat them,' she murmured in a heart-broken tone. 'I want—I want—something—something—to—to live with.'

"I was on the point of crying at her, 'Don't you hear them?' The dusk was repeating them in a persistent whisper all around us, in a whisper that seemed to swell menacingly like the first whisper of a rising wind. 'The horror! The horror!'

"'His last word—to live with,' she insisted. 'Don't you understand I loved him—I loved him—I loved him!'

"I pulled myself together and spoke slowly.

"'The last word he pronounced was—your name.'

"I heard a light sigh, and then my heart stood still, stopped dead short by an exulting and terrible cry, by the cry of inconceivable triumph and of unspeakable pain. 'I knew it—I was sure!' . . . She knew. She was sure. I heard her weeping; she had hidden her face in her hands. It seemed to me that the house would collapse before I could escape, that the heavens would fall upon my head. But nothing happened. The heavens do not fall for such a trifle. Would they have fallen, I wonder, if I had rendered Kurtz that justice which was his due? Hadn't he said he wanted only justice? But I couldn't. I could not tell her. It would have been too dark—too dark altogether. . . ."

Marlow ceased, and sat apart, indistinct and silent, in the pose of a meditating Buddha. Nobody moved for a time. "We have lost the first of the ebb," said the Director, suddenly. I raised my head. The offing was barred by a black bank of clouds, and the tranquil waterway leading to the uttermost ends of the earth flowed somber under an overcast sky—seemed to lead into the heart of an immense darkness.

QUESTIONS

1. Analyze the character of Marlow and discuss how his character may shape and influence our perception of the events he describes.

2. How would you describe Marlow's attitudes toward the colonial enterprise? Does he support imperialist ideals? Point to specific passages.

3. What specific practices and attitudes does Marlow criticize or condemn? What practices and attitudes does he approve of?

4. Marlow seems to draw a distinction between Belgian and British colonial practices. What are these distinctions? Are they valid?

5. In what senses do Europeans regard Africa as the "dark continent"? What meanings of *dark* are found in the story?

6. Is Marlow racist? Use details from the story to support your answer.

7. Do you perceive this story as supporting imperialism or condemning it?

8. In all three of the long stories included in this collection—"The Beach of Falesá," "The Man Who Would Be King," and "Heart of Darkness"—the white narrators comment frequently and significantly on the natives' religion or "superstition." Compare these comments across the three stories. What do these comments reveal about European attitudes toward non-Christian religions? What part do these attitudes play in justifying colonialism or imperialism?

Flora Annie Steel

(1847–1929)

The name of Flora Annie Steel is inevitably linked with that of Rudyard Kipling, just as her fiction is often and favorably compared with his. Unlike Kipling, however, Flora Webster was born in England and raised there and later in Scotland. Her early years of unusual freedom in Scotland, together with her unorthodox home schooling, may have shaped her into the independent woman she later became. Moreover, the news of the Indian Mutiny of 1857 may have permanently influenced her view of the Raj, which she steadfastly supported.

In 1867, she married Henry William Steel, and almost immediately the young couple embarked for India, where she lived and worked with her husband until 1889. Henry Steel's postings in the Indian Civil Service were to remote areas of northern India, where Mrs. Steel was often the only European woman. Partly for this reason, but also because of her innate curiosity and energy, she escaped the stultifying life of a memsahib (a respectful term used by Indians to address white European women). Steel threw herself into Indian affairs, often to the consternation of British officials. She learned several Indian languages, championed the cause of Indian women (though she defended arranged marriages), and in 1874 founded a girls' school at Kasur. Accompanying her husband on his rounds, she encouraged Indians to relate their folktales and stories, a collection of which she published in 1884. A year before leaving India, she and a coauthor wrote and published *The Complete Indian Housekeeper*, giving detailed directions to European women on all aspects of household management in India. This book is still valuable for its insights into Anglo-Indian life and attitudes.

It was not until her return to Scotland that Steel began to write the fiction for which she is best remembered. Beginning with stories for *Macmillan's Magazine*, she eventually published five volumes of short stories about India, novels (including her best, *On the Face of the Waters*, 1896), and nonfiction, culminating in her autobiography. Steel's fiction provides a view of Indian life that Kipling's does not. For one thing, as a woman she could go behind the purdah into the hidden world of Indian women, whose education and dignity she championed in her stories and in life. She was also sympathetic to and understanding of Indian culture in ways that Kipling and others were not. She saw much to admire in the Indian way of life, though abuses like those of the village moneylenders she attacked vigorously. She understood the plight of small farmers, sympathized with widowed women (especially child-bride widows), and appreciated, as few other Europeans did, that Indian ways and European ideas were often incompatible.

For postcolonial critics, however, Steel's persistent support for the British Raj and her opposition to Indian independence make her a problematic figure in Anglo-Indian literature and postcolonial studies. Those who read "At the Great

Durbar," however, will certainly recognize that she was a woman who, more so than most of her contemporaries, saw matters from the Indians' point of view and chastised the injustices perpetrated by a colonial system over which they had no control.

At the Great Durbar 1897

He sat, cuddled up in a cream-coloured cotton blanket, edged with crimson, shooing away the brown rats from the curved cobs of Indian corn. The soft mists of a northern November hung over the landscape in varying density: heavy over the dank sugarcane patch by the well, lighter on the green fodder crop, dewy among the moisture-loving leaves of the sprouting vetches, and here, in the field of ripening maize, scarcely visible between the sparse stems. He was an old man with a thin white beard tucked away behind his ears, and a kindly look on his high-featured face. Every now and then he took up a little clod of earth from the dry, crumbling ridge of soil which divided the field he was watching from the surrounding ones, and threw it carefully among the maize, saying in a gentle, grumbling voice, "*Ari,* brothers! Does no shame come to you?"

It had no perceptible effect on the rats, who, owing to the extreme sparsity of the crop, could be seen every here and there deliberately climbing up a swaying stem to seat themselves on a cob and begin breakfast systematically. In the calm, windless silence you could almost hear the rustle and rasp of their sharp white teeth. But Nanuk Singh—as might have been predicted from his seventy and odd years of life in the fields—was somewhat hard of hearing, somewhat near of vision also. For when so many years have been spent watching the present furrow cling to the curves of the past one, in sure and certain hope of similar furrows in the future, or in listening to the endless lamentations of a water-wheel ceasing not by day or night to proclaim an eternity of toil and harvest, both eyes and ears are apt to grow dull towards new sights and sounds. Nanuk's had, at any rate, even though the old familiar ones no longer occupied them, fate having decreed that in his old age the peasant farmer should have neither furrows nor water-wheel of his own. How this had come about needs a whole statute-book of Western laws to understand. Nanuk himself never attempted the task. To him it was, briefly, the will of God. His district officer, however, when the case fell under his notice by reason of the transfer of the land, thought differently; and having a few minutes' leisure from office drudgery to spare for really important work, made yet one more representation regarding the scandalous rates of interest, the cruelty of time-foreclosures, and the general injustice of applying the maxim "*caveat emptor*"[1] to transactions in which one party is practically a child and the other a Jew. A futile representation, of course, since the Government, so experts

---

1 *"caveat emptor":* "Let the buyer beware." Here and in the following paragraph, Steel alludes to the high interest rates charged by village moneylenders.

affirm, is not strong enough to attack the Frankenstein monster of Law which it has created.

In a measure, nevertheless, old Nanuk was right in attributing his ruin to fate, since it had followed naturally from the death of his three sons: one, the eldest, dying of malarial fever in the prime of life, leaving, alas! a young family of girls; another, the youngest, swept off by cholera just as his hand began to close firmly round his dead brother's plough-handle; the third, when on the eve of getting his discharge from a frontier regiment in order to take his brothers' places by his father's side, being struck down ingloriously in one of the petty border raids of which our Punjab peasant soldiers have always to bear the brunt.

And this loss of able hands led inevitably to the loss of ill-kept oxen; while from the lack of well-cattle[2] came that gradual shrinkage of the irrigated area where some crop is certain—rain or no rain—which means a less gradual sinking further and further into debt, until, as had been the case with Nanuk, the owner loses all right in the land save the doubtful one of toil. Even this had passed from the old man's slackening hold after his wife died, and the daughters-in-law, with starvation staring them in the face, had drifted away back to their own homes, leaving him to live as best he could on the acre or so of unirrigated land lent to him out of sheer charity. For public opinion still has some power over the usurer in a village of strong men, and all his fellows respected old Nanuk, who stood six feet two, barefoot, and had tales to tell of the gentle art of singlestick as applied to the equitable settling of accounts in the old days, before western laws had taken the job out of the creditor's hands.

Strangely enough, however, Nanuk, as he sat coping inadequately with the brown rats, felt less resentment against the usurer who had robbed him, or the law which permitted the robbery, than he did against the weather. The former had made no pretence of favouring him; the latter, year after year, had tempted his farmer's soul to lavish sowings by copious rain at seedtime, and thereinafter withheld the moisture necessary for a bare return of measure for measure. Briefly, he had gambled in grain, and he had lost. Lost hopelessly in this last harvest of maize, since, when the sound cobs should be separated from those which the wanton teeth had spoilt, they would not yield the amount of Government revenue which the old man had to pay; certainly would not do so if the cobs became scarcer day by day and the rats more numerous. In fact, the necessity for action ere matters grew worse appeared to strike Nanuk, making him, after a time, draw out a small sickle and begin to harvest the remaining stalks one by one.

"*Bullah!* Neighbour Nanuk," cried the new man, who, better equipped for the task with sons and cattle, was driving the wheel and curving the furrows for the usurer, "I would, for thy sake, the task was harder. And as if the crop were not poor enough, the dissolute rats must needs play the wanton with the half of it. But, 'tis the same all over the land, and between them and the revenue we poor folk of the plough will have no share."

---

2 **well-cattle:** Cattle used to draw water from wells.

Nanuk stood looking meditatively at a very fine cob out of which a pair of sharp white teeth were taking a last nibble, while a pair of wicked black eyes watched him fearlessly.

"They are God's creatures also, and have a right to live on the soil as we others," he said slowly.

"Then they should pay the revenue," grumbled Dittu. "Why should *you*, who have no crop whereon to pay? O infamous one!" he added sharply to one of the oxen he was driving to their work, "sleepest thou? And the well silent! Dost want to bring me to Nanuk's plight?"

So, with a prod of the goad, he passed on, leaving old Nanuk still looking at the brown rat on the corn-cob. Why, indeed, should he have to pay for God's other creatures? In the old days justice would have been meted out to such as he. The crop would have been divided into heaps, so many for the owner of the soil, so many for the tiller, so many for the State. Then if *Purmeshwar*[3] sent rats instead of rain, the heaps were smaller. That was all. And if the equity of this had been patent to those older rulers, who had scarcely given a thought in the other ways to the good of their subjects, why should it not be patent to those new ones who—God keep them!— gave justice without respect of persons, so far as in them lay? There must be a mistake somewhere; the facts could not have been properly placed before the *Lat-sahib*—that vice-regent of God upon earth. This conviction came home slowly to the old man as he finished his harvesting; slowly but surely, so that when he had spread the cobs out to dry on his cotton blanket he walked over to the well, and, between the whiffs of the general pipe, hinted that he thought of laying the matter before the authorities. "I will take the produce of my field," he said, "in my hand—it will not be more than five *seers*[4] when the good is sifted from the bad—and I will say to the *Lat-sahib*, 'This is because *Purmeshwar* sent rats instead of rain. Take your share, and ask no more.'"

Dittu, the new man, laughed scornfully. "Better take a rat also, since all parties to the case must be present by the law."

He intended it as a joke, but Nanuk took it quite seriously. "That is true," he assented; "I will take a rat also; then there can be no mistake."

That evening, when he sat with his cronies on the mud dais beneath the peepul tree, where he was welcome to a pull out of anybody's pipe, he spoke again of his intention. The younger folk laughed, but the seniors thought that it could at least do no harm. Nanuk's case was a hard one; it was quite clear he could not pay the revenue, and it was better to go to the fountainhead in such matters, since underlings could do nothing but take fees. So, while the stars came out in the evening sky, they sat and told tales of Nausherwan,[5] and many another worthy whose memory lingers in native minds by reason of perfectly irrational acts of despotic clemency, such as even Socialists do not dream of nowadays. The corn-cobs then being harvested,

---

3 **Purmeshwar:** God.
4 **seers:** Units of weight equal to just over two pounds each.
5 **Nausherwan:** Nausherwan Audil, a King of Persia, renowned for justice.

dried, and shelled, he set to work with the utmost solemnity on rat-traps; but here at once he realised his mistake. By harvesting his own crop he had driven the little raiders farther afield; and though he could easily have caught one in his neighbour's patch, a desire to deal perfectly fairly with those who, in his experience, dealt perfectly fairly with facts, made him stipulate for a rat out of his own.

This necessitated the baiting of his property with some of the corn in order to attract the wanton creatures again; and even then, though he sat for hours holding the cord by which an earthen dish was to be made to fall upon the unsuspecting intruder, he was unsuccessful.

"Trra! Not catch rats!" cried a most venerable old pantaloon[6] to whom he applied for advice, remembering him in his boyhood as one almost god-like in his supreme knowledge of such things. "Wait a while; 'tis a trick—a mere trick—but when you once know it you cannot forget it." All that day the old men sat together in the sunshine, profoundly busy, and towards evening they went forth together to the field, chattering and laughing like a couple of schoolboys. It was long after dusk ere they returned, full of mutual recrimination. The one had coughed too much, the other had wheezed perpetually; there was no catching of rats possible under such circumstances. Then the old pantaloon went a-hunting by himself, full of confidence, only to return dejected; then Nanuk, full of determination, sat up all one moonlit night in the field where—now that he had no crop to benefit by it—the night-dew gathered heavily on every leaf and blade—on Nanuk, too, as he sat crouched up in his cotton blanket, thinking of what he should say to the *Lat-sahib* when the rat was caught, which it was not. Finally, with angry misgivings as to the capabilities of the present generation of boys, the old pantaloon suggested the offering of one whole anna for the first rat captured in Nanuk's maize-field. Before the day was over a score or two of the village lads, long-limbed, bright-eyed, were vociferously maintaining the prior claims of as many brown rats, safely confined in little earthen pipkins[7] with a rag tied round the top. They stood in a row, like an offering of sweets to some deity, round Nanuk's bed, for—as was not to be wondered at after his night-watch—he was down with an attack of the chills. That was nothing new. He had had them every autumn since he was born; but he was not accustomed to be surrounded on such occasions by brown rats appealing to him for justice. It ended in his giving, with feverish hands, one anna to each of the boys, and reserving his selection until he was in a more judicial frame of mind. Still, it would not do to starve God's creatures, so every morning while the fever lingered—for it had got a grip on him somehow—he went round the pipkins and fed the rats with some of the maize. And every morning, rather to his relief, there were fewer of them to feed, since they nibbled their way out once they discovered that the top of their prison was but cloth. So as he lay, sometimes hot, sometimes cold, the idea came to him, foolishly enough, that this was a process of divine selection, and that if he only waited the day when

6 **pantaloon:** A foolish old man.
7 **pipkins:** Small pots with horizontal handles.

but one rat should remain, his mission would bear the seal of success. An idea like this only needs presentation to a mind, or lack of mind, like old Nanuk's. So what with the harvesting and the rat-catching, and the fever and the omen-awaiting, it was close on the new year when, with a brown rat, now quite tame, tied up in a pipkin, some five *seers* of good grain tied up in the corner of his cotton blanket, and Heaven knows what a curious conglomeration of thought bound up in his still feverish brain, the old man set out from his village to find the *Lat-sahib*. Such things are still done in India, such figures are still to be seen, making some civilised people stand out of the road bareheaded, as they do to a man on his way to the grave—a man who has lived his life, whose day is past.

Owing also to the fever and the paying for rats, etc., old Nanuk's pockets were ill-provided for the journey, but that mattered little in a country where a pilgrimage on foot is in itself presumptive evidence of saintship. Besides, the brown rat—which Nanuk had attached a string lest one of the parties to the suit might escape him on the road—was a perpetual joy to the village children, who scarcely knew if it was greater fun to peep at it in its pipkin, or see it peeping out of the old man's cotton blanket, when in the evenings it nibbled away at its share of Nanuk's dinner. They used to ask endless questions as to why he carried it about, and what he was going to do with it, until, half in jest, half in earnest, he told them he was the *muda-ee* (plaintiff) and the rat the *mudee-ala* (defendant) in a case they were going to lay before the *Lat-sahib;* an explanation perfectly intelligible to even the babes and sucklings, who in a Punjabi village nowadays lisp in numbers of petitions and pleaders.

So the *muda-ee* and *mudee-ala* tramped along together amicably, sometimes by curving wheel-tracks among the furrows—ancient rights-of-way over the wide fields, as transient yet immutable as the furrows themselves; and there, with the farmer's eye-heritage of generations, he noted each change of tint in the growing wheat, from the faintest yellowing to the solid dark green with its promise of a full ear to come. Sometimes by broad lanes, telling yet once more the strange old Indian tale of transience and permanence, of death and renewed birth, in the deep grass-set ruts through which the traffic of centuries had passed rarely, yet inevitably. And here with the same knowledgeable eye he would mark the homing herds of village cattle, and infer from their condition what the unseen harvest had been which gave them their fodder. Finally, out upon the hard, white highroad, so different from the others in its self-sufficient straightness, its squared heaps of nodular limestone ready for repairs, its elaborate arrangements for growing trees where they never grew before, and where even western orders will not make them grow. And here Nanuk's eyes still found something familiar in the great wains[8] creaking along in files to add their quota of corn sacks to the mountain of wheat cumbering the railway platforms all along the line. Yet even this was in its essence new, provoking the wonder in his slow brain how it could be that the increased demand for wheat and its enhanced price should have gone hand-in-hand with the financial ruin of the grower.

8 **wains:** Wagons.

To say sooth, however, such problems as these flitted but vaguely through the old man's thought, and even his own spoliation was half forgotten in the one great object of that long journey which, despite his cheerful patience, had sapped his strength sadly. To find the *Lat-sahib*, to make his *salaam*, and bid the *mudee-ala-jee* do so likewise, to lay the produce of the field at the Sahib's feet, and say that *Purmeshwar* had sent rats instead of rain—that in itself was sufficient for the old man as he trudged along doggedly, his eyes becoming more and more dazed by unfamiliar sights, as he neared the big city.

"*Bullah!*" said the woman of whom he begged a night's lodging. "If we were to house and feed the wanderers on this road, we should have to starve ourselves. And thou art a Sikh. Go to thine own people. 'Tis each for each in this world." That was a new world to Nanuk.

"Doth thy rat do tricks?" asked the children critically. "What, none? Trra! We can see rats of that mettle any day in the drains, and there was a man here yesterday whose rat cooked bread and drew water. Ay! and his goat played the drum. That was a show worth seeing."

So Nanuk trudged on.

"See the *Lat-sahib*," sneered the yellow-legged police constable when, after much wandering through bewildering crowds, the old Sikh found himself at a meeting of roads, each one of which was barred by a baton. "Which *Lat-sahib*—the big one or the little?"

"The big one," replied Nanuk stoutly. There was no good in underlings; *that* he knew.

Police Constable number Seventy-five called over to his crony, number Ninety-six, on the next road.

"Ho, brother! Here is another *durbari*.[9] Canst let him in on thy beat? I have no room on mine." And then they both laughed, whereat old Nanuk, taking courage, moved on a step, only to be caught and dragged back, hustled, and abused. What! Was the Great Durbar for the like of him—the Great Durbar on which lakhs and crores[10] had been spent—the Great Durbar all India had been thinking of for months? *Wah!* Whence had he come if he had not heard of the Great Durbar, and what had he thought was the meaning of the Venetian masts and triumphal arches, the flags and the watered roads? Did he think such things were always? If it came to such ignorance as that, mayhap he would not know what *this* was coming along the road.

It was a disciplined tramp of feet, an even glitter of bayonets, a straight line of brown faces, a swing and a sweep, as a company of the Guides came past in their khaki and crimson uniform. Old Nanuk looked at it wistfully.

"Nay, brother," he said, "I know that. 'Twas my son's regiment, God rest him!"

"Thou shouldst sit down, old man," said a bystander kindly. "Of a truth thou canst go no farther till the show is over. Hark! There are the guns again. 'Twill be Bairanpore likely, since Hurriana has gone past. *Wah!* It is a show—a rare show!"

---

9 *durbari:* A durbar is an Indian court; the policeman's reference is sarcastic.
10 **lakhs and crores:** A lakh is 100,000 rupees; a crore is 100 lakhs or 10 million rupees.

So down the watered road, planted out in miserable attempts at decoration with barbers' poles unworthy of a slum in the East End, came a bevy of Australian horses, wedged at a trot between huge kettledrums, which were being whacked barbarically by men who rose in their stirrups with the conscientious precision of a newly imported *competition-wallah*.[11] Then more Australian horses again in an *orfévré* barouche[12] lined with silver, where, despite the glow of colour, the blinding flash of diamonds in an Indian sun, despite even the dull wheat-green glitter of the huge emerald tiara about the turban, the eye forgot these things to fix itself upon the face which owned them all; a face haggard, sodden, superlatively handsome even in its soddenness; indifferent, but with an odd consciousness of the English boy who—dressed as for a flower show—sat silently beside his charge. Behind them with a clatter and flutter of pennons came a great trail of wild horsemen, showing, as they swept past, dark, lowering faces among the sharp spearpoints.

And the guns beat on their appointed tale, till, with the last, a certain satisfaction came to that sodden face, since there were none short in the salute—*as yet.* The measure of his misdoings was not full *as yet.*[13]

The crowd ebbed and flowed irregularly to border the straight white roads, where at intervals the great tributary chiefs went backwards and forwards to pay their State visits, but Nanuk and his rat—the plaintiff and the defendant—waited persistently for their turn to pass on. It was long in coming; for even when the last flash and dash of barbaric splendour had disappeared, the roar of cannon began louder, nearer, regular to a second in its even beat.

"That is the *Lat* salute,"[14] said one man to another in the crowd. "Let us wait and see the *Lat,* brother, ere we go."

Nanuk overheard the words, and looked along the road anxiously, then stood feeling more puzzled than ever; for there was nothing to see here but a plain closed carriage with a thin red and gold trail of the bodyguard behind it and before. The sun was near to its setting, and sent a red, angry flare upon a bank of clouds which had risen in the east, and the dust of many feet swept past in whirls before a rising wind.

"It will rain ere nightfall," declared the crowd contentedly, as it melted away citywards. "And the crops will be good, praise to God."

Once more Nanuk overheard, and this time a glad recognition seemed to rouse him from a dream. Yes! The crops would be good. Down by the well, on the land he and his had ploughed for so many years, the wheat would be green—green as those emeralds above that sodden face.

"The *Lat* has gone out," joked Constable Seventy-five as he went off duty; "but there are plenty of other things worth seeing to such an ignoramus as thou."

True; only by this time Nanuk was almost past seeing aught save that all things were unfamiliar in those miles and miles of regiments and rajahs, electric lights and newly macadamised roads, tents and make-believe gardens, all pivoted, as it were,

11 **competition-wallah:** A wallah is a person associated with or engaged in a service.
12 *orfévré* **barouche:** A four-wheeled open carriage, seating two.
13 A reduction in the number of guns is the first punishment for bad administration. [Steel's note.]
14 **Lat salute:** Salute to a high government official.

round the Royal Standard of England, which was planted out in the centre of the Viceroy's camp. As he wandered aimlessly about the vast canvas city, hustled here, sent back there, the galloping orderlies, the shuffling elephants, the carriages full of English ladies, the subalterns cracking their tandem whips, and the native outriders had but one word for him.

"*Hut! Hut!*" ("Stand back! Stand back!")

A heavy drop of rain came as a welcome excuse to his dogged perseverance for sheltering awhile under a thorn bush. He was more tired than hungry, though he had not tasted food that day; and it needed a sharp nip from the defendant's teeth, as it sought for something eatable in the folds of his blanket, to remind him that others of God's creatures had a better appetite than he. But what was he to give? There was the five *seers* of grain still, of course; but who was to apportion the shares? Who was to say, 'This much for the plaintiff, this much for the defendant, this much for the State?' The familiar idea seemed to give him support in the bewildering inrush of new impressions, and he held to it as a drowning man in a waste of unknown waters clutches at a straw.

Nevertheless, the parties to the suit must not be allowed to starve meanwhile, and if they took equal shares surely that would be just.

The rain now fell in torrents, and the bush scarcely gave him any shelter as, with a faint smile, he sat watching the brown rat at work upon the corn, and counting the number of grains the wanton teeth appropriated as their portion. For so much, and no more, would be his also. It was not a sumptuous repast, but uncooked maize requires mastication, and that took up time. So that it was dark ere he stood up, soaked through to the skin, and looked perplexedly at the long lines of twinkling lights which had sprung up around him. And hark! What was that? It was the dinner bugle at a mess close by, followed, as by an echo, by another and another and another—quite a chorus of cheerful invitations to dinner. But Nanuk knew nothing of such feasts as were spread there in the wilderness. He had lived all his life on wheat and lentils, though, being a Sikh, he would eat wild boar or deer if it could be got, or take a tot of country spirits on occasion to make life seem less dreary. He stood listening, shivering a little with the cold, and then went on his way, since *Lat-sahib* must be found, the case decided, before this numbing forgetfulness crept over everything.

Sometimes he inquired of those he met. More often he did not, but wandered on aimlessly through the maze of light, driven and hustled as he had been by day. And as he wandered the bands of the various camps were playing, say, the march in *Tannhäuser*, or "Linger longer, Loo." But sooner or later they all paused to break suddenly into a stave or two of another tune, as the colonel gave "The Queen"[15] to his officers.

Of all this, again, Nanuk knew nothing. Even at the best of times, he had been ignorant as a babe unborn of anything beyond his fields, and now he remembered nothing save that he and the brown rat were suitors in a case against *Purmeshwar* and the State.

So the night passed. It was well on into the chilliest time before the dawn, when the slumber which comes to all the world for that last dead hour of darkness having

---

15 **"The Queen":** The soldiers' toast to Queen Victoria.

rid him of all barriers, he found himself beneath what had been the goal of his hopes ever since he had first seen its strange white rays piercing the night—the great ball of electric light which crowned the flagstaff whereon the Standard of England hung dank and heavy; for the wind had dropped, the rain had ceased, and a thick white mist clung close even to the round bole of the mast, which was set in the centre of a stand of chrysanthemums. The colours of the blossoms were faintly visible in the downward gleam of the light spreading in a small circle through the mist.

So far so good. This was the "*Standard of Sovereignty,*" no doubt—the "*Lamp of Safety*"—the guide by day and night to faithful subjects seeking justice before the king. This Nanuk understood; this he had heard of in those tales of Nausherwan and his like, told beneath the village peepul tree.

Here, then, he would stay—he and the defendant—till the dawn brought a hearing. He sat down, his back to the flowers, his head buried in his knees. And as he sat, immovable, the mist gathered upon him as it had gathered in the field. But he was not thinking now what he should say to the *Lat-sahib.* He was past that.

He did not hear the jingle and clash of arms which, after a time, came through the fog, or the voice which said cheerfully—

"Appy Noo Year to you, mate!"

"Same to you, Tommy, and many of 'em; but it's rather you nor I, for it's chillin' to the vitals."

They were changing guards on this New Year's morning, and Private Smith, as he took his first turn under the long strip of canvas stretched as a sun-shelter between the two sentry-boxes, acknowledged the truth of his comrade's remark by beating his arms upon his breast like any cabman. Yet he was hot enough in his head, for he had been singing 'Auld Lang Syne' and drinking rum for the greater part of the night, and, though sufficiently sober to pass muster on New Year's Eve, was drunk enough to be intensely patriotic. So, as he walked up and down, there was a little lilt in his step which attempted to keep time to the stave of "God Save our Gracious Queen" which he was whistling horribly out of tune. On the morrow—or, rather, today, since the dawn was at hand—there was to be the biggest review in which he had ever taken part: six-and-twenty thousand troops marching up to the Royal Standard and saluting! They had been practising it for weeks, and the thrill of it, the pride and power of it, had somehow got into Private Smith's head—with the rum. It made him take a turn beyond that strip of canvas, round the flagstaff he was supposed to guard.

"'Alt! 'oo goes there?"

The challenge rang loudly, rousing Nanuk from a dream which was scarcely less unreal than the past twelve hours of waking had been to his ignorance. He stumbled up stiffly—a head taller than the sentry—and essayed a *salaam.*

"'Ullo! What the devil are you doin' here? *Hut,* you! Goramighty! Wot's that?"

It was the defendant, which Nanuk had brought out to *salaam* also, and which, alarmed at the sudden introduction, began darting about wildly at the end of its string. Private Smith fell back a step, and then pulled himself together with a violent effort, uncertain if the rat were real; but the cold night air was against him.

"Wash'er-mean?—Wash'er doin'-'ere?—Wash'er-got?" he asked conglomerately; and Nanuk, understanding nothing, went down on his knees the better to untie the knot in the corner of his blanket. *"Poggle,"* commented Private Smith, recovering himself as he looked down at the heap of maize, the defendant, and the old man talking about *Purmeshwar.* Then, being in a benevolent mood, he wagged his head sympathetically. "Pore old Johnny! Wot's 'e want, with 'is rat and 'is popcorn? Fine lookin' old chap, though—but we licked them Sickies,[16] and, by gum! we'll lick 'em again, if need be!"

The thought made him begin to whistle once more as he bent unsteadily to look at something which glittered faintly as the old man laid it on the top of the pile of corn.

It was his son's only medal.

"Hillo!" said Private Smith, bringing himself up with a lurch, "so that is it, eh, mate? Gor-save-a-Queen! Now wot's up, sonny? 'Orse Guards been a-doing wot they didn't ought to 'ave done? Well, that ain't no noos, is it, comrade? But we'll drink the old Lady's 'elth all the same. Lordy! If you've bin doin' extra dooty on the rag all night you won't mind a lick o' the lap—eh? Lor' bless you!—I don' want it. I've 'ad as mush as me and Lee-Metford can carry 'ome without takin' a day-tour by orderly room—Woy! You won't, won't yer? Come now, Johnny, don't be a fool—it's rum, I tell yer, and you Sickies ain't afraid o' rum. Wot! You won't drink 'er 'elth, you mutineering nigger? Then I'll make yer. Feel that—now then, ''Ere's a 'elth unto'w her Majesty.'"

Perhaps it was the unmistakable prick of a bayonet in his stomach, perhaps it was the equally unmistakable smell of the liquor arousing a craving for comfort in the old man, but he suddenly seized the flask which Private Smith had dragged from his pocket, and, throwing his head back, poured the contents down his throat, the action—due to his desire not to touch the bottle with his lips—giving him an almost ludicrous air of eagerness.

Private Smith burst into a roar of laughter.

"Gor-save-the-Queen!" And as he spoke the first gun of the hundred and one which are fired at daybreak on the anniversary of her Most Gracious Majesty's assumption of the title *Kaiser-i-Hind* boomed out sullenly through the fog.

But Nanuk did not hear it. He had stumbled to his feet and fallen sideways to the ground.

"I gather, then," remarked the surgeon-captain precisely, "that before gun-fire this morning you found the old man in a state of collapse below the flagstaff—is this so?"

Private Smith, sober to smartness and smart to stiffness, saluted; but there was an odd trepidation on his face. "Yes, sir—I done my best for 'im, sir. I put 'im in the box, sir, and give 'im my greatcoat, and I rub 'is 'ands and feet, sir. I done my level best for 'im, not being able, you see, sir, to go off guard. I couldn't do no more."

"You did very well, my man; but if you had happened to have some stimulant—any alcohol, for instance."

---

16 **Sickies:** Sikhs, followers of the Sikh denomination of Hinduism. Many of them, like Nanuk's son, served in the British army and were valued as especially brave fighters.

Private Smith's very smartness seemed to leave him in a sudden slackness of relief. "Which it were a tot of rum, sir, as I 'appened to 'ave in my greatcoat pocket. It done 'im no 'arm, sir, did it?"

The surgeon-captain smiled furtively. "It saved his life, probably; but you might have mentioned it before. How much did he take?"

"About 'arf a pint, sir—more nor less." Private Smith spoke under his breath with an attempt at regret; then he became loquacious. "Beggin' your pardon, sir, but I was a bit on myself, and 'e just poured it down like as it was milk, an' then 'e tumbled over and I thought 'e was dead, and it sobered me like. So I done my level best for 'im all through."

Perhaps he had; for old Nanuk Singh found a comfortable spot in which to spend his remaining days when the regimental coolie carried him that New Year's morning from the flagstaff to the hospital. He lay ill of rheumatic fever for weeks, and when he recovered it was to find himself and his rat quite an institution among the gaunt, listless convalescents waiting for strength in their long dressing-gowns. The story of how the old Sikh had drunk the Queen's health had assumed gigantic proportions under Private Smith's care, and something in the humour and the pathos of it tickled the fancy of his hearers, who, when the unfailing phrase, "An' so I done my level best for him, I did," came to close the recital, would turn to the old man and say—

"Pore old Johnny—an' Gord knows what 'e wanted with 'is rat and 'is popcorn!"

That was true, since Nanuk Singh did not remember even the name of his own village; and, though he still talked about the plaintiff and the defendant, *Purmeshwar* and the State, he was apparently content to await his chance of hearing at another and greater durbar.

QUESTIONS:

1. What hardships and deprivations have reduced Nanuk to poverty? What is his attitude toward these?

2. Is Nanuk a pathetic figure? A ludicrous one? A sympathetic one? Explain your answer.

3. What measures does Nanuk take to be sure that the defendant rat is treated fairly? What do these measures tell you about Nanuk and his sense of justice?

4. Why does Steel describe the British parade and the New Year's celebrations in such detail? What do these descriptions add to the story?

5. What attitudes toward Indians do the two British soldiers reveal?

6. Overall, what does the story say about the possibilities of justice within the British Raj?

Alice Perrin

(1867–1934)

Alice Robinson Perrin was an almost exact contemporary of Rudyard Kipling's, and indeed, Perrin's early works were often compared favorably to his. Like Kipling, she was born in India, but her roots in the country extended back to her grandfather, who had been a director in the East India Company. Her father, John Robinson, was a major general in the Bengal calvary. Typical of her generation, she was sent to England for her education, returning to India when her schooling was complete, where she married Charles Perrin, an engineer in the Indian Public Works Department. During her twenty-five years with her husband in India, she traveled widely, observing the country's people and institutions, and of course her Anglo-Indian counterparts. Generally speaking, her earlier stories are among her best. Those written after she and her husband retired to Switzerland in the 1920s are less vividly realized and more conventional in content than her earlier work.

Perrin began writing short stories in 1892 and a novel two years later, in all producing three collections of stories and seventeen novels. Her fiction focuses on the people she knew best—Indian and English men and women living in India or of Anglo-Indian background. Many of her stories center on romantic love or domestic issues, and like most Victorian and Edwardian authors, she often overtly moralizes. On the whole, she supports the British Raj and accepts the conventional wisdom that European values and ways are superior to those of India. But she is not blinded by these conventional ideas and often dramatizes the misunderstandings that arise between ruler and ruled and the mistakes that the British can make, however good their intentions.

"Justice" is an attempt to see the Raj from an Indian point of view. Whether the story represents what Indians "really" thought of the English is debatable, but it does examine the assumption that British justice is intrinsically superior to India's. This was already a central issue in the tensions between the British and the Indians, and it became increasingly so as the movement for independence gained momentum. Nor is it an issue whose relevance has passed: Revenge codes remain a deeply divisive issue in many contemporary societies and cultures, making the debate as urgent today as it was a century ago.

Justice

ca. 1901

The long day's work in field and jungle was over, the sunset meal had been prepared and eaten, and the dusty little Indian village lay quiet save for a monotonous murmur of voices, and the lowing of cattle penned into safety for the night. Light wreaths of smoke from fires that had cooked the rice and chupattis[1] hung to the mud walls, twined among the branches of the old pipal tree, and mingled with the pungent fumes of the hookah[2] that was being passed around the group of villagers squatted about the giant roots.

To-day this jungle hamlet, that lay far from the life of great cities and populous districts, had been stirred to intense excitement by the rare visit of an English official, whose camp now gleamed white in the mango-grove half a mile away. The head-man and elders of the village had spent busy hours in front of the great square tent wherein the magistrate had sat and received their petitions, examined accounts, listened to complaints, and administered justice.

Now the evening talk over the evening hookah on the spot that constituted the public meeting-place, club-house, and council-chamber of the village, was of the sahib and his curious habits, his strange clothing, the furniture in the tent, his judgments and decisions, and the offensiveness of his swaggering Mahomedan butler, who had demanded eggs and milk for his master's table.

Abstract questions concerning the white people were also earnestly discussed, such as how far the theory was correct that poison lay under their nails, which compelled them to eat with knives and forks instead of with their fingers like reasonable beings. Also whether the existence of "the Momiai-walla sahib" was an actual fact— that dreaded Government official whose reputed duty it was to obtain plump native victims for the purpose of distilling from their brains the magic essence known as "Momiai," which is said to heal all injuries.

"Truly the ways of the English are beyond comprehension," said the head-man conclusively; "did'st remark how the sahib entered his camp on foot this morning, having his horse led after him? Who but an Englishman would walk when he might ride?"

He offered the hookah politely to a very old man who sat huddled beside him, wrapped in a grimy cotton sheet, and having a mummy's withered shrunken visage, though the black eyes that twinkled deep in the shrivelled face were very much alive.

"Thou, Narain Singh," continued the head-man to him courteously, "hast lived longer and must therefore have seen more of the sahib-people and their customs than any of us here. What thinkest thou of their rule, and their manner of distributing justice?"

That morning, Narain Singh, the patriarch, had travelled many miles across country from his village, on a pony that was little more than a foal, for the purpose of interviewing the Government representative concerning a question of land assessment that affected his little property. He had obtained audience of the sahib, attention and investigation had been promised him, and he was therefore elated in spirit, and disposed to be garrulously agreeable to his hosts. He took a bubbling pull at the

---

1 **chupattis:** A flat bread made of wheat.
2 **hookah:** A bubble pipe for smoking tobacco.

hookah through his closed fist, for none of the company touched the mouthpiece directly with their lips.

"Without doubt the sahib-people mean well," he said graciously, "and endeavour to be just in their judgements, but 'the weevil is ground up with the flour,' and at times they can be stupid as owls and make big mistakes." He paused, with effect, and the entire attention of a respectful audience became his. "Many times have I been concerned with litigation—as witness, as defendant, as plaintiff, and again as onlooker only. And I have come to know that there is one thing which the Government with all its truth, and wisdom, and justice, can seldom understand, and that is the heart of a dark man towards an enemy."

A murmur of interrogation went round the little circle, mingled with the gurgle of the hookah.

"Proof have I seen of this not once but often," continued the quavering voice reminiscently. "Dost recall the case of Mirat, son of Atchari, in my village?" turning to the head-man.

"Somewhat do I recall concerning it, though but faintly. Surely it was many years back? Was it not Mirat who slew his neighbour's mother, and so was hanged?"

The old man chuckled. "Truly was Mirat hanged though he slew not the woman, and I alone have knowledge of the truth! Throughout the years have I kept silence, but now, brothers, if it please thee, will I tell how it came to pass that Mirat was hanged for the murder of old Bitia, mother of Mulloo, because the Sirkar was unable to comprehend the feeling of the dark ones towards an enemy."

"Speak, Father!" said the head-man, voicing the general wish.

The old man settled his back more comfortably against the trunk of the pipil tree. "Then it happened thus. The fields of Mirat adjoined mine own fields, and I knew him well. He was young, and gay, and handsome, and thought much of himself. He found favour in the sight of the village girls—aye, and in the sight of the older women also. Many times have I beheld him coming forth early in the mornings to work on his land, driving his plough with the small white bullocks, his skin shining brown in the sun, and a yellow marigold set above his ear. And as he worked he would sing in a voice that was high, and sweet, and carried far. He was clever too with his tongue, and in the evenings when the day's work was done, and we sat beneath our village pipal tree, he would tell tales and sing songs. So the neighbours favoured him—all save one, and this was Mulloo, who hated him. And the two were enemies.

"Now Mulloo was stupid and of an evil countenance, and always had he been jealous because the village favoured Mirat, and because Mirat's fields and cattle prospered; whereas Mulloo was disliked, and season after season had his crops failed and his cattle died. Some there were who held that this bad fortune was only to be expected because Bitia, the mother of Mulloo, was a widow and, it was said, a witch also. Moreover, she had but one eye, which all know is a mark of ill-omen and will cause disaster.

"The quarrel between Mirat and Mulloo arose concerning a field that divided their dwelling-places, and which was claimed by both. First Mulloo would begin to cultivate it, and Mirat would destroy the work and commence to plough for himself. Then Mulloo would also undo the labour of Mirat and turn his cattle on to the land.

Thus it went on, and nothing was permitted to flourish in the plot because of the ill-feeling between these two. When they met they would revile one another from opposite ends of the fields, but there was no fighting or beating till Mirat's best bullock fell sick, and died as though by magic. The next morning, in the village, Mirat fell upon Mulloo as one possessed of an evil spirit, and beat him sorely, crying out that Bitia, the hag, had overlooked his beast with her one eye and so caused its death—for had he not beheld her crossing his field the night before, and in an hour from then was not his bullock dead? The anger of Mirat was hot and swift, and I and others that stood by saw the fierce light of it in his eyes, and heard him swear that he would kill the old woman, and her son, and all their relations, should any of them so much as come nigh the field again. Mulloo was in fear of his life. He covered his head and ran to a place of safety, and from thence he abused his enemy with a loud voice, and took an oath to be avenged.

"But Mirat, having cooled his anger by beating Mulloo, went on his way with laughter, repeating the saying that 'Though an enemy's words may be terrible, death still comes at the appointed time,' and from that hour he tilled the field undisturbed in the early mornings and sowed his seed, singing of love, and battle, and riches, in his strong young voice. And Mulloo listened with a dark face behind his mud boundary wall, and whispered that his day of reckoning was yet to come. Then Mulloo brought an action against Mirat in the Civil Courts, and after many months he lost his case and was well-nigh ruined. The field was adjudged to belong to Mirat, and Mulloo hated his enemy more bitterly than before, while Mirat laughed and triumphed.

"It was at this time that I took Lachmi, the girl widow, to dwell in my house, for my wife was old, and the work of the spinning and cooking and milking was heavy. It was at the urging of Chunia, my wife, that I took to myself a younger woman to be her co-wife and helpmeet. She was a girl whose husband had died in infancy and she was young and fair, with a face like the moon at its full, and limbs that were rounded and smooth. At first was she all humility and gratitude, and she worked well and did as she was bid by my wife; and the sweetness of her warmed my heart that was growing chill, even then, with advancing years. She would laugh, and sing, and her little hands were soft to the touch, and her eyes bright and tender as a fawn's. I loved her as I had loved Chunia, my wife, in the days when she came to me as a bride.

"Ai! little did I suspect of the trick that was to be played on me by Mirat who was my neighbour—Mirat the bold, the handsome, with the ringing voice, and the fierce temper. Little did I guess of the treachery of Lachmi, when Mirat cast eyes of desire upon her; and I knew not that her caresses had grown false, or that the lips she gave me were yet hot with the kisses of her lover, until the evening when I beheld the two with mine own eyes in the mango grove, clasped in each other's arms.

"Behind the trunk of a tree did I wait and watch, and I heard their words of love, their mockery of me, the old man, and their arrangement for the next meeting, which was to be that night in the field of Mirat when all in my house should be sleeping. I waited and saw Mirat leave her with many a backward look of longing, whilst Lachmi gathered up the bundle of fodder she had been sent into the jungle to cut, and, raising it to her head, passed on alone into the open fields. I did not strike her down as she stood, I did not follow her to kill her, my wrath was no flame like that of Mirat my neighbour, but a slow, steady fire that does not die. With Lachmi I meant presently to deal as is the custom with such light women who are false to their homes. That night would I cut off her nose, so that neither Mirat nor any other man should desire to look upon her twice, and henceforth should she drudge for the household in her shame, eating the leavings of the meals, sleeping on the ground, wearing once more the coarse garments of the outcast.

"With Mirat did I plan to deal in mine own way. And that night, when the punishment of Lachmi was accomplished, and she lay in a corner of the cow-shed bleeding and moaning, did I go forth (though somewhat weakened with the struggle, for the girl was young and strong), bearing my muzzle-loading gun, for which I held a permit from the Government so that I might protect my crops from the deer and wild pigs. The moon was rising, and in the field that had caused the enmity between Mirat and Mulloo a crop of pulse,[3] tall and vigorous as the sower thereof, showed black and thick, save where, in the corner, a patch was left uncultivated as a refuge for the spirits. I went on to the edge of this crop where the shadow was darkest, and sat down on my heels to await the coming of Mirat, who thought to meet Lachmi in his field when all in my house should be safely sleeping. And as I sat I beheld a man who crept along the boundary wall like a wild beast that fears the hunter, bearing something in his arms. Often did he stop and look round, and I could hear his breathing. He saw me not, though he passed near to where I sat, for I was in the shadow of the pulse-crop. The man was Mulloo, and the thing that he carried in his arms was the body of old Bitia his mother, and her head hung over to one side as though she were dead.

"I watched him cross the field, stealing along the edge of the crop, and presently he stopped. I saw him push the body of Bitia, the old woman, in amongst the pulse, and then he came back like a jackal, bending low to the ground, and looking swiftly to the right and to the left. When he reached his boundary wall he climbed it as though he were pursued by a devil, and I heard his footsteps quick and short as he ran to his hut on the other side.

"I sat on, and turned over in my mind the thing that I had seen; and understanding came to me. I knew then that Mulloo had murdered his mother and placed her body in the pulse-field, that Mirat his enemy might be accused of her death and so hanged. Had we not all heard the words of Mirat when he swore he would slay Bitia, or any of the people of Mulloo who set foot upon his land? I sat and pondered, and presently, as I had expected, Mirat came forth from his dwelling-place and stood at the top of the field in the moonlight, singing softly to himself. But 'Singing songs and making a bower is all unseemly without a lover': and he was waiting for Lachmi, I hid my face in my wrapper and laughed, for I knew that Lachmi was lying in the cow-shed with her beauty gone for ever, and that never more would she seek her lover in the field, or the mango-grove, or anywhere else. Whilst he stood there, singing and waiting, I crept back in the shadow of the crop to my home, knowing

---

3 **pulse:** A food crop resembling peas or beans.

that I had only to keep silent for Mirat to be punished, without trouble to myself, for the injury he had wrought me, his neighbour.

"And so it happened. Old Bitia was found next morning, strangled, in the crop of pulse, and Mirat was arrested; for the field was his, and his words were remembered, and I, being called as one of the witnesses, spoke truth when I testified that Mirat had threatened to kill the old woman. Also I gave evidence that having risen on the night of the murder to scare wild pigs from my crops, had I beheld Mirat standing in the moonlight at the top of his field, near to where the body was found.

"As I spoke in the Court I met the eyes of the man who had stolen from me the love of Lachmi the widow, and he understood full well that there was more that I could tell if I would, but that I meant to keep silence: 'The lizard was as wide as the snake was long!'

"His defence was that Mulloo had slain the woman and placed her body in the field to bring trouble upon him, the two being at enmity; and the district judge, who had seen much, and knew more than most *Feringhees*[4] concerning the hearts of black people, said that it might well be. And so the case went up to the High Court, while Mirat remained in prison. The judge-sahibs of the High Court ruled that such a thing was not possible; that no man, black or white, would murder his own mother to be avenged on his neighbour, and the evidence being strong against Mirat, they sentenced him to be hanged.

"On the morning when Mirat was to die, Lachmi went forth as usual into the jungle to cut grass for the beasts, and she never returned. What became of her I know not to this day, nor did it greatly matter, for there are widows in plenty, and Chunia my wife chose another woman who was strong and faithful, but neither young nor fair.

"As for Mulloo, now that the evil influence of his mother's one eye had been removed, his crops flourished and his cattle prospered; also he purchased the field that had been Mirat's, which yielded a rich return, so that when he died, full of years, his son and his son's sons inherited wealth.

"So it is true what I have said—that there are few white men who can see into the heart of a dark man desiring to be avenged on an enemy; and that though the sahib-people mean well, and endeavour to be just and sound in their judgments, sometimes can they be stupid as owls and make mistakes. But though Mirat had not killed Bitia, the old woman, still had he tricked me, Narain Singh, his neighbour, and defiled the honour of my house; and 'It is sin whether you steal oil or sugar.' Therefore, to my mind, was he deservedly punished—and without further trouble or undertaking on my part. What sayest thou, O my brothers?"

A chorus of approval arose from the little crowd of listeners, and the hookah gurgled freely as it passed from hand to hand.

"It were well done," said the head-man graciously; and at the same time he drew his wrapper closer about his shoulders. "The night grows chilly," he added, restraining a yawn, "and the hour of crow-caw will soon be at hand. Come, let us sleep."

4 *Feringhees:* A foreigner; a European.

QUESTIONS

1. What ways of the English are beyond comprehension? What "normal" practices are implied by these criticisms?

2. What ways of the Indians do you find odd or perplexing in the story?

3. What "superstitions" do the participants in the story hold? How do you react to them?

4. By Western standards, is justice served by the hanging of Mirat? Why or why not?

5. What standards of justice seem to be held by the narrator and his audience?

6. What does the story say about the possibilities of imperial rule? About the fairness of foreign justice?

John Buchan

(1875–1940)

John Buchan is best known today for his mystery novel *The Thirty-nine Steps* (1915), which Alfred Hitchcock filmed in 1935. In the late nineteenth and early twentieth centuries, however, Buchan was a well-known adventure writer, editor, and statesman who entertained millions of readers, adult and juvenile, with his exciting stories of danger, daring, and conquest.

Like Robert Louis Stevenson, Buchan was born in Scotland. After being educated at Glasgow University and Oxford, he set his mind on a literary career. Buchan was already a successful author when, in 1901, he became a lawyer and secretary to Lord Milner, high commissioner for South Africa. Buchan spent the next two years in South Africa, where he absorbed a great many impressions and experiences that later found their way into his fiction.

Upon his return to England in 1903, Buchan became a fiction reader for the publisher Thomas Nelson and Sons and wrote regularly for the *Spectator.* Until 1910, most of Buchan's writing was nonfiction, but in 1910 he published *Prester John,* an adventure novel for young readers, which signaled a new direction. Yet another new interest emerged the following year when he entered politics. During World War I, Buchan served on the staff at British headquarters, subsequently writing a multivolume history of the conflict for Nelson and Sons. By 1920, he retired from Nelson and devoted himself completely to his own projects. The result was a stream of books—novels, short stories, histories, biographies, essays. Moreover, his political activities continued; he was a member of Parliament from 1927–1935 and then governor general of Canada.

Buchan wrote in all the popular genres—adventure, mystery, science fiction—and it is as a popular writer that he is still known today. He aimed more at entertainment than art, but never pandered to his audience. His heroes are marked more by common sense than dash and daring, and beneath the exciting surface of his stories there are often characters of substance and interest.

"The Kings of Orion" combines realism and outlandish adventure, and centers on a character more memorable for his incompetence and vivid imagination than his skill. Written at or near the height of the British Empire, it reveals perhaps more than Buchan intended about the imperialist spirit and the assumptions that underlay its easy self-confidence.

The Kings of Orion   1902

"An ape and a lion lie side by side in the heart of a man."

PERSIAN PROVERB.

Spring-fishing in the North is a cold game for a man whose blood has become thin in gentler climates. All afternoon I had failed to stir a fish, and the wan streams of the Laver, swirling between bare grey banks, were as icy to the eye as the sharp gusts of hail from the north-east were to the fingers. I cast mechanically till I grew weary, and then with an empty creel and a villainous temper set myself to trudge the two miles of bent to the inn. Some distant ridges of hill stood out snow-clad against the dun sky, and half in anger, half in a dismal satisfaction, I told myself that fishing tomorrow would be as barren as to-day.

At the inn door a tall man was stamping his feet and watching a servant lifting rod-cases from a dog-cart.[1] Hooded and wrapped though he was, my friend Thirlstone was an unmistakable figure in any landscape. The long, haggard, brown face, with the skin drawn tightly over the cheek-bones, the keen blue eyes finely wrinkled round the corners with staring at many suns, the scar which gave his mouth a humorous droop to the right, made up a whole which was not easily forgotten. I had last seen him on the quay at Funchal[2] bargaining with some rascally boatman to take him after mythical wild goats in the Desertas. Before that we had met at an embassy ball in Vienna, and still earlier at a hill station in Persia to which I had been sent post-haste by an anxious and embarrassed government. Also I had been at school with him, in those far-away days when we rode nine stone[3] and dreamed of cricket averages. He was a soldier of note, who had taken part in two little wars and one big

1 **dog-cart:** A light two-wheeled carriage with back-to-back seats.
2 **Funchal:** A port city in Portugal.
3 **nine stone:** A stone is 14 pounds; hence 126 pounds.

one; had himself conducted a political mission through a hard country with some success, and was habitually chosen by his superiors to keep his eyes open as a foreign attaché in our neighbours' wars. But his fame as a hunter had gone abroad into places where even the name of the British army is unknown. He was the hungriest shikari[4] I have ever seen, and I have seen many. If you are wise you will go forth-with to some library and procure a little book entitled *Three Hunting Expeditions,* by A. W. T. It is a modest work, and the style is that of a leading article, but all the lore and passion of the Red Gods are in its pages.

The sitting-room at the inn is a place of comfort, and while Thirlstone warmed his long back at the fire I sank contentedly into one of the well-rubbed leather arm-chairs. The company of a friend made the weather and the scarcity of salmon less the intolerable grievance they had seemed an hour ago than a joke to be laughed at. The landlord came in with whisky, and banked up the peats[5] till they glowed beneath a pall of blue smoke.

"I hope to goodness we are alone," said Thirlstone, and he turned to the retreating landlord and asked the question.

"There's naebody bidin' the nicht forbye yoursels," he said, "but the morn there's a gentleman comin'. I got a letter frae him the day. Maister Wiston, they ca' him. Maybe ye ken him?"

I started at the name, which I knew very well. Thirlstone, who knew it better, stopped warming himself and walked to the window, where he stood pulling his moustache and staring at the snow. When the man had left the room, he turned to me with the face of one whose mind is made up on a course but uncertain of the best method.

"Do you know this sort of weather looks infernally unpromising? I've half a mind to chuck it and go back to town."

I gave him no encouragement, finding amusement in his difficulties.

"Oh, it's not so bad," I said, "and it won't last. To-morrow we may have the day of our lives."

He was silent for a little, staring at the fire. "Anyhow," he said at last, "we were fools to be so far up the valley. Why shouldn't we go down to the Forest Lodge? They'll take us in, and we should be deucedly comfortable, and the water's better."

"There's not a pool on the river to touch the stretch here," I said. "I know, for I've fished every inch of it."

He had no reply to this, so he lit a pipe and held his peace for a time. Then, with some embarrassment but the air of having made a discovery, he announced that his conscience was troubling him about his work, and he thought he ought to get back to it at once. "There are several things I have forgotten to see to, and they're rather important. I feel a beast behaving like this, but you won't mind, will you?"

"My dear Thirlstone," I said, "what is the good of hedging? Why can't you say you won't meet Wiston?"

4 **shikari:** Big-game hunter.
5 **peats:** Carbonized vegetable matter, burned as fuel in Scotland and Ireland.

His face cleared. "Well, that's the fact—I won't. It would be too infernally unpleasant. You see, I was once by way of being his friend, and he was in my regiment. I couldn't do it."

The landlord came in at the moment with a basket of peats. "How long is Capt—Mr. Wiston staying here?" I asked.

"He's no bidin' ony time. He's just comin' here in the middle o' the day for his denner, and then drivin' up the water to Altbreac. He has the fishin' there."

Thirlstone's face showed profound relief. "Thank God!" I heard him mutter under his breath, and when the landlord had gone he fell to talking of salmon with enthusiasm. "We must make a big day of it to-morrow, dark to dark, you know. Thank Heaven, our beat's downstream, too." And thereafter he made frequent excursions to the door, and bulletins on the weather were issued regularly.

Dinner over, we drew our chairs to the hearth, and fell to talk and the slow consumption of tobacco. When two men from the ends of the earth meet by a winter fire, their thoughts are certain to drift overseas. We spoke of the racing tides off Vancouver, and the lonely pine-clad ridges running up to the snow peaks of the Selkirks,[6] to which we had both travelled once upon a time in search of sport. Thirlstone on his own account had gone wandering to Alaska, and brought back some bear-skins and a frost-bitten toe as trophies, and from his tales had consorted with the finest band of rogues which survived unhanged on this planet. Then some casual word took our thoughts to the south, and our memories dallied with Africa. Thirlstone had hunted in Somaliland and done mighty slaughter; while I had spent some never-to-be-forgotten weeks long ago in the hinterland of Zanzibar, in the days before railways and game preserves. I had gone through life with a keen eye for the discovery of earthly paradises, to which I intend to retire when my work is over, and the fairest I thought I had found above the Rift valley,[7] where you have a hundred miles of blue horizon and the weather of Scotland. Thirlstone, not having been there, naturally differed, and urged the claim of a certain glen in Kashmir, where you may hunt two varieties of bear and three of buck in thickets of rhododendron, and see the mightiest mountain-wall on earth from your tent door. The mention of the Indian frontier brought us back to our professions, and for a little we talked "shop," with the unblushing confidence of those who know each other's work and approve it. As a very young soldier Thirlstone had gone shooting in the Pamirs[8] and had blundered into a Russian party of exploration which contained Kuropatkin.[9] He had in consequence grossly outstayed his leave, having been detained for a fortnight by an arbitrary hospitality; but he had learned many things, and the experience had

6 **Selkirks:** Mountains in British Columbia, Canada.
7 **Rift valley:** The Great Rift Valley, a depression running from the Jordan River south to Mozambique, Africa.
8 **Pamirs:** Mountain region in central Asia.
9 **Kuropatkin:** Alexei Nikolaievich Kuropatkin, Russian general who took part in operations in Turkistan in 1876 and again in 1881.

given him strong views on frontier questions. Half an hour was devoted to a masterly survey of the East, until a word pulled us up.

"I went there in '99," Thirlstone was saying,—"the time Wiston and I were sent—" and then he stopped, and his eager face clouded. Wiston's name cast a shadow over our reminiscences.

"What did he actually do?" I asked after a short silence.

"Pretty bad! He seemed a commonplace, good sort of fellow, popular, fairly competent, a little bad-tempered perhaps. And then suddenly he did something so extremely blackguardly that everything was at an end. It's no good repeating details, and I hate to think about it. We know little about our neighbours, and I'm not sure that we know much about ourselves. There may be appalling depths of iniquity in every one of us, only most people are fortunate enough to go through the world without meeting anything to wake the devil in them. I don't believe Wiston was bad in the ordinary sense. Only there was something else in him—*somebody else,* if you like,—and in a moment it came uppermost, and he was a branded man. Ugh! it's a gruesome thought."

Thirlstone had let his pipe go out, and was staring moodily into the fire.

"How do you explain things like that?" he asked. "I have an idea of my own about them. We talk glibly of ourselves and our personality and our conscience, as if every man's nature were a smooth, round, white thing, like a chuckiestone. But I believe there are two men—perhaps more—in every one of us. There's our ordinary self, generally rather humdrum; and then there's a bit of something else, good, bad, but never indifferent—and it is that something else which may make a man a saint or a great villain."

"'The Kings of Orion[10] have come to earth,'" I quoted.

Something in the words struck Thirlstone, and he asked me what was the yarn I spoke of.

"It's an old legend," I explained. "When the kings were driven out of Orion, they were sent to this planet and given each his habitation in some mortal soul. There were differences of character in that royal family, and so the *alter ego* which dwells alongside of us may be virtuous or very much the reverse. But the point is that he is always greater than ourselves, for he has been a king. It's a foolish story, but very widely believed. There is something of the sort in Celtic folk-lore, and there's a reference to it in Ausonius.[11] Also the bandits in the Bakhtiari[12] have a version of it in a very excellent ballad."

"Kings of Orion," said Thirlstone musingly. "I like that idea, Good or bad, but always great! After all, we show a kind of belief in it in our daily practice. Every man is always making fancies about himself; but it is never his workaday self, but something else. The bank clerk who pictures himself as a financial Napoleon knows that

10 **Orion:** A constellation named for the giant hunter killed by Artemis of Greek legend.
11 **Ausonius:** Fourth-century Latin poet.
12 **Bakhtiari:** Nomadic tribes of Iran.

his own thin little soul is incapable of it; but he knows, too, that it is possible enough for that other bigger thing which is not his soul, but yet in some odd way is bound up with it. I fancy myself a field-marshal in a European war; but I know perfectly well that if the job were offered me, I should realise my incompetence and decline. I expect you rather picture yourself now and then as a sort of Julius Cæsar and empire-maker, and yet, with all respect, my dear chap, I think it would be rather too much for you."

"There was once a man," I said, "an early Victorian Whig, whose chief ambitions were to reform the criminal law and abolish slavery. Well, this dull, estimable man in his leisure moments was Emperor of Byzantium. He fought great wars and built palaces, and then, when the time for fancy was past, went into the House of Commons and railed against militarism and Tory extravagance. That particular king from Orion had a rather odd sort of earthly tenement."

Thirlstone was all interest. "A philosophic Whig and the throne of Byzantium. A pretty rum mixture! And yet—yet," and his eyes became abstracted. "Did you ever know Tommy Lacelles?"

"The man who once governed Deira? Retired now, and lives somewhere in Kent? Yes, I've met him once or twice. But why?"

"Because," said Thirlstone solemnly, "unless I'm greatly mistaken, Tommy was another such case, though no man ever guessed it except myself. I don't mind telling you the story, now that he is retired and vegetating in his ancestral pastures. Besides, the facts are all to his credit, and the explanation is our own business. . . .

"His wife was my cousin, and when she died Tommy was left a very withered, disconsolate man, with no particular object in life. We all thought he would give up the service, for he was hideously well off; and then one fine day, to our amazement, he was offered Deira, and accepted it. I was short of a job at the time, for my battalion was at home, and there was nothing going on anywhere, so I thought I should like to see what the East Coast of Africa was like, and wrote to Tommy about it. He jumped at me, cabled offering me what he called his Military Secretaryship, and I got seconded, and set off. I had never known him very well, but what I had seen I had liked; and I suppose he was glad to have one of Maggie's family with him, for he was still very low about her loss. I was in pretty good spirits, for it meant new experiences, and I had hopes of big game.

"You've never been to Deira? Well, there's no good trying to describe it, for it's the only place in the world like itself. God made it and left it to its own devices. The town is pretty enough, with its palms and green headland, and little scrubby islands in the river's mouth. It has the usual half-Arab, half-Portugee look—white green-shuttered houses, flat roofs, sallow little men in duck, and every type of nigger from the Somali to the Shangaan. There are some good buildings, and Government House was the mansion of some old Portugee seigneur, and was built when people in Africa were not in such a hurry as to-day. Inland there's a rolling forest country, beginning with decent trees and ending in mimosa-thorn, when the land begins to rise to the stony hills of the interior; and that poisonous yellow river rolls through it all, with a denser native population along its banks than you will find anywhere else north of the Zambesi. For about two months in the year the climate is Paradise, and for the rest you live in a Turkish bath, with every known kind of fever hanging about. We cleaned out the town and improved the sanitation, so there were few epidemics, but there was enough ordinary malaria to sicken a crocodile.

"The place was no special use to us. It had been annexed in spite of a tremendous Radical[13] outcry, and, upon my soul, it was one of the few cases where the Radicals had something to say for themselves. All we got by it was half a dozen of the nastiest problems an unfortunate governor can have to face. Ten years before it had been a decaying strip of coast, with a few trading firms in the town, and a small export of ivory and timber. But some years before Tommy took it up there had been a huge discovery of copper in the hills inland, a railway had been built, and there were several biggish mining settlements at the end of it. Deira itself was filled with offices of European firms, it had got a Stock Exchange of its own, and it was becoming the usual cosmopolitan playground. It had a knack, too, of getting the very worst breed of adventurer. I know something of your South African and Australian mining towns, and with all their faults they are run by white men. If they haven't much morals, they have a kind of decency which keeps them fairly straight. But for our sins we got a brand of Levantine Jew who was fit for nothing but making money and making trouble. They were always defying the law, and then, when they got into a hole, they squealed to Government for help, and started a racket in the home papers about the weakness of the Imperial power. The crux of the whole difficulty was the natives, who lived along the river and in the foothills. They were a hardy race of Kaffirs,[14] sort of far-away cousins to the Zulu, and till the mines were opened they had behaved well enough. They had arms, which we had never dared to take away, but they kept quiet and paid their hut-taxes like men. I got to know many of the chiefs, and liked them, for they were upstanding fellows to look at and heaven-born shikaris. However, when the Jews came along they wanted labour, and, since we did not see our way to allow them to add to the imported coolie population, they had to fall back upon the Labonga. At first things went smoothly. The chiefs were willing to let their men work for good wages, and for a time there was enough labour for everybody. But as the mines extended, and the natives, after making a few pounds, wanted to get back to their kraals,[15] there came a shortage; and since the work could not be allowed to slacken, the owners tried other methods. They made promises which they never intended to keep, and they stood on the letter of a law which the natives did not understand, and they employed touts who were little better than slave-dealers. They got the labour, of course, but soon they had put the Labonga into a state of unrest which a very little would turn into a rising.

"Into this kettle of fish Tommy was pitchforked, and when I arrived he was just beginning to understand how unpleasant it was. As I said before, I did not know him very well, and I was amazed to find how bad he was at his job. A more curiously

---

13 **Radical:** A British politician opposed to colonial expansion.
14 **Kaffirs:** In India, Hindus; but here, dark-skinned people, Africans.
15 **kraals:** Villages.

incompetent person I never met. He was a long, thin man, with a grizzled moustache, and a mild sleepy eye—not an impressive figure, except on a horse; and he had an odd lisp which made even a shrewd remark sound foolish. He was the most industrious creature in the world, and a model of official decorum. His papers were always in order, his dispatches always neat and correct, and I don't believe anyone ever caught him tripping in office work. But he had no more conception than a child of the kind of trouble that was brewing. He never knew an honest man from a rogue, and the result was that he received all unofficial communications with a polite disbelief. I used to force him to see people—miners, prospectors, traders, anyone who had something to say worth listening to, but it all glided smoothly off his mind. He was simply the most incompetent being ever created, living in the world as not being of it, or rather creating a little official world of his own, where all events happened on lines laid down by the Colonial Office, and men were like papers, to be rolled into packets and properly docketed. He had an Executive Council of people like himself, competent officials and blind bats at anything else. Then there was a precious Legislative Council, intended to represent the different classes of the population. There were several good men on it—one old trader called Mackay, for instance, who had been thirty years in the country—but most were nominees of the mining firms, and very seedy rascals at that. They were always talking about the rights of the white man, and demanding popular control of the government, and similar twaddle. The leader was a man who hailed from Hamburg, and called himself Le Foy—descended from a Crusader of the name of Levi—who was a jackal of one of the chief copper firms. He overflowed with Imperialist sentiment, and when he was not waving the flag he used to gush about the beauties of English country life and the grandeur of the English tradition. He hated me from the start, for when he talked of going 'home' I thought he meant Hamburg, and said so; and then a thing happened which made him hate me worse. He was infernally rude to Tommy, who, like the dear sheep he was, never saw it, and, if he had, wouldn't have minded. But one day I chanced to overhear some of his impertinences, so I hunted out my biggest sjambok[16] and lay in wait for Mr. Le Foy. I told him that he was a representative of the sovereign people, that I was a member of an effect bureaucracy, and that it would be most painful if unpleasantness arose between us. But, I added, I was prepared, if necessary, to sacrifice my official career to my private feelings, and if he dared to use such language again to his Majesty's representative I would give him a hiding he would remember till he found himself in Abraham's bosom. Not liking my sjambok, he became soap and butter at once, and held his tongue for a month or two.

"But though Tommy was no good at his job, he was a tremendous swell at other things. He was an uncommonly good linguist, and had always about a dozen hobbies which he slaved at; and when he found himself at Deira with a good deal of leisure, he became a bigger crank than ever. He had a lot of books which used to follow him about the world in zinc-lined boxes—your big paper-backed German

16 **sjambok:** A heavy whip made of hippopotamus hide.

books which mean research—and he was a Fellow of the Royal Society, and corresponded with half a dozen foreign shows. India was his great subject, but he had been in the Sudan and knew a good deal about African races. When I went out to him, his pet hobby was the Bantu, and he had acquired an amazing amount of miscellaneous learning. He knew all about their immigration from the North, and the Arab and Phœnician trade-routes, and the Portuguese occupation, and the rest of the history of that unpromising seaboard. The way he behaved in his researches showed the man. He worked hard at the Labonga language—which, I believe, is a linguistic curiosity of the first water—from missionary books and the conversation of tame Kaffirs. But he never thought of paying them a visit in their native haunts. I was constantly begging him to do it, but it was not Tommy's way. He did not care a straw about political expedience, and he liked to look at things through the medium of paper and ink. Then there were the Phœnician remains in the foothills where the copper was mined—old workings, and things which might have been forts or temples. He knew all that was to be known about them, but he had never seen them, and never wanted to. Once only he went to the hills, to open some new reservoirs and make the ordinary Governor's speech; but he went in a special train and stayed two hours, most of which was spent in lunching and being played to by brass bands.

"But, oddly enough, there was one thing which stirred him with an interest that was not academic. I discovered it by accident one day when I went into his study and found him struggling with a map of Central Asia. Instead of the mild, benevolent smile with which he usually greeted my interruptions, he looked positively furtive, and, I could have sworn, tried to shuffle the map under some papers. Now it happens that Central Asia is the part of the globe that I know better than most men, and I could not help picking up the map and looking at it. It was a wretched thing, and had got the Oxus two hundred miles out of its course. I pointed this out to Tommy, and to my amazement he became quite excited. 'Nonsense,' he said. 'You don't mean to say it goes south of that desert. Why, I meant to—' and then he stammered and stopped. I wondered what on earth he had meant to do, but I merely observed that I had been there, and knew. That brought Tommy out of his chair in real excitement. 'What!' he cried, 'you! You never told me,' and he started to fire off a round of questions, which showed that if he knew very little about the place, he had it a good deal in his mind. I drew some sketch-plans for him, and left him brooding over them.

"That was the first hint I got. The second was a few nights later, when we were smoking in the billiard-room. I had been reading Marco Polo, and the talk got on to Persia and drifted all over the north side of the Himalaya. Tommy, with an abstracted eye, talked of Alexander and Timour and Genghis Khan, and particularly of Prester John,[17] who was a character that took his fancy. I had told him that the natives in the Pamirs were true Persian stock, and this interested him greatly. 'Why was

---

17 **Alexander . . . Prester John:** Alexander the Great, fourth-century B.C.E. King of Macedonia and military conqueror whose conquests took him as far east as India; Timour, also known as Tamburlaine, fourteenth-century Tartar conqueror; Genghis Khan, twelfth-century Mongol conqueror; Prester John, mythical Christian ruler of a vast empire in central Asia.

there never a great state built up in those valleys?' he asked. 'You get nothing but a few wild conquerors rushing east and west, and then some squalid khanates. And yet all the materials were there—the stuff for a strong race, a rich land, the traditions of an old civilisation, and natural barriers against invasion.'

" 'I suppose they never found the man,' I said.

"He agreed. 'Their princes were sots, or they were barbarians of genius who could devastate to the gates of Peking or Constantinople, but could never build. They did not recognise their limits, and so they went out in a whirlwind. But if there had been a man of solid genius he might have built up the strongest nation on the globe. In time he could have annexed Persia and nibbled at China. He would have been rich, for he could tap all the inland trade-routes of Asia. He would have had to be a conqueror, for his people would be a race of warriors, but first and foremost he must have been a statesman. Think of such a civilisation, *the* Asian civilisation, growing up mysteriously behind the deserts and the ranges! That's my idea of Prester John. Russia would have been confined to the line of the Urals. China would have been absorbed. There would have been no Japan. The whole history of the world for the last few hundred years would have been different. It is the greatest of all the lost chances in history.' Tommy waxed pathetic over the loss.

"I was a little surprised at his eloquence, especially when he seemed to remember himself and stopped all of a sudden. But for the next week I got no peace with his questions. I told him all I knew of Bokhara, and Samarkand, and Tashkend, and Yarkand. I showed him the passes in the Pamirs and the Hindu Kush. I traced out the rivers, and I calculated distances; we talked over imaginary campaigns, and set up fanciful constitutions. It was a childish game, but I found it interesting enough. He spoke of it all with a curious personal tone which puzzled me, till one day when we were amusing ourselves with a fight on the Zarafshan, and I put in a modest claim to be allowed to win once in a while. For a second he looked at me in blank surprise. 'You can't,' he said; 'I've got to enter Samarkand before I can' . . . and he stopped again, with a glimmering sense in his face that he was giving himself away. And then I knew that I had surprised Tommy's secret. While he was muddling his own job, he was salving his pride with fancies of some wild career in Asia, where Tommy, disguised as the lord knows what Mussulman grandee, was hammering the little states into an empire.

"I did not think then as I think now, and I was amused to find so odd a trait in a dull man. I had known something of the kind before. I had met fellows who after their tenth peg[18] would begin to swagger about some ridiculous fancy of their own—their little private corner of soul showing for a moment when the drink had blown aside their common sense. True, I had never known the thing appear in cold blood and everyday life, but I assumed the case to be the same. I thought of it only as a harmless fancy, never imagining that it had anything to do with character. I put it down to that kindly imagination which is the old opiate for failures. So I played up

---

18 **peg:** Drink, usually whisky.

to Tommy with all my might, and though he became very discreet after the first betrayal, having hit upon the clue, I knew what to look for, and I found it. When I told him that the Labonga were in a devil of a mess, he would look at me with an empty face and change the subject; but once among the Turcomans his eye would kindle, and he would slave at his confounded folly with sufficient energy to reform the whole East Coast. It was the spark that kept the man alive. Otherwise he would have been as limp as a rag, but this craziness put life into him, and made him carry his head in the air and walk like a free man. I remember he was very keen about any kind of martial poetry. He used to go about crooning Scott and Macaulay to himself, and when we went for a walk or a ride he wouldn't speak for miles, but keep smiling to himself and humming bits of songs. I dare say he was very happy—far happier than your stolid, competent man, who sees only the one thing to do, and does it. Tommy was muddling his particular duty, but building glorious palaces in the air.

"One day Mackay, the old trader, came to me after a sitting of the precious Legislative Council. We were very friendly, and I had done all I could to get the Government to listen to his views. He was a dour, ill-tempered Scotsman, very anxious for the safety of his property, but perfectly careless about any danger to himself.

"'Captain Thirlstone,' he said, 'that Governor of yours is a damned fool.'

"Of course I shut him up very brusquely, but he paid no attention. 'He just sits and grins, and lets yon Pentecostal crowd we've gotten here as a judgment for our sins do what they like wi' him. God kens what'll happen. I would go home tomorrow, if I could realise without an immoderate loss. For the day of reckoning is at hand. Maark my words, Captain—at hand.'

"I said I agreed with him about the approach of trouble, but that the Governor would rise to the occasion. I told him that people like Tommy were only seen at their best in a crisis, and that he might be perfectly confident that when it arrived he would get a new idea of the man. I said this, but of course I did not believe a word of it. I thought Tommy was only a dreamer, who had rotted any grit he ever possessed by his mental opiates. At that time I did not understand about the Kings from Orion.

"And then came the thing we had all been waiting for—a Labonga rising. A week before I had got leave and had gone up country, partly to shoot, but mainly to see for myself what trouble was brewing. I kept away from the river, and therefore missed the main native centres, but such kraals as I passed had a look I did not like. The chiefs were almost always invisible, and the young bloods were swaggering about and bukking to each other, while the women were grinding maize as if for some big festival. However, after a bit the country seemed to grow more normal, and I went into the foothills to shoot, fairly easy in my mind. I had got up to a place called Shimonwe, on the Pathi River, where I had ordered letters to be sent, and one night coming in from a hard day after kudu[19] found a post-runner half-dead of fatigue with

19 **kudu:** African antelope.

a chit from Utterson, who commanded a police district twenty miles nearer the coast. It said simply that all the young men round about him had cleared out and appeared to be moving towards Deira, that he was in a devil of a quandary, and that, since the police were under the Governor, he would take his orders from me.

"It looked as if the heather were fairly on fire at last, so I set off early next morning to trek back. About midday I met Utterson, a very badly scared little man, who had come to look for me. It seemed that his policemen had bolted in the night and gone to join the rising, leaving him with two white sergeants, barely fifty rounds of ammunition, and no neighbour for a hundred miles. He said that the Labonga chiefs were not marching to the coast, as he had thought, but north along the eastern foothills in the direction of the mines. This was better news, for it meant that in all probability the railway would remain open. It was my business to get somehow to my chief, and I was in the deuce of a stew how to manage it. It was no good following the line of the natives' march, for they would have been between me and my goal, and the only way was to try and outflank them by going due east, in the Deira direction, and then turning north, so as to strike the railway about half-way to the mines. I told Utterson we had better scatter, otherwise we should have no chance of getting through a densely populated native country. So, about five in the afternoon, I set off with my chief shikari, who, by good luck, was not a Labonga, and dived into the jungly bush which skirts the hills.

"For three days I had a baddish time. We steered by the stars, travelling chiefly by night, and we showed extraordinary skill in missing the water-holes. I had a touch of fever and got light-headed, and it was all I could do to struggle through the thick grass and wait-a-bit thorns. My clothes were torn to rags, and I grew so footsore that it was agony to move. All the same we travelled fast, and there was no chance of our missing the road, for any route due north was bound to cut the railway. I had the most sickening uncertainty about what was to come next. Hely, who was in command at Deira, was a good enough man, but he had only three companies of white troops, and the black troops were as likely as not to be on their way to join the rebels. It looked as if we should have a Cawnpore[20] business on a small scale, though I thanked Heaven there were no women in the case. As for Tommy, he would probably be repeating platitudes in Deira and composing an intelligent dispatch on the whole subject.

"About four in the afternoon of the third day I struck the line near a little station called Palala. I saw by the look of the rails that trains were still running, and my hopes revived. At Palala there was a coolie stationmaster, who gave me a drink and a little food, after which I slept heavily in his office till wakened by the arrival of an up train. It contained one of the white companies and a man Davidson, of the 101st, who was Hely's second in command. From him I had news that took away my breath. The Governor had gone up the line two days before with an A.D.C.[21] and old

20 **Cawnpore:** Site of a bitter and bloody conflict during the Indian Mutiny of 1857.
21 **A.D.C.:** Aide-de-camp.

Mackay. 'The sportsman has got a move on him at last,' said Davidson, 'but what he means to do Heaven only knows. The Labonga are at the mines, and a kind of mine-guard has been formed for defence. The joke of it is that most of the magnates are treed up there, for the railway is cut and they can't get away. I don't envy your chief the job of schooling that nervous crowd.'

"I went on with Davidson, and very early next morning we came to a broken culvert and had to stop. There we stuck for three hours till the down train arrived, and with it Hely. He was for ordinary a stolid soul, but I never saw a man in such a fever of excitement. He gripped me by the arm and fairly shook me. 'That old man of yours is a hero,' he cried. 'The Lord forgive me! and I have always crabbed him.'

"I implored him in Heaven's name to tell me what was up, but he would say nothing till he had had his pow-wow with Davidson. It seemed that he was bringing all his white troops up the line for some great demonstration that Tommy had conceived. Davidson went back to Deira, while we mended the culvert and got the men transferred to the other train. Then I screwed the truth out of Hely. Tommy had got up to the mines before the rebels arrived, and had found as fine a chaos as can be imagined. He did not seem to have had any doubts what to do. There were a certain number of white workmen, hard fellows from Cornwall mostly, with a few Australians, and these he got together with Mackay's help and organised into a pretty useful corps. He set them to guard the offices, and gave them strict orders to shoot at sight anyone attempting to leave. Then he collected the bosses and talked to them like a father. What he said Hely did not know, except that he had damned their eyes pretty heartily, and told them what a set of swine they were, making trouble which they had not the pluck to face. Whether from Mackay, or from his own intelligence, or from a memory of my neglected warnings, he seemed to have got a tight grip on the facts at last. Meanwhile, the Labonga were at the doors, chanting their battle-songs half a mile away, and shots were heard from the far pickets. If they had tried to rush the place then, all would have been over, but, luckily, that was never their way of fighting. They sat down in camp to make their sacrifices and consult their witch-doctors, and presently Hely arrived with the first troops, having come in on the northern flank when he found the line cut. He had been in time to hear the tail-end of Tommy's final address to the mine-owners. He told them, in words which Hely said he could never have imagined coming from his lips, that they would be well served if the Labonga cleaned the whole place out. Only, he said, that would be against the will of Britain, and it was his business, as a loyal servant, to prevent it. Then, after giving Hely his instructions, he had put on his uniform, gold lace and all, and every scrap of bunting he possessed—all the orders and 'Golden Stars' of half a dozen Oriental States where he had served. He made Ashurst, the A.D.C., put on his best Hussar's kit, and Mackay rigged himself out in a frock-coat and a topper;[22] and the three set out on horseback for the Labonga. 'I believe he'll bring it off,' said Hely, with wild eyes, 'and, by Heaven, if he does, it'll be the best thing since John Nicholson!'

22 **frock-coat and a topper:** A long, double-breasted coat and a top hat.

"For the rest of the way I sat hugging myself with excitement. The miracle of miracles seemed to have come. The old, slack, incompetent soul in Tommy seemed to have been driven out by that other spirit, which had hitherto been content to dream of crazy victories on the Oxus. I cursed my folly in having missed it all, for I would have given my right hand to be with him among the Labonga. I envied that young fool Ashurst his luck in being present at that queer transformation scene. I had not a doubt that Tommy would bring it off all right. The Kings from Orion don't go into action without coming out on top. As we got near the mines I kept my ears open for the sound of shots; but all was still—not even the kind of hubbub a native force makes when it is on the move. Something had happened, but what it was no man could guess. When we got to where the line was up, we made very good time over the five miles to the mines. No one interfered with us, and the nearer we got the greater grew my certainty. Soon we were at the pickets, who had nothing to tell us; and then we were racing up the long sandy street to the offices, and there, sitting smoking on the doorstep of the hotel, surrounded by everybody who was not on duty, were Mackay and Ashurst.

"They were an odd pair. Ashurst still wore his uniform; but he seemed to have been rolling about in it on the ground; his sleek hair was wildly ruffled, and he was poking holes in the dust with his sword. Mackay had lost his topper, and wore a disreputable cap, his ancient frock-coat was without buttons, and his tie had worked itself up behind his ears. They talked excitedly to each other, now and then vouchsafing a scrap of information to an equally excited audience. When they saw me they rose and rushed for me, and dragged me between them up the street, while the crowd tailed at our heels.

"'Ye're a true prophet, Captain Thirlstone,' Mackay began, 'and I ask your pardon for doubting you. Ye said the Governor only needed a crisis to behave like a man. Well, the crisis has come; and if there's a man alive in this sinful world, it's that chief o' yours.' And then his emotion overcame him, and, hard-bitten devil as he was, he sat down on the ground and gasped with hysterical laughter, while Ashurst, with a very red face, kept putting the wrong end of a cigarette in his mouth and swearing profanely.

"I never remember a madder sight. There was the brassy blue sky and reddish granite rock and acres of thick red dust. The scrub had that metallic greenness which you find in all copper places. Pretty unwholesome it looked, and the crowd, which had got round us again, was more unwholesome still. Fat Jew boys, with diamond rings on dirty fingers and greasy linen cuffs, kept staring at us with twitching lips; and one or two smarter fellows in riding-breeches, mine managers and suchlike, tried to show their pluck by nervous jokes. And in the middle was Mackay, with his damaged frocker, drawling out his story in broad Scots.

"'He made this laddie put on his braws,[23] and he commandeered this iniquitous garment for me. I've raxed its seams, and it'll never look again on the man that owns

---

23 **braws**: Best clothes.

it. Syne he arrayed himself in purple and fine linen till he was like the king's daughter, all glorious without; and says he to me, "Mackay," he says, "we'll go and talk to these uncovenanted deevils in their own tongue. We'll visit them at home, Mackay," he says. "They're none such bad fellows, but they want a little humouring from men like you and me." So we got on our horses and started the procession—the Governor with his head in the air, and the laddie endeavouring to look calm and collected, and me praying to the God of Israel and trying to keep my breeks from working up above my knees. I've been in Kaffir wars afore, but I never thought I would ride without weapon of any kind into such a black Armageddon. I am a peaceable man for ordinair', and a canny one, but I wasna myself in that hour. Man, Thirlstone, I was that overcome by the spirit of your chief, that if he had bidden me gang alone on the same errand, I wouldna say but what I would have gone.

" 'We hadna ridden half a mile before we saw the indunas and their men, ten thousand if there was one, and terrible as an army with banners. I speak feeguratively, for they hadna the scrap of a flag among them. They were beating the war-drums, and the young men were dancing with their big skin-shields and wagging their ostrich feathers, so I saw they were out for business. I'll no' say but what my blood ran cold, but the Governor's eye got brighter and his back stiffer. "Kings may be blest," I says to myself, "but thou art glorious."

" 'We rode straight for the centre of the crowd, where the young men were thickest and the big war-drums lay. As soon as they saw us a dozen lifted their spears and ran out to meet us. But they stopped after six steps. The sun glinted on the Governor's gold lace and my lum hat, and no doubt they thought we were heathen deities descended from the heavens. Down they went on their faces, and then back like rabbits to the rest, while the drums stopped, and the whole body awaited our coming in a silence like the tomb.

" 'Never a word we spoke, but just jogged on with our chins cocked up till we were forenent the big drum, where yon old scoundrel Umgazi was standing with his young men looking as black as sin. For a moment their spears were shaking in their hands, and I heard the click of a breech-bolt. If we had winked an eye we would have become pincushions that instant. But some unearthly power upheld us. Even the laddie kept a stiff face, and for me I forgot my breeks in watching the Governor. He looked as solemn as an archangel, and comes to a halt opposite Umgazi, where he glowers at the old man for maybe three minutes, while we formed up behind him. Their eyes fell before his, and by and by their spears dropped to their sides. "The father has come to his children," says he in their own tongue. "What do the children seek from their father?"

" 'Ye see the cleverness of the thing. The man's past folly came to help him. The natives had never seen the Governor before till they beheld him in gold lace and a cocked hat on a muckle horse, speaking their own tongue and looking like a destroying angel. I tell you the Labonga's knees were loosed under them. They durstna speak a word until the Governor repeated the question in the same quiet, steely voice. "You seek something," he said, "else you had not come out to meet me in your numbers. The father waits to hear the children's desires."

"'Then Umgazi found his tongue and began an uneasy speech. The mines, he said, truly enough, were the abode of devils, who compelled the people to work under the ground. The crops were unreaped and the buck went unspeared, because there were no young men left to him. Their father had been away or asleep, they thought, for no help had come from him; therefore it had seemed good to them, being freemen and warriors, to seek help for themselves.

"'The Governor listened to it all with a set face. Then he smiled at them with supernatural assurance. They were fools, he said, and people of little wit, and he flung the better part of the Book of Job at their heads. The Lord kens where the man got his uncanny knowledge of the Labonga. He had all their heathen customs by heart, and he played with them like a cat with a mouse. He told them they were damned rascals to make such a stramash, and damned fools to think they could frighten the white man by their demonstrations. There was no brag about his words, just a calm statement of fact. At the same time, he said, he had no mind to let anyone wrong his children, and if any wrong had been done it should be righted. It was not meet,[24] he said, that the young men should be taken from the villages unless by their own consent, though it was his desire that such young men as could be spared should have a chance of earning an honest penny. And then he fired at them some stuff about the British Empire and the King, and you could see the Labonga imbibing it like water. The man in a cocked hat might have told them that the sky was yellow, and they would have swallowed it.

"'"I have spoken," he says at last, and there was a great shout from the young men, and old Umgazi looked pretty foolish. They were coming round our horses to touch our stirrups with their noses, but the Governor stopped them.

"'"My children will pile their weapons in front of me," says he, "to show me how they have armed themselves, and likewise to prove that their folly is at an end. All except a dozen," says he, "whom I select as a bodyguard." And there and then he picked twelve lusty savages for his guard, while the rest without a cheep stacked their spears and guns forenent the big drum.

"'Then he turned to us and spoke in English. "Get back to the mines hell-for-leather, and tell them what's happening, and see that you get up some kind of a show for to-morrow at noon. I will bring the chiefs, and we'll feast them. Get all the bands you can, and let them play me in. Tell the mines fellows to look active, for it's the chance of their lives." Then he says to the Labonga, "My men will return," he says, "but as for me I will spend the night with my children. Make ready food, but let no beer be made, for it is a solemn occasion."

"'And so we left him. I will not describe how I spent last night mysel', but I have something to say about this remarkable phenomenon. I could enlarge on the triumph of mind over matter. . . .'

"Mackay did not enlarge. He stopped, cocked his ears, and looked down the road, from which came the strains of *Annie Laurie*, played with much spirit but

---

24 **meet:** Proper; appropriate.

grievously out of tune. Followed *The British Grenadiers,* and then an attempt at *The March of the Priests.* Mackay rose in excitement and began to crane his disreputable neck, while the band—a fine scratch collection of instruments—took up their stand at the end of the street, flanked by a piper in khaki who performed when their breath failed. Mackay chuckled with satisfaction. 'The deevils have entered into the spirit of my instructions,' he said. 'In a wee bit the place will be like Falkirk Tryst for din.'

"Punctually at twelve there came a great hullabaloo up the road, the beating of drums and the yelling of natives, and presently the procession hove in sight. There was Tommy on his horse, and on each side of him six savages with feather head-dress, and shields and war-paint complete. After him trooped about thirty of the great chiefs, walking two by two, for all the world like an Aldershot parade.[25] They carried no arms, but the bodyguard shook their spears, and let yells out of them that would have scared Julius Cæsar. Then the band started in, and the piper blew up, and the mines people commenced to cheer, and I thought the heavens would fall. Long before Tommy came abreast of me I knew what I should see. His uniform looked as if it had been slept in, and his orders were all awry. But he had his head flung back, and his eyes very bright and his jaw set square. He never looked to right or left, never recognised me or anybody, for he was seeing something quite different from the red road and the white shanties and the hot sky."

The fire had almost died out. Thirlstone stooped for a moment and stirred the peats.

"Yes," he said, "I knew that in his fool's ear the trumpets of all Asia were ringing, and the King of Bokhara was entering Samarkand."

QUESTIONS

1. Does the opening frame tale serve any thematic or artistic purpose? Explain your answer.

2. The ostensible subject of Thirlstone's story is the unexpected bravery of Tommy Lacelles. Is this the real subject of the story?

3. How are Africans portrayed in Thirlstone's story?

4. What does the story say about the relationship between British colonial officers and Africans? Point to specific passages to support your answer.

5. In what ways does the story reinforce ideas of racial superiority and inferiority? Point to specific passages to support your answer.

6. Compare "Heart of Darkness" with Buchan's "The Kings of Orion." Are there significant differences in the attitudes of their respective narrators? In their depictions of Africans? In their depictions of whites?

---

25 **Aldershot parade:** A parade of the Queen's personal bodyguard.

Leonard Woolf

(1880–1969)

If Leonard Woolf is known at all today among students of literature, it is primarily as the husband of the novelist Virginia Woolf, or perhaps as the founder of the Hogarth Press or as a member of the Bloomsbury Group of artists, writers, and scholars. But in his own time and among those who study British social and political history, Woolf earned a solid reputation as a political thinker, activist, essayist, editor, and public servant.

He was born into upper-middle-class privilege, the son of a successful lawyer, Sidney Woolf, and his wife Marie, who was born in Holland. The Woolfs were reformed Jews in a country that still harbored significant anti-Semitism. Tragically, Sidney Woolf died when Leonard was only twelve, leaving Marie to raise ten children on a barely adequate inheritance. Nevertheless, Leonard was sent to St. Paul's School and later to Trinity College, Cambridge, where among his classmates were luminaries such as the philosopher G. E. Moore, the writer Lytton Strachey, and the economist John Maynard Keynes.

Upon leaving university, Woolf joined many of his fellow graduates by tying his fortunes to those of the Empire, joining the Ceylon (present-day Sri Lanka) Service in 1904. Unlike most of his contemporaries, however, Woolf rose rapidly through the colonial ranks, becoming an assistant agent in charge of the Uva Province on the south coast of the island in 1908. Woolf's years in Ceylon brought him into daily and intimate contact with the workings of the Empire, and like George Orwell, he was frequently appalled by the beatings, executions, and oppressions of imperialism. In 1911, he qualified for a year's leave in England and at the end of that time resigned his post, partly in response to his feelings about the Empire, but also because he had fallen in love with Virginia, whom he married in 1912.

Woolf's first attempts at writing were fiction, including *Stories of the East* (1921), from which "Pearls and Swine" is taken. But fiction paid too poorly to support the young couple, so Leonard turned to journalism. Just as he had become disillusioned with the Empire, so was he becoming increasingly aware of Britain's social and economic inequalities, and his contacts with other liberal thinkers of the day, particularly Beatrice and Sidney Webb, turned him to socialism, a cause that he championed for most of his life. Books on social and political issues followed rapidly, such as *The Framework for a Lasting Peace* (1917), *Empire and Commerce in Africa* (1919), and *Mandates and Empire* (1920). Woolf also became one of the best and most influential editors of his time, editing the *Contemporary Review* (1920–1922), *Nation and Athenaeum* (1923–1930), and *Political Quarterly* (1931–1959).

"Pearls and Swine" is based directly on Woolf's experiences in Ceylon. The second volume of his autobiography, *Growing* (1961), which chronicles the years 1904–1911, contains photographs of scenes that come directly from the story; indeed, reversing the usual practice of memoir writers, he quotes from the fictional story as a way of illustrating his experiences. The manner of the story is Kiplingesque, but there is little ambiguity about the narrator's attitude toward the ideas of his listeners, who represent all too accurately many of the "hard line" views of the Empire's supporters in the early years of the twentieth century.

_____

Pearls and Swine   1915

I had finished my hundred up[1]—or rather he had—with the Colonel and we strolled into the smoking room for a smoke and a drink round the fire before turning in. There were three other men already round the fire and they widened their circle to take us in. I didn't know them, hadn't spoken to them or indeed to anyone except the Colonel in the large gaudy uncomfortably comfortable hotel. I was run down, out of sorts generally, and—like a fool, I thought now—had taken a week off to eat, or rather to read the menus of interminable table d'hote dinners, to play golf and to walk on the "front" at Torquay.[2]

I had only arrived the day before, but the Colonel (retired) a jolly tubby little man—with white moustaches like two S's lying side by side on the top of his stupid red lips and his kind choleric eyes bulging out on a life which he was quite content never for a moment to understand—made it a point, my dear Sir, to know every new arrival within one hour after he arrived.

We got our drinks and as, rather forgetting that I was in England, I murmured the Eastern formula, I noticed vaguely one of the other three glance at me over his shoulder for a moment. The Colonel stuck out his fat little legs in front of him, turning up his neatly shoed toes before the blaze. Two of the others were talking, talking as men so often do in the comfortable chairs of smoking rooms between ten and eleven at night, earnestly, seriously, of what they call affairs, or politics or questions. I listened to their fat, full-fed assured voices in that heavy room which smelt of solidity, safety, horsehair furniture, tobacco smoke, and the faint civilized aroma of whisky and soda. It came as a shock to me in that atmosphere that they were discussing India and the East: it does you know every now and again. Sentimental? Well, I expect one is sentimental about it, having lived there. It doesn't seem to go with solidity and horsehair furniture: the fifteen years come back to one in one moment all in a heap. How one hated it and how one loved it!

I suppose they had started on the Durbar and the King's visit.[3] They had got on to Indian unrest, to our position in India, its duties, responsibilities, to the problem

_____

1 **hundred up:** The narrator and the Colonel have been playing billiards.
2 **Torquay:** A resort town on the south coast of England.
3 **Durbar and the King's visit:** A durbar is a great ceremonial occasion. The visit is probably that of King George V, who held a coronation durbar in Delhi in December 1911.

of East and West. They hadn't been there of course, they hadn't even seen the brothel and cafe chantant at Port Said suddenly open out into that pink and blue desert that leads you through Africa and Asia into the heart of the East. But they knew all about it, they had solved, with their fat voices and in their fat heads, riddles, older than the Sphinx, of peoples remote and ancient and mysterious whom they had never seen and could never understand. One was, I imagine, a stock jobber,[4] plump and comfortable with a greasy forehead and a high colour in his cheeks, smooth shiny brown hair and a carefully grown small moustache: a good dealer in the market: sharp and confident, with a loud voice and shifty eyes. The other was a clergyman: need I say more? Except that he was more of a clergyman even than most clergymen, I mean that he wore tight things—leggings don't they call them? or breeches?—round his calves. I never know what it means: whether they are bishops or rural deans or archdeacons or archimandrites. In any case I mistrust them even more than the black trousers: they seem to close the last door for anything human to get in through the black clothes. The dog collar[5] closes up the armour above, and below, as long as they *were* trousers, at any rate some whiff of humanity might have eddied up the legs of them and touched bare flesh. But the gaiters button them up finally, irremediably, for ever.

I expect he was an archdeacon; he was saying: "You can't impose Western civilization upon an Eastern people—I believe I'm right in saying that there are over two hundred millions in our Indian Empire—without a little disturbance. I'm a Liberal you know. I've been a Liberal my whole life—family tradition—though I grieve to say I could not follow Mr. Gladstone on the Home Rule question.[6] It seems to me a good sign, this movement, an awakening among the people. But don't misunderstand me, my dear Sir, I am not making any excuses for the methods of the extremists. Apart from my calling—I have a natural horror of violence. Nothing can condone violence, the taking of human life, it's savagery, terrible, terrible."

"They don't put it down with a strong enough hand," the stock jobber was saying almost fiercely. "There's too much Liberalism in the East, too much namby-pambyism. It is all right here, of course, but it's not suited to the East. They want a strong hand. After all they owe us something: we aren't going to take all the kicks and leave them all the halfpence. Rule' em, I say, rule 'em, if you're going to rule 'em. Look after 'em, of course: give 'em schools, if they want education—schools, hospitals, roads, and railways. Stamp out the plague, fever, famine. But let 'em know you are top dog. That's the way to run an eastern country. I am a white man, you're black; I'll treat you well, give you courts and justice; but I'm the superior race, I'm master here."

The man who had looked round at me when I said "Here's luck!" was fidgeting about in his chair uneasily. I examined him more carefully. There was no mistaking

4 **stock jobber:** Stock broker.
5 **dog collar:** Slang term for a clergyman's collar.
6 **Home Rule question:** William Gladstone, four-time prime minister of England between 1868 and 1894, twice proposed independence for Ireland, but was defeated by the House of Commons.

the cause of his irritation. It was written on his face, the small close-cut white mustache, the smooth firm cheeks with the red-and-brown glow on them, the innumerable wrinkles round the eyes, and above all the eyes themselves, that had grown slow and steady and unastonished, watching that inexplicable, meaningless march of life under blazing suns. He had seen it, he knew. "Ah," I thought, "he is beginning to feel his liver. If he would only begin to speak, we might have some fun."

H'm, h'm, said the archdeacon. "Of course there's something in what you say. Slow and sure. Things may be going too fast, and, as I say, I'm entirely for putting down violence and illegality with a strong hand. And after all, my dear Sir, when you say we're the superior race you imply a duty. Even in secular matters we must spread the light. I believe—devoutly—I am not ashamed to say so—that we are. We're reaching the people there, it's the cause of the unrest, we set them an example. They desire to follow. Surely, surely we should help to guide their feet. I don't speak without a certain knowledge. I take a great interest, I may even say that I play my small part, in the work of one of our great missionary societies. I see our young men, many of them risen from the people, educated often, and highly educated (I venture to think), in Board Schools.[7] I see them go out full of high ideals to live among those poor people. And I see them when they come back and tell me their tales honestly, unostentatiously. It is always the same, a message of hope and comfort. We are getting at the people, by example, by our lives, by our conduct. They respect us."

I heard a sort of groan, and then quite loud, these strange words:

"Kasimutal Rameswaramvaraiyil terintavan."

"I beg your pardon," said the Archdeacon, turning to the interrupter.

"I beg yours. Tamil, Tamil, proverb. Came into my mind. Spoke without thinking. Beg yours."

"Not at all. Very interesting. You've lived in India? Would you mind my asking you for a translation?"

"It means 'he knows everything between Benares and Rameswaram.' Last time I heard it, an old Tamil, seventy or eighty years old, perhaps—he looked a hundred—used it of one of your young men. The young man, by the bye, had been a year and a half in India. D'you understand?"

"Well, I'm not sure I do: I've heard, of course, of Benares, but Rameswaram, I don't seem to remember the name."

I laughed; I could not help it; the little Anglo-Indian looked so fierce. "Ah!" he said, "you don't recollect the name. Well, it's pretty famous out there. Great temple—Hindu—right at the southern tip of India. Benares, you know, is up north. The old Tamil meant that your friend knew everything in India after a year and a half: *he* didn't you know, after seventy, after seven thousand years. Perhaps you also don't recollect that the Tamils are Dravidians? They've been there since the beginning of time, before we came, or the Dutch or Portuguese or the Muhammadans, or our cousins, the other Aryans. Uncivilized, black? Perhaps, but, if they're black, after all

---

7 **Board Schools:** Public schools established by the 1870 Education Act.

it's *their* suns, through thousands of years, that have blackened them. They ought to know, if anyone does: but they don't, they don't pretend to. But you two gentlemen, you seem to know everything between Kasimutal—that's Benares—and Rameswaram, without having seen the sun at all."

"My dear sir," began the Archdeacon pompously, but the jobber interrupted him. He had had a number of whiskies and sodas, and was quite heated. "It's very easy to sneer: it doesn't mean because you've lived a few years in a place . . ."

"I? Thirty. But they—seven thousand at least."

"I say, it doesn't mean because you've lived thirty years in a place that you know all about it. Ramisram, or whatever the damned place is called, I've never heard of it and don't want to. You do, that's part of your job, I expect. But I read the papers, I've read books too, mind you, about India. I know what's going on. One knows enough—enough—data: East and West and the difference: I can form an opinion— I've a right to it even if I've never heard of Ramis what d'you call it. You've lived there and you can't see the wood for the trees. We see it because we're out of it—see it at a distance."

"Perhaps," said the Archdeacon "there's a little misunderstanding. The discussion—if I may say so—is getting a little heated—unnecessarily, I think. We hold our views. This gentleman has lived in the country. He holds others. I'm sure it would be most interesting to hear them. But I confess I didn't quite gather them from what he said."

The little man was silent: he sat back, his eyes fixed on the ceiling. Then he smiled.

"I won't give you views," he said. "But if you like I'll give you what you call de-tails, things seen, facts. Then you can give me *your* views on 'em."

They murmured approval.

"Let's see, it's fifteen, seventeen years ago. I had a district then about as big as England. There may have been twenty Europeans in it, counting the missionaries, and twenty million Tamils and Telegus. I expect nineteen million of the Tamils and Telegus never saw a white man from one year's end to the other, or if they did, they caught a glimpse of me under a sun helmet riding through their village on a flea-bitten grey Indian mare. Well, Providence had so designed it that there was a stretch of coast in that district which was a barren wilderness of sand and scrubby thorn jungle—and nothing else—for three hundred miles; no towns, no villages, no water, just sand and trees for three hundred miles. O, and sun, I forget that, blazing sun. And in the water off the shore at one place there were oysters, millions of them lying and breeding at the bottom, four or five fathoms down. And in the oysters, or some of them, were pearls.

Well, we rule India and the sea, so the sea belongs to us, and the oysters are in the sea and the pearls are in the oysters. Therefore of course the pearls belong to us. But they lie in five fathoms. How to get 'em up, that's the question. You'd think being progressive we'd dredge for them or send down divers in diving dresses. But we don't, not in India. They've been fishing up the oysters and the pearls there ever since the beginning of time, naked brown men diving feet first out of long wooden boats into the blue sea and sweeping the oysters off the bottom of the sea into baskets slung to their sides. They were doing it centuries and centuries before we came, when—as someone said—our ancestors were herding swine on the plains of Norway. The Arabs of the Persian Gulf came down in dhows[8] and fished up pearls which found their way to Solomon and the Queen of Sheba. They still come, and the Tamils and Moormen of the district come, and they fish 'em up in the same way, diving out of long wooden boats shaped and rigged as in Solomon's time, as they were centuries before him and the Queen of Sheba. No difference, you see, except that we—Government I mean—take two-thirds of all the oysters fished up: the other third we give to the diver, Arab or Tamil or Moorman, for his trouble in fishing 'em up.

We used to have a Pearl Fishery about once in three years. It lasted six weeks or two months just between the two monsoons, the only time the sea is calm there. And I had, of course, to go and superintend it, to take Government's share of oysters, to sell them, to keep order, to keep out K.D.'s—that means Known Depredators—and smallpox and cholera. We had what we called a camp, in the wilderness remember, on the hot sand down there by the sea: it sprang up in a night, a town, a big town of thirty or forty thousand people, a little India, Asia almost, even a bit of Africa. They came from all districts: Tamils, Telegus, fat Chetties, Parsees, Bombay merchants, Sinhalese from Ceylon, the Arabs and their negroes, Somalis probably, who used to be their slaves. It was an immense gamble; everyone bought oysters for the chance of the prizes in them: it would have taken fifty white men to superintend that camp properly: they gave me one, a little boy of twenty-four fresh-cheeked from England, just joined the service. He had views, he had been educated in a Board School, won prizes, scholarships, passed the Civil Service 'Exam.' Yes, he had views; he used to explain them to me when he first arrived. He got some new ones I think before he got out of that camp. You'd say he only saw details, things happen, facts, data. Well, he did that too. He saw men die—he hadn't seen that in his Board School—die of plague or cholera, like flies, all over the place, under the trees, in the boats, outside the little door of his own little hut. And he saw flies, too, millions, billions of them all day long buzzing, crawling over everything, his hands, his little fresh face, his food. And he smelt the smell of millions of decaying oysters all day long and all night long for six weeks. He was sick four or five times a day for six weeks; the smell did that. Insanitary? Yes, very. Why is it allowed? The pearls, you see, the pearls: you must get them out of the oysters as you must get the oysters out of the sea. And the pearls are very often small and embedded in the oyster's body. So you put all the oysters, millions of them, in dug-out canoes in the sun to rot. They rot very well in that sun, and the flies come and lay eggs in them, and maggots come out of the eggs and more flies come out of the maggots; and between them all, the maggots and the sun, the oysters' bodies disappear, leaving the pearls and a little sand at the bottom of the canoe. Unscientific? Yes, perhaps; but after all it's our camp, our fishery,—just as it was in

---

8 **dhows:** Arabic boats with triangular sails.

Solomon's time? At any rate, you see, it's the East. But whatever it is, and whatever the reason, the result involves flies, millions of them and a smell, a stench—Lord! I can smell it now.

There was one other white man there. He was a planter, so he said, and he had come to 'deal' in pearls. He dropped in on us out of a native boat at sunset on the second day. He had a red face and a red nose, he was unhealthily fat for the East: the whites of his eyes were rather blue and rather red: they were also watery. I noticed that his hand shook, and that he first refused and then took a whisky and soda—a bad sign in the East. He wore very dirty white clothes and a vest[9] instead of a shirt: he apparently had no baggage of any sort. But he was a white man, and so he ate with us that night and a good many nights afterwards.

In the second week he had his first attack of D.T.[10] We pulled him through, Robson and I, in the intervals of watching over the oysters. When he hadn't got D.T., he talked: he was a great talker, he also had views. I used to sit in the evenings—they were rare—when the fleet of boats had got in early and the oysters had been divided, in front of my hut and listen to him and Robson settling India and Asia, Africa too probably. We sat there in our long chairs on the sand looking out over the purple sea, towards a sunset like blood shot with gold. Nothing moved or stirred except the flies which were going to sleep in a mustard tree close by; they hung in buzzing clusters, billions of them on the smooth leaves and little twigs: literally it was black with them. It looked as if the whole tree had suddenly broken out all over into some disease of living black currants. Even the sea seemed to move with an effort in the hot, still air; only now and again a little wave would lift itself up very slowly, very wearily, poise itself for a moment, and then fall with a weary little thud on the sand.

I used to watch them, I say, in the hot still air and the smell of dead oysters—it pushed up against your face like something solid talking, talking in their long chairs, while the sweat stood out in little drops on their foreheads and trickled from time to time down their noses. There wasn't, I suppose, anything wrong with Robson, he was all right at bottom, but he annoyed me, irritated me in that smell. He was too cocksure altogether, of himself, of his Board School education, of life, of his 'views.' He was going to run India on new lines, laid down in some damned Manual of Political Science out of which they learn life in Board Schools and extension lectures. He would run his own life, I dare say, on the same lines, laid down in some other text book or primer. He hadn't seen anything, but he knew exactly what it was all like. There was nothing curious, astonishing, unexpected, in life, he was ready for any emergency. And we were all wrong, all on the wrong tack in dealing with natives! He annoyed me a little, you know, when the thermometer stood at 99, at 6 p.m., but what annoyed me still more was that they—the natives!—were all wrong too. They too had to be taught how to live—and die, too, I gathered.

9 **vest:** Sleeveless undershirt.
10 **D.T.:** Delirium tremens, violent tremors brought on by alcohol abuse.

But his views were interesting, very interesting—especially in the long chairs there under the immense Indian sky, with the camp at our hands—just as it had been in the time of Moses and Abraham—and behind us the jungle for miles, and behind that India, three hundred millions of them listening to the piping voice of a Board School boy, are the inferior race, these three hundred millions—mark race, though there are more races in India than people in Peckham—and we, of course, are superior. They've stopped somehow on the bottom rung of the ladder of which we've very nearly, if not quite, reached the top. They've stopped there hundreds, thousands of years: but it won't take any time to lead 'em up by the hand to our rung. It's to be done like this: by showing them that they're our brothers, inferior brothers; by reason, arguing them out of their superstitions, false beliefs; by education by science, by example, yes, even he did not forget example, and White, sitting by his side with his red nose and watery eyes, nodded approval. And all this must be done scientifically, logically, systematically: if it were, a Commissioner could revolutionize a province in five years, turn it into a Japanese India, with all the ryots as well as all the vakils[11] and students running up the ladder of European civilization to become, I suppose, glorified Board School angels at the top. 'But you've none of you got clear plans out here,' he piped, 'you never work on any system; you've got no point of view. The result is'—here, I think, he was inspired, by the dead oysters, perhaps—'instead of getting hold of the East, it's the East which gets hold of you.'

And White agreed with him, solemnly, at any rate when he was sane and sober. And I couldn't complain of his inexperience. He was rather reticent at first, but afterwards we heard much—too much—of his experiences—one does, when a man gets D.T. He said he was a gentleman, and I believe it was true; he had been to a public school; Cheltenham or Repton. He hadn't, I gathered, succeeded as a gentleman at home, so they sent him to travel in the East. He liked it, it suited him. So he became a planter in Assam. That was fifteen years ago, but he didn't like Assam: the luck was against him—it always was—and he began to roll; and when a man starts rolling in India, well—He had been a clerk in merchants' offices; he had served in a draper's shop in Calcutta; but the luck was always against him. Then he tramped up and down India, through Ceylon, Burma; he had got at one time or another to the Malay States, and when he was very bad one day, he talked of cultivating camphor in Java. He had been a sailor on a coasting tramp; he had sold horses (which didn't belong to him) in the Deccan somewhere; he had tramped day after day begging his way for months in native bazaars; he had lived for six months with, and on, a Tamil woman in some little village down in the south. Now he was 'dealing in' pearls. 'India's got hold of me,' he'd say, 'India's got hold of me and the East.'

He had views too, very much like Robson's, with additions. 'The strong hand' came in, and 'rule.' We ought to govern India more; we didn't now. Why, he had been in hundreds of places where he was the first Englishman that the people had ever seen. (Lord! think of that!). He talked a great deal about the hidden wealth of India

---

11 **ryots . . . vakils:** Peasants . . . lawyers.

and exploitation. He knew places where there was gold—workable too—only one wanted a little capital—coal probably and iron—and then there was this new stuff, radium. But we weren't go-ahead, progressive, the Government always put difficulties in his way. They made 'the native' their stalking-horse against European enterprise. He would work for the good of the native, he'd treat him firmly but kindly—especially, I thought, the native women, for this teeth were sharp and pointed and there were spaces between each, and there was something about his chin and jaw—*you* know the type, I expect.

As the fishing went on we had less time to talk. We had to work. The divers go out in the fleet of three hundred or four hundred boats every night and dive until midday. Then they sail back from the pearl banks and bring all their oysters into an immense Government enclosure where the Government share is taken. If the wind is favourable all the boats got back by 6 p.m. and the work is over at 7. But if the wind starts blowing off shore, the fleet gets scattered and boats drop in one by one all night long. Robson and I had to be in the enclosure as long as there was a boat out, ready to see that, as soon as it did get in, the oysters were brought to the enclosure and Government got its share.

Well, the wind never did blow favourably that year. I sat in that enclosure sometimes for forty-eight hours on end. Robson found managing it rather difficult, so he didn't like to be left there alone. If you get two thousand Arabs, Tamils, Negroes, and Moormen, each with a bag or two of oysters, into an enclosure a hundred and fifty yards by a hundred and fifty yards, and you only have thirty timid native 'subordinates' and twelve native policemen to control them—well, somehow or other he found a difficulty in applying his system of reasoning to them. The first time he tried it, we very nearly had a riot; it arose from a dispute between some Arabs and Tamils over the ownership of three oysters which fell out of a bag. The Arabs didn't understand Tamil and the Tamils didn't understand Arabic, and, when I got down there, fetched by a frightened constable, there were sixty or seventy men fighting with great poles—they had pulled up the fence of the enclosure for weapons—and on the outskirts was Robson running round like a distracted hen with a white face and tears in his blue eyes. When we got the combatants separated, they had only killed one Tamil and broken nine or ten heads. Robson was very upset by that dead Tamil, he broke down utterly for a minute or two, I'm afraid.

Then White got his second attack. He was very bad: he wanted to kill himself, but was worse than that, before killing himself, he wanted to kill other people. I hadn't been to bed for two nights and I knew I should have to sit up another night in that enclosure as the wind was all wrong again. I had given White a bed in my hut: it wasn't good to let him wander in the bazaar. Robson came down with a white face to tell me he had 'gone mad up there again.' I had to knock him down with the butt end of a rifle; he was a big man and I hadn't slept for forty eight hours, and then there were the flies and the smell of those dead oysters.

It sounds unreal, perhaps a nightmare, all this told here to you behind blinds and windows in this—" he sniffed—"in this smell of—of—horsehair furniture and paint and varnish. The curious thing is it didn't seem a nightmare out there. It was too real. Things happened, anything might happen, without shocking or astonishing. One just did one's work, hour after hour, keeping things going in that sun which stung one's bare hands, took the skin off even my face, among the flies and the smell. It wasn't a nightmare, it was just a few thousand Arabs and Indians fishing up oysters from the bottom of the sea. It wasn't even new, one felt; it was old, old as the Bible, old as Adam, so the Arabs said. One hadn't much time to think, but one felt it and watched it, watched the things happen quietly, unastonished, as men do in the East. One does one's work,—forty eight hours at a stretch doesn't leave one much time or inclination for thinking,—waiting for things to happen. If you can prevent people from killing one another or robbing one another, or burning down the camp, or getting cholera or plague or small-pox, and if one can manage to get one night's sleep in three, one is fairly satisfied; one doesn't much worry about having to knock a mad gentleman from Repton on the head with the butt end of a rifle between-whiles.

I expect that's just what Robson would call 'not getting hold of India but letting India get hold of you.' Well, I said I wouldn't give you views and I won't: I'm giving you facts: what I want, you know, too is to give you the feeling of facts out there. After all that is data for your views, isn't it? Things here feel so different; you seem so far from life, with windows and blinds and curtains always in between, and then nothing ever happens, you never wait for things to happen, never watch things happening here. You are always doing things somehow—Lord knows what they are—according I suppose to systems, views, opinions. But out there you live so near to life, every morning you smell damp earth if you splash too much in your tin bath. And things happen slowly, inexorably by fate, and you—you don't do things, you watch with the three hundred millions. You feel it there in everything, even in the sunrise and sunset, every day, the immensity, inexorableness, mystery of things happening. You feel the whole earth waking up or going to sleep in a great arch of sky; you feel small, not very powerful. But who ever felt the sun set or rise in London or Torquay either? It doesn't: you just turn on or turn off the electric light.

White was very bad that night. When he recovered from being knocked down by the rifle, I had to tie him down to the bed. And then Robson broke down—nerves, you know. I had to go back to the enclosure and I wanted him to stay and look after White in the hut—it wasn't safe to leave him alone even tied down with cord to the camp bed. But this was apparently another emergency to which the manual system did not apply. He couldn't face it alone in the hut with that man tied to the bed. White was certainly not a pretty sight writhing about there, and his face—have you ever seen a man in the last stages of D.T? I beg your pardon. I suppose you haven't. It isn't nice, and White was also seeing things, not nice either: not snakes you know as people do in novels when they get D.T., but things which had happened to him, and things which he had done—they weren't nice either—and curious ordinary things distorted in a most unpleasant way. He was very much troubled by snipe: hundreds of them kept on rising out of the bed from beside him with that shrill 'cheep! cheep!' of theirs: he felt their soft little feathered bodies against his bare skin as they fluttered up from under him somewhere and flew out of the window. It threw him into paroxysms of fear, agonies: It made one, I admit, feel chilly round the heart to hear him pray one to stop it.

And Robson was also not a nice sight. I hate seeing a sane man break down with fear, mere abject fear. He just sat down at last on a cane-bottomed chair and cried like a baby. Well, that did him some good, but he wasn't fit to be left alone with White. I had to take White down to the enclosure, and I tied him to a post with coir rope near the table at which I sat there. There was nothing else to do. And Robson came too and sat there at my side through the night watching White, terrified but fascinated.

Can you picture that enclosure to yourself down on the sandy shore with its great fence of rough poles cut in the jungle, lighted by a few flares, torches dipped in coconut oil: and the white man tied to a pole raving, writhing in the flickering light which just showed too Robson's white scared little face? And in the intervals of taking over oysters and settling disputes between Arabs and Somalis and Tamils and Moormen, I sat at the table writing a report (which had to go by runner next morning) on a proposal to introduce the teaching of French in 'English schools' in towns. That wasn't a very good report. White gave us the whole history of his life between ten p.m. and four a.m. in the morning. He didn't leave much to the imagination; a parson would have said that in that hour the memory of his sins came upon him— O, I beg your pardon. But really I think they did. I thought I had lived long enough out there to have heard without a shock anything that men can do and do—especially white men who have 'gone under.' But I hadn't: I couldn't stomach the story of White's life told by himself. It wasn't only that he had robbed and swindled himself through India up and down for fifteen years. That was bad enough for there wasn't a station where he hadn't swindled and bamboozled his fellow white men. But it was what he had done when he got away 'among the natives'—to men, and women too, away from 'civilization,' in the jungle villages and high up in the mountains. God! the cold, civilized, corrupted cruelty of it. I told you, I think, that his teeth were pointed and spaced out in his mouth.

And his remorse was the most horrible thing, tied to that post there, writhing under the flickering light of the flare: the remorse of fear—fear of punishment, of what was coming of death, of the horrors, real horrors and the phantom horrors of madness.

Often during the night there was nothing to be heard in the enclosure but his screams, curses, hoarse whispers of fear. We seemed alone there in the vast stillness of the sky: only now and then a little splash from the sea down on the shore. And then would come a confused murmur from the sea and a little later perhaps the wailing voice of one man calling to another from boat to boat across the water 'Abdulla! Abdulla!' And I would go out on to the shore. There were boats, ten, fifteen, twenty, perhaps, coming in from the banks, sad, mysterious, in the moonlight, gliding in with the little splashings of the great round oars. Except for the slow moving of the oars one would have thought they were full of the dead, there was not a movement on board, until the boats touched the sand. Then the dark shadows, which lay like dead men about the boats, would leap into life—there would rise a sudden din of hoarse voices, shouting, calling, quarrelling. The boats swarmed with shadows running about, gesticulating, staggering under sacks of oysters, dropping one after the other over the boats' sides into the sea. The sea was full of them and soon the shore too, Arabs, Negroes, Tamils, bowed under the weight of the sacks. They came up dripping from the sea. They burst with a roar into the enclosure: they flung down their sacks of oysters with a crash. The place was full of swaying struggling forms: of men calling to one another in their different tongues: of the smell of the sea.

And above everything one could hear the screams and prayers of the madman writhing at the post. They gathered about him, stared at him. The light of the flares fell on their dark faces, shining and dripping from the sea. They looked calm, impassive, stern. It shone too on the circle of eyes: one saw the whites of them all round him: they seemed to be judging him, weighing him: calm patient eyes of men who watched unastonished the procession of things. The Tamils' squat black figures nearly naked watched him silently, almost carelessly. The Arabs in their long dirty, night-shirts, black-bearded, discussed him earnestly together with their guttural voices. Only an enormous negro, towering up to six feet six at least above the crowd, dressed in sacks and an enormous ulster,[12] with ten copper coffee pots slung over his back and a pipe made of a whole coconut with an iron tube stuck in it in his hand, stood smiling mysteriously.

And White thought they weren't real, that they were devils of Hell sent to plague and torture him. He cursed them, whispered at them, howled with fear. I had to explain to them that the Sahib was not well, that the sun had touched him, that they must move away. They understood. They salaamed quietly, and moved away slowly, dignified.

I don't know how many times this didn't happen during the night. But towards morning White began to grow very weak. He moaned perpetually. Then he began to be troubled by the flesh. As dawn showed grey in the east, he was suddenly shaken by convulsions horrible to see. He screamed for someone to bring him a woman, and, as he screamed, his head fell back: he was dead. I cut the cords quickly in a terror of haste, and covered the horror of the face. Robson was sitting in a heap in his chair. He was sobbing, his face in his hands.

At that moment I was told I was wanted on the shore. I went quickly. The sea looked cold and grey under the faint light from the East. A cold little wind just ruffled the surface of the water. A solitary boat stood out black against the sky, just throbbing slowly up and down on the water close in shore. They had a dead Arab on board, he had died suddenly while diving, they wanted my permission to bring the body ashore. Four men waded out to the boat: the corpse was lifted out and placed upon their shoulders. They waded back slowly: the feet of the dead man stuck out, toes pointing up, very stark over the shoulders of the men in front. The body was laid on the sand. The bearded face of the dead man looked very calm, very dignified in the faint light. An Arab, his brother, sat down upon the sand near his head. He

---

12 **ulster:** A long, baggy overcoat of heavy material.

covered himself with sackcloth. I heard him weeping. It was very silent, very cold and still on the shore in the early dawn.

A tall figure stepped forward, it was the Arab sheik, the leader of the boat. He laid his hand on the head of the weeping man and spoke to him calmly, eloquently, compassionately. I didn't understand Arabic, but I could understand what he was saying. The dead man had lived, had worked, had died. He had died working, without suffering, as men should desire to die. He had left a son behind him. The speech went on calmly, eloquently, I heard continually the word Khallas—all is over, finished. I watched the figures outlined against the grey sky—the long lean outline of the corpse with the toes sticking up so straight and stark, the crouching huddled figure of the weeping man and the tall upright sheik standing by his side. They were motionless, sombre, mysterious, part of the grey sea, of the grey sky.

Suddenly the dawn broke red in the sky. The sheik stopped, motioned silently to the four men. They lifted the dead man on to their shoulders. They moved away down the shore by the side of the sea which began to stir under the cold wind. By their side walked the sheik, his hand laid gently on the brother's arm. I watched them move away, silent, dignified. And over the shoulders of the men I saw the feet of the dead man with the toes sticking up straight and stark.

Then I moved away too, to make arrangements for White's burial: it had to be done at once."

There was silence in the smoking-room. I looked round The Colonel had fallen asleep with his mouth open. The jobber tried to look bored, the Archdeacon was, apparently, rather put out.

"It's too late, I think," said the Archdeacon, "to—Dear me, dear me, past one o'clock." He got up. "Don't you think you've chosen rather exceptional circumstances, out of the ordinary case?"

The Commissioner was looking into the few red coals that were all that was left of the fire.

"There's another Tamil proverb," he said: "When the cat puts his head into a pot, he thinks all is darkness."

QUESTIONS

1. Compare the opening paragraphs of this story with the opening of Joseph Conrad's "Heart of Darkness." What similarities do you find, and why might these be significant?

2. What segments of British society and ranges of political opinion are represented by the men who listen to the story? Why might Woolf have chosen to include these particular aspects of society?

3. The Anglo-Indian who narrates the story says that he is providing "facts." What is the significance of these facts to the frame discussion that precedes his story? What point do you think the narrator is attempting to make?

4. Analyze the characters Robson and White. What does their presence add to the story? How are they relevant to it?

5. Contrast the death of White with that of the Arab. What is the significance of these two deaths?

George Orwell

(1903–1950)

George Orwell (the pen name of Eric Blair) is the only major English writer to serve in the British colonial civil service and to write about that experience.

He was born in Motihari, Bengal (now the Indian province of Bihar), where his father served in the colonial administration, but returned as an infant to England with his mother and was sent to St. Cyprian's boarding school at age eight, an experience that he thoroughly hated. From there he entered prestigious Eton College and again endured and witnessed the cruelties of England's snobbish class system, becoming increasingly aware (as he said he had already done at St. Cyprian's) of the injustices perpetrated by those who wield power. It is perhaps ironic, then, that in 1921 Orwell enrolled not in a university but in the Burmese branch of the Indian Imperial Police, later the basis of his first novel, *Burmese Days* (1934). "A Hanging" is also based on those five years (1922–1927) during which Orwell's distaste for authority was in constant tension with the need to exercise it.

Upon returning to England, Orwell investigated the lives of England's poor and unemployed by becoming one of them, later working as a dishwasher in Paris's restaurants, experiences he chronicled in *Down and Out in Paris and London* (1933). By this time, the effects of worldwide depression were being keenly felt in Europe as well as in the United States, and many intellectuals were turning to socialism and communism for solutions to the economic injustices of capitalism. His novels *A Clergyman's Daughter* (1935) and *Keep the Aspidistra Flying* (1936) brought him to the attention of Victor Gollancz, the left-leaning publisher of the New Left Book Club. The result was *The Road to Wigan Pier* (1937), a nonfiction account of his life among miners and factory workers, and *Homage to Catalonia* (1938), based on his experiences fighting Fascists during Spain's civil war. Characteristically, however, Orwell refused to dogmatize, criticizing England's socialists and Spain's Republicans almost as severely as their right-wing enemies.

The outbreak of World War II in 1939 brought out Orwell's patriotic side, and in radio broadcasts aimed at Asia, he was torn between his newly found nationalism and the independence claims of Britain's colonies. His two most famous novels, *Animal Farm* (1945) and *1984* (1949), resumed Orwell's attacks on dictatorships in general and Stalin's in particular. These made him appear a conservative in the eyes of some, but Orwell's consistent target was authoritarianism in any form, whether of the left or right. His positions on other issues, such as colonialism, varied with the times and his perception of the moment's dangers, so that generalizing about his thought from any single piece is dangerous. His equivocal position in "A Hanging" is perhaps in this respect suggestive of the tensions in his thought as a whole.

A Hanging   1931

It was in Burma, a sodden morning of the rains. A sickly light, like yellow tinfoil, was slanting over the high walls into the jail yard. We were waiting outside the condemned cells, a row of sheds fronted with double bars, like small animal cages. Each cell measured about ten feet by ten and was quite bare within except for a plank bed and a pot for drinking water. In some of them brown silent men were squatting at the inner bars, with their blankets draped round them. These were the condemned men, due to be hanged within the next week or two.

One prisoner had been brought out of his cell. He was a Hindu, a puny wisp of a man, with a shaven head and vague liquid eyes. He had a thick, sprouting moustache, absurdly too big for his body, rather like the moustache of a comic man on the films. Six tall Indian warders were guarding him and getting him ready for the gallows. Two of them stood by with rifles and fixed bayonets, while the others handcuffed him, passed a chain through his handcuffs and fixed it to their belts, and lashed his arms tight to his sides. They crowded very close about him, with their hands always on him in a careful, caressing grip, as though all the while feeling him to make sure he was there. It was like men handling a fish which is still alive and may jump back into the water. But he stood quite unresisting, yielding his arms limply to the ropes, as though he hardly noticed what was happening.

Eight o'clock struck and a bugle call, desolately thin in the wet air, floated from the distant barracks. The superintendent of the jail, who was standing apart from the rest of us, moodily prodding the gravel with his stick, raised his head at the sound. He was an army doctor, with a grey toothbrush moustache and a gruff voice. "For God's sake hurry up, Francis," he said irritably. "The man ought to have been dead by this time. Aren't you ready yet?"

Francis, the head jailer, a fat Dravidian[1] in a white drill suit and gold spectacles, waved his black hand. "Yes sir, yes sir," he bubbled. "All iss satisfactorily prepared. The hangman iss waiting. We shall proceed."

"Well, quick march, then. The prisoners can't get their breakfast till this job's over."

We set out for the gallows. Two warders marched on either side of the prisoner, with their rifles at the slope; two others marched close against him, gripping him by

1 **Dravidian:** A resident of southern India.

arm and shoulder, as though at once pushing and supporting him. The rest of us, magistrates and the like, followed behind. Suddenly, when we had gone ten yards, the procession stopped short without any order or warning. A dreadful thing had happened—a dog, come goodness knows whence, had appeared in the yard. It came bounding among us with a loud volley of barks, and leapt round us wagging its whole body, wild with glee at finding so many human beings together. It was a large woolly dog, half Airedale, half Pariah. For a moment it pranced round us, and then, before anyone could stop it, it had made a dash for the prisoner and, jumping up, tried to lick his face. Everyone stood aghast, too taken aback even to grab at the dog.

"Who let that bloody brute in here?" said the superintendent angrily. "Catch it, someone!"

A warder, detached from the escort, charged clumsily after the dog, but it danced and gambolled just out of his reach, taking everything as part of the game. A young Eurasian jailer picked up a handful of gravel and tried to stone the dog away, but it dodged the stones and came after us again. Its yaps echoed from the jail walls. The prisoner, in the grasp of the two warders, looked on incuriously, as though this was another formality of the hanging. It was several minutes before someone managed to catch the dog. Then we put my handkerchief through its collar and moved off once more, with the dog still straining and whimpering.

It was about forty yards to the gallows. I watched the bare brown back of the prisoner marching in front of me. He walked clumsily with his bound arms, but quite steadily, with that bobbing gait of the Indian who never straightens his knees. At each step his muscles slid neatly into place, the lock of hair on his scalp danced up and down, his feet printed themselves on the wet gravel. And once, in spite of the men who gripped him by each shoulder, he stepped slightly aside to avoid a puddle on the path.

It is curious, but till that moment I had never realised what it means to destroy a healthy, conscious man. When I saw the prisoner step aside to avoid the puddle I saw the mystery, the unspeakable wrongness, of cutting a life short when it is in full tide. This man was not dying, he was alive just as we are alive. All the organs of his body were working—bowels digesting food, skin renewing itself, nails growing, tissues forming—all toiling away in solemn foolery. His nails would still be growing when he stood on the drop, when he was falling through the air with a tenth of a second to live. His eyes saw the yellow gravel and the grey walls, and his brain still remembered, foresaw, reasoned—reasoned even about puddles. He and we were a party of men walking together, seeing, hearing, feeling, understanding the same world; and in two minutes, with a sudden snap, one of us would be gone—one mind less, one world less.

The gallows stood in a small yard, separate from the main grounds of the prison, and overgrown with tall prickly weeds. It was a brick erection like three sides of a shed, with planking on top, and above that two beams and a crossbar with the rope dangling. The hangman, a grey-haired convict in the white uniform of the prison, was waiting beside his machine. He greeted us with a servile crouch as we entered. At a word from Francis the two warders, gripping the prisoner more closely than ever, half led, half pushed him to the gallows and helped him clumsily up the ladder. Then the hangman climbed up and fixed the rope round the prisoner's neck.

We stood waiting, five yards away. The warders had formed in a rough circle round the gallows. And then, when the noose was fixed, the prisoner began crying out to his god. It was a high, reiterated cry of "Ram! Ram! Ram! Ram!"[2] not urgent and fearful like a prayer or a cry for help, but steady, rhythmical, almost like the tolling of a bell. The dog answered the sound with a whine. The hangman, still standing on the gallows, produced a small cotton bag like a flour bag and drew it down over the prisoner's face. But the sound, muffled by the cloth, still persisted, over and over again: "Ram! Ram! Ram! Ram! Ram!"

The hangman climbed down and stood ready, holding the lever. Minutes seemed to pass. The steady, muffled crying from the prisoner went on and on, 'Ram! Ram! Ram!' never faltering for an instant. The superintendent, his head on his chest, was slowly poking the ground with his stick; perhaps he was counting the cries, allowing the prisoner a fixed number — fifty, perhaps, or a hundred. Everyone had changed colour. The Indians had gone grey like bad coffee, and one or two of the bayonets were wavering. We looked at the lashed, hooded man on the drop, and listened to his cries — each cry another second of life; the same thought was in all our minds: oh, kill him quickly, get it over, stop that abominable noise!

Suddenly the superintendent made up his mind. Throwing up his head he made a swift motion with his stick. "*Chalo!*" he shouted almost fiercely.

There was a clanking noise, and then dead silence. The prisoner had vanished, and the rope was twisting on itself. I let go of the dog, and it galloped immediately to the back of the gallows; but when it got there it stopped short, barked, and then retreated into a corner of the yard, where it stood among the weeds looking timorously out at us. We went round the gallows to inspect the prisoner's body. He was dangling with his toes pointed straight downwards, very slowly revolving, as dead as a stone.

The superintendent reached out with his stick and poked the bare brown body; it oscillated slightly. "*He's* all right," said the superintendent. He backed out from under the gallows, and blew out a deep breath. The moody look had gone out of his face quite suddenly. He glanced at his wristwatch. "Eight minutes past eight. Well, that's all for this morning thank God."

The warders unfixed bayonets and marched away. The dog, sobered and conscious of having misbehaved itself, slipped after them. We walked out of the gallows yard, past the condemned cells with their waiting prisoners, into the big central yard of the prison. The convicts, under the command of warders armed with *lathis*[3] were already receiving their breakfast. They squatted in long rows, each man holding a tin panikin, while two warders with buckets marched round ladling out rice; it seemed quite a homely, jolly scene, after the hanging. An enormous relief had come upon us

---

2 **Ram!:** A supplication to the Hindu god Rama.
3 *lathis:* Long bamboo poles, sometimes tipped with metal, used by Indian troops and police in crowd control.

now that the job was done. One felt an impulse to sing, to break into a run, to snig-ger. All at once everyone began chattering gaily.

The Eurasian boy walking beside me nodded towards the way we had come, with a knowing smile: "Do you know, sir, our friend (he meant the dead man) when he heard his appeal had been dismissed, he pissed on the floor of his cell. From fright. Kindly take one of my cigarettes, sir. Do you not admire my new silver case, sir? From the boxwallah, two rupees eight annas. Classy European style."

Several people laughed—at what, nobody seemed certain.

Francis was walking by the superintendent, talking garrulously: "Well, sir, all hass passed off with the utmost satisfactoriness. It was all finished—flick! like that. It iss not always so—oah, no! I have known cases where the doctor wass obliged to go beneath the gallows and pull the prissoner's legs to ensure decease. Most disagree-able!"

"Wriggling about, eh? That's bad," said the superintendent.

"Ach, sir, it iss worse when they become refractory! One man, I recall, clung to the bars of his cage when we went to take him out. You will scarcely credit, sir, that it took six warders to dislodge him, three pulling at each leg. We reasoned with him. 'My dear fellow,' we said, 'think of all the pain and trouble you are causing to us!' But no, he would not listen! Ach, he wass very troublesome!"

I found that I was laughing quite loudly. Everyone was laughing. Even the su-perintendent grinned in a tolerant way. "You'd better all come out and have a drink," he said quite genially. "I've got a bottle of whisky in the car. We could do with it."

We went through the big double gates of the prison into the road. "Pulling at his legs!" exclaimed a Burmese magistrate suddenly, and burst into a loud chuckling. We all began laughing again. At that moment Francis' anecdote seemed extraordinarily funny. We all had a drink together, native and European alike, quite amicably. The dead man was a hundred yards away.

QUESTIONS

1. This selection has been called both a story and an essay. In what ways does it re-semble a story? In what ways does it resemble an essay? Does it matter how we categorize it? Why or why not?

2. If, as Orwell says, the condemned man is so small and weak, why is he so heavily guarded? What point might Orwell be making about power? About the rela-tionship between the condemned man and the Empire?

3. What is the effect of the dog's presence in the story? Why might Orwell have in-cluded these apparently trivial, even irrelevant, details and events?

4. Note carefully how everyone behaves after the execution. Why was there such "enormous relief"? Why does everyone laugh at Francis's remarks?

5. What point or points might this story be making about empire and impe-rialism?

William Plomer

(1903–1973)

William Plomer was an early manifestation of a phenomenon that became increasingly common in the twentieth century—a writer of no one nationality whose experiences and writing transcend political boundaries.

He was born of British parents in Pietersburg, South Africa, but was sent to England at age five to attend school, an experience that made him feel like an outsider for the rest of his life. Returning to South Africa in 1911, he attended St. John's College (high school) for a brief but idyllic period until the family moved to England and enrolled him in Beechmont, which he hated. He was admitted to the prestigious Rugby school in 1917 and prospered there for a year, but the family returned to South Africa, where he finished his schooling at St. John's.

Deciding not to attend university, Plomer spent 1920 to 1922 as an apprentice sheep farmer in the eastern cape, then joined his father in Entumeni in a venture to trade with the Zulus, whom he grew to admire. He began writing poetry and made an important friendship with poet Roy Campbell, who in 1926 invited him to join the staff of *Voorslag,* a liberal literary magazine. These experiences, and the fact that Plomer's parents were free of racial prejudice, imbued William with ideas of racial equality that were unusual at that time. They found effective expression in Plomer's first and probably most famous novel, *Turbott Wolfe* (1926), which savagely satirizes British claims of racial superiority. His first book of short stories, *I Speak of Africa,* came out the following year and is based largely on his experiences in sheep farming.

The association with *Voorslag* ended after only a few months, but it led to Plomer's being invited to Japan, where he taught at the Tokyo School of Foreign Languages and then at a private school. He stayed three years, learning as much as an outsider could about Japanese life and culture. His experiences there are chronicled in *Paper Houses* (1929). Eventually disillusioned by Japan's imperial tendencies, he returned to England and then toured Europe, using some of these experiences, together with his African memories, in *The Child of Queen Victoria and Other Stories* (1933). Four years later, Plomer settled in England, becoming chief reader for publisher Jonathan Cape and turning his creative hand to poetry, nonfiction, opera librettos (with Benjamin Brittain), and another volume of stories. He was made Commander of the British Empire in 1968.

"The Child of Queen Victoria" is highly autobiographical and one of Plomer's most memorable stories. Its vivid descriptions of the African scene, shrewd characterization of the naive, eager, and sexually repressed young protagonist, and tragic ending give poignancy and context to the love story that cannot end happily because of the gulf separating Frant and Seraphina.

The Child of Queen Victoria   *1933*

1

A Ford car, rattling its way up a rough road in Lembuland[1] in the most brilliant sunshine, carried two very different people—a hard-bitten colonial of Scotch descent, a trader, MacGavin by name, nearer thirty than forty, with a sour red face, and a young Englishman called Frant who had just left school. It was really very awkward. They did not know what to say to each other. MacGavin thought his passenger was despising him simply for being what he was, and Frant, feeling foolish and useless in contrast with this sunburnt, capable man, made a painful effort to be hearty, and looked inquiringly at the country. The road wound in and out, climbing through grassy hills, with patches of virgin forest here and there, especially in the hollows. There were outcrops of rock, and small tilled fields of red earth, and any number of beehive-shaped huts perched here and there in twos and threes. And there were always natives in sight, with herds of bony cattle and ragged goats. It did not need a specially acute eye to see that the landscape, though picturesque, was over-crowded, and that the whites, coveting the lowlands for sugarcane, had gradually squeezed the natives up into these heights which were poor in soil, coarse in pasturage, and too full of ups and downs to afford space for any proper attempts at cultivation. Frant looked at the natives, naturally, with some curiosity. He wondered what they were like when you got to know them, and then he wondered if he couldn't say something suitable to MacGavin about them. At last he said:

"It seems a pity that the natives haven't got a higher standard of living, then there would be so much more money to be made out of them."

MacGavin looked at him with the savage expression sometimes to be seen on the faces of the ignorant when confronted with what seems to them a new and difficult and rather mad idea.

"The black bastards!" he exclaimed. "There's bloody little to be made out of *them,* as you'll pretty soon find out."

And he violently changed gear. As the car began to strain its way up a steep hill, Frant, vibrating by his side, was glad that the noise of the engine destroyed what would have been a painful silence.

Sons of the "new poor," young wasters, retrenched civil servants or Indian Army officers, and other mostly misguided wretches, they went to settle overseas—one even heard of suicides, because not everybody is tough enough to stand an absolute change of environment, or frightful isolation in some magnificent landscape. And Frant, lured by advertisements, driven by enterprise, encouraged by supposedly responsible persons, went out like them, only fresh from a public school.

---

1 **Lembuland:** A fictitious African country.

His incipient relationship with MacGavin was not made easier by the practical basis on which it rested, for Frant came to him neither as a partner, nor as a servant, nor as a guest, nor had he paid one penny by way of premium. A committee in London had picked out MacGavin's name as that of a person who had declared himself willing to give a young Englishman free board and lodging and two or three years' training in the art of trading with the Lembus in exchange for nothing but that young stranger's "services." MacGavin was in some ways a practical man, and the chance of obtaining a responsible white servant who need be paid no wages seemed to him a good one. Frant had been brought up to be eager to oblige. And that was how they started.

Frant was young—so young that, bumping adventurously along into the heart of Lembuland, he could not help thinking of his former schoolfellows and of how they would have envied him if they could have seen him at that moment. A fatal eagerness possessed him. He was flying in the face of the world, as the young are apt to do, with the finest of ambitions. For some of us when young it does not seem so important that we should be successful in a worldly sense and at once enjoy money and comfort, as that we should try and become our true selves. We want to blossom out and fulfil our real natures. The process is complex, and is obviously conditioned by our approaches to the work we mean to do or have to do in life, by the way our heredity and upbringing make us react to our environment, and especially by our relations with other people. In the long run this affair of becoming a grown-up person, a real person (for that is what it amounts to) is, for most of us, an affair of the heart. We hear a great deal about sex nowadays; it is possible to overestimate its importance, because there are always people who pay it little attention or who apparently manage, like Sir Isaac Newton, to get along, without giving it a thought. But Frant came of a susceptible family. He arrived in Lembuland with a pretty appetite for life, and little knew what he was letting himself in for.

2

The trading station at Madumbi occupied the top of a slope a little back from the road, or track rather, and consisted of two main buildings, the store and the house, about fifty yards apart, and a number of ramshackle outhouses. In front, there had been some attempt at a garden—not much of an attempt, for cows and chickens always roamed about in it, and it was now and then invaded by monkeys. At the back, there was some rough grazing land and a patch of forest that went with the place. The buildings themselves were made of corrugated iron, painted khaki and lined with deal boards, looking out, curiously hideous, on the land which sloped away from them on all sides with streams, and clumps of trees, and grassy spaces like a well-planned park. But Mr. and Mrs. MacGavin, in settling at Madumbi, had been little influenced by the scenery.

The store itself was lighted only by two small windows and the open door, and as you came in from the strong sunlight it was at first difficult to get your bearings.

The place was so crowded with goods that it looked like a cave crowded with all sorts of plunder. Your head bumping against a suspended trek-chain or storm-lantern, you looked up and saw that the ceiling was almost entirely hidden in festoons of kettles and baskets, hanks of Berlin wool, enormous bouquets of handkerchiefs of all sizes and colours, bunches of tunics and trousers interspersed with camisoles, frying-pans, wreaths of artificial forget-me-nots, hatchets and matchets, necklaces and ploughshares. As for the shelves, they were entirely crammed with different kinds of goods, for the production of which a hundred factories had smoked and roared in four continents. All kinds of shoddy clothing and showy piece-goods, brittle ironmongery and chinaware, the most worthless patent medicines, the gaudiest cheap jewellery, the coarsest groceries, bibles, needles, pipes, celluloid collars, soup tureens, hair-oil, notebooks, biscuits and lace curtains rose in tiers and patterns on every side. Certain shelves were full of refuse left over from the war—grey cotton socks made in Chicago for American recruits who had never enlisted, khaki tunics and breeches, puttees, Balaclava helmets[2] and so forth, all ugly and serviceable, made and carried by machinery to contribute to a scene of universal murder, produced in too great quantities, by contract instead of by necessity or impulse, and at last deposited here, so that a profit might be made out of the pleasure these things, by their novelty, gave to the blacks. The whole world seemed to have conspired to make a profit on this lonely Lembu hilltop.

Two doors at the back of the store itself gave access to two other rooms. One was large, and was used for storing reserves of bulky goods—sacks of salt, sugar and grain; ironware; boxes of sweets and soap; besides a profusion of bunches of Swazi tobacco leaves, at least two feet long, their fragrance preserved by an occasional sprinkling with water. It was the custom to give away a leaf or two of tobacco to each adult shopper, and to the young a handful of the cheapest sweets, their virulent pinks and greens and acid chemical flavours promising a quick decay to strong white teeth. The other and smaller room was used as an office, and contained a table, a chair, a safe, and a great accumulation of MacGavin's papers. The window, which received the afternoon sun, would not open, and was always buzzing with flies and hornets in various stages of fatigue. A flea-bitten dog was usually asleep on a pile of unpaid bills in the corner, while the ink, from standing so much in the sun, was always evaporating, so that when one had occasion to write one had to use a pencil.

But all that was only the background. The space before the counter was often thronged with Lembus of all ages and both sexes. The noise was overpowering. They would all be talking at once, some laughing, some arguing, some gossiping, some bargaining, while all the time a peculiarly strident gramophone was playing records of Caruso and Clara Butt.[3] Sometimes an old black woman, nearly blind and nearly naked, her last peppercorns of hair grizzled to a pepper-and-salt colour, and her dry old dugs so long that she could comfortably tuck the ends of them into her belt,

---

2 **puttees, Balaclava helmets:** Puttees are leather or cloth leggings covering the ankle to the knee; Balaclava helmets are knit caps covering the head and neck.
3 **Caruso and Clara Butt:** Enrico Caruso, Italian operatic tenor; Clara Butt, English contralto.

might be seen listening to it, with her head on one side, for the first time, uttering occasional exclamations of incredulity ("*Abantu! Inkosi yami! Maye babo!*") and slapping her scrawny thighs, as she demanded whether the voice was the voice of a spirit.

In another part of the room the only vacant space on the wall was occupied by a pier-glass, before which a group of very fat girls were fond of comparing their charms, to the accompaniment of shrieks of delight. Their main wish was to observe the reflection of their bottoms, partly out of pure curiosity and partly with a view to interesting the men present. Standing among the older customers there were always some children, patiently awaiting their turn to be served with threepennyworths of this and that. Some brought eggs or wild fruit to trade, which they carried in small bowl-shaped baskets on their heads. One might have a fowl under her arm, and a little boy of seven would perhaps bring an enormous scarlet lily, complete with leaves and root.

To say that all this was strange to Frant would be an understatement. It was a new world. Into this exotic atmosphere he was plunged; this was where he had to work; this was what he had to learn. What is called adaptability is little more than freshness and keenness and readiness to learn, and Frant, who had been brought up to obey, made himself completely and at first willingly subservient to MacGavin's instructions. He didn't like MacGavin, and it was plain that he never would do so, but it was also plain that MacGavin knew his business, and Frant's presence at Madumbi was, in theory, a business matter. So he rose early and retired late, working hours that no trade union would approve at a job that needed endless patience and good humour, with diligence and imagination as well. He struggled with a strange language, did accounts, avoided cheating or being cheated (he had been brought up to be honest) and toiled morning, noon and night, without haste, without rest, never for a moment questioning what he conceived to be his duty. And MacGavin, finding that he had to do with an honest and docile and responsible person, confided to his wife that the plan was succeeding beyond his hopes. Very soon, he felt, he would be able to leave Frant in entire charge of the proceedings, while he himself attended to other money-making operations out of doors. Mrs. MacGavin was pleased too, because she found she was less often required to help in the store, and could spend more time in the house. Though God knows the store was the pleasanter building of the two.

On his very first afternoon Frant had been given tea on the veranda of the house, in order to afford Mrs. MacGavin an early chance of sizing him up, but after that his tea was always sent over to the store. Apart from that he had meals in the house, and he slept in it, and spent part of his Sunday leisure in it as well. There were only four rooms. Frant's own room, nine feet by seven, was oppressively hot, was never properly cleaned, and had a disagreeable smell. The living-room, not large in itself, was so crammed with furniture that one person could with difficulty turn round in it, whereas three people were supposed to eat and sleep and rest in it, quite in addition to the fact that, the house lacking either hall or passage, it had to serve as both. Thus the pattern on the linoleum was in places quite worn away, and behind the front door was a rack bulging with hats, coats and mackintoshes, which gave off a greenish odour of stale sweat, cheap rubber and mildew. The middle of the room was occupied by a large table covered with a khaki mohair table-cloth with bobbles[4] round the edges, and in the middle of that stood a large oil-lamp with a shade of crinkly pink paper. A sideboard held a load of worthless ornaments, and on the walls faded wedding-groups in bamboo Oxford frames alternated with dusty paper fans, cuckoo clocks and fretwork brackets supporting electro-plated vases containing dusty everlasting flowers in process of perishing from dry-rot. With difficulty it was possible to make one's way to a small bookcase which stood beneath a reproduction of a problem picture, showing a woman in evening dress in the fashion of 1907 kneeling on the floor before a man in a dinner-jacket, the whole suffused in a red glow from a very hot-looking fire in the background, and called 'The Confession'. Among the books were several by Marie Corelli,[5] a brochure on the diseases of cattle, and a girlish album of Mrs. MacGavin's, in which her friends had written or attempted to draw personal tributes and pleasantries. Had this album been a little more vulgar, it might have been almost a curiosity, but the commonness of colonial schoolgirls in the second decade of this century has scarcely even a period interest. It must be admitted, however, that one contributor had written the following very appropriate wisecrack:

> Roses are red and violets blue,
> Pickles are sour and so are you.

"Fond of reading?" MacGavin, in an expansive moment, once asked Frant. "No time myself."

"Yes and no," said Frant, who was trying to make up for his education and had a copy of *The Brothers Karamazov* in his bedroom. "It depends."

On the table in that front room there was nearly always a fly-haunted still-life consisting of a teapot and some dirty cups, for Mrs. MacGavin drank very strong tea seven times daily, a habit which no doubt accounted partly for the state of her complexion. But all day long and most evenings the double doors on to the veranda were open, and there was the view. As the trading station was on the top of a hill and partly surrounded with groves of mimosa trees, the outlook was very fine. Beyond the trees, it could be seen that every depression in the landscape had its rivulet and patch of forest, and that in every sheltered and elevated place there was a kraal[6] of beehive-shaped huts with small fields of grain and roots; cattle were grazing here and there; and in the distance rose range upon range of blue mountains. At first sight it seemed, like so many African landscapes, a happy mixture of the pastoral and the magnificent, but those who lived under its influence came to feel gradually a mingled sense of uneasiness and sorrow, so that what at first seemed grand became

---

4 **bobbles:** Small balls of fabric used as decoration.
5 **Marie Corelli:** Popular romantic novelist.
6 **kraal:** Village, but also a cattle pen or corral.

indifferent or menacing, what at first seemed peaceful was felt to be brooding, and stillness and quietness seemed to be an accumulation of repressed and troubled forces, like the thunderclouds that often hung over the horizon of an afternoon. Those sunny hills seemed to be possessed by a spirit that nursed a grievance.

3

Frant's approach to the natives was complicated by his character and education, which in some ways helped and in some ways hindered him. As a polite person, he treated them with a good-humoured consideration which they were quite unused to receiving from the whites, but then the whites in Lembuland are an unusually discouraging lot—the way they behave to one another is proof of that. A natural quick sympathy and warmth in his character immediately attracted the natives, who are uncannily quick at character, but at the same time they found a certain reserve in him. It was not that he stood on his dignity with them, but simply that he was a little too conscientious. There were certain vague ideas about the white man's prestige and so on which made him rather careful in his behaviour. He imagined that if he let himself go at all he might in some way damage MacGavin's standing and do harm to the trade, and of course MacGavin, in teaching him the trade, was careful to try and instil various principles about treating the natives firmly. And to MacGavin's credit it may be added that he insisted on the natives being treated as fairly as possible, though this was a matter of business rather than principle with him. And after all, there was no need to tell Frant to be fair—it was clear that though a trifle priggish, he was no swindler. This priggishness of his was easy to account for. It was partly in his nature, but also he had been brought up with certain rigid English ideas about being a gentleman, playing the game, and all that sort of thing, and until now he had had no reason to doubt that they were right. The effect of being abruptly transferred to a completely new environment; of being cut off from those familiar companions and surroundings which had enabled his principles to be taken for granted; and of associating with Mr. and Mrs. MacGavin, was not to make him doubt those principles but to convince him that they were right. And to be all by oneself and to think oneself right is really rather fatal, especially if one naturally tends to be both straightforward and severe. Already he would receive some of the opinions of MacGavin and his wife in a silence that was even stronger in its effect than the quiet and smiling "Oh, I'm afraid I can't quite agree with you" which he often had to use in conversation with them.

"He always thinks he's right," MacGavin remarked to his wife, "but it doesn't matter about that. What's more important is that the niggers like him. There's a slight improvement in the takings this month, and I shouldn't be surprised if it's partly due to him. He does what he's told for the most part, and I shouldn't be surprised if he turns out a good salesman when he knows the lingo a bit better."

The Lembu language presents no great difficulties, and it is surprising what good use one can make of a language as soon as one has a small working vocabulary and a few colloquial turns of phrase. Frant enjoyed speaking it, because it is one of those Bantu languages[7] which, to be spoken well, have to be spoken with gusto, and it can be both sonorous and elegant. His progress in the language naturally made his work more easy and pleasant, but it had other effects—it drew him closer into sympathy with the Lembus, and showed him how little they liked the whites. In fact, he began to realize that the remains of the white man's prestige, in Lembuland at least, rested mainly on fear—fear of the white man's money, his mechanical genius and his ruthless and largely joyless energy—and not on love or respect. And since he himself had very little money, no mechanical genius and a certain joyful vitality, he felt that there must be something rather "un-white" about himself. This discovery acted directly upon his pride—it made him resolve to treat the natives with as much kindness and dignity as were consonant with his odd position (the ruling race behind the counter!), as if to show that there were still white men who knew how to behave humanely. This made him think himself better than MacGavin and the few other whites with whom he came in touch, and shut him up in a small cell of his own (as it were) closely barred with high principles.

He did not pretend to himself that the Lembus were paragons of virtue. The very fact that as customers in a shop they had a certain right to order the shopkeepers about, added to the fact that these shopkeepers were nominally their 'superiors', was a temptation to some of the natives to be tiresome, cheeky or even insolent, and that was one reason why a great deal of persevering good temper was needed in dealing with them. By the time they had convinced themselves that Frant was both patient and cheerful he had already begun to get a good name amongst them. They were used to MacGavin, whom they thought of as a beast, but a just beast, and finding Frant just without being a beast, and youthful and personable as well, they undoubtedly began to come to Madumbi in greater numbers.

At first he had been much struck by the extreme suspiciousness and diffidence of the customers. They never entered the place with that air of cheerful confidence which, in the dreams of good shopkeepers, is found on every customer's face. On the contrary, they always seemed to come in expecting the worst. Many an old, wild woman, skirted in skins, smeared with fat and ochre, hung with charms, a bladder or an antelope's horn suspended at her neck, her hair dressed high and stuck with bone ornaments, a snuff-box at her waist, perhaps having about her too a couple of pounds, every penny of which she meant to spend, would pause in the doorway with a roving eye and an expression of extreme disillusionment and contempt, as though she found herself there unwillingly and by chance. After some time she would perhaps help herself to a cupful of water from a tank that stood at the door, and would then sit down in the shade and take a lot of snuff with immense deliberation, the expression on her face seeming to say, "Well, here I am, and I don't give a damn for anybody. I haven't lived all these years for nothing. Experience has taught me to expect the worst of every situation and every person, particularly if he or she happens

---

7 **Bantu languages:** Languages spoken in Kenya and Cameroons.

to be white. If I condescend to do any shopping here, I mean to see everything, and to have exactly what I want or nothing at all. Don't think you can swindle me, because you can't. However, I shall proceed on the assumption that you mean to try, that all your goods are damaged, that you're a cunning profiteer, and that you think I'm a fool." And when at last she deigned to enter the store, she would proceed accordingly.

But it was not only old women who were so much on their guard. Many and many a customer would show the same symptoms of a deep and cynical mistrust, walking in as if they were threading their way among mantraps all carefully set for them. Even children would show plainly how they had been forewarned, repeating innocently the last parental injunctions, and carefully counting their change from sixpence. And all this was not due to MacGavin but to the reputation which the white overlords of Lembuland had managed, in the course of two or three decades, to build up for themselves.

If for Frant this unpleasant relationship between the two races was one of his earliest and most enduring impressions, even stronger was that of the immediate physical presence of the Lembus. So many more or less naked bodies of men and women, coloured a warm brown, smooth-skinned and mostly graceful, with white teeth, straight backs and easy manners, do not leave one, when one is young and susceptible and unfamiliar with them, exactly indifferent.

"Don't worry about the stink," MacGavin had said. "You'll get used to it."

Stink? The whites always say that the blacks have a bad smell. Well, there at Madumbi was a confined space usually tightly packed with natives, but although the weather was hot and the air sometimes scarcely moving, it could not have been said that the smell was much more than strange, though to Frant it was heady, like the very smell of life itself, and excited him with a promise of joys not yet tasted. The wholesome smell of an out-of-door race cannot in any case seem unpleasant, except to diseased nerves, and the lightly clad or unclad bodies of the Lembus are continually exposed to sun, air and water, while they are almost as vegetarian as their flocks and herds. If some of the old women were a little inclined to accumulate several layers of ochre and fat all over them by way of skin treatment, they were quite amusing enough in their manners and conversation, and had quite enough natural style, to make up for it. At Madumbi there was a far more oppressive smell than that of the natives, and that was the combined aroma of the dressing that stiffened the calicoes of Osaka and Manchester into a dishonest stoutness, and, to speak figuratively, of the sand in the sugar.

4

In places like Madumbi, time seems more of a thief and enemy than in crowded cities or even in circles where the months are frittered away in useless leisure. In that part of Lembuland the changing of the seasons is less marked than in the highlands, and at Madumbi life was a packed routine; work began at half-past five or six in the morning; fatigue often precluded thought; and the tired eyes, turning towards clock or calendar, would close in sleep. Sometimes all sense of chronological sequence was lost; sometimes it seemed almost as if time were going backwards; and now and again Frant would realize with a shock how many weeks or months had slipped by since this or that trifling break in his existence. But he was not discontented, for he was interested in his work, not so much for its own sake as for the close contact with some of the realities of human nature into which it brought him.

There were certain things which he could never sell without a smile. Now and then a young Lembu would come in and say rather furtively, "*Amafuta wemvubu akona na?*" That is to say, "Have you got any hippopotamus fat?" Whereupon Frant used to go to the small showcase in which the medicines were kept, and produce a small bottle with a label bearing a Lembu inscription, and underneath, in very small letters, PEDERSEN'S GENUINE HIPPO FAT. This commodity looked like ordinary lard, probably was ordinary lard, was put up by a Norwegian chemist in Dunnsport, and sold for a shilling a bottle. It was used for a love philtre, and helped the manufacturer to maintain his son at a theological seminary in Oslo. But other "lines" were more lucrative than hippo fat. Love philtres, after all, were usually only required by the young and romantically inclined, whereas PEDERSEN'S BLUE WONDERS, as another Lembu inscription testified, were indispensable to both young and old. Certainly they were always in demand. Pills as large as peas and the colour of gun-metal, they were not merely an infallible, but a powerful aphrodisiac. When MacGavin happened to be asked for either of these medicines, he would never sell them without a clumsy pleasantry, a habit which had resulted in a falling-off of the sales of the hippo fat, for the younger natives, though their morals, according to some standards, were not above reproach, had their finer feelings. However, his misplaced humour did not much affect the demand for Blue Wonders, which were usually bought by customers of a coarser fibre. Mrs. MacGavin herself came to lend a hand in the store when business was brisk, and it would sometimes happen that she would be called upon to serve a customer with these things, which she would do with the grimmest face in the world—her expression might well have suggested a subject for an allegorical picture, "Avarice overcoming Chastity." But still, out of all the hotch-potch that the store contained, there was one kind of goods which she would neither buy nor sell. The male natives of those parts were in the habit of using a peculiar kind of *cache-sexe*[8] made of the leaves of the wild banana. At Madumbi these were made, in assorted sizes, by an old vagabond of a native who sold them to MacGavin at wholesale prices. When he came to the store it was always at some odd time, when there was nobody else about, either on a very hot afternoon or just after the store had been locked up, or at dawn, or when the moon was rising. If he saw MacGavin, the business was soon settled. If he encountered Mrs. MacGavin, he would wave his bundle of unmentionables right under her nose, saluting her with his free hand and uttering all sorts of high-flown and wholly ironical compliments before crying the

8 *cache-sexe:* Evidently an herbal mixture supposed to function as an aphrodisiac.

virtues of his wares. Nothing annoyed her more, as he very well knew. She always told him rudely to wait for her husband. If it was Frant he chanced to find, he would say with real politeness, "*Sa' ubona, umtwana ka Kwini Victoli!*" Greetings, child of Queen Victoria! This became shortened later to "Child of the Queen" and at last simply to "Child." The very first time he had seen Frant he had said, "Ah, I can see you're a real Englishman from *over there,*" and since England suggested Queen Victoria to him more than anything else it was not hard to account for the complimentary title. The old man, to whom Frant always gave an extra large leaf or two of tobacco, was also fond of saying that the *amaBhunu,* the Boers, were "no good," which was partly his real opinion and meant partly as a piece of indirect flattery, though as Frant had not had anything to do with any Dutch people it was not particularly effectual.

"How can you allow that dirty old swine to call you 'child'!" exclaimed MacGavin.

"Why, he's old enough to be my grandfather!" Frant retorted.

Frant's point of view seemed so fantastic to MacGavin that he laughed a short, harsh laugh.

"My advice is, don't stand any cheek from any nigger," he said.

He isn't cheeky to *me,*" said Frant. "Only friendly."

And with an irritable grunt from MacGavin the conversation was closed. It seemed extraordinary how full of prejudice the trader was. He was fond of generalizations about the natives which were not even remotely true, such as that they were incapable of gratitude (as if they had such a lot to be grateful for!) and he seemed to have a fixed idea that every black is determined to try and score off every white, under any conditions whatsoever. And when, as occasionally happened, a native addressed him politely in English, it made him so furious that he was no longer master of himself—it seemed to him a suggested assumption of equality between the races!

The MacGavins were amazed at Frant's continued progress, and if they welcomed his popularity with the natives as being good for trade, they resented a little that a stranger and a *rooinek*[9] should be able to beat them at their own game. As to what went on in his mind, they knew and cared nothing. They neither knew nor cared that neither work nor fatigue could prevent him from feeling at times an overwhelming loneliness and an intolerable hunger for experiences which his youth, the climate and the glorious suggestiveness of his surroundings did everything to sharpen, while its satisfaction was firmly forbidden by circumstances—or so it seemed to Frant. Already esteemed by the natives, he valued their good opinion of him too much to take chances with it, and in the background of his thoughts, in spite of the MacGavins, or perhaps because of them, there still presided that tyrannical spectre, the "white man's prestige." What it is to be an ex-prefect[10] of an English public school!

---

9 *rooinek:* "Red neck." Dutch nickname for Englishman. [Plomer's note.]
10 **ex-prefect:** A monitor in an English public (that is, private) school.

5

It was bound to happen that sooner or later his attention would become centred in some individual out of the hundreds he had to do with in the course of a week. One drowsy afternoon, when he was alone behind the counter and there was nobody in the store but a couple of gossips and a child, a young woman came in rather shyly and stood near the door, hesitating to speak. He couldn't see her very well because of the bright sunshine behind her, but he asked her what she wanted and she made a small purchase.

"Do you remember me?" she asked suddenly in a very quiet voice, looking at him gravely while she spoke.

He was surprised. He didn't remember ever having seen her before, but not wishing to offend her, he said in a slightly ironical tone of voice:

"Oh, when I've once seen people, *just once,* I never forget them."

"Well!" she exclaimed, and uttered a little peal of laughter, partly because she was surprised at his ready answer and amused at his white man's accent; partly because, as a Lembu, she could appreciate irony; and partly because it made her happy that he should talk to her. But as soon as she had uttered that little laugh she grew shamefaced and cast down her eyes with the incomparable grace of a young woman with whom modesty is natural, and not a mere device of coquetry. There was more sadness than usual in her expression, because she had at once understood that he did not remember her, and no woman likes to be forgotten by any young man. She had moved now, and the diffused radiance reflected from the sunburnt hilltop outside shone full upon her through the open door. Her hair was dressed in a cylinder on the crown of her head, stained with red ochre, and stuck with a long bone pin at the broad end of which was a minute incised design; she wore no ornament but a flat necklace of very small blue beads and a few thin bangles and anklets of silver and copper wire. She was dressed in a single piece of dark red stuff which was supported by her pointed young breasts and fastened under the arms—it fell in straight, classical folds almost to her feet, and at the sides it did not quite join but revealed a little her soft flanks. From bearing weights on her head from early childhood she carried herself very erect; she was slender, and an awareness of her graceful nubility gave every movement the value of nature perfectly controlled by art. The fineness of her appearance may have been due to some remote Arab strain in her blood, for though unmistakably negroid, her features were in no sense exaggerated. Her nose, for example, though the nostrils were broad, was very slightly aquiline; her skin was unusually light in tone; and the modelling of her cheeks and temples could only be described as delicate. Her mouth was good-humoured, her eyes were lustrous, and though one side of her face was marked with a long scar, this only drew closer attention to its beauty.

"You don't come here very often, do you?" said Frant, leaning on the counter, partly because he did not want their conversation to be overheard by anybody else, and partly because he felt somehow weak in the legs. He was in the grip of an unaccustomed shyness, he felt unsure of himself, and so excited that his heart was beating very quickly.

"No," she said, avoiding his eyes. "I don't live very near."

"Where do you live?"

"Down there—down in the valley," she said, extending an exquisite arm and looking out through the open doorway with a vague and dreamy air. He noticed the light colour of the insides of her hands. "Near the river," she said.

"That's not very far away," he said.

"You've been there, then?" she said. "You know the place?"

"No, but I don't think it's very far."

"The hill is long and steep," she said.

Frant suddenly remembered two lines of verse—

> Does the road wind uphill all the way?
> Yes, to the very end.

"I don't know your name," he said.

She looked at him quickly and uttered an exclamation of surprise.

"What's the matter?" he said.

"Why do you want to know my name?" she asked anxiously, for the use of names is important in witchcraft.

"I'm just asking. I just want to know it."

"My name is Seraphina," she said, with a mixture of modesty and seductiveness.

"*What?*"

"Seraphina."

"How on earth did you get a name like that? It's not a Lembu name! You're not a Christian, are you?"

She laughed, as though the idea of her being a Christian was absolutely ridiculous—which indeed it was.

"No!" she said. "A missionary gave it to me when I was a child. He made magic water on my head and said that Christ wanted me to be called Seraphina."

This time Frant laughed.

"Christ chose well," he said. "But none of your family are Christians, are they?"

"No, it just happened like that."

He laughed again.

"You don't know my name," he said.

"Yes, I do," she said, and pronounced it "Front," and they both laughed.

Just then some noisy customers arrived, and he had to leave her. Suddenly bold, he said:

"Good-bye, go in peace. Please come again. I like talking with you."

He couldn't possibly have dared to speak so directly of his feelings in English, but somehow in Lembu it was easier. Besides, he was stirred as he had never been stirred before.

"Good-bye," she said, smiling. "Stay in peace."

She turned to go, and looked like some virgin in an archaic frieze saying farewell to the world. As for Frant, his hands were trembling, and there was a wild gladness in his heart.

6

His tortures now began in earnest. His dreams and waking thoughts were haunted by the image of the black girl, tantalizing and yet infinitely remote. As his desire for her increased, so did its fulfilment seem to recede. He knew little or nothing of her; he knew little enough of her language and nothing at all of her situation in life. He had been so busy learning to make a profit out of the natives that he had had little chance of learning much about their customs, the way they lived and thought. Supposing, he said to himself, for the sake of argument, this girl were to become my mistress? First of all, is it possible? I am certain that to some extent she reciprocates my feelings, but to what extent? What would she expect of me? What would her family think of her? How would the affair be possible in any case? How am I to communicate with her? And then the MacGavins—presumably his success in his trading depends to some extent on the fact that he is not one of these white men who get mixed up with the natives; and if I were to become the lover of Seraphina, should I not damage his livelihood, besides ruining my own? Whatever happened, everybody would know about it, of course. And how could we live together? Are we to meet furtively in the forest? And have I the right to take this black girl? How can I pretend to myself that I love her? Is it not simply that I want to sleep with her, to touch, kiss, embrace and caress her? He found no answers to his questions, but the very fact that he could ask them was significant. His loneliness and his difficulties had taught him one of the very things that his education had been evolved to prevent—the habit of introspection. He was being Hamletized by circumstances.

Of the numerous forms of anguish which Providence has designed for her creatures few can be more intense than the state of mind and body of a man who is young, sensual by nature and sexually repressed; and who, instead of yielding to the voluptuous provocations of his surroundings, tries to exorcize them with the public-school spirit. When he might well have acted with boldness, he found himself filled with doubts, scruples and equivocations, in addition to the ordinary fears of a lover. And he had nobody to turn to, there was nobody who would say to him what so much needed to be said, "Well, go ahead and have the woman. You will have your pleasure and she will have hers, and you will both be a bit the wiser and possibly the happier for the experience. You will treat her with consideration, because it is your nature to be considerate. You are in no danger of 'going native,' because you aren't the sort of person who goes native. And as for worrying about the MacGavins, do you imagine they worry at all about you, or are likely to do so as long as you rake in the bawbees[11] for them? Be a man! *Carpe diem,*[12] etc." Lacking such an adviser, Frant continued to torment himself.

Each day he got up with Seraphina in his thoughts. Day followed day, and Seraphina did not appear. Round the trading station, meanwhile, Africa unrolled her

11 **bawbees:** English half-pennies.
12 *Carpe diem:* Latin, meaning "Seize the day" (that is, live for the present).

splendours and her cruelties. The seasons did not assert themselves overmuch. One waited for the rains to stop, or one suddenly noticed buds among thorns. One was aware, all too aware, of the spring, the season of trouble, when more people die, in all countries, than at any other time of the year. The sap was troubled, and the heart with it. All the mimosa trees at Madumbi broke into pollenous clouds of blossom, creaming in a light wind against the cobalt morning sky. Glossy toucans with scarlet bills nested in them, swooping among the boughs, and uttering the most touching matingcries. Fireflies went through their luminous rites under a coral-tree; crested hoopoes, the colour of cinnamon, pursued their fitful flight across the clear green of dawn; on long, sultry afternoons a group of turkey-bustards, as grave as senators, would plod grumbling across some grassy plateau, looking carefully for the snakes which they could kill at a blow; raindrops pattered down on leaves as large as tables, magenta-veined; and on dry, tranquil afternoons, when the days were still short and some solitary voice was singing far away, an aromatic smell of burning sweet-grass sometimes drifted through the air, the clear light, and the music, and the odour all playing together on the nerves, and inducing an emotion inexpressibly painful and delicious.

When he was free, Frant could not bear to stay near the house: but in roaming about, which became his habit, he was none the less a prisoner. Fettered by scruples and afflicted with a kind of moral impotence, he wandered in a lovely world from which he was barred almost as effectually as if he were literally in a steel cage on wheels. His troubled eyes turned to the natural scenes around him but found no rest in them, and his repression might just have gone on increasing in morbidity had not a number of unexpected things happened.

Now the arrival of Frant at Madumbi had put a check on certain of MacGavin's habits. At one time, when the Scotchman was alone in the store, in the afternoons for instance, when the weather was hot or wet and business slack, or when his wife was busy in the house, he had not been disinclined for a little amusement at the expense of some of the coarser Lembu girls who came to deal with him. Joking with them in order to try and convert their apprehensive titters into abandoned fits of giggling, he had sometimes gone so far as to pinch their breasts and slap their behinds in order to win their confidence. The bolder ones had quickly taken advantage of his susceptibilities in order to try and get something for nothing, and pointing to this or that, had copied the horseleech's daughters and cried, "Give, give!" When MacGavin so far overcame his sense of commercial fitness as to give them a string of beads or a damaged jews' harp, they immediately asked for more, determined to lose nothing for the want of asking. He would then refuse, but they would not go away, leaning on the counter and repeating their requests over and over again in a whining voice until he began to fear that his wife might come in. Whereupon he would suddenly fly into a raging temper. Purple in the face and trembling with anger, he would hammer on the counter with his fists and utter violent threats and abuse, and if that did not frighten the young women away he would hustle them out. One or two in particular loved to provoke him to the utmost, and then fly screaming with laughter down the road, their large naked breasts wobbling and flapping and tears running out of their eyes. But he had grown tired of these scenes, and even before Frant's arrival had abstained from inducing them. With the arrival of Frant he determined to behave himself, at least in Frant's presence, as he wanted the young man to concentrate on business and not begin his stay by getting obsessed with black women. But now that he had found Frant what he would have called "steady," he was about to revert to his old habits, and it cannot be said that his wife, that freckled virago,[13] with her ever-increasing indigestion and her less and less amiable moods, acted exactly as a strong deterrent.

But the first time Frant saw MacGavin behaving familiarly with a gross fat girl it gave him a shock—not because he was prudish by nature, but because it was something he was not used to, and the discovery that MacGavin did not always practise what he preached seemed likely to modify his own behaviour. The thought immediately occurred to him that MacGavin might abuse the modesty of Seraphina, and the idea that the trader's bloodshot and slightly protuberant eye might focus itself upon her natural elegance produced in him a most violent reaction. He said nothing. After MacGavin's wench had departed he came up to Frant and said:

"You'll excuse my saying so, Frant, but don't you feel you want a woman sometimes?"

The effect of this remark upon the young man was extraordinary.

"I do," he answered at once in a quiet voice, "but not a black one."

And he launched into a flood of abuse! He said that he would rather do anything than touch a black woman; he said that they were dirty, that they stank, that they were no better than animals; he said that the blacks and whites were in his opinion races apart, and that on no account should they mix in any way; he said that white men ought to be respected by black ones, and that that could only be possible if they treated them as inferiors, absolute inferiors. He grew white with passion and the heat of his denunciation. His words almost choked him.

MacGavin was astonished beyond measure. He did not know whether to take it all as an attack on himself, or whether Frant had not gone a little out of his mind.

"Well, you do surprise me," he said, in what was meant to be a sarcastic tone of voice. "You've always given me the impression of being a bit too fond of the niggers, and treating them a bit too much as if they were really human beings."

"I get a bit sick of the sight of them at times," said Frant in a much quieter voice, not in the least meaning and indeed hardly knowing what he said. Then he turned away, and the incident was closed, except that MacGavin confided to his wife that he thought Frant was getting a bit restless, and perhaps needed a change or a holiday.

"He can surely wait till Christmas," she said in an aggrieved whisper, for the walls of the house were thin. "We could take him away with us then for a couple of days. But if you ask me, he's unsociable and disagreeable by nature."

"Don't forget that the takings showed another increase last month," said Mac-Gavin.

"That's just why I don't want him to go away now," she said.

---

13 **virago:** A shrewish woman.

It was a brilliant moonlight night, as quiet as the grave, and in his little room Frant was asking himself what on earth could have made him say a whole lot of things he did not mean, what on earth had made him lose control of himself. He felt he had come to the end of everything, that he could not bear this impossible kind of life any longer, and would have to go away. His head was hot, he could not sleep, and he rolled uneasily on his bed. Suddenly, somewhere in a tree, a galago[14] began to scream. Its screams filled the naked air and the heavy silence, the African silence; scream after scream, like prophecies of endless and unthinkable supernatural horrors, uttered by a furred and furtive little creature, hidden large-eyed among moon-drenched branches. Frant got up from his bed and drew back the curtains on a world chalk-white like the face of a clown or pierrot,[15] silent and heartless, and with a sense of terror, of madness almost, let them fall back again.

And the next day Seraphina appeared.

7

There she stood, balancing on her head a light bundle tied with grass. Her arms hung by her side, and when she turned her head authority and resignation, patience and sensibility were in the movement.

> Nowhere but here did ever meet
> Sweetness so sad, sadness so sweet.

Before the coming of the white man the Lembus lived under a system of strict discipline and formality, which did not, however, fail to allow various channels for the various passions of the Lembu heart. It was a system which recognized that some of life's best rewards are best appreciated by those who have not been able to win them too easily. In those days they were all warriors under a mad military autocrat, who believed that too easy an access to heterosexual pleasures might impair the morale and efficiency of his regiments; he trammelled them with a hundred taboos and would not allow them to marry young, while adultery was punished by pushing the guilty parties over separate cliffs of no small height. As for the girls and women, they had a most clearly prescribed course of life, and each stage in their development was made to conform to strict rules. The later relaxation of tribal ethics, for which the white man offered little substitute but calico drawers and hyms Ancient & Modern,[16] rapidly weakened the fibre of the race. But it still happened that there were members of it who managed to live lives not wholly devoid of order and dignity, there were still families 'of the old school' who from the force of heredity or a kind of good breeding managed to do homage to the ghosts of the beliefs of their fore-

---

14 **galago:** Small nocturnal monkey.
15 **pierrot:** Stock character in French comedy, usually made up with a white face and wearing a loose white costume.
16 **hyms A. and M.:** *Hymns Ancient and Modern*, title of a popular Christian hymnal.

fathers. And such a family was Seraphina's. Both its ancient pride and its present obscurity had gone to the making of her features, and its vigour and vitality as well.

They were alone together in the space before the counter.

"Greeting, Seraphina."

"Greeting, my white-man."

Frant could hardly speak, he was so agitated. His heart seemed to fill the whole of his breast with its leaping, and he could scarcely recognize the sound of his own voice as he asked:

"Why have you been so long returning?"

"Do I know?" she said. "Perhaps I was afraid."

She had reason to be afraid—of gossip, of her family, of herself, of Frant, of consequences. With an unhurried movement she took down the bundle from her head and laid it on the floor without bending her knees. Then she untied the grass ropes that held it together and began to open it.

"A snakeskin!" said Frant.

It was a broad snakeskin, and crackled stiffly as it was unrolled. She put her foot on the tail to hold it down while Frant unrolled it. Fully opened, it was at least fifteen feet long, and a great part of it was quite two feet in width. It was the skin of a python, and there were two large rents in the middle of the back as if a spear had killed it. It was not often that the natives traded such things.

"How much are you asking for it?" said Frant in a caressing voice most unsuitable for a commercial transaction.

"I am not selling it," said Seraphina without looking at him. "I am giving it."

"Giving it! To me?"

"To you."

"I thank you very much indeed," he said. In Lembu the same word means to thank and to praise.

There was a pause, then he said:

"Where did it come from? Who killed it?"

"I was hoeing in a maize-field near the river, and it disturbed me. Besides, two of the children were with me. So I killed it."

"You killed it! What with?"

"With my hoe."

When he had got over his astonishment he said, his face shining with admiration:

"But you mustn't give it to me. I must give you some money for it."

"I don't want money," she said, and looked at him with troubled, almost angry eyes.

"I thank you very much," he said again, with the humility and the pride of a lover, and hardly knowing what he was doing he caught hold of her and kissed her on the mouth.

She uttered a cry of surprise and sprang away from him. She simply did not understand him, and was afraid. Natives do not make love as we do. She laughed, just a trifle hysterically.

"What are you doing?" she said.

"What's the matter?" said Frant, approaching again. "I won't hurt you."

"How do I know?" she said.

And he would have answered "Because I love you" (which would have been so hard to say in English and was so easy in Lembu) had they not just at that moment been interrupted.

"Come again soon," Frant said hurriedly. "I want to see you."

And he stooped down and rolled up his snakeskin. When he had finished she was gone.

In the evening he nailed up the skin on the walls of his bedroom. It was so long that it took up the whole of two sides. And very late, before putting out his light, he lay in bed looking at it. Like a banner it hung there to celebrate the intensity of his happiness; it hung like a trophy—the skin of the dragon of his misery, killed by Seraphina as she hoed her father's field of maize.

The next day at noon Mrs. MacGavin said:

"Oh, Mr. Frant, that skin in your room—it gave me such a nasty turn when I went in there this morning!"

"Isn't it a beauty? You don't mind my putting it up, I suppose?"

"Oh, *I* don't mind," she said, "though I couldn't bear to have such a thing over *my* bed. If there's one thing I can't stand it's snakes, alive or dead."

It was nearly Christmas time and the MacGavins told Frant they thought a holiday would do him good, and that they would take him with them to the nearest town. The trading station would be closed for three days, and would be quite safe in the care of the servants. They were extremely surprised when he refused—not because he wanted to help to guard their property, but because the nearest town, of which he had had a few glimpses, did not attract him, and because he had other plans in mind. He felt no inclination to attend the gymkhana[17] or the dance at which, in an atmosphere of false bonhomie and commonplace revelry, the white inhabitants tried annually to forget for a time all about the white man's burden.[18] The MacGavins thought him almost mad for refusing.

"Whatever will you do with yourself?" they said.

"I shall be quite happy," he said.

They felt that something was amiss.

"What, are you 'going native' or something?" cried MacGavin. "You need a change, you know."

He always did his work well, and on account of his natural air of independence they both respected and feared him a little. They gave up trying to argue with him and murmured to each other instead. Then on Christmas Eve the Ford car, newly washed, went rattling away, leaving behind it a cloud of blue smoke and a stink, both of which soon vanished. After the MacGavins had gone Frant felt greatly relieved. It

17 **gymkhana:** A festival featuring athletic contests and games.
18 **white man's burden:** An allusion to Rudyard Kipling's famous phrase, urging Europeans to raise the level of civilization among "heathen" people.

was such a blessing to be free to see and hear what was going on round him instead of being haunted by those harsh stupid voices, that sour red face and that pasty drab one, which had already got on his nerves. Unlike most white men alone in native territories, he had neither a gun nor alcohol in his possession. He did not feel the want of them. For the first time in his life he was to spend Christmas by himself. There would be no exchange of presents; no heavy meals; no forced gaiety; no stuck-up relations. His time, for once, was his own.

8

On Christmas morning he stood on the veranda and stretched his arms, filled with a delicious sense of anticipation. Then he felt in his pocket for a cigarette, and failing to find one took a key and went to fetch a packet from the store. The atmosphere in that building, so closely shuttered at holiday times, was more than oppressive. It was a brilliant morning, and the heat of the sun on the corrugated-iron roof made the interior like an oven. He found some cigarettes, and paused a moment in the doorway to look round at the place where his days were spent. He shuddered slightly, then went out, locking the door behind him. Enjoying his cigarette, and the sun, and the shade, and the peacefulness of not having to look at *those* faces, of not having to listen to *those* voices, he took a path which led through a deserted garden, on the site of the first settlement at Madumbi, towards the forest. In the old garden the foundations of the earlier house remained, but the whole place was now a tangle of vegetation. The hardier growths had survived, and some still withstood the wildings that struggled to oust them. Thickets of ragged junipers and berberis made a forbidding fence which few ever sought to penetrate, and indeed the natives thought the place haunted. Snake apples, those cruel trees, with every bud a barb, and every fruit an ugly bulb filled with dry and poisonous powder, extended their angry foliage over crumbling brickwork. Rankly growing mimosas split with their coarse-grained roots what had once been a path, and month by month in the summer raised their smooth bark and feathery foliage perceptibly higher into the air. A solitary yucca, survivor of several, had produced a single spire thickly hung with white bells, which the mountain wind shook together as if they were made of paper. Tendrils of Christ-thorn put out here and there a few sticky scarlet flowers, and passion flowers hung in unexpected places, in the grass or high up among the junipers, together with the oval, dented granadillas into which they too would change.

Leaving the garden, Frant followed the path to the forest. Then, forcing his way through the undergrowth, parting lianas and monkey-ropes, breaking cobwebs so thick that their breaking was audible, being scratched by thorns, sinking up to the ankles in leaf-mould, he reached a glade he had been to before in times of unhappiness. In the middle of the glade there was a shallow stream of very clear water gliding over sand, and it was sheltered by the vast indigenous trees from the heat of the day.

Here, as he had done before, he threw himself on the breast of earth, surrendering himself to the trees, the water and the quietness. He lay on his back and looked up through half-closed eyes at the topmost branches, watching the fall of a leaf, hearing the call of a bird, the lapse of water, and the thin cries of insects. Under his hand lay a skeleton leaf, over his head a few epiphytic orchids lolled their greenish mouths open over the ancient, rotting bough that gave them life, and at times the wind brought a hint of the perfume of a hidden syringa or laurustinus. A clump of clivia lilies were blooming in deep shadow—they were living and dying in secret, without argument, and untroubled by eyes and voices. A humming-bird appeared from nowhere, and poising itself on the wing before every open flower, whirred there like a moth, gleamed like a jewel, darting its thin curved beak, as sharp as a needle, into each for honey. Nature is inevitable—this stone lies on that one, because it must; fronds uncurl from the hairy trunk of a tree-fern; each new growth and decay seems spontaneous and impersonal; there is a kind of harmony of conflict, and it may have been some sense of that harmony that brought Frant to a decision he might, had he not been so solitary, have taken long before. He was roused. He would act boldly. He would give up caution, discretion, doubt, hesitation, he would forget all about the MacGavins, the trade, the future, he would give up all fear of gossip, of crisis, of reputation, he would break through the bars of his prison. He would go that very day down into the valley and visit the home of Seraphina. He would behave with candour, he would be open in his dealings. He had proved in commerce that he was 'a white man'; he would now be bold, and prove it in love.

Such was his resolution, but the enterprise was not entirely successful. He set out early in the afternoon, carrying a camera, and a stick in case he should meet snakes. He walked as fast as if he were in a more temperate climate, and felt the heat. The first part of the journey took him across an undulating plateau, through country much like that immediately round Madumbi. But after about an hour he came to the top of a hill which marked the end of an escarpment ("The hill is long and steep," Seraphina had said) and he began to follow a downward path winding among rocks and thorn trees. This brought him out on to a platform or small tableland and before him lay suddenly open an immense view. Directly below lay the valley of the Umgazi river, where Seraphina lived, and he sat down under a bean tree to rest and to gaze at the scene.

Somebody was coming up the hill. It was a young man. He was a typical Lembu, naked except for a fur codpiece and some bead ornaments, upright, slender and vigorous. He came striding along, singing joyfully as he went, glistening with oil and sweat, his movements full of natural pride. He was holding a tiny shield, a stick and a knobkerrie[19] in one hand, and in the other a large black cotton Brummagem umbrella, to shelter himself from the sun. When he saw Frant he looked surprised and then saluted him with a large and cheerful gesture. Frant knew him by sight and responded cordially.

"What are you doing here?" said the young man. "Are you out on holiday?"

"Yes," said Frant, "I am just out on holiday."

"Why aren't you riding?"

"I have no horse."

19 **knobkerrie:** Short wooden club with a knot at one end.

"But white men don't walk!"

"I like walking."

The native expressed surprise.

"Is that a camera?" he said.

"Yes, it's a camera."

"Will you take my picture?"

"All right. Go and stand over there. But you must close your umbrella."

"What, must I close my umbrella?"

So Frant stood under the bean tree with his feet among the open pods and little black-and-scarlet beans that had fallen from it, and took a photograph of the native, who stood smiling and glistening in the sun.

"Do you know me?" said the young man.

"Yes," said Frant.

"Do you know Seraphina?"

Frant was startled.

"Yes," he said, unable to conceal his surprise.

"She is my sister."

"What! You're her brother?"

"Yes."

"Fancy that!"

"Seraphina likes you," said her brother. But, thought Frant, is he really her brother? The natives used such terms somewhat loosely. Was this perhaps a rival trying to warn him off? He put the thought out of his mind, for the native was so friendly. "Seraphina likes you," he said. But in Lembu the same word means to like and to love, so perhaps he meant "Seraphina loves you."

"I like Seraphina," said Frant.

"It is not good," said the native, "when a white man likes a black girl."

There was no condemnation in his tone, no threat, no high moral purpose. He smiled as he spoke what he no doubt regarded as a self-obvious truism.

"Why?" said Frant.

"Do I know? It is so."

Frant wanted to say "Would you be angry if your sister married a white man?" but he had no wish to suggest any such thing. And it seemed too crude to say "Would you be angry if your sister slept with a white man?" So he said:

"We are all people."

"Yes, we are all people, but we are different."

"I like natives," said Frant.

"I know you do. But you live in Lembuland, and there are no white people near here for you to like."

This was really unanswerable.

"There are Mr. MacGavin and his wife," said Frant.

Seraphina's brother (if he was Seraphina's brother) laughed.

"Nobody likes *them!*" he said.

"What is your name?" said Frant.

"Me? Umlilwana."

"And where do you live?"

"Down there," said Umlilwana, pointing to the valley.

The river Umgazi, which seemed to consist mostly of a broad bed of stones, with only a small stream of water in the middle, curved in a gigantic S-shaped bend just below where they stood. And on some slightly raised ground in one of the curves of the S were a group of grass domes, which were huts, and a cattle kraal made of thorn trees and brushwood, and a few patches of maize and millet and sweet potatoes. And that was the home of Seraphina. It looked the most peaceful place in the world.

"Will you take me there?" said Frant.

"Take you there! What would you do there?"

"I want to see your home. I want to see Seraphina."

"Seraphina is not there."

"Not there! Where is she?"

"She has gone on a journey to the mountains for several days with our mother and father to see our cousins. There's nobody down there but an old woman and some children."

"Oh," said Frant, and was silent a moment. "I am sorry," he said then. "I wanted to see Seraphina."

And suddenly everything seemed utterly remote. The view was like a view in a dream. Seraphina (*could* that be her name?) seemed only an idea and her cousins like characters in a myth. And even the friendly smiling Umlilwana seemed utterly strange and unapproachable.

"Yes, I am sorry," Frant repeated in a dull voice. "But I should like some day to visit your home and take photographs of Seraphina—and of all your family."

Umlilwana was a little suspicious of this, but he said Frant would be welcome.

"Will you do something for me?" said Frant. "Will you come and tell me when Seraphina returns? Tell Seraphina I want to see her. Tell her I want to see her again."

"All right," said Umlilwana in English and with great affability. It was about all the English he knew.

"Umlilwana, you are my friend."

"All right, will you give me some cigarettes?"

Frant smiled, and gave him all he had. Umlilwana was loud in thanks.

Some children could be seen playing near Seraphina's kraal. They looked as small as ants. The distant mountains looked infinitely blue and remote, with the shadows of a few light clouds patterning their peaks. There was nothing to do but to return to Madumbi.

9

Frant returned to Madumbi. So, a couple of days later, did the MacGavins, both with a touch of righteous indignation at Frant's oddness in not having gone with them, and Mrs. MacGavin with more than a touch of dyspepsia. Life then resumed its usual course. But things were not quite the same. First of all, Frant was in a far more cheerful frame of mind. Not only had he begun to act with some initiative, not only had he seen Seraphina's home and made friends with her brother, but he had told somebody of his love for her. As soon as she returned he meant to bring matters to a head, even though he and she were "different." And if her continued absence was a great trial to his patience, he got up every morning in hopes of a visit and news from Umlilwana in the course of the day. But day followed day, and Umlilwana did not appear. Frant played with the idea of sending him a message, but as it would have to be a verbal one, he thought it more prudent not to do so. And when he once ventured to inquire about Umlilwana, and to ask if he were really Seraphina's brother, the people he spoke to said they had never heard of either of them. And at night he lay naked and sweating on his bed, tortured continually with the image of Seraphina, remembering her gestures, her "sadness so sweet", and the touch of her flesh.

"Frant should have gone away with us," MacGavin remarked to his wife. "He's quite liverish now at times."

"This weather's enough to make anybody liverish,"[20] said she. "I always did say that January was the worst month of the year. It's bilious weather. But it's not his liver, if you ask me, it's his nerves."

January was certainly a bad month at Madumbi, and that year it was more trying than ever. There had been no rain for weeks, and things were beginning to look parched. The heat was dry and intense. And then, day after day, clouds would collect in the morning and accumulate in the afternoon, thunder was occasionally heard and once even a few drops of rain fell in the dust, as if a few devils had spat from a great height. Every morning seemed to promise a thunderstorm, and one began to imagine how the earth would smell after rain, and how cool the air would be, and how the flying ants would come out in the twilight, but every evening the clouds dispersed and left a hot moon to glare down on the veld,[21] or the glittering arrogance of the stars. And every morning Frant said to himself, "Umlilwana will come, or Seraphina herself," but every evening he found himself alone again, exhausted and restless. Even the natives, in their anxiety about their crops, were beginning to get on one another's nerves. The air seemed charged with electricity, it seemed to brace one's very muscles against a shock which was not forthcoming, and to leave them at once taut and tired. Even MacGavin took to glancing often at the sky, at the great cumulus clouds that hung in it all the afternoon, and he would say, "It'll be serious if something doesn't happen soon."

It was like waiting for an earthquake, a revolution, the day of judgment almost. There was an awful mixture of certainty that something was going to happen, and of uncertainty as to when it would happen. "We only want a storm to clear the air," Mrs. MacGavin repeated every day until Frant almost felt that he could murder her.

20 **liverish:** Peevish; irritable.
21 **veld:** Grassland, with some shrubs and trees.

The sweat ran down inside his shirt, his overheated blood inflamed his overstrained imagination, he found it more and more difficult to sleep and eat. Trade grew slack, because few could endure to climb up the slopes to Madumbi, and when the store was empty it was far less tolerable than when it was full. The morning sun beat down on the corrugated iron and the interior grew so hot that it failed to cool down during the night. Strange stories came in—that some grass had caught fire simply from the heat of the sun shining through an empty bottle, and several huts had been burnt in consequence; that a young crocodile had come right up one of the little tributaries of the Umgazi and had been found less than a mile from Madumbi itself, an occurrence never before known; and that a native woman had been arrested for killing a new-born baby with six fingers on one hand, in the belief that this deformity was keeping the rain away. Where was Umlilwana? Where was Seraphina? "I will wait till next Sunday," said Frant to himself, "and if neither of them has come by then I shall go down to the kraal itself on the pretext of wanting to take photographs." But he did not have to wait till Sunday, for the weather broke.

The worst day of all was the fourteenth of the month.

"Well, this is the worst we've had yet," said Mrs. MacGavin at supper time.

"You've said that for the last four days," observed her husband.

All the doors and windows were wide open. The sky was completely overcast and nothing was stirring but the moths and other insects which flew in from the garden and bumped against the paper lampshade, or against the glass which covered "The Confession," or fell into the soup, the powder from their wings mingling with the film of grease which already covered that liquid. The rays of lamplight lay on the creepers of the veranda itself and on the path, but beyond them was utter silence and hot, heavy darkness.

"Hark! Was that thunder?" said Mrs. MacGavin.

"You always say that at supper time," remarked her husband.

"It *was* thunder," she said, her head on one side, as she pushed a stray wisp of hair out of her eye.

Yes, it *was* thunder. They all heard it. Low, continuous thunder.

"That's up in the mountains," said MacGavin. "It's a bad sign if it begins up there. If there *is* a storm, it'll probably miss us altogether . . . Ah, did you see the lightning? Yes, that's where it is. I bet it's pouring up there already. And I don't like a dry storm. It's much more dangerous. More likely to strike the trees."

Frant's heart was beating loud and fast as if in anticipation of some personal, not a meteorological event. He walked alone to the bottom of the garden and stood there watching the play of lightning in the distance, but it did not seem much more than on previous nights. He came in and tried to read a paper, lighted several cigarettes in succession, throwing one or two away half-smoked, paced up and down in the garden, glancing up at the darkness, and then retired to his room where he lay on his bed without undressing. His hands were clenched, the nails dug into the palms, and he was conscious of little but the beating of his heart. He couldn't hear the MacGavins talking anywhere, or any natives, and had lost all sense of the time. He put out his light, and like a convict without a crime, in a prison that was not locked, for a sentence of indeterminate duration, he just lay there sweating.

At last he got up and went to the window. The moon was out again. It was almost full, and stood high in the sky, flooding the landscape with light. To the south, vast banks of cloud were ranged above the forest, and among them, now and then, a worm of lightning played, followed by a distant roll of thunder. Not a leaf seemed to be stirring, when he noticed that a light breeze was rising and feathering the tops of the distant trees. Very soon the tops of the mimosas near the house bowed, lightly swaying towards the moon, and a tremor ran through the grass as if an invisible hand had stroked it. The wind rose, the clouds towered and toppled upwards, the moon was caught in a web of flying mist, the thunder grew louder, and the flashes of lightning more frequent. A greenish light seemed to emanate from the moon, and as the sky grew more heavily loaded, the forest, by contrast, appeared more ethereal, the heavy boscage and the trunks of the huge indigenous trees appearing in great detail, all dry and luminous and lurid, the foliage beginning to churn and writhe slowly on the topmost boughs. The tenseness of the atmosphere, the expectancy of nature, and the way in which the whole landscape, the very buildings and their shadows, seemed to take part in the great symphony of the impending storm, combined to produce an effect so dramatic as to seem almost supernatural.

The rolling of the thunder was now continuous. All the mountain country was overhung with the incessant play of sheet-lightning, as if a curtain of fire, continually agitated by unseen forces, hung over half the world. The wind began to howl round the house, leaves and twigs to fly from the trees, a pile of timber was blown over, and the moon was half hidden in a swirl of clouds. Chains and forks of lightning, steely-blue and sulphurous red, larger and brighter and more frequent than Frant had ever seen, lighted everything with a continuous, shaken glare. Thunder pealed almost overhead, phalanxes of cloud advanced like avenging armies, the house shook, the windows rattled, and he put his hand to his burning and throbbing head. His pulses raced, sweat poured down his face and body, and he felt as if his veins would burst. Suddenly he caught sight of a white horse, which had broken loose from heaven knows where, and was careering madly, its mane and tail flying, its halter trailing, along the slope of the nearest hill. It seemed a creature of fire as it tossed its head, swerved at sudden obstacles, and galloped up to the ridge. There for a moment it stood, quivering with fear and exertion in the quivering glare of the lightning, and then, made splendid by freedom, disappeared from view.

"I can't stay in the house an instant longer!" Frant said aloud to himself, and taking up an electric torch,[22] he stepped out into the garden. A strong refreshing breeze was blowing, but not a drop of rain had fallen. "It looks as though MacGavin was right—the storm seems to have missed us altogether . . ." He wondered what on earth he had brought the torch for, since the lightning was quivering incessantly, like a network of luminous nerves.

"Is that you, Frant?"

It was MacGavin calling from the house.

---

22 **electric torch:** Flashlight.

"Yes. I can't sleep. I'm going for a walk. It's much fresher out now."

"A walk! At this time! Don't go far. It's risky. And if it *should* come on to rain . . ."

"I'll be all right, thanks. Good night."

He disappeared from view, and instinctively found himself taking the path he had taken on Christmas Day. He was frightened of the night, of losing his way, of the storm. He had at first no thought of going far, but when he paused to try and calculate how far he had already come he was almost as afraid to turn back as to go on, so he went on. He had got an idea that he must get to the bean tree, and he kept telling himself that it was not really very far. The wind was behind him now, and its freshness gave him energy. The glare and racket of the storm grew no less—it now seemed to be everywhere except immediately overhead. He hurried on, stumbling now and again, for the path was in places rough and narrow. He saw lights once or twice but did not meet a soul. And back at Madumbi MacGavin had grown anxious about him.

Before he came to the escarpment there was a loud detonation just overhead, and it began to rain. He had come too far now to turn back, so he hurried on, vaguely imagining that he would ask for shelter at Seraphina's. Near the top of the hill he realized that the worst of the weather was in front of him. The lightning revealed a thick grey veil of rain beyond the valley, and he could hear a tremendous steady downpour in the distance. The nearer he got to the top the louder the tumult grew, and he thought, "The river must be a lot fuller by now than when I last saw it." He was going downhill at last, but not so fast as he wanted, for it was raining pretty hard now and the paths were getting slippery. A feeling of terror seized him. He felt that he would never get down to the valley, that the storm would beat him, that it was no good thinking of turning back.

There was no doubt as to what he could hear now. The river must be in flood. And he suddenly thought, would the kraal be safe? Hardly . . . He was running now, to reach the bean tree. He was soaked to the skin, and his feet kept slipping. He missed the way twice and found it again, and then, waiting for the lightning to show him where he was, he found he was only a few yards from the tree.

And just at that moment, exactly as before, he saw a man coming towards him. Only this time the man was running. And this time it was not Umlilwana he saw. And this time he was terrified.

The man didn't see Frant until he almost ran into him, and he was too frightened.

"*Au!*" cried a familiar voice. "*Umtwana ka Kwini!* Child of the Queen! What are you doing here? Where are you going? Child! My child! Have you *seen*? Look, look!"

He dragged Frant over the slippery rocks to the very edge of the tableland.

"Look!" he cried.

A prolonged flash of lightning lit up the whole valley with a tremulous, pale violet glare like the light of some hellish arclamp, and in a few seconds Frant had understood. Gone was the S-shaped bend, gone were the grassy domes, the kraal and little fields! There was nothing where they had been but a gigantic swirl of greyish water, in which trunks of trees could be seen travelling, spinning and half raising themselves above the surface like animate things.

"Seraphina!" cried Frant. "Do you know Seraphina?"

He had caught hold of the little old man, who was shivering with fear and cold and seemed the only reality left in the world.

"Seraphina!" cried Frant. "Do you know her? Did she come back? Was she at home?"

"She was at home for two weeks, *umtwana*," said the old man, shaking like a leaf. "The cattle are drowned!" he cried in the voice of Job and of Lear. "The houses, the people—all are drowned!"

"Drowned?" cried Frant, shining his torch full in the old man's face. "Why? Why are they drowned?"

"The water came like a wall, my child," said the old man, and the torchlight made the raindrops running down his face look as if it was covered with tears. He was shivering violently from top to toe, and his old tunic clung to his skin.

"Umlilwana," said Frant. "Was Umlilwana her brother?"

"Umlilwana?" said the old man. "Umlilwana wasn't her brother! She was going to marry Umlilwana."

In the lightning-glare he saw Frant's face.

"All is finished!" he cried, putting out a black and bony claw, as if to defend himself from some unknown danger. In Lembu the same word means to be finished or to be destroyed. "Are you bewitched?"

Yes, all was finished, all was destroyed. Already the rolling of the thunder was increasing in volume, but the roar of the flood seemed to grow louder, and the rain was coming down like whips of ice and steel. It was like the coming of the deluge itself. It was like the end of the world.

Something in Frant urged him to leave the old man and run down the hill and plunge into those maddened waters and lose himself, but something stronger told him that he must return to Madumbi, to the store, to the MacGavins, to the making of a livelihood, to the fashioning of a way of life, to a roll of undeveloped negatives, and to a python skin nailed to a wall like a banner, with two large holes in it cut by a girl with a hoe.

"I must go back!" he said to the old man, and gripped his shoulder for an instant. Then he made off in the direction of Madumbi, flashing the torch on the path. The old man called after him to take care, but he was at once out of earshot in the downpour. After he had stumbled a short way one spasmodic sob escaped from him, and he began to run.

QUESTIONS

1. What is the significance of the title?

2. Characterize relations between whites and Africans in this story. Does Plomer appear to be neutrally describing these relations, or is he passing judgment?

3. How do you interpret the author's remarks about Frant's background and education? Is he approving, disapproving, satirical, harshly critical, or something else?

4. How do descriptions of weather and landscape contribute to the story?

5. Is the author's description of Seraphina admiring? Racist? Neutral?

6. How does Frant grow and change in the course of the story?

Doris Lessing

ability to change the nature, appearance, & / behavior

(b. 1919)

Doris Lessing is a powerful and protean voice in modern literature, a writer whose intellectual interests and ideas are as varied and provocative as her personal background.

She was born Doris May Tayler in Kermanshah, Persia (present-day Iran), where her father worked in a bank. In 1924 the family joined other white settler-farmers in Southern Rhodesia to raise corn and tobacco and pan for gold, but the search for fortune found only hard work and poverty. Doris attended a convent school and then a public girls' school in Salisbury (now Harare), but she left school permanently at age twelve because of eye problems. At sixteen she went to work as a typist for a phone company and eventually for the *Guardian* newspaper in Cape Town, South Africa. She married Frank Wisdom in 1939, with whom she had two children before divorcing him in 1943. Two years later she married Gottfried Lessing, with whom she had a son, but again the marriage ended in divorce. In 1949, she moved to London, where, apart from travels, she has lived ever since. Africa, however, left an indelible impression on Lessing as a woman and a writer, and many of her political ideas and activities have sprung from the racial injustices she witnessed while living and working there.

The horrors of apartheid formed the basis for her first novel, *The Grass Is Singing* (1950), one of the first fictional works to treat the subject honestly. The next year saw the publication of her first collection of short stories, *This Was the Old Chief's Country*, which dealt with problems of race but also with the larger issue of power and its uses or misuses. In some of the stories, the perspective is that of a young girl observing the injustices around her. In 1952 Lessing published *Martha Quest*, the first of a five-book series of autobiographically based novels. Lessing's most famous work is *The Golden Notebook* (1962), a complex novel whose central character, Anna Wulf, struggles with writer's block and keeps several notebooks that comment on various social, political, and sexual issues. The book earned Lessing a reputation as a feminist, a label she rejects—as she does all others—as limiting.

In addition to writing novels, Lessing has written short stories, poetry, essays, drama, and science fiction. The settings of her stories have often moved away from Africa, just as coming-of-age stories have given way to those focusing on older characters. Two of her most famous, "To Room Nineteen" and

"A Woman on the Roof," have reinforced the idea that Lessing is primarily a feminist writer, but this ignores her interests in and commitment to a wide variety of social and political issues. Always an experimentalist, Lessing's accomplishments in various genres and with a variety of formal structures and stylistic devices make her one of the most difficult of modern writers to categorize and one of the most interesting to read. Critics sometimes complain that she is too polemical, that her ideas get in the way of artistic expression. This may be true on occasion, but Lessing's constantly changing interests and viewpoints neutralize such criticism, as does the urgency of the issues she writes about.

The Old Chief Mshlanga
1951

They were good, the years of ranging the bush over her father's farm which, like every white farm, was largely unused, broken only occasionally by small patches of cultivation. In between, nothing but trees, the long sparse grass, thorn and cactus and gully, grass and outcrop and thorn. And a jutting piece of rock which had been thrust up from the warm soil of Africa unimaginable eras of time ago, washed into hollows and whorls by sun and wind that had travelled so many thousands of miles of space and bush, would hold the weight of a small girl whose eyes were sightless for anything but a pale willowed river, a pale gleaming castle—a small girl singing: "Out flew the web and floated wide, the mirror cracked from side to side . . ."[1]

Pushing her way through the green aisles of the mealie stalks,[2] the leaves arching like cathedrals veined with sunlight far overhead with the packed red earth underfoot, a fine lace of red-starred witchweed would summon up a black bent figure croaking premonitions: the Northern witch, bred of cold Northern forests, would stand before her among the mealie fields, and it was the mealie fields that faded and fled, leaving her among the gnarled roots of an oak, snow falling thick and soft and white, the woodcutter's fire glowing red welcome through crowding tree trunks.

A white child, opening its eyes curiously on a sun-suffused landscape, a gaunt and violent landscape, might be supposed to accept it as her own, to take the msasa trees and the thorn trees as familiars, to feel her blood running free and responsive to the swing of the seasons.

This child could not see a msasa tree, or the thorn, for what they were. Her books held tales of alien fairies, her rivers ran slow and peaceful, and she knew the shape of the leaves of an ash or an oak, the names of the little creatures that lived in English streams, when the words "the veld" meant strangeness, though she could remember nothing else.

Because of this, for many years, it was the veld that seemed unreal; the sun was a foreign sun, and the wind spoke a strange language.

---

1 **"Out . . . side . . .":** Lines 114–15 of Alfred Lord Tennyson's "The Lady of Shalott."
2 **Mealie stalks:** Corn stalks

The black people on the farm were as remote as the trees and the rocks. They were an amorphous black mass, mingling and thinning and massing like tadpoles, faceless, who existed merely to serve, to say "Yes, Baas," take their money and go. They changed season by season, moving from one farm to the next, according to their outlandish needs, which one did not have to understand, coming from perhaps hundreds of miles North or East, passing on after a few months—where? Perhaps even as far away as the fabled gold mines of Johannesburg, where the pay was so much better than the few shillings a month and the double handful of mealie meal twice a day which they earned in that part of Africa.

The child was taught to take them for granted: the servants in the house would come running a hundred yards to pick up a book if she dropped it. She was called "Nkosikaas"—Chieftainess, even by the black children her own age.

Later, when the farm grew too small to hold her curiosity, she carried a gun in the crook of her arm and wandered miles a day, from vlei to vlei, from kopje to kopje,[3] accompanied by two dogs: the dogs and the gun were an armour against fear. Because of them she never felt fear.

If a native came into sight along the kaffir paths half a mile away, the dogs would flush him up a tree as if he were a bird. If he expostulated (in his uncouth language which was by itself ridiculous) that was cheek. If one was in a good mood, it could be a matter for laughter. Otherwise one passed on, hardly glancing at the angry native in the tree.

On the rare occasions when white children met together they could amuse themselves by hailing a passing native in order to make a buffoon of him; they could set the dogs on to him and watch him run; they could tease a small black child as if he were a puppy—save that they would not throw stones and sticks at a dog without a sense of guilt.

Later still, certain questions presented themselves in the child's mind; and because the answers were not easy to accept, they were silenced by an even greater arrogance of manner.

It was even impossible to think of the black people who worked about the house as friends, for if she talked to one of them, her mother would come running anxiously: "Come away; you mustn't talk to natives."

It was this instilled consciousness of danger, of something unpleasant, that made it easy to laugh out loud, crudely, if a servant made a mistake in his English or if he failed to understand an order—there is a certain kind of laughter that is fear, afraid of itself.

One evening, when I was about fourteen, I was walking down the side of a mealie field that had been newly ploughed, so that the great red clods showed fresh and tumbling to the vlei beyond, like a choppy red sea; it was that hushed and listening hour, when the birds send long sad calls from tree to tree, and all the colours of earth and sky and leaf are deep and golden. I had my rifle in the curve of my arm, and the dogs were at my heels.

---

3 **vlei . . . kopje:** A shallow pool of water or a patch of low lying ground . . . small hill on the African veld.

In front of me, perhaps a couple of hundred yards away, a group of three natives came into sight around the side of a big antheap. I whistled the dogs close in to my skirts and let the gun swing in my hand, and advanced, waiting for them to move aside, off the path, in respect for my passing. But they came on steadily, and the dogs looked up at me for the command to chase. I was angry. It was "cheek" for a native not to stand off a path, the moment he caught sight of you.

In front walked an old man, stooping his weight on to a stick, his hair grizzled white, a dark red blanket slung over his shoulders like a cloak. Behind him came two young men, carrying bundles of pots, assegais,[4] hatchets.

The group was not a usual one. They were not natives seeking work. These had an air of dignity, of quietly following their own purpose. It was the dignity that checked my tongue. I walked quietly on, talking softly to the growling dogs, till I was ten paces away. Then the old man stopped, drawing his blanket close.

"'Morning, Nkosikaas," he said, using the customary greeting for any time of the day.

"Good morning," I said. "Where are you going?" My voice was a little truculent.

The old man spoke in his own language, then one of the young men stepped forward politely and said in careful English: "My Chief travels to see his brothers beyond the river."

A Chief! I thought, understanding the pride that made the old man stand before me like an equal—more than an equal, for he showed courtesy, and I showed none.

The old man spoke again, wearing dignity like an inherited garment, still standing ten paces off, flanked by his entourage, not looking at me (that would have been rude) but directing his eyes somewhere over my head at the trees.

"You are the little Nkosikaas from the farm of Baas Jordan?"

"That's right," I said.

"Perhaps your father does not remember," said the interpreter for the old man, "but there was an affair with some goats. I remember seeing you when you were . . ." The young man held his hand at knee level and smiled.

We all smiled.

"What is your name?" I asked.

"This is Chief Mshlanga," said the young man.

"I will tell my father that I met you," I said.

The old man said: "My greetings to your father, little Nkosikaas."

"Good morning," I said politely, finding the politeness difficult, from lack of use.

"'Morning, little Nkosikaas," said the old man, and stood aside to let me pass.

I went by, my gun hanging awkwardly, the dogs sniffing and growling, cheated of their favourite game of chasing natives like animals.

Not long afterwards I read in an old explorer's book the phrase: "Chief Mshlanga's country." It went like this: "Our destination was Chief Mshlanga's country, to the

---

4 **assegais:** Spears.

north of the river; and it was our desire to ask his permission to prospect for gold in his territory."

The phrase "ask his permission" was so extraordinary to a white child, brought up to consider all natives as things to use, that it revived those questions, which could not be suppressed: they fermented slowly in my mind.

On another occasion one of those old prospectors who still move over Africa looking for neglected reefs, with their hammers and tents, and pans for sifting gold from crushed rock, came to the farm and, in talking of the old days, used that phrase again: "This was the Old Chief's country," he said. "It stretched from those mountains over there way back to the river, hundreds of miles of country." That was his name for our district: "The Old Chief's Country"; he did not use our name for it—a new phrase which held no implication of usurped ownership.

As I read more books about the time when this part of Africa was opened up, not much more than fifty years before, I found Old Chief Mshlanga had been a famous man, known to all the explorers and prospectors. But then he had been young; or maybe it was his father or uncle they spoke of—I never found out.

During that year I met him several times in the part of the farm that was traversed by natives moving over the country. I learned that the path up the side of the big red field where the birds sang was the recognized highway for migrants. Perhaps I even haunted it in the hope of meeting him: being greeted by him, the exchange of courtesies, seemed to answer the questions that troubled me.

Soon I carried a gun in a different spirit; I used it for shooting food and not to give me confidence. And now the dogs learned better manners. When I saw a native approaching, we offered and took greetings; and slowly that other landscape in my mind faded, and my feet struck directly on the African soil, and I saw the shapes of tree and hill clearly, and the black people moved back, as it were, out of my life: it was as if I stood aside to watch a slow intimate dance of landscape and men, a very old dance, whose steps I could not learn.

But I thought: this is my heritage, too; I was bred here; it is my country as well as the black man's country; and there is plenty of room for all of us, without elbowing each other off the pavements and roads.

It seemed it was only necessary to let free that respect I felt when I was talking with old Chief Mshlanga, to let both black and white people meet gently, with tolerance for each other's differences: it seemed quite easy.

Then, one day, something new happened. Working in our house as servants were always three natives: cook, houseboy, garden boy. They used to change as the farm natives changed: staying for a few months, then moving on to a new job, or back home to their kraals.[5] They were thought of as "good" or "bad" natives; which meant; how did they behave as servants? Were they lazy, efficient, obedient, or disrespectful? If the family felt good-humoured, the phrase was: "What can you expect from raw black savages?" If we were angry, we said: "These damned niggers, we would be much better off without them."

5 **kraals:** Villages, but also the corrals used to pen farm animals.

One day, a white policeman was on his rounds of the district, and he said laughingly: "Did you know you have an important man in your kitchen?"

"What!" exclaimed my mother sharply. "What do you mean?"

"A Chief's son." The policeman seemed amused. "He'll boss the tribe when the old man dies."

"He'd better not put on a Chief's son act with me," said my mother.

When the policeman left, we looked with different eyes at our cook: he was a good worker, but he drank too much at weekends—that was how we knew him.

He was a tall youth, with very black skin, like black polished metal, his tightly-growing black hair parted white man's fashion at one side, with a metal comb from the store stuck into it; very polite, very distant, very quick to obey an order. Now it had been pointed out, we said: "Of course, you can see. Blood always tells."

My mother became strict with him now she knew about his birth and prospects. Sometimes, when she lost her temper, she would say: "You aren't the Chief yet, you know." And he would answer her very quietly, his eyes on the ground: "Yes, Nkosikaas."

One afternoon he asked for a whole day off, instead of the customary half-day, to go home next Sunday.

"How can you go home in one day?"

"It will take me half an hour on my bicycle," he explained.

I watched the direction he took; and next day I went off to look for this kraal; I understood he must be Chief Mshlanga's successor: there was no other kraal near enough our farm.

Beyond our boundaries on that side the country was new to me. I followed unfamiliar paths past kopjes that till now had been part of the jagged horizon, hazed with distance. This was Government land, which had never been cultivated by white men; at first I could not understand why it was that it appeared, in merely crossing the boundary, I had entered a completely fresh type of landscape. It was a wide green valley, where a small river sparkled, and vivid water-birds darted over the rushes. The grass was thick and soft to my calves, the trees stood tall and shapely.

I was used to our farm, whose hundreds of acres of harsh eroded soil bore trees that had been cut for the mine furnaces and had grown thin and twisted, where the cattle had dragged the grass flat, leaving innumerable criss-crossing trails that deepened each season into gullies, under the force of the rains.

This country had been left untouched, save for prospectors whose picks had struck a few sparks from the surface of the rocks as they wandered by; and for migrant natives whose passing had left, perhaps, a charred patch on the trunk of a tree where their evening fire had nestled.

It was very silent: a hot morning with pigeons cooing throatily, the midday shadows lying dense and thick with clear yellow spaces of sunlight between and in all that wide green park-like valley, not a human soul but myself.

I was listening to the quick regular tapping of a woodpecker when slowly a chill feeling seemed to grow up from the small of my back to my shoulders, in a constricting spasm like a shudder, and at the roots of my hair a tingling sensation began and ran down over the surface of my flesh, leaving me goosefleshed and cold, though I was damp with sweat. Fever? I thought; then uneasily, turned to look over my shoulder; and realized suddenly that this was fear. It was extraordinary, even humiliating. It was a new fear. For all the years I had walked by myself over this country I had never known a moment's uneasiness; in the beginning because I had been supported by a gun and the dogs, then because I had learnt an easy friendliness for the natives I might encounter.

I had read of this feeling, how the bigness and silence of Africa, under the ancient sun, grows dense and takes shape in the mind, till even the birds seem to call menacingly, and a deadly spirit comes out of the trees and the rocks. You move warily, as if your very passing disturbs something old and evil, something dark and big and angry that might suddenly rear and strike from behind. You look at groves of entwined trees, and picture the animals that might be lurking there; you look at the river, running slowly, dropping from level to level through the vlei, spreading into pools where at night the buck come to drink, and the crocodiles rise and drag them by their soft noses into underwater caves. Fear possessed me. I found I was turning round and round, because of that shapeless menace behind me that might reach out and take me; I kept glancing at the files of kopjes which, seen from a different angle, seemed to change with every step so that even known landmarks, like a big mountain that has sentinelled my world since I first became conscious of it, showed an unfamiliar sunlit valley among its foothills. I did not know where I was. I was lost. Panic seized me. I found I was spinning round and round, staring anxiously at this tree and that, peering up at the sun which appeared to have moved into an eastern slant, shedding the sad yellow light of sunset. Hours must have passed! I looked at my watch and found that this state of meaningless terror had lasted perhaps ten minutes.

The point was that it was meaningless. I was not ten miles from home: I had only to take my way back along the valley to find myself at the fence; away among the foothills of the kopjes gleamed the roof of a neighbour's house, and a couple of hours walking would reach it. This was the sort of fear that contracts the flesh of a dog at night and sets him howling at the full moon. It had nothing to do with what I thought or felt; and I was more disturbed by the fact that I could become its victim than of the physical sensation itself: I walked steadily on, quietened, in a divided mind, watching my own pricking nerves and apprehensive glances from side to side with a disgusted amusement. Deliberately I set myself to think of this village I was seeking, and what I should do when I entered it—if I could find it, which was doubtful, since I was walking aimlessly and it might be anywhere in the hundreds of thousands of acres of bush that stretched about me. With my mind on that village, I realized that a new sensation was added to the fear: loneliness. Now such a terror of isolation invaded me that I could hardly walk; and if it were not that I came over the crest of a small rise and saw a village below me, I should have turned and gone home. It was a cluster of thatched huts in a clearing among trees. There were neat patches of mealies and pumpkins and millet, and cattle grazed under some trees at a distance. Fowls scratched among the huts, dogs lay sleeping on the grass, and goats friezed a kopje that jutted up beyond a tributary of the river lying like an enclosing arm round the village.

As I came close I saw the huts were lovingly decorated with patterns of yellow and red and ochre mud on the walls; and the thatch was tied in place with plaits of straw.

This was not at all like our farm compound, a dirty and neglected place, a temporary home for migrants who had no roots in it.

And now I did not know what to do next. I called a small black boy, who was sitting on a log playing a stringed gourd, quite naked except for the strings of blue beads round his neck, and said: "Tell the Chief I am here." The child stuck his thumb in his mouth and stared shyly back at me.

For minutes I shifted my feet on the edge of what seemed a deserted village, till at last the child scuttled off, and then some women came. They were draped in bright cloths, with brass glinting in their ears and on their arms. They also stared, silently; then turned to chatter among themselves.

I said again: "Can I see Chief Mshlanga?" I saw they caught the name; they did not understand what I wanted. I did not understand myself.

At last I walked through them and came past the huts and saw a clearing under a big shady tree, where a dozen old men sat crosslegged on the ground, talking. Chief Mshlanga was leaning back against the tree, holding a gourd in his hand, from which he had been drinking. When he saw me, not a muscle of his face moved, and I could see he was not pleased: perhaps he was afflicted with my own shyness, due to being unable to find the right forms of courtesy for the occasion. To meet me, on our own farm, was one thing; but I should not have come here. What had I expected? I could not join them socially: the thing was unheard of. Bad enough that I, a white girl, should be walking the veld alone as a white man might: and in this part of the bush where only Government officials had the right to move.

Again I stood, smiling foolishly, while behind me stood the groups of brightly-clad, chattering women, their faces alert with curiosity and interest, and in front of me sat the old men, with old lined faces, their eyes guarded, aloof. It was a village of ancients and children and women. Even the two young men who kneeled beside the Chief were not those I had seen with him previously: the young men were all away working on the white men's farms and mines, and the Chief must depend on relatives who were temporarily on holiday for his attendants.

"The small white Nkosikaas is far from home," remarked the old man at last.

"Yes," I agreed, "it is far." I wanted to say: "I have come to pay you a friendly visit, Chief Mshlanga." I could not say it. I might now be feeling an urgent helpless desire to get to know these men and women as people, to be accepted by them as a friend, but the truth was I had set out in a spirit of curiosity: I had wanted to see the village that one day our cook, the reserved and obedient young man who got drunk on Sundays, would one day rule over.

"The child of Nkoss Jordan is welcome," said Chief Mshlanga.

"Thank you," I said, and could think of nothing more to say. There was a silence, while the flies rose and began to buzz around my head; and the wind shook a little in the thick green tree that spread its branches over the old men.

"Good morning," I said at last. "I have to return now to my home."

"Morning, little Nkosikaas," said Chief Mshlanga.

I walked away from the indifferent village, over the rise past the staring amber-eyed goats, down through the tall stately trees into the great rich green valley where the river meandered and the pigeons cooed tales of plenty and the woodpecker tapped softly.

The fear had gone; the loneliness had set into sniff-necked stoicism; there was now a queer hostility in the landscape, a cold, hard, sullen indomitability that walked with me, as strong as a wall, as intangible as smoke; it seemed to say to me: you walk here as a destroyer. I went slowly homewards, with an empty heart: I had learned that if one cannot call a country to heel like a dog, neither can one dismiss the past with a smile in an easy gush of feeling, saying: I could not help it, I am also a victim.

I only saw Chief Mshlanga once again.

One night my father's big red land was trampled down by small sharp hooves, and it was discovered that the culprits were goats from Chief Mshlanga's kraal. This had happened once before, years ago.

My father confiscated all the goats. Then he sent a message to the old Chief that if he wanted them he would have to pay for the damage.

He arrived at our house at the time of sunset one evening, looking very old and bent now, walking stiffly under his regally-draped blanket, leaning on a big stick. My father sat himself down in his big chair below the steps of the house; the old man squatted carefully on the ground before him, flanked by his two young men.

The palaver was long and painful, because of the bad English of the young man who interpreted, and because my father could not speak dialect, but only kitchen kaffir.

From my father's point of view, at least two hundreds pounds worth of damage had been done to the crop. He knew he could not get the money from the old man. He felt he was entitled to keep the goats. As for the old Chief, he kept repeating angrily: "Twenty goats! My people cannot lose twenty goats! We are not rich, like the Nkosi Jordan, to lose twenty goats at once."

My father did not think of himself as rich, but rather as very poor. He spoke quickly and angrily in return, saying that the damage done meant a great deal to him, and that he was entitled to the goats.

At last it grew so heated that the cook, the Chief's son, was called from the kitchen to be interpreter, and now my father spoke fluently in English, and our cook translated rapidly so that the old man could understand how very angry my father was. The young man spoke without emotion, in a mechanical way, his eyes lowered, but showing how he felt his position by a hostile uncomfortable set of the shoulders.

It was now in the late sunset, the sky a welter of colours, the birds singing their last songs, and the cattle, lowing peacefully, moving past us towards their sheds for the night. It was the hour when Africa is most beautiful; and here was this pathetic, ugly scene, doing no one any good.

At last my father stated finally: "I'm not going to argue about it. I am keeping the goats."

The old Chief flashed back in his own language: "That means that my people will go hungry when the dry season comes."

"Go to the police, then," said my father, and looked triumphant.

There was, of course, no more to be said.

The old man sat silent, his head bent, his hands dangling helplessly over his withered knees. Then he rose, the young men helping him, and he stood facing my father. He spoke once again, very stiffly; and turned away and went home to his village.

"What did he say?" asked my father of the young man, who laughed uncomfortably and would not meet his eyes.

"What did he say?" insisted my father.

Our cook stood straight and silent, his brows knotted together. Then he spoke. "My father says: All this land, this land you call yours, is his land, and belongs to our people."

Having made this statement, he walked off into the bush after his father, and we did not see him again.

Our next cook was a migrant from Nyasaland, with no expectations of greatness.

Next time the policeman came on his rounds he was told this story. He remarked: "That kraal has no right to be there; it should have been moved long ago. I don't know why no one has done anything about it. I'll have a chat to the Native Commissioner next week. I'm going over for tennis on Sunday, anyway."

Some time later we heard that Chief Mshlanga and his people had been moved two hundred miles east, to a proper native reserve; the Government land was going to be opened up for white settlement soon.

I went to see the village again, about a year afterwards. There was nothing there. Mounds of red mud, where the huts had been, had long swathes of rotting thatch over them, veined with the red galleries of the white ants. The pumpkin vines rioted everywhere, over the bushes, up the lower branches of trees so that the great golden balls rolled underfoot and dangled overhead: it was a festival of pumpkins. The bushes were crowding up, the new grass sprang vivid green.

The settler lucky enough to be allotted the lush warm valley (if he chose to cultivate this particular section) would find, suddenly, in the middle of a mealie field, the plants were growing fifteen feet tall, the weight of the cobs dragging at the stalks, and wonder what unsuspected vein of richness he had struck.

QUESTIONS

1. Trace in detail the narrator's changing attitudes toward Africans.

2. How does the narrator's view of the African landscape change as the story progresses?

3. After visiting the Old Chief in his village, the narrator says, "I could not help it, I am also a victim." Is she a victim? If so, in what sense? Who or what has victimized her?

4. When the narrator's father decides to keep the goats that have trampled his crop, is he acting justly? Why or why not?

5. What are the implications of the last paragraph of the story?

6. In what ways might this be considered a coming-of-age story?

Ireland

Issues of conflict and colonialism between England and Ireland began almost nine centuries ago. The first conflict, characteristically motivated by religion, was Henry II's invasion of Ireland in 1171. Encouraged by the Pope to bring Irish religious practices into line with those of Rome, Henry (r. 1154–1189) conquered most of Ireland and secured Irish conformity in 1172. This conquest and its religious motivation remained the basis for England's claim to hegemony over Ireland until 1541, when Henry VIII (r. 1509–1547) broke with the Roman church and attempted to establish himself as head of the church in England and Ireland. Ireland, unlike England, never assented to the Protestant reformation, and religious strife remains today an important source of conflict between Ireland and England and within Ireland itself. Elizabeth I (r. 1558–1603) extended British control of Ireland, in spite of Ireland's alliances with Catholic Italy and Spain. Revolts in 1567, 1580, 1594, and 1603 led to defeats that resulted in the subjugation of Ireland by England and the establishment of colonial rule.

As part of her colonial policy, Elizabeth I suppressed the native Irish language, Gaelic, which had a centuries-long history of oral and written literature. She removed the native Irish aristocracy and replaced its members with English-speaking, Protestant lords. As a result, the patronage for Gaelic bards disappeared, and both the Irish oral and written languages began their long slow decline into near oblivion.

In 1607 the "flight of the earls" from the north of Ireland led to the "plantation" of English and Irish Protestants on the best land in Ulster (now the province of Northern Ireland). Under Oliver Cromwell, this policy was forcibly extended, partly in response to Irish "massacres" of Protestants in 1641. The result was that Protestant control of northern Ireland was fully established, relegating the native Gaelic and Catholic population to peasant status. A brief period of hope for the Irish came under the sympathetic rule of James II (r. 1685–1688), a Catholic, but his ouster, the 1689 coronation of William and Mary (r. 1689–1702), and the defeat of James II's followers at the Battle of the Boyne (1690) effectively sealed the Protestants' rule of Ulster.

From this point on, the Irish Parliament was effectively controlled by Episcopalian members of the Church of Ireland, disenfranchising and impoverishing both Catholics in the south and Presbyterians in the north. The eighteenth century was dominated by the Ascendancy—aristocratic British sympathizers. One result of

England's political, social, and economic domination of Ireland was that native Irish literature increasingly gave way to works written in English, some of which were overtly or covertly critical of English rule. Among the most famous of these Anglo-Irish writers was Jonathan Swift, whose essay, "A Modest Proposal," savagely ridiculed England's harsh treatment of the Irish. But perhaps the most important flowering of Anglo-Irish writers was in drama, for the English theater after Shakespeare is rather meagre if one subtracts the contributions of Irish dramatists such as William Congreve, George Farquar, Oliver Goldsmith, Richard Brinsley Sheridan, Oscar Wilde, and George Bernard Shaw.

Fears raised by revolutions in the American colonies (1776) and France (1789) led Prime Minister William Pitt to propose the abolition of Ireland's Parliament in an Act of Union that would make Ireland, like Scotland and Wales, part of Great Britain. The scheme, which took effect in 1801, sent Irish members of Parliament to Westminster, shifting the political and social center of Ireland from Dublin to London, with disastrous consequences for the Irish economy. But if the Act of Union was a disaster for the Irish, the Great Famine of 1845–1850 can only be termed a catastrophe. The already-impoverished Irish peasantry was barely subsisting on tiny plots of land and living almost entirely on potatoes, when a fungus blown in from the United States by the prevailing winds wiped out the potato crop in 1846 and 1847. An estimated 1 million Irish died, and another 1 million emigrated. Population decline because of emigration continued throughout the nineteenth century. The combined devastation of the Irish through death and emigration led to the near-extinction of Irish as a spoken, let alone a literary, language.

Perhaps the best hopes for Irish emancipation and home rule following the Great Famine came in the combined forces of Michael Davitt's agrarian movement and Charles Stewart Parnell's brilliant parliamentary tactics. In fact, Prime Minister Gladstone was persuaded to introduce an Irish home rule bill in 1886, but dissension among Gladstone's party members, opposition by the House of Lords, and finally Parnell's disgrace over his affair with Mrs. Kitty O'Shea dashed Ireland's hopes for independence. Meanwhile, a growing nationalist movement revived the Irish language, culminating in the formation of the Gaelic League in 1893, and led to the establishment of military-political movement, Sinn Fein (Gaelic for "Ourselves Alone").

Reviving Gaelic as a literary vehicle, however, proved to be enormously difficult. Perhaps the most successful genre in Gaelic was the short story as represented by Padraic O'Conaire, Mairtin O'Cadhain, and Liam O'Flaherty. Concurrently, some Irish writers were crafting stories in English. Among them was William Carlton, who was strongly influenced by Gaelic oral tradition and whose stories focused on Irish peasant life. Succeeding generations of Anglo-Irish writers were aided in no small measure by the founding of two important magazines, *The Nation,* a nationalist periodical, and *Dublin University Magazine,* edited in the 1860s by Joseph Sheridan LeFanu, regarded by many as Ireland's foremost practitioner of the ghost story.

By 1912, home rule again seemed assured, but this time opposition arose from a new quarter—the Ulster Unionists. Fearing domination in a largely Catholic Ireland independent of Great Britain, northern Irish Protestants supported by British conservatives stockpiled arms and openly defied Parliament. A home rule bill was passed in 1912, but it exempted Ulster. The outbreak of World War I in 1914, however, temporarily shelved the home rule issue. Nevertheless, growing Irish opposition to British rule could not be squelched, even by the Great War. Events culminated in the Easter Rebellion of 1916, when a small group of armed rebels including nationalist leader Michael Collins occupied the post office and a few other buildings in the heart of Dublin. The British response was swift and deadly, resulting in the rapid defeat of the insurgents and the execution of their leaders, including Patrick Pearse and James Connolly. As is so often the case, the executed became instant martyrs, and their cause was furthered when in 1918 the British government under Lloyd George tried to force conscription on the Irish. Sinn Fein consequently swept the election of 1918, and military conflict soon followed. Both sides in the 1919–1921 war were brutal, but British irregulars who came to be known as the Black and Tans were particularly so. Though neither side won outright victory, the treaty signed in 1921 gave independence to southern Ireland but allowed the six northern counties to remain part of Great Britain. Ironically, the decision to partition Ireland led to further violence, including the assassination of Michael Collins.

The responses of short story writers to these tumultuous events were complex, even contradictory. As early as 1830, William Carleton acknowledged the tragedy of internecine violence in "Wildgoose Lodge." The heartbreak of Irish emigrants is the focus of stories by George Moore, James Joyce, and Liam O'Flaherty, while both Frank O'Connor and Sean O'Faolain portray the difficulties faced by those Irish who, whatever their feelings about British rule and occupation, found it difficult to ally themselves wholeheartedly with the Irish Republican Army (IRA) a paramilitary guerrilla unit formed to oppose the British presence in Ireland. The stories set in Northern Ireland by Mary Beckett and Colum McCann analyze the complex divisions within a society still essentially an English colony deeply divided by religion and national identity. Irish writers, most famously James Joyce, have dealt frequently with the tension between their love for their native land and their anger and disgust at its blind loyalty to the Catholic Church and its cultural backwardness and moral puritanism.

By 1937, the creation of the Irish Free State (Eire) ended the last vestiges of British rule in southern Ireland, but a kind of colonialism persisted in the north. There the Protestant majority supported by the British government held effective political and economic control over the Catholic minority, which chafed under harshly discriminatory treatment at the hands of Protestants. Inspired by the U.S. civil rights movement in the 1960s, Roman Catholics in Northern Ireland agitated for increased civil rights. Their efforts met stiff opposition from Protestants under the leadership of Reverend Ian Paisley. In 1969, following attacks by extreme Protestants, the IRA and civil rights groups in Londonderry joined forces to create a "Free Derry" zone, permitting only residents of the traditionally Catholic area called Bogside to enter or leave. In response, the British sent 3,000 "peacekeepers" (British troops) to restore order, a number that soon swelled to over 11,000. Home rule was suspended, and cycles of violence, terrorism, and harsh reprisals became commonplace. (Mary Beckett's story, "A Belfast Woman," reflects this period.) Various attempts to restore home rule and create power-sharing governments with both Protestants and Catholics represented foundered as positions on both sides hardened and grievances mounted. The politics of Northern Ireland since 1969 have been dominated by violence, with the IRA using terrorist-style bombings against Protestant targets and British troops, while militant Protestants have responded in kind against Catholics and doggedly held onto economic and political power.

A temporary breakthrough occurred in 1994 when the IRA announced a cease-fire. Although it lasted less than two years, this relatively peaceful interlude set the stage for continued negotiations, resulting in a peace accord in April 1998. Since then, both Catholics and Protestants have caused sporadic violence, and Northern Ireland has frequently teetered on the edge of renewed civil war. Whether the Easter Accord of 1998 will lead to permanent peace in Northern Ireland remains to be seen.

Throughout the centuries, the Irish talent for oral and written storytelling has reflected and recorded the effects of English colonial rule. In many ways, Ireland was the prototype for British colonialism everywhere—the imposition of minority British rule on a reluctant, even rebellious, indigenous population. As in Africa, India, and the Caribbean, English has largely replaced the native tongue as the primary literary vehicle in Ireland. Furthermore, the political aftermath of British rule in Ireland reflects what has happened and continues to happen elsewhere. In Ireland's case, partition into north and south shows two possible long-range results, for currently the Irish Republic in the south is enjoying the fruits of democracy, self-rule, and a thriving economy. In the north, conversely, sporadic sectarian violence continues, even as the majority on both sides hopes for a permanent and peaceful end to centuries of strife.

William Carleton

(1794–1869)

William Carleton's life and work, though the earliest of the writers included here as postcolonial, exemplifies many of the conflicts and features that we now recognize as typical.

Born to an impoverished northern Irish peasant family in County Tyrone, Carleton grew up knowing firsthand the people about whom he later wrote. His father evidently bequeathed to William a talent for storytelling, for James Carleton could regale audiences in both Irish and English with folklore, tales, poems, and superstitions housed in a memory so capacious that it was said to hold the whole of the Old and New Testaments as well. His mother, though less fluent in English than her husband, was another source of Irish lore and language, as she was known for her beautiful voice and sang traditional songs at wakes, weddings, and festivals.

Charleton's early life was largely one of poverty, hardship, and triumph over great obstacles. His education was spotty at best, much of it taking place in the hedge schools of rural Ireland, so-called because they were often held literally under the shelter of a hedge. At seventeen, disappointed in love and devastated by the death of his father, Carleton left northern Ireland for the south in search of education, finding it temporarily in Munster as a "poor scholar." Dissatisfied at the cruel treatment he received there, he spent two years in Glasslough and there joined the Ribbon Society, a secret pro-Catholic society intended to counter the ruling Protestants. Improbably inspired by the fictional adventures he read about in the French novel *Gil Blas* (1715–1735), Carleton again took to the road and eventually found that he could earn dinner and a night's lodging by telling stories. It was during this time that he encountered the corpse in the gibbet that later inspired "Wildgoose Lodge."

Carleton eventually landed a job as a tutor and in 1822 married his employer's niece. From there he was hired as a teacher at a Protestant school and was encouraged to submit some essays for publication. Ironically, his early work appeared in a violently anti-Catholic publication before being collected in *Traits and Stories of the Irish Peasantry* (1830). This was followed by *Tales of Ireland* (1834) and by subsequent expanded editions of *Traits and Stories*. Besides stories, Carleton published poems, essays, and five novels.

Carleton's strengths as a writer are his understanding of the Irish peasantry, his gift for capturing the idioms of the Irish language in English, and his uncompromising realism. Though he relies too heavily on verisimilitude as the justification for his stories, they are nevertheless powerful fictional realizations of the experiences they contain. Moreover, Carleton is credited as being among the first truly national Irish writers in English, for he remained in Ireland and wrote to Irish audiences about national issues, using indigenous materials and forms. His primary downfall was a lack of attention to form, with the result that his work is very uneven in quality. Even so, his writing was a powerful antidote to the stereotyped depiction of the Irish peasant as an ignorant, inferior, and feckless character given to strong drink and outlandish superstition.

Carleton's apparently divided attitude toward the religious conflicts of his country can perhaps best be explained as arising first out of his need to escape poverty through publication and by his recognition that both sides in the conflict were irrational, bigoted, and violent. "Wildgoose Lodge" exposes these qualities in the Catholics, but Carleton was equally harsh on their Protestant counterparts. "Wildgoose Lodge" is a chilling tale, almost Gothic in its depiction of irrational religious hatred and violent retribution.

Wildgoose Lodge   *ca. 1830*

I had read the anonymous summons, but, from its general import, I believed it to be one of those special meetings convened for some purpose affecting the usual objects and proceedings of the body; at least, the terms in which it was conveyed to me had nothing extraordinary or mysterious in them beyond the simple fact that it was not to be a general but a select meeting: this mark of confidence flattered me, and I determined to attend punctually. I was, it is true, desired to keep the circumstance entirely to myself; but there was nothing startling in this, for I had often received summonses of a similar nature. I therefore resolved to attend, according to the letter of my instructions, "on the next night, at the solemn hour of midnight, to deliberate and act upon such matters as should then and there be submitted to my consideration." The morning after I received this message I arose and resumed my usual occupations; but, from whatever cause it may have proceeded, I felt a sense of approaching evil hang heavily upon me: the beats of my pulse were languid, and an undefinable feeling of anxiety pervaded my whole spirit; even my face was pale, and my eye so heavy that my father and brothers concluded me to be ill; an opinion which I thought at the time to be correct, for I felt exactly that kind of depression which precedes a severe fever. I could not understand what I experienced, nor can I yet, except by supposing that there is in human nature some mysterious faculty by which, in coming calamities, the dread of some fearful evil is anticipated, and that it is possible to catch a dark presentiment of the sensations which they subsequently produce. For my part, I can neither analyze nor define it; but on that day I knew it by painful experience, and so have a thousand others in similar circumstances.

It was about the middle of winter. The day was gloomy and tempestuous almost beyond any other I remember: dark clouds rolled over the hills about me, and a close, sleet-like rain fell in slanting drifts that chased each other rapidly towards the earth on the course of the blast. The outlying cattle sought the closest and calmest corners of the fields for shelter; the trees and young groves were tossed about, for the wind was so unusually high that it swept in hollow gusts through them with that hoarse murmur which deepens so powerfully on the mind the sense of dreariness and desolation.

As the shades of night fell, the storm, if possible, increased. The moon was half gone, and only a few stars were visible by glimpses, as a rush of wind left a temporary opening in the sky. I had determined, if the storm should not abate, to incur any penalty rather than attend the meeting; but the appointed hour was distant, and I resolved to be decided by the future state of the night.

Ten o'clock came, but still there was no change; eleven passed, and on opening the door to observe if there were any likelihood of its clearing up, a blast of wind, mingled with rain, nearly blew me off my feet. At length it was approaching to the hour of midnight; and on examining a third time, I found it had calmed a little, and no longer rained.

I instantly got my oak stick, muffled myself in my great coat, strapped my hat about my ears, and, as the place of meeting was only a quarter of a mile distant, I presently set out.

The appearance of the heavens was lowering and angry, particularly in that point where the light of the moon fell against the clouds, from a seeming chasm in them, through which alone she was visible. The edges of this chasm were faintly bronzed, but the dense body of the masses that hung piled on each side of her was black and impenetrable to sight. In no other point of the heavens was there any part

of the sky visible: a deep veil of clouds overhung the horizon, yet was the light sufficient to give occasional glimpses of the rapid shifting which took place in this dark
canopy, and of the tempestuous agitation with which the midnight storm swept to
and fro beneath it.

At length I arrived at a long slated house, situated in a solitary part of the neighbourhood; a little below it ran a small stream, which was now swollen above its
banks, and rushing with mimic roar over the flat meadows beside it. The appearance
of the bare slated[1] building in such a night was particularly sombre, and to those,
like me, who knew the purpose to which it was usually devoted, it was, or ought to
have been, peculiarly so. There it stood, silent and gloomy, without any appearance
of human life or enjoyment about or within it. As I approached, the moon once
more had broken out of the clouds, and shone dimly upon the wet, glittering slates
and windows with a death-like lustre, that gradually faded away as I left the point of
observation and entered the folding-door. It was the parish chapel.

The scene which presented itself here was in keeping not only with the external
appearance of the house, but with the darkness, the storm, and the hour, which was
now a little after midnight. About eighty persons were sitting in dead silence upon
the circular steps of the altar. They did not seem to move; and as I entered and advanced the echo of my footsteps rang through the building with a lonely distinctness, which added to the solemnity and mystery of the circumstances about me. The
windows were secured with shutters on the inside, and on the altar a candle was
lighted, which burned dimly amid the surrounding darkness, and lengthened the
shadow of the altar itself, and those of six or seven persons who stood on its upper
steps, until they mingled in the obscurity which shrouded the lower end of the
chapel. The faces of the men who sat on the altar steps were not distinctly visible, yet
their prominent and more characteristic features were in sufficient relief, and I observed that some of the most malignant and reckless spirits in the parish were assembled. In the eyes of those who stood at the altar, and whom I knew to be invested
with authority over the others, I could perceive gleams of some latent and ferocious
purpose, kindled, as I soon observed, into a fiercer expression of vengeance by the
additional excitement of ardent spirits,[2] with which they had stimulated themselves
to a point of determination that mocked at the apprehension of all future responsibility, either in this world or the next.

The welcome which I received on joining them was far different from the boisterous good-humour that used to mark our greetings on other occasions: just a nod
of the head from this or that person, on the part of those *who sat,* with a *ghud
dhemur tha thu?*[3] in a suppressed voice, even below a common whisper: but from the
standing group, who were evidently the projectors of the enterprise, I received a convulsive grasp of the hand, accompanied by a fierce and desperate look, that seemed
to search my eye and countenance, to try if I were a person not likely to shrink from

1 **slated:** With a slate roof.
2 **ardent spirits:** Strong drink; whisky.
3 ***ghud dhemur tha thu:*** "How are you?" [Carleton's note.]

whatever they had resolved to execute. It is surprising to think of the powerful expression which a moment of intense interest or great danger is capable of giving to the eye, the features, and the slightest actions, especially in those whose station in society does not require them to constrain nature, by the force of social courtesies, into habits that conceal their natural emotions. None of the standing group spoke; but as each of them wrung my hand in silence, his eye was fixed on mine with an expression of drunken confidence and secrecy, and an insolent determination not to be gainsayed without peril. If looks could be translated with certainty, they seemed to say, "We are bound upon a project of vengeance, and if you do not join us, remember that we *can* revenge." Along with this grasp they did not forget to remind me of the common bond by which we were united, for each man gave me the secret grip of Ribbonism in a manner that made the joints of my fingers ache for some minutes afterwards.

There was one present, however—the highest in authority—whose actions and demeanour were calm and unexcited. He seemed to labour under no unusual influence whatever, but evinced a serenity so placid and philosophical that I attributed the silence of the sitting group, and the restraint which curbed in the out-breaking passions of those who *stood*, entirely to his presence. He was a schoolmaster, who taught his daily school in that chapel, and acted also, on Sunday, in the capacity of clerk to the priest—an excellent and amiable old man, who knew little of his illegal connections and atrocious conduct.

When the ceremonies of brotherly recognition and friendship were past, the captain (by which title I shall designate the last-mentioned person) stooped, and raising a jar of whisky on the corner of the altar, held a wine-glass to its neck, which he filled, and, with a calm nod, handed it to me to drink. I shrunk back, with an instinctive horror at the profaneness of such an act, in the house, and on the altar, of God, and peremptorily refused to taste the proffered draught. He smiled mildly at what he considered my superstition, and added quietly, and in a low voice, "You'll be wantin' it, I'm thinkin', afther the wettin' you got."

"Wet or dry," said I——

"Stop, man!" he replied, in the same tone: "spake low. But why wouldn't you take the whisky? Sure there's as holy people to the fore as you: didn't they all take it? An' I wish we may never do worse nor dhrink a harmless glass o' whisky to keep the cowld out, anyway."

"Well," said I, "I'll jist trust to God and the consequences for the cowld, Paddy, ma bouchal; but a blessed dhrop of it won't be crossin' my lips, avick; so no more ghosther about it—dhrink it yourself, if you like. Maybe you want it as much as I do; wherein I've the patthern of a good big coat upon me, so thick, your sowl, that if it was rainin' bullocks a dhrop wouldn't get under the nap of it."

He gave me a calm but keen glance, as I spoke.

"Well, Jim," said he, "it's a good comrade you've got for the weather that's in it; but, in the manetime, to set you a dacent patthern, I'll just take this myself"—saying which, with the jar still upon its side, and the forefinger of his left hand in its neck, he swallowed the spirits. "It's the first I dhrank to-night," he added, "nor would I dhrink it now, only to show you that I've heart an' spirit to do the thing that we're all bound an' sworn to, when the proper time comes;" after which he laid down the glass, and turned up the jar, with much coolness, upon the altar.

During our conversation those who had been summoned to this mysterious meeting were pouring in fast; and as each person approached the altar he received from one to two or three glasses of whisky, according as he chose to limit himself; but, to do them justice, there were not a few of those present who, in spite of their own desire, and the captain's express invitation, refused to taste it in the house of God's worship. Such, however, as were scrupulous he afterwards recommended to take it on the outside of the chapel door, which they did, as, by that means, the sacrilege of the act was supposed to be evaded.

About one o'clock they were all assembled except six; at least, so the captain asserted, on looking at a written paper.

"Now, boys," said he, in the same low voice, "we are all present except the thraitors whose names I am goin' to read to you; not that we are to count thim thraitors, till we know whether or not it was in their power to come. Anyhow, the night's terrible—but, boys, you're to know that neither fire nor wather is to prevint yees, when duly summoned to attind a meeting—particularly whin the summons is widout a name, as you have been told that there is always something of consequence to be done *thin*."

He then read out the names of those who were absent, in order that the real cause of their absence might be ascertained, declaring that they would be dealt with accordingly. After this, with his usual caution, he shut and bolted the door, and having put the key in his pocket, ascended the steps of the altar, and for some time traversed the little platform, from which the priest usually addresses the congregation.

Until this night I had never contemplated the man's countenance with any particular interest; but as he walked the platform I had an opportunity of observing him more closely. He was slight in person, apparently not thirty; and, on a first view, appeared to have nothing remarkable in his dress or features. I, however, was not the only person whose eyes were fixed upon him at that moment; in fact, everyone present observed him with equal interest, for hitherto he had kept the object of the meeting perfectly secret, and of course we all felt anxious to know it. It was while he traversed the platform that I scrutinised his features with a hope, if possible, to glean from them some evidence of what was passing within him. I could, however, mark but little, and that little was at first rather from the intelligence which seemed to subsist between him and those whom I have already mentioned as *standing* against the altar than from any indication of his own. Their gleaming eyes were fixed upon him with an intensity of savage and demon-like hope which blazed out in flashes of malignant triumph, as, upon turning, he threw a cool but rapid glance at them, to intimate the progress he was making in the subject to which he devoted the undivided energies of his mind. But in the course of his meditation I could observe, on one or two occasions, a dark shade come over his countenance, that contracted his brow into a deep furrow, and it was then, for the first time, that I saw the Satanic expression of which his face, by a very slight motion of its muscles, was capable. His hands, during this silence, closed and opened convulsively; his eyes shot out two or three baleful glances, first to his confederates, and afterwards vacantly into the deep gloom of the lower part of the chapel; his teeth ground against each other like those of a man whose revenge burns to reach a distant enemy, and finally, after having wound himself up to a certain determination, his features relapsed into their original calm and undisturbed expression.

At this moment a loud laugh, having something supernatural in it, rang out wildly from the darkness of the chapel: he stopped, and putting his open hand over his brows, peered down into the gloom, and said calmly, in Irish, "*Bee dhu husth; ha nihl anam inh*—hold your tongue, it is not yet the time."

Every eye was now directed to the same spot, but, in consequence of its distance from the dim light on the altar, none could perceive the person from whom the laugh proceeded. It was, by this time, near two o'clock in the morning.

He now stood for a few moments on the platform, and his chest heaved with a depth of anxiety equal to the difficulty of the design he wished to accomplish.

"Brothers," said he—"for we are all brothers—sworn upon all that's blessed an' holy to obey whatever them that's over us, *manin' among ourselves,*[4] wishes us to do—are you now ready, in the name of God, upon whose althar I stand, to fulfil yer oaths?"

The words were scarcely uttered, when those who had *stood* beside the altar during the night sprang from their places, and descending its steps rapidly, turned round, and raising their arms, exclaimed, "By all that's sacred an' holy, we're willin'."

In the meantime, those who *sat* upon the steps of the altar instantly rose, and following the example of those who had just spoken, exclaimed after them, "To be sure—by all that's sacred an' holy, we're willin'."

"Now boys," said the captain, "ar'n't yees big fools for your pains? an' one of yees doesn't know what I mane."

"You're our captain," said one of those who had stood at the altar, "an' has yer ordhers from higher quarthers; of coorse, whatever ye command upon us we're bound to obey you in."

"Well," said he, smiling, "I only wanted to thry yees; an' by the oath yees tuck, there's not a captain in the county has as good a right to be proud of his min as I have. Well, yees won't rue it, maybe, when the right time comes; and for that same rason every one of yees must have a glass from the jar; thim that won't dhrink it *in* the chapel can dhrink it *widout;* an' here goes to open the door for them."

He then distributed another glass to every man who would accept it, and brought the jar afterwards to the chapel door, to satisfy the scruples of those who would not drink within. When this was performed, and all duly excited, he proceeded:

"Now, brothers, you are solemnly sworn to obey me, and I'm sure there's no thraithur here that ud parjure himself for a thrifle; but *I'm* sworn to obey them that's

---

4 **manin' among ourselves:** In opposition to the constituted authorities. [Carleton's note.]

above me, manin' still among ourselves; an' to show you that I don't scruple to do it, here goes!"

He then turned round, and taking the Missal[5] between his hands, placed it upon the altar. Hitherto every word was uttered in a low, precautionary tone; but on grasping the book he again turned round, and looking upon his confederates with the same Satanic expression which marked his countenance before, exclaimed, in a voice of deep determination:

"By this sacred an' holy book of God, I will perform the action which we have met this night to accomplish, be that what it may; an this I swear upon God's book an' God's althar!"

On concluding he struck the book violently with his open hand.

At this moment the candle which burned before him went suddenly out, and the chapel was wrapped in pitchy darkness; the sound as if of rushing wings fell upon our ears, and fifty voices dwelt upon the last words of his oath with wild and supernatural tones, that seemed to echo and to mock what he had sworn. There was a pause, and an exclamation of horror from all present: but the captain was too cool and steady to be disconcerted. He immediately groped about until he got the candle, and proceeding calmly to a remote corner of the chapel, took up a half-burned turf[6] which lay there, and after some trouble, succeeded in lighting it again. He then explained what had taken place; which indeed was easily done, as the candle happened to be extinguished by a pigeon which sat directly above it. The chapel, I should have observed, was at this time, like many country chapels, unfinished inside, and the pigeons of a neighbouring dove-cote had built nests among the rafters of the unceiled roof; which circumstance also explained the rushing of the wings, for the birds had been affrighted by the sudden loudness of the noise. The mocking voices were nothing but the echoes, rendered naturally more awful by the scene, the mysterious object of the meeting, and the solemn hour of the night.

When the candle was again lighted, and these startling circumstances accounted for, the persons whose vengeance had been deepening more and more during the night rushed to the altar in a body, where each, in a voice trembling with passionate eagerness, repeated the oath, and as every word was pronounced, the same echoes heightened the wildness of the horrible ceremony by their long and unearthly tones. The countenances of these human tigers were livid with suppressed rage: their knit brows, compressed lips, and kindled eyes fell under the dim light of the taper with an expression calculated to sicken any heart not absolutely diabolical.

As soon as this dreadful rite was completed we were again startled by several loud bursts of laughter, which proceeded from the lower darkness of the chapel, and the captain, on hearing them, turned to the place, and reflecting for a moment, said in Irish, "*Gutsho nish, avohelhee*—come hither now, boys."

---

5 **Missal:** The book containing the words of all the Roman Catholic masses and services for the year.
6 **turf:** Peat, used for fuel.

A rush immediately took place from the corner in which they had secreted themselves all the night; and seven men appeared, whom we instantly recognised as brothers and cousins of certain persons who had been convicted, some time before, for breaking into the house of an honest poor man in the neighbourhood, from whom, after having treated him with barbarous violence, they took away such fire-arms as he kept for his own protection.

It was evidently not the captain's intention to have produced these persons until the oath should have been generally taken, but the exulting mirth with which they enjoyed the success of his scheme betrayed them, and put him to the necessity of bringing them forward somewhat before the concerted moment.

The scene which now took place was beyond all power of description; peals of wild, fiend-like yells rang through the chapel, as the party which *stood* on the altar, and that which had crouched in the darkness, met; wringing of hands, leaping in triumph, striking of sticks and fire-arms against the ground and the altar itself, dancing and cracking of fingers, marked the triumph of some hellish determination. Even the captain for a time was unable to restrain their fury; but at length he mounted the platform before the altar once more, and, with a stamp of his foot, recalled their attention to himself and the matter in hand.

"Boys," said he, "enough of this, and too much; an' well for us it is that the chapel is in a lonely place, or our foolish noise might do us no good. Let thim that swore so manfully jist now stand a one side, till the rest kiss the book, one by one."

The proceedings, however, had by this time taken too fearful a shape for even the captain to compel them to a blindfold oath; the first man he called flatly refused to answer until he should hear the nature of the service that was required. This was echoed by the remainder, who, taking courage from the firmness of this person, declared generally that until they first knew the business they were to execute none of them would take the oath. The captain's lip quivered slightly, and his brow again became knit with the same hellish expression, which I have remarked gave him so much the appearance of an embodied fiend; but this speedily passed away, and was succeeded by a malignant sneer, in which lurked, if there ever did in a sneer, "a laughing devil," calmly, determinedly atrocious.

"It wasn't worth yer whiles to refuse the oath," said he, mildly, "for the truth is, I had next to nothing for yees to do. Not a hand, maybe, would have to *rise,* only jist to look on, an' if any resistance would be made, to show yourselves; yer numbers would soon make them see that resistance would be no use whatever in the present case. At all evints, the oath of *secrecy must* be taken, or woe be to him that will refuse *that;* he won't know the day, nor the hour, nor the minute, when he'll be made a spatchcock[7] ov."

He then turned round, and placing his right hand on the Missal, swore, "In the presence of God, and before his holy altar, that whatever might take place that night he would keep secret from man or mortal, except the priest, and that neither bribery, nor imprisonment, nor death would wring it from his heart."

7 **spatchcock:** A fowl, split open and grilled.

Having done this, he again struck the book violently, as if to confirm the energy with which he swore, and then calmly descending the steps, stood with a serene countenance, like a man conscious of having performed a good action. As this oath did not pledge those who refused to take the other to the perpetration of any specific crime, it was readily taken by all present. Preparations were then made to execute what was intended; the half-burned turf was placed in a little pot; another glass of whisky was distributed; and the door being locked by the captain, who kept the key as parish clerk and master, the crowd departed silently from the chapel.

The moment those who lay in the darkness during the night made their appearance at the altar, we knew at once the persons we were to visit; for, as I said before, they were related to the miscreants whom one of those persons had convicted, in consequence of their midnight attack upon himself and his family. The captain's object in keeping them unseen was that those present, not being aware of the duty about to be imposed on them, might have less hesitation about swearing to its fulfilment. Our conjectures were correct, for on leaving the chapel we directed our steps to the house in which this devoted man resided.

The night was still stormy, but without rain; it was rather dark, too, though not so as to prevent us from seeing the clouds careering swiftly through the air. The dense curtain which had overhung and obscured the horizon was now broken, and large sections of the sky were clear, and thinly studded with stars that looked dim and watery, as did indeed the whole firmament; for in some places black clouds were still visible, threatening a continuance of tempestuous weather. The road appeared washed and gravelly; every dike was full of yellow water; and every little rivulet and larger stream dashed its hoarse music in our ears; every blast, too, was cold, fierce, and wintry, sometimes driving us back to a standstill, and again, when a turn in the road would bring it in our backs, whirling us along for a few steps with involuntary rapidity. At length the fated dwelling became visible, and a short consultation was held in a sheltered place between the captain and the two parties who seemed so eager for its destruction. The fire-arms were now loaded, and their bayonets and short pikes, the latter shod and pointed with iron, were also got ready. The live coal which was brought in the small pot had become extinguished; but to remedy this two or three persons from a remote part of the county entered a cabin on the wayside, and under pretence of lighting their own and their comrades' pipes, procured a coal of fire, for so they called a lighted turf. From the time we left the chapel until this moment a profound silence had been maintained, a circumstance which, when I considered the number of persons present, and the mysterious and dreaded object of their journey, had a most appalling effect upon my spirits.

At length we arrived within fifty perches[8] of the house, walking in a compact body, and with as little noise as possible; but it seemed as if the very elements had conspired to frustrate our design, for on advancing within the shade of the farm-hedge, two or three persons found themselves up to the middle in water, and on

---

8 **perches:** One perch equals one rod, a measure of distance equaling 16.5 feet.

stooping to ascertain more accurately the state of the place, we could see nothing but one immense sheet of it—spread like a lake over the meadows which surrounded the spot we wished to reach.

Fatal night! The very recollection of it, when associated with the fearful tempests of the elements, grows, if that were possible, yet more wild and revolting. Had we been engaged in any innocent or benevolent enterprise, there was something in our situation just then that had a touch of interest in it to a mind imbued with a relish for the savage beauties of nature. There we stood, about a hundred and thirty in number, our dark forms bent forward, peering into the dusky expanse of water, with its dim gleams of reflected light, broken by the weltering of the mimic waves into ten thousand fragments, whilst the few stars that overhung it in the firmament appeared to shoot through it in broken lines, and to be multiplied fifty-fold in the gloomy mirror on which we gazed.

Over us was a stormy sky, and around us a darkness through which we could only distinguish, in outline, the nearest objects, whilst the wind swept strongly and dismally upon us. When it was discovered that the common pathway to the house was inundated, we were about to abandon our object and return home. The captain, however, stooped down low for a moment, and, almost closing his eyes, looked along the surface of the waters, and then, raising himself very calmly, said, in his usual quiet tone, "Yees needn't go back, boys, I've found a way; jist follow me."

He immediately took a more circuitous direction, by which we reached a causeway that had been raised for the purpose of giving a free passage to and from the house during such inundations as the present. Along this we had advanced more than half way, when we discovered a breach in it, which, as afterwards appeared, had that night been made by the strength of the flood. This, by means of our sticks and pikes, we found to be about three feet deep and eight yards broad. Again we were at a loss how to proceed, when the fertile brain of the captain devised a method of crossing it.

"Boys," said he, "of coorse you've all played at leap-frog; very well, strip and go in, a dozen of you, lean one upon the back of another from this to the opposite bank, where one must stand facing the outside man, both their shoulders agin one another, that the outside man may be supported. Then *we* can creep over you, an' a dacent bridge you'll be, anyway."

This was the work of only a few minutes, and in less than ten we were all safely over.

Merciful heaven! how I sicken at the recollection of what is to follow! On reaching the dry bank, we proceeded instantly, and in profound silence, to the house; the captain divided us into companies, and then assigned to each division its proper station. The two parties who had been so vindictive all the night he kept about himself; for of those who were present they only were in his confidence, and knew his nefarious purpose: their number was about fifteen. Having made these dispositions, he, at the head of about five of them, approached the house on the windy side, for the fiend possessed a coolness which enabled him to seize upon every possible advantage. That he had combustibles about him was evident, for in less than fifteen minutes nearly one-half of the house was enveloped in flames. On seeing this, the others rushed over to the spot where he and his gang were standing, and remonstrated earnestly, but in vain; the flames now burst forth with renewed violence, and as they flung their strong light upon the faces of the foremost group, I think hell itself could hardly present anything more Satanic than their countenances, now worked up into a paroxysm of infernal triumph at their own revenge. The captain's look had lost all its calmness, every feature started out into distinct malignity, the curve in his brow was deep, and ran up to the root of the hair, dividing his face into two segments, that did not seem to have been designed for each other. His lips were half open, and the corners of his mouth a little brought back on each side, like those of a man express-ing intense hatred and triumph over an enemy who is in the death struggle under his grasp. His eyes blazed from beneath his knit eyebrows with a fire that seemed to be lighted up in the infernal pit itself. It is unnecessary and only painful to describe the rest of his gang; demons might have been proud of such horrible visages as they ex-hibited: for they worked under all the power of hatred, revenge, and joy; and these passions blended into one terrible scowl, enough almost to blast any human eye that would venture to look upon it.

When the others attempted to intercede for the lives of the inmates, there were at least fifteen guns and pistols levelled at them.

"Another word," said the captain, "an' you're a corpse where you stand, or the first man who will dare to spake for them; no, no, it wasn't to spare them we came here. 'No mercy' is the password for the night, an' by the sacred oath I swore beyant in the chapel, anyone among yees that will attempt to show it will find none at my hand. Surround the house, boys, I tell ye, I hear them stirring. 'No quarther—no mercy,' is the ordher of the night."

Such was his command over these misguided creatures, that in an instant there was a ring round the house to prevent the escape of the unhappy inmates, should the raging element give them time to attempt it; for none present durst withdraw themselves from the scene, not only from an apprehension of the captain's present vengeance, or that of his gang, but because they knew that, even had they then es-caped, an early and certain death awaited them from a quarter against which they had no means of defence. The hour now was about half-past two o'clock. Scarcely had the last words escaped from the captain's lips, when one of the windows of the house was broken, and a human head, having the hair in a blaze, was descried, ap-parently a woman's, if one might judge by the profusion of burning tresses, and the softness of the tones, notwithstanding that it called, or rather shrieked aloud, for help and mercy. The only reply to this was the whoop from the captain and his gang of "No mercy—no mercy!" and that instant the former and one of the latter rushed to the spot, and ere the action could be perceived the head was transfixed with a bay-onet and a pike, both having entered it together. The word mercy was divided in her mouth; a short silence ensued; the head hung down on the window, but was in-stantly tossed back into the flames!

This action occasioned a cry of horror from all present, except the *gang* and their leader, which startled and enraged the latter so much that he ran towards one of them, and had his bayonet, now reeking with the blood of its innocent victim, raised to plunge it in his body, when, dropping the point, he said in a piercing whisper, that hissed in the ears of all, "It's no use *now,* you know; if one's to hang, all will hang; so our safest way, you persave, is to lave none of them to tell the story. Ye *may* go now, if you wish; but it won't save a hair of your heads. You cowardly set! I knew if I had tould yees the sport, that none of yees, except my *own* boys, would come, so I jist played a thrick upon you; but remimber what you are sworn to, and stand to the oath ye tuck."

Unhappily, notwithstanding the wetness of the preceding weather, the materials of the house were extremely combustible; the whole dwelling was now one body of glowing flame, yet the shouts and shrieks within rose awfully above its crackling and the voice of the storm, for the wind once more blew in gusts and with great violence. The doors and windows were all torn open, and such of those within as had escaped the flames rushed towards them, for the purpose of further escape, and of claiming mercy at the hands of their destroyers; but whenever they appeared the unearthly cry of "NO MERCY" rung upon their ears for a moment, and for a moment only, for they were flung back at the points of the weapons which the demons had brought with them to make the work of vengeance more certain.

As yet there were many persons in the house whose cry for life was strong as despair, and who clung to it with all the awakened powers of reason and instinct. The ear of man could hear nothing so strongly calculated to stifle the demon of cruelty and revenge within him as the long and wailing shrieks which rose beyond the elements in tones that were carried off rapidly upon the blast, until they died away in the darkness that lay behind the surrounding hills. Had not the house been in a solitary situation, and the hour the dead of night, any person sleeping within a moderate distance must have heard them, for such a cry of sorrow rising into a yell of despair was almost sufficient to have awakened the dead. It was lost, however, upon the hearts and ears that heard it: to them, though in justice be it said, to only comparatively a few of them, it was as delightful as the tones of soft and entrancing music.

The claims of the surviving sufferers were now modified; they supplicated merely to suffer death *by the weapons of their enemies;* they were willing to bear that, provided they should be allowed to escape from the flames; but no—the horrors of the conflagration were calmly and malignantly gloried in by their merciless assassins, who deliberately flung them back into all their tortures. In the course of a few minutes a man appeared upon the side-wall of the house, nearly naked; his figure, as he stood against the sky in horrible relief, was so finished a picture of woe-begone agony and supplication that it is yet as distinct in my memory as if I were again present at the scene. Every muscle, now in motion by the powerful agitation of his sufferings, stood out upon his limbs and neck, giving him an appearance of desperate strength, to which by this time he must have been wrought up; the perspiration poured from his frame, and the veins and arteries of his neck were inflated to a surprising thickness. Every moment he looked down into the flames which were rising to where he stood; and as he looked the indescribable horror which flitted over his features might have worked upon the devil himself to relent. His words were few.

"My child," said he, "is still safe; she is an infant, a young crathur that never harmed you nor anyone—she is still safe. Your mothers, your wives, have young innocent childhre like it. Oh, spare her; think for a moment that it's one of your own: spare it, as you hope to meet a just God, or if you don't, in mercy shoot me first—put an end to me before I see her burned!"

The captain approached him coolly and deliberately. "You'll prosecute no one now, you bloody informer," said he: "you'll convict ro more boys for takin' an ould gun an' pistol from you, or for givin' you a neighbourly knock or two into the bargain."

Just then, from a window opposite him, proceeded the shrieks of a woman, who appeared at it with the infant in her arms. She herself was almost scorched to death; but, with the presence of mind and humanity of her sex, she was about to put the little babe out of the window. The captain noticed this, and, with characteristic atrocity, thrust, with a sharp bayonet, the little innocent, along with the person who endeavoured to rescue it, into the red flames, where they both perished. This was the work of an instant. Again he approached the man. "Your child is a coal now," said he, with deliberate mockery; "I pitched it in myself, on the point of this"—showing the weapon—"an' now is your turn"—saying which he clambered up, by the assistance of his gang, who stood with a front of pikes and bayonets bristling to receive the wretched man, should he attempt, in his despair, to throw himself from the wall. The captain got up, and placing the point of his bayonet against his shoulder, flung him into the fiery element that raged behind him. He uttered one wild and terrific cry as he fell back, and no more. After this nothing was heard but the crackling of the fire and the rushing of the blast: all that had possessed life within were consumed, amounting either to eleven or fifteen persons.

When this was accomplished, those who took an active part in the murder stood for some time about the conflagration; and as it threw its red light upon their fierce faces and rough persons, soiled as they now were with smoke and black streaks of ashes, the scene seemed to be changed to hell, the murderers to spirits of the damned, rejoicing over the arrival and the torture of some guilty soul. The faces of those who kept aloof from the slaughter were blanched to the whiteness of death: some of them fainted, and others were in such agitation that they were compelled to lean on their comrades. They became actually powerless with horror; yet to such a scene were they brought by the pernicious influence of Ribbonism.[9]

It was only when the last victim went down that the conflagration shot up into the air with most unbounded fury. The house was large, deeply thatched, and well furnished; and the broad red pyramid rose up with fearful magnificence towards the sky. Abstractedly it had sublimity, but now it was associated with nothing in my mind but blood and terror. It was not, however, without a purpose that the captain and his gang stood to contemplate its effect. "Boys," said he, "we had better be

9 **Ribbonism:** A Ribbon Society was a secret Roman Catholic league formed to counter Protestant Orange societies.

sartin that all's safe; who knows but there might be some of the sarpents crouchin' under a hape o' rubbish, to come out an' gibbet us to-morrow or next day; we had betther wait awhile, anyhow, if it was only to see the blaze."

Just then the flames rose majestically to a surprising height. Our eyes followed their direction; and we perceived, for the first time, that the dark clouds above, together with the intermediate air, appeared to reflect back, or rather to have caught, the red hue of the fire. The hills and country about us appeared with an alarming distinctness; but the most picturesque part of it was the effect or reflection of the blaze on the floods that spread over the surrounding plains. These, in fact, appeared to be one broad mass of liquid copper, for the motion of the breaking waters caught from the blaze of the high waving column, as reflected in them, a glaring light, which eddied, and rose, and fluctuated as if the flood itself had been a lake of molten fire.

Fire, however, destroys rapidly. In a short time the flames sank—became weak and flickering—by-and-by they shot out only in fits—the crackling of the timbers died away—the surrounding darkness deepened—and, ere long, the faint light was overpowered by the thick volumes of smoke that rose from the ruins of the house and its murdered inhabitants.

"Now, boys," said the captain, "all is safe—we may go. Remember, every man of you, what you've sworn this night on the book an' altar of God—not on a heretic Bible. If you perjure yourselves, you may hang us; but let me tell you, for your comfort, that if you do there is them livin' that will take care the lase of your own lives will but short."

After this we dispersed every man to his own home.

Reader, not many months elapsed ere I saw the bodies of this captain, whose name was Patrick Devann, and all those who were actively concerned in the perpetration of this deed of horror, withering in the wind, where they hung gibbetted[10] near the scene of their nefarious villainy; and while I inwardly thanked heaven for my own narrow and almost undeserved escape, I thought in my heart how seldom, even in this world, justice fails to overtake the murderer, and to enforce the righteous judgment of God—that "whoso sheddeth man's blood, by man shall his blood be shed."

This tale of terror is, unfortunately, too true. The scene of hellish murder detailed in it lies at Wildgoose Lodge, in the county of Louth, within about four miles of Carrickmacross, and nine of Dundalk. No such multitudinous murder has occurred, under similar circumstances, except the burning of the Sheas in the county of Tipperary. The name of the family burned in Wildgoose Lodge was Lynch. One of them had, shortly before this fatal night, prosecuted and convicted some of the neighbouring Ribbonmen, who visited him with severe marks of their displeasure in consequence of his having refused to enrol himself as a member of their body.

The language of the story is partly fictitious; but the facts are pretty closely such as were developed during the trial of the murderers. Both parties were Roman

10 **gibbetted:** Hanged on a gallows and left unburied.

Catholics. There were, if the author mistake not, either twenty-five or twenty-eight of those who took an active part in the burning hanged and gibbetted in different parts of the county of Louth. Devann, the ringleader, hung for some months in chains, within about a hundred yards of his own house, and about half a mile from Wildgoose Lodge. His mother could neither go into or out of her cabin without seeing his body swinging from the gibbet. Her usual exclamation on looking at him was, "God be good to the sowl of my poor marthyr!" The peasantry, too, frequently exclaimed, on seeing him, "Poor Paddy!" a gloomy fact that speaks volumes.

QUESTIONS

1. Why does the narrator attend the meeting, even though he says he does not want to?

2. What devices does the leader use to keep the group together and implicate everyone in the crime?

3. What part does the weather play in the story?

4. In spite of the horrible violence of the story, there is a kind of beauty in the description of the fire and its reflection on the water. What is the effect of this description? How does it affect our perception of the events?

5. What comment, direct or indirect, does this story make on the occupation of Ireland by England? Is it a protest against colonial rule?

James Joyce

(1882–1941)

"I'm sick of my own country, sick of it!" cries Gabriel Conroy, the protagonist of Joyce's final story in *Dubliners*, "The Dead." Gabriel might have been speaking for Joyce, who in the guise of Stephen Daedalus vows to live outside Ireland by "silence, exile, and cunning" as a way of breaking free of the barriers of Irish religion, politics, and morality. Indeed, Joyce lived most of his adult life on the European continent, but the subject of his fiction was always and obsessively Ireland.

Joyce was born into a relatively prosperous family, but already at the time of his birth his improvident father's fortunes were declining. After spending 1888–1891 at the Clongowes Wood College boarding school, Joyce was forced to return to Dublin and fortunate to enroll in Belvedere College at no cost, thanks to the patronage of a kindly priest. Joyce was an excellent student, especially at languages, and graduated in 1902 from the University of Dublin, where he riled both the authorities and his puritanical fellow students with his defense of the controversial Norwegian dramatist, Henrik Ibsen. A month after graduating, he left for Paris, but returned after a few months to be at the bedside of his dying mother.

In 1904, Joyce returned to the continent, already at work on his first novel and the stories that later formed his only collection, *Dubliners* (1914). Publishing *Dubliners* was an artistic and moral victory for Joyce because of the barriers constantly raised by his publisher, Grant Richards, who rightly feared the public's reaction to some of the language and descriptions in the stories. What Joyce claims he set out to accomplish was "to betray the soul of that hemiplogia or paralysis which many consider a city." The city, of course, was Dublin, and the paralysis Joyce perceived was the moral conformity and blindness of its people. So successful was Joyce in this book that he helped to reshape the twentieth-century short story in his own image, just as he forever influenced the novel with his masterwork, *Ulysses* (1922).

Joyce is often credited with perfecting the "stream of consciousness" technique in his novels. In the stories, he is less experimental and more in line with the kind of realism pioneered by the Russian author Anton Chekhov. Stories are not so much plotted as built of descriptions and incidents, in language that often rises to the symbolic suggestiveness of poetry. Sometimes Joyce's characters undergo what he would call an "epiphany"—a moment of revelation. At other times, the revelation comes to the reader, not in a flash so much as in the accumulation of significant details. "Eveline" depicts the life of its protagonist through just such tiny details while simultaneously delineating the paralysis they exert on the psyche of one trying to escape, as Joyce did, the stifling effects of Dublin.

———————————

Eveline   1914

She sat at the window watching the evening invade the avenue. Her head was leaned against the window curtains and in her nostrils was the odour of dusty cretonne.[1] She was tired.

Few people passed. The man out of the last house passed on his way home; she heard his footsteps clacking along the concrete pavement and afterwards crunching on the cinder path before the new red houses. One time there used to be a field there in which they used to play every evening with other people's children. Then a man from Belfast bought the field and built houses in it—not like their little brown houses but bright brick houses with shining roofs. The children of the avenue used to play together in that field—the Devines, the Waters, the Dunns, little Keogh the cripple, she and her brothers and sisters. Ernest, however, never played: he was too

———————————

1 **cretonne:** Sturdy cotton or linen cloth used primarily for curtains or upholstery.

grown up. Her father used often to hunt them in out of the field with his blackthorn stick[2] but usually little Keogh used to keep nix[3] and call out when he saw her father coming. Still they seemed to have been rather happy then. Her father was not so bad[4] then, and besides her mother was alive. That was a long time ago; she and her brothers and sisters were all grown up; her mother was dead. Tizzie Dunn was dead, too, and the Waters had gone back to England. Everything changes. Now she was going to go away like the others, to leave her home.

Home! She looked round the room reviewing all its familiar objects which she had dusted once a week for so many years, wondering where on earth all the dust came from. Perhaps she would never see again those familiar objects from which she had never dreamed of being divided. And yet during all those years she had never found out the name of the priest whose yellowing photograph hung on the wall above the broken harmonium beside the coloured print of the promises made to Blessed Margaret Mary Alacoque. He had been a school friend of her father's. Whenever he showed the photograph to a visitor her father used to pass it with a casual word:

—He is in Melbourne now.

She had consented to go away, to leave her home. Was that wise? She tried to weigh each side of the question. In her home anyway she had shelter and food; she had those whom she had known all her life about her. Of course she had to work hard both in the house and at business. What would they say of her in the stores when they found out that she had run away with a fellow? Say she was a fool, perhaps; and her place would be filled up by advertisement. Miss Gavan would be glad. She had always had an edge on her, especially whenever there were people listening.

—Miss Hill, don't you see these ladies are waiting?

—Look lively, Miss Hill, please.

She would not cry many tears at leaving the stores.

But in her new home, in a distant unknown country, it would not be like that. Then she would be married—she, Eveline. People would treat her with respect then. She would not be treated as her mother had been. Even now, though she was over nineteen, she sometimes felt herself in danger of her father's violence. She knew it was that that had given her the palpitations. When they were growing up he had never gone for her, like he used to go for Harry and Ernest, because she was a girl; but latterly he had begun to threaten her and say what he would do to her only for her dead mother's sake. And now she had nobody to protect her. Ernest was dead and Harry, who was in the church decorating business, was nearly always down somewhere in the country. Besides, the invariable squabble for money on Saturday nights had begun to weary her unspeakably. She always gave her entire wages—seven shillings[5]—and Harry always sent up what he could but the trouble was to get any

2 **blackthorn stick:** A walking stick made of blackthorn, a very hard wood.
3 **keep nix:** Keep watch; keep out of sight.
4 **not so bad:** Not so frequently drunk.
5 **seven shillings:** With twenty shillings to the pound, Eveline's weekly wage was very low.

money from her father. He said she used to squander the money, that she had no head, that he wasn't going to give her his hard earned money to throw about the streets and much more for he was usually fairly bad of a Saturday night. In the end he would give her the money and ask her had she any intention of buying Sunday's dinner. Then she had to rush out as quickly as she could and do her marketing, holding her black leather purse tightly in her hand as she elbowed her way through the crowds and returning home late under her load of provisions. She had hard work to keep the house together and to see that the two young children who had been left to her charge went to school regularly and got their meals regularly. It was hard work—a hard life—but now that she was about to leave it she did not find it a wholly undesirable life.

She was about to explore another life with Frank. Frank was very kind, manly, openhearted. She was to go away with him by the night boat to be his wife and to live with him in Buenos Ayres where he had a home waiting for her. How well she remembered the first time she had seen him; he was lodging in a house on the main road where she used to visit. It seemed a few weeks ago. He was standing at the gate, his peaked cap pushed back on his head and his hair tumbled forward over a face of bronze. Then they had come to know each other. He used to meet her outside the stores every evening and see her home. He took her to see the *Bohemian Girl* and she felt elated as she sat in an unaccustomed part of the theatre with him. He was awfully fond of music and sang a little. People knew that they were courting and when he sang about the lass that loves a sailor she always felt pleasantly confused. He used to call her Poppens out of fun. First of all it had been an excitement for her to have a fellow and then she had begun to like him. He had tales of distant countries. He had started as a deck boy at a pound a month on a ship of the Allan line going out to Canada. He told her the names of the ships he had been on and the names of the different services. He had sailed through the Straits of Magellan and he told her stories of the terrible Patagonians.[6] He had fallen on his feet in Buenos Ayres, he said, and had come over to the old country just for a holiday. Of course, her father had found out the affair and had forbidden her to have anything to say to him:

—I know these sailor chaps, he said.

One day he had quarrelled with Frank and after that she had to meet her lover secretly.

The evening deepened in the avenue. The white of two letters in her lap grew indistinct. One was to Harry, the other was to her father. Ernest had been her favourite but she liked Harry too. Her father was becoming old lately, she noticed; he would miss her. Sometimes he could be very nice. Not long before, when she had been laid up for a day, he had read her out a ghost story and made toast for her at the fire. Another day, when their mother was alive, they had all gone for a picnic to the Hill of Howth. She remembered her father putting on her mother's bonnet to make the children laugh.

---

6 **Patagonians:** Inhabitants of an area of southern Argentina and Chile.

Her time was running out but she continued to sit by the window, leaning her head against the window curtain, inhaling the odour of dusty cretonne. Down far in the avenue she could hear a street organ playing. She knew the air.[7] Strange that it should come that very night to remind her of the promise to her mother, her promise to keep the home together as long as she could. She remembered the last night of her mother's illness; she was again in the close dark room at the other side of the hall and outside she heard a melancholy air of Italy. The organ player had been ordered to go away and given sixpence. She remembered her father strutting back into the sickroom saying:

—Damned Italians! coming over here!

As she mused the pitiful vision of her mother's life laid its spell on the very quick of her being—that life of commonplace sacrifices closing in final craziness. She trembled as she heard again her mother's voice saying constantly with foolish insistence:

—Derevaun Seraun! Derevaun Seraun!

She stood up in a sudden impulse of terror. Escape! She must escape! Frank would save her. He would give her life, perhaps love too. But she wanted to live. Why should she be unhappy? She had a right to happiness. Frank would take her in his arms, fold her in his arms. He would save her.

She stood among the swaying crowd in the station at the North Wall. He held her hand and she knew that he was speaking to her, saying something about the passage over and over again. The station was full of soldiers with brown baggages. Through the wide doors of the sheds she caught a glimpse of the black mass of the boat lying in beside the quay wall, with illumined portholes. She answered nothing. She felt her cheek pale and cold and out of a maze of distress she prayed to God to direct her, to show her what was her duty. The boat blew a long mournful whistle into the mist. If she went, tomorrow she would be on the sea with Frank, steaming towards Buenos Ayres. Their passage had been booked. Could she still draw back after all he had done for her? Her distress awoke a nausea in her body and she kept moving her lips in silent fervent prayer.

A bell clanged upon her heart. She felt him seize her hand:

—Come!

All the seas of the world tumbled about her heart. He was drawing her into them: he would drown her. She gripped with both hands at the iron railing.

—Come!

No! No! No! It was impossible. Her hands clutched the iron in frenzy. Amid the seas she sent a cry of anguish.

—Eveline! Evvy!

He rushed beyond the barrier and called to her to follow. He was shouted at to go on but he still called to her. She set her white face to him, passive, like a helpless animal. Her eyes gave him no sign of love or farewell or recognition.

7 **air:** Song.

QUESTIONS

1. Describe Eveline's situation. Why does she want to leave Ireland?

2. What is Eveline's relationship with her father?

3. Why does Eveline seem reluctant to leave Ireland? Why does she change her mind at the last moment?

4. Are there hints early in the story that Eveline will not in fact leave Ireland? Point to specific details to support your answer.

5. Is this story only about one young woman's dilemma, or can her situation be seen as representing a wider problem? Can Eveline be interpreted as Ireland itself? Why or why not?

6. What does the story say about the position of women in Ireland at the time? Point to specific details to support your answer.

Liam O'Flaherty

(1896–1984)

Liam O'Flaherty was born on Inishmore, a remote and bleak island in the group off the western coast of Ireland known collectively as the Aran Islands. These are tiny patches of barren, rocky soil, lashed by winds off the Atlantic and populated by hardy peasants who wrest a living from the thin soil and the unforgiving ocean. Early recognized as a promising student, O'Flaherty was sent to Dublin in 1914 to study for the priesthood, but his independent spirit and political radicalism could not long tolerate priestly discipline. During World War I, he joined the English army and was badly traumatized on the Belgian front. After a period of travel in Europe and North America, he returned to Ireland in 1920 and joined the Republican forces against the Irish Free State. Narrowly escaping arrest, he fled to England in 1923 and there published his first short story, "The Sniper," based on his experiences in the civil war.

Encouraged by the famed editor, Edward Garnett, O'Flaherty flourished in the 1920s, producing two novels and three fine collections of stories in that decade alone. His work then and later was strongly influenced by the passions and natural forces he observed on his native island. His characters tend to be irrationally driven by strong emotions they cannot control, and their enemy is either a rigid society controlled by the church and an inflexible class system, or the unyielding forces of hostile nature. This approach to life and literature, often labeled naturalism, gives O'Flaherty's stories raw power and immediate impact, but even their occasional passages of lyrical beauty cannot always overcome the simplistic brutality that too often robs them of subtlety and nuance.

By the 1930s, O'Flaherty had largely abandoned writing short stories for the more lucrative (and in his eyes more prestigious) novel. His 1925 novel, *The Informer*, was filmed by John Ford in 1935 and won four Academy Awards. Story collections did appear in 1948 and 1953, the latter including stories originally written in Irish and then translated into English. Throughout his career, O'Flaherty excelled in stories written from an animal's point of view, using the same plain style and naturalistic philosophy as in his stories of human beings. By the 1950s, O'Flaherty's most creative period was over, though he continued writing novels, political material, and finally his autobiography.

"Going into Exile" is one of O'Flaherty's less melodramatic and violent tales, but it treats a theme that recurs frequently in Irish literature—that of emigrants leaving Ireland for North America. Even in O'Flaherty's time, the stifling social conditions and grinding poverty that James Joyce had written about a generation earlier were still causing young Irish men and women to seek greater opportunities abroad. There is little overt drama in this depiction of the party celebrating the emigration of Mary and Michael, but the story bursts with repressed emotion, fear of the unknown, and urgency.

Going into Exile   1929

Patrick Feeney's cabin was crowded with people. In the large kitchen men, women, and children lined the walls, three deep in places, sitting on forms, chairs, stools, and on one another's knees. On the cement floor three couples were dancing a jig and raising a quantity of dust, which was, however, soon sucked up the chimney by the huge turf[1] fire that blazed on the hearth. The only clear space into the kitchen was the corner to the left of the fireplace, where Pat Mullaney sat on a yellow chair, with his right ankle resting on his left knee, a spotted red handkerchief on his head that reeked with perspiration, and his red face contorting as he played a tattered old accordion. One door was shut and the tins hanging on it gleamed in the firelight. The opposite door was open and over the heads of the small boys that crowded in it and outside it, peering in at the dancing couples in the kitchen, a starry June sky was visible and, beneath the sky, shadowy grey crags and misty, whitish fields lay motionless, still and sombre. There was a deep, calm silence outside the cabin and within the cabin, in spite of the music and dancing in the kitchen and the singing in the little room to the left, where Patrick Feeney's eldest son Michael sat on the bed with three other young men, there was a haunting melancholy in the air.

The people were dancing, laughing and singing with a certain forced and boisterous gaiety that failed to hide from them the real cause of their being there, dancing, singing and laughing. For the dance was on account of Patrick Feeney's two children, Mary and Michael, who were going to the United States on the following morning.

---

1 **turf:** Peat burned for fuel.

Feeney himself, a black-bearded, red-faced, middle-aged peasant, with white ivory buttons on his blue frieze[2] shirt and his hands stuck in his leather waist belt, wandered restlessly about the kitchen, urging the people to sing and dance, while his mind was in agony all the time, thinking that on the following day he would lose his two eldest children, never to see them again perhaps. He kept talking to everybody about amusing things, shouted at the dancers and behaved in a boisterous and abandoned manner. But every now and then he had to leave the kitchen, under the pretence of going to the pigsty to look at a young pig that was supposed to be ill. He would stand, however, upright against his gable and look gloomily at some star or other, while his mind struggled with vague and peculiar ideas that wandered about in it. He could make nothing at all of his thoughts, but a lump always came up his throat, and he shivered, although the night was warm.

Then he would sigh and say with a contraction of his neck: "Oh, it's a queer world this and no doubt about it. So it is." Then he would go back to the cabin again and begin to urge on the dance, laughing, shouting and stamping on the floor.

Towards dawn, when the floor was crowded with couples, arranged in fours, stamping on the floor and going to and fro, dancing the "Walls of Limerick," Feeney was going out to the gable when his son Michael followed him out. The two of them walked side by side about the yard over the grey sea pebbles that had been strewn there the previous day. They walked in silence and yawned without need, pretending to be taking the air. But each of them was very excited. Michael was taller than his father and not so thickly built, but the shabby blue serge suit that he had bought for going to America was too narrow for his broad shoulders and the coat was too wide around the waist. He moved clumsily in it and his hands appeared altogether too bony and big and red, and he didn't know what to do with them. During his twenty-one years of life he had never worn anything other than the homespun clothes of Inverara, and the shop-made clothes appeared as strange to him and as uncomfortable as a dress suit worn by a man working in a sewer. His face was flushed a bright red and his blue eyes shone with excitement. Now and again he wiped the perspiration from his forehead with the lining of his grey tweed cap.

At last Patrick Feeney reached his usual position at the gable end. He halted, balanced himself on his heels with his hands in his waist belt, coughed and said, "It's going to be a warm day." The son came up beside him, folded his arms and leaned his right shoulder against the gable.

"It was kind of Uncle Ned to lend the money for the dance, father," he said. "I'd hate to think that we'd have to go without something or other, just the same as everybody else has. I'll send you that money the very first money I earn, father . . . even before I pay Aunt Mary for my passage money. I should have all that money paid off in four months, and then I'll have some more money to send you by Christmas."

And Michael felt very strong and manly recounting what he was going to do when he got to Boston, Massachusetts. He told himself that with his great strength

---

2 **frieze:** A heavy, rough wool fabric.

he would earn a great deal of money. Conscious of his youth and his strength and lusting for adventurous life, for the moment he forgot the ache in his heart that the thought of leaving his father inspired in him.

The father was silent for some time. He was looking at the sky with his lower lip hanging, thinking of nothing. At last he sighed as a memory struck him. "What is it?" said the son. "Don't weaken, for God's sake. You will only make it hard for me." "Fooh!" said the father suddenly with pretended gruffness. "Who is weakening? I'm afraid that your new clothes make you impudent." Then he was silent for a moment and continued in a low voice: "I was thinking of that potato field you sowed alone last spring the time I had the influenza. I never set eyes on the man that could do it better. It's a cruel world that takes you away from the land that God made you for."

"Oh, what are you talking about, father?" said Michael irritably. "Sure what did anybody ever got out of the land put poverty and hard work and potatoes and salt?"

"Ah yes," said the father with a sigh, "but it's your own, the land, and over there"—he waved his hand at the western sky—"you'll be giving your sweat to some other man's land, or what's equal to it."

"Indeed," muttered Michael, looking at the ground with a melancholy expression in his eyes, "it's poor encouragement you are giving me."

They stood in silence fully five minutes. Each hungered to embrace the other, to cry, to beat the air, to scream with excess of sorrow. But they stood silent and sombre, like nature about them, hugging their woe. Then they went back to the cabin. Michael went into the little room to the left of the kitchen, to the three young men who fished in the same curragh[3] with him and were his bosom friends. The father walked into the large bedroom to the right of the kitchen.

The large bedroom was also crowded with people. A large table was laid for tea in the centre of the room and about a dozen young men were sitting at it, drinking tea and eating buttered raisin cake. Mrs Feeney was bustling about the table, serving the food and urging them to eat. She was assisted by her two younger daughters and by another woman, a relative of her own. Her eldest daughter Mary, who was going to the United States that day, was sitting on the edge of the bed with several other young woman. The bed was a large four poster bed with a deal[4] canopy over it, painted red, and the young women were huddled together on it. So that there must have been about a dozen of them there. They were Mary Feeney's particular friends, and they stayed with her in that uncomfortable position just to show how much they liked her. It was a custom.

Mary herself sat on the edge of the bed with her legs dangling. She was a pretty, dark-haired girl of nineteen, with dimpled, plump, red cheeks and ruminative brown eyes that seemed to cause little wrinkles to come and go in her little low forehead. Her nose was soft and small and rounded. Her mouth was small and the lips were red and open. Beneath her white blouse that was frilled at the neck and her

---

3 **curragh:** A small, light fishing boat.
4 **deal:** Wide, rough boards.

navy blue skirt that outlined her limbs as she sat on the edge of the bed, her body was plump, soft, well-moulded and in some manner exuded a feeling of freshness and innocence. So that she seemed to have been born to be fondled and admired in luxurious surroundings instead of having been born a peasant's daughter, who had to go to the United States that day to work as a servant or maybe in a factory.

And as she sat on the edge of the bed crushing her little handkerchief between her palms, she kept thinking feverishly of the United States, at one moment with fear and loathing, at the next with desire and longing. Unlike her brother she did not think of the work she was going to do or the money that she was going to earn. Other things troubled her, things of which she was half ashamed, half afraid, thoughts of love and of foreign men and of clothes and of houses where there were more than three rooms and where people ate meat every day.

She was fond of life, and several young men among the local gentry had admired her in Inverara. But . . .

She happened to look up and she caught her father's eyes as he stood silently by the window with his hands stuck in his waist belt. His eyes rested on hers for a moment and then he dropped them without smiling, and with his lips compressed he walked down into the kitchen. She shuddered slightly. She was a little afraid of her father, although she knew that he loved her very much and he was very kind to her. But the winter before he had whipped her with a dried willow rod, when he caught her one evening behind Tim Hernon's cabin after nightfall, with Tim Hernon's son Bartly's arms around her waist and he kissing her. Ever since, she always shivered slightly when her father touched her or spoke to her. "Oho!" said an old peasant who sat at the table with a saucer full of tea in his hand and his grey flannel shirt open at his thin, hairy, wrinkled neck. "Oho! indeed, but it's a disgrace to the island of Inverara to let such a beautiful woman as your daughter go away, Mrs Feeney. If I were a young man, I'll be flayed alive if I'd let her go."

There was a laugh and some of the women on the bed, said: "Bad cess to you, Patsy Coyne, if you haven't too much impudence, it's a caution." But the laugh soon died. The young men sitting at the table felt embarrassed and kept looking at one another sheepishly, as if each tried to find out if the others were in love with Mary Feeney.

"Oh, well, God is good," said Mrs Feeney, as she wiped her lips with the tip of her bright, clean, check apron. "What will be must be, and sure there is hope from the sea, but there is no hope from the grave. It is sad and the poor have to suffer, but . . ." Mrs Feeney stopped suddenly, aware that all these platitudes meant nothing whatsoever. Like her husband she was unable to think intelligibly about her two children going away. Whenever the reality of their going away, maybe for ever, three thousand miles into a vast unknown world, came before her mind, it seemed that a thin bar of some hard metal thrust itself forward from her brain and rested behind the wall of her forehead. So that almost immediately she became stupidly conscious of the pain caused by the imaginary bar of metal and she forgot the dread prospect of her children going away. But her mind grappled with the things about her busily and efficiently, with the preparation of food, with the entertaining of her guests, with the numerous little things that have to be done in a house where there is a party and which only a woman can do property. These little things, in a manner, saved her, for the moment at least, from bursting into tears whenever she looked at her daughter and whenever she thought of her son, whom she loved most of all her children, because perhaps she nearly died giving birth to him and he had been very delicate until he was twelve years old. So she laughed down in her breast a funny laugh she had that made her heave, where her check apron rose out from the waist band in a deep curve. "A person begins to talk," she said with a shrug of her shoulders sideways, "and then a person says foolish things."

"That's true," said the old peasant, noisily pouring more tea from his cup to his saucer.

But Mary knew by her mother laughing that way that she was very near being hysterical. She always laughed that way before she had one of her fits of hysterics. And Mary's heart stopped beating suddenly and then began again at an awful rate as her eyes became acutely conscious of her mother's body, the rotund, short body with the wonderful mass of fair hair, growing grey at the temples and the fair face with the soft liquid brown eyes, that grew hard and piercing for a moment as they looked at a thing and then grew soft and liquid again, and the thin-lipped small mouth with the beautiful white teeth and the deep perpendicular grooves in the upper lip and the tremor that always came in the corner of the mouth, with love, when she looked at her children. Mary became acutely conscious of all these little points, as well as of the little black spot that was on her left breast below the nipple and the swelling that came now and again in her legs and caused her to have hysterics and would one day cause her death. And she was stricken with horror at the thought of leaving her mother and at the selfishness of her thoughts. She had never been prone to thinking of anything important but now, somehow for a moment, she had a glimpse of her mother's life that made her shiver and hate herself as a cruel, heartless, lazy, selfish wretch. Her mother's life loomed up before her eyes, a life of continual misery and suffering, hard work, birth pangs, sickness and again hard work and hunger and anxiety. It loomed up and then it fled again, a little mist came before her eyes and she jumped down from the bed, with the jaunty twirl of her head that was her habit when she set her body in motion.

"Sit down for a while, mother," she whispered toying with one of the black ivory buttons on her mother's brown bodice. "I'll look after the table." "No, no," murmured the mother with a shake of her whole body, "I'm not a bit tired. Sit down, my treasure. You have a long way to travel today."

And Mary sighed and went back to the bed again. At last somebody said: "It's broad daylight." And immediately everybody looked out and said: "So it is, and may God be praised." The change from the starry night to the grey, sharp dawn was hard to notice until it had arrived. People looked out and saw the morning light sneaking over the crags silently, along the ground, pushing the mist banks upwards. The stars were growing dim. A long way off invisible sparrows were chirping in their ivied perch in some distant hill or other. Another day had arrived and even as the people looked at it, yawned and began to search for their hats, caps and shawls preparing to go home, the day grew and spread its light and made things move and give voice. Cocks crew, blackbirds carolled, a dog let loose from a cabin by an early riser chased madly after an imaginary robber, barking as if his tail were on fire. The people said good-bye and began to stream forth from Feeney's cabin. They were going to their homes to see to the morning's work before going to Kilmurrage to see the emigrants off on the steamer to the mainland. Soon the cabin was empty except for the family.

All the family gathered into the kitchen and stood about for some minutes talking sleepily of the dance and of the people who had been present. Mrs Feeney tried to persuade everybody to go to bed, but everybody refused. It was four o'clock and Michael and Mary would have to set out for Kilmurrage at nine. So tea was made and they all sat about for an hour drinking it and eating raisin cake and talking. They talked of the dance and of the people who had been present.

There were eight of them there, the father and mother and six children. The youngest child was Thomas, a thin boy of twelve, whose lungs made a singing sound every time he breathed. The next was Bridget, a girl of fourteen, with dancing eyes and a habit of shaking her short golden curls every now and then for no apparent reason. Then there were the twins, Julia and Margaret, quiet, rather stupid, flat-faced girls of sixteen. Both their upper front teeth protruded slightly and they were both great workers and very obedient to their mother. They were all sitting at the table, having just finished a third large pot of tea, when suddenly the mother hastily gulped down the remainder of the tea in her cup, dropped the cup with a clatter to her saucer and sobbed once through her nose.

"Now mother," said Michael sternly, "what's the good of this work?"

"No, you are right, my pulse,"[5] she replied quietly. "Only I was just thinking how nice it is to sit here surrounded by all my children, all my little birds in my nest, and then two of them going to fly away made me sad." And she laughed, pretending to treat it as a foolish joke.

"Oh, that be damned for a story," said the father, wiping his mouth on his sleeve; "there's work to be done. You Julia, go and get the horse. Margaret, you milk the cow and see that you give enough milk to the calf this morning." And he ordered everybody about as if it were an ordinary day of work.

But Michael and Mary had nothing to do and they sat about miserably conscious that they had cut adrift from the routine of their home life. They no longer had any place in it. In a few hours they would be homeless wanders. Now that they were cut adrift from it, the poverty and sordidness of their home life appeared to them under the aspect of comfort and plenty.

So the morning passed until breakfast time at seven o'clock. The morning's work was finished and the family was gathered together again. The meal passed in a dead silence. Drowsy after the sleepless night and conscious that the parting would come in a few hours, nobody wanted to talk. Everybody had an egg for breakfast in honour of the occasion. Mrs Feeney, after her usual habit, tried to give her egg first

---

5 **my pulse:** My life.

to Michael, then to Mary, and as each refused it, she ate a little herself and gave the remainder to little Thomas who had the singing in his chest. Then the breakfast was cleared away. The father went to put the creels[6] on the mare so as to take the luggage into Kilmurrage. Michael and Mary got the luggage ready and began to get dressed. The mother and the other children tidied up the house. People from the village began to come into the kitchen, as was customary, in order to accompany the emigrants from their home to Kilmurrage.

At last everything was ready. Mrs Feeney had exhausted all excuses for moving about, engaged on trivial tasks. She had to go into the big bedroom where Mary was putting on her new hat. The mother sat on a chair by the window, her face contorting on account of the flood of tears she was keeping back. Michael moved about the room uneasily, his two hands knotting a big red handkerchief behind his back. Mary twisted about in front of the mirror that hung over the black wooden mantelpiece. She was spending a long time with the hat. It was the first one she had ever worn, but it fitted her beautifully, and it was in excellent taste. It was given to her by the schoolmistress, who was very fond of her, and she herself had taken it in a little. She had an instinct for beauty in dress and deportment.

But the mother, looking at how well her daughter wore the cheap navy blue costume and the white frilled blouse, and the little round black hat with a fat, fluffy, glossy curl covering each ear, and the black silk stockings with blue clocks[7] in them, and the little black shoes that had laces of three colours in them, got suddenly enraged with. . . She didn't know with what she got enraged. But for the moment she hatred her daughter's beauty, and she remembered all the anguish of giving birth to her and nursing her and toiling for her, for no other purpose than to lose her now and let her go away, maybe to be ravished wantonly because of her beauty and her love of gaiety. A cloud of mad jealousy and hatred against this impersonal beauty that she saw in her daughter almost suffocated the mother, and stretched out her hands in front of her unconsciously and then just as suddenly her anger vanished like a puff of smoke, and she burst into wild tears, waiting: "My children, oh, my children, far over the sea you will be carried from me, your mother." And she began to rock herself and she threw her apron over her head.

Immediately the cabin was full of the sound of bitter wailing. A dismal cry rose from the women gathered in the kitchen. "Far over the sea they will be carried," began woman after woman, and they all rocked themselves and hid their heads in their aprons. Michael's mongrel dog began to howl on the hearth. Little Thomas sat down on the hearth beside the dog and, putting his arms around him, he began to cry, although he didn't know exactly why he was crying, but he felt melancholy on account of the dog howling and so many people being about.

In the bedroom the son and daughter, on their knees, clung to their mother, who held their heads between her hands and rained kisses on both heads ravenously.

---

6 **creels:** Wicker baskets.
7 **clocks:** Ornaments in the stockings, at the ankle.

After the first wave of tears she had stopped weeping. The tears still ran down her cheeks, but her eyes gleamed and they were dry. There was a fierce look in them as she searched all over the heads of her two children with them, with her brows contracted, searching with a fierce terror-stricken expression, as if by the intensity of her stare she hoped to keep a living photograph of them before her mind. With her quivering lips she made a queer sound like "im-m-m-m" and she kept kissing. Her right hand clutched at Mary's left shoulder and with her left she fondled the back of Michael's neck. The two children were sobbing freely. They must have stayed that way a quarter of an hour.

Then the father came into the room, dressed in his best clothes. He wore a new frieze waistcoat, with a grey and black front and a white back. He held his soft black felt hat in one hand and in the other hand he had a bottle of holy water. He coughed and said in a weak gentle voice that was strange to him, as he touched his son: "Come now, it is time."

Mary and Michael got to their feet. The father sprinkled them with holy water and they crossed themselves. Then, without looking at their mother, who lay in the chair with her hands clasped on her lap, looking at the ground in a silent tearless stupor, they left the room. Each hurriedly kissed little Thomas, who was not going to Kilmurrage, and then, hand in hand, they left the house. As Michael was going out the door he picked a piece of loose white-wash from the wall and put it in his pocket. The people filed out after them, down the yard and on to the road, like a funeral procession. The mother was left in the house with little Thomas and two old peasant women from the village. Nobody spoke in the cabin for a long time.

Then the mother rose and came into the kitchen. She looked at the two women, at her little son at the hearth, as if she was looking for something she had lost. Then she threw her hands into air and ran out into the yard.

"Come back," she screamed; "come back to me."

She looked wildly down the road with dilated nostrils, her bosom heaving. But there was nobody in sight. Nobody replied. There was a crooked stretch of limestone road, surrounded by grey crags that were scorched by the sun. The road ended in a hill and then dropped out of sight. The hot June day was silent. Listening foolishly for an answering cry, the mother imagined she could hear the crags simmering under the hot rays of the sun. It was something in her head that was singing.

The two old women led her back into the kitchen. "There is nothing that time will not cure," said one. "Yes. Time and patience," said the other.

QUESTIONS

1. Why does the title use the word *exile*? What does the word imply?

2. What conditions does the story reveal that would explain why Mary and Michael feel they must leave Ireland?

3. What emotions do the family members, including Mary and Michael, feel during the party?

4. What fears are expressed by the family members about Mary and Michael's future in the United States? Were these fears well founded?

5. Is the Feeney family a victim of British colonial policies? Why or why not?

Frank O'Connor

(1903–1966)

Anyone who has read Frank McCourt's memoir *Angela's Ashes* (1996) or seen the film based on the book will have a fair idea of Frank O'Connor's childhood. He was christened Michael Francis O'Donovan, Jr., son of the handsome, feckless, and drunken Michael O'Donovan, who soon came to regard his frail and bookish son as a weakling and sissy. Naturally, the boy turned for solace to his mother, Minnie, who encouraged his reading and desire for education, believing learning to be the only road out of the squalid poverty of Cork's slums. Michael, Jr.'s interest in literature and art alienated him not only from his father; the other boys shunned him as well, with the result that he retreated further and further into the world of books and the life of the imagination.

The world, however, is not always kind to romantic dreamers. Young Michael lost his first jobs because employers caught him daydreaming during working hours. Seeking to educate himself, Michael luckily found a mentor in his former schoolteacher, Daniel Corkery, who introduced him to Sean O'Faolain and set both of them to reading the great Russians—Nikolai Gogol, Ivan Turgenev, and Anton Chekhov, among others—all masters of the modern short story. Michael was only thirteen when the Easter Rebellion erupted in 1916, and nineteen when the Irish Republican Army rebelled against the treaty with Britain that established the Irish Free State. Full of romantic notions of Irish independence and the glory of war, he joined the IRA in 1922 and soon came to realize that war is anything but heroism and glory. Captured by the Free State, he witnessed the brutal beating and execution of a fellow IRA member, then endured the taunts and isolation imposed by his fellow prisoners as he grappled with the morality and self-destruction of civil war. Out of these experiences came his beliefs that humor is a corrective to fanaticism, and that war brutalizes and destroys rather than ennobles and creates.

Released from prison in 1924, he turned first to teaching in rural schools and then became a librarian in a succession of cities. After ending up in Dublin, he was encouraged by the editor of *The Irish Statesman*, George Russell (also known as "AE"), and introduced to the leading writers of the time, including William Butler Yeats. During this time, he took the pen name Frank O'Connor, combining his middle name with his mother's maiden name. O'Connor's early stories appeared in Russell's magazine, and his first collection, *Guests of the Nation*, appeared in 1931, following the publication in January of that year of the title story in the famous U.S. magazine, *The Atlantic Monthly*. O'Connor eventually became known primarily as a short story writer, but in the 1930s he considered himself a poet. With Yeats's backing, O'Connor also directed the famous Abbey Theatre in Dublin during the 1937–1938 season.

Like many other Irish writers, O'Connor made himself unpopular with his fellow Irish by criticizing Ireland's parochialism, narrow-mindedness, and backwardness. Several of his books were banned in Ireland in the 1940s and 1950s, with the result that he emigrated in 1951 to lecture in U.S. universities. He visited nearly every year, however, and when a stroke disabled him in 1961, he returned permanently.

O'Connor's rich legacy of short stories is now a significant part of Ireland's literary heritage, and none of his stories has surpassed the popularity and importance of his first success, "Guests of the Nation." Set not during the civil war of 1922–1923 but during the rebellion of 1916–1919, the story turns a minor example of war's inhumanity into a powerful synecdoche for the nature of war itself.

———————————

Guests of the Nation $\qquad$ *1931*
——

At dusk the big Englishman Belcher would shift his long legs out of the ashes and ask, "Well, chums, what about it?" and Noble or me would say, "As you please, chum" (for we had picked up some of their curious expressions), and the little Englishman 'Awkins would light the lamp and produce the cards. Sometimes Jeremiah Donovan would come up of an evening and supervise the play, and grow excited over 'Awkins's cards (which he always played badly), and shout at him as if he was one of our own, "Ach, you divil you, why didn't you play the tray?"[1] But, ordinarily, Jeremiah was a sober and contented poor devil like the big Englishman Belcher, and was looked up to at all only because he was a fair hand at documents, though slow enough at these, I vow. He wore a small cloth hat and big gaiters over his long pants, and seldom did I perceive his hands outside the pockets of that pants. He reddened when you talked to him, tilting from toe to heel and back and looking down all the while at his big farmer's feet. His uncommon broad accent was a great source of jest to me, I being from the town as you may recognize.

I couldn't at the time see the point of me and Noble being with Belcher and 'Awkins at all, for it was and is my fixed belief you could have planted that pair in any untended spot from this to Claregalway and they'd have stayed put and flourished like a native weed. I never seen in my short experience two men that took to the country as they did.

They were handed on to us by the Second Battalion to keep when the search for them became too hot, and Noble and myself, being young, took charge with a

———————————

1 **the tray:** The three.

natural feeling of responsibility. But little 'Awkins made us look right fools when he displayed he knew the countryside as well as we did and something more. "You're the bloke they calls Bonaparte?" he said to me. "Well, Bonaparte, Mary Brigid Ho'Connell was arskin abaout you and said 'ow you'd a pair of socks belonging to 'er young brother." For it seemed, as they explained it, that the Second used to have little evenings of their own, and some of the girls of the neighborhood would turn in, and seeing they were such decent fellows, our lads couldn't well ignore the two Englishmen, but invited them in and were hail-fellow-well-met with them. 'Awkins told me he learned to dance "The Walls of Limerick" and "The Siege of Ennis" and "The Waves of Tory" in a night or two, though naturally he could not return the compliment, because our lads at that time did not dance foreign dances on principle.

So whatever privileges and favors Belcher and 'Awkins had with the Second they duly took with us, and after the first evening we gave up all pretense of keeping a close eye on their behavior. Not that they could have got far, for they had a notable accent and wore khaki tunics and overcoats with civilian pants and boots. But it's my belief they never had an idea of escaping and were quite contented with their lot.

Now, it was a treat to see how Belcher got off with the old woman of the house we were staying in. She was a great warrant to scold, and crotchety even with us, but before ever she had a chance of giving our guests, as I may call them, a lick of her tongue, Belcher had made her his friend for life. She was breaking sticks at the time, and Belcher, who hadn't been in the house for more than ten minutes, jumped up out of his seat and went across to her.

"Allow me, madam," he says, smiling his queer little smile; "please allow me," and takes the hatchet from her hand. She was struck too parlatic[2] to speak, and ever after Belcher would be at her heels carrying a bucket, or basket, or load of turf,[3] as the case might be. As Noble wittily remarked, he got into looking before she leapt, and hot water or any little thing she wanted Belcher would have it ready for her. For such a huge man (and though I am five foot ten myself I had to look up to him) he had an uncommon shortness—or should I say lack—of speech. It took us some time to get used to him walking in and out like a ghost, without a syllable out of him. Especially because 'Awkins talked enough for a platoon, it was strange to hear big Belcher with his toes in the ashes come out with a solitary "Excuse me, chum," or "That's right, chum." His one and only abiding passion was cards, and I will say for him he was a good card-player. He could have fleeced me and Noble many a time; only if we lost to him, 'Awkins lost to us, and 'Awkins played with the money Belcher gave him.

'Awkins lost to us because he talked too much, and I think now we lost to Belcher for the same reason. 'Awkins and Noble would spit at one another about religion into the early hours of the morning; the little Englishman as you could see worrying the soul out of young Noble (whose brother was a priest) with a string of questions that

---

2 **parlatic:** paralytic: paralyzed.
3 **turf:** Peat, used as fuel.

would puzzle a cardinal. And to make it worse, even in treating of these holy subjects, 'Awkins had a deplorable tongue; I never in all my career struck across a man who could mix such a variety of cursing and bad language into the simplest topic. Oh, a terrible man was little 'Awkins, and a fright to argue! He never did a stroke of work, and when he had no one else to talk to he fixed his claws into the old woman.

I am glad to say that in her he met his match, for one day when he tried to get her to complain profanely of the drought she gave him a great comedown by blaming the drought upon Jupiter Pluvius[4] (a deity neither 'Awkins nor I had ever even heard of, though Noble said among the pagans he was held to have something to do with rain). And another day the same 'Awkins was swearing at the capitalists for starting the German war,[5] when the old dame laid down her iron, puckered up her little crab's mouth and said, "Mr. 'Awkins, you can say what you please about the war, thinking to deceive me because I'm an ignorant old woman, but I know well what started the war. It was that Italian count that stole the heathen divinity out of the temple in Japan, for believe me, Mr. 'Awkins, nothing but sorrow and want follows them that disturbs the hidden powers!" Oh, a queer old dame, as you remark!

So one evening we had our tea together, and 'Awkins lit the lamp and we all sat in to cards. Jeremiah Donovan came in too, and sat down and watched us for a while. Though he was a shy man and didn't speak much, it was easy to see he had no great love for the two Englishmen, and I was surprised it hadn't struck me so clearly before. Well, like that in the story, a terrible dispute blew up late in the evening between 'Awkins and Noble, about capitalists and priests and love for your own country.

"The capitalists," says 'Awkins, with an angry gulp, "the capitalists pays the priests to tell you all abaout the next world, so's you won't notice what they do in this!"

"Nonsense, man," says Noble, losing his temper, "before ever a capitalist was thought of people believed in the next world."

'Awkins stood up as if he was preaching a sermon. "Oh, they did, did they?" he says with a sneer. "They believed all the things you believe, that's what you mean? And you believe that God created Hadam and Hadam created Shem and Shem created Jehoshophat?[6] You believe all the silly hold fairy-tale abaout Heve and Heden and the happle? Well, listen to me, chum. If you're entitled to 'old to a silly belief like that, I'm entitled to 'old to my own silly belief—which is, that the fust thing your God created was a bleedin' capitalist with mirality and Rolls Royce complete. Am I right, chum?" he says then to Belcher.

"You're right, chum," says Belcher, with his queer smile, and gets up from the table to stretch his long legs into the fire and stroke his mustache. So, seeing that

4 **Jupiter Pluvius:** Jupiter is the Roman name for the Greek god Zeus, god of the sky. *Pluvius* means "relating to rain." The combination however is comical.

5 **German war:** World War I.

6 **Hadam . . . Jehoshophat:** Hawkins's garbled version of the many "begat" genealogies in the Old Testament. Hadam is Adam.

Jeremiah Donovan was going, and there was no knowing when the conversation about religion would be over, I took my hat and went out with him. We strolled down towards the village together, and then he suddenly stopped, and blushing and mumbling, and shifting, as his way was, from toe to heel, he said I ought to be behind keeping guard on the prisoners. And I, having it put to me so suddenly, asked him what the hell he wanted a guard on the prisoners at all for, and said that so far as Noble and me were concerned we had talked it over and would rather be out with a column. "What use is that pair to us?" I asked him.

He looked at me for a spell and said, "I thought you knew we were keeping them as hostages." "Hostages—?" says I, not quite understanding. "The enemy," he says in his heavy way, "have prisoners belong' to us, and now they talk of shooting them. If they shoot our prisoners we'll shoot theirs, and serve them right." "Shoot them?" said I, the possibility just beginning to dawn on me. "Shoot them exactly," said he. "Now," said I, "wasn't it very unforeseen of you not to tell me and Noble that?" "How so?" he asks. "Seeing that we were acting as guards upon them, of course." "And hadn't you reason enough to guess that much?" "We had not, Jeremiah Donovan, we had not. How were we to know when the men were on our hands so long?" "And what difference does it make? The enemy have our prisoners as long or longer, haven't they?" "It makes a great difference," said I. "How so?" said he sharply; but I couldn't tell him the difference it made, for I was struck too silly to speak. "And when may we expect to be released from this anyway?" said I. "You may expect it tonight," says he. "Or tomorrow or the next day at latest. So if it's hanging round here that worries you, you'll be free soon enough."

I cannot explain it even now, how sad I felt, but I went back to the cottage, a miserable man. When I arrived the discussion was still on, 'Awkins holding forth to all and sundry that there was no next world at all and Noble answering in his best canonical style that there was. But I saw 'Awkins was after having the best of it. "Do you know what, chum?" he was saying, with his saucy smile. "I think you're jest as big a bleedin' hunbeliever as I am. You say you believe in the next world and you know jest as much abaout the next world as I do, which is sweet damn-all. What's 'Eaven? You dunno. Where's 'Eaven? You dunno. Who's in 'Eaven? You dunno. You know sweet damn-all! I arsk you again, do they wear wings?"

"Very well then," says Noble, "they do; is that enough for you? They do wear wings." "Where do they get them then? Who makes them? 'Ave they a fact'ry for wings? 'Ave they a sort of store where you 'ands in your chit[7] and tikes your bleedin' wings? Answer me that."

"Oh, you're an impossible man to argue with," says Noble. "Now listen to me—" And off the pair of them went again.

It was long after midnight when we locked up the Englishmen and went to bed ourselves. As I blew out the candle I told Noble what Jeremiah Donovan had told me. Noble took it very quietly. After we had been in bed about an hour he asked me

---

7 **chit:** A voucher.

did I think we ought to tell the Englishmen. I having thought of the same thing my-self (among many others) said no, because it was more than likely the English wouldn't shoot our men, and anyhow it wasn't to be supposed the Brigade who were always up and down with the Second Battalion and knew the Englishmen well would be likely to want them bumped off. "I think so," says Noble. "It would be sort of cruelty to put the wind up them now." "It was very unforeseen of Jeremiah Dono-van anyhow," says I, and by Noble's silence I realized he took my meaning.

So I lay there half the night, and thought and thought, and picturing myself and young Noble trying to prevent the Brigade from shooting 'Awkins and Belcher sent a cold sweat out through me. Because there were men on the Brigade you daren't let nor hinder without a gun in your hand, and at any rate, in those days disunion be-tween brothers seemed to me an awful crime. I knew better after.[8]

It was next morning we found it so hard to face Belcher and 'Awkins with a smile. We went about the house all day scarcely saying a word. Belcher didn't mind us much; he was stretched into the ashes as usual with his usual look of waiting in quietness for something unforeseen to happen, but little 'Awkins gave us a bad time with his audacious gibing and questioning. He was disgusted at Noble's not answer-ing him back. "Why can't you tike your beating like a man, chum?" he says. "You with your Hadam and Heve! I'm a Communist—or an Anarchist. An Anarchist, that's what I am." And for hours after he went round the house, mumbling when the fit took him "Hadam and Heve! Hadam and Heve!"

I don't know clearly how we got over that day, but get over it we did, and a great relief it was when the tea things were cleared away and Belcher said in his peaceable manner, "Well, chums, what about it?" So we all sat round the table and 'Awkins pro-duced the cards, and at that moment I heard Jeremiah Donovan's footsteps up the path, and a dark presentiment crossed my mind. I rose quietly from the table and laid my hand on him before he reached the door. "What do you want?" I asked him. "I want those two soldier friends of yours," he says reddening. "Is that the way it is, Jeremiah Donovan?" I ask. "That's the way. There were four of our lads went west[9] this morning, one of them a boy of sixteen." "That's bad, Jeremiah," says I.

At that moment Noble came out, and we walked down the path together talking in whispers. Feeney, the local intelligence officer, was standing by the gate. "What are you going to do about it?" I asked Jeremiah Donovan. "I want you and Noble to bring them out: you can tell them they're being shifted again; that'll be the quietest way." "Leave me out of that," says Noble suddenly. Jeremiah Donovan looked at him hard for a minute or two. "All right so," he said peaceably. "You and Feeney collect a few tools from the shed and dig a hole by the far end of the bog. Bonaparte and I'll be after you in about twenty minutes. But whatever else you do, don't let anyone see you with the tools. No one must know but the four of ourselves."

8 **I knew better after:** A reference to the civil war that broke out later between the Irish Free State and the Irish Republican Army.
9 **went west:** Died; was executed.

We saw Feeney and Noble go round to the houseen[10] where the tools were kept, and sidled in. Everything if I can so express myself was tottering before my eyes, and I left Jeremiah Donovan to do the explaining as best he could, while I took a seat and said nothing. He told them they were to go back to the Second. 'Awkins let a mouthful of curses out of him at that, and it was plain that Belcher, though he said nothing, was duly perturbed. The old woman was for having them stay in spite of us, and she did not shut her mouth until Jeremiah Donovan lost his temper and said some nasty things to her. Within the house by this time it was pitch dark, but no one thought of lighting the lamp, and in the darkness the two Englishmen fetched their khaki topcoats and said good-bye to the woman of the house. "Just as a man mikes a 'ome of a bleedin' place," mumbles 'Awkins, shaking her by the hand, "some bastard at Headquarters thinks you're too cushy and shunts you off." Belcher shakes her hand very hearty. "A thousand thanks, madam," he says, "a thousand thanks for everything . . ." as though he'd made it all up.

We go round to the back of the house and down towards the fatal bog. Then Jeremiah Donovan comes out with what is in his mind. "There were four of our lads shot by your fellows this morning so now you're to be bumped off." "Cut that stuff out," says 'Awkins, flaring up. "It's bad enough to be mucked about such as we are without you plying at soldiers." "It's true," says Jeremiah Donovan, "I'm sorry, 'Awkins, but 'tis true," and comes out with the usual rigmarole about doing our duty and obeying our superiors. "Cut it out," says 'Awkins irritably. "Cut it out!"

Then, when Donovan sees he is not being believed he turns to me, "Ask Bonaparte here," he says. "I don't need to arsk Bonaparte. Me and Bonaparte are chums." "Isn't it true, Bonaparte?" says Jeremiah Donovan solemnly to me. "It is," I say sadly, "it is." 'Awkins stops. "Now, for Christ's sike. . . ." "I mean it, chum," I say. "You daon't saound as if you mean it. You knaow well you don't mean it." "Well, if he don't I do," says Jeremiah Donovan. "Why the 'ell sh'd you want to shoot me, Jeremiah Donovan?" "Why the hell should your people take out four prisoners and shoot them in cold blood upon a barrack square?" I perceive Jeremiah Donovan is trying to encourage himself with hot words.

Anyway, he took little 'Awkins by the arm and dragged him on, but it was impossible to make him understand that we were in earnest. From which you will perceive how difficult it was for me, as I kept feeling my Smith and Wesson and thinking what I would do if they happened to put up a fight or ran for it, and wishing in my heart they would. I knew if only they ran I would never fire on them. "Was Noble in this?" 'Awkins wanted to know, and we said yes. He laughed. But why should Noble want to shoot him? Why should we want to shoot him? What had he done to us? Weren't we chums (the word lingers painfully in my memory)? Weren't we? Didn't we understand him and didn't he understand us? Did either of us imagine for an instant that he'd shoot us for all the so-and-so brigadiers in the so-and-so British Army? By this time I began to perceive in the dusk the desolate edges of the bog that

10 **houseen:** Shed.

was to be their last earthly bed, and, so great a sadness overtook my mind, I could not answer him. We walked along the edge of it in the darkness, and every now and then 'Awkins would call a halt and begin again, just as if he was wound up, about us being chums, and I was in despair that nothing but the cold and open grave made ready for his presence would convince him that we meant it all. But all the same, if you can understand, I didn't want him to be bumped off.

At last we saw the unsteady glint of a lantern in the distance and made towards it. Noble was carrying it, and Feeney stood somewhere in the darkness behind, and somehow the picture of the two of them so silent in the boglands was like the pain of death in my heart. Belcher, on recognizing Noble, said " 'Allo, chum" in his usual peaceable way, but 'Awkins flew at the poor boy immediately, and the dispute began all over again, only that Noble hadn't a word to say for himself, and stood there with the swaying lantern between his gaitered legs.[11]

It was Jeremiah Donovan who did the answering. 'Awkins asked for the twentieth time (for it seemed to haunt his mind) if anybody thought he'd shoot Noble. "You would," says Jeremiah Donovan shortly. "I wouldn't, damn you!" "You would if you knew you'd be shot for not doing it." "I wouldn't, not if I was to be shot twenty times over; he's my chum. And Belcher wouldn't—isn't that right, Belcher?" "That's right, chum," says Belcher peaceably. "Damned if I would. Anyway, who says Noble'd be shot if I wasn't bumped off? What d'you think I'd do if I was in Noble's place and we were out in the middle of a blasted bog?" "What would you do?" "I'd go with him wherever he was going. I'd share my last bob[12] with him and stick by 'im through thick and thin."

"We've had enough of this," says Jeremiah Donovan, cocking his revolver. "Is there any message you want to send before I fire?" "No, there isn't, but . . ." "Do you want to say your prayers?" 'Awkins came out with a cold-blooded remark that shocked even me and turned to Noble again. "Listen to me, Noble," he said. "You and me are chums. You won't come over to my side, so I'll come over to your side. Is that fair? Just you give me a rifle and I'll go with you wherever you want."

Nobody answered him.

"Do you understand?" he said. "I'm through with it all. I'm a deserter or anything else you like, but from this on I'm one of you. Does that prove to you that I mean what I say?" Noble raised his head, but as Donovan began to speak he lowered it again without answering. "For the last time have you any messages to send?" says Donovan in a cold and excited voice.

"Ah, shut up, you, Donovan; you don't understand me, but these fellows do. They're my chums; they stand by me and I stand by them. We're not the capitalist tools you seem to think us."

---

11 **gaitered legs:** Gaiters are cloth or leather coverings over the ankle and calf.
12 **bob:** Shilling, one-twentieth of a British pound, or twelve pence.

I alone of the crowd saw Donovan raise his Webley to the back of 'Awkins's neck, and as he did so I shut my eyes and tried to say a prayer. 'Awkins had begun to say something else when Donovan let fly, and, as I opened my eyes at the bang, I saw him stagger at the knees and lie out flat at Noble's feet, slowly, and as quiet as a child, with the lantern light falling sadly upon his lean legs and bright farmer's boots. We all stood very still for a while watching him settle out in the last agony.

Then Belcher quietly takes out a handkerchief, and begins to tie it about his own eyes (for in our excitement we had forgotten to offer the same to 'Awkins), and, seeing it is not big enough, turns and asks for a loan of mine. I give it to him and as he knots the two together he points with his foot at 'Awkins. " 'E's not quite dead," he says, "better give 'im another." Sure enough 'Awkins's left knee as we see it under the lantern is rising again. I bend down and put my gun to his ear; then, recollecting myself and the company of Belcher, I stand up again with a few hasty words. Belcher understands what is in my mind. "Give 'im 'is first," he says. "I don't mind. Poor bastard, we dunno what's 'appening to 'im now." As by this time I am beyond all feeling I kneel down again and skilfully give 'Awkins the last shot so as to put him forever out of pain.

Belcher who is fumbling a bit awkwardly with the handkerchiefs comes out with a laugh when he hears the shot. It is the first time I have heard him laugh, and it sends a shiver down my spine, coming as it does so inappropriately upon the tragic death of his old friend. "Poor blighter," he says quietly, "and last night he was so curious abaout it all. It's very queer, chums, I always think. Naow, 'e knows as much abaout it as they'll ever let 'im know, and last night 'e was all in the dark."

Donovan helps him to tie the handkerchiefs about his eyes. "Thanks, chum," he says. Donovan asks him if there are any messages he would like to send. "Naow, chum," he says, "none for me. If any of you likes to write to 'Awkins's mother you'll find a letter from 'er in 'is pocket. But my missus left me eight years ago. Went away with another fellow and took the kid with her. I likes the feelin' of a 'ome (as you may 'ave noticed) but I couldn't start again after that."

We stand around like fools now that he can no longer see us. Donovan looks at Noble and Noble shakes his head. Then Donovan raises his Webley again and just at that moment Belcher laughs his queer nervous laugh again. He must think we are talking of him; anyway, Donovan lowers his gun. " 'Scuse me, chums," says Belcher, "I feel I'm talking the 'ell of a lot . . . and so silly . . . abaout me being so 'andy abaout a 'ouse. But this thing come on me so sudden. You'll forgive me, I'm sure." "You don't want to say a prayer?" asks Jeremiah Donovan. "No, chum," he replies, "I don't think that'd 'elp. I'm ready if you want to get it over." "You understand," says Jeremiah Donovan, "it's not so much our doing. It's our duty, so to speak." Belcher's head is raised like a real blind man's, so that you can only see his nose and chin in the lamplight. "I never could make out what duty was myself," he said, "but I think you're all good lads, if that's what you mean. I'm not complaining." Noble, with a look of desperation, signals to Donovan, and in a flash Donovan raises his gun and fires. The big man goes over like a sack of meal, and this time there is no need of a second shot.

I don't remember much about the burying, but that it was worse than all the rest, because we had to carry the warm corpses a few yards before we sunk them in the windy bog. It was all mad lonely, with only a bit of lantern between ourselves and the pitch blackness, and birds hooting and screeching all round disturbed by the guns. Noble had to search 'Awkins first to get the letter from his mother. Then having smoothed all signs of the grave away, Noble and I collected our tools, said good-bye to the others, and went back along the desolate edge of the treacherous bog without a word. We put the tools in the houseen and went into the house. The kitchen was pitch black and cold, just as we left it, and the old woman was sitting over the hearth telling her beads.[13] We walked past her into the room, and Noble struck a match to light the lamp. Just then she rose quietly and came to the doorway, being not at all so bold or crabbed as usual.

"What did ye do with them?" she says in a sort of whisper, and Noble took such a mortal start the match quenched in his trembling hand. "What's that?" he asks without turning round. "I heard ye," she said. "What did you hear?" asks Noble, but sure he wouldn't deceive a child the way he said it. "I heard ye. Do you think I wasn't listening to ye putting the things back in the houseen?" Noble struck another match and this time the lamp lit for him. "Was that what ye did with them?" she said, and Noble said nothing—after all what could he say?

So then, by God, she fell on her two knees by the door, and began telling her beads, and after a minute or two Noble went on his knees by the fireplace, so I pushed my way out past her, and stood at the door, watching the stars and listening to the damned shrieking of the birds. It is so strange what you feel at such moments, and not to be written afterwards. Noble says he felt he seen everything ten times as big, perceiving nothing around him but the little patch of black bog with the two Englishmen stiffening into it; but with me it was the other way, as though the patch of bog where the two Englishmen were was a thousand miles away from me, and even Noble mumbling just behind me and the old woman and the birds and the bloody stars were all far away, and I was somehow very small and very lonely. And anything that ever happened me after I never felt the same about again.

QUESTIONS

1. What irony is there in the story's title?

2. What role does humor play in the story? Point to specific passages or incidents.

3. How does O'Connor individualize each character in the story? What details serve to make each person appear unique?

4. What is the significance of the religious debate between Hawkins and Noble? What role does it play in the story?

13 **telling her beads:** Praying the rosary.

5. Why, when they are about to be executed, does Hawkins stress that he is a Communist? Why does he think this appeal will be effective with his Irish captors?

6. Who are the victims in this story? To what extent could it be said that Britain's colonial occupation of Ireland is responsible for this situation?

Mary Beckett

(b. 1926)

Mary Beckett faced the difficulties women often encounter when trying to balance their lives as wives and mothers with their lives as writers. Beckett was born to Sean and Catherine Beckett in Belfast, Northern Ireland. Both of her parents were schoolteachers, a profession Beckett followed also from age nineteen until 1956, when she was married. During her years as a teacher in the poor Ardoyne area of Dublin, Beckett began writing short stories, in part, she said later, because she never saw Catholics portrayed in books. Her first success came with "The Excursion," which won a British Broadcasting Corporation competition. Beckett continued publishing stories in Irish magazines during the 1940s and 1950s, but after she married and began having children, she found little time for writing. Moreover, the magazines that had printed her stories were rapidly going out of business, and having moved with her husband to Dublin, where the dialect was no longer that of her native Belfast, Beckett felt cut off from the speech that had nourished her fiction.

For the next twenty years, Beckett's creative energies were directed toward raising her family. Then she received a phone call from an editor who had read her stories at university. He urged her to write again, and since the renewed "Troubles" in Northern Ireland were weighing on her conscience, she added "A Belfast Woman" to those stories she had published twenty years earlier. A volume of stories, also titled *A Belfast Woman*, was issued in 1980 to very favorable reviews. Her novel, *Give Them Stones*, followed in 1987, and *A Literary Woman* four years after that. She has since written a number of children's books.

Beckett is often praised for giving voice to the ordinary people of Northern Ireland, especially women. "A Belfast Woman" takes place against the sectarian conflict that broke out in the 1970s and that continues sporadically today. Though herself a Roman Catholic, Beckett deplores the violence on both sides and chronicles the devastating effects it has on all those it touches, both directly and indirectly.

A Belfast Woman

1980

I mind well the day the threatening letter came. It was a bright morning, and warm, and I remember thinking while I was dressing myself that it would be nice if the Troubles[1] were over so that a body could just enjoy the feel of a good day. When I came down the stairs the hall was dark but I could see the letter lying face down. I lifted it and just my name was on the envelope, "Mrs. Harrison" in red felt pen. I knew what it was. There was a page of an exercise book inside with "Get out or we'll burn you out" all in red with bad printing and smeared. I just went in and sat at the kitchen table with the note in front of me. I never made myself a cup of tea even. It was a shock, though God knows I shouldn't have been surprised.

One of the first things I remember in my life was wakening up with my mother screaming downstairs when we were burnt out in 1921. I ran down in my nightgown and my mother was standing in the middle of the kitchen with her hands up to her face screaming and screaming and the curtains were on fire and my father was pulling them down and stamping on them with the flames catching the oilcloth on the floor. Then he shouted: "Sadie, the children", and she stopped screaming and said: "Oh God, Michael, the children," and she ran upstairs and came down with the baby in one arm and Joey under the other, and my father took Joey in his arms and me by the hand and we ran out along the street. It was a warm summer night and the fires were crackling all over the place and the street was covered with broken glass. It wasn't until we got into my grandmother's house that anybody noticed that I had nothing on but my nightie and nothing on my feet and they were cut. It was all burnt, every-thing they had. My mother used to say she didn't save as much as a needle and thread. I wasn't able to sleep for weeks, afraid I'd be wakened by that screaming.

We stayed in my grandmother's house until 1935 and my grandmother was dead by that time and my father too for he got T.B. like many another then. He used to say "When you have no house and no job sure what use are you?" and then he'd get fits of coughing. In 1935 when we got the letter threatening to burn us out I said to my mother "We'll gather our things and we'll go." So we did and like all the rest of them in our street we went up to Glenard to the new houses. When we showed our "Get out or we'll burn you out" note they gave us a house and we'd enough out to get things fixed up. We got new jobs in another mill, my mother and Patsy and me. Only my mother never liked it there. She always said the air was too strong for her. It was cold right enough, up close to the mountains. But when I was getting married to William, and his aunt who was a Protestant gave him the key of her house in this street, my mother was in a terrible state—"Don't go into that Protestant street, Mary, or you'll be a sorry girl," and she said we could live with her. But I didn't want

---

1 **the Troubles:** The euphemism for the conflict between Protestant and Catholic factions in Northern Ireland. Belfast was especially torn by violence on both sides. The story is set in the 1970s. The narra-tor's family is Roman Catholic.

William to pine like my poor father, so here we came and not a day's trouble until the note came.

Mind you, the second night we were here there was trouble in the Catholic streets across the road. We heard shots first and then the kind of rumbling, roaring noises of all the people out on the streets. I wanted to get up and run out and see what was wrong but William held on to me in bed and he said: "They don't run out on the street here. They stay in." And it was true. They did. I was scared lying listening to the noise the way I never was when I was out with my neighbours. It turned out some poor young lad had stayed at home when he should have gone back to the British army and they sent the police for him. He got out of the back window and ran down the entry and the police ran after him and shot him dead. They said their gun went off by accident but the people said they beat him up. When I went over the next day I saw him laid out in the wee room off the kitchen and his face had all big yellowy-greenish blotches on it. I never mentioned it to my new neighbours and they never mentioned it to me.

I couldn't complain about them. They were good decent people. They didn't come into the house for a chat or a loan of tea or milk or sugar like the neighbours in Glenard or North Queen Street but they were ready to help at any time. I didn't know the men much because they had work so they didn't stand around the corners the way I was used to. But when Liam was born they all helped and said what a fine baby he was. He was too. Nine pounds with black hair and so strong he could lift his head and look round at a week old. They were always remarking on his mottled skin—purply kind of measles when he'd be up out of the pram[2]—and said it was the sign of a very strong baby. At that time I had never seen a baby with any other colour of skin—I suppose Catholic babies had to be strong to get by. But when Eileen was born a year and ten months later she was different. She had beautiful creamy skin. She was plump and perfect and I loved her more than Liam, God forgive me, and more than William and more than anybody in the world and I wanted everything to be right for her. I thought to myself if I was a Protestant now we'd have just the two and no more and I'd be able to look after them and do well for them. So I didn't act fair[3] with William at all.

Then I started having trouble. I looked as if I was expecting again and my stomach was hard and round but I had bleeding and I could feel no life so I was afraid. I went to the doctor and he said "No, Mrs. Harrison, you're not pregnant. There is something here we shall have to look into." And I said "Is it serious, doctor?" and he said "I can't tell you that, can I, until you go into hospital and have it investigated" and I said "Do you mean an operation?" and he said "I do, Mrs. Harrison." I came home saying to myself it's cancer and who will rear my Eileen and Liam. I remembered hearing it said that once they put the knife into you, you were dead in six

2 **pram:** Short for *perambulator,* or baby buggy.
3 **act fair:** She refused to have sex with her husband because Irish Catholics were strictly forbidden to practice artificial birth control.

months so I made up my mind I'd have no operation and I'd last out as long as I could. Every year I was able to look after them would be a year gained and the bigger they were the better they'd be able to do without me. But oh dear it was terrible hard on everybody. I told William and my mother and Patsy there was nothing at all the matter with me but they knew to look at me it wasn't true. I was a real blay[4] colour and I was so tired I was ready to drop. I'd sit down by the fire at night when the children were in bed and my eyes would close and if I opened them I'd see William staring at me with such a tortured look on his face I'd have to close them again so that I wouldn't go and lean my head against him and tell him the whole thing. I knew if I did that he'd make me go back to the doctor and I'd be done for. At times I'd see against my closed eyes the white long roots of the cancer growing all over my inside and I'd remember the first time William brought me to see his father in the country.

He had a fine labourer's cottage for he was a Protestant and was head ploughman to some rich farmer down there. He was a good man. William's mother was a Catholic and she died when William was a wee boy but they brought him up a Catholic because it had been promised. He was cross-looking though, and I was a bit nervous of him. He had his garden all planted in rows and squares and he was digging clods in one corner and breaking them up fine and I could see all the long white roots and threads he was shaking the mud out of and he turned to us and he said: "Sitfast and scutch! Sitfast and scutch![5] They're the plague of my life. No matter how much I weed there's more in the morning." I told him about my grandfather and the big elderberry tree that grew behind the wee house he'd got in the country when he was burnt out in Lisburn. It wasn't there when he went into the house and when he noticed it first it was only a wee bit of a bush but it grew so quickly it blocked out all the light from his back window. Then one summer it was covered with black slimy kind of flies so he cut it down to the stump, but it started growing again straight away. One day when my father took Patsy and Joey and me down to visit him he had dug all around the stump and he was trying to pull it out with a rope. He told my father to pull with him. My father tried but then he leaned against the wall with his face pale and covered with sweat. My grandfather said: "Are you finished, Michael," and my father said "I'm clean done," and my grandfather said "God help us all" and brought us into the house and gave us lemonade. It was just after that my father went into the sanatorium and my mother was all the time bringing him bottles of lemonade. At the funeral I asked my grandfather if he got the stump out and he didn't know for a minute what I was talking about. Then he said "No, no. Indeed the rope's still lying out there. I must bring it in or it'll rot." I never saw him again, never saw the wee house either. My mother never was one for the country.

She wasn't old herself when she died—not that much over fifty, but she looked an old woman. She wore a shawl at times and not many did that any more. She was

---

4 **blay:** Lead colored; gray.
5 **Sitfast, scutch:** Weeds, but sitfast is also the name of a tumor that grows on horses.

always fussing about my health and me going to the doctor but I managed fine without. I didn't look much. I had this swollen stomach and I got into the way of hiding it with my arms. But every year I got through I'd say to myself wasn't I right to stick it out. When the war finished and the free health[6] came, everybody thought I'd get myself seen to, and my mother was at me she'd mind Liam and Eileen. Of course there were no more children but I kept those two lovely. There was no Protestant child better fed or better dressed than those two, and I always warned them to fight with nobody, never to get into trouble. If any of the children started to shout at them about being Catholics or Fenians or Teagues[7] they were just to walk away, not to run mind you, but just walk home. And Liam was the best boy ever. He wasn't great at his lessons but the masters said how pleasant and good he was. Eileen was inclined to be a bit bold and that was the cause of the only terrible thing I ever did. I can't believe even now how I came to do it. It was the week after my mother had died.

I blamed myself for what happened to my mother. I should have seen in time that she wasn't well and made her mind herself and she'd have lasted better. She came into my house one day with her shawl on and I was going to say I wished she'd wear a coat and not have my neighbours passing remarks, but she hung the shawl up on the back of the door and she looked poorly. She said she'd had a terrible pain in her chest and she had been to the doctor and he'd told her it was her heart. She was to rest and take tablets. She had other wee tablets to put under her tongue if she got a pain and she was not to go up hills. She looked so bad I put her to bed in the wee room off the kitchen. She never got up again. She had tense crushing pains and the tablets did no good. Sometimes the sip of Lourdes water[8] helped her. The doctor said he could do nothing for her unless she went into hospital and she wouldn't hear of that. "Ah no, no. I'm just done, that's all." Every now and again she'd say this would never have happened if she hadn't been burnt out of her home down near the docks and had to go half roads up the mountains with all the hills and the air too strong for her. "And your father wouldn't ever have got consumption if he hadn't had to move in with my mother and spend his days at the street corner. You wouldn't remember it, Mary. You were too small" she'd say and I never contradicted her, "but we hadn't left as much as a needle and thread. The whole block went up. Nothing left." She was buried from our house even though she kept saying she must go home. She had a horror of my Protestant neighbours even though she liked well enough the ones she met. But at her funeral, better kinder decenter neighbours you could not get. When it was over, all I could do was shiver inside myself as if my shelter had been taken away. William was good to me, always good to me, but I had to keep a bit of myself to myself with him.

---

6 **free health:** After World War II, Britain enacted National Health legislation, which provided free health care to all citizens, which included Northern Ireland.

7 **Fenians or Teagues:** Fenians were Irish rebels attempting to overthrow the British government; Teague is a generic name for the Irish, perhaps implying Irish nationalists.

8 **Lourdes water:** Lourdes is the famous shrine in France, whose waters are claimed by the faithful to have healing powers.

My mother never looked for anything from me. I'd tell her what I needed to tell her and she'd listen but she never interfered. And she was as proud of Liam and Eileen as I was. I'd see the way she looked at them.

The week after she died Eileen came home from school crying. She was ten years of age and she didn't often cry. She showed me the mark on her legs where the head-teacher had hit her with a cane. A big red mark it was right across the back of her legs. And she had lovely skin on her legs, lovely creamy skin. When I think of it I can still see that mark. I didn't ask her what happened. I just lifted my mother's shawl from where it was still hanging on the back of the kitchen door and I flung it round me and ran down to the school. I knocked the door and she opened it herself, the head-teacher, because the most of the school had gone home. She took one look at me and ran away back into a classroom. I went after her. She ran into another room off it and banged the door. My arm stuck in through the glass panel and I pulled it out with a big deep cut from my wrist to my elbow. She didn't come out of the door and I never spoke to her at all. There were a couple of other teachers over a bit and a few children about but I couldn't say anything to anybody and they just stood. To stop the blood pouring so much I held my arm up out of my mother's shawl as I went back up the street. There was a woman standing at her door near the top of the street. She was generally at her door knitting, that woman. She had very clever children and some of them did well. One got to be a teacher, another was in the Post Office which is about as far as a clever poor Catholic can get. She asked me what happened but when I couldn't answer she said "You'd need to get to the hospital Mrs. I'll get my coat and go with you." I didn't want to go to any hospital. I just wanted to go home and wash off all the blood but my head was spinning so I let myself be helped on the bus. They stitched it up and wanted me so stay in for the night but I was terrified they'd operate on me just when I was managing so well. I insisted I couldn't because the children were on their own and Mrs. O'Reilly came with me right to the end of my own street. "If your neighbours ask what happened, just tell them you fell off the bus," she told me. "You don't want them knowing all about your business." I've heard she was from the west of Ireland.

When I went into the kitchen I was ready to drop but Eileen started screaming and crying and saying how ashamed of me she was and that she'd never go back to school again. Liam made me a cup of tea and stood looking worried at me. When William came in from work he helped me to bed and was kind and good but I could see by the cut of his mouth that he was shocked and offended at me. It took a long time to heal and the scar will never leave me. The story went around the parish in different ways. Some said I hit the teacher. Some said she knifed me. I was too ashamed ever to explain.

Eileen never was touched in school after that, though, and when she left she learned shorthand and typing and got an office job. She grew up lovely, and I used to think, watching her going out in the morning in the best of clothes with her hair shining that she could have gone anywhere and done herself credit. She wasn't contented living where we did. At first I didn't understand what she wanted. I thought she wanted a better house in a better district. I didn't know how we could manage it but I made up my mind it would have to be done. I went for walks up round the avenues where there were detached houses[9] with gardens and when I saw an empty house I'd peer in through the windows. Then one day a woman from the parish, who worked cleaning one of those houses, saw me and asked me in because the people of the house were out all day. Seeing it furnished with good solid shining furniture I knew we'd never manage it. In the sitting-room there was an old-fashioned copper canopy[10] and when I looked into it I could see the whole room reflected smaller like a fairytale with flowers and books and pictures and plates on the wall. I knew it wasn't for us. How could I go in and out there? William and Liam wouldn't look right in their working clothes. Only Eileen would fit in. I was a bit sad but relieved because at no time could I see where the money would have come from. I told her that night when she came in but she looked at me all puzzled. "But that wasn't what I meant, Mammy," she said. "I have to get away from everything here. There's no life for me here. I'm thinking of going to Canada." That was before any trouble at all here. People now would say that was in the good times when you could get in a bus and go round the shops or into the pictures and nothing would have happened by the time you came home except that the slack would have burnt down a bit on the fire.

Off she went anyway and got a job and wrote now and again telling us how well off she was. In no time at all she was married and was sending photographs first of this lovely bungalow and then of her two wee girls with the paddling pool in her garden or at their swing when they were a bit bigger. I was glad she was doing so well. It was the kind of life I had reared her for and dreamed of for her only I wished she and her children were not so far away. I kept inviting her home for a visit but I knew it would cost far too much money. Only I thought if she was homesick it would help her to know we wanted to see her too. Once the troubles came I stopped asking her.

Liam at that time was getting on well too. He was always such a nice pleasant big fellow that a plumber in the next street to ours asked him to join in his business at putting in fireplaces and hot water pipes. He put in a lovely fireplace for me with a copper canopy like the one I'd seen years before and built me a bathroom and hot water and put in a sink unit for me till I was far better off than any of my neighbours even though a lot of them had their houses very nice too. They were able to get paint from the shipyard of course, and marble slabs and nice bits of mahogany. He got married to a nice wee girl from the Bone and they got a house up in one of the nice streets in Ardoyne[11]—up the far end in what they call now a mixed area. It's all gone now, poor Liam's good way of living. When that street of houses up there was put on fire in 1972 his wife Gemma insisted on coming back to the Bone and squatting in

---

9 **detached houses:** Individual houses, as opposed to row houses or semidetached houses (duplexes). A detached house is a sign of middle-class prosperity.

10 **canopy:** A decorative hood over the fireplace.

11 **Ardoyne:** A road in North Belfast that marked an "interface" area where both Protestants and Catholics lived. It remains the scene of much sectarian tension and violence.

an empty house. They did their best to fix it up but it's old and dark. Then when the murders got bad his partner asked him not to come back to work any more because he'd been threatened for working with a Catholic. I was raging when Liam told me, raging about what a coward the plumber was but then as Liam said, you can't blame a man for not wanting to be murdered. So there he is—no work and no house and a timid wife and a family of lovely wee children. He had plenty to put up with. But where else could I go when I got the note. I sat looking round my shining kitchen and the note said "Get out or we'll burn you out" and where could I go for help but to Liam.

Still I was glad William was dead before it happened. He would have been so annoyed. He felt so ashamed when the Protestants did something nasty. I could swallow my own shame every time the I.R.A.[12] disgraced us. I lived with it the same as I lived with the memory of my own disgrace when I went for the teacher and ripped my arm. But William had always been such a good upright man, he could never understand wickedness. Even the way he died showed it. He was a carter all his days, always in steady work but for a while before he died they were saying to him that nobody had horses any more and they were changing to a lorry.[13] He could never drive a lorry. He was afraid he'd be on the dole.[14] It wasn't the money he was worrying about for I kept telling him it would make little difference to us—just the two of us, what did it matter. It was his pride that was upset. For years there was a big notice up on a corner shop at the bottom of the Oldpark Road. It said: "Drivers, dismount. Don't overload your horses going up the hill." He used to remark on it. It irked him if he didn't obey it. So one day in March when there was an east wind he collapsed on the hill and died the next day in hospital with the same disease as my mother.

There was a young doctor in the hospital asked me did I need a tranquilliser or a sleeping tablet or something to get over the shock. I told him no that I never took any tablets, that I had had cancer when I was in my twenties and that I was still alive in my fifties with never a day in bed. He was curious and he asked me questions and then he said, "Mrs. Harrison, of course I can't be absolutely sure, but I'd say it was most unlikely you had cancer. Maybe you needed a job done on your womb. Maybe you even needed your womb removed but I would be very, very surprised if you had cancer. You wouldn't be here now if you had." So I went in and knelt down at William's side. He still had that strained, worried look, even then. All I could think was: "Poor William. Poor William. Poor, poor, poor William."

It wasn't that I was lonely without him for I'd kept him at a distance for a long time, but the days had no shape to them. I could have my breakfast, dinner and tea whatever time I liked or I needn't have them at all. For a while I didn't bother cooking for myself, just ate tea and bread. Then Liam's wife, Gemma, said the butcher told her that I hadn't darkened his door since William died and that if I wouldn't

---

12 **I.R.A.:** Irish Republican Army, a militant Catholic group attempting to free Northern Ireland from British control.
13 **lorry:** A large truck.
14 **the dole:** Public welfare.

cook for myself I'd have to come and have my dinner with them. So I thought to my-self I wasn't being sensible and I'd only be a nuisance to them if I got sick so I fixed everything to the clock as if there was no such thing as eternity. Until that morning the note came and then I just sat, I didn't look at the clock. I didn't make a cup of tea. I didn't know how long I stayed. I felt heavy, not able to move. Then I thought maybe Liam could get somebody with a van to take out my furniture and I could think later where to go. I took my Rosary beads from under my pillow and my hand-bag with my money and my pension book and Eileen's letters and the photographs of her children and I shut the door behind me. There wasn't a soul in the street but there was nothing odd about that. You'll always know you're in a Protestant street if it's deserted. When I went across the road to get to Liam's house there were children playing and men at the corner and women standing at the doors in the sun and a squad of nervous-looking soldiers down at the other end.

Liam wasn't in but Gemma and the children were. The breakfast table wasn't cleared and Gemma was feeding the youngest. When he finished she stood him up on her lap and he reached over her shoulder trying to reach the shiny new handle Liam had put on the door. He was sturdy and happy and he had a warm smell of milk and baby-powder. I wanted to hold him but I was afraid of putting her out of her routine. Sometimes I wonder if she has a routine—compared to the way I reared mine. Nothing was allowed to interrupt their feeding times and sleeping times. Maybe I was wrong and I'll never know what way Eileen managed hers. I would have liked to do the dishes too but I was afraid it might look like criticising. After a wee while chatting Gemma got up to put the child in his pram and make us a cup of tea. "You don't look great, Granny," she said. "Are you minding yourself at all?" I opened my bag and showed her the note.

She screamed and put her hands up to her face and the baby was startled and cried and bounced up and down in his pram with his arms up to be lifted. I said "Don't scream, Gemma. Don't ever scream, do you hear me," and I unstrapped the baby and hugged him. She stared at me, surprised, and it stopped her. "You'll have to come and stay here," she said. "We'll fit you in." She gave a kind of a look around and I could see her thinking where on earth she could fit me in. Still, where could I go? "All I wanted was for Liam to get a van and take out my stuff," I explained. "Maybe my sister Patsy would have more room than you." She took the baby and gave me my cup of tea. "You'll come here," she said. "You'll count this your home and we'll be glad to have you." She was a good kind girl, Gemma, and when Liam came in he was the same; only anxious to make me welcome and he went off to get the van.

After a while Gemma said. "Write to Eileen straight away. She's the one you should be living with anyway—not all alone over yonder. All her money and her grand house. She's the one should have you." I laughed but it hurt me a bit to hear it said. "What would I do in Eileen's grand house in Canada? How would I fit in?" And Gemma said: "You could keep her house all shining. She'd use you for that. Where would you see the like of your own house for polish! You'd do great for Eileen." I looked round her own few bits and pieces—no look on anything, and a pile of chil-dren's clothes on the floor waiting to be washed and the children running in and out and knocking things over. Mary, my wee Godchild, came and stood leaning against my knees, sucking her thumb. She was wearing one of the dresses I make for them. In the spring when I was fitting it on her I was noticing how beautiful her skin was with little pinprick freckles on the pink and white and I was thinking when she's so lovely what must Eileen's children be like. Then she turned her head and looked at me and her eyes were full of love—for me! I couldn't get over it. Since then sometimes she'd just hold my hand. When Liam came back I said, "Liam, I'm going home. I'm sorry about the bother. I just got frightened but you can cancel the van. I'm going home and I'm staying home. I've a Protestant house to the right of me and a Protestant house to the left of me. They'll not burn me out." They argued with me and they were a bit upset but I knew they were relieved and I stuck to it.

Liam insisted on going back to the house with me although since the murders started I had never let him come down my side of the road. There was a land-rover with soldiers in it not far from my door and no flames, no smoke. But when I opened the door, such a mess. There was water spouting out of a broken pipe in the wall where they had pulled out my sink. The Sacred Heart statute and the wee red lamp were broken on the floor. My copper canopy was all dinged. The table had big hatchet marks on it. The cover on the couch was ripped and the stuffing pulled out. And filth. For months I thought I could get the smell of that filth. I wouldn't let Liam turn off the water until I had it washed away. We cleaned up a bit but Liam said he'd have to get help before he could do much and not to touch the electric because the water had got into it. He had been very quiet so I jumped when he shouted at the soldiers once he went out the door. They drove up very slowly and he was shouting and waving his arms and calling them names. One of them looked into the house and started to laugh. Liam yelled at him about me being a widow woman living alone and that they were here to protect me but one of them said, "You've got it wrong. We're here to wipe out the I.R.A."

"Oh, Liam," I said, "go home. Go home before harm befalls you," and he shook his fist at the soldiers and shouted, "I'm going now but I'll be back and I won't be on my own then. Just look out. I'm warning you." He turned and ran off down the street and the soldier turned and looked after him and I thought he was lifting up his gun and I grabbed at his arm and the gun went off into the air and I begged, "Don't shoot at him. Oh don't shoot him." He said, "Mrs. I have no intention . . ." and then I fell against the wall and when I came to they were making me drink whiskey out of a bottle. It made me cough and splutter but it brought me round. They weren't bad to me I must admit. When I was on my feet they corked up the bottle and put it back in the landrover and drove off. Not one of my neighbours came out and all evening when I worked at tidying up and all night when I sat up to keep watch, not one of them knocked at my door.

Next day Liam brought back two other lads and they fixed up the electricity and the water. It took a while to get everything decent again but they were in and out every day, sometimes three or four of them and it never cost me a penny. Then a queer thing happened. My neighbours began moving out. The woman next door told me out of the side of her mouth that they had all been threatened. I didn't understand how a whole Protestant area could be threatened but out they all went. Of course I know they can always get newer better houses when they ask for them and indeed there was a lot of shooting and wrecking on the front of the road, but still I often wondered what was the truth of it. Maybe I'm better off not knowing. As they left, Catholics from across the road moved in—mostly older people and I have good friends among them although it took us a while to get used to each other. I didn't take easy to people expecting to open my door and walk in at any hour of the day. They thought I was a bit stiff. I have no time for long chats and I never liked gossip. But Mrs. Mulvenna, next door now, has a son in Australia—farther away than my Eileen and I think sons are even worse at writing home. I listen to her and I feel for her and I show her my photographs. I didn't tell her when Eileen wrote about how ashamed she was of us all and how she didn't like to let on she was Irish. I see talk like that in the papers too. It's not right to put the blame on poor powerless people. The most of us never did anything but stay quiet and put up with things the way they were. And we never taught our children to hate the others nor filled their heads with their wrongs the way it's said we did. When all the young people thought they could fix everything with marches and meetings I said it wouldn't work and they laughed at me. "All you old ones are awful bitter," they said and they jeered when Hannah in the shop and I were warning them "It'll all lead to shooting and burning and murder."

Still, last November a man came round here trying to sell Venetian blinds. Some of the houses have them but I said no I liked to see out. I pointed to the sunset behind Divis—bits of red and yellow in the sky and a sort of mist all down the mountain that made it nearly see-through. The man looked at it for a minute and then he said, "Do you know Belfast has the most beautiful sunsets in the whole world?" I said I didn't because I'd never been any place close to look at sunsets and he said, "They tell me Belfast has the best and do you know why? It's because of all the smoke and dirt and dust and pollution. And it seems to me," he said, "it seems to me that if the dirt and dust and smoke and pollution of Belfast just with the help of the sun can make a sky like that, then there's hope for all of us." He nodded and winked and touched his hat and went off and I went in and sat down at the table. And thinking of it I started to laugh, for it's true. There is hope for all of us. Well, anyway, if you don't die you live through it, day in, day out.

QUESTIONS

1. The narrator, Mrs. Harrison, is a Roman Catholic. What difficulties, problems, and persecutions have she and her family members suffered because they are Roman Catholic?

2. How are the British soldiers depicted?

3. What is the relevance, if any, of Mrs. Harrison's conflict with the schoolteacher?

4. Politically and religiously, Mrs. Harrison differs from Protestants, but how does she feel about them personally? Is there, in other words, a division between the political and the personal?

5. How do you interpret the last paragraph of the story? Does it point toward genuine hope?

Colum McCann

(b. 1965)

Colum McCann represents some of the common features of writers (and others) of the "Irish diaspora": having fled Ireland, he continues to write about it and its "troubles." Since the potato famine of the 1840s, young Irish men and women have left their native land to escape its limited possibilities and seek their fortunes in North America, Australia—indeed around the world. For McCann, however, exile was less a matter of economic necessity than a desire to see and experience the world.

He was born into a solid middle-class family, and a writing one at that. His father, Sean McCann, was a successful journalist and author who actively discouraged his son from entering the field. But enter it he did, after a successful academic career at St. Joseph's Clonkeen College, by studying journalism at Rathmine's College. He first traveled to the United States in 1983 while still a student, but after a short period as a journalist in Dublin, he returned to the States to write fiction. Like so many native U.S. writers, McCann embarked on a cross-country trip to gather material for his writing, all the while reading the Beat writers (for example, Jack Kerouac and Allen Ginsberg). Along the way he spent from 1988 to 1990 in Texas teaching survival techniques to delinquent boys. He left that job to enroll in the University of Texas to study English, and began publishing poems and short stories. One of these stories, "Sisters," was selected for two *Best Short Stories* collections, and by 1994 he had enough stories for a volume, *Fishing the Sloe-Black River.* This was followed by two novels and another collection, *Everything in This Country Must* (2000).

McCann's "exile" has taken him well beyond the United States. After marrying in 1992, he and his wife taught English in Japan and later traveled around Asia. Reflecting these travels, his stories and novels include a wide range of characters in a variety of settings, including Northern Ireland, which he visited every summer as a boy and which is the setting for "Everything in This Country Must." Set during some indefinite time when British soldiers occupied the country, the story delves into the bitterness one farmer feels over the loss of his son—a bitterness so deep he cannot accept the help given him by the soldiers.

McCann's promising career may mark a new stage in Irish literature as the island flourishes under its newfound prosperity (especially in the south) and the promise of a lasting peace clings precariously in the north.

Everything in This Country Must

2000

It was a summer flood when our draft horse was caught in the river and the river smashed against stones. The sound of it to me was like the turning of locks. It was silage[1] time, and the water smelled of grass. The draft horse, Father's favorite, had stepped in the river for a sniff maybe, and she was caught, couldn't move, her foreleg trapped between rocks. Father found her and called, *Katie!* above the wailing of the rain. I was in the barn, waiting for drips on my tongue from the ceiling hole. I ran out past the farmhouse into the field. At the river the horse stared wild through the rain; maybe she remembered me. Father moved slow and scared, like someone traveling deep in snow except there was no snow, just flood, and Father was frightened of water, always frightened. Father told me, *Out on the rock there, girl.* He gave me the length of rope with the harness clip, and I knew what to do. I am taller than Father since my last birthday, fifteen. I stretched wide like love and put one foot on the rock in the river middle and one hand on the tree branch above it and swung out over the river flood.

Behind me Father said, *Careful now hai.* The water ran warm and fast, like girl blood, and I held the tree branch, still able to lean down from the rock and put the rope to the halter of the lovely draft horse.

The trees went down to the river in a whispering, and they hung their long branches over the water, and the horse jerked quick and sudden, and I felt there would be a dying, but I pulled the rope up to keep her neck above water.

Father was shouting, *Hold it, girl!* and I could see his teeth clenched and his eyes wide and all the traveling of veins in his neck, the same as when he walks the ditches of our farm, many cows, hedgerows, fences. Father is always full of ditches and fright for the losing of Mammy and Fiachra and now his horse, his favorite, a big Belgian mare that cut fields once in the peaceful dark soil of long ago.

The river split at the rock and jumped fast into sprays coming up above my feet into my dress. But I held tight to the rope, held it like Father sometimes holds his last Sweet Afton cigarette at mealtime before prayers. Father was shouting, *Keep it there, girl, good!* He was looking at the water as if Mammy was there, as if Fiachra was there, and he gulped air and down he went in the water until he was gone so long he made me wail to the sky for being alone. He kept a strong hold of one tree root but all the rest of his body went away under the quick brown water.

The night had started stars. They were up through the branches. The river was spraying in them.

Father came up splutter spluttering for air with his eyes all horsewild and his cap lost down the river. The rope was jumping in my hands and burning like oven rings, and he was shouting, *Hold it, girl, hold it, for the love of God hold it, please!*

Father went down in the water again but came up early, no longer enough in his lungs to keep down. He stayed in the river holding the root, and the water was hitting his shoulders and he was sad watching the draft horse die like everything

---

1 **silage:** Coarse material (such as grain stalks) made into animal food by fermentation.

does, but still I pulled on the halter rope so it would not, because Molly in the sweet shop told me it is not always so.

One more try, Father said in a sad voice like his voice over Mammy and Fiachra's coffins long ago.

Father dipped under and he stayed down as long as yesterday's yesterday, and then some headlights came sweeping up the town road. The lights made a painting of the rain way up high and they put shadows on the hedgerows and ditches. Father's head popped out of the water and he was breathing heavy, so he didn't see the light. His chest was wide and jumping. He looked at the draft horse and then at me. I pointed up the road and he turned in the flood and stared. Father smiled, maybe thinking it was Mack Devlin with his milk truck or Molly coming home from the sweet shop or someone come to help save his favorite horse. He dragged on the tree root and out-struggled from the river and stood on the bank, and his arms went up in the air like he was waving, shouting, *Over here over here hai!*

Father's shirt was wet under his overalls and it was very white when the headlights hit it. The lights got close close closer, and in the brightening we heard shouts and then the voices came clear. They sounded like they had swallowed things I never swallowed. I looked at Father and he looked at me all of a sudden with the strangest of faces, like he was lost, like he was punched, like he was the river cap floating, like he was a big alone tree desperate for forest. Someone shouted out, *Hey, mate, what's goin' on?* in a strange strange way, and Father said, *Nothing,* and his head dropped to his chest and he looked across the river at me and I think what he was telling me was *Drop the rope, girl,* but I didn't. I kept it tight, holding the draft horse's neck above the water, and all the time Father was saying but not saying, *Drop it, please, Katie, drop it, let her drown.*

They came right quick through the hedge, with no regard for the uniforms that hide them. One took off his helmet while he was running, and his hair was the color of winter ice. One had a moustache that looked like long grasses, and one had a scar on his cheek like the bottom end of Father's barn hay knife.

HayKnife was first to the edge of the river, and his rifle banged against his hip when he jumped out to the rock where I was halter holding. *Okay, love, you're all right now,* he said to me, and his hand was rain-wet at my back, and he took the halter and shouted things to the other soldiers, what to do, where to stand. He kept ahold of the halter and passed me back to LongGrasses, who caught my hand and brought me safely to the riverbank. There were six of them now, all guns and helmets. Father didn't move. His eyes were steady looking at the river, maybe seeing Mammy and Fiachra in each eye of the draft horse, staring back.

One soldier was talking to him loud and fast, but Father was like a Derry shopwindow dummy, and the soldier threw up his arms and turned away through the rain and spat a big spit into the wind.

HayKnife was all balance on the rock with the halter, and he didn't even hold the branch above his head. IceHair was taking off his boots and gun and shirt and he looked not like boys from town who come to the barn for love, he looked not like Father when Father cuts hay without his shirt, no, he looked not like anybody; he was very skinny and strong with ribs like sometimes a horse has after a long day in the field. He didn't dive like I think now I would have liked him to, he just stepped into the water very slow and not show-offy and began making his way across, arms high in the air getting lower. But the river got too deep and HayKnife shouted from the rock, saying, *Stay high, Stevie, stay high side, mate.*

And Stevie gave a thumb up to HayKnife and then he was down under the water and the last thing was the kick of the feet.

LongGrasses was standing beside me and he put Stevie's jacket on my shoulders to warm me, but then Father came over and pushed LongGrasses away. Father pushed hard. He was smaller than LongGrasses, but LongGrasses bashed against the trunk of the tree. LongGrasses took a big breath and stared hard at him. Father said, *Leave her alone, can't you see she's just a child?* I covered my face for shame, like in school when they put me in class at a special desk bigger than the rest, not the wooden ones with lifting lids, except I don't go to school anymore since Mammy and Fiachra died. I felt shame like the shame of that day, and I covered my face and peeped through my fingers.

Father was giving a bad look to LongGrasses. LongGrasses stared at Father for a long time too and then shook his head and walked away to the riverbank where Stevie was still down in the water.

Father's hands were on my shoulders, keeping me warm, and he said, *It'll be all right now, love,* but I was only thinking about Stevie and how long he was under water. HayKnife was shouting at the top of his voice and staring down into the water, and I looked up and saw the big army truck coming through the hedgerow fence and the hedge was broken open with a big hole and Father screamed *No!* The extra lights of the truck were on and they were lighting up all the river. Father screamed again, *No!* but stopped when one of the soldiers stared at him. *Your horse or your bloody hedge, mate.*

Father sat down on the riverbank and said, *Sit down, Katie,* and I could hear in Father's voice more sadness than when he was over Mammy's and Fiachra's coffins, more sadness than the day after they were hit by the army truck down near the Glen, more sadness than the day the judge said, *Nobody is guilty, it's just a tragedy,* more sadness than even that day and all the other days that follow.

Bastards, Father said in a whisper, *bastards,* and he put his arm around me and sat watching until Stevie came up from the water swimming against the current to stay in one place. He shouted up at HayKnife, *Her leg's trapped,* and then, *I'm gonna try and get the hoof out.* Stevie took four big gulps of air and HayKnife was pulling on the halter rope and the draft horse was screaming like I never heard a horse before or after. Father was quiet and I wanted to be back in the barn alone, waiting for drips on my tongue. I was wearing Stevie's jacket but I was shivering and wet and cold and scared, because Stevie and the draft horse were going to die, since everything in this country must.

Father likes his tea without bags, like Mammy used to make, and so there is a special way for me to make it. Put cold cold water in the kettle, and only cold, and boil it, and then put a little boiling water in the teapot and swish it around until the bottom of the teapot is warm. Then put in tea leaves, not bags, and then the boiling water, and stir it all very slowly and put on the tea cozy,[2] and let it stew on the stove for five minutes, making sure the flame is not too high so the tea cozy doesn't catch flame and burn. Then pour milk into the cups and then the tea, followed at last by the sugar all spooned around into a careful mixture.

My tea fuss made the soldiers smile, even Stevie, who had a head full of blood pouring down from where the draft horse kicked him above his eye. Father's face went white when Stevie smiled, but Stevie was very polite. He took a towel from me because he said he didn't want to get blood on the chair. He smiled at me two times when I put my head around the kitchen door, and held up one finger, meaning *One sugar, please,* and a big O from fingers for *No milk, please.* Some blood was drying in his hair, and his eyes were bright like the sky should be, and I could feel my belly sink way down until it was there like love in the barn, and he smiled at me number three.

Everyone felt good for saving a life, even a horse life, maybe even Father, but Father was silent in the corner. He was angry at me for asking the soldiers to tea, and his chin was long to his chest and there was a puddle at his feet. Everybody was towel-drying except Father and me, because we had not enough towels.

LongGrasses sat in the armchair and said, *Good thing ya had heat lamps, guvnor.*
Father just nodded.

How was it under the water, Stevie? LongGrasses said.

Wet, Stevie said, and everybody laughed but not Father. He stared at Stevie and then looked away.

The living room is always dark with Father grim, but it was brighter now. I liked the green of the uniforms and even the red of Stevie's blood. But Stevie's head from the horse kick must have been very sore. The other soldiers were talking about how maybe the army truck should take Stevie straight off to hospital and not get dry, just get stitches, and not get tea, just come back later to see about the draft horse if she survives under the heat lamps. But Stevie said, *I'm okay, guys, it's just a scrape. I'd kill for a cuppa.*

The tea was good-tasting from long brewing, and we had biscuits[3] for special visitors. I fetched them from the pantry. I tasted one to make sure they were fresh-tasting and I carried out the tray.

I was sneezing but I was very careful to sneeze away from the tray so as to have politeness like Stevie. Stevie said, *God bless you* in his funny funny way, and we were

---

2 **tea cozy:** A quilted or knitted cover for a tea pot to keep the tea warm.
3 **biscuits:** Cookies.

all quiet as we sipped on the tea, but I sneezed again three four five times, and HayKnife said, *You should change out of them wet clothes, love.*

Father put down his teacup very heavy on the saucer and it was very quiet.

Everyone, even the soldiers, looked at the floor, and the mantelpiece clock was ticking and Mammy's picture was staring down from the wall, and Fiachra when he was playing football,[4] and the soldiers didn't see them but Father did. The long silence was longer and longer until Father called me over, *Come here, Katie,* and he stood me by the window and he took the long curtain in his hands. He turned me around and wrapped the curtain around me and he took my hair and started rubbing not tender but hard. Father is good; he was just wanting to dry my hair because I was shivering even in Stevie's jacket. From under the curtain I could see the soldiers and I could see most of all Stevie. He sipped from his tea and smiled at me, and Father coughed real loud and the clock ticked some more until HayKnife said, *Here, guv, why don't you use my towel for her?*

Father said, *No, thanks.*

HayKnife said, *Go on, guv,* and he put the towel in a ball and made about to throw it.

Father said, *No!*

Stevie said, *Take it easy.*

Take it easy? HayKnife said.

Maybe you should all leave, Father said.

HayKnife changed his face and threw the towel on the ground at Father's feet, and HayKnife's cheeks were outpuffing and he was breathing hard and he was saying, *Fat lot of fuckin thanks we get from your sort, mister.*

HayKnife was up on his feet now and pointing at Father, and the light shone off his boots well polished, and his face was twitching so the scar looked like it was cutting his face. LongGrasses and Stevie stood up from the chairs and were holding HayKnife back, but HayKnife was saying, *Risk our fuckin lives and save your fuckin horse and that's all the thanks we get, eh?*

Father held me very tight with the curtain wrapped around me, and he seemed scared and small and trembly. HayKnife was shouting lots and his face was red and scrunched. Stevie kept him back. Stevie's face was long and sad and I knew he knew because he kept looking at Mammy and Fiachra on the mantelpiece beside the ticking clock. Stevie dragged HayKnife out from the living room and at the kitchen door he let go. HayKnife turned over Stevie's shoulder one last time and looked at Father with his face all twisted, but Stevie grabbed him again and said, *Forget it, mate.*

Stevie took HayKnife out through the kitchen door and into the yard toward the army truck, and still the rain was coming down outside, and then the living room was quiet except for the clock.

I heard the engine of the army truck start.

4 **football:** Soccer.

Father stood away from me and put his head on the mantelpiece near the photos. I stayed at the window still in Stevie's jacket, which Stevie forgot and hasn't come back for yet.

I watched the truck as it went down the laneway, and the red lights on the green gate as it stopped and then turned into the road past where the draft horse was lifted from the river. I didn't hear anything then, just Father starting low noises in his throat, and I didn't turn from the window because I knew he would be angry for me to see him. Father was sniff sniffling. Maybe he forgot I was there. It was going right down into him and it came in big gulps like I never heard before. I stayed still, but Father was trembling big and fast. He took out a handkerchief and moved away from the mantelpiece. I didn't watch him because I knew he would be shamed for his crying.

The army truck was near out of sight, red lights on the hedgerows.

I heard the living room door shut, then the kitchen door, then the pantry door where Father keeps his hunting rifle, then the front door, and I heard the sounds of the clicker on the rifle and him still crying going farther and farther away until they were gone, and he must have been in the courtyard standing in the rain.

The clock on the mantelpiece sounded very loud, so did the rain, so did my breathing, and I looked out the window.

It was all near empty on the outside road, and the soldiers were going around the corner when I heard the sounds, not like bullets, more like pops one two three and the echo of them came loud to me.

The clock still ticked.

It ticked and ticked and ticked.

The curtain was wet around me, but I pulled it tight. I was scared, I couldn't move. I waited it seemed like forever.

When Father came in from outside I knew what it was. His face was like it was cut from a stone and he was not crying anymore and he didn't even look at me, just went to sit in the chair. He picked up his teacup and it rattled in his fingers, so he put it down again and put his face in his hands and stayed like that. The ticking was gone from my mind, and all was quiet everywhere in the world, and I held the curtain like I held the sound of the bullets going into the draft horse's head, his favorite, in the barn, one two three, and I stood at the window in Stevie's jacket and looked and waited and still the rain kept coming down outside one two three one two three one two three and I was thinking oh, what a small sky for so much rain.

QUESTIONS

1. What verb finishes the phrase in the story title?

2. Is it significant that Katie narrates the story? Would the story be the same if the narrator were a fifteen-year-old boy? Why or why not?

3. What event has made father angry at the British soldiers?

4. Why does Father kill his favorite horse?

5. What does the story suggest about the relations between Ireland and England?

Canada

In about 13,000 B.C.E. (the period of the last great Ice Age), groups of early humans crossed the Bering Strait from Asia and settled in the Bluefish Caves in what is currently the Yukon. Anthropological evidence suggests that by the time Christopher Columbus landed in the West Indies, the descendants of these people had spread throughout North, Central, and South America. There is no evidence that any great civilizations comparable to those formed in Central and South America by the Incas, Aztecs, and Mayans ever developed in Canada, largely due to the diverse nature of the landscape and climate as well as the immense distances between the various native groups.

Canada was settled by six distinct ethnic groups. First were the Arctic People. The second were the Sub-Arctic Tribes who settled in Newfoundland and northern British Columbia. Third were the Eastern Woodland Tribes, who settled along the Great Lakes and along the St. Lawrence River. The Plains People settled in the areas that today encompass the provinces of Saskatchewan, Manitoba, and parts of eastern Alberta. Fifth were the mountain-dwelling Plateau People who populated the central and southern parts of British Columbia. Finally, there were the Northwest Peoples who settled around modern-day Vancouver and along the coast as far north as Alaska.

Those people who are considered native Canadians, the Inuit people, actually arrived from Asia in about 1000 C.E., significantly later than the arrival of various North American Indian tribes. One estimate concludes that by 1250 there were 25,000 Inuit peoples populating the Arctic regions of Canada; they were a largely peaceful and isolated group and were the last to give up their traditional lifestyle. The first European contact between the Norse Vikings (who had set up small communities in what is now Newfoundland in 1000) and the Inuit probably occurred around 1250 when Viking hunters arriving from the Norse colonies in southwest Greenland and Newfoundland expanded their hunting camps and small communities. By 1425, probably due to the harsh climate, these Norse colonies had disappeared, and the Inuit controlled all of Arctic Canada.

EUROPEAN EXPLORATION AND SETTLEMENT

The French were the first explorers of a major European power to make a claim in Canada. In 1534, Jacques Cartier reached the Gulf of St. Lawrence and declared the land for Francis I (r. 1515–1547). Cartier may have chosen the name Canada from a Huron-Iroquois term meaning "small community." Whatever the derivation, the name stuck and became the name of the northerly part of the continent. Nearly a half century later, the English explorer Sir Martin Frobisher, who was leading an expedition to find the Northwest Passage, landed on Baffin Island and skirmished with the Inuit. Nevertheless, the Inuit carried on their traditional lifestyle until the early nineteenth century. During this period, the Inuit became fur traders and whalers. To live closer to the trading posts, they moved to permanent campsites along the coasts, where they contracted infectious diseases from which they had little immunity. Further, the arrival of Christian missionaries altered their spiritual beliefs and traditions. The little that remained of the Inuit's traditional lifestyle was finally eroded away by the onset of European and U.S. technology.

The French did not bother much with their new territory for the rest of the sixteenth century; but by the middle part of the next century, Samuel de Champlain explored and settled a large portion of what today is Quebec. By 1640, both Quebec City and Montreal were established as outposts for the Catholic priests who were being sent from France to baptize members of the indigenous population whom the French Catholics regarded as heathens. At this period, the rich interior of Canada was filled with wild animals whose furs protected them from the harshness of the Canadian winter. These furs were immediately seen as an asset for stimulating the economy; as a result, trading posts sprung up all through the region, and by 1663 New France (Canada) had over 60,000 French settlers.

As is the case with nearly all imperialist justifications, in Canada, the native peoples were depicted as the enemies of the developers, and wars were waged against any perceived obstructions to what was deemed social progress or economic expansion. Throughout the seventeenth century, the French fought battles with the native peoples. To protect their economic investments, the French built a string of fortresses along the St. Lawrence River, across the Great Lakes, and as far south as New Orleans at the mouth of the Gulf of Mexico. By 1730, largely under the leadership of Pierre Vereines, a series of forts was built across the south of Ontario and as far west as Saskatchewan.

The British too had interests in the area. In 1670, the Hudson Bay Company was formed to expand British trading interests throughout the world. By 1713, the company was established along the east coast of North America, primarily in what is today Nova Scotia and Newfoundland. By 1745, the British attacked and captured the French area of Acadia (now part of Nova Scotia); this action brought about the first major European conflict to North America, the French and Indian War (1754–1763). The single most symbolic event of that war was the storming of Quebec City by the British General Wolfe in 1759. The victory at the Plains of Abraham ensured that Canada would fall into English hands, and at the Treaty of Paris in 1763, Canada was ceded to the British. The British realized that the largely French Canadian settlers would need to be ruled benevolently because the English were having problems with their upstart colonies to the south. In 1774, just a year before the American Revolution began, the Quebec Act ensured the French Canadians freedom of religion as well as their own legal structure. It is perhaps ironic that the American War of Independence also influenced the early years of British stewardship in Canada. Many British loyalists not wishing to live in the newly formed federation of states fled the thirteen colonies and settled in Canada during the period between 1776 and 1783. This rush of British loyalists into Canada helped balance the number of French and English settlers in Canada, which at that time consisted of what are today the provinces of Ontario and Quebec. This influx of new Canadians also pushed the boundaries of the new country westward. After the War of 1812, in which Canadians and British fought U.S. soldiers to a stalemate, a large number of British soldiers who had been brought to Canada to fight for the mother country elected to stay in southern Ontario, and the population balance shifted significantly in favor of English speakers. By 1840, the two regions of Upper and Lower Canada (Ontario and Quebec) shared a unified government, and in 1867 the British North America Act created the Dominion of Canada, which brought self-government to the new Dominion. John A. MacDonald was elected the first prime minister of this nation of 3.5 million people, most of whom were eastern city dwellers or immigrant farmers in the western regions.

THE DEVELOPMENT OF CANADIAN LITERATURE

Canadian literature has two major strands: English and French. Questions of bilingualism, biculturalism, and multiculturalism still permeate Canadian society. This anthology is dedicated to examining the Anglo-Canadian tradition in short fiction, but it is important to point out that the French Canadian tradition is as vibrant and as varied as the English Canadian one. It also shares similarities with English Canadian literature; the indifference of nature to human endeavors, for example, is a theme in both traditions. Nearly all of Canada labors under the extremes of a harsh climate. The winters are long and cold, and the summers are hot and muggy. To overlook the significant role that nature plays in Canadian literature is a serious oversight. Further, eastern Canada was explored largely by boat; long winding rivers and massive lakes cover the Canadian landscape. The west is dominated by the Rockies, and the vast plains of the middle of the country appear endless. Canadian settlers regularly faced the vastness of space, the indifference of nature, and the impediments of geography. Whether French or English, much of the early writing about Canada was focused on survival against nature and landscape.

In the first half of the nineteenth century, many English writers were influenced by the romantic poetry of William Wordsworth and Samuel Coleridge. Part of that tradition included a pantheistic vision of the world where man was seen to be in harmony with benevolent nature. Early English writers in Canada such as Charles Sangster, Charles Mair, William Kirby, and Alexander MacLachlan depicted the Canadian landscape dressed up like a rolling English hillside rather than as an honest depiction of harsh Canadian topography. It took fictional accounts of characters coping with the landscape for readers to have a real awareness of the climatic and geographical severity of the country.

Thomas McCulloch and Thomas Chandler Haliburton established a tradition of writing short fiction in various Halifax newspapers as early as the 1830s. These stories were largely sketches of local life and events with an absence of detailed plot development; however, the stories often offered a satiric view of U.S. or Nova Scotian manners and behavior. The taste for the genre was firmly established and exploited by subsequent writers such as Susanna Moodie, whose collection of sketches, *Roughing It in the Bush* (1852), described the complications involved in settling the area north of Peterborough, Ontario. Here, the struggles of the new settlers were depicted as battles against an unforgiving environment and also an awareness of the losses of a familiar social and cultural world left behind. For Moodie, Canada offered a series of hopeful expectations, but the realization of those promises was never fully achieved. Moodie's depiction of Canada is far different from her sister's. In *The Backwoods of Canada* (1836), Catherine Parr Traill describes her first two years in the Peterborough area. Traill's depiction of pioneer life is largely idealized, and the overriding sentiment one takes from the book is that hard work and a good-humored attitude can overcome most unpleasantry in the wilderness.

In the 1850s, following Moodie's literary success, a number of female writers began publishing regularly not only in Canadian journals but in New York and Boston ones as well. May Agnes Fleming, the first Canadian mystery writer; Rosanna Leprohon, a romantic novelist and short story writer; Sara Jeanette Duncan, journalist and political writer; and Susie Frances Harrison, Anglophone commentator on French Canadian life, all successfully published short fiction in the middle of the century. What all of these female writers had in common was the predominance of Canadian natural settings in their work. And while one would hesitate to call these writers local colorists in the tradition of Mark Twain or Sarah Orne Jewett, the utilizing of Canadian surroundings and society for a backdrop was more than coincidence. The absence of significant male writers during the period is dismissed with the argument that the men were using their energies in developing the country's political and economic base instead of following an artistic track.

With the western expansion, European immigrants began moving rapidly into the lands of the native peoples. The Indian Act of 1880 attempted to ensure that the native peoples were treated fairly under the law. Although the act was only partially successful, the concept was quite enlightened by Victorian standards. As the Europeans continued to push westward, the most symbolic act of nationhood was the completion of the Trans Canada Railway in 1885. Not only did the completion of the railway link markets thousands of miles apart, but it made communication between isolated parts of the country possible. By 1912, every part of the country was linked by rail and road.

It was not until the 1880s that male writers began to contribute regularly to the short story genre. Edward William Thomson published countless stories about Canada and its people, but when his most famous short story, "The Privilege of Limits," appeared in *Harper's Weekly* in 1891, the legitimacy of the Canadian short story was assured. His *Old Man Savarin and Other Stories* (1895) epitomized what was expected in contemporary Canadian short fiction at the time. The volume affirms that by the end of the nineteenth and beginning of the twentieth centuries, very little had changed thematically in Canadian literature since Moodie's reflections a half century earlier.

Gilbert Parker was another popular writer in the 1890s. His melodramatic tales first appeared in *Pierre and His People* (1892). Parker's stories concern the hardships of natural life in Canada as well as the positive implications of imperialism. His stories were exceedingly popular throughout the Empire, and he may have been one of the first Canadian writers with an international reputation.

By the turn of the twentieth century, however, with the contributions of writers such as Duncan Campbell Scott with his *In the Village of Viger* (1896) and Stephen Leacock with *Sunshine Sketches of a Little Town* (1912), a new, almost urbane flavor began to pervade the Canadian short story form. When Leacock described his beloved Orillia, Ontario (called Mariposa in the book), he was able to satirize the social life, the business world, the idealism, and the narrowness of religious values in his region with a maturity and humanism that places his tales of Mariposa alongside those of the English writer Arnold Bennett's Five Towns in Staffordshire.

Canada achieved its nationhood in the trial by fire called World War I. Throughout Canada, monuments commemorate the sacrifice of brave young Canadians who fought alongside the British and other Commonwealth soldiers against the Central Powers. But while the war was seen to be against a common enemy, many French Canadians saw the battle as primarily a British one and did not want to get involved. Nevertheless, French Canadians were drafted and often reluctantly took part in military operations. This enforced service sparked the flames of suppressed disagreement between English- and French-speaking citizens of Canada, a resentment that continues to the present.

With the publication of novelist, short story writer, and poet John Raymond Knister's edition of *Canadian Short Stories* in 1928, many critics felt the experimental era of the genre had been fulfilled. The collection clearly delineated between the traditional tale and the emerging modernist concerns in the genre. Knister's, Thomas Murtha's, and Morley Callaghan's works all represented a new departure in Canadian short fiction. Callaghan was by far the most influential practitioner of the genre in the period before World War II, and his stories are often compared favorably to those written by Ernest Hemingway. His collections *A Native Argosy* (1929) and *Now That April's Here and Other Short Stories* (1936) capture the emerging flavor and style of contemporary Canadian short fiction. Callaghan's stories in the later collection are set in Toronto during the 1920s. Here urban Canada is depicted in brushstrokes that are redolent of T. S. Eliot's *The Waste Land*. In "Silk Stockings," for example, the painful love of a young man for the landlady's daughter, who unfortunately loves another, is dissected with a deft touch. The stories in the collection are populated with characters who are psychologically unable to overcome their self-inertia and reflect the modernist conundrum of how to achieve self-actualization despite fractured egos.

At the same time, writers such as Frederick Philip Grove, whose "Snow" (1932) is a classic piece of Canadian short fiction, and Sinclair Ross were publishing short stories in magazines. However, the financial ramifications of the onset of the Great Depression and the political implications of Canadian involvement in World War II slowed the development of the short story genre considerably. Many small magazines folded during the 1930s, and paper was at a premium during the austere years of the war. Both Grove and Ross, for example, had to wait over thirty years before their short stories were collected and presented to the Canadian public.

Canada officially became a member of the Commonwealth in 1931 and steadfastly stood beside England and the European Allies during World War II. The aftermath of the war spawned an incredible interest in Canada. Many of the displaced people of Europe felt they could not return to their own country for both political and economic reasons. Canada, with a reasonably open immigration policy (there are allegations that Prime Minister Mackenzie King was anti-Semitic and discouraged Jewish immigration after the war), became the country of choice for many people. From 1945 onwards, waves of European immigrants flooded into the country. Canada was envisioned as a land of opportunity, and throughout the 1950s, the country grew rapidly.

It was not until World War II concluded that Canadian literature regained the impetus it had enjoyed before the Great Depression. Surprisingly, the impetus began in French-speaking Montreal, where two English literary journals, *Preview* and *First Statement,* merged to become *Northern Review.* In that journal, Canadian poetry and fiction of the highest quality began to reappear. Talented writers such as Mavis Gallant, who had published powerfully evocative stories such as "Three Brick Walls" and "Good Morning and Goodbye" in the early 1940s in *Preview,* offered more mature pieces for the *Northern Review.* One of her better stories, "Varieties of Exile," introduces Frank Cairns, an Englishman who joins the Canadian forces to fight the Germans in World War II. Gallant explores the tension between the handsome man in uniform and the riddled corpse that he becomes on the battlefield. The tragedy of war and its ramifications are examined with a universality of Erich Maria Remarque's *All Quiet on the Western Front* (1929) or Siegfried Sassoon's *Memoirs of George Sherston* (1937).

In 1947, Desmond Pacey's *A Book of Canadian Stories* demonstrated to an audience hungering for a voice that Canadian literature was on the rise, and many of the writers who appeared in the anthology continued to explore Canadian themes throughout the 1950s. Hugh Garner's *The Yellow Sweater* (1952) and Gallant's *The Other Paris* (1955) were well reviewed, and these collections helped to convince the Canadian Broadcasting Corporation that radio programs dedicated to reading short stories would capture listening audiences. By the mid-1950s, a number of radio spots were dedicated to short story readings and literary discussions; this helped to stimulate the publishing of anthologies of Canadian short fiction. By 1958, when the highly influential *Tamarack Review* replaced the *Northern Review,* new writers such as Mordecai Richler, Alice Munro, Hugh Hood, Jack Ludwig, and David Godfrey had become national figures in literary circles. By the mid-1960s, the short story genre was well established, and small presses such as Oberon Press in Ottawa were publishing younger writers. This trend was repeated throughout the country, and new publishing houses such as House of Anansi and Coach House Press in Toronto and Talonbooks in Vancouver were established.

These independent publishing houses were reflective of a nationalistic movement, a "Canada first" movement, in the mid-1960s fostered by the policies of Prime Minister Pierre Trudeau. Canada made great strides in establishing its national identity and solving the socioeconomic problems that had been festering beneath the surface. As is true in any nation where dynamic change needs to be implemented, some Canadians did not feel comfortable with the way in which the federal government was making policy to unify the country and press for adjustments to the status quo. The 1970s proved to be a time of regional change and unrest, with Quebec demanding a separate status from the other provinces and the west feeling quite buoyant with its newly found oil revenues.

This regional emphasis was one of the more important influences in the proliferation of new publishing houses throughout Canada. In fact, the literary focus shifted dramatically from the east of Canada to the west coast. Almost overnight, there were new presses publishing writers outside the traditional publishing centers. In 1981, for example, western publishers produced Edna Alford's *A Sleep Full of Dreams,* which dealt with a nursing home for the aged; Joan Clark's Alberta-based *From a High Thin Wire* (1982) and Sandra Birdsell's *Night Travellers* (1982) caused a stir; Margaret Laurence's *A Bird in the House* (1970) was set in Manitoba; and Jack Hodgins's *Spit Delaney's Island* (1976) and *The Barclay Family Theatre* (1981) take place in a mythic world set amidst the lushness of Vancouver Island.

This is not to say that regionalism developed only in the west; the exploration of the Canadian experience was nationwide in scope. Alistair MacLeod's grim tales of Cape Breton in *The Lost Salt Gift of Blood* (1976) or Hugh Hood's celebration of urban Montreal in *Around the Mountain* (1967) reflect the same fascination with Canadian settings. Mordecai Richler's studies of Jewish ghetto life in *The Street* (1969), Howard O'Hagan's tales of the mountain country of western Canada, and Alden Nowlan's stories of New Brunswick life are all reflective of this regional impulse.

It was out of the political problems faced during these emotive issues that Canada began to achieve a sense of identity. Until then, Canada identified itself almost always in negative constructs: It was not England and it certainly was not the United States. But the answer to what exactly constituted a Canadian experience was not apparent. Eventually, Canada defined itself as a "vertical mosaic," which loosely meant that it was a nation of immigrants who were allowed to find their own way into this nebulous Canadian society. Diversity was to be celebrated and enjoyed. John Porter's book *The Vertical Mosaic* (1965) went a long way to prove that this contention was a myth, but the concept of a free-flowing classless society is one that, in theory at least, Canadians support.

In the 1970s, the issue of regionalist writing received further stimulation with the large influx of immigrants to Canada. And while Canadian Margaret Laurence had been publishing short stories about Ghana as early as the 1960s, many of these new stories were written by the immigrants themselves. These short stories might be categorized under the term *ethnic realism,* for these stories captured the experience of newly arrived minorities into the largely white urban centers in Canada. Perhaps the most visible of these writers was Austin Clarke, who arrived from Barbados. His collection *When He Was Free and Young and He Used to Wear Silks* (1971) was set in Toronto and examined the struggle of West Indians learning to survive in Toronto. The collection exposed racial exploitation by white Canadians and exposed the need for the West Indian to discover strategies of adaptation in order to gain some level of material success in Canada. Clark Blaise, who was born in North Dakota of a French Canadian father and English Canadian mother, brought a similar perspective in his two major collections of short fiction: *A North American Education* (1973) and *Tribal Justice* (1974). Blaise's stories were concerned with the victimization of blacks in Canada, but also explored their attempts to acquire a sense of racial unity against a system that they found oppressive and demeaning.

By the 1980s, Canadian short fiction had achieved international recognition. Not only were anthologies and magazines publishing short stories, but the issues argued in the works caught the mood of a Canadian public who were still uncertain about questions of national identity and what living in Canada meant to the large immigrant population. One of the most powerful subjects in Canadian fiction was the suffering of new immigrants as they struggled to find their way in the Canadian society. Whether they originated from Trinidad, Jamaica, India, or the emergent African nations, the struggle of relocation is reiterated. The most evocative immigrant collections include Neil Bissoondath's *Digging Up the Mountains* (1985) and *On the Eve of Uncertain Tomorrows* (1990), which concerns the plight of West Indian immigrants. The Trinidadian André Alexis uses the freshness of magic realism to describe the Kafkaesque nature of governmental bureaucracy in *Despair and Other Stories of Ottawa* (1994).

Rohinton Mistry's *Tales from Firozsha Baag* (1987) are a linked collection of stories that carry an immigrant from an apartment complex in Bombay to taking up residence in Canada. M. G. Vassanji's *Uhuru Street* (1992) chronicles the frustrations and tribulations of a group of Asians in Tanzania who hope to come to North America. Dionne Brand's *Sans Souci* (1989) offers dramatic insights into the endeavors of a Jamaican woman both in her homeland and after arrival in Canada.

Many feminist writings began to appear regularly at this time as well. And while much of the writing comes from the pen of immigrant female writers exposing patriarchal corruption in their homelands and the need to escape into a freer environment such as Canada, Canadian writers such as Elizabeth Brewster, Veronica Ross, Audrey Thomas, Zsuzsi Gartner, Jennifer Duncan, Robyn Sarah, Elyse Gasco, Diane Schompererleon, Elizabeth Hay, and Bronwen Wallace all deal with the struggle within Western culture between male and female expectations. Perhaps the writer who has most effectively dissected the changing gender roles over the last thirty years is Margaret Atwood. And while Atwood is best known for her novel writing, her collections of short stories *Bluebeard's Egg* (1983), *Wilderness Tips* (1990), and *Good Bones* (1992) all examine preoccupations with female-male relationships.

In the mid-1980s, another marginalized voice from the forgotten peoples of Canada discovered that the short story form was an apt vehicle for alerting readers to their causes. First Nation writer Lee Maracle argues in *Sojourner's Truth* (1990) that Eurocentric literary discourse is not capable of explaining native peoples' story-telling techniques. Beth Brant in her two collections, *Mohawk Trail* (1985) and *Food and Spirits* (1991), writes stories that not only voice the concerns of the native peoples but also add a feminist perspective that is unique to the genre.

The Canadian literary critic Geoff Hancock intimates in his various journal articles that the 1990s was when many Canadian writers challenged what was perceived as the traditional presentation of Canadian fiction. Suddenly, the impulse in modern Canadian fiction moved inward and dramatized internal conflicts. This new mood of expression can be observed in Canadian literature in the final years of the twentieth century. Examples of this change of direction can be found in Brian Fawcett's *Capital Tales* (1984) or *The Secret Journal of Alexander Mackenzie* (1985) or Monty Reid's *Dog Sleeps: Irritated Texts* (1993). These collections move away from social considerations and play with the postmodern dilemma as depicted in nearly all Western literary experimentations in fiction during this period.

In Canada then, the short story genre reflects the immense changes the twentieth century brought to the country both historically and socially. This twenty-first century should continue to hold out many challenges for the Canadian writer since social hypocrisies, immigrants' struggles, conflicts with nature, the search for a national identity (including a movement supporting independence for French-speaking Canada), and a rift between conservative and liberal movements that contributed to the January 2006 election of numerous Conservative Party members, including the prime minister, are still much in evidence in today's Canadian society. The exploration and the solving of these problems through literature promise a rich vein of ore in which to mine the gold of Canadian literature.

Despite its challenges, as a nation Canada has entered the twenty-first century as one of the most enlightened and forward-looking social democracies in the world. Although it has faced internal stresses such as those named above, Canada is often seen internationally as a voice of reason in an unsettled period. Canada's contribution to United Nations peace-keeping initiatives, Third World engagement, and ecology concerns such as the Kyoto Accord have established it as a progressive force in the postmodern world.

Sinclair Ross

(1908–1996)

Sinclair Ross grew up on a large farm near Shelbrooke, Saskatchewan. He reportedly left school in eleventh grade and subsequently found work in banks throughout Saskatchewan and Manitoba, where he settled in Winnipeg in 1933. While there, Ross became interested in writing fiction, and he published nearly two dozen short stories in *Queen's Quarterly*. These stories were collected later in *The Lamp at Noon and Other Stories* (1968) and *The Race and*

Other Stories (1982). Ross's stories are set on the prairies during the period of the Great Depression and reflect the grim realities of financial hardship and natural disaster that plagued the inhabitants. His first novel, *As for Me and My House* (1941), with its evocation of prairie life during the Depression, was not valued when it appeared, but subsequently was recognized as a major contributor in the development of Canadian fiction.

Ross served with the Canadian army in London during World War II, and in 1946 he returned briefly to Winnipeg before settling in Montreal, where he continued in banking until his retirement in 1968. He wrote three more novels—*The Well* (1958), *Whir of Gold* (1970), and *Sawbones Memorial* (1974)—all of which deal with day-to-day struggles implicit in Canadian prairie life. Ross retired to Greece and Spain before returning to Canada, where he died in Vancouver.

The story that follows was published in 1939 during the height of the Depression in Canada. It explores the harshness of married life in isolated Saskatchewan.

The Painted Door
1939

Straight across the hills it was five miles from John's farm to his father's. But in winter, with the roads impassable, a team had to make a wide detour and skirt the hills, so that from five the distance was more than trebled to seventeen.

"I think I'll walk," John said at breakfast to his wife. "The drifts in the hills wouldn't hold a horse, but they'll carry me all right. If I leave early I can spend a few hours helping him with his chores, and still be back by suppertime."

She went to the window, and thawing a clear place in the frost with her breath, stood looking across the snowswept farmyard to the huddle of stables and sheds. "There was a double wheel around the moon last night," she countered presently. "You said yourself we could expect a storm. It isn't right to leave me here alone. Surely I'm as important as your father."

He glanced up uneasily, then drinking off his coffee tried to reassure her. "But there's nothing to be afraid of—even supposing it does start to storm. You won't need to go near the stable. Everything's fed and watered now to last till night. I'll be back at the latest by seven or eight."

She went on blowing against the frosted pane, carefully elongating the clear place until it was oval-shaped and symmetrical. He watched her a moment or two longer, then more insistently repeated, "I say you won't need to go near the stable. Everything's fed and watered, and I'll see that there's plenty of wood in. That will be all right, won't it?"

"Yes—of course—I heard you—" It was a curiously cold voice now, as if the words were chilled by their contact with the frosted pane. "Plenty to eat—plenty of wood to keep me warm—what more could a woman ask for?"

"But he's an old man—living there all alone. What is it, Ann? You're not like yourself this morning."

She shook her head without turning. "Pay no attention to me. Seven years a farmer's wife—it's time I was used to staying alone."

Slowly the clear place on the glass enlarged: oval, then round, then oval again. The sun was risen above the frost mists now, so keen and hard a glitter on the snow that instead of warmth its rays seemed shedding cold. One of the two-year-old colts that had cantered away when John turned the horses out for water stood covered with rime at the stable door again, head down and body hunched, each breath a little plume of steam against the frosty air. She shivered, but did not turn. In the clear, bitter light the long white miles of prairie landscape seemed a region alien to life. Even the distant farmsteads she could see served only to intensify a sense of isolation. Scattered across the face of so vast and bleak a wilderness it was difficult to conceive them as a testimony of human hardihood and endurance. Rather they seemed futile, lost, to cower before the implacability of snow-swept earth and clear pale sun-chilled sky.

And when at last she turned from the window there was a brooding stillness in her face as if she had recognized this mastery of snow and cold. It troubled John. "If you're really afraid," he yielded, "I won't go today. Lately it's been so cold, that's all. I just wanted to make sure he's all right in case we do have a storm."

"I know—I'm not really afraid." She was putting in a fire now, and he could no longer see her face. "Pay no attention. It's ten miles there and back, so you'd better get started."

"You ought to know by now I wouldn't stay away," he tried to brighten her. "No matter how it stormed. Before we were married—remember? Twice a week I never missed and we had some bad blizzards that winter too."

He was a slow, unambitious man, content with his farm and cattle, naïvely proud of Ann. He had been bewildered by it once, her caring for a dull-witted fellow like him; then assured at last of her affection he had relaxed against it gratefully, unsuspecting it might ever be less constant than his own. Even now, listening to the restless brooding in her voice, he felt only a quick, unformulated kind of pride that after seven years his absence for a day should still concern her. While she, his trust and earnestness controlling her again:

"I know. It's just that sometimes when you're away I get lonely . . . There's a long cold tramp in front of you. You'll let me fix a scarf around your face."

He nodded. "And on my way I'll drop in at Steven's place. Maybe he'll come over tonight for a game of cards. You haven't seen anybody but me for the last two weeks."

She glanced up sharply, then busied herself clearing the table. "It will mean another two miles if you do. You're going to be cold and tired enough as it is. When you're gone I think I'll paint the kitchen woodwork. White this time—you remember we got the paint last fall. It's going to make the room a lot lighter. I'll be too busy to find the day long."

"I will though," he insisted, "and if a storm gets up you'll feel safer, knowing that he's coming. That's what you need, maybe—someone to talk to besides me."

She stood at the stove motionless a moment, then turned to him uneasily. "Will you shave then, John—now—before you go?"

He glanced at her questioningly, and avoiding his eyes she tried to explain, "I mean—he may be here before you're back—and you won't have a chance then."

"But it's only Steven—we're not going anywhere."

"He'll be shaved, though—that's what I mean—and I'd like you too to spend a little time on yourself."

He stood up, stroking the heavy stubble on his chin. "Maybe I should—only it softens up the skin too much. Especially when I've got to face the wind."

She nodded and began to help him dress, bringing heavy socks and a big woollen sweater from the bedroom, wrapping a scarf around his face and forehead. "I'll tell Steven to come early," he said, as he went out. "In time for supper. Likely there'll be chores for me to do, so if I'm not back by six don't wait."

From the bedroom window she watched him nearly a mile along the road. The fire had gone down when at last she turned away, and already through the house there was an encroaching chill. A blaze sprang up again when the draughts were opened, but as she went on clearing the table her movements were furtive and constrained. It was the silence weighing upon her—the frozen silence of the bitter fields and sun-chilled sky—lurking outside as if alive, relentlessly in wait, mile-deep between her now and John. She listened to it, suddenly tense, motionless. The fire crackled and the clock ticked. Always it was there. "I'm a fool," she whispered, rattling the dishes in defiance, going back to the stove to put in another fire. "Warm and safe—I'm a fool. It's a good chance when he's away to paint. The day will go quickly. I won't have time to brood."

Since November now the paint had been waiting warmer weather. The frost in the walls on a day like this would crack and peel it as it dried, but she needed something to keep her hands occupied, something to stave off the gathering cold and loneliness. "First of all," she said aloud, opening the paint and mixing it with a little turpentine, "I must get the house warmer. Fill up the stove and open the oven door so that all the heat comes out. Wad something along the window-sills to keep out the draughts. Then I'll feel brighter. It's the cold that depresses."

She moved briskly, performing each little task with careful and exaggerated absorption, binding her thoughts to it, making it a screen between herself and the surrounding snow and silence. But when the stove was filled and the windows sealed it was more difficult again. Above the quiet, steady swishing of her brush against the bedroom door the clock began to tick. Suddenly her movements became precise, deliberate, her posture self-conscious, as if someone had entered the room and were watching her. It was the silence again, aggressive, hovering. The fire spat and crackled at it. Still it was there. "I'm a fool," she repeated. "All farmers' wives have to stay alone. I mustn't give in this way. I mustn't brood. A few hours now and they'll be here."

The sound of her voice reassured her. She went on: "I'll get them a good supper—and for coffee after cards bake some of the little cakes with raisins that he likes . . . Just three of us, so I'll watch, and let John play. It's better with four, but at least we can talk. That's all I need—someone to talk to. John never talks. He's stronger—doesn't need to. But he likes Steven—no matter what the neighbours say. Maybe he'll have him come again, and some other young people too. It's what we need, both of us, to help keep young ourselves . . . And then before we know it we'll be into March. It's cold still in March sometimes, but you never mind the same. At least you're beginning to think about spring."

She began to think about it now. Thoughts that outstripped her words, that left her alone again with herself and the ever-lurking silence. Eager and hopeful first, then clenched, rebellious, lonely. Windows open, sun and thawing earth again, the urge of growing, living things. Then the days that began in the morning at half-past four and lasted till ten at night; the meals at which John gulped his food and scarcely spoke a word; the brute-tired stupid eyes he turned on her if ever she mentioned town or visiting.

For spring was drudgery again. John never hired a man to help him. He wanted a mortgage-free farm; then a new house and pretty clothes for her. Sometimes, because with the best of crops it was going to take so long to pay off anyway, she wondered whether they mightn't better let the mortgage wait a little. Before they were worn out, before their best years were gone. It was something of life she wanted, not just a house and furniture; something of John, not pretty clothes when she would be too old to wear them. But John of course couldn't understand. To him it seemed only right that she should have the clothes—only right that he, fit for nothing else, should slave away fifteen hours a day to give them to her. There was in his devotion a baffling, insurmountable humility that made him feel the need of sacrifice. And when his muscles ached, when his feet dragged stolidly with weariness, then it seemed that in some measure at least he was making amends for his big hulking body and simple mind. Year after year their lives went on in the same little groove. He drove his horses in the field; she milked the cows and hoed potatoes. By dint of his drudgery he saved a few months' wages, added a few dollars more each fall to his payments on the mortgage; but the only real difference that it all made was to deprive her of his companionship, to make him a little duller, older, uglier than he might otherwise have been. He never saw their lives objectively. To him it was not what he actually accomplished by means of the sacrifice that mattered, but the sacrifice itself, the gesture—something done for her sake.

And she, understanding, kept her silence. In such a gesture, however futile, there was a graciousness not to be shattered lightly. "John," she would begin sometimes, "you're doing too much. Get a man to help you—just for a month—" but smiling down at her he would answer simply, "I don't mind. Look at the hands on me. They're made for work." While in his voice there would be a stalwart ring to tell her that by her thoughtfulness she had made him only the more resolved to serve her, to prove his devotion and fidelity.

They were useless, such thoughts. She knew. It was his very devotion that made them useless, that forbade her to rebel. Yet over and over, sometimes hunched still before their bleakness, sometimes her brush making swift sharp strokes to pace the chafe and rancour that they brought, she persisted in them.

This now, the winter, was their slack season. She could sleep sometimes till eight, and John till seven. They could linger over their meals a little, read, play cards, go visiting the neighbours. It was the time to relax, to indulge and enjoy themselves; but instead, fretful and impatient, they kept on waiting for the spring. They were compelled now, not by labour, but by the spirit of labour. A spirit that pervaded their lives and brought with idleness a sense of guilt. Sometimes they did sleep late, sometimes they did play cards, but always uneasily, always reproached by the thought of more important things that might be done. When John got up at five to attend to the fire he wanted to stay up and go out to the stable. When he sat down to a meal he hurried his food and pushed his chair away again, from habit, from sheer work-instinct, even though it was only to put more wood in the stove, or go down cellar to cut up beets and turnips for the cows.

And anyway, sometimes she asked herself, why sit trying to talk with a man who never talked? Why talk when there was nothing to talk about but crops and cattle, the weather and the neighbours? The neighbours, too—why go visiting them when still it was the same—crops and cattle, the weather and the other neighbours? Why go to the dances in the schoolhouse to sit among the older women, one of them now, married seven years, or to waltz with the work-bent, tired old farmers to a squeaky fiddle tune? Once she had danced with Steven six or seven times in the evening, and they had talked about it for as many months. It was easier to stay at home. John never danced or enjoyed himself. He was always uncomfortable in his good suit and shoes. He didn't like shaving in the cold weather oftener than once or twice a week. It was easier to stay at home, to stand at the window staring out across the bitter fields, to count the days and look forward to another spring.

But now, alone with herself in the winter silence, she saw the spring for what it really was. This spring—next spring—all the springs and summers still to come. While they grew old, while their bodies warped, while their minds kept shrivelling dry and empty like their lives. "I mustn't," she said aloud again. "I married him—and he's a good man. I mustn't keep on this way. It will be noon before long, and then time to think about supper . . . Maybe he'll come early—and as soon as John is finished at the stable we can all play cards."

It was getting cold again, and she left her painting to put in more wood. But this time the warmth spread slowly. She pushed a mat up to the outside door, and went back to the window to pat down the woollen shirt that was wadded along the sill. Then she paced a few times round the room, then poked the fire and rattled the stove lids, then paced again. The fire crackled, the clock ticked. The silence now seemed more intense than ever, seemed to have reached a pitch where it faintly moaned. She began to pace on tiptoe, listening, her shoulders drawn together, not realizing for a while that it was the wind she heard, thin-strained and whimpering through the eaves.

Then she wheeled to the window, and with quick short breaths thawed the frost to see again. The glitter was gone. Across the drifts sped swift and snakelike little tongues of snow. She could not follow them, where they sprang from, or where they disappeared. It was as if all across the yard the snow were shivering awake—roused by the warnings of the wind to hold itself in readiness for the impending storm. The sky had become a sombre, whitish grey. It, too, as if in readiness, had shifted and lay close to earth. Before her as she watched a mane of powdery snow reared up breast-high against the darker background of the stable, tossed for a moment angrily, and then subsided again as if whipped down to obedience and restraint. But another followed, more reckless and impatient than the first. Another reeled and dashed itself against the window where she watched. Then ominously for a while there were only the angry little snakes of snow. The wind rose, creaking the troughs that were wired beneath the eaves. In the distance, sky and prairie now were merged into one another linelessly. All round her it was gathering; already in its press and whimpering there strummed a boding of eventual fury. Again she saw a mane of snow spring up, so dense and high this time that all the sheds and stables were obscured. Then others followed, whirling fiercely out of hand; and, when at last they cleared, the stables seemed in dimmer outline than before. It was the snow beginning, long lancet shafts of it, straight from the north, borne almost level by the straining wind. "He'll be here soon," she whispered, "and coming home it will be in his back. He'll leave again right away. He saw the double wheel—he knows the kind of storm there'll be."

She went back to her painting. For a while it was easier, all her thoughts half-anxious ones of John in the blizzard, struggling his way across the hills; but petulantly again she soon began, "I knew we were going to have a storm—I told him so—but it doesn't matter what I say. Big stubborn fool—he goes his own way anyway. It doesn't matter what becomes of me. In a storm like this he'll never get home. He won't even try. And while he sits keeping his father company I can look after his stable for him, go ploughing through snowdrifts up to my knees—nearly frozen—"

Not that she meant or believed her words. It was just an effort to convince herself that she did have a grievance, to justify her rebellious thoughts, to prove John responsible for her unhappiness. She was young still, eager for excitement and distractions; and John's steadfastness rebuked her vanity, made her complaints seem weak and trivial. She went on, fretfully, "If he'd listen to me sometimes and not be so stubborn we wouldn't still be living in a house like this. Seven years in two rooms—seven years and never a new stick of furniture . . . There—as if another coat of paint could make it different anyway."

She cleaned her brush, filled up the stove again, and went back to the window. There was a void white moment that she thought must be frost formed on the window-pane; then, like a fitful shadow through the whirling snow, she recognized the stable roof. It was incredible. The sudden, maniac raging of the storm struck from her face all its pettishness. Her eyes glazed with fear a little; her lips blanched. "If he starts for home now," she whispered silently—"But he won't—he knows I'm safe—he knows Steven's coming. Across the hills he would never dare."

She turned to the stove, holding out her hands to the warmth. Around her now there seemed a constant sway and tremor, as if the air were vibrating with the shudderings of the walls. She stood quite still, listening. Sometimes the wind struck with sharp, savage blows. Sometimes it bore down in a sustained, minute-long blast, silent with effort and intensity; then with a foiled shriek of threat wheeled away to gather and assault again. Always the eave-troughs creaked and sawed. She stared towards the window again, then detecting the morbid trend of her thoughts, prepared fresh coffee and forced herself to drink a few mouthfuls. "He would never dare," she whispered again. "He wouldn't leave the old man anyway in such a storm. Safe in here— there's nothing for me to keep worrying about. It's after one already. I'll do my baking now, and then it will be time to get supper ready for Steven."

Soon, however, she began to doubt whether Steven would come. In such a storm even a mile was enough to make a man hesitate. Especially Steven, who was hardly the one to face a blizzard for the sake of someone else's chores. He had a stable of his own to look after anyway. It would be only natural for him to think that when the storm blew up John had turned again for home. Another man would have—would have put his wife first.

But she felt little dread or uneasiness at the prospect of spending the night alone. It was the first time she had been left like this on her own resources, and her reaction, now that she could face and appraise her situation calmly, was gradually to feel it a kind of adventure and responsibility. It stimulated her. Before nightfall she must go to the stable and feed everything. Wrap up in some of John's clothes—take a ball of string in her hand, one end tied to the door, so that no matter how blinding the storm she could at least find her way back to the house. She had heard of people having to do that. It appealed to her now because suddenly it made life dramatic. She had not felt the storm yet, only watched it for a minute through the window.

It took nearly an hour to find enough string, to choose the right socks and sweaters. Long before it was time to start out she tried on John's clothes, changing and rechanging, striding around the room to make sure there would be play enough for pitching hay and struggling over snowdrifts; then she took them off again, and for a while busied herself baking the little cakes with raisins that he liked.

Night came early. Just for a moment on the doorstep she shrank back, uncertain. The slow dimming of the light clutched her with an illogical sense of abandonment. It was like the covert withdrawal of an ally, leaving the alien miles unleashed and unrestrained. Watching the hurricane of writhing snow rage past the little house she forced herself, "They'll never stand the night unless I get them fed. It's nearly dark already, and I've work to last an hour."

Timidly, unwinding a little of the string, she crept out from the shelter of the doorway. A gust of wind spun her forward a few yards, then plunged her headlong against a drift that in the dense white whirl lay invisible across her path. For nearly a minute she huddled still, breathless and dazed. The snow was in her mouth and nostrils, inside her scarf and up her sleeves. As she tried to straighten a smothering scud flung itself against her face, cutting off her breath a second time. The wind struck from all sides, blustering and furious. It was as if the storm had discovered her, as if all its forces were concentrated upon her extinction. Seized with panic suddenly she threshed out a moment with her arms, then stumbled back and sprawled her length across the drift.

But this time she regained her feet quickly, roused by the whip and batter of the storm to retaliative anger. For a moment her impulse was to face the wind and strike back blow for blow; then, as suddenly as it had come, her frantic strength gave way to limpness and exhaustion. Suddenly, a comprehension so clear and terrifying that it struck all thoughts of the stable from her mind, she realized in such a storm her puniness. And the realization gave her new strength, stilled this time to a desperate persistence. Just for a moment the wind held her, numb and swaying in its vice; then slowly, buckled far forward, she groped her way again towards the house.

Inside, leaning against the door, she stood tense and still a while. It was almost dark now. The top of the stove glowed a deep, dull red. Heedless of the storm, self-absorbed and self-satisfied, the clock ticked on like a glib little idiot. "He shouldn't have gone," she whispered silently. "He saw the double wheel—he knew. He shouldn't have left me here alone."

For so fierce now, so insane and dominant did the blizzard seem, that she could not credit the safety of the house. The warmth and lull around her was not real yet, not to be relied upon. She was still at the mercy of the storm. Only her body pressing hard like this against the door was staving it off. She didn't dare move. She didn't dare ease the ache and strain. "He shouldn't have gone," she repeated, thinking of the stable again, reproached by her helplessness. "They'll freeze in their stalls—and I can't reach them. He'll say it's all my fault. He won't believe I tried."

Then Steven came. Quickly, startled to quietness and control, she let him in and lit the lamp. He stared at her a moment, then flinging off his cap crossed to where she stood by the table and seized her arms. "You're so white—what's wrong? Look at me—" It was like him in such little situations to be masterful. "You should have known better—for a while I thought I wasn't going to make it here myself—"

"I was afraid you wouldn't come—John left early; and there was the stable—"

But the storm had unnerved her, and suddenly at the assurance of his touch and voice the fear that had been gripping her gave way to an hysteria of relief. Scarcely aware of herself she seized his arm and sobbed against it. He remained still a moment unyielding, then slipped his other arm around her shoulder. It was comforting and she relaxed against it, hushed by a sudden sense of lull and safety. Her shoulders trembled with the easing of the strain, then fell limp and still. "You're shivering,"—he drew her gently towards the stove. "It's all right—nothing to be afraid of. I'm going to see to the stable."

It was a quiet, sympathetic voice, yet with an undertone of insolence, a kind of mockery even, that made her draw away quickly and busy herself putting in a fire. With his lips drawn in a little smile he watched her till she looked at him again. The smile too was insolent, but at the same time companionable; Steven's smile, and therefore difficult to reprove. It lit up his lean, still-boyish face with a peculiar kind of arrogance: features and smile that were different from John's, from other men's—wilful and derisive, yet naïvely so—as if it were less the difference itself he was conscious of, than the long-accustomed privilege that thereby fell his due. He was erect, tall, square-shouldered. His hair was dark and trim, his lips curved soft and full. While John, she made the comparison swiftly, was thick-set, heavy-jowled, and stooped. He always stood before her helpless, a kind of humility and wonderment in his attitude. And Steven now smiled on her appraisingly with the worldly-wise assurance of one for whom a woman holds neither mystery nor illusion.

"It was good of you to come, Steven," she responded, the words running into a sudden, empty laugh. "Such a storm to face—I suppose I should feel flattered."

For his presumption, his misunderstanding of what had been only a momentary weakness, instead of angering quickened her, roused from latency and long disuse all the instincts and resources of her femininity. She felt eager, challenged. Something was at hand that hitherto had always eluded her, even in the early days with John, something vital, beckoning, meaningful. She didn't understand, but she knew. The texture of the moment was satisfyingly dreamlike: an incredibility perceived as such, yet acquiesced in. She was John's wife—she knew—but also she knew that Steven standing here was different from John. There was no thought or motive, no understanding of herself as the knowledge persisted. Wary and poised round a sudden little core of blind excitement she evaded him. "But it's nearly dark—hadn't you better hurry if you're going to do the chores? Don't trouble—I can get them off myself—"

An hour later when he returned from the stable she was in another dress, hair rearranged, a little flush of colour in her face. Pouring warm water for him from the kettle into the basin she said evenly, "By the time you're washed supper will be ready. John said we weren't to wait for him."

He looked at her a moment. "You don't mean you're expecting John tonight? The way it's blowing—"

"Of course." As she spoke she could feel the colour deepening in her face. "We're going to play cards. He was the one that suggested it."

He went on washing, and then as they took their places at the table, resumed, "So John's coming. When are you expecting him?"

"He said it might be seven o'clock—or a little later." Conversation with Steven at other times had always been brisk and natural, but now all at once she found it strained. "He may have work to do for his father. That's what he said when he left. Why do you ask, Steven?"

"I was just wondering—it's a rough night."

"You don't know John. It would take more than a storm to stop him."

She glanced up again and he was smiling at her. The same insolence, the same little twist of mockery and appraisal. It made her flinch, and ask herself why she was pretending to expect John—why there should be this instinct of defence to force her. This time, instead of poise and excitement, it brought a reminder that she had changed her dress and rearranged her hair. It crushed in a sudden silence, through which she heard the whistling wind again, and the creaking saw of the eaves. Neither spoke now. There was something strange, almost frightening, about this Steven and his quiet, unrelenting smile; but strangest of all was the familiarity: the Steven she had never seen or encountered, and yet had always known, always expected, always waited for. It was less Steven himself that she felt than his inevitability. Just as she had felt the snow, the silence and the storm. She kept her eyes lowered, on the window past his shoulder, on the stove, but his smile now seemed to exist apart from him, to merge and hover with the silence. She clinked a cup—listened to the whistle of the storm—always it was there. He began to speak, but her mind missed the meaning of his words. Swiftly she was making comparisons again; his face so different to John's, so handsome and young and clean-shaven. Swiftly, helplessly, feeling the imperceptible and relentless ascendancy that thereby he was gaining over her, sensing sudden menace in this new, more vital life, even as she felt drawn towards it.

The lamp between them flickered as an onslaught of the storm sent shudderings through the room. She rose to build up the fire again and he followed her. For a long time they stood close to the stove, their arms almost touching. Once as the blizzard creaked the house she spun around sharply, fancying it was John at the door; but quietly he intercepted her. "Not tonight—you might as well make up your mind to it. Across the hills in a storm like this—it would be suicide to try."

Her lips trembled suddenly in an effort to answer, to parry the certainty in his voice, then set thin and bloodless. She was afraid now. Afraid of his face so different from John's—of his smile, of her own helplessness to rebuke it. Afraid of the storm, isolating her here alone with him. They tried to play cards, but she kept starting up at every creak and shiver of the walls. "It's too rough a night," he repeated. "Even for John. Just relax a few minutes—stop worrying and pay a little attention to me."

But in his tone there was a contradiction to his words. For it implied that she was not worrying—that her only concern was lest it really might be John at the door.

And the implication persisted. He filled up the stove for her, shuffled the cards—won—shuffled—still it was there. She tried to respond to his conversation, to think of the game, but helplessly into her cards instead she began to ask, Was he right? Was that why he smiled? Why he seemed to wait, expectant and assured?

The clock ticked, the fire crackled. Always it was there. Furtively for a moment she watched him as he deliberated over his hand. John, even in the days before they were married, had never looked like that. Only this morning she had asked him to shave. Because Steven was coming—because she had been afraid to see them side by side—because deep within herself she had known even then. The same knowledge, furtive and forbidden, that was flaunted now in Steven's smile. "You look cold," he said at last, dropping his cards and rising from the table. "We're not playing, anyway. Come over to the stove for a few minutes and get warm."

"But first I think we'll hang blankets over the door. When there's a blizzard like this we always do." It seemed that in sane, commonplace activity there might be release, a moment or two in which to recover herself. "John has nails to put them on. They keep out a little of the draught."

He stood on a chair for her, and hung the blankets that she carried from the bedroom. Then for a moment they stood silent, watching the blankets sway and tremble before the blade of wind that spurted around the jamb. "I forgot," she said at last, "that I painted the bedroom door. At the top there, see—I've smeared the blankets."

He glanced at her curiously, and went back to the stove. She followed him, trying to imagine the hills in such a storm, wondering whether John would come. "A man couldn't live in it," suddenly he answered her thoughts, lowering the oven door and drawing up their chairs one on each side of it. "He knows you're safe. It isn't likely that he'd leave his father, anyway."

"The wind will be in his back," she persisted. "The winter before we were married—all the blizzards that we had that year—and he never missed—"

"Blizzards like this one? Up in the hills he wouldn't be able to keep his direction for a hundred yards. Listen to it a minute and ask yourself."

His voice seemed softer, kindlier now. She met his smile a moment, its assured little twist of appraisal, then for a long time sat silent, tense, careful again to avoid his eyes.

Everything now seemed to depend on this. It was the same as a few hours ago when she braced the door against the storm. He was watching her, smiling. She dared not move, unclench her hands, or raise her eyes. The flames crackled, the clock ticked. The storm wrenched the walls as if to make them buckle in. So rigid and desperate were all her muscles set, withstanding, that the room around her seemed to swim and reel. So rigid and strained that for relief at last, despite herself, she raised her head and met his eyes again.

Intending that it should be for only an instant, just to breathe again, to ease the tension that had grown unbearable—but in his smile now, instead of the insolent appraisal that she feared, there seemed a kind of warmth and sympathy. An understanding that quickened and encouraged her—that made her wonder why but a moment ago she had been afraid. It was as if the storm had lulled, as if she had suddenly found calm and shelter.

Or perhaps, the thought seized her, perhaps instead of his smile it was she who had changed. She who, in the long, wind-creaked silence, had emerged from the increment of codes and loyalties to her real, unfettered self. She who now felt his air of appraisal as nothing more than an understanding of the unfulfilled woman that until this moment had lain within her brooding and unadmitted, reproved out of consciousness by the insistence of an outgrown, routine fidelity.

For there had always been Steven. She understood now. Seven years—almost as long as John—ever since the night they first danced together.

The lamp was burning dry, and through the dimming light, isolated in the fastness of silence and storm, they watched each other. Her face was white and struggling still. His was handsome, clean-shaven, young. Her eyes were fanatic, believing desperately, fixed upon him as if to exclude all else, as if to find justification. His were cool, bland, drooped a little with expectancy. The light kept dimming, gathering the shadows round them, hushed, conspiratorial. He was smiling still. Her hands again were clenched up white and hard.

"But he always came," she persisted. "The wildest, coldest nights—even such a night as this. There was never a storm—"

"Never a storm like this one." There was a quietness in his smile now, a kind of simplicity almost, as if to reassure her. "You were out in it yourself for a few minutes. He'd have it for five miles, across the hills . . . I'd think twice myself, on such a night before risking even one."

Long after he was asleep she lay listening to the storm. As a check on the draught up the chimney they had left one of the stove lids partly off, and through the open bedroom door she could see the flickerings of flame and shadow on the kitchen wall. They leaped and sank fantastically. The longer she watched the more alive they seemed to be. There was one great shadow that struggled towards her threateningly, massive and black and engulfing all the room. Again and again it advanced, about to spring, but each time a little whip of light subdued it to its place among the others on the wall. Yet though it never reached her still she cowered, feeling that gathered there was all the frozen wilderness, its heart of terror and invincibility.

Then she dozed for a while, and the shadow was John. Interminably he advanced. The whips of light still flickered and coiled, but now suddenly they were the swift little snakes that this afternoon she had watched twist and shiver across the snow. And they too were advancing. They writhed and vanished and came again. She lay still, paralysed. He was over her now, so close that she could have touched him. Already it seemed that a deadly tightening hand was on her throat. She tried to scream but her lips were locked. Steven beside her slept on heedlessly.

Until suddenly as she lay staring up at him a gleam of light revealed his face. And in it was not a trace of threat or anger—only calm, and stonelike hopelessness.

That was like John. He began to withdraw, and frantically she tried to call him back. "It isn't true—not really true—listen, John—" but the words clung frozen to her lips. Already there was only the shriek of wind again, the sawing eaves, the leap and twist of shadow on the wall.

She sat up, startled now and awake. And so real had he seemed there, standing close to her, so vivid the sudden age and sorrow in his face, that at first she could not make herself understand she had only been dreaming. Against the conviction of his presence in the room it was necessary to insist over and over that he must still be with his father on the other side of the hills. Watching the shadows she had fallen asleep. It was only her mind, her imagination, distorted to a nightmare by the illogical and unadmitted dread of his return. But he wouldn't come. Steven was right. In such a storm he would never try. They were safe, alone. No one would ever know. It was only fear, morbid and irrational; only the sense of guilt that even her new-found and challenged womanhood could not entirely quell.

She knew now. She had not let herself understand or acknowledge it as guilt before, but gradually through the wind-torn silence of the night his face compelled her. The face that had watched her from the darkness with its stonelike sorrow—the face that was really John—John more than his features of mere flesh and bone could ever be.

She wept silently. The fitful gleam of light began to sink. On the ceiling and wall at last there was only a faint dull flickering glow. The little house shuddered and quailed, and a chill crept in again. Without wakening Steven she slipped out to build up the fire. It was burned to a few spent embers now, and the wood she put on seemed a long time catching light. The wind swirled through the blankets they had hung around the door, and then, hollow and moaning, roared up the chimney again, as if against its will drawn back to serve still longer with the onrush of the storm.

For a long time she crouched over the stove, listening. Earlier in the evening, with the lamp lit and the fire crackling, the house had seemed a stand against the wilderness, a refuge of feeble walls wherein persisted the elements of human meaning and survival. Now, in the cold, creaking darkness, it was strangely extinct, looted by the storm and abandoned again. She lifted the stove lid and fanned the embers till at last a swift little tongue of flame began to lick around the wood. Then she replaced the lid, extended her hands, and as if frozen in that attitude stood waiting.

It was not long now. After a few minutes she closed the draughts, and as the flames whirled back upon each other, beating against the top of the stove and sending out flickers of light again, a warmth surged up to relax her stiffened limbs. But shivering and numb it had been easier. The bodily well-being that the warmth induced gave play again to an ever more insistent mental suffering. She remembered the shadow that was John. She saw him bent towards her, then retreating, his features pale and overcast with unaccusing grief. She re-lived their seven years together and, in retrospect, found them to be years of worth and dignity. Until crushed by it all at last, seized by a sudden need to suffer and atone, she crossed to where the draught was bitter, and for a long time stood unflinching on the icy floor.

The storm was close here. Even through the blankets she could feel a sift of snow against her face. The eaves sawed, the walls creaked, and the wind was like a wolf in howling flight.

And yet, suddenly she asked herself, hadn't there been other storms, other blizzards? And through the worst of them hadn't he always reached her?

Clutched by the thought she stood rooted a minute. It was hard now to understand how she could have so deceived herself—how a moment of passion could have quieted within her not only conscience, but reason and discretion too. John always came. There could never be a storm to stop him. He was strong, inured to the cold. He had crossed the hills since his boyhood, knew every creek-bed and gully. It was madness to go on like this—to wait. While there was still time she must waken Steven, and hurry him away.

But in the bedroom again, standing at Steven's side, she hesitated. In his detachment from it all, in his quiet, even breathing, there was such sanity, such realism. For him nothing had happened; nothing would. If she wakened him he would only laugh and tell her to listen to the storm. Already it was long past midnight; either John had lost his way or not set out at all. And she knew that in his devotion there was nothing foolhardy. He would never risk a storm beyond endurance, never permit himself a sacrifice likely to endanger her lot or future. They were both safe. No one would ever know. She must control herself—be sane like Steven.

For comfort she let her hand rest a while on Steven's shoulder. It would be easier were he awake now, with her, sharing her guilt; but gradually as she watched his handsome face in the glimmering light she came to understand that for him no guilt existed. Just as there had been no passion, no conflict. Nothing but the sane appraisal of their situation, nothing but the expectant little smile, and the arrogance of features that were different from John's. She winced deeply, remembering how she had fixed her eyes on those features, how she had tried to believe that so handsome and young, so different from John's, they must in themselves be her justification.

In the flickering light they were still young, still handsome. No longer her justification—she knew now—John was the man—but wistfully still, wondering sharply at their power and tyranny, she touched them a moment with her fingertips again.

She could not blame him. There had been no passion, no guilt; therefore there could be no responsibility. Looking down at him as he slept, half-smiling still, his lips relaxed in the conscienceless complacency of his achievement, she understood that thus he was revealed in his entirety—all there ever was or ever could be. John was the man. With him lay all the future. For tonight, slowly and contritely through the day and years to come, she would try to make amends.

Then she stole back to the kitchen, and without thought, impelled by overwhelming need again, returned to the door where the draught was bitter still. Gradually towards morning the storm began to spend itself. Its terror blast became a feeble, worn-out moan. The leap of light and shadow sank, and a chill crept in again. Always the eaves creaked, tortured with wordless prophecy. Heedless of it all the clock ticked on in idiot content.

They found him the next day, less than a mile from home. Drifting with the storm he had run against his own pasture fence and overcome had frozen there, erect still, both hands clasping fast the wire.

"He was south of here," they said wonderingly when she told them how he had come across the hills. "Straight south—you'd wonder how he could have missed the buildings. It was the wind last night, coming every way at once. He shouldn't have tried. There was a double wheel around the moon."

She looked past them a moment, then as if to herself said simply, "If you knew him, though—John would try."

It was later, when they had left her a while to be alone with him, that she knelt and touched his hand. Her eyes dimmed, it was still such a strong and patient hand; then, transfixed, they suddenly grew wide and clear. On the palm, white even against its frozen whiteness, was a little smear of paint.

QUESTIONS

1. What effect does the harsh climate of the Canadian prairies have on human relationships in this story?

2. What does Ross suggest is missing from Ann's life, and how is she representative of many Canadian women on the prairies during the Great Depression?

3. How would you characterize the relationship between Ann and Steven? What does he represent in her life?

4. How do you interpret the true cause of John's death?

Hugh Garner

(1913–1979)

Hugh Garner was born in Yorkshire, England. When he was six, his family emigrated to Toronto. His father deserted his mother and left her to raise their four children in the Cabbagetown area of the city. Garner later wrote of his experiences in this poverty-laden section of Toronto in his novel *Cabbagetown* (1950). Garner left school at sixteen just as the Great Depression spawned economic chaos throughout the world. To survive, he worked a series of unskilled jobs and rode freight trains across North America. He worked as a harvest hand, made cemetery flower-pot holders, became a housing inspector, managed a grocery store, and wrote a newspaper column. In 1937, he joined the Abraham Lincoln Battalion of the International Brigade and went to Spain to fight alongside the Republicans in the Spanish civil war. During World War II, he served in the Canadian navy and in 1949 wrote about his experiences in a novel entitled *Storm Below*. The story followed the men aboard a naval vessel for six days during the war. When the war ended, Garner pursued a writing career. Starting as a freelance journalist, by the mid-1950s, he was one of Canada's most prolific magazine writers. His first volume of short stories appeared in 1952; *The Yellow Sweater and Other Stories* was not a commercial success, but a few of the stories, including "The Yellow Sweater," a tale about a middle-aged salesman's sexual temptation when he picks up an attractive female hitchhiker, have become Canadian classics. He wrote several novels about his adopted home in Toronto, including *The Silence on the Shore* (1962), a novel about characters in a boarding house, and *The Intruders* (1976), a novel about the gentrification of the city.

In 1963, he was awarded the Governor General's Award for *Hugh Garner's Best Stories*, from which "One-Two-Three Little Indians" is taken. Following in the realist mode of Sinclair Ross, Garner's stories tend to focus on the outsiders in modern society. He writes about the despair of an alcoholic, a traveling preacher who has lost his faith, and a poor displaced tobacco worker trying to find his way back into the world after the devastation of World War II. In the story that follows, a poor Indian family is struggling to survive on the fringes of white society in northern Ontario. Garner wrote two further collections of short stories: *Men and Women* (1966) and *Violation of the Virgins* (1971).

Garner was a man of action, a Canadian Ernest Hemingway so to speak. As a result, his literary interest reflected his taste in people and events, and this predilection often led to stories concerning the struggles of inner-city life. Several of his novels have been overlooked by critics because of the potboiler nature of his writing; *Waste No Tears* (1950), *Present Reckoning* (1951), and his trilogy of mystery novels written in the 1970s are cases in point. In 1973, Garner wrote a memoir of his nonconformist life and attitudes; *One Damn*

Thing After Another suggests Garner would not have been much bothered by this critical neglect.

———————————

One-Two-Three Little Indians   *1963*

After they had eaten, Big Tom pushed the cracked and dirty supper things to the back of the table and took the baby from its high chair carefully, so as not to spill the flotsam of bread crumbs and boiled potatoes from the chair to the floor.

He undressed the youngster, talking to it in the old dialect, trying to awaken its interest. All evening it had been listless and fretful by turns, but now it seemed to be soothed by the story of Po-chee-ah, and the Lynx, although it was too young to understand him as his voice slid awkwardly through the ageless folk-tale of his people.

For long minutes after the baby was asleep he talked on, letting the victorious words fill the small cabin so that they shut out the sounds of the Northern Ontario night: the buzz of mosquitoes, the far-off bark of a dog, the noise of the cars and transport trucks passing on the gravelled road.

The melodious hum of his voice was like a strong soporific, lulling him with the return of half-forgotten memories, strengthening him with the knowledge that once his people had been strong and brave, men with a nation of their own, encompassing a million miles of teeming forest, lake and tamarack[1] swamp.

When he halted his monologue to place the baby in the big brass bed in the corner the sudden silence was loud in his ears, and he cringed a bit as the present suddenly caught up with the past.

He covered the baby with a corner of the church-donated patchwork quilt, and lit the kerosene lamp that stood on the mirrorless dressing table beside the stove. Taking a broom from a corner he swept the mealtime debris across the doorsill.

This done, he stood and watched the headlights of the cars run along the trees bordering the road, like a small boy's stick along a picket fence. From the direction of the trailer camp a hundred yards away came the sound of a car engine being gunned, and the halting note-tumbles of a clarinet from a tourist's radio. The soft summer smell of spruce needles and wood smoke blended with the evening dampness of the earth, and felt good in his nostrils, so that he filled his worn lungs until he began to cough. He spat the resinous phlegm into the weed-filled yard.

It had been this summer smell, and the feeling of freedom it gave which had brought him back to the woods after three years in the mines during the war. But only part of him had come back, for the mining towns and the big money had done more than etch his lungs with silica: they had also brought him pain and distrust, and a wife who had learned to live in gaudy imitation of the boomtown life.

When his coughing attack subsided he peered along the path, hoping to catch a glimpse of his wife Mary returning from her work at the trailer camp. He was

———————————

1 **tamarack:** The American larch tree.

becoming worried about the baby, and her presence, while it might not make the baby well, would mean that there was someone else to share his fears. He could see nothing but the still blackness of the trees, their shadows interwoven in a sombre pattern across the mottled ground.

He re-entered the cabin and began washing the dishes, stopping once or twice to cover the moving form of the sleeping baby. He wondered if he could have transmitted his own wasting sickness to the lungs of his son. He stood for long minutes at the side of the bed, staring, trying to diagnose the child's restlessness into something other than what he feared.

His wife came in and placed some things on the table. He picked up a can of pork-and-beans she had bought and weighed it in the palm of his hand. "The baby seems pretty sick," he said.

She crossed the room, and looked at the sleeping child. "I guess it's his teeth."

He placed the pork-and-beans on the table again and walked over to his chair beside the empty stove. As he sat down he noticed for the first time that his wife was beginning to show her pregnancy. Her squat form had sunk lower, and almost filled the shapeless dress she wore. Her brown ankles were puffed above the broken-down heels of the dirty silver dancing pumps she was wearing.

"Is the trailer camp full?" he asked.

"Nearly. Two more Americans came about half an hour ago."

"Was Billy Woodhen around?"

"I didn't see him, only Elsie," she answered. "A woman promised me a dress to-morrow if I scrub out her trailer."

"Yeh." He saw the happiness rise over her like a colour as she mentioned this. She was much younger than he was—twenty-two years against his thirty-nine—and her dark face had a fullness that is common to many Indian women. She was no longer pretty, and as he watched her he thought that wherever they went the squalor of their existence seemed to follow them.

"It's a silk dress," Mary said, as though the repeated mention of it brought it nearer.

"A silk dress is no damn good around here. You should get some overalls," he said, angered by her lack of shame in accepting the cast-off garments of the trailer women.

She seemed not to notice his anger. "It'll do for the dances next winter."

"A lot of dancing you'll do," he said pointing to her swollen body. "You'd better learn to stay around here and take care of the kid."

She busied herself over the stove, lighting it with newspapers and kindling. "I'm going to have some fun. You should have married a grandmother."

He filled the kettle with water from an open pail near the door. The baby began to cough, and the mother turned it on its side in the bed. "As soon as I draw my money from Cooper I'm going to get him some cough syrup from the store," she said.

"It won't do any good. We should take him to the doctor in town tomorrow."

"I can't. I've got to stay here and work."

He knew the folly of trying to reason with her. She had her heart set on earning the silk dress the woman had promised.

After they had drunk their tea he blew out the light, and they took off some of their clothes and climbed over the baby into the bed. Long after his wife had fallen asleep he lay in the darkness listening to a ground moth beating its futile wings against the glass of the window.

They were awakened in the morning by the twittering of a small colony of tree sparrows who were feasting on the kitchen sweepings of the night before. Mary got up and went outside, returning a few minutes later carrying a handful of birch and poplar stovewood.

He waited until the beans were in the pan before rising and pulling on his pants. He stood in the doorway scratching his head and absorbing the sunlight through his bare feet upon the step.

The baby awoke while they were eating their breakfast.

"He don't look good," Big Tom said as he dipped some brown sauce from his plate with a hunk of bread.

"He'll be all right later," his wife insisted. She poured some crusted tinned milk from a tin into a cup and mixed it with water from the kettle.

Big Tom splashed his hands and face with cold water, and dried himself on a soiled shirt that lay over the back of a chair. "When you going to the camp, this morning?"

"This afternoon," Mary answered.

"I'll be back by then."

He took up a small pile of woven baskets from a corner and hung the handles over his arm. From the warming shelf of the stove he pulled a bedraggled band of cloth, into which a large goose feather had been sewn. Carrying this in his hand he went outside and strode down the path toward the highway.

He ignored the chattering sauciness of a squirrel that hurtled up the green ladder of a tree beside him. Above the small noises of the woods could be heard the roar of a transport truck braking its way down the hill from the burnt-out sapling covered ridge to the north. The truck passed him as he reached the road, and he waved a desultory greeting to the driver, who answered with a short blare of the horn.

Placing the baskets in a pile on the shoulder of the road he adjusted the corduroy band on his head so that the feather stuck up at the rear. He knew that by so doing he became a part of the local colour, "a real Indian with a feather'n everything," and also that he sold more baskets while wearing it. In the time he had been living along the highway he had learned to give them what they expected.

The trailer residents were not yet awake, so he sat down on the wooden walk leading to the shower room, his baskets resting on the ground in a half circle behind him.

After a few minutes a small boy descended from the door of a trailer and stood staring at him. Then he leaned back inside the doorway and pointed in Big Tom's direction. In a moment a man's hand parted the heavy curtains on the window and a bed-mussed unshaven face stared out. The small boy climbed back inside.

A little later two women approached on the duckboard walk, one attired in a pair of buttock-pinching brown slacks, and the other wearing a blue chenille dressing gown. They circled him warily and entered the shower room. From inside came the buzz of whispered conversation and the louder noises of running water.

During the rest of the morning several people approached and stared at Big Tom and the baskets. He sold two small ones to an elderly woman. She seemed surprised when she asked him what tribe he belonged to, and instead of answering in a monosyllable he said, "I belong to the Algonquins,[2] Ma'am." He also got rid of one of his big forty-five cent baskets to the mother of the small boy who had been the first one up earlier in the day.

A man took a series of photographs of him with an expensive-looking camera, pacing off the distance and being very careful in setting his lens openings and shutter speeds.

"I wish he'd look into the camera," the man said loudly to a couple standing nearby, as if he were talking about an animal in a cage.

"You can't get any good picshus around here. Harold tried to get one of the five Dionney kids, but they wouldn't let him. The way they keep them quints hid you'd think they was made of china or somep'n," a woman standing by said.

She glanced at her companion for confirmation.

"They want you to *buy* their picshus," the man said. "We was disappointed in 'em. They used to look cute before, when they was small, but now they're just five plain-looking kids."

"Yeah. My Gawd, you'd never believe how homely they got, would you, Harold? An' everything's pure robbery in Callander. You know, Old Man Dionney's minting money up there. Runs his own souvenir stand."

"That's durin' the day, when he's got time," her husband said.

The man with the camera, and the woman, laughed.

After lunch Big Tom watched Cooper prepare for his trip to North Bay. "Is there anybody going fishing, Mr Cooper?" he asked.

The man took the radiator cap off the old truck he was inspecting, and peered inside.

"Mr Cooper!"

"Hey?" Cooper turned and looked at the Indian standing behind him, hands in pockets, his manner shy and deferential. He showed a vague irritation as though he sensed the overtone of servility in the Indian's attitude.

"Anybody going fishing?" Big Tom asked again.

"Seems to me Mr Staynor said he'd like to go," Cooper answered. His voice was kind, with the amused kindness of a man talking to a child.

---

2 **Algonquins:** Any of various Native American peoples inhabiting the Ottawa River valley of Quebec and Ontario.

The big Indian remained standing where he was, saying nothing. His old second-hand army trousers drooped around his lean loins, and his plaid shirt was open at the throat, showing a grey high-water mark of dirt where his face washing began and ended.

"What's the matter?" Cooper asked. "You seem pretty anxious to go today."

"My kid's sick. I want to make enough to take him to the doctor."

Cooper walked around the truck and opened one of the doors, rattling the handle in his hand as if it was stuck. "You should stay home with it. Make it some pine-sap syrup. No need to worry, it's as healthy as a bear cub."

Mrs Cooper came out of the house and eased her bulk into the truck cab. "Where's Mary?" she asked.

"Up at the shack," answered Big Tom.

"Tell her to scrub the washrooms before she does anything else. Mrs Anderson, in that trailer over there, wants her to do her floors." She pointed across the lot to a large blue and white trailer parked behind a Buick.

"I'll tell her," he answered.

The Coopers drove between the whitewashed stones marking the entrance to the camp, and swung up the highway, leaving behind them a small cloud of dust from the pulverized gravel of the road.

Big Tom fetched Mary and the baby from the shack. He gave his wife Mrs Cooper's instructions, and she transferred the baby from her arms to his. The child was feverish, its breath noisy and fast.

"Keep him warm," she said. "He's been worse since we got up. I think he's got a touch of the 'flu."

Big Tom placed his hand inside the old blanket and felt the baby's cheek. It was dry and burning to his palm. He adjusted the baby's small weight in his arm and walked across the camp and down the narrow path to the shore of the lake where the boats were moored.

A man sitting in the sternsheets of a new-painted skiff looked up and smiled at his approach. "You coming out with me, Tom?" he asked.

The Indian nodded.

"Are you bringing the papoose along?"

Big Tom winced at the word "papoose," but he answered, "He won't bother us. The wife is working this afternoon."

"O.K. I thought maybe we'd go over to the other side of the lake today and try to get some of them big fellows at the creek mouth. Like to try?"

"Sure," the Indian answered, placing the baby along the wide seat in the stern, and unshipping the oars.

He rowed silently for the best part of an hour, the sun beating through his shirt causing the sweat to trickle coldly down his back. At times his efforts at the oars caused a constriction in his chest, and he coughed and spat into the water.

When they reached the mouth of the creek across the lake, he let the oars drag and leaned over to look at the baby. It was sleeping restlessly, its lips slightly blue and its breath laboured and harsh. Mr Staynor was busy with his lines and tackle in the bow of the boat.

Tom picked the child up and felt its little body for sweat.

The baby's skin was bone dry. He picked up the bailing can from the boat bottom and dipped it over the side. With the tips of his fingers he brushed some of the cold water across the baby's forehead. The child woke up, looked at the strange surroundings, and smiled up at him. He gave it a drink of water from the can. Feeling reassured now he placed the baby on the seat and went forward to help the man with his gear.

Mr Staynor fished for a half hour or so, catching some small fish and a large black bass, which writhed in the bottom of the boat. Big Tom watched its gills gasping its death throes, and noted the similarity between the struggles of the fish and those of the baby lying on the seat in the blanket.

He became frightened again after a time, and he turned to the man in the bow and said, "We'll have to go pretty soon. I'm afraid my kid's pretty sick."

"Eh! We've hardly started," the man answered. "Don't worry, there's not much wrong with the papoose."

Big Tom lifted the child from the seat and cradled it in his arms. He opened the blanket, and shading the baby's face, allowed the warm sun to shine on its chest. He thought, if I could only get him to sweat; everything would be all right then.

He waited again as long as he dared, noting the blueness creeping over the baby's lips, before he placed the child again on the seat and addressed the man in the bow. "I'm going back now. You'd better pull in your line."

The man turned and felt his way along the boat. He stood over the Indian and parted the folds of the blanket, looking at the baby. "My God, he is sick, Tom! You'd better get him to a doctor right away!" He stepped across the writhing fish to the bow and began pulling in the line. Then he busied himself with his tackle, stealing glances now and again at the Indian and the baby.

Big Tom turned the boat around, and with long straight pulls on the oars headed back across the lake. The man took the child in his arms and blew cooling drafts of air against its fevered face.

As soon as they reached the jetty below the tourist camp, Tom tied the boat's painter[3] to a stump and took the child from the other man's arms.

Mr Staynor handed him the fee for a full afternoon's work. "I'm sorry the youngster is sick, Tom," he said. "Don't play around. Get him up to the doctor in town right away. We'll try her again tomorrow afternoon."

Big Tom thanked him. Then, carrying the baby and unmindful of the grasping hands of the undergrowth, he climbed the path through the trees. On reaching the parked cars and trailers he headed in the direction of the large blue and white one where his wife would be working.

---

3 **painter:** A rope attached to the bow of a boat and used for tying up, as when docking or towing.

When he knocked, the door opened and a woman said, "Yes?" He recognized her as the one who had been standing nearby in the morning while his picture was being taken.

"Is my wife here?" he asked.

"Your wife. Oh, I know who you mean. No, she's gone. She went down the road in a car a few minutes ago."

The camp was almost empty, most of the tourists having gone to the small bathing beach farther down the lake. A car full of bathers was pulling away to go down to the beach. Big Tom hurried over and held up his hand until it stopped. "Could you drive me to the doctor in town?" he asked. "My baby seems pretty sick."

There was a turning of heads within the car. A woman in the back seat began talking about the weather. The driver said, "I'll see what I can do, Chief, after I take the girls to the beach."

Big Tom sat down at the side of the driveway to wait. After a precious half hour had gone by and they did not return, he got to his feet and started up the highway in the direction of town.

His long legs pounded on the loose gravel of the road, his anger and terror giving strength to his stride. He noticed that the passengers in the few cars he met were pointing at him and laughing, and suddenly he realized that he was still wearing the feather in the band around his head. He reached up, pulled it off, and threw it in the ditch.

When a car or truck came up from behind him he would step off the road and raise his hand to beg a ride. After several passed without pausing he stopped this useless time-wasting gesture and strode ahead, impervious to the noise of their horns as they approached him.

Now and again he placed his hand on the baby's face as he plodded along, reassuring himself that it was still alive. It had been hours since it had cried or shown any other signs of consciousness.

Once, he stepped off the road at a small bridge over a stream, and making a crude cup with his hands, tried to get the baby to drink. He succeeded only in making it cough, harshly, so that its tiny face became livid with its efforts to breathe.

It was impossible that the baby should die. Babies did not die like this, in their father's arms, on a highway that ran fifteen miles north through a small town, where there was a doctor and all the life-saving devices to prevent their deaths.

The sun fell low behind the trees and the swarms of black flies and mosquitoes began their nightly forage. He waved his hand above the fevered face of the baby, keeping them off, while at the same time trying to waft a little air into the child's tortured lungs.

But suddenly, with feelings as black as hell itself, he knew that the baby was dying. He had seen too much of it not to know now, that the child was in an advanced stage of pneumonia. He stumbled along as fast as he could, his eyes devouring the darkening face of his son, while the hot tears ran from the corners of his eyes.

With nightfall he knew that it was too late. He looked up at the sky where the first stars were being drawn in silver on a burnished copper plate, and he cursed them, and cursed what made them possible.

To the north-west the clouds were piling up in preparation for a summer storm. Reluctantly he turned and headed back down the road in the direction he had come.

It was almost midnight before he felt his way along the path through the trees to his shack. It was hard to see anything in the teeming rain, and he let the water run from his shoulders in an unheeded stream, soaking the sodden bundle he still carried in his arms.

When he reached the shanty he opened the door and fell inside. He placed the body of his son on the bed in the corner. Then, groping around the newspaper-lined walls, he found some matches in a pocket of his mackinaw and lit the lamp. With a glance around the room he knew that his wife had not yet returned, so he placed the lamp on the table under the window and headed out again into the rain.

At the trailer camp he sat down on the rail fence near the entrance to wait. Some lights shone from the small windows of the trailers and from Cooper's house across the road. The illuminated sign said: COOPER'S TRAILER CAMP—Hot And Cold Running Water, Rest Rooms. FISHING AND BOATING—INDIAN GUIDES.

One by one, as he waited, the lights went out, until only the sign lit up a small area at the gate. He saw the car's headlights first, about a hundred yards down the road. When it pulled to a stop he heard some giggling, and Mary and another Indian girl, Elsie Woodhen, staggered out into the rain.

A man's voice shouted through the door, "See you again, sweetheart. Don't forget next Saturday night." The voice belonged to one of the French-Canadians who worked at a creosote[4] camp across the lake.

Another male voice shouted, "Wahoo!"

The girls clung to each other, laughing drunkenly, as the car pulled away.

They were not aware of Big Tom's approach until he grasped his wife by the hair and pulled her backwards to the ground. Elsie Woodhen screamed, and ran away in the direction of the Cooper house. Big Tom bent down as if he was going to strike at Mary's face with his fist. Then he changed his mind and let her go.

She stared into his eyes and saw what was there. Crawling to her feet and sobbing hysterically she left one of her silver shoes in the mud and limped along towards the shack.

Big Tom followed behind, all the anguish and frustration drained from him, so that there was nothing left to carry him into another day. Heedless now of the coughing that tore his chest apart, he pushed along in the rain, hurrying to join his wife in the vigil over their dead.

4 **creosote:** Wood tar oil.

QUESTIONS

1. Why did Garner choose the title of this story?

2. In what way is this tale about the clash of two cultures? Characterize the nature of these conflicts.

3. Describe the relationship between Big Tom and Mary.

4. How is this story as much about economics as it is about racial divisions and perceptions?

5. What makes the conclusion of this tale so powerful?

Clark Blaise

(b. 1940)

Clark Blaise was born in Fargo, North Dakota, of Canadian parents. He grew up in the U.S. South and graduated from high school in Pittsburgh. He spent periods of time during his youth in Winnipeg, but decided to attend university at Denison University in Ohio, where he studied English and began to write creatively. He attended summer writing schools at Harvard and graduated with an MFA from Iowa Writers Workshop in 1964. He moved to Montreal at age twenty-five and founded the graduate writing program at Concordia University, which allowed him to travel and teach throughout the world. Blaise has published five collections of short stories, *A North American Education* (1973), *Tribal Justice* (1974), *Southern Stories* (2000), *Pittsburgh Stories* (2001), and *Montreal Stories* (2003); two novels, *Lunar Attractions* (1979) and *Lusts* (1983); one autobiographical travel memoir with his wife, *Days and Nights in Calcutta* (1977); one book containing autobiographical fragments and short tales, *Resident Alien* (1986); and one piece of investigative journalism, *The Sorrow and the Terror: The Haunting Legacy of the Air India Tragedy* (1987).

Blaise's fictional work almost always deals with the problem of identity and being an outsider. As Blaise portrays him, the outsider is often a person with two conflicting streams in his culture or personality. In Blaise's case, the conflict is between his U.S. self and his Canadian parents or between the French and English strains in Canadian history and culture. His writing appears to be very personal (like it is happening to himself), but the creative part of his fiction is the way Blaise shapes the raw material from his life and retells it in new and original perspectives. In the story that follows, the Blaisian hero, Norman Dyer, reflects fondly on the important role he plays as a language teacher in the life of new immigrants to Montreal. Before the teaching evening is complete, the third-person narrator shows the reader the absurdity of that contention.

A Class of New Canadians   1973

Norman Dyer hurried down Sherbrooke Street, collar turned against the snow. "Superb!" he muttered, passing a basement gallery next to a French bookstore. Bleached and tanned women in furs dashed from hotel lobbies into waiting cabs. Even the neon clutter of the side streets and the honks of slithering taxis seemed remote tonight through the peaceful snow. *Superb,* he thought again, waiting for a light and backing from a slushy curb: a word reserved for wines, cigars, and delicate sauces; he was feeling superb this evening. After eighteen months in Montreal, he still found himself freshly impressed by everything he saw. He was proud of himself for having steered his life north, even for jobs that were menial by standards he could have demanded. Great just being here no matter what they paid, looking at these buildings, these faces, and hearing all the languages. He was learning to be insulted by simple bad taste, wherever he encountered it.

Since leaving graduate school and coming to Montreal, he had sampled every ethnic restaurant downtown and in the old city, plus a few Levantine[1] places out in Outremont. He had worked on conversational French and mastered much of the local dialect, done reviews for local papers, translated French-Canadian poets for Toronto quarterlies, and tweaked his colleagues for not sympathizing enough with Quebec separatism. He attended French performances of plays he had ignored in English, and kept a small but elegant apartment near a colony of *émigré* Russians just off Park Avenue. Since coming to Montreal he'd witnessed a hold-up, watched a murder, and seen several riots. When stopped on the street for directions, he would answer in French or accented English. To live this well and travel each long academic summer, he held two jobs. He had no intention of returning to the States. In fact, he had begun to think of himself as a semi-permanent, semi-political exile.

Now, stopped again a few blocks farther, he studied the window of Holt-Renfrew's exclusive men's shop. Incredible, he thought, the authority of simple good taste. Double-breasted chalk-striped suits he would never dare to buy. Knitted sweaters, and fifty-dollar shoes. One tanned mannequin was decked out in a brash checkered sportscoat with a burgundy vest and dashing ascot. Not a price tag under three hundred dollars. Unlike food, drink, cinema, and literature, clothing had never really involved him. Some day, he now realized, it would. Dyer's clothes, thus far, had all been bought in a chain department store. He was a walking violation of American law, clad shoes to scarf in Egyptian cottons, Polish leathers, and woollens from the People's Republic of China.

---

1 **Levantine:** An inhabitant of the region of the Eastern Mediterranean comprising modern-day Lebanon, Israel, and parts of Syria and Turkey.

He had no time for dinner tonight; this was Wednesday, a day of lectures at one university, and then an evening course in English as a Foreign Language at McGill, beginning at six. He would eat afterwards.

Besides the money, he had kept this second job because it flattered him. There was to Dyer something fiercely elemental, almost existential, about teaching both his language and his literature in a foreign country—like Joyce in Trieste, Isherwood and Nabokov in Berlin, Beckett in Paris. Also it was necessary for his students. It was the first time in his life that he had done something socially useful. What difference did it make that the job was beneath him, a recent Ph.D., while most of his colleagues in the evening school at McGill were idle housewives and bachelor civil servants? It didn't matter, even, that this job was a perversion of all the sentiments he held as a progressive young teacher. He was a god two evenings a week, sometimes suffering and fatigued, but nevertheless an omniscient, benevolent god. His students were silent, ignorant, and dedicated to learning English. No discussions, no demonstrations, no dialogue.

I love them, he thought. They need me.

He entered the room, pocketed his cap and ear muffs, and dropped his briefcase on the podium. Two girls smiled good evening.

They love me, he thought, taking off his boots and hanging up his coat; I'm not like their English-speaking bosses.

I love myself, he thought with amazement even while conducting a drill on word order. I love myself for tramping down Sherbrooke Street in zero weather just to help them with noun clauses. I love myself standing behind this podium and showing Gilles Carrier and Claude Veilleux the difference between the past continuous and the simple past; or the sultry Armenian girl with the bewitching half-glasses that "put on" is not the same as "take on"; or telling that dashing Mr Miguel Mayor, late of Madrid, that simple futurity can be expressed in four different ways, at least.

This is what mastery is like, he thought. Being superb in one's chosen field, not merely in one's mother tongue. A respected performer in the lecture halls of the major universities, equipped by twenty years' research in the remotest libraries, and slowly giving it back to those who must have it. Dishing it out suavely, even wittily. Being a legend. Being loved and a little feared.

"Yes, Mrs David?"

A *sabra:* freckled, reddish hair, looking like a British model, speaks with a nifty British accent, and loves me.

"No," he smiled, "I *were* is not correct except in the present subjunctive, which you haven't studied yet."

The first hour's bell rang. The students closed their books for the intermission. Dyer put his away, then noticed a page of his Faulkner lecture from the afternoon class. *Absalom, Absalom!* his favourite.

"Can anyone here tell me what the *impregnable citadel of his passive rectitude* means?"

"What, sir?" asked Mr Vassilopoulos, ready to copy.

"What about *the presbyterian and lugubrious effluvium of his passive vindictiveness?*" A few girls giggled. "O.K.," said Dyer, "take your break."

* * *

In the halls of McGill they broke into the usual groups. French Canadians and South Americans into two large circles, then the Greeks, Germans, Spanish, and French into smaller groups. The patterns interested Dyer. Madrid Spaniards and Parisian French always spoke English with their New World co-linguals. The Middle Europeans spoke German together, not Russian, preferring one occupier to the other. Two Israeli men went off alone. Dyer decided to join them for the break.

Not *sabras*, Dyer concluded, not like Mrs David. The shorter one, dark and wavy-haired, held his cigarette like a violin bow. The other, Mr Weinrot, was tall and pot-bellied, with a ruddy face and thick stubby fingers. Something about him suggested truck-driving, perhaps of beer, maybe in Germany. Neither one, he decided, could supply the name of a good Israeli restaurant.

"This is really hard, you know?" said Weinrot.

"Why?"

"I think it's because I'm not speaking much of English at my job."

"French?" asked Dyer.

"French? Pah! All the time Hebrew, sometimes German, sometimes little Polish. Crazy thing, eh? How long you think they let me speak Hebrew if I'm working in America?"

"Depends on where you're working," he said.

"Hell, I'm working for the Canadian government, what you think? Plant I work in—I'm engineer, see—makes boilers for the turbines going up North. Look. When I'm leaving Israel I go first to Italy. Right away-bamm I'm working in Italy I'm speaking Italian like a native. Passing for a native."

"A native Jew," said his dark-haired friend.

"Listen to him. So in Rome they think I'm from Tyrol—that's still native, eh? So I speak Russian and German and Italian like a Jew. My Hebrew is bad, I admit it, but it's a lousy language anyway. Nobody likes it. French I understand but English I'm talking like a bum. Arabic I know five dialects. Danish fluent. So what's the matter I can't learn English?"

"It'll come, don't worry," Dyer smiled. *Don't worry, my son;* he wanted to pat him on the arm. "Anyway, that's what makes Canada so appealing. Here they don't force you."

"What's this *appealing*? Means nice? Look, my friend, keep it, eh? Two years in a country I don't learn the language means it isn't a country."

"Come on," said Dyer. "Neither does forcing you."

"Let me tell you a story why I come to Canada. Then you tell me if I was wrong, O.K.?"

"Certainly," said Dyer, flattered.

In Italy, Weinrot told him, he had lost his job to a Communist union. He left Italy for Denmark and opened up an Israeli restaurant with five other friends. Then the six Israelis decided to rent a bigger apartment downtown near the restaurant. They found a perfect nine-room place for two thousand kroner a month, not bad shared six ways. Next day the landlord told them the deal was off. "You tell me why," Weinrot demanded.

No Jews? Dyer wondered. "He wanted more rent," he finally said.

"More—you kidding? More we expected. *Less* we didn't expect. A couple with eight kids is showing up after we're gone and the law in Denmark says a man has a right to a room for each kid plus a hundred kroner knocked off the rent for each kid. What you think of that? So a guy who comes in *after* us gets a nine-room place for a thousand kroner *less*. Law says no way a bachelor can get a place ahead of a family, and bachelors pay twice as much."

Dyer waited, then asked, "So?"

"So, I make up my mind the world is full of communismus, just like Israel. So I take out applications next day for Australia, South Africa, U.S.A., and Canada. Canada says come right away, so I go. Should have waited for South Africa."

"How could you?" Dyer cried. "What's wrong with you anyway? South Africa is fascist. Australia is racist."

The bell rang, and the Israelis, with Dyer, began walking to the room.

"What I was wondering, then," said Mr Weinrot, ignoring Dyer's outburst, "was if my English is good enough to be working in the United States. You're American, aren't you?"

It was a question Dyer had often avoided in Europe, but had rarely been asked in Montreal. "Yes," he admitted, "your English is probably good enough for the States or South Africa, whichever one wants you first."

He hurried ahead to the room, feeling that he had let Montreal down. He wanted to turn and shout to Weinrot and to all the others that Montreal was the greatest city on the continent, if only they knew it as well as he did. If they'd just break out of their little ghettos.

At the door, the Armenian girl with the half-glasses caught his arm. She was standing with Mrs David and Miss Parizeau, a jolly French-Canadian girl that Dyer had been thinking of asking out.

"Please, sir," she said, looking at him over the tops of her tiny glasses, "what I was asking earlier—*put on*—I heard on the television. A man said *You are putting me on* and everybody laughed. I think it was supposed to be funny but *put on* we learned means get dressed, no?"

"Ah—*don't put me on*," Dyer laughed.

"I yaven't erd it neither," said Miss Parizeau.

"To put some*body* on means to make a fool of him. To put some*thing* on is to wear it. O.K.?" He gave examples.

"Ah, now I know," said Miss Parizeau. "Like bullshitting somebody. Is it the same?"

"Ah, yes," he said, smiling. French Canadians were like children learning the language. "Your example isn't considered polite. 'Put on' is very common now in the States."

"Then maybe," said Miss Parizeau, "we'll ave it ere in twenty years."

The Armenian giggled.

"No—I've heard it here just as often," Dyer protested, but the girls had already entered the room.

He began the second hour with a smile which slowly soured as he thought of the Israelis. America's anti-communism was bad enough, but it was worse hearing it echoed by immigrants, by Jews, here in Montreal. Wasn't there a psychological type who chose Canada over South Africa? Or was it just a matter of visa and slow adjustment? Did Johannesburg lose its Greeks, and Melbourne its Italians, the way Dyer's students were always leaving Montreal?

And after class when Dyer was again feeling content and thinking of approaching one of the Israelis for a restaurant tip, there came the flood of small requests: should Mrs Papadopoulos go into a more advanced course; could Mr Perez miss a week for an interview in Toronto; could Mr Giguère, who spoke English perfectly, have a harder book; Mr Coté an easier one?

Then as he packed his briefcase in the empty room, Miguel Mayor, the vain and impeccable Spaniard, came forward from the hallway.

"Sir," he began, walking stiffly, ready to bow or salute. He wore a loud grey checkered sportscoat this evening, blue shirt, and matching ascot-handkerchief, slightly mauve. He must have shaved just before class, Dyer noticed, for two fresh daubs of antiseptic cream stood out on his jaw, just under his earlobe.

"I have been wanting to ask *you* something, as a matter of fact," said Dyer. "Do you know any good Spanish restaurants I might try tonight?"

"There are not any good Spanish restaurants in Montreal," he said. He stepped closer. "Sir?"

"What's on your mind, then?"

"Please—have you the time to look on a letter for me?"

He laid the letter on the podium.

"Look *over* a letter," said Dyer. "What is it for?"

"I have applied," he began, stopping to emphasize the present perfect construction, "for a job in Cleveland, Ohio, and I want to know if my letter will be good. Will an American, I mean—"

"Why are you going there?"

"It is a good job."

"But Cleveland—"

"They have a blackman mayor, I have read. But the job is not in Cleveland."

"Let me see it."

Most honourable Sir: I humbly beg consideration for a position in your grand company . . .

"Who are you writing this to?"

"The president," said Miguel Mayor.

I am once a student of Dr Ramiro Gutierrez of the Hydraulic Institute of Sevilla, Spain . . .

"Does the president know this Ramiro Gutierrez?"

"Oh, everybody is knowing him," Miguel Mayor assured, "he is the most famous expert in all Spain."

"Did he recommend this company to you?"

"No—I have said in my letter, if you look—"

An ancient student of Dr Gutierrez, Salvador del Este, is actually a boiler expert who is being employed like supervisor is formerly a friend of mine . . .

"Is he still your friend?"

Whenever you say come to my city Miguel Mayor for talking I will be coming. I am working in Montreal since two years and am now wanting more money than I am getting here now . . .

"Well . . ." Dyer sighed.

"Sir—what I want from you is knowing in good English how to interview me by this man. The letters in Spanish are not the same to English ones, you know?"

I remain humbly at your orders . . .

"Why do you want to leave Montreal?"

"It's time for a change."

"Have you ever been to Cleveland?"

"I am one summer in California. Very beautiful there and hot like my country. Montreal is big port just like Barcelona. Everybody mixed together and having no money. It is just a place to land, no?"

"Montreal? Don't be silly."

"I thought I come here and learn good English but where I work I get by in Spanish and French. It's hard, you know?" he smiled. Then he took a few steps back and gave his cuffs a gentle tug, exposing a set of jade cufflinks.

Dyer looked at the letter again and calculated how long he would be correcting it, then up at his student. How old is he? My age? Thirty? Is he married? Where do the Spanish live in Montreal? He looks so prosperous, so confident, like a male model off a page of *Playboy*. For an instant Dyer felt that his student was mocking him, somehow pitting his astounding confidence and wardrobe, sharp chin and matador's bearing against Dyer's command of English and mastery of the side streets, bistros, and ethnic restaurants. Mayor's letter was painful, yet he remained somehow competent. He would pass his interview, if he got one. What would he care about America, and the odiousness he'd soon be supporting? It was as though a superstructure of exploitation had been revealed, and Dyer felt himself abused by the very people he wanted so much to help. It had to end someplace.

He scratched out the second "humbly" from the letter, then folded the sheet of foolscap. "Get it typed right away," he said. "Good luck."

"Thank you, sir," said his student, with a bow. Dyer watched the letter disappear in the inner pocket of the checkered sportscoat. Then the folding of the cashmere scarf, the draping of the camel's hair coat about the shoulders, the easing of the fur hat down to the rims of his ears. The meticulous filling of the pigskin gloves. Mayor's patent leather galoshes glistened.

"Good evening, sir," he said.

"*Buenas noches,*" Dyer replied.

He hurried now, back down Sherbrooke Street to his daytime office where he could deposit his books. Montreal on a winter night was still mysterious, still magical. Snow blurred the arc lights. The wind was dying. Every second car was now a taxi, crowned with an orange crescent. Slushy curbs had hardened. The window of

Holt-Renfrew's was still attractive. The legless dummies invited a final stare. He stood longer than he had earlier, in front of the sporty mannequin with a burgundy waistcoat, the mauve and blue ensemble, the jade cufflinks.

Good evening, sir, he could almost hear. The ascot, the shirt, the complete outfit, had leaped off the back of Miguel Mayor. He pictured how he must have entered the store with three hundred dollars and a prepared speech, and walked out again with everything off the torso's back.

I want that.

What, sir?

That.

The coat, sir?

Yes.

Very well, sir.

And *that.*

Which, sir?

All that.

"Absurd man!" Dyer whispered. There had been a moment of fear, as though the naked body would leap from the window, and legless, chase him down Sherbrooke Street. But the moment was passing. Dyer realized now that it was comic, even touching. Miguel Mayor had simply tried too hard, too fast, and it would be good for him to stay in Montreal until he deserved those clothes, that touching vanity and confidence. With one last look at the window, he turned sharply, before the clothes could speak again.

QUESTIONS

1. What is particularly exciting to Norman about Montreal life and culture?

2. How would you characterize the immigrants who take English lessons with Norman?

3. Is there a difference between the new immigrants' perception of the United States and that of Norman? Discuss the nature of the perceptions.

4. Why does Norman allow Miguel Mayor to send a poorly written letter of application for the job in Cleveland?

George Bowering

(b. 1935)

George Bowering was born in Penticton, British Columbia, and attended high school on the west coast. After graduating from high school, he enlisted in the

Royal Canadian Air Force as an aerial photographer from 1954 to 1957. He started a degree course in history at the University of British Columbia and completed an MA in English in 1963. With a group of similar avant-garde writers in British Columbia, Bowering founded *TISH* magazine, which was influenced by U.S. writers of the Black Mountain School. He taught at several Canadian universities including Calgary and Concordia, but finished his career in 2001 at Simon Fraser University. In 2002, Bowering was appointed the first Canadian resident poet to Parliament Hill.

Bowering is a prolific writer, having published over forty volumes of poetry, novels, and short stories, not to mention his many historical studies, young adult fictions, plays, biography, criticism, memoirs, and essays. He is also an editor and a unionized radio performer. His first novel, *Mirror on the Floor* (1967), was published after he had written five volumes of poetry.

His third novel, *Burning Water* (1980), won the Governor General's Award for fiction. The story is ostensibly about George Vancouver's exploration of the west coast of North America in the late eighteenth century. But more than that, it is an exercise in historical reconstruction, a study of the imagination, and a postmodern essay. Bowering's other novels include *Caprice* (1988) and *Shoot!* (1994). He has written a number of short story volumes including *Flycatcher & Other Stories* (1974), *Concentric Circles* (1977), *Protective Footwear* (1978), *A Place to Die* (1983), and *The Rain Barrel* (1994).

The short story in this collection depicts the arrival of George Vancouver into British Columbia. Two Indians muse about this European civilization that will soon replace their own. Their rather comic conclusions prove not only the failure of their imaginations but also the innocence with which they view the world.

Bring Forth a Wonder   1980

Whatever it was, the vision, came out of the far fog and sailed right into the sunny weather of the inlet. It was June 10, 1792.

It could have been June 20 for all the two men who watched from the shore could care. The shore was rocks and scrubby trees right to the high tide water line. The two men were Indians, and they knew enough to blend in with the rocks and trees, for the time being at least.

"It is the first time in my life that I have seen a vision," said the first Indian.

"A vision?" said the second Indian.

"The old folks told me about them. They said you went alone to the woods with no food for a week or two, and you would see visions. Well, maybe I have not been eating much lately."

The second Indian, who was about ten years older, a world-weary man with scars here and there, sighed.

"You have had no particular problem with eating," he said. "You eat more than I do, though I carry more than you do."

"I am still growing. Surely you would not deny me the nourishment I require to take my place as a full man of the tribe?"

These young ones could be pretty tiresome. Full man of the tribe. Talk talk talk. The second Indian looked over at his companion, who was now leaning back on a bare patch of striped granite, idly picking at his navel. And now he is seeing visions.

"I will make certain that I give you half of my fish tonight, before you start hinting for it this time. Meanwhile I might as well tell you about this vision you are seeing."

The first Indian looked up from his belly as if he had forgotten about the vision. He held his hand up, palm downward, sheltering his eyes as he gazed out over the silver water, where another vision or whatever had joined the first. When it got close enough it would be seen to be larger than the first one. The first Indian put his fishing gear down on a flat rock and climbed a little closer down to the water. Much further and he would fall in and the second Indian would have to rescue him from drowning for the second time in a week. I am an artist, he had said the first time, what do I know about swimming? To which his lifeguard had replied: or about fishing?

"Okay, what do you see?"

"I see two immense and frighteningly beautiful birds upon the water."

"Birds?"

"Giant birds. They can only be spirits. Their huge shining wings are folded and at rest. I have heard many of the stories about bird visions, the one who cracks your head open and eats your brains . . ."

"Hoxhok."[1]

"And others who alight from the mountains and the skies and take away unsuspecting children and people with bad personalities. Also the one with the hopelessly long name who eats eyeballs. But never anything quite like this."

"Maybe, then, it is a vision that rightly belongs to another people entirely," suggested the second Indian.

"An interesting thought, but the fact is that it has been revealed, in the present case, to *us*."

"Then you do think there is something to facts?"

"Of course. But the facts can only lead us to visions. Some of us, at least, were born to see visions."

"That is perhaps why you have so much difficulty getting a fish to leave the sea and come home with you. He is a fact whether he is hidden under the surface, or changing colours on the rocks. To make this fact your fact, you need skill and a well-made hook."

"But a vision is not a fish, my old ironic friend."

"I was perhaps making that very point in its opposite order," said he.

---

1 **Hoxhok:** A powerful bird spirit.

"But look yonder, how the late afternoon sun has picked out the true aspect of those wings at rest. Now they are revealed to be gold, and we are two lucky men to have seen this. We will camp here tonight, and while the visions remain I will watch them . . ."

"You'll be asleep a minute after it gets dark."

"I will watch them until they have flown back into their sky or heaven or home-land up in the air. Then I will open my mind to the Great Spirit, and create a song, and the song will reveal the meaning of the vision, and I will take it back with me to the tribe, where I will be accepted and welcomed as . . ."

"A full man of the tribe."

He stopped writing and went out for a while in the Triestino[2] sunlight. When he came back this all seemed crazy.

"Yes, a full man of the tribe. You should not sneer. That is perhaps more than you think I am, but it is also perhaps more than you feel need of for yourself."

The second Indian spat in the direction of those two giant swans or whatever they were.

"You see those visions of yours?"

"Yes, I see them. Oh, I get it. Very clever. But I do see them and so do you, so that takes care of your precious facts, too."

"Not quite." Now he was going to get the brash little squirrel. Little prick. "Those are boats."

"Haw haw haw!"

"Two large dugouts from another people, as I said."

"Oh sure, dugouts with wings."

"Those wings are made of thick cloth. They catch the wind as we are supposed to catch fish in our nets, and travel far out to sea."

"You are only trying to discredit me."

"No, I am discrediting only your fancy. Your fancy would have the fish leap from the water into your carrying bag. But the imagination, now that is another matter. Your imagination tells you where to drop your hooks."

The first Indian looked from his companion to the contraptions and back again. He turned full around, and looked at the second Indian as suddenly as he could, fishing for a truth perhaps swimming in the shadow of a rock.

"You know, I do not want to believe you, but I find it hard not to. I have been bred to believe you."

"Though you were born to see visions."

The artist turned from his older friend with hurt pride and feigned derision. His friend put his hand on his deerskin-covered shoulder and turned him around.

---

2 **Triestino:** Belonging to the city of Trieste in northern Italy.

"They are boats. Your fancy cannot dissemble that much. You must allow your senses to play for your imagination. Now, look at the highest point at the rear of the larger dugout. What do you see there?"

The first Indian looked with his very good eyes.

"It looks like a man."

"Yes?"

"In outlandish clothes. Like no clothes ever seen on this sea. He must be a god, he . . ."

The second Indian squeezed tight on his shoulder.

"That is your fancy speaking. That can be very dangerous for people such as us. You must never believe that you have seen a god when you have seen a man on a large boat."

"You have perhaps seen them before?"

"I have."

"Up close?"

"Closer. The vision is made of wood. Hard, smooth, shiny, painted wood. The figures wear peculiar clothes, all right, and some have hair on their faces. Can you imagine a god with hair on his face?"

"Did you hear them speak?"

"No, my imagination did not take me that close. A friend who did hear one speak a year ago said these people come from far in the south, and they call them-selves *Narvaez*."[3]

In Trieste, it was raining most of the time, and he would bump other umbrellas with his own on his way down to the piazza, where he would look out at the fog that had drifted in across the northern end of the Adriatic.

It was his idea, crazed in all likelihood, that if he was going to write a book about that other coast as it was two hundred years ago, he would be advised to move away in space too.

It was a neat-sounding idea, but it didn't hold any water at all. In fact it was probably informed by the malaise that had been responsible for a decade of waiting around for a shape to appear out of the fog.

And while there were certainly some people who cared very much whether George Vancouver[4] came back over the ocean with his maps, there wasn't anyone who cared whether *he* ever showed up in Vancouver with a novel written there or elsewhere.

He had thought he would write the book nine thousand miles east because there the weather would be too poor to promote lying on a beach, the city so dull that one day's walk would take care of the sightseeing, and he didn't know a soul

---

3 *Narvaez:* A Spanish explorer who was sent to Mexico after Hernando Cortés; said to have been one of the first Europeans to explore Florida.

4 **George Vancouver:** British sea captain who led an expedition to explore the inland waters of the Burrell Inlet in what today is British Columbia.

(or body) within a thousand miles, and knew only a close relative of the language. He would be ineluctably driven to the manuscript because there would be no telephone to summon his voice for a lecture in a prison, no mail to petition his name for a young writer's attempt to secure a grant to go and write a novel somewhere else, no pub to call for his anticipation Thursday, his body Friday night, and his aching head all day Saturday. No distractions, he said, meaning partly that *she* couldn't get him to change a light bulb or listen to a dream while he should be, as he habitually put it to himself, sitting down in that chair in that tax write-off study, producing.

. . . The name of the larger of the two dragon-bird-visions was HMS *Discovery*, that of the smaller was HMS *Chatham*. Thirteen years earlier, HMS *Discovery* had appeared at Nootka, under the command of the yet uneaten Captain James Cook. Captain Cook has come down in the British historical imagination as a great seaman and superior Englishman. This is so because he told the Admiralty a lot of wonderful things. On one occasion, after the boats had spent days and days in a large inlet far to the north, he said to young Vancouver, his twenty-one-year-old pre-officer, "You see how far we have proceeded inland? This is clearly the largest river in the New World."

"It looks like an inlet, sir."

"You are inexperienced, George. It is the great river we have been waiting to find."

"Shouldn't we wait a little longer to make sure, sir? I mean to say we have been mistaken before now. We thought the strait between the great island and the mainland might be the way east. We called it the Great Inland Sea, you remember?"

. . . It had been Cook's purpose and responsibility to claim whatever lands he found for the British Crown. Vancouver had no such mission. He was supposed to chart the coast, be friendly but firm with the Spanish, and if he had any time left over, keep an eye open for gold and the North-West Passage.

But Vancouver loved to jump out of a boat, stride a few paces up the beach, and announce: "I claim this new-found land for his Britannic Majesty in perpetuity, and name it New Norfolk!"

Usually the officers and men stood around fairly alertly, holding flags and oars and looking about for anyone who did not agree.

Vancouver thought about Champlain and de Maisonneuve,[5] who got to climb hills with big crosses and plant Christ in the soil of a new world. He wished that there were some Frenchmen around to fight. It had looked, when they left home, as if there would be another colourful war with the French navy, and a great military career was what he wanted to leave behind for his family.

Instead, they sent him as far away as they could, exploring, serving science.

5 **Champlain and de Maisonneuve:** French explorers of North America.

The only Frenchman around had been Etienne Marchand, that little pecker, in the *Solide*. Marchand had taken one look, had seen no way of getting the beaver from the Russians and the Spanish, and gone on home.

. . . Well, that's the way he was. He thought and knew that he was the best surveyor around, the best navigator in the world. So he hated a lot of people, as the best often do. He hated fakers, as we have seen. He hated people who were satisfied with sloppy jobs. He hated Frenchmen and all other republicans. Yet he was not all that taken with the king, though he himself was the king, and that was something.

Most of all, on this trip, he hated the scientists. Especially Menzies,[6] that godforsaken Scotchman. Oh yes, he wasn't very strong on Scotchmen.

The little fucker has the deck cluttered up with his stuff, and he is taking over more and more space every day. First there were those contraptions of wood and glass, through which he was going to advise the captain on longitude! Then there were the plants, bushes and trees and weeds from New Holland, New Zealand, the Sandwiches, the Societies, and now the North Coast. I cannot set anchor but the little porridge-eater is off in one of my boats, having commandeered two of my men, to dig up another obnoxious weed, to make a home for it upon *my* planks, and to sequester yet more canvas to make it a roof from the rain, as if it had never felt the rain in this desert!

The vessel is ninety-nine feet long, and he hopes to cover all of it, I'm certain.

. . . In Trieste there was no mail. Vancouver, BC, was proceeding day by day independent of his help or even knowledge. Was his wife alive? Was his daughter? Did his house stand?

James Cook spent his time at home with Mrs Cook and their three sons, an excellent salary and praise every day in the *Gazette*. After his strange and distant death there was a family as well as a nation to mourn him, publicly and in the dark hours after windows went dim along the street.

Who would have remembered longer than the news if George Vancouver had been cooked and eaten somewhere in the other hemisphere? This moment he could quietly slip his legs over the side and let his body fall into the retreating tide, and the world of affairs or the parlours of Albion would never notice the splash.

Even that wouldn't make much of a story.

He wanted to be a famous story very much, the kind of story that is known before you read it. He wanted his name and exploits to be a part of the world any Englishman would walk through.

So he wrote all over the globe. He laid the names of his officers on mountains at north 50° and south 40°. That was a kind of love. He put the names of his sisters on New Albion. He inscribed the names of every officer he had ever respected or

---

6 **Menzies:** Archibald Menzies, famous Scots botanist.

needed up and down the coast. But most of all he loved to give abstract names to coves and headlands and passages. They would perhaps write his feelings, so seldom displayed any other way, all over the long-living geography of the southwestern half of the world. Being aboard the *Discovery* probably helped him decide upon Port Discovery, as well as Port Conclusion, Port Decision, Cape Quietude, Hesitation Harbour, The Straits of Inconsistency. He never wrote down on his charts any names that were there before he got there. He didn't imagine that one should.

And certainly (for novelists have the privilege of knowing everything) he thought a great deal about readers far in the future, as far as London and Lisbon, about what they would read when they uncovered his charts. They would read the depth of water, the true configuration of the shoreline, and the name that pressed through his exact head at the exact time that he was required to set ink to surface.

If they did not love him they would not be able to avoid him.

He had even allowed his own name to be affixed to a rock in the antipodes and a mountain in New Norfolk, as far from the common eye as possible, of a certainty.

. . . "Did you notice something odd about the *Mamathni*?" asked the first Indian the next day.

Mamathni was the Nootka word for the Europeans. In the Chickliset tongue it meant "their houses move over the water". The Indians plied canoes just about as long as the *Chatham* but they had never conceived the notion of placing chairs and tables and beds in them. Of course in their circumnavigation of the watery globe, the Englishmen, as well, one supposes, as the Spaniards, the Russians, and the French, were accustomed to being called many varied and fanciful names. A hundred miles north of here they were called *Yets-Haida,* which translated as Iron Men, a way of calling them very rich, not quite gods, but certainly permitted by the gods a favoured position in life.

"Of course," replied the second Indian now. "One cannot help noticing many odd things about them. They have, for instance, a profusion of hair upon their faces, which suggests their relationship with beasts such as the bear and the wolf. Yet they have magic glasses that make the distance near."

"Well, I mean something more basic, something one has never noticed about any other distant tribes."

"They have, of course, that thin transparent skin. I remember many years ago when I was even younger than you are now, my friends and I seized one of them and scrubbed him till the blood came. We thought they were painted pink, you see, as the northerners paint themselves grey. We got into serious trouble, but at least we found out. They are real inside and pink on the surface. It is perhaps as if their exterior skin has been removed from them, and they are compelled to face the world with their inner skin. How they must suffer in a cold wind! It is an explanation of why they wear those heavy garments covered with pieces of shining metal."

All the while these words were being said, the first Indian was fidgeting, his fingers and toes moving out of sequence, and his mouth slightly open. At last he was able to get some Nootka words in edgewise.

"In my own short lifetime I have seen over a hundred *Mamathni*. You have seen many more than I have. Our people have seen them every summer for twenty years at least."

"There are stories that our great grandfathers saw them. At least that is the most common interpretation these days of their stories about flame-bearded gods who sailed here from the sun."

The second Indian loved being middle-aged. It meant that he could be the one who passes on the stories from the old people to the young people, while still being able to pursue most of the young people's duties and pleasures. One also was credited with a certain store of wisdom. He thought he knew what his young friend was going to point out.

"What I would like to point out, if it has to be left to me," said the first Indian, "is that the *Mamathni* are all male."

That wasn't it. The second Indian was really taken aback. But it was true. There were boys on their houses that moved over the water, and there were men as old as himself. But there were no old men, and there were no females at all. It was a thought very difficult to assimilate.

"Now that you mention it, I see it. The pink people are all men. In that regard, the strangest race of people we have ever encountered. Nowhere else in nature have I ever met such a thing."

He was a truly disoriented middle-aged man for the moment.

"How do they make more of themselves, then?" asked the first Indian, as they sat on the rocks looking toward the cove where the buttoned people had last been seen.

"Perhaps they fall from the sky with the rain, as frogs do," said the second Indian.

"One of their number is often in the forest or the meadows, drawing pictures of plants, and taking plants to their floating house," said the lad. "Is it possible that they have in some way learned to mate with the plants to produce more of their kind?"

"Such a thing seems too fanciful for the imagination."

The second Indian was a little bashful for some reason, but he continued. "I have been thinking about it, and it seems to me that we should cleave to the simple line of reason."

"So you always say."

"Facts are facts."

"But the large winged craft on the sea bring us new facts in great numbers."

"Logic demands that we begin with these facts: the *Mamathni* are men, not gods; men like to fuck, but the *Mamathni* have no females in their species. Therefore, it seems plain that they fuck each other."

"Thus producing children?"

"So it would seem. You said yourself that their floating houses bring countless new facts. If a people can live with no permanently fixed home but rather houses that are nearly always in motion, they can probably produce children in their own way too."

The first Indian was playing with the scissors that had been part of the deal for the dream of the large eastern sea. He cut the leaves one by one from a salmonberry bush.

"We have our own men who like to fuck each other," he said at last.

"But they are not many. They are a minority, an exception to our ways. They are usually artists and designers and sometimes teachers. The *Mamathni* are presumably all that way."

"Maybe when men fuck men all the time it makes their skin turn pink."

"Maybe when men fuck men all the time they learn the lore that takes them great distances on winged homes filled with useful objects made of iron."

QUESTIONS

1. What does Bowering suggest about the dimension of spirituality among First Nation peoples? How do the First Nation peoples look upon the Europeans?

2. What comment is Bowering putting forth about the nature of appearance and reality?

3. What motivates Captain Vancouver in his explorations?

Jane Rule

(b. 1931)

Born in Plainfield, New Jersey, Jane Rule moved around the United States during her childhood. She graduated from Mills College in California in 1952 and attended University College, London, in 1953. After a brief teaching career in Massachusetts, Rule began writing and moved to Vancouver in 1956. She took a position at the University of British Columbia's International House and taught occasionally in UBC's creative writing program.

Her first novel, *The Desert of the Heart* (1964), is set in Reno, Nevada, and chronicles the struggle of a female university professor to accept her powerful love impulse for another woman. The exploration of lesbian relationships as well as the complexities of children with gay parents are major concerns in Rule's fiction. Her *Contract with the World* (1980) is a novel about artists who are required to make decisions and accept responsibility for their sexuality and consequent life choices. She has written three collections of short stories including *Theme for Diverse Instruments* (1975), *Outlander* (1981), and *Inland Passage* (1985), all of which concern themselves with issues faced by gays and lesbians.

"The End of Summer" comes from the *Inland Passage* collection and deals with the strained marriage of a couple who are heading toward separation and divorce. On a deeper level, the story is one of a growing awareness by Judith of the difference between the sexes. The climax is tauntingly abstract, and Judith's realization informs much of Rule's fictional attitudes toward men in general.

The End of Summer

1985

Canchek arrived promptly at eight in the morning in what looked like a new work shirt and trousers, boots that had been carefully cleaned. Even his beard looked freshly laundered. So well covered by hair and cloth, his age was readable only in his eyes, young enough still for consternation and hope.

"Your holiday's done you good," Judith Thornburn said.

"Got her pumped out?" he asked, ignoring her civility in a way she didn't mind. He was a man who didn't like wasting other people's money.

"Yes, they've just left. They couldn't see any cracks in it. Neither could I."

"You looked in it yourself?" he asked, surprised.

"I wanted to know," she answered.

Judith had been waiting for nearly a month to get this last of the summer problems solved before she closed the house for another year. There had been too many of them, a leaky skylight, a failed pump, and finally this seeping septic tank, whose pungent odours had driven her guests off the new back terrace with its lovely view. One man had dug down to it.

"It's cracked," he told her. "You'll probably have to get it replaced."

When she called Canchek in urgent concern, he said, "I'm going sailing for three weeks. She probably just needs patching. I'll do her when I get back."

There was only one other man who could be called about such things, Thompson, but, once you'd had one work for you, the other wouldn't come back unless you made it clear that you were switching sides. Thompson was an older man, garrulous, who told the widows and grass widows he worked for, "Don't go looking for trouble. Just don't put no paper down her, and don't clean your sinks with nothing to interfere with the natural process. These old places, they don't like to be disturbed any more than you do. Old plumbing is old plumbing."

"He's a harmless old coot, and at least he's friendly," those who sided with Thompson would say, and they'd add, "And he'll take a neighbourly drink and he doesn't still live with his mother."

Canchek wouldn't and Canchek did. Judith wasn't old enough yet, in her mid-thirties as Canchek was, to appreciate Thompson's vulgarity. And she was a person who liked to look for trouble, get to the bottom of it, and solve it. Canchek was her man even if she had to wait.

They walked around the house together, she carrying the trowel she had been using when he arrived.

"I thought I might lift some of the plants if you show me where you have to dig."

"Don't know yet," he said, flashing a light into the tank.

"It's odd," she said. "I even saw the cracks when we uncovered the outside, right about there, and I would have sworn they went right through. Fiberglass isn't that thick."

Canchek blew out his breath harshly before he spoke. "Not cracked," he said, and then he walked down the sodden earth below the tank, "but she's been leaking all right, for quite a while."

"Is that why that plum tree looks so sick?"

"Lost two of my own apples just to run off. Probably." He put a sympathetic hand on the trunk as he looked up to the blackened rather than turning leaves. "They're only drawn to so much water. Not like a man."

Even Canchek people said he was a dour, silent man, but good at what he did, hardworking and reliable. Perhaps that's why she valued these small attempts at conversation. They made her know that Canchek liked her, or at least didn't disapprove of her as she suspected he did a lot of people, even those who chose to be his particular customers. She didn't know why he did. She drank and smoked, both of which would probably be against his beliefs. Nobody seemed quite sure what sect it was he and his mother were the lonely representatives of. He was willing to drive a truck; he even did emergency work on Sunday, but his beard looked more like a religious than a personal choice. Judith knew so little about religious choices, she wasn't sure what anybody believed or was supposed to believe. She was not yet divorced, but the prospect seemed more and more likely. Surely Canchek wouldn't approve of that. He could easily have heard the gossip, if he listened to such things, about the Thornburn woman, out here most of the summer by herself. Husband bought her the place to get her out of the way, as so many of them did. A fancy car, a boat, whatever else she wanted or he wanted for her to show that she was well provided for. He didn't give her the one thing a man ought to give a woman: a child. Maybe, in a world increasingly both careless and frantic about money, Canchek liked her simply because the Thornburns were willing to pay the cost promptly of having things fixed.

"You can save the daisies," he said, pointing. "I'll save only some of the bulbs." Did he notice her regret when he added, "but bulbs just turn up, don't they?"

She wanted to save what flowers she could, but she also felt less guilty about asking him, or anyone, to do such an unpleasant job if she didn't flinch from it herself, and worked along with him.

"Funny thing," Canchek said as he began to dig in the area she'd indicated. "Man's the only animal that doesn't like his own smell."

Judith heard the lines, "And all is seared with trade; bleared, smeared with toil:/ And wears man's smudge and shares man's smell." Certainly Hopkins[1] didn't like it.

It was warm enough, now that the early morning fog was burning off, for another workman to take off his shirt. Canchek would not. Judith had to imagine his shoulders, the muscles of his back. She was not so much attracted to him as curious.

1 **Hopkins:** Gerard Manley Hopkins, English Jesuit priest and poet.

The skin on her husband's back already began to feel like the skin of a puppy which would grow into a large dog.

Judith supposed he still made love to her the way he still paid the bills, as a responsibility. He hadn't said anything about a divorce yet. When he first became involved with another woman and Judith confronted him, he said he expected her to be civilized about it. In front of him, she was. Alone her hysterical crying fits and destructive rages so humiliated her that he was the last person she'd subject to them. Judith hadn't even spoken to her close friends because her grief and her shame were both so boring and so predictable, as was her fantasy of being his mistress instead of his wife, the one he ran away to. This last summer, in fact, he was occasionally running away from his mistress to Judith or the quiet life she provided at what they called "the cottage." It was a good-sized house, set in some acres of woods, just across the road from the sea. His mistress was not being civilized, or she owned a vicious cat.

"At this point, my dear," said a friend Judith hadn't confided in, "they go back to their wives."

Judith couldn't see why. There were no children for whose sake things should be done. For herself, he didn't any longer seem much of a prize for her good behaviour: "Home is the sailor, home from the sea, and the hunter home from the hill." She would never expel him from the world he had paid for, but she would not move out once he'd left either.

"Look," Canchek said, "This must be the crack you saw."

She walked over and looked at the exposed curve of a badly damaged septic tank.

"That's it," she agreed.

"Well, she's not yours. She's another one."

"Really?"

"They must of broken this one putting her in, just smashed her up a bit more and put in this other one."

"Why didn't they take the broken one out?"

"Couldn't be bothered maybe. These guys with machines won't get off them. Some of them don't even own a shovel."

Canchek pulled great pieces of fibreglass out of the soil until he and she could have played at a giant jigsaw puzzle, but he was not interested in the wreckage. He wanted to find out what was leaking. As he dug, he occasionally grunted in discovery and disgust.

"There's no septic field here at all, nothing but some tile and mud. I'll have to get pipe."

He had done enough work around the place for her to know he begrudged any purchase of new material if what was around could be used. Whether it belonged to the rich or the pensioned, money was money.

"We'll need some rocks," he said, kicking about in the tall grass where cultivation ended.

"There's a pile over here," she offered. "They came out of the garden."

He did not look up or acknowledge her offer, intent on his own search which seemed to her odd. Judith would not have looked for rocks like Easter eggs in the field grass.

Canchek grunted and sank down on his haunches, like a hunter checking prints and droppings, only the crest of his dark hair visible among the tassle tops. Then he stood up, shaking his head.

"You know, there's as sure a wrong way to do it as there is a right way. Look at this."

Judith followed his path to where he stood, and there spreading out beside him was a sprawling pile of stones nearly uniform in size, hidden in the tall grass. She remembered having seen it in spring, matted over with last year's rot before new grass began to grow again.

"Why do they even dump it on the site if they don't intend to use it?" he asked himself and then gave his answer. "They call in the inspector just before they're going to lay the pipe. He sees the trenches. He sees the pile of rock, says, 'Okay, boys, that's good.' And the minute he turns his back, they bulldoze the trenches and go home. What did I tell you? Not a shovel to their name!"

It was a long speech for Canchek. He walked over to the collapsed septic tank and dragged it over to his van.

"I'll take this to the dump on my way to get the pipe," he said.

"You can fix it then?" she asked.

"Sure, today," he answered and smiled at her slumping relief.

Judith had had her frugal lunch before Canchek returned, knowing he would have stopped for a man's lunch with his mother, a woman Judith had never met. Mrs Canchek spoke only enough English to call her son to the phone or say when he would be back. As far as Judith knew, she never left the place, a well-made log cabin in a clearing as neat and bare as a table top between meals. Canchek did their shopping. Occasionally Mrs Canchek could be seen behind the high deer fence around the vegetable garden, hoeing, drab kerchief around her head, skirts to the ground, a peasant in a painting. There were neither chickens nor dog to keep her company. The only sign of companionability was a bird feeder outside what was probably a kitchen window. No one was ever invited in.

Judith did not go out at once to greet him. She stayed at her own kitchen table and watched him work, shoveling new trenches away from the uncovered septic tank, like fingers stretching away from a palm, down hill. It was hot now, and, though the tank had been emptied, the soil he dug in must be putrid with clogging waste. Yet he was taking time, like a man not reckoning the hours, to sift what good bulbs he found and pile them for her to replant in the restored bed. As son to woman, obedient to her love of flowers, though there were none in his own beaten and swept yard. Was he, in fact, good to his mother? Or did he go home and sit sullen with the burden she was to him and let her bring him servile offerings?

The phone rang. Judith let it ring six times before she answered it.

"Outdoors, were you?" her husband asked, his dictating cheerfulness always freshly insulting her.

Judith wanted to answer truthfully, but instead said, "I'm digging out the septic tank with Canchek."

"My God, Judy, martyrdom doesn't have to go that far. Surely, the man is paid enough—if I recall the last bill correctly—to do it himself."

"I wanted to save the bulbs," she answered defensively.

"Buy more; buy a carload."

Is there any point? Is there going to be a next year, she wanted to ask him, but she didn't.

"One of the reasons Canchek's so expensive is that he's too cheap to buy himself machinery. Is he out there with a shovel? I bet he is."

"He says it's the only way to do it properly," Judith answered.

"Once a shit shoveller, always a shit shoveller. Is he going to get it done by the week-end?"

"He said he'd be finished today."

"Good. I'll be down then, tomorrow."

"Driving?"

"No, I'm beat. I'll take the early train."

He didn't ask her to meet him any more than he would ask to come down. At first, she had cancelled whatever other plans she had made either to go out, which he wouldn't want to do, or have friends in, because she didn't trust herself to keep up the façade with an attentive audience. Lately, she had not made week-end plans, a time she spent either in relieved loneliness or in nervous dread that this would be the last time. By now, she was equally afraid that he would decide to re-establish himself in their life or end it.

Canchek was now kneeling, replacing the terracotta tiles he had dug up. It would have been no use or terrible use to have had a son, if not materially bound to her as Canchek was to his mother, still guilty to leave her as his father had done before him. People said it was harder for a man to leave when there were children. Was it? Sometimes Judith imagined her husband regretting his refusal to be a father, easier to leave her in children's distracting company than alone. But that allowed him some concern for her feelings. He didn't want to know she had any.

Canchek was now laying the long black perforated pipe along a trench, his feet planted on either side, walking backwards. She envied him a task to be absorbed in, then remembered the stench of it for a man whose only known pleasure was sailing, the freshening breeze taking him far out from shore until salt purified the odours of earth and the far horizon promised nothing, nothing at all.

He was standing at the back door.

"Have you got a bucket?" he asked.

His eyes were darker than they had been in the morning, as if they had absorbed the colour of earth. He had put on a sweat band. It pressed at his hairline, forcing his hair to stand up like a dark crop.

She found two buckets and went out with him to gather stones from the pile he had found. A wheelbarrow would have been more efficient, and there was one in the garden shed, but she did not want to think her husband's thoughts. A breeze had come up from shore with the faintest bite of autumn in it, cooling the afternoon, making their harvesting of rock easier. Sometimes he stopped to shovel dirt over the rock they had strewn, leaving her to haul by herself, and alone with her own job she felt more companionable with him, as if he accepted a simple partnership.

It was nearly six o'clock when they finished, the light nearly gone. She washed out the buckets while he collected scraps and tools.

"May I get you something?" Judith asked. "Coffee? A cold drink?"

"Fill her up as soon as you can," he said. "I'll cover her up tomorrow, some time before dark."

She nodded but waited, keeping the question between them.

"Her," he said finally, nodding his head in a downward direction.

An apology, an excuse. Was that how her husband left his woman with that grunted female pronoun and a nod in the direction of the sea? Perhaps Canchek preferred a mother to a woman with more ambiguous needs and motives. Nothing bound him really but his acceptance of the bond.

"Thank you," she said. "I'm so glad it could be done."

"There's always a way to do it right," he said.

Canchek had not returned by the time Judith left to meet her husband's train. There was still an hour of daylight. To defend Canchek, she wanted him to have come and gone before she returned. For herself, she wanted him to be there when she got back, she couldn't say why. Canchek could not prevent anything from happening or make it happen, a dark figure in the dusk, shovelling.

"He doesn't look quite human," her husband observed out the kitchen window, pouring himself a drink.

"He said yesterday, 'Man's the only animal that doesn't like his own smell.'"

"What's that supposed to mean?" her husband asked.

"Just that, to him," Judith answered.

"To you?" her husband asked, and she heard in his tone what she had been waiting for, hopefully, then dreadfully, for months.

"A reason for being civilized?" she suggested mildly.

He took a long drink and set the glass down. There wasn't a trace of summer in his face, of sea or earth. He was bleached with tiredness. She couldn't offer him anything either. He had, in his own house, helped himself.

"I've appreciated it," he said flatly.

The months' long fuse of her fury sputtered up toward an explosion right behind her eyes. The second before it ignited, Canchek's fist on the back door banged it out.

"She's done," he said.

"Come have a drink," Judith's husband suggested, humanly enough, "after a stinking job like that."

But Canchek had turned away quickly after his announcement and was gone. Judith stood in the doorway, looking out at the buried tank, its now secret fingers also properly rock-and-earth-covered, the surface carefully raked to prepare for bulbs, the old ones Canchek had saved and the carload her husband wanted her to buy. They would camouflage and be nourished by man's "smudge and smell," which Canchek, and perhaps all men, called by the name of "she," as they did ships which would bear them away. Judith turned back to her husband.

"Thank you," he said.

"You're welcome," Judith answered, seeing him for the first time in months as clearly as she saw Canchek, but this man was her husband, at home.

QUESTIONS

1. What does the character of Canchek in the story represent?

2. Judith Thornburn's economic situation has been determined by her relationship with her husband. How does this dependency affect her actions?

3. Compare and contrast Judith's husband and Canchek.

4. What is the significance of the title of the story?

5. What causes Judith's near angry explosion at her husband just before Canchek knocks at the door suddenly?

Austin Clarke

(b. 1934)

Born in poverty on the island of Barbados, Clarke was well educated in a British school system on the island. In his memoir, *Growing Up Stupid Under the Union Jack* (1980), Clarke may be critical of some of the aspects of his education, but when he graduated from Harrison College in 1952, he was well enough educated in English to teach at a rural school. Clarke came to Trinity College, University of Toronto, in 1955 to study economics, but dropped out, married, and took a number of menial jobs that allowed him time to practice writing. Eventually he took a job as a journalist in northern Ontario. In 1962, he began work on what would become three of his most important works: *The Survivors of the Crossing* (1964), *Amongst Thistles and Thorns* (1965), and *The Meeting Point* (1967). He worked as a freelance broadcaster for Canadian Broadcasting Corporation in the mid-1960s, commenting on black issues in North America and England.

Clarke's strength resides in his ability to use humor to make some serious comments on the struggle of poor blacks in both Barbados and North America. For example, *Amongst Thistles and Thorns* is a lively and amusing novel telling how a couple of Barbados cane-cutters try to start a revolution. In the late 1960s and 1970s, Clarke taught at a number of U.S. universities and was the cultural attaché to the Barbadian embassy in Washington. During this period he wrote three very powerful novels exploring the difficulties of Caribbean immigrants in Toronto. The Caribbean characters in *The Meeting Point* (1966), *Storm of Fortune* (1971), and *The Bigger Light* (1975) are believable because of the language and situations they confront. Clarke's depiction of racism and economic exploitation is vivid and disturbing.

In 1977, Clarke returned to Canada and sat on a number of community boards and continued to write fiction about the struggle of immigrants into Canada, many of which were short stories. His second collection, *When He Was Free and Young and He Used to Wear Silks* (1971), contains the story that follows. He wrote four subsequent volumes: *When Women Rule* (1985), *Nine Men Who Laughed* (1986), *In This City* (1992), and *There Are No Elders* (1993). In all these selections, Caribbean characters struggle against the hostility in Canada, but also among themselves. Clarke's most recent novel, *The Polished Hoe*, won the Giller Prize for fiction in 2002.

"Griff!" deals with environmental rootlessness and the psychological and emotional problems this presents for immigrants to Toronto. Griff's wife knows that her husband has serious problems adjusting to Canadian life, but she is unable to reach him, for she is limited by her artificial English gentility.

Griff!   *1985*

Griff was a black man from Barbados who sometimes denied he was black. Among black Americans who visited Toronto, he was black: "Right on!" "Peace and love, Brother!" and "Power to the people!" would suddenly become his vocabulary. He had emigrated to Toronto from Britain, and as a result, thought of himself as a black Englishman. But he was blacker than most immigrants. In colour, that is. It must have been this double indemnity of being British and black that caused him to despise his blackness. To his friends, and his so-called friends, he flaunted his British experience, and the "civilized" bearing that came with it; and he liked being referred to as a West Indian who had lived in London, for he was convinced that he had an edge, in breeding, over those West Indians who had come straight to Canada from the canefields in the islands. He had attended Ascot[1] many times and he had seen the Queen in her box. He hated to be regarded as just black.

"Griff, but you're blasted black, man," Clynn said once, at a party in his own home, "and the sooner you realize that fact, the more rass-hole wiser you would be!" Clynn usually wasn't so honest, but that night he was drunk.

What bothered Griff along with his blackness was that most of his friends were "getting through": cars and houses and "swinging parties" every Friday night, and a

---

1 **Ascot:** Famous fashionable horseracing track in England near London.

yearly trip back home for Christmas and for Carnival. Griff didn't have a cent in the bank. "And you don't even have *one* blasted child, neither!" Clynn told him that same night.

But Griff was the best-dressed man present. They all envied him for that. And nobody but his wife really knew how poor he was in pocket. Griff smiled at them from behind his dark-green dark glasses. His wife smiled too, covering her embarrassment for her husband. She never criticized him in public, by gesture or by attitude, and she said very little to him about his ways, in their incensed apartment. Nevertheless, she carried many burdens of fear and failure for her husband's apparent ambitionless attitudes. England had wiped some British manners on her, too. Deep down inside, Griff was saying to Clynn and the others, *godblindyougodblindyou!*

"Griffy, dear, pour your wife a Scotch, darling. I've decided to enjoy myself." She was breathing as her yoga teacher had taught her to do.

And Griffy said, *godblindyougodblindyou!* again, to Clynn; poured his wife her drink, poured himself a large Scotch on the rocks, and vowed, *I am going to drink all your Scotch tonight, boy!* This was his only consolation. Clynn's words had become wounds. Griff grew so centred around his own problems that he did not, for one moment, consider any emotion coming from his wife. "She's just a nice kid," he told Clynn once, behind her back. He had draped his wife in an aura of sanctity; and he would become angry to the point of violence, and scare anybody, when he thought his friends' conversation had touched the cloud and virginity of sanctity in which he had clothed her: like taking her out on Friday and Saturday nights to the Cancer Calypso Club, in the entrails of the city, where pimps and doctors and lonely immigrants hustled women and brushed reputations in a brotherhood of illegal liquor. And if the Club got too crowded, Griff would feign a headache, and somehow make his wife feel the throbbing pain of his migraine, and would take her home in a taxi, and would recover miraculously on his way back along Sherbourne Street, and with the tact of a good barrister, would make tracks back to the Cancer and dance the rest of the limp-shirt night with a woman picked from among the lonely West Indian stags: his jacket let loose to the sweat and the freedom, his body sweet with the music rejoicing in the happy absence of his wife in the sweet presence of this woman.

But after these hiatuses of dance, free as the perspiration pouring down his face, his wife would be put to bed around midnight, high up in the elevator, high off the invisible hog of credit, high up on the Chargex Card, and Griff would be tense, for days. It was a tenseness which almost gripped his body in a paralysis, as it strangled the blood in his body when the payments of loans for furniture and for debts approached, and they always coincided with the approaching of his paycheque, already earmarked against its exact face value. In times of this kind of stress, like his anxiety at the racetrack, when the performance of a horse contradicted his knowledge of the Racing Form and left him broke, he would grumble, "Money is *naught* all."

Losing his money would cause him to ride on streetcars, and he hated any kind of public transportation. He seemed to realize his blackness more intensely; white people looking at him hard—questioning his presence, it seemed. It might be nothing more than the way his colour changed colour, going through a kaleidoscope of tints and shades under the varying ceiling lights of the streetcar. Griff never saw it this way. To him, it was staring. And his British breeding told him that to look at a person you didn't know (except she was a woman) was *infra dig.*[2] *Infra dig* was the term he chose when he told Clynn about these incidents of people staring at him on the streetcars. The term formed itself on his broad thin lips, and he could never get the courage to spit it at the white people staring at him.

When he lost his money, his wife, after not having had dinner nor the money to buy food (the landlord locked the apartment door with a padlock one night while they were at a party), would smile in that half-censuring smile, a smile that told you she had been forced against the truth of her circumstances, to believe with him, that money was "not all, at-all." But left to herself, left to the ramblings of her mind and her aspirations and her fingers over the new broadloom in her girl-friend's home, where her hand clutched the tight sweating glass of Scotch on the rocks, her Scotch seeming to absorb her arriving unhappiness with the testimony of her friend's broadloom, or in Clynn's recreation room, which she called a "den"; in her new sponge of happiness, fabricated like the house in her dreams, she would put her smile around her husband's losses, and in the embrace they would both feel higher than anybody present, because, "Griffy, dear, you were the only one there with a Master of Arts."

"I have more brains than *any one* there. They only coming-on strong. But I don't have to come on strong, uh mean, I don't *have* to come on strong, but . . ."

One day, at Greenwood Race Track, Griff put his hand into his pocket and pulled out five twenty-dollar bills, and put them on one race: he put three twenty-dollar bills on Number Six, on *the fucking nose—to win! Eh?* (he had been drinking earlier at the Pilot Tavern); and he also put two twenty-dollar bills on Number Six, *to show.* He had studied the Racing Form like a man studying his torts: he would put it into his pocket, take it out again, read it in the bathroom as he trimmed his moustache; he studied it on the sweet-smelling toilet bowl, he studied it as he might have studied laws in Britain; and when he spoke of his knowledge in the Racing Form, it was as if he had received his degrees in the Laws of Averages, and not in English Literature and Language.

And he "gave" a horse to a stranger that same day at Greenwood. "Buy Number Three, man. I read the Form for three days, taking notes. It *got* to be Number Three!" The man thanked him because he himself was no expert; and he spent five dollars (more than he had ever betted before) on Number Three, to *win.* "I read the Form like a blasted book, man!" Griff told him. He slipped away to the wicket farthest away; and like a thief, he bought his own tickets: "Number Six! Sixty on the nose! forty to show!" and to himself he said, smiling, "Law o' averages, man, law of averages."

Tearing up Number Six after the race, he said to the man who had looked for him to thank him, and who thanked him and shook his hand and smiled with him,

2 *infra dig:* Latin for "beneath one's dignity."

"I don't have to come on strong, man, I *mastered* that Form." He looked across the field to the board at the price paid on Number Three, and then he said to the man, "Lend me two dollars for the next race, man. I need a bet."

The man gave him three two-dollar bills and told him, "*Any* time, pardner, any time! Keep the six dollars. Thank *you!*"

Griff was broke. Money is *naught* all, he was telling the same man who, seeing him waiting by the streetcar stop, had picked him up. Griff settled himself back into the soft leather of the new Riviera, going west, and said again to the man, "Money is naught all! But I don't like to come on strong. Uh mean, you see how I mastered the *Form,* did you?"

"You damn right, boy!" the man said, adjusting the tone of the tape-deck. "How you like my new car?"

The elevator was silent that evening, on the way up to the twenty-fifth floor; and he could not even lose his temper with it: "This country is uncivilized—even the elevators—they make too much noise a man can't even think in them; this place only has money but it doesn't have any culture or breeding or style so everybody is grabbing for money money money." The elevator that evening didn't make a comment. And neither did his wife: she had been waiting for him to come from work, straight, with the money untouched in his monthly paycheque. But Griff had studied the Racing Form thoroughly all week, and had worked out the laws and averages and notations in red felt-pen ink; had circled all the "long shots" in green, and had moved through the "donkeys" (the slow horses) with waves of blue lines; had had three "sure ones" for that day; and had averaged his wins against heavy bets against his monthly salary, it was such a "goddamn cinch"! He had developed a migraine headache immediately after lunch, slipped through the emergency exit at the side, holding his head in his hand, his head full of tips and cinches, and had caught the taxi which miraculously had been waiting there, with the meter ticking; had run through the entrance of the racetrack, up the stairs, straight for the wicket to be on the Daily Double; had invested fifty dollars on a "long shot" (worked out scientifically from his red-marked, green-and-blue wavy-line Form), and had placed "two goddamn dollars" on the favourite—just to be sure!—and went into the clubhouse. The favourite won. Griff lost fifty dollars by the first race. But had won two dollars on his two-dollar bet.

"I didn't want to come on strong," he told the man who was then a stranger to him. The man could not understand what he was talking about: and he asked for no explanation. "I didn't want to come on strong, but I worked out all the winners today, since ten o'clock last night. I *picked* them, man. I can pick them. But I was going for the 'long shot.' Hell, what is a little bread? Fifty dollars! Man, that isn't no bread, at all. If I put my hand in my pocket now, look . . . *this is* bread! . . . five *hundred* dollars. I can lose, man, I can afford to lose bread. Money don't mean anything to me, man, money is no *big* thing! . . . money is *naught* all."

His wife remained sitting on the Scandinavian couch, which had the habit of whispering to them, once a month, "Fifty-nine thirty-five owing on me!" in payments. She looked up at Griff as he gruffed through the door. She smiled. Her face did not change its form, or its feeling, but she smiled. Griff grew stiff at the smile. She got up from the couch. She brushed the anxiety of time from her waiting miniskirt ("My wife must dress well, and look *sharp,* even in the house!"), she tidied the already-tidy hairdo she had just got from Azans, and she went into the kitchen, which was now a wall separating Griff from her. Griff looked at the furniture, and wished he could sell it all in time for the races tomorrow afternoon: the new unpaid-for living-room couch, desk, matching executive chair, the table and matching chairs where they ate, desk pens thrown in, into the bargain the salesman swore he was giving them, ten Friday nights ago down Yonge Street, scatter rugs, Scandinavian-type settee with its matching chairs, like Denmark in the fall season, in style and design; he looked at the motto, CHRIST IS THE HEAD OF THIS HOME, which his wife had insisted upon taking as another "bargain"; and he thought of how relaxed he felt driving in the man's new Riviera. He took the new Racing Form, folded in half and already no-tated, from his breast pocket, and sat on the edge of the bed, in the wisteria-smelling bedroom. His wife had been working, he said to himself, as he noticed he was sitting on his clean folded pyjamas. But he left them there and perused the handicaps and histories of the horses. The bundle buggy for shopping was rolling over the polished wood of the living-room floor. The hinges of the doors of the clothes cupboard in the hallway were talking. A clothes hanger dropped on the skating rink of the floor. The cupboard door was closed. The bundle buggy rolled down from its prop against the cupboard and jangled onto the hardboard ice. Griff looked up and saw a smooth brown, black-maned horse standing before him. It was his wife.

"Griffy, dear? I am ready." She had cleaned out her pocketbook of old papers, useless personal and business cards accumulated over drinks and at parties; and she had made a budget of her month's allowance, allowing a place in the tidied wallet section for her husband's arrival. The horse in Griff's mind changed into a donkey. "Clynn called. He's having a party tonight. Tennish. After the supermarket, I want to go round to the corner, to the cleaners' and stop off at the liquor store for a bottle of wine. My sisters're coming over for dinner, and they're bringing their boy-friends. I want to have a roast. Should I also buy you a bottle of Black-and-White, Griffy, dear?": *they're at post! they're off! . . . as they come into the backstretch, moving for the wire . . . it's Phil Kingston by two lengths, Crimson Admiral, third, True Willie . . . Phil Kingston, Crimson Admiral, True Willie . . .* but Griff had already moved downstairs, in the direction of the cashiers' wicket: "Long shot in your arse! Uh got it, this time, old man!" *True Willie is making a move. True Willie! . . . Phil Kingston now by one length, True Willie is coming on the outside! True Willie! It's True Willie!*

"It's almost time for the supermarket to close, Griff dear, and I won't like to be running about like a race horse, sweating and perspiring. I planned my housework and I tried to finish all my housework on time so I'll be fresh for when you came home. I took my time, too, doing my housework and I took a shower so I won't get excited by the time my sisters come and I didn't bother to go to my yoga class" *it's True Willie by a neck! True Willie! What a run, ladies and gentlemen! what a run! True Willie's the winner, and it's now official!* "and I even made a promise to budget this month so we'll have some money for all these bills we have to pay. We have to pay these bills and we never seem to be paying them off and the rent's due in two days, no, today! oh, I forgot to tell you that the bank manager called about your loan, to say that" *it's True Willie, by a neck!*

Griff smashed all the furniture in the apartment in his mind, and then walked through the door. "Oh Griffy, dear! Stooly called to say he's getting a lift to the races tomorrow and if you're going he wants you to . . ."

Griff was standing in the midst of a group of middle-aged West Indians, all of whom pretended through the amount of liquor they drank, and the "gashes they lashed" that they were still young black studs.

"Man, when I entered that door, she knew better than to open her fucking mouth to me! To *me? Me?*" The listening red eyes understood the unspoken chastisement in his threatening voice. "Godblindyou! she knew better than, *that*; me? if she'd only opened her fucking mouth, I would have . . ." They raised their glasses, all of them, to their mouths, not exactly at the same time, but sufficiently together, to make it a ritualistic harmony among men. "As man!" Griff said, and then wet his lips. They would, each of them, have chastised their women in precisely the same way that Griff was boasting about disciplining his. But he never did. He could never even put his hand to his wife's mouth to stop her from talking. And she was not the kind of woman you would want to beat: she was much too delicate. The history of their marriage had coincided with her history of a woman's illness which had been kept silent among them; and its physical manifestation, in the form of a large scar that crawled halfway around her neck, darker in colour than the natural shade of her skin, had always, from the day of recovery after the operation, been covered by a neckline on each of her dresses. And this became her natural style and fashion in clothes. Sometimes, in more daring moods, she would wear a silk scarf to hide the scar. "If my wife wasn't so blasted sickly, I would've put my hand in her arse, *many times!* I've thought o' putting my hand in her arse, after a bad day at the races!" He had even thought of doing something drastic about her smile and about his losses at the track and at poker. It was not clearly shaped in his mind: and at times, with this violent intent, he could not think of whom he would perform this drastic act on. After a bad day at the track, the thought of the drastic act, like a cloud over his thoughts, would beat him down and take its toll out of his slim body which itself seemed to refuse to bend under the great psychological pressure of losing, all the time. He had just lost one hundred dollars at Woodbine Race Track, when one evening as he entered Clynn's living-room, for the usual Friday night party of Scotch and West Indian peas and rice and chicken, which Clynn's Polish wife cooked and spoiled and learned how to cook as she spoiled the food, he had just had time to adjust his shoulders in the over-sized sports jacket, when he said, braggingly, "I just dropped a hundred. At Woodbine." He wet his lips and smiled.

"Dollars?" It was Clynn's voice, coming from the dark corner where he poured drinks. Clynn was a man who wouldn't lend his sister, nor his mother—if she was still alive—more than five dollars at one time.

"Money don't mean anything, man."

"A *hundred* dollars?" Clynn suddenly thought of the amount of Scotch Griff had been drinking in his house.

"Money is *naught* all."

"You're a blasted . . . boy, do you lose *just* for fun or wha'?" Clynn sputtered. "Why the arse you don't become a *groom,* if you like racehorse so much? Or you's a . . . a *paffological* loser?"

"Uh mean, I don't like to come on strong, or anything, but, money is *naught* all . . ."

"Rass-hole put down my Scotch, then! You drinking my fucking Scotch!"

And it rested there. It rested there because Griff suddenly remembered he was among men who knew him: who knew his losses both in Britain and Canada. It rested there also, because Clynn and the others knew that his manner and attitude towards money, and his wife's expressionless smile, were perhaps lying expressions of a turbulent inner feeling of failure. "He prob'ly got rass-hole ulcers, too!" Clynn said, and then spluttered into a laugh. Griff thought about it, and wondered whether he had indeed caused his wife to be changed into a different woman altogether. But he couldn't know that. Her smile covered a granite of silent and apparent contentment. He wondered whether he hated her, to the bone, and whether she hated him. He felt a spasm through his body as he thought of her hating him, and not knowing about it. For so many years living together, both here and in Britain; and she was always smiling. Her constancy and her cool exterior, her smiles, all made him wonder now, with the Scotch in his hand, about her undying devotion to him, her faithfulness, pure as the sheets in their sweet-smelling bedroom; he wondered whether "I should throw my hand in her arse, *just* to see what she would do." But Clynn had made up his own mind that she was, completely, destroyed inside: her guts, her spirit, her aspirations, her procreative mechanism, "Hysterectomy all shot to pieces!" Clynn said cruelly, destroyed beyond repair, beneath the silent consolation and support which he saw her giving to her husband; at home among friends and relations, and in public among his sometimes silently criticizing friends. "I don't mean to come on strong, but . . ."

"You really want to know what's wrong with Griff?" Clynn's sister, Princess, asked one day. "He want a *stiff* lash in his backside! He don't know that he's gambling-'way his wife's life? He doesn't know that? Look, he don't have chick nor child! Wife working in a good job, for *decent* money, and they don't even live in a decent apartment that you could say, well, rent eating out his sal'ry. Don't own no record-player. *Nothing.* And all he doing is walking 'bout Toronto with his blasted head high in the air! He ain' know this is Northamerica? Christ, he don't even speak to poor people. He ain' have no motto-car, like some. Well, you tell me then, what the hell is Griff doing with thirteen-thousand Canadian dollars a year? Supporting race-horse? No, man, you can't tell me that, 'cause not even the *most* wutless o' Wessindians living in Toronto, could gamble-'way thirteen thousand dollars! Jesuschrist! that is twenty-six thousand back in Barbados! Think o' the land he could buy back home wid thirteen-thousand Canadian dollars. And spending it 'pon a race-horse? What the hell is a race-horse? *Thirteen thousand?* But lissen to me! One o' these mornings, that wife o' his going get up and tell him that she with-child, that she *pregnunt . . .*" ("She can't get pregnunt, though, Princess, 'cause she already had one o' them operations!") "Anyhow, if his wife was a diff'rent person, she would 'ave walked-out on his arse *long ago!* Or else, break his two blasted hands! and she won't spend a *day* in jail!"

When Griff heard what Princess had said about him, he shrugged his shoulders and said, "I don't have to come on strong, but if I was a different man, I would really show these West Indian women something . . ." He ran his thin, long, black fingers over the length of his old-fashioned slim tie, he shrugged the grey sports jacket that was a size too large, at the shoulders, into shape and place, wet his lips twice, and said, "Grimme another Scotch, man." While Clynn fixed the Scotch, he ran his thumb and index finger of his left hand down the razor edge of his dark brown trouser seams. He inhaled and tucked his shirt and tie neatly beneath the middle button of his sports jacket. He took the Scotch, which he liked to drink on the rocks, and he said, "I don't have to come on strong, but I am going to tell you something . . ."

The next Friday night was the first day of fête in the long weekend. There hadn't been a long weekend in Canada for a long time. Everybody was tired of just going to work, coming home, watching CBC television, bad movies on the TV, and then going to bed. "There ain' no action in this fucking town," Clynn was saying for days, before the weekend appeared like raindrops on a farmer's dry-season head. And everybody agreed with him. It was so. Friday night was here, and the boys, their wives, their girl-friends, and their "outside women" were noisy and drunk and happy. Some of the men were showing off their new bell-bottom trousers and broad leather belts worn under their bulging bellies, to make them look younger. The women, their heads shining like wet West Indian tar roads, the smell from the cosmetics and grease that went into their kinky hair and on their faces, to make them look sleek and smooth, all these smells and these women mixed with the cheap and domestic perfumes they used, whenever Avon called; and some women, wives who husbands "were getting through," were wearing good-looking dresses, in style and fashion; others were still back home in their style, poured in against their wishes and the better judgement of their bulging bodies; backsides big, sometimes too big, breasts bigger, waists fading into the turbulence of middle age and their be-hinds, all poured against the shape of their noisy bodies, into evil-fitting, shiny material, made on sleepy nights after work, on a borrowed sewing machine. But everybody was happy. They had all forgotten now, through the flavour of the ca-lypso and the peas and the rice, the fried chicken, the curry-chicken, that they were still living in a white man's country; and it didn't seem to bother them now, nor touch them now. Tonight, none of them would tell you that they hated Canada; that they wanted to go back home; that they were going "to make a little money, first"; that they were only waiting till then; that they were going to go back before the "blasted Canadian tourisses buy-up the blasted Caribbean"; they wouldn't tell you tonight that they all suffered some form of racial discrimination in Canada, and that that was to be expected, since "there are certain things with this place that are not just right"; not tonight. Tonight, Friday night, was forgetting night. West Indian night. And they were at the Cancer Club to forget and to drink and to get drunk. To make plans for some strange woman's (or man's) body and bed, to spend "some time" with a real West Indian "thing," to eat her boiled mackerel and green bananas, which their wives and women had, in their ambitions to be "decent" and Canadian, forgotten how to cook, and had left out of their diets, especially when Canadian friends were coming to dinner, because that kind of food was "plain West Indian stupidness." Tonight, they would forget and drink, forget and dance, and dance to forget.

"Oh-Jesus-Christ, Griff!" Stooly shouted, as if he was singing a calypso. He greeted Griff this way each time he came to the Club, and each time it was as if Stooly hadn't seen Griff in months, although they might have been together at the track the same afternoon. It was just the way Stooly was. "Oh-Jesus-Christ, Griff!" he would shout, and then he would rush past Griff, ignoring him, and make straight for Griff's wife. He would wrap his arms round her slender body (once his left hand squeezed a nipple, and Griff saw, and said to himself, "Uh mean, I won't like to come on strong about it, but . . ."; and did nothing about it), pulling up her new minidress above the length of decency, worn for the first time tonight, exposing the expensive lace which bordered the tip of her slip. The veins of her hidden age, visible only at the back of her legs, would be exposed to Griff, who would stand and stare and feel "funny," and feel, as another man inquired with his hands all over his wife's body, the blood and the passion and the love mix with the rum in his mouth. Sometimes, when in a passion of brandy, he would make love to his wife as if she was a different woman, as if she was no different from one of the lost women found after midnight on the crowded familiar floor of the Cancer.

"Haiii! How?" the wife would say, all the time her body was being crushed. She would say, "Haiii! How?" every time it happened; and it happened every time; and every time it happened, Griff would stand and stare, and do nothing about it, because his memory of British breeding told him so; but he would feel mad and helpless afterwards, all night; and he would always want to kill Stooly, or kill his wife for doing it; but he always felt she was so fragile. He would want to kill Stooly more than he would want to kill his wife. But Stooly came from the same island as his wife. Griff would tell Clynn the next day, on the telephone, that he should have done something about it; but he "didn't want to come on strong." Apparently, he was not strong enough to rescue his wife from the rape of Stooly's arms, as he rubbed his body against hers, like a dog scratching its fleas against a tree.

Once, a complete stranger saw it happen. Griff had just ordered three drinks: one for his wife, one for himself, and one for Stooly, his friend. Griff looked at the man, and in an expansive mood (he had made the "long shot" in the last race at Woodbine that afternoon), he asked the stranger, "What're you drinking?"

"Rum, sah!"

"I am going to buy you a goddamn drink, just because I like you, man."

The stranger did not change the mask on his face, but stood there, looking at Griff's dark-green lenses. Then he said, "You isn' no blasted man at all, man!" He then looked behind: Stooly was still embracing Griff's wife. It looked as if he was feeling her up. The man took the drink from Griff, and said, "You is no man, sah!"

Griff laughed; but no noise came out of his mouth. "Man, that's all right. They went to school together in Trinidad."

"In *my* books, you still ain' no fucking man, boy!" The stranger turned away from Griff: and when he got to the door of the dance floor, he said, "Thanks for the drink, *boy*."

The wife was standing beside Griff now, smiling as if she was a queen parading through admiring lines of subjects. She looked, as she smiled, like she was under the floodlights of some première performance she had prepared herself for a long time. She smiled, although no one in particular expected a smile from her. Her smiling went hand in hand with her new outfit. It had to be worn with a smile. It looked good, as usual, on her; and it probably understood that it could only continue to look good and express her personality if she continued smiling. At intervals, during the night, when you looked at her, it seemed as if she had taken the smile from her handbag, and had then powdered it onto her face. She could have taken it off any time, but she chose to wear it the whole night. "Griffy, dear?" she said, although she wasn't asking him anything, or telling him anything, or even looking in his direction. "Haiii! How?" she said to a man who brushed against her hips as he passed. The man looked suddenly frightened, because he wanted his advance to remain stealthy and masculine. When he passed back from the bar, with five glasses of cheap rum-and-Cokes in his hands, he walked far from her.

Griff was now leaning on the bar, facing the part-time barman, and talking about the results of the last race that day; his wife, her back to the bar, was looking at the men and the women, and smiling; when someone passed, who noticed her, and lingered in the recognition, she would say, "Haiii! How?"

A large, black, badly dressed Jamaican (he was talking his way through the crowd) passed. He stared at her. She smiled. He put out his calloused construction hand, and with a little effort, he said, "May I have this dance, gal?" Griff was still talking. But in his mind he wondered whether his wife would dance with the Jamaican. He became ashamed with himself for thinking about it. He went back to talking, and got into an argument with the part-time barman, Masher, over a certain horse that was running in the feature race the next day at Greenwood. Masher, ever watchful over the women, especially other men's, couldn't help notice that the calloused-hand Jamaican was holding on to Griff's wife's hand. With his shark-eyes he tried to get Griff's attention off horses and onto his wife. But Griff was too preoccupied. His wife placed her drink on the counter beside him, her left hand still in the paws of the Jamaican construction worker, whom nobody had seen before, and she said, "Griffy, dear?" The man's hand on her manicured fingers had just come into his consciousness, when he wheeled around to give her her drink. He was upset. But he tried to be cool. It was the blackness of the Jamaican. And his size. Masher knew he was upset. The Jamaican reminded Griff of the "Congo-man" in one of Sparrow's calypsos. Masher started to laugh in his spitting kee-kee laugh. And when Griff saw that everybody was laughing, and had seen the Congojamaican walk off with his wife, he too decided to laugh.

"It's all right, man," he said, more than twice, to no one in particular, although he could have been consoling the Jamaicancongo man, or Masher, or the people nearby, or himself.

"I sorry, suh," the Jamaican said. He smiled to show Griff that he was not a rough fellow. "I am sorry, suh. I didn't know you was with the missis. I thought the missis was by-sheself, tonight, again, suh."

"It's no *big* thing, man," Griff said, turning back to talk to Masher, who by now had lost all interest in horses. Masher had had his eyes on Griff's wife, too. But Griff was worried by something new now: the man had said, "*by-sheself, tonight, again, suh*"; and that could mean only one thing: that his wife went places, like this very Club, when he wasn't with her; and he had never thought of this, and never even imagined her doing a thing like this; and he wasn't sure that it was not merely the bad grammar of the Jamaican, and not the accusation in that bad grammar, "*but language is a funny thing, a man could kill a person with language, and the accusation can't be comprehended outside of the structure of the language . . . wonder how you would parse this sentence, Clynn . . . a Jamaican fella told me last night, 'by-sheself, tonight, again, suh'; now, do you put any emphasis on the position of the adverb, more than the conditional phrase?*" Griff was already dozing off into the next day's dreams of action, thinking already of what he would tell Clynn about the accident: "*Which is the most important word in that fellow's sentence structure? 'By-sheself,' 'again,' or 'tonight'?*"

"Never mind the fellow looks like a canecutter, he's still a brother," Griff said to Masher, but he could have been talking into the future, the next day, to Clynn; or even to himself. "I don't want to come on strong, but he's a brother." The CBC television news that night dealt with the Black Power nationalism in the States. The Jamaican man and Griff's wife were now on the dance floor. Griff stole a glimpse at them, to make sure the man was not holding his wife in the same friendly way Stooly, who was a friend, would hold her. He thought he would be able to find the meaning of "*by-sheself,*" "*again,*" and "*tonight*" in the way the man held his wife. Had the Jamaican done so, Griff would have had to think even more seriously about the three words. But the Jamaican was about two hundred and fifty pounds of muscle and mackerel and green bananas. "Some other fellow would have come on strong, just because a rough-looking chap like him, held on . . ."

"Man, Griff, you's a rass-hole idiot, man!" Masher said. He crept under the bar counter, came out, faced Griff, broke into his sneering laugh, and said, "You's a rass-hole!" Griff laughed too, in his voiceless laugh. "You ain' hear that man say, '*by-sheself,*' '*tonight,*' '*again*'? If I had a woman like that, I would kiss her arse, by-Christ, just for *looking* at a man like that Jamaikianman!" Masher laughed some more, and walked away, singing the calypso the amateur band was trying to play: "*Oh Mister Walker, Uh come to see your daughter . . .*"

Griff wet his lips. His bottom lip disappeared inside his mouth, under his top lip; then he did the same thing with his top lip. He adjusted his dark glasses, and ran his right hand, with a cigarette in it, over his slim tie. His right hand was trembling. He shrugged his sports jacket into place and shape on his shoulders . . . "*Oh, Mister*

Walker, uh come to see ya daughterrrrr . . ." He stood by himself in the crowd of West Indians at the door, and he seemed to be alone on a sun-setting beach back home. Only the waves of the calypsonian, and the rumbling of the congo drum, and the whispering, the loud whispering in the breakers of the people standing nearby, were with him. He was like the sea. He was like a man in the sea. He was a man at sea . . . *"tell she is the man from Sangre Grande . . ."*

The dance floor was suddenly crowded, jam-packed. Hands were going up in the air, and some under dresses, in exuberance after the music; the words in the calypso were tickling some appetites; he thought of his wife's appetite and of the Jamaican's, who could no longer be seen in the gloom of the thick number of black people; and tomorrow was races, and he had again mastered the Form. And Griff suddenly became terrified about his wife's safety and purity, and the three words came back to him: *"by-sheself," "tonight," "again."* Out of the crowd, he could see Masher's big red eyes and his teeth, skinned in mocking laugh. Masher was singing the words of the calypso: *"Tell she I come for she . . ."* The music and the waves on the beach, when the sun went behind the happy afternoon, came up like a gigantic sea, swelling and roaring as it came to where he was standing in the wet white sand; and the people beside him, whispering like birds going home to branches and rooftops, some whispering, some humming like the sea, fishing for fish and supper and for happiness, no longer in sight against the blackening dusk . . . *"she know me well, I had she already! . . ."* Stooly walked in front of him, like the lightning that jigsawed over the rushing waves; and behind Stooly was a woman, noisy and Trinidadian, "this part-tee can't done till morning come!" like an empty tin can tied to a motor car bumper. All of a sudden, the fishermen and the fishing boats were walking back to shore, climbing out of their boats, laden with catches, their legs wet up to their knees; and they walked with their boats up to the brink of the sand. In their hands were fish. Stooly still held the hand of a woman who laughed and talked loud, "Fête for so!" She was like a barracuda. Masher, raucous and happy, and harmless, and a woman he didn't know, were walking like Siamese twins. One of his hands could not be seen. Out of the sea, now resting from the turbulent congo drumming of the waves in the calypso, came the Jamaicancongoman, and his wife.

"Thank you very much, suh" he said, handing Griff his wife's hand. With the other hand, she was pulling her miniskirt into place. "She is a first class dancer, suh."

"Don't have to come on *strong,* man."

"If I may, some other time, I would like to . . ." the man said, smiling and wiping perspiration from his face with a red handkerchief. His voice was pleasant and it had an English accent hidden somewhere in it. But all the words Griff heard were "I know she well, I had she already." . . . *"by-sheself," "again," "tonight"* . . . and there were races tomorrow. His wife was smiling, smiling like the everlasting sea at calm.

"Haiii!" she said, and smiled some more. The Jamaicanman moved back into the sea for some more dancing and fish. The beach was still crowded; and in Griff's mind it was crowded, but there was no one but he standing among the broken forgotten pieces of fish: heads and tails, and empty glasses and cigarette butts, and some scales broken off in a bargain, or by chance, and the ripped-up tickets of wrong bets.

Masher appeared and said in his ear, "If she was my wife, be-Christ, I tell you . . ." and he left the rest for the imagination.

Griff's wife's voice continued, "Griffy, dear?"

Masher came back from the bar with a Coke for the woman he was with. When he got close to Griff, he said in his ear, "Even if she was only just a screw like that one I have there . . ."

"Griffy, dear, let's go home, I am feeling . . ."

". . . and if you was *something*," Masher was now screaming down the stairs after them. Griff was thinking of the three little words which had brought such a great lump of weakness within the pit of his stomach.

"Masher seems very happy tonight, eh, Griffy, dear? I never quite saw Masher so happy."

". . . you, *boy!* you, *boy!* . . ."

"Masher, Haiii! How?"

"If it was mine," Masher shouted, trying to hide the meaning of his message, "if it was mine, and I had put only a two-dollar bet 'pon that horse, that horse that we was talking about, and, and that horse *behave' so*, well, I would have to *lash* that horse, till . . . *unnerstan?*"

"Griffy, dear? Masher really loves horses, doesn't he, eh?"

They were around the first corner, going down the last flight of stairs, holding the rails on the right-hand side. Griff realized that the stairs were smelling of stale urine, although he could not tell why. His wife put her arm round his waist. It was the first for the day. "I had a *great* time, a real ball, a *lovely* time!" Griff said nothing. He was tired, but he was also tense inside; still he didn't have the strength or the courage, whichever it was he needed, to tell her how he felt, how she had humiliated him, in that peculiar West Indian way of looking at small matters, in front of all those people, he could not tell her how he felt each time he watched Stooly put his arms round her slender body; and how he felt when the strange Jamaican man, with his cluttered use of grammar broken beyond meaning and comprehending, had destroyed something, like a dream, which he had had about her for all these fifteen years of marriage. He just couldn't talk to her. He wet his lips and ran his fingers over the slim tie. All she did (for he wanted to know that he was married to a woman who could, through all the years of living together, read his mind, so he won't have to talk) was smile. That goddamn smile, he cursed. The sports jacket shoulders were shrugged into place and shape.

"Griffy, dear? Didn't you enjoy yourself?" Her voice was like a flower, tender and caressing. The calypso band, upstairs, had just started up again. And the quiet waltz-like tune seemed to have been chosen to make him look foolish, behind his back. He could hear the scrambling of men and crabs trying to find dancing partners. He could imagine himself in the rush of fishermen after catches. He was thinking of getting his wife home quickly and coming back, to face Stooly and the Jamaican man; and he wished that if he did come back, that they would both be gone, so he won't have to come on strong; but he was thinking more of getting rid of his wife and coming back to dance and discuss the Racing Form; and tomorrow was races, again.

He imagined the large rough Jamaican man searching for women again. He saw Stooly grabbing some woman's hand, some woman whom he had never seen before. But it was *his* Club. He saw Masher, his eyes bulging and his mouth wide open, red and white, in joy. And Griff found himself not knowing what to do with his hands. He took his hands out of his jacket pockets, and his wife, examining her minidress in the reflection of the glass in the street door they were approaching, and where they always waited for the taxicab to stop for them, removed her arm from his waist. Griff placed his hand on her shoulder, near the scar, and she shuddered a little, and then he placed both hands on her shoulders; and she straightened up, with her smile on her face, waiting for the kiss (he always kissed her like that), which would be fun, which was the only logical thing to do with his hands in that position around her neck, which would be fun and a little naughty for their ages like the old times in Britain; and his wife, expecting this reminder of happier nights in unhappy London, relaxed, unexcited, remembering both her doctor and her yoga teacher, and in the excitement of her usually unexcitable nature, relaxed a little, and was about to adjust her body to his, and lean her scarred neck just a little bit backward to make it easy for him, to get the blessing of his silent lips, (she remembered then that the Jamaican held her as if he was her husband) when she realized that Griff's hands had walked up from her shoulders, and were now caressing the hidden bracelet of the scar on her neck, hidden tonight by a paisley scarf. She shuddered in anticipation. He thought of Stooly, as she thought of the Jamaican, as he thought of Masher, as he squeezed, and of the races—tomorrow the first race goes at 1:45 P.M. And the more he squeezed the less he thought of other things, and the less those other things bothered him, and the less he thought of the bracelet of flesh under his fingers, the bracelet which had become visible, as his hands rumpled the neckline. He was not quite sure what he was doing, what he wanted to do; for he was a man who always insisted that he didn't like to come on strong, and to be standing up here in a grubby hallway killing his wife, would be coming on strong: he was not sure whether he was wrapping his hands round her neck in a passionate embrace imitating the Jamaican, or whether he was merely kissing her.

But she was still smiling, the usual smile. He even expected her to say, "Haiii! How?" But she didn't. She couldn't. He didn't know where his kiss began and ended; and he didn't know where his hands stopped squeezing her neck. He looked back up the stairs, and he wanted so desperately to go back up into the Club and show them, or talk to them, although he did not, at the moment, know exactly why, and what he would have done had he gone back into the Club. His wife's smile was still on her body. Her paisley scarf was falling down her bosom like a rich spatter of baby food, pumpkin and tomato sauce; and she was like a child, propped against a corner, in anticipation of its first step, toddling into movement. But there was no movement. The smile was there, and that was all. He was on the beach again, and he was looking down at a fish, into the eye of reflected lead, a fish left by a fisherman on the beach. He thought he saw the scales moving up and down, like small billows, but there was no movement. He had killed her. But he did not kill her smile. He wanted to kill her smile more than he wanted to kill his wife.

Griff wet his lips, and walked back up the stairs. His wife was standing against the wall by the door, and she looked as if she was dead, and at the same time she looked as if she was living. It must have been the smile. Griff thought he heard her whisper, "Griffy, dear?" as he reached the door. Stooly, with his arm round a strange woman's body, took away his arm, and rushed to Griff, and screamed as if he was bellowing out a calypso line, "Oh-Jesus-Christ-Griff!"

Masher heard the name called, and came laughing and shouting, "Jesus-Christ, boy! You get rid o' the wife real quick, man! As man, *as man.*" Griff was wetting his lips again; he shrugged his sports jacket into place, and his mind wandered . . . "show me the kiss-me-arse Racing Form, man. We going to the races tomorrow . . ."

QUESTIONS

1. How does Clarke depict the nature of the lifestyle of the West Indian immigrants in the story?

2. Characterize the relationship between Griff and his wife in the story.

3. Why is Griff so ambiguous about his identity and race?

4. How are many of the characters in this story forced to play so many roles?

5. Ultimately, what events in the story cause Griff to murder his wife? What is his response to her death?

Neil Bissoondath

(b. 1955)

Neil Bissoondath comes from an East Indian family of writers. His grandfather was Seepersad Naipaul, the famous Trinidadian short story writer and father of writers V. S. and Shiva Naipaul. Bissoondath's father owned a variety store, but Bissoondath's uncle V. S. Naipaul wrote him a letter when he was a teenager advising him to migrate to Canada if he wanted to become a writer. The Trinidad that Bissoondath grew up in was not particularly suitable in the sense that most Marxists in the region placed the concerns of African Caribbeans over those of East Indians. At eighteen, Bissoondath left for Toronto and attended York University to study French, which he was able to teach in language schools. Bissoondath now teaches as a visiting professor at Laval University in Quebec City.

In his first book of short stories, *Digging Up the Mountains* (1985), Bissoondath refers to the Caribbean as a "carnival of radicals and madmen." In this work, out of which the story below is taken, his characters often find the transition to Canadian life more difficult than they imagine and return home. But

Bissoondath's vision is not as one-sided as some writers'; he sees that often the immigrants themselves are to blame for the difficulties they face. His characters often come to Canada with postcolonial chips on their shoulders and see every difficulty as the legacy of colonialism.

Bissoondath has published another collection of short stories, *On the Eve of Uncertain Tomorrows* (1990), and three novels, *A Casual Brutality* (1988), *The Innocence of Age* (1993), and *Doing the Heart Good* (2002). In 1994, he published a controversial book condemning multiculturalism in Canada and alienating a good many of his former countrymen who accused him of turning his back on his people. *Selling Illusions: The Cult of Multiculturalism in Canada* sparked an intense public debate in Canada about whose responsibility it is to preserve culture: the family or the government.

"Digging Up the Mountains" is a story filled with distorted nationalism. Here, a Caribbean businessman, Hari Beharry, wishes desperately to return to his home country, but realizes that his old world is now filled with political corruption and violence. Everything in this new world is uncertain; there is no stability.

Digging Up the Mountains   *1985*

1.

Hari Beharry lived a comfortable life, until, citing the usual reasons of national security, the government declared a State of Emergency.

"National security, my ass," Hari mumbled. "Protecting their own backsides, is all."

His wife, anguished, said, "Things really bad, hon."

"*Things really bad, hon,*" Hari mimicked her. He sucked his teeth. "Looking after their own backsides."

"The milk gone sour and the honey turn sugary." She gave a wry little smile.

Hari sucked his teeth once more. "Don't give me none of that stupid nonsense. 'Land a milk and honey,' my ass."

"You used to call it that."

"That was a long time ago."

"Rangee used to blame it on independence. He used to blame the British for—"

"I know what Rangee used to say. It ain't get him very far, eh? Shut up about Rangee, anyway. I don't want to talk about him."

"Again? Still? Faizal? They tried to help you."

"Why you like to talk about dead people so much?" he demanded irritably.

"Because you don't. You ain't mentioned their names once in the last two weeks."

"Why should I?"

"Because you might be next."

"Don't talk nonsense."

"Because *we* might be next, me and the children."

"Shut up, woman!"

Hari stalked angrily out to the back porch. The evening air, cooled by the higher ground which made the area so desirable to those who could afford it, tempered the heat of the day. The bulk of the mountains, cutting jagged against the inky sky, allowed only the faintest glow of the last of the sunset.

In those mountains, Hari had once found comfort. His childhood had been spent in the shadow of their bulk and it was through them, through their brooding permanence, that he developed an attachment to this island, an attachment his father had admitted only in later life when, as strength ebbed and distances grew larger, inherited images of mythic India dipped into darkness.

The island, however, was no longer that in which his father had lived. Its simplicity, its unsophistication, had vanished over the years and had been replaced by the cynical politics of corruption that plagued all the urchin nations scrambling in the larger world. Independence—written ever since with a capital I, small i being considered a spelling mistake at best, treason at worst—had promised the world. It had failed to deliver, and the island, in its isolation, blamed the world.

Hari's father had died on Independence night and Hari had sought consolation in the mountains. He'd received it that night and continued to receive it many nights after. Now things had changed: the mountains spoke only of threat. He didn't know if he could trust them anymore.

The emergency legislation had shut his stores. Hari was idle, and the sudden idleness made him irritable. If only he had someone with whom he could discuss the situation, someone who would make him privy to state secrets, as his old friends used to do. But the government had changed, his friends were no longer ministers, and the new ministers were not his friends. He could no longer say, "Eh, eh, you know what the Minister of National Security tell me yesterday?" The former Minister of National Security was in prison, put there by the new Minister for State Security. No one was left to show Hari the scheme of things; he was left to grapple alone, his wife useless, whining, demanding escape.

The darkness of the evening deepened. Hari felt a constriction in his throat. In the sky the first stars appeared. Hari reached into his back pocket and took out a large grey revolver. Its squared bulk fit nicely into his hand, its weight intimated power. He raised his arm with deliberation, keeping the elbow locked, and fired a shot at the sky. His arm, still locked, moved rapidly down and left; he fired another shot, at the mountains. The reports mingled and echoed away into the depths of the hidden gully.

"Come, you bastards, just try and come."

Only the barking of the German Shepherds answered him.

2.

It had started—when? Five, six, seven months before? He couldn't be sure. So much had happened, and in so short a time, event superseding grasp, comprehension exhausted. And it had all begun, quietly, with rumour: a whisper that had rapidly bred of itself, engendering others, each wilder, more speculative, and, so, more frightening than the last; rumour of trouble in the Ferdinand Pale, the shanty area to the east of the town.

Hari had dismissed the rumours: "Trouble, my ass. Shoot two or three of them and bam!—no more trouble."

But it hadn't worked out that way. The police had shot several people and had arrested dozens more, yet the rumours and the troubles persisted.

Hari had obtained a pistol from his friend, the Minister of National Security.

Hari said to the minister, "To protect the shops, you know, boy."

And to his wife, Hari said, "Let them come here. This is my land and my house. Let them come. It's bullet in their backside."

But no backsides presented themselves. Occasionally Hari would go out to the back porch and brandish his pistol: "Let them see what they walking into," he would say to his children who stood in the doorway staring wide-eyed at him. And to the darkness he would say, "Come, come and try."

Unexpectedly, the rumours dried up. Tension abated and fears were packed away. Life resumed. Hari called in the contractor, and gardeners—dark, sullen men of the Pale—started putting the yard in order, tugging out rocks and stones and laying out the drainage, preparing the ground for the topsoil.

Hari spent much of his free time overseeing this activity. Constantly followed by the children, he stalked around the yard nodding and murmuring and giving the occasional order, his tall rubber boots sinking deep into the convulsed earth. Slowly, at intervals less frequent than promised by the contractor, trucks arrived with loads of topsoil. Hari railed at the contractor: "But at this rate, man, it going to take five years to cover the whole yard!" The contractor, a fat man with red, wet eyes and a shirt that strained at the buttons, replied with exasperation: "But what I going to do, boss? The boys don't want to work, half of them ain't even show their face around the office since the little trouble in the Pale." The soil that did arrive was dumped into one corner of the yard under Hari's direction. He had it furrowed and combed, and had holes dug for the small grove of shade trees he would plant.

He started thinking about giving the place a name, like a ranch: Middlemarch, Rancho Rico, Golden Bough. He tossed the names about in his mind, playing with them, trying to picture how each would look on the personal stationery he was having printed up. He asked his wife's opinion. She suggested Bombay Alley. He stomped away, angry.

Twice he beat his son for playing with the gardeners' tools. "Look here, boy," he said, "I have enough troubles without you giving me more."

Still, the progress of the lawn pleased Hari. The contractor managed to hire additional men; trucks dumped their loads of topsoil at regular intervals. In less than a month, there swept from the base of the house to the base of the wrought-iron fence neatly raked stretches of an opulent brown. Hari, pleased, decided to order the grass.

He was on the phone arguing with the contractor about the price of the grass—it would mean sending three men and a truck to the country to dig up clumps of shoots; the contractor wanted more money than Hari was offering—when the music on the radio was interrupted by the announcement of a sudden call to elections. Hari understood immediately: the government, taking advantage of the apathy that followed the troubles, hoped to catch the opposition, such as it was, off-balance. Hari told the contractor he would call him back.

He poured himself a large whisky and listened to the Prime Minister's deep, bored voice as he spoke of a renewed mandate, of the confidence of the people. Hari thought the use of the island accent a little overdone. Did this election switch from Oxford drawl to island lilt really fool those at whom it was aimed? Did they really believe him to be one of them?

He dialled the number of his friend, the Minister of National Security: "Since when all-you care about mandate, boy? Is a new word you pick up in New York, or what?" Hari laughed. "Or maybe the Americans want a little reassurance before they hand over the loan cheque?" Hari laughed again, and his friend laughed with him.

But things went wrong. It was not a matter of political miscalculation; it was simply the plight of the small country: nothing went as planned, the foreseen never came into sight, and possibilities were quickly exhausted. The government lost. The opposition, on the verge of illegality only weeks before, took power.

Hari was untroubled. Life continued. He had, through it all, remained a financial contributor to both parties; and he liked the new Prime Minister, the scion of an old, respected island family that, adapting itself to the times, often publicly decried its slave-owning roots. The new Prime Minister considered himself a man truly of the people, for in him flowed the blood of master and slave alike.

The Americans handed over the cheque. The Prime Minister, serious and handsome, with a sallow island whiteness, went on television: ". . . the land of milk and honey . . . new loans from the World Bank . . . stimulation of industry and agriculture . . . a socialist economy . . ." This became known as the Milk and Honey speech. It was printed in pamphlet form and distributed to all the schools in the island. It was reported on the BBC World Service news.

The rumours started once more about a month later: trouble in the Ferdinand Pale. There were reports of shootings. Death threats were made against the new Prime Minister. Hari, without knowing why, sensed the hand of his friend, the former Minister of National Security. Pamphlets began appearing in the streets, accusing several businessmen of collusion with "imperialists." Hari's name cropped up time and time again. Letters—typed askew on good-quality paper, words often misspelt—began arriving at the house. Occasionally the phone would ring in the middle of the night, giving Hari the fearful vision of sudden death in the family. But always the same voice with the lazy island drawl would say in a conversational tone: "Damned exploitationist . . . Yankee slave . . ."

Hari complained to the police. The sergeant was apologetic: there was nothing they could do, their hands were full with the Ferdinand Pale.

The letters, less accusatory, more threatening, continued; the phone calls increased to three and four a night. Hari bought a whistle and blasted it into the phone. The next night the caller returned the favour. Hari's wife said, "You ask for that, you damn fool."

Hari complained directly to the Minister for State Security. He was called in; the minister wanted to see him.

Hari had never met the minister, and the new title, more sinister, less British, worried him. Before he entered the cream-coloured colonial building on Parliament Square, Hari noticed that his shirt was sticking to his back with perspiration. He wished he could dash back home to change it.

The minister was cordial. A big black man with a puffy face and clipped beard, he explained that his men were investigating the threats—a man of Mr Beharry's standing deserved "the full attention of the security forces"—but that it was a slow process, it would take time. "Processes," the minister said, and Hari noticed he seemed to smack his lips when he pronounced the word, as if relishing it, "processes take a long time, they are established by law, there's paperwork. You understand?"

Hari nodded. He thought: How can I trust this man? The minister used to be what was called a "fighter for social justice." He had studied in the United States and Canada, until he was expelled from Canada for his part in the destruction of the computer centre at Sir George Williams College in Montreal. He had returned to the island as a hero. The papers had said he'd struck a blow for freedom and racial equality. In Hari's circle he'd been considered a common criminal; the former Minister of National Security had said at a party, "We have a cell reserved for that one." Now here he was, Minister for State Security, growing pudgy, wearing a suit.

The minister offered a drink.

Hari asked for Scotch. "Straight."

"Imported or local?"

"Imported." Then he changed his mind. "Local."

The minister buzzed his secretary. "Pour us some whisky, Charlene. Local for Mr Beharry, imported for me." The minister smiled. He said to Hari, "I never drink the local stuff, disagrees with my stomach."

Hari said, "Too bad. It's good." And he knew instantly that he was grovelling.

The minister swung his chair around and stood up. A big man, he towered over Hari. "Mr Beharry, you are a well-known man here in our happy little island. You are an *important* man. You own a chain of stores, the Good Look Boutiques, not so? You are a rich man, you have a nice family. In short, Mr Beharry, you have a stake in this island." He paused as the secretary came in with the drinks. As Hari took his glass, he noticed a tremble in his hand, and he was aware that the minister too had noticed it. The minister smiled, raised his glass briefly at Hari, and sipped at the whisky. Then he continued: "It is because of all this, Mr Beharry, that I want you to trust me. I am responsible for the security of this island. Trust between people like us is vital. And that is why, right now, I am going to reveal to you a state secret: in a few days we are going to ask everybody to turn in their guns, you included. It's the best way we know how to clean up the island. This violence must stop."

Hari's palm became sweaty on the glass. He said, "But is my gun, there's no law—"

"The law will be pushed through Parliament tomorrow. No one can stop us, you know that."

Hari, suddenly emboldened by the minister's smugness, said, "You know better than me. I never went to university."

The minister, unchastened, said, "That's right, Mr Beharry."

Then they drank their Scotch and talked soccer. Hari knew nothing about soccer. The minister talked. Hari listened.

A few days later, Hari turned in his gun. Before handing it over at the police station, he jammed a piece of wood down the barrel.

The letters and phone calls were still coming. Hari threw the letters out unopened and put the telephone into a drawer. His wife, constantly worried, asked him, "How we going to defend ourselves now, hon?"

Hari said, "Don't worry."

That night, he went to his parents' old house, locked up and deserted. He hadn't been there in months. The place hadn't changed: the furniture was where it had always been, his parents' clothes still hung in the closets. Dust lay everywhere. Thieves, assuming the house contained nothing, had never bothered to break in. The air was musty, the familiar smells of childhood gone forever. Those smells, of food frying, of milk boiling, of his mother's perfumes and powders, had lingered several months after his mother's death and given Hari a haunted feeling. It was because of them that he'd stayed away so long, leaving the house and its ghosts to their own devices.

He went into his parents' bedroom. The bed had never been stripped and the sheets, now discoloured by dust, lay as they had been thrown by the undertakers who'd taken his mother's body away. He wondered if the impression left by the body in its attitude of death could still be seen. He rejected the thought as morbid but couldn't help taking a look: he saw only dusty, rumpled sheets.

Ignoring the dust, he lowered himself to the floor and felt around under the bed with his hand. He found what he was looking for: a rectangular wooden box the size of a cookie can. He opened it and took out a large grey revolver, the kind worn by American officers during the war. His father had bought it off an American soldier stationed on the island in 1945. After so many years of lying around, of being considered a toy, it would finally find a use.

Hari slipped the revolver into his pocket—it was bigger and heavier than the one he'd turned in and didn't fit as snugly into his pocket—and left the house. He didn't bother to lock the door.

Later that same night, Rangee, Hari's closest friend, telephoned. Hari was in bed, the revolver on the headboard just above him; and the ring of the telephone, startling in the semi-darkness, caused him to reach first for the revolver.

Rangee said, "Listen, Hari, things really bad in the Pale, but watch out. Is not the Ferdinand Pale you have to fear, is the other pale."

Before Hari could ask what he was talking about, the phone went dead. Hari assumed it was another of the frequent malfunctions of the telephone system.

Rangee was found the next day, shot twice in the head, the receiver still clutched in his hand. The police said it had been a robber: Rangee's watch and wallet were missing. Nothing else in his house had been touched.

Hari returned from the morgue. So many had already left, gone to lands unfamiliar beyond the seas, that he took Rangee's death as just another departure. He froze Rangee in his mind, as he'd done with the others. He was determined never to mention them again; they were like a challenge to him. He sat at the kitchen table, his son and daughter, large-eyed, across from him, and cleaned and oiled the American's revolver. It needed little work: the mechanism clicked sharply, precisely, the magazine full. Hari marvelled at American ingenuity.

About a week after Rangee's death—later, Hari would have difficulty separating events: which came first? which second?—Faizal, another friend and business partner, came to see Hari. Faizal had connections in the army and liked to show off his knowledge of things military. Once, after a dinner party, Hari had told his wife, "Faizal went on and on. I feel as if I just finish planning the whole D-Day invasion."

Seated in the darkened black porch, glass poised between restless fingers, Faizal appeared nervous. He talked about the weather, about business, about the Ferdinand Pale. His eyes, agitated, traced the bulky silhouette of the mountains against the star-strewn sky. He related the story of the Battle of Britain and explained the usefulness of the Dieppe raid.

Hari felt that Faizal was trying to say something important but that he had to work up the courage. He didn't push him.

Faizal left without saying anything. Despite all the alcohol he had consumed, he left as nervous as he'd arrived. Hari assumed he was just upset over Rangee's death, and he was thankful that Faizal had said nothing about it.

Faizal was shot three days later. He'd received two bullets in the head; his watch and wallet were missing. The police concluded it was another case of robbery.

Hari, steeled, said, "Damn strange robbers. All they take is watches and wallets when they could empty the house."

The night after Faizal's death, one of Hari's stores was destroyed by fire. The fire department, an hour late in responding to the call, said it was arson. Then the fire marshal changed his mind: the final report spoke of old wiring and electrical shorts.

It was after this that Hari obtained two German Shepherds and started firing his warning shots into the evening sky.

The troubles in the Ferdinand Pale erupted into riots. Two policemen were killed. The government declared a State of Emergency and sent the army into the streets. Hari said, "Faizal would have been thrilled." It was the last time he mentioned Faizal's name. Members of the former government, including Hari's friend the former Minister of National Security, were arrested, for agitation, for treason. Stores and schools were closed, the airport and ports cordoned off.

It was only after watching the Prime Minister announce the Emergency on television that the meaning of Rangee's strange last words clicked in Hari's mind. The announcement had included news of an offer, at once accepted, of fraternal aid from Cuba. The Prime Minister, exhausted, had looked very, very pale.

3.

The day after the Emergency proclamation, the labourers didn't turn up, as was to be expected. Hari, restless, walked around the yard pretending to inspect the progress of the lawn. There had been problems obtaining the grass. The contractor, once more, complained of the workmen, their laziness, drunkenness. But Hari guessed at the real problem: whatever was seething in the Pale had seized them. Only one load of grass had been delivered, and the soil was beginning to harden in spots, to bind to itself.

Hari, feeling the heaviness of the revolver in his back pocket, let his eyes roam over the few rows of grass that had been planted, scraggly little shoots not quite in straight lines. Looking at them he found it difficult to picture the thick, carpet-like lawn he'd envisaged. His eyes moved on, past the ugliness of incomplete lawn, past several piles of wood left over from the construction of the house and not yet carted away, to the deep gully where his wife, if she got the chance, would start to plant her nursery, to the wall of forest, dank and steamy, to the mountains beyond, a great distance away yet ever present, like a dead loved one.

Just let them try to take it away. Let them try!

"Hari," his wife called from the kitchen window, "we need milk, you better go to the plaza."

"For sour milk?"

"We need milk, Hari." She sounded tired. Her anxiety had distilled to fatigue. She had given up dreams of a nursery; she wanted only flight—to Toronto, Vancouver, Miami.

He looked at her and said, "This is my island. My father born here, I born here, you born here, our children born here. Nobody can make me leave, nobody can take it away."

"All right, Hari. But we still need milk."

His son came to the door. He was so small that Hari, when drunk, doubted his parentage. His son said, "I want chocolate milk."

His daughter, plump, more like Hari, echoed, "I want chocolate milk too."

Hari sucked his teeth and brushed roughly past them into the house. He snatched up the car keys from the kitchen counter and started to remove the revolver from his pocket. Then he paused and let it fall back, an ungainly lump in his trousers. It was a calculated risk: what if the police stopped him? They could shoot him and announce that Mr Hari Beharry, well-known businessman, had died of a heart attack during a road-block search; an illegal revolver had been the source of his anxiety. Bullet holes? If the government said he'd died of a heart attack, he'd died of a heart attack. Hari had lived here too long, been too close to the former government, to delude himself. He knew the way of the island: nowhere was truth more relative.

It occurred to him only afterwards that they might have simply shot him, then claimed he had shot first. But this was too simple, the island didn't seek simplicity. With the obvious evidence, it would have been smarter to claim a heart attack: it was more brazen, it would be admired.

He braked at the driveway and glanced into the rearview mirror: the house, white, brilliant in the sun, the windows and doors of mahogany lending a touch of simple elegance, filled the glass. His wife had surprised him with her suggestion of mahogany: he hadn't thought her capable of such taste. With all the trimmings, he'd ended up sinking over a hundred thousand dollars into the house. It was the investment of a lifetime and one that would have caused his father both pride and anguish: pride that the family could spend so vast a sum on a house, anguish that they would. It was in this house that Hari planned to entertain his grandchildren and their children, to this house that he would welcome future Beharry hordes, from this house that he would be buried. The house spoke of generations.

But now, as he drove along the serpentine road, verges broken and nibbled by wild grass, his dreams all managed to elude him. Those scenes of future familial joy that he had for so long caressed had, almost frighteningly, become like a second, parallel, life. And now they had gone out of reach: he could no longer conjure up a future and what did come to him, in little snippets, like wayward pieces of film negative, caused him to shudder.

It wasn't yet ten o'clock but the sun was already high, radiating a merciless heat. Hari could feel the mounting degrees pressing down on him from the car roof. He could see waves rising like insubstantial cobras from the asphalt paving; he dripped with perspiration. The wind rushing in through the window did little to relieve his discomfort. He wiped away a drop of perspiration that had settled in the deep cleft between his nose and upper lip and shifted in his seat, trying to get used to the feel of the revolver under him.

The plaza was only a short distance away but already Hari could sense the change of atmosphere. At the house the heat was manageable. It suggested comfort, security; it was like the heat of the womb. Outside, away from the house, under the blue of a sky so expansive, so untrammelled that it seemed to expose him, to strip him, the heat became tangible, held menace, was suggestive of physical threat. It conjured not a desire for beach and sea but an awareness of the lack of cover, a sense of nothing to hide behind. The familiar of the outside world had undergone an irrevocable transformation.

The revolver, he realized with a twinge of disappointment, gave no comfort. He used to be able to picture himself blazing away at blurry figures, but his image had been the result of too many paperback westerns. The blurry figures had unexpect-edly taken on more substance. What had once seemed epic now seemed absurd.

He drove past several empty lots, wild grass punctuated occasionally by the rusting hulks of abandoned cars. In the distance, on both sides, beyond the land that had been cleared for an aborted agricultural scheme (money had disappeared, as had the minister responsible), he could see the indistinct line of forest, recalling a smudged, green watercolour: government land, guerrilla land. And far away to the left, beyond and above forest, the mountains, sturdy, mottled green, irregularly irri-gated by vertical streams of white smoke: signs, some said, of guerrilla camps, signs, others said, of the immemorial bush fires.

At last the plaza came into sight, low stucco buildings with teak panelling and light fixtures imported from Switzerland. The fixtures were broken and in several places were marked only by the forlorn ends of electrical wire. The teak had been scratched and gouged, some pieces ripped from the wall for a bonfire that had been lit at the entrance to the bookstore. The stucco, unrecognizable, had been defaced by slo-gans, both sexual and political, and crude paintings and election posters and askew copies of the Emergency proclamation, unglued corners hanging limply in the hot air.

In front of the barricaded shops, in the shadow of the overhang, lounged a line of black youths, wool caps pulled down tightly over their heads, impenetrable sun-glasses masking their eyes.

Hari couldn't separate his fear from his quick anger.

"We need milk, must have milk, chocolate milk," he muttered, vexed, as he pulled into the parking lot. He could hear their voices, his wife, his son, his daughter, and they were like mockery, demanding and insistent, ignorant of his problems and worries.

He pulled carefully into a parking space, stopping neatly in the middle equidis-tant from the white lines on either side of the car. An unnecessary vanity, the lot was deserted. He sucked his teeth with irritation and tugged the keys out of the ignition. With the engine dead, an anticlimactic silence fell over the plaza. None of the youths moved and Hari couldn't tell whether they were looking at him. He wished he knew.

He opened the door—it squeaked a little, disturbing the quiet like a fingernail scraping a blackboard—and put one leg out onto the scorching asphalt. Heat waves tickled up his pant leg, sending a spasm through him. Faintly, from the shadow of the overhang, came the sound of a radio, disturbingly gay, the music local, proud, threatening.

Hari let his foot rest on the asphalt and sat still, trying to discern where the music was coming from. As he looked around, it occurred to him that the milk store would be closed, everything was closed by the Emergency; it was a wasted trip. He noted, as if from a distance, a curious lack of emotion within him: it was as if all feel-ing had dried up.

"Wha' you doin' here, boss?"

The voice startled Hari. Four black faces were at his door, sunglasses scrutiniz-ing him. He could see his reflection in the black lenses, his strained face eight times, each a caricature of himself.

He heard his voice reply, "I come to get milk, *bredda.* For the children. You know. They need milk. They just small." He wondered if the men were hot under those wool caps, but they were part of the uniform.

"Look like you out of luck, boss. The milk store close." He was the leader, the others deferred to him.

"Yeah, I just remember that myself."

Another of the men said, "You better get out of the car, boss."

Hari didn't move.

The leader said, "My friend like your car, boss."

Hari didn't hear him. He was wondering if the leader had bought his pink dashiki[1] at his store.

Hari said, "You buy that dashiki at the Good Look Boutique?"

One of the men said, "What business that is of yours?"

Hari said, "I own the Good Look."

Fingering the dashiki, the leader said, "I know that, boss. And no. My wife make the dashiki for me. You like it? How much you'd sell that for, boss?"

Hari's heart sank.

"Get out of the car."

"Look, all-you know who I am?"

"Yes, Boss Beharry, we know you. Get out of the car."

"What you want, *bredda*?"

"Get out. I not going to ask you again."

Hari stumbled out. The men crowded in. Hari reached for the revolver, levelled it at the leader, and pulled the trigger. The hammer clicked emptily. Hari's vision fogged; the world went into a tilt: he had drained the clip at the sky and mountains.

The leader said, "Well, well, boss. So the Americans supplying you with guns now, eh?" He knocked the revolver from Hari's hand with an easy, fluid blow.

"What you want, *bredda*?"

"The keys."

Hari gave the car keys to the leader. Hari noticed he was wearing a large silver ring marked U.S. Air Force Academy, the kind advertised in comic books.

"The money."

"Money?" A sudden presence of mind gripped Hari. The heat scorched his skin, the asphalt solidified beneath his feet, the world righted itself.

Hari said, "Give me room, *bredda,* I'll give you the money." He reached into his pocket and pulled out a thick wad of bills. With a quick movement of the wrist, he flung it high and away. The bills scattered like confetti.

The leader looked perplexed. No one moved. Then suddenly everyone was running, the youths from the shadow of the overhang to the money, the robbers from the car to the money. Only the leader remained; Hari pushed him, hard. The man stumbled and fell. Hari started to run.

---

1 **dashiki:** A usually bright colored loose-fitting pullover garment.

At the corner of the farthest building, he looked quickly back. No one was following him. The leader, standing casually by the car, was dusting himself off and smoothing the creases in his pink dashiki. It was a strangely domestic sight.

Hari had just finished watering the little patch of lawn when the police came to return his car. All the windows had been smashed into tiny crystal diamonds. Glittering in the sunlight, they littered the seats and floor like so many water droplets. The body had been badly dented in several places and the paint maliciously gouged with an icepick. Hari could make out the letters CA but only deep gouges followed, as if the vandal had gotten into a sudden rage. This, more than anything, frightened Hari: it was an elegant, hieroglyphic statement.

"We find it on a back road," the policeman said, cocking his military-style helmet to one side. In the old days Hari might have pulled him up for sloppiness; now he said nothing. "We didn't find no money. The keys was in the ignition."

Hari said, "You didn't find the—" He stopped short, remembering he had had the revolver illegally.

The policeman said, "What?"

Hari said, "Nothing. The men. You know."

The policeman said, "No, nothing. We'll call if we find anything."

Hari took the keys and thanked him. The policeman turned and walked away, up the driveway into a waiting jeep. Four men were sitting in the back of the jeep; they all wore police uniforms and sported impenetrable sunglasses.

As the jeep pulled away, one of the men waved at Hari.

Hari waved back.

A second man raised his arm; in his hand fluttered a pink dashiki. The man shouted, "Thanks, boss."

Hari pulled the children inside and bolted the door.

That evening the Minister for State Security telephoned. He said, "Mr Beharry, I hear you are leaving our happy little island. That's too bad."

Hari said, "Well, I—"

The minister said, "Are you going to visit your American friends?"

Hari said nothing.

The minister said, "You know if you are out of the island for more than six months, your property reverts to the people, who are its rightful owners."

Hari put the phone down.

Flight had become necessary, and it would be a penniless flight. The government controlled the flow of money. Friends had been caught smuggling; some had had their life savings confiscated. He could leave with nothing. It was the price for years of opulent celebrity in a little place going wrong.

His wife, stabbing at her eyes with a tissue, said, "At least we not dead."

Hari said, "We're not?"

He went out into the back yard. The sun was beginning to set behind the mountains and random dark clouds diffused the light into a harsh yellowness. It would probably rain tomorrow.

Hari went to the tool shed and got a fork. The earth around the patch of lawn was loose and damp. The grass shoots had not yet begun to root; they popped out easily under the probing prongs. In a few minutes, the work was done. Hari looked up. The sun had already sunk behind the mountains: Hari wished he could dig them up too.

QUESTIONS

1. How is Hari an insider or outsider in this work?

2. Describe the political situation on the island.

3. Why doesn't Hari and his family simply leave the island when the "troubles" come?

4. How is the United States viewed in this short story?

Dionne Brand

(b. 1953)

Born in Guayaguayare, Trinidad, Dionne Brand was educated at Naparima Girl's School and graduated in 1970. Upon graduation, she immediately moved to Toronto, where she began community work. She completed her BA in English and philosophy at the University of Toronto in 1975 and received a graduate degree in education in 1988. While an undergraduate student she began a writing career, first as an editor and then as a writer for newspapers and journals. Her experiences working as a counselor at the Immigrant Women's Centre and the Black Youth Hotline certainly influenced her worldview and made her a social activist. She worked for a revolution in Grenada and in 1986 was a founding member of a community newspaper called *Our Lives*. Brand has taught writing at several Canadian universities and was recently writer-in-residence at the University of Guelph. She lives in Toronto.

Brand is both a poet and a fiction writer. To date she has published eight volumes of poetry. Her first volume, *'Fore Day Morning*, was published in 1978; her seventh volume, *Land to Light On* (1997), won the Governor General's Award for poetry. Her latest volume of poetry, *Thirsty* (2002), concerns an immigrant who is shot by police while in his front yard. The contrast between the violence of his murder and the inside of the man's mind makes this another of the long line of critical attacks on the soulless nature of modern urban life.

Brand has published a number of books on racism and on black women's history. *Sans Souci and Other Stories* (1988) details with great force the reality behind blacks' lives in Canada and the Caribbean, and the stories demonstrate the effect that poverty has on those lives. The narrative voice in the stories is often an interior monologue trying to understand how it has come to this situation. Characters are buffeted by racism, sexism, and inhumanity at every turn—and in the title story, rape becomes the central focus of this unjust contemporary world. Brand also explores the survival mechanisms that keep people afloat in this sea of madness.

Brand's first novel, *In Another Place, Not Here* (1996), explores two modern women's inner selves as they struggle against their colonial legacy. Her second novel, *At the Full and Change of the Moon* (1999), follows six generations of descendants of Marie Ursule, the queen of militant slaves who plan a mass suicide. She saves her daughter Bola, and her children and grandchildren are instilled with Ursule's passions.

Sans Souci[1]

1989

Rough grass asserted itself everywhere, keeping the earth damp and muddy. It inched its way closer and closer to doorsteps and walls until some hand, it was usually hers, ripped it from its tendrilled roots. But it soon grew back again. It kept the woman in a protracted battle with its creeping mossyness. She ripping it out; shaking the roots of earth. It grew again the minute she turned her back. The house, like the others running up and down the hill, could barely be seen from the struggling road, covered as it was by lush immortelle trees with coarse vine spread among them so that they looked like women with great bushy hair, embracing.

In Sans Souci, the place was called, they said that the people were as rough as the grass.

She may have looked that way but it was from walking the hills and tearing out the grass which grew until she was afraid of it covering her. It hung like tattered clothing from her hips, her breasts, her whole large body. Even when her arms were lifted to carry water to the small shack, she felt weighed down by the bush. Great green patches of leaves, bougainvillea, almond, karili vine fastened her ankles to her wrists. She kept her eyes to the floor of the land. Her look tracing, piercing the bush and marking her steps to the water, to the tub, to the fire, to the road, to the land. The woman turning into a tree, though she was not even old yet. As time went on she felt her back harden like a crab's, like the bark of a tree, like its hard brown meat. A man would come often, but it was difficult to know. When she saw him coming, she would never know him until he said her name, "Claudine." Then she would remember him vaguely. A bee near her ear, her hand brushing it away. Sometimes she let the bush grow as tall as it wanted. It overwhelmed her. Reaching at her each new spore or shoot burdened her. Then someone would pass by and not see the house and say that she was minding snakes. Then she would cut it down.

---

1 **Sans Souci:** French for "without care."

She climbed the hill often when the bush was low around the house. Then she went for water, or so it seemed because she carried a pot. Reaching the top, her feet caking with mud, she would sit on the ground near the edge of the cliff. Then she would look down into the sea and rehearse her falling—a free fall, a dive into the sea. How fast the sea would come toward her—probably not—the cliff was not vertical enough. Her body would hit tufts of grass before reaching the bottom. She could not push off far enough to fall into the water. Musing on whether it would work or not she would lie down on the ground, confused. Spread out, the pot beneath her head, she would be faced by the sky. Then her eyes would close, tired of the blue of the sky zooming in and out at her gaze, and she would be asleep. She never woke up suddenly. Always slowly, as if someone else was there moving in on her sleep. Even when it rained a strong rain which pushed her into the ground or when she slept till the sky turned purple.

Her children knew where she was. They would come up the hill when they did not see her or go to their grandmother's. She never woke up suddenly here, even when the three of them screamed her name—"Claudine!" The boy with his glum face turning cloudier and the girl and the little boy looking hungry.

Three of them. In the beginning she had bathed them and oiled their skins in coconut and dressed them in the wildest and brightest of colours and played with them and shown them off to the other inhabitants of the place. Then they were not good to play with any more. They cried and felt her hands. They cried for the roughness of her hands and the slap. If he was there he would either say "don't hit them" or "why don't you hit those children?" His ambiguity caused her to hesitate before each decision on punishment. Then she decided not to touch the children, since either instruction he gave, he gave in an angry and distant voice and for her the two had to be separate thoughts, clear opposites. So after a time the children did not get bathed and dressed and after a time they did not get beaten either.

The people around spoke well of him, described his physical attributes which were in the main two cheloidal[2] scars on his chin and face. When he came he told them of his escapades on the bigger island. Like the time he met the famous criminal Weapon and he and Weapon spent the night drinking and touring the whore houses and the gambling dens and Weapon stuck a knife into the palm of a man who touched his drink. He brought new fashions to the place. The wearing of a gold ring on his little finger and the growing of an elegant nail to set it off. The men, they retold his stories until he came with new ones. They wore copper rings on their little fingers.

If she wasn't careful they would come into the house and tell her what to do again. The shacks up and down the hill were arranged like spiders crawling towards her. One strong rain and they'd be inside of her house which was not at the bottom of the hill so there was no real reason to think that it would actually happen. Looking at them, the other people, they made gestures towards her as they did to each

---

2 **cheloidal:** Marked by skin lesions.

other, to everyone else. They brought her things and she gave them things and they never noticed, nor did she, that she was not her mother's child nor her sister's sister nor an inhabitant of the place, but the woman turning into a tree. They had pressed her with their eyes and their talk and their complicit winks first into a hibiscus switch then into a shrub and now this . . . a tree.

He didn't live there. The dirt path beside the house ran arbitrarily up the hill. Whenever he came he broke a switch with which to scare the children. This was his idea of being fatherly. Coming through the path, he made his stern face up to greet the children and the woman. He came and went and the people in the place expected him to come for her and made excuses when he did not. They expected her to be his. They assumed this as they assumed the path up the hill, the steady rain in March. He is a man, you're a woman, that's how it is.

Those times, not like the first, he would sit on her bed—a piece of wood, his face blunt in the air, dense and unmoving, he had no memory, almost like the first, his breathing and his sweat smelling the same furry thickness as before. Like something which had walked for miles with rain falling and insects biting and the bush and trees slapping some green and murky scent onto its body, a scent rough from years of instinct, and horrible. Now he grew his fingernails and splashed himself with cheap scent but sometimes when he lifted his arm she recalled and forgot quickly. And sometimes she saw his face as before. Always, in and out of seeing him and not seeing him; or wondering who he was and disbelieving when she knew.

Those times he would sit on her bed and tell her about a piece of land which his maternal grandmother had left him. He was just waiting for the day that they built the road across Sans Souci and that was the day that he was going to be a rich man. Because it was good agricultural land and only a road was holding it back. He went on about how he would work the land and how he was really a man of the earth. She listened even though she knew that his mouth was full of nonsense. He had said that for the last many years.

How many . . . was he the same as the first . . . somehow she had come to be with him. Not if he was the first, not him.

His hands with their long fingernails, the elegant long nail on the right finger could never dig into the soil. She listened to him even though she knew that he was lying. But he really wasn't lying to deceive her. He liked to hear himself. He liked to think that he sounded like a man of ideas, like a man going somewhere. Mostly he repeated some phrase which he heard in a popular reggae song about having the heights of jah-jah[3] or something he had heard at the occasional north-american evangelist meeting. He had woven these two into a thousand more convolutions than they already were and only he could understand them. He, the other men in the place and Claudine who couldn't really understand either but liked the sound of him. The sound confused her, it was different, not like the pig squealing that sorrowful squealing as it hung in front of the knife nor its empty sound as it hung for days . . . years . . .

3 **jah-jah:** Rastafarian call for redemption.

its white belly bloodless when it hung with no one seeing it. None around except the air of the yard folding and sealing pockets of flesh, dying. The sound covered an afternoon or so for her above the chorus of the pig's squeal at once mournful and brief in its urgency. The startling incidence of its death mixed with commonplaceness and routine. She liked to have him sit with her as if they were husband and wife.

II

She had met uncle Ranni on the Carenage,[4] she never thought that he would ever get old, he used to be quick and smooth, with golden rings on his fingers. Each time he smiled or laughed that challenging sweet laugh of his the sun would catch the glint of his rings and throw it onto his teeth so that they looked yellow. He would throw his head way back revealing the gold nugget on his thick chain. He was a small man really but you would never know, looking at him when he laughed.

Then even when he talked of killing a man he laughed that sweet laugh, only his eyes were different.

They cut across your face for the briefest of moments like the knife that he intended to use. Once he even threatened to kill his father and his father believed him and slapped his face and never spoke with him again. She poured everything out to him now hoping he would kill the man this time.

Everything about Prime's exhortations and his lies. It came out of her mouth and she didn't know who was saying it. Uncle Ranni's laugh only changed slightly. No one in the family ever really believed that he'd ever kill anyone but no one ever dared not to believe either. Something about his laugh said that he'd never kill a man if he didn't have to and if he did, it would be personal. With a knife or a machete, never with a gun, but close so that the dying man would know who had killed him and why. She'd caught a glimpse of him once, under a tamarind tree, talking about cutting a man's head off and the eyes of the head open, as it lay apart from its body in the dirt. He had told it and the men around, kicking the dust with their toes, had laughed, weakly. Claudine told him everything, even some things that she only thought happened, but happened. These didn't make the case against Prime any worse, they just made her story more lyrical—inspiring the challenging laugh from Ranni. "This man don't know who your uncle is, or what?" This only made her say more, Prime had lied to her and left her with three children to feed.

The new child, the fourth, moved in her like the first, it felt green and angry. Her flesh all around it, forced to hang there protecting this green and angry thing. It reached into her throat sending up bubbles and making her dizzy all the time. It was not that she hated it, she only wanted to be without it. Out, out, out, out, never to have happened. She wanted to be before it, to never know or have known about it. He had said that the land was in her name, he had even shown her papers which said

4 **Carenage:** Village in northwest Trinidad outside the former U.S. naval base near Port-of-Spain.

so and now he had run off, taken a boat to St Croix.[5] "St Croix? It don't have a place that man can hide; he don't know me," uncle Ranni said. Claudine got more and more frightened and more and more excited as she talked the story. It would serve Prime right to have uncle Ranni chop him up with a knife, she would like to see it herself. Uncle Ranni was old now. Sixty-four, but when he laughed like that she could see his mouth still full of his white teeth. It surprised her.

Her mother's brother—he had looked at her once back then as if she had made it happen. Looked at her as if she were a woman and contemptible, but it passed quickly like his other looks.

She'd only been talking to an old man about her trouble. She had not been paying attention. His old face had lit up briefly with that look and his teeth were as white as when he was young. His skin was tight and black as she remembered it years ago. He seemed to laugh out of a real joy. She remembered liking to hear him laugh and see his white teeth against his beautiful skin. He would spit afterward as if there was something too sweet in his mouth. Now when she'd first seen him on the Carenage she had seen an old man with grey eyelashes and a slight stubble of grey on parts of his skin and face. She had told him everything in a surge of relief and nostalgia, never expecting him to do anything but it was he, uncle Ranni, she had told. She almost regretted saying anything but she needed to say it to someone.

The look across her face as before, cutting her eyes away, cutting her lips, her head, slicing her, isolating sections of her for scrutiny and inevitable judgment. Her hand reached to touch her face, to settle it, dishevelled as it was, to settle it on her empty chest. All that she had said was eaten up by the old man's face, and thrown at her in a transient lacerating look which he gave back. Her eyes sniffed the quickly sealed cut and turned, fell on a wrecked boat in the Carenage.

A little boy jumped off the end not submerged in the water. The glum-faced boy at home came to her. She hurriedly made excuses to uncle Ranni about having to go and ran with a kind of urgency toward the tied-up boat to Cast Island. Disappearing into its confusion of provisions, vegetables and goats. She did what she always had to do. She pretended to live in the present. She looked at the awful sky. She made its insistent blueness define the extent of what she could see. Before meeting uncle Ranni she had walked along pretending that the boat was not there; that she did not have to go; wishing she could keep walking; that the Carenage would stretch out into the ocean, that the water of the ocean was a broad floor and the horizon a shelf which divided and forgot. An end to things completely. Where she did not exist. The line of her eyes' furthest look burned her face into the sunset of yellow, descending. The red appearing behind her eyelids, rubbing the line with her head. She had wished that the water between the jetty and the lapping boat was wider and fit to drink so that she could drink deeply, become like sand, change places with the bottom of the ocean, sitting in its fat-legged deepness and its immutable width.

5 **St Croix:** Largest island of the U.S. Virgin Islands, situated in the West Indies.

III

After the abortion, she went to Mama's Bar, even though she was in pain and even though she knew that she should lie down. Mama's was a wooden house turned into a restaurant and bar and Mama was a huge woman who had an excellent figure. Mama dominated the bar; she never shouted; she raised her eyebrows lazily when challenged. There were other women in the bar, regulars, who imitated Mama's walk and Mama's eyelids but deferred to Mama and faded, when Mama was in the bar. Mama always sat with her back to the door, which proved just how dangerous she was.

The walls of the bar, at unaccounted intervals, had psychedelic posters in fluorescent oranges and blues. One of them was of an aztec-like mountain—dry, mud brown, cracked, strewn with human bones. Nothing stood on it except bones of feet and ribs and skulls. It would be a foreboding picture if it weren't so glossy. Instead it looked sickly and distant. It was printed by someone in California and one of Mama's visitors had bought it at a head shop in San Diego. Mama thought that it was high art and placed it so that people entering the bar could see it immediately.

Claudine walked down the steps to the bar, closed her eyes anticipating the poster then opened them too soon and felt her stomach reach for her throat.

Mama's eyes watched her walk to the counter, ask for a rum, down it and turning to leave bump into the man with the limp. A foamy bit of saliva hung onto the stubble on his face. He grabbed Claudine to save himself from falling and then they began dancing to Mama's crackling stereo.

They danced until lunch time, until the saliva from the limping man's face stretched onto the shoulder of Claudine's dress. Mama had not moved either. She controlled all of it with her eyes and when they told Claudine to leave, she sat the man with the limp onto a stool and left. Going somewhere, averting her stare from the mountain strewn with human bones.

IV

She went to the address on the piece of paper someone had given her—29 Ponces Road. When she got to the street there was no number on any of the houses. She didn't know the woman's name. It was best in these situations not to know anyone's name or to ask anyone where. She walked up and down the street looking at the houses. Some were back from the curb and faced the next street over so there was no way of telling. Maybe something about the house would tell her—what does a house where a woman does that look like, she asked herself— she walked up and down the street thinking that maybe it was this one with the blue veranda or that one with the dog tied to a post. No, she couldn't tell. Maybe this was a sign or something. She gave up, suddenly frightened that it may be just a sign—holy mary mother of god—and bent her head walking very fast up the street for the last time.

She passed a house with nine or ten children in the yard. Most of them were chasing after a half-dressed little boy. They were screaming and pointing at something he was chewing. She hadn't seen the woman on the wooden veranda until one of the children ran towards her saying something breathless and pointing to the woman on the veranda. Then she saw her as the woman on the veranda reached out into the yard and hit a flying child. It didn't seem as if she wanted to hit this one in particular or any one in particular. The group of children gave a common flinch (accustomed to these random attacks on their chasing and rushing around), then continued after the boy. Faced with finally doing this Claudine didn't know anymore. She hesitated, looked at the woman's face for some assurance. But nothing. The woman looked unconcerned waiting for her, and then turning and walking into the ramshackle house, her back expecting Claudine to follow. Claudine walked toward the yard not wanting to stand in the street. Now she moved because of the smallest reasons, now she was trapped by even tinier steps, by tinier reasons. She moved so that her feet would follow each other, so that she could get away from the road, so that she could make the distance to the house, so that it would be over. Nothing had come from the woman's face, no sign of any opinion. Claudine had seen her face, less familiar than a stranger's. Later when she tried she would never remember the face, only as a disquieting and unresolved meeting. Like waking in between sleep and catching a figure, a movement in the room.

#

He had raped her. That is how her first child was born. He had grabbed her and forced her into his little room and covered her mouth so that his mother would not hear her screaming. She had bitten the flesh on his hand until there was blood and still he had exploded her insides, broken her. His face was dense against her crying. He did it as if she was not there, not herself, not how she knew herself. Anyone would have seen that he was killing her but his dense face told her that he saw nothing. She was thirteen, she felt like the hogs that were strung on the limbs of trees and slit from the genitals to the throat. That is how her first child was born. With blood streaming down her legs and feeling broken and his standing up and saying "Nothing is wrong, go home and don't tell anyone." And when she ran through the bush crying that she would tell her mother and stood at the stand pipe to wash the blood off her dress and to cool the pain between her thighs, she knew she could tell no one.

Up the hill to the top overlooking the water, she wanted to dive into the sea. The water would hit her face, it would rush past her ears quickly it would wash her limbs and everything would be as before and this would not have happened—a free fall, a dive into the sea. Her body would hit the tuft of grass before reaching the bottom and it would hurt even more. She could not push off far enough to fall into the water.

She said nothing. She became sick and puffy. And her stepfather told her mother that she was pregnant and she begged her mother not to believe him, it was a lie, and her mother sent her to the doctor and told her not to come back home if it was true. When the doctor explained the rape, he said "Someone put a baby in your belly." And she could not go home. And when it was dark that night and she was alone on the road because everyone—her aunt first and then her grandmother had said "go home," she saw her mother on the road coming down with a torchlight. Her mother, rakish and holding her skirt coming toward her. Both of them alone on the road. And she walked behind her all the way home silent, as her mother cursed and told her that she'd still have to do all the work and maybe more. Every day until the birth her mother swore and took care of her.

He denied it when the child was coming and she screamed it was "you, you, you!" loud and tearing so that the whole village could hear, that it was he. He kept quiet after that and his mother bore his shame by feeding her and asking her "How're things?"

From then, everyone explained the rape by saying that she was his woman. In fact they did not even say it, they did not have to. Only they made her feel as if she was carrying his body around. In their looking at her and their smiles which moved to one side of the cheek and with their eyelids, uncommonly demurring, or round and wide and gazing she came into the gaze of all of them no longer a child, much less a child who had been raped, now—a man's body. All she remembered was his face as if he saw nothing when he saw her and his unusual body resembling the man who slaughtered pigs for the village—so gnarled and horrible, the way he moved. Closing her eyes he seemed like a tamarind tree—sour and unclimbable—her arms could not move, pinned by his knotted hands and she could not breathe, her breathing took up all the time and she wanted to scream, not breathe—more screaming than breathing.

That is how her first child with him was born. Much as she tried her screaming did not get past the bush and the trees even though she tried to force it through the blades of grass and the coarse vines. Upon every movement of the bush her thin and piercing voice grabbed for the light between but the grass would move the other way making the notes which got through dissonant and unconnected, not like the sound of a killing.

QUESTIONS

1. What do the trees and grass symbolize in the story?

2. Define the manner in which Claudine's life has been determined by the patriarchal values instilled in Prime and her uncle Ranni.

3. What is Claudine's attitude toward motherhood?

4. Is there any way for Claudine to escape her situation? Why or why not?

Margaret Atwood

(b. 1939)

As one of Canada's most famous poets and novelists, Margaret Atwood's works defy easy categorization. She was born in Ottawa, moved at age six to Sault Ste. Marie, and then to Toronto the following year. Because her father was an entomologist, she spent her summers in the Canadian bush and was back in the city for the rest of the year. This duality between city and country played an important part in her development. She received her BA from the University of Toronto in 1961 and an MA from Radcliffe the following year. In 1961, she published her first volume of poems and within five years won the Governor General's Award for poetry with *The Circle Game* (1966). Throughout the 1960s, Atwood taught at a series of Canadian universities. Once her writing career was established, Atwood traveled throughout North America and the world; she now lives in Toronto and is married to the novelist Graeme Gibson.

Although most noted for her fiction writing, she has published her poetry in magazines as varied as the *Tamarack Review, The Canadian Forum, The New Yorker, The Atlantic Monthly, Poetry (Chicago), Kayak, Quarry,* and *Prism.* Her most recent volume of poems, *Morning in the Burned House* (1995), is about observing life around her. She is concerned with the manifold ways in which the ugliness in the world appears beautiful. Her fiction is wide-ranging, but certain tendencies can be detected. Often, feminist issues are in the forefront of her writings. In *The Handmaid's Tale* (1985), for example, she writes of a dystopia in the United States where the moral majority gains ultimate power. These religious fanatics impose a rigid series of regulations on women, and Offred, the handmaiden, has the task of having sex once a month with her master with the sole purpose of having his children. The gradual awakening of Offred to the flaws in the system is analogous to what happened to women in the last half of the twentieth century. Some of her more important novels include *The Edible Woman* (1969), *Surfacing* (1972), *Lady Oracle* (1976), *Cat's Eye* (1988), and *The Blind Assassin* (2000). *The Blind Assassin,* like many of her novels, is set in Canada and explores through the reminiscences of an old woman, Iris Chase, who comes to understand herself by examining the events around the suicide of her sister just after World War II. The novel explores the complications of decision making in the restrictive Canadian society and how the ramifications of those decisions can affect those involved throughout their lives.

Atwood has published five volumes of short stories, *Dancing Girls* (1977), *Murder in the Dark* (1983), *Bluebeard's Egg* (1983), *Wilderness Tips* (1991), and *Good Bones* (1992). The story below is from the *Wilderness Tips* collection. The story examines the protagonist's musings about the discovery of a long-deceased Arctic explorer's body in the ice and the death of her best friend Vincent. Her reflections cause her to examine the nature of their relationship and the emptiness of her generation. Atwood's tale offers a stirring condemnation of the modern world, which is built on material acquisition and selfish decisions.

The Age of Lead   *1991*

The man has been buried for a hundred and fifty years. They dug a hole in the frozen gravel, deep into the permafrost, and put him down there so the wolves couldn't get to him. Or that is the speculation.

When they dug the hole the permafrost was exposed to the air, which was warmer. This made the permafrost melt. But it froze again after the man was covered up, so that when he was brought to the surface he was completely enclosed in ice. They took the lid off the coffin and it was like those maraschino cherries you used to freeze in ice-cube trays for fancy tropical drinks: a vague shape, looming through a solid cloud.

Then they melted the ice and he came to light. He is almost the same as when he was buried. The freezing water has pushed his lips away from his teeth into an astonished snarl, and he's a beige colour, like a gravy stain on linen, instead of pink, but everything is still there. He even has eyeballs, except that they aren't white but the light brown of milky tea. With these tea-stained eyes he regards Jane: an indecipherable gaze, innocent, ferocious, amazed, but contemplative, like a werewolf meditating, caught in a flash of lightning at the exact split second of his tumultuous change.

Jane doesn't watch very much television. She used to watch it more. She used to watch comedy series, in the evenings, and when she was a student at university she would watch afternoon soaps about hospitals and rich people, as a way of procrastinating. For a while, not so long ago, she would watch the evening news, taking in the disasters with her feet tucked up on the chesterfield, a throw rug over her legs, drinking a hot milk and rum to relax before bed. It was all a form of escape.

But what you can see on the television, at whatever time of day, is edging too close to her own life; though in her life, nothing stays put in those tidy compartments, comedy here, seedy romance and sentimental tears there, accidents and violent deaths in thirty-second clips they call *bites,* as if they were chocolate bars. In her life, everything is mixed together. *Laugh, I thought I'd die,* Vincent used to say, a very long time ago in a voice imitating the banality of mothers; and that's how it's getting to be. So when she flicks on the television these days, she flicks it off again soon enough. Even the commercials, with their surreal dailiness, are beginning to look sinister, to suggest meanings behind themselves, behind their facade of cleanliness, lusciousness, health, power, and speed.

Tonight she leaves the television on, because what she is seeing is so unlike what she usually sees. There is nothing sinister behind this image of the frozen man. It is entirely itself. *What you sees is what you gets,* as Vincent also used to say, crossing his eyes, baring his teeth at one side, pushing his nose into a horror-movie snout. Although it never was, with him.

The man they've dug up and melted was a young man. Or still is: it's difficult to know what tense should be applied to him, he is so insistently present. Despite the distortions caused by the ice and the emaciation of his illness, you can see his youthfulness, the absence of toughening, of wear. According to the dates painted carefully onto his nameplate, he was only twenty years old. His name was John Torrington. He was, or is, a sailor, a seaman. He wasn't an able-bodied seaman though; he was a petty officer, one of those marginally in command. Being in command has little to do with the ableness of the body.

He was one of the first to die. This is why he got a coffin and a metal nameplate, and a deep hole in the permafrost—because they still had the energy, and the piety, for such things, that early. There would have been a burial service read over him, and prayers. As time went on and became nebulous and things did not get better, they must have kept the energy for themselves; and also the prayers. The prayers would have ceased to be routine and become desperate, and then hopeless. The later dead ones got cairns of piled stones, and the much later ones not even that. They ended up as bones, and as the soles of boots and the occasional button, sprinkled over the frozen stony treeless relentless ground in a trail heading south. It was like the trails in fairy tales, of bread crumbs or seeds or white stones. But in this case nothing had sprouted or lit up in the moonlight, forming a miraculous pathway to life; no rescuers had followed. It took ten years before anyone knew even the barest beginnings of what had been happening to them.

All of them together were the Franklin Expedition. Jane has seldom paid much attention to history except when it has overlapped with her knowledge of antique furniture and real estate—"19th C. pine harvest table," or "Prime location Georgian centre hall, impeccable reno"—but she knows what the Franklin Expedition was. The two ships with their bad-luck names have been on stamps—the *Terror,* the *Erebus.* Also she took it in school, along with a lot of other doomed expeditions. Not many of those explorers seemed to have come out of it very well. They were always getting scurvy, or lost.

What the Franklin Expedition was looking for was the Northwest Passage, an open seaway across the top of the Arctic, so people, merchants, could get to India from England without going all the way around South America. They wanted to go that way because it would cost less and increase their profits. This was much less exotic than Marco Polo or the headwaters of the Nile; nevertheless, the idea of exploration appealed to her then: to get onto a boat and just go somewhere, somewhere mapless, off into the unknown. To launch yourself into fright; to find things out. There was something daring and noble about it, despite all of the losses and failures, or perhaps because of them. It was like having sex, in high school, in those days before the Pill, even if you took precautions. If you were a girl, that is. If you were a boy, for whom such a risk was fairly minimal, you had to do other things: things with weapons or large amounts of alcohol, or high-speed vehicles, which at her suburban Toronto high school, back then at the beginning of the sixties, meant switchblades, beer, and drag races down the main streets on Saturday nights.

Now, gazing at the television as the lozenge of ice gradually melts and the outline of the young sailor's body clears and sharpens, Jane remembers Vincent, sixteen and with more hair then, quirking one eyebrow and lifting his lip in a mock sneer and saying, "Franklin, my dear, I don't give a damn." He said it loud enough to be heard, but the history teacher ignored him, not knowing what else to do. It was hard for the teachers to keep Vincent in line, because he never seemed to be afraid of anything that might happen to him.

He was hollow-eyed even then; he frequently looked as if he'd been up all night. Even then he resembled a very young old man, or else a dissipated child. The dark circles under his eyes were the ancient part, but when he smiled he had lovely small white teeth, like the magazine ads for baby foods. He made fun of everything, and was adored. He wasn't adored the way other boys were adored, those boys with surly lower lips and greased hair and a studied air of smouldering menace. He was adored like a pet. Not a dog, but a cat. He went where he liked, and nobody owned him. Nobody called him Vince.

Strangely enough, Jane's mother approved of him. She didn't usually approve of the boys Jane went out with. Maybe she approved of him because it was obvious to her that no bad results would follow from Jane's going out with him: no heartaches, no heaviness, nothing burdensome. None of what she called *consequences*. Consequences: the weightiness of the body, the growing flesh hauled around like a bundle, the tiny frill-framed goblin head in the carriage. Babies and marriage, in that order. This was how she understood men and their furtive, fumbling, threatening desires, because Jane herself had been a consequence. She had been a mistake, she had been a war baby. She had been a crime that had needed to be paid for, over and over.

By the time she was sixteen, Jane had heard enough about this to last her several lifetimes. In her mother's account of the way things were, you were young briefly and then you fell. You plummeted downwards like an over-ripe apple and hit the ground with a squash; you fell, and everything about you fell too. You got fallen arches and a fallen womb, and your hair and teeth fell out. That's what having a baby did to you. It subjected you to the force of gravity.

This is how she remembers her mother, still: in terms of a pendulous, drooping, wilting motion. Her sagging breasts, the downturned lines around her mouth. Jane conjures her up: there she is, as usual, sitting at the kitchen table with a cup of cooling tea, exhausted after her job clerking at Eaton's department store, standing all day behind the jewellery counter with her bum stuffed into a girdle and her swelling feet crammed into the mandatory medium-heeled shoes, smiling her envious, disapproving smile at the spoiled customers who turned up their noses at pieces of glittering junk she herself could never afford to buy. Jane's mother sighs, picks at the canned spaghetti Jane has heated up for her. Silent words waft out of her like stale talcum powder. *What can you expect,* always a statement, never a question. Jane tries at this distance for pity, but comes up with none.

As for Jane's father, he'd run away from home when Jane was five, leaving her mother in the lurch. That's what her mother called it—"running away from home"—as if he'd been an irresponsible child. Money arrived from time to time, but that was the sum total of his contribution to family life. Jane resented him for it, but she didn't blame him. Her mother inspired in almost everyone who encountered her a vicious desire for escape.

Jane and Vincent would sit out in the cramped backyard of Jane's house, which was one of the squinty-windowed little stuccoed wartime bungalows at the bottom of the hill. At the top of the hill were the richer houses, and the richer people: the girls who owned cashmere sweaters, at least one of them, instead of the Orlon and lambswool so familiar to Jane. Vincent lived about halfway up the hill. He still had a father, in theory.

They would sit against the back fence, near the spindly cosmos flowers[1] that passed for a garden, as far away from the house itself as they could get. They would drink gin, decanted by Vincent from his father's liquor hoard and smuggled in an old military pocket flask he'd picked up somewhere. They would imitate their mothers.

"I pinch and I scrape and I work my fingers to the bone, and what thanks do I get?" Vincent would say peevishly. "No help from you, Sonny Boy. You're just like your father. Free as the birds, out all night, do as you like and you don't care one pin about anyone else's feelings. Now take out that garbage."

"It's love that does it to you," Jane would reply, in the resigned, ponderous voice of her mother. "You wait and see, my girl. One of these days you'll come down off your devil-may-care high horse." As Jane said this, and even though she was making fun, she could picture love, with a capital L, descending out of the sky towards her like a huge foot. Her mother's life had been a disaster, but in her own view an inevitable disaster, as in songs and movies. It was Love that was responsible, and in the face of Love, what could be done? Love was like a steamroller. There was no avoiding it, it went over you and you came out flat.

Jane's mother waited, fearfully and uttering warnings, but with a sort of gloating relish, for the same thing to happen to Jane. Every time Jane went out with a new boy her mother inspected him as a potential agent of downfall. She distrusted most of these boys; she distrusted their sulky, pulpy mouths, their eyes half-closed in the up-drifting smoke of their cigarettes, their slow, sauntering manner of walking, their clothing that was too tight, too full: too full of their bodies. They looked this way even when they weren't putting on the sulks and swaggers, when they were trying to appear bright-eyed and industrious and polite for Jane's mother's benefit, saying goodbye at the front door, dressed in their shirts and ties and their pressed heavy-date suits. They couldn't help the way they looked, the way they were. They were

---

1 **cosmos flowers:** Colorful flowers from the aster family.

hel]
slee

goi
app
bat
ery
Vir
car
goi
do
to
bo

get
sh
fal
th
ch
m
lu
th
th
w

m
b
k

"]
al
e
st
tl

u
ti
a

l

2

Jane and Vincent wandered off to different cities. They wrote each other post-cards. Jane did this and that. She ran a co-op food store in Vancouver, did the financial stuff for a diminutive theatre in Montreal, acted as managing editor for a small publisher, ran the publicity for a dance company. She had a head for details and for adding up small sums—having to scrape her way through university had been instructive—and such jobs were often available if you didn't demand much money for doing them. Jane could see no reason to tie herself down, to make any sort of soul-stunting commitment, to anything or anyone. It was the early seventies; the old heavy women's world of girdles and precautions and consequences had been swept away. There were a lot of windows opening, a lot of doors: you could look in, then you could go in, then you could come out again.

She lived with several men, but in each of the apartments there were always cardboard boxes, belonging to her, that she never got around to unpacking; just as well, because it was that much easier to move out. When she got past thirty she decided it might be nice to have a child, some time, later. She tried to figure out a way of doing this without becoming a mother. Her own mother had moved to Florida, and sent rambling, grumbling letters, to which Jane did not often reply.

Jane moved back to Toronto, and found it ten times more interesting than when she'd left it. Vincent was already there. He'd come back from Europe, where he'd been studying film; he'd opened a design studio. He and Jane met for lunch, and it was the same: the same air of conspiracy between them, the same sense of their own potential for outrageousness. They might still have been sitting in Jane's garden, beside the cosmos flowers, drinking forbidden gin and making fun.

Jane found herself moving in Vincent's circles, or were they orbits? Vincent knew a great many people, people of all kinds; some were artists and some wanted to be, and some wanted to know the ones who were. Some had money to begin with, some made money; they all spent it. There was a lot more talk about money, these days, or among these people. Few of them knew how to manage it, and Jane found herself helping them out. She developed a small business among them, handling their money. She would gather it in, put it away safely for them, tell them what they could spend, dole out an allowance. She would note with interest the things they bought, filing their receipted bills: what furniture, what clothing, which *objets.* They were delighted with their money, enchanted with it. It was like milk and cookies for them, after school. Watching them play with their money, Jane felt responsible and indulgent, and a little matronly. She stored her own money carefully away, and eventually bought a townhouse with it.

All this time she was with Vincent, more or less. They'd tried being lovers but had not made a success of it. Vincent had gone along with this scheme because Jane had wanted it, but he was elusive, he would not make declarations. What worked with other men did not work with him: appeals to his protective instincts, pretences at jealousy, requests to remove stuck lids from jars. Sex with him was more like a musical workout. He couldn't take it seriously, and accused her of being too solemn about it. She thought he might be gay, but was afraid to ask him; she dreaded feeling irrelevant to him, excluded. It took them months to get back to normal.

He was older now, they both were. He had thinning temples and a widow's peak, and his bright inquisitive eyes had receded even farther into his head. What went on between them continued to look like a courtship, but was not one. He was always bringing her things; a new, peculiar food to eat, a new grotesquerie to see, a new piece of gossip, which he would present to her with a sense of occasion, like a flower. She in her turn appreciated him. It was like a yogic exercise, appreciating Vincent; it was like appreciating an anchovy, or a stone. He was not everyone's taste.

There's a black-and-white print on the television, then another: the nineteenth century's version of itself, in etchings. Sir John Franklin, older and fatter than Jane had supposed; the *Terror* and the *Erebus,* locked fast in the crush of the ice. In the high Arctic, a hundred and fifty years ago, it's the dead of winter. There is no sun at all, no moon; only the rustling northern lights, like electronic music, and the hard little stars.

What did they do for love, on such a ship, at such a time? Furtive solitary gropings, confused and mournful dreams, the sublimation of novels. The usual, among those who have become solitary.

Down in the hold, surrounded by the creaking of the wooden hull and the stale odours of men far too long enclosed, John Torrington lies dying. He must have known it; you can see it on his face. He turns toward Jane his tea-coloured look of puzzled reproach.

Who held his hand, who read to him, who brought him water? Who, if anyone, loved him? And what did they tell him about whatever it was that was killing him? Consumption, brain fever, Original Sin. All those Victorian reasons, which meant nothing and were the wrong ones. But they must have been comforting. If you are dying, you want to know why.

In the eighties, things started to slide. Toronto was not so much fun any more. There were too many people, too many poor people. You could see them begging on the streets, which were clogged with fumes and cars. The cheap artists' studios were torn down or converted to coy and upscale office space; the artists had migrated elsewhere. Whole streets were torn up or knocked down. The air was full of wind-blown grit.

People were dying. They were dying too early. One of Jane's clients, a man who owned an antique store, died almost overnight of bone cancer. Another, a woman who was an entertainment lawyer, was trying on a dress in a boutique and had a heart attack. She fell over and they called the ambulance, and she was dead on arrival. A theatrical producer died of AIDS, and a photographer; the lover of the photographer shot himself, either out of grief or because he knew he was next. A friend of a friend died of emphysema, another of viral pneumonia, another of hepatitis picked up on a tropical vacation, another of spinal meningitis. It was as if they had been weakened by some mysterious agent, a thing like a colourless gas, scentless and invisible, so that any germ that happened along could invade their bodies, take them over.

He d
uprooted
meadows
water ver
bridges, t
the water
talking. I
many ho
more dro
another l
ten. The
all over a
In o
family is
have gra
taings. T
had lace
nearer to
"W
"No
He
went slo
verted f
"W
We
green, y
in trees
Ge
farm w
eyes, a
rounde
under
under
the sm
them a
W
below.
as it d
cross v
"I
a Jew.
M
Georg

man in a T-shirt brought a dog, a terrier, on a leash. Then he let him go into the shallows. Under an umbrella a young woman was breast-feeding a baby. Nearer to the water a tall woman with white skin and red hair was lying on her back, topless. People were changing using large coloured towels . . . while the continual sound of the low surf as it came in breaking over the pebbles and sliding back.

I had brought a picnic: bread, a hard-boiled egg, cheese, tomatoes, a pear. And a can of cider to wash it down. After I had eaten I took off my shirt, shoes, socks, and lay down on the stones.

A loud noise woke me. It was two boys running over the stones between my head and the cliffs. I sat up. I didn't know how long I had been asleep. The surface of the water sparkled. The click of the boules was still going. From somewhere a dog was barking. The cliffs, a few yards behind me and on both sides, had light green streaks in the massive white grey. And high up, on the very top, a thin layer of grass.

The tide was coming in. I put on shirt, socks, and shoes, and walked over the pebbles to a paved slope that led from the beach to the road. I could now see a narrow opening between the cliffs. And as I walked up the slope the opening fanned out to show a suburb of houses with gardens, green lawns, and trees. As I came to the top of the paved slope I saw, across the road, on a stone, in French and English:

> On this beach
> Officers and Men of the
> Royal Regiment of Canada
> Died at Dawn 19 August 1942
> Striving to Reach the Heights Beyond
>
> You who are alive on this beach
> remember that these men died far from home
> that others here and everywhere might freely
> enjoy life in God's mercy.

When I got back to the hotel the "full" sign had been taken down. Madame greeted me with a smile.

"You have caught the sun. I have surprise for you."

She soon re-appeared with a thin blonde girl of about twelve or thirteen.

"This is Jean. She is from Canada," Madame said proudly. "From Alberta."

"Where from in Alberta?" I asked.

"Edmonton," the girl replied in a quiet voice.

"How long will you be in Dieppe?"

"I live here. I go to school."

"When were you in Edmonton?"

"Three weeks ago."

"Is your father there?"

"No, he is somewhere else. He travels. I'm with my mother."

"Can you speak French as well as you can English?"

"I can speak it better," she said.

country and come to the city for a visit. Their observations allow the reader to understand the temptations and shallowness of urban life. In "A Brief Conversion," an adolescent confronts conflicting definitions of manhood and through the struggle comes to learn dignity and respect for himself and others.

The question of being an outsider in the mainstream of West Indian fiction is also germane when examining writing by Indo-Caribbean and Creole writers as well as women. The most well-known "outsider" is the Trinidadian-born Vidiadhar Surajprasad Naipaul. Son of the short story writer Seepersad Naipaul, V. S. Naipaul moved to the capital when he was six and was encouraged to write by his father. In 1950, Naipaul went to study at Oxford, but he had a very difficult time adjusting to English life. After a suicide attempt, Naipaul realized he could alchemize his unhappiness into fictional gold. His first novel was published in 1959, and like many of his contemporaries' fiction, it examined his upbringing in Trinidad. A few years later, his masterpiece, *A House for Mr. Biswas* (1961), appeared. Based largely on his father's life, the novel chronicles the struggles of a young determined man to gain his independence in a world of poverty and prejudice. Naipaul's pessimistic views of life and his abhorrence of imperialism color his fiction works, but his premier place in Caribbean literature was assured with the awarding of the Nobel Prize for literature in 2001. His most popular collection of short fiction, *A Flag on the Island* (1967), concerns the problems of racial tension and class distinction in Trinidad; the story "The Night Watchman's Occurrence Book" is a typical example of how well Naipaul captures these nuances.

In the 1960s, the movement for self-determination in the Caribbean took root. With national liberationist figures such as Marcus Garvey in Jamaica, Frantz Fanon in Martinique, and Eric Williams in Trinidad, the colonial powers realized they could not deny nationhood to the various islands any longer. Barbados was granted internal autonomy in 1961; Jamaica gained full independence in 1962, as did Trinidad and Tobago. But these developing countries soon discovered that independence is not in itself a guarantee of success. In the 1960s, poverty, inflation, unemployment, and racial tensions between Afro- and Indo-Caribbeans made self-determination a complicated issue. As a result of the growing pains of new nationhood and the political problems arising out of it, the literature analyzed the new society and the failed promises of nationhood and social democracy. These issues continue to permeate the short fiction and novels of the Indies.

Only since the 1980s have West Indian women writers been judged to deserve critical attention. Since then, the flourishing richness of their voices has been amazingly profuse. Delineating the unity of the women of the English-speaking Caribbean fiction writers from any standpoint is exceedingly difficult. In Mary Condé's introduction to *Caribbean Women Writers* (1999), she points out that if one looked only at the major Guyana women writers in the last half of the twentieth century, one would have a very different set of experiences on which to base fiction: Beryl Gilroy was one of those early Afro-Caribbean expatriates who left her birthplace for Britain in the 1960s. Poet and fiction writer Grace Nichols, of African

Caribbean background, left Guyana in 1977 and works in Sussex, England. Meiling Jin's *Song of the Boatwoman* (1996) examines with humor and realism the lives of Chinese women not only in Guyana, but also in England, the United States, China, and Malaysia. Narmala Shewcharan, of Indian descent; Pauline Melville, of African, Dutch, and Amerindian heritage; Joan Cambridge, who set her novel *Clarise Cumberbatch Want to Go Home* (1987) in New York; and Norma DeHaarte, now of Canada, all write from different stances and out of exceedingly different backgrounds.

The eclectic nature of culture and background is valid across the whole of the Caribbean, but certain themes do occur consistently enough in the women's works to draw an important conclusion. In most Caribbean women's writing, a strong strain of nostalgia for the home country as it existed in the past can be found. The enforced exile, whether it be for economic or educative reasons, almost always finds a tension between the culture embraced and the culture remembered. The most poignant example of this tension can be observed in Velma Pollard's "Gran," from her short story collection *Considering Women* (1989). Pollard's grandmother was a woman who, after her husband died, raised seven children alone by working a sugar-cane farm. The evocation of this stalwart Jamaican woman into fiction, a woman whose fundamental determination cannot be denied, is an act of dedication with the past. Erna Brodber (Jamaica), Olive Senior (Jamaica), Merle Hodge (Trinidad), Beryl Gilroy (Guyana), Zee Edgell (Belize), Paule Marshall (Barbados), Michelle Cliff (Jamaica), and Dionne Brand (Trinidad) are the leading lights of a wonderfully diverse number of female writers who in the past twenty years have offered glimpses into the often silenced female existence in the Caribbean.

The Caribbean woman's struggle against the past as well as the present is highly visible in contemporary life and literature. She has taken on the issues of self-determination, cultural limitations, patriarchy, racism, and repressive culture values. These struggles are chronicled by some of the most talented individuals mentioned above. By the end of the last century, Caribbean women writers had joined forces with Caribbean men to offer an exciting and vibrant literary experience in English. Currently, West Indian writing has become academically accepted, and a postcolonial agenda has been foisted upon it. Ironically, much of the criticism of the West Indian fiction came from North America or England, where now most of the writers reside.

One burning question in Caribbean literature at the moment is, Who are the West Indian writers addressing: an audience of academics with theoretical expectations built along a postcolonial agenda, or their own people, the people of the Caribbean islands who are the true inheritors of the culture? The debate continues into the twenty-first century.

Samuel Dickson Selvon

(TRINIDAD, 1923–1994)

A child of East Indian parents, Samuel Dickson Selvon was born in San Fernando, Trinidad, and was educated at Naparima College, Trinidad. While serving in the Royal Navy during World War II, he began to think seriously about writing as a career. This decision led him to take up the position of the fiction editor for the Trinidad *Guardian* newspaper when he left the military. This career allowed him to pursue a creative writing interest, and between 1945 and 1950 he published not only fiction but also poetry and critical reviews in Caribbean magazines. In 1950, he migrated to England, where, as a freelance writer, many of his stories were published in prestigious literary magazines such as *The London Magazine*, *The New Statesman*, and *Nation*. His first novel, *A Brighter Sun* (1952), was published in England; this novel is characteristic of many of Selvon's literary concerns. The novel is set in Trinidad and looked into the many cultural changes and their ramifications in a rural Indo-Caribbean community. The story chosen for this collection, "The Cricket Match," is set in London and presents in a humorous fashion the nature of English preconceived notions about West Indians. The story turns on the West Indians' sense of pride and love of overstatement, but the purport of the story focuses on how little the English and the West Indians understand one another.

Throughout the 1950s, Selvon published novels and short story collections about life in Trinidad and then about the lonely existence of West Indian expatriates in England. In the 1960s, Selvon began work for the British Broadcasting Company (BBC) and produced radio plays, television scripts, and even a film version of his 1956 novel, *The Lonely Londoners*. He received a number of academic fellowships and held positions at Canadian, British, and U.S. universities. In 1978, Selvon moved to Alberta to continue writing his strongly critical ironic studies of the dissimilarity between the British and the West Indian lifestyles and cultures. His *Moses Ascending* (1975) and *Moses Migrating* (1983) are playful and subversive revisitings of the colonial relationships and power structures of Robinson Crusoe and Friday set in 1970s London. *Moses Migrating* follows the protagonist of *The Lonely Londoners* and *Moses Ascending* back to his birthplace in Trinidad where he joins the annual celebrations.

Selvon received an honorary doctorate from the University of Warwick in 1989 and was posthumously awarded the Trinidad and Tobago Gold Medal for Literature (1995). Selvon's stories are alive with energy and vitality; in his works the West Indians are not victims but rather are participants in a struggle for equality and freedom. Often his migrant characters are disillusioned and depressed as they struggle against the odds for their rightful place in their host society while at the same time remaining true to their own heritage.

The Cricket Match

1957

The time when the West Indies cricket eleven come to England to show the Englishmen the finer points of the game, Algernon was working in a tyre factory down by Chiswick way, and he lambast them English fellars for so.

"That is the way to play the game," he tell them, as the series went on and West Indies making some big score and bowling out them English fellars for duck[1] and thing, "you thought we didn't know how to play the game, eh? That is cricket, lovely cricket."

And all day he singing a calypso that he make up about the cricket matches that play, ending up by saying that in the world of sport, is to wait until the West Indies report.

Well in truth and in fact, the people in this country believe that everybody who come from the West Indies at least like the game even if they can't play it. But you could take it from me that it have some tests that don't like the game at all, and among them was Algernon. But he see a chance to give the Nordics tone and he get all the gen[2] on the matches and players, and come like an authority in the factory on cricket. In fact, the more they ask him the more convinced Algernon get that perhaps he have the talent of a Walcott[3] in him only waiting for a chance to come out.

They have a portable radio hide away from the foreman and they listening to the score every day. And as the match going on you should hear Algernon: "Yes, lovely stroke," and "That should have been a six," and so on. Meanwhile, he picking up any round object that near to hand and making demonstration, showing them how Ramadhin[4] does spin the ball.

"I bet you used to play a lot back home," the English fellars tell him.

"Who, me?" Algernon say. "Man, cricket is breakfast and dinner where I come from. If you want to learn about the game you must go down there. I don't want to brag," he say, hanging his head a little, "but I used to live next door to Ramadhin, and we used to teach one another the fine points."

But what you think Algernon know about cricket in truth? The most he ever play was in the street, with a bat make from a coconut branch, a dry mango seed for ball, and a pitchoil tin for wicket. And that was when he was a boy, and one day he get lash with the mango seed and since that time he never play again.

But all day long in the factory, he and another West Indian fellar name Roy getting on as if they invent the game, and the more the West Indies eleven score, the more they getting on. At last a Englisher name Charles, who was living in the suburbs, say to Algernon one morning:

---

1 **for duck:** Without scoring a single run.
2 **gen:** Information.
3 **Walcott:** Clyde Walcott, famous Guyana cricket player.
4 **Ramadhin:** Sonny Ramadhin, famous West Indian spin bowler.

"You chaps from the West Indies are really fine cricketers. I was just wondering . . . I play for a side where I live, and the other day I mentioned you and Roy to our captain, and he said why don't you organize an eleven and come down our way one Saturday for a match? Of course," Charles went on earnestly, "we don't expect to be good enough for you, but still, it will be fun."

"Oh," Algernon say airily, "I don't know. I uses to play in first-class matches, and most of the boys I know accustom to a real good game with strong opposition. What kind of pitch you have?"

"The pitch is good," Charles say. "Real English turf."

Algernon start to hedge. He scratch his head. He say, "I don't know. What you think about the idea, Roy?"

Roy decide to hem and leave Algernon to get them out of the mooch.[5] He say, "I don't know, either. It sound like a good idea, though."

"See what you can do," Charles say, "and let me know this week."

Afterwards in the canteen having elevenses Roy tell Algernon: "You see what your big mouth get us into."

"*My* big mouth!" Algernon say. "Who it is say he bowl four top bats for duck one after the other in a match in Queen's Park oval in Port of Spain? Who it is say he score two hundred and fifty not out in a match against Jamaica?"

"Well to tell you the truth Algernon," Roy say, now that they was down to brass tacks, "I ain't play cricket for a long time. In fact, I don't believe I could still play."

"Me too, boy," Algernon say. "I mean, up here in England you don't get a chance to practise or anything. I must be out of form."

They sit down there in the canteen cogitating on the problem.

"Anyway," Roy say, "it look as if we will have to hustle an eleven somehow. We can't back out of it now."

"I studying," Algernon say, scratching his head. "What about Eric, you think he will play?"

"You could ask him, he might. And what about Williams? And Wilky? And Heads? Those boys should know how to play."

"Yes, but look at trouble to get them! Wilky working night and he will want to sleep. Heads is a man you can't find when you want. And Williams—I ain't see him for a long time, because he owe me a pound and he don't come my way these days."

"Still," Roy say, "we will have to manage to get a side together. If we back out of this now them English fellars will say we are only talkers. You better wait for me after work this evening, and we will go around by some of the boys and see what we could do."

That was the Monday, and the Wednesday night about twelve of the boys get together in Algernon room in Kensal Rise, and Algernon boiling water in the kettle and making tea while they discuss the situation.

---

5 **mooch:** An obligation, usually of an unwelcome sort.

3. What does the reverence for the West Indian cricket team by the exiles tell you about the nature of their exile?

4. Why is there a strong sense of irony in the conclusion of the story?

Karl Sealy

(BARBADOS, b. ca. 1932)

Karl Sealy was born in Barbados and was influenced greatly by the poverty and lack of educational potential there after World War II. Sealy's short stories are generally concerned with the question of poverty such as "The Pieces of Silver," which describes how poor boys at a local school are expected to donate money toward a teacher's retirement present. Cleverly, one student earns enough money by singing to pay for the entire contribution, saving his schoolmates from further hardship.

"My Fathers Before Me" comes from the collection entitled *West Indian Stories* (1960), edited by Andrew Salkey. It originally appeared in *Bim* and was broadcast on the BBC radio program *Caribbean Voices*. The story captures very powerfully the upheaval that emigrating to the United Kingdom has upon a small tight-knit family, all of whom have been torn apart for generations by having their men leave Barbados. Its theme is one of Sealy's major concerns: the problem of his people leaving Barbados to find new and better lives in the United Kingdom or North America.

My Fathers Before Me   1958

Dick, the yard man, took the big Rhode Island cock from the run and, tucking it under his arm, went back to the kitchen steps where he had been sitting.

He held the cock fast between his legs and, squeezing its mouth open with his left hand, took a pinch of ashes from the small heap beside him, between right thumb and forefinger. This he rubbed on to the bird's tongue, and began to peel the hard, horny growth from the tongue's end.

His grandmother, who had spent most of her usefulness with the family, came shambling from the house behind him, eating cassava farina[1] soaked in water and sugar. She stood looking down at him for some time, her eyes, the colour of dry bracken, tender, before she took a spoonful of farina from the glass and, bending with the stiffness of years, put it from behind into his mouth. Through the farina in his mouth Dick said, like a man continuing his thought in speech:

---

1 **cassava farina:** A food similar to tapioca, made from the roots of the cassava plant.

"And your age, Granny? You've spent a lifetime here. How many summers have you seen?"

"More than you'll ever see if you go to England," she said, letting herself down on the step above him. "Eighty-four years come October, God spare life. Whole fourteen above-and-beyond what the good Lord says."

"Hmm," Dick said, and taking the cock to the run, returned with a hen as white as a swan.

The old woman said: "Just think of it, Dick, just think of it. Come this time to-morrow you'll be miles away, with oceans of water separating you from everybody who loves you, and going to a land where you ent got a bird in the cotton tree, where nobody'll care a straw whether you sink or swim, and where black ent altogether liked." She scraped the last of the farina from the glass, and once more put the spoon to his mouth.

"You ent mind leaving us, Dick?" she said. "You ent mind leaving your poor old Granny and Ma? And Vere? What about Vere? You ent got no feelings in that belly of ye'n, Dick?"

Sucking farina from his teeth with his tongue, Dick said: "I'll send for Vere as soon as I can. Maybe Ma, too."

The old woman continued as though she had not heard: "No more Dick about the house to put your hands 'pon. Maybe some lazy wringneck governor in your place whose only interest'll be his week's pay."

"Time enough too, and welcome," Dick said.

From an upstairs window, whose curtains she had been pulling against the evening sun, Bessie saw her mother sitting on the concrete step above Dick. Going down to the servants' room she took a cushion from the sofa and went out to where they were sitting. She said:

"Up, Ma. Think you're young, sitting on this cold step?"

The old woman raised herself a few inches, and Bessie pushed the cushion under her.

"I's just been telling Dick, Bessie, how no good ent ever come to our family leaving our land and going into nobody else country."

"True enough," said Bessie. "Look at my Dick and Panama."

Then the old woman asked: "Ever teach you who the Boers[2] was at school, Dick?"

"I ent ever learn for sure who the Boers were," said Dick, "save that they couldn't stand up to bayonets."

"That's right," Bessie said. " 'At the bayonet charge the Boers surrender.' "

"British bayonets," Dick remarked.

"Don't you let nobody fool you with that, Dick," said the old woman. "There wasn't all no British bayonets. Your gran'dad's bayonet was there, too."

"Oh, well, we're all British. At least that's the way I look at it."

---

2 **Boers:** South African settlers of Dutch descent who fought against the British in South Africa from 1899 to 1901.

"No use, nuh?" said the old woman. "Hm."

Vere said, sitting up and half-turning so that her words might be taken in by both women:

"You two had husbands, *husbands* mind you, and nothing you could say or do could stop them from going away once their minds was made up. I ent see how I's been more foolish than either of you 'cause I ent been able to stop Dick here from going."

Dick executed a long stretch before he said: "My father was sick of cleaning up the mess that Miss Barbara's dogs made in the morning, sick of watering the gardens under the big evergreen, sick of cleaning pips off these stupid fowls, sick of waiting for the few paltry shillings at the end of the week, just as heartily sick of the whole deuced show as I am myself now.

"And so when the chance of going to Panama came along nothing nobody could say could stop him from going, just as nothing nobody can say will stop me from going to England. My grandfather and dad didn't go because they were foolish, but because they were brave. They didn't go because they wanted to be rid of their wives and children. They didn't go because they wanted an easy life. They didn't go for a spree. They went because their souls cried out for better opportunities and better breaks. And just like them, I'm going for the same thing."

Bessie was still standing there her hands akimbo, looking down at Dick. When Dick finished speaking her eyes switched their measure to Vere, and with a fleeting lightening of her harsh face which none of the others saw she decided to play her last card.

"Still, Vere," said Bessie, "you're a foolish girl."

Vere pouted: "Say it again. A hundred times. Till you're tired."

"What're you straightening your hair so for?" Bessie asked.

"'Cause other girls do," said Vere.

"And rouging your face, and plastering that red thing on to your mouth?"

"'Cause other girls do." Vere hugged her knees, rocking herself back and forth on the step.

"You was always a rude brazen little girl. All the same, I hope you's got something else to make Dick stick by you. He going to England where he'll see hundreds of girls with real straight hair and really red cheeks and mouths natural like roses. Ten to one, one of them will get him."

Vere sprang to her feet, her eyes dilated.

"And I'd spend the last cent getting to England, and wherever they was I'd find them out and tear the last straight hair from her head. I'd tear the flesh from her red cheeks to the bone!

"I'd beat her rosy mouth to a bloody pulp! Oh Christ, I'd . . ."

She caught at her breath in a long racking sob, snatched the basket from the ground and ran into the house.

The other three were all standing now, and in the understanding of Vere's love, had drawn involuntarily closer to one another.

The old woman said, knocking a beetle from Dick's shirt with her spoon: "And will you still go to England, Dick?"

Their ears just barely caught the one word from his lips.

The women turned and, mounting the steps in the settling dusk, made their way together into the house.

The old woman said: "It's the same with him as it was with them, Bessie. Nothing will ever stop him."

"No. Nothing," said Bessie.

QUESTIONS

1. What is the origin of the conflict in this story?

2. What do you think is the "one word" that comes from Dick's lips at the conclusion of the tale? How do you know that?

3. Why are the historical references to the building of the Panama Canal and the Boer War relevant to the story?

4. Why is Bessie so opposed to Vere's hair-straightening and use of cosmetics? What does this reveal about gender and gender identities in the story and of the time?

5. What is at the core of the struggle between Dick and Bessie in the story?

Jean Rhys

(DOMINICA, ca. 1890–1979)

Jean Rhys was born Ella Rees Williams in Roseau on the British colony of Dominica in the West Indies. Her Welsh father was a doctor, and her mother was the granddaughter of James Potter Lockhart, who had bought the Geneva estate on Dominica in 1824. The estate's decline is depicted in Rhys's most popular novel, *Wide Sargasso Sea* (1966), which was completed and published when she was seventy-six. Rhys's childhood experiences on Dominica as a member of the Creole (white elite) class left her with a very mixed legacy; her sense of isolation and of being an outsider clashed with her admiration for the vibrancy and "cultural richness" of the native Dominicans. Much of her fiction is an attempt to align herself with the black women she had met in her life, but somehow the sterility of her Englishness stands in her way.

Rhys left Dominica in 1907 to attend the Perse School in Cambridge, and subsequently came back only once, briefly, in 1936; nevertheless, she never forgot her experiences there. The impact Dominica had on Rhys can be ascertained from her autobiographical memoir, *Smile Please* (1979), which was published posthumously. In her early twenties, Rhys attended a drama college in London, where she began to write creatively. In 1919, she married a Dutch novelist and had two children, one of whom died three weeks after birth. She had an affair with the British novelist Ford Madox Ford in 1924, and her first novel, *Quartet: A Novel* (1929), is a fictional record of this experience. The novel's development of the character of Marya Zelli introduces the typical Rhys heroine: alluring yet dependent on those around her for support. Her first book of short stories, *The Left Bank and Other Stories* (1927), shows the developing Rhys heroine as well.

In the 1930s, Rhys wrote three very powerful novels: *After Leaving Mr Mackenzie* (1931), *Voyage in the Dark* (1934), and *Good Morning, Midnight* (1939). These novels gained her literary and financial success; however, by 1950, Rhys was living in poverty, divorced and remarried, and an alcoholic. She visited Dominica with her second husband in 1936. While the journey awakened her interest in Caribbean themes, she felt the guilt of a member of the imperialist class returning to a world to which she really did not belong. Many of the notes from this experience were later used for the writing of *Wide Sargasso Sea*.

Rhys's literary fortunes were revived when the BBC dramatized her *Good Morning, Midnight* in 1958 and her novel *Wide Sargasso Sea* was published in 1966. The popularity of her novel, inspired by Charlotte Brontë's *Jane Eyre*, propelled her into the public eye and eventual acceptance in her adopted country. Rhys lived her final years accepted by the society that had found her work unconventional and controversial during most of her writing career.

The story that follows, "The Day They Burnt the Books," shows the cruel, uneducated nature of the narrow-minded colonials in the Caribbean and how their attitudes tried to shape the native peoples into something they could never be. Rhys also examined the nature of sexual repression and awakenings in stories such as "Goodbye Marcus, Goodbye Rose." The important point here is that Rhys was continually influenced by her early upbringing, and her short stories are strongly autobiographical in nature.

The Day They Burnt the Books   1960

My friend Eddie was a small, thin boy. You could see the blue veins in his wrists and temples. People said that he had consumption and wasn't long for this world. I loved, but sometimes despised him.

His father, Mr Sawyer, was a strange man. Nobody could make out what he was doing in our part of the world at all. He was not a planter or a doctor or a lawyer or a banker. He didn't keep a store. He wasn't a schoolmaster or a government official. He wasn't—that was the point—a gentleman. We had several resident romantics who had fallen in love with the moon on the Caribees—they were all gentlemen and quite unlike Mr Sawyer who hadn't an "h" in his composition. Besides, he detested the moon and everything else about the Caribbean and he didn't mind telling you so.

He was an agent for a small steamship line which in those days linked up Venezuela and Trinidad with the smaller islands, but he couldn't make much out of that. He must have a private income, people decided, but they never decided why he had chosen to settle in a place he didn't like and to marry a coloured woman. Though a decent, respectable, nicely educated coloured woman, mind you.

Mrs Sawyer must have been very pretty once but, what with one thing and another, that was in days gone by.

When Mr Sawyer was drunk—this often happened—he used to be very rude to her. She never answered him.

"Look at the nigger showing off," he would say; and she would smile as if she knew she ought to see the joke but couldn't. "You damned, long-eyed gloomy half-caste, you don't smell right," he would say; and she never answered, not even to whisper, "You don't smell right to me, either."

The story went that once they had ventured to give a dinner party and that when the servant, Mildred, was bringing in coffee, he had pulled Mrs Sawyer's hair. "Not a wig, you see," he bawled. Even then, if you can believe it, Mrs Sawyer had laughed and tried to pretend that it was all part of the joke, this mysterious, obscure, sacred English joke.

But Mildred told the other servants in the town that her eyes had gone wicked, like soucriant's[1] eyes, and that afterwards she had picked up some of the hair he pulled out and put it in an envelope, and that Mr Sawyer ought to look out (hair is obeah[2] as well as hands).

Of course, Mrs Sawyer had her compensations. They lived in a very pleasant house in Hill Street. The garden was large and they had a fine mango tree, which bore prolifically. The fruit was small, round, very sweet and juicy—a lovely, red-and-yellow colour when it was ripe. Perhaps it was one of the compensations, I used to think.

Mr Sawyer built a room on to the back of this house. It was unpainted inside and the wood smelt very sweet. Bookshelves lined the walls. Every time the Royal Mail steamer came in it brought a package for him, and gradually the empty shelves filled.

Once I went there with Eddie to borrow *The Arabian Nights*. That was on a Saturday afternoon, one of those hot, still afternoons when you felt that everything had gone to sleep, even the water in the gutters. But Mrs Sawyer was not asleep. She put

---

1 **soucriant:** A much feared supernatural female figure in the Caribbean. She sheds her skin at night and travels through the air in a ball of fire searching for sleeping victims from which to suck blood. She is stopped by a circle of rice around the bed, which she must stop and eat.

2 **obeah:** An African-derived matrix of cultural and magical practices; here it is a charm with magical powers.

her head in at the door and looked at us, and I knew that she hated the room and hated the books.

It was Eddie with the pale blue eyes and straw-coloured hair—the living image of his father, though often as silent as his mother—who first infected me with doubts about "home," meaning England. He would be so quiet when others who had never seen it—none of us had ever seen it—were talking about its delights, gesticulating freely as we talked—London, the beautiful, rosy-cheeked ladies, the theatres, the shops, the fog, the blazing coal fires in winter, the exotic food (whitebait eaten to the sound of violins), strawberries and cream—the word "strawberries" always spoken with a guttural and throaty sound which we imagined to be the proper English pronunciation.

"I don't like strawberries," Eddie said on one occasion.

"You *don't like* strawberries?"

"No, and I don't like daffodils either. Dad's always going on about them. He says they lick the flowers here into a cocked hat and I bet that's a lie."

We were all too shocked to say, "You don't know a thing about it." We were so shocked that nobody spoke to him for the rest of the day. But I for one admired him. I also was tired of learning and reciting poems in praise of daffodils, and my relations with the few "real" English boys and girls I had met were awkward. I had discovered that if I called myself English they would snub me haughtily: "You're not English; you're a horrid colonial." "Well, I don't much want to be English," I would say. "It's much more fun to be French or Spanish or something like that—and, as a matter of fact, I am a bit." Then I was too killingly funny, quite ridiculous. Not only a horrid colonial, but also ridiculous. Heads I win, tails you lose—that was the English. I had thought about all this, and thought hard, but I had never dared to tell anybody what I thought and I realized that Eddie had been very bold.

But he was bold, and stronger than you think. For one thing, he never felt the heat; some coldness in his fair skin resisted it. He didn't burn red or brown, he didn't freckle much.

Hot days seem to make him feel especially energetic. "Now we'll run twice round the lawn and then you can pretend you're dying of thirst in the desert and that I'm an Arab chieftain bringing you water."

"You must drink slowly," he would say, "for if you're very thirsty and you drink quickly you die."

So I learnt the voluptuousness of drinking slowly when you are very thirsty—small mouthful by small mouthful, until the glass of pink, iced Coca-Cola was empty.

Just after my twelfth birthday, Mr Sawyer died suddenly, and as Eddie's special friend I went to the funeral, wearing a new white dress. My straight hair was damped with sugar and water the night before and plaited into tight little plaits, so that it should be fluffy for the occasion.

When it was all over everybody said how nice Mrs Sawyer had looked, walking like a queen behind the coffin and crying her eyeballs out at the right moment, and wasn't Eddie a funny boy? He hadn't cried at all.

After this Eddie and I took possession of the room with the books. No one else ever entered it, except Mildred to sweep and dust in the mornings, and gradually the ghost of Mr Sawyer pulling Mrs Sawyer's hair faded though this took a little time. The blinds were always half-way down and going in out of the sun was like stepping into a pool of brown-green water. It was empty except for the bookshelves, a desk with a green baize top and a wicker rocking-chair.

"My room," Eddie called it. "My books," he would say, "my books."

I don't know how long this lasted. I don't know whether it was weeks after Mr Sawyer's death or months after, that I see myself and Eddie in the room. But there we are and there, unexpectedly, are Mrs Sawyer and Mildred. Mrs Sawyer's mouth tight, her eyes pleased. She is pulling all the books out of the shelves and piling them into two heaps. The big, fat glossy ones—the good-looking ones, Mildred explains in a whisper—lie in one heap. The *Encyclopedia Britannica, British Flowers, Birds and Beasts,* various histories, books with maps, Froude's *English in the West Indies* and so on—they are going to be sold. The unimportant books, with paper covers or damaged covers or torn pages, lie in another heap. They are going to be burnt—yes, burnt.

Mildred's expression was extraordinary as she said that—half hugely delighted, half-shocked, even frightened. And as for Mrs Sawyer—well, I knew bad temper (I had often seen it). I knew rage, but this was hate. I recognized the difference at once and stared at them curiously. I edged closer to her so that I could see the titles of the books she was handling.

It was the poetry shelf. *Poems,* Lord Byron, *Poetical Works,* Milton, and so on. Vlung, vlung, vlung—all thrown into the heap that were to be sold. But a book by Christina Rossetti, though also bound in leather, went into the heap that was to be burnt, and by a flicker in Mrs Sawyer's eyes I knew that worse than men who wrote books were women who wrote books—infinitely worse. Men could be mercifully shot; women must be tortured.

Mrs Sawyer did not seem to notice that we were there, but she was breathing free and easy and her hands had got the rhythm of tearing and pitching. She looked beautiful, too—beautiful as the sky outside which was a very dark blue, or the mango tree, long sprays of brown and gold.

When Eddie said "No," she did not even glance at him.

"No," he said again in a high voice. "Not that one. I was reading that one."

She laughed and he rushed at her, his eyes starting out of his head, shrieking, "Now I've got to hate you too. Now I hate you too."

He snatched the book out of her hand and gave her a violent push. She fell into the rocking-chair.

Well, I wasn't going to be left out of all this, so I grabbed a book from the condemned pile and dived under Mildred's outstretched arm.

Then we were both in the garden. We ran along the path, bordered with crotons.[3] We pelted down the path, though they did not follow us and we could hear

---

3 **crotons:** Tropical plant, like a shrub.

Mildred laughing—kyah, kyah, kyah, kyah. As I ran I put the book I had taken into the loose front of my brown holland dress. It felt warm and alive.

When we got into the street we walked sedately, for we feared the black children's ridicule. I felt very happy, because I had saved this book and it was my book and I would read it from the beginning to the triumphant words "The End." But I was uneasy when I thought of Mrs Sawyer.

"What will she do?" I said.

"Nothing," Eddie said. "Not to me."

He was white as a ghost in his sailor suit, a blue-white even in the setting sun, and his father's sneer was clamped on his face.

"But she'll tell your mother all sorts of lies about you," he said. "She's an awful liar. She can't make up a story to save her life, but she makes up lies about people all right."

"My mother won't take any notice of her," I said. Though I was not at all sure.

"Why not? Because she's . . . because she isn't white?"

Well, I knew the answer to that one. Whenever the subject was brought up—people's relations and whether they had a drop of coloured blood or whether they hadn't—my father would grow impatient and interrupt. "Who's white?" he would say. "Damned few."

So *I* said, "Who's white? Damned few."

"You can go to the devil," Eddie said. "She's prettier than your mother. When she's asleep her mouth smiles and she has curling eyelashes and quantities and quantities and *quantities* of hair."

"Yes," I said truthfully. "She's prettier than my mother."

It was a red sunset that evening, a huge, sad, frightening sunset.

"Look, let's go back," I said. "If you're sure she won't be vexed with you, let's go back. It'll be dark soon."

At the gate he asked me not to go. "Don't go yet, don't go yet."

We sat under the mango tree and I was holding his hand when he began to cry. Drops fell on my hand like the water from the drip-stone in the filter in our yard. Then I began to cry too and when I felt my own tears on my hand I thought, "Now perhaps we're married."

"Yes, certainly, now we're married," I thought. But I didn't say anything. I didn't say a thing until I was sure he had stopped. Then I asked, "What's your book?"

"It's *Kim*," he said. "But it got torn. It starts at page twenty now. What's the one you took?"

"I don't know; its too dark to see," I said.

When I got home I rushed into my bedroom and locked the door because I knew that this book was the most important thing that had ever happened to me and I did not want anybody to be there when I looked at it.

But I was very disappointed, because it was in French and seemed dull. *Fort Comme La Mort*,[4] it was called . . .

---

4 **Fort Comme La Mort:** "Strong as Death," a short story by Guy de Maupassant about a mysterious passion and how it lasts beyond the grave.

QUESTIONS

1. How does Rhys's status as an outsider inform this story?

2. Discuss the importance of race in this story.

3. What motivates Mrs. Sawyer to burn the books?

4. Looking specifically at the narrator's comments, why is the discovery of the French book at the conclusion of the story so ironic?

C. L. R. James

(TRINIDAD, 1901–1989)

C. L. R. James was not only a fine writer, but also a historian, a Marxist social critic, and an activist whose insights and interpretations significantly shaped the Afro-Caribbean struggle for self-governance. James was born into an educated family in Tunapuna, in colonial Trinidad. In 1910, James won a scholarship to Queen's Royal College in Port-of-Spain, Trinidad, and graduated in 1918. He was kept on to teach and subsequently worked at the Government Training College for Teachers. While there, he met Alfred Mendes, and together they formed a group of progressive thinkers, the ideas from which James began to turn into literature. His short story "La Divina Pastora" was published by the British *Saturday Review of Literature,* and James's depiction of the poverty-stricken cocoa worker brought him international attention.

"Triumph" was James's next published work. It appeared in *Trinidad,* a literary journal published between 1929 and 1930 and coedited by James and Mendes. The story is important because it is an early example of what became known as "Yard Fiction." Yards are communal dwelling places and communities based around shared facilities and close proximity; they are particularly associated with working-class habitation. Further, the depictions of female characters here became models of female characters who appeared in subsequent male-dominated short fiction of the Caribbean. James's story introduces the large and sexually alluring, but rather indolent woman who dominates the local scene. James's woman is able to outwit her suitors and keep her independence against the odds.

While in England during the 1930s as a sports writer for the *Manchester Guardian,* James became enamored of Leon Trotsky's thinking and embraced a Marxist agenda that called for Caribbean independence. But James was not an idle dreamer. In his *Minty Alley* (1936), he discussed the complications of bringing self-rule into a society that was largely uneducated. With the invasion of Ethiopia by Fascist Italy in 1935, James became involved in a Pan African movement and wrote the influential play *Toussaint L'Ouverture* (1936), concerning the revolution in Haiti in 1801. James moved to the United States in the 1940s and promoted an Afro-American Worker's Party, which stood for equality and socialist values. After the war, James was detained by the U.S. government for disseminating Communist propaganda and wrote a severe condemnation of U.S. democracy entitled *Mariners, Renegades, and Castaways: The Story of Herman Melville and the World We Live In* (1953).

On his expulsion from the United States, James returned to Trinidad to work for a pro-independence group, but he fell out of favor for his radical stance. He moved to England and continued to write and lecture. After a brief teaching appointment in the United States, he moved back to London, where he died.

Triumph   1965

Where people in England and America say slums, Trinidadians say barrack-yards. Probably the word is a relic of the days when England relied as much on garrisons of soldiers as on her fleet to protect her valuable sugar-producing colonies. Every street in Port-of-Spain[1] proper can show you numerous examples of the type: a narrow gateway leading into a fairly big yard, on either side of which run long low buildings, consisting of anything from four to eighteen rooms, each about twelve feet square. In these live, and have always lived the porters, prostitutes, carter-men, washer-women, and domestic servants of the city.

In one corner of the yard is the hopelessly inadequate water-closet, unmistakable to the nose if not to the eye; sometimes there is a structure with the title of bath-room: a courtesy title, for he or she who would wash in it with decent privacy must cover the person as if bathing on the Lido[2]; the kitchen happily presents no difficulty: never is there one and each barrack-yarder cooks before her door. In the centre of the yard is a heap of stones. On these the half-laundered clothes are bleached before being finally spread out to dry on the wire lines which in every yard cross and recross each other in all directions. Not only to Minerva have these stones been dedicated. Time was when they would have had an honoured shrine in a local temple to Mars, for they were the major source of ammunition for the homicidal strife which in times past so often flared up in barrack-yards. As late as 1915, the local bard, practising his band for the annual carnival (which still flourishes in Trinidad alone of the British West Indian islands)—as late as 1915 he could sing:

> When the rumour went round the town
> That the Germans was comin' to blow us down,
> When the rumour went round the town
> That the Germans was comin' to blow us down,
> Some like cowards remain at home

---

1 **Port-of-Spain:** Capital of Trinidad and Tobago on the Gulf of Paria.
2 **Lido:** A fashionable beach in Venice, Italy.

Others come forth with bottle and stone
Old lady couldn't bring stone but she come with the pot-chambre.

The stones from "the bleach" were to help even in the repelling of the German invader. A poetic idea, and as is not uncommon with poetry, an anachronism. No longer do the barrack-yarders live the picturesque life of twenty-five years ago. Then, practising for the carnival, rival singers, Will, Jean, and Freddie, porter, wharf-man, or loafer, in ordinary life, but for that season ennobled by some such striking sobriquet as The Duke of Normandy or The Lord Invincible, and carrying with dignity homage such as young aspirants to literature would pay to Mr Kipling or Mr Shaw, thirty years ago. They sang in competition from seven in the evening until far into the early morning, stimulated by the applause of their listeners and the excellence and copiousness of the rum; night after night the stick-men practised their dangerous and skilful game; the "pierrots," after elaborate preface of complimentary speech, belaboured each other with riding whips; while around the performers the spectators pressed thick and good-humoured, until mimic warfare was transformed into real, and stones from "the bleach" flew thick. But today that life is dead. All carnival practice must cease at ten o'clock. The policeman is to the stick-fighter and "pierrot" as the sanitary inspector to mosquito larvae. At nights the streets are bright with electric light, the arm of the law is longer, its grip stronger. Gone are the old lawlessness and picturesqueness. Barrack-yard life has lost its savour. Luckily, prohibition in Trinidad is still but a word. And life, dull and drab as it is in comparison, can still offer its great moments.

On a Sunday morning in one of the rooms of a barrack in Abercromby Street sat Mamitz. Accustomed as is squalid adversity to reign unchallenged in these quarters, yet in this room it was more than usually triumphant, sitting, as it were, high on a throne of royal state, so depressed was the woman and depressing her surroundings.

The only representatives of the brighter side of life were three full-page pictures torn from illustrated periodicals, photographs of Lindbergh, Bernard Shaw, and Sargent's "Portrait of a Woman," and these owed their presence solely to the fact that no pawnshop would have accepted them. They looked with unseeing eyes upon a room devoid of furniture save for a few bags spread upon the floor to form a bed. Mamitz sat on the door-step talking to, or rather being talked to, by her friend Celestine who stood astride the concrete canal which ran in front of the door.

"Somebody do you something," said Celestine with conviction. "Nobody goin' to change my mind from that. An' if you do what I tell you, you will t'row off this black spirit that on you. A nice woman like you, and you carn' get a man to keep you! You carn' get nothing to do!"

Mamitz said nothing. Had Celestine said the exact opposite, Mamitz's reply would have been the same.

She was a black woman, too black to be pure negro, probably with some Madrasi[3] East Indian blood in her, a suspicion which was made a certainty by the

---

3 **Madrasi:** A person born in Madras, capital of Tamil Nadu state in southeast India on the Bay of Bengal.

"Jesu, lover of my soul," "Onward! Christian soldiers." Celestine and Irene sang so-
prano and Irene sang well. Mamitz was a naturally fine contralto and had a fine ear,
while Nathan who was a Barbadian and consequently knew vocal music used to sing
bass whenever he happened to be in. The singing would put him in a good mood
and he would send off to buy more rum and everything would be peaceful and
happy. But Irene was a jealous woman, not only jealous of her man, but jealous of
Mamitz's steady three dollars a week and Celestine's policeman with his twenty-
eight dollars at the end of the month. She lived with a cab-man whose income,
though good enough was irregular. And he was a married man, with a wife and children to support. Irene had to do washing to help her out, while Mamitz and Celestine did nothing, merely cooked and washed clothes for their men. So gradually a
state of dissatisfaction arose. Then one damp evening, Mamitz passing near the
bamboo pole which supported a clothes line overburdened with Irene's clothes,
brought it down with her broad expansive person. The line burst, and night-gowns,
sheets, pillowcases, white suits, and tablecloths fluttered to the mud. It had been a
rainy week with little sun, and already it would have been difficult to get the clothes
ready in time for Saturday morning; after this it was impossible. And hot and fiery
was the altercation. Celestine who tried to make peace was drawn into the quarrel by
Irene's comprehensive and incendiary invective.

"You comin' to put you' mouth in this. You think because you livin' with a policeman you is a magistrate. Mind you' business, woman, mind you' business. The
two o' all you don't do nothing for you' livin'. You only sittin' down an' eatin' out the
men all you livin' wid. An' I wo'k so hard an' put out me clo'es on the line. And this
one like some blame cab-horse knock it down, and when I tell 'er about it you
comin' to meddle! Le' me tell you . . ."

So the wordy warfare raged, Celestine's policeman coming in for rough treatment at the tongue of Irene. Celestine, even though she was keeping herself in check,
was a match for any barrack-yard woman Port-of-Spain could produce, but yet it
was Mamitz who clinched the victory.

"Don't min' Celestine livin' with a policeman. You will be glad to get 'im for
you'self. An' it better than livin' wid any stinkin' so'-foot man."

For Irene's cab-man had a sore on his foot, which he had had for thirty years
and would carry with him to the grave even if he lived for thirty years more.
Syphilis, congenital and acquired, and his copious boozing would see to it that there
was no recovery. Irene had stupidly hoped that nobody in the yard knew. But in
Trinidad when His Excellency the Governor and his wife have a quarrel, the street
boys speak of it the day after, and Richard's bad foot had long been a secret topic of
conversation in the yard. But it was Mamitz who had made it public property, and
Irene hated Mamitz with a virulent hatred, and had promised to "do" for her. Three
days before, Nathan, the tram-conductor had given Mamitz the first beating; but
even at the time of the quarrel there was no hint of his swift defection and Mamitz's
rapid descent to her present plight. So that Celestine, an errant but staunch religion-
ist, was convinced that Mamitz's troubles were due to Irene's trafficking with the
devil, if not personally, at least through one of his numerous agents who ply their

profitable trade in every part of Port-of-Spain. Secure of her own immunity from any thing that Irene might "put on her," she daily regretted that she couldn't rip the woman to pieces. "Oh Jesus! If it wasn't for Jimmy I'd tear the wretch lim' from lim'." But the energy that she could not put into the destruction of Irene she spent in upholding Mamitz. The fiery Celestine had a real affection for the placid Mamitz, whose quiet ways were so soothing. But, more than this, she was determined not to see Mamitz go down. In the bitter antagonism she nursed against Irene, it would have been a galling defeat if Mamitz went to the wall. Further, her reputation as a woman who knew things and could put crooked people straight was at stake. Once she had seen to Jimmy's food and clothes and creature comforts she set herself to devise ways and means of supporting the weak, easily crushed Mamitz.

Celestine's policeman being on duty that night, she herself was off duty and free to attend to her own affairs. At mid-night with the necessary rites and ceremonies, Ave Marias and Pater Nosters, she bathed Mamitz in a large bath-pan full of water prepared with gully-root, fever-grass, lime leaves, gueerir tout, herbe a femmes, and other roots, leaves, and grasses noted for their efficacy, (when properly applied) against malign plots and influences.

QUESTIONS

1. What elements of this story reflect James's concern with realism and local fiction?

2. How is life in the barrack-yard depicted?

3. What insights about the lives of Mamitz, Celestine, and Irene are exposed as the story unfolds?

4. How does this story offer the reader insights into explicit issues of class, race, sex roles, and the complexities of Caribbean identity?

V. S. Naipaul

(TRINIDAD, b. 1932)

Probably the most important writer of English literature in the Caribbean and winner of the Nobel Prize for literature in 2001, V. S. Naipaul may also be one of the sternest critics of both Indo-Caribbean people and their society. He was born in Trinidad into a family of Indian Brahmin heritage. His father was a journalist for the *Trinidad Guardian* and a short story writer, and he encouraged his son to be a writer. Naipaul was educated at Queen's Royal College in Port-of-Spain and went to study at Oxford in 1950. Although he tried to commit suicide while at Oxford, he eventually graduated and took a position as a

Noted. *Chas. Ethelbert Hillyard*

November 25. Midnight Bar close and 12.23 a.m. Barman left leaving Mr Wills and others in Bar. Mr Owen take 5 bottles Carib, Mr Wilson 6 Bottles Heineken, Mr Wills 18 Carib and they left at 2.52 a.m. Nothing unusual. Mr Wills was helpless, I don't see how anybody could drink so much, eighteen one man alone, this work enough to turn anybody Seventh Day Adventist, and another man come in the bar, I dont know his name, I hear they call him Paul, he assist me because the others couldn't do much, and we take Mr Wills up to his room and take off his boots and slack his other clothes and then we left. Don't know sir if they did take more while I was away, nothing was mark on the Pepsi Cola board, but they was drinking still, it look as if they come back and take some more, but with Mr Wills I want some extra assistance sir.

Mr Manager, the clock break I find it break when I come back from Mr Wills room sir. It stop 3.19 sir. *Chas. E. Hillyard*

> More than 2 lbs of veal were removed from the Fridge last night, and a cake that was left in the press was cut. It is your duty, Night Watchman Hillyard, to keep an eye on these things. I ought to warn you that I have also asked the Police to check on all employees leaving the hotel, to prevent such occurrences in the future. *W. A. G. Inskip*

Mr Manager, I don't know why people so anxious to blame servants sir. About the cake, the press lock at night and I dont have the key sir, everything safe where I am concern sir. *Chas. Hillyard*

November 26. Midnight Bar close and Barman left. Mr Wills didn't come, I hear he at the American base tonight, all quiet, nothing unusual.

Mr Manager, I request one thing. Please inform the Barman to let me know sir when there is a female guest in the hotel sir. *C. E. Hillyard*

> This morning I received a report from a guest that there were screams in the hotel during the night. You wrote All Quiet. Kindly explain in writing.
> *W. A. G. Inskip*
>   Write Explanation here:

EXPLANATION. Not long after midnight the telephone ring and a woman ask for Mr Jimminez. I try to tell her where he was but she say she cant hear properly. Fifteen minutes later she came in a car, she was looking vex and sleepy, and I went up to call him. The door was not lock, I went in and touch his foot and call him very soft, and he jump up and begin to shout. When he come to himself he said he had Night Mere, and then he come down and went away with the woman, was not necessary to mention.

Mr Manager, I request you again, please inform the Barman to let me know sir when there is a female guest in the hotel. *C. Hillyard*

November 27. 1 a.m. Bar close, Mr Wills and a American 19 Carib and 2.30 a.m. a Police come and ask for Mr Wills, he say the American report that he was robbed of

$200.00¢, he was last drinking at C— with Mr Wills and others. Mr Wills and the Police ask to open the Bar to search it, I told them I cannot open the Bar for you like that, the Police must come with the Manager. Then the American say it was only joke he was joking, and they try to get the Police to laugh, but the Police looking the way I feeling. Then laughing Mr Wills left in a garage car as he couldn't drive himself and the American was waiting outside and they both fall down as they was getting in the car, and Mr Wills saying any time you want a overdraft you just come to my bank kiddo. The Police left walking by himself. *C. Hillyard*

> Night Watchman Hillyard: "Was not necessary to mention"!! You are not to decide what is necessary to mention in this night watchman's occurrence book. Since when have you become sole owner of the hotel as to determine what is necessary to mention? If the guest did not mention it I would never have known that there were screams in the hotel during the night. Also will you kindly tell me who Mr Jimminez is? And what rooms he occupied or occupies? And by what right? You have been told by me personally that the names of all hotel guests are on the slate next to the light switches. If you find Mr Jimminez's name on this slate, or could give me some information about him, I will be most warmly obliged to you. The lady you ask about is Mrs Roscoe, Room 12, as you very well know. It is your duty to see that guests are not pestered by unauthorized callers. You should give no information about guests to such people, and I would be glad if in future you could direct such callers straight to me. *W. A. G. Inskip*

Sir was what I ask you two times, I dont know what sort of work I take up, I always believe that nightwatchman work is a quiet work and I dont like meddling in white people business, but the gentleman occupy Room 12 also, was there that I went up to call him, I didn't think it necessary to mention because was none of my business sir. *C.E.H.*

November 28. 12 Midnight Bar close and Barman left at 12.20 a.m. leaving Mr Wills and others, and they all left at 1.25 a.m. Mr Wills 8 Carib, Mr Wilson 12, Mr Percy 8, and the man they call Paul 12. Mrs Roscoe join the gentlemen at 12.33 a.m., four gins, everybody calling her Minnie from Trinidad, and then they start singing that song, and some others. Nothing unusual. Afterwards there were mild singing and guitar music in Room 12. A man come in and ask to use the phone at 2.17 a.m. and while he was using it about 7 men come in and wanted to beat him up, so he put down the phone and they all ran away. At 3 a.m. I notice the padlock not on the press, I look inside, no cake, but the padlock was not put on in the first place sir. Mr Wills come down again at 6 a.m. to look for his sweet, he look in the Fridge and did not see any. He took a piece of pineapple. A plate was covered in the Fridge, but it didn't have anything in it. Mr Wills put it out, the cat jump on it and it fall down and break. The garage bulb not burning. *C.E.H.*

> You will please sign your name at the bottom of your report. You are in the habit of writing Nothing Unusual. Please take note and think before

making such a statement. I want to know what is meant by nothing unusual. I gather, not from you, needless to say, that the police have fallen into the habit of visiting the hotel at night. I would be most grateful to you if you could find the time to note the times of these visits. *W. A. G. Inskip*

Sir, nothing unusual means everything usual. I dont know, nothing I writing you liking. I don't know what sort of work this night watchman work getting to be, since when people have to start getting Cambridge certificate to get night watchman job, I ain't educated and because of this everybody think they could insult me. *Charles Ethelbert Hillyard*

November 29. Midnight Bar close and 12.15 Barman left leaving Mr Wills and Mrs Roscoe and others in the Bar. Mr Wills and Mrs Roscoe left at 12.30 a.m. leaving Mr Wilson and the man they call Paul, and they all left at 1.00 a.m. Twenty minutes to 2 Mr Wills and party return and left again at 5 to 3. At 3.45 Mr Wills return and take bread and milk and olives and cherries, he ask for nutmeg too, I said we had none, he drink 2 Carib, and left ten minutes later. He also collect Mrs Roscoe bag. All the drinks, except the 2 Carib, was taken by the man they call Paul. I don't know sir I don't like this sort of work, you better hire a night barman. At 5.30 Mrs Roscoe and the man they call Paul come back to the bar, they was having a quarrel, Mr Paul saying you make me sick, Mrs Roscoe saying I feel sick, and then she vomit all over the floor, shouting I didn't want that damned milk. I was cleaning up when Mr Wills come down to ask for soda water, we got to lay in more soda for Mr Wills but I need extra assistance with Mr Wills Paul and party sir.

The police come at 2, 3.48 and 4.52. They sit down in the bar a long time. Firearms discharge 2 times in the back yard. Detective making inquiries. I don't know sir, I thinking it would be better for me to go back to some other sort of job. At 3 I hear somebody shout Thief, and I see a man running out of the back, and Mr London, Room 9, say he miss 80 cents and a pack of cigarettes which was on his dressing case. I don't know when the people in this place does sleep. *Chas. Ethelbert Hillyard*

> Night Watchman Hillyard: A lot more than 80 cents was stolen. Several rooms were in fact entered during the night, including my own. You are employed to prevent such things occurring. Your interest in the morals of our guests seems to be distracting your attention from your duties. Save your preaching for your roadside prayer meetings. Mr Pick, Room 7, reports that in spite of the most pressing and repeated requests, you did not awaken him at 5. He has missed his plane to British Guiana as a result. No newspapers were delivered to the rooms this morning. I am again notifying you that papers must be handed personally to Doorman Vignales. And the messenger's bicycle, which I must remind you is the property of the hotel, has been damaged. What do you *do* at nights? *W. A. G. Inskip*

Please don't ask me sir.

Relating to the damaged bicycle: I left the bicycle the same place where I meet it, nothing took place so as to damage it. I always take care of all property sir. I dont know how you could think I have time to go out for bicycle rides. About the papers, sir, the police and them read it and leave them in such a state that I didn't think it would be nice to give them to guests. I wake up Mr Pick, room 7, at 4.50 a.m. 5 a.m. 5.15 a.m. and 5.30. He told me to keep off, he would not get up, and one time he pelt a box of matches at me, matches scatter all over the place I always do everything to the best of my ability sir but God is my Witness I never find a night watchman work like this, so much writing I dont have time to do anything else, I dont have four hands and six eyes and I want this extra assistance with Mr Wills and party sir. I am a poor man and you could abuse me, but you must not abuse my religion sir because the good Lord sees All and will have His revenge sir, I don't know what sort of work and trouble I land myself in, all I want is a little quiet night work and all I getting is abuse. *Chas. E. Hillyard*

November 30. 12.25 a.m. Bar close and Barman left 1.00 a.m. leaving Mr Wills and party in Bar. Mr Wills take 12 Carib Mr Wilson 6, Mr Percy 14. Mrs Roscoe five gins. At 1.30 a.m. Mrs Roscoe left and there were a little singing and mild guitar playing in Room 12. Nothing unusual. The police come at 1.35 and sit down in the bar for a time, not drinking, not talking, not doing anything except watching. At 1.45 the man they call Paul come in with Mr McPherson of the SS Naparoni, they was both falling down and laughing whenever anything break and the man they call Paul say Fireworks about to begin tell Minnie Malcolm coming the ship just dock. Mr Wills and party scatter leaving one or two bottles half empty and then the man they call Paul tell me to go up to Room 12 and tell Minnie Roscoe that Malcolm coming. I don't know how people could behave so the thing enough to make anybody turn priest. I notice the padlock on the bar door break off it hanging on only by a little piece of wood. And when I went up to Room 12 and tell Mrs Roscoe that Malcolm coming the ship just dock the woman get sober straight away like she dont want to hear no more guitar music and she asking me where to hide where to go. I dont know, I feel the day of reckoning is at hand, but she not listening to what I saying, she busy straightening up the room one minute packing the next, and then she run out into the corridor and before I could stop she run straight down the back stairs to the annexe. And then 5 past 2, still in the corridor, I see a big man running up to me and he sober as a judge and he mad as a drunkard and he asking me where she is where she is. I ask whether he is a authorized caller, he say you don't give me any of that crap now, where she is, where she is. So remembering about the last time and Mr Jimminez I direct him to the manager office in the annexe. He hear a little scuffling inside Mr Inskip room and I make out Mr Inskip sleepy voice and Mrs Roscoe voice and the red man run inside and all I hearing for the next five minutes is bam bam bodow bodow bow and this woman screaming. I dont know what sort of work this night watchman getting I want something quiet like the police. In time things quiet down and the red man drag Mrs Roscoe out of the annexe and they take a taxi, and the Police sitting down quiet in the bar. Then Mr Percy and the others come back one by one to the bar and they talking quiet and they not drinking and they left 3 a.m. 3.15 Mr Wills return and take one whisky and 2 Carib. He asked for pineapple or some sweet fruit but it had nothing.

6 a.m. Mr Wills came in the bar looking for soda but it aint have none. We have to get some soda for Mr Wills sir.

6.30 a.m. the papers come and I deliver them to Doorman Vignales at 7 a.m. *Chas. Hillyard*

> Mr Hillyard: In view of the unfortunate illness of Mr Inskip, I am temporarily in charge of the hotel. I trust you will continue to make your nightly reports, but I would be glad if you could keep your entries as brief as possible. *Robt. Magnus, Acting Manager*

December 1 10.30 p.m. C. E. Hillyard take over duty at C— Hotel all corrected 12 Midnight Bar close 2 a.m. Mr Wills 2 Carib, 1 bread 6 a.m. Mr Wills 1 soda 7 a.m. Night Watchman Hillyard hand over duty to Mr Vignales with one torch light 2 Fridge keys and Room Keys 1, 3, 6 and 12. Bar intact all corrected no report. *C.E.H.*

QUESTIONS

1. What advantages does the narrative form of this story offer the reader?

2. What different characteristics between Hillyard and Inskip are developed during the story?

3. How do the strained relationships between the two races (Indian and African) manifest themselves in the stories?

4. Ultimately, the conclusion of this tale mirrors its beginning. Is this a comment about Trinidadian society? What comment is being made?

Jamaica Kincaid

(ANTIGUA, b. 1949)

Jamaica Kincaid was born Elaine Potter Richardson on the island of Antigua; she was raised by her mother, a political activist, and her stepfather, a carpenter, until age sixteen, when she was sent to work as an au pair in New York state. In addition to working as an au pair, she worked as a receptionist and a magazine writer. While in the United States, she completed her education, studying photography at the New York School for Social Research and attending Franconia College in New Hampshire. In 1973, she wrote a series of articles for *Ingenue* magazine; she published under the pseudonym of Jamaica Kincaid because of family pressure. These early pieces brought her to the attention of the editor of the *New Yorker,* and she began to publish fiction through the 1970s and 1980s.

Many of the stories she published in the *New Yorker* were collected and published under the title *At the Bottom of the River* (1983). The collection caused quite a stir when published; the stories were lyrically breathtaking and startlingly original. The tales often concern the tension between mother and daughter, and the importance of this relationship to build an independent bonding amidst the prevalence of a male-dominated world. The story in this anthology explores the definition of what it is like to be black, both physically and metaphysically.

In 1985 Kincaid revisited Antigua, which had gained independence from Great Britain in 1981, and was angered by the vestiges of colonial legacy as well as the failure of the Antiguan people to build on the positive aspects of colonial rule. She wrote *A Small Place* (1988), a vituperative look at the colonial British rule in Antigua and its aftermath. Kincaid is also very critical of the values of capitalism and materialism that Antiguans had bought into through mass tourism and trade. More recently, she published a touching memory of her brother who died of AIDS, *My Brother* (1997), and an eclectic series of essays about gardening, botany, and colonialism and the New World entitled *My Garden: Book* (1999).

Blackness   1983

How soft is the blackness as it falls. It falls in silence and yet it is deafening, for no other sound except the blackness falling can be heard. The blackness falls like soot from a lamp with an untrimmed wick. The blackness is visible and yet it is invisible, for I see that I cannot see it. The blackness fills up a small room, a large field, an island, my own being. The blackness cannot bring me joy but often I am made glad in it. The blackness cannot be separated from me but often I can stand outside it. The blackness is not the air, though I breathe it. The blackness is not the earth, though I walk on it. The blackness is not water or food, though I drink and eat it. The blackness is not my blood, though it flows through my veins. The blackness enters my many-tiered spaces and soon the significant word and event recede and eventually vanish: in this way I am annihilated and my form becomes formless and I am absorbed into a vastness of free-flowing matter. In the blackness, then, I have been erased. I can no longer say my own name. I can no longer point to myself and say "I." In the blackness my voice is silent. First, then, I have been my individual self, carefully banishing randomness from my existence, then I am swallowed up in the blackness so that I am one with it . . .

There are the small flashes of joy that are present in my daily life: the upturned face to the open sky, the red ball tumbling from small hand to small hand, as small voices muffle laughter; the sliver of orange on the horizon, a remnant of the sun setting. There is the wide stillness, trembling and waiting to be violently shattered by impatient demands.

("May I now have my bread without the crust?"

"But I long ago stopped liking my bread without the crust!")

All manner of feelings are locked up within my human breast and all manner of events summon them out. How frightened I became once on looking down to see an oddly shaped, ash-colored object that I did not recognize at once to be a small part of my own foot. And how powerful I then found that moment, so that I was not at one with myself and I felt myself separate, like a brittle substance dashed and shattered, each separate part without knowledge of the other separate parts. I then clung fast to a common and familiar object (my lamp, as it stood unlit on the clean surface of my mantelpiece), until I felt myself steadied, no longer alone at sea in a small rowboat, the waves cruel and unruly. What is my nature, then? For in isolation I am all purpose and industry and determination and prudence, as if I were the single survivor of a species whose evolutionary history can be traced to the most ancient of ancients; in isolation I ruthlessly plow the deep silences, seeking my opportunities like a miner seeking veins of treasure. In what shallow glimmering space shall I find what glimmering glory? The stark, stony mountainous surface is turned to green, rolling meadow, and a spring of clear water, its origins a mystery, its purpose and beauty constant, draws all manner of troubled existence seeking solace. And again and again, the heart—buried deeply as ever in the human breast, its four chambers exposed to love and joy and pain and the small shafts that fall with desperation in between.

I sat at a narrow table, my head, heavy with sleep, resting on my hands. I dreamed of bands of men who walked aimlessly, their guns and cannons slackened at their sides, the chambers emptied of bullets and shells. They had fought in a field from time to time and from time to time they grew tired of it. They walked up the path that led to my house and as they walked they passed between the sun and the earth; as they passed between the sun and the earth they blotted out the daylight and night fell immediately and permanently. No longer could I see the blooming trefoils, their overpowering perfume a constant giddy delight to me; no longer could I see the domesticated animals feeding in the pasture; no longer could I see the beasts, hunter and prey, leading a guarded existence; no longer could I see the smith moving cautiously in a swirl of hot sparks or bent over anvil and bellows. The bands of men marched through my house in silence. On their way, their breath scorched some flowers I had placed on a dresser, with their bare hands they destroyed the marble columns that strengthened the foundations of my house. They left my house, in silence again, and they walked across a field, opposite to the way they had come, still passing between the sun and the earth. I stood at a window and watched their backs until they were just a small spot on the horizon.

I see my child arise slowly from her bed. I see her cross the room and stand in front of the mirror. She looks closely at her straight, unmarred body. Her skin is without color, and when passing through a small beam of light, she is made transparent. Her eyes are ruby, revolving orbs, and they burn like coals caught suddenly in a gust of wind. This is my child! When her jaws were too weak, I first chewed her food, then fed it to her in small mouthfuls. This is my child! I must carry a cool liquid in my flattened breasts to quench her parched throat. This is my child sitting in the shade, her head thrown back in rapture, prolonging some moment of joy I have created for her.

My child is pitiless to the hunchback boy; her mouth twists open in a cruel smile, her teeth becoming pointed and sparkling, the roof of her mouth bony and ridged, her young hands suddenly withered and gnarled as she reaches out to caress his hump. Squirming away from her forceful, heated gaze, he seeks shelter in a grove of trees, but her arms, which she can command to grow to incredible lengths, seek him out and tug at the long silk-like hairs that lie flattened on his back. She calls his name softly and the sound of her voice shatters his eardrum. Deaf, he can no longer heed warnings of danger and his sense of direction is destroyed. Still, my child has built for him a dwelling hut on the edge of a steep cliff so that she may watch him day after day flatten himself against a fate of which he knows and yet cannot truly know until the moment it consumes him.

My child haunts the dwelling places of the useless-winged cormorants, so enamored is she of great beauty and ancestral history. She traces each thing from its meager happenstance beginnings in cool and slimy marsh, to its great glory and dominance of air or land or sea, to its odd remains entombed in mysterious alluviums. She loves the thing untouched by lore, she loves the thing that is not cultivated, and yet she loves the thing built up, bit carefully placed upon bit, its very beauty eclipsing the deed it is meant to commemorate. She sits idly on a shore, staring hard at the sea beneath the sea and at the sea beneath even that. She hears the sounds within the sounds, common as that is to open spaces. She feels the specter, first cold, then briefly warm, then cold again as it passes from atmosphere to atmosphere. Having observed the many differing physical existences feed on each other, she is beyond despair or the spiritual vacuum.

Oh, look at my child as she stands boldly now, one foot in the dark, the other in the light. Moving from pool to pool, she absorbs each special sensation for and of itself. My child rushes from death to death, so familiar a state is it to her. Though I have summoned her into a fleeting existence, one that is perilous and subject to the violence of chance, she embraces time as it passes in numbing sameness, bearing in its wake a multitude of great sadnesses.

I hear the silent voice; it stands opposite the blackness and yet it does not oppose the blackness, for conflict is not a part of its nature. I shrug off my mantle of hatred. In love I move toward the silent voice. I shrug off my mantle of despair. In love, again, I move ever toward the silent voice. I stand inside the silent voice. The silent voice enfolds me. The silent voice enfolds me so completely that even in memory the blackness is erased. I live in silence. The silence is without boundaries. The pastures are unfenced, the lions roam the continents, the continents are not separated. Across the flat lands cuts the river, its flow undammed. The mountains no longer rupture. Within the silent voice, no mysterious depths separate me; no vision is so distant that longing is stirred up in me. I hear the silent voice—how softly now it falls, and all of existence is caught up in it. Living in the silent voice, I am no longer "I." Living in the silent voice, I am at last at peace. Living in the silent voice, I am at last erased.

QUESTIONS

1. How important are colonially determined gender roles in this story?

2. How does Kincaid describe the female subject and femininity?

3. Is the speaker alienated from her culture?

4. Why does Kincaid choose to tell this story in a prose poem form? What does the experimental, antirealist mode contribute to the story's effect?

5. How does the narrator's consciousness develop in the progression of the story?

Paule Marshall

(BARBADOS, b. 1929)

Born in Brooklyn to immigrant parents from Barbados, Paule Marshall was raised in a West Indian communal setting. She claims that in her childhood she used to listen to the women talking around the kitchen table, and this experience offered her a great many hints on how to write a successful narrative. This ability to tell a good tale is apparent in Marshall's use of the lyrical images of her West Indian heritage, which tell the stories of how the survivors of the African diaspora learn to exist in a different culture. Her stories highlight the African sense of time in contrast to the Western sense of linear progression. Her stories are cyclical in structure and celebrate dualities over fixity. Ultimately, her stories do demonstrate the hopefulness of diasporic trajectories, despite all the separations and losses incurred.

Marshall has written five novels, her first being *Brown Girl, Brownstones* (1959), which many black feminist critics consider to be the beginning of contemporary African American women's writings. She has also published two collections of short stories, including *Reena and Other Short Stories* (1983) and *Merle: A Novella and Other Stories* (1985), from which this story originates. Marshall's characters often reconsider their African roots as positive features in a not-so-positive world. Western values are often portrayed as dry, featureless, and arid of meaning, whereas the values inculcated by the Afro-Caribbean experiences are far richer in humanistic values and transcendent experience. In

print dr
encased
as they
loused h
big-big
tell you,
Da-
while. "
from 'A'
wunna.
know. Y
We
flour, c
gifts. W
real pro
tle lim
mourn
balanc
wore to
their fe
the hea
D
my ha
fear o
held o
A
aroun
marl
pretty
T
the is
pine
that v
the c
throu
Broo
out g
frien

cane
take

1 Bri

this story, the narrator's mother's desire to return home and to hold on to her cultural identity is in stark contrast to her father's rejection of the old ways and desire to embrace the U.S. lifestyle.

Marshall's other novels include *The Chosen Place, the Timeless People* (1969), *Praisesong for the Widow* (1983), and *The Fisher King* (2000). She has taught creative writing at several U.S. universities.

To Da-duh, in Memoriam

1985

> "... *Oh Nana! all of you is not involved in this evil business*
> *Death, Nor all of us in life.*"
>
> —FROM "AT MY GRANDMOTHER'S GRAVE,"
> BY LEBERT BETHUNE

I did not see her at first I remember. For not only was it dark inside the crowded disembarkation shed in spite of the daylight flooding in from outside, but standing there waiting for her with my mother and sister I was still somewhat blinded from the sheen of tropical sunlight on the water of the bay which we had just crossed in the landing boat, leaving behind us the ship that had brought us from New York lying in the offing. Besides, being only nine years of age at the time and knowing nothing of islands I was busy attending to the alien sights and sounds of Barbados, the unfamiliar smells.

I did not see her, but I was alerted to her approach by my mother's hand which suddenly tightened around mine, and looking up I traced her gaze through the gloom in the shed until I finally made out the small, purposeful, painfully erect figure of the old woman headed our way.

Her face was drowned in the shadow of an ugly rolled-brim brown felt hat, but the details of her slight body and of the struggle taking place within it were clear enough—an intense, unrelenting struggle between her back which was beginning to bend ever so slightly under the weight of her eighty-odd years and the rest of her which sought to deny those years and hold that back straight, keep it in line. Moving swiftly toward us (so swiftly it seemed she did not intend stopping when she reached us but would sweep past us out the doorway which opened onto the sea and like Christ walk upon the water!), she was caught between the sunlight at her end of the building and the darkness inside—and for a moment she appeared to contain them both: the light in the long severe old-fashioned white dress she wore which brought the sense of a past that was still alive into our bustling present and in the snatch of white at her eye; the darkness in her black high-top shoes and in her face which was visible now that she was closer.

It was as stark and fleshless as a death mask, that face. The maggots might have already done their work, leaving only the framework of bone beneath the ruined skin and deep wells at the temple and jaw. But her eyes were alive, unnervingly so for one so old, with a sharp light that flicked out of the dim clouded depths like a

True to her word Da-duh took me with her the following day out into the ground. It was a fairly large plot adjoining her weathered board and shingle house and consisting of a small orchard, a good-sized canepiece and behind the canes, where the land sloped abruptly down, a gully. She had purchased it with Panama money sent her by her eldest son, my uncle Joseph, who had died working on the canal. We entered the ground along a trail no wider than her body and as devious and complex as her reasons for showing me her land. Da-duh strode briskly ahead, her slight form filled out this morning by the layers of sacking petticoats she wore under her working dress to protect her against the damp. A fresh white cloth, elaborately arranged around her head, added to her height, and lent her a vain, almost roguish air.

Her pace slowed once we reached the orchard, and glancing back at me occasionally over her shoulder, she pointed out the various trees.

"This here is a breadfruit," she said. "That one yonder is a papaw. Here's a guava. This is a mango. I know you don't have anything like these in New York. Here's a sugar apple." (The fruit looked more like artichokes than apples to me.) "This one bears limes. . . ." She went on for some time, intoning the names of the trees as though they were those of her gods. Finally, turning to me, she said, "I know you don't have anything this nice where you come from." Then, as I hesitated: "I said I know you don't have anything this nice where you come from. . . ."

"No," I said and my world did seem suddenly lacking.

Da-duh nodded and passed on. The orchard ended and we were on the narrow cart road that led through the canepiece, the canes clashing like swords above my cowering head. Again she turned and her thin muscular arms spread wide, her dim gaze embracing the small field of canes, she said—and her voice almost broke under the weight of her pride, "Tell me, have you got anything like these in that place where you were born?"

"No."

"I din' think so. I bet you don't even know that these canes here and the sugar you eat is one and the same thing. That they does throw the canes into some damn machine at the factory and squeeze out all the little life in them to make sugar for you all so in New York to eat. I bet you don't know that."

"I've got two cavities and I'm not allowed to eat a lot of sugar."

But Da-duh didn't hear me. She had turned with an inexplicably angry motion and was making her way rapidly out of the canes and down the slope at the edge of the field which led to the gully below. Following her apprehensively down the incline amid a stand of banana plants whose leaves flapped like elephants ears in the wind, I found myself in the middle of a small tropical wood—a place dense and damp and gloomy and tremulous with the fitful play of light and shadow as the leaves high above moved against the sun that was almost hidden from view. It was a violent place, the tangled foliage fighting each other for a chance at the sunlight, the branches of the trees locked in what seemed an immemorial struggle, one both necessary and inevitable. But despite the violence, it was pleasant, almost peaceful in the gully, and beneath the thick undergrowth the earth smelled like spring.

This time Da-duh didn't even bother to ask her usual question, but simply turned and waited for me to speak.

"No," I said, my head bowed. "We don't have anything like this in New York."

"Ah," she cried, her triumph complete. "I din' think so. Why, I've heard that's a place where you can walk till you near drop and never see a tree."

"We've got a chestnut tree in front of our house," I said.

"Does it bear?" She waited. "I ask you, does it bear?"

"Not anymore," I muttered. "It used to, but not anymore."

She gave the nod that was like a nervous twitch. "You see," she said. "Nothing can bear there." Then, secure behind her scorn, she added, "But tell me, what's this snow like that you hear so much about?"

Looking up, I studied her closely, sensing my chance, and then I told her, describing at length and with as much drama as I could summon not only what snow in the city was like, but what it would be like here, in her perennial summer kingdom.

". . . And you see all these trees you got here," I said. "Well, they'd be bare. No leaves, no fruit, nothing. They'd be covered in snow. You see your canes. They'd be buried under tons of snow. The snow would be higher than your head, higher than your house, and you wouldn't be able to come down into this here gully because it would be snowed under. . . ."

She searched my face for the lie, still scornful but intrigued. "What a thing, huh?" she said finally, whispering it softly to herself.

"And when it snows you couldn't dress like you are now," I said. "Oh no, you'd freeze to death. You'd have to wear a hat and gloves and galoshes and ear muffs so your ears wouldn't freeze and drop off, and a heavy coat. I've got a Shirley Temple coat with fur on the collar. I can dance. You wanna see?"

Before she could answer I began, with a dance called the Truck which was popular back then in the 1930's. My right forefinger waving, I trucked around the nearby trees and around Da-duh's awed and rigid form. After the Truck I did the Suzy-Q, my lean hips swishing, my sneakers sidling zigzag over the ground. "I can sing," I said and did so, starting with "I'm Gonna Sit Right Down and Write Myself a Letter," then without pausing, "Tea For Two," and ending with "I Found a Million Dollar Baby in a Five and Ten Cent Store."

For long moments afterwards Da-duh stared at me as if I were a creature from Mars, an emissary from some world she did not know but which intrigued her and whose power she both felt and feared. Yet something about my performance must have pleased her, because bending down she slowly lifted her long skirt and then, one by one, the layers of petticoats until she came to a drawstring purse dangling at the end of a long strip of cloth tied round her waist. Opening the purse she handed me a penny. "Here," she said half-smiling against her will. "Take this to buy yourself a sweet at the shop up the road. There's nothing to be done with you, soul."

From then on, whenever I wasn't taken to visit relatives, I accompanied Da-duh out into the ground, and alone with her amid the canes or down in the gully I told her about New York. It always began with some slighting remark on her part: "I know they don't have anything this nice where you come from," or "Tell me, I hear those foolish people in New York does do such and such. . . ." But as I answered, re-creating my towering world of steel and concrete and machines for her, building the city out of words, I would feel her give way. I came to know the signs of her surren-der: the total stillness that would come over her little hard dry form, the probing gaze that like a surgeon's knife sought to cut through my skull to get at the images there, to see if I were lying; above all, her fear, a fear nameless and profound, the same one I had felt beating in the palm of her hand that day in the lorry.

Over the weeks I told her about refrigerators, radios, gas stoves, elevators, trolley cars, wringer washing machines, movies, airplanes, the cyclone at Coney Island, sub-ways, toasters, electric lights: "At night, see, all you have to do is flip this little switch on the wall and all the lights in the house go on. Just like that. Like magic. It's like turning on the sun at night."

"But tell me," she said to me once with a faint mocking smile, "do the white peo-ple have all these things too or it's only the people looking like us?"

I laughed. "What d'ya mean," I said. "The white people have even better." Then: "I beat up a white girl in my class last term."

"Beating up white people!" Her tone was incredulous.

"How you mean!" I said, using an expression of hers. "She called me a name."

For some reason Da-duh could not quite get over this and repeated in the same hushed, shocked voice, "Beating up white people now! Oh, the lord, the world's changing up so I can scarce recognize it anymore."

One morning toward the end of our stay, Da-duh led me into a part of the gully that we had never visited before, an area darker and more thickly overgrown than the rest, almost impenetrable. There in a small clearing amid the dense bush, she stopped before an incredibly tall royal palm which rose cleanly out of the ground, and drawing the eye up with it, soared high above the trees around it into the sky. It appeared to be touching the blue dome of sky, to be flaunting its dark crown of fronds right in the blinding white face of the late morning sun.

Da-duh watched me a long time before she spoke, and then she said very qui-etly, "All right, now, tell me if you've got anything this tall in that place you're from."

I almost wished, seeing her face, that I could have said no. "Yes," I said. "We've got buildings hundreds of times this tall in New York. There's one called the Empire State building that's the tallest in the world. My class visited it last year and I went all the way to the top. It's got over a hundred floors. I can't describe how tall it is. Wait a minute. What's the name of that hill I went to visit the other day, where they have the police station?"

"You mean Bissex?"

"Yes, Bissex. Well, the Empire State Building is way taller than that."

"You're lying now!" she shouted, trembling with rage. Her hand lifted to strike me.

"No, I'm not," I said. "It really is, if you don't believe me I'll send you a picture postcard of it soon as I get back home so you can see for yourself. But it's way taller than Bissex."

All the fight went out of her at that. The hand poised to strike me fell limp to her side, and as she stared at me, seeing not me but the building that was taller than the highest hill she knew, the small stubborn light in her eyes (it was the same amber as the flame in the kerosene lamp she lit at dusk) began to fail. Finally, with a vague gesture that even in the midst of her defeat still tried to dismiss me and my world, she turned and started back through the gully, walking slowly, her steps groping and uncertain, as if she were suddenly no longer sure of the way, while I followed triumphant yet strangely saddened behind.

The next morning I found her dressed for our morning walk but stretched out on the Berbice chair in the tiny drawing room where she sometimes napped during the afternoon heat, her face turned to the window beside her. She appeared thinner and suddenly indescribably old.

"My Da-duh," I said.

"Yes, nuh," she said. Her voice was listless and the face she slowly turned my way was, now that I think back on it, like a Benin[2] mask, the features drawn and almost distorted by an ancient abstract sorrow.

"Don't you feel well?" I asked.

"Girl, I don't know."

"My Da-duh, I goin' boil you some bush tea," my aunt, Da-duh's youngest child, who lived with her, called from the shed roof kitchen.

"Who tell you I need bush tea?" she cried, her voice assuming for a moment its old authority. "You can't even rest nowadays without some malicious person looking for you to be dead. Come girl," she motioned me to a place beside her on the old-fashioned lounge chair, "give us a tune."

I sang for her until breakfast at eleven, all my brash irreverent Tin Pan Alley songs, and then just before noon we went out into the ground. But it was a short, dispirited walk. Da-duh didn't even notice that the mangoes were beginning to ripen and would have to be picked before the village boys got to them. And when she paused occasionally and looked out across the canes or up at her trees it wasn't as if she were seeing them but something else. Some huge, monolithic shape had imposed itself, it seemed, between her and the land, obstructing her vision. Returning to the house she slept the entire afternoon on the Berbice chair.

She remained like this until we left, languishing away the mornings on the chair at the window gazing out at the land as if it were already doomed; then, at noon, taking the brief stroll with me through the ground during which she seldom spoke, and afterwards returning home to sleep till almost dusk sometimes.

On the day of our departure she put on the austere, ankle length white dress, the black shoes and brown felt hat (her town clothes she called them), but she did not go with us to town. She saw us off on the road outside her house and in the midst of my mother's tearful protracted farewell, she leaned down and whispered in my ear, "Girl, you're not to forget now to send me the picture of that building, you hear."

---

2 **Benin:** Ancient African kingdom whose masks were especially prized by European ethnographers, museum curators, and artists in the late nineteenth and early twentieth centuries.

By the time I mailed her the large colored picture postcard of the Empire State building she was dead. She died during the famous '37 strike which began shortly after we left. On the day of her death England sent planes flying low over the island in a show of force—so low, according to my aunt's letter, that the downdraft from them shook the ripened mangoes from the trees in Da-duh's orchard. Frightened, everyone in the village fled into the canes. Except Da-duh. She remained in the house at the window so my aunt said, watching as the planes came swooping and screaming like monstrous birds down over the village, over her house, rattling her trees and flattening the young canes in her field. It must have seemed to her lying there that they did not intend pulling out of their dive, but like the hard-back beetles which hurled themselves with suicidal force against the walls of the house at night, those menacing silver shapes would hurl themselves in an ecstasy of self-immolation onto the land, destroying it utterly.

When the planes finally left and the villagers returned they found her dead on the Berbice chair at the window.

She died and I lived, but always, to this day even, within the shadow of her death. For a brief period after I was grown I went to live alone, like one doing penance, in a loft above a noisy factory in downtown New York and there painted seas of sugar-cane and huge swirling Van Gogh suns and palm trees striding like brightly-plumed Tutsi[3] warriors across a tropical landscape, while the thunderous tread of the machines downstairs jarred the floor beneath my easel, mocking my efforts.

QUESTIONS

1. How does this story reflect the inescapable reality of colonialism in West Indian daily life?

2. What are some of the apparent political realities in the story?

3. How is the physical landscape represented in this tale? More specifically, what is the tension between the forces of nature and human-shaped time?

4. Can one reduce this story to a simple formula: Barbados represents nature and New York the sterility of Western artificial life? Explain your answer.

5. What does the snow symbolize in the story?

6. What qualities of kinship does Da-duh recognize in her granddaughter, the narrator?

---

3 **Tutsi:** One of the main ethnic groups of the part of Africa that is now the country of Rwanda.

Olive Senior

(JAMAICA, b. 1941)

Olive Senior was born in rural Jamaica to peasant parents and was schooled in Montego Bay where she lived with well-off relatives. This dichotomy of lifestyles was to pay dividends in her early fiction. When she finished high school, she went to live in the capital, Kingston, but she described her real home as the mountains of Jamaica. She studied at Carleton University in Ottawa, Canada, as well as at the Thomson Foundation in the United Kingdom. In Jamaica, she edited two of the Caribbean's leading journals—*Social and Economic Studies* at the University of the West Indies and *Jamaica Journal*, published by the Institute of Jamaica Publications, of which she was also managing director. Since about 1993, Senior has lived in Toronto; however, her writings, both poetry and prose, have remained focused on the Caribbean experience.

Senior is the author of two books of poetry, four of nonfiction, and three of short stories. It is her short story collections—*Summer Lightning and Other Stories* (1987), *Arrival of the Snake-Woman and Other Stories* (1989), and *Discerner of Hearts* (1995)—on which her reputation stands. The short story that follows is from the *Summer Lightning* collection, and it tells of an eleven-year-old girl's obstinacy in the face of societal disapproval. Here the voice of the long-silenced Caribbean female is heard in the delightful exchange between the Archdeacon and little Rebecca. And while the tone of this story is light and full of humor, the message is far deeper than the surface story.

In some of her recent short fiction, Senior writes less about herself and more about West Indian society. This change can be observed in "The View from the Terrace," a dispassionate third-person narrative about race and class in Jamaica. In the story she is critical of Jamaican society and where it is headed. At the moment, Senior is revising her nonfiction book, *A–Z of Jamaican Heritage* (1983), a study on the natural and social history of her homeland. She is on the faculty of the Humber School for Writers at Humber College, Toronto.

Do Angels Wear Brassieres?   1986

Beccka down on her knees ending her goodnight prayers and Cherry telling her softly, "And Ask God to bless Auntie Mary." Beccka vex that anybody could interrupt her private conversation with God so, say loud loud, "No. Not praying for nobody that tek weh mi best glassy eye marble."

"Beccka!" Cherry almost crying in shame, "Shhhhh! She wi hear you. Anyway she did tell you not to roll them on the floor when she have her headache."

"A hear her already"—this is the righteous voice of Auntie Mary in the next room—"But I am sure that God is not listening to the like of she. Blasphemous little wretch."

She add the last part under her breath and with much lifting of her eyes to heaven she turn back to her nightly reading of the Imitations of Christ.

"Oooh Beccka, Rebecca, see what yu do," Cherry whispering, crying in her voice.

Beccka just stick out her tongue at the world, wink at God who she know right now in the shape of a big fat anansi[1] in a corner of the roof, kiss her mother and get into bed.

As soon as her mother gone into Auntie Mary room to try make it up and the whole night come down with whispering, Beccka whip the flashlight from off the dressing table and settle down under the blanket to read. Beccka reading the Bible in secret from cover to cover not from any conviction the little wretch but because everybody round her always quoting that book and Beccka want to try and find flaw and question she can best them with.

Next morning Auntie Mary still vex. Auntie Mary out by the tank washing clothes and slapping them hard on the big rock. Fat sly-eye Katie from the next yard visiting and consoling her. Everybody visiting Auntie Mary these days and consoling her for the crosses she have to bear (that is Beccka they talking about). Fat Katie have a lot of time to walk bout consoling because ever since hard time catch her son and him wife a town they come country to cotch with Katie. And from the girl walk through the door so braps! Katie claim she too sickly to do any washing or house-work. So while the daughter-in-law beating suds at her yard she over by Auntie Mary washpan say she keeping her company. Right now she consoling about Beccka who (as she telling Auntie Mary) every decent-living upright Christian soul who is every-body round here except that Dorcas Waite about whom one should not dirty one's mouth to talk yes every clean living person heart go out to Auntie Mary for with all due respect to a sweet mannersable child like Cherry her daughter is the devil own pickney. Not that anybody saying a word about Cherry God know she have enough trouble on her head from she meet up that big hard back man though young little gal like that never shoulda have business with no married man. Katie take a breath long enough to ask question:

"But see here Miss Mary you no think Cherry buck up the devil own self when she carrying her? Plenty time that happen you know. Remember that woman over Allside that born the pickney with two head praise Jesus it did born dead. But see here you did know one day she was going down river to wash clothes and is the devil own self she meet. Yes'm. Standing right there in her way. She pop one big bawling before she faint weh and when everybody run come not a soul see him. Is gone he gone. But you no know where he did gone? No right inside that gal. Right inna her

---

1 **anansi:** The trickster god in West African folklore; he is chameleon-like and can take on the shape of many animals.

belly. And Miss Mary I telling you the living truth, just as the baby borning the midwife no see a shadow fly out of the mother and go right cross the room. She frighten so till she close her two eye tight and is so the devil escape."

"Well I dont know about that. Beccka certainly dont born with no two head or nothing wrong with her. Is just hard ears she hard ears."

"Den no so me saying?"

"The trouble is, Cherry is too soft to manage her. As you look hard at Cherry herself she start cry. She was never a strong child and she not a strong woman, her heart just too soft."

"All the same right is right and there is only one right way to bring up a child and that is by bus' ass pardon my french Miss Mary but hard things call for hard words. That child should be getting blows from the day she born. Then she wouldn't be so force-ripe now. Who cant hear must feel for the rod and reproof bring wisdom but a child left to himself bringeth his mother to shame. Shame, Miss Mary."

"Is true. And you know I wouldn't mind if she did only get into mischief Miss Katie but what really hurt me is how the child know so much and show off. Little children have no right to have so many things in their brain. Guess what she ask me the other day nuh?—if me know how worms reproduce."

"Say what, maam?"

"As Jesus is me judge. Me big woman she come and ask that. Reproduce I say. Yes Auntie Mary she say as if I stupid. When the man worm and the lady worm come together and they have baby. You know how it happen?—Is so she ask me."

"What you saying maam? Jesus of Nazareth!"

"Yes, please. That is what the child ask me. Lightning come strike me dead if is lie I lie. In my own house. My own sister pickney. So help me I was so frighten that pickney could so impertinent that right away a headache strike me like autoclaps. But before I go lie down you see Miss Katie, I give her some licks so hot there she forget bout worm and reproduction."

"In Jesus name!"

"Yes. Is all those books her father pack her up with. Book is all him ever good for. Rather than buy food put in the pickney mouth or help Cherry find shelter his only contribution is book. Nuh his character stamp on her. No responsibility that man ever have. Look how him just take off for foreign without a word even to his lawful wife and children much less Cherry and hers. God knows where it going to end."

"Den Miss M. They really come to live with you for all time?"

"I dont know my dear. What are they to do? You know Cherry cant keep a job from one day to the next. From she was a little girl she so nervous she could never settle down long enough to anything. And you know since Papa and Mama pass away is me one she have to turn to. I tell you even if they eat me out of house and home and the child drive me to Bellevue I accept that this is the crosses that I put on this earth to bear ya Miss Katie."

"Amen. Anyway dont forget what I was saying to you about the devil. The child could have a devil inside her. No pickney suppose to come facety and force-ripe so. You better ask the Archdeacon to check it out next time he come here."

"Well. All the same Miss Katie she not all bad you know. Sometime at night when she ready to sing and dance and make up play and perform for us we laugh so till! And those times when I watch her I say to myself, this is really a gifted child."

"Well my dear is your crosses. If is so you see it then is your sister child."

"Aie. I have one hope in God and that is the child take scholarship exam and God know she so bright she bound to pass. And you know what, Miss Katie, I put her name down for the three boarding school them that furthest from here. Make them teacher deal with her. That is what they get paid for."

Beccka hiding behind the tank listening to the conversation as usual. She think about stringing a wire across the track to trip fat Katie but she feeling too lazy today. Fat Katie will get her comeuppance on Judgement Day for she wont able to run quick enough to join the heavenly hosts. Beccka there thinking of fat Katie huffing and puffing arriving at the pasture just as the company of the faithful in their white robes are rising as one body on a shaft of light. She see Katie a-clutch at the hem of the gown of one of the faithful and miraculously, slowly, slowly, Katie start to rise. But her weight really too much and with a tearing sound that spoil the solemn moment the hem tear way from the garment and Katie fall back to earth with a big buff, shouting and wailing for them to wait on her. Beccka snickering so hard at the sight she have to scoot way quick before Auntie Mary and Katie hear her. They think the crashing about in the cocoa walk is mongoose.

Beccka in Auntie Mary room—which is forbidden—dress up in Auntie Mary bead, Auntie Mary high heel shoes, Auntie Mary shawl, and Auntie Mary big floppy hat which she only wear to wedding—all forbidden. Beccka mincing and prancing prancing and mincing in front of the three-way adjustable mirror in Auntie Mary vanity she brought all the way from Cuba with her hard earned money. Beccka seeing herself as a beautiful lady on the arms of a handsome gentleman who look just like her father. They about to enter a night club neon sign flashing for Beccka know this is the second wickedest thing a woman can do. At a corner table lit by Chinese lantern soft music playing Beccka do the wickedest thing a woman can do—she take a drink. Not rum. One day Beccka went to wedding with Auntie Mary and sneak a drink of rum and stay sick for two days. Beccka thinking of all the bright-colour drink she see advertise in the magazine Cherry get from a lady she use to work for in town a nice yellow drink in a tall frosted glass . . .

"Beccka, Rebecca O My god!" That is Cherry rushing into the room and wailing. "You know she wi mad like hell if she see you with her things you know you not to touch her things."

Cherry grab Auntie Mary things from off Beccka and fling them back into where she hope is the right place, adjust the mirror to what she hope is the right angle, and pray just pray that Auntie Mary wont find out that Beccka was messing with her things. Again. Though Auntie Mary so absolutely neat she always know if a pin out of place. "O God Beccka," Cherry moaning.

Beccka stripped of her fancy clothes dont pay no mind to her mother fluttering about her. She take the story in her head to the room next door though here the mirror much too high for Beccka to see the sweep of her gown as she does the third wickedest thing a woman can do which is dance all night.

Auntie Mary is a nervous wreck and Cherry weeping daily in excitement. The Archdeacon is coming. Auntie Mary so excited she cant sit cant stand cant do her embroidery cant eat she forgetting things the house going to the dog she dont even notice that Beccka been using her lipstick. Again. The Archdeacon coming Wednesday to the churches in the area and afterwards—as usual—Archdeacon sure to stop outside Auntie Mary gate even for one second—as usual—to get two dozen of Auntie Mary best roses and a bottle of pimento dram save from Christmas. And maybe just this one time Archdeacon will give in to Auntie Mary pleading and step inside her humble abode for tea. Just this one time.

Auntie Mary is due this honour at least once because she is head of Mothers Union and though a lot of them jealous and back-biting her because Archdeacon never stop outside their gate even once let them say anything to her face.

For Archdeacon's certain stop outside her gate Auntie Mary scrub the house from top to bottom put up back the freshly laundered Christmas Curtains and the lace tablecloth and the newly starch doilies and the antimacassars clean all the windows in the house get the thick hibiscus hedge trim so you can skate across the top wash the dog whitewash every rock in the garden and the trunk of every tree paint the gate polish the silver and bring out the crystal cake-plate and glasses she bring from Cuba twenty-five years ago and is saving for her old age. Just in case Archdeacon can stop for tea Auntie Mary bake a fruitcake a upside-down cake a three-layer cake a chocolate cake for she dont know which he prefer also some coconut cookies for although the Archdeacon is an Englishman dont say he dont like his little Jamaican dainties. Everything will be pretty and nice for the Archdeacon just like the American lady she did work for in Cuba taught her to make them.

The only thing that now bothering Auntie Mary as she give a last look over her clean and well ordered household is Beccka, dirty Beccka right now sitting on the kitchen steps licking out the mixing bowls. The thought of Beccka in the same house with Archdeacon bring on one of Auntie Mary headache. She think of asking Cherry to take Beccka somewhere else for the afternoon when Archdeacon coming but poor Cherry work so hard and is just excited about Archdeacon coming. Auntie Mary dont have the courage to send Beccka to stay with anyone for nobody know what that child is going to come out with next and a lot of people not so broadmind as Auntie Mary. She pray that Beccka will get sick enough to have to stay in bed she—O God forgive her but is for a worthy cause—she even consider drugging the child for the afternoon. But she dont have the heart. And anyway she dont know how. So Auntie Mary take two asprin and a small glass of tonic wine and pray hard that Beccka will vanish like magic on the afternoon that Archdeacon visit.

Now Archdeacon here and Beccka and everybody in their very best clothes. Beccka thank God also on her best behaviour which can be very good so far in fact she really look like a little angel she so clean and behaving.

In fact Archdeacon is quite taken with Beccka and more and more please that this is the afternoon he decide to consent to come inside Auntie Mary parlour for one little cup of tea. Beccka behaving so well and talking so nice to the Archdeacon Auntie Mary feel her heart swell with pride and joy over everything. Beccka behaving so beautiful in fact that Auntie Mary and Cherry dont even think twice about leaving her to talk to Archdeacon in the parlour while they out in the kitchen preparing tea.

By now Beccka and the Archdeacon exchanging Bible knowledge. Beccka asking him question and he trying his best to answer but they never really tell him any of these things in theological college. First he go ask Beccka if she is a good little girl. Beccka say yes she read her Bible every day. Do you now say the Archdeacon, splendid. Beccka smile and look shy.

"Tell me my little girl, is there anything in the Bible you would like to ask me about?"

"Yes sir. Who in the Bible wrote big?"

"Who in the Bible wrote big. My dear child!"

This wasn't the kind of question Archdeacon expecting but him always telling himself how he have rapport with children so he decide to confess his ignorance.

"Tell me, who?"

"Paul!" Beccka shout.

"Paul?"

"Galations six eleven 'See with how large letters I write onto you with mine own hands.'"

"Ho Ho Ho Ho" Archdeacon laugh.—"Well done. Try me with another one."

Beccka decide to ease him up this time.

"What animal saw an angel?"

"What animal saw an angel? My word. What animal . . . of course. Balaam's Ass."

"Yes you got it."

Beccka jumping up and down she so excited. She decide to ask the Archdeacon trick questions her father did teach her.

"What did Adam and Eve do when they were driven out of the garden?"

"Hm," the Archdeacon sputtered but could not think of a suitable answer.

"Raise Cain ha ha ha ha ha."

"They raised Cain Ho Ho Ho Ho Ho."

The Archdeacon promise himself to remember that one to tell the Deacon. All the same he not feeling strictly comfortable. It really dont seem dignified for an Archdeacon to be having this type of conversation with an eleven-year-old girl. But Beccka already in high gear with the next question and Archdeacon tense himself.

"Who is the shortest man in the Bible?"

Archdeacon groan.

"Peter. Because him sleep on his watch. Ha Ha Ha."

"Ho Ho Ho Ho Ho."

"What is the smallest insect in the Bible?"

"The widow's mite," Archdeacon shout.

"The wicked flee," Beccka cry.

"Ho Ho Ho Ho Ho Ho."

Archdeacon laughing so hard now he starting to cough. He cough and cough till the coughing bring him to his senses. He there looking down the passage where Auntie Mary gone and wish she would hurry come back. He sputter a few time into his handkerchief, wipe his eye, sit up straight and assume his most religious expression. Even Beccka impress.

"Now Rebecca. Hm. You are a very clever very entertaining little girl. Very. But what I had in mind were questions that are a bit more serious. Your aunt tells me you are being prepared for confirmation. Surely you must have some questions about doctrine hm, religion, that puzzle you. No serious questions?"

Beccka look at Archdeacon long and hard. "Yes," she say at long last in a small voice. Right away Archdeacon sit up straighter.

"What is it my little one?"

Beccka screwing up her face in concentration.

"Sir, what I want to know is this for I cant find it in the Bible. Please sir, do angels wear brassieres?"

Auntie Mary just that minute coming through the doorway with a full tea tray with Cherry carrying another big tray right behind her. Enough food and drink for ten Archdeacon. Auntie Mary stop braps in the doorway with fright when she hear Beccka question. She stop so sudden that Cherry bounce into her and spill a whole pitcher of cold drink all down Auntie Mary back. As the coldness hit her Auntie Mary jump and half her tray throw way on the floor milk and sugar and sandwiches a rain down on Archdeacon. Archdeacon jump up with his handkerchief and start mop himself and Auntie Mary at the same time he trying to take the tray from her. Auntie Mary at the same time trying to mop up the Archdeacon with a napkin in her mortification not even noticing how Archdeacon relieve that so much confusion come at this time. Poor soft-hearted Cherry only see that her sister whole life ruin now she dont yet know the cause run and sit on the kitchen stool and throw kitchen cloth over her head and sit there bawling and bawling in sympathy.

Beccka win the scholarship to high school. She pass so high she getting to go to the school of Auntie Mary choice which is the one that is furthest away. Beccka vex because she dont want go no boarding school with no heap of girl. Beccka dont want to go to no school at all.

Everyone so please with Beccka. Auntie Mary even more please when she get letter from the headmistress setting out Rules and Regulation. She only sorry that the list not longer for she could think of many things she could add. She get another letter setting out uniform and right away Auntie Mary start sewing. Cherry take the bus to town one day with money coming from God know where for the poor child dont have no father to speak of and she buy shoes and socks and underwear and hair ribbon and towels and toothbrush and a suitcase for Beccka. Beccka normally please like puss with every new thing vain like peacock in ribbons and clothes. Now she hardly look at them. Beccka thinking. She dont want to go to no school. But how to get out of it. When Beccka think done she decide to run away and find her father who like a miracle have job now in a circus. And as Beccka find him so she get job in the circus as a tight-rope walker and in spangles and tights lipstick and powder (her own) Beccka perform every night before a cheering crowd in a blaze of light. Beccka and the circus go right round the world. Every now and then, dress up in furs and hats like Auntie Mary wedding hat Beccka come home to visit Cherry and Auntie Mary. She arrive in a chauffeur-driven limousine pile high with luggage. Beccka shower them with presents. The whole village. For fat Katie Beccka bring a years supply of diet pill and a exercise machine just like the one she see advertise in the magazine the lady did give to Cherry.

Now Beccka ready to run away. In the books, the picture always show children running away with their things tied in a bundle on a stick. The stick easy. Beccka take one of the walking stick that did belong to Auntie Mary's dear departed. Out of spite she take Auntie Mary silk scarf to wrap her things in for Auntie Mary is to blame for her going to school at all. She pack in the bundle Auntie Mary lipstick Auntie Mary face powder and a pair of Auntie Mary stockings for she need these for her first appearance as a tight rope walker. She take a slice of cake, her shiny eye marble and a yellow nicol which is her best taa in case she get a chance to play in the marble championship of the world. She also take the Bible. She want to find some real hard question for the Archdeacon next time he come to Auntie Mary house for tea.

When Auntie Mary and Cherry busy sewing her school clothes Beccka take off with her bundle and cut across the road into the field. Mr O'Connor is her best friend and she know he wont mind if she walk across his pasture. Mr O'Connor is her best friend because he is the only person Beccka can hold a real conversation with. Beccka start to walk toward the mountain that hazy in the distance. She plan to climb the mountain and when she is high enough she will look for a sign that will lead her to her father. Beccka walk and walk through the pasture divided by stone wall and wooden gates which she climb. Sometime a few trees tell her where a pond is. But it is very lonely. All Beccka see is john crow and cow and cattle egret blackbird and parrotlets that scream at her from the trees. But Beccka dont notice them. Her mind busy on how Auntie Mary and Cherry going to be sad now she gone and she composing letter she will write to tell them she safe and she forgive them everything. But the sun getting too high in the sky and Beccka thirsty. She eat the cake but she dont have water. Far in the distance she see a bamboo clump and hope is round a spring with water. But when she get to the bamboo all it offer is shade. In fact the dry bamboo leaves on the ground so soft and inviting that Beccka decide to sit and rest for a while. Is sleep Beccka sleep. When she wake she see a stand above her four horse leg and when she raise up and look, stirrups, boots, and sitting atop the horse her best friend, Mr O'Connor.

"Well Beccka, taking a long walk?"

"Yes sir."

"Far from home eh?"

"Yes sir."

"Running away?"

"Yes sir."

"Hm. What are you taking with you?"

Beccka tell him what she have in the bundle. Mr O'Connor shock.

"What, no money?"

"Oooh!"

Beccka shame like anything for she never remember anything about money.

"Well you need money for running away you know. How else you going to pay for trains and planes and taxis and buy ice cream and pindar cake?"

Beccka didn't think about any of these things before she run away. But now she see that is sense Mr O'Connor talking but she dont know what to do. So the two of them just stand up there for a while. They thinking hard.

"You know Beccka if I was you I wouldnt bother with the running away today. Maybe they dont find out you gone yet. So I would go back home and wait until I save enough money to finance my journey."

Beccka love how that sound. To finance my journey. She think about that a long time. Mr O'Connor say, "Tell you what. Why dont you let me give you a ride back and you can pretend this was just a practice and you can start saving your money to run away properly next time."

Beccka look at Mr O'Connor. He looking off into the distance and she follow where he gazing and when she see the mountain she decide to leave it for another day. All the way back riding with Mr O'Connor Beccka thinking and thinking and her smile getting bigger and bigger. Beccka cant wait to get home to dream up all the tricky question she could put to a whole school full of girl. Not to mention the teachers. Beccka laughing for half the way home. Suddenly she say—

"Mr Connor, you know the Bible?"

"Well Beccka I read my Bible every day so I should think so."

"Promise you will answer a question."

"Promise."

"Mr Connor, do angels wear brassieres?"

"Well Beccka, as far as I know only the lady angels need to."

Beccka laugh cant done. Wasnt that the answer she was waiting for?

QUESTIONS

1. Why does Senior use the Jamaican children's creole or national language to tell the story?

2. How are the indigenous population and foreigners distinguished in this story?

3. Where does Senior demonstrate a lament for past values and heritage in the tale?

4. How would this story be different if it were written in standard English?

5. How is humor used to make a thematic point in the story?

Regiment. Now we've got war memorials like exclamation marks. I remember a pink dirty crushed ration card on the shelf in the pantry which we had to show the commisserie man to get sugar, rice, and coconut oil. In the streets the calypsonians were singing "Chiney never had a VJ Day," and in dark places where the sun shone hot and strong, in red dirt backyards with governor plum trees, music came from dustbin covers, and oil drums were fashioned and tempered in that same fire behind the fence we were trying to put out.

Now I think of it no one ever told me when I was small, smaller than him in the snapshot, that six million people had been gassed by civilized Europeans. Only, on Good Friday, at the Mass of the Pre-Sanctified, we said special prayers for the conversion of pagans, heretics, and Jews. And, during the Stations of the Cross, I wondered why the Barbadians had nailed Jesus to the cross.

On the radio in the drawing-room: "Hiroshima . . . Nagasaki . . ."

"We will have to pay for this," his mother said when she heard the news. "We'll have to pay for this." Hiroshima, Nagasaki. Far away headlines in *The Gazette*.

We were in the shadow of America a long time, a long time. Like under a big umbrella. ". . . rum and Coca-Cola . . . working for the Yankee dollar."

You see, you start telling the story about a guy and then you get to telling the story of a time, a place, a people, and a world. Then I start getting into the story. Well I made that choice early. I remember him well, the all-American-kinda-looking guy on the steps of the sugar-cane estate bungalow with Mutt his dog. Broad shouldered, his stare holds Baboolal: the white French creole with the Indian boy.

It was one night out on the sugar estate . . .

He was still at home, lifting weights under the house in the afternoon. He was the last of the boys to leave home. That's what she (my, and his mother, she who said, "We will have to pay for this") always said: "He was the last of the boys to leave home," with that look in her eyes which knew that we all had to go eventually and leave her alone with her husband. It wasn't true that he had been the last of the boys to leave. I was. But for her there were always the boys, my sister, and me. So, he was the last of the boys to leave. Then she had me to speak to, had me there, not like a child but more like a lover, a changeling companion, a mirror, a fairy child, a Peter Pan—but that's another tale. Then I left and she and her husband were alone and she was always wanting us to come back, looking out of the window down the gravel road. He always did, dropping in with the jitney to do a message, carrying something, have a coffee with her at the edge of the dining-room table, pulled by her, she listening, reaching out to touch his arm on the table with raised veins, listening, feeling proud. When he came, there would have to be a leg of lamb and macaroni pie. She wouldn't have siesta if he was going to drop in for tea, or might. She would bake a sponge cake and be tired in the evening and have to have a whisky and soda. He would have a slice of the cake for her sake between cigarettes and black coffee, not tea. She would look at him with half a look of owning and half a look of relinquishing and then call him over to the side of the drawing-room to have a talk about his job. He marvelled, we all did, how she could talk of cars and mechanics when it was cars and mechanics, and later about oil derricks, bits, blow outs, and cementing. Then she would let him go to his father on the verandah. She liked the idea that her boys were close to their father. It was just an idea. The man said little and the boys were left yearning and looking elsewhere, dreaming the dream of their ancestors, El Dorado. His memory was the dawn, horses and Baboolal.

. . . But maybe it was on one of those nights when he had already left home and there was a leg of lamb and macaroni pie. Out of the blue he bet me I would not run down into the yard in the dark, down behind the hibiscus hedge into the savannah and touch the trunk of the big silk cotton tree under which a coolie man was buried and a jumbie[2] lived. If I did he would take me to the pictures there and then, night-time pictures there and then, that night. He bet it not as a threat or something to demean me, that I might not be able to do, but rather as a warm reaching-out challenge to my boyish youth and his own, spoken across the wide polished oval dining-room table like a mirror for us to see ourselves and the servants passing out and coming in through the pantry door when my mother rang the little brass bell. He spoke it with affection and warmth and with an endless desire for adventure. "Come, boy, let we go." He wanted me to have an adventure and he wished to be the one to offer it. I leapt out of my chair and went out into the dark, not pretending, through the hibiscus hedge, across the gravel road, down into the gully and the savannah to the base and trunk of the silk cotton tree where the coolie man was buried and my heart jumping for the jumbie that might be. I touched the tree. I did what he had said and ran all the way back up to the bungalow, up the back steps, through the pantry. There, I had done it, and off, at once, because we were late and my mother said that we wouldn't make it on time. We went to the cinema. Theatre.

Time would stop for us in the jitney round the bend by Palmiste where the bull gouged out the overseer's stomach in the savannah, over the potholed roads, through the kerosene flambeaux-lit villages, through the dark to the Gaiety Theatre in Mucurapo Street, warm and alive with talk, car horns, roast corn, peanuts, and channa from vendors with tin stands lit by flambeaux burning through perforated holes made with an ice pick in an old biscuit tin. Palms warm with hot groundnuts in small brown-paper bags, throwing the shells on the ground. Night-time theatre.

My memories kept by a memory of him. I longed for him on a horse, held in front, too small to straddle the strong back, to rub those sweating flanks, with him and Baboolal's thin brown legs flying in the wind.

It was a double: *The Wild One* with Marlon Brando, and *Rebel Without a Cause* with James Dean. Looking at the snapshot it is James Dean who was always young that I remember. I remember his chiselled cheekbones, his sad soft eyes dreaming of an early death: and him in the snapshot, his sad soft eyes, sitting with Mutt on the steps of the bungalow.

They were all of a time, mixed up in memory. A decade of heroes and gods. Brando, James Dean, and a little later Elvis. He of the snapshot liked Frank Sinatra,

2 **jumbie:** Ghost.

and Frankie Laine singing "I believe." Singing, "I believe in every drop of rain that falls," and "When you hear a new-born baby cry, I believe." Mario Lanza's "Ave Maria." He tried to crack the glass in the bathroom window like him when he took a shower.

We weren't American, but we lived in the shadow of America a long time, a long time . . . "Working for the Yankee dollar."

Hiroshima, Nagasaki. Like a big parasol.

"They will have to pay for this," she said.

Yes, gods: Brando, Dean. The way they walked. The way they talked. Bigger than life on the big screen: John Wayne, Errol Flynn, Rock Hudson, heroes of the 12.30 matinée. Heroes for him in the snapshot, for the black tess[3] on the pavement, the badjohn on the sidewalk under the rum shop. Like them he had an odyssey weaving the gravelled traces with his motor-bike, skidding the corners at the Wallerfield American Base Camp in the motor-car rally on two wheels, the white promise of the carnival-queen beauty-show cat walk screaming at the curb, shaking their pony tails.

Twice they woke her, madonna mother, prayer of rosaries and novenas for her boys all night, while her husband snored forgetting that he had begotten sons. In the next room in the troubled house her débutante daughter asleep under the picture of guardian angels set in battle array. Twice they woke her, his pardner messenger at the front door with the news. His car was in the ravine. He had been snatched from death, tugged to life with a string of rosary beads, whispered novenas and ejaculations to Saint Christopher.

She had kept on believing; so had he.

"He is a religious boy. He has a natural religious feeling. He always prays. Always thinking of God. The Man Upstairs he calls Him. If I think of any of my boys being religious I think of him. He used to wake early and take me to the First Friday morning mass. He always had his rosary in his pocket. He had a strong sense of right and wrong. Always went to confession and communion, a religious boy, pious. Used his missal."

That was her creed. Although they always, the boys, followed mass from the back porch of the church and smoked cigarettes during the sermon leaning up against their cars in the churchyard. But, they were the boys. I, blent with her in prayer, kneeling side by her under the statue of Saint Thérèse of Lisieux, The Little Flower. Taking it all in.

You try to put it all down before it passes away. Sing the ballad for the heroes of the new world. Heroes of the dawn, he and Baboolal.

Do you remember that James Dean walk? The way he kicked a stone in *East of Eden*? The way he hung his head and the way he suddenly bounded out of himself up the stairs to find his mysterious mother? The way he would hold back, hang back in there, inside himself with his sad soft eyes dreaming of an early death, and then hit out, want to hit someone, hit himself, pound the ribs of the house with his fists?

3 **black tess:** Streetwalker.

He was like that, a badjohn. He had to hit someone. He would have to cuff someone down.

There was this mixture in him of sadness and softness, tenderness and hardness all blent in one, this religious boy who was the last of the boys to leave home. I see him now, he begins to change ". . . rum and Coca-Cola . . . working for . . . the Yankee dollar." Grog.

White shirt, collar, and tie when he used to sell motor-cars in San Fernando for his uncle. He quit that. He had to make more money. He had to prove himself otherwise he would have to hit somebody. Big car time.

Cocoa and sugar dead. Motor-cars

oil

the decades pass.

Now Texaco is written where the British Oil Company used to be. The history book says they sucked the orange dry.

Later in his khaki pants, unshaven, bare-backed, brow stained, smelling of cigarettes and black coffee, rum, his hands smelling of oil, we would go for a drive alone to see where he worked. Alone, driving through the bush to the clearing in the forest where the oil well stood, the derrick pumping out oil, piping stacked on the sides. I learnt about drilling a hole, cementing, bits, blow outs, and the whole adventure, the whole far-flung adventure of his—American, British, French, Dutch, Spanish here again for El Dorado the sixteenth-century myth.

There was no stopping him. He said it himself, "I am a self-made man." He still liked to ride his motor-bike for the hell of it, back from the beach with a carnival queen riding pillion in the dusk, in the amber of the dusk and rum. Madonna mother prayed all the while for him and the parish priest came to bless the office when he formed his own company and hanged the picture of "The Sacred Heart"[4] over his desk.

He went from there to become a millionaire. He made himself, he said, and said it again, "I'm a self-made man," forgetting (if he ever knew) what whiteness meant. What did it cost him? He had collected houses, cars, companies, registered companies.

The story begins to fade as I begin to lose him as he enters dreams, his hallucinations, *folies de grandeur,* the old madness of the ancestors of the savannahs of Monagas, the pampas of Bolivar. They dreamt of horses and the building of large houses and eternal gardens, dreaming of a grandeur they thought they once had.

He lost his James Dean rebel smile. His broad shoulders caved in. His sad soft eyes stared blindly without anger or dreams.

"If only Baboolal could see me now. If only Baboolal could see me now . . . If only he could see this lake with ice, this land with conifers," (the dream of Christmas in a tropic mind). "Baboolal never see ice, except he see it by the USE ICE factory San Fernando roundabout, or shave ice on the promenade."

---

4 **The Sacred Heart:** A depiction of Jesus Christ with his heart exposed.

* * *

It all came rushing back, this ballad for the heroes of the new world as we sat in a little Spanish restaurant in the old world.

"I going away," he said.

"Go to a hot country," I said.

"Maybe hot, maybe cold," he said.

I paid the cheque (unusually) for the last time.

As he stares now through amber at the green dream of green canefields in the sun, he remembers the East Indian boy Baboolal barebacked with him on horses cantering the gravelled traces.

If Baboolal could see him now, I thought.

". . . rum and Coca-Cola, down Point Cumana . . . working for the Yankee Dollar."

QUESTIONS

1. What evidence can you find about the perspective and point of view of the narrator in this story?

2. How has the corruption of the "Yankee dollar" directly affected the characters in this story?

3. Discuss the nature and causes of the thwarted desire and repressed passion evident in this story.

4. What has the narrator concluded about the New World heroes by the conclusion of the story?

Sasenarine Persaud

(GUYANA, b. 1957)

Sasenarine Persaud was born in Guyana of Indo-Caribbean descent and has lived for the last twenty years in Canada. He is known for his insightful literary criticism and his own creative writing. He has published three volumes of poetry, two novels, and a collection of short stories entitled *Canada Geese and Apple Chatney* (1998).

Much of Persaud's writing is centered on the adjustments that Guyanese immigrants to North America must make. The title of his short story collection and its title story is a clever pair of images that puts the Guyanese immigrant's struggle to understand the North American mind in focus. For the immigrant, the mystery of why the Canadian people have denied themselves the joy of indulging in a succulent feast of wild Canadian geese, which are prevalent throughout Canada, is unfathomable. Along with that, the Guyanese new-comer to Canada learns quickly that a fairly tasty version of mango chutney can be made out of the wasted green apples that go unpicked or unused in the late Canadian summer. What Persaud is suggesting in his title is that the immi-grants, who are already alienated by the harshness of the Canadian climate and customs, must learn to adjust and adapt to these ways.

Persaud's collection is full of comparisons between the two cultures. In one story he looks at the manner in which both the Canadian and Guyanese atti-tudes toward animals differ and at the infiltration of Western feminist agendas into traditional Indian families. In "Canada Geese and Apple Chatney," which may be the most difficult story to read and grasp in this book's Caribbean sec-tion, the story turns on three friends' discussion about the nature of writing. The friends criticize the Indo-Caribbean writer V. S. Naipaul for being critical of the traditional Hindu religion and values. Later, they realize that Naipaul's vi-sion has a much more universal application and that criticism is not always hateful—it can be constructive.

Canada Geese and Apple Chatney — 1997

Bai dhem time something else—rough—rough like rass. And was no laughter. Yuh want hear about dhem time? Leh me tell yuh. And don't bother with Writerji. He's mih friend but remember he's a writer. He change-up everything, mix-up people and place so nobody could tell who is who, and what what. And if yuh ain't know, all sound like true. But dhat is because Writerji good. Well he always good. Yuh see dhat story about running from immigration officer which set in New York. Dhat same thing happen here in Toronto to he. And was he, me, and Hermit sharing a apart-ment at the same time. Yuh know how Anand get dhat name Writerji? Is me give he, me and Hermit. Ask Hermit when yuh see he.

And dhat bai Hermit is something else. A holiday—was Christmas. Just the three ah we in the apartment. Snow like ass outside. Prem and Kishore invite we over but Hermit old car ain't starting, and anyway too much snow. And Prem and Kishore ain't gat car—dhey living in the east end, somewhere behind gaad back near Morningside. In dhem days, once people know yuh illegal, nobady want see yuh, nobady invite yuh at them house. Even yuh own relative—people come hey and change. Money, money, money. Mih own uncle don't call me. And when he ass going to UG he staying at we place, five years—mih mother neva tek a cent from he. When yuh illegal everybady think yuh want money, or something. Yuh don't let people know you situation—yuh laugh outside. So is just dhe three a we. Snow tearing tail and we putting lash on some Johnnie Walker Black Label. Hermit bring out he big tape and we playing some Mukesh and Rafi. Suddenly the tape finish. Is a eerie si-lence. Fat snow flakes khat khat khat on dhe window pane.

relax, my friend. Ah know yuh hungry. Well, this meat defrost. I will cook some—curry?"

"Nah, how about some bunjal geese," Hermit laughed, "and a bake one—come, I'll come and help you. Put on dhat Sundar-Popo[4] tape, Jones." Hermit turn to me a bit unsteady. He nicknamed me Jones because I see Jim Jones[5] when he first land in Guyana, and because I went and see he fraud miracle in Sacred Heart Church lang before all them murders. Well, I start one big laugh. And Hermit start laughing too.

I tell yuh, times was tough. Hermit just come down from Montreal—he just get he landed and want make a new start—he give too many false name and false social insurance number in Montreal, and dhem Frenchie getting more racial—I coming up from GT[6] and illegal, then baps, Writerji landing down on we. See how things happen! Remember dhem time when government thugs try to break up we meeting at Kitty Market Square[7] and dhey get beat up and run in the police station for help. Was me, Cuffy and Akkara, and some other bais from Buxton. They shoot Akkara in dhe gardens and seh he had gun fuh overthrow dhe government, and dhey beat up Cuffy in he garage and put a AK-47 in he car trunk and seh he about to resist arrest, that he commit suicide in jail. All this just after Rodney[8] assassination. Well, I ain't wait around. Them days yuh didn't had to get visa to come to Canada. Next flight I in Toronto. But mih uncle and he wife meking all sort a remark. If I bathe two times a day—that was a summer hotter than anything in Guyana—they complaining I bathe too lang and too often, I go to the toilet too often—is money water cost. This nat Guyana! Yuh pay fuh water here! Well, a meet Hermit in Knob Hill Farms one day and he seh he gat same prablem, he went through same thing—leh we rent a two-bedroom. I ain't gat no wuk yet, you know. He seh, man, no prablem. He get a social insurance number and a name fuh mih. Some Indian name. The man dead and one a Hermit girlfriend get the name and number. Frank Sharma. See how Frank stick. All yuh must be think that I change mih name, become Frank instead of Ramesh because I want become Canadian duck. Nah. This coolie ain't shame he name. Anyway I Frank Sharma now. And frighten like ass when I go any place to wuk and I gat to say I name Frank Sharma. I trembling but trying to look bold, hoping I ain't say meh real name.

Yuh think is three cents we go though! Well, I ain't gat no wuk yet and Hermit just pick up a thing in a factory. Although he just get he landed, money still small. Almost a month and I ain't get nothing, then I walk in a factory at Steeles and

---

4 **Sundar-Popo:** Icon of Trinidad and Tobago's Indian songs; died in 2000 to much lamenting.
5 **Jim Jones:** Leader of a U.S. fundamentalist religious cult that moved to Guyana in 1977. In November 1978, Jones ordered the group's members to commit mass suicide by drinking cyanide-laced Kool-Aid. Over 900 members died, including Jones.
6 **GT:** Georgetown, capital of Guyana.
7 **Kitty Market Square:** Main square of Georgetown.
8 **Rodney:** Walter Rodney, assassinated Guyanese Marxist activist.

Bathurst desperate—and get tek on. The supervisor want a forklift operator. Man, I neva drive a donkey-cart yet, much less forklift. I tell the man, with experience, I could manage dhe forklift, anything. Lucky for me the forklift break down, and the forklift driver who didn't show up, turn up next day. The supervisor find wuk for me packing boxes. And next two weeks, bam, Writerji turn up in the apartment lobby. He dhe last man to land in Canada before Canadian immigration decide yuh gat to get visa from Guyana, too much Guyanese fulling up Toronto. We bunking on dhe ground, can't afford a bed or even mattress, in a room and squeezing cents. Hermit trying to get a name and number for Writerji.

Well, Writerji waiting fuh he name and number but he ain't wasting time. He want learn about Toronto and Canada. He find library and reading up about Canada, about trees and birds. Whenever we go out anyway he pointing out birch, spruce, oak, cedar, weeping willow, pussy willow, ash, he pointing out bluejay, red-start, sparrow, starling, cardinal. He teking walk in park—yuh want know which park? Is at Eglinton and Jane street—Eglinton Flats. Autumn coming and Writerji want experience Canadian fall—colours radiant over all dhem trees. Geese coming in to land sweet sweet like plane. Every afternoon he coming home and writing poems. A night he writing a poem and suddenly he buss out one big laugh. He seh we thinking money scarce and cutting we tail and food all over dhe place. All them geese nice and fat, heading south fuh winter. He seh if is Guyana yuh think all them duck could deh so nice and lazy all over dhe place, preening themself like majesty and nobady own them, and people starving? And other people feeding them bread and fattening them up fuh we!

He seh why we don't catch some a dhem geese and stock up for winter. Them geese heading south to get away from the cold and now is dhe right time. And he tell we how in England dhem bai do dhe same thing and some Trini writer name Selvon[9] write about this thing in a book call *The Lonely Londoners*. Hermit remember he hear this someway but he laugh and seh nobady neva write this—and how he know? Tell yuh the truth, I see them geese and I thinking same thing—how dhem bais in Guyana woulda done wuk them down.

"Is how I know? I'm a writer man!"

"So Hermit is Gandhi like Gandhiji and yuh is Writer—like Writerji," I buss out one laugh.

Well, Hermit still ain't believe that this thing write down, so Writerji and we gone to St Dennis library near Weston Road and Eglinton corner and he get Hermit to borrow *The Lonely Londoners* and *Ways of Sunlight* by Sam Selvon. As soon as we get home he find the page and start read how hunger washing Cap tail and Cap decided to ketch seagull and eat them. We laugh good. And dhat is how he get dhe name Writerji. From dhat night we call he Writerji. But he done plan this thing. We could buy expire bread, and night time head down to Eglinton Flats Park. Them geese sleeping right next to a little culvert and all over the grass behind them trees.

---

9 **Selvon:** Sam Selvon, Trinidadian writer. The episode of Cap and the pigeon in *The Lonely Londoners* is intertextual with this story and is mentioned later on this page.

Two a-we could catch ducks and one man swipe dhe neck. Hermit get excited. He want try this thing. Well, is me and Hermit end up catching all them ducks and geese. I holding them and Hermit swiping them neck. All Writerji doing is holding bag and keeping lookout. Just like he since schooldays. He always thinking up something and me and Hermit doing the wuk. A trunk full a ducks in large double garbage bags. We skin them when we get home. Writerji saying we ain't stupid like Cap and we dispose of them feathers and skin real good. Nobody could catch we. Well them geese taste good.

Hermit seh next weekend let we take some fuh Prem and Kishore. They apartment overlooking Morningside Park and them maple trees flaming with colours. Writerji want tek a walk in the park and see this thing near. I want see too—was mih first autumn—but I playing I ain't care before them bai start laugh at me and call me Newfie and Pole and Balgobin-come-to-town. Writerji ain't care about who laugh he, he want see this thing close, hold them leaves. So we laughing he, asking if he really want size up more geese because it gat geese in that park. We teking a drink on a picnic table in the park and Writerji disappear. Next thing he coming back with he hand full a them small sour apple. He can't believe all them apple falling on the grass and wasting. People wasteful in Canada, he muttering over and over. Writerji want help to pick some nice green apple on them tree. Why? He thinking just like how yuh use green mango, or bilimbi, or barahar to make achaar and chatney, why not green apple. And right then mango scarce in Toronto, cost a fortune. Them days was not like nowadays when you gat West Indian store every corner. Them days you only get fruits from the West Indies when anybody coming. But that apple chatney taste good with them geese we bring for Prem and Kishore. Writerji didn't make no chatney though. He gat all dhem ideas but is me, Hermit, and Prem and Kishore in they apartment making apple chatney! Not three cents dhat bai Writerji.

Anyway just after new year Hermit get a number for Writerji and same time a Vietnamese girl get pregnant and quit. So I talk to dhe boss and Writerji get tek on. Well, is a factory making knockdown cardboard cartons up in Concorde by Steeles and Bathurst and is winter. We getting up five in the morning to reach for seven. Writerji get easy job. How he manage I ain't know. See, I working on line. As fast as them boxes come off the line we gat to pack them on a crate. Yuh ain't even gat time to blow you nose or scratch yuh balls. If you tek a break while machine working, cardboard pile up on you. Bai, we only glad when machine break down every other day so we get an extra half hour or hour break. And them thing heavy. All Writerji gat to do is move them crates and strap them cardboard tight. Is not easy work but he could control things at he own pace. Dhe man whistling and singing while he working as though nuthing bother he. Lunch time he finding time to talk with them Vietnamese girls. Since I working in dhat factory them Vietnamese don't mix with nobody. At break time at nine they sit in a group one side in the factory, lunchtime they sit there, and afternoon break they sit there. Them two Vietnamese men watching Writerji carefully but soon he gat them girls laughing, and they saying hello now when they passing, and he know all they name. Writerji dressing smart and comb he hair everytime he go to the toilet, soon he in the office talking to dhe payroll clerk, Annette, who uncle own dhe factory. She really pretty and she rarely come into the factory until Writerji start talking with she now and again during lunchtime. The office mek with plexiglass and them office people could see everything happening in the factory. Soon she lending Writerji book. He just smiling when I ask he and saying is just literature. He trying to catch up on Canadian Literature.

Don't let mih tell yuh, dhem white man in the factory vex. They gat all them forklift and checker and loader and supervisor and manager jobs but Annette ain't bothering with dhem. Lunchtime and break time them big-bais alone in the lunch room. Only Ravi with them. Ravi come from Sri Lanka and he is senior floor hand—them supervisor give he order and he give we order. And he feel superior. He working there long and feel he is white man too. He don't mix with we. All them floor hands Guyanese or Trini Indians, Sri Lankans or Vietnamese—and it look like everybody refugee. Soon the foreman start finding extra work for Writerji. As soon as Writerji finish strapping, he gat to come and help we on line, help with the forklift, clean up the factory floor, help with checking, help with dhis and dhat. Writerji still smiling but he hardly talking to Annette except when he gat to go and collect he paycheque from she every Friday afternoon. She and he talking on phone nighttime, and weekend she coming for Writerji and they going for lunch or dinner. Writerji ain't going no place except work if he ain't get car. April coming and every morning at dhe bus stop Writerji grumbling about dhe blasted Canadian cold—and how dhe blasted foreman picking on he.

This lunchtime Writerji just done eating and he can't bear it. He walk straight in dhe office and give Annette a book, and spend two minutes chatting with she. And everybody could see what happening with dhem. Is love like first time. As soon as he come out dhe office and sit down next to me, the foreman come out the lunch room.

"Anand—this lunch room need cleaning and sweeping. Go and give it a clean out."

"I'm on lunchbreak now Tony." Writerji sounding sharp and everybody listening. The factory silent, nat a machine working. You know how in a factory everything close down because everybody get break same time.

"Well, things slack now. . . ."

Writerji cut him off and speaking louder. "Listen, Tony, I said I'm on my lunch break. Talk to me after my break. Do you understand simple English?"

"You Paki teaching me about English?"

"I'm not a Paki. See, you don't even know geography!"

"All right, smart ass. Clean and sweep this lunch room after break—here's the broom."

Writerji jump up and I get up too. I thinking he gun knock the foreman. "Let me tell you something, Tony. You can take that broom and shove it. I don't eat in that lunch room. Let the pigs who eat in there clean it up."

"You're fired, man. You're fired."

Writerji laugh loud and touch he waist. "O course I'm fired! Jealous son-of-a-bitch! And you think I'm scared, yeh! I had enough, yeh. I quit anyway, yeh!" He imitating the Canadian accent perfect perfect. I want laugh, but I thinking about meself so I hold in till Tony rush to the office. Writerji pick up he things and walk to dhe office, everybody watching as he bend down and whisper something in Annette ear and kiss she cheek. And she get up and follow he to dhe door. Night time Writerji tell me and Hermit he thinking about heading for New York. Same time Hermit lawyer just file my papers and he seh things look good fuh mih so I holding on. Writerji seh he ain't able with this cold and stupid Canadians, and he jus call he cousin in New York. New York warmer and things easier. The biggest joke is that he cousin give he two names in Toronto to contact in the "backtrack" ring to smuggle he across dhe border and one a dhe people is Hermit self!

Well, next day late winter storm—one foot snow and cold cold. Minus fifteen degrees and with wind chill like minus thirty. Confusion on dhem road. People hardly go to wuk. I stay home. Writerji said he cut right card. He going to New York, he ain't staying for next Canadian winter. Two days later, is Friday, and everything running. Temperature warm up to minus two and road salted and clear, sunshine. Friday afternoon after work Annette come and she and Writerji gone out. Dhe man feel free like a bird. He stap grumbling about Canadian cold now he decide to head south. Half past five and place dark already. Me and Hermit done eat and looking news when, bam bam bam on dhe door. We think Writerji come back, forget he key or something. Is good thing is Hermit open dhe door. Two immigration officer get tip that an illegal alien name Anand living here. Man I nearly get heart attack. Hermit checking dhem ID and talking to them officer like is he own buddy and he invite them officer in for coffee—cold night for this work, he telling them. Hermit say is just the two a-we live there. He show dhem ID and tell them how lawyer file paper fuh me. I not working, he say, just waiting for my case, and he send me for mih passport and immigration papers. I sweating and praying dhat Writerji don't turn up then. After he tell dhem I ain't working I feeling better. I afraid I might say something wrang.

Finally them officer gone—apologize to we, man them men nice and pleasant and apologize. Hermit seh when dhem gane, don't let them smile fool yuh. Well, is time to move Writerji. When Writerji come home is late. We looking TV and waiting fuh he but is he and Annette come in quiet quiet. Writerji laugh when he see we up. Well, we gat to wait till next morning. We done know why dhem come in so quiet quiet like fowl thief. We mek excuse and hustle to bed closing we room door and left them on dhe settee.

Next morning Writerji blue when we give he dhe lowdown. He seh he certain is Tony. Yuh think Writerji would lie low after this! Dhat bai now get bad to go out. And Annette teking day off from work. . . .

Yuh think is lil story we go through nuh. When Writerji ready fuh leave, is how you think he cross the border. Well, a gun tell you, but still secret. Yuh think Writerji can write dhis? Is in a container truck. Special container, forty-foot container.

Them bai moving genuine shipment of furniture and personal effects to the States. Yuh know people always moving back and forth to States legally. A separate section in dhe front of dhe container conceal real good—double wall—to hold four people. That is how. Can't give more details as dhem bai still using dhe route. And Hermit seh less I know, less I talk. Well he didn't figure on Writerji. Writerji disappear underground in New York and is years we hear nothing about he. Next thing we know is novel out set in Guyana, and then dhem "Underground Stories" by a writer name S. T. Writerji! He mixing up place and incident between New York and Canada— who can tell what is what? But them thing real and only we know who is who. Writerji send Hermit book to mih house. When Hermit, Lena, and them children come over Hermit quiet quiet. Is summer and we barbecuing in the backyard and dhem children running around, just like now. He find a corner and read that book right out. Nat a man disturb he. Lena surprise but nat me, dhat is dhe Hermit I know. When he done he shake he head and come over and tek a drink. Ask Lena and Katie. We drinking in mih house. Tears run down he eyes. No, that bai nat like Naipaul, he seh. He mek we proud! Dhem days, dhem days right hey, mixup and sanaay, sanaay good like rice and daal, and nice hot seven curry with hot chatney. I read dhat book out, right out dhe night before, and was same way I feel. Hermit tek a next drink—I gat a special bottle 12 Year Old Demerara Gold—and he come and sit next to me. Ask he when yuh see he. And he point to dhe front page. Writerji mek dedication—

> *To Hermit and Jones*

—and he seh, "dhem days, bai, dhem days is something else. See what we gain from dhem!" He close dhe book—just so and tears run down he face. Ask he, ask Hermit when yuh see him, ask him about dhat, about Writerji, about we.

QUESTIONS

1. How are the typical immigrant themes of fear, uncertainty, and hope handled in Persaud's story?

2. What constitutes the transitional experience for the Guyanese immigrants to Canada? Give supporting examples.

3. What does the making of chatney from rotting green apples instead of mangos symbolize in the tale?

4. How do the Guyanese immigrants view the unmolested sanctuary given to Canadian geese when they themselves are finding it hard to make money to eat anything?

5. How important to the story's effect is its use of creole or nation language voices? What would be lost if the story had been written in standard English?

John Stewart

(TRINIDAD, b. 1933)

John Stewart was born in Trinidad and left to pursue university study in the United States when he was twenty-two. After graduating, he took an interest in developing black studies programs in the United States and is still credited with being one of the founding fathers of that movement. He has authored six books, including *Last Cool Days* (1971), a novel that was awarded London's Royal Society of Literature prize. He has also published two collections of short stories, *Curving Road* (1975) and *Looking for Josephine and Other Stories* (1998). Currently he is professor of African American and African studies at the University of California, Davis. He has taught at Cal State Fresno, the Ohio State University, and the University of Illinois, where he was the director of the Afro American studies program. He completed a PhD in anthropology and has made fine contributions in fiction and anthropology, as well as the ethnology of his birthplace, Trinidad. His research investigates the interrelationships among people, land, agriculture, and religion.

Curving Road, the collection from which this story originates, is a book that is full of poignant vignettes of experience. The stories are full of Stewart's perceptions of culture, music, and people. In "Pablo's Blues," the eponymous main character wanders through town with the beat of Miles Davis's bluesy jazz song playing in the background. His "a-day-in-the-life" depiction of Pablo's life offers the contrast between the traditional lifestyle confronting head-on the complicated Western lifestyle imposing itself on the Trinidadian way of life. In the story that follows, the expatriate Trinidadian narrator at first is appalled at the poor roads and scanty dwellings he observes when he returns to his former neighborhood in Princes Town. He cannot believe he has ever existed in this kind of environment. But as he wanders around and remembers his childhood and youth, his perceptions begin to change and a nostalgia for what he has lost overcomes him.

The Old Men Used to Dance   1998

It had never dawned on him all through the years that Trinidad was a narrow place. Now that Simon is retired from his teaching appointment in the Miami district and is spending his days as a tourist his views have changed. When he drove around Miami going from school to school teaching, coaching, demonstrating how to play the steelpan, he dearly loved everything about Trinidad. Now, since he has toured in Vancouver and Toronto, Hollywood, and Albuquerque New Mexico, his feelings have changed.

One of the things he likes about the western places he's seen is the streets. The roads. Their spaciousness, their direct lines. Whoever laid them out did so with a large plan and clear goals in mind, the desire to facilitate great deeds and leave access to them for all who come behind. This year he's back home to tour the four corners of Trinidad, and the contrast between roads here at home and the roads on which he has toured abroad strikes him as humiliating.

Of course he's accustomed to the murderous potholes that go on for miles: all Trinidadians are, and he had more or less prepared himself to deal with that. The sharp, flat curves that invite oncoming drivers to ignore the lanes and drive a straight line, that too. The corrugated paving that shook his stomach into mild nausea at times, that too. Concrete abutments and canals where there should be shoulder, all of that. He was prepared to handle all the conditions for which Trinidad roads are well known, including the intemperate taxi drivers who overtake, stop, start, cut in oblivious to the heart-jolting jeopardy in which they place other drivers.

But here he is after five days—since he'd taken time to overnight in San Fernando, Point Fortin, Moruga, Mayaro—in the last hours of his tour, on his way to see the old house in Princes Town, and only now awakening to an impaling circumstance that must have been there before his eyes all along without his recognizing it. Too often when he got off the main road to pass through little villages and towns he decided to see for the first time he found there was simply no easy way to get through. Too often he found that the road just runs out, or that side or back streets are too thin and narrow, that they curve and twist without reason, hump and sink into open drains, slide tiredly into the muck of a pasture, or expire at the base of some concrete wall topped with barbed wire or pointed shards of broken glass ready to eviscerate the sky itself, were it so malicious as to come down any closer.

Manzanilla, Sangre Grande, Toco, Valencia, more of the same. Of course Trinidad is not a big country rich enough to afford boulevards and avenues (although one sees the sign "avenue" often enough where there's nothing but a narrow lane) but surely we have imagination and energy aplenty (just look at carnival!), and the material (La Brea[1] has been shipping pitch for roads to Europe and elsewhere in the world for nearly a century and the pitchlake still brims) and the manpower to conceive a plan, lay down a "plat" for a decent network of roadways that didn't run us into unmarked dead ends or run us into fields where cows graze.

This treacherous and frustrating passageway is not the result of sporadic and self-indulgent irrationalities, however. It may seem so, but the thing happens too regular for there not to be a hand behind it all, he thinks. Our roads say, the mission here will be limited. No matter what the spirit invested in this place, the mission will be limited, the power to do things awarded grudgingly, at times suspended, or even withdrawn. The forces that carved out towns and villages in Trinidad were grudgingly awarded and suspended here and there through whimsy.

---

1 **La Brea:** Tar pits near San Fernando in the south of Trinidad.

Now that he's taken time to travel through his homeland, from Cumuto, Tacarigua, Tunupuna, to Curepe, he sees the same hand mingy with space for passing, the same atmosphere armed with an aggressive narrowness. It offends him. The press of open drains and abutted concrete curbs, the unexpected ditch that must be skirted with great care between close, menacing walls offend him. Overseas the drains are all placed underground: why couldn't such care be taken here? The press of other drivers impatiently cutting and squeezing in their knowledge of the local terrain offends him. Why couldn't things be more orderly here? Why couldn't street signs be posted at a level where drivers may easily read them?

He finally finds the correct street leading back to the main road out of San Juan. And once he gets through the tangled maze of taxis, buses, trucks and vans back onto the dual highway he breathes again with ease. This is more like it. This is how it should be: dual lane space, shoulders, no concrete abutments. This is how it should be everywhere from the beginning.

He knows, he can understand. He is not a scholar but he's been a teacher and he enjoys reading history. He knows that streets in the towns of Trinidad were not laid out with the automobile in mind. These streets were made for walking, for the bicycle, for a time when the country was a more friendly place. A jovial place, with lilies and hibiscus blossoms dancing in the breeze, and people in their graceful country walk taking time to stop here and there and talk to one another. Even from his own childhood he could remember the warmth and neighborliness of the streets in St Joseph, Barataria, Laventille, people walking to church or market, men on their bicycles to and from work, everyone with time to see and recognize each other on the road, time to stand up in the grass or in a gap and talk, time to walk or ride slowly with friends or someone who would soon be a friend. Sunday walks around the savannah, when old and young, the well-off and the poor joined in casual strolls around the bandstand. Motor car changed all that. They demand space to turn, to park, to roll past each other without bouncing. They are not made to negotiate lanes, be carried across gutters, or up the track where paved streets peter into rocky paths between the neighbors' yards. Not that he harbors any preference for the old days, he likes having the motor car. What grinds him is the slowness or absence of effort to adapt the streets themselves to civil use of the motor car. The slowness to have streets that reflect the new order—well marked and spacious, not corrugated—the deadlock this brings around every narrow town square, the tension of driving in defence against unmarked deadends.

On the dual carriage highway there is still a bicycle or two as he crosses the flat plain of Caroni. He enters the hilly terrain at the heart of the Naparima district thinking no one back then when he was young forecast the crush of squeezing, noisy, exhaust-belching machines forcing themselves into deadlock around every market center, or the hurried and careless fashion in which people shoulder by each other in their shopping. Nothing in his childhood foresaw how rusty and dilapidated shops that once housed books, and cloths, and favours of all kinds from various countries would become. Of course, there were the new buildings too. Straight-up concrete boxes with glass louvred windows. Like the new streets they no doubt were reasonably functional but they made no statement. They were no evidence that so-and-so was once here. Anybody could have thrown them up.

He had to face it now. This touring of his homeland is in no way innocent. He had come back primed to see Lloyd, and Sheila, Earl and Hugh and reconstruct the times they used to have dancing, laughing, being in the company of each other. He had come back primed to see Gregory and the boys, to play with them, and get immersed again in the sound and feeling of those days. He was hungry for the sound and feeling of those days. No denying that. He had come back exactly as they used to say islanders always come back, hungry for sweet life after all the false and shallow hurried-up living done abroad. No denying. But even so, even if he had not come back with a probably over-burdening romantic desire, there was still much here to make return a disappointment.

The young Indian family who apparently owned what used to be the ice-cream shop on High Street, once he got in to Princes Town, were not selling ice-cream and peanut punch. The small counter behind which they gathered was greasy and taken up mostly with a glass case of cooked meats. The atmosphere was strong with sweet curry. "Can you tell me which street it is the Pompeys live on?" he asked the young girl serving as the cashier.

"Pompey? I don't know no Pompey here in Princes Town."

"They used to live on Centenary Street. I passed by there but somebody else in the house said they had moved. You don't know the Pompeys?"

"I never hear about no Pompeys living here. The person in the house couldn't tell you?"

"Said she's just moved in and didn't know. He used to be the light-heavy weight champion of the empire."

"No, I never hear about nobody by the name of Pompey. But let me ask."

She went to the rear of the shop from where steam and the smells were coming, then came back. "No. We don't know of no Pompeys. Ask next door by the bank. Somebody there might be able to help you."

Next door at the bank the clerks were all young Indians. They had never heard of Pompey. But "Ask the guard there by the door," one young man with pomaded hair and an executive power tie said. "He's an old-timer. He might know."

And that's how a world champion ranks in the esteem of these new citizens. Something an old-timer might remember.

The old-timer at the door was not at the door. He was in a small room next to the manager's office making coffee. He was grey, tall, and had the lean hard look of a former fighter himself. "Pompey?" he said. "Pompey dead. You enh hear that? Pompey dead long time. You must be from away?"

"I used to live here."

"Well you must be away long time because Pompey dead and bury so long, plenty young people nowadays don't even know nothing about him."

He did not ask about Gregory.

Market Street was crowded, with vendors and shoppers locked in a haggling noise he didn't want to hear. It grated against the two solos he carried in his head. He had two. One for Gregory, and one for himself saying maybe thanks to this place where he had first learned to hear and reach the big pulse, the heart that was in everybody. That's what drummers do. Reach the big heart in everybody. And he had learned that here, in a place less noisy, crowded and complacent.

The old men used to dance outside the rumshop near the warden's office. And Gregory was their favourite drummer. Gregory had the gift, they used to say, and when he played, if you were man you knew there was nothing you couldn't do. He used to watch Gregory play, watch the old fighters dance, and feel the awesome stir that made their faces sweet and fierce at the same time. "Bois!" he could still hear the voices, the solemn, chanting men's voices singing their best to tame the drums and in absolute self-confidence sending their own exclamations to the sky, "Bois!"

He had two solos, one for Gregory, one for the boy who had never left this town of sloping yards with their flower gardens, zaboca, teke, and mora trees, and the rolling fields of sugar-cane covering the distance. This boy in him who had come home to find the market square a muddle with small heaps of white chicken feathers, broken boxes and stale produce in the drains, and vendors crowded everywhere, their cloths spread in the street itself, all hawking the same tomatoes, melongene, bhodi, ochro, pumpkin, bananas, spices. No one offered flowers. And the haggle of voices was no chant. No one seemed the least bit concerned with the sky, and he reasoned with the boy inside that this was so because times change, things change, people change, all in time becomes the jettison of a drama taking place somewhere else. He reasoned with the boy.

QUESTIONS

1. How has Simon's life in Miami changed his superficial perceptions of Trinidad?

2. Are Simon's negative reactions and criticisms of Trinidad justified in any way?

3. What was the purpose of Simon's return home? Is this purpose ever achievable?

4. What does Simon's experience in trying to locate Pompey demonstrate to him?

5. How does the story treat the theme of memory?

India / Pakistan

At the same time that Elizabeth I (r. 1558–1603) was consolidating her control over Ireland, she unwittingly set in motion forces that centuries later resulted in England's control of India—the "jewel in the crown" of the British Empire. On the last day of the year 1600, Elizabeth signed a document granting a group of adventurers led by Thomas Smythe exclusive rights for fifteen years to the potentially lucrative trade in Indian spices. England's foray into this new commercial venture had been made possible twelve years earlier by her defeat of the Spanish Armada, which opened trade routes previously controlled by Spain and Portugal.

What the British found when they arrived on the west coast of India was the still powerful Muslim (or Mughal) empire, then at the height of its power under Akbar "the Great" (r. 1556–1605). Like the Portuguese, the British established well-fortified warehouses on India's coast and hired Indian sepoys (police) to guard them. For their part, Akbar and his successors were content to replace the Spanish and Portuguese, whose missionaries were constantly trying to convert his subjects to Christianity, with British traders whose only aim was profitable commerce.

India at the time of these early contacts with Europe was a rich and highly cultured subcontinent, whose civilization was older by centuries and more accomplished in nearly every respect than Europe's. The famous Taj Mahal, for example, was built by the Mughal emperor Shāh Jahān (r. 1628–1658) within fifty years of England's first contact. But long before this architectural wonder, Indian literature had achieved unrivaled heights of beauty and sophistication. Earliest are the four Vedas, the basic sacred texts of Hinduism, probably completed about 500 B.C.E. The Sanskrit epic *Mahabharata* (which contains the famous *Bhagavad Gita*) achieved its present form ca. 200 B.C.E. to 200 C.E., while the *Ramayana* was composed probably in the third century B.C.E. Indian drama was well established by the sixth century C.E., when the theater in Europe, after its flowering in Greece and Rome, had ceased to exist.

For the century and a quarter following England's initial contact with India, most of Europe's colonial and religious conflicts were waged on the continent or in the New World. This is not to say that Europe's contacts with India remained purely commercial and mutually beneficial. The spice trade gradually was joined by commerce in cotton cloth, a relatively new commodity to Europe made cheap by abundant Indian labor, some of it slave. During this time, the descendants of Akbar spent much of their time and resources fighting dynastic battles, warding-off enemies on their borders, and attempting to extend the empire. As a result, by the close of the reign of Aurangzeb in 1707, the Mughal empire was in decline. It would last for another century and a half as a power to be reckoned with, but it was nevertheless losing sway to more powerful forces, primarily internal ones. An important external threat, however, was to emerge from the French. Joseph Francois Dupleix perceived that internal Indian conflicts could be exploited for European gain; when Dupleix was recalled to France, Robert Clive of the British East India Company stepped up the company's efforts at extending its control and ejecting the French. It must be remembered that no part of India was as yet a British colony in the sense that America was until its revolution. Britain's interests were still represented by the East India Company, supported by British troops and regulated (in theory at least) by Parliament. The situation was similar with regard to the other European powers with interests in India—France, Portugal, and Holland. European "colonies" in India consisted mainly of fortified trading centers dotted around the Indian coasts.

This situation changed in 1756 when the Indian ruler of Bengal, Sirāj-ud-Dawlah, attacked the British in Calcutta and imprisoned 145 Brits overnight in a small room measuring only 18 by 14 feet. All but 23 died of suffocation and dehydration—a tragedy caused more by negligence than malice—but this so-called black hole incident gave Clive an excuse to retaliate, and by a combination of treachery and boldness he defeated Sirāj-ud-Dawlah. In a phony ceremony, the East India Company was adopted into the Mughal hierarchy, and Bengal thus became the foundation of the British Empire in India. Further British victories over the French in India were paralleled by similar conquests in North America and the Caribbean. This so-called Seven Years' War concluded with the Treaty of Paris in 1763, and Britain suddenly found itself the foremost colonial power in the world.

This did not spell the end of British expansionism. By the early nineteenth century, British victories in a series of conflicts had extended its control to nearly a third of India: Bengal and provinces northwest of it, plus a strip extending southwest from Calcutta along the coast to and including much of the "tip" of India. By 1820, following the so-called Maratha Wars, it controlled nearly half of the subcontinent. All of this expansion caused a change in Britain's role in India, for the costs of maintaining a large army (most of it Indian) far outstripped the profits that the East India Company could make by trade. Consequently, revenues became increasingly dependent upon taxes. Much of this expansion was accomplished by treaty and annexation, but military force played its part as well. The next stage in Britain's expansion was brutally aggressive. Fearing (rightly or wrongly) that Russia intended to expand southward toward India, Britain waged a series of bloody and costly wars to conquer what is now Afghanistan and Pakistan.

By 1850, the East India Company's expansions and its accompanying technological innovations had transformed India. Economically, the ending of the Company's monopoly in 1813 and the opening of Indian markets to all comers devastated Indian cotton weavers, as manufactured goods from England's industrial north swept the market. Modern communications and travel, however, in the form of the telegraph, the "penny post," and railroads began the process of unifying India. The Company congratulated itself on bringing good government in the wake of conquest and, unlike previous conquerors, of respecting indigenous religious institutions. Indeed, the Company veiled its rule behind the facade of traditional rajas and nawabs. But while eighteenth-century Company administrators had attempted to learn India's languages (and indeed, sometimes did great service by extolling and preserving Indian literature and art), nineteenth-century rulers adopted a different course. Acting on the recommendations of Thomas Babington Macaulay, British policy in India after 1835 promoted the education of Indians in English language, literature, and culture. The idea was that upper-caste Indian men would be British educated so as to be able to serve in the company's civil service ranks. Like everything else, this proved to be a double-edged sword. On the one hand, it eventually provided India with one of its national languages—English; on the other, it deemphasized the study of traditional Sanskrit and Persian literatures and cast Indian students and civil servants as "wannabe" Englishmen.

At about the same time as Macaulay was introducing his radical and indeed epoch-making educational changes, another momentous social change was occurring in India's small European community: the arrival of significant numbers of European women. Previous to this, European men had freely mixed with Indian women, sometimes taking them as mistresses, sometimes marrying them. The offspring of these unions usually were given preferential treatment in employment and society; in essence, they were treated as equals (or near-equals) in Indo-European society. Interestingly, this practice was exactly the opposite of what happened to the children of mixed-race unions in the New World, where those with any African blood were consigned to slavery. But the arrival of significant numbers of European women as brides or prospective brides for European men changed all this. In a relatively short time, mixed-race unions, indeed mixed-race relations of almost any kind, became taboo, and the offspring of Anglo-Indian unions were shunned. Within a generation, the meeting of Indians and Europeans as social equals became nearly impossible, and the notion that whites were by nature and culture superior to Indians became the dominant social and political ideology. The social and political divide that opened would never be repaired.

The year 1850 marks the approximate date of other important cultural and political shifts. By this date, the fiction that the East India Company was in charge of Indian affairs had largely evaporated in the heat of governmental intervention and military conquest. Native rulers were openly replaced with British administrators. Simultaneously, pressures by British evangelical Protestants to convert Hindus and Muslims to Christianity had opened the country to floods of missionaries eager to wean Hindus especially from their "idolatrous" ways. Laws were passed as early as 1829 to abolish suttee (the burning of widows on their husbands' funeral pyres) and thuggery (ritual highway robbery and murder). Confident of their scientific, technological, military, cultural, and religious superiority, the British set out to remake India in their own image. Indians of every caste chafed under the slights and humiliations of British presumptions.

Thus the stage was set for the single most important event in nineteenth century India: the so-called Mutiny of 1857–1859, known to Indians as the First War of Independence. The proximate cause was the introduction of the new Enfield rifle to

sentenced to six years. The Hindu-Muslim coalition he had held together collapsed, but independence agitation continued, aided by British blunders. At the 1929 Congress meeting, Jawaharlal Nehru succeeded in proclaiming India's official goal of independence. Until 1950, January 26, 1930, was observed as Independence Day. Since 1950, it has been observed as Republic Day.

The period between the declaration and India's actual independence in 1947 was marked by continued civil strife—Gandhi's ingenious boycott of British-taxed salt, for example. But as the inevitability of independence drew ever nearer, fractures in the apparently unified Indian front began to appear. Gandhi's nonviolent movement was countered by Nehru's socialist tendencies, while the leader of the Muslim League, Quaid-i-Azam M. A. Jinnah, led a movement for a separate Muslim state. Ironically, the success and power of the Indian National Congress had raised fears among various non-Hindu minorities of a "Congress Raj"—dominance by the Congress Party. The outbreak of World War II in 1939 brought other complications and delays. Once again, Indians rallied to Britain's cause, but this time in fewer numbers, and some advocated overt cooperation with Japan. Fear of Muslim defection from Britain's side prompted the British to support Jinnah's separatist idea, and this was made official in the agreement that secured India's independence in 1947.

There had been Hindu-Muslim violence before independence—for example, in the riots in Bengal in August 1946 that left at least 4,000 people dead. But no one was prepared for the carnage that followed independence and the formation of Pakistan, a divided country with territory both in the north (present-day Pakistan) and in the east (present-day Bangladesh). Fear became hysteria as Muslims fleeing Hindu domination moved westward toward Pakistan, while Hindus fearing Muslims fled toward India. Hysteria turned into madness as murders, massacres, rapes, looting, and burning raged out of control. Perhaps 1 million people died in the months of atrocities, in spite of Gandhi's direct appeals for peace and tolerance. A lasting effect of the hastily drawn borders of 1947 is the continuing tension between India and Pakistan over the former princely state of Kashmir. Another casualty of these conflicts was Gandhi himself, who was assassinated in January 1948.

Independence and the new republican constitution adopted in 1949 did not end India's centuries-long problems nor bring immediate peace and prosperity. Although politically unified under its constitution, India remains divided by language (fifteen constitutionally recognized languages, plus many others), religion, geography, educational and economic levels, political philosophy, geographic region, and a widening gulf between educated, cosmopolitan urban dwellers and tradition-bound rural peoples. As the world's largest democracy with a population of 1 billion people, homogeneity and cultural unity are hardly to be expected. Externally, India's most pressing problem remains its dispute with Pakistan over Kashmir, which erupted into war in 1947 and 1965 and threatens to do so again. The fact that both India and Pakistan have nuclear weapons gives this conflict international significance.

Nevertheless, the India of the twenty-first century is emerging as an international political and economic force, capturing high-tech jobs in computer-related industries and services and providing stiff competition for the European powers that for centuries exploited India's wealth.

THE SHORT STORY IN INDIA

While England's merchants and armies were constructing the empire "on which the sun never set," her writers were largely preoccupied with domestic matters. Considering the scope and importance of Britain's colonial expansion, relatively little of its literature deals directly with this development, although postcolonial critics have revealed the ways in which many literary works (for example, Jane Austen's *Mansfield Park* and Charles Dickens's *Great Expectations*) use the existence of the colonies as major plot ingredients. Novels and poetry dominated the British literary scene in the nineteenth century, with the short story gradually emerging after 1880. Simultaneously, the curriculum for India inaugurated by Macaulay's reforms in 1835 stressed traditional canonical English literature—Shakespeare, Milton, and later the romantic poets. Indian students read almost no British fiction in school or university until very late in the century. Of course, Britons stationed in India read the novels of the day, and eventually there arose in India British fiction writers who depicted their lives as colonials or wrote about the "exotic" natives they saw around them. Anglo-Indian authors such as Rudyard Kipling, Flora Annie Steele, and Alice Perrin explored the life of India and the relations between the British who lived there and the Indians who served, were exploited by, and, yes, opposed them.

Meanwhile, Indian students were being exposed to European literature, ideas, and literary forms, including the novel. Bankim Chandra Chatterjee is generally regarded as India's first novelist, writing historical romances in the vein of Sir Walter Scott. But by the turn of the century, European novelists and short story writers in the realistic mode were influencing Indian writers to abandon the traditional emphasis on supernatural characters, marvelous events, and florid style in favor of fiction that described current people and situations in India. As a result, a distinctively new Indian fiction arose, first in the novel, and then in the short story, and fiction both in English and in indigenous languages became not only a medium of imaginative expression but also a form of political and social protest.

Curiously, it was not British but European writers such as Anton Chekhov and Guy de Maupassant who inspired Indian writers to take up the short story. Who wrote the "first" Indian short story is impossible to determine, but one candidate is Rabindranath Tagore, a Bengali who published several volumes of stories in a variety of modes beginning in 1895. Honors for the first stories in English by an Indian may belong to Cornelia Sorabji, whose *Love and Life Behind the Purdah* was published in 1901. The short story quickly became a vehicle of social protest; in fact, *Passion for the Fatherland* (first published in Urdu in 1908) by Premchand, was seized and burned by British officials as seditious. As pressures for self-government grew during the late nineteenth century and throughout the early decades of the twentieth, Indian writers frequently expressed the nation's political and social aspirations, often using English as the language that could transcend regional limitations and reach the world at large.

Tagore's stories are seldom overtly anticolonial, but Premchand often attacked British institutions and practices and, like Tagore, used fiction to criticize indigenous social problems such as the caste system and the treatment of widows. The same tendencies are found in the "big three" writers of the early Indian short story in English—Mulk Raj Anand, R. K. Narayan, and Raja Rao. Anand's first story collection, *The Barber's Trade Union and Other Stories* (1944), began his literary career, but it was his earlier novel, *Untouchable* (1935), that established his reputation as a social critic. Moreover, Anand can be credited with treating even the lowliest of his characters as complex human beings. Narayan, the least overtly political of the three, sets his stories and novels in the imaginary village of Malgudi, which serves as a microcosm of the larger world. In his hands, the people of Malgudi and their problems, triumphs, and everyday lives become deeply humanized. Rao's short fiction uses the particulars of Indian social life to comment on Indian society at large. More than any other of his contemporaries, Rao sought to bend English to the Indian idiom, to make it less a foreign language than one capable of expressing Indian realities. By the mid-twentieth century, these writers, and many others influenced by them, had established the short story genre in many languages and the short story in English as an important cultural force in India and beyond.

Just as India has emerged as a world political and economic power since its independence, so has it become prominent culturally, especially through its literature and film. After independence, a new generation of writers emerged. Many of them excelled in the short story, and the *Nayi Kahani* or "new story" movement of the 1950s and 1960s reenergized the genre with sharper realism and sometimes with experimental techniques. New story writers include Krushwant Singh and Attia Hosain. More recently, women writers have emerged to bring feminist concerns and sensibilities to the short story, while writers of the "Indian diaspora" (for example, V. S. Naipaul, Ruth Prawer Jhabvala, and Rohinton Mistry) have tackled the problems faced by Indian emigrants in England, the Caribbean, and North America. In the 1980s, Indian literature exploded on the world scene with the publication of such novels as Salman Rushdie's *Satanic Verses* (1988) and Anita Desai's *Baumgartner's Bombay* (1988), opening the way for still further best-selling authors such as Arundhati Roy (*The God of Small Things,* 1997) and Zadie Smith (*White Teeth,* 2000, and *On Beauty,* 2005). Indian writing in English is now a dominant force in postcolonial literature and, like Indian film and the burgeoning Indian economy, is making itself felt throughout the world.

Raja Rao

(b. 1908)

Like many writers of his generation, Raja Rao was born into an intellectual family, his father a professor, his mother an actress. Unlike many of his peers, however, Rao was educated not in England but in the United States (Hunter College in New York) and France (Universities of Montpelier and the Sorbonne). In substance, too, his education was unusual, for although a Hindu, he studied at Muslim schools in India and then focused on Christian theology and history at university. In 1931 he married a French woman and shortly thereafter began writing short stories in French and English. When his marriage ended in 1939, he returned to India and joined the resistance against British rule. His first novel, *Kanthapura* (1938), takes a Gandhian approach to opposing the Raj, as does his collection of stories, *The Cow of the Barricades* (1947).

After India's independence in 1947, Rao left the country and traveled widely, including a visit to the United States in 1950. In 1965 he married U.S. actress Katherine Jones and began lecturing on Indian philosophy at the University of Texas at Austin, where he remained until 1983. The novels Rao wrote during these years—*The Serpent and the Rope* (1960) and *The Cat and Shakespeare* (1965)—reflect his abiding interest in spiritual and philosophical issues. Another volume of stories, *The Policeman and the Rose*, appeared in 1978, followed by nonfiction works of history and literary criticism. In 1988 he was awarded the Neustadt International Prize for literature.

Although Rao was educated in the West and spent much of his life in Europe and the United States, his fiction is thoroughly Indian in outlook. The influence of Mulk Raj Anand may be visible in Rao's novels and stories, which are often set in Indian villages. "The Cow of the Barricades" is evidently set during the "quit India" campaign and is typical of Rao's Gandhian influence with its emphasis on the Master's spirituality and the uncanny nature of Gauri, the cow, which seems almost ghost-like in her mysterious movements and habits. Readers are left to decide for themselves what Gauri signifies and whether the story advocates peaceful or violent resistance.

The Cow of the Barricades   1947

They called her Gauri for she came every Tuesday evening before sunset to stand and nibble at the hair of the Master. And the Master touched her and caressed her and he said: "How are you, Gauri?" and Gauri simply bent her legs and drew back her tongue and, shaking her head, ambled round him and disappeared among the bushes. And till Tuesday next she was not to be seen. And the Master's disciples gathered grain and grass and rice-water to give her every Tuesday, but she refused it all and took only the handful of grain the Master gave. She munched it slowly and carefully as one articulates a string of holy words, and when she had finished eating, she knelt again, shook her head and disappeared. And the Master's disciples said: "This is a strange creature," and they went to the Cotton Street and the Mango Street, and they went by the Ginning Mills and through the Weavers' Lines, but Gauri was nowhere to be seen. She was not even a god-dedicated cow, for never had a shopkeeper caught her eating the grams nor was she found huddled in a cattle-pound. People said, "Only the Master could have such strange visitors," and they went to the Master and said: "Master, can you tell us who this cow may be?" And the Master smiled with unquenchable love and fun and he said: "She may be my baton-armed mother-in-law. Though she may be the mother of one of you. Perhaps, she is the great Mother's vehicle."[1] And like to a mother, they put kumkum[2] on her forehead and till Tuesday next they waited for Gauri.

But people heard of it here and people heard of it there, and they came with grain and hay and kumkum water saying, "We have a strange visitor, let us honour her." And merchants came saying, "Maybe she's Lakshmi,[3] the Goddess, and we may have more money next harvest," and fell at her feet. And students came to touch her head and touch her tail, saying, "Let me pass the examinations this year!" And young girls came to ask for husbands and widows to ask for purity, and the childless to ask for children. And so every Tuesday there was a veritable procession of people at the Master's hermitage. But Gauri would pass by them all like a holy wife among men, and going straight to the Master, would nibble at his hair and disappear among the bushes. People unable to take back the untouched offerings gave them to the river and the fishes jumped to eat them as at a festival; but the crocodile had disappeared from the whirls of the deep waters. And one fine morning the Master woke in his bed to hear the snake and the rat playing under him, for when the seeker finds harmony, the jackal and the deer and the rat and the serpent become friends. And Gauri was no doubt a fervent soul who had sought the paths of this world to be born a sage in the next, for she was so compassionate and true.

And people were much affrighted, and they took the women and the children to the fields beyond and they cooked food beneath the trees and lived there—for the army of the Government was going to take the town and no woman or child would be spared. And doors were closed and clothes and vessels and jewels were hidden away, and only the workmen and the men ruled the city, and the Master was the head of them all, and they called him President. Patrols of young men in khadi[4] and Gandhi cap[5] would go through the streets, and when they saw the old or the miserly peeping from behind the doors they called them and talked to them and led them to

---

1 **great Mother's vehicle:** In the *Rigveda*, the cow is referred to as a goddess and identified with Aditi, the mother of the gods.
2 **kumkum:** The red powder used to mark the foreheads of Hindu women.
3 **Lakshmi:** Goddess of fortune and wife of Krishna.
4 **khadi:** Homespun cotton cloth, advocated by Gandhi.
5 **Gandhi cap:** Close-fitting hat worn by followers of Gandhi.

the camp by the fields, for the Master said there was danger and nobody could stay but the strong and the young. Grass grew beneath the eaves and the dust of the monsoon swept along the streets while the red men's trains brought army after army and everybody could see them for the station was down below and the town upon a hill. Barricades lay on the streets like corpse-heaps after the last plague, but the biggest of them all was in the Suryanarayana Street. It was as big as a chariot.

Men were hidden behind it and waited for the battle. But the Master said, "No, there shall be no battle, brothers." But the workmen said again, "It is not with, 'I love you, I love you,' that you can change the grinding heart of this Government," and they brought picks and scythes and crowbars, and a few Mohammedans brought their swords and one or two stole rifles from the mansions, and there was a regular fighting army ready to fall on the red man's men. And the Master went and said this and the Master went and said that, but the workmen said, "We'll fight," and fight they would. So deep in despair the Master said, "I resign from the presidentship," and he went and sat in meditation and rose into the worlds from which come light and love, in order that the city might be saved from bloodshed. And when people heard this they were greatly angered against the workmen, but they knew the workmen were right and the Master was right, and they did not know which way the eye should turn. Owls hovered about even in midday light, and when dusk fell, all the stars hung so low that people knew that that night would see the fight.

But everybody looked at the empty street-corners and said, "Where is she— Gauri?"

At ten that night the first war-chariots were heard to move up, and cannons and bayonets and lifted swords rushed in assault.

And what happened afterwards people remember to this very day. There she was, Gauri, striding out of the Oil Lane and turning around Copper Seenayya's house towards the Suryanarayana Street, her head held gently bent and her ears pressed back like plaits of hair, and staggering like one going to the temple with fruits and flowers to offer to the Goddess. And she walked fast, and when people saw her they ran behind her, and crowd after crowd gathered round her and torch and lantern in hand they marched through the Brahmin Street and the Cotton Street and past the Venkatalakshmamma Well, and the nearer she came to the barricades the faster she walked, though she never ran. And people said, "She will protect us. Now it's sure she will save us," and bells were brought and rung and camphors were lit and coconuts were broken at her feet, but she neither shuddered nor did she move her head; she walked on. And the workmen who were behind the barricades, saw this and they were sore furious with it, and they said, "Here, they send the cow instead of coming to help us." Some swore and others laughed, and one of them said, "We'll fire at her, for if the crowd is here and the red man's army on the other side it will be terrible." But they were afraid, for the crowd chanted "Vande Mataram"[6] and they were all uplifted and sure, and Gauri marched onwards her eyes raised towards the

6 **Vande Mataram:** National song of India.

barricades. And as she came near the temple square the workmen laid down their arms, as she came by the Tulsi Well they folded their hands, and as she was beneath the barricades they fell prostrate at her feet murmuring, "Goddess, who may you be?" And they formed two rings, and between them passed Gauri, her left foreleg first, then her back right leg, once on the sandbag, once on the cart-wheel, and with the third move men pushed her up and she was on top of the barricades. And then came a rich whispering like a crowd at evening worship, but the red man's army cried from the other side of the barricades, "Oh, what's this? Oh, what's this?" and they rushed towards the barricades thinking it was a flag of truce. But when they saw the cow and its looks and the tear, clear as a drop of the Ganges, they shouted out, "Victory to the Mahatma! Mahatma Gandhi ki jai!" and joined up with the crowd. But their chief, the red man, saw this and fired a shot. It went through Gauri's head, and she fell a vehicle of God among lowly men.

But they said blood did not gush out of the head but only between the forelegs, from the thickness of her breast.

Peace has come back to us now. Seth Jamnalal Dwarak Chand bought the two houses on either side of the barricades, cut a loop road through them, and in the middle he erected a metal statue for Gauri. Our Gauri was not so tall nor was she stiff, for she had a very human look. But we all offer her flowers and honey and perfumed sweetmeats and the first green grass of spring. And our children jump over the railings and play between her legs, and putting their mouths to the hole in the breast—for this was made too—shout out resounding booms. And never have our carpenters had gayer times than since Gauri died, for our children do not want their baswanna-bulls but only ask for Gauris. And to this day hawkers cry them about at the railway station, chanting, "Gauris of Gorakhpur! Polished, varnished and on four wheels!" and many a child from the Himalayas to the seas of the South pulls them through the dusty streets of Hindustan.

But even now when we light our sanctum lights at night, we say, "Where is she, Gauri?" Only the Master knows where she is. He says: "Gauri is waiting in the Middle Heavens[7] to be born. She will be reborn when India sorrows again before she is free."

Therefore it is said, "The Mahatma may be all wrong about politics, but he is right about the fullness of love in all creatures—the speechful and the mute."

QUESTIONS

1. Gauri eats only the grain given by the Master. Is this significant? What might it suggest?

2. What do people other than the Master expect from Gauri? What does this suggest?

---

7 **Middle Heavens:** In Hindu cosmology, there are seven levels of the heavens.

3. Why do women and children leave the village? What signs, natural and super-natural, tell them to leave?

4. What aspects of Gauri suggest that she is an ordinary cow? What aspects suggest that she is in some ways supernatural or spiritual?

5. Twice the story offers paradoxical comment: "they knew the workmen were right and the Master was right" and similarly in the last sentence of the story. Can these paradoxes be resolved? Are both sides of these paradoxes equally true within the story, or does the story itself favor one side or the other? Cite specific passages in support of your answer.

6. How does the story comment on the possibilities of passive resistance as a political tool? How does it reveal the conflicts and issues surrounding independence movements?

Krishan Chander

(1914–1976)

A prolific short story writer in Urdu, Krishan Chander was a long-time secretary-general of the Progressive Writers Association in India. As such, he left his mark on a whole generation of young writers, making them conscious of social reality. Among his better-known collections of short stories are *Talism-i-Khyal, Nazzare, Anna Data, Zindigi ke Mod Par*, and *Ajanta se Aage. Ham Wahshi Hain* is the title of his collection of short stories devoted exclusively to the theme of partition. He also wrote novels and a large number of radio plays. Some of these radio plays are collected in an anthology called *Ek Rupya EkPhool.*

Peshawar[1] *Express*   *ca. 1950*

TRANSLATED BY K. S. DUGGAL

When I left Peshawar, I heaved a sigh of relief. All my bogies[2] were occupied mainly by Hindus. They came from Peshawar itself and from Mardan, Kohat and Char Sadda, from Khyber and Landi Kotal, Bannu and Naushehra. Finding themselves unsafe in Pakistan, they were fleeing their home towns. There were strict security measures at the railway station: the army personnel appeared quite fastidious.

---

1 **Peshawar:** City in the Northwest Province of India. The path of the train can be followed on a map as it moves north to south, from Muslim majority Pakistan to Hindu majority India.
2 **bogies:** Cars; carriages.

Every compartment had two fully armed Baluchi soldiers[3] to ensure their safety. The soldiers with their peacock *turrahs*[4] at the back of their turbans gazed at the well-preserved womenfolk of the evacuees and made rude comments.

The passengers in the train were shedding tears of blood in their heart of hearts. They were leaving the land of their birth, the land that had made them hardy. They had drunk deep at its salubrious springs. And today they had become strangers to it. It had shut its doors on them.

They were proceeding to an unknown country. When they thought of its parched plains and its scorching sun their hearts sank. But they must go to save themselves, to protect the honour of their wives and daughters.

Still, their eyes were riveted on the ancient plateau—their own. They wanted to know why they were being thrown out, why the land of their birth no longer belonged to them. As I gathered speed, the passengers occupying the various compartments were trying to cling to the familiar sights of hills and meadows, valleys and orchards. Seeing them feel so forlorn, my spirits sank and I felt weak in the knees. I feared I might collapse any minute.

I reached Hasan Abdal. The passengers continued to be morose and depressed. At Hasan Abdal—also known as Panja Sahib, the Temple of Guru's Palm—they were joined by Sikhs[5] with their swords. It appeared they had been decimated with their own weapons. Rather than bring relief, they only added to the gloom. The moment they entered, they started exchanging notes with the old passengers. It was the same story. Their houses had been burnt and property looted; they could escape just in the clothes they were wearing. They told their tales of misery to fellow-passengers and won their sympathy. The Baluchi soldiers guarding the compartments with loaded guns heard it too and felt merely amused.

At Taxila railway station, the halt was unusually long. I could not understand the reason. Maybe they were waiting for the non-Muslim evacuees to arrive from the surrounding villages. When the train guard asked the station-master again and again, the latter replied in desperation: "The train won't go any further." Another hour passed in uncertainty. The people pulled out their tiffin boxes[6] and began eating. The children stopped crying, the young girls began peering out of the windows, the *hookahs*[7] of the old started an uninterrupted hubble-bubble. Suddenly a noise and beating of drums was heard in the air.

I thought it must be the non-Muslim evacuees anxious to escape Pakistan. The passengers craned their necks out of the windows to see them approach. As they came close, there was a firing of guns. The passengers quickly pulled themselves in.

---

3 **Baluchi soldiers:** Soldiers from Baluchistan, which became part of Pakistan.

4 *turrahs:* Ornamental tassel or crest fitted to the turban.

5 **Sikhs:** Followers of Guru Nanak, founder of a nonsectarian faith advocating the fundamental truth of all religions; Sikhs later became known for military prowess. The sword or dagger is part of their required dress code.

6 **tiffin boxes:** Three-tiered lunch boxes.

7 *hookahs:* Water pipes for smoking tobacco; the sound made by the smoke passing through water is often represented by "hubble-bubble."

They were indeed Hindus, being brought by Muslims from the nearby villages. But they were now mere corpses of *kafirs*[8] on the backs of their Muslim neighbours. Their crime? They had tried to flee their villages!

The Muslims nonchalantly handed over the dead bodies to the Baluchi soldiers for safe conveyance to India. The Baluchis took their charge dutifully, and the corpses were evenly distributed to the various compartments: fifteen corpses to every compartment. Having done the job, the Muslims fired a volley of shots in the air and signalled the station-master to let me proceed. I had hardly moved when I was stopped again. It occurred to the leader of the mob that with two hundred Hindus lost to their villages, they would be left desolate. Moreover, they would incur economic losses, having lost so many hands. He must have two hundred passengers detrained to replace them. Accordingly, two hundred passengers, not one more nor one less, were detrained and handed over to the leader by the Baluchi soldiers.

The leader of the mob then roared, "Fall into line, you *kafirs*." He was the biggest *jagirdar*[9] of the region. He heard the echoes of the holy crusade in the flow of the blood in his veins.

The *kafirs* stood still, fear-stricken. They couldn't move. They were physically lifted and made to stand in a row. They were like living corpses with their frozen faces and stony looks swimming in the air.

The Baluchis this time gave the lead. Fifteen people were brought down at the first volley.

It was Taxila.

Then another twenty fell.

It was Asia's biggest university where thousands of students studied and benefited from it.

Fifty more were gunned down.

The Taxila museum has the most wonderful specimens of sculpture reflecting the glory of this ancient land.

Yet another fifty were slaughtered now.

In the background are the ruins of the palaces of Sircopo and an extensive sports stadium in a town sprawling for miles and miles.

Thirty more joined the dead.

Kanishka[10] *ruled over this land and taught people to live in peace and amity.*

Another twenty-five were shot dead.

It was here that the Buddha's call for compassion echoed and re-echoed and his followers carried his message far and near.

The remainder were finished.

It was at Taxila that the Muslim flag of brotherhood and love was hoisted for the first time on the soil of India.

8 **kafirs:** Nonbelievers, i.e., non-Muslims.
9 **jagirdar:** Landlord.
10 **Kanishka:** Illustrious first-century C.E. king of Kushan.

All two hundred were dead. The entire platform was smeared with blood. There was blood on the railway tracks. When I moved, my wheels started wobbling. I feared I might tumble down any minute and also finish those left in the compartment.

Death was hovering in every compartment. The living corpses sat around the dead bodies. The Baluchi soldiers saw all this and smiled. At times, a child would start whimpering, or an old woman would articulate a wail. Or, maybe, a widowed young girl would curse her fate. I moved on hooting and whistling and arrived at Rawalpindi station.

No one entrained here except fifteen *burqa*[11]-clad women escorted by two armed young men. However, a lot of firearms, including machine guns and revolvers, were loaded in a luggage van.

I was made to stop between Gujar Khan and Jhelum. The Muslim men escorting the *burqa*-clad ladies stepped down from the train. Just then one of the women tore open her veil and began shouting: "We are Hindus and Sikhs. We are being kidnapped." The other women joined in the cry and pleaded for help, but none was forthcoming. The Muslim escort just laughed and pulled them out and drove them away.

A Hindu boy from the Frontier jumped out of the train and tried to escape. He was instantly gunned down by the Baluchi soldiers. Some fifteen Hindus made a vain attempt to run away while the train was stationary. They, in turn, were surrounded by armed Muslim *goondas*[12] and killed. The kidnapped girls were prodded with rifles and forced into a jungle. I shut my eyes and ran as fast as I could, belching black smoke that looked like clouds of doom hovering on the horizon. I felt that I was going to lose my breath soon and the red flames of fire raging in my belly would in a twinkling of an eye burn to ashes the entire jungle that had devoured the fifteen girls.

When I reached Lala Musa the dead bodies had started putrefying. The foul stink was becoming oppressive. The Baluchi soldiers would order a passenger to pick up a corpse and take it to the door of the compartment. They would then push the passenger along with the dead body from the running train. Before long, all the corpses were disposed of and along with them an equal number of passengers. There was now room in the train for the remaining passengers to stretch themselves a little.

After Lala Musa I arrived at Wazirabad Junction. Wazirabad town is known for manufacturing knives and daggers. It was here that Hindus and Muslims celebrated the festival of *Baisakhi*[13] every year and feasted each other. The platform was literally littered with dead bodies. Maybe they had assembled there to participate in the *Baisakhi* celebrations. It had turned out to be a festival of corpses. Thick smoke continued to spiral from the town towards the sky. Then a band was heard being played near the railway station. It was followed by a cheering crowd. A little later the proces-

11 *burqa:* The garment worn by strict Muslim women that covers the body head to toe, including the face.
12 *goondas:* Hired thugs; hooligans.
13 *Baisakhi:* A harvest festival.

sion entered the railway platform. It was led by folk dancers. They were followed by a host of naked women, old and young, married and unmarried, mothers and daughters, virgins and those pregnant. They were all Hindus and Sikhs. The men following and jeering at them were Muslims. Evidently, this is how they had celebrated *Baisakhi* this year. The women had bruises on their naked bodies. With hair falling loosely on their shoulders, they walked straight as if they had wrapped themselves in thousands of folds. The anguish in their eyes reminded one of Draupadi.[14]

Someone from the crowd shouted "Pakistan *Zindabad,* Islam *Zindabad,* Qaid-i-Azam *Zindabad.*"[15]

The procession came close to the compartments. The passengers started pulling down the shutters of their windows. The womenfolk began to cover their faces with their *dupattas.*[16]

The Baluchi soldiers forbade the passengers from bringing down the shutters— it was getting stuffy in the compartments. But no one would listen to them. So they began firing their rifles. Nevertheless, all the shutters were pulled down, though some of the evacuees lost their lives. The naked women were forced to sit with the passengers.

And then amidst the slogans of Pakistan *Zindabad* and *Qaid-i-Azam Zindabad,* I pulled out of the station.

A child in one of the compartments went over to an old woman and staring at her naked body, asked: "You had your bath?"

"Yes, child, I was given a bath today by the sons of my motherland." And tears gushed into her eyes.

"But where are your clothes?"

"They were stained with the *sindoor*[17] of a wedded wife, they have taken them away to wash them."

In the meanwhile, two naked young girls jumped out of the running train. I did not stop: whistling and hooting I reached Lahore.

I was diverted to Platform 1. There was another train stationed at Platform 2. It had arrived from Amritsar with Muslim refugees. A little while later, a band of Muslim *mujahids*[18] started searching my compartments. They collected all the jewellery, cash and other valuables they could find with the evacuees. They picked out four hundred of them and made them stand on the platform. They were to be slaughtered because the train that had just steamed in from Amritsar had arrived minus four hundred Muslim refugees. And no less than fifty women had also been

---

14 **Draupadi:** Beautiful heroine of the Indian epic *Mahabharata;* she had numerous husbands and was the victim of intended rape.
15 *Zindabad:* "Long live Pakistan; long live Islam; long live Mohammed Ali Jinnah" (also known as Qaid-I-Azam, or "Great Leader"). Jinnah was the man largely responsible for creating Pakistan as a Muslim state.
16 *dupattas:* Head scarves worn by women of northern India.
17 *sindoor:* The red coloring in the part of a Hindu wife's hair.
18 *mujahids:* Warriors.

kidnapped. It was therefore decided to detrain fifty Hindu women so that the balance in the population of both India and Pakistan could be maintained.

The Muslim volunteers surrounded the four hundred Hindu evacuees standing on the platform and started stabbing them. Before long they finished the whole lot.

I was now allowed to leave the station. Every bit of my body was stinking. I felt unclean all over. I felt as if I had been thrown out of hell and despatched straight to Punjab. When I reached Atari, the whole atmosphere changed. The Baluchi guards had already been replaced at Mughalpura by the Dogra[19] and the Sikh soldiers. At Atari, there were so many dead bodies of Muslim evacuees that the Hindu refugees now felt exhilarated. I was now entering Independent India. Where else could one find such an air of freedom? As I reached Amritsar, my ears were splitting with the slogans shouted by the Sikhs and the Hindus. Here, too, there were piles of corpses, but of Muslim evacuees. The Sikh *jats*[20] wielding swords came and peeped into every compartment in search of *shikar.*[21]

A little while later, four persons looking like Hindu brahmins[22] entered a compartment. They sported proper Hindu *chotis,*[23] each one of them. And they wore their *dhotis*[24] in the typical caste Hindu fashion. They said they were going to Hardwar.

At Amritsar, a number of Sikh *jats* had fanned themselves out into the compartments in search of *shikar.* One of them got a bit suspicious and asked one of the four brahmins where he was going.

"To Hardwar on pilgrimage."

"Is it Hardwar or Pakistan you are going to?"

"Allah forbid," blurted the man.

The Sikh laughed and then pounced on him with his axe. The Sikh's companions overpowered the other three "brahmins".

"You all must be medically examined before you are allowed to go to Hardwar," said the Sikh.

The four "brahmins" were stripped of their clothes, found to be circumcised Muslims, and done to death.

I left Amritsar and was proceeding at top speed when I was stopped in a thick jungle. The moment I came to a halt, the Sikh *jats* and Hindus got out and pounced upon Muslim evacuees hiding behind trees and bushes. Shouting slogans of *Sat Sri Akal*[25] and *Har Har Mahadev*[26] they surrounded the helpless men and women and murdered them brutally. A Sikh *jat* held a baby on the point of his spear and shouted: "*Ai Baisakhi oh jat, Ai Baisakhi*"[27]

---

19 **Dogra:** A well-known Indian army regiment from northwest India (now Pakistan).
20 *jats:* An ethnic group of northwest India, mainly farmers.
21 *shikar:* Sport in the sense of hunting or shooting.
22 **brahmins:** Originally the priestly caste of Hinduism; now, more generally, the highest caste.
23 *chotis:* Tufts of hair worn by orthodox Hindus.
24 *dhotis:* Loincloths worn by Indian men.
25 *Sat Sri Akal:* "God is truth," a Sikh slogan.
26 *Har Har Mahadev:* "Mahadev is God," a Hindu slogan.
27 *Ai . . . Baisakhi:* "The festival of Baisakhi (a harvest festival) is here."

Before entering Jullundar there was a Pathan[28] village. I was stopped here again and everyone in the train, the refugees and the local *jats,* came out and attacked the village. The Pathans put up a brave resistance, but to no avail. Men and children were killed, and it was now the turn of their womenfolk. They were assembled in the open *maidan*[29] outside the village. Here they harvested their crop. Here they assembled on festival days and sang and danced, and made merry. Here fifty Pathan beauties found themselves in the clutches of five hundred ruffians. Fifty sheep and five hundred wolves. Having completed their task they carried some of the dead bodies to their compartments. When we passed over a canal, the bodies were thrown into it. One by one, as the compartments came over the canal bridge, they would hurl the dead bodies into the water. Having got rid of the corpses, the Sikh *jats* started drinking country liquor. I moved on puffing the smoke of blood and hatred.

Reaching Ludhiana, the refugees and their escorts traced out Muslim localities and began looting and massacring. They returned to the train about four hours later, duly laden with booty. This was repeated several times before I reached Ambala. At every wayside station they slaughtered as many Muslims as they could lay their hands on and relieved them of their few possessions.

I had wounds all over my body. My soul was bruised. I badly needed a bath. But I knew it was not in my lot to get one during the current journey.

At Ambala, a Muslim Deputy Commissioner and his family entered and occupied a first class compartment. After midnight when the train left Ambala, it was stopped at a distance of about ten miles from the city. Sikhs and Hindus broke into the Deputy Commissioner's compartment and massacred the entire family save his charming young daughter. They carried the girl and her jewellery box to a nearby jungle. She was so captivating that they did not know what to do with her.

The girl pleaded: "Why must you kill me? You may convert me to Hinduism. One of you can even marry me. What good will it do you to kill me?"

"She is right," said one.

Another stepped forward and stabbing the girl in the stomach, remarked: "What is this sentimental nonsense? We have work to do; let us go back to the train."

The girl lay dying on the grass. In her hand she was clutching a book on socialism, its theory and practice.

She must have been an intelligent girl with dreams of serving her people and her country. She must have wanted to belong to someone, to be a mother and to rear children. She was a young girl. She was a darling. She was a mother, the creator, carrying the secret of the universe in her bosom. And here she was lying in a desolate jungle—her virginal body a feast for the vultures and wild animals.

I moved on. People were drinking and shouting the slogan—"Long live Mahatma Gandhi!" And then, finally, I arrived at Bombay.

---

28 **Pathan:** Tribal people living on the borders between India and Afghanisthan.
29 *maidan:* Open space or parade ground.

I have since been given a thorough bath and parked in a shed. Occasionally, I am reminded of the harrowing time I have had, and I tremble all over. I would now like to get out and make a journey to the Punjab only when there are rich crops and its people are singing the songs of love and good neighbourliness.

I am made of wood and steel. There is no life in me. And yet, rather than witness bloodshed and be burdened with dead bodies, I want to carry grain to the famine stricken areas. I want to visit coal mines, steel mills and fertiliser plants. And transport in my compartments happy and carefree peasants. Women with their eyes longing for their menfolk. Children with smiles on their faces. People who would salute the brave new world where there would be no Hindu and no Muslim. They would be all peasants and workers. Just human beings.

QUESTIONS

1. Why might the author have chosen to have the train narrate his story? What advantages does this voice offer? Are there any disadvantages? Cite specific passages that show how the train has been personified.

2. Follow the reactions of the Baluchi soldiers. What do the soldiers' reactions and actions convey?

3. Analyze the tone of the narrative voice. How would you describe it? Cite specific passages to support your answer.

4. At some points the narrator contrasts the usual activities of a certain place with the atrocities occurring on this occasion. What is the effect of these comparisons?

5. Compare events in this story with nonfiction descriptions of the events following the partition of India. Does the story exaggerate the atrocities or depict them accurately?

Attia Hosain

(1913–1998)

Attia Hosain was born and raised in Lucknow to a highly traditional Taluqdari, or Muslim, family. Although she was raised in a household where *purdah* was kept, she attended a local convent school and had an English governess. By her own admission she was a "cheeky" or saucy child who resisted traditional restraints and the idea of an arranged marriage. She was the first woman of a Taluqdari family to further her education, attending Isabelle Thoburn College where she absorbed the liberal arts tradition that complemented her traditional training in Persian, Urdu, and Arabic. She graduated in 1933. Still, she lacked the freedom of her brothers, who attended university in England. Already she was a woman who had experienced two very different worlds, both literally and through her reading of British writers such as the Brontës, Jane Austen, and George Eliot (Mary Jane Evans). At the suggestion of Mulk Raj Anand, she expanded her reading to include modern writers such as James Joyce and Virginia Woolf. He also encouraged her to keep a journal that he hoped would expand into an autobiography. She even attended a Progressive Writers' Conference held in Lucknow and later the All India Woman's Conference. Her articles began appearing in the Indian journals, *The Pioneer* and *The Statesman.*

When independence came to India in 1947, and with it the horrors of Indian-Pakistani partition, she and her husband and two children, then living in Bombay, moved to London. Her own family had been torn apart by partition. Although postwar Britain was not entirely hospitable to immigrant Indians, Hosain was able to exercise her talents in a variety of ways. She presented an Eastern women's radio program for the British Broadcasting Company's overseas service, lectured on Indian and Western culture, and appeared frequently on television and even on the London stage. During this time, she was also writing the stories that were later published in *Phoenix Fled* (1953); later came her only but highly autobiographical and influential novel, *Sunlight on a Broken Column* (1961).

_____

The First Party   1953

After the dimness of the verandah, the bewildering brightness of the room made her stumble against the unseen doorstep. Her nervousness edged towards panic, and the darkness seemed a forsaken friend, but her husband was already steadying her into the room.

"My wife," he said in English, and the alien sounds softened the awareness of this new relationship.

The smiling, tall woman came towards them with outstretched hands and she put her own limply into the other's firm grasp.

"How d'you do?" said the woman.

"How d'you do?" said the fat man beside her.

"I am very well, thank you," she said in the low voice of an uncertain child repeating a lesson. Her shy glance avoided their eyes.

They turned to her husband, and in the warm current of their friendly ease she stood coldly self-conscious.

"I hope we are not too early," her husband said.

"Of course not; the others are late. Do sit down."

She sat on the edge of the big chair, her shoulders drooping, nervously pulling her sari over her head as the weight of its heavy gold embroidery pulled it back.

"What will you drink?" the fat man asked her.

"Nothing, thank you."

"Cigarette?"

"No, thank you."

Her husband and the tall woman were talking about her, she felt sure. Pinpoints of discomfort pricked her and she smiled to hide them.

The woman held a wineglass in one hand and a cigarette in the other. She wondered how it felt to hold a cigarette with such self-confidence; to flick the ash with such assurance. The woman had long nails, pointed and scarlet. She looked at her own—unpainted, cut carefully short—wondering how anyone could eat, work, wash with those claws dipped in blood. She drew her sari over her hands, covering her rings and bracelets, noticing the other's bare wrists, like a widow's.

"Shy little thing, isn't she, but charming," said the woman as if soothing a frightened child.

"She'll get over it soon. Give me time," her husband laughed. She heard him and blushed, wishing to be left unobserved and grateful for the diversion when other guests came in.

She did not know whether she was meant to stand up when they were being introduced, and shifted uneasily in the chair, half rising; but her husband came and stood by her, and by the pressure of his hand on her shoulder she knew she must remain sitting.

She was glad when polite formality ended and they forgot her for their drinks, their cigarettes, their talk and laughter. She shrank into her chair, lonely in her strangeness yet dreading approach. She felt curious eyes on her and her discomfort multiplied them. When anyone came and sat by her she smiled in cold defence, uncertainty seeking refuge in silence, and her brief answers crippled conversation. She found the bi-lingual patchwork distracting, and its pattern, familiar to others, with allusions and references unrelated to her own experiences, was distressingly obscure. Overheard light chatter appealing to her woman's mind brought no relief of understanding. Their different stresses made even talk of dress and appearance sound unfamiliar. She could not understand the importance of relating clothes to time and place and not just occasion; nor their preoccupation with limbs and bodies, which should be covered, and not face and features alone. They made problems about things she took for granted.

Her bright rich clothes and heavy jewellery oppressed her when she saw the simplicity of their clothes. She wished she had not dressed so, even if it was the custom, because no one seemed to care for customs, or even know them, and looked at her as if she were an object on display. Her discomfort changed to uneasy defiance, and she stared at the strange creatures around her. But her swift eyes slipped away in timid shyness if they met another's.

Her husband came at intervals that grew longer with a few gay words, or a friend to whom he proudly presented "My wife." She noticed the never-empty glass in his hand, and the smell of his breath, and from shock and distress she turned to disgust and anger. It was wicked, it was sinful to drink, and she could not forgive him.

She could not make herself smile any more but no one noticed and their unconcern soured her anger. She did not want to be disturbed and was tired of the persistent "Will you have a drink?" "What will you drink?" "Sure you won't drink?" It seemed they objected to her not drinking, and she was confused by this reversal of values. She asked for a glass of orange juice and used it as protection, putting it to her lips when anyone came near.

They were eating now, helping themselves from the table by the wall. She did not want to leave her chair, and wondered if it was wrong and they would notice she was not eating. In her confusion she saw a girl coming towards her, carrying a small tray. She sat up stiffly and took the proffered plate with a smile.

"Do help yourself," the girl said and bent forward. Her light sari slipped from her shoulder and the tight red silk blouse outlined each high breast. She pulled her own sari closer round her, blushing. The girl, unaware, said, "Try this sandwich, and the olives are good."

She had never seen an olive before but did not want to admit it, and when she put it in her mouth she wanted to spit it out. When no one was looking, she slipped it under her chair, then felt sure someone had seen her and would find it.

The room closed in on her with its noise and smoke. There was now the added harsh clamour of music from the radiogram. She watched, fascinated, the movement of the machine as it changed records; but she hated the shrieking and moaning and discordant noises it hurled at her. A girl walked up to it and started singing, swaying her hips. The bare flesh of her body showed through the thin net of her drapery below the high line of her short tight bodice.

She felt angry again. The disgusting, shameless hussies, bold and free with men, their clothes adorning nakedness not hiding it, with their painted false mouths, that short hair that looked like the mad woman's whose hair was cropped to stop her pulling it out.

She fed her resentment with every possible fault her mind could seize on, and she tried to deny her lonely unhappiness with contempt and moral passion. These women who were her own kind, yet not so, were wicked, contemptible, grotesque mimics of the foreign ones among them for whom she felt no hatred because from them she expected nothing better.

She wanted to break those records, the noise from which they called music.

A few couples began to dance when they had rolled aside the carpet. She felt a sick horror at the way the men held the women, at the closeness of their bodies, their vulgar suggestive movements. That surely was the extreme limit of what was possible in the presence of others. Her mother had nearly died in childbirth and not moaned lest the men outside hear her voice, and she, her child, had to see this exhibition of . . . her outraged modesty put a leash on her thoughts.

This was an assault on the basic precept by which her convictions were shaped, her life was controlled. Not against touch alone, but sound and sight, had barriers been raised against man's desire.

A man came and asked her to dance and she shrank back in horror, shaking her head. Her husband saw her and called out as he danced, "Come on, don't be shy; you'll soon learn."

She felt a flame of anger as she looked at him, and kept on shaking her head until the man left her, surprised by the violence of her refusal. She saw him dancing with another girl and knew they must be talking about her, because they looked towards her and smiled.

She was trembling with the violent complexity of her feelings, of anger, hatred, jealousy and bewilderment, when her husband walked up to her and pulled her affectionately by the hand.

"Get up. I'll teach you myself."

She gripped her chair as she struggled, and the violence of her voice through clenched teeth, "Leave me alone," made him drop her hand with shocked surprise as the laughter left his face. She noticed his quick embarrassed glance round the room, then the hard anger of his eyes as he left her without a word. He laughed more gaily when he joined the others, to drown that moment's silence, but it enclosed her in dreary emptiness.

She had been so sure of herself in her contempt and her anger, confident of the righteousness of her beliefs, deep-based on generation-old foundations. When she had seen them being attacked, in her mind they remained indestructible, and her anger had been a sign of faith; but now she saw her husband was one of the destroyers; and yet she knew that above all others was the belief that her life must be one with his. In confusion and despair she was surrounded by ruins.

She longed for the sanctuary of the walled home from which marriage had promised an adventurous escape. Each restricting rule became a guiding stone marking a safe path through unknown dangers.

The tall woman came and sat beside her and with affection put her hand on her head.

"Tired, child?" The compassion of her voice and eyes was unbearable.

She got up and ran to the verandah, put her head against a pillar and wet it with her tears.

QUESTIONS

1. What specific actions and attitudes does the young wife object to? Why?

2. Is she justified in her feelings, or is she being inflexible or prudish?

3. When values and cultures clash, who should compromise or change? Why?

4. The story is written from the point of view of the wife. How would it be different if written from the husband's point of view?

5. Pressures from Western countries to adopt "modern" attitudes, values, and customs are sometimes seen as cultural imperialism. Does the West have a right,

perhaps even an obligation, to spread its values to other countries and cultures? Consider not only the kinds of values discussed in this story, but other values, such as democracy, free markets, and women's rights.

Mulk Raj Anand

(1905–2004)

Mulk Raj Anand's life encompasses the vital period of the Indian independence movement, from the "quit India" days just before World War I through the campaigns of Nehru and Gandhi and of course after independence itself. Born in Peshawar, the son of a coppersmith and soldier, Anand formed his early sympathies with India's poor—a natural connection that was influenced by his mother's peasant background. Educated at the University of Punjab, University College (London), and Cambridge, Anand has written short and long fiction, children's stories, art and literary criticism, and has edited numerous magazines and journals, most importantly *Marg*. An activist as well as intellectual, he fought in the Spanish civil war (1937–1938), helped to found India's progressive writer's movement, worked as a broadcaster and script writer, and has served on a variety of important boards and councils. He is frequently grouped with R. K. Narayan and Raja Rao as the fountainhead of Indian literature in English, both in form and thematic content.

One of Anand's important contributions to Indian literature was to focus attention for the first time on India's poorest people. His first novel, *Untouchable* (1935), which sympathetically portrays a member of India's lowest and most despised caste, set the tone for much of his subsequent writing, including his short stories. His realistic, even naturalistic, approach to poverty and injustice invites comparisons with the great English and French novelists of the nineteenth century, whose objective, "scientific" manner exposed injustice by describing accurately the people and institutions around them. But Anand's humanism goes beyond muckraking for its own sake. Behind his exposures of the hardships endured by working people and peasants is a respect for their dignity, hard work, and integrity. Along the way he also explodes the myth that India's poor are content in their backwardness and misery. In many ways, his stories invite comparisons with those of Anton Chekhov, Guy de Maupassant, Sean O'Faolain, and Frank O'Connor. In spite of his emphasis on life's hardships and injustices, Anand remains optimistic about man's possibilities.

"The Cobbler and the Machine" raises a number of questions relating to economic development, the relationship between handicrafts and machines, and the influence of Western practices and ideas on developing countries and cultures.

The Cobbler and the Machine   1959

(To Arthur and Ara Calder Marshall)

Apart from the innocence of old age and youth, Saudagar, the cobbler of my village, and I shared in common a passion for the machine.

Saudagar, of course, was interested in only one machine, the small sewing-machine which the village tailor wielded very ostentatiously on the footboard of his cavernous shop before the gaping rustics, who had often travelled fifty miles from their homes in the hills to see it—a grimy, black hand-machine in a casket, decorated with a tracery of leaves in yellow paint, that nibbled at the yards of cloth like a slimy rat, at terrific speed. But I liked all kinds of machines which I saw in the town where I went to school every morning; the great big railway-engine, whose phuff-phuff I had learned to imitate when we played at trains at the recess hour; the phonograph from which I hope to hear my own voice one day; the motor-car in which my father was given a lift by Lalla Sain Das when there was an election; the push-bike on which our second master came to school from his bungalow; the intricate mass of wheels and pistons which lay hiccuping in the power-house at the junction of the two canals; and the roaring monsters of iron and steel that converted the cotton and wool of our village into cloth at the Dhariwal mills. And even of sewing-machines I had seen at least two varieties other than the one that Saudagar knew, and yet a third—a pedal-machine, adjusted to a chair with a leather belt across it, to which I used to see Baha-ud-din, the tailor in the Main Bazaar in the town, glued all day, and a similar upright contraption on which one of the employees in the Bhalla shoe shop sat sewing boots.

"Uncle Saudagar," I said to the cobbler one day as I sat idly at the door of his dark straw hut while he stared across the street at Bhagirath, the tailor, revolving the handle of his sewing-machine with amazing alacrity. "Do you know you waste so much of your time sewing pieces of leather to the soles of people's shoes and then they complain that you don't sew them well and that the water gets into them? Why, you could have a machine like Bhagirath's, even superior, with a seat attached to it like the chairs the Sahibs[1] sit on. I have seen a man in the Bhalla shoe shop sewing boots on one."

"Is there a machine like that, son?" said Saudagar incredulously, and yet vaguely convinced, as he had been for months since the tailor brought his casket machine, that there must be a contrivance for sewing leather as there was one for sewing cloth.

"Yes, uncle," I said enthusiastically, for to me all machines were still toys and playthings, rather than "chariots which men could ride." "There are wonderful machines in the town if only you will go and see, but you never stir out of this hovel. Didn't you go to see the great exhibition at Lahore? My father tells me there was a great big boot there all sewn by machine in which people could play hide-and-seek."

---

1 **Sahibs** People of high rank; often used to refer to any Englishman.

I had seen the wonders of science in the school laboratory and the marvels in the streets of the town and wished rather too eagerly that they could come to my village, so convinced was I of the superiority of modernity over the old ways of the countryside.

"Well, son," said the old man kindly, "I have heard that there is a machine which can do the work of my hand, but I have never seen it. Ever since I saw the ready-made saddles, reins and collars in the stables of Thakur Mahan Chand, I knew they were made by a defter hand than that of man. And when the son of the landlord sent me the black leather boots which he bought in town to mend I knew that they couldn't have been sewn by any human being. And truly, I have been looking at Bhagirath's sewing-machine and wondering if there is a similar contraption for sewing shoes. But I am old and I have not been to town these ten years. So I have not seen what this machine looks like. One day I must make a trip to see it. But, of course, I am too poor ever to be able to buy it. And perhaps God would curse my fingers and those of my pupils, and make them incapable of sewing at all, if I began to use this machine."

"But, Uncle Saudagar," I said, "I tell you will like this machine if you see it. And you will look like a Sahib sitting on the chair which is adjusted to it. You will only need a basket-hat to complete your life and you will begin to eat and drink on a raised platform automatically. I wish my mother would let me convert that broken pitcher we have into a chair and I could use the manger of the cows for a table always."

"I am an outcast, son," Saudagar said. "How can I presume to eat like the Sahibs or be like them? And won't people laugh at me if they see me seated in a chair, sewing shoes?"

"But these people are fools, Uncle," I said. "They regard the Sahibs as outcasts, too, even though the Sahibs are clean. And these rustics have no idea of modern times. They are old fogies with jungly habits. They are oxen. They have no idea of the new life."

"Yes, son, perhaps you are right," said the older cobbler. "God has created iron in the mountains. I suppose He means us to make machines with it."

"I have got a beautiful bolt I found in the playground, Uncle," I said. "I will show it to you, if you like."

"I would like to see it, son," said Saudagar indulgently. "Now run along and go home. Your father might come this way and abuse you for wasting your time sitting in an outcast's shop. Run along and play with your fellows."

"I will also bring you a picture of the sewing-machine, if you like, Uncle," I said, making an overture of friendship so as to win more easily the privilege of fidgeting round the cobbler's shop, for ordinarily he discouraged children from flocking round the door of his hovel and robbing his dim eyes of the little natural light that trickled through the aperture of the door.

"All right," he said. "All right, son. You must show me a picture if you can, though I don't know what use it is to show a man the likeness of a bunch of grapes when he will never be able to eat the fruit."

But the spark that had failed to kindle a devouring flame in the heart of old Saudagar lit my flesh with the warmth of a new delight, for the echo of the old cobbler of my village handling a new machine reverberated in my brain like the voice of a wish that had become father to the thought. I ran towards home as if I were possessed by more than a love of the new toy that would be Saudagar's machine. I had a feeling that there might come to be in my village the atmosphere of a splendid, gorgeous wonder-house, in which great big iron frames, with a thousand screws and knobs assembled through the ingenuity of a man like my science master, created the power to achieve miracles.

I persuaded my class-fellows when we were coming home from school the next day to climb a high wall near the Railway Station and pull off a poster which showed an English-woman, with a bun on the top of her head, wielding a Singer sewing-machine embossed on a steel plate in the shape of the letter S. And I brought it to Saudagar.

"This, Uncle," I said, "is the kind of machine which I told you you should have. Only this is for sewing cloth. But, the one for sewing leather which the man in the Bhalla shoe shop plies is like it in appearance, except that it has a thicker needle."

The old cobbler looked at the picture in wide-eyed wonder. I could see from the loving way in which he passed his hand over the surface of the steel that his imagination had caught fire from the picture of the sewing-machine, bigger than Bhagirath's, which seemed to make him firmly believe in the existence of a similar machine for sewing leather though he hadn't seen it.

And so charmed was he by the novelty of the instrument of which I had shown him the picture, that he asked us to bring the steel plate which we had stolen into his shop and leave it there for a decoration. And he gave us a pice[2] each as compensation for our trouble.

It seemed to me that he had not kept the advertisement for the Singer Sewing machine merely for decorative purposes, but because he wanted to see the likeness of the object which he had set his heart on buying one day. And my feeling was confirmed by the fact that whenever I went to his hovel now he would always say something about the shape of the needle in the picture not being quite clear, and of his inability to understand how one could get into the habit of pressing the pedal with the feet while one was sewing something on top.

"And the stool seems too small," he said. "It may be all right for the "lendis" to sit on, but how will such a crude old bottom as mine balance on it?"

"Don't you care," I said, with an emphasis that gained weight from the earnestness and zeal I felt at the prospect of seeing the cobbler of my village achieve the dexterity of the man in the Bhalla shoe shop. "A little practice and you will learn to wield it better than anyone else, and as for your old posterior, why, I have seen the heavy-bottomed Mem Sahib,[3] who is the wife of the City Engineer, balanced on a

2 **pice** A coin worth one-fourth of an anna; an anna is one-sixteenth of a rupee. Hence, a coin of very little value.
3 **Mem Sahib** A female Sahib; often used to refer to any Englishwoman.

stool like that in the verandah of her bungalow, as if she were seated on a comfortable horse."

A look of wonder lit his dim eyes and, glancing at me with the tenderness of humility, he traced the curves of the steel plate on the picture of the machine printed in black-and-white against the green. And then he would close his eyes and, smiling, shake his head as if he were surcharged with the ecstasy of a knowledge in the hollows of his brain where phantasmagoric visions of himself at work on the new machine swirled in a mad delirium, the edges of enchanting top-boots, splendid, well-polished shoes, and strong-soled country shoes creating and destroying each other in an irrelevant disorder.

"But anyhow, the trouble is, son, where am I to get the money to buy the machine?" the old man would then say with a sigh, and continue: "I don't know how I shall get it, and where it is to be got even if I had the money, which I shall never have."

The grim sagacity of his practical argument defeated my intelligence, for I had no idea how many rupees the machine cost and where Saudagar was to get the money, but, of course, the address of the Singer Sewing Machine Company, England, was printed at the bottom of the picture, and I speculated that if that company manufactured sewing-machines for cloth, surely they made those for sewing leather, and I said: "It is made in Vilayat, and can be had from there, or perhaps through a commission agent in Lahore or Bombay, if not in our district."

"Vilayat is very far away," Saudagar said, "and I shall never cross the seven seas even when I go to Heaven, because I have not done enough good deeds to earn the privilege of being able to travel in my next life. As for Lahore and Bombay, if anyone is going there from our parts we will make inquiries."

But for days and weeks and months no one from our parts was going to Lahore, Delhi, or Bombay, and I hugged the desparate enthusiasm for Saudagar's sewing-machine in my heart till the cool waters of a placid existence had washed off the bright edges of my dreams. I went to see the cobbler as usual in the afternoons, but the topic of the machine was seldom mentioned, and instead the old man bent over the shoes he was mending, brushed his beard, and, with a mischievous light in his eyes, told me a story about some ogre or wild animal, or the witchery of an old maiden who died without ever being married.

One day, however, when I was waiting at the usual hour for my friends to emerge from their homes to play in a maidan near Saudagar's house, he called me and, with a weird chuckle that rose above the curve of his usual silence into a jerky shriek like the convulsive laugh of a madman, he said: "Come here, son, and guess what has happened."

"What is it, then?" I asked, at first completely taken aback but then warming to the happy glare in his eyes with a sensation that the cause of Saudagar's sudden happiness was somehow connected with our project about the machine.

"You know, son, that Lalla Sain Das, the notary and cotton dealer, has gone to Vilayat on business. Well, he asked me to make him some gold-worked shoes to give as present to his clients beyond the seas. When he came to collect them he asked me politely whether he could do something for me while he was away. And I asked him to fetch a machine for sewing leather. He was very kind and said he would bring the machine most unwillingly. And what is more, that since he knew I was a poor man who couldn't pay him for the thing at once, he would buy the machine at his own expense and let me use it and pay for it by and by exactly as if it were a loan with a small interest attached to it. Now I have had this letter from the rail office and the Munshi read it and he says that it is the voucher for the sewing-machine which Lalla Sain Das has sent from Vilayat and which is lying in the railway godown. So, please God, I shall have the machine after all. I am going to distribute sugar-plums among the brotherhood to celebrate the auspicious occasion when the machine comes, and I will make you a pair of Angrezi boots,[4] since it was really you who told me about it."

I clapped my hands with joy, breathed some breaths quickly, and stimulated my being with shouts of "Marvellous! Marvellous!" And, either because I easily whipped myself into a kind of elemental buoyancy, or because it was the natural colour of my temperament, I danced in my mind to the cadence of a rhythm I could feel in the working of the machines, in its contours, in its dainty, intricate contrivances, its highly ingenious purpose, in the miracle it was to me, an architecture embodying mysteries which not only represented the exact formula of science and mathematics, but was the magnificent toy, the plaything. And, of course, Saudagar's offer of a pair of Angrezi boots, such as I had been persuading my father to buy for me for years, made me hysterically happy, for I felt that I could rise in the estimation of all my fellows by possessing footwear which was worn only by the Sahib and the rich folk.

"When will you actually get the machine, Uncle?" I asked eagerly.

"I shall go and get it to-morrow, son," he said. "It is after eleven years that I am going to town."

"If you are in town, then, go and get the advice of the cobbler in the Bhalla shoe shop as to how to work it."

"That is a good idea," Saudagar said. "Yes, I will do that. And since you have been so good to me, child, I shall take your measurements now and start sewing your shoes first on the machine."

I would have stayed and talked about the possibilities of the new wonder to Saudagar if my friends had not been calling incessantly, but that afternoon I was too preoccupied by my ardour to put my heart into playing Kabadi, and I couldn't sleep in the night for the sheer excitement of sharing the glory of having inspired the old cobbler. In the morning I ran along to school bound up in the curves of a rich stillness, the radiant exultation of a child whose fantastic dreams have, for the first time, achieved the guise of visible truths. And all day I was full of mischief—the tingling shadow of an ingrown largeness in my being played havoc with every mundane fact, the vastness of the creator laughed at people, and the depths of a realized truth mocked at impossibilities.

4 **Angrezi boots** English-style boots, i.e., high-topped shoes.

Off I went to Saudagar's shop immediately after I returned from school and, true as the very colour of my dream, even truer because harder, the sewing-machine was before me, with the old cobbler seated on the stool adjusted to it, sewing a piece of leather, with beads of perspiration on his forehead, as his two pupils and a number of other people of low and high castes crowded into the hovel to see the wizardry.

"Come, son," Saudagar said, lifting his eyes and breathing a mouthful of stale breath. "This is the upper part of the boots I am going to sew for you, since you must have the first-fruits of my acquisition."

I smiled awkwardly and then felt a sudden urge to touch the wonderful new thing which was exactly like the sewing-machine of which I had brought Saudagar the picture, except that it had no casket to enclose the upper part, but an anvil into which the needle darted like a shaft, probing the leather in between the cotton in its eye. But I curbed my childish desire as, just then, Saudagar brushed aside the crowd which was clamouring to touch it, and I only asked: "When will my shoes be ready, Uncle?"

"You shall have them by and by," Saudagar said. "I will sew them at any odd times I get, because all the rest of my time must be devoted to turning out enough work to pay off the debt I owe on the machine to Lalla Sain Das, who is coming back to-morrow."

My visits to the cobbler's shop became more frequent since I could always excuse myself to my parents by saying that I was going to the outcast's quarter to see how the boots that Saudagar had promised to make me were getting on. And as my old Indian shoes made of crude hide were wearing out and my parents would have had to buy me a new pair if Saudagar had not offered me the gift, I was allowed to go and waste as much time as I liked.

Saudagar had added a pattern of stitches to the shoes he intended for me during the first few days, but then he had hung them up as a sample on the door of his hut, and was mainly busy turning out Indian shoes by the dozen to defray the interest that accrued at the rate of fifteen per cent on the sum of one thousand rupees, which Sain Das had declared to be the cost of the machine plus freightage and taxes. Every time I went the old man would pick up the sample and contemplate it with an air of absorption and say: "Well, son, I believe I shall begin to sew the lining to them next week, and then I must send Majitha to get some leather for the soles and heels. Or would you like rubber soles instead?"

"No, I want leather soles and rubber heels, Uncle," I said, swinging from the first disappointment of seeing the shoes no further advanced to a sudden excitement.

"You can't have both, son," Saudagar would say kindly.

"I want to set the fashion," I replied.

"But, son, let me make you an ordinary pair first," said the old man, "and then later—"

"When will they be ready?" I would ask impatiently.

"To-morrow, by the grace of God, to-morrow I shall do something to them...."

But to-morrow and to-morrow and to-morrow came and went, and as my old Indian shoes were completely worn out and discarded, I trudged barefoot to and from school, and cursed both my parents for not buying me a new pair of Angrezi shoes and Saudagar for not completing the pair he had promised me.

I couldn't realize that my parents were poor and could not afford to buy me a pair of English boots, and I was too obstinate to accept a cheap pair of Indian shoes. But Saudagar's work was pledged to Lalla Sain Das for the money the cobbler had borrowed to buy the machine, and I was disgusted.

"Let me buy a good pair of shoes like your old ones," my mother said.

"No," I replied stubbornly. "I want English shoes and you needn't bother because Saudagar is making them for me."

" 'Never trust a washerman's promise, nor a goldsmith's nor a cobbler's,' " she quoted the proverb.

But mine was the faith that would have moved mountains but for the fact that an act of God intervened. Saudagar, the old cobbler, fell ill and was unable to work for days, and when he got up from his illness he had to clear arrears of debt and work so hard on his ordinary job that he had no time left even to think of the shoes he had so lovingly cut and on which he had sewn the first stitches. And considering that he had not been able to pay up even the arrears of interest on the cost of the machine, there was little prospect of his ever completing the job for me.

I looked at the old man bending over the machine and working patiently as the sweat poured from his face on to his neck and then on to the earth, and I felt constrained not to trouble him with my demands. And the mixture of resentment and pity I felt for the old man became transformed into feeling of hate for the machine, for, as it stood hard, hard and unbending, it seemed to have become a barrier between Saudagar and me and the thing which had emphasized his self-interest so that he never seemed to put a stitch on anyone's shoes without insisting on being paid for it. And as he sat tied to the chariot wheels of doom, he also began to be more and more reticent, as if he were turning in upon himself to drink his own blood in the silent places of his heart, and the illumination of his natural manner disappeared behind a pale, shadowy face that was always dirty and grimy with a layer of scum on the sweat-covered beard. And still the sample shoes of English design meant for me stood unfinished, while he and his assistants worked furiously to produce enough to pay off the debt on the machine.

I shook the roots of hope from their foundation in my heart and rarely visited Saudagar's shop, thinking he would call me one day when the remorse of his unfulfilled promise had prompted him to finish making my boots.

But that day never came, for, worn out by the fatigue of producing many more shoes than he had ever sewn to pay off his debt, drained of his life-blood by the sweat that was always pouring off his body, he fell stone dead one evening as he recited the devotional verse:

"The days of your life are ending

And you have not made your accounts with God."

In the amorphous desert of my familiar thoughts I felt the pain of a silent guilt, as I knew that I had to some extent been the cause of his death. If only I had known then that it was not enough for Saudagar and his pupils to love the machine and

work it, but to own it, I could have defied the verdict of the v⟶
Saudagar was killed by the devil disguised in the image of the sev⟶

QUESTIONS

1. Who is the narrator? What is his perspective on the events related by

2. What is the narrator's attitude toward the British? How do you know? Point to specific passages to support your answer.

3. What is the narrator's attitude toward India? How do you know? Point to specific passages to support your answer.

4. At the end of the story, the narrator blames himself for contributing to the cobbler's death. Is he responsible? Why or why not?

5. What do you think the story is saying about "progress," machinery, debt, and imperialism? Give specific reasons for your answers, pointing to particular passages in the story to support your response.

R. K. Narayan

(1906–2001)

R. K. Narayan was born in the small town of Chennapatna, Madras—a town not unlike the fictional Malgudi where he has set most of his 15 novels and 200 short stories. By his own admission, he was a poor student but a voracious reader who took full advantage of the fact that his father was a school headmaster, hence providing access to the school's library. Nevertheless, he failed his high school exams, though this did not prevent his attending Maharaja College in Mysore. After graduation in 1930, he worked briefly as a teacher and then tried freelance journalism, but his articles were returned by every editor to whom he sent them.

The story is told that he invented Malgudi on a September day in 1930 with a sentence that began, "It was Monday morning. . . ." Somehow, he imagined a small railway station, and around it grew the fictional town that would serve as a microcosm for India and indeed the world. The novel that was begun that day, *Swami and Friends* (1935), recounts the adventures of a gang of schoolboys. It, too, was rejected by numerous publishers until a friend showed the manuscript to novelist Graham Greene. Greene recommended that the book be published and that its author shorten his name from Rasipuram Krishnaswami Ayyar Narayanswami to its present form. Narayan's college experiences formed the basis of *Bachelor of Arts* (1937), followed by *The Dark Room*

(1938) and *Mysore* (1939). Although his novels brought critical praise, Narayan struggled to support himself until *The English Teacher* (1945) scored a popular success. He was also very active during this time as a short story writer, publishing four collections in the 1940s and returning to the form with at least one volume every decade until the very end of his life.

Unlike many postcolonial authors, Narayan has always felt comfortable writing in English. His style is clear and simple, with a slight Indian accent. By his own admission, "I was never aware that I was using a different, a foreign language when I wrote in English, because it came to me very easily." Also unlike many of his Indian contemporaries, Narayan took little interest in politics or social reform. He focuses instead on characters, whom he sets in a particular environment and then watches as they struggle with their own hopes and aspirations and interact with those around them. Narayan's attitude toward them is often that of sympathetic irony, tinged with humor. They often end with a surprise or reversal, reminiscent of O. Henry without the sentimentality or moralizing. Human relations are what interest Narayan.

Critics respond variously to his work. Some find in Malgudi and its residents the universals of human nature expressed in a style that is limpid and supple, evocative but never extravagant. Others regard him as lacking in the imaginative capacity and thematic range that would place him in the first rank of writers. "A Horse and Two Goats" is among his finest short stories, exhibiting all the qualities of simplicity, irony, pathos, and comedy that have earned Narayan a reputation as one of India's foremost writers of the twentieth century.

A Horse and Two Goats

1965

Of the seven hundred thousand villages dotting the map of India, in which the majority of India's five hundred million live, flourish, and die, Kritam was probably the tiniest, indicated on the district survey map by a microscopic dot, the map being meant more for the revenue official out to collect tax than for the guidance of the motorist, who in any case could not hope to reach it since it sprawled far from the highway at the end of a rough track furrowed up by the iron-hooped wheels of bullock carts. But its size did not prevent its giving itself the grandiose name Kritam, which meant in Tamil "coronet" or "crown" on the brow of this subcontinent. The village consisted of less than thirty houses, only one of them built with brick and cement. Painted a brilliant yellow and blue all over with gorgeous carvings of gods and gargoyles on its balustrade, it was known as the Big House. The other houses, distributed in four streets, were generally of bamboo thatch, straw, mud, and other unspecified material. Muni's was the last house in the fourth street, beyond which stretched the fields. In his prosperous days Muni had owned a flock of forty sheep and goats and sallied forth every morning driving the flock to the highway a couple of miles away. There he would sit on the pedestal of a clay statue of a horse while his cattle grazed around. He carried a crook at the end of a bamboo pole and snapped foliage from the avenue trees to feed his flock; he also gathered faggots and dry sticks, bundled them, and carried them home for fuel at sunset.

His wife lit the domestic fire at dawn, boiled water in a mud pot, threw into it a handful of millet flour, added salt, and gave him his first nourishment for the day. When he started out, she would put in his hand a packed lunch, once again the same millet cooked into a little ball, which he could swallow with a raw onion at midday. She was old, but he was older and needed all the attention she could give him in order to be kept alive.

His fortunes had declined gradually, unnoticed. From a flock of forty which he drove into a pen at night, his stock had now come down to two goats, which were not worth the rent of a half rupee a month the Big House charged for the use of the pen in their backyard. And so the two goats were tethered to the trunk of a drum-stick tree[1] which grew in front of his hut and from which occasionally Muni could shake down drumsticks. This morning he got six. He carried them in with a sense of triumph. Although no one could say precisely who owned the tree, it was his because he lived in its shadow.

She said, "If you were content with the drumstick leaves alone, I could boil and salt some for you."

"Oh, I am tired of eating those leaves. I have a craving to chew the drumstick out of sauce, I tell you."

"You have only four teeth in your jaw, but your craving is for big things. All right, get the stuff for the sauce, and I will prepare it for you. After all, next year you may not be alive to ask for anything. But first get me all the stuff, including a mea-sure of rice or millet, and I will satisfy your unholy craving. Our store is empty today. Dhal,[2] chilli, curry leaves, mustard, coriander, gingili oil, and one large potato. Go out and get all this." He repeated the list after her in order not to miss any item and walked off to the shop in the third street.

He sat on an upturned packing case below the platform of the shop. The shop-man paid no attention to him. Muni kept clearing his throat, coughing, and sneezing until the shopman could not stand it anymore and demanded, "What ails you? You will fly off that seat into the gutter if you sneeze so hard, young man." Muni laughed inordinately, in order to please the shopman, at being called "young man." The shop-man softened and said, "You have enough of the imp inside to keep a second wife busy, but for the fact the old lady is still alive." Muni laughed appropriately again at this joke. It completely won the shopman over; he liked his sense of humor to be appreciated. Muni engaged his attention in local gossip for a few minutes, which always ended with a reference to the postman's wife, who had eloped to the city some months before.

The shopman felt most pleased to hear the worst of the postman, who had cheated him. Being an itinerant postman, he returned home to Kritam only once in

---

1 **drumstick tree:** Bears drumstick-shaped pods.
2 **Dhal:** Lentil soup.

ten days and every time managed to slip away again without passing the shop in the third street. By thus humoring the shopman, Muni could always ask for one or two items of food, promising repayment later. Some days the shopman was in a good mood and gave in, and sometimes he would lose his temper suddenly and bark at Muni for daring to ask for credit. This was such a day, and Muni could not progress beyond two items listed as essential components. The shopman was also displaying a remarkable memory for old facts and figures and took out an oblong ledger to support his observations. Muni felt impelled to rise and flee. But his self-respect kept him in his seat and made him listen to the worst things about himself. The shopman concluded, "If you could find five rupees and a quarter, you will have paid off an ancient debt and then could apply for admission to *swarga*.[3] How much have you got now?"

"I will pay you everything on the first of the next month."

"As always, and whom do you except to rob by then?"

Muni felt caught and mumbled. "My daughter has sent word that she will be sending me money."

"Have you a daughter?" sneered the shopman. "And she is sending you money! For what purpose, may I know?"

"Birthday, fiftieth birthday," said Muni quietly.

"Birthday! How old are you?"

Muni repeated weakly, not being sure of it himself, "Fifty." He always calculated his age from the time of the great famine when he stood as high as the parapet around the village well, but who could calculate such things accurately nowadays with so many famines occurring? The shopman felt encouraged when other customers stood around to watch and comment. Muni thought helplessly, "My poverty is exposed to everybody. But what can I do?"

"More likely you are seventy," said the shopman. "You also forget that you mentioned a birthday five weeks ago when you wanted castor oil for your holy bath."

"Bath! Who can dream of a bath when you have to scratch the tank bed for a bowl of water? We would all be parched and dead but for the Big House, where they let us take a pot of water from their well." After saying this Muni unobtrusively rose and moved off.

He told his wife, "That scoundrel would not give me anything. So go out and sell the drumsticks for what they are worth."

He flung himself down in a corner to recoup from the fatigue of his visit to the shop. His wife said, "You are getting no sauce today, nor anything else. I can't find anything to give you to eat. Fast till the evening, it'll do you good. Take the goats and be gone now," she cried and added, "Don't come back before the sun is down." He knew that if he obeyed her she would somehow conjure up some food for him in the evening. Only he must be careful not to argue and irritate her. Her temper was undependable in the morning but improved by evening time. She was sure to go out and work—grind corn in the Big House, sweep or scrub somewhere, and earn enough to buy foodstuff and keep a dinner ready for him in the evening.

3 *swarga:* Heaven.

Unleashing the goats from the drumstick tree, Muni started out, driving them ahead and uttering weird cries from time to time in order to urge them on. He passed through the village with his head bowed in thought. He did not want to look at anyone or be accosted. A couple of cronies lounging in the temple corridor hailed him, but he ignored their call. They had known him in the days of affluence when he lorded over a flock of fleecy sheep, not the miserable gawky goats that he had today. Of course he also used to have a few goats for those who fancied them, but real wealth lay in sheep; they bred fast and people came and bought the fleece in the shearing season; and then that famous butcher from the town came over on the weekly market days bringing him betel leaves,[4] tobacco, and often enough some bhang,[5] which they smoked in a hut in the coconut grove, undisturbed by wives and well-wishers. After a smoke one felt light and elated and inclined to forgive everyone, including that brother-in-law of his who had once tried to set fire to his home. But all this seemed like the memories of a previous birth. Some pestilence afflicted his cattle (he could of course guess who had laid his animals under a curse), and even the friendly butcher would not touch one at half the price . . . and now here he was left with the two scraggly creatures. He wished someone would rid him of their company too. The shopman had said that he was seventy. At seventy, one only waited to be summoned by God. When he was dead what would his wife do? They had lived in each other's company since they were children. He was told on their day of wedding that he was ten years old and she was eight. During the wedding ceremony they had had to recite their respective ages and names. He had thrashed her only a few times in their career, and later she had the upper hand. Progeny, none. Perhaps a large progeny would have brought him the blessing of the gods. Fertility brought merit. People with fourteen sons were always so prosperous and at peace with the world and themselves. He recollected the thrill he had felt when he mentioned a daughter to that shopman; although it was not believed, what if he did not have a daughter?—his cousin in the next village had many daughters, and any one of them was as good as his; he was fond of them all and would buy them sweets if he could afford it. Still, everyone in the village whispered behind their backs that Muni and his wife were a barren couple. He avoided looking at anyone; they all professed to be so high up, and everyone else in the village had more money than he. "I am the poorest fellow in our caste and no wonder that they spurn me, but I won't look at them either," and so he passed on with his eyes downcast along the edge of the street, and people left him also very much alone, commenting only to the extent, "Ah, there he goes with his two goats; if he slits their throats, he may have more peace of mind." "What has he to worry about anyway? They live on nothing and have none to worry about." Thus people commented when he passed through the village. Only on the outskirts did he lift his head and look up. He urged and bullied the goats until they meandered along to the foot of the horse statue on the edge of the village. He sat on

---

4 **betel leaves:** Wrapped around pieces of nut, lime, or tobacco and chewed.
5 **bhang:** Marijuana.

its pedestal for the rest of the day. The advantage of this was that he could watch the highway and see the lorries[6] and buses pass through to the hills, and it gave him a sense of belonging to a larger world. The pedestal of the statue was broad enough for him to move around as the sun traveled up and westward; or he could also crouch under the belly of the horse, for shade.

The horse was nearly life-size, molded out of clay, baked, burnt, and brightly colored, and reared its head proudly, prancing its forelegs in the air and flourishing its tail in a loop; beside the horse stood a warrior with scythe-like mustachios, bulging eyes, and aquiline nose. The old image-makers believed in indicating a man of strength by bulging out his eyes and sharpening his mustache tips, and also decorated the man's chest with beads which looked today like blobs of mud through the ravages of sun and wind and rain (when it came), but Muni would insist that he had known the beads to sparkle like the nine gems at one time in his life. The horse itself was said to have been as white as a dhobi-washed[7] sheet, and had had on its back a cover of pure brocade of red and black lace, matching the multicolored sash around the waist of the warrior. But none in the village remembered the splendor as no one noticed its existence. Even Muni, who spent all his waking hours at its foot, never bothered to look up. It was untouched even by the young vandals of the village who gashed tree trunks with knives and tried to topple off milestones and inscribed lewd designs on all walls. This statue had been closer to the population of the village at one time, when this spot bordered the village; but when the highway was laid through (or perhaps when the tank and wells dried up completely here) the village moved a couple of miles inland.

Muni sat at the foot of the statue, watching his two goats graze in the arid soil among the cactus and lantana bushes. He looked at the sun; it had tilted westward no doubt, but it was not the time yet to go back home; if he went too early his wife would have no food for him. Also he must give her time to cool off her temper and feel sympathetic, and then she would scrounge and manage to get some food. He watched the mountain road for a time signal. When the green bus appeared around the bend he could leave, and his wife would feel pleased that he had let the goats feed long enough.

He noticed now a new sort of vehicle coming down at full speed. It looked like both a motor car and a bus. He used to be intrigued by the novelty of such spectacles, but of late work was going on at the source of the river on the mountain and an assortment of people and traffic went past him, and he took it all casually and described to his wife, later in the day, everything he saw. Today, while he observed the yellow vehicle coming down, he was wondering how to describe it later to his wife when it sputtered and stopped in front of him. A red-faced foreigner, who had been driving it, got down and went around it, stooping, looking, and poking under the vehicle; then he straightened himself up, looked at the dashboard, stared in Muni's direction, and approached him. "Excuse me, is there a gas station nearby, or do I

6 **lorries:** Large trucks.
7 **dhobi-washed:** Washed by a dhobi, a lower-caste Hindu.

have to wait until another car comes—" He suddenly looked up at the clay horse and cried, "Marvelous," without completing his sentence. Muni felt he should get up and run away, and cursed his age. He could not readily put his limbs into action; some years ago he could outrun a cheetah, as happened once when he went to the forest to cut fuel and it was then that two of his sheep were mauled—a sign that bad times were coming. Though he tried, he could not easily extricate himself from his seat, and then there was also the problem of the goats. He could not leave them behind.

The red-faced man wore khaki clothes—evidently a policeman or a soldier. Muni said to himself, "He will chase or shoot if I start running. Some dogs chase only those who run—oh, Shiva[8] protect me. I don't know why this man should be after me." Meanwhile the foreigner cried, "Marvelous!" again, nodding his head. He paced around the statue with his eyes fixed on it. Muni sat frozen for a while, and then fidgeted and tried to edge away. Now the other man suddenly pressed his palms together in a salute, smiled, and said, "*Namaste!* How do you do?"

At which Muni spoke the only English expressions he had learned, "Yes, no." Having exhausted his English vocabulary, he started in Tamil: "My name is Muni. These two goats are mine, and no one can gainsay it—though our village is full of slanderers these days who will not hesitate to say that what belongs to a man doesn't belong to him." He rolled his eyes and shuddered at the thought of evil-minded men and women peopling his village.

The foreigner faithfully looked in the direction indicated by Muni's fingers, gazed for a while at the two goats and the rocks, and with a puzzled expression took out his silver cigarette case and lit a cigarette. Suddenly remembering the courtesies of the season, he asked, "Do you smoke?" Muni answered, "Yes, no." Whereupon the red-faced man took a cigarette and gave it to Muni, who received it with surprise, having had no offer of a smoke from anyone for years now. Those days when he smoked bhang were gone with his sheep and the large-hearted butcher. Nowadays he was not able to find even matches, let alone bhang. (His wife went across and borrowed a fire at dawn from a neighbor.) He had always wanted to smoke a cigarette; only once did the shopman give him one on credit, and he remembered how good it had tasted. The other flicked the lighter open and offered a light to Muni. Muni felt so confused about how to act that he blew on it and put it out. The other, puzzled but undaunted, flourished his lighter, presented it again, and lit Muni's cigarette. Muni drew a deep puff and started coughing; it was racking, no doubt, but extremely pleasant. When his cough subsided he wiped his eyes and took stock of the situation, understanding that the other man was not an Inquisitor of any kind. Yet, in order to make sure, he remained wary. No need to run away from a man who gave him such a potent smoke. His head was reeling from the effect of one of those strong American cigarettes made with roasted tobacco. The man said, "I come from New York," took out a wallet from his hip pocket, and presented his card.

---

8 **Shiva:** One of the three gods of the Hindu trinity; a male depicted with three eyes representing past, present, and future.

Muni shrank away from the card. Perhaps he was trying to present a warrant and arrest him. Beware of khaki, one part of his mind warned. Take all the cigarettes or bhang or whatever is offered, but don't get caught. Beware of khaki. He wished he weren't seventy as the shopman had said. At seventy one didn't run, but surrendered to whatever came. He could only ward off trouble by talk. So he went on, all in the chaste Tamil for which Kritam was famous. (Even the worst detractors could not deny that the famous poetess Avvaiyar was born in this area, although no one could say whether it was in Kritam or Kuppam, the adjoining village.) Out of this heritage the Tamil language gushed through Muni in an unimpeded flow. He said, "Before God, sir, Bhagwan,[9] who sees everything, I tell you, sir, that we know nothing of the case. If the murder was committed, whoever did it will not escape. Bhagwan is all-seeing. Don't ask me about it. I know nothing." A body had been found mutilated and thrown under a tamarind tree at the border between Kritam and Kuppam a few weeks before, giving rise to much gossip and speculation. Muni added an explanation. "Anything is possible there. People over there will stop at nothing." The foreigner nodded his head and listened courteously though he understood nothing.

"I am sure you know when this horse was made," said the red man and smiled ingratiatingly.

Muni reacted to the relaxed atmosphere by smiling himself, and pleaded, "Please go away, sir, I know nothing. I promise we will hold him for you if we see any bad character around, and we will bury him up to his neck in a coconut pit if he tries to escape; but our village has always had a clean record. Must definitely be the other village."

Now the red man implored, "Please, please, I will speak slowly, please try to understand me. Can't you understand even a simple word of English? Everyone in this country seems to know English. I have gotten along with English everywhere in this country, but you don't speak it. Have you any religious or spiritual scruples against English speech?"

Muni made some indistinct sounds in his throat and shook his head. Encouraged, the other went on to explain at length, uttering each syllable with care and deliberation. Presently he sidled over and took a seat beside the old man, explaining, "You see, last August, we probably had the hottest summer in history, and I was working in shirtsleeves in my office on the fortieth floor of the Empire State Building. We had a power failure one day, you know, and there I was stuck for four hours, no elevator, no air conditioning. All the way in the train I kept thinking, and the minute I reached home in Connecticut, I told my wife, Ruth, 'We will visit India this winter, it's time to look at other civilizations.' Next day she called the travel agent first thing and told him to fix it, and so here I am. Ruth came with me but is staying back at Srinagar, and I am the one doing the rounds and joining her later."

Muni looked reflective at the end of this long oration and said, rather feebly, "Yes, no," as a concession to the other's language, and went on in Tamil, "When I was this high"—he indicated a foot high—"I had heard my uncle say . . ."

9 **Bhagwan:** God, especially Vishnu (preserver and destroyer) and Shiva.

No one can tell what he was planning to say, as the other interrupted him at this stage to ask, "Boy, what is the secret of your teeth? How old are you?"

The old man forgot what he had started to say and remarked, "Sometimes we too lose out cattle. Jackals or cheetahs may sometimes carry them off, but sometimes it is just theft from over in the next village, and then we will know who has done it. Our priest at the temple can see in the camphor flame the face of the thief, and when he is caught . . ." He gestured with his hands a perfect mincing of meat.

The American watched his hands intently and said, "I know what you mean. Chop something? Maybe I am holding you up and you want to chop wood? Where is your axe? Hand it to me and show me what to chop. I do enjoy it, you know, just a hobby. We get a lot of driftwood along the backwater near my house, and on Sundays I do nothing but chop wood for the fireplace. I really feel different when I watch the fire in the fireplace, although it may take all the sections of the Sunday *New York Times* to get a fire started." And he smiled at this reference.

Muni felt totally confused but decided the best thing would be to make an attempt to get away from this place. He tried to edge out, saying, "Must go home," and turned to go. The other seized his shoulder and said desperately, "Is there no one, absolutely no one here, to translate for me?" He looked up and down the road, which was deserted in this hot afternoon; a sudden gust of wind churned up the dust and dead leaves on the roadside into a ghostly column and propelled it towards the mountain road. The stranger almost pinioned Muni's back to the statue and asked, "Isn't this statue yours? Why don't you sell it to me?"

The old man now understood the reference to the horse, thought for a second, and said in his own language, "I was an urchin this high when I heard my grandfather explain this horse and warrior, and my grandfather himself was this high when he heard his grandfather, whose grandfather—"

The other man interrupted him. "I don't want to seem to have stopped here for nothing. I will offer you a good price for this," he said, indicating the horse. He had concluded without the least doubt that Muni owned this mud horse. Perhaps he guessed by the way he sat on its pedestal, like other souvenir sellers in this country presiding over their wares.

Muni followed the man's eyes and pointing fingers and dimly understood the subject matter and, feeling relieved that the theme of the mutilated body had been abandoned at least for the time being, said again, enthusiastically, "I was this high when my grandfather told me about this horse and the warrior, and my grandfather was this high when he himself . . ." and he was getting into a deeper bog of reminiscence each time he tried to indicate the antiquity of the statue.

The Tamil that Muni spoke was stimulating even as pure sound, and the foreigner listened with fascination. "I wish I had my tape recorder here," he said, assuming the pleasantest expression. "Your language sounds wonderful. I get a kick out of every word you utter, here"—he indicated his ears—"but you don't have to waste your breath in sales talk. I appreciate the article. You don't have to explain its points."

"I never went to a school, in those days only Brahmin[10] went to schools, but we had to go out and work in the fields morning till night, from sowing to harvest time . . . and when Pongal[11] came and we had cut the harvest, my father allowed me to go out and play with others at the tank, and so I don't know the Parangi language you speak, even little fellows in your country probably speak the Parangi language, but here only learned men and officers know it. We had a postman in our village who could speak to you boldly in your language, but his wife ran away with someone and he does not speak to anyone at all nowadays. Who would if a wife did what she did? Women must be watched; otherwise they will sell themselves and the home." And he laughed at his own quip.

The foreigner laughed heartily, took out another cigarette, and offered it to Muni, who now smoked with ease, deciding to stay on if the fellow was going to be so good as to keep up his cigarette supply. The American now stood up on the pedestal in the attitude of a demonstrative lecturer and said, running his finger along some of the carved decorations around the horse's neck, speaking slowly and uttering his words syllable by syllable, "I could give a sales talk for this better than anyone else. . . . This is a marvelous combination of yellow and indigo, though faded now. . . . How do you people of this country achieve these flaming colors?"

Muni, now assured that the subject was still the horse and not the dead body, said, "This is our guardian, it means death to our adversaries. At the end of Kali Yuga,[12] this world and all other worlds will be destroyed, and the Redeemer will come in the shape of a horse called 'Kalki'; this horse will come to life and gallop and trample down all bad men." As he spoke of bad men the figures of his shopman and his brother-in-law assumed concrete forms in his mind, and he reveled for a moment in the predicament of the fellow under the horse's hoof: served him right for trying to set fire to his home. . . .

While he was brooding on this pleasant vision, the foreigner utilized the pause to say, "I assure you that this will have the best home in the U.S.A. I'll push away the bookcase, you know I love books and am a member of five book clubs, and the choice and bonus volumes mount up to a pile really in our living room, as high as this horse itself. But they'll have to go. Ruth may disapprove, but I will convince her. The T.V. may have to be shifted too. We can't have everything in the living room. Ruth will probably say what about when we have a party? I'm going to keep him right in the middle of the room. I don't see how that can interfere with the party— we'll stand around him and have our drinks."

Muni continued his description of the end of the world. "Our pundit discoursed at the temple once how the oceans are going to close over the earth in a huge wave and swallow us—this horse will grow bigger than the biggest wave and carry on its back only the good people and kick into the floods the evil ones—plenty

10 **Brahmin:** High-caste Hindus; the priestly caste.
11 **Pongal:** The Tamil festival of the New Year, celebrated in January.
12 **Kali Yuga:** In Hindu thought, the present age, the Age of Action.

of them about—" he said reflectively. "Do you know when it is going to happen?" he asked.

The foreigner now understood by the tone of the other that a question was being asked and said, "How am I transporting it? I can push the seat back and make room in the rear. That van can take in an elephant"—waving precisely at the back of the seat.

Muni was still hovering on visions of avatars[13] and said again, "I never missed our pundit's discourses at the temple in those days during every bright half of the month, although he'd go on all night, and he told us that Vishnu is the highest god. Whenever evil men trouble us, he comes down to save us. He has come many times. The first time he incarnated as a great fish, and lifted the scriptures on his back when the floods and sea waves . . ."

"I am not a millionaire, but a modest businessman. My trade is coffee."

Amidst all this wilderness of obscure sound Muni caught the word "coffee" and said, "If you want to drink 'kapi,' drive farther up, in the next town, they have Friday market, and there they open 'kapi-otels'—so I learn from passersby. Don't think I wander about. I go nowhere and look for nothing." His thoughts went back to the avatars. "The first avatar was in the shape of a little fish in a bowl of water, but every hour it grew bigger and bigger and became in the end a huge whale which the seas could not contain, and on the back of the whale the holy books were supported, saved and carried." Once he had launched on the first avatar, it was inevitable that he should go on to the next, a wild boar on whose tusk the Earth was lifted when a vicious conqueror of the Earth carried it off and hid it at the bottom of the sea. After describing this avatar Muni concluded, "God will always save us whenever we are troubled by evil beings. When we were young we staged at full moon the story of the avatars. That's how I know the stories; we played them all night until the sun rose, and sometimes the European collector would come to watch, bringing his own chair. I had a good voice and so they always taught me songs and gave me the women's roles. I was always Goddess Lakshmi[14] and they dressed me in a brocade sari, loaned from the Big House. . . ."

The foreigner said, "I repeat I am not a millionaire. Ours is a modest business; after all, we can't afford to buy more than sixty minutes of T.V. time in a month, which works out to two minutes a day, that's all, although in the course of time we'll maybe sponsor a one-hour show regularly if our sales graph continues to go up. . . ."

Muni was intoxicated by the memory of his theatrical days and was about to explain how he had painted his face and worn a wig and diamond earrings when the visitor, feeling that he had spent too much time already, said, "Tell me, will you accept a hundred rupees or not for the horse? I'd love to take the whiskered soldier also but no space for him this year. I'll have to cancel my air ticket and take a boat home, I suppose. Ruth can go by air if she likes, but I will go with the horse and keep him in

---

13 **avatars:** Incarnations of the gods in human form.
14 **Lakshmi:** Goddess of good fortune.

my cabin all the way if necessary." And he smiled at the picture of himself voyaging across the seas hugging this horse. He added, "I will have to pad it with straw so that it doesn't break. . . ."

"When we played *Ramayana*,[15] they dressed me as Sita,[16] added Muni. "A teacher came and taught us the songs for the drama and we gave him fifty rupees. He incarnated himself as Rama, and He alone could destroy Ravana, the demon with ten heads who shook all the worlds; do you know the story of *Ramayana?*"

"I have my station wagon as you see. I can push the seat back and take the horse in if you will just lend me a hand with it."

"Do you know *Mahabharata?*[17] Krishna was the eighth avatar of Vishnu, incarnated to help the Five Brothers regain their kingdom. When Krishna was a baby he danced on the thousand-hooded giant serpent and trampled it to death; and then he suckled the breasts of the demoness and left them flat as a disc though when she came to him her bosoms were large, like mounds of earth on the banks of a dug-up canal." He indicated two mounds with his hands. The stranger was completely mystified by the gesture. For the first time he said, "I really wonder what you are saying because your answer is crucial. We have come to the point when we should be ready to talk business."

"When the tenth avatar comes, do you know where you and I will be?" asked the old man.

"Lend me a hand and I can lift off the horse from its pedestal after picking out the cement at the joints. We can do anything if we have a basis of understanding."

At this stage the mutual mystification was complete, and there was no need even to carry on a guessing game at the meaning of words. The old man chattered away in a spirit of balancing off the credits and debits of conversational exchange, and said in order to be on the credit side, "O honorable one, I hope God has blessed you with numerous progeny. I say this because you seem to be a good man, willing to stay beside an old man and talk to him, while all day I have none to talk to except when somebody stops by to ask for a piece of tobacco. But I seldom have it, tobacco is not what it used to be at one time, and I have given up chewing. I cannot afford it nowadays." Noting the other's interest in his speech, Muni felt encouraged to ask, "How many children have you?" with appropriate gestures with his hands. Realizing that a question was being asked, the red man replied, "I said a hundred," which encouraged Muni to go into details. "How many of your children are boys and how many girls? Where are they? Is your daughter married? Is it difficult to find a son-in-law in your country also?"

In answer to these questions the red man dashed his hand into his pocket and brought forth his wallet in order to take immediate advantage of the bearish trend in the market. He flourished a hundred-rupee currency note and said, "Well, this is what I meant."

---

15 *Ramayana:* An epic poem in the ancient Sanskrit language.
16 **Sita:** An incarnation of Lakshmi.
17 *Mahabharata:* One of the Puaranas, or great Sanskrit epics by Vyasa.

The old man now realized that some financial element was entering their talk. He peered closely at the currency note, the like of which he had never seen in his life; he knew the five and ten by their colors although always in other people's hands, while his own earning at any time was in coppers and nickels. What was this man flourishing the note for? Perhaps asking for change. He laughed to himself at the notion of anyone coming to him for changing a thousand- or ten-thousand-rupee note. He said with a grin, "Ask our village headman, who is also a money-lender; he can change even a lakh[18] of rupees in gold sovereigns if you prefer it that way; he thinks nobody knows, but dig the floor of his puja[19] room and your head will reel at the sight of the hoard. The man disguises himself in rags just to mislead the public. Talk to the headman yourself because he goes mad at the sight of me. Someone took away his pumpkins with the creeper and he, for some reason, thinks it was me and my goats . . . that's why I never let my goats be seen anywhere near the farms." His eyes traveled to his goats nosing about, attempting to wrest nutrition from minute greenery peeping out of rock and dry earth.

The foreigner followed his look and decided that it would be a sound policy to show an interest in the old man's pets. He went up casually to them and stroked their backs with every show of courteous attention. Now the truth dawned on the old man. His dream of a lifetime was about to be realized. He understood that the red man was actually making an offer for the goats. He had reared them up in the hope of selling them someday and, with the capital, opening a small shop on this very spot. Sitting here, watching towards the hills, he had often dreamed how he would put up a thatched roof here, spread a gunnysack out on the ground, and display on it fried nuts, colored sweets, and green coconut for the thirsty and famished wayfarers on the highway, which was sometimes very busy. The animals were not prize ones for a cattle show, but he had spent his occasional savings to provide them some fancy diet now and then, and they did not look too bad. While he was reflecting thus, the red man shook his hand and left on his palm one hundred rupees in tens now, suddenly realizing that this was what the old man was asking. "It is all for you or you may share it if you have a partner."

The old man pointed at the station wagon and asked, "Are you carrying them off in that?"

"Yes, of course," said the other, understanding the transportation part of it.

The old man said, "This will be their first ride in a motor car. Carry them off after I get out of sight, otherwise they will never follow you, but only me even if I am traveling on the path to Yama Loka." He laughed at his own joke, brought his palms together in a salute, turned round and went off, and was soon out of sight beyond a clump of thicket.

The red man looked at the goats grazing peacefully. Perched on the pedestal of the horse, as the westerly sun touched off the ancient faded colors of the statue with

18 **lakh:** 100,000.
19 **puja room:** Room where religious rites are performed.

a fresh splendor, he ruminated, "He must be gone to fetch some help, I suppose!" and settled down to wait. When a truck came downhill, he stopped it and got the help of a couple of men to detach the horse from its pedestal and place it in his station wagon. He gave them five rupees each, and for a further payment they siphoned off gas from the truck, and helped him to start his engine.

Muni hurried homeward with the cash securely tucked away at his waist in his dhoti.[20] He shut the street door and stole up softly to his wife as she squatted before the lit oven wondering if by a miracle food would drop from the sky. Muni displayed his fortune for the day. She snatched the notes from him, counted them by the glow of the fire, and cried, "One hundred rupees! How did you come by it? Have you been stealing?"

"I have sold our goats to a red-faced man. He was absolutely crazy to have them, gave me all this money and carried them off in his motor car!"

Hardly had these words left his lips when they heard bleating outside. She opened the door and saw the two goats at her door. "Here they are!" she said. "What's the meaning of all this?"

He muttered a great curse and seized one of the goats by its ears and shouted, "Where is that man? Don't you know you are his? Why did you come back?" The goat only wriggled in his grip. He asked the same question of the other too. The goat shook itself off. His wife glared at him and declared, "If you have thieved, the police will come tonight and break your bones. Don't involve me. I will go away to my parents. . . ."

QUESTIONS

1. How would you describe the narrator's tone in this story? Does the narrator pity Muni's poverty? Regard it matter of factly? Humorously?

2. What forces and conditions have brought about Muni's poverty and kept him poor?

3. What do the incidental and descriptive details reveal about village life? Be specific.

4. Apart from language, what divides the U.S. tourist and Muni? What differing assumptions and ideas interfere with communication?

5. Do you regard the ending of the story as comic or tragic? Why?

6. What does the story reveal, if anything, about the relations between rich nations and poor ones? Can it be read allegorically or symbolically?

---

20 **dhoti:** The loincloth worn by members of the respectable Hindu castes.

Ruth Prawer Jhabvala

(b. 1927)

Ruth Prawer Jhabvala epitomizes the contemporary international author who is impossible to place by nationality. In an interview, she was once asked about her roots and replied, "I don't have any." Born to Jewish Polish parents in Cologne, she and her family fled Hitler's Germany in 1939 and settled in England, eventually residing in London. In 1951, she completed a master's degree in English literature at London University and married architect Cyrus Jhabvala, who moved the family to Delhi, India. In 1955, Jhabvala published the first of her many novels, *To Whom She Will*, and there followed a steady stream of novels set in India and based on her experiences there. Her early books were bright and upbeat in tone, but increasingly, the novels darken in outlook and shift from a focus on Indian characters to the experiences of expatriate Europeans reacting to the country. Because of the novels and short stories of this period, Jhabvala is often regarded as an Indian writer, though she denies the validity of that label. Indeed, the authors to whom she is most often compared are the English novelists, Jane Austen, Charles Dickens, and William Makepeace Thackeray.

The family lived in India until 1975, but finally left for the United States. As she explains in an essay in *An Experience of India* (1971), the land that she at first found beautiful and entrancing finally became oppressive in its dirt and irremediable poverty. After moving, Jhabvala gradually shifted the setting of her fiction from India to the United States, though many of her characters are Indians attempting to negotiate the difficult transition to living in the West. Another consistent theme in her fiction is the search for spiritual fulfillment.

Even before leaving India, however, Jhabvala formed what would be one of the most important partnerships of her creative life—a relationship with the filmmakers James Ivory and Ismail Merchant. She was at first reluctant when the filmmakers called her in 1963 to write a screenplay of her novel, *The House-holder* (1960), but since then Jhabvala's success at writing screenplays of other writers' novels has been little short of phenomenal, with substantial films like *The Bostonians* (1984), *A Room with a View* (1986), and perhaps most notably E. M. Forster's *Howards End* (1992). She has won two Academy Awards for screenwriting, and some critics note that her later fiction is informed by some of the techniques of film.

Jhabvala's main accomplishments as a writer probably remain her memorable pictures of Indian life and the depth and sensitivity with which she examines the complexities and ambiguities of cross-cultural encounters. Whether she is writing about the problems of Indians in the period after colonization, the difficulties faced by Europeans in Southeast Asia, or the complexities of adapting oneself to the demands of Western culture, Jhabvala always brings fresh insights and nuanced thinking to her fiction. "Miss Sahib" is but one story in a large opus of such writing.

Miss Sahib   *1968*

The entrance to the house in which Miss Tuhy lived was up a flight of stairs between a vegetable shop and a cigarette and cold-drink one. The stairs were always dirty, and so was the space around the doorway, with rotted bits of vegetable and empty cigarette packets trampled into the mud. Long practice had taught Miss Tuhy to step around this refuse, smilingly and without rancour, and as she did so she always nodded friendly greetings to the vegetable-seller and the cold-drink man, both of whom usually failed to notice her. Everyone in the neighbourhood had got used to her, for she had lived there, in that same house, for many years.

It was not the sort of place in which one would have expected to find an Englishwoman like Miss Tuhy, but the fact was, she was too poor to live anywhere else. She had nothing but her savings, and these, in spite of her very frugal way of life, could not last for ever; and of course there was always the vexed question of how long she would live. Once, in an uncharacteristically realistic moment, she had calculated that she could afford to go on for another five years, which would bring her up to sixty-five. That seemed fair enough to her, and she did not think she had the right to ask for more. However, most of the time these questions did not arise for she tended to be too engrossed in the present to allow fears of the future to disturb her peace of mind.

She was, by profession and by passionate inclination, a teacher, but she had not taught for many years. She had first come to India thirty years ago to take up a teaching post at a school for girls from the first families, and she had taught there and at various other places for as long as she had been allowed. She did it with enthusiasm, for she loved the country and her students. When Independence came and all the other English teachers went home, it never for a moment occurred to her to join them, and she went on teaching as if nothing had changed. And indeed, as far as she was concerned, nothing did change for a number of years, and it was only at the end of that time that it was discovered she was not sufficiently well qualified to go on teaching in an Indian high school. She bowed her head to this decision, for she knew she wasn't; not compared with all those clever Indian girls who held M.A. degrees in politics, philosophy, psychology, and economics. As a matter of fact, even though they turned out to be her usurpers, she was proud of these girls; for wasn't it she and those like her who had educated them and made them what they now were—sharp, emancipated, centuries ahead of their mothers and grandmothers? So it was not difficult for her to cede to them with a good grace, to enjoy her farewell party, cry a bit at the speeches, and receive with pride and a glow in her heart the silver model of the Taj Mahal which was presented to her as a token of appreciation. After that, she sailed for England—not because she in the least wanted to, but because it was what everyone seemed to expect of her.

She did not stay long. True, no one here said she was not well qualified enough to teach and she had no difficulty in getting a job; but she was not happy. It was not the same. She liked young people always, and so she liked the young people she was teaching here; but she could not love them the way she had loved her Indian pupils. She missed their playfulness, their affection, their sweetness—by comparison the English children struck her as being cool and distant. And not only the children but everyone she met, or only saw in streets and shops: they seemed a colder people somehow, politer perhaps and more considerate than the Indians among whom she had spent so many years, but without (so she put it to herself) *real love*. Even physically the English looked cold to her, with their damp white skins and pale blue eyes, and she longed again to be surrounded by those glowing coloured skins; and those eyes! the dark, large, liquid Indian eyes! and hair that sprang with such abundance from their heads. And besides the people, it was everything else as well. Everything was too dim, too cold. There was no sun, the grass was not green, the flowers not bright enough, and the rain that continually drizzled from a washrag sky was a poor substitute for the silver rivers that had come rushing in torrents out of immense, dark-blue, monsoon clouds.

So she and her savings returned, improvidently, to India. Everyone still remembered her and was glad to see her again but, once the first warm greetings were over, they were all too busy to have much time to spare for her. She didn't mind, she was just happy to be back; and in any case she had to live rather a long way away from her friends because, now that she had no job, she had to be where rents were cheaper. She found the room in the house between the vegetable-seller and the cold-drink shop and lived there contentedly all the week round, only venturing forth on Sundays to visit her former colleagues and pupils. As time went on, these Sunday visits became fewer and further between, for everyone always seemed to be rather busy; anyway, there was less to say now, and also she found it was not always easy to spare the bus-fare to and fro. But it didn't matter, she was even happier staying at home because all her life was there now, and the interest and affection she had formerly bestowed on her colleagues and pupils, she now had as strongly for the other people living in the house, and even for the vegetable-seller and the cold-drink man though her contact with them never went further than smiles and nods.

The house was old, dirty, and inward-looking. In the centre was a courtyard which could be overlooked like a stage from the galleries running all the way round the upper storeys. The house belonged to an old woman who lived on the ground floor with her enormous family of children and grandchildren; the upper floors had been subdivided and let out to various tenants. The stairs and galleries were always crowded, not only with the tenants themselves but with their servants. Everyone in the house except Miss Tuhy kept a servant, a hill-boy, who cleaned and washed and cooked and was frequently beaten and frequently dismissed. There seemed to be an unending supply of these boys; they could be had very cheaply, and slept curled up on the stairs or on a threshold, and ate what was left in the pot.

Miss Tuhy was a shy person who loved other people but found it difficult to make contact with them. On the second floor lived an Anglo-Indian nurse with her grown-up son, and she often sought Miss Tuhy out, to talk in English with her, to ask questions about England, to discuss her problems and those of her son (a rather insipid young man who worked in an airlines office). She felt that she and Miss Tuhy should present a united front against the other neighbours, who were all Hindus and whom she regarded with contempt. But Miss Tuhy did not feel that way. She liked and was interested in everyone, and it seemed a privilege to her to be near them and to be aware of what seemed to her their fascinating, their passionate lives.

Down in the courtyard the old landlady ruled her family with a rod of iron. She kept a tight hold of everything and doled out little sums of pocket-money to her forty-year-old sons. She could often be heard abusing them and their wives, and sometimes she beat them. There was only one person to whom she showed any indulgence—who, in fact, could get away with anything—and that was Sharmila, one of her granddaughters. When Miss Tuhy first came to live in the house, Sharmila was a high-spirited, slapdash girl of twelve, with big black eyes and a rapidly developing figure. Although she had reached the age at which her sisters and cousins were already beginning to observe that reticence which, as grown women, would keep them away from the eyes of strangers, Sharmila still behaved with all the freedom of the smaller children, running round the courtyard and up and down the stairs and in and out of the homes of her grandmother's tenants. She was the first in the house to establish contact with Miss Tuhy, simply by bursting into the room where the English lady lived and looking round and touching things and lifting them up to examine them—"What's that?"—all Miss Tuhy's treasures: her mother-of-pearl penholder, the photograph of her little niece as a bridesmaid, the silver Taj Mahal. Decorating the mantel-piece was a bowl of realistically shaped fruits made of plaster-of-paris, and before leaving Sharmila lifted a brightly-coloured banana out of the bowl and held it up and said, "Can I have it?" After that she came every day, and every day, just before leaving, helped herself to one more fruit until they were all finished and then she took the bowl.

Sharmila was lazy at school all the year round, but she always panicked before her class-promotion exams and came running for help to Miss Tuhy. These were Miss Tuhy's happiest times, for not only was she once again engaged in the happy pursuit of teaching, but she also had Sharmila sitting there with her all day long, bent ardently over her books and biting the tip of her tongue in her eagerness to learn. Miss Tuhy would have dearly loved to teach her the whole year round, and to teach her everything she knew, and with that end in view she had drawn up an ambitious programme for Sharmila to follow; but although sometimes the girl consented to submit to this programme, it was evident that once the terror of exams was past her interest sharply declined, so that sometimes, when Miss Tuhy looked up from a passionate reading of the romantic poets, she found her pupil fiddling with the strands of hair which always managed to escape from her sober pigtail and her mouth wide open in a yawn she saw no reason to disguise. And indeed Miss Tuhy had finally to admit that Sharmila was right; for what use would all this learning ever be to her when her one purpose in life, her sole duty, was to be married and give satisfaction to the husband who would be chosen for her and to the in-laws in whose house she would be sent to live?

She was just sixteen when she was married. Her grandmother, who usually hated spending money, excelled herself that time and it was a grand and memorable occasion. A big wedding marquee was set up in the courtyard and crammed tight with wedding-guests shimmering in their best clothes; all the tenants were invited too, including Miss Tuhy in her good dress (white dots on a chocolate brown background) and coral necklace. Like everyone else, she was excitedly awaiting the arrival of the bridegroom and his party. She wondered what sort of a boy they had chosen for her Sharmila. She wanted a tall, bold boy for her, a soldier and a hero; and she had heightened, almost mythological visions of the young couple—decked out in jewels and gorgeous clothes—gaily disporting themselves in a garden full of brightly-coloured flowers. But when at last the band accompanying the bridegroom's party was heard, and everyone shouted 'They have come!' and rushed to the entrance to get the first glimpse, then the figure that descended from the horse amid the jubilation of the trumpets was not, in spite of his garlands and his golden coat, a romantic one. Not only was Sharmila's bridegroom stocky and ill at ease, but he was also no longer very young. Miss Tuhy, who had fought her way to the front with the best of them, turned away in bitter disappointment. There were tears in her eyes. She knew it would not turn out well.

Sharmila came every day to visit her old home. At first she came in order to boast, to show off the saris and shawls and jewellery presented to her on her marriage, and to tell about her strange new life and the house she lived in and all her new family. She was brimming over with excitement and talked non-stop and danced round the courtyard. Some time later she came with different stories, about what her mother-in-law had said to her and what she had answered back, about her sisters-in-law and all the other women, how they tried to get the better of her but how she soon showed them a trick or two: she tucked in her chin and talked in a loud voice and was full of energy and indignation. Sometimes she stayed for several days and did not return till her husband came to coax her back. After a year the first baby arrived, and a year later the second, and after a few more years a third. Sharmila became fat and matronly, and her voice was louder and more raucous. She still came constantly, now with two of the children trailing behind her and a third riding on her hip, and she stayed longer than before, often refusing to go back even when her husband came to plead with her. And in the end she seemed to be there all the time, she and her children, so that, although nothing much was said on the subject, it was generally assumed that she had left her husband and her in-laws' house and had come back to live with her grandmother.

She was a little heavy now to go running up and down the stairs the way she used to: but she still came up to Miss Tuhy's room, and the English lady's heart still beat in the same way when she heard her step on the stair, though it was a different step now, heavier, slower, and accompanied by children's tiny shuffle and patter. "Miss Sahib!" Sharmila would call from the landing, and Miss Tuhy would fling her door wide open and stand there beaming. Now it was the children who moved from object to object, touching everything and asking to know what it was, while Sharmila, panting a little from her climb up the stairs, flung herself on the narrow bed and allowed Miss Tuhy to tuck a pillow behind her back. When the children had examined all the treasures, they began to play their own games, they crawled all over the floor and made a lot of noise. Their mother lay on the bed and sometimes she laughed and sometimes she sighed and talked about everything that came into her head. They always stayed for several hours, and when they left at last, Miss Tuhy, gorged with bliss, shut the door and carefully cleaned out her little room which the children had so delightfully disordered.

When she didn't feel like going upstairs, Sharmila stood in the middle of the courtyard and shouted "Miss Sahib!" in her loud voice. Miss Tuhy hurried downstairs, smoothing her dress and adjusting her glasses. She sat with Sharmila in the courtyard and helped her to shell peas. The old grandmother watched them from her bed inside the room: that terrible old woman was bedridden now and quite unable to move, a huge helpless shipwreck wrapped in shawls and blankets. Her speech was blurred and could be understood only by Sharmila who had become her interpreter and chief functionary. It was Sharmila, not one of the older women of the household, who carried the keys and distributed the stores and knew where the money was kept. While she sat with Miss Tuhy in the courtyard, every now and again the grandmother would make calling noises and then Sharmila would get up and go in to see what she wanted. Inside the room it was dark and smelled of sickness and old age, and Sharmila was glad to come out in the open again.

"Poor old Granny," she said to Miss Tuhy, who nodded and also looked sad for Granny because she was old and bedridden: as for herself, she did not feel old at all but a young girl, sitting here like this shelling peas and chatting with Sharmila. The children played and sang, the sun shone, along the galleries upstairs the tenants went to and fro hanging out their washing; there was the sound of voices calling and of water running, traffic passed up and down on the road outside, a near-by flour-mill chucked and chucked. "Poor old Granny," Sharmila said again. "When she was young, she was like a queen—tall, beautiful, everyone did what she wanted. If they didn't she stamped her foot and screamed and waved her arms in the air—like this," Sharmila demonstrated, flailing her plump arms with bangles up to the elbow and laughing. But then she grew serious and put her face closer to Miss Tuhy's and said in a low, excited voice: "They say she had a lover, a jeweller from Dariba. He came at nights when everyone was asleep and she opened the door for him." Miss Tuhy blushed and her heart beat faster; though she tried to check them, a thousand impressions rippled over her mind.

"They say she was a lot like me," said Sharmila, smiling a little and her eyes hazy with thought. She had beautiful eyes, very large and dark with heavy brows above them; her lips were full and her cheeks plump and healthy. When she was thoughtful or serious, she had a habit of tucking in her chin so that several chins were formed, and this too somehow was attractive, especially as these chins seemed to merge and swell into her very large, tight bust.

But her smile became a frown, and she said, "Yes, and now look at her, how she is. Three times a day I have to change the sheets under her. This is the way it all ends. Hai," and she heaved a sigh and a brooding look came on her face. The children, who had been chasing each other round the courtyard, suddenly began to quarrel in loud voices; at that Sharmila sprang up in a rage and caught hold of the biggest child and began to beat him with her fist, but hardly had he uttered the first cry when she stopped and instead lifted him in her arms and held him close, close to her bosom, her eyes shut in rapturous possessiveness as if he were all that she had.

It was one of the other tenants who told Miss Tuhy that Sharmila was having an affair with the son of the Anglo-Indian nurse from upstairs. The tenant told it with a lot of smiles, comments, and gestures, but Miss Tuhy pretended not to understand, she only smiled back at the informer in her gentle way and said "Good morning," in English and shut the door of her room. She was very much excited. She thought about the young man whom she had seen often and sometimes talked to: a rather colourless young man, with brown hair and Anglo-Indian features, who always dressed in English clothes and played cricket on Sunday mornings. It seemed impossible to connect him in any way with Sharmila; and how his mother would have hated any such connection! The nurse, fully opening her heart to Miss Tuhy, never tired of expressing her contempt for the other tenants in the house who could not speak English and also did not know how to live decently. She and her son lived very decently, they had chairs and a table in their room and linoleum on the floor and a picture of the Queen of England on the wall. They ate with knife and fork. "Those others, Miss Tuhy, I wouldn't like you to see," she said with pinched lips (she was a thin woman with matchstick legs and always wore brown shoes and stockings). "The dirt. Squalor. You would feel sick, Miss Tuhy. And the worst are those downstairs, the—" and she added a bad word in Hindi (she never said any bad words in English, perhaps she didn't know any). She hated Sharmila and the grandmother and that whole family. But she was often away on night-duty, and then who knew—as the other tenant had hinted—what went on?

Miss Tuhy never slept too well at nights. She often got up and walked round her room and wished it were time to light the fire and make her cup of tea. Those night hours seemed very long, and sometimes, tired of her room, she would go out on the stairs and along the galleries overlooking the courtyard. How silent it was now with everyone asleep! The galleries and the courtyard, so crowded during the day, were empty except where here and there a servant-boy lay sleeping huddled in a corner. There was no traffic on the road outside and the flour-mill was silent. Only the sky seemed alive, with the moon sliding slowly in and out of patches of mist. Miss Tuhy thought about the grandmother and the jeweller for whom she had opened the door when it was like this silent and empty at nights. She remembered conversations she had heard years ago among her English fellow-teachers. They had always had a lot to say about sensuality in the East. They whispered to each other how some of the older boys were seen in the town entering certain disreputable alleys, while boys who came from princely or landowner families were taught everything there was to know by women on their fathers' estates. And as for the girls—well, they whispered, one had only to look at them, how quickly they ripened: could one ever imagine an English girl so developed at thirteen? It was, they said, the climate; and of course the food they ate, all those curries and spices that heated the blood. Miss Tuhy wondered: if she had been born in India, had grown up under this sun and had eaten the food, would she have been different? Instead of her thin, inadequate, English body, would she have grown up like the grandmother who had opened the door to the jeweller, or like Sharmila with flashing black eyes and a big bust?

Nothing stirred, not a sound from anywhere, as if all those lively people in the house were dead. Miss Tuhy stared and stared down at Sharmila's door and the courtyard washed in moonlight, and wondered was there a secret, was something going on that should not be? She crept along the gallery and up the stairs towards the nurse's door. Here too everything was locked and silent, and if there was a secret, it was being kept. She put her ear to the door and stayed there, listening. She did not feel in the least bad or guilty doing this, for what she wanted was nothing for herself but only to have proof that Sharmila was happy.

She did not seem happy. She was getting very bad-tempered and was for ever fighting with her family or with the other tenants. It was a not uncommon sight to have her standing in the middle of the courtyard, arms akimbo, keys at her waist, shouting insults in her loud, somewhat raucous voice. She no longer came to visit Miss Tuhy in her room, and once, when the English lady came to be with her downstairs, she shouted at her that she had enough with one old woman on her hands and did not have time for any more. But that night she came upstairs and brought a little dish of carrot halwa which Miss Tuhy tried to refuse, turning her face away and saying primly that thank you, she was not hungry. "Are you angry with me, Missie Sahib?" coaxed Sharmila with a smile in her voice, and she dug her forefinger into the halwa and then brought it to Miss Tuhy's lips, saying "One little lick, just one, for Sharmila," till Miss Tuhy put out her tongue and shyly slid it along Sharmila's finger. She blushed as she did so, and anger and hurt melted out of her heart.

"There!" cried Sharmila, and then she flung herself as usual on the bed. She began to talk, to unburden herself completely. Tears poured down her cheeks as she spoke of her unhappy life and all the troubles brought down upon her by the grandmother who did not give her enough money and treated her like a slave, the other family members who were jealous of her, the servants who stole from her, the shopkeepers who cheated her—"If it weren't for my children," she cried, "why should I go on? I'd make an end of it and get some peace at last."

"Sh," said Miss Tuhy, shocked and afraid.

"Why not? What have I got to live for?"

"*You?*" said Miss Tuhy with an incredulous laugh, and looked at that large, full-bloomed figure sprawled there on the narrow bed and rumpling the bedcover from which the embroidery (girls carrying baskets of apples and pansies on their arms) had almost completely faded.

Sharmila said, "Did I ever tell you about that woman, two doors away from the coal-merchant's house? She was a widow and they treated her like a dog, so one night she took a scarf and hung herself from a hook on the stairs. We all went to have a look at her. Her feet were swinging in the air as if there was a wind blowing. I was only four but I still remember."

There was an eerie little pause which Miss Tuhy broke as briskly as she could: "What's the matter with you? A young woman like you with all your life before you—I wonder you're not ashamed."

"I want to get away from here! I'm so sick of this *house!*"

"Yes, Miss Tuhy," said the Anglo-Indian nurse a few days later, when the English lady had come to pay her a visit and they both sat drinking tea under the tinted portrait of the Queen, "I'm just sick and tired of living here, that I can tell you. If I could get out tomorrow, I would. But it's not so easy to find a place, not these days with the rents.' She sighed and poured the two of them strong tea out of an earthenware pot. She drank in as refined a way as Miss Tuhy, without making any noise at all. 'My boy's wanting to go to England, and why not? No future for us here, not with these people."

Miss Tuhy gave a hitch to her wire-framed glasses and smiled ingratiatingly: "No young lady for him yet?" she asked, and her voice quavered like an inefficient spy's.

"Oh, he goes with the odd girl or two. Nothing serious. There's time yet. We're not like those others—hurry-curry, muddle-puddle, marry them off at sixteen, and they never even see each other's face! No wonder there's trouble afterwards." She put her bony brown hand on Miss Tuhy's knee and brought her face close: "Like that one downstairs, the she-devil. It's so disgusting. I don't even like to tell you." But her tongue was already wiping round her pale lips in anticipation of the telling.

Miss Tuhy got up abruptly. She dared not listen, and for some unknown reason tears had sprung into her eyes. She went out quickly but the nurse followed her. It was dark on the stairs and Miss Tuhy's tears could not be seen. The nurse clung to her arm: "With servants," she whispered into Miss Tuhy's ear. "She gets them in at night when everyone's asleep. Mary Mother," said the nurse and crossed herself. Instantly a quotation rose to Miss Tuhy's lips: "Her sins are forgiven, for she loved much. But to whom little is forgiven, the same loveth little." The nurse was silent for a moment and then she said, "*She's* not Christian," with contempt. Miss Tuhy freed her arm and hurried to her own room. She sat in her chair with her hands folded in her lap and her legs trembling. A procession of servants filed through her mind: undersized hill-boys with naked feet and torn shirts, sickly but tough, bent on survival. She heard their voices as they called to each other in their weird hill-accents and laughed with each other, showing pointed teeth. Every few years one of them in the neighbourhood went berserk and murdered his master and ran away with the jewellery and cash, only to be caught the next day on a wild spree at cinemas and country liquor shops. Strange wild boys, wolf-boys: Miss Tuhy had always liked them and felt sorry for them. But now she felt most sorry for Sharmila, and prayed for it not to be true.

It could not be true. Sharmila had such an innocent nature. She was a child. She loved sweet things to eat, and when the bangle-seller came, she was the first to run to meet him. She was also very fond of going to the cinema, and when she came home she told Miss Tuhy the story. She acted out all the more important scenes, especially the love-scenes—"Just as their lips were about to meet, quick as a flash, with her veil flying in the wind, she ran to the next tree and called to him—Arjun!—and he followed her and he put his arms round the tree and this time she did not run away— no, they stood looking at each other, eating each other up with their eyes, and then the music—oh, Missie, Missie, Missie!" she would end and stretch her arms into the air and laugh with longing.

Once, on her little daily shopping trip to the bazaar, Miss Tuhy caught sight of Sharmila in the distance. And seeing her like that, unexpectedly, she saw her as a stranger might, and realized for the first time that the Sharmila she knew no longer existed. Her image of Sharmila was two-fold, one superimposed on the other yet also simultaneous, the two images merged in her mind: there was the hoyden schoolgirl, traces of whom still existed in her smile and in certain glances of her eyes, and then there was Sharmila in bloom, the young wife dancing round the courtyard and boasting about her wedding presents. But the woman she now saw in the bazaar was fat and slovenly; the end of her veil, draped carelessly over her breasts, trailed a little in the dust, and the heel of her slipper was trodden over to one side so that she seemed to be dragging her foot when she walked. She was quarrelling with one of the shopkeepers, she was gesticulating and using coarse language; the other shopkeepers leaned out of their stalls to listen, and from the way they grinned and commented to each other, it was obvious that Sharmila was a well-known figure and the scene she was enacting was one she had often played before. Miss Tuhy, in pain, turned and walked away in the opposite direction, even though it meant a longer way home. For the first time she failed to greet the vegetable-seller and the cold-drink man as she passed between their two shops on her way into the house, and when she had to step round the refuse trodden into the mud, she felt a movement of distaste and thought irritably to herself why it was that no one ever took the trouble to clean the place. The stairs of the house too were dirty, and there was a bad smell of sewage. She reached her room with a sigh of relief, but it seemed as if the bad smell came seeping in from under the closed door. Then she heard again Sharmila's anguished voice crying, "I want to get away! I'm so sick of this *house!*" and she too felt the same anguish to get away from the house and from the streets and crowded bazaars around it.

That night she said to Sharmila, in a bright voice, "Why don't we all go away somewhere for a lovely holiday?"

Sharmila, who had never had occasion to leave the city she was born in, thought it was a joke and laughed. But Miss Tuhy was very much in earnest. She remembered all the holidays she had gone on years ago when she was still teaching. She had always gone to the Simla hills and stayed in an English boarding-house, and she had taken long walks every day and breathed in the mountain air and collected pine cones. She told Sharmila all about this, and Sharmila too began to get excited and said, "Let's go," and asked many more questions.

"Sausages and bacon for breakfast every morning," Miss Tuhy reminisced, and Sharmila, who had never eaten either, clapped her hands with pleasure and gave an affectionate squeeze to her youngest child playing in her lap: "You'll like that, Munni, na? Shaushage? Hmmm!"

"They'll get wonderful red cheeks up there," said Miss Tuhy, "real English apple cheeks," and she smiled at the sallow city-child dressed in dirty velvet. "And there'll be pony-rides and wild flowers to pick and lovely cool water from the mountain streams."

"Let's go!" cried Sharmila with another hug to her child.

"We'll go by train," said Miss Tuhy. "And then a bus'll take us up the mountains."

Sharmila suddenly stopped smiling: "Yes, and the money? Where's that to come from? You think *she*'d ever give?" and she tossed her head towards the room where her grandmother lay, immobile and groaning but still a power to be reckoned with.

Miss Tuhy waved her aside: "This'll be *my* treat," she said.

And why not? The money was there, and what pleasure it would be to spend it on a holiday with Sharmila and the children! She brutally stifled all thoughts of caution, of the future. Money was there to be spent, to take pleasure with, not to eke out a miserable day by day existence which, in any case, might end—who knew?—tomorrow or the day after. And then what use would it ever be to her? Her glasses slipped and lay crooked on her nose, her face was flushed: she looked drunk with excitement. 'You'll get such a surprise,' she said. "When we're sitting in the bus, and it's going up up up, higher and higher, and you'll see the mountains before you, more beautiful than anything you've ever dreamed of."

Unfortunately Sharmila and the children were all very sick in the bus that carried them up the mountains, and so could not enjoy the scenery. Sharmila, in between retching with abandon, wept loudly that she was dying and cursed the fate that had brought her here instead of leaving her quietly at home where she belonged and was happy. However, once the bus had stopped and they had reached their destination, they began to enjoy themselves. They were amused by the English boarding-house, and at meal-times were lost in wonder not only at the food, the like of which they had never eaten, but also at the tablecloths and the cutlery. Their first walk was undertaken with great enthusiasm, and they collected everything they found on the way—pine cones and flowers and leaves and stones and empty cigarette packets. As Miss Tuhy had promised, they rode on ponies: even Sharmila, gasping and giggling and letting out loud cries of fright, was hoisted on to the back of a pony but had to be helped down again, dissolving in fits of laughter, because she was too heavy. Miss Tuhy revelled in their enjoyment; and for herself she was happy too to be here again among the familiar smells of pine and wood-fires and cold air. She loved the pale mists that rose from the mountainside and the rain that rained down so softly. She wished they could stay for ever. But after the third day Sharmila and the children began to get bored and kept asking when they were going home. They no longer cared to go for walks or ride on ponies. When it rained, all four of them sat mournfully by the window, and sighed and moaned and kept asking, what shall we do now? and Sharmila wondered how human beings could bear to live in a place like this; speaking for herself, it was just the same as being dead. Miss Tuhy had to listen not only to their complaints but also to those of the management, for Sharmila and the children were behaving badly—especially in the dining-room where, after the third day, they began demanding pickles and chapattis, and the children spat out the unfamiliar food on the tablecloth while Sharmila abused the hotel servants in bazaar language.

So they went home again earlier than they had intended. They had been away less than ten days, but their excitement on seeing the old places again was that of long-time voyagers. They had hired a tonga[1] at the station and, as they neared home, they began to point out familiar landmarks to each other; by the time they had got to their own neighbourhood bazaar, the children were bobbing up and down so much that they were in danger of falling off the carriage, and Sharmila shouted cordial greetings to the shopkeepers with whom she would be fighting again tomorrow. And at home all the relatives and friends crowded into the courtyard to receive them, and there was much kissing and embracing and even a happy tear or two, and the tenants and servants thronged the galleries upstairs to watch the scene and call down their welcome to the travellers. It was a great homecoming.

Only Miss Tuhy was not happy. She did not want to be back. She longed now for the green mountains and the clean, cool air; she also missed the boarding-house with its English landlady and very clean stairs and bathrooms. It was intensely hot in the city and dust-storms were blowing. The sky was covered with an ugly yellow heat haze, and all day hot, restless winds blew dust about. Loudspeaker vans were driven through the streets to advise people to be vaccinated against the current outbreak of smallpox. Miss Tuhy hardly left her room. She felt ill and weak, and contrary to her usual custom, she often lay down on her bed, even during the day. She kept her doors and windows shut, but nevertheless the dust seeped in, and so did the smells and the noise of the house. She no longer went on her daily shopping and preferred not to eat. Sharmila brought food up for her, but Miss Tuhy did not want it, it was too spicy for her and too greasy. "Just a little taste," Sharmila begged and brought a morsel to her lips. Miss Tuhy pushed her hand away and cried out, "Go away! I can't stand the smell!" She meant not only the smell of the food, but also that of Sharmila's heavy, perspiring body.

It was in these days of terrible heat that the grandmother at last managed to die. Miss Tuhy dragged herself up from her bed in order to attend the funeral on the bank of the river. It was during the hottest part of the day, and the sun spread such a pall of white heat that, seen through it, the flames of the pyre looked colourless and quite harmless as they first licked and then rose higher and enveloped the body of the grandmother. The priest chanted and the eldest son poured clarified butter to feed the fire. All the relatives shrieked and wailed and beat their thighs in the traditional manner. Sharmila shrieked the loudest—she tore open her breast and, beating it with her fists, demanded to be allowed to die, and then she tried to fling herself on the pyre and had to be held back by four people. Vultures swayed overhead in the dust-laden sky. The river had dried up and the sand burned underfoot. Everything

1 **tonga:** A two-wheeled, horse-drawn vehicle, common in India.

was white, desolate, empty, for miles and miles and miles around, on earth and, apart from the vultures, in the sky. Sharmila suddenly flung herself on Miss Tuhy and held her in a stifling embrace. She wept that now only she, Miss Tuhy, was left to her, and promised to look after her and tend and care for her as she had done for her dear, dead granny. Miss Tuhy gasped for air and tried to free herself, but Sharmila only clung to her the tighter and her tears fell on and smeared Miss Tuhy's cheeks.

Miss Tuhy's mother had died almost forty years ago, but Miss Tuhy could still vividly recall her funeral. It had drizzled, and rich smells of damp earth had mixed with the more delicate smell of tuberoses and yew. The clergyman's words brought ease and comfort, and weeping was restrained; birds sang cheerfully from out of the wet trees. That's the way to die, thought Miss Tuhy, and bitterness welled up into her hitherto gentle heart. The trouble was, she no longer had the fare home to England, not even on the cheapest route.

QUESTIONS

1. How do you regard the title? Is it descriptive or ironic?

2. Analyze Miss Tuhy's attitude toward Indians. How does her attitude change as the story progresses? What does she like about India and Indians? What does she dislike?

3. Postcolonial criticism frequently analyzes what happens to people from previously colonized countries who emigrate to the United States, Canada, or Britain. Can such techniques be applied to Miss Tuhy? If so, what do they reveal about her and her relationship to India and Indians?

4. How are we to understand Miss Tuhy? Is she representative of English sentimentality about the Raj? Is she just a foolish individual who can't adjust to new realities? Is she, in spite of her professed fondness for India and its people, a racist?

5. Ultimately, is Miss Tuhy a tragic or simply pathetic woman?

Anita Desai

(b. 1937)

Anita Desai is among India's outstanding contemporary authors, with a world-wide audience for her novels and short stories, which focus primarily on the problems and issues of modern India and frequently on women's issues.

She was born north of Delhi, the daughter of a Bengali businessman, D. N. Mazumdar, and his wife of German extraction, Toni Nime. Desai spoke German and Hindi at home, learning English at school in Delhi. In 1957, she graduated from the University of Delhi with a degree in English and the following year married businessman Ashrin Desai. She and her family came to the United States in 1987, where she has taught at several universities, most recently at the Massachusetts Institute of Technology.

Desai began writing stories at an early age, her earliest models being the writers she studied at university—Virginia Woolf and D. H. Lawrence. Later she was drawn to Russian models, Fyodor Dostoyevsky and Anton Chekhov, and then to Japanese and Russian poetry. Her first published book was the novel *Cry, the Peacock* (1963). Since then she has published nine novels, several juvenile books, and two collections of short stories. Her characters have been described as coming from the Anglicized middle classes of India, those who have benefited most directly and fully from independence and its aftermath. Although not consciously a social critic, her studies of family life and individuals on the fringes of society nevertheless imply or suggest attitudes toward society. Many of her characters are suspicious of the traps of everyday life—conformity, social convention, the preassigned roles that can entrap anyone.

Studies in the Park   1978

—Turn it off, turn it off, turn it off! First he listens to the news in Hindi. Directly after, in English. Broom—brroom—brrroom—the voice of doom roars. Next, in Tamil. Then in Punjabi. In Gujarati. What next, my god, what next? Turn it off before I smash it onto his head, fling it out of the window, do nothing of the sort of course, nothing of the sort.

—And my mother. She cuts and fries, cuts and fries. All day I hear her chopping and slicing and the pan of oil hissing. What all does she find to fry and feed us on, for God's sake? Eggplants, potatoes, spinach, shoe soles, newspapers, finally she'll slice me and feed me to my brothers and sisters. Ah, now she's turned on the tap. It's roaring and pouring, pouring and roaring into a bucket without a bottom.

—The bell rings. Voices clash, clatter and break. The tin-and-bottle man? The neighbours? The police? The Help-the-Blind man? Thieves and burglars? All of them, all of them, ten or twenty or a hundred of them, marching up the stairs, hammering at the door, breaking in and climbing over me—ten, twenty or a hundred of them.

—Then, worst of all, the milk arrives. In the tallest glass in the house. "Suno, drink your milk. Good for you, Suno. You need it. Now, before the exams. Must have it, Suno. Drink." The voice wheedles its way into my ear like a worm. I shudder. The table tips over. The milk runs. The tumbler clangs on the floor. "Suno, Suno, how will you do your exams?"

—That is precisely what I ask myself. All very well to give me a room—Uncle's been pushed off on a pilgrimage to Hardwar[1] to clear a room for me—and to bring me milk and say, "Study, Suno, study for your exam." What about the uproar around me? These people don't know the meaning of the word Quiet. When my mother fills buckets, sloshes the kitchen floor, fries and sizzles things in the pan, she thinks she is being Quiet. The children have never even heard the word, it amazes and puzzles them. On their way back from school they fling their satchels in at my door, then tear in to snatch them back before I tear them to bits. Bawl when I pull their ears, screech when mother whacks them. Stuff themselves with her fries and then smear the grease on my books.

So I raced out of my room, with my fingers in my ears, to scream till the roof fell down about their ears. But the radio suddenly went off, the door to my parents' room suddenly opened and my father appeared, bathed and shaven, stuffed and set up with the news of the world in six different languages—his white *dhoti*[2] blazing, his white shirt crackling, his patent leather pumps glittering. He stopped in the doorway and I stopped on the balls of my feet and wavered. My fingers came out of my ears, my hair came down over my eyes. Then he looked away from me, took his watch out of his pocket and enquired, "Is the food ready?" in a voice that came out of his nose like the whistle of a punctual train. He skated off towards his meal, I turned and slouched back to my room. On his way to work, he looked in to say, "Remember, Suno, I expect good results from you. Study hard, Suno." Just behind him, I saw all the rest of them standing, peering in, silently. All of them stared at me, at the exam I was to take. At the degree I was to get. Or not get. Horrifying thought. Oh study, study, study, they all breathed at me while my father's footsteps went down the stairs, crushing each underfoot in turn. I felt their eyes on me, goggling, and their breath on me, hot with earnestness. I looked back at them, into their open mouths and staring eyes.

"Study," I said, and found I croaked. "I know I ought to study. And how do you expect me to study—in this mad-house? You run wild, *wild*. I'm getting out," I screamed, leaping up and grabbing my books, "I'm going to study outside. Even the street is quieter," I screeched and threw myself past them and down the stairs that my father had just cowed and subjugated so that they still lay quivering, and paid no attention to the howls that broke out behind me of "Suno, Suno, listen. Your milk— your studies—your exams, Suno!"

At first I tried the tea shop at the corner. In my reading I had often come across men who wrote at café tables—letters, verse, whole novels—over a cup of coffee or a

---

1 **Hardwar:** A sacred place of pilgrimage in Uttar Pradesh, where a bath in the Ganges is considered purifying.
2 ***dhoti:*** Loincloth worn by Hindu men.

glass of absinthe[3] I thought it would be simple to read a chapter of history over a cup of tea. There was no crowd in the mornings, none of my friends would be there. But the proprietor would not leave me alone. Bored, picking his nose, he wandered down from behind the counter to my table by the weighing machine and tried to pass the time of day by complaining about his piles,[4] the new waiter and the high prices. "And sugar," he whined. "How can I give you anything to put in your tea with sugar at four rupees a kilo? There's rationed sugar, I know, at two rupees, but that's not enough to feed even an ant. And the way you all sugar your tea—*hai, hai,*" he sighed, worse than my mother. I didn't answer. I frowned at my book and looked stubborn. But when I got rid of him, the waiter arrived. "Have a biscuit?" he murmured, flicking at my table and chair with his filthy duster. "A bun? Fritters? Make you some hot fritters?" I snarled at him but he only smiled, determined to be friendly. Just a boy, really, in a pink shirt with purple circles stamped all over it—he thought he looked so smart. He was growing sideburns, he kept fingering them. "I'm a student, too," he said, "sixth class, fail. My mother wanted me to go back and try again, but I didn't like the teacher—he beat me. So I came here to look for a job. Lala-*ji* had just thrown out a boy called Hari for selling lottery tickets to the clients so he took me on. I can make out a bill . . ." He would have babbled on if Lala-*ji* had not come and shoved him into the kitchen with an oath. So it went on. I didn't read more than half a chapter that whole morning. I didn't want to go home either. I walked along the street, staring at my shoes, with my shoulders slumped in the way that makes my father scream, "What's the matter? Haven't you bones? A spine?" I kicked some rubble along the pavement, down the drain, then stopped at the iron gates of King Edward's Park.

"Exam troubles?" asked a *gram*[5] vendor who sat outside it, in a friendly voice. Not insinuating, but low, pleasant. "The park's full of boys like you," he continued in that sympathetic voice. "I see them walk up and down, up and down with their books, like mad poets. Then I'm glad I was never sent to school," and he began to whistle, not impertinently but so cheerfully that I stopped and stared at him. He had a crippled arm that hung out of his shirt sleeve like a leg of mutton dangling on a hook. His face was scarred as though he had been dragged out of some terrible accident. But he was shuffling hot *gram* into paper cones with his one hand and whistling like a bird, whistling the tune of, "We are the *bul-buls*[6] of our land, our land is Paradise." Nodding at the greenery beyond the gates, he said, "The park's a good place to study in," and, taking his hint, I went in.

I wonder how it is I never thought of the park before. It isn't far from our house and I sometimes went there as a boy, if I managed to run away from school, to lie on a bench, eat peanuts, shy stones at the chipmunks that came for the shells, and drink

3 **absinthe:** A liqueur.
4 **piles:** Hemorrhoids.
5 *gram:* Chickpeas or similar legume.
6 *bul-buls:* Birds of the thrush family, known for their sweet song.

from the fountain. But then it was not as exciting as playing marbles in the street or stoning rats with my school friends in the vacant lot behind the cinema. It had straight paths, beds of flapping red flowers—cannas, I think—rows of palm trees like limp flags, a dry fountain and some green benches. Old men sat on them with their legs far apart, heads drooping over the tops of sticks, mumbling through their dentures or cackling with that mad, ripping laughter that makes children think of old men as wizards and bogey-men. Bag-like women in grey and fawn *saris* or black *borkhas*[7] screamed, just as grey and fawn and black birds do, at children falling into the fountain or racing on rickety legs after the chipmunks and pigeons. A madman or two, prancing around in paper caps and bits of rags, munching banana peels and scratching like monkeys. Corners behind hibiscus bushes stinking of piss. Iron rails with rows of beggars contentedly dozing, scratching, gambling, with their sackcloth backs to the rails. A city park.

What I hadn't noticed, or thought of, were all the students who escaped from their city flats and families like mine to come and study here. Now, walking down a path with my history book tucked under my arm, I felt like a gatecrasher at a party or a visitor to a public library trying to control a sneeze. They all seemed to belong here, to be at home here. Dressed in loose pyjamas, they strolled up and down under the palms, books open in their hands, heads lowered into them. Or they sat in twos and threes on the grass, reading aloud in turns. Or lay full length under the trees, books spread out across their faces—sleeping, or else imbibing information through the subconscious. Opening out my book, I too strolled up and down, reading to myself in a low murmur.

In the beginning, when I first started studying in the park, I couldn't concentrate on my studies. I'd keep looking up at the boy strolling in front of me, reciting poetry in a kind of thundering whisper, waving his arms about and running his bony fingers through his hair till it stood up like a thorn bush. Or at the chipmunks that fought and played and chased each other all over the park, now and then joining forces against the sparrows over a nest or a paper cone of *gram*. Or at the madman going through the rubble at the bottom of the dry fountain and coming up with a rubber shoe, a banana peel or a piece of glittering tin that he appreciated so much that he put it in his mouth and chewed it till blood ran in strings from his mouth.

It took me time to get accustomed to the ways of the park. I went there daily, for the whole day, and soon I got to know it as well as my own room at home and found I could study there, or sleep, or daydream, as I chose. Then I fell into its routine, its rhythm, and my time moved in accordance with its time. We were like a house-owner and his house, or a turtle and its shell, or a river and its bank—so close. I resented everyone else who came to the park—I thought they couldn't possibly share my feeling for it. Except, perhaps, the students.

---

7 **saris** and **borkhas:** A sari is the traditional Hindu dress for women, consisting of a single piece of cloth, wrapped at the waist and draped over the shoulder. The borkha or burkha is the head-to-toe dress of traditional Muslim women, covering everything but the eyes.

The park was like an hotel, or an hospital, belonging to the city but with its own order and routine, enclosed by iron rails, laid out according to prescription in rows of palms, benches and paths. If I went there very early in the morning. I'd come upon a yoga class. It consisted of young body-builders rippling their muscles like snakes as well as old crack-pots determined to keep up with the youngest and fittest, all sitting cross-legged on the grass and displaying *hus-mukh* to the sun just rising over the palms: the Laughing Face pose it was called, but they looked like gargoyles with their mouths torn open and their thick, discoloured tongues sticking out. If I were the sun, I'd feel so disgusted by such a reception I'd just turn around and go back. And that was the simplest of their poses—after that they'd go into contortions that would embarrass an ape. Once their leader, a black and hirsute man like an aborigine, saw me watching and called me to join them. I shook my head and ducked behind an oleander. You won't catch me making an ass of myself in public. And I despise all that body-beautiful worship anyway. What's the body compared to the soul, the mind?

I'd stroll under the palms, breathing in the cool of the early morning, feeling it drive out, or wash clean, the stifling dark of the night, and try to avoid bumping into all the other early morning visitors to the park—mostly aged men sent by their wives to fetch the milk from the Government dairy booth just outside the gates. Their bottles clinking in green cloth bags and newspapers rolled up and tucked under their arms, they strutted along like stiff puppets and mostly they would be discussing philosophy. "Ah but in Vedanta it is a different matter," one would say, his eyes gleaming fanatically, and another would announce, "The sage Shanakaracharya showed the way," and some would refer to the Upanishads[8] or the Bhagavad Puranas,[9] but in such argumentative, hacking tones that you could see they were quite capable of coming to blows over some theological argument. Certainly it was the mind above the body for these old coots but I found nothing to admire in them either. I particularly resented it when one of them disengaged himself from the discussion long enough to notice me and throw me a gentle look of commiseration. As if he'd been through exams, too, long long ago, and knew all about them. So what?

Worst of all were the athletes, wrestlers, Mr Indias and others who lay on their backs and were massaged with oil till every muscle shone and glittered. The men who massaged them huffed and puffed and cursed as they climbed up and down the supine bodies, pounding and pummelling the men who lay there wearing nothing but little greasy clouts, groaning and panting in a way I found obscene and disgusting. They never looked up at me or at anyone. They lived in a meaty, sweating world of their own—massages, oils, the body, a match to be fought and won—I kicked up dust in their direction but never went too close.

The afternoons would be quiet, almost empty. I would sit under a tree and read, stroll and study, doze too. Then, in the evening, as the sky softened from its blank

8 **Upanishads:** Books of ancient, mystic Hindu philosophy.
9 **Bhagavad Puranas:** The Puranas are Sanskrit texts giving legendary accounts of ancient times; the *Bhagavad Purana* is the most famous of these. It stresses the need for faith and devotion.

white glare and took on shades of pink and orange and the palm trees rustled a little in an invisible breeze, the crowds would begin to pour out of Darya Ganj, Mori Gate, Chandni Chowk and the Jama Masjid bazaars and slums. Large families would come to sit about on the grass, eating peanuts and listening to a transistor radio placed in the centre of the circle. Mothers would sit together in flocks like screeching birds while children jumped into the dry fountains, broke flowers and terrorized each other. There would be a few young men moaning at the corners, waiting for a girl to roll her hips and dart her fish eyes in their direction, and then start the exciting adventure of pursuit. The children's cries would grow more piercing with the dark; frightened, shrill and exalted with mystery and farewell. I would wander back to the flat.

The exams drew nearer. Not three, not two, but only one month to go. I had to stop daydreaming and set myself tasks for every day and remind myself constantly to complete them. It grew so hot I had to give up strolling on the paths and staked out a private place for myself under a tree. I noticed the tension tightening the eyes and mouths of other students—they applied themselves more diligently to their books, talked less, slept less. Everyone looked a little demented from lack of sleep. Our books seemed attached to our hands as though by roots, they were a part of us, they lived because we fed them. They were parasites and, like parasites, were sucking us dry. We mumbled to ourselves, not always consciously. Chipmunks jumped over our feet, mocking us. The *gram* seller down at the gate whistled softly "I'm glad I never went to school, I am a *bul-bul*, I live in Paradise . . ."

My brains began to jam up. I could feel it happening, slowly. As if the oil were all used up. As if everything was getting locked together, rusted. The white cells, the grey matter, the springs and nuts and bolts. I yelled at my mother—I think it was my mother—"What do you think I am? What do you want of me?" and crushed a glass of milk between my hands. It was sticky. She had put sugar in my milk. As if I were a baby. I wanted to cry. They wouldn't let me sleep, they wanted to see my light on all night, they made sure I never stopped studying. Then they brought me milk and sugar and made clicking sounds with their tongues. I raced out to the park. I think I sobbed as I paced up and down, up and down, in the corner that stank of piss. My head ached worse than ever. I slept all day under the tree and had to work all night.

My father laid his hand on my shoulder. I knew I was not to fling it off. So I sat still, slouching, ready to spring aside if he lifted it only slightly. "You must get a first[10] Suno," he said through his nose, "must get a first, or else you won't get a job. Must get a job, Suno," he sighed and wiped his nose and went off, his patent leather pumps squealing like mice. I flung myself back in my chair and howled. Get a first, get a first, get a first—like a railway engine, it went charging over me, grinding me down, and left me dead and mangled on the tracks.

---

10 **a first:** English examination results are divided into "firsts," the highest mark, "seconds," and "thirds."

Everything hung still and yellow in the park. I lay sluggishly on a heap of waste paper under my tree and read without seeing, slept without sleeping. Sometimes I went to the water tap that leaked and drank the leak. It tasted of brass. I spat out a mouthful. It nearly went over the feet of the student waiting for his turn at that dripping tap. I stepped aside for him. He swilled the water around his mouth and spat, too, carefully missing my feet. Wiping his mouth, he asked, "B.A?"

"No, Inter.[11]

"Hu," he burped. "Wait till you do your B.A. Then you'll get to know." His face was like a grey bone. It was not unkind, it simply had no expression. "Another two weeks," he sighed and slouched off to his own lair.

I touched my face. I thought it would be all bone, like his. I was surprised to find a bit of skin still covering it. I felt as if we were all dying in the park, that when we entered the examination hall it would be to be declared officially dead. That's what the degree was about. What else was it all about? Why were we creeping around here, hiding from the city, from teachers and parents, pretending to study and prepare? Prepare for what? We hadn't been told. Inter, they said, or B.A, or M.A. These were like official stamps—they would declare us dead. Ready for a dead world. A world in which ghosts went about, squeaking or whining, rattling or rustling. Slowly, slowly we were killing ourselves in order to join them. The ball-point pen in my pocket was the only thing that still lived, that still worked. I didn't work myself any more—I mean physically, my body no longer functioned. I was constipated, I was dying. I was lying under a yellow tree, feeling the dust sift through the leaves to cover me. It was filling my eyes, my throat. I could barely walk. I never strolled. Only on the way out of the park, late in the evening, I crept down the path under the palms, past the benches.

Then I saw the scene that stopped it all, stopped me just before I died.

Hidden behind an oleander was a bench. A woman lay on it, stretched out. She was a Muslim, wrapped in a black *borkha*. I hesitated when I saw this straight, still figure in black on the bench. Just then she lifted a pale, thin hand and lifted her veil. I saw her face. It lay bared, in the black folds of her *borkha*, like a flower, wax-white and composed, like a Persian lily or a tobacco flower at night. She was young. Very young, very pale, beautiful with a beauty I had never come across even in a dream. It caught me and held me tight, tight till I couldn't breathe and couldn't move. She was so white, so still, I saw she was very ill—with anaemia, perhaps, or t.b. Too pale, too white—I could see she was dying. Her head—so still and white it might have been carved if it weren't for this softness, this softness of a flower at night—lay in the lap of a very old man. Very much older than her. With spectacles and a long grey beard like a goat's, or a scholar's. He was looking down at her and caressing her face—so tenderly, so tenderly, I had never seen a hand move so gently and tenderly. Beside them, on the ground, two little girls were playing. Round little girls, rather dirty,

11 **Inter:** Intermediate, roughly equivalent to high school.

drawing lines in the gravel. They stared at me but the man and the woman did not notice me. They never looked at anyone else, only at each other, with an expression that halted me. It was tender, loving, yes, but in an inhuman way, so intense. Divine, I felt, or insane. I stood, half-hidden by the bush, holding my book, and wondered at them. She was ill, I could see, dying. Perhaps she had only a short time to live. Why didn't he take her to the Victoria Zenana Hospital, so close to the park? Who was this man—her husband, her father, a lover? I couldn't make out although I watched them without moving, without breathing. I felt not as if I were staring rudely at strangers, but as if I were gazing at a painting or a sculpture, some work of art. Or seeing a vision. They were still and I stood still and the children stared. Then she lifted her arms above her head and laughed. Very quietly.

I broke away and hurried down the path, in order to leave them alone, in privacy. They weren't a work of art, or a vision, but real, human and alive as no one else in my life had been real and alive. I had only that glimpse of them. But I felt I could never open my books and study or take degrees after that. They belonged to the dead, and now I had seen what being alive meant. The vision burnt the surfaces of my eyes so that they watered as I groped my way up the stairs to the flat. I could hardly find my way to the bed.

It was not just the examination but everything else had suddenly withered and died, gone lifeless and purposeless when compared with this vision. My studies, my family, my life—they all belonged to the dead and only what I had seen in the park had any meaning.

Since I did not know how to span the distance between that beautiful ideal and my stupid, dull existence, I simply lay still and shut my eyes. I kept them shut so as not to see all the puzzled, pleading, indignant faces of my family around me, but I could not shut out their voices.

"Suno, Suno," I heard them croon and coax and mourn.

"Suno, drink milk."

"Suno, study."

"Suno, take the exam."

And when they tired of being so patient with me and I still would not get up, they began to crackle and spit and storm.

"Get up, Suno."

"Study, Suno."

"At once, Suno."

Only my mother became resigned and gentle. She must have seen something quite out of the ordinary on my face to make her so. I felt her hand on my forehead and heard her say, "Leave him alone. Let him sleep tonight. He is tired out, that is what it is—he has driven himself too much and now he must sleep."

Then I heard all of them leave the room. Her hand stayed on my forehead, wet and smelling of onions, and after a bit my tears began to flow from under my lids.

"Poor Suno, sleep," she murmured.

* * *

I went back to the park of course. But now I was changed. I had stopped being a student—I was a "professional." My life was dictated by the rules and routine of the park. I still had my book open on the palms of my hands as I strolled but now my eyes strayed without guilt, darting at the young girls walking in pairs, their arms linked, giggling and bumping into each other. Sometimes I stopped to rest on a bench and conversed with one of the old men, told him who my father was and what examination I was preparing for, and allowing him to tell me about his youth, his politics, his philosophy, his youth and again his youth. Or I joked with the other students, sitting on the grass and throwing peanut shells at the chipmunks, and shocking them, I could see, with my irreverence and cynicism about the school, the exam, the system. Once I even nodded at the yoga teacher and exchanged a few words with him. He suggested I join his class and I nodded vaguely and said I would think it over. It might help. My father says I need help. He says I am hopeless but that I need help. I just laugh but I know that he knows I will never appear for the examination, I will never come up to that hurdle or cross it—life has taken a different path for me, in the form of a search, not a race as it is for him, for them.

Yes, it is a search, a kind of perpetual search for me and now that I have accepted it and don't struggle, I find it satisfies me entirely, and I wander about the park as freely as a prince in his palace garden. I look over the benches, I glance behind the bushes, and wonder if I shall ever get another glimpse of that strange vision that set me free. I never have but I keep hoping, wishing.

QUESTIONS

1. How does the author create a sense of desperation in the opening paragraphs? Point to specific words and phrases that contribute to this feeling.

2. To what extent does this mood change when Suno discovers the park? Why does it change?

3. How does the sight of the ill Muslim woman affect Suno? What events in the story lead up to this moment and its aftermath?

4. Suno says that "They [books] belonged to the dead, and now I had seen what being alive meant." What do you think he means by "being alive"?

5. Why does Suno rebel against books and school? Is this just typical adolescent rebellion, or is something more important at work?

6. In your view, does the park represent a larger world that Suno is entering, or is it an escape from the world?

7. Considering that the Indian system of education is based on the English system, is this story a protest against the colonial legacy? Explain your answer.

Chitra Banerjee Divakaruni

(b. 1957)

Chitra Banerjee was born in Calcutta and earned a BA in English from Calcutta University. She then emigrated to the United States, where she earned an MA at Wright State in 1978 and a PhD at the University of California, Berkeley, in 1985. While attending college and graduate school, she held a variety of odd jobs—babysitting, clerking in an Indian boutique and later a bakery, and serving in a university dining hall. A crucial event occurred the day after she arrived in Chicago: She was attacked with snowballs and racial epithets by young men. It emphasized for her that people of color would always be regarded by Americans as "outsiders." She married S. Murthy Divakaruni in 1979. In 1991, she and a group of friends established a hotline for South Asian women who were victims of domestic abuse; she has also volunteered at Chinmaya Mission, where she taught Sunday school. Although a successful teacher of creative writing in U.S. universities, she now devotes full time to writing and to women's issues.

Divakaruni's best-known work is her first novel, *The Mistress of Spices* (1997), whose heroine is an Indian woman with magical powers. Her one collection of short stories, *Arranged Marriage* (1995), won the American Book Award for 1996 because of its finely crafted studies of young women involved in arranged marriages, a custom she believes is still valid, even though her own marriage was not arranged. The subject has intrinsic interest, but it is also a locus for the clash of cultural values that divides so many South Asian families and creates psychological and emotional difficulties for many of the young people involved. Unlike many brides, however, Mita in "Clothes" is pleased with her family's choice, and what begins as a tentative relationship soon blossoms into passion.

Divakaruni's other recent books include *The Unknown Errors of Our Lives* (short stories, 2001) and *Queen of Dreams* (novel, 2004). In spite of the magical realism in *The Mistress of Spices*, Divakaruni traces her literary influences to the nineteenth-century realists like Charles Dickens and Thomas Hardy, but also credits the emotion in her writing to Bengali tales and myths, and to the Indian epics, the *Mahabharata* and *Ramayana*.

Clothes   *1990*

The water of the women's lake laps against my breasts, cool, calming. I can feel it beginning to wash the hot nervousness away from my body. The little waves tickle my armpits, make my sari float up around me, wet and yellow, like a sunflower after rain. I close my eyes and smell the sweet brown odor of the *ritha* pulp[1] my friends Deepali and Radha are working into my hair so it will glisten with little lights this evening. They scrub with more vigor than usual and wash it out more carefully, because today is a special day. It is the day of my bride-viewing.

"Ei, Sumita! Mita! Are you deaf?" Radha says. "This is the third time I've asked you the same question."

"Look at her, already dreaming about her husband, and she hasn't even seen him yet!" Deepali jokes. Then she adds, the envy in her voice only half hidden, "Who cares about friends from a little Indian village when you're about to go live in America?"

I want to deny it, to say that I will always love them and all the things we did together through my growing-up years—visiting the *charak*[2] fair where we always ate too many sweets, raiding the neighbor's guava tree[3] summer afternoons while the grown-ups slept, telling fairy tales while we braided each other's hair in elaborate patterns we'd invented. *And she married the handsome prince who took her to his kingdom beyond the seven seas.* But already the activities of our girlhood seem to be far in my past, the colors leached out of them, like old sepia photographs.

His name is Somesh Sen, the man who is coming to our house with his parents today and who will be my husband "if I'm lucky enough to be chosen," as my aunt says. He is coming all the way from California. Father showed it to me yesterday, on the metal globe that sits on his desk, a chunky pink wedge on the side of a multicolored slab marked *Untd. Sts. of America.* I touched it and felt the excitement leap all the way up my arm like an electric shock. Then it died away, leaving only a beaten-metal coldness against my fingertips.

For the first time it occurred to me that if things worked out the way everyone was hoping, I'd be going halfway around the world to live with a man I hadn't even met. Would I ever see my parents again? *Don't send me so far away,* I wanted to cry, but of course I didn't. It would be ungrateful. Father had worked so hard to find this match for me. Besides, wasn't it every woman's destiny, as Mother was always telling me, to leave the known for the unknown? She had done it, and her mother before her. *A married woman belongs to her husband, her in-laws.* Hot seeds of tears pricked my eyelids at the unfairness of it.

"Mita Moni, little jewel," Father said, calling me by my childhood name. He put out his hand as though he wanted to touch my face, then let it fall to his side. "He's a good man. Comes from a fine family. He will be kind to you." He was silent for a while. Finally he said, "Come, let me show you the special sari I bought in Calcutta for you to wear at the bride-viewing."

"Are you nervous?" Radha asks as she wraps my hair in a soft cotton towel. Her parents are also trying to arrange a marriage for her. So far three families have come to see her, but no one has chosen her because her skin-color is considered too dark. "Isn't it terrible, not knowing what's going to happen?"

1 *ritha* **pulp:** A fruit that, when soaked in water, gives a soapy suds. Used for washing and shampooing.
2 *charak:* A festival in Bengal during April.
3 **guava tree:** A tropical tree that bears green or yellow fruit.

I nod because I don't want to disagree, don't want to make her feel bad by saying that sometimes it's worse when you know what's coming, like I do. I knew it as soon as Father unlocked his mahogany *almirah*[4] and took out the sari.

It was the most expensive sari I had ever seen, and surely the most beautiful. Its body was a pale pink, like the dawn sky over the women's lake. The color of transition. Embroidered all over it were tiny stars made out of real gold *zari* thread.[5]

"Here, hold it," said Father.

The sari was unexpectedly heavy in my hands, silk-slippery, a sari to walk carefully in. A sari that could change one's life. I stood there holding it, wanting to weep. I knew that when I wore it, it would hang in perfect pleats to my feet and shimmer in the light of the evening lamps. It would dazzle Somesh and his parents and they would choose me to be his bride.

When the plane takes off, I try to stay calm, to take deep, slow breaths like Father does when he practices yoga. But my hands clench themselves on to the folds of my sari and when I force them open, after the *fasten seat belt* and *no smoking* signs have blinked off, I see they have left damp blotches on the delicate crushed fabric.

We had some arguments about this sari. I wanted a blue one for the journey, because blue is the color of possibility, the color of the sky through which I would be traveling. But Mother said there must be red in it because red is the color of luck for married women. Finally, Father found one to satisfy us both: midnight-blue with a thin red border the same color as the marriage mark I'm wearing on my forehead.

It is hard for me to think of myself as a married woman. I whisper my new name to myself, Mrs. Sumita Sen, but the syllables rustle uneasily in my mouth like a stiff satin that's never been worn.

Somesh had to leave for America just a week after the wedding. He had to get back to the store, he explained to me. He had promised his partner. The store. It seems more real to me than Somesh—perhaps because I know more about it. It was what we had mostly talked about the night after the wedding, the first night we were together alone. It stayed open twenty-four hours, yes, all night, every night, not like the Indian stores which closed at dinnertime and sometimes in the hottest part of the afternoon. That's why his partner needed him back.

The store was called *7-Eleven*. I thought it a strange name, exotic, risky. All the stores I knew were piously named after gods and goddesses—*Ganesh Sweet House, Lakshmi Vastralaya for Fine Saris*—to bring the owners luck.

The store sold all kinds of amazing things—apple juice in cardboard cartons that never leaked; American bread that came in cellophane packages, already cut up; canisters of potato chips, each large grainy flake curved exactly like the next. The large refrigerator with see-through glass doors held beer and wine, which Somesh said were the most popular items.

4 *almirah:* A tall cupboard or wardrobe.
5 *zari* **thread:** Gold thread for brocade work.

"That's where the money comes from, especially in the neighborhood where our store is," said Somesh, smiling at the shocked look on my face. (The only places I knew of that sold alcohol were the village toddy shops, "dark, stinking dens of vice," Father called them.) "A lot of Americans drink, you know. It's a part of their culture, not considered immoral, like it is here. And really, there's nothing wrong with it." He touched my lips lightly with his finger. "When you come to California, I'll get you some sweet white wine and you'll see how good it makes you feel. . . ." Now his fingers were stroking my cheeks, my throat, moving downward. I closed my eyes and tried not to jerk away because after all it was my wifely duty.

"It helps if you can think about something else," my friend Madhavi had said when she warned me about what most husbands demanded on the very first night. Two years married, she already had one child and was pregnant with a second one.

I tried to think of the women's lake, the dark cloudy green of the *shapla*[6] leaves that float on the water, but his lips were hot against my skin, his fingers fumbling with buttons, pulling at the cotton night-sari I wore. I couldn't breathe.

"Bite hard on your tongue," Madhavi had advised. "The pain will keep your mind off what's going on down there."

But when I bit down, it hurt so much that I cried out. I couldn't help it although I was ashamed. Somesh lifted his head. I don't know what he saw on my face, but he stopped right away. "Shhh," he said, although I had made myself silent already. "It's OK, we'll wait until you feel like it." I tried to apologize but he smiled it away and started telling me some more about the store.

And that's how it was the rest of the week until he left. We would lie side by side on the big white bridal pillow I had embroidered with a pair of doves for married harmony, and Somesh would describe how the store's front windows were decorated with a flashing neon Dewar's sign and a lighted Budweiser waterfall *this big*. I would watch his hands moving excitedly through the dim air of the bedroom and think that Father had been right, he was a good man, my husband, a kind, patient man. And so handsome, too, I would add, stealing a quick look at the strong curve of his jaw, feeling luckier than I had any right to be.

The night before he left, Somesh confessed that the store wasn't making much money yet. "I'm not worried, I'm sure it soon will," he added, his fingers pleating the edge of my sari. "But I just don't want to give you the wrong impression, don't want you to be disappointed."

In the half dark I could see he had turned toward me. His face, with two vertical lines between the brows, looked young, apprehensive, in need of protection. I'd never seen that on a man's face before. Something rose in me like a wave.

"It's all right," I said, as though to a child, and pulled his head down to my breast. His hair smelled faintly of the American cigarettes he smoked. "I won't be disappointed. I'll help you." And a sudden happiness filled me.

---

6 *shapla:* A type of water lily.

That night I dreamed I was at the store. Soft American music floated in the background as I moved between shelves stocked high with brightly colored cans and elegant-necked bottles, turning their labels carefully to the front, polishing them until they shone.

Now, sitting inside this metal shell that is hurtling through emptiness, I try to remember other things about my husband: how gentle his hands had been, and his lips, surprisingly soft, like a woman's. How I've longed for them through those drawn-out nights while I waited for my visa to arrive. He will be standing at the customs gate, and when I reach him, he will lower his face to mine. We will kiss in front of everyone, not caring, like Americans, then pull back, look each other in the eye, and smile.

But suddenly, as I am thinking this, I realize I cannot recall Somesh's face. I try and try until my head hurts, but I can only visualize the black air swirling outside the plane, too thin for breathing. My own breath grows ragged with panic as I think of it and my mouth fills with sour fluid the way it does just before I throw up.

I grope for something to hold on to, something beautiful and talismanic from my old life. And then I remember. Somewhere down under me, low in the belly of the plane, inside my new brown case which is stacked in the dark with a hundred others, are my saris. Thick Kanjeepuram silks in solid purples and golden yellows, the thin hand-woven cottons of the Bengal countryside, green as a young banana plant, gray as the women's lake on a monsoon morning. Already I can feel my shoulders loosening up, my breath steadying. My wedding Benarasi,[7] flame-orange, with a wide *palloo*[8] of gold-embroidered dancing peacocks. Fold upon fold of Dhakais[9] so fine they can be pulled through a ring. Into each fold my mother has tucked a small sachet of sandalwood powder to protect the saris from the unknown insects of America. Little silk sachets, made from *her* old saris—I can smell their calm fragrance as I watch the American air hostess wheeling the dinner cart toward my seat. It is the smell of my mother's hands.

I know then that everything will be all right. And when the air hostess bends her curly golden head to ask me what I would like to eat, I understand every word in spite of her strange accent and answer her without stumbling even once over the unfamiliar English phrases.

Late at night I stand in front of our bedroom mirror trying on the clothes Somesh has bought for me and smuggled in past his parents. I model each one for him, walking back and forth, clasping my hands behind my head, lips pouted, left hip thrust out just like the models on TV, while he whispers applause. I'm breathless with suppressed laughter (Father and Mother Sen must not hear us) and my cheeks are hot with the delicious excitement of conspiracy. We've stuffed a towel at the bottom of the door so no light will shine through.

---

7 **Benarasi:** A sari made in the city of that name, known for its silk saris.
8 *palloo:* End of the sari that goes over the shoulder.
9 **Dhakais:** Fine muslin or silk cloth made in Dhaka, Bangladesh.

I'm wearing a pair of jeans now, marveling at the curves of my hips and thighs, which have always been hidden under the flowing lines of my saris. I love the color, the same pale blue as the *nayantara*[10] flowers that grow in my parents' garden. The solid comforting weight. The jeans come with a close-fitting T-shirt which outlines my breasts.

I scold Somesh to hide my embarrassed pleasure. He shouldn't have been so extravagant. We can't afford it. He just smiles.

The T-shirt is sunrise-orange—the color, I decide, of joy, of my new American life. Across its middle, in large black letters, is written *Great America.* I was sure the letters referred to the country, but Somesh told me it is the name of an amusement park, a place where people go to have fun. I think it a wonderful concept, novel. Above the letters is the picture of a train. Only it's not a train, Somesh tells me, it's a roller coaster. He tries to explain how it moves, the insane speed, the dizzy ground falling away, then gives up. "I'll take you there, Mita sweetheart," he says, "as soon as we move into our own place."

That's our dream (mine more than his, I suspect)—moving out of this two-room apartment where it seems to me if we all breathed in at once, there would be no air left. Where I must cover my head with the edge of my Japan nylon sari (my expensive Indian ones are to be saved for special occasions—trips to the temple, Bengali New Year) and serve tea to the old women that come to visit Mother Sen, where like a good Indian wife I must never address my husband by his name. Where even in our bed we kiss guiltily, uneasily, listening for the giveaway creak of springs. Sometimes I laugh to myself, thinking how ironic it is that after all my fears about America, my life has turned out to be no different from Deepali's or Radha's. But at other times I feel caught in a world where everything is frozen in place, like a scene inside a glass paperweight. It is a world so small that if I were to stretch out my arms, I would touch its cold unyielding edges. I stand inside this glass world, watching helplessly as America rushes by, wanting to scream. Then I'm ashamed. Mita, I tell myself, you're growing westernized. Back home you'd never have felt this way.

We must be patient. I know that. Tactful, loving children. That is the Indian way. "I'm their life," Somesh tells me as we lie beside each other, lazy from lovemaking. He's not boasting, merely stating a fact. "They've always been there when I needed them. I could never abandon them at some old people's home." For a moment I feel rage. You're constantly thinking of them, I want to scream. But what about me? Then I remember my own parents, Mother's hands cool on my sweat-drenched body through nights of fever, Father teaching me to read, his finger moving along the crisp black angles of the alphabet, transforming them magically into things I knew, water, dog, mango tree. I beat back my unreasonable desire and nod agreement.

Somesh has bought me a cream blouse with a long brown skirt. They match beautifully, like the inside and outside of an almond. "For when you begin working," he says. But first he wants me to start college. Get a degree, perhaps in teaching. I

---

10 *nayantara:* A flower with small petals.

picture myself in front of a classroom of girls with blond pigtails and blue uniforms, like a scene out of an English movie I saw long ago in Calcutta. They raise their hands respectfully when I ask a question. "Do you really think I can?" I ask. "Of course," he replies.

I am gratified he has such confidence in me. But I have another plan, a secret that I will divulge to him once we move. What I really want is to work in the store. I want to stand behind the counter in the cream-and-brown skirt set (color of earth, color of seeds) and ring up purchases. The register drawer will glide open. Confident, I will count out green dollars and silver quarters. Gleaming copper pennies. I will dust the jars of gilt-wrapped chocolates on the counter. Will straighten, on the far wall, posters of smiling young men raising their beer mugs to toast scantily clad redheads with huge spiky eyelashes. (I have never visited the store—my in-laws don't consider it proper for a wife—but of course I know exactly what it looks like.) I will charm the customers with my smile, so that they will return again and again just to hear me telling them to have a nice day.

Meanwhile, I will the store to make money for us. Quickly. Because when we move, we'll be paying for two households. But so far it hasn't worked. They're running at a loss, Somesh tells me. They had to let the hired help go. This means most nights Somesh has to take the graveyard shift (that horrible word, like a cold hand up my spine) because his partner refuses to.

"The bastard!" Somesh spat out once. "Just because he put in more money he thinks he can order me around. I'll show him!" I was frightened by the vicious twist of his mouth. Somehow I'd never imagined that he could be angry.

Often Somesh leaves as soon as he has dinner and doesn't get back till after I've made morning tea for Father and Mother Sen. I lie mostly awake those nights, picturing masked intruders crouching in the shadowed back of the store, like I've seen on the police shows that Father Sen sometimes watches. But Somesh insists there's nothing to worry about, they have bars on the windows and a burglar alarm. "And remember," he says, "the extra cash will help us move out that much quicker."

I'm wearing a nightie now, my very first one. It's black and lacy, with a bit of a shine to it, and it glides over my hips to stop outrageously at mid-thigh. My mouth is an O of surprise in the mirror, my legs long and pale and sleek from the hair remover I asked Somesh to buy me last week. The legs of a movie star. Somesh laughs at the look on my face, then says, "You're beautiful." His voice starts a flutter low in my belly.

"Do you really think so," I ask, mostly because I want to hear him say it again. No one has called me beautiful before. My father would have thought it inappropriate, my mother that it would make me vain.

Somesh draws me close. "Very beautiful," he whispers. "The most beautiful woman in the whole world." His eyes are not joking as they usually are. I want to turn off the light, but "Please," he says, "I want to keep seeing your face." His fingers are taking the pins from my hair, undoing my braids. The escaped strands fall on his face like dark rain. We have already decided where we will hide my new American clothes—the jeans and T-shirt camouflaged on a hanger among Somesh's pants, the skirt set and nightie at the bottom of my suitcase, a sandalwood sachet tucked between them, waiting.

I stand in the middle of our empty bedroom, my hair still wet from the purification bath, my back to the stripped bed I can't bear to look at. I hold in my hands the plain white sari I'm supposed to wear. I must hurry. Any minute now there'll be a knock at the door. They are afraid to leave me alone too long, afraid I might do something to myself.

The sari, a thick voile that will bunch around the waist when worn, is borrowed. White. Widow's color, color of endings. I try to tuck it into the top of the petticoat, but my fingers are numb, disobedient. It spills through them and there are waves and waves of white around my feet. I kick out in sudden rage, but the sari is too soft, it gives too easily. I grab up an edge, clamp down with my teeth and pull, feeling a fierce, bitter satisfaction when I hear it rip.

There's a cut, still stinging, on the side of my right arm, halfway to the elbow. It is from the bangle-breaking ceremony. Old Mrs. Ghosh performed the ritual, since she's a widow, too. She took my hands in hers and brought them down hard on the bedpost, so that the glass bangles I was wearing shattered and multicolored shards flew out in every direction. Some landed on the body that was on the bed, covered with a sheet. I can't call it Somesh. He was gone already. She took an edge of the sheet and rubbed the red marriage mark off my forehead. She was crying. All the women in the room were crying except me. I watched them as though from the far end of a tunnel. Their flared nostrils, their red-veined eyes, the runnels of tears, salt-corrosive, down their cheeks.

It happened last night. He was at the store. "It isn't too bad," he would tell me on the days when he was in a good mood. "Not too many customers. I can put up my feet and watch MTV all night. I can sing along with Michael Jackson as loud as I want." He had a good voice, Somesh. Sometimes he would sing softly at night, lying in bed, holding me. Hindi songs of love, *Mere Sapnon Ki Rani,* queen of my dreams. (He would not sing American songs at home out of respect for his parents, who thought they were decadent.) I would feel his warm breath on my hair as I fell asleep.

Someone came into the store last night. He took all the money, even the little rolls of pennies I had helped Somesh make up. Before he left he emptied the bullets from his gun into my husband's chest.

"Only thing is," Somesh would say about the night shifts, "I really miss you. I sit there and think of you asleep in bed. Do you know that when you sleep you make your hands into fists, like a baby? When we move out, will you come along some nights to keep me company?"

My in-laws are good people, kind. They made sure the body was covered before they let me into the room. When someone asked if my hair should be cut off, as they sometimes do with widows back home, they said no. They said I could stay at the apartment with Mrs. Ghosh if I didn't want to go to the crematorium. They asked

Dr. Das to give me something to calm me down when I couldn't stop shivering. They didn't say, even once, as people would surely have in the village, that it was my bad luck that brought death to their son so soon after his marriage.

They will probably go back to India now. There's nothing here for them anymore. They will want me to go with them. You're like our daughter, they will say. Your home is with us, for as long as you want. For the rest of your life. *The rest of my life.* I can't think about that yet. It makes me dizzy. Fragments are flying about my head, multicolored and piercing sharp like bits of bangle glass.

I want you to go to college. Choose a career. I stand in front of a classroom of smiling children who love me in my cream-and-brown American dress. A faceless parade straggles across my eyelids: all those customers at the store that I will never meet. The lace nightie, fragrant with sandalwood, waiting in its blackness inside my suitcase. The savings book where we have $3605.33. *Four thousand and we can move out, maybe next month.* The name of the panty hose I'd asked him to buy me for my birthday: sheer golden-beige. His lips, unexpectedly soft, woman-smooth. Elegant-necked wine bottles swept off shelves, shattering on the floor.

I know Somesh would not have tried to stop the gunman. I can picture his silhouette against the lighted Dewar's sign, hands raised. He is trying to find the right expression to put on his face, calm, reassuring, reasonable. *OK, take the money. No, I won't call the police.* His hands tremble just a little. His eyes darken with disbelief as his fingers touch his chest and come away wet.

I yanked away the cover. I had to see. *Great America, a place where people go to have fun.* My breath roller-coasting through my body, my unlived life gathering itself into a scream. I'd expected blood, a lot of blood, the deep red-black of it crusting his chest. But they must have cleaned him up at the hospital. He was dressed in his silk wedding *kurta.*[11] Against its warm ivory his face appeared remote, stern. The musky aroma of his aftershave lotion that someone must have sprinkled on the body. It didn't quite hide that other smell, thin, sour, metallic. The smell of death. The floor shifted under me, tilting like a wave.

I'm lying on the floor now, on the spilled white sari. I feel sleepy. Or perhaps it is some other feeling I don't have a word for. The sari is seductive-soft, drawing me into its folds.

Sometimes, bathing at the lake, I would move away from my friends, their endless chatter. I'd swim toward the middle of the water with a lazy backstroke, gazing at the sky, its enormous blueness drawing me up until I felt weightless and dizzy. Once in a while there would be a plane, a small silver needle drawn through the clouds, in and out, until it disappeared. Sometimes the thought came to me, as I floated in the middle of the lake with the sun beating down on my closed eyelids, that it would be so easy to let go, to drop into the dim brown world of mud, of water weeds fine as hair.

---

11 **kurta:** A loose-fitting shirt worn by men.

Once I almost did it. I curled my body inward, tight as a fist, and felt it start to sink. The sun grew pale and shapeless; the water, suddenly cold, licked at the insides of my ears in welcome. But in the end I couldn't.

They are knocking on the door now, calling my name. I push myself off the floor, my body almost too heavy to lift up, as when one climbs out after a long swim. I'm surprised at how vividly it comes to me, this memory I haven't called up in years: the desperate flailing of arms and legs as I fought my way upward; the press of the water on me, heavy as terror; the wild animal trapped inside my chest, clawing at my lungs. The day returning to me as searing air, the way I drew it in, in, in, as though I would never have enough of it.

That's when I know I cannot go back. I don't know yet how I'll manage, here in this new, dangerous land. I only know I must. Because all over India, at this very moment, widows in white saris are bowing their veiled heads, serving tea to in-laws. Doves with cut-off wings.

I am standing in front of the mirror now, gathering up the sari. I tuck in the ripped end so it lies next to my skin, my secret. I make myself think of the store, although it hurts. Inside the refrigerated unit, blue milk cartons neatly lined up by Somesh's hands. The exotic smell of Hills Brothers coffee brewed black and strong, the glisten of sugar-glazed donuts nestled in tissue. The neon Budweiser emblem winking on and off like a risky invitation.

I straighten my shoulders and stand taller, take a deep breath. Air fills me—the same air that traveled through Somesh's lungs a little while ago. The thought is like an unexpected, intimate gift. I tilt my chin, readying myself for the arguments of the coming weeks, the remonstrations. In the mirror a woman holds my gaze, her eyes apprehensive yet steady. She wears a blouse and skirt the color of almonds.

QUESTIONS

1. By Western standards, many of the attitudes and ideas that the narrator expresses, especially early in the story, seem old-fashioned, even antifeminist. Cite some of these details. What about them specifically seems antithetical to Western ways and values?

2. How do the narrator's ideas and values change as the story progresses? Why do they change? Do they change for the better?

3. What is the relevance of this story's title? How are clothes used in the story? Why are clothes important to the narrator and to others in the story?

4. Color symbolism is often referred to in the story: Pink, for example, is the "color of transition." Note other examples of color symbolism. How does Indian color symbolism differ from Western?

5. The narrator regards her husband's 7-Eleven store as something exotic and romantic. How does her attitude affect your reaction to her character? To her view of the United States?

6. What does Somesh's death suggest about the United States? Does his death mean that his coming to the States was a mistake? Was the narrator mistaken to come to the States with him?

7. Overall, in your view, what comment does the story make on the Indian diaspora?

Salman Rushdie

(b. 1947)

People who have never read a word of Salman Rushdie's know that the publication of his novel, *The Satanic Verses* (1988), so angered Muslim fundamentalists that the Ayatollah Khomeini of Iran proclaimed a *fatwa* or death sentence on the author, compelling him to go into hiding for several years. Faithful Muslims were admonished to kill anyone involved in the book's publication and a reward for Rushdie eventually reached $2.5 million. For his part, Rushdie was raised a "relaxed" Muslim and contends that the book should offend no one except those he calls the "thought police" of Islam.

Rushdie was born in Bombay, son of Anis Ahmed Rushdie, a businessman, and Negin Rushdie, who worked in publishing. He attended Rugby (a famous English prep school) and then graduated with honors from King's College, Cambridge, in 1968 with an MA in history. His family lived in England from 1962 to 1964, and then moved to Pakistan, where Rushdie worked for a while in television and publishing, but government censorship drove him back to London, where he continued in advertising while working on his first novels. *Grimus*, a science fiction parody, was published in 1975, but it was *Midnight's Children* (1981) that established his reputation. Always the provocateur, Rushdie attacks a variety of targets in his fiction: Hindu fundamentalists, colonialism and its legacy, politicians (including India's former prime minister, Indira Gandhi), racial and religious intolerance. Like many postmodern writers, he often plays with language and regards "truth" as more a function of power than of objective reality—hence his often highly unreliable narrators, experimental language, and fantastic story lines.

Rushdie's complicated heritage underscores the difficulty of classifying postcolonial authors. Although born in India, he has lived much of his life in England, and his seven-year exile from India occasioned by the *fatwa* reinforced his feelings of isolation and marginality. Writing in English, he acknowledges, is both a compromise and a necessity. But his use of English suggests that like India itself, he has appropriated it for his own purposes and put his own stamp on it. Some of the linguistic issues of his novels arise, usually with comic effect, in "The Courter," from Rushdie's only collection of stories, *East, West* (1994). Three of these stories are set in India, three in Europe, and three (including "The Courter") in England. Like the young narrator of the story, Rushdie would say that "I, too, have ropes around my neck, I have them to this day, pulling me this way and that, East and West, the nooses tightening, commanding, *choose, choose.*" But this is just one theme in this multilayered story, with its family politics, love stories, racism, violence, and the complexities of cross-cultural encounters.

Rushdie has pursued the complexities and dislocations of postcolonial life in other media and genres—essays, travel writing, film, and a children's book. In one way or another, most of his characters are forced to negotiate the boundaries of race, culture, and nationality, often in the face of uncomprehending others and hostile social and political climates. His fiction thus reflects not only his personal reality but the experiences of millions who have encountered his fictional world in real life.

The Courter   1994

1

Certainly-Mary was the smallest woman Mixed-Up the hall porter had come across, dwarfs excepted, a tiny sixty-year-old Indian lady with her greying hair tied behind her head in a neat bun, hitching up her redhemmed white sari in the front and negotiating the apartment block's front steps as if they were Alps. "No," he said aloud, furrowing his brow. What would be the right peaks. Ah, good, that was the name. "Ghats," he said proudly. Word from a schoolboy atlas long ago, when India felt as far away as Paradise. (Nowadays Paradise seemed even further away but India, and Hell, had come a good bit closer.) "Western Ghats, Eastern Ghats, and now Kensington Ghats," he said, giggling. "Mountains."

She stopped in front of him in the oak-panelled lobby. "But ghats in India are also stairs," she said. "Yes yes certainly. For instance in Hindu holy city of Varanasi, where the Brahmins sit taking the filgrims' money is called Dasashwamedh-ghat. Broad-broad staircase down to River Ganga. O, most certainly! Also Manikarnika-ghat. They buy fire from a house with a tiger leaping from the roof—yes certainly, a statue tiger, coloured by Technicolor, what are you thinking?—and they bring it in a box to set fire to their loved ones' bodies. Funeral fires are of sandal. Photographs not allowed; no, certainly not."

He began thinking of her as Certainly-Mary because she never said plain yes or no; always this O-yes-certainly or no-certainly-not. In the confused circumstances that had prevailed ever since his brain, his one sure thing, had let him down, he could hardly be certain of anything any more; so he was stunned by her sureness, first into nostalgia, then envy, then attraction. And attraction was a thing so long forgotten that when the churning started he thought for a long time it must be the Chinese dumplings he had brought home from the High Street carry-out.

English was hard for Certainly-Mary, and this was a part of what drew damaged old Mixed-Up towards her. The letter p was a particular problem, often turning into an f or a c; when she proceeded through the lobby with a wheeled wicker shopping basket, she would say, "Going shocking," and when, on her return, he offered to help lift the basket up the front ghats, she would answer, "Yes, fleas." As the elevator lifted her away, she called through the grille: "Oé, courter! Thank you, courter. O, yes, certainly." (In Hindi and Konkani, however, her p's knew their place.)

So: thanks to her unexpected, somehow stomach-churning magic, he was no longer porter, but courter. "Courter," he repeated to the mirror when she had gone. His breath made a little dwindling picture of the word on the glass. "Courter courter caught." Okay. People called him many things, he did not mind. But this name, this courter, this he would try to be.

2

For years now I've been meaning to write down the story of Certainly-Mary, our ayah,[1] the woman who did as much as my mother to raise my sisters and me, and her great adventure with her 'courter' in London, where we all lived for a time in the early Sixties in a block called Waverley House; but what with one thing and another I never got round to it.

Then recently I heard from Certainly-Mary after a longish silence. She wrote to say that she was ninety-one, had had a serious operation, and would I kindly send her some money, because she was embarrassed that her niece, with whom she was now living in the Kurla district of Bombay, was so badly out of pocket.

I sent the money, and soon afterwards received a pleasant letter from the niece, Stella, written in the same hand as the letter from "Aya"—as we had always called Mary, palindromically dropping the "h." Aya had been so touched, the niece wrote, that I remembered her after all these years. "I have been hearing the stories about you folks all my life," the letter went on, "and I think of you a little bit as family. Maybe you recall my mother, Mary's sister. She unfortunately passed on. Now it is I who write Mary's letters for her. We all wish you the best."

This message from an intimate stranger reached out to me in my enforced exile from the beloved country of my birth and moved me, stirring things that had been buried very deep. Of course it also made me feel guilty about having done so little for Mary over the years. For whatever reason, it has become more important than ever to set down the story I've been carrying around unwritten for so long, the story of Aya and the gentle man whom she renamed—with unintentional but prophetic

---

1 **ayah**: Aunt.

overtones of romance—"the courter." I see now that it is not just their story, but ours, mine, as well.

3

His real name was Mecir: you were supposed to say Mishirsh because it had invisible accents on it in some Iron Curtain language in which the accents had to be invisible, my sister Durré said solemnly, in case somebody spied on them or rubbed them out or something. His first name also began with an m but it was so full of what we called Communist consonants, all those z's and c's and w's walled up together without vowels to give them breathing space, that I never even tried to learn it.

At first we thought of nicknaming him after a mischievous little comic-book character, Mr Mxyztplk from the Fifth Dimension, who looked a bit like Elmer Fudd and used to make Superman's life hell until ole Supe could trick him into saying his name backwards, Klptzyxm, whereupon he disappeared back into the Fifth Dimension; but because we weren't too sure how to say Mxyztplk (not to mention Klptzyxm) we dropped that idea. "We'll just call you Mixed-Up," I told him in the end, to simplify life. "Mishter Mikshed-Up Mishirsh." I was fifteen then and bursting with unemployed cock and it meant I could say things like that right into people's faces, even people less accommodating than Mr Mecir with his stroke.

What I remember most vividly are his pink rubber washing-up[2] gloves, which he seemed never to remove, at least not until he came calling for Certainly-Mary . . . At any rate, when I insulted him, with my sisters Durré and Muneeza cackling in the lift, Mecir just grinned an empty good-natured grin, nodded, 'You call me what you like, okay,' and went back to buffing and polishing the brasswork. There was no point teasing him if he was going to be like that, so I got into the lift and all the way to the fourth floor we sang *I Can't Stop Loving You* at the top of our best Ray Charles voices, which were pretty awful. But we were wearing our dark glasses, so it didn't matter.

4

It was the summer of 1962, and school was out. My baby sister Scheherazade was just one year old. Durré was a beehived fourteen; Muneeza was ten, and already quite a handful. The three of us—or rather Durré and me, with Muneeza trying desperately and unsuccessfully to be included in our gang—would stand over Scheherazade's cot and sing to her. 'No nursery rhymes,' Durré had decreed, and so there were none, for though she was a year my junior she was a natural leader. The infant Scheherazade's lullabies were our cover versions of recent hits by Chubby Checker, Neil Sedaka, Elvis and Pat Boone.

---

2 **washing-up:** Dish-washing gloves, i.e., rubber gloves.

"Why don't you come home, Speedy Gonzales?" we bellowed in sweet dishar-mony: but most of all, and with actions, we would jump down, turn around and pick a bale of cotton. We would have jumped down, turned around and picked those bales all day except that the Maharaja of B—— in the flat below complained, and Aya Mary came in to plead with us to be quiet.

"Look, see, it's Jumble-Aya who's fallen for Mixed-Up," Durré shouted, and Mary blushed a truly immense blush. So naturally we segued right into a quick me-oh-my-oh; son of a gun, we had big fun. But then the baby began to yell, my father came in with his head down bull-fashion and steaming from both ears, and we needed all the good luck charms we could find.

I had been at boarding school in England for a year or so when Abba took the decision to bring the family over. Like all his decisions, it was neither explained to nor discussed with anyone, not even my mother. When they first arrived he rented two adjacent flats in a seedy Bayswater mansion block called Graham Court, which lurked furtively in a nothing street that crawled along the side of the ABC Queensway cinema towards the Porchester Baths. He commandeered one of these flats for himself and put my mother, three sisters and Aya in the other; also, on school holidays, me. England, where liquor was freely available, did little for my fa-ther's *bonhomie,*[3] so in a way it was a relief to have a flat to ourselves.

Most nights he emptied a bottle of Johnnie Walker Red Label and a soda-siphon.[4] My mother did not dare to go across to "his place" in the evenings. She said: "He makes faces at me."

Aya Mary took Abba his dinner and answered all his calls (if he wanted any-thing, he would phone us up and ask for it). I am not sure why Mary was spared his drunken rages. She said it was because she was nine years his senior, so she could tell him to show due respect.

After a few months, however, my father leased a three-bedroom fourth-floor apartment with a fancy address. This was Waverley House in Kensington Court, W8. Among its other residents were not one but two Indian Maharajas, the sporting Prince P—— as well as the old B—— who has already been mentioned. Now we were jammed in together, my parents and Baby Scare-zade (as her siblings had affec-tionately begun to call her) in the master bedroom, the three of us in a much smaller room, and Mary, I regret to admit, on a straw mat laid on the fitted carpet in the hall. The third bedroom became my father's office, where he made phone-calls and kept his *Encyclopaedia Britannica,* his *Reader's Digests,* and (under lock and key) the television cabinet. We entered it at our peril. It was the Minotaur's[5] lair.

---

3 **bonhomie:** Good heartedness.
4 **soda-siphon:** A device for making and dispensing carbonated water.
5 **Minotaur:** The half-man, half-bull monster of Greek mythology.

One morning he was persuaded to drop in at the corner pharmacy and pick up some supplies for the baby. When he returned there was a hurt, schoolboyish look on his face that I had never seen before, and he was pressing his hand against his cheek.

"She hit me," he said plaintively.

"Hai! Allah-tobah! Darling!" cried my mother, fussing. "Who hit you? Are you injured? Show me, let me see."

"I did nothing," he said, standing there in the hall with the pharmacy bag in his other hand and a face as pink as Mecir's rubber gloves. "I just went in with your list. The girl seemed very helpful. I asked for baby compound, Johnson's powder, teething jelly, and she brought them out. Then I asked did she have any nipples, and she slapped my face."

My mother was appalled. "Just for that?" And Certainly-Mary backed her up. "What is this nonsense?" she wanted to know. "I have been in that chemist's shock, and they have flenty nickels, different sizes, all on view."

Durré and Muneeza could not contain themselves. They were rolling round on the floor, laughing and kicking their legs in the air.

"You both shut your face at once," my mother ordered. "A madwoman has hit your father. Where is the comedy?"

"I don't believe it," Durré gasped. "You just went up to that girl and said," and here she fell apart again, stamping her feet and holding her stomach, " 'have you got any nipples?' "

My father grew thunderous, empurpled. Durré controlled herself. "But Abba," she said, at length, "here they call them teats."

Now my mother's and Mary's hands flew to their mouths, and even my father looked shocked. "But how shameless!" my mother said. "The same word as for what's on your bosoms?" She coloured, and stuck out her tongue for shame.

"These English," sighed Certainly-Mary. "But aren't they the limit? Certainly-yes; they are."

I remember this story with delight, because it was the only time I ever saw my father so discomfited, and the incident became legendary and the girl in the pharmacy was installed as the object of our great veneration. (Durré and I went in there just to take a look at her—she was a plain, short girl of about seventeen, with large, unavoidable breasts—but she caught us whispering and glared so fiercely that we fled.) And also because in the general hilarity I was able to conceal the shaming truth that I, who had been in England for so long, would have made the same mistake as Abba did.

It wasn't just Certainly-Mary and my parents who had trouble with the English language. My schoolfellows tittered when in my Bombay way I said "brought-up" for upbringing (as in "where was your brought-up?") and "thrice" for three times and "quarter-plate" for side-plate and "macaroni" for pasta in general. As for learning the difference between nipples and teats, I really hadn't had any opportunities to increase my word power in that area at all.

5

So I was a little jealous of Certainly-Mary when Mixed-Up came to call. He rang our bell, his body quivering with deference in an old suit growth too loose, the trousers tightly gathered by a belt; he had taken off his rubber gloves and there were roses in his hand. My father opened the door and gave him a withering look. Being a snob, Abba was not pleased that the flat lacked a separate service entrance, so that even a porter had to be treated as a member of the same universe as himself.

"Mary," Mixed-Up managed, licking his lips and pushing back his floppy white hair. "I, to see Miss Mary, come, am."

"Wait on," Abba said, and shut the door in his face.

Certainly-Mary spent all her afternoons off with old Mixed-Up from then on, even though that first date was not a complete success. He took her "up West"[6] to show her the visitors' London she had never seen, but at the top of an up escalator at Piccadilly Circus, while Mecir was painfully enunciating the words on the posters she couldn't read—*Unzip a banana,* and *Idris when I's dri*—she got her sari stuck in the jaws of the machine, and as the escalator pulled at the garment it began to unwind. She was forced to spin round and round like a top, and screamed at the top of her voice, "O BAAP! BAAPU–RÉ! BAAP–RÉ–BAAP–RÉ–BAAP!" It was Mixed-Up who saved her by pushing the emergency stop button before the sari was completely unwound and she was exposed in her petticoat for all the world to see.

"O, courter!" she wept on his shoulder. "O, no more escaleater, courter, nevermore, surely not!"

My own amorous longings were aimed at Durré's best friend, a Polish girl called Rozalia, who had a holiday job at Faiman's shoe shop on Oxford Street. I pursued her pathetically throughout the holidays and, on and off, for the next two years. She would let me have lunch with her sometimes and buy her a Coke and a sandwich, and once she came with me to stand on the terraces at White Hart Lane to watch Jimmy Greaves's first game for the Spurs.[7] "Come on you whoi-oites," we both shouted dutifully. "Come on you *Lily-whoites.*" After that she even invited me into the back room at Faiman's, where she kissed me twice and let me touch her breast, but that was as far as I got.

And then there was my sort-of-cousin Chandni, whose mother's sister had married my mother's brother, though they had since split up. Chandni was eighteen months older than me, and so sexy it made you sick. She was training to be an Indian classical dancer, Odissi as well as Natyam,[8] but in the meantime she dressed in tight black jeans and a clinging black polo-neck jumper and took me, now and then, to

6 **up West:** London's theater and restaurant district.
7 **Spurs:** Tottenham Hot Spurs, one of London's professional soccer teams.
8 **Odissi . . . Natyam:** Forms of Indian classical dance.

hang out at Bunjie's, where she knew most of the folk-music crowd that frequented the place, and where she answered to the name of Moonlight, which is what *chandni* means. I chain-smoked with the folkies and then went to the toilet to throw up.

Chandni was the stuff of obsessions. She was a teenage dream, the Moon River come to Earth like the Goddess Ganga,[9] dolled up in slinky black. But for her I was just the young greenhorn cousin to whom she was being nice because he hadn't learned his way around.

She-E-rry, won't you come out tonight? yodelled the Four Seasons. I knew exactly how they felt. *Come, come, come out toni-yi-yight.* And while you're at it, love me do.

6

They went for walks in Kensington Gardens. "Pan," Mixed-Up said, pointing at a statue. "Los' boy.[10] Nev' grew up." They went to Barkers and Pontings and Derry & Toms and picked out furniture and curtains for imaginary homes. They cruised supermarkets and chose little delicacies to eat. In Mecir's cramped lounge they sipped what he called 'chimpanzee tea' and toasted crumpets in front of an electric bar fire.

Thanks to Mixed-Up, Mary was at last able to watch television. She liked children's programmes best, especially *The Flintstones.* Once, giggling at her daring, Mary confided to Mixed-Up that Fred and Wilma reminded her of her Sahib and Begum Sahiba upstairs; at which the courter, matching her audaciousness, pointed first at Certainly-Mary and then at himself, grinned a wide gappy smile and said, "Rubble."

Later, on the news, a vulpine Englishman with a thin moustache and mad eyes declaimed a warning about immigrants, and Certainly-Mary flapped her hand at the set: "Khali-pili bom marta," she objected, and then, for her host's benefit translated: "For nothing he is shouting shouting. Bad life! Switch it off."

They were often interrupted by the Maharajas of B—— and P——, who came downstairs to escape their wives and ring other women from the call-box in the porter's room.

"Oh, baby, forget that guy," said sporty Prince P——, who seemed to spend all his days in tennis whites, and whose plump gold Rolex was almost lost in the thick hair on his arm. "I'll show you a better time than him, baby; step into my world."

The Maharaja of B—— was older, uglier, more matter-of-fact. "Yes, bring all appliances. Room is booked in name of Mr Douglas Home. Six forty-five to seven fifteen. You have printed rate card? Please. Also a two-foot ruler, must be wooden. Frilly apron, plus."

9 **Goddess Ganga:** Goddess of the sacred river Ganges.
10 **Los' boy:** Statues depicting the Lost Boys from *Peter Pan*, who in the story remain boys forever.

This is what has lasted in my memory of Waverley House, this seething mass of bad marriages, booze, philanderers and unfulfilled young lusts; of the Maharaja of P—— roaring away towards London's casinoland every night, in a red sports car with fitted blondes, and of the Maharaja of B—— skulking off to Kensington High Street wearing dark glasses in the dark, and a coat with the collar turned up even though it was high summer; and at the heart of our little universe were Certainly-Mary and her courter, drinking chimpanzee tea and singing along with the national anthem of Bedrock.

But they were not really like Barney and Betty Rubble at all. They were formal, polite. They were . . . courtly. He courted her, and, like a coy, ringleted ingénue with a fan, she inclined her head, and entertained his suit.

7

I spent one half-term weekend in 1963 at the home in Beccles, Suffolk of Field Marshal Sir Charles Lutwidge-Dodgson, an old India hand and a family friend who was supporting my application for British citizenship. "The Dodo," as he was known, invited me down by myself, saying he wanted to get to know me better.

He was a huge man whose skin had started hanging too loosely on his face, a giant living in a tiny thatched cottage and forever bumping his head. No wonder he was irascible at times; he was in Hell, a Gulliver trapped in that rose-garden Lilliput of croquet hoops, church bells, sepia photographs and old battle-trumpets.

The weekend was fitful and awkward until the Dodo asked if I played chess. Slightly awestruck at the prospect of playing a Field Marshal, I nodded; and ninety minutes later, to my amazement, won the game.

I went into the kitchen, strutting somewhat, planning to boast a little to the old soldier's long-time house-keeper, Mrs Liddell. But as soon as I entered she said: "Don't tell me. You never went and won?"

"Yes," I said, affecting nonchalance. "As a matter of fact, yes, I did."

"Gawd," said Mrs Liddell. "Now there'll be hell to pay. You go back in there and ask him for another game, and this time make sure you lose."

I did as I was told, but was never invited to Beccles again.

Still, the defeat of the Dodo gave me new confidence at the chessboard, so when I returned to Waverley House after finishing my O levels,[11] and was at once invited to play a game by Mixed-Up (Mary had told him about my victory in the Battle of Beccles with great pride and some hyperbole), I said: "Sure, I don't mind." How long could it take to thrash the old duffer, after all?

There followed a massacre royal. Mixed-Up did not just beat me; he had me for breakfast, over easy. I couldn't believe it—the canny opening, the fluency of

---

11 **O levels:** Exams at the end of high school. A-levels are university qualifying exams; O levels (ordinary levels) are lesser qualifications.

his combination play, the force of his attacks, my own impossibly cramped, strangled positions—and asked for a second game. This time he tucked into me even more heartily. I sat broken in my chair at the end, close to tears. *Big girls don't cry,* I reminded myself, but the song went on playing in my head: *That's just an alibi.*

"Who are you?" I demanded, humiliation weighing down every syllable. "The devil in disguise?"

Mixed-Up gave his big, silly grin. "Grand Master," he said. "Long time. Before head."

"You're a Grand Master," I repeated, still in a daze. Then in a moment of horror I remembered that I had seen the name Mecir in books of classic games. "Nimzo-Indian," I said aloud. He beamed and nodded furiously.

"That Mecir?" I asked wonderingly.

"That," he said. There was saliva dribbling out of a corner of his sloppy old mouth. This ruined old man was in the books. He was in the books. And even with his mind turned to rubble he could still wipe the floor with me.

"Now play lady," he grinned. I didn't get it. "Mary lady," he said. "Yes yes certainly." She was pouring tea, waiting for my answer. "Aya, you can't play," I said, bewildered. "Learning, baba," she said. "What is it, na? Only a game."

And then she, too, beat me senseless, and with the black pieces, at that. It was not the greatest day of my life.

8

From *100 Most Instructive Chess Games* by Robert Reshevsky, 1961:

> *M. Mecir—M. Najdorf*
> *Dallas 1950, Nimzo-Indian Defense*
> The attack of a tactician can be troublesome to meet—that of a strategist even more so. Whereas the tactician's threats may be unmistakable, the strategist confuses the issue by keeping things in abeyance. He threatens to threaten!
>
> Take this game for instance: Mecir posts a Knight at Q6 to get a grip on the center. Then he establishes a passed Pawn on one wing to occupy his opponent on the Queen side. Finally he stirs up the position on the Kingside. What does the poor bewildered opponent do? How can he defend everything at once? Where will the blow fall?
>
> Watch Mecir keep Najdorf on the run, as he shifts the attack from side to side!

Chess had become their private language. Old Mixed-Up, lost as he was for words, retained, on the chessboard, much of the articulacy and subtlety which had vanished from his speech. As Certainly-Mary gained in skill—and she had learned with astonishing speed, I thought bitterly, for someone who couldn't read or write or pronounce the letter p—she was better able to understand, and respond to, the wit of the reduced maestro with whom she had so unexpectedly forged a bond.

He taught her with great patience, showing-not-telling, repeating openings and combinations and endgame techniques over and over until she began to see the meaning in the patterns. When they played, he handicapped himself, he told her her best moves and demonstrated their consequences, drawing her, step by step, into the infinite possibilities of the game.

Such was their courtship. "It is like an adventure, baba," Mary once tried to explain to me. "It is like going with him to his country, you know? What a place, baap-ré! Beautiful and dangerous and funny and full of fuzzles. For me it is a big-big discovery. What to tell you? I go for the game. It is a wonder."

I understood, then, how far things had gone between them. Certainly-Mary had never married, and had made it clear to old Mixed-Up that it was too late to start any of that monkey business at her age. The courter was a widower, and had grown-up children somewhere, lost long ago behind the ever-higher walls of Eastern Europe. But in the game of chess they had found a form of flirtation, an endless renewal that precluded the possibility of boredom, a courtly wonderland of the ageing heart.

What would the Dodo have made of it all? No doubt it would have scandalised him to see chess, chess of all games, the great formalisation of war, transformed into an art of love.

As for me: my defeats by Certainly-Mary and her courter ushered in further humiliations. Durré and Muneeza went down with the mumps, and so, finally, in spite of my mother's efforts to segregate us, did I. I lay terrified in bed while the doctor warned me not to stand up and move around if I could possibly help it. "If you do," he said, "your parents won't need to punish you. You will have punished yourself quite enough."

I spent the following few weeks tormented day and night by visions of grotesquely swollen testicles and a subsequent life of limp impotence—finished before I'd even started, it wasn't fair!—which were made much worse by my sisters' quick recovery and incessant gibes. But in the end I was lucky; the illness didn't spread to the deep South. "Think how happy your hundred and one girlfriends will be, bhai," sneered Durré, who knew all about my continued failures in the Rozalia and Chandni departments.

On the radio, people were always singing about the joys of being sixteen years old. I wondered where they were, all those boys and girls of my age having the time of their lives. Were they driving around America in Studebaker convertibles? They certainly weren't in my neighbourhood. London, W8 was Sam Cooke country that summer. *Another Saturday night* . . . There might be a mop-top love-song stuck at number one, but I was down with lonely Sam in the lower depths of the charts, how-I-wishing I had someone, etc., and generally feeling in a pretty goddamn dreadful way.

9

"Baba, come quick."

It was late at night when Aya Mary shook me awake. After many urgent hisses, she managed to drag me out of sleep and pull me, pajama'ed and yawning, down the hall. On the landing outside our flat was Mixed-Up the courter, huddled up against a wall, weeping. He had a black eye and there was dried blood on his mouth.

"What happened?" I asked Mary, shocked.

"Men," wailed Mixed-Up. "Threaten. Beat."

He had been in his lounge earlier that evening when the sporting Maharaja of P—— burst in to say, "If anybody comes looking for me, okay, any tough-guy type guys, okay, I am out, okay? Oh you tea. Don't let them go upstairs, okay? Big tip, okay?"

A short time later, the old Maharaja of B—— also arrived in Mecir's lounge, looking distressed.

"Suno, listen on," said the Maharaja of B——. "You don't know where I am, samajh liya? Understood? Some low persons may inquire. You don't know. I am abroad, achha? On extended travels abroad. Do your job, porter. Handsome recompense."

Late at night two tough-guy types did indeed turn up. It seemed the hairy Prince P—— had gambling debts. "Out," Mixed-Up grinned in his sweetest way. The tough-guy types nodded, slowly. They had long hair and thick lips like Mick Jagger's. "He's a busy gent. We should of made an appointment," said the first type to the second. "Didn't I tell you we should of called?"

"You did," agreed the second type. "Got to do these things right, you said, he's royalty. And you was right, my son, I put my hand up, I was dead wrong. I put my hand up to that."

"Let's leave our card," said the first type. "Then he'll know to expect us."

"Ideal," said the second type, and smashed his fist into old Mixed-Up's mouth. "You tell him," the second type said, and struck the old man in the eye. "When he's in. You mention it."

He had locked the front door after that; but much later, well after midnight, there was a hammering. Mixed-Up called out, "Who?"

"We are close friends of the Maharaja of B——" said a voice. "No, I tell a lie. Acquaintances."

"He calls upon a lady of our acquaintance," said a second voice. "To be precise."

"It is in that connection that we crave audience," said the first voice.

"Gone," said Mecir. "Jet plane. Gone."

There was a silence. Then the second voice said, "Can't be in the jet set if you never jump on a jet, eh? Biarritz, Monte, all of that."

"Be sure and let His Highness know," said the first voice, "that we eagerly await his return."

"With regard to our mutual friend," said the second voice. "Eagerly."

* * *

What does the poor bewildered opponent do? The words from the chess book popped unbidden into my head. *How can be defend everything at once? Where will the blow fall? Watch Mecir keep Najdorf on the run, as he shifts the attack from side to side!*

Mixed-Up returned to his lounge and on this occasion, even though there had been no use of force, he began to weep. After a time he took the elevator up to the fourth floor and whispered through our letterbox to Certainly-Mary sleeping on her mat.

"I didn't want to wake Sahib," Mary said. "You know his trouble, na? And Begum Sahiba is so tired at end of the day. So now you tell, baba, what to do?"

What did she expect me to come up with? I was sixteen years old. "Mixed-Up must call the police," I unoriginally offered.

"No, no, baba," said Certainly-Mary emphatically. "If the courter makes a scandal for Maharaja-log, then in the end it is the courter only who will be out on his ear."

I had no other ideas. I stood before them feeling like a fool, while they both turned upon me their frightened, supplicant eyes.

"Go to sleep," I said. "We'll think about it in the morning." *The first pair of thugs were tacticians,* I was thinking. *They were troublesome to meet. But the second pair were scarier; they were strategists. They threatened to threaten.*

Nothing happened in the morning, and the sky was clear. It was almost impossible to believe in fists, and menacing voices at the door. During the course of the day both Maharajas visited the porter's lounge and stuck five-pound notes in Mixed-Up's waistcoat pocket. "Held the fort, good man," said Prince P——, and the Maharaja of B—— echoed those sentiments: "Spot on. All handled now, achha? Problem over."

The three of us—Aya Mary, her courter, and me—held a council of war that afternoon and decided that no further action was necessary. The hall porter was the front line in any such situation, I argued, and the front line had held. And now the risks were past. Assurances had been given. End of story.

"End of story," repeated Certainly-Mary doubtfully, but then, seeking to reassure Mecir, she brightened. "Correct," she said. "Most certainly! All-done, finis." She slapped her hands against each other for emphasis. She asked Mixed-Up if he wanted a game of chess; but for once the courter didn't want to play.

10

After that I was distracted, for a time, from the story of Mixed-Up and Certainly-Mary by violence nearer home.

My middle sister Muneeza, now eleven, was entering her delinquent phase a little early. She was the true inheritor of my father's black rage, and when she lost control it was terrible to behold. That summer she seemed to pick fights with my father on purpose; seemed prepared, at her young age, to test her strength against his. (I intervened in her rows with Abba only once, in the kitchen. She grabbed the kitchen scissors and flung them at me. They cut me on the thigh. After that I kept my distance.)

As I witnessed their wars I felt myself coming unstuck from the idea of family itself. I looked at my screaming sister and thought how brilliantly self-destructive she was, how triumphantly she was ruining her relations with the people she needed most.

And I looked at my choleric, face-pulling father and thought about British citizenship. My existing Indian passport permitted me to travel only to a very few countries, which were carefully listed on the second right-hand page. But I might soon have a British passport and then, by hook or by crook, I would get away from him. I would not have this face-pulling in my life.

At sixteen, you still think you can escape from your father. You aren't listening to his voice speaking through your mouth, you don't see how your gestures already mirror his; you don't see him in the way you hold your body, in the way you sign your name. You don't hear his whisper in your blood.

On the day I have to tell you about, my two-year-old sister Chhoti Scheherazade, Little Scare-zade, started crying as she often did during one of our family rows. Amma and Aya Mary loaded her into her push-chair and made a rapid getaway. They pushed her to Kensington Square and then sat on the grass, turned Scheherazade loose and made philosophical remarks while she tired herself out. Finally, she fell asleep, and they made their way home in the fading light of the evening. Outside Waverley House they were approached by two well-turned-out young men with Beatle haircuts and the buttoned-up, collarless jackets made popular by the band. The first of these young men asked my mother, very politely, if she might be the Maharani of B——.

"No," my mother answered, flattered.

"Oh, but you are, madam," said the second Beatle, equally politely. "For you are heading for Waverley House and that is the Maharaja's place of residence."

"No, no," my mother said, still blushing with pleasure. "We are a different Indian family."

"Quite so," the first Beatle nodded understandingly, and then, to my mother's great surprise, placed a finger alongside his nose, and winked. "Incognito, eh. Mum's the word."

"Now excuse us," my mother said, losing patience. "We are not the ladies you seek."

The second Beatle tapped a foot lightly against a wheel of the push-chair. "Your husband seeks ladies, madam, were you aware of that fact? Yes, he does. Most assiduously, may I add."

"Too assiduously," said the first Beatle, his face darkening.

"I tell you I am not the Maharani Begum," my mother said, growing suddenly alarmed. "Her business is not my business. Kindly let me pass."

The second Beatle stepped closer to her. She could feel his breath, which was minty. "One of the ladies he sought out was our ward, as you might say," he explained. "That would be the term. Under our protection, you follow. Us, therefore, being responsible for her welfare."

"Your husband," said the first Beatle, showing his teeth in a frightening way, and raising his voice one notch, "damaged the goods. Do you hear me, Queenie? He damaged the fucking goods."

"Mistaken identity, fleas," said Certainly-Mary. "Many Indian residents in Waverley House. We are decent ladies; *fleas.*"

The second Beatle had taken out something from an inside pocket. A blade caught the light. "Fucking wogs," he said. "You fucking come over here, you don't fucking know how to fucking behave. Why don't you fucking fuck off to fucking Wogistan? Fuck your fucking wog arses. Now then," he added in a quiet voice, holding up the knife, "unbutton your blouses."

Just then a loud noise emanated from the doorway of Waverley House. The two women and the two men turned to look, and out came Mixed-Up, yelling at the top of his voice and windmilling his arms like a mad old loon.

"Hullo," said the Beatle with the knife, looking amused. "Who's this, then? Oh oh fucking seven?"

Mixed-Up was trying to speak, he was in a mighty agony of effort, but all that was coming out of his mouth was raw, unshaped noise. Scheherazade woke up and joined in. The two Beatles looked displeased. But then something happened inside old Mixed-Up; something popped, and in a great rush he gabbled, "Sirs sirs no sirs these not B—— women sirs B—— women upstairs on floor three sirs Maharaja of B—— also sirs God's truth mother's grave swear."

It was the longest sentence he had spoken since the stroke that had broken his tongue long ago.

And what with his torrent and Scheherazade's squalls there were suddenly heads poking out from doorways, attention was being paid, and the two Beatles nodded gravely. "Honest mistake," the first of them said apologetically to my mother, and actually bowed from the waist. "Could happen to anyone," the knife-man added, ruefully. They turned and began to walk quickly away. As they passed Mecir, however, they paused. "I know you, though," said the knife-man. " '*Jet plane. Gone.*' " He made a short movement of the arm, and then Mixed-Up the courter was lying on the pavement with blood leaking from a wound in his stomach. "All okay now," he gasped, and passed out.

11

He was on the road to recovery by Christmas; my mother's letter to the landlords, in which she called him a "knight in shining armour," ensured that he was well looked after, and his job was kept open for him. He continued to live in his little ground-floor cubby-hole, while the hall porter's duties were carried out by shift-duty staff. "Nothing but the best for our very own hero," the landlords assured my mother in their reply.

The two Maharajas and their retinues had moved out before I came home for the Christmas holidays, so we had no further visits from the Beatles or the Rolling Stones. Certainly-Mary spent as much time as she could with Mecir; but it was the look of my old Aya that worried me more than poor Mixed-Up. She looked older, and powdery, as if she might crumble away at any moment into dust.

"We didn't want to worry you at school," my mother said. "She has been having heart trouble. Palpitations. Not all the time, but."

Mary's health problems had sobered up the whole family. Muneeza's tantrums had stopped, and even my father was making an effort. They had put up a Christmas tree in the sitting-room and decorated it with all sorts of baubles. It was so odd to see a Christmas tree at our place that I realised things must be fairly serious.

On Christmas Eve my mother suggested that Mary might like it if we all sang some carols. Amma had made song-sheets, six copies, by hand. When we did *O come, all ye faithful* I showed off by singing from memory in Latin. Everybody behaved perfectly. When Muneeza suggested that we should try *Swinging on a Star* or *I Wanna Hold Your Hand* instead of this boring stuff, she wasn't really being serious. So this is family life, I thought. This is it.

But we were only play-acting.

A few weeks earlier, at school, I'd come across an American boy, the star of the school's Rugby football team, crying in the Chapel cloisters. I asked him what the matter was and he told me that President Kennedy had been assassinated. 'I don't believe you,' I said, but I could see that it was true. The football star sobbed and sobbed. I took his hand.

"When the President dies, the nation is orphaned," he eventually said, broken-heartedly parroting a piece of cracker-barrel wisdom he'd probably heard on Voice of America.

"I know how you feel," I lied. "My father just died, too."

Mary's heart trouble turned out to be a mystery; unpredictably, it came and went. She was subjected to all sorts of tests during the next six months, but each time the doctors ended up by shaking their heads: they couldn't find anything wrong with her. Physically, she was right as rain; except that there were these periods when her heart kicked and bucked in her chest like the wild horses in *The Misfits,* the ones whose roping and tying made Marilyn Monroe so mad.

Mecir went back to work in the spring, but his experience had knocked the stuffing out of him. He was slower to smile, duller of eye, more inward. Mary, too, had turned in upon herself. They still met for tea, crumpets and *The Flintstones,* but something was no longer quite right.

At the beginning of the summer Mary made an announcement.

"I know what is wrong with me," she told my parents, out of the blue. "I need to go home."

"But, Aya," my mother argued, "homesickness is not a real disease."

"God knows for what-all we came over to this country," Mary said. "But I can no longer stay. No. Certainly not." Her determination was absolute.

So it was England that was breaking her heart, breaking it by not being India. London was killing her, by not being Bombay. And Mixed-Up? I wondered. Was the courter killing her, too, because he was no longer himself? Or was it that her heart, roped by two different loves, was being pulled both East and West, whinnying and rearing, like those movie horses being yanked this way by Clark Gable and that way by Montgomery Clift, and she knew that to live she would have to choose?

"I must go," said Certainly-Mary. "Yes, certainly. *Bas.* Enough."

That summer, the summer of '64, I turned seventeen. Chandni went back to India. Durré's Polish friend Rozalia informed me over a sandwich in Oxford Street that she was getting engaged to a "real man," so I could forget about seeing her again, because this Zbigniew was the jealous type. Roy Orbison sang *It's Over* in my ears as I walked away to the Tube, but the truth was that nothing had really begun.

Certainly-Mary left us in mid-July. My father bought her a one-way ticket to Bombay, and that last morning was heavy with the pain of ending. When we took her bags down to the car, Mecir the hall porter was nowhere to be seen. Mary did not knock on the door of his lounge, but walked straight out through the freshly polished oak-panelled lobby, whose mirrors and brasses were sparkling brightly; she climbed into the back seat of our Ford Zodiac and sat there stiffly with her carry-on grip on her lap, staring straight ahead. I had known and loved her all my life. *Never mind your damned courter,* I wanted to shout at her, *what about me?*

As it happened, she was right about the homesickness. After her return to Bombay, she never had a day's heart trouble again; and, as the letter from her niece Stella confirmed, at ninety-one she was still going strong.

Soon after she left, my father told us he had decided to "shift location" to Pakistan. As usual, there were no discussions, no explanations, just the simple fiat. He gave up the lease on the flat in Waverley House at the end of the summer holidays, and they all went off to Karachi, while I went back to school.

I became a British citizen that year. I was one of the lucky ones, I guess, because in spite of that chess game I had the Dodo on my side. And the passport did, in many ways, set me free. It allowed me to come and go, to make choices that were not the ones my father would have wished. But I, too, have ropes around my neck, I have them to this day, pulling me this way and that, East and West, the nooses tightening, commanding, *choose, choose.*

I buck, I snort, I whinny, I rear, I kick. Ropes, I do not choose between you. Lassoes, lariats, I choose neither of you, and both. Do you hear? I refuse to choose.

A year or so after we moved out I was in the area and dropped in at Waverley House to see how the old courter was doing. Maybe, I thought, we could have a game of chess, and he could beat me to a pulp. The lobby was empty, so I knocked on the door of his little lounge. A stranger answered.

"Where's Mixed-Up?" I cried, taken by surprise. I apologised at once, embarrassed. "Mr Mecir, I meant, the porter."

"I'm the porter, sir," the man said. "I don't know anything about any mix-up."

QUESTIONS

1. People's names often become rather distorted, either on purpose or because of language difficulties. What is the significance of these name changes?

2. Is the narrator poking fun at Mary's difficulties with English? Is he laughing with her or at her?

3. What is the significance of the many references to U.S. popular culture?

4. What is the significance of chess to the story? In what way or ways does it contribute to the story's overall effects?

5. How does the language of the major characters differ from that of the London thugs? Is articulateness always a matter of speaking one's native tongue?

6. Why does the narrator compare himself to the horse in *The Misfits*?

7. What does the story suggest about the immigrant experience? About the problems of identity and nationality?

Bapsi Sidhwa

(b. 1938)

Bapsi Sidhwa was born in Karachi, Pakistan, into a Parsi family, descendants of those practicing Zoroastrianism. (This religion, which began in Iran during the first millennium B.C.E., came to India when Islam swept through the Middle East in the seventh century C.E., expelling many of Zoroaster's adherents). Sidhwa attended Kinnaird College for women in Lahore, Pakistan, and began writing at age twenty-six, inspired by an account she heard about a young girl who married a tribal clansman. After the wedding, the girl ran away, and thus became subject to an ancient code of honor that dictated she be killed. The short story Sidhwa sat down to write about this incident became her first attempt at a novel, *The Bride*. However, it was her second novel, *The Crow Eaters* (1978), which she self-published, that placed her among the very few Pakistani writers of the time to write in English. Publication of *The Bride* followed in 1984. Both novels dealt with women's issues as they manifest themselves in patriarchal Pakistan. Critics have since noted that Sidhwa's writing paved the way for the blend of magic and fantasy with history that was to become the trade-mark of subcontinental fiction in the 1980s and 1990s. Her best-known work, *Cracking India,* came out in 1991. This time the author turned her attention to the horrific events of the 1947 partition. Hailed as a notable book for that year by the *New York Times,* it was later made into the film *Earth,* directed by Deepa Mehta. Her most recent novel, *An American Brat* (1993), deals with the difficulties of coming to age as an immigrant of divided loyalties. Sara Suleri Goodyear said in her introduction to *Cracking India,* "Her work has certainly created a framework for such indebted novelists as Salman Rushdie, Anrundhati Roy and Parsi novelist Rohinton Mistry. When the postcolonial novel from the Indian subcontinent is evaluated, Bapsi Sidhwa will figure as one of its most startling progenitors."

While writing and publishing these books, Sidhwa was also lecturing and teaching in the United States. She has taught at Columbia, Brandeis, and Mt. Holyoke, and been a postcolonial teaching fellow in Southampton, England, and a Bunting fellow at Radcliffe and Harvard (1986–1987). She has received numerous awards, among them the Lila Wallace–Reader's Digest Writers' Award (1993).

Although she has lived in the United States since the 1980s, Sidhwa has remained actively engaged with her native Pakistan, serving as an advisor to Prime Minister Benazir Bhutto on women's issues and as a representative of the Punjab at the Asian Women's Conference at Alma Ata, Kazakhstan.

"Serahbai's Story" is published here for the first time, though its author hopes it will soon become part of a collection. At once humorous and touching, realistic and fantastic, this mother-daughter story reveals both the particularities of a culture and the transnational themes that color so many such relationships.

Serahbai's Story   *2004*

Serahbai suffered a stroke two years ago. She goes through phases of intense reminiscence. She is aware that her mind is reliving an old memory, yet the memory is so immediate that all the emotions that accompanied her then are with her now. Sometimes an unbearable hurt surfaces, and her poor forehead all crinkles up with her inability to cope with the rage, or guilt, or the sadness that swamps her.

When Ruby notices this, and she is not unduly rushed, she holds her mother's wasted body. Often she rubs her face against Serahbai's and strokes her chest beneath the collarbone to calm her as she listens to her mother. At such times Serahbai might unburden an old pain her mind has brutally resurrected, and they discuss the episode as if it has present currency. They structure new strategies to cope with the situation until Serahbai feels more in control of the events that had rendered her so helpless then.

And, almost as often, she preens—gloating at her wit in putting down some past rival, or her charm in vanquishing an ancient foe. At such times, like a Geisha expertly flipping open a delicately wrought fan, Serahbai audaciously unfurls the radiant spectrum of her vanished beauty. It is unbearably poignant. This 72-year-old woman, propped up with pillows, pinned by paralysis to her bed, recalling the sun-lit moments that peaked amidst the darkened hollows of her life like snow-capped mountains.

Late one December evening, when Ruby wheels her mother from the living room to her bedroom, Serahbai is in a chirpy mood. Ruby is exhausted. They've just watched *Fawlty Towers*. It has been Serahbai's favorite show ever since it suddenly popped up on Pakistan TV screens in the 1980's. Tonight they watched John Cleese stomp his wacky way through a roomful of befuddled guests in the hotel he runs with such lunatic abandon. Alternately supporting her stomach and wiping tears of mirth from her eyes, Serahbai hooted with laughter. She is not ready for bed. "I want to talk for a bit," she says when Ruby removes her headscarf and shawl. "I know I won't be able to sleep." The night-nurse has already placed her hot-water-bag in her bed and is turning down the comforter.

Ruby stands before her mother's wheelchair, her hands hanging helplessly down her sides. "Can we talk tomorrow? I'm ready to drop."

"Nonsense," says Serahbai. "Wait till you hear what I've to say; it'll refresh you, I promise! Please?" she pleads.

The sprightly gleam in her mother's eye warns Ruby. She knows from past experience that Serahbai will keep the house awake unless she is permitted to have her say. The night-nurse turns from stacking and smoothing the pillows to raise resigned eyebrows. She shrugs her trim shoulders and throws Ruby an amused glance.

Ruby capitulates. "Oh all right," she says, wearily, as if indulging a capricious child, and wraps the old shahtoos shawl back around Serahbai's legs. She sits down on her mother's bed and the nurse positions the wheelchair closer to her. The bed is raised on bricks to make it easier for them to lay her down. "So? What do we talk about?" Ruby asks as the nurse quietly leaves the room and shuts the door behind her.

Pointy chin and toothless mouth parodying the prim grave expression of her youth, Serahbai tells her daughter: "Whenever I went to the Central Bank in Nila Gumbad, it was '*pens-down*' time. You never knew that, did you?"

Ruby is puzzled. The Parsees, the tiny community she belongs to, have a tedious reputation for loyalty and hard work. This was especially so during the days of the British Raj that her mother is harking back to.

Because of their small numbers in Lahore the bank could employ only a sprinkling of Parsees in key positions. Stern exemplars of a favored community, the Parsee bankers were hardly the type to abandon their duty or their loyalty and lay down their pens. Nor were the Hindu and Sikh bankers who fled Lahore at Partition likely to; or the staff of Muslims who replaced them after 1947.

Ruby recalls childhood visits with her mother to the cavernous, neon-lit Central Bank hall, segmented like a hive by shallow mahogany paneling, with legions of brown men bent over enormous ledgers like so many drones. In summer their shirt pockets bore ink stains and were stuffed with pens and pencil stubs.

Was her mother some kind of covert and slickly packaged labor activist in her youth? Fomenting sedition in the shape of a pens-down strike among the dependable colony of bank accountants? It was fashionable in Serahbai's days to be a Marxist. But that was a preserve of intellectuals. Although Ruby has become adept at pouring her mother into different moulds to correspond with Serahbai's images of her past, she finds she cannot accommodate this image. Serahbai was intelligent, yes. At times formidably so. But there was little impulse in her towards intellectualism or Communism.

"Pens-down time?" Ruby asks, frowning over the rim of her glasses, peering suspiciously into her mother's sanguine, gimlet eye.

"Yes," says Serahbai, girlishly prim, exactly as she would have spoken at that time she refers to as her "heyday." "Jal Jeriwalla gave them the permission to . . . Pesi Cooper too, when he became Bank Manager. Whenever I walked into the Bank, the men were permitted to put down their pens!"

"But what on earth for?" Ruby asks, feigning astonishment, although by this time she's cottoned on to her mother's drift.

"So they could stop working to look at me! What else!"

And, eyes twinkling, flung-back face all lit-up in a mischievously breaking series of magical smiles and silent laughter, that ignited sparks of unruly joy in their hearts and eyes and kept attracting her children and grandchildren to Serahbai's bedside like expectant honeybees, she added, "I freshened their eyes."

"O, mumm, you're too much," says Ruby, laughing despite her earlier inclination to remain indifferent. She bends forward to nuzzle her face against her mother's headscarf. Serahbai has married her daughter's earlier contention about being "too tired" to her own contrary assertion that what she has to say will "refresh" her, and given them narrative context. That's sharper than anything Ruby could ever conjure up at such short notice.

"I told you I'd freshen you up," says Serahbai gleefully, and her conceited smile stretches her mouth until it breaks in a triumphant chortle.

Ruby kisses the top of her head. "You did," she says, "I'm so freshened I won't be able to sleep." They chat for almost an hour until, finally, Ruby calls the nurse and together they lift Serahbai into bed.

"How many boyfriends did you have, Grannums?" Perin asks. She is besotted by her grandmother.

"None. We didn't have boyfriends in my days," says Grannums firmly. "Your grandfather was my first boyfriend. Not even kissy-koty allowed before marriage." A touch of mischief lifts her tone and she adds: "But when the family went to the cinema, and it was dark, he would hold my hand."

"And after marriage? How many boyfriends did you kissy-koty with?"

Although Serahbai indulges her granddaughter brazenly, there is a limit to the familiarity she will permit. She stops short of allowing it to totally undermine her

hospitable, and less contrary. The Jariwallas are persuaded to stay to lunch and Serahbai is brought to sit at the head of the table.

Ruby believes Mr. Jariwalla was one of her mother's earliest admirers, and like most of that elite coterie, her confidant.

Mr. Jariwalla has always carried his integrity in the fixed contours of his boyish face and his cosmopolitan genes in the Chinese slant of his liquid eyes. Although his pink skin bears testimony to the Parsee claim to Aryan ancestry, his small features and hairless skin signify a Mongolian mixture. Well into his eighties by now, the retired banker still retains his trim form and straight bearing, and his precise and soft-spoken ways.

Hirabai, his plump consort, as loosely fleshed as he is tightly wrought, is his laughing-Buddha, his lucky talisman. Originally from Calcutta, she shimmied through her years in Lahore like an even-keeled boat cruising bright waters, and has arrived at the calm shore of an arthritic and liver-spotted old age without rancor. She is helped to the other end of the table by Ruby and sits there in her flame-red sari, cracking jokes and giggling like a palsied strawberry set in a Jell-O of infectious merriment. A contagion that lodged in a goatish and incurable twinkle in the apple of her spouse's adoring eye ever since the day Jal J. first met his 13 year old fiancé at their engagement ceremony in Calcutta.

"He plucked the words right off her lips . . . he granted her littlest wish," says Serahbai after they leave. "When your husband is that good to you, you don't care about anything else . . . you don't care what goes on in the rest of your life." And later that evening, when they gather round her bed, she is still in a philosophical mood. "He kept her so happy Hirabai didn't even care all that much when her only son died." Serahbai's eyes become glazed and ruminative, and she sighs. "That is how it is when your husband is devoted to you. It cushions life's blows."

"Did Grandpums make you happy?" asks Perin. "Did he pluck the words right off your lips?"

"He was deaf when I spoke," says Serahbai with equanimity. "He never heard me."

"But Grandpums was devoted to you," asserts Perin protectively, as if she was around when her grandfather was alive.

"Yes," says Serahbai. "In his own way he was devoted to me." Although her voice is confident, her eyes, diffident, shift to Ruby.

"Of course, he was devoted to her," affirms Ruby.

Ruby accompanied her mother to the Central Bank ever since she could remember. Mr. Jariwalla was Chairman of the bank. Mr. Cooper was Chairman after him.

Whether she was going to the locker to change her jewelry, or with ledgers and files on some business errand assigned to her by Keki, the trip to the bank was a formal occasion. And as befits formal occasions, it was heralded by certain rites.

Serah bolted the bedroom doors and removing the massive middle drawer from her cupboard, staggering under its wooden bulk, dumped it on one of the beds. She then pushed open the little doors of the secret chambers cunningly concealed on either side of the vacated spaces in the cupboard. When Ruby grew older she helped her mother remove the drawer and fetch the precious contents of the secret chambers.

Perched sideways on the bed Serah opened the little boxes lined with velvet to examine the diamond and emerald necklaces and earrings, the gold and ruby choker set, the colorful meena-work[2] sets, the cloth pouches so heavy with gold guineas[3] Ruby needed both hands to lift them, the heavy hand-wrought 22 carat gold chains, belts, bracelets and dangling earrings. Serah would ponder them and set aside the items she might chose to wear at forthcoming events. The gold guineas, embossed with Queen Victoria's profile, were always at hand to give as wedding, Navjote[4] and new-born baby gifts. The jewelry Serahbai decided to relinquish to the bank locker she would wrap in a silk scarf and pack into a leather handbag reserved for the occasion.

Tucked beneath her arm the bloated handbag is inadequately concealed by the scarf of Serahbai's sari as, Ruby in tow, she swishes solemnly across the dusty black-and-white squares of the bank floor. Her purposeful air and the preoccupied pucker of her lips indicates the enormity of the task she is about to accomplish—a transaction that is, at the very least, commensurate with the stature of her husband's standing.

No one was fooled, not even the handsome turbaned Pathan chowkidar[5] from the Khyber Pass who stood double barreled guard outside the entrance and militarily salaamed[6] when mother and daughter entered the building. As they put down their pens the bankers sighed: and the sighing bankers knew that whatever worldly airs she might put on, no matter what important reason she might assign her mission—whether she'd come to balance a discrepancy in her husband's ledgers or to remove jewelry, Serahbai was there to distract them from their drudgery and to refresh their eyes.

As they ogle the goddess carting gold to the bank's steely vault they hope she will exchange a few words with them on her way out. But when Serah arrives bearing ledgers, memos and files, they know their turn will surely come. Sooner or later, courting help, Chanel scented, she will spread the ponderous ledgers before them and, listing forward, follow their clever pens as they make the requisite entries, adjustments and corrections—a hair's breath from her charmingly packaged butt and bosom.

But first. Swishing across the black-and-white floor Serah heads headlong for the Chairman's door, which the salaaming chaprasi[7] opens with adroit timing. Flashing her splendid teeth in a winsome smile Serah breezes in just as Jal J., flushed of face and ears, dapper in his pin-stripe suit, courteously stands up behind his mahogany desk. He welcomes her with a glad and indulgent eye and, with

2 **meena-work:** Gold jewelry stained with blue, green, red, or purple.
3 **guineas:** British coins worth 21 shillings.
4 **Navjote:** A Zoroastrian/Parsi initiation ceremony performed just before puberty.
5 **chowkidar:** Security guard.
6 **salaamed:** Bowed.
7 **chaprasi:** An odd-job servant who performs menial tasks.

compact movements of his arms and head, graciously indicates the two chairs opposite him.

Serah, as is her wont, plants her globular rump on his desk instead. Ruby, her presence barely noted, primly parks herself on a cane-bottomed chair.

With practiced movements of her hands and shoulders Serah adjusts her sari across her chest and, leaning back on the heels of her hands, placing one svelte sari-sheathed knee over the other, swings her leg with its pretty shoe.

Swinging her shoe right under his nose she chatters away, engaging Jal J. in a discourse leavened by innuendo and repartee, and an occasional exuberant laugh that penetrates the bank corridors and echoes in its lofty halls.

"Why weren't you and Hirabai at the Lawrence gardens last evening? I missed you so much . . ." she might ask with a flirtatious glance from the corner of her eyes, and then add, "I missed both of you."

"If I knew you were coming I'd have come too." Jal J.'s caressing murmur implies a double-entendre Ruby is too young to fathom, and Serah too old not to. "I'd have—"

"Hired a band?" Serahbai interrupts, and her tart tone implies a warning: there is a line he may not cross.

"That too," murmurs the chastened banker, his pale skin lightly flushed. "But I would have certainly brought you chocolate cake."

His proprieties once again intact, smiling neatly beneath his goatish gaze, the impeccably behaved and soft-spoken banker matches his client's wit, and continues to first back with commendable cool.

"And what about now? What will you get me now?" Serah leans forward to accommodate her cleavage to Jal J.'s stealthy gaze.

"Anything . . . Anything you want."

"*Anything* I want? What will Hirabai have to say to that?"

"She will say: Give her the stars and the moon . . . Give her chicken sandwiches . . ."

"And mango juice."

Just as Ruby begins to wonder about the curious puffiness around the snug fit of Jal J.'s trousers, Mr. Jariwalla buttons up his coat and primly sits down. Ringing for the chaprasi he asks him to bring chicken sandwiches from Shezan and two bottles of mango juice for Serah and Ruby, adding: "Use your bicycle and be quick about it."

Is there an impropriety in viewing one's mother as a sex object, even if she is an ex-sex object? But that is the only way Ruby knows to view her. The mold of her mother's body and the voluptuous wallop it packed could no more be ignored than the sudden puffiness that formed behind Jal J.'s fly whenever they were alone in his office . . . or the clear split in her mother's dual nature that could express an exuberance so contrary to the reserve she displayed to her children.

Serahbai had an enormous gift for friendship, and although she produced three children, little talent for motherhood.

It is a balmy afternoon on New Year's day. Decked out in a lemony house-gown, cocooned in shawls, supported by Ruby, Serahbai is brought out to the verandah to greet visitors. Level with the lawn, the verandah is lined with stunted palms and curling chrysanthemums in clay pots. A green thicket of nasturtium leaves swells from Serahbai's feet to flow over a rising rockery. The garden is fragrant with flowers, and the scent from neighboring gardens.

Mr. and Mrs. Cooper call. Col. Manzoor and the Phailbuses from across the street call, and 4 committee members of the Parsee Anjuman bring Serahbai a pineapple cake with "Happy 1995 To Our President" written on it. More chairs are brought out and the circle spills over onto the lawn.

By the time Aunty Tamy drops by laden with Indian sweets and curried chicken, and raucously announcing her presence with her customary "Where is my Serahbai? How is my Sheroo-veroo?" it is late afternoon and they have moved indoors.

Exhausted and peevish Serahbai barely countenances her friend's hearty New Year's greetings and cheerful chatter. Aunty Tamy is not related to them, in fact she is not even a Parsee, but she is one of Serahbai's closest surviving friends. She is also the house's favorite and most faithful visitor. No one has ever seen her lose her temper. She is a few years younger than Serahbai and still a handsome woman with lazy-lidded hazel eyes, softly curving cheekbones and lips the shape of lipstick advertisements. Brown hair, streaked with gray, frames her oval face in becoming sweeps before it is coiled in a large bun at the back.

Aunty Tamy accompanies her taciturn friend as Serahbai, too tired to walk, is wheeled to her room and prepared for bed.

"Arrey wah! Look at the gorgeous gown madam's wearing," she exclaims, when the shawls are removed and the splendor of the cruell-stitch embroidery on Serahbai's housecoat is revealed. She tells Perin: "Why is your grandma sitting at home? Take her to the Bert Institute's ball!" Still frequented by Anglo-Indians, and the more westernized among the Indian Christians, the Club is no longer the posh hangout it was during the Raj. Aunty Tamy turns to Serahbai: "If you go dancing in that dress you'll be the bell of the ball."

The cords on Serahbai's neck thicken and grow rigid. She turns away her angry face.

"What's the matter with my friend?" Aunty Tamy inquires affectionately of her friend, and at the same time casts a concerned glance at the others.

"We've had visitors all day," explains Ruby. "She's exhausted, I guess."

"I don't like you," says Serahbai sternly to Aunty Tamy. "You say one thing but you mean another. You were making fun of me. You are cruel."

"Arrey Serhroo, you know I'd never make fun of you if I thought it angered you," says Aunty Tamy matching her friend's solemn demeanor.

"You think I can go dancing? You think anyone will look at me?" Serahbai's tone is scathing.

"Alley-alley," says Aunty Tamy instead of *arrey-arrey,* and leans over to embrace her friend. "I've hurt my Sehroo-veroo's feelings . . . I'm velly velly sorry."

"Don't talk to me like that," says Serahbai glaring at her friend. "Don't talk to me as if I'm a baby."

"You know I'm joking," says Aunty Tamy. "If I can't joke with my friend, who can I joke with?"

Serahbai's eyes become sly slits. She makes a sudden grab at the pashmina shawl wrapped round Aunty Tamy's shoulders and tries to snatch it away. In doing so she has gotten hold also of the silk sari beneath it. As Aunty Tamy almost topples on her friend her arms shoot out and she grabs the wheelchair just in time to prevent an injury to herself or Serahbai.

Seizing her unexpected advantage as her friend teeters inches from her face, Serahbai hisses: "Give it back to me . . . you sly-loocchi!"

Ruby and Perin rush to intervene, but regaining her balance Aunty Tamy tidies her sari with slightly trembling fingers and at the same time assists her friend unwind the shawl. Clutched triumphantly by Serahbai, the shawl lies in a heap on her lap.

"It is your shawl," says Aunty Tamy. "You gave it to me in Murree Hills years ago, remember?"

"I know I gave it to you," says Serahbai. "Do you think I've forgotten? I want it back."

"Keep it," says Aunt Tamy.

"Mum, you can't take it back," says Ruby trying to pry the shawl lose from her mother's talon-like grip. "You gave it to her."

"I can," says Serahbai," hanging onto the shawl as if her life depended on it.

"Let Grannums keep it," intercedes Perin protectively, and winks at Aunty Tamy behind Serahbai's back.

"Yes," agrees Serahbai promptly. "Your daughter has more sense than you." She adds: "If you mind so much, give the *Currenty* one of yours."

"Mumma! How can you say that," cries Ruby, almost ill with embarrassment. *Currenty* is an unpardonable and obnoxious pejorative applied to Indian Christians and Anglo Indians. "I'll bring you another shawl Aunty Tamy," she says apologetically, "You'll freeze."

"Let the whore freeze," says Serahbai.

Aunty Tamy leaves. Ruby and Perin see her to her car. It is dark outside and the mercury has dropped below freezing. Aunty Tamy has covered her head with Ruby's Kashmiri shawl and wrapped it round her throat and overcoat. "I'm sorry this happened," says Ruby. "It's these Halcyon tablets the doctor's given her. Instead of tranquilizing her they make her abusive."

"Don't worry. I don't mind," says Aunty Tamy. "My poor friend, I know how she feels; she's trapped by her sickness."

A few months after her stroke, when she was still herself and her personality had not changed so much, Serahbai had said, "I'm in a cage . . . caged like a canary." Another time she'd fretted: "My body has become my jail . . . I want to be free." Ruby had assured her the daily physiotherapy would soon restore her control over her body.

"You're so right," says Ruby gratefully. "She's trapped in her body. You understand her so well."

"We've been through a lot together," says Aunty Tamy getting into her little Suzuki, for once serious. "Shared a lot—good-times bad-times. She knows everything about me . . . and I know everything about her."

Ruby shuts the car door and as Perin moves to one side, the light from the porch ignites the wet on Aunty Tamy's cheeks. "My God, you're crying," says Ruby, wiping the tears with icy fingers. "I'm so sorry . . . She can be horrid but she doesn't mean it . . . she doesn't know what she's saying."

"Oh, that doesn't bother me," says Aunty Tamy. "My friend can say anything she wants to me. But I can't bear to see her like this . . . God should have spared my friend this . . . she was so beautiful."

Aunty Tamy reverses up the drive. She does not require glasses even at night. Perin, standing hunched in the cold, scoots inside the moment the Suzuki's out of the gates. Ruby walks slowly back. Aunty Tamy's husband died about eight months back. Uncle Ahmed was a Muslim and Aunty Tamy, although distantly related to him, was Christian. They had sidestepped the hurdles to their marriage—raised by both sets of relatives—by eloping. Uncle Ahmed belonged to an old land-owning family with deep tentacles in politics. They had not been very kind to Aunt Tamy. Aunt Tamy belonged to distinguished Brahmin Christian family that had stocked Lahore's colleges with a sturdy brood of professors. Many in her family had moved to England and some to Canada. Aunt Tamy must miss him, thought Ruby. She doesn't show it, so they think she's over it and we don't consider her feelings. Uncle Ahmed had insisted on visiting Serahbai even while he was recovering from his heart attack and his doctor had advised him to stay home and rest.

Instead of the low-keyed day of respite Ruby had hoped for, the next day starts on a disconcertingly unruly note. Early that morning Serahbai slapped her night-nurse. Had Ruby not nimbly skipped back, she would've been slapped too. After a lunch calculated to neutralize the excess of the previous day—a mishmash of chicken soup and rice followed by banana and Jell-O, Serahbai's mood switches direction and she shifts into a state of agitated dejection. She is restless. She wants to be taken out. When she's out she wants to be brought in. She wants to visit her friend Najamai. Najamai is one of the few remaining friends who still welcomes her. Najamai is out. Serahbai wishes to visit friends in Laxmi Mansions: her friends in Laxmi Mansions are dead. She wants to go to Anarkali, which throngs with jostling shoppers, and to Temple Road. "Why Temple Road?' asks Ruby surprised. "You don't know anyone on Temple Road."

"I have my reasons," says Serahbai fiercely. "Who are you to question me?"

And when, exhausted, Ruby flees to her room Serahbai's insistent cry pursues her up the stairs: "Ruby! Come here! Ruby! Ruby! Ruby!"

Ruby covers her ears with her pillows. She recalls a story. A kind youth offers to carry a feeble old man home, but when they get there the old man's grip grows supernaturally strong and he never lets go. Ruby feels like that. Serahbai's climbed on her back and she'll never be rid of her burden. Ruby wishes fervently she were back in America.

One of the more poignant dilemmas of migration is the care of the people one leaves behind. "Abandons," Ruby had thought, when her conflict between her concern for her mother and her responsibility to her family in America had made a

will see *Janoo's* Morris parked right behind your good friend Begum Jalil Ahmed's car in her house."

Begum Jalil Ahmed is Aunty Tamy. The agony of that instant, the betrayal, is etched on Serahbai's crushed face. Ruby is shocked. How can it be Aunty Tamy? Her mother's staunchest friend? She and Uncle Jalil Ahmed were among the new lot of friends—landlords, lawyers, politicians, judges—her parents socialized with when her father suddenly burgeoned into a wealthy man and required a battery of lawyers to protect his interests. He also ventured briefly into politics. Along with most of the others the Jalil Ahmeds had remained lifelong friends.

"Did you go?" Ruby asks

"She was my best friend." Serahbai emits a strange series of guttural sounds. Misled for a moment Ruby think she's laughing sardonically. She's not. She's sobbing, her mouth wide open in a way Ruby has never seen her cry.

"I'm so sorry to hear this mum. So sorry . . ." Ruby gently runs her hand over Serahbai's cheek to sooth and console her. The peculiar sobbing stops. "Did you go, mum?" she asks again.

"My legs and hands were trembling. Still, I quickly-quickly tried to put on my sari . . . I couldn't get the pleats right and I bunched the sari into the petticoat any-old-how. Ayah[8] was sleeping in your room and the phone must have awakened her. She helped me dress." Breathless with the rush of words that are pouring from her, Serahbai is panting. "It was freezing that night. I ran to the car and Ayah ran out with the coat and made me put it on. 'Should I come with you bibiji?'[9] she asked. I told her 'Stay with the children.' "

Serahbai is quiet for a stretch. Ruby remains silent—let her mother relay the experience at the pace that suits her. She wonders which ayah Serahbai is referring to. It must be that tall thin ayah with that narrow, delicate face they had when she was about seven. She was a refugee from across the border in India. One of the women who had been kidnapped and raped by the opposing religious group during the Partition riots. She had not been accepted back by her family because she had been dishonored. The ayah told her stories about giantesses with breasts as long and fat as Queens Road.

Serahbai starts speaking again and interrupts her thoughts. She appears to have come to terms with some aspects of her feelings and her narration is more orderly. Although she is calmer her words appear to well up from a cocoon of sadness that envelopes Ruby with its melancholy. "There was a thick fog that night," Serahbai says, her voice again evoking the dread ambiance of that night. "I couldn't see the sidewalks or the rain-ditches . . . I was so hyper I could have driven through a stone wall. There was no traffic. I drove fast, like a madwoman. From Queens Road, through Mozang to Temple Road. I took the turns by instinct. The gate was open—it was one of those cheap tin-sheet gates—and I could see up the drive. Either there

---

8 **Ayah:** Nanny.
9 **bibiji:** A term of affection and respect.

was less fog, or my vision suddenly became sharper. Tamy's car was parked in the porch. Your father's car was parked right behind it."

Ruby lies down alongside her mother and gingerly wrapping an arm around her slack body presses as close to her as she can without discomforting her. Whispering endearments and solace she presses her face against her mother's. Serahbai's old skin is still velvety and Ruby is loath to separate from its silk.

Serahbai's expression is surprisingly composed, but her chest is heaving and tears are sliding down both sides of her face and into her ears. Ruby props herself on an elbow to open the buttons on Serahbai's flannel nightgown. She strokes her chest beneath the collarbone and down between the sagging ruins of her breasts. She knows it will sooth her. She waits.

When Serahbai doesn't say anything Ruby asks: "Did you recognize the man's voice?"

"No," Serahbai whispers. "I'd go to the Gymkhana Club tennis courts and I'd inspect all the men playing tennis, and wonder which one it was. I'd go to the Central Bank and imagine it was one of the bank clerks. It was terrible. I'd play bridge at the Cosmopolitan Club and think my partner could be the man, or my opponent, or a man playing rummy or flush at the other table. I never knew who he was: he had disguised his voice thoroughly."

"He must have been in love with you himself," says Ruby, attempting to tease Serahbai out of the grip of her malaise. "Otherwise why would he do a thing like that? Go to such lengths?"

"No. People in love don't hurt the people they love."

"Don't they, mum," asks Ruby wryly.

'Your father loved me," asserts Serahbai with startling certitude. "He would never deliberately hurt me."

Ruby is not about to argue with her. She remains quiet.

"I know you don't believe me," Serahbai says. "He wasn't the type to show it, but I was the only one he loved. The only one he trusted. He could have left his estate to a trust, but he left everything to me. He knew I would do as he wished."

Ruby thought back to those times when Mother needed her complicity in handling Father. They would gang up on him. It used to be either to help Mother unearth something he had hidden, or to wheedle money out of him. Those were happy, lighthearted occasions, devoid of the tension and the state of alertness Father's presence in the house increasingly generated. In fact they were instants of great release—akin to bolts of lightening dispelling negative charges. Father might have hidden a bracelet or ring Mother had neglected to put away, or he was being coy parting with the money. Her mother's dire need gave her an unerring instinct—Serah always knew when Keki stepped over the threshold with cash. Not small change, but substantial sums from the provisions store, or from some deal in scrap metal, or cotton, he had struck. Then it was "Janoo, don't tease me . . . I know you've brought money: where is it? You've hidden it!" and they'd go through his pockets, which were more numerous in winter, and launch a search of the rooms under his wary, almost mischievous eyes. The moment they were "hot," Keki would jump to the rescue of his secreted loot.

When unhappy, Serah took to her bed. Ruby recalls a long stretch—a period, perhaps, of some months—when her mother stayed in bed most of the day. With intuitive certitude Ruby links it to the horror of that anonymous phone call in the dead of might. She must be about 7 then. It occurs to her Dr. Bharucha visited their house so frequently during that time that he was more a friend to her parents than physician. Serahbai emerged from this period of semi-hibernation as from a cocoon. Changed.

But it wasn't Serah who had so abruptly changed, Ruby now realizes—it was her father who was transformed.

Moderate looking in all respects, neither tall nor broad or fair of face, and at one time unappealing to all women save his wife, Keki had suddenly blossomed into a creature of irresistible attraction when it became known that he had, with characteristic quietude and reticence, become one of the wealthiest men in the land.

Faced with his unforeseen and formidable attraction—as Serah's once almost unappetizing husband burgeoned with allure and confusing appetite—Serah rallied with wherewithal: and whatever random means she had at hand. Nature had already endowed her with a provocative figure and a lovely face and, rising to the occasion, she acquired an American bra through an American friend. It was a special, crossover, Maidenform bra and the satin bands of the bra crisscrossed in a way that left Serahbai's nipples uncovered. The snug fit of Serahbai's sari-bodices accomplished the desired effect. Artfully embellishing her various attributes with similar ingenuity Serahbai succeeded in invoking a spectacular aura of glamour. Thinking back Ruby believes what made her mother so irresistible to the endless line of valorous men who befriended her was not just her beauty and glamour but their auspicious conjunction with the childish innocence and make-believe that formed the bedrock of her personality.

For the more mesmeric Keki's hooded eyes became behind their thick rimless glasses, and the more they compelled other lotus-eyed women to lure him to their beds, the more seductively Serahbai's innocence bloomed, and the better it engaged illustrious men of immaculate reputation to abandon themselves to their discrete passion to help and befriend her mother.

That she was often distressed, Ruby knew. But as to its cause—she didn't have a clue. Becoming adept at shielding her daughter from her worries her young mother withdrew from her. Withdrew into herself. So that even in her happier moments, even when her splendid teeth flashed in duplicitous smiles, she concealed herself from Ruby. Ruby inhabited the same joyless house with an aloof, remote and beautiful woman who was so wrapped up in the excess of her misery—and the desperate stratagems she deployed to hang on to her increasingly mute, unassailable and furtive husband—that she had little time or energy to spare for her daughter. Except at a most rudimentary and perfunctory level. But kept from this knowledge by the neurotic, thrift-driven austerity of their lives, and an unyielding rectitude that voided all conversation within the family, Ruby had no means of understanding what was happening around her.

How did she view her mother then? From the distanced and yet necessarily foreshortened perspective of a scrawny and angular child looking up at the radiant flesh and face of a beautiful and inaccessible woman. A mysterious woman who cried out some nights "Janoo, you can't go to her. I won't let you." A child who heard the muted bursts of hushed altercations accompanied by ominous thuds—as if heavy objects were being flung about in the dark. The thump-thump of what she grew up to realize were furtive blows.

Mr. Jariwalla's visits—with their aura of concealed intimacy—can also be dated to that period.

Of unimpeachable repute and principled character the confidant of the moment sits by Serah's bed. He leans forward on the Spartan desk chair he has brought from the writing desk to hear her better—and the better to be heard. Serah and Jal J. converse in low voices so as not to be overheard by servants or children. Little Ruby hears only an indecipherable stream of sibilant whispers, an interminable murmur that issues from the bedroom like the burble and hiss of some unspecified animal. Once she heard Mr. J say: "You must pull yourself together, Serah . . . brooding on such thoughts can destroy you . . . plunge you into depression you may never get out of." His voice was unexpectedly strong, sustaining. So uncharacteristic of him that it had made an impression.

Did he actually say the words she recalls so clearly, or was it Dr. Bharucha? Is her memory playing tricks?

Although Serahbai's bedroom door was often shut it was seldom locked. It was locked only when she opened the secret compartment in her cupboard to stash away jewelry, or the documents and cash Keki might have instructed her to. Occasionally there was a lull in the conversation, or it was carried out in such low voices that Ruby, thinking her mother was alone, blundered into the room. She always found her mother as she might have expected to: decently clad, covered by a sheet, discretely made-up and fetchingly prostrate with misery.

At such times Ruby's sudden appearances put a stop to the discourse and, depending on her reception, whether she was greeted heartily or hollowly, she beat a hasty—or a slightly less hasty—and awkward retreat. She could tell, of course, from the expression on their faces and the intimate gloom-doom ambiance of the curtained room—hushed confidences still lurking among the shadowy rafters of the receding 20 foot tall ceiling—that Serah's select advocate of the moment had been gravely listening, offering comfort and sage advise.

Sometimes Jal J. dragged the square ottoman-stool—which still squats in a corner next to the door—and pressed it into service by Serah's bed. Its stuffed lid opens on an array of sewing-thread reels. Wood rises about 6 inches on either side to proffer armrests—provided the sitter is narrow-hipped enough to fit—which Mr. Jariwalla still is, and Dr. Bharucha wasn't.

And later, in their turn, Mr. Bankwalla? Or Mr. Singh? Or Cooper? Or Shabbir? Or Adenwalla? Ruby imagines it would be a snug fit for them all—except for Mr. Cooper who is as slight as Dr. Bharucha and Mr. King were corpulent.

So successfully did Serah shield her daughter from her distress, so discretely did she deploy her ploys, that Ruby had felt shut out of her mother's life. And in her progressively bewildered isolation, shut out of life itself. By the time Ruby turned 11, she had migrated to the charged world of romance tinctured fantasy.

Did she judge her mother harshly then? Not then. She did not have the experience or a standard of comparison by which to judge—if one is ever qualified to do so.

But later, yes.

It takes decades, and a illness that causes Serahbai to confide the emotional turmoil of her past, that Ruby is at last able to unravel the mystery of her mother's despair; to decode the preoccupation that appeared to turn her mother cold and remote and absent from her.

And now? How does Ruby view her now? From the condescending and bullying perspective of a woman trundling an aged mother in a wheelchair?

Serahbai was having tea on the front verandah with Mrs. Cooper when Mrs. Cooper shouted: "Ruby! Ruby! Come at once. Something's happened to Serahbai."

Ruby rushed down the stairs to see her mother sitting on the wicker chair, her head flung back and her hand circling the air as if pointing out something on the ceiling. And she was babbling.

Ruby had cried when her mother was in hospital, and she cried after she came home. She cried in the bathroom during the day, and at night in her bedroom upstairs. Her friends tried to console her but they didn't know why she was crying. Does anyone know why others mourn? She mourned that her mother had been taken from her just when they had made their peace. She had returned from America to be with Serahbai and Serahbai looked forward to do things with her. She took Serahbai shopping, to the hairdressers and to Chinese restaurants. They parked before the city's unsanitary lean-tos and were served flaming kebabs and curries through their car windows. They licked their fingers clean. They called on Serahbai's friends, and invited her friends to lunch. Perhaps they were bonding only because she had moved so far away, Ruby thought. Resentments nursed since childhood had evaporated as if they were nothing. Ruby was flooded by feelings of tenderness and love. She was gratified to do all the little things Serahbai asked of her, and Serahbai beamed her pleasure and her approval. Ruby's existence was cushioned by a contentment that was akin to the very threshold of joy. Isn't that what children want? No matter what their age? Their mother's praise and approval?

And the stroke came along and snatched her mother away. Serahbai was drifting away from her, again withdrawing, and this time with a finality that would not be denied.

QUESTIONS

1. How are we to regard Serahbai's accounts of her own past? Is she exaggerating her beauty and charms or reporting accurately? Support your answer with details from the story.

2. Describe the relationship between Serahbai and Ruby.

3. At one point, Serahbai says, "When your husband is that good to you, you don't care about anything else . . . you don't care what goes on in the rest of your life." Is she speaking truthfully? Does the rest of the story bear out what she says here?

4. Serahbai flirts openly with various men, while her husband takes a mistress. How are we to understand these differing infidelities? Are they reflections of differing personalities, opportunities, status? Is Serahbai a victim of the "colonized" status of women in many societies?

5. What provokes the argument between Serahbai and Aunty Tamy?

6. What effects do the parents' conflicts have on Ruby? How does Serahbai's death affect her?

Africa

A frica is so large a continent and so varied in its geography and peoples that generalizing about it is nearly impossible. As the second largest continent, covering 11.5 million square miles, it is almost four times the size of the United States (3.6 million square miles) and nearly nine times the size of India (1.3 million square miles). In geography and climate, it ranges from the massive Sahara Desert to tropical jungles, from grassy plains to mountain ranges topped by Kilimanjaro at 19,000 feet. Its people are equally various, ranging from desert nomads and traditional villagers to sophisticated urbanites in such cities as Cairo, Nairobi, Lagos, and Johannesburg.

EARLY HISTORY

European contacts with North Africa date back at least to 800 B.C.E., when the Carthaginians plied the Mediterranean. European invasion and occupation began ca. 631 B.C.E. with Greek settlements, followed by Rome's conquest of Carthage in three series of Punic Wars from 218 to 74 B.C.E. Islamic conquests and conversions began in the seventh century C.E. and covered most of North Africa and later the Sudan. European colonization in the modern sense, however, did not begin until the Portuguese began to explore the western coast under the impetus of Prince Henry the Navigator (1394–1460). The earliest settlements were merely fortified trading outposts, beginning with Elmina on the Gold Coast in 1481. Over the next century, Portugal's main expansion was along the west coast, moving steadily southward, then up the east coast. When Portugal and Spain conquered South America in the sixteenth century, the demand for slaves created a need for more permanent settlements in West Africa, particularly in the area of the Niger River. (Previous to this, the African slave market, run by indigenous Africans and Muslims, had sent its human cargo mainly into North Africa and the Middle East.)

Nor surprisingly, Portugal's success in Africa encouraged competition from its European rivals—first Spain, then Holland, England, France, and eventually Germany, Belgium, and others. By and large, the rivalry was commercial, with competing countries establishing trading outposts very close to one another along the west coast. Gold, slaves, spices, and gum arabic were among the most sought-after commodities. Britain did not establish trading stations until the mid-seventeenth century, by which time its own holdings in the New World brought the country into the notorious slave trade. European interests in Africa remained confined to coastal trading stations until the late seventeenth century.

Two forces converged to alter this purely commercial relationship between Europe and Africa. The first, ironically, was motivated by the European antislavery movement, beginning in 1788 with the establishment of a colony of former British West Indian slaves at Sierra Leone. A similar colony was founded by Americans in 1821 next door to Sierra Leone in Liberia. The second factor was Europe's interest in exploring the African interior, spearheaded by Britain's African Association (1788). Explorers seeking to trace the course of Africa's largest rivers—the Nile, Congo, Niger, and Zambezi—not only aroused the public's curiosity about the interior of Africa, but also opened up its major waterways to commercial exploitation and military conquest.

EUROPEAN ATTITUDES, AFRICAN REALITIES

Europe's ideas about Africa and Africans in the nineteenth and early twentieth centuries can be summarized in a three-word phrase: *the dark continent.* This phrase has two important meanings. First, the term referred to the fact that the interior of sub-Saharan Africa was largely unexplored and unknown to Europeans (though not of course, to Africans). Marlow alludes to this in "Heart of Darkness" when he recalls that the maps he studied as a boy depicted the African interior as a blank place. By the end of the nineteenth century, European explorers had filled in the geographical details and thereby rendered this first sense obsolete, but the term had a second and more sinister connotation: Africa as an unenlightened, uncivilized, heathen, backward, and primitive land needing the civilizing, uplifting, and Christianizing benefits of European progress. Much of the darkness perceived by Europeans was the result of their own narrow and prejudicial views of the people and institutions they encountered. These views, bolstered by misapplied ideas from biological evolution, cultural anthropology, and linguistics, held that Africans as a race were less highly evolved, less naturally intelligent and moral, and less fully developed than Europeans.

There is neither time nor space in this brief overview of African history to refute these charges in detail, but before proceeding further, it is imperative to dispel the myth that Africa was a dark continent in this second sense of the term. Long before Europeans penetrated beyond the coastal trading posts and into the interior, Africans had developed highly complex and sophisticated systems of government and trade. The Ashanti, for example, had developed a complex political democracy by the mid-seventeenth century, one far more advanced in many respects than contemporary political systems in Europe. Similarly, by the close of the eighteenth century, the Zulus had invented a highly effective and magnificently coordinated military strategy that enabled them to conquer large portions of South Africa and, when the time came, to mount effective resistance against European conquerors. Not all African societies were as advanced as the Ashantis and Zulus, but similar examples could be multiplied.

In intellectual and cultural matters, too, Africans were hardly the benighted people Europeans thought them to be. The Bantu, for example, had a highly complex legal system long before the colonial period, and even at the village level, procedures for handling disputes of every kind were well established and effective. In the arts, Africa's best-known forms of expression were sculpture, music, dance, and oral literature. Although seldom appreciated by colonists, African sculpture had a profound effect on European artists at the turn of the twentieth century, influencing such artists as Pablo Picasso and Henri Matisse to abandon strict realism for freer and more abstract forms. The bronze castings of the Benin peoples made a huge impact in late-nineteenth-century Europe. European music, with its emphasis on melody and harmony, deals in relatively simple rhythms, whereas African music and dance may overwhelm the untrained ear with its complex rhythms, frequently five or more at one time, and occasionally as many as a dozen. African dance is equally complicated in its rhythms and movements. Most directly relevant for this book is the refined art of African oral literature. Often reduced to mere plot summary by collectors, African oral literature consists not merely of short legends and anecdotes but of long, complex, interactive performances involving a skilled narrator and an appreciative and participating audience.

Of course, Africans had not developed the kind of science and technology that Europeans possessed in the late nineteenth century, with the result that they were easily conquered and exploited by armies wielding automatic rifles and machine guns. But technological advancement is hardly the only or even the best means for assessing the achievements of a civilization. Far from being the dark continent of European prejudice, Africa was in many ways a highly sophisticated collection of successful civilizations thriving in a harsh environment. That we in the West have only recently begun to understand and appreciate African achievements says more about us than about Africans.

THE ANTISLAVERY MOVEMENT

Denmark was first to outlaw slavery in its territories in 1792, and the United States outlawed participation in the trade in 1794 and the importation of slaves in 1808. Britain prohibited its citizens and ships from slave trading in 1807, and all the European powers had followed suit by 1836, although enforcement of these prohibitions was difficult and often ineffectual. Europe's sincerity in this endeavor is also open to question, as none of the major European powers seriously challenged slavery as a practice in the Americas. Moreover, these legal measures and the attempts to enforce them applied only to the trans-Atlantic trade; slavery itself continued in Africa, the Middle East, and the New World colonies. Antislavery groups in Britain, the United States, and elsewhere continued to press for the abolition of slavery itself and for suppression of the illegal trade, which had degenerated into practices of unimaginable brutality. Slaves were packed into ships and chained to the floor, forced to lie in airless holds and their own excrement, ill fed, and without medical care. Death during this "middle passage" was a daily affair and considered simply part of the cost of doing business. Britain's efforts to enforce its antislavery laws led to the establishment in

1851 of a permanent military base on Lagos Island, near the mouth of the Niger River. Three years later, the French began to establish themselves in Senegal. These posts later served as the starting points for colonization.

The motives of antislavery and scientific discovery were joined with those of missionary zeal as a third colonizing force. Their interconnectedness is well illustrated by the activities of Scotland's David Livingstone, who began as a missionary in what is now South Africa in 1840, but by 1852 had shifted his main activity to exploration. His early travels took him to Lake Ngami, across the Kalahari Desert, and up the Zambezi River to Victoria Falls. His published books on these travels were best sellers, arousing great interest in Africa and righteous indignation at the evils of the internal African slave trade. From 1865–1871 he explored Tanganyika, during which time his whereabouts were of such international interest that the *New York Herald* commissioned H. M. Stanley to find him. Stanley did find Livingstone and briefly joined his expeditions, but dysentery eventually killed the already-weakened Livingstone. Livingstone was one among many explorers who inspired still others (including Stanley, who mapped the Congo River) to follow in their footsteps, with the result that Africa was not only mapped and its plants and animals catalogued, but also that access to its interior was made increasingly possible. Gradually, coastal holdings were expanded to spheres of influence over interior territories, which soon became protectorates, then permanent dependencies or de facto colonies. With each change came increasingly direct European control.

THE SCRAMBLE FOR AFRICA, 1876–1900

Historians debate the motivations behind Europe's colonial expansion in Africa. Marxists argue that Europe needed African markets and materials for capitalist expansion, but other historians stress such factors as national prestige, the desire to maintain a balance of power among the various countries, or the jockeying for strategic position. Some look to the ambitious machinations of Belgium's King Leopold II as the instigator of what historians call "the scramble for Africa."

The "scramble" is often said to have begun in 1876, when King Leopold called a conference in Brussels to establish the International Association for the Exploration and Civilization of Africa. Ostensibly, the proposal was to create an international body to regulate trade and cooperate in scientific and humanitarian ventures; in reality, the conference was a smoke screen for Leopold's colonial ambitions. In 1877, Stanley completed his exploration of the Congo and was anxious to see it developed commercially. By 1880, the French were competing with Belgium in the region, and within a few years, Portugal and Britain also expressed interest. Britain was solidifying and expanding its holdings in South Africa, which had existed since 1814 to ensure the safety and refitting of British ships on their way to India. Still, in 1880, Europe held sway over only 10 percent of Africa: Turkey had the largest claim, ruling Egypt and part of what is now Libya. France held coastal Algeria and Senegal; the Portuguese controlled coastal Angola and Mozambique; and Britain ruled South

Africa and the Transvaal. Clearly, Leopold's desire for international cooperation (if that is what it was) had not borne fruit.

After 1880, competition intensified. To settle disputes and establish ground rules, a conference was held in Berlin in 1884–1885. It addressed a number of issues, including free trade and the abolition of slavery, but it also formalized the process by which countries could establish their spheres of influence, and it recognized Belgium's claim to the Congo, which shortly thereafter became Leopold's private domain and remained so until 1908. Over the next fifteen years, a series of bilateral treaties literally carved Africa into European colonies, with Britain emerging as a significant power. An important factor in British expansion, and perhaps an instigating force in the "scramble," was Britain's annexation of Egypt. In 1869, the French completed the Suez Canal, which created a direct link between the Mediterranean and the Red Sea, cutting weeks from the journey between Europe and the East. For Britain, this was a crucial link to India, and in 1875 it purchased a 40 percent interest in the canal. An Egyptian rebellion against the local khedive (ruler) in 1881 gave Britain an excuse to take control of Egypt and hence protect its interests in the canal, which it effectively held from 1883 to 1956. Thus, by the time of World War I, all of Africa except Ethiopia and Liberia was controlled by Europeans, with the French having the largest share in its control of Morocco, Algeria, and French West Africa. Britain, however, occupied Egypt and ruled the Sudan, Uganda, British East Africa (Kenya), Nigeria, Northern and Southern Rhodesia, Becuanaland, and South Africa, plus the Gold Coast and Sierra Leone. Significantly, this division had been accomplished without a major military battle between European powers; all the aggression was directed at Africans.

COLONIALISM: THREE CASE STUDIES

Nigeria

To trace in detail the progress of Britain's conquests in Africa is well beyond the limits of this brief outline, but developments in Nigeria may serve as one example. As with India, Britain began its takeover indirectly, through the United African Company (1879), later called the Royal Niger Company (1886). Charged with opening trade in the interior of Nigeria and with eradicating the largely Arab-controlled slave trade and other barbarous practices, the company secured treaties with existing African chiefs. Both company constables and British military forces were used to combat slave trading and to extort economic concessions. Not surprisingly, they encountered resistance, chiefly from the Yoruba tribe. In 1900, the company sold its assets to the British government, which appointed Frederick Lugard as high commissioner. Lugard's goal was to establish control over the entire region, using treaties when possible, force when necessary. Once control was established, Lugard used local emirs as rulers, paid by the British. In effect, traditional African rule was simply capped by an overarching British authority. Simultaneously, railroads were built to the interior to facilitate trade in tin, cotton, and peanuts, while Christian missionaries provided schools and medical care. By 1914, northern and southern Nigeria were united under British administration. Wisely, the British largely respected local values and religions—Muslim in the north, Christian in the south—with due allowance made for local customs and practices not at odds with "civilized" behavior. Lugard's successor, Hugh Clifford, pressed for a more centralized scheme, but was only partially successful. The constitution adopted in 1922 largely reaffirmed the principle of indirect rule

Kenya

In east Africa, Kenya eventually became an important British holding. In the seventeenth century, Mombasa was the center of intense competition between Portuguese and Arab traders, a battle eventually won late in the century by the Arabs. But interest in abolishing the slave trade brought Britain into the picture in 1822, even though the first Europeans to explore the interior were German missionaries. One reason for the slow expansion of European interests was the existence of the powerful and rapidly expanding Masai peoples, but their influence abated in the 1880s due largely to widespread disease among their cattle and the ravages of smallpox. By 1888, much of Kenya was controlled by the Imperial British East Africa Company. The need for communication and trade spurred the development of the Uganda Railway, which in turn led to the importing of some 20,000 Asian Indian workers, with whose labor the railroad was completed in 1903. Meanwhile, the British government had taken over from the East Africa Company, much as it had done in India after the 1857 uprising. Perceiving that much of the rich pasture and farmland formerly controlled by the Masai was now deserted owing to the smallpox epidemic, the British encouraged white settlements, at first with little success. However, by the outbreak of World War I in 1914, white settlers had increased to the point that they were asking for legislative representation. Kenya officially became a British colony in 1920, with much of its indigenous population dispossessed of its land, which had been turned into farmland and coffee and cotton plantations.

South Africa

South Africa provides a third example worth considering in some detail. As noted previously, Britain established naval bases in South Africa early in the nineteenth century, but the Dutch had preceded them in this by nearly two hundred years. What began as merely a supply station for Dutch merchant ships soon expanded into a white settlement of farmers and traders supported by imported slaves. By the end of the eighteenth century, some 20,000 Europeans and their 25,000 slaves had settled in the southwestern tip of the continent. In 1814, Britain bought out the Dutch and assumed control of the territory. Among their early acts, the British expanded white settlements by seizing land from the native Xosha people, established a circuit court system that treated blacks as equal to whites, and imported English farmers, thus exacerbating an already acute shortage of farmland. Britain's decision to forbid slavery increased tensions between the British and the Dutch settlers, known as Boers. Meanwhile, in the eastern and northern parts of South Africa, four powerful native states arose, the most famous being the Zulus.

In 1836, Boers, dissatisfied with British policies on slavery and the treatment of Africans generally, reacted by migrating north and east, which brought them into direct conflict with the previously mentioned African states. War between the Voortrekkers (pioneers) and the Africans resulted in the establishment of Natal in 1839, which the British annexed. Further waves of Boer pioneers created two independent republics, the Orange Free State (northeast of the Orange River) and the South African Republic (northeast of the Vaal River, or Transvaal). By 1870, therefore, there were two British and two Boer colonies. The economy being primarily agricultural and not especially profitable, the white population stabilized at about 200,000 in the British areas and another 50,000 in the Boer holdings.

Just as matters seemed reasonably stable, however, diamonds were discovered in 1867 where the Orange and Vaal rivers intersect, and within a few years, the rush was on. In 1886, vast deposits of gold were found near present-day Johannesburg, and another rush ensued. By 1900, the white population of Cape Colony (or the Cape of Good Hope) had doubled to 400,000. Mining completely transformed the economy, politics, and racial tensions in South Africa. A key figure in these developments was Cecil Rhodes, who rivaled Leopold II as an instigator of imperialism at its worst.

Rhodes, whose name has become synonymous with "muscular Christianity," ironically was driven by ill health to join his older brother, a farmer in Natal, in 1870. Within a year, Rhodes had recovered his health in the hot dry climate and become one of the earliest successes in the Kimberley diamond mines. Already rich at nineteen, he toured the Transvaal and Bechuanaland (present-day Botswana), where his imagination became fired by the possibilities of the country and, as he saw it, the necessity of Britain's extending its Empire. During the following decade, Rhodes earned a degree from Oxford University and consolidated the diamond business into the DeBeers Company, which is still the largest diamond cartel in the world. In 1881, Rhodes entered South African politics and over the next five years maneuvered a reluctant Britain into annexing Bechuanaland. But Rhodes wanted more—in fact, the whole of east Africa up to Cairo. He formed the British Chartered Company and through it swindled Lobengula, chief of the Matebele, into ceding territory. A war and two native rebellions later and Rhodes had extended the Empire further north with a country christened Rhodesia (subsequently Southern Rhodesia, currently Zimbabwe). This was in 1889; the following year Rhodes became prime minister—in practice, dictator—of Cape Colony, a position he held for six years until forced to resign over his part in the Jameson Raid, a military maneuver that appeared to be largely motivated by Rhodes's own greed.

Another Matabele rebellion resulted in a military stalemate, which Rhodes almost singlehandedly resolved by earning the complete trust of the chiefs. The result was Northern Rhodesia, which extended Britain's holdings to the southern shore of Lake Tanganika. At the same time, the British concluded a series of treaties with Germany that yielded Kenya, and in 1900 Britain negotiated with Africans for effective control of what is now Uganda. Thus, Rhodes's dream of an uninterrupted line of British control from the Cape to Cairo had nearly been completed. But Rhodes's other dream, that of a united South Africa that would include both English and Boer possessions, was not to be realized in his lifetime. Worse, in 1899 war erupted between the English and the Boers, essentially over the issue of who was to control South Africa. England eventually won, but not before the Boers had inflicted humiliation and heavy casualties on the numerically superior British. It is a war that some in hindsight have called "Britain's Vietnam."

The story of South Africa is incomplete, however, without at least a brief account of the development of the apartheid ("apartness") system. The huge influx of Europeans stimulated by diamond and gold mining resulted in stresses on available land and a perceived need for cheap labor. The first of these issues was settled by a series of wars against the remaining African tribes, which dispossessed them of their land by the mid-1880s. The desire for cheap labor was fulfilled by a series of repressive laws that deprived Africans of the vote, restricted their movements by requiring them to carry identification passes, segregated them from white society by zoning restrictions, and denied them access to education. African resistance arose early through such groups as the Native Education Association, the founding of black newspapers, and the activities of black churches, but the struggle against apartheid continued until black majority rule was achieved in 1994.

COLONIALISM: BREAKUP AND AFTERMATH

The carving up of Africa was achieved in a period of only about thirty-five years, and colonial rule in most African colonies lasted only fifty or sixty years. In that relatively brief time, however, the whole face of a continent was changed. European governments were fond of calling their conquests "pacification," "civilizing," or "subduing native resistance." In fact, the violence was often brutal and systematic, pitting European rifles and machine guns against the natives' antiquated muskets or flimsy shields and spears. European commanders frequently bragged in their letters and memoirs about the numbers of Africans slaughtered in battle, and often women and children were killed along with the warriors. Those not killed outright died in other ways— from overwork, starvation, or the importation of European diseases such as smallpox against which Africans had no immunity. Of course, there were protests from Christian missionaries, native groups, and in particular a scathing report on atrocities in King Leopold's Congo by a remarkable African American named George Washington Williams, but this was the period during which the United States' own westward expansion was killing, dispossessing, and exploiting Native Americans. What protests there were against such practices went largely unnoticed. With nearly all European countries and the United States implicated in some form of colonial expansion and exploitation, there was a virtual conspiracy of silence.

Britain's Empire reached its zenith just before the outbreak of World War I in 1914. After that war, in which many of Britain's colonies supported the country, the process of dismantling the Empire began, slowly and tentatively in some places, rapidly and aggressively in others. Again, Nigeria, Kenya, and South Africa may be selected as illustrating the forces at work.

NIGERIAN INDEPENDENCE

The national boundaries of Nigeria, like those of every other colony in Africa, were drawn arbitrarily, with no regard for traditional tribal loyalties or even geographical features. As noted above, Nigeria was divided along religious lines into the Muslim north and the Christian south, with many competing ethnic groups within these broad divisions. Nigerian nationalism, therefore, took many forms and involved many interest groups—professional organizations like those involving teachers and lawyers, ethnic groups like the Igbo and the Yoruba, youth and student movements, and labor unions, to name just a few. After World War II, a series of constitutions yielded increasing power to Nigerian civil servants and elected officials. These constitutions attempted to acknowledge ethnic differences by creating three regional states, but in some respects, this practice intensified tensions and weakened the idea of Nigeria as a unified country. Elections held in 1964 were marred by irregularities, charges of corruption, and subsequent disorder, including riots. In 1966, the military intervened and took control under Major General Ironsi, who promised to restore order and respect ethnic sensibilities, but ethnic-inspired violence killed thousands, and in May 1967, the southeastern portion of the country attempted to secede, calling itself Biafra. The ensuing war lasted thirty months and crushed Biafran independence. An estimated 1 to 3 million civilian and military casualties resulted. Reunification was relatively peaceful and successful, but the war had taken a heavy toll.

Economically, Nigeria was traditionally agricultural, with cocoa, peanuts, and palm oil as its chief exports. In the late 1960s, however, oil became the leading export, and by 1971, Nigeria was the seventh largest producer in the world. Unfortunately, oil exports did little to raise the general standard of living, and Nigeria's former self-sufficiency in agriculture suffered as rural people left their land for what they hoped would be success in the big cities. Nevertheless, there was progress toward a new economy based on manufacturing, in spite of corruption, inefficiencies, and high unemployment. The plight of ordinary people was hardly helped by periodic lurches from military government to civilian rule and back again. The continued plight of the Igbo grabbed the international spotlight when Ken Saro-Wiwa, a well-known writer and political activist, was executed on trumped-up charges arising from his opposition to military rule and the government's mishandling of the country's oil wealth.

Debates over oil revenues, the distribution of the wealth derived from oil, and the generally poor state of Nigeria's economy continue to divide this potentially successful country, already riven by racial, religious, and ethnic tensions. With oil supplies from the Middle East increasingly threatened, Nigeria's strategic position and oil revenues could help bring it out of poverty—or plunge it into civil strife.

KENYAN INDEPENDENCE

The decades between the two world wars saw the further development of infrastructure (primarily railroads) and increased agitation by all groups (whites, Indians, and blacks) for legislative representation—in other words, a struggle for political power, though two Africans were included in the legislature in 1944. Shortly after World War II, in 1952, the so-called Mau-Mau rebellion launched a violent campaign against European settlers. Although this insurrection was eventually put down, it was instrumental in helping to achieve independence for Kenya. By 1962, two political parties had emerged, the Kenya African National Union (KANU) and the Kenya African Democratic Union (KADU). KANU won the first election in May 1963, so that when Kenya became independent in December of that year, its first president was Jomo Kenyatta, the leader of KANU. Land reform in the early days of the country returned much white-owned land to Africans, as Europeans voluntarily left the country.

It is often noted that the most important election in a democracy is not its first but its second, for this is when a democracy is really tested. The maxim is true for Kenya, for in the years following independence, Kenyatta consistently increased the power of the presidency at the expense of the legislature and successfully defeated all attempts by other leaders to challenge his power. When Kenyatta died in 1978, he was succeeded by Daniel Arap Moi, his vice president who, like Kenyatta, allied himself with the West. At the insistence of Western powers, multiparty elections were held in 1992, but Moi was reelected. As a result, Kenya has remained a one-party state with an enfeebled legislature and powerful central government that controls virtually every aspect of Kenya's politics. Kenya is thus a relatively stable African nation, but hardly a democratic one.

SOUTH AFRICA: APARTHEID AND INDEPENDENCE

Nigeria and Kenya represent the path of European colonies controlled by the colonizing power. South Africa represents a considerably different development—dominion status within the British Empire. In 1910, the two Afrikaner and two British states came together as the Union of South Africa. Although technically under Britain's parliament and monarch, dominion states (including Canada and Australia) exercised control over their internal and external affairs, making them for all practical purposes sovereign countries. Immediately, South African whites strengthened the steps taken earlier to ensure domination politically and economically, prompting educated blacks to form the African National Congress (ANC) in 1912. Power struggles between English and Afrikaners focused on language issues (English versus Dutch as official languages) and became particularly heated during World War II, when many Afrikaners supported Germany and its ideas of white supremacy. Nevertheless, after the war, the Dutch-based right-wing political parties successfully gained control of the government, and apartheid became even more pronounced than previously, classifying everyone on the basis of race and strictly segregating whites, coloreds (mixed-race people), Indians, and native or Bantu peoples. Under these laws, legalized segregation was more rigorously enforced than even in the southern United States: everything from interracial marriage to separate (and unequal) education to special job categories for each race was enforced by law. Police powers were expanded to squelch even the slightest dissent. But even these draconian measures could not prevent dissent by the ANC and others: Strikes, boycotts, and peaceful protests that sometimes erupted in violence prompted thousands of arrests. Predictably, too, the ineffectiveness of peaceful and lawful protests spurred more militant and violent organizations to appear. In 1963, much of this resistance was squashed, and many leaders, including Nelson Mandela, were imprisoned for life. To further reinforce apartheid and to forestall protest, the white government created homelands or reserves for blacks, moving some 3.5 million of them between 1963 and 1985 under the fiction of allowing them self-government.

The pacification of African protests against apartheid spurred new investment and white immigration to South Africa, but it also bred a new generation of black activists, the most important of whom was Steve Biko and the South African Students' Organisation. Biko preached nonviolence, but when the government tried to enforce Afrikaans as the official language in schools, protests erupted in Soweto in 1976 and turned violent, with hundreds killed. That same year, Biko was found dead of massive head wounds while in police custody. Because of the protests against apartheid from within and political pressures from without, by the mid-1970s, apartheid was beginning to crack. South Africa was overwhelmingly black in population, and the economy depended upon black labor. As country after country in Africa threw off white rule, South Africa became increasingly isolated. Opinion among whites became ever more divided, some directly or indirectly supporting antiapartheid forces.

In 1984, the government tried to accommodate pressures for reform by rewriting the constitution to include representation from coloreds and black, but few nonwhites accepted the arrangement. Peaceful and violent opposition continued, especially in the townships, where black police and other officials were attacked and sometimes killed as "collaborators." International pressures were mounting as well, and calls for countries to withdraw aid and for investors to divest themselves of South African stocks became effective. Finally, in 1990, President F. W. de Klerk released Nelson Mandela, legalized the ANC and other organizations, and began the systematic dismantling of apartheid and white minority rule. Despite opposition from many sides and continued violence, de Klerk persevered, and many provisions of the apartheid system were repealed in 1991. Elections open to all parties and races were held in 1994 under a new constitution, with the ANC winning nearly two-thirds of the vote. The National Assembly elected Mandela president.

In the years since white minority rule came to an end, progress toward racial harmony has been problematic but steady. Truth and Reconciliation commissions have been instrumental in keeping violence to a minimum. Decades will pass before South Africa's blacks emerge from the ravages of colonial conquest and white minority rule, but South Africa, even with its large areas of grinding poverty, is among the most successful and prosperous of Africa's decolonized countries.

THE AFRICAN SHORT STORY

Until the advent of missionary schools, written literature was nearly unknown in sub-Saharan Africa, except in Muslim areas, where Arabic was the language of religion and culture. Missionaries recorded many African languages and translated the Bible into native tongues, but in most missionary schools, English was the language of instruction. Throughout Africa, literature outside of the schools was transmitted orally as a part of traditional culture. Songs, stories, and proverbs transmitted knowledge, values, religious rites, and cultural practices from generation to generation. African lore is rich in folktales, legends, and fables—all precursors to the short story.

As in India and elsewhere, government schools gradually augmented missionary schools with the aim of providing Africans with the skills and values they needed to serve as effective colonial administrators, and much of the curriculum therefore followed British models, including British literature. Following independence, governments assumed responsibility for formal education, and opportunities expanded rapidly, especially at the primary level. In Nigeria, for example, by 1985, approximately half of the children attended school, and about half of these went on to secondary level. Universities and technical institutions of higher education proliferated in the late twentieth century, but by 1990 only 1 percent of the population was enrolled in any form of postsecondary institution. Basic literacy, therefore, was relatively widespread in Nigeria as it was elsewhere, creating an audience for literature of all types, including the short story. Literacy rates among whites, of course, were much higher than for blacks, with the result that most of the writing coming out of Africa early in its colonial history was written by whites. Among the early short story collections were R. Hodge's *The Settler in South Africa and Other Tales* (1860) and Olive Schreiner's *Dreams* (South Africa, 1891). This tradition is represented in the present collection by the stories of William Plomer and Doris Lessing, which are included in the chapter on England.

Because of its relatively late start in Western-style education, indigenous written literature was late to bloom in Africa. In most cases, little was published by way of imaginative literature in English until just before or after independence—about 1950 or so. Among these early collections were Es'kia Mphahlele's *Man Must Live and Other Stories* (1947). During this early period, the short story was often the dominant literary form, circulating through magazines like South Africa's *Drum,* because magazines could be produced and circulated more cheaply and easily than books. The short story quickly spread in popularity and readership; moreover, its close affiliation to traditional African oral modes made it seem a familiar genre. Many African writers, in fact, used traditional ideas, customs, and spiritual elements to explore the tensions between Western ideas and practices and indigenous ones.

The short story form could also easily be adopted to local conditions and could quickly respond to current political and social issues. Many of the stories in this collection illustrate the ways in which the short story was used to criticize corrupt practices, question social trends, explore gender issues, expose racial and economic injustice, and probe the tensions between rural and urban ways.

The short story tradition in Africa is relatively new, and its critical and historical literature is just beginning to be written. For the moment, it is safe to say that most of Africa's short fiction has come out of the realist tradition, except for those stories that explore traditional themes and ideas and for some modernist and postmodernist experiments by authors like Taban lo Liyong and Amos Tutuola. These movements, although related to European traditions, have been given a specifically African twist in which traditional oral devices like exaggeration and fantasy express the absurd or satirize "reality." The world now has its eye on African literature, and the continent's writers are responding with fiction that is finding a worldwide and appreciative audience.

Grace Ogot

(KENYA, b. 1930)

Grace Ogot has enjoyed a varied career as teacher, nurse, United Nations delegate, member of the Kenyan parliament, cabinet minister, broadcaster, and writer. She was the first African woman writer to publish short stories in English.

She was born Grace Akinyi in Butere, Kenya, daughter of a teacher in a missionary school. Her education began at Ng'iya Girls' School and Butere High School, after which she trained as a nurse and midwife at the Missionary Society's Maseno Hospital and in England. From 1955–1958, she was a script writer and announcer for the British Broadcasting Company in London. She returned to Kenya and there married Dr. Bethwell Ogot, a historian, returning to England with him from 1959–1961. When the Ogots returned to Kenya, Grace taught nursing and continued writing fiction, which she had begun publishing in 1962. Her first novel, *The Promised Land,* appeared in 1966, followed by three volumes of short stories: *Land Without Thunder* (1968), *The Other Woman* (1976), and *The Island of Tears* (1980).

Ogot's writing career has continued, but much of her energy since 1975 has been directed into government service and politics. She served as Kenya's UN delegate beginning in 1975 and in 1983 was appointed to fill a vacant seat in Kenya's parliament, to which she was elected on her own in 1985. She joined the cabinet three years later. She remains active in Kenya's politics and is known as an advocate for women's rights.

Much of Ogot's fiction attempts to negotiate the difficult transition between Africa's rural, oral culture and its modern urban, written culture. Her early stories were written in Luo, her mother's language, and later in Kiswahili and English, Kenya's official languages. Moreover, she often incorporates aspects of traditional folktales in her short stories or refers to traditional customs and practices. Kenya's history is another source of inspiration, with the conflict between tradition and innovation being a recurring theme.

The Green Leaves

1968

It was a dream. Then the sounds grew louder. Nyagar threw the blanket off his ears and listened. Yes, he was right. Heavy footsteps and voices were approaching. He turned round to wake up his wife. She was not there. He got up and rushed to the door. It was unlocked. Where was Nyamundhe? "How could she slip back to her hut so quietly?" he wondered. "I've told her time and again never to leave my hut without waking me up to bolt the door. She will see me tomorrow!"

"*Ero, ero,* there, there!" The noise was quite close now—about thirty yards away. Nyagar put a sheet round his well-developed body, fumbled for his spear and club, and then left the hut.

"*Piti, piti. Piti, piti.*" A group was running towards his gate. He opened the gate and hid by the fence. Nyagar did not want to meet the group directly, as he was certain some dangerous person was being pursued.

Three or four men ran past the gate, and then a larger group followed. He emerged from his hiding-place and followed them.

"These bastards took all my six bulls," he heard one voice cursing.

"Don't worry—they will pay for it," another voice replied.

Nyagar had caught up with the pursuing crowd. He now realised that the three or four men he had seen run past his gate were cattle thieves. They rounded a bend. About thirty yards away were three figures who could only be the thieves.

"They must not escape," a man shouted.

"They will not," the crowd answered in chorus.

The gap was narrowing. The young moon had disappeared, and it was quite dark.

"Don't throw a spear," an elder warned. "If it misses, they can use it against us."

The thieves took the wrong turning. They missed the bridge across the River Opok, which separated the people of Masala from those of Mirogi. Instead they turned right. While attempting to cross the river, they suddenly found themselves in a whirlpool. Hastily they scrambled out of the water.

"*Ero, ero,*" a cry went out from the pursuers.

Before the thieves could find a safe place at which to cross the river, the crowd was upon them. With their clubs they smote the thieves to the ground. The air was filled with the howls of the captured men. But the crowd showed no mercy.

During the scuffle, one of the thieves escaped and disappeared into the thick bush by the river.

"Follow him! Follow him!" someone shouted.

Three men ran in the direction in which he had disappeared, breathing heavily. The bush was thick and thorny. They stood still and listened. There was no sound. They beat the bush around with their clubs—still no sound. He had escaped.

Another thief took out his knife and drove it into the shoulder-blade of one of the pursuers, who fell back with the knife still sticking in him. In the ensuing confusion, the thief got up and made straight for the whirlpool. To everybody's amazement, he was seen swimming effortlessly across it to the other side of the river.

Nyagar plucked the knife out from Omoro's shoulder and put his hand over the wound to stop the bleeding. Omoro, still shaken, staggered to his feet and leaned on Nyagar. Streaks of blood were still running along his back, making his buttocks wet.

One thief was lying on the grass, groaning. As the other two had escaped, the crowd were determined to make an example of this one. They hit him several times on the head and chest. He groaned and stretched out his arms and legs as if giving up the ghost.

"Aa, aa," Omoro raised his voice. "Let not the enemy die in your hands. His spirit would rest upon our village. Let him give up the ghost when we have returned to our huts."

The crowd heeded Omoro's warning. They tore green leaves from nearby trees and covered the victim completely with them. They would call the entire clan in the morning to come and bury him by the riverside.

The men walked back home in silence. Omoro's shoulder had stopped bleeding. He walked, supported by two friends who volunteered to take him home. It was still not light, but their eyes were by now accustomed to the darkness. They reached Nyagar's home—the gate was still ajar.

"Remember to be early tomorrow," a voice told him. "We must be on the scene before the women start going to the river, to stop them."

Nyagar entered his home, while the others walked on without looking back. The village was hushed in quiet. The women must have been awake, but they dared not talk to their husbands. Whatever had happened, they thought, they would hear about it in the morning. Having satisfied themselves that their husbands were safely back, they turned over and slept.

Nyagar entered his hut, searched for his medicine bag and found it in a corner. He opened it, and pulled out a bamboo container. He uncorked the container, and then scooped out some ash from it. He placed a little on his tongue, mixed it well with saliva and then swallowed. He put some on his palm and blew it in the direction of the gate. As he replaced the bamboo container in the bag, his heart felt at peace.

He sat on the edge of his bed. He started to remove his clothes. Then he changed his mind. Instead he just sat there, staring vacantly into space. Finally he made up his mind to go.

He opened the door slowly, and then closed it quietly after him. No one must hear him.

He did not hesitate at the gate, but walked blindly on.

"Did I close the gate?" he wondered. He looked back. Yes, he had closed it—or it looked closed.

"He must have a lot of money in his pocket," Nyagar [thought.]

Apart from a sinister sound which occasionally rolled through the night, everything was silent. Dawn must have been approaching. The faint and golden gleams of light which usually herald the birth of a new day could be seen in the east shooting skywards from the bowels of the earth, he said aloud. He knew that stock thieves sold stolen cattle at the earliest opportunity.

"The others were foolish not to have searched him." He stopped and listened. Was somebody coming? No. He was merely hearing the echo of his own footsteps.

"Perhaps the other two thieves who had escaped are now back at the scene," he thought nervously. "No, they can't be there—they wouldn't be such idiots as to hang around there."

The heap of green leaves came in sight. A numb paralysing pain ran through his spine. He thought his heart had stopped beating. He stopped to check. It was still beating, all right. He was just nervous. He moved on faster, and the echo of his footsteps bothered him.

When Nyagar reached the scene of murder, he noticed that everything was exactly as they had left it earlier. He stood there for a while, undecided. He looked in all directions to ensure that no-one was coming. There was nobody. He was all alone with the dead body. He now felt nervous. "Why should you disturb a dead body?" his inner voice asked him. "What do you want to do with money? You have three wives and twelve children. You have many cattle and enough food. What more do you want?" the voice persisted. He felt even more nervous, and was about to retreat when an urge stronger than his will egged him on.

"You have come all this far for one cause only, and the man is lying before you. You only need to put your hand in his pockets, and all the money will be yours. Don't deceive yourself that you have enough wealth. Nobody in the world has enough wealth."

Nyagar bent over the dead man, and hurriedly removed the leaves from him. His hand came in contact with the man's arm which lay folded on his chest. It was still warm. A chill ran through him again, and he stood up. It was unusual for a dead person to be warm, he thought. However, he dismissed the thought. Perhaps he was just nervous and was imagining things. He bent over the man again, and rolled him on his back. He looked dead all right.

He fumbled quickly to find the pockets. He dipped his hand into the first pocket. It was empty. He searched the second pocket—that, too, was empty. A pang of disappointment ran through his heart. Then he remembered that cattle traders often carried their money in a small bag stringed with a cord round their neck.

He knelt beside the dead man and found his neck. Sure enough there was a string tied around his neck, from which hung a little bag. A triumphant smile played at the corners of his mouth. Since he had no knife with which to cut the string, he decided to remove it over the man's head. As Nyagar lifted the man's head, there was a crashing blow on his right eye. He staggered for a few yards and fell unconscious to the ground.

The thief had just regained consciousness and was still very weak. But there was no time to lose. He managed to get up on his feet after a second attempt. His body was soaked in blood, but his mind was now clear. He gathered all the green leaves and heaped them on Nyagar. He then made for the bridge which he had failed to locate during the battle.

He walked away quickly—the spirit should not leave the body while he was still on the scene. It was nearly dawn. He would reach the river Migua in time to rinse the blood off his clothes.

Before sunrise, the clan leader Olielo sounded the funeral drum to alert the people. Within an hour more than a hundred clansmen had assembled at the foot of the *Opok* tree where the elders normally met to hear criminal and civil cases. Olielo then addressed the gathering.

"Listen, my people. Some of you must have heard of the trouble we had in our clan last night. Thieves broke into Omogo's kraal[1] and stole six of his ploughing oxen."

"Oh!" the crowd exclaimed.

Olielo continued, "As a result, blood was shed, and we now have a body lying here."

"Is this so?" one elder asked.

"Yes, it is so," Olielo replied. "Now, listen to me. Although our laws prohibit any wanton killing, thieves and adulterers we regard as animals. If anyone kills one of them he is not guilty of murder. He is looked upon as a person who has rid society of an evil spirit, and in return society has a duty to protect him and his children. You all know that such a person must be cleansed before he again associates with other members of society. But the white man's laws are different. According to his laws, if you kill a man because you find him stealing your cattle or sleeping in your wife's hut, you are guilty of murder—and therefore you must also be killed. Because he thinks his laws are superior to ours, we should handle him carefully. We have ancestors—the white man has none. That is why they bury their dead far away from their houses.

"This is what we should do. We shall send thirty men to the white man to tell him that we have killed a thief. This group should tell him that the whole clan killed the thief. Take my word, my children. The white man's tricks work only among a divided people. If we stand united, none of us will be killed."

"The old man has spoken well," they shouted. Thirty men were elected, and they immediately left for the white man's camp.

More people, including some women, had arrived to swell the number of the group. They moved towards the river where the dead thief lay covered in leaves, to await the arrival of the white man.

---

1 **kraal:** Pen or corral for keeping animals.

Nyamundhe moved near her co-wife. "Where is Nyagar? My eye has not caught him,"

His co-wife peered through the crowd, and then answered, "I think he has gone with the thirty. He left home quite early. I woke up very early this morning, but the gate was open. He had left the village."

Nyamundhe recollected that as they entered the narrow path which led to the river, their feet felt wet from the morning dew. And bending across the path as if saying prayers to welcome the dawn, were long grasses which were completely overpowered by the thick dew. She wanted to ask her co-wife where their husband could have gone but, noticing her indifference, she had decided to keep quiet.

"I did not like that black cat which dashed in front of us when we were coming here," Nyamundhe said to her co-wife.

"Yes, it is a bad sign for a black cat to cross one's way first thing in the morning."

They heard the sound of a lorry. They looked up and saw a cloud of dust and two police lorries approaching.

The two lorries pulled up by the heap of green leaves. A European police officer and four African officers stepped down. They opened the back of one of the lorries and the thirty men who had been sent to the police station by the clan came out.

"Where is the clan elder?" the white officer demanded.

Olielo stepped forward.

"Tell me the truth. What happened? I don't believe a word of what these people are saying. What did you send them to tell me?"

Olielo spoke sombrely and slowly in Dholuo, pronouncing every word distinctly. His words were translated by an African police officer.

"I sent them to inform you that we killed a thief last night."

"What! You killed a man?" the white man moved towards Olielo. The other policemen followed him.

"You killed a man?" the white officer repeated.

"No, we killed a thief." Olielo maintained his ground.

"How many times have I told you that you must abandon this savage custom of butchering one another? No-one is a thief until he has been tried in a court of law and found guilty. Your people are deaf." The white man pointed at Olielo with his stick in an ominous manner.

"This time I shall show you how to obey the law. Who killed him?" the white officer asked angrily.

"All of us," answered Olielo, pointing at the crowd.

"Don't be silly. Who hit him first?"

The crowd was getting restless. The people surged forward menacingly towards the five police officers.

"We all hit the thief," they shouted.

"If you want to arrest us, you are free to do so. You'd better send for more lorries."[2]

2 **lorries:** Large trucks.

"Where is the dead man?" the white man asked Olielo.

"There," Olielo replied, pointing at the heap of leaves.

The police moved towards the heap. The crowd also pushed forward. They wanted to get a glimpse of him before the white man took him away.

The last time a man had been killed in the area, the police took the corpse to Kisumu where it was cut up into pieces and then stitched up again. Then they returned it to the people saying, "Here is your man—bury him." Some people claimed that bile is extracted from such bodies and given to police tracker dogs; and that is why the dogs can track a thief to his house. Many people believed such stories. They were sure that this body would be taken away again by the police.

The European officer told the other police officer to uncover the body. They hesitated for a while, and then obeyed.

Olielo looked at the body before them unbelievingly. Then he looked at his people, and at the police. Was he normal? Where was the thief? He looked at the body a second time. He was not insane. It was the body of Nyagar, his cousin, who lay dead, with a sizable wooden stick driven through his right eye.

Nyamundhe broke loose from the crowd and ran towards the dead body. She fell on her husband's body and wept bitterly. Then turning to the crowd, she shouted, "Where is the thief you killed? Where is he?"

As the tension mounted, the crowd broke up into little groups of twos and threes. The women started to wail; and the men who had killed the thief that night looked at one another in complete disbelief. They had left Nyagar entering his village while they walked on. They could swear to it. Then Olielo, without any attempt to conceal his tear-drenched face, appealed to his people with these words, "My countrymen, the evil hand has descended upon us. Let it not break up our society. Although Nyagar is dead, his spirit is still among us."

But Nyamundhe did not heed the comforts of *Jaduong'* Olielo nor did she trust the men who swore that they had seen Nyagar enter his village after the incident with the thieves. She struggled wildly with the police who carried the corpse of her husband and placed it at the back of the lorry to be taken to Kisumu for a *post mortem*. A police officer comforted her with the promise that a village-wide inquiry would start at once into the death of her husband.

But Nyamundhe shook her head. "If you say you will give him back to me alive, then I will listen."

Nyamundhe tore her clothes and stripped to the waist. She walked slowly behind the mourners, weeping and chanting, her hands raised above her head.

> My lover the son of Ochieng'
> The son of Omolo
> The rains are coming down
> Yes, the rains are coming down
> The nights will be dark
> The nights will be cold and long.
> Oh! the son-in-law of my mother
> I have no heart to forgive,

I have no heart to pardon
All these mourners cheat me now
Yes, they cheat me
But when the sun goes to his home and
Darkness falls, they desert me.
In the cold hours of the night
Each woman clings to her man
There is no-one among them
There is none
There is no woman who will lend me a
Husband for the night
Ah, my lover, the son of Ochieng'
The son-law of my mother.

QUESTIONS

1. Postcolonial authors writing for a Western audience often must explain certain customs or translate native words for their readers. Find instances in this story where Ogot has supplied information perhaps necessary to non-African readers but probably unnecessary for an African readership. Do these explanations weaken the story in any way? Are they skillfully or clumsily integrated?

2. Is Nyagar's death a case of poetic justice? Does he "deserve" to die for his greed?

3. Whose system of justice does the story favor? Are the Africans justified in killing the thief? Are the white policemen justified in believing that their system of justice is superior?

4. In what other ways do the ideas, values, and practices of the Africans differ from those of Westerners? Point to specific passages or incidents.

5. When Nyagar is struck by the thief, the author describes him as "unconscious." Later, the police find him dead, "a sizable wooden stake driven through his right eye." Has the author contrived a trick ending, or has she used a legitimate device for suspense?

6. What does the story reveal about the place of women in this society?

Ama Ata Aidoo

(GHANA, b. 1942)

Ama Ata Aidoo's father was chief of Abeadzi Kyiakor, where she was born in 1942. Both parents were politically aware and active; indeed, her grandfather was imprisoned, tortured, and eventually killed by the British. After attending

Ghanaian schools, she graduated from the University of Ghana in Lagon with an honors degree in English in 1964. While at university, her play, *The Dilemma of a Ghost,* was produced. Her institution also appointed her a research fellow in African studies, after which she studied creative writing at Stanford University in the United States. From 1970–1982, she lectured in English at the University of Cape Coast, after which she served as Ghana's minister of education for a year. Meanwhile, her writing career was blossoming, beginning with a prize-winning story first published in *Black Orpheus.* In 1970, she published both a play, *Anowa,* and a collection of stories, *No Sweetness Here.* Since then, novels, poems, a children's book, and another collection of stories, *The Girl Who Can and Other Stories* (1997), have followed at regular intervals.

Like many writers of her generation, Aidoo writes about the effects of sexism and colonialism. Her work, therefore, is keenly aware of the past and present and of the problems facing post-colonial Africans. Pain and suffering are common features of the life she describes. The psychological effects of colonialism complicate the lives of her characters, causing many of them to be uncertain and confused. Stylistically, her narrative and dramatic talents merge; dialogue is almost as essential to her fiction as it is to her plays. She is also influenced by African oral traditions and claims that her stories are written as much to be heard as read.

"Two Sisters," like Chinua Achebe's "Girls at War," explores the relation between the personal and the political.

Two Sisters   1970

As she shakes out the typewriter cloak and covers the machine with it, the thought of the bus she has to hurry to catch goes through her like a pain. It is her luck, she thinks. Everything is just her luck. Why, if she had one of those graduates for a boyfriend, wouldn't he come and take her home every evening? And she knows that a girl does not herself have to be a graduate to get one of those boys. Certainly, Joe is dying to do exactly that—with his taxi. And he is as handsome as anything, and a good man, but you know . . . Besides there are cars and there are cars. As for the possibility of the other actually coming to fetch her—oh well. She has to admit it will take some time before she can bring herself to make demands of that sort on *him.* She has also to admit that the temptation is extremely strong. Would it really be so dangerously indiscreet? Doesn't one government car look like another? The hugeness of it? Its shaded glass? The uniformed chauffeur? She can already see herself stepping out to greet the dead-with-envy glances of the other girls. To begin with, she will insist on a little discretion. The driver can drop her under the neem trees in the morning and pick her up from there in the evening . . . anyway, she will have to wait a little while for that and it is all her luck.

There are other ways, surely. One of these, for some reason, she has sworn to have nothing of. Her boss has a car and does not look bad. In fact the man is alright.

But she keeps telling herself that she does not fancy having some old and dried-out housewife walking into the office one afternoon to tear her hair out and make a row. ... Mm, so for the meantime, it is going to continue to be the municipal bus with its grimy seats, its common passengers and impudent conductors. ... Jesus! She doesn't wish herself dead or anything as stupidly final as that. Oh no. She just wishes she could sleep deep and only wake up on the morning of her glory.

The new pair of black shoes are more realistic than their owner, though. As she walks down the corridor, they sing:

> Count, Mercy, count your blessings
> Count, Mercy, count your blessings
> Count, count, count your blessings.

They sing along the corridor, into the avenue, across the road and into the bus. And they resume their song along the gravel path, as she opens the front gate and crosses the cemented courtyard to the door.

"Sissie!" she called.

"*Hei* Mercy," and the door opened to show the face of Connie, big sister, six years or more older and now heavy with her second child. Mercy collapsed into the nearest chair.

"Welcome home. How was the office today?"

"Sister, don't ask. Look at my hands. My fingers are dead with typing. Oh God, I don't know what to do."

"Why, what is wrong?"

"You tell me what is right. Why should I be a typist?"

"What else would you be?"

"What a strange question. Is typing the only thing one can do in this world? You are a teacher, are you not?"

"But ... but ..."

"But what? Or you want me to know that if I had done better in the exams, I could have trained to be a teacher too, eh, sister? Or even a proper secretary?"

"Mercy, what is the matter? What have I done? What have I done? Why have you come home so angry?"

Mercy broke into tears.

"Oh I am sorry. I am sorry, Sissie. It's just that I am sick of everything. The office, living with you and your husband. I want a husband of my own, children. I want ... I want ..."

"But you are so beautiful."

"Thank you. But so are you."

"You are young and beautiful. As for marriage, it's you who are postponing it. Look at all these people who are running after you."

"Sissie, I don't like what you are doing. So stop it."

"Okay, okay, okay."

And there was a silence.

"Which of them could I marry? Joe is—mm, fine—but, but I just don't like him."

"You mean . . ."

"Oh, Sissie!"

"Little sister, you and I can be truthful with one another."

"Oh yes."

"What I would like to say is that I am not that old or wise. But still I could advise you a little. Joe drives someone's car now. Well, you never know. Lots of taxi drivers come to own their taxis, sometimes fleets of cars."

"Of course. But it's a pity you are married already. Or I could be a go-between for you and Joe!"

And the two of them burst out laughing. It was when she rose to go to the bedroom that Connie noticed the new shoes.

"*Ei,* those are beautiful shoes. Are they new?"

From the other room, Mercy's voice came interrupted by the motions of her body as she undressed and then dressed again. However, the uncertainty in it was due to something entirely different.

"Oh, I forgot to tell you about them. In fact, I was going to show them to you. I think it was on Tuesday I bought them. Or was it Wednesday? When I came home from the office, you and James had taken Akosua out. And later, I forgot all about them."

"I see. But they are very pretty. Were they expensive?"

"No, not really." This reply was too hurriedly said.

And she said only last week that she didn't have a penny on her. And I believed her because I know what they pay her is just not enough to last anyone through any month, even minus rent. . . . I have been thinking she manages very well. But these shoes. And she is not the type who would borrow money just to buy a pair of shoes, when she could have gone on wearing her old pairs until things get better. Oh I wish I knew what to do. I mean I am not her mother. And I wonder how James will see these problems.

"Sissie, you look worried."

"Hmm, when don't I? With the baby due in a couple of months and the government's new ruling on salaries and all. On top of everything, I have reliable information that James is running after a new girl."

Mercy laughed.

"Oh Sissie. You always get reliable information on these things."

"But yes. And I don't know why."

"Sissie, men are like that."

"They are selfish."

"No, it's just that women allow them to behave the way they do instead of seizing some freedom themselves."

"But I am sure that even if we were free to carry on in the same way, I wouldn't make use of it."

"But why not?"

"Because I love James. I love James and I am not interested in any other man." Her voice was full of tears. But Mercy was amused.

"O God. Now listen to that. It's women like you who keep all of us down."

"Well, I am sorry but it's how the good God created me."

"Mm. I am sure that I can love several men at the same time."

"Mercy!"

They burst out laughing again. And yet they are sad. But laughter is always best.

Mercy complained of hunger and so they went to the kitchen to heat up some food and eat. The two sisters alone. It is no use waiting for James. And this evening, a friend of Connie's has come to take out the baby girl, Akosua, and had threatened to keep her until her bedtime.

"Sissie, I am going to see a film." This from Mercy.

"Where?"

"The Globe."

"Are you going with Joe?"

"No."

"Are you going alone?"

"No."

Careful Connie.

"Whom are you going with?"

Careful Connie, please. Little sister's nostrils are widening dangerously. Look at the sudden creasing-up of her mouth and between her brows. Connie, a sister is a good thing. Even a younger sister. Especially when you have no mother or father.

"Mercy, whom are you going out with?"

"Well, I had food in my mouth! And I had to swallow it down before I could answer you, no?"

"I am sorry." How softly said.

"And anyway, do I have to tell you everything?"

"Oh no. It's just that I didn't think it was a question I should not have asked."

There was more silence. Then Mercy sucked her teeth with irritation and Connie cleared her throat with fear.

"I am going out with Mensar-Arthur."

As Connie asked the next question, she wondered if the words were leaving her lips.

"Mensar-Arthur?"

"Yes."

"Which one?"

"How many do you know?"

Her fingers were too numb to pick up the food. She put the plate down. Something jumped in her chest and she wondered what it was. Perhaps it was the baby.

"Do you mean that member of Parliament?"

"Yes."

"But Mercy . . ."

Little sister only sits and chews her food.

"But Mercy . . ."

Chew, chew, chew.

"But Mercy . . ."

"What?"

She startled Connie.

"He is so old."

Chew, chew, chew.

"Perhaps, I mean, perhaps that really doesn't matter, does it? Not very much anyway. But they say he has so many wives and girl-friends."

Please little sister. I am not trying to interfere in your private life. You said yourself a little while ago that you wanted a man of your own. That man belongs to so many women already. . . .

That silence again. Then there was only Mercy's footsteps as she went to put her plate in the kitchen sink, running water as she washed her plate and her hands. She drank some water and coughed. Then as tears streamed down her sister's averted face, there was the sound of her footsteps as she left the kitchen. At the end of it all, she banged a door. Connie only said something like, "O Lord, O Lord," and continued sitting in the kitchen. She had hardly eaten anything at all. Very soon Mercy went to have a bath. Then Connie heard her getting ready to leave the house. The shoes. Then she was gone. She needn't have carried on like that, eh? Because Connie had not meant to probe or bring on a quarrel. What use is there in this old world for a sister, if you can't have a chat with her? What's more, things like this never happen to people like Mercy. Their parents were good Presbyterians. They feared God. Mama had not managed to give them all the rules of life before she died. But Connie knows that running around with an old and depraved public man would have been considered an abomination by the parents.

A big car with a super-smooth engine purred into the drive. It actually purrs: this huge machine from the white man's land. Indeed, its well-mannered protest as the tyres slid on to the gravel seemed like a lullaby compared to the loud thumping of the girl's stiletto shoes. When Mensar-Arthur saw Mercy, he stretched his arm and opened the door to the passenger seat. She sat down and the door closed with a civilised thud. The engine hummed into motion and the car sailed away.

After a distance of a mile or so from the house, the man started conversation.

"And how is my darling today?"

"I am well," and only the words did not imply tragedy.

"You look solemn today, why?"

She remained silent and still.

"My dear, what is the matter?"

"Nothing."

"Oh . . ." he cleared his throat again. "Eh, and how were the shoes?"

"Very nice. In fact, I am wearing them now. They pinch a little but then all new shoes are like that."

"And the handbag?"

"I like it very much too. . . . My sister noticed them. I mean the shoes." The tragedy was announced.

"Did she ask you where you got them from?"

"No."

He cleared his throat again.

"Where did we agree to go tonight?"

"The Globe, but I don't want to see a film."

"Is that so? Mm, I am glad because people always notice things."

"But they won't be too surprised."

"What are you saying, my dear?"

"Nothing."

"Okay, so what shall we do?"

"I don't know."

"Shall I drive to the Seaway?"

"Oh yes."

He drove to the Seaway. To a section of the beach they knew very well. She loves it here. This wide expanse of sand and the old sea. She has often wished she could do what she fancied: one thing she fancies. Which is to drive very near to the end of the sands until the tyres of the car touched the water. Of course it is a very foolish idea as he pointed out sharply to her the first time she thought aloud about it. It was in his occasional I-am-more-than-old-enough-to-be-your-father tone. There are always disadvantages. Things could be different. Like if one had a younger lover. Handsome, maybe not rich like this man here, but well-off, sufficiently well-off to be able to afford a sports car. A little something very much like those in the films driven by the white racing drivers. With tyres that can do everything . . . and they would drive exactly where the sea and the sand meet.

"We are here."

"Don't let's get out. Let's just sit inside and talk."

"Talk?"

"Yes."

"Okay. But what is it, my darling?"

"I have told my sister about you."

"Good God. Why?"

"But I had to. I couldn't keep it to myself any longer."

"Childish. It was not necessary at all. She is not your mother."

"No. But she is all I have. And she has been very good to me."

"Well, it was her duty."

"Then it is my duty to tell her about something like this. I may get into trouble."

"Don't be silly," he said, "I normally take good care of my girl-friends."

"I see," she said and for the first time in the one month since she agreed to be this man's lover, the tears which suddenly rose into her eyes were not forced.

"And you promised you wouldn't tell her." It was father's voice now.

"Don't be angry. After all, people talk so much, as you said a little while ago. She was bound to hear it one day."

"My darling, you are too wise. What did she say?"

"She was pained."

"Don't worry. Find out something she wants very much but cannot get in this country because of the import restrictions."

"I know for sure she wants an electric motor for her sewing machine."

"Is that all?"

"That's what I know of."

"Mm. I am going to London next week on some delegation, so if you bring me the details on the make of the machine, I shall get her the motor."

"Thank you."

"What else is worrying my Black Beauty?"

"Nothing."

"And by the way, let me know as soon as you want to leave your sister's place. I have got you one of the government estate houses."

"Oh . . . oh," she said, pleased, contented for the first time since this typically ghastly day had begun, at half-past six in the morning.

Dear little child came back from the playground with her toe bruised. Shall we just blow cold air from our mouth on it or put on a salve? Nothing matters really. Just see that she does not feel unattended. And the old sea roars on. This is a calm sea, generally. Too calm in fact, this Gulf of Guinea. The natives sacrifice to him on Tuesdays and once a year celebrate him. They might save their chickens, their eggs and their yams. And as for the feast once a year, he doesn't pay much attention to it either. They are always celebrating one thing or another and they surely don't need him for an excuse to celebrate one day more. He has seen things happen along these beaches. Different things. Contradictory things. Or just repetitions of old patterns. He never interferes in their affairs. Why should he? Except in places like Keta where he eats houses away because they leave him no choice. Otherwise he never allows them to see his passions. People are worms, and even the God who created them is immensely bored with their antics. Here is a fifty-year-old "big man" who thinks he is somebody. And a twenty-three-year-old child who chooses a silly way to conquer unconquerable problems. Well, what did one expect of human beings? And so as those two settled on the back seat of the car to play with each other's bodies, he, the Gulf of Guinea, shut his eyes with boredom. It is right. He could sleep, no? He spread himself and moved further ashore. But the car was parked at a very safe distance and the rising tides could not wet its tyres.

James has come home late. But then he has been coming back late for the past few weeks. Connie is crying and he knows it as soon as he enters the bedroom. He hates tears, for like so many men, he knows it is one of the most potent weapons in women's bitchy and inexhaustible arsenal. She speaks first.

"James."

"Oh, you are still awake?" He always tries to deal with these nightly funeral parlour doings by pretending not to know what they are about.

"I couldn't sleep."

"What is wrong?"

"Nothing."

So he moves quickly and sits beside her.

"Connie, what is the matter? You have been crying again."

"You are very late again."

"Is that why you are crying? Or is there something else?"

"Yes."

"Yes to what?"

"James, where were you?"

"Connie, I have warned you about what I shall do if you don't stop examining me, as though I were your prisoner, every time I am a little late."

She sat up.

"A little late! It is nearly two o'clock."

"Anyway, you won't believe me if I told you the truth, so why do you want me to waste my breath?"

"Oh well." She lies down again and turns her face to the wall. He stands up but does not walk away. He looks down at her. So she remembers every night: they have agreed, after many arguments, that she should sleep like this. During her first pregnancy, he kept saying after the third month or so that the sight of her tummy the last thing before he slept always gave him nightmares. Now he regrets all this. The bed creaks as he throws himself down by her.

"James."

"Yes."

"There is something much more serious."

"You have heard about my newest affair?"

"Yes, but that is not what I am referring to."

"Jesus, is it possible that there is anything more important than that?"

And as they laugh they know that something has happened. One of those things which, with luck, will keep them together for some time to come.

"He teases me on top of everything."

"What else can one do to you but tease when you are in this state?"

"James! How profane!"

"It is your dirty mind which gave my statement its shocking meaning."

"Okay! But what shall I do?"

"About what?"

"Mercy. Listen, she is having an affair with Mensar-Arthur."

"Wonderful."

She sits up and he sits up.

"James, we must do something about it. It is very serious."

"Is that why you were crying?"

"Of course."

"Why shouldn't she?"

"But it is wrong. And she is ruining herself."

"Since every other girl she knows has ruined herself prosperously, why shouldn't she? Just forget for once that you are a teacher. Or at least, remember she is not your pupil."

"I don't like your answers."

"What would you like me to say? Every morning her friends who don't earn any more than she does wear new dresses, shoes, wigs and what-have-you to work. What would you have her do?"

"The fact that other girls do it does not mean that Mercy should do it too."

"You are being very silly. If I were Mercy, I am sure that's exactly what I would do. And you know I mean it too."

James is cruel. He is terrible and mean. Connie breaks into fresh tears and James comforts her. There is one point he must drive home though.

"In fact, encourage her. He may be able to intercede with the Ministry for you so that after the baby is born they will not transfer you from here for some time."

"James, you want me to use my sister!"

"She is using herself, remember."

"James, you are wicked."

"And maybe he would even agree to get us a new car from abroad. I shall pay for everything. That would be better than paying a fortune for that old thing I was thinking of buying. Think of that."

"You will ride in it alone."

"Well . . ."

That was a few months before the *coup*. Mensar-Arthur did go to London for a conference and bought something for all his wives and girl-friends, including Mercy. He even remembered the motor for Connie's machine. When Mercy took it to her she was quite confused. She had wanted this thing for a long time, and it would make everything so much easier, like the clothes for the new baby. And yet one side of her said that accepting it was a betrayal. Of what, she wasn't even sure. She and Mercy could never bring the whole business into the open and discuss it. And there was always James supporting Mercy, to Connie's bewilderment. She took the motor with thanks and sold even her right to dissent. In a short while, Mercy left the house to go and live in the estate house Mensar-Arthur had procured for her. Then, a couple of weeks later, the *coup*. Mercy left her new place before anyone could evict her. James never got his car. Connie's new baby was born. Of the three, the one who greeted the new order with undisguised relief was Connie. She is not really a demonstrative person but it was obvious from her eyes that she was happy. As far as she was concerned, the old order as symbolised by Mensar-Arthur was a threat to her sister and therefore to her own peace of mind. With it gone, things could return to normal. Mercy would move back to the house, perhaps start to date someone more— ordinary, let's say. Eventually, she would get married and then the nightmare of those past weeks would be forgotten. God being so good, he brought the *coup* early before the news of the affair could spread and brand her sister. . . .

The arrival of the new baby has magically waved away the difficulties between James and Connie. He is that kind of man, and she that kind of woman. Mercy has not been seen for many days. Connie is beginning to get worried. . . .

James heard the baby yelling—a familiar noise, by now—the moment he opened the front gate. He ran in, clutching to his chest the few things he had bought on his way home.

"We are in here."

"I certainly could hear you. If there is anything people of this country have, it is a big mouth."

"Don't I agree? But on the whole, we are well. He is eating normally and every-thing. You?"

"Nothing new. Same routine. More stories about the overthrown politicians."

"What do you mean, nothing new? Look at the excellent job the soldiers have done, cleaning up the country of all that dirt. I feel free already and I am dying to get out and enjoy it."

James laughed mirthlessly.

"All I know is that Mensar-Arthur is in jail. No use. And I am not getting my car. Rough deal."

"I never took you seriously on that car business."

"Honestly, if this were in the ancient days, I could brand you a witch. You don't want me, your husband, to prosper?"

"Not out of my sister's ruin."

"Ruin, ruin, ruin! Christ! See Connie, the funny thing is that I am sure you are the only person who thought it was a disaster to have a sister who was the girl-friend of a big man."

"Okay; now all is over, and don't let's quarrel."

"I bet the *coup* could have succeeded on your prayers alone."

And Connie wondered why he said that with so much bitterness. She won-dered if . . .

"Has Mercy been here?"

"Not yet, later, maybe. Mm. I had hoped she would move back here and start all over again."

"I am not surprised she hasn't. In fact, if I were her, I wouldn't come back here either. Not to your nagging, no thank you, big sister."

And as the argument progressed, as always, each was forced into a more aggres-sive defensive stand.

"Well, just say what pleases you, I am very glad about the soldiers. Mercy is my only sister, brother; everything. I can't sit and see her life going wrong without feel-ing it. I am grateful to whatever forces there are which put a stop to that. What pains me now is that she should be so vague about where she is living at the moment. She makes mention of a girlfriend but I am not sure that I know her."

"If I were you, I would stop worrying because it seems Mercy can look after her-self quite well."

"Hmm," was all she tried to say.

Who heard something like the sound of a car pulling into the drive? Ah, but the footsteps are unmistakably Mercy's. Are those shoes the old pair which were new a couple of months ago? Or are they the newest pair? And here she is herself, the pretty one. A gay Mercy.

"Hello, hello, my clan!" and she makes a lot of her nephew.

"Dow-dah-dee-day! And how is my dear young man today? My lord, grow up fast and come to take care of Auntie Mercy."

Both Connie and James cannot take their eyes off her. Connie says, "He says to Auntie Mercy he is fine."

Still they watch her, horrified, fascinated and wondering what it's all about. Because they both know it is about something.

"Listen people, I brought a friend to meet you. A man."

"Where is he?" from James.

"Bring him in," from Connie.

"You know, Sissie, you are a new mother. I thought I'd come and ask you if it's all right."

"Of course," say James and Connie, and for some reason they are both very nervous.

"He is Captain Ashey."

"Which one?"

"*How many do you know?*"

James still thinks it is impossible. "Eh . . . do you mean the officer who has been appointed the . . . the . . ."

"Yes."

"Wasn't there a picture in *The Crystal* over the week-end about his daughter's wedding? And another one of him with his wife and children and grandchildren?"

"Yes."

"And he is heading a commission to investigate something or other?"

"Yes."

Connie just sits there with her mouth open that wide. . . .

QUESTIONS

1. Note carefully the shifts in point of view as the story progresses. What is the effect of these shifts? What do they allow the author to do that a fixed point of view would prohibit?

2. What kinds of official corruption are revealed in the story?

3. What does the story imply about men? Point to specific details to support your answer.

4. Is Connie right to oppose Mercy's behavior? Is James right to defend it?

5. In general, does official morality affect private morality? Does corruption at the top "trickle down" through society? Does private immorality disqualify someone for public office? Why or why not? How might the story reflect on these questions?

Charles Mungoshi

(ZIMBABWE, b. 1947)

Charles Mungoshi's life and work have spanned the period when African countries moved from colonial status to independence, and black African literature has progressed from protest and suppression to worldwide significance and recognition.

He was born in a village south of what was then Salisbury, Southern Rhodesia (present-day Harare, Zimbabwe) and spent his early childhood tending his father's cattle and absorbing the oral culture of his people, especially the tales told by his grandmother. After attending local schools, he left home to attend high school, where his writing talents were encouraged. He published his first short story in 1966. His first job was with the Forestry Commission, but he later worked as a clerk with a textbook company. In 1970 he published his first novel in Shona, the native language, and two years later released his first collection of short stories in English, *Coming of the Dry Season,* which was banned from 1974–1978 because one of its stories was deemed racially subversive by white authorities.

During the 1970s, Rhodesia was torn by civil war, as black Africans attempted to wrest control of the country from the white minority. This struggle, as well as other tensions in African society, are reflected in Mungoshi's best-known novel in English, *Waiting for the Rain* (1975), and his second novel in Shona (translated as *How Time Passes,* 1975). That same year, he left his job to become an editor for the Rhodesia Literature Bureau, whose purpose was to encourage but also control literature by black Africans in their native tongues. This new position put him in touch with other writers. In 1980, Zimbabwe became independent, and Mungoshi published his second volume of stories, *Some Kinds of Wounds and Other Stories,* which deal with the physical, psychic, and social wounds inflicted by war.

With independence came increased interest in Mungoshi's work, as he was recognized as a major national author and his books were widely read in schools. Perhaps in response, Mungoshi wrote increasingly in Shona, producing a play in 1980 and a new novel (translated as *Is Silence Not a Form of Speech?* 1983). These works reflect postindependence issues—the tension between rural and city life, problems of family division and discord, the impossible position many villagers felt as they were caught between government forces and rebel soldiers, and the increasing alienation of Africans from their traditional roots.

In addition to novels, short stories, and plays, Mungoshi has written highly acclaimed poetry and has most recently turned to film scripts and film production. His many honors include two P.E.N. International Awards, the Commonwealth Literature Prize for Africa, and the Noma Award for African Writing.

Shadows on the Wall   1972

Father is sitting just inside the hut near the door and I am sitting far across the hut near the opposite wall, playing with the shadows on the wall. Bright sunlight comes in through the doorway now and father, who blocks most of it, is reproduced in caricature on the floor and half-way up the wall. The wall and floor are bare, so he looks like a black scarecrow in a deserted field after the harvest.

Outside, the sun drops lower and other shadows start creeping into the hut. Father's shadow grows vaguer and climbs further up the wall like a ghost going up to heaven. His shadow moves behind sharper wriggling shadows like the presence of a tired old woman in a room full of young people, or like that creepy nameless feeling in a house of mourning.

He has tried five times to talk to me but I don't know what he wants. Now he talks about his other wife. He wants me to call her 'mother' but I can't because something in me cries each time I say it. She isn't my mother and my real mother is not dead. This other woman has run away. It is now the fourth time she has run away and tomorrow he is going to cycle fifty miles to her home to collect her. This will be the fourth time he has had to cycle after her. He is talking. I am not listening. He gives up.

Now the sun shines brilliantly before going down. The shadows of bushes and grass at the edge of the yard look as if they are on fire and father's features are cut more sharply and exaggerated. His nose becomes longer each time he nods because now he is sleeping while sitting, tired of the silence.

Father dozes, wakes up; dozes, wakes up and the sun goes down. His shadow expands and fades. Now it seems all over the wall, behind the other shadows, moving silently like a cold wind in a bare field. I look at him. There is still enough light for me to see the grey stubble sticking up untidily all over his face. His stubble, I know, is as stiff as a porcupine's, but as the light wanes now, it looks fleecy and soft like the down on a dove's nestling.

I was in the bush, long ago, and I came upon two dove nestlings. They were still clumsy and blind, with soft pink vulnerable flesh planted with short scattered grey feathers, their mouths open, waiting for their mother. I wished I had corn to give them. As it was, I consoled myself with the thought that their mother was somewhere nearby, coming home through the bush in the falling dark with food in her mouth for her children.

Next day I found the nestlings dead in their nest. Somewhere out in the bush or in the yellow ripe unharvested fields, someone had shot their mother in mid-flight home.

Not long after that, I was on my father's shoulders coming home from the fields at dusk. Mother was still with us then, and father carried me because she had asked him to. I had a sore foot and couldn't walk and mother couldn't carry me because she was carrying a basket of mealies,[1] for our supper on her head and pieces of

1 **mealies:** Cobs of corn.

firewood in her arms. At first father grumbled. He didn't like to carry me and he didn't like receiving orders from mother: she was there to listen to him always, he said. He carried me all the same although he didn't like to, and worse, I didn't like him to carry me. His hands were hard and pinchy and his arms felt as rough and barky as logs. I preferred mother's soft warm back. He knew, too, that I didn't want him to carry me because I made my body stiff and didn't relax when he rubbed his hard chin against my cheek. His breath was harsh and foul. He wore his battered hat and stank of dirt, sweat and soil. He was trying to talk to me but I was not listening to him. That was when I noticed that his stubble looked as vulnerable as the unprotected feathers on a dove's nestling. Tears filled my eyes then and I tried to respond to his teasing, but I gave it up because he immediately began picking on mother and made her tense and tight and this tension I could feel in me also.

After this he always wanted me to be near him and he made me ignore mother. He taught me to avoid mother. It was hard for me but he had a terrible way of making mother look despicable and mean. She noticed this and fought hard to make me cheerful, but I always saw father's threatening shadow hunched hawkishly over me. Instead of talking to either of them I became silent. I was no longer happy in either's presence. And this was when I began to notice the shadows on the wall of our hut.

One day the eternal quarrel between mother and father flared up to an unbelievable blaze. Mother went away to her people. After an unsuccessful night full of nightmares with father in the hut, he had to follow her. There had been a hailstorm in the night and everything looked sad in the dripping chill of the next day. The small mealie plants in the yard had been destroyed by the storm; all the leaves torn off except the small hard piths which now stood about in the puddles like nails in a skull. Father went away without a word and I was alone.

I lay under the blankets for a long time with the door of the hut open. One by one, our chickens began to come in out of the cold.

There is something in a cold chicken's voice that asks for something you don't know how to give, something more than corn.

I watched them come into the hut and I felt sorry for them. Their feathers were still wet and they looked smaller and sicklier than normal. I couldn't shoo them out. They came and crowded by the fire, their little bird voices scarcely rising above the merest whisper. My eyes left them and wandered up and down the walls.

At first I couldn't see them but when one chicken made a slight move I noticed that there were shadows on the wall.

These shadows fascinated me. There were hundreds of them. I spent the whole day trying to separate them, to isolate them, but they were as elusive and liquid as water in a jar. After a long time looking at them, I felt that they were talking to me. I held my breath and heard their words distinctly, a lullaby in harmony: sleep, sleep, you are all alone, sleep and don't wake up, ever again.

I must have fallen asleep because I remember seeing later on that the sky had turned all dark and a thin chilly drizzle was falling. The chickens, which must have gone out feeling hungry, were coming in again, wet, their forlorn voices hardly audible above the sound of the rain. I knew by the multitude of shadows on the wall that night was falling. I felt too weak to wake up and for a long time watched the shadows multiply and fade, multiply, mingle and fade, and listened to their talk. Again I must have fallen asleep because when I woke up I was well tucked in and warm. The shadows were now brilliant and clear on the wall because there was a fire on the hearth.

Mother and father had come in and they were silent. Seeing them, I felt as if I were coming from a long journey in a strange country. Mother noticed that I was awake and said,

"How do you feel?"

"He's just lazy," father said.

"He is ill," mother said. "His body is all on fire." She felt me.

"Lies. He is a man and you want to turn him into a woman."

After this I realized how ill I was. I couldn't eat anything: there was no appetite and I wasn't hungry.

I don't know how many days I was in bed. There seemed to be nothing. No light, no sun, to show it was day or darkness to show it was night. Mother was constantly in but I couldn't recognize her as a person. There were only shadows, the voices of the shadows, the lonely cries of the dripping wet fowls shaking the cold out of their feathers by the hearth, and the vague warm shadow that must have been mother. She spoke to me often but I don't remember if I answered anything. I was afraid to answer because I was alone on a solitary plain with the dark crashing of thunder and lightning always in my ears, and there was a big frightening shadow hovering above me so that I couldn't answer her without its hearing me. That must have been father.

They might have had quarrels—I am sure they had lots of them—but I didn't hear them. Everything had been flattened to a dim depthless grey landscape and the only movement on it was of the singing shadows. I could see the shadows and hear them speak to me, so I wasn't dead. If mother talked to me at all, her voice got lost in the vast expanse of emptiness between me and the shadows. Later, when I was beginning to be aware of the change of night into day, her voice was the soft pink intrusion like cream on the hard darkness of the wall. This turned later into a clear urgent sound like the lapping of water against boulders in the morning before sunrise. I noticed too that she was often alone with me. Father was away and must have been coming in late after I had fallen asleep.

The day I saw father, a chill set in the hut.

There was another hailstorm and a big quarrel that night. It was the last quarrel.

When I could wake up again mother was gone and a strange woman had taken her place in the house.

This woman had a shrill strident voice like a cicada's that jarred my nerves. She did all the talking and father became silent and morose. Instead of the frightful silences and sudden bursts of anger I used to know, he now tried to talk softly to me. He preferred to talk to me rather than to his new wife.

But he was too late. He had taught me silence and in that long journey between mother's time and this other woman's, I had given myself to the shadows.

So today he sits just inside the hut with the sun playing with him: cartooning him on the bare cold floor and the bare dark walls of the hut, and me watching and listening to the images on the wall. He cannot talk to me because I don't know how to answer him, his language is too difficult for me. All I can think of, the nearest I can come to him, is when I see that his tough grey stubble looks like the soft unprotected feathers on a dove's nestling; and when I remember that the next morning the nestlings were dead in their nest because somebody had unknowingly killed their mother in the bush on her way home, I feel the tears in my eyes.

It is all—all that I feel for my father; but I cannot talk to him. I don't know how I should talk to him. He has denied me the gift of language.

QUESTIONS

1. How is time handled in the story? When does the story begin? When does it end?

2. The language of the story is richly descriptive and full of images. What use does the author make of images and descriptions of shadows? Of birds? Of the weather?

3. Compare the way the narrator describes his father and the way he describes his mother. What is conveyed by the descriptions in each case?

4. What does the narrator mean when he says, "I had given myself to the shadows"?

5. In what sense has his father "denied [him] the gift of language"?

6. What ideas about marriage and man-woman relations lie behind the story?

7. How has the father changed by the end of the story? What has changed him?

Chinua Achebe

(NIGERIA, b. 1930)

Seldom has an author burst on the world scene with more immediate and lasting impact than Chinua Achebe did with his first novel, *Things Fall Apart* (1958). Achebe's fictional treatment of the clash between traditional Igbo villagers and Victorian colonizers was both an artistic and a political success, opening the world's eyes to African literature in general and the issues of colonialism and its aftermath. Since that first novel, Achebe has extended and solidified his reputation in a series of novels, short stories, juvenile books, poetry, and essays that collectively trace and comment on the situation in Nigeria in particular and sub-Saharan Africa in general as it has evolved since the nineteenth century.

Achebe was born a member of the Igbo people in Agidi, Nigeria, the son of mission teachers. After completing his secondary education and studying at University College, Ibadan, in Nigeria, he completed his BA degree in 1953. He spent the next several years in broadcasting, first for the Nigerian Broadcasting Company, and then for the British Broadcasting Company in England. He left broadcasting in 1966 to teach at the University of Nigeria and, in the following year, also served as a diplomat for Biafra during the 1967–1970 civil war. Since then, he has divided his time between teaching at various American, British, and Nigerian universities and in several positions in public administration, including president of the Ogidi town union since 1986. His writings have won numerous national and international prizes.

Achebe's fiction began by criticizing the devastating effects of European colonialism on Africa's traditional societies, and he continues to lay much of the blame for Africa's problems on European racism, which he traces in part to Joseph Conrad's depiction of Africa in "Heart of Darkness." But Achebe is equally hard on African politicians and officials, whose corruption and lust for power have led to cynicism among ordinary people toward political institutions and to millions of deaths through civil strife. For Achebe, these are not merely social or political problems but spiritual issues as well. The death of traditional African ways and values lies at the heart of these problems, though Achebe does not advocate a nostalgic return to the past but rather a wise reconciliation to the realities of change. The tension between old and new is reflected in his ambivalence about the English language, which must be confronted as a fact, even while lamented as a usurper of native tongues.

Achebe is an outspoken critic of Nigeria's political leaders and was active in the attempt by Biafra to secede from the Nigerian Federation. In 1983, he was elected to a prominent position in the People's Redemption Party. He has also used his success as a writer to champion the efforts of younger authors and artists, in part by editing a bilingual literary journal.

"Girls at War" (1972) is Achebe's most famous and frequently anthologized story. Set during the Biafran struggle for independence from Nigeria (1967–1970), it chronicles the sufferings war inflicts on soldiers and civilians, but more importantly raises the question what integrity can mean when physical and psychological survival are at stake.

Girls at War   *1972*

The first time their paths crossed nothing happened. That was in the first heady days of warlike preparation when thousands of young men (and sometimes women too) were daily turned away from enlistment centres because far too many of them were coming forward burning with readiness to bear arms in defence of the exciting new nation.[1]

The second time they met was at a check-point at Awka. Then the war had started and was slowly moving southwards from the distant northern sector. He was driving from Onitsha to Enugu and was in a hurry. Although intellectually he approved of thorough searches at road-blocks, emotionally he was always offended whenever he had to submit to them. He would probably not admit it but the feeling people got was that if you were put through a search then you could not really be one of the big people. Generally he got away without a search by pronouncing in his deep, authoritative voice: "Reginald Nwankwo, Ministry of Justice." That almost always did it. But sometimes either through ignorance or sheer cussedness the crowd at the odd check-point would refuse to be impressed. As happened now at Awka. Two constables carrying heavy Mark 4 rifles were watching distantly from the road-side leaving the actual searching to local vigilantes.

"I am in a hurry," he said to the girl who now came up to his car. "My name is Reginald Nwankwo, Ministry of Justice."

"Good afternoon, sir. I want to see your trunk."

"O Christ! What do you think is in the trunk?"

"I don't know, sir."

He got out of the car in suppressed rage, stalked to the back, opened the trunk and holding the lid up with his left hand he motioned with the right as if to say: After you!

"Are you satisfied?" he demanded.

"Yes, sir. Can I see your pigeon-hole?"

"Christ Almighty!"

"Sorry to delay you, sir. But you people gave us this job to do."

"Never mind. You are damn right. It's just that I happen to be in a hurry. But never mind. That's the glovebox. Nothing there as you can see."

"All right, sir, close it." Then she opened the rear door and bent down to inspect under the seats. It was then he took the first real look at her, starting from behind. She was a beautiful girl in a breasty blue jersey, khaki jeans and canvas shoes with the newstyle hair-plait which gave a girl a defiant look and which they called—for reasons of their own—"air force base"; and she looked vaguely familiar.

"I am all right, sir," she said at last meaning she was through with her task. "You don't recognize me?"

"No. Should I?"

"You gave me a lift to Enugu that time I left my school to go and join the militia."

"Ah, yes, you were the girl. I told you, didn't I, to go back to school because girls were not required in the militia. What happened?"

"They told me to go back to my school or join the Red Cross."

---

1 **new nation:** Biafra.

"You see I was right. So, what are you doing now?"

"Just patching up with Civil Defence."

"Well, good luck to you. Believe me you are a great girl."

That was the day he finally believed there might be something in this talk about revolution. He had seen plenty of girls and women marching and demonstrating before now. But somehow he had never been able to give it much thought. He didn't doubt that the girls and the women took themselves seriously; they obviously did. But so did the little kids who marched up and down the streets at the time drilling with sticks and wearing their mothers' soup bowls for steel helmets. The prime joke of the time among his friends was the contingent of girls from a local secondary school marching behind a banner: WE ARE IMPREGNABLE!

But after that encounter at the Awka check-point he simply could not sneer at the girls again, nor at the talk of revolution, for he had seen it in action in that young woman whose devotion had simply and without self-righteousness convicted him of gross levity. What were her words? We are doing the work you asked us to do. She wasn't going to make an exception even for one who once did her a favour. He was sure she would have searched her own father just as rigorously.

When their paths crossed a third time, at least eighteen months later, things had got very bad. Death and starvation having long chased out the headiness of the early days, now left in some places blank resignation, in others a rock-like, even suicidal, defiance. But surprisingly enough there were many at this time also who had no other desire than to corner whatever good things were still going and to enjoy themselves to the limit. For such people *a strange normalcy* had returned to the world. All those nervous check-points disappeared. Girls became girls once more and boys boys. It was a tight, blockaded and desperate world but none the less a world—with some goodness and some badness and plenty of heroism which, however, happened most times far, far below the eye-level of the people in this story—in out-of-the-way refugee camps, in the damp tatters,[2] in the hungry and bare-handed courage of the first line of fire.

Reginald Nwankwo lived in Owerri then. But that day he had gone to Nkwerri in search of relief. He had got from Caritas[3] in Owerri a few heads of stockfish, some tinned meat, and the dreadful American stuff called Formula Two which he felt certain was some kind of animal feed. But he always had a vague suspicion that not being a Catholic put one at a disadvantage with Caritas. So he went now to see an old friend who ran the WCC depot at Nkwerri to get other items like rice, beans and that excellent cereal commonly called Gabon gari.

He left Owerri at six in the morning so as to catch his friend at the depot where he was known never to linger beyond 8:30 for fear of air-raids. Nwankwo was very fortunate that day. The depot had received on the previous day large supplies of new stock as a result of an unusual number of plane landings a few nights earlier. As his

2 **tatters:** Tattered clothing, rags.
3 **Caritas:** A Roman Catholic relief agency.

driver loaded tins and bags and cartons into his car the starved crowds that perpetually hung around relief centres made crude, ungracious remarks like "War Can Continue!" meaning the WCC! Some-body else shouted "Irevolu!" and his friends
replied "shum!" "Irevolu!" "shum!" "Isofeli?" "shum!" "Isofeli?" "Mba!"

Nwankwo was deeply embarrassed not by the jeers of this scarecrow crowd of
rags and floating ribs but by the independent accusation of their wasted bodies and
sunken eyes. Indeed he would probably have felt much worse had they said nothing,
simply looked on in silence, as his trunk was loaded with milk, and powdered egg
and oats and tinned meat and stockfish. By nature such singular good fortune in the
midst of a general desolation was certain to embarrass him. But what could a man
do? He had a wife and four children living in the remote village of Ogbu and completely dependent on what relief he could find and send them. He couldn't abandon
them to kwashiokor.[4] The best he could do—and did do as a matter of fact—was to
make sure that whenever he got sizeable supplies like now he made over some of it
to his driver, Johnson, with a wife and six, or was it seven? children and a salary of
ten pounds a month when gari in the market was climbing to one pound per cigarette cup. In such a situation one could do nothing at all for crowds; at best one
could try to be of some use to one's immediate neighbours. That was all.

On his way back to Owerri a very attractive girl by the roadside waved for a lift.
He ordered the driver to stop. Scores of pedestrians, dusty and exhausted, some military, some civil, swooped down on the car from all directions.

"No, no, no," said Nwankwo firmly. "It's the young woman I stopped for. I have
a bad tyre and can only take one person. Sorry."

"My son, please," cried one old woman in despair, gripping the door-handle.

"Old woman, you want to be killed?" shouted the driver as he pulled away, shaking her off. Nwankwo had already opened a book and sunk his eyes there. For at
least a mile after that he did not even look at the girl until she finding, perhaps, the
silence too heavy said:

"You've saved me today. Thank you."

"Not at all. Where are you going?"

"To Owerri. You don't recognize me?"

"Oh yes, of course. What a fool I am . . . You are . . ."

"Gladys."

"That's right, the militia girl. You've changed, Gladys. You were always beautiful
of course, but now you are a beauty queen. What do you do these days?"

"I am in the Fuel Directorate."

"That's wonderful."

It was wonderful, he thought, but even more it was tragic. She wore a high-
tinted wig and a very expensive skirt and low-cut blouse. Her shoes, obviously from
Gabon, must have cost a fortune. In short, thought Nwankwo, she had to be in the
keep of some well-placed gentleman, one of those piling up money out of the war.

---

4 **kwashiokor:** Severe malnutrition caused by a lack of protein.

"I broke my rule today to give you a lift. I never give lifts these days."

"Why?"

"How many people can you carry? It is better not to try at all. Look at that old woman."

"I thought you would carry her."

He said nothing to that and after another spell of silence Gladys thought maybe he was offended and so added: "Thank you for breaking your rule for me." She was scanning his face, turned slightly away. He smiled, turned, and tapped her on the lap.

"What are you going to Owerri to do?"

"I am going to visit my girlfriend."

"Girlfriend? You sure?"

"Why not? . . . If you drop me at her house you can see her. Only I pray God she hasn't gone on weekend today; it will be serious."

"Why?"

"Because if she is not at home I will sleep on the road today."

"I pray to God that she is not at home."

"Why?"

"Because if she is not at home I will offer you bed and breakfast . . . What is that?" he asked the driver who had brought the car to an abrupt stop. There was no need for an answer. The small crowd ahead was looking upwards. The three scrambled out of the car and stumbled for the bush, necks twisted in a backward search of the sky. But the alarm was false. The sky was silent and clear except for two high-flying vultures. A humourist in the crowd called them Fighter and Bomber and everyone laughed in relief. The three climbed into their car again and continued their journey.

"It is much too early for raids," he said to Gladys, who had both her palms on her breast as though to still a thumping heart. "They rarely come before ten o'clock."

But she remained tongue-tied from her recent fright. Nwankwo saw an opportunity there and took it at once.

"Where does your friend live?"

"250 Douglas Road."

"Ah! That's the very centre of town—a terrible place. No bunkers, nothing. I won't advise you to go there before 6 p.m.; it's not safe. If you don't mind I will take you to my place where there is a good bunker and then as soon as it is safe, around six, I shall drive you to your friend. How's that?"

"It's all right," she said lifelessly. "I am so frightened of this thing. That's why I refused to work in Owerri. I don't even know who asked me to come out today."

"You'll be all right. We are used to it."

"But your family is not there with you?"

"No," he said. "Nobody has his family there. We like to say it is because of air-raids but I can assure you there is more to it. Owerri is a real swinging town and we live the life of gay bachelors."

"That is what I have heard."

"You will not just hear it; you will see it today. I shall take you to a real swinging party. A friend of mine, a Lieutenant-Colonel, is having a birthday party. He's hired the Sound Smashers to play. I'm sure you'll enjoy it."

He was immediately and thoroughly ashamed of himself. He hated the parties and frivolities to which his friends clung like drowning men. And to talk so approvingly of them because he wanted to take a girl home! And this particular girl too, who had once had such beautiful faith in the struggle and was betrayed (no doubt about it) by some man like him out for a good time. He shook his head sadly.

"What is it?" asked Gladys.

"Nothing. Just my thoughts."

They made the rest of the journey to Owerri practically in silence.

She made herself at home very quickly as if she was a regular girl friend of his. She changed into a house dress and put away her auburn wig.

"That is a lovely hair-do. Why do you hide it with a wig?"

"Thank you," she said leaving his question unanswered for a while. Then she said: "Men are funny."

"Why do you say that?"

"You are now a beauty queen," she mimicked.

"Oh, that! I mean every word of it." He pulled her to him and kissed her. She neither refused nor yielded fully, which he liked for a start. Too many girls were simply too easy those days. War sickness, some called it.

He drove off a little later to look in at the office and she busied herself in the kitchen helping his boy with lunch. It must have been literally a look-in, for he was back within half an hour, rubbing his hands and saying he could not stay away too long from his beauty queen.

As they sat down to lunch, she said: "You have nothing in your fridge."

"Like what?" he asked, half-offended.

"Like meat," she replied undaunted.

"Do you still eat meat?" he challenged.

"Who am I? But other big men like you eat."

"I don't know which big men you have in mind. But they are not like me. I don't make money trading with the enemy or selling relief or . . ."

"Augusta's boyfriend doesn't do that. He just gets foreign exchange."

"How does he get it? He swindles the government—that's how he gets foreign exchange, whoever he is. Who is Augusta, by the way?"

"My girlfriend."

"I see."

"She gave me three dollars last time which I changed to forty-five pounds. The man gave her fifty dollars."

"Well, my dear girl, I don't traffic in foreign exchange and I don't have meat in my fridge. We are fighting a war and I happen to know that some young boys at the front drink gari and water once in three days."

"It is true," she said simply. "Monkey de work, baboon de chop."

"It is not even that; it is worse," he said, his voice beginning to shake. "People are dying every day. As we talk now somebody is dying."

"It is true," she said again.

"Plane!" screamed his boy from the kitchen.

"My mother!" screamed Gladys. As they scuttled towards the bunker of palm stems and red earth, covering their heads with their hands and stooping slightly in their flight, the entire sky was exploding with the clamour of jets and the huge noise of homemade anti-aircraft rockets.

Inside the bunker she clung to him even after the plane had gone and the guns, late to start and also to end, had all died down again.

"It was only passing," he told her, his voice a little shaky. "It didn't drop anything. From its direction I should say it was going to the war front. Perhaps our people who are pressing them. That's what they always do. Whenever our boys press them, they send an SOS to the Russians and Egyptians to bring the planes." He drew a long breath.

She said nothing, just clung to him. They could hear his boy telling the servant from the next house that there were two of them and one dived like this and the other dived like that.

"I see dem well well," said the other with equal excitement. "If no to say de ting de kill porson e for sweet for eye. To God."

"Imagine!" said Gladys, finding her voice at last. She had a way, he thought, of conveying with a few words or even a single word whole layers of meaning. Now it was at once her astonishment as well as reproof, tinged perhaps with grudging admiration for people who could be so light-hearted about these bringers of death.

"Don't be so scared," he said. She moved closer and he began to kiss her and squeeze her breasts. She yielded more and more and then fully. The bunker was dark and unswept and might harbour crawling things. He thought of bringing a mat from the main house but reluctantly decided against it. Another plane might pass and send a neighbour or simply a chance passerby crashing into them. That would be only slightly better than a certain gentleman in another air-raid who was seen in broad daylight fleeing his bedroom for his bunker stark-naked pursued by a woman in a similar state!

Just as Glady had feared, her friend was not in town. It would seem her powerful boyfriend had wangled for her a flight to Libreville[5] to shop. So her neighbours thought anyway.

"Great!" said Nwankwo as they drove away. "She will come back on an arms plane loaded with shoes, wigs, pants, bras, cosmetics and what have you, which she will then sell and make thousands of pounds. You girls are really at war, aren't you?"

---

5 **Libreville:** Port city in Gabon.

She said nothing and he thought he had got through at last to her. Then suddenly she said, "That is what you men want us to do."

"Well," he said, "here is one man who doesn't want you to do that. Do you remember that girl in khaki jeans who searched me without mercy at the checkpoint?"

She began to laugh.

"That is the girl I want you to become again. Do you remember her? No wig. I don't even think she had any earrings . . ."

"Ah, na lie-o. I had earrings."

"All right. But you know what I mean."

"That time done pass. Now everybody want survival. They call it number six. You put your number six; I put my number six. Everything all right."

The Lieutenant-Colonel's party turned into something quite unexpected. But before it did things had been going well enough. There was goat-meat, some chicken and rice and plenty of home-made spirits. There was one fiery brand nicknamed "tracer" which indeed sent a flame down your gullet. The funny thing was looking at it in the bottle it had the innocent appearance of an orange drink. But the thing that caused the greatest stir was the bread—one little roll for each person! It was the size of a golf ball and about the same consistency too! But it was real bread. The band was good too and there were many girls. And to improve matters even further two white Red Cross people soon arrived with a bottle of Courvoisier and a bottle of Scotch! The party gave them a standing ovation and then scrambled to get a taste. It soon turned out from his general behaviour, however, that one of the white men had probably drunk too much already. And the reason it would seem was that a pilot he knew well had been killed in a crash at the airport last night, flying in relief in awful weather.

Few people at the party had heard of the crash by then. So there was an immediate damping of the air. Some dancing couples went back to their seats and the band stopped. Then for some strange reason the drunken Red Cross man just exploded.

"Why should a man, a decent man, throw away his life. For nothing! Charley didn't need to die. Not for this stinking place. Yes, everything stinks here. Even these girls who come here all dolled up and smiling, what are they worth? Don't I know? A head of stockfish, that's all, or one American dollar and they are ready to tumble into bed."

In the threatening silence following the explosion one of the young officers walked up to him and gave him three thundering slaps—right! left! right!—pulled him up from his seat and (there were things like tears in his eyes) shoved him outside. His friend, who had tried in vain to shut him up, followed him out and the silenced party heard them drive off. The officer who did the job returned dusting his palms.

"Fucking beast!" said he with an impressive coolness. And all the girls showed with their eyes that they rated him a man and a hero.

"Do you know him?" Gladys asked Nwankwo.

He didn't answer her. Instead he spoke generally to the party.

"The fellow was clearly drunk," he said.

"I don't care," said the officer. "It is when a man is drunk that he speaks what is on his mind."

"So you beat him for what was on his mind," said the host, "that is the spirit, Joe."

"Thank you, sir," said Joe, saluting.

"His name is Joe," Gladys and the girl on her left said in unison, turning to each other.

At the same time Nwankwo and a friend on the other side of him were saying quietly, very quietly, that although the man had been rude and offensive what he had said about the girls was unfortunately the bitter truth, only he was the wrong man to say it.

When the dancing resumed Captain Joe came to Gladys for a dance. She sprang to her feet even before the word was out of his mouth. Then she remembered immediately and turned round to take permission from Nwankwo. At the same time the Captain also turned to him and said, "Excuse me."

"Go ahead," said Nwankwo, looking somewhere between the two.

It was a long dance and he followed them with his eyes without appearing to do so. Occasionally a relief plane passed overhead and somebody immediately switched off the lights saying it might be the Intruder. But it was only an excuse to dance in the dark and make the girls giggle, for the sound of the Intruder was well known.

Gladys came back feeling very self-conscious and asked Nwankwo to dance with her. But he wouldn't. "Don't bother about me," he said, "I am enjoying myself perfectly sitting here and watching those of you who dance."

"Then let's go," she said, "if you won't dance."

"But I never dance, believe me. So please, enjoy yourself."

She danced next with the Lieutenant-Colonel and again with Captain Joe, and then Nwankwo agreed to take her home.

"I am sorry I didn't dance," he said as they drove away. "But I swore never to dance as long as this war lasts."

She said nothing.

"When I think of somebody like that pilot who got killed last night. And he had no hand whatever in the quarrel. All his concern was to bring us food . . ."

"I hope that his friend is not like him," said Gladys.

"The man was just upset by his friend's death. But what I am saying is that with people like that getting killed and our own boys suffering and dying at the war fronts I don't see why we should sit around throwing parties and dancing."

"You took me there," said she in final revolt. "They are your friends. I don't know them before."

"Look, my dear, I am not blaming you. I am merely telling you why I personally refuse to dance. Anyway, let's change the subject . . . Do you still say you want to go back tomorrow? My driver can take you early enough on Monday morning for you to go to work. No? All right, just as you wish. You are the boss."

She gave him a shock by the readiness with which she followed him to bed and by her language.

"You want to shell?" she asked. And without waiting for an answer said, "Go ahead but don't pour in troops!"

He didn't want to pour in troops either and so it was all right. But she wanted visual assurance and so he showed her.

One of the ingenious economics taught by the war was that a rubber condom could be used over and over again. All you had to do was wash it out, dry it and shake a lot of talcum powder over it to prevent its sticking; and it was as good as new. It had to be the real British thing, though, not some of the cheap stuff they brought in from Lisbon which was about as strong as a dry cocoyam leaf in the harmattan.[6]

He had his pleasure but wrote the girl off. He might just as well have slept with a prostitute, he thought. It was clear as daylight to him now that she was kept by some army officer. What a terrible transformation in the short period of less than two years! Wasn't it a miracle that she still had memories of the other life, that she even remembered her name? If the affair of the drunken Red Cross man should happen again now, he said to himself, he would stand up beside the fellow and tell the party that here was a man of truth. What a terrible fate to befall a whole generation! The mothers of tomorrow!

By morning he was feeling a little better and more generous in his judgments. Gladys, he thought, was just a mirror reflecting a society that had gone completely rotten and maggoty at the centre. The mirror itself was intact; a lot of smudge but no more. All that was needed was a clean duster. "I have a duty to her," he told himself, "the little girl that once revealed to me our situation. Now she is in danger, under some terrible influence."

He wanted to get to the bottom of this deadly influence. It was clearly not just her good-time girlfriend, Augusta, or whatever her name was. There must be some man at the centre of it, perhaps one of these heartless attack-traders who traffic in foreign currencies and make their hundreds of thousands by sending young men to hazard their lives bartering looted goods for cigarettes behind enemy lines, or one of those contractors who receive piles of money daily for food they never deliver to the army. Or perhaps some vulgar and cowardly army officer full of filthy barrack talk and fictitious stories of heroism. He decided he had to find out. Last night he had thought of sending his driver alone to take her home. But no, he must go and see for himself where she lived. Something was bound to reveal itself there. Something on which he could anchor his saving operation. As he prepared for the trip his feeling towards her softened with every passing minute. He assembled for her half of the food he had received at the relief centre the day before. Difficult as things were, he

6 **harmattan:** A dusty wind that blows into Africa from the Atlantic.

thought a girl who had something to eat would be spared, not all, but some of the temptation. He would arrange with his friend at the WCC to deliver something to her every fortnight.

Tears came to Gladys's eyes when she saw the gifts. Nwankwo didn't have too much cash on him but he got together twenty pounds and handed it over to her.

"I don't have foreign exchange, and I know this won't go far at all, but . . ."

She just came and threw herself at him, sobbing. He kissed her lips and eyes and mumbled something about victims of circumstance, which went over her head. In deference to him, he thought with exultation, she had put away her high-tinted wig in her bag.

"I want you to promise me something," he said.

"What?"

"Never use that expression about shelling again."

She smiled with tears in her eyes. "You don't like it? That's what all the girls call it."

"Well, you are different from all the girls. Will you promise?"

"O.K."

Naturally their departure had become a little delayed. And when they got into the car it refused to start. After poking around the engine the driver decided that the battery was flat. Nwankwo was aghast. He had that very week paid thirty-four pounds to change two of the cells and the mechanic who performed it had promised him six months' service. A new battery, which was then running at two hundred and fifty pounds, was simply out of the question. The driver must have been careless with something, he thought.

"It must be because of last night," said the driver.

"What happened last night?" asked Nwankwo sharply, wondering what insolence was on the way. But none was intended.

"Because we use the headlight."

"Am I supposed not to use my light, then? Go and get some people and try pushing it." He got out again with Gladys and returned to the house while the driver went over to neighboring houses to seek the help of other servants.

After at least half an hour of pushing it up and down the street, and a lot of noisy advice from the pushers, the car finally spluttered to life, shooting out enormous clouds of black smoke from the exhaust.

It was eight-thirty by his watch when they set out. A few miles away a disabled soldier waved for a lift.

"Stop!" screamed Nwankwo. The driver jammed his foot on the brakes and then turned his head toward his master in bewilderment.

"Don't you see the soldier waving? Reverse and pick him up!"

"Sorry, sir," said the driver. "I don't know Master want to pick him."

"If you don't know you should ask. Reverse back."

The soldier, a mere boy, in filthy khaki drenched in sweat, lacked his right leg from the knee down. He seemed not only grateful that a car should stop for him but greatly surprised. He first handed in his crude wooden crutches, which the driver arranged between the two front seats, then painfully he levered himself in.

"Thanks, sir," he said, turning to look at the back and completely out of breath. "I am very grateful. Madame, thank you."

"The pleasure is ours," said Nwankwo. "Where did you get your wound?"

"At Azumini, sir. On tenth of January."

"Never mind. Everything will be all right. We are proud of you boys and will make sure you receive your due reward when it is all over."

"I pray God, sir."

They drove in silence for the next half hour or so. Then as the car sped down a slope toward a bridge somebody screamed—perhaps the driver, perhaps the solder—"They have come!" The screech of the brakes merged into the scream and the shattering of the sky overhead. The doors flew open even before the car had come to a stop and they were fleeing blindly to the bush. Gladys was a little ahead of Nwankwo when they heard through the drowning tumult the solder's voice crying: "Please come and open for me!" Vaguely he saw Gladys stop; he pushed past her, shouting to her at the same time to come on. Then a high whistle descended like a spear through the chaos and exploded in a vast noise and motion that smashed up everything. A tree he had embraced flung him through the bush. Then another terrible whistle starting high up and ending again in a monumental crash of the world; and then another, and Nwankwo heard no more.

He woke up to human noises and weeping and the smell and smoke of a charred world. He dragged himself up and staggered toward the source of the sounds.

From afar he saw his driver running toward him in tears and blood. He saw the remains of his car smoking and the entangled remains of the girl and the soldier. And he let out a piercing cry and fell down again.

QUESTIONS

1. Describe the internal conflicts Nwankwo faces. What contradictory forces does he grapple with?

2. How successful is Nwankwo at dealing with the moral dilemmas he faces?

3. How do you judge Nwankwo? Is he hypocritical? Weak? A normal human being facing difficult choices? An opportunist? Simply immoral?

4. How do you regard Gladys? Is she a failed idealist, or one who has come to deal realistically with life? Is she justified in using her looks to survive?

5. What is the story saying about the moral effects of war? Are the issues raised in this war unique to it, or are they endemic to war itself?

6. Is Gladys a hero or a fool for running back to the car to help the soldier?

Ngugi wa Thiong'o

(KENYA, b. 1938)

Ngugi wa Thiong'o has emerged as one of Africa's leading voices of protest against European colonialism and its continuing effects on the continent and its people. In particular, he has been an outspoken critic of Christian missionaries, the use of English, and the repressive regimes that followed the collapse of colonial rule.

He was born James Ngugi in Limuru, Kenya. His father was a landless peasant farmer with four wives and twenty-eight children—landless because his property was taken away under the British Imperial Land Act of 1915. At age eight, James entered a missionary school, but two years later was sent to a school sponsored by Gikuyu nationalists. With the outbreak of the so-called Mau-Mau rebellion in 1952, these schools were closed, and he was transferred to an official school, where instruction was in English. In 1955, he entered the prestigious Alliance High School and read widely in English writers, especially Robert Louis Stevenson, but he also reacted against an education that he believed was aimed at producing obedient colonial servants. In 1959, he entered Makerere University College to study English, but it was his independent reading in African and West Indian authors like Chinua Achebe who fired his imagination and led him to begin writing his own stories. In 1964 he worked toward an MA at Leeds University in England, where he fell under the influence of Karl Marx and Frantz Fanon. Returning to Africa, he became a schoolteacher and then joined the faculty of the University of Nairobi, where he persuaded officials to change the English Department into the Department of African Languages and Literatures. He also changed his given name to its present form in the Gikuyu language.

Ngugi's early published novel (*Weep Not, Child,* 1969) and stories (*Secret Lives,* 1974) were in English, but in 1977, he vowed to write in Gikuyu or Swahili. That same year, his outspoken criticism of Kenya's repressive regime led to his arrest and imprisonment without trial. He spent 1978 in a maximum security prison, secretly writing *Detained: A Writer's Prison Diary* (1981) on toilet paper. Although released from prison, he had lost his university position and was prevented from finding other employment. He turned to writing plays on political and anticolonial themes, but performances were halted and his theater troupe banned. Fearing further action by the government, he fled Kenya in 1982 and has spent most of his time since in London.

From his exile in London, Ngugi has continued to write novels and essays. His critics argue that political ideology too frequently dominates his fiction at the expense of aesthetic and structural concerns, but others defend his work as containing the most potent and insightful criticisms of African politics and society, past and present. The essays collected in *Decolonising the Mind* (1986), together with his novels in Gikuyu, form powerful statements against the cultural devastation wrought by colonialism's effects, especially its imposition of English on Africans. He continues to be an effective champion for African culture, women's rights, democracy, and economic justice.

Minutes of Glory   1975

Her name was Wanjiru. But she liked better her Christian one, Beatrice. It sounded more pure and more beautiful. Not that she was ugly; but she could not be called beautiful either. Her body, dark and full fleshed, had the form, yes, but it was as if it waited to be filled by the spirit. She worked in beer halls where sons of women came to drown their inner lives in beer cans and froth. Nobody seemed to notice her. Except, perhaps, when a proprietor or an impatient customer called out her name, Beatrice; then other customers would raise their heads briefly, a few seconds, as if to behold the bearer of such a beautiful name, but not finding anybody there, they would resume their drinking, their ribald jokes, their laughter and play with the other serving girls. She was like a wounded bird in flight: a forced landing now and then but nevertheless wobbling from place to place so that she would variously be found in Alaska, Paradise, The Modern, Thome and other beer-halls all over Limuru. Sometimes it was because an irate proprietor found she was not attracting enough customers; he would sack her without notice and without a salary. She would wobble to the next bar. But sometimes she was simply tired of nesting in one place, a daily witness of familiar scenes; girls even more decidedly ugly than she were fought over by numerous claimants at closing hours. What do they have that I don't have? She would ask herself, depressed. She longed for a bar-kingdom where she would be at least one of the rulers, where petitioners would bring their gifts of beer, frustrated smiles and often curses that hid more lust and love than hate.

She left Limuru town proper and tried the mushrooming townlets around. She worked at Ngarariga, Kamiritho, Rironi and even Tiekunu and everywhere the story was the same. Oh, yes, occasionally she would get a client; but none cared for her as she would have liked, none really wanted her enough to fight over her. She was always a hard-up customer's last resort. No make-believe even, not for her that sweet pretence that men indulged in after their fifth bottle of Tusker.[1] The following night or during a pay-day, the same client would pretend not to know her; he would be trying his money-power over girls who already had more than a fair share of admirers.

She resented this. She saw in every girl a rival and adopted a sullen attitude. Nyagūthiī especially was the thorn that always pricked her wounded flesh. Nyagūthiī, arrogant and aloof, but men always in her courtyard; Nyagūthiī, fighting with men, and to her they would bring propitiating gifts which she accepted as of right. Nyagūthiī could look bored, impatient, or downright contemptuous and still

1 **Tusker:** A well-known Kenyan lager beer.

men would cling to her as if they enjoyed being whipped with biting words, curled lips and the indifferent eyes of a free woman. Nyagũthiĩ was also a bird in flight, never really able to settle in one place, but in her case it was because she hungered for change and excitement: new faces and new territories for her conquest. Beatrice resented her very shadow. She saw in her the girl she would have liked to be, a girl who was both totally immersed in and yet completely above the underworld of bar violence and sex. Wherever Beatrice went the long shadow of Nyagũthiĩ would sooner or later follow her.

She fled Limuru for Ilmorog in Chiri District. Ilmorog had once been a ghost village, but had been resurrected to life by that legendary woman, Nyang'endo, to whom every pop group had paid their tribute. It was of her that the young dancing Muthuu and Muchun g' wa sang:

> When I left Nairobi for Ilmorog
> Never did I know
> I would bear this wonder-child mine
> Nyang'endo.

As a result, Ilmorog was always seen as a town of hope where the weary and the down-trodden would find their rest and fresh water. But again Nyagũthiĩ followed her.

She found that Ilmorog, despite the legend, despite the songs and dances, was not different from Limuru. She tried various tricks. Clothes? But even here she never earned enough to buy herself glittering robes. What was seventy-five shillings[2] a month without house allowance, *posho,* without salaried boy-friends? By that time, Ambi had reached Ilmorog, and Beatrice thought that this would be the answer. Had she not, in Limuru, seen girls blacker than herself transformed overnight from ugly sins into white stars by a touch of skin-lightening creams? And men would ogle them, would even talk with exaggerated pride of their newborn girl friends. Men were strange creatures, Beatrice thought in moments of searching analysis. They talked heatedly against Ambi, Butone, Firesnow, Moonsnow, wigs, straightened hair; but they always went for a girl with an Ambi-lightened skin and head covered with a wig made in imitation of European or Indian hair. Beatrice never tried to find the root cause of this black self-hatred, she simply accepted the contradiction and applied herself to Ambi with a vengeance. She had to rub out her black shame. But even Ambi she could not afford in abundance; she could only apply it to her face and to her arms so that her legs and her neck retained their blackness. Besides there were parts of her face she could not readily reach—behind the ears and above the eye-lashes, for instance—and these were a constant source of shame and irritation to her Ambi-self.

She would always remember this Ambi period as one of her deepest humiliation before her later minutes of glory. She worked in Ilmorog Starlight Bar and Lodging. Nyagũthiĩ, with her bangled hands, her huge earrings, served behind the counter.

---

2 **Seventy-five shillings:** With 20 shillings to the pound, this equals just over 3 pounds, a low wage.

The owner was a good Christian soul who regularly went to church and paid all his dues to *Harambee*[3] projects. Pot-belly. Grey hairs. Soft-spoken. A respectable family man, well known in Ilmorog. Hardworking even, for he would not leave the bar until the closing hours, or more precisely, until Nyagūthiī left. He had no eyes for any other girl; he hung around her, and surreptitiously brought her gifts of clothes without receiving gratitude in kind. Only the promise. Only the hope for tomorrow. Other girls he gave eighty shillings a month. Nyagūthiī had a room to herself. Nyagūthiī woke up whenever she liked to take the stock. But Beatrice and the other girls had to wake up at five or so, make tea for the lodgers, clean up the bar and wash dishes and glasses. Then they would hang around the bar in shifts until two o'clock when they would go for a small break. At five o'clock, they had to be in again, ready for customers whom they would now serve with frothy beers and smiles until twelve o'clock or for as long as there were customers thirsty for more Tuskers and Pilsners. What often galled Beatrice, although in her case it did not matter one way or another, was the owner's insistence that the girls should sleep in Starlight. They would otherwise be late for work, he said. But what he really wanted was for the girls to use their bodies to attract more lodgers in Starlight. Most of the girls, led by Nyagūthiī, defied the rule and bribed the watchman to let them out and in. They wanted to meet their regular or one-night boy-friends in places where they would be free and where they would be treated as not just barmaids. Beatrice always slept in. Her occasional one-night patrons wanted to spend the minimum. Came a night when the owner, refused by Nyagūthiī, approached her. He started by finding fault with her work; he called her names, then as suddenly he started praising her, although in a grudging almost contemptuous manner. He grabbed her, struggled with her, pot-belly, grey hairs, and everything. Beatrice felt an unusual revulsion for the man. She could not, she would not bring herself to accept that which had so recently been cast aside by Nyagūthiī. My God, she wept inside, what does Nyagūthiī have that I don't have? The man now humiliated himself before her. He implored. He promised her gifts. But she would not yield. That night she too defied the rule. She jumped through a window; she sought a bed in another bar and only came back at six. The proprietor called her in front of all the others and dismissed her. But Beatrice was rather surprised at herself.

She stayed a month without a job. She lived from room to room at the capricious mercy of the other girls. She did not have the heart to leave Ilmorog and start all over again in a new town. The wound hurt. She was tired of wandering. She stopped using Ambi. No money. She looked at herself in the mirror. She had so aged, hardly a year after she had fallen from grace. Why then was she scrupulous, she would ask herself. But somehow she had a horror of soliciting lovers or directly bartering her body for hard cash. What she wanted was decent work and a man or several men who cared for her. Perhaps she took that need for a man, for a home and for a child with her to bed. Perhaps it was this genuine need that scared off men who

---

3 *Harambee:* A business club promoting Kenya's international trade.

wanted other things from barmaids. She wept late at nights and remembered home. At such moments, her mother's village in Nyeri seemed the sweetest place on God's earth. She would invest the life of her peasant mother and father with romantic illusions of immeasurable peace and harmony. She longed to go back home to see them. But how could she go back with empty hands? In any case the place was now a distant landscape in the memory. Her life was here in the bar among this crowd of lost strangers. Fallen from grace, fallen from grace. She was part of a generation which would never again be one with the soil, the crops, the wind and the moon. Not for them that whispering in dark hedges, not for her that dance and love-making under the glare of the moon, with the hills of Tumu Tumu rising to touch the sky. She remembered that girl from her home village who, despite a life of apparent glamour being the kept mistress of one rich man after another in Limuru, had gassed herself to death. This generation was not awed by the mystery of death, just as it was callous to the mystery of life; for how many unmarried mothers had thrown their babies into latrines rather than lose that glamour? The girl's death became the subject of jokes. She had gone metric—without pains, they said. Thereafter, for a week, Beatrice thought of going metric. But she could not bring herself to do it.

She wanted love; she wanted life.

A new bar was opened in Ilmorog. Treetop Bar, Lodging and Restaurant. Why Treetop, Beatrice could not understand unless because it was a storied building: teashop on the ground floor and beer-shop in a room at the top. The rest were rooms for five-minute or one-night lodgers. The owner was a retired civil servant but one who still played at politics. He was enormously wealthy with business sites and enterprises in every major town in Kenya. Big shots from all over the country came to his bar. Big men in Mercedez. Big men in their Bentleys. Big men in their Jaguars and Daimlers. Big men with uniformed chauffeurs drowsing with boredom in cars waiting outside. There were others not so big who came to pay respects to the great. They talked politics mostly. And about their work. Gossip was rife. Didn't you know? Indeed so and so has been promoted. Really? And so and so has been sacked. Embezzlement of public funds. So foolish you know. Not clever about it at all. They argued, they quarrelled, sometimes they fought it out with fists, especially during the elections campaign. The only point on which they were all agreed was that the Luo community[4] was the root cause of all the trouble in Kenya; that intellectuals and University students were living in an ivory tower of privilege and arrogance; that Kiambu had more than a lion's share of developments; that men from Nyeri and Muranga had acquired all the big business in Nairobi and were even encroaching on Chiri District; that African workers, especially those on the farms, were lazy and jealous of 'us' who had sweated ourselves to sudden prosperity. Otherwise each would hymn his own praises or return compliments. Occasionally in moments of drunken ebullience and self-praise, one would order two rounds of beer for each man present

4 **Luo community:** A region and language in Kenya. The Luo people constitute about 14 percent of Kenya's population.

in the bar. Even the poor from Ilmorog would come to Treetop to dine at the gates of the *nouveaux riches.*

Here Beatrice got a job as a sweeper and bedmaker. Here for a few weeks she felt closer to greatness. Now she made beds for men she had previously known as names. She watched how even the poor tried to drink and act big in front of the big. But soon fate caught up with her. Girls flocked to Treetop from other bars. Girls she had known at Limuru, girls she had known at Ilmorog. And most had attached themselves to one or several big men, often playing a hide-and-not-to-be-found game with their numerous lovers. And Nyagūthiī was there behind the counter, with the eyes of the rich and the poor fixed on her. And she, with her big eyes, bangled hands and earrings maintained the same air of bored indifference. Beatrice as a sweeper and bedmaker became even more invisible. Girls who had fallen into good fortune looked down upon her.

She fought life with dreams. In between putting clean sheets on beds that had just witnessed a five-minute struggle that ended in a half-strangled cry and a pool, she would stand by the window and watch the cars and the chauffeurs, so that soon she knew all the owners by the number plates of their cars and the uniforms of their chauffeurs. She dreamt of lovers who would come for her in sleek Mercedes sports cars made for two. She saw herself linking hands with such a lover, walking in the streets of Nairobi and Mombasa, tapping the ground with high heels, quick, quick short steps. And suddenly she would stop in front of a display glass window, exclaiming at the same time; Oh darling, won't you buy me those . . . ? Those what, he would ask, affecting anger. Those stockings, darling. It was as an owner of several stockings, ladderless[5] and holeless, that she thought of her well-being. Never again would she mend torn things. Never, never, never. Do you understand? Never. She was next the proud owner of different coloured wigs, blonde wigs, brunette wigs, Redhead wigs, Afro wigs, wigs, wigs, all the wigs in the world. Only then would the whole earth sing hallelujah to the one Beatrice. At such moments, she would feel exalted, lifted out of her murky self, no longer a floor sweeper and bedmaker for a five-minute instant love, but Beatrice, descendant of Wangu Makeri who made men tremble with desire at her naked body bathed in moonlight, daughter of Nyang'endo, the founder of modern Ilmorog, of whom they often sang that she had worked several lovers into impotence.

Then she noticed him and he was the opposite of the lover of her dreams. He came one Saturday afternoon driving a big five-ton lorry. He carefully parked it beside the Benzes, the Jaguars and the Daimlers, not as a lorry, but as one of those sleek cream-bodied frames, so proud of it he seemed to be. He dressed in a baggy grey suit over which he wore a heavy khaki military overcoat. He removed the overcoat, folded it with care, and put it in the front seat. He locked all the doors, dusted himself a little, then walked round the lorry as if inspecting it for damage. A few steps before he entered Treetop, he turned round for a final glance at his lorry dwarfing

5 **Ladderless:** Without "runs."

the other things. At Treetops he sat in a corner and, with a rather loud defiant voice, ordered a Kenya one. He drank it with relish, looking around at the same time for a face he might recognize. He indeed did recognize one of the big ones and he immediately ordered for him a quarter bottle of Vat 69.[6] This was accepted with a bare nod of the head and a patronizing smile; but when he tried to follow his generosity with a conversation, he was firmly ignored. He froze, sank into his Muratina. But only for a time. He tried again: he was met with frowning faces. More pathetic were his attempts to join in jokes; he would laugh rather too loudly, which would make the big ones stop, leaving him in the air alone. Later in the evening he stood up, counted several crisp hundred shilling notes and handed them to Nyagūthiī behind the counter ostensibly for safekeeping. People whispered; murmured; a few laughed, rather derisively, though they were rather impressed. But this act did not win him immediate recognition. He staggered towards room no. 7 which he had hired. Beatrice brought him the keys. He glanced at her, briefly, then lost all interest.

Thereafter he came every Saturday. At five when most of the big shots were already seated. He repeated the same ritual, except the money act, and always met with defeat. He nearly always sat in the same corner and always rented room 7. Beatrice grew to anticipate his visits and, without being conscious of it, kept the room ready for him. Often after he had been badly humiliated by the big company, he would detain Beatrice and talk to her, or rather he talked to himself in her presence. For him, it had been a life of struggles. He had never been to school although getting an education had been his ambition. He never had a chance. His father was a squatter in the European settled area in the Rift Valley. That meant a lot in those colonial days. It meant among other things a man and his children were doomed to a future of sweat and toil for the white devils and their children. He had joined the freedom struggle and like the others had been sent to detention. He came from detention the same as his mother had brought him to this world. Nothing. With independence he found he did not possess the kind of education which would have placed him in one of the vacancies at the top. He started as a charcoal burner, then a butcher, gradually working his own way to become a big transporter of vegetables and potatoes from the Rift Valley and Chiri districts to Nairobi. He was proud of his achievement. But he resented that others, who had climbed to their present wealth through loans and a subsidized education, would not recognize his like. He would rumble on like this, dwelling on education he would never have, and talking of better chances for his children. Then he would carefully count the money, put it under the pillow, and then dismiss Beatrice. Occasionally he would buy her a beer but he was clearly suspicious of women whom he saw as money-eaters of men. He had not yet married.

One night he slept with her. In the morning he scratched for a twenty shilling note and gave it to her. She accepted the money with an odd feeling of guilt. He did this for several weeks. She did not mind the money. It was useful. But he paid for her body as he would pay for a bag of potatoes or a sack of cabbages. With the one

---

6 **Vat 69:** An expensive brand of whisky.

instance. There were rules about what, how and when to eat. You must even walk like a Christian lady. You must never be seen with boys. Rules, rules all the way. One day instead of returning home from school, I and another girl from a similar home ran away to Eastleigh. I have never been home once this last four years. That's all."

Another silence. Then they looked at one another in mutual recognition.

"One more question, Nyagūthiī. You need not answer it. But I have always thought that you hated me, you despised me."

"No, no, Beatrice, I have never hated you. I have never hated anybody. It is just that nothing interests me. Even men do not move me now. Yet I want, I need instant excitement. I need the attention of those false flattering eyes to make me feel myself, myself. But you, you seemed above all this—somehow you had something inside you that I did not have."

Beatrice tried to hold her tears with difficulty.

Early the next day, she boarded a bus bound for Nairobi. She walked down Bazaar street looking at the shops. Then down Government Road, right into Kenyatta Avenue, and Kimathi street. She went into a shop near Hussein Suleman's street and bought several stockings. She put on a pair. She next bought herself a new dress. Again she changed into it. In a Bata Shoeshop, she bought high heeled shoes, put them on and discarded her old flat ones. On to an Akamba kiosk, and she fitted herself with earrings. She went to a mirror and looked at her new self. Suddenly she felt enormous hunger as if she had been hungry all her life. She hesitated in front of Moti Mahal. Then she walked on, eventually entering Fransae. There was a glint in her eyes that made men's eyes turn to her. This thrilled her. She chose a table in a corner and ordered Indian curry. A man left his table and joined her. She looked at him. Her eyes were merry. He was dressed in a dark suit and his eyes spoke of lust. He bought her a drink. He tried to engage her in conversation. But she ate in silence. He put his hand under the table and felt her knees. She let him do it. The hand went up and up her thigh. Then suddenly she left her unfinished food and her untouched drink and walked out. She felt good. He followed her. She knew this without once turning her eyes. He walked beside her for a few yards. She smiled at herself but did not look at him. He lost his confidence. She left him standing sheepishly looking at a glass window outside Gino's. In the bus back to Ilmorog, men gave her seats. She accepted this as of right. At Treetops bar she went straight to the counter. The usual crowd of big men was there. Their conversations stopped for a few seconds at her entry. Their lascivious eyes were turned to her. The girls stared at her. Even Nyagūthiī could not maintain her bored indifference. Beatrice bought them drinks. The manager came to her, rather unsure. He tried a conversation. Why had she left work? Where had she been? Would she like to work in the bar, helping Nyagūthiī behind the counter? Now and then? A barmaid brought her a note. A certain big shot wanted to know if she would join their table. More notes came from different big quarters with the one question; would she be free tonight? A trip to Nairobi even. She did not leave her place at the counter. But she accepted their drinks as of right. She felt a new power, confidence even.

She took out a shilling, put it in the slot and the juke box boomed with the voice of Robinson Mwangi singing Hūnyū wa Mashambani. He sang of those despised girls who worked on farms and contrasted them with urban girls. Then she played a Kamaru and a D.K. Men wanted to dance with her. She ignored them, but enjoyed their flutter around her. She twisted her hips to the sound of yet another D.K. Her body was free. She was free. She sucked in the excitement and tension in the air.

Then suddenly at around six, the man with the five-ton lorry stormed into the bar. This time he had on his military overcoat. Behind him was a policeman. He looked around. Everybody's eyes were raised to him. But Beatrice went on swaying her hips. At first he could not recognize Beatrice in the girl celebrating her few minutes of glory by the juke box. Then he shouted in triumph. "That is the girl! Thief! Thief!"

People melted back to their seats. The policeman went and handcuffed her. She did not resist. Only at the door she turned her head and spat. Then she went out followed by the policeman.

In the bar the stunned silence broke into hilarious laughter when someone made a joke about sweetened robbery without violence. They discussed her. Some said she should have been beaten. Others talked contemptuously about 'these bar girls.' Yet others talked with a concern noticeable in unbelieving shakes of their heads about the rising rate of crime. Shouldn't the Hanging Bill be extended to all thefts of property? And without anybody being aware of it the man with the five-ton lorry had become a hero. They now surrounded him with questions and demanded the whole story. Some even bought him drinks. More remarkable, they listened, their attentive silence punctuated by appreciative laughter. The averted threat to property had temporarily knit them into one family. And the man, accepted for the first time, told the story with relish.

But behind the counter Nyagūthiī wept.

QUESTIONS

1. How is Wanjiru (Beatrice) presented? Is she admirable? Pathetic? An innocent victim? A loser?

2. What does the story say about the nature of British colonial rule?

3. What does the story reveal about Kenyan society of the time?

4. What is the significance of Beatrice's relationship with Nyagūthiī? How does her conversation with Nyagūthiī change her attitude and behavior?

5. Is it only the new clothes that transform Beatrice into a desirable woman? What else might have happened to bring about her transformation?

6. Why is the lorry driver suddenly acknowledged by the other men after he has Beatrice arrested? What does his sudden acceptance suggest about the relations between men and women?

7. Overall, what does the story reveal about the status of women in this part of African society? Have Western-style attitudes and values helped to liberate women in this story, or have they only helped to create a new kind of dependency and subservience?

Bessie Head

(SOUTH AFRICA, 1937–1986)

Bessie Amelia (née Emery) Head was born in a mental hospital in Pietermaritzburg, South Africa, where her white, upper-class mother had been committed because she had become pregnant by a black stable hand. As a result, Bessie was raised by foster parents to age thirteen and then in an orphanage, attending missionary school and eventually becoming a teacher in 1955. She married journalist Harold Head in 1960, but the marriage ended in divorce. In 1964, she left teaching to write for *The Gold City Post* until personal problems forced her and her son Howard to leave South Africa and become refugees in Botswana, where Bessie remained for fifteen years. Her experiences reflect those of many Africans displaced by civil war, poverty, or natural disaster. In spite of poverty and bouts of mental instability, Head turned to fiction writing and published her first novel, *When Rain Clouds Gather*, in 1968. Its themes of innocence to experience and personal fulfillment against a backdrop of political oppression and corruption set the pattern for much of her subsequent writing. As an outsider, Head became involved in various community projects, but her fiery temper and unpredictability often alienated those around her, including her literary agents. That she was able to continue writing and publishing in spite of such difficulties (some self-inflicted) is a testament to her tenacity.

Although she eschewed the label "political writer" (she claimed to dislike politics, as well as organized religion), Head writes tellingly of alienation and oppression, often the oppression experienced by women in a racist and patriarchal society. Racism, of course, is endemic to the South Africa of her birth, whereas patriarchy was also part of traditional African culture. "The Wind and a Boy" is taken from her only collection of stories, *The Collector of Treasures and Other Botswana Village Tales* (1977). Its casual narrative style and simple language suggest the methods of traditional oral storytelling, but beneath the apparently uncomplicated surface is a complex structure based on contrasts, subtly presented as almost incidental details.

Head's last two published books were more historical chronicles than fiction, and at the time of her death, she was at work on an autobiography. Although her output was not large, Head is widely considered to be among the most important African writers of her generation.

The Wind and a Boy   1977

Like all the village boys, Friedman had a long wind blowing for him, but perhaps the enchanted wind that blew for him, filled the whole world with magic.

Until they became ordinary, dull grown men, who drank beer and made babies, the little village boys were a special set all on their own. They were kings whom no one ruled. They wandered where they willed from dawn to dusk and only condescended to come home at dusk because they were afraid of the horrible things in the dark that might pounce on them. Unlike the little girls who adored household chores and drawing water, it was only now and then that the boys showed themselves as useful attachments to any household. When the first hard rains of summer fell, small dark shapes, quite naked except for their loin-cloths, sped out of the village into the bush. They knew that the first downpour had drowned all the wild rabbits, moles, and porcupines in their burrows in the earth. As they crouched down near the entrances to the burrows, they would see a small drowned nose of an animal peeping out; they knew it had struggled to emerge from its burrow, flooded by the sudden rush of storm water and as they pulled out the animal, they would say, pityingly:

"Birds have more sense than rabbits, moles and porcupines. They build their homes in trees." But it was hunting made easy, for no matter how hard a boy and his dog ran, a wild rabbit ran ten times faster; a porcupine hurled his poisonous quills into the body; and a mole stayed where he thought it was safe—deep under the ground. So it was with inordinate pride that the boys carried home armfuls of dead animals for their families to feast on for many days. Apart from that, the boys lived very much as they pleased, with the wind and their own games.

Now and then, the activities of a single family could captivate the imagination and hearts of all the people of their surroundings; for years and years, the combination of the boy, Friedman and his grandmother, Sejosenye, made the people of Ga-Sefete-Molemo ward, smile, laugh, then cry.

They smiled at his first two phases. Friedman came home as a small bundle from the hospital, a bundle his grandmother nursed carefully near her bosom and crooned to day and night with extravagant care and tenderness.

"She is like that," people remarked, "because he may be the last child she will ever nurse. Sejosenye is old now and will die one of these days; the child is a gift to keep her heart warm."

Indeed, all Sejosenye's children were grown, married, and had left home. Of all her children, only her last-born daughter was unmarried and Friedman was the result of some casual mating she had indulged in, in a town a hundred miles away where she had a job as a typist. She wanted to return to her job almost immediately, so she handed the child over to her mother and that was that; she could afford to forget him as he had a real mother now. During all the time that Sejosenye haunted the hospital, awaiting her bundle, a friendly foreign doctor named Friedman took a fancy to her maternal, grandmotherly ways. He made a habit of walking out of his path to talk to her. She never forgot it and on receiving her bundle she called the baby, Friedman.

They smiled at his second phase, a small dark shadow who toddled silently and gravely beside a very tall grandmother; wherever the grandmother went, there went Friedman. Most women found this phase of the restless, troublesome toddler tedious; they dumped the toddler onto one of their younger girls and were off to weddings and visits on their own.

"Why can't you leave your handbag at home some times, granny?" they said.

"Oh, he's no trouble," Sejosenye would reply.

They began to laugh at his third phase. Almost overnight he turned into a tall, spindly-legged, graceful gazelle with large, grave eyes. There was an odd, musical lilt to his speech and when he teased, or was up to mischief, he moved his head on his long thin neck from side to side like a cobra. It was he who became the king of kings of all the boys in his area; he could turn his hand to anything and made the best wire cars with their wheels of shoe polish tins. All his movements were neat, compact, decisive, and for his age he was a boy who knew his own mind. They laughed at his knowingness and certainty on all things, for he was like the grandmother who had had a flaming youth all her own too. Sejosenye had scandalized the whole village in her days of good morals by leaving her own village ward to live with a married man in Ga-Sefete-Molemo ward. She had won him from his wife and married him and then lived down the scandal in the way only natural queens can. Even in old age, she was still impressive. She sailed through the village, head in the air, with a quiet, almost expressionless face. She had developed large buttocks as time went by and they announced their presence firmly in rhythm with her walk.

Another of Sejosenye's certainties was that she was a woman who could plough, but it was like a special gift. Each season, in drought or hail or sun, she removed herself to her lands. She not only ploughed but nursed and brooded over her crops. She was there all the time till the corn ripened and the birds had to be chased off the land, till harvesting and threshing were done; so that even in drought years with their scanty rain, she came home with some crops. She was the envy of all the women of the surroundings.

"Sejosenye always eats fine things in her house," they said. "She ploughs and then sits down for many months and enjoys the fruits of her labour."

The women also envied her beautiful grandson. There was something special there, so that even when Friedman moved into his bad phase, they forgave him crimes other boys received a sound thrashing for. The small boys were terrible thieves who harassed people by stealing their food and money. It was all a part of the games they played but one which people did not like. Of them all, Friedman was the worst thief, so that his name was mentioned more and more in any thieving that had been uncovered.

"But Friedman showed us how to open the window with a knife and string," the sobbing, lashed boys would protest.

"Friedman isn't as bad as you," the parents would reply, irrationally. They were hypnotised by a beautiful creature. The boy Friedman, who had become a real nuisance by then, also walked around as though he were special. He couldn't possibly be a thief and he added an aloof, offended, disdainful expression to his pretty face. He wasn't just an ordinary sort of boy in Ga-Sefete-Molemo ward. He was . . .

It happened, quite accidentally, that his grandmother told him all those stories about the hunters, warriors, and emissaries of old. She was normally a quiet, absent-minded woman, given to dreaming by herself but she liked to sing the boy a little song now and then as they sat by the outdoor fire. A lot of them were church songs and rather sad; they more or less passed as her bed-time prayer at night—she was one of the old church-goers. Now and then she added a quaint little song to her repertoire and as the night-time, fire-light flames flickered between them, she never failed to note that this particular song was always well received by the boy. A little light would awaken in his eyes and he would bend forward and listen attentively.

"Welcome, Robinson Crusoe, welcome," she would sing, in clear, sweet tones. "How could you stay, so long away, Robinson how could you do so?"

When she was very young, Sejosenye had attended the mission school of the village for about a year; made a slight acquaintance with the ABC and one, two, three, four, five, and the little song about Robinson Crusoe. But girls didn't need an education in those days when ploughing and marriage made up their whole world. Yet Robinson Crusoe lived on as a gay and out-of-context memory of her school-days. One evening the boy leaned forward and asked:

"Is that a special praise-poem song for Robinson Crusoe, grandmother?"

"Oh yes," she replied, smiling.

"It appears that the people liked Robinson Crusoe much," the boy observed. "Did he do great things for them?"

"Oh yes," she said, smiling.

"What great things did he do?" the boy asked, pointedly.

"They say he was a hunter who went by Gweta side and killed an elephant all by himself," she said, making up a story on the spot. "Oh! In those days, no man could kill an elephant by himself. All the regiments had to join together and each man had to thrust his sword into the side of the elephant before it died. Well, Robinson Crusoe was gone many days and people wondered about him: 'Perhaps he has been eaten by a lion,' they said. 'Robinson likes to be a solitary person and do foolish things. We won't ever go out into the bush by ourselves because we know it is dangerous.' Well, one day, Robinson suddenly appeared in their midst and people could see that he had a great thing on his mind. They all gathered around him. He said: 'I have killed an elephant for all the people.' The people were surprised: 'Robinson!' they said. 'It is impossible! How did you do it? The very thought of an elephant approaching the village makes us shiver!' And Robinson said: 'Ah, people, I saw a terrible sight! I was standing at the feet of the elephant. I was just a small ant. I could not see the world any more. Elephant was above me until his very head touched the sky and his ears spread out like great wings. He was angry but I only looked into one eye which was turning round and round in anger. What to do now? I thought it better to put that eye out. I raised my spear and threw it at the angry eye. People! It went right inside. Elephant said not a word and he fell to one side. Come I will show you what I have done.' Then the women cried in joy: 'Loo-loo-loo!' They ran to fetch their containers as some wanted the meat of the elephant; some wanted the fat. The men made their knives sharp. They would make shoes and many things from the skin and bones. There was something for all the people in the great work Robinson Crusoe did."

QUESTIONS

1. What tensions does the story illustrate between traditional and "modern" ways? How are these tensions portrayed in the characters of Friedman and Sejosenye?

2. Similarly, how does the story explore the tensions between the individual and society?

3. What does the story say about the relative positions of men and women, boys and girls, in this society? What is the narrator's attitude toward these differences?

4. Why is Friedman able to get away with tricks and thievery that other boys are not?

5. What effect does the story of Robinson Crusoe have on Friedman?

6. Why is Friedman killed? Is he responsible for his own death?

7. Is the last paragraph of the story a logical extension of the story itself, or is it "tacked on" to the story to point a moral? If the last paragraph were eliminated, how would the story be different? With the last paragraph, do previous events in the story take on any new significance?

Ken Saro-Wiwa

(NIGERIA, 1941–1995)

Ken Saro-Wiwa was born Kenule Beeson Saro-Wiwa into the Ogoni tribe in Bori, southeastern Nigeria. His father was a tribal chief and civil servant, which enabled young Kenule to attend a native elementary school, then the Government College (high school), and finally the University of Ibadan, where he studied German, French, and English literatures.

After several years of teaching and further studies of drama, he became a government bureaucrat and wrote his first play, *The Transistor Radio* (1972). He rose steadily in government ranks until the governor of Rivers State objected to his play, *Eneka*, and he was forced to resign. He spent most of the 1970s in the family's grocery business and later founded Saros International Publishers to publish his own work. During the 1980s, he wrote a popular soap opera for Nigerian television called *Basi and Company*, which boldly satirized corruption in Nigeria's government. This was followed by a book of poems and his most successful novel, *Sozaboy* (*Soldier Boy*, 1985).

From this point on, Saro-Wiwa's outlook became increasingly radical and antiestablishment. While investigating the oral traditions of his ancestral Ogoni tribe, Saro-Wiwa became outraged at the treatment of the Ogoni and their land, which was being devastated economically and environmentally by international oil companies, aided by the Nigerian government and its succession of military dictators, culminating in General Sani Abacha. Saro-Wiwa's Movement for the Survival of the Ogoni People, founded in 1990, brought this situation to international attention, with the result that Saro-Wiwa was arrested in 1993 for treason. Briefly released, he and seven others were rearrested on trumped-up murder charges, and in spite of protests by international human rights, environmental, and literary organizations, he was hanged with the others in 1995. The fact that the inept hangman botched the execution attempt five times further inflamed international opinion and made Saro-Wiwa even more a martyr, in spite of the fact that not all of his political activities were selfless or saintly. Nevertheless, Saro-Wiwa has become an international symbol for Third World victims of rapacious First World multinationals and domestic tyrants, while Nigeria itself can be seen as typical of post-colonial Africa's plight.

Saro-Wiwa wrote in so many styles and genres—children's stories, television scripts, novels, essays, poetry, and short stories—that it is impossible to single out a representative selection. The epistolary form of "Africa Kills Her Sun" is unusual, and some readers may regard it less as a story than as an essay or even diatribe. But political as the story is, it is affecting emotionally. The mixture of bravado and fear, anger and pathos, comedy and tragedy, bitterness and tenderness, awareness and sleep (among other qualities) take it beyond mere manifesto—important as this is—to the tragic human element that can too easily be overlooked by abstract political considerations.

Africa Kills Her Sun   1989

Dear Zole,

You'll be surprised, no doubt, to receive this letter. But I couldn't leave your beautiful world without saying goodbye to you who are condemned to live in it. I know that some might consider my gesture somewhat pathetic, as my colleagues, Sazan and Jimba, do, our finest moments having been achieved two or three weeks ago. However, for me, this letter is a celebration, a final act of love, a quality which, in spite of my career, in spite of tomorrow morning, I do possess in abundance, and cherish. For I've always treasured the many moments of pleasure we spent together in our youth when the world was new and fishes flew in golden ponds. In the love we then shared have I found happiness, a true resting place, a shelter from the many storms that have buffeted my brief life. Whenever I've been most alone, whenever I've been torn by conflict and pain, I've turned to that love for the resolution which has sustained and seen me through. This may surprise you, considering that this love was never consummated and that you may possibly have forgotten me, not having seen me these ten years gone. I still remember you, have always remembered you, and it's logical that on the night before tomorrow, I should write you to ask a small favor of you. But more important, the knowledge that I have unburdened myself to you will make tomorrow morning's event as pleasant and desirable to me as to the thousands of spectators who will witness it.

I know this will get to you because the prison guard's been heavily bribed to deliver it. He should rightly be with us before the firing squad tomorrow. But he's condemned, like most others, to live, to play out his assigned role in your hell of a world. I see him burning out his dull, uncomprehending life, doing his menial job for a pittance and a bribe for the next so many years. I pity his ignorance and cannot envy his complacency. Tomorrow morning, with this letter and our bribe in his pocket, he'll call us out, Sazan, Jimba and I. As usual, he'll have all our names mixed up: he always calls Sazan "Sajim" and Jimba "Samba." But that won't matter. We'll obey him, and as we walk to our death, we'll laugh at his gaucherie, his plain stupidity. As we laughed at that other thief, the High Court Judge.

You must've seen that in the papers too. We saw it, thanks to our bribe-taking friend, the prison guard, who sent us a copy of the newspaper in which it was reported. Were it not in an unfeeling nation, among a people inured to evil and taking sadistic pleasure in the loss of life, some questions might have been asked. No doubt, many will ask the questions, but they will do it in the safety and comfort of their homes, over the interminable bottles of beer, uncomprehendingly watching their boring, cheap television programs, the rejects of Europe and America, imported to fill their vacuity. They will salve their conscience with more bottles of beer, wash the answers down their gullets and pass question, conscience and answer out as waste into their open sewers choking with concentrated filth and murk. And they will forget.

I bet, though, the High Court Judge himself will never forget. He must remember it the rest of his life. Because I watched him closely that first morning. And I can't describe the shock and disbelief which I saw registered on his face. His spectacles fell to his table and it was with difficulty he regained composure. It must have been the first time in all his experience that he found persons arraigned on a charge for which the punishment upon conviction is death, entering a plea of guilty and demanding that they be sentenced and shot without further delay.

Sazan, Jimba and I had rehearsed it carefully. During the months we'd been remanded in prison custody while the prosecutors prepared their case, we'd agreed we weren't going to allow a long trial, or any possibility that they might impose differing sentences upon us: freeing one, sentencing another to life imprisonment and the third to death by firing squad.

Nor did we want to give the lawyers in their funny black funeral robes an opportunity to clown around, making arguments for pleasure, engaging in worthless casuistry. No. We voted for death. After all, we were armed robbers, bandits. We knew it. We didn't want to give the law a chance to prove itself the proverbial ass. We were being honest to ourselves, to our vocation, to our country and to mankind.

"Sentence us to death immediately and send us before the firing squad without further delay," we yelled in unison. The Judge, after he had recovered from his initial shock, asked us to be taken away that day, "for disturbing my court." I suppose he wanted to see if we'd sleep things over and change our plea. We didn't. When they brought us back the next day, we said the same thing in louder voice. We said we had robbed and killed. We were guilty. Cool. The Judge was bound hand and foot and did what he had to. We'd forced him to be honest to his vocation, to the laws of the country and to the course of justice. It was no mean achievement. The court hall was stunned; our guards were utterly amazed as we walked out of court, smiling. "Hardened criminals." "Bandits," I heard them say as we trooped out of the court. One spectator actually spat at us as we walked into the waiting Black Maria![1]

And now that I've confessed to banditry, you'll ask why I did it. I'll answer that question by retelling the story of the young, beautiful prostitute I met in St. Pauli in Hamburg when our ship berthed there years back. I've told my friends the story several times. I did ask her, after the event, why she was in that place. She replied that some girls chose to be secretaries in offices, others to be nurses. She had chosen prostitution as a career. Cool. I was struck by her candor. And she set me thinking. Was I in the Merchant Navy by choice or because it was the first job that presented itself to me when I left school? When we returned home, I skipped ship, thanks to the prostitute of St. Pauli, and took a situation as a clerk in the Ministry of Defense.

It was there I came face-to-face with the open looting of the national treasury, the manner of which I cannot describe without arousing in myself the deepest, basest emotions. Everyone was busy at it and there was no one to complain to. Everyone to whom I complained said to me: "If you can't beat them, join them." I was not about to join anyone; I wanted to beat them and took it upon myself to wage a war against them. In no time they had gotten rid of me. Dismissed me. I had no option but to join them then. I had to make a choice. I became an armed robber, a bandit. It was my choice, my answer. And I don't regret it.

Did I know it was dangerous? Some girls are secretaries, others choose to be prostitutes. Some men choose to be soldiers and policemen, others doctors and lawyers; I chose to be a robber. Every occupation has its hazards. A taxi driver may meet his death on the road; a businessman may die in an air crash; a robber dies before a firing squad. It's no big deal. If you ask me, the death I've chosen is possibly more dramatic, more qualitative, more eloquent than dying in bed of a ruptured liver from overindulgence in alcohol. Yes? But robbery is antisocial, you say? A proven determination to break the law. I don't want to provide an alibi. But just you think of the many men and women who are busy breaking or bending the law in all coasts and climes. Look for a copy of *The Guardian* of 19th September. That is the edition in which our plea to the Judge was reported. You'll find there the story of the Government official who stole over seven million naira.[2] Seven million. Cool. He was antisocial, right? How many of his type do you know? And how many more go undetected? I say, if my avocation was antisocial, I'm in good company. And that

---

1 **Black Maria:** Police van for transporting prisoners.
2 **naira:** Nigeria's currency.

company consists of Presidents of countries, transnational organizations, public servants high and low, men and women. The only difference is that while I'm prepared
to pay the price for it all, the others are not. See?

I'm not asking for your understanding or sympathy. I need neither, not now nor
hereafter. I'm saying it as it is. Right? Cool. I expect you'll say that armed robbery
should be the special preserve of the scum of society. That no man of my education
has any business being a bandit. To that I'll answer that it's about time well-endowed
and well-trained people took to it. They'll bring to the profession a romantic quality,
a proficiency which will ultimately conduce to the benefit of society. No, I'm not
mad. Truly. Time was when the running and ruining of African nations was in the
hands of half-literate politicians. Today, well-endowed and better-trained people
have taken over the task. And look how well they're doing it. So that even upon that
score, my conscience sleeps easy. Understand?

Talking about sleep, you should see Sazan and Jimba on the cold, hard prison
floor, snoring away as if life itself depends on a good snore. It's impossible, seeing
them this way, to believe that they'll be facing the firing squad tomorrow. They're
men of courage. Worthy lieutenants. It's a pity their abilities will be lost to society
forever, come tomorrow morning. Sazan would have made a good Army General
any day, possibly a President of our country in the mold of Idi Amin or Bokassa.[3]
The Europeans and Americans would have found in him a useful ally in the progressive degradation of Africa. Jimba'd have made an excellent Inspector-General of Police, so versed is he in the ways of the Police! You know, of course, that Sazan is a
dismissed Sergeant of our nation's proud army. And Jimba was once a Corporal in
the Police Force. When we met, we had similar reasons for pooling our talents. And a
great team we did make. Now here we all are in the death cell of a maximum security
prison and they snoring away the last hours of their lives on the cold, smelly floor.
It's exhilarating to find them so disdainful of life. Their style is the stuff of which history is made. In another time and in another country, they'd be Sir Francis Drake,
Cortés or Sir Walter Raleigh.[4] They'd have made empires and earned national honors. But here, our life is one big disaster, an endless tragedy. Heroism is not in our
star. We are millipedes crawling on the floor of a dank, wet forest. So Sazan and
Jimba will die unsung. See?

One thing, though. We swore never to kill. And we never did. Indeed, we didn't
take part in the particular "operation" for which we were held, Sazan, Jimba and I.
That operation would've gone quite well if the Superintendent of Police had fulfilled
his part of the bargain. Because he was in it with us. The Police are involved in every
single robbery that happens. They know the entire gang, the gangs. We'd not succeed
if we didn't collaborate with them. Sazan, Jimba and I were the bosses. We didn't go
out on "operations." The boys normally did. And they were out on that occasion.

3 **Idi Amin or Bokassa:** Idi Amin was president of Uganda (1971–1979) and a brutal dictator. Jean Bedal
Bokassa was ruler of the Central African Republic (1966–1979).
4 **Sir ... Raleigh:** Famous sixteenth-century explorers; Sir Francis Drake and Walter Raleigh were English;
Hernán Cortés was Spanish.

The Superintendent of Police was supposed to keep away the police escorts from the vehicle carrying workers' salaries that day. For some reason, he failed to do so. And the policeman shot at our boys. The boys responded and shot and killed him and the Security Company guards. The boys got the money all right. But the killing was contrary to our agreement with the Police. We had to pay. The Police won't stand for any of their men being killed. They took all the money from us and then they went after the boys. We said no. The boys had acted on orders. We volunteered to take their place. The Police took us in and made a lot of public noises about it. The boys, I know, will make their decisions later. I don't know what will happen to the Superintendent of Police. But he'll have to look to himself. So, if that is any comfort to you, you may rest in the knowledge that I spilt no blood. No, I wouldn't. Nor have I kept the loot. Somehow, whatever we took from people—the rich ones—always was shared by the gang, who were almost always on the bread line. Sazan, Jimba and I are not wealthy.

Many will therefore accuse us of recklessness, or of being careless with our lives. And well they might. I think I speak for my sleeping comrades when I say we went into our career because we didn't see any basic difference between what we were doing and what most others are doing throughout the land today. In every facet of our lives—in politics, in commerce and in the professions—robbery is the base line. And it's been so from time. In the early days, our forebears sold their kinsmen into slavery for minor items such as beads, mirrors, alcohol and tobacco. These days, the tune is the same, only the articles have changed into cars, transistor radios and bank accounts. Nothing else has changed, and nothing will change in the foreseeable future. But that's the problem of those of you who will live beyond tomorrow, Zole.

The cock crows now and I know dawn is about to break. I'm not speaking figuratively. In the cell here, the darkness is still all-pervasive, except for the flickering light of the candle by which I write. Sazan and Jimba remain fast asleep. So is the prison guard. He sleeps all night and is no trouble to us. We could, if we wanted, escape from here, so lax are the guards. But we consider that unnecessary, as what is going to happen later this morning is welcome relief from burdens too heavy to bear. It's the guard and you the living who are in prison, the ultimate prison from which you cannot escape because you do not know that you are incarcerated. Your happiness is the happiness of ignorance and your ignorance is it that keeps you in the prison, which is your life. As this night dissolves into day, Sazan, Jimba and I shall be free. Sazan and Jimba will have left nothing behind. I shall leave at least this letter, which, please, keep for posterity.

Zole, do I rant? Do I pour out myself to you in bitter tones? Do not lay it to the fact that I'm about to be shot by firing squad. On second thoughts, you could, you know. After all, seeing death so clearly before me might possibly have made me more perspicacious? And yet I've always seen these things clearly in my mind's eye. I never did speak about them, never discussed them. I preferred to let them weigh me down. See?

So, then, in a few hours we shall be called out. We shall clamber with others into the miserable lorry which they still call the Black Maria. Notice how everything

Jimba says to ask my girl to shed him a tear if she can so honor a complete stranger. They both chuckle and withdraw to a corner of the cell and I'm left alone to end my letter.

Now, I was telling you about my statue. My corpse will not be available to you. You will make a grave for me, nonetheless. And place the statue on the gravestone. And now I come to what I consider the most important part of this letter. My epitaph.

I have thought a lot about it, you know. Really. What do you say about a robber shot in a stadium before a cheering crowd? That he was a good man who strayed? That he deserved his end? That he was a scallywag? A ragamuffin? A murderer whose punishment was not heavy enough? "Here lies X, who was shot in public by firing squad for robbing a van and shooting the guards in broad daylight. He serves as an example to all thieves and would-be thieves!"

Who'd care for such an epitaph? They'd probably think it was a joke. No. That wouldn't carry. I'll settle for something different. Something plain and commonsensical. Or something truly cryptic and worthy of a man shot by choice in public by firing squad.

Not that I care. To die the way I'm going to die in the next hour or two is really nothing to worry about. I'm in excellent company. I should find myself recorded in the annals of our history. A history of violence, of murder, of disregard for life. Pleasure in inflicting pain—sadism. Is that the word for it? It's a world I should be pleased to leave. But not without an epitaph.

I recall, many years ago as a young child, reading in a newspaper of an African leader who stood on the grave of a dead lieutenant and through his tears said: "Africa kills her sons." I don't know what he meant by that, and though I've thought about it long enough, I've not been able to unravel the full mystery of those words. Now, today, this moment, they come flooding back to me. And I want to borrow from him. I'd like you to put this on my gravestone, as my epitaph: "Africa Kills Her Sun." A good epitaph, eh? Cryptic. Definite. A stroke of genius, I should say. I'm sure you'll agree with me. "Africa Kills Her Sun!" That's why she's been described as the Dark Continent? Yes?

So, now, dear girl, I'm done. My heart is light as the daylight which seeps stealthily into our dark cell. I hear the prison guard jangle his keys, put them into the keyhole. Soon he'll turn it and call us out. Our time is up. My time here expires and I must send you all my love. Goodbye.

Yours forever,

Bana

QUESTIONS

1. Bana calls his letter to Zole a "love letter." Is it? If so, in what sense is it a love letter? If not, what is it?

2. Why is Bana's encounter with the prostitute important to him?

3. On what grounds does Bana defend his choice to become a robber? Are his reasons logical and sound, or is he rationalizing?

4. Why is Bana contemptuous of ordinary people? Is he right to be contemptuous of them?

5. Do you admire Bana, Sazan, and Jimba for their bravery, or do you consider them foolhardy for admitting their guilt and demanding the death penalty?

6. Can Bana, Sazan, and Jimba be compared to Robin Hood and his merry men? Why or why not?

7. What does Bana's epitaph "Africa Kills Her Sun" mean? Why does he change the word from *son* to *sun*?

Nadine Gordimer

(SOUTH AFRICA, b. 1923)

Like many other writers represented in this anthology, Nadine Gordimer was born into a life of uncertain identity. Her father was a Jewish watch repairman who owned a small jewelry store in Springs, a town just outside of Johannesburg; her mother was English. When Gordimer was born, South Africa was not yet mired in the apartheid system against which she would later protest, but in any case, her social contacts were severely circumscribed when she was taken from school at age eleven for what her mother deemed were health reasons. For the next five years, Gordimer studied with a private tutor, read constantly, and went with her mother to tea parties and with both her parents to restaurants. She called herself at that stage, "a little old woman." But she has also stated that books saved her from thinking like everyone else. By the age of nine she had begun writing and by fourteen had published her first story. Her formal schooling ended at sixteen, until 1945 when she studied for just one year at the University of the Witwatersrand.

Gordimer's career as a professional writer began with the publication of short stories, her first collection appearing in 1949 and another collection following in 1952—both books already showing her mastery of dialogue and her concern with the plights of both whites and blacks under apartheid. Since these early story collections, Gordimer has produced a steady stream of story collections, novels, and nonfiction, culminating in the Nobel Prize for literature in 1991, just three years before the collapse of the apartheid system she had spent her life opposing.

The problem for an artist living in a blatantly segregationist and repressive society is how to express one's opposition to the status quo. For many of her black and white contemporaries, the path in the 1950s was to try to ignore racial separation in their personal lives and hope by this example to tear down the barriers. For Gordimer, this was not enough, and many of her white fictional characters live with the contradictions and compromises of such a strategy. When liberal intellectuals turned violent in the 1960s, Gordimer turned her critical gaze on them. But not all her fiction is overtly political: Often in the stories especially, she explores simply what it means to be human and to reach out for genuine relationships. In her speculative, almost idealistic novel of 1987, *A Sport of Nature*, she attempts to imagine a society free of prejudice, united in a common humanity. Nevertheless, much of her late fiction advocates the necessity of activism against immoral policies.

The story included here, "Amnesty," is from *Jump and Other Stories* (1991), published in the year she was awarded the Nobel Prize. Like a great many of her stories, it has its roots in the political and social situation of its time, and as usual, Gordimer approaches her material in the realistic manner, paying careful attention to the details of everyday life and the plausibility of the story's events. But also like much of her fiction, the perspective is humanistic, focusing on those basic impulses of love, marriage, and home that inform so much of Western literature. In these ways only, perhaps, is this story "typical" of Gordimer, a writer whose output is so various and whose perspectives are so honestly and compellingly multiple that no one work can stand for the whole.

Amnesty   1991

W hen we heard he was released I ran all over the farm and through the fence to our people on the next farm to tell everybody. I only saw afterwards I'd torn my dress on the barbed wire, and there was a scratch, with blood, on my shoulder.

He went away from this place nine years ago, signed up to work in town with what they call a construction company—building glass walls up to the sky. For the first two years he came home for the weekend once a month and two weeks at Christmas; that was when he asked my father for me. And he began to pay. He and I thought that in three years he would have paid enough for us to get married. But then he started wearing that T-shirt, he told us he'd joined the union, he told us about the strike, how he was one of the men who went to talk to the bosses because some others had been laid off after the strike. He's always been good at talking, even in English—he was the best at the farm school, he used to read the newspapers the Indian wraps soap and sugar in when you buy at the store.

There was trouble at the hostel where he had a bed, and riots over paying rent in the townships[1] and he told me—just me, not the old ones—that wherever people were fighting against the way we are treated they were doing it for all of us, on the farms as well as the towns, and the unions were with them, he was with them, making speeches, marching. The third year, we heard he was in prison. Instead of getting married. We didn't know where to find him, until he went on trial. The case was heard in a town far away. I couldn't go often to the court because by that time I had passed my Standard 8 and I was working in the farm school. Also my parents were short of money. Two of my brothers who had gone away to work in town didn't send home; I suppose they lived with girl-friends and had to buy things for them. My father and other brother work here for the Boer[2] and the pay is very small, we have two goats, a few cows we're allowed to graze, and a patch of land where my mother can grow vegetables. No cash from that.

When I saw him in the court he looked beautiful in a blue suit with a striped shirt and brown tie. All the accused—his comrades, he said—were well-dressed. The union bought the clothes so that the judge and the prosecutor would know they weren't dealing with stupid *yes-baas* black men who didn't know their rights. These things and everything else about the court and trial he explained to me when I was allowed to visit him in jail. Our little girl was born while the trial went on and when I brought the baby to court the first time to show him, his comrades hugged him and then hugged me across the barrier of the prisoners' dock and they had clubbed together to give me some money as a present for the baby. He chose the name for her, Inkululeko.

Then the trial was over and he got six years. He was sent to the Island.[3] We all knew about the Island. Our leaders had been there so long. But I have never seen the sea except to colour it in blue at school, and I couldn't imagine a piece of earth surrounded by it. I could only think of a cake of dung, dropped by the cattle, floating in a pool of rain-water they'd crossed, the water showing the sky like a looking-glass, blue. I was ashamed only to think that. He had told me how the glass walls showed the pavement trees and the other buildings in the street and the colours of the cars and the clouds as the crane lifted him on a platform higher and higher through the sky to work at the top of a building.

He was allowed one letter a month. It was my letter because his parents didn't know how to write. I used to go to them where they worked on another farm to ask what message they wanted to send. The mother always cried and put her hands on her head and said nothing, and the old man, who preached to us in the veld[4] every

---

1 **townships:** Rural areas to which urban Africans were sent; notorious for their poverty, lack of infrastructure, and resources.

2 **Boer:** "Farmer." Slang term for Dutch-speaking settlers of South Africa and their descendants.

3 **the Island:** Robben Island Prison, about four miles off the coast of South Africa, near Cape Town. The most famous inmate of this notorious prison was Nelson Mandela.

4 **veld:** Grassland with scattered trees and shrubs.

Sunday, said tell my son we are praying, God will make everything all right for him. Once he wrote back, That's the trouble—our people on the farms, they're told God will decide what's good for them so that they won't find the force to do anything to change their lives.

After two years had passed, we—his parents and I—had saved up enough money to go to Cape Town to visit him. We went by train and slept on the floor at the station and asked the way, next day, to the ferry. People were kind; they all knew that if you wanted the ferry it was because you had somebody of yours on the Island.

And there it was—there was the sea. It was green *and* blue, climbing and falling, bursting white, all the way to the sky. A terrible wind was slapping it this way and that; it hid the Island, but people like us, also waiting for the ferry, pointed where the Island must be, far out in the sea that I never thought would be like it really was.

There were other boats, and ships as big as buildings that go to other places, all over the world, but the ferry is only for the Island, it doesn't go anywhere else in the world, only to the Island. So everybody waiting there was waiting for the Island, there could be no mistake we were not in the right place. We had sweets and biscuits, trousers and a warm coat for him (a woman standing with us said we wouldn't be allowed to give him the clothes) and I wasn't wearing, any more, the old beret pulled down over my head that farm girls wear, I had bought relaxer cream from the man who comes round the farms selling things out of a box on his bicycle, and my hair was combed up thick under a flowered scarf that didn't cover the gold-coloured rings in my ears. His mother had her blanket tied round her waist over her dress, a farm woman, but I looked just as good as any of the other girls there. When the ferry was ready to take us, we stood all pressed together and quiet like the cattle waiting to be let through a gate. One man kept looking round with his chin moving up and down, he was counting, he must have been afraid there were too many to get on and he didn't want to be left behind. We all moved up to the policeman in charge and everyone ahead of us went onto the boat. But when our turn came and he put out his hand for something, I didn't know what.

We didn't have a permit. We didn't know that before you come to Cape Town, before you come to the ferry for the Island, you have to have a police permit to visit a prisoner on the Island. I tried to ask him nicely. The wind blew the voice out of my mouth.

We were turned away. We saw the ferry rock, bumping the landing where we stood, moving, lifted and dropped by all that water, getting smaller and smaller until we didn't know if we were really seeing it or one of the birds that looked black, dipping up and down, out there.

The only good thing was one of the other people took the sweets and biscuits for him. He wrote and said he got them. But it wasn't a good letter. Of course not. He was cross with me; I should have found out, I should have known about the permit. He was right—I bought the train tickets, I asked where to go for the ferry, I should have known about the permit. I have passed Standard 8. There was an advice office to go to in town, the churches ran it, he wrote. But the farm is so far from town, we on the farms don't know about these things. It was as he said; our ignorance is the way we are kept down, this ignorance must go.

We took the train back and we never went to the Island—never saw him in the three more years he was there. Not once. We couldn't find the money for the train. His father died and I had to help his mother from my pay. For our people the worry is always money, I wrote. When will we ever have money? Then he sent such a good letter. That's what I'm on the Island for, far away from you, I'm here so that one day our people will have the things they need, land, food, the end of ignorance. There was something else—I could just read the word 'power' the prison had blacked out. All his letters were not just for me; the prison officer read them before I could.

He was coming home after only five years!

That's what it seemed to me, when I heard—the five years were suddenly disappeared—nothing!—there was no whole year still to wait. I showed my—our—little girl his photo again. That's your daddy, he's coming, you're going to see him. She told the other children at school, I've got a daddy, just as she showed off about the kid goat she had at home.

We wanted him to come at once, and at the same time we wanted time to prepare. His mother lived with one of his uncles; now that his father was dead there was no house of his father for him to take me to as soon as we married. If there had been time, my father would have cut poles, my mother and I would have baked bricks, cut thatch, and built a house for him and me and the child.

We were not sure what day he would arrive. We only heard on my radio his name and the names of some others who were released. Then at the Indian's store I noticed the newspaper, *The Nation,* written by black people, and on the front a picture of a lot of people dancing and waving—I saw at once it was at that ferry. Some men were being carried on other men's shoulders. I couldn't see which one was him. We were waiting. The ferry had brought him from the Island but we remembered Cape Town is a long way from us. Then he did come. On a Saturday, no school, so I was working with my mother, hoeing and weeding round the pumpkins and mealies, my hair, that I meant to keep nice, tied in an old *doek.* A combi came over the veld and his comrades had brought him. I wanted to run away and wash but he stood there stretching his legs, calling, hey! hey! with his comrades making a noise around him, and my mother started shrieking in the old style aie! aie! and my father was clapping and stamping towards him. He held his arms open to us, this big man in town clothes, polished shoes, and all the time while he hugged me I was holding my dirty hands, full of mud, away from him behind his back. His teeth hit me hard through his lips, he grabbed at my mother and she struggled to hold the child up to him. I thought we would all fall down! Then everyone was quiet. The child hid behind my mother. He picked her up but she turned her head away to her shoulder. He spoke to her gently but she wouldn't speak to him. She's nearly six years old! I told her not to be a baby. She said, That's not him.

The comrades all laughed, we laughed, she ran off and he said, She has to have time to get used to me.

He has put on weight, yes; a lot. You couldn't believe it. He used to be so thin his feet looked too big for him. I used to feel his bones but now—that night—when he lay on me he was so heavy, I didn't remember it was like that. Such a long time. It's strange to get stronger in prison; I thought he wouldn't have enough to eat and would come out weak. Everyone said, Look at him!—he's a man, now. He laughed and banged his fist on his chest, told them how the comrades exercised in their cells, he would run three miles a day, stepping up and down on one place on the floor of that small cell where he was kept. After we were together at night we used to whisper a long time but now I can feel he's thinking of some things I don't know and I can't worry him with talk. Also I don't know what to say. To ask him what it was like, five years shut away there; or to tell him something about school or about the child. What else has happened, here? Nothing. Just waiting. Sometimes in the daytime I do try to tell him what it was like for me, here at home on the farm, five years. He listens, he's interested, just like he's interested when people from the other farms come to visit and talk to him about little things that happened to them while he was away all that time on the Island. He smiles and nods, asks a couple of questions and then stands up and stretches. I see it's to show them it's enough, his mind is going back to something he was busy with before they came. And we farm people are very slow; we tell things slowly, he used to, too.

He hasn't signed on for another job. But he can't stay at home with us; we thought, after five years over there in the middle of that green and blue sea, so far, he would rest with us a little while. The combi or some car comes to fetch him and he says don't worry, I don't know what day I'll be back. At first I asked, what week, next week? He tried to explain to me: in the Movement it's not like it was in the union, where you do your work every day and after that you are busy with meetings; in the Movement you never know where you will have to go and what is going to come up next. And the same with money. In the Movement, it's not like a job, with regular pay—I know that, he doesn't have to tell me—it's like it was going to the Island, you do it for all our people who suffer because we haven't got money, we haven't got land—look, he said, speaking of my parents', my home, the home that has been waiting for him, with his child: look at this place where the white man owns the ground and lets you squat in mud and tin huts here only as long as you work for him—*Baba* and your brother planting his crops and looking after his cattle, Mama cleaning his house and you in the school without even having the chance to train properly as a teacher. The farmer owns us, he says.

I've been thinking we haven't got a home because there wasn't time to build a house before he came from the Island; but we haven't got a home at all. Now I've understood that.

I'm not stupid. When the comrades come to this place in the combi to talk to him here I don't go away with my mother after we've brought them tea or (if she's made it for the weekend) beer. They like her beer, they talk about our culture and there's one of them who makes a point of putting his arm around my mother, calling her the mama of all of them, the mama of Africa. Sometimes they please her very much by telling her how they used to sing on the Island and getting her to sing an old song we all know from our grandmothers. Then they join in with their strong voices. My father doesn't like this noise travelling across the veld; he's afraid that if the Boer finds out my man is a political, from the Island, and he's holding meetings on the Boer's land, he'll tell my father to go, and take his family with him. But my brother says if the Boer asks anything just tell him it's a prayer meeting. Then the singing is over; my mother knows she must go away into the house.

I stay, and listen. He forgets I'm there when he's talking and arguing about something I can see is important, more important than anything we could ever have to say to each other when we're alone. But now and then, when one of the other comrades is speaking I see him look at me for a moment the way I will look up at one of my favourite children in school to encourage the child to understand. The men don't speak to me and I don't speak. One of the things they talk about is organizing the people on the farms—the workers, like my father and brother, and like his parents used to be. I learn what all these things are: minimum wage, limitation of working hours, the right to strike, annual leave, accident compensation, pensions, sick and even maternity leave. I am pregnant, at last I have another child inside me, but that's women's business. When they talk about the Big Man, the Old Men, I know who these are: our leaders are also back from prison. I told him about the child coming; he said, And this one belongs to a new country, he'll build the freedom we've fought for! I know he wants to get married but there's no time for that at present. There was hardly time for him to make the child. He comes to me just like he comes here to eat a meal or put on clean clothes. Then he picks up the little girl and swings her round and there!—it's done, he's getting into the combi, he's already turning to his comrade that face of his that knows only what's inside his head, those eyes that move quickly as if he's chasing something you can't see. The little girl hasn't had time to get used to this man. But I know she'll be proud of him, one day!

How can you tell that to a child six years old. But I tell her about the Big Man and the Old Men, our leaders, so she'll know that her father was with them on the Island, this man is a great man, too.

On Saturday, no school and I plant and weed with my mother, she sings but I don't; I think. On Sunday there's no work, only prayer meetings out of the farmer's way under the trees, and beer drinks at the mud and tin huts where the farmers allow us to squat on their land. I go off on my own as I used to do when I was a child, making up games and talking to myself where no one would hear me or look for me. I sit on a warm stone in the late afternoon, high up, and the whole valley is a path between the hills, leading away from my feet. It's the Boer's farm but that's not true, it belongs to nobody. The cattle don't know that anyone says he owns it, the sheep—they are grey stones, and then they become a thick grey snake moving—don't know. Our huts and the old mulberry tree and the little brown mat of earth that my mother dug over yesterday, way down there, and way over there the clump of trees round the chimneys and the shiny thing that is the TV mast of the farmhouse—they are nothing, on the back of this earth. It could twitch them away like a dog does a fly.

I am up with the clouds. The sun behind me is changing the colours of the sky and the clouds are changing themselves, slowly, slowly. Some are pink, some are white, swelling like bubbles. Underneath is a bar of grey, not enough to make rain. It gets longer and darker, it grows a thin snout and long body and then the end of it is a tail. There's a huge grey rat moving across the sky, eating the sky.

The child remembered the photo; she said *That's not him.* I'm sitting here where I came often when he was on the Island. I came to get away from the others, to wait by myself.

I'm watching the rat, it's losing itself, its shape, eating the sky, and I'm waiting. Waiting for him to come back.

Waiting.

I'm waiting to come back home.

QUESTIONS

1. Analyze the effects on family life that are caused when the men leave the townships and go to the cities to work. Cite specific passages to illustrate these effects.

2. What specific injustices is "the movement" attempting to correct? Cite specific passages.

3. Gordimer has chosen to narrate her story through a naive speaker. What are the effects of having the wife tell the story? Are there disadvantages?

4. Does the narrator change or learn during the course of the story? If so, in what specific ways? Cite specifics to support your answer.

5. Is the narrator's husband irresponsible in his treatment of his wife and children? Explain your answer.

6. What is the significance of the rat-shaped cloud that the narrator describes at the end of the story?

Alexander Kanengoni

(ZIMBABWE, b. 1951)

Alexander Kanengoni may well be the most controversial author included in this anthology—not for what he has written, but for the political stance he has taken since 2001.

He was born in Chivhu in what was then Southern Rhodesia, one of the last white-minority states in Africa. He was educated in a mission school and later trained to be a teacher at St. Paul's Teacher Training College and at the University of Zimbabwe. When open rebellion against the white government broke out in 1974, Kanengoni joined the African National Union, headed by Robert

Mugabe. Independence was achieved in 1980 with Mugabe as the country's first black president, and in 1983, Kanengoni began working for the Ministry of Education and Culture. Five years later, he was named head of Research Services for the Zimbabwe Broadcasting Corporation. In 2002, Mugabe began the controversial program of seizing land from white owners and distributing it to his supporters, many of them, like Kanengoni, ignorant of farming.

In the same year that he joined the Ministry of Education and Culture, Kanengoni published *Vicious Circle,* a novel for young readers that depicts the difficulties civilians faced during the war for independence. This was followed by an adult novel on a similar theme, *When the Rainbird Cries* (1987). His third novel, *Echoing Silences* (1997), also deals with the civil war, especially the infighting among rebel factions and the postindependence political scene, which Kanengoni sees as dominated by lies and silence. "Effortless Tears" is the title story of his only collection (1993). Unlike the novels, it explores the other great ravagers of Africa—disease and famine.

Given Kanengoni's artistic vision, it is difficult for many to understand his unwavering support for Robert Mugabe, one of the most ruthless and deadly of Africa's current dictators. He has recently been quoted as admiring the dictator because, "Robert Mugabe has always been guided by his beliefs and visions." In his view, the restoration of land to Zimbabweans brings the colonial/post-colonial process full circle, putting himself and others once again in touch with their heritage.

Effortless Tears *1993*

We buried my cousin, George Pasi, one bleak windswept afternoon: one of those afternoons that seem fit for nothing but funerals. Almost everyone there knew that George had died of an AIDS-related illness but no one mentioned it. What showed was only the fear and uncertainty in people's eyes; beyond that, silence.

Even as we traveled from Harare[1] on that hired bus that morning, every one of us feared that at last AIDS had caught up with us. In the beginning, it was a distant, blurred phenomenon which we only came across in the newspapers and on radio and television, something peculiar to homosexuals. Then we began hearing isolated stories of people dying of AIDS in far-flung districts. After that came the rumors of sealed wards at Harare and Parirenyatwa, and of other hospitals teeming with people suffering from AIDS. But the truth is that it still seemed rather remote and did not seem to have any direct bearing on most of us.

When AIDS finally reached Highfield and Zengeza, and started claiming lives in the streets where we lived, that triggered the alarm bells inside our heads. AIDS had finally knocked on our doors.

---

1 **Harare:** Capital of Zimbabwe.

referred to it in indirect terms: that animal, that phantom, that creature, that beast. It was not out of any respect for George. It was out of fear and despair.

"Whatever this scourge is"—George's father chuckled—"it has claimed more lives than all my three years in the Imperial Army against Hitler." He chuckled again helplessly.

"It seems as if these endless funerals have taken the place of farming."

"They are lucky, the ones who are still getting decent burials," chipped in someone from out of the dark. "Very soon, there will be no one to bury anybody."

The last glowing ember in the collected heap of ashes grew dimmer and finally died away. George's grandfather asked for an ox-hide drum and began playing it slowly at first and then with gathering ferocity. Something in me snapped.

Then he began to sing. The song told of an unfortunate woman's repeated pregnancies which always ended in miscarriages. I felt trapped.

When at last the old man, my father, stood up and began to dance, stamping the dry earth with his worn-out car-tire sandals, I knew there was no escape. I edged George's grandfather away from the drum and began a futile prayer on that moonless night. The throbbing resonance of the drum rose above our voices as we all became part of one great nothingness. Suddenly I was crying for the first time since George's death. Tears ran from my eyes like rivers in a good season. During those years, most of us firmly believed that the mighty Save River would roll on forever, perhaps until the end of time.

But not now, not any longer.

QUESTIONS

1. What conflicting cultural, spiritual, and medical ideas do you find in the story? What do these conflicting ideas tell you about Zimbabwe and its people?

2. In addition to the scourge of AIDS, what images and descriptions of death and desolation do you find in the story? What is the cumulative effect of these?

3. In what ways does AIDS differ from other threats to life and prosperity?

4. Do you regard the dancing at the end of the story a sign of renewed hope or a sign of defeat and despair? Explain.

Sindiwe Magona

(SOUTH AFRICA, b. 1943)

Sindiwe Magona was born in Tsolo, a village in the Transkei region of the Kingdom of Lesotho, South Africa. The family later moved to Guguletu, Cape Town. After primary and secondary school, she earned a teaching certificate in

1961 and then furthered her studies at the University of London, completing her degree in history and psychology at the University of South Africa. She taught primary school in Cape Town from 1967–1980 and the Xhosa language in high school, 1977–1981. She again left Africa to earn an MS degree in organizational social work from Columbia University in New York (1983) and thereafter became a press officer at the United Nations. She has since returned to South Africa.

Magona's first published works, *Mother to Mother* and *Forced to Grow* (both 1998), are autobiographical and grow out of her desire to encourage other African women to make the transition from oral to written narrative. African women have always passed on their stories via oral tradition, but Magona believes that the time has come not to abandon oral transmission, but to complement it with the written word. Just as she was inspired by Maya Angelou's *I Know Why the Caged Bird Sings* (1969), she hopes to inspire other women to make the transition to writing.

Another motivation lies in her desire to help her people transcend the effects of generations of apartheid. Although apartheid has officially ended, its effects linger in every aspect of black Africans' lives. Knowing both the hardships of their history and the strength required to survive will help her countrymen find the means to move forward. Magona's own life illustrates that one can overcome poverty and racism, which is why much of her writing has been autobiographical.

"I'm Not Talking About That, Now" captures in a short story much of the pain and ambiguity of her novel, *Mother to Mother*, which grew out of the murder in 1993 of Fulbright scholar Amy Elizabeth Biehl, one of whose killers was the child of a friend. The incident, she said in an interview, forced her to look at murder from a different point of view, and she used fiction to try to explain how difficult life was for parents of children growing up under apartheid, without in any way attempting to justify the crime. While apartheid itself was a terrible evil, those fighting it often faced moral dilemmas of their own, and its effects on families could be devastating.

I'm Not Talking About That, Now   *1996*

Mamvulane lay very still, her eyes wide open, staring unseeingly into nowhere. She listened to her husband snore softly beside her.

A big bold orange band lay on the carpet—painted there by the strong dawn light pouring through the bright orange-curtained window.

Reluctantly, she focused her eyes. Her head was throbbing. She glanced at the alarm clock on the dressing table. God, it wasn't even five o'clock yet. How was she going to survive this day? she asked herself. Her right eye felt as though someone was poking a red-hot iron rod into it from the back of her head, where he'd first drilled a hole.

Irritatedly, she pushed her husband onto his side. Immediately, the snoring stopped. She listened to the drilling inside her head, assuming that with the noise of Mdlangathi's snoring gone, the pain would subside. And, indeed, it did appear to be in abeyance if not completely vanished.

She took a deep and noisy inward draw of breath. Cruel fancy played her tricks. She could swear the air was faintly laced with the barest soupçon of the bittersweet smell of coffee. Mmmhh! What she wouldn't give for just one cup. Just one.

Her stomach growled. Swiftly, she placed one hand on her still girlishly flat tummy. She felt the quick ripples of air bubbles in her bowels. When last had she eaten? And what had she had then?

Mdlangathi, her husband, lying next to her, mumbled something in his sleep and turned over to lie, once more, facing the ceiling, his distinctly discernible paunch hilling the blankets.

Immediately, the snoring resumed, provoking swift and righteous retaliation from his wife, reflex by now, after all the years with him and his snoring.

Mamvulane dug an elbow into his side, grumbling, "*Uyarhona, Mdlangathi, Uyarhona!*" for habits die hard. In their more than twenty years of marriage, among the constants in their relationship was his snoring whenever he lay "like a rat suffering from acute heartburn," her talking to him as though he were awake and the answers he never failed to mumble—pearls from an ancient oracle. She always chided herself that she actually listened, paid attention to the barely audible ramblings of a snoring man who'd gone to bed drunk. But she always did. And tonight not only was he drunk when he went to bed, Mamvulane told herself, but she had never seen him so agitated. Would she never learn?

Last night, however, was the worst she'd ever seen him. He'd returned positively excited, ranting and raving about the gross lack of respect of today's young people.

"*Baqalekisiwe, ndifung' uTat' ekobandayo. Baqalekisiw' aba bantwana, Mamvulane.*"

"What children are cursed?" his wife wanted to know.

And that is when he told her of the curse the actions of today's children would surely invite onto their heads.

"Why do you say such a terrible thing?" his wife wanted to know.

"Now, now, just as the sun set, I was on my way here from the single men's zones,[1] where I'd gone to get a little something to wet my parched throat. What do you think I should come across? Mmhhmh?" He stopped and considered her with his bleary eyes.

His wife conceded ignorance. "I'm sure I don't know. Why don't you tell me," she said. She wanted to scrape together what food there was in the house. And try to prepare a meal.

---

1 **single men's zones:** Under apartheid, African men who worked in mines or factories were required to live in male-only accommodations—even if they were married with families.

"Do you know that a group of boys accosted a man? A grown man, who was circumcised? Boys laid their filthy hands on such a man . . . a man old enough to be their father?"

"Where was this?" asked Mamvulane, not sure how much of Mdlangathi's ramblings she should take seriously.

"You ask me something I have already told you. Where are your ears, woman? Or else, you think I'm drunk and pay no attention to what I tell you? No wonder your children are as bad as they are, where would they learn to listen and obey since you, our wives, who are their mothers, have stopped doing that? Mmhhh?"

"Are you telling me the story or should I go about my business?" retorted Mamvulane. She was taking a risk, for she did want to hear the story. But she also knew that her husband rather fancied the sound of his own voice.

"If you want to hear the story, then pay attention. I told you I was from the zones. On my way here, I came across a group of boys, you know, these little rascals who are always passing by here, pretending to be visiting your son, Mteteli, when you full know it's your daughter they want. And they were manhandling one of their fathers."

"Who was that?"

"Now, you make me laugh. You imagine I stopped and asked them for their *dompasses?*[2] Am I mad? Or do you think I am a fool? Or is it your hurry to be a widow that is putting those stupid words into your mouth? Mmhh?"

With great deliberateness, Mdlangathi attended to the business of picking his teeth. First, he took out a match. Then he took out his jackknife and started whittling slowly on the tiny match, chiseling it till the back had a sharp point.

"When a woman told me what those dogs were doing, I knew enough to mind my own business, my friend. Today's children show no respect for their fathers.

"This man, the woman said to me, had had too much to drink. Now, mind you," quickly, he went to the defense of his fallen comrade, "the man drank from his own pocket, he didn't ask those silly boys to buy him his liquor. So what is his sin? Tell me, what is this man's sin when he has drunk liquor he bought with his own money? Why should these mad children make that their business, mmhhmh?"

"What did they do?"

"These little devils," bellowed Mdlangathi, eyes flashing. "Don't they force the sad man to drink down a solution of *Javel?*[3] *Javel*, Mamvulane! Do you hear me? What do you think *Javel* does to a man's throat? To his stomach? I ask you, what do you think it does to those things? Just visit and make jokes with them, heh?"

He glowered at her as though she were one of the "little devils" and he was itching to teach her a lesson.

Bang! went his fist on the table.

---

2 **dompasses:** The identification pass every African was required to carry, containing the person's photograph and fingerprint and information on his or her access to white areas.
3 **Javel:** Chlorine bleach.

"A grown man, no less! The boys make him drink that poison. They tell him, 'We are helping you, Tata, not killing you!' Then, when they see that his belly is well extended from all that liquid, they give him a feather from a cock's tail and force him to insert it into his throat, '. . . deep down the path the poison traveled,' they say to him.

"The man does as he is told. Only he is so enfeebled by the heaviness of his stomach and what he'd had before he drank the *Javel* solution that his attempts do not immediately bring the required results. Whereupon the urchins take matters into their hands.

"'This poison crushes Africa's seed!' they say, one of them taking the feather from his trembling hand and pushing it down the man's gullet himself.

"Do you hear what I'm telling you, Mamvulane? Even a witchdoctor does not put his own hand into the throat of the man he is helping to bring up poison from his craw.

"But that is what these wretched children did. Put their dirty hands down the throats of their fathers and forced them to regurgitate the liquor they had drunk."

None too sober himself, Mdlangathi embarked upon a bitter tirade directed at all of today's children, miserable creatures who had no respect for their elders.

Recalling last night's events or the account her husband had given her, Mamvulane now looked down at him, asleep still by her side. Poor Mdlangathi. So vulnerable in the soft early-morning light. Poor Mdlangathi. He must have got the fright of his life, she thought, shaking her head in dumb disbelief at the things that were happening these days in their lives.

Her immediate problem, however, was what were they all going to eat once they got out of bed? She had all but scraped the bottom of the barrel last night. Her mind made an inventory of all the food they had in the house: a potato, by no means gigantic; two small onions; a quarter packet of beans but no samp,[4] there was no salt; a cup or a cup and a half of mealie meal[5] . . . And then there was no paraffin[6] with which to cook whatever she might have, far from adequate as that itself was.

Three weeks now, the consumer boycott had been going on. Three weeks, they had been told not to go to the shops. She was at her wit's end. Mdlangathi and the children expected to eat—boycott or no boycott. Whether she had gone to the shops or not didn't much concern them. All they understood, especially the younger children, was that their tummies were growling and they wanted something to eat. And their unreasonableness, conceded Mamvulane, was understandable. Now, her husband's case was cause for vexation to her. Wasn't Mdlangathi another thing altogether? A grown man. With all that was happening. But still, he wanted and expected no changes in his life. Didn't he still go to work every day? That's what he'd asked her when she told him they were running out of food. What did she do with the money he gave her? As though, in these mad and crazy days, money were the only issue, the

4 **samp:** Coarse hominy (corn) or a cooked cereal made from it.
5 **mealie meal:** Corn meal.
6 **paraffin:** Kerosene.

sole consideration. And not the very shopping itself—the getting of the food. With the comrades guarding every entry point in Guguletu. And neighbor informing on neighbor. People sprouting eyes at the back of their heads so that they could go and curry favor with the comrades, giving them information about others, especially those with whom they did not see eye to eye about things. Yes, it was so. For the very people who denounced others to the comrades were not above turning a blind eye to the same things . . . when the actors were people they favored. But did her very reasonable, understanding, and loving husband, who always gave her his wages, understand that? No. He thought she should just hop on a bus and go to Claremont and there go to Pick 'n Pay! Mdlangathi was something else, concluded Mamvulane, shaking her head slowly like one deep in thought. How did he arrive at thinking, at a time like this, that food shopping was still a simple matter of whether one had money in one's pocket?

The very thought of getting up was too much for her to entertain this morning. Hunger has that effect. Her anger mounted with the growing realization that she faced a hard day with no answers to the questions it raised, that she had to feed her family and had nothing at all that she could put together to make a meal.

It's all very well for the comrades to stop people from going to the shops, she fumed. They were fighting the businessmen, they said. But as far as she could see, it was only people like herself, poor people in the township,[7] who were starving. The businessmen were eating. So were their families. They were getting fatter and fatter by the day. They had meat and bread and fruit and vegetables and milk for their babies. They put heavily laden plates on their tables . . . not just once a day, as most people like herself did in good times, no, but each time they had a meal—several times a day. Oh, no, the businessmen the comrades were fighting were in no danger of dying from starvation. It was not their bowels that had nothing but the howling air in them. And not their children whose ribs one could count.

Midafternoon that same day, Mamvulane said, "*I have to do something today!*" As there was no one else in the house, she was talking to herself. Thereafter, without a word even to her very good neighbor and friend, Nolitha, she made her way out of her yard. Looking neither left nor right, away she hurried.

She had her day clothes on, complete with apron and back-flattened slippers. The pale of her rather large heels showing, she flip-flopped down the road. Anyone seeing her thus attired would have assumed she wasn't going any farther than perhaps fifty or so meters from her very own doorstep.

It was a little after three—time to start the evening meal. For those who could do that. Not me, thought Mamvulane bitterly. Not poor me, she said under her breath, walking away as nonchalantly as you please.

NY 74 is a crescent street with three exit points: north, west, and south. Mamvulane's family lived directly opposite the western exit, separated from it by two large buildings, the Community Center in front of her house and plumb in the center of

---

7 **township:** An area outside the main city where Africans were forced to live.

the circle, and the Old Apostolic Church behind it. In reality, therefore, from her house she could not see anyone coming or leaving from that exit which lay on NY 65. The other two exits were clearly visible from her house. And usually those were the ones she favored because, until she disappeared altogether, she could always turn back and yell for one of the children to bring her anything she might have forgotten.

But this day she slowly made her way toward NY 65, soon losing sight of her house. "*Andizi kubukel' abantwana bam besifa yindlala.*" And thus emboldened by her own thoughts, she went on her way. No, she was not going to watch her children starve to death.

Her plan was simple. And daring. Straight through NY 65 she walked. Into the zones, she went, her gait slow and steady, not once hesitating. Past the zones and into the Coloured township of Mannenberg. She'd gained enough anonymity, she deemed. Along Hanover Road she made her way until she found a bus stop. With a sigh, she stopped and leaned against the electric pole marking the stop.

Into her breast her hand fished for the little bundle, the handkerchief wherein lay her stash. Money. Bus fare and much more.

Carefully, she extricated enough for the fare and put the rest back where it had been, securely tied it into a knot at one corner of the handkerchief. And then back went the purse, safe and secure.

Her wait wasn't long. A bus came. She clambered on—one of only a few still making their way to the shopping suburb at that time of day, and definitely the only woman from Guguletu (or any of the other African townships, for that matter) on that bus. The buses coming back from Claremont were full with workers and shoppers returning home.

Mamvulane found a seat easily. Her heart was quite calm. Her chin quite firm. Her head held high. She was amazed at how unbelievably easily she had accomplished her mission thus far. But she knew that the real difficulty lay ahead . . . in Claremont? Or would it be harder for her back in Guguletu? *Ndakubona ngoko.* That stubborn thought planted itself in her mind. *I'll cross that bridge when I get to it.*

At Pick 'n Pay the aisles were full. She began to wonder whether the boycott had been lifted and she and her neighbors were maintaining a boycott long past because they had not heard the good news. But a closer look told her the people milling about there were not from the African townships. They were from everywhere else. And what they were doing there, they were doing quite openly—freely and without one little qualm.

Soon, her own timidity left her. She forgot that what she was doing was forbidden. Once more, it had become, to her too, a normal and very ordinary activity. Only the unusual exhilaration she felt, silent laughter of parched gardens drinking in rain after a drought, gave any indication of her deprivation. That, and the serious weighing of choices, which items to select, which to discard, and which to ignore completely. Deep down, on another level of knowing, she knew that she had to travel very light.

Her purchases made and paid for, Mamvulane went to the train station. There was a toilet there that she could use. She had put back a lot of the articles that, at first impulse, she'd grabbed and thrown into her trolley. Not unaware of the dangers that lay in her homeward-bound journey, she saw the virtue of ridding herself of most of what she wished for. It would be stupid to make her venture that obvious that she ended up losing all she had risked her neck for. The problem of packaging was of prime importance.

With her two Pick 'n Pay plastic bags, Mamvulane entered the toilet at the railway station. Fortunately, there was no one there. In her mind, all the way from her house, on the bus, and in the store itself, she had turned and turned the problem of what to do with her purchases and now that the time had come it was as though she had actually rehearsed the whole thing. Several times over.

In less than ten minutes, Mamvulane left the toilet. She now carried only one plastic bag. And it was not from Pick 'n Pay. To any eyes happening on her, she was just a rather shabby African woman who might have gone to buy some clothing, not much, from Sales House. For that is what the bag she was carrying said now: SALES HOUSE. And everyone knew Sales House was a clothing and drapery store. Indeed, since the bag had long lost its crispness it could be taken that she was a domestic worker carrying home goodies her madam had given her.

Deliberately avoiding the Guguletu bus line, Mamvulane made a beeline for the Nyanga bus. The line was not that long. Soon she would be home. Soon. Soon.

When the bus came she was one of the last to board it. But still found a seat, for most workers were already back in their houses, the time being half past six.

Ordinarily, she would have been concerned that her husband might get home before her. That was something he didn't particularly care for. Mdlangathi liked to get home and find his wife waiting supper for him, so that, should he feel in the mood for it, he could go back out again to get a drink from one of the *shebeens*[8] nearby. To make matters worse, Mamvulane reminded herself, in her haste and caution, she had not told even one of her children where she was going. Ahh, silently she told herself, I'm sure when he sees where I've been he will not only understand; he will be mighty pleased.

The Nyanga bus passes Guguletu on its way to Nyanga, for the two townships are neighbors, with Nyanga lying east of Guguletu. Somewhere in the indistinct border between the two, there is an area neither in the one nor in the other, a kind of administratively forgotten no-man's-land. And there one finds all sorts of people, including some not classified as Africans or as Coloured—those who somehow escaped government classification. Some of them work, others don't. No one really knows what does happen in that place, which has come to be called *kwaBraweni*. How it got to be Brown's Place is a mystery, or perhaps a myth awaiting excavation.

Mamvulane let the bus ride past Guguletu with her, making no sign at all that that was where she was headed. Only when the bus came to *kwaBraweni* did she ring the bell, indicating to the driver that her stop approached.

---

8 *shebeens:* Unlicensed bars or liquor stores.

From the bus stop where she got off, it was less than a kilometer or so to her house. But Mamvulane was well aware that that was where the greatest challenge lay. In covering that distance that seemed insignificant and easy.

There was a shortcut through a thicket. Avoiding the road, where she risked running into people, she chose the shortcut. Here and there she had to use her hands to separate entangled branches of trees so she could pass. Dry twigs scratched her bare legs and she kept her eyes peeled for dog and human shit. Her slippers were old and torn and anything on which she trod would certainly get intimate with her feet.

In the middle of the woods, when she was halfway home, she heard voices, loud enough but still a distance away. Quickly, she stepped away from the path and went deeper into the woods. When she was a good few meters away from the path, she chose a well-leafed shrub and squatted in its shadow. In the case of prying eyes, she would look like someone relieving herself or digging up some root to use for an ailment. Either way, she should be left alone—unless the passersby happened to be people with more on their minds than she bargained for.

The foursome, two young men escorting their girlfriends somewhere, from the look of things, passed along. They were so engrossed in their discussion that they hardly paid her any heed. If, indeed, they saw her at all.

After they had gone past, Mamvulane resumed her journey, which was without event until she had almost cleared the thicket. She could plainly see the houses to the back of her own, on NY 72, when suddenly her ears picked up a not too faraway buzzing.

She stopped to hear better from which side it came. But even as she stood, her ears straining hard to pinpoint the source of the disturbance, the sound grew to a cacophony, discordant and threatening.

Right about the time her ears told her to look a little toward her left, in the bushes hiding Fezeka High School from view, her eyes picked up tumultuous movement.

She stood as though rooted to the spot. From sheer terror.

Mesmerized, Mamvulane watched as the unruly throng crowded in on her. Leading the rabble were a few women and one elderly man. She realized then that a few of those whose heels were chasing their heads were not just ahead of the group—they were actually fleeing from it.

She needed no further notice. Turning from the spectacle approaching her, she ran toward the houses, now so desperately near.

Mamvulane ran. The other women and the old man with them ran also. They all ran. But the army of young people at their heels had speed born of youth on their side.

Just as she came to the T-junction, where NY 74 joins NY 72, she found her way blocked. Some of her pursuers had taken a shortcut by jumping over fences from NY 75 to NY 74 and were now ahead of her. In seconds, she was completely surrounded.

Without further ado, someone snatched her plastic bag from her. "Let us see what you have in that bag, Mama?" he said, ripping it open.

Out spilled her groceries. And as each packet tumbled onto the hard, concrete road, it split or tore open, spilling its guts onto the sand, and there joined other debris that had long made its home there.

Happy and willing feet did the rest. Stamping and kicking at her food so that everything got thoroughly mixed up with the sand and with other food items. The samp and the mealie meal and the sugar and the dried milk and the coffee and the broken candles and the paraffin—everything became one thing. All those things, mixed together, became nothing. Nothing she or anyone else could use.

"*Sigqibile ngawe ke ngoku, Mama.* We are finished with you," announced her tormentors.

Walking home, her knees weak from the encounter, Mamvulane met one of her neighbors, attracted by the noise. "Mvulane, what is happening? Why are all these people staring at you?"

"I can't talk now, Mandaba," answered the other, not pausing in her unsteady walk. Mandaba, suspecting the cause of her neighbor's reticence and disheveled appearance, remarked, "*Hayi,* you are naughty, Mamvulane." To which the latter said not a word but just continued walking to her home as though the other had not spoken at all.

When she got to her gate, Mamvulane shooed away the straggling group, mostly curious children and one or two adults, that was following her. What the comrades had done to her had disarranged her. But her heart grieved. And that was definitely not on their account. About the comrades, she supposed she should be grateful they had done her no bodily harm. She remembered the man Mdlangathi had told her about the previous evening—the man the comrades had forced to drink *Javel.* That man, after he had brought up little chunks of meat, and of course the liquor that had caused him all the trouble to start with, had eventually brought up blood. His own. So, when all is said and done, I suppose I'm lucky, Mamvulane told herself after she had calmed down some. At her home. But, her eyes smarting, she could feel her heart bleed. Because of the other thing.

Her husband was home when she got there. "What happened to you?" he asked, seeing her disheveled appearance. For although she had not been beaten, she had been manhandled.

Mamvulane recounted her experience while her husband listened to her in dumb silence. And then she told him, ". . . and among the comrades who did this to me, there was Mteteli, our son." There, it was out in the open. She had mentioned the despicable, unmentionable thing that had gnawed at her heart since the comrades had fallen upon her.

When she said that, mentioned Mteteli as one of her attackers, she burst out crying. Mdlangathi started up and for a moment his wife thought he was going to go out of the house in search of their son right there and then.

But no, after two or three hesitant, halfhearted steps, he sat down again and quietly inquired, "You saw him? With your own eyes, I mean?"

"Oh, why wouldn't I know my own child, even in a crowd."

"Mmmhhmh." That is what Mdlangathi said. Only that and nothing more. On being told that his son was part of the crowd that had spilled his wife's groceries on the sand, all that was heard from him was that sigh. That is all.

Mamvulane waited for more reaction from her husband, usually so easy to reach boiling point. But no, not today. Today he kept so calm that his wife became resentful of exactly that calmness that she had so frequently and desperately sought from him. Today, when she least expected it or welcomed it for that matter, here was her priceless husband displaying remarkable sangfroid.

"I'm glad, Father of Fezeka, to see that you appreciate the risk I took, nearly getting myself killed by these unruly children, so that you would have something to eat." She spoke in a quiet voice. Inside, however, she was seething. What did he think! That she had gone to Claremont only so that she could buy a loaf of bread and stuff it down her own gullet? That would have saved her all the trouble and bad name she, no doubt, had earned herself.

But Mdlangathi would not be drawn to a fight and, after seeing that, Mamvulane soon found her anger dissipate.

When she had rested a little and was sure there would be no follow-up action on the part of the comrades, Mamvulane went to her bedroom and closed the door. When she emerged, in her hand was a tray full of sausage. There were also two loaves of bread and a plastic packet of powdered milk.

"That is all I was able to save," she told her husband, showing him her spoils. "To think I spent more than fifty rands[9] at Pick 'n Pay . . . and that is all that I was able to save!"

"But how?" he wanted to know.

And she knew he wasn't talking about the money she had spent.

For the first time since she had come into the house, harassed and agitated, Mamvulane allowed a slow smile to appear on her face. Her eyes widening in mock disbelief, she exclaimed, "*Tyhini, Tata kaFezeka!* Don't you think that a woman should have some secrets?" And refused to divulge how she had achieved the miracle.

As she prepared the meal, she wondered what he would say if she were to tell him that she had girdled the sausage around her waist, put the packet of milk in the natural furrow between her breasts and carried the loaves of bread flattened in the hollow of her back, one atop the other so that they formed a pipe. Ah, Mdlangathi, she thought, feeling the smile in her heart, these are not times for one to be squeamish.

But thinking about the whole *indaba* later as she stirred her pots, now and then peering into this one and then, a moment later, the other one, she was a bit miffed. Mdlangathi had been more upset about the drunkard the comrades had forced to regurgitate his beer than over what they had done to her. Imagine that! A man to have more sympathy for someone like that than for his own wife. She was sure she didn't know what to make of it. His lack of indignation on her behalf galled her, though.

---

9 **rands:** Currency of South Africa.

On the other hand, she had to admit relief that he had not carried on the way he had about the stupid drunk. A fight might have broken out between father and son. Mteteli had become quite cheeky with this new thing of children who had secrets from their parents and went about righting all the wrongs they perceived in society. Yes, she told herself, perhaps it was just as well his father said nothing to the boy, or didn't show anger on her behalf. Anger that he had participated in her humiliating attack, which had resulted in the loss of her groceries.

Mamvulane dished up and father and children fell on the food as camels coming upon an oasis after crossing a vast desert.

As usual, Mteteli had missed dinner—out attending meetings. "Wife, times have truly changed," said the husband. "Do you realize that all over Guguletu and Nyanga and Langa, not just here in our home, people are having dinner, with their children only God knows where?"

"You are quite right," replied his wife. But seeing that he was getting angry, she added, "But you must remember that our children live in times very different to what ours were when we were their age."

"And that means we must eat and go to bed not knowing where this boy is?"

Although he didn't name names, she knew he meant Mteteli, for he was the only one of the children not in. The girl, Fezeka, for some reason that wasn't clear to the mother, was not that involved in the doings of the students, although she was the older by three years.

"Well, that is what is happening in all homes now. What can one do?"

"Mamvulane, do you hear yourself? Are those words that should be coming from a parent's mouth? 'What can I do?' Talking about the behavior of her own child?"

"He is your child too, you know. But all these children are the same. They don't listen to anyone except each other."

"*Hayi!* You are right, my wife. I don't know why I argue with you when what you say is the Gospel Truth. Here I am, having dinner when I do not know the whereabouts of one of my own children. Very soon, dishes will be washed. Then we will say our evening prayers and go to bed. And still we will have no idea where Mteteli is. And you tell me there is nothing to be done about that. Not that I disagree with you, mind you."

"Well, what could you do, even if you knew where he was right now. What could you possibly do?" Mamvulane stood up, gathered the dishes, and took them to the kitchen, where Fezeka and the two youngest children were having their meal.

When Mamvulane returned to the dining room, Mdlangathi, who was smoking his pipe, said, "Do you know what's wrong with the world today?" And quickly answered himself, "All of us parents are very big cowards. The biggest cowards you have ever seen."

She hummed her agreement with what he was saying. But in her heart she didn't believe that what he said was wholly true. Powerless, perhaps. That is what she thought parents were—overwhelmed by a sense of powerlessness in the face of the children's collective revolt, where the mildest child had become a stranger: intransigent, loud of voice, and deadly bold of action.

"*Mama, kuph' okwam ukutya?* Where is my food, Mama?" asked a grumpy voice in the dark. It was Mteteli, all right. The mother knew at once. Only *he* had not had supper. Only *he* would come in the middle of the night, demanding food when no one had sent him on an errand anywhere that he should have been absent during dinner.

"My son," replied Mamvulane without bothering to strike a match and light the candle standing on a small round table next to the bed. "I am surprised you should ask me for food when *you* know what happened to the groceries I went to get in Claremont."

"Are you telling me that no one has had food tonight, here at home?" His tone had become quite belligerent.

Before the mother said a word in reply, Mdlangathi roared at his son: "*Kwedini!* What gives you the right to go about causing mischief that I, your father, have not asked you to perform and then, as though that were not grief enough to your poor mother here, come back here in the middle of the night and wake us up with demands of food? Where were you when we were having dinner?"

"*Awu,* Tata, what is this that you are asking me? Do you not know that a war is going on? That we are fighting the hateful apartheid government?"

"Since when is this woman lying next to me the government? Is this not the woman you and your friends attacked this evening?"

"Mama was not attacked. She was disciplined for . . ."

But Mdlangathi sprang out of bed and, in the dark, groped his way toward the door, where he judged his son was standing. Grabbing him by the scruff of his neck, he bellowed, "She was *whaat?* Are you telling me you have a hand to discipline your mother? What has happened to your senses? Have they been eaten away by intoxicating drugs?"

By now, Mteteli's teeth were chattering from the shaking he was receiving at the hands of his father.

Quickly, Mamvulane lit the candle.

Startled by the light, the two grappling figures sprang apart. Both were breathing heavily.

"Are you fighting me?" quietly, the father asked his son.

"You are beating me."

"I asked you a direct question. Are you lifting a hand, fighting with me, your father?"

"All I want is my food. I'm not fighting anyone," said Mteteli sullenly.

"I suggest you get out of my house and go and seek your food elsewhere. I do not work hard so that I shall feed thugs."

"Now I am a thug because I want my food?"

Mdlangathi had had enough of sparring with Mteteli. Abruptly, he told him, "Go and look for your food from the sand, where you threw it away when you took it from your mother by force." Fuming, he got back into bed and covered himself with the blankets till not even his hair could be seen.

"Yes, Mteteli," Mamvulane added. "Remember all the sand, and samp you and your group threw down onto the sand, *that* was to be your supper. You spilled your supper on the sand out there—birds will feast on it on the morrow."

"*Andithethi loo nto mna, ngoku.*"

"Mteteli, your father goes to work tomorrow morning. Leave us alone and let us have some sleep. You are the one who doesn't have time for doing this or that, you come and go as you please, but don't let that become a nuisance to us now, please."

"Mama, I don't know what all this fuss is about. All I said I want, and still want, is my food. Where is my food?" Mteteli had now raised his voice so high people three doors away put on their candles. The whole block heard there were angry words being exchanged at Mdlangathi's house.

Mteteli, angry at the reception he was getting, and hungry, having gone the whole day without eating anything substantial, approached his parents' bed and stood towering over them, his bloodshot eyes trained on his mother.

"*Hee, kwedini,*" came the muffled sound of his father's voice from under the blankets. "What exactly do you want my wife to do for you, at this time of night?"

"I want my food."

"That we tell you it is where you spilled it on the sand doesn't satisfy you?" Mdlangathi stuck his head out of the blankets again.

"*Andithethi loo nto mna, ngoku.* I'm not talking about that, now."

Under his bed, Mdlangathi kept a long, strong, well-seasoned knobkerrie.[10] A flash of bare arm shot out of the blankets. A heave, and he'd strained and reached the stick.

Before Mteteli fully grasped what his father was up to, his father had leapt out of bed and, in one swoop, landed the knobkerrie on Mteteli's skull.

"CRRAA-AA-AAKK!"

The sound of wood connecting with bone. The brightest light he had ever seen flashed before Mteteli's startled eyes. A strong jet of red. The light dimmed, all at once. A shriek from the mother. In a heap, the young man collapsed onto the vinyl-covered floor.

"*Umosele!*" That is what people said afterwards. One of those cruel accidents. How often does one stroke of a stick, however strong, end up in a fatality? He must have ruptured a major artery.

The boy bled to death before help could get to him, others said.

Yes, the mother tried to get one of the neighbors to take him to the hospital, you know ambulances had stopped coming to the townships because they had been stoned by the comrades. But the neighbor refused, saying, "Your son can ask some-one who doesn't drink to take him to hospital." Apparently, he was one of the men the comrades had forced to bring up, forcing them to make themselves sick because they had "*drunk the white man's poison that kills Africa's seed.*"

---

10 **knobkerrie:** A short, wooden club with a knot at one end; traditional Zulu weapon.

Of course, later, some people condemned the man who had refused to take Mteteli to the hospital. But others said he taught the comrades a lesson long overdue. And others still pointed at the father and said, "Why should someone else bother about a dog whose father wouldn't even ask for permission to come to his funeral?"

Yes, many wondered about that. About the fact that Mdlangathi was not denied permission to come to bury his son but had not requested that permission from the prison officials. That was something even Mamvulane found hard to understand. Harder still for her to swallow was his answer when she'd asked him about his reasons for the omission.

"*Andifuni.*" That was all he would say. "I do not want to."

However, so did she fear being bruised even more by events that seemed to her to come straight out of the house of the devil himself that she could not find the courage to ask what he meant: whether what he did not want was to come to the funeral or to ask to be allowed to attend the funeral. She did not know which would hurt her more. And did not dare find out.

QUESTIONS

1. How would you describe the relationship between Mamvulane and Mdlangathi?

2. Why is Mdlangathi so upset by the young men's treatment of the drunken man?

3. Are the young people right in calling for and enforcing the boycott? If so, why? If not, what alternative form of protest or political action should they have taken?

4. Can you account for Mteteli's apparently contradictory behavior? How can he help enforce the boycott on the one hand and demand food from his family on the other? What might his situation say about the intersection of the personal and the political?

5. Why does Mdlangathi strike his son with the club? What forces and circumstances cause him to react so violently to his son's demand for food?

Australia

M any anthropologists believe that the Aboriginal people first settled Australia approximately 40,000 years ago, most likely emigrating from southeast Asia. It is estimated that it took these Asiatic groups about 10,000 years to populate the continent. By 1788, when the first European settlers came to the continent, probably just under a million people were dotted throughout the area. These various tribes were as diverse as the continent itself, but archeological evidence suggests some common features of Aboriginal life: a strong sense of community, a respect for the land, and a strong sense of ritual and religious significance. Further, the native people of Australia, much like their counterparts in North America and New Zealand, had a long tradition of oral storytelling. Although some of these tales have been transcribed in recent years, written culture did not occur on the continent until Europeans began to settle in the area.

The first Europeans to see Australia were most likely the Portuguese explorers in the sixteenth century; the Dutch followed shortly afterwards in the following century. In fact, the first "settlers" may have been two Dutch mutineers from the wrecked Dutch ship, the *Batavia,* who were left in Australia as punishment for their part in the mutiny. Much like the fate of the small community of settlers in Roanoke, Virginia, these two men were never heard of again.

In 1642, the crew of the Dutch captain Abel Tasman discovered and claimed for the Dutch what eventually became Tasmania (first called Van Dieman's Land) in the southern tip of eastern Australia. This was followed by the English captain William Dampier's explorations around the northwest coast of the continent in 1688. This voyage brought English claims to the continent, which were reinforced when Captain James Cook explored the east coast in 1770. The report of Cook's voyage ensured that within twenty years the country would be settled by the English.

Many of the original colonists were convicts who had been sent out of Great Britain for repeated criminal offenses or soldiers, many of whom had been court-martialed for military crimes. The new colony they formed, started at Botany Bay in 1788, eventually became known as New South Wales. A disproportionate number of Irish were sent to Australia as well, and their presence resulted in tensions between the English and Irish settlers throughout the twentieth century. In general, those sent to New South Wales were poorly educated, poorly clothed, poorly equipped, and generally unprepared for the pioneering life.

Free settlers did trickle into the new settlement from as early as 1792 because of generous land grants and cheap convict labor offered by the British government. These various inducements were especially welcome after the Napoleonic War

(1815), when it became clear that advancement opportunities for the second and third sons of the gentry were lessened. In 1829, the British government designed the Swan River Colony in Western Australia to entice a more refined group of people to Australia; the project succeeded moderately. The smattering of free colonists created a dichotomy between what is conveniently called high and popular culture in Australia.

It was during this period that the first written depiction of Australian life appeared in the form of letters and reports. Much early fiction that was produced in Australia was based on the facts and history expressed in these documents.

Not surprisingly, the most common themes in these correspondences reiterate the same concerns that appeared in the early creative fiction. The struggle of men and women to adjust to a distinctively different environment is a recurring motif in the early prose works. Much material compares life in the new country to that in England, and generally the comparison favors the old world. These new settlers longed for the familiar, and the loneliness of being so far from friends and family was heartfelt. The concept of a continent with great expanses of inhospitable land was also the subject that filled volumes.

One of the earliest semifictional memoirs in Australia is *The Memoirs of James Hardy Vaux* (1819), a book that discusses in part the transportation of prisoner Hardy Vaux to Australia. The literary quality of the book is reminiscent of Tobias Smollett's picaresque novels of eighteenth-century England. Memoirs appeared throughout the period, and Charles Rowcroft's *Tales of the Colonies* (1843) and Henry Savey's *Quintus Servinton* (1850) depicted the hardships of immigrant life in the rough-and-tumble pioneer settlements in the middle of the nineteenth century.

The first flood of voluntary Australian immigrants arrived in the 1840s and 1850s as a result of economic failure in Scotland and the Irish potato famine. By the 1850s, the need for enforced immigration had lessened significantly. However, many religious nonconformists who found their non-Anglican beliefs held them back from both educational and social acceptance in Victorian England came to the area near Adelaide and established a new life. This tradition of nonconformity and political liberalism is still reflected in the literature of Australia.

These two diverse streams of Australian fiction, the societal and the bush, can be observed in two novels from the 1850s. It must have come as a surprise to the new settlers when, in 1854, C. H. Spence published her novel of manners, *Clara Morison*. The novel makes little or no attempt to romanticize the bush life; instead, it is a novel about civilized people struggling to bring Western culture to the growing city of Adelaide. The novel's tone and sentiments directly contrast with those expressed by Henry Kingsley's *The Recollections of Geoffry Hamlyn* (1859). His novel celebrates the masculine accomplishments of the Australian pioneer. For Kingsley, the bushman is a hero, a depiction that became the model for the ideal male in Australian fiction well into the 1950s. Geoffry Hamlyn's world is lived in the vastness of the interior; he has no contact with Spence's Victorian world of manners and choreographed behavior.

In the 1850s, the immigrant population of the country had reached half a million people, and the settlements were beginning to take shapes recognizable today. New South Wales and Victoria were recognized as governing units; Tasmania and Queensland states soon followed. With the discovery of gold in Victoria in 1851, prospectors and miners arrived in droves. Shiploads of women came from Britain with both religious and more earthly considerations on their minds; the Australian economy moved forward with great speed as more and more Europeans came to try their luck at generating a fortune from gold. Many Chinese also came to the new country as workers and pioneers.

Marcus Clarke was a short story writer whose short tales of Australian bush life and settlement towns are a romantic mix of humor and tragedy, but the stories are convincing portrayals of the pioneering spirit during this period of rapid growth. His Bullochtown stories are realistic in scope, and the narrator's tendency to laugh at himself and the townspeople is not unlike the narrative irony utilized by O. Henry and Stephen Crane in the United States. One of the tropes that Clarke discovers with considerable skill in "Pretty Dick," the "lost in the bush" theme, continues to be a popular one in modern Australian fiction.

Many of the concerns and themes of subsequent Australian literature were already in place during this period. The tension between laboring-class expectations and middle-class values became obvious and unavoidable. These problems had their roots in the convict versus free immigrant histories, but they had religious implications as well. Further, the frontier male values often conflicted with the civilizing influence of female values, and this struggle, too, affected the way in which the female voice in literature was marginalized until the 1960s. The reality of racial prejudice was already well established by this period. The native peoples' rights were often overlooked, and little concern was shown for their rights of autonomy or equality of opportunity in the nineteenth and most of the twentieth centuries.

Throughout the nineteenth century, Australians saw themselves largely as dependents of the United Kingdom. When Britain entered the Boer War in 1899, Australians saw themselves as natural allies and partners in Britain's empire building. More than 15,000 Australians participated in the war. One outcome of this partnering in empire was that the simmering republican movement was put to rest. However, the sense of empire brought with it several new considerations: The most important was that of national defense against perceived enemies, which was quickened by the Russo-Japanese War of 1905. The completeness of the Japanese victory spawned fears of an invasion and hastened the call for a standing army and compulsory military service for men. The rising sense of nationalism also ensured a closed immigration policy and a suspicion of any culture that did not conform to European standards.

As Australian cities grew and matured, societal fiction continued to act as a counterweight to the bush fiction. By the 1880s and 1890s, female writers such as Tasma (Mrs. Jesse Couvreur), Ada Cambridge, and Mrs. Campbell Praed all were examining the nature of the bourgeois classes with sentiment and humor. The social

because it would be cowardly to do otherwise. He valued, above all, things Australian and did not like foreigners and foreign ways. His figure dominated Australian popular literature between the two world wars. The manly Australian digger is portrayed in the figure of Crocodile Dundee played by Paul Hogan in the film of that name.

Intriguingly, important though World War I was in the development of Australian nationhood, there was very little literary response to this traumatic event. Perhaps because the war was too remote, too far removed from the daily Australian experience, it never achieved the importance it deserved in the nation's literary history. Instead, the literature recycled stories about life in the bush and reasserted bush values. The frontier was celebrated, and stories about the Northern Territory and Queensland began appearing regularly in journals and magazines. Vance and Netty Palmer's *Bulletin* published stories with slice-of-life realism predominating, but they also attempted to intellectualize the offerings with bits of modernism borrowed from the U.S. and European traditions. This foreign influence was largely resisted. On the home front, Katharine Susannah Prichard attempted solitarily to capture the essence of the Aboriginal culture, but the insular attitudes espoused by artists such as Norman Lindsey were more in touch with Australian tastes and attitudes.

The most noticeable effect of World War I on Australian fiction writers was to isolate them from the rest of the world and to turn their queries inward toward exploration of the self. As the country counted its dead after the war, a growing sense of nationalism involved a revisionism in fact and in fiction. For example, partially out of pique for being brought into a European war where Australia's contribution was undervalued, Australian authors penned tales of transported criminals who were unfairly treated by the peccadillos of a class-ridden British justice system. The characters of these criminals were often romanticized into hard old pioneers and cranky squatters who were filled with qualities of resilience and independence; in essence, they were made into cult heroes with anti-British biases. Unfortunately for Australian letters, this self-indulgence cut many writers off from overseas writing, and their works suffered from limited or even negligible access to international cross-currents. Clearly, talented fiction writers such as Katharine Susannah Prichard, Alan Marshall, and Kylie Tennant were disadvantaged by this isolationist trend.

The case of Vance Palmer offers a lesson about too much isolation. He published his first volume of short stories in 1915; *The World of Men* was full of masculine values and heroic stances. Twenty years later, however, in his *Separate Lives* (1931) and *Sea and Spinifex* (1934), his short fiction was still promoting the same values: The heroes all show fortitude, will power, leadership, and restraint, but they are one-dimensional. In contrast, Prichard's fiction may be "Australia focused," but she examines the social and economic changes the country requires to progress as a democracy. Her stories are concerned with the exploitation of the immigrants; her "Coonardoo" deals with the taboo topic of an Aboriginal woman's love for a white station boss. The story also develops the issue of the native peoples' spiritual tie with the land. In "The Cooboo" and "The Grey Horse," she takes a poke at Australian smugness and complacency. As interesting and topical as Prichard's stories are, however, they lack the transcendent quality that produces great literature.

In many artists' minds, the importance of high culture became diminished in a society where lowbrow popular cultural pursuits such as sport, popular music, and literature were the accepted forms of value. The result was a considerable expatriation of writers and artists from Australia. Many went to Europe for inspiration: Martin Boyd, Christina Stead, and Henry Richardson are examples of this diaspora. Many of these writers never returned, and the loss was significant. For example, Stead's powerful novel, *The Man Who Loved Children* (1940), was a stinging portrait of a dysfunctional family; however, while Stead drew on her own life growing up in Australia, she set her novel in the United States, the country where she died.

On September 3, 1939, Australian Prime Minister Robert Menzies announced that his nation was entering the war against the Axis powers. As relationships with Japan degenerated and fears of an Asiatic invasion became a reality with the fall of Singapore in February 1942, Australia turned to the United States for advice and assistance. General Douglas MacArthur landed in Australia in March 1942, and the country became a base for the eventual successful counteroffensive against Japan. The war turned Australian fiction inward; it focused on the individual's perception of self rather than on the external conditions of existence. Writers such as Christina Stead, Martin Boyd, and Patrick White all concentrated on internal nuances and queries. Their themes were familiar ones: the ambiguous attitudes toward landscape and its effect on the individual psyche; the concerns about how one sustains an active intellectual life in a vast nation with few people; and the ways in which distance and isolation play upon the minds of the intellectuals. By the time the war finished, Australians found themselves concerned with social progressiveness. With the publication of *Coast to Coast,* a short story journal published annually, writers reaffirmed 1930s working-class values and cries for greater social reform.

After World War II, a conservative immigration policy ensured that the country remained largely European and British, but as the economy grew, many southern Europeans flooded into Australia. As might be expected, the cultural clash between the new immigrants and the conservative traditionalists was inevitable. In this new Australia, there was still a strong feeling that conformity was essential and that the new immigrants had better realize that they needed to fit into Australian society. John O'Grady's novel, *They're a Weird Mob* (1957), written under the pen name Nino Culotta, is an example of the expectations of many Australians of the period.

> There is no better way of life in the world than that of the Australian. I firmly believe this. The grumbling, growling, cursing, profane, laughing, beer drinking, abusive, loyal-to-his-mates Australian is one of the few free men left on this earth. He fears no one, crawls to no one, bludges on no one, and acknowledges no master. Learn his way. Learn his language. Get yourself accepted as one of him; and you will enter a world that you never dreamed existed. And once you have entered it, you will never leave it.

With the tide of immigrants moving to Australia in the 1950s, fiction began to reflect some of these urban settling-in experiences. David Martin's *The Young Wife* (1962) concerns itself with the lives of Greek migrants in Melbourne and sets the stage for a number of writers to explore life in the urban centers—that of both newly arrived immigrants and native Australians from the interior. John Morrison's exploration of characters in a restrictive situation appears in two collections of short stories: *Black Cargo* (1955) and *Twenty-Three* (1962). *Black Cargo* is a collection based on a true story chronicling a dockers' strike in Sydney where two political ideologies collide: traditional conservative values meet foreign values.

Hal Porter appears to welcome the conflict engendered in the clash of values with broad humor and a gift of satire that, in the spirit of the 1960s, debunks the very nature of the Australian value structure and its heroic figures. His *A Bachelor's Children* (1962) and *The Cats of Venice* (1967) mark an end to the idealistic vision of nationalistic sentiment in the country's fiction. Shirley Hazzard, an expatriate Australian writer, published her collection of short stories, *The Cliffs of Fall,* in 1963. These stories are memorable because her use of irony adds a perspective that dominates most of Australian short story writing even today. Hazzard's stories concern the fickleness of love and its regrets. Like the famous contemporary Australian novelist Patrick White, she delves into the inner consciousness, but what she sees is more of an ironic recognition of the detached nature of love from other kinds of experience. Australian readers in the 1960s broadened their range of acceptance, as the fiction of Thomas Keneally, Morris Lurie, David Ireland, and even the radical tales of Peter Mathers such as "A Knight of Teeth" demonstrate. When Frank Moorhouse published *Futility and Other Animals* (1969), the floodgates of literature critical of the monocultural nature of Australia began to shift quite rapidly. Moorhouse's work is essential reading because his stories deal with the loneliness and isolation that the postwar world has inflicted on its denizens. Moorhouse also chronicles the pressing issues of the period, such as Australia's involvement in the Vietnam War and the reason for U.S. presence on the continent. His stories belie the Australian myth of a cohesive and happy society; instead, he uncovers the sexual tensions that attend most marriages and shows the inadequacy of culture's stereotyped sex roles.

The 1970s proved to be a period of significant change in Australia. With the election of a Labour Party prime minister, Gough Whitlam, the government embarked on an extensive program of reform. Whitlam abolished mandatory National Service (conscription), and all conscientious objectors were released from the nation's prisons. Whitlam ordered the withdrawal of remaining Australian troops from Vietnam, and in 1973, his government also abolished the White Australia Policy. As a result, Australia became a much more liberal country in the 1970s, as reflected in the short stories of Frank Moorhouse and Michael Wilding written in the first half of the decade. In their writing, the urban voice of modern Australia is distinctly heard. Through the use of irony and broad comedy respectively, both writers herd their tales around Sydney, where they provoke the acceptance of insularity in middle-class life and celebrate inner-city rogues and survivors. Moorhouse pokes fun at modern-day politics as well. In his short story collection, *Conference-ville* (1976), the left-wing radicals, as a result of the fall of the Whitlam government, come together to engender a new political doctrine. The collection of stories makes light of Marxist, feminist, anarchistic, and even academic agendas and their makers. Wilding, although British born, and at one time a communist, does not use as much irony as Moorhouse; his view of the urban confusion is largely that of detached amusement.

From the 1980s onward, it became apparent that Australian practitioners of the short story were far more radical than the novelists; even the novelists tended to be more experimental and freer when writing short stories than when writing novels. Peter Carey is a case in point. His 1974 collection of short fiction, *The Fat Man in History,* and his *War Crimes* (1979) capture the essence of the international power struggle. But Carey's world is that of fantasy (an Australian version of magic realism perhaps), and his fiction is wildly allegorical and symbolic, verging on science fiction in places. In the later part of the century, short fiction writers such as Judah Waten, Eric Schlunke, Thelma Forshaw, and Elizabeth Jolley have taken postmodern concerns and experimented greatly with issues of identity and gender roles, and the results have been very positive.

During the last two decades of the twentieth century, Australia struggled with problems generated by the global economy. Inflation increased and large corporations controlled greater portions of what were once government-owned and -operated utilities and services. The nation also became more aware of the environment, largely because of the depletion of the ozone layer, increased rates of skin cancer, and scientific evidence of global warming.

Australia's long-ignored problem of dealing with its native peoples has also required its attention. Despite the High Court of Australia's confirmation of the Mabo ruling in 1992, a decision that argued that Aboriginals were the first human occupants of Australia, very little progress has been made in redressing their serious maltreatment. "A Very Brief History of Australia" (at http://www.showroom.com.au/aushistory.htm) offers typical examples of the ways in which Australian attitudes toward the Aboriginal peoples were racist and unfeeling. By 1967, the 60,000 Aboriginals were given voting rights as full Australian citizens, but even in the twenty-first century, despite talk of reconciliation and reconsideration, nothing specific has been done to address the systematic alienation of these people from their own lands. And while immigration policy has been liberalized considerably, the incident of the detention centers for boat people from Asia in 2002 suggests that some of Australians' xenophobia and fears of losing their essential culture still persist.

Sadly too, Aboriginal writers have not been drawn to the short story genre. In 1929, David Unalpon's publication of *Native Legends* offered a glimpse into the potential of what the form could offer. Some of the potential was realized in *Paperbark* (1990), which was a collection of black Australian writings; however, the short fiction offerings were few and slight.

Today, Australia is no longer the obscure outback. Australian soldiers keep the peace in United Nations forces in all corners of the globe; the bicentennial of 1988 and the success of the Sydney Olympics in 2000 catapulted the nation into the forefront of the world. Its filmmakers, artists, musicians, and writers are accessible throughout the world. In just over two centuries, the last habitable continent has housed a vibrant nation that has found its place in the sun.

Henry Lawson

(1867–1922)

Henry Lawson was born near the Grenfell goldfields in New South Wales; the son of a failed gold prospector and women's rights advocate, he grew up in poverty in the Mudgee district. An ear infection led to deafness by the time he was fourteen, making the already solitary child grow even more introverted. His upbringing was marked by poverty, divorce, and insecurity. His rough life and relationship to the bush life paid large dividends from a literary standpoint because it allowed him to accurately describe the harshness of the lifestyle and to explore how it affects characters.

Lawson was first published in the *Bulletin,* a magazine with a decidedly clear vision of what constituted an Australian. In many ways Lawson felt very comfortable with this vision, for most of his characters and poems celebrate egalitarianism, unionism, and republicanism. However, within this stereotype was also the idolization of mateship (a strong form of male bonding), a lack of interest in family life, a distrust of established religion, a fondness for alcohol and gambling, and a celebration of brute strength and endurance over intellectual attainment. Nearly all of Lawson's stories celebrate this kind of hero and depict the hardship of the early settlers to Australia. Criticized at the time as being too provincial, Lawson's stories and poetry caught the imagination of Australians and made him the voice of a large segment of the society.

Lawson never wrote any novels, but his two most popular collections of short stories are *While the Billy Boils* (1896) and *Joe Wilson and His Mates* (1901). Although Lawson emphasized the Australian traits of toughness and mateship, he also demonstrated that the harsh Australian landscape could overpower those who lacked the endurance and will to keep their spirits alive amidst this powerful natural force. Today's critics understand that he was writing about the "dark side" of the Australian experience. In "Water Them Geraniums," for example, Mrs. Spicer moves with her husband and large family into the bush; her only joy is watching her planted geraniums blossom in the desert. But this attempt at beautifying her environment is not enough, and she dies worn out by the struggle of raising a family in the harsh outback climate.

Lawson died of alcoholism, having never really come to terms with the changing values and cultural mores that began to creep into Australia as the twentieth century advanced. The two stories that follow, "The Union Buries Its Dead" and "The Drover's Wife," are from *While the Billy Boils.* The first captures with seemingly little effort the way in which the Australian "mate brotherhood" celebrates the death of one of their own. There is a stoicism and acceptance of death in the outback, but a camaraderie of sorts over a fellow union worker who has drowned while crossing the river. Both stories demonstrate the harshness of colonial life and the importance of self-reliance and stoic behavior against the forces of nature.

The Union Buries Its Dead   1896

While out boating one Sunday afternoon on a billabong[1] across the river, we saw a young man on horse-back driving some horses along the bank. He said it was a fine day, and asked if the water was deep there. The joker of our party said it was deep enough to drown him, and he laughed and rode further up. We didn't take much notice of him.

Next day a funeral gathered at a corner pub and asked each other in to have a drink while waiting for the hearse. They passed away some of the time dancing jigs to a piano in the bar parlour. They passed away the rest of the time sky-larking and fighting.

The defunct was a young union labourer, about twenty-five, who had been drowned the previous day while trying to swim some horses across a billabong of the Darling.

He was almost a stranger in town, and the fact of his having been a union man accounted for the funeral. The police found some union papers in his swag,[2] and called at the General Labourers' Union Office for information about him. That's how we knew. The secretary had very little information to give. The departed was a "Roman," and the majority of the town were otherwise—but unionism is stronger than creed. Drink, however, is stronger than unionism; and, when the hearse presently arrived, more than two-thirds of the funeral were unable to follow. They were too drunk.

The procession numbered fifteen, fourteen souls following the broken shell of a soul. Perhaps not one of the fourteen possessed a soul any more than the corpse did—but that doesn't matter.

Four or five of the funeral, who were boarders at the pub, borrowed a trap which the landlord used to carry passengers to and from the railway station. They were strangers to us who were on foot, and we to them. We were all strangers to the corpse.

A horseman, who looked like a drover[3] just returned from a big trip, dropped into our dusty wake and followed us a few hundred yards, dragging his pack-horse behind him, but a friend made wild and demonstrative signals from a hotel verandah—hooking at the air in front with his right hand and jobbing his left thumb over his shoulder in the direction of the bar—so the drover hauled off and didn't catch up to us any more. He was a stranger to the entire show.

We walked in twos. There were three twos. It was very hot and dusty; the heat rushed in fierce dazzling rays across every iron roof and light coloured wall that was turned to the sun. One or two pubs closed respectfully until we got past. They closed their bar doors and the patrons went in and out through some side or back entrance

---

1 **billabong:** Waterhole; offshoot of a river.
2 **swag:** Personal belongings sack.
3 **drover:** Someone who herds cattle or sheep from one place to another.

for a few minutes. Bushmen seldom grumble at an inconvenience of this sort, when it is caused by a funeral. They have too much respect for the dead.

On the way to the cemetery we passed three shearers sitting on the shady side of a fence. One was drunk—very drunk. The other two covered their right ears with their hats, out of respect for the departed—whoever he might have been—and one of them kicked the drunk and muttered something to him.

He straightened himself up, stared, and reached helplessly for his hat, which he shoved half off and then on again. Then he made a great effort to pull himself together—and succeeded. He stood up, braced his back against the fence, knocked off his hat, and remorsefully placed his foot on it—to keep it off his head till the funeral passed.

A tall sentimental drover, who walked by my side, cynically quoted Byronic verses suitable to the occasion—to death—and asked with pathetic humour whether we thought the dead man's ticket would be recognised "over yonder." It was a G.L.U. ticket, and the general opinion was that it would be recognised.

Presently my friend said:

"You remember, when we were in the boat yesterday, we saw a man driving some horses along the bank?"

"Yes."

He nodded at the hearse and said:

"Well, that's him."

I thought awhile.

"I didn't take any particular notice of him," I said. "He said something, didn't he?"

"Yes; said it was a fine day. You'd have taken more notice if you'd known that he was doomed to die in the hour and that those were the last words he would say to any man in this world."

"To be sure," said a full voice from the rear. "If ye'd known that ye'd have prolonged the conversation."

We plodded on across the railway line and along the hot, dusty road which ran to the cemetery, some of us talking about the accident, and lying about the narrow escapes we had had ourselves. Presently someone said:

"There's the Devil."

I looked up and saw a priest standing in the shade of the tree by the cemetery gate.

The hearse was drawn up and the tail-boards were opened. The funeral extinguished its right ear with its hat as four men lifted the coffin out and laid it over the grave. The priest—a pale, quiet young fellow—stood under the shade of a sapling which grew at the head of the grave. He took off his hat, dropped it carelessly on the ground, and proceeded to business. I noticed that one or two heathens winced slightly when the holy water was sprinkled on the coffin. The drops quickly evaporated, and the little round black spots they left were soon dusted over; but the spots showed, by contrast, the cheapness and shabbiness of the cloth with which the coffin was covered. It seemed black before;—now it looked a dusky grey.

Just here man's ignorance and vanity made a farce of the funeral. A big bull-necked publican, with heavy, blotchy features, and a supremely ignorant expression, picked up the priest's straw hat and held it about two inches over the head of his reverence during the whole of the service. The father, be it remembered, was standing in the shade. A few shoved their hats on and off uneasily, struggling between their disgust for the living and their respect for the dead. The hat had a conical crown and a brim sloping down all round like a sunshade, and the publican held it with his great red claw spread over the crown. To do the priest justice, perhaps he didn't notice the incident. A stage priest or parson in the same position might have said, "Put the hat down, my friend; is not the memory of our departed brother worth more than my complexion?" A wattlebark[4] layman might have expressed himself in stronger language, none the less to the point. But my priest seemed unconscious of what was going on. Besides, the publican was a great and important pillar of the church. He couldn't, as an ignorant and conceited ass, lose such a good opportunity of asserting his faithfulness and importance to his church.

The grave looked very narrow under the coffin, and I drew a breath of relief when the box slid easily down. I saw a coffin get stuck once, at Rookwood, and it had to be yanked out with difficulty, and laid on the sods at the feet of the heart-broken relations, who howled dismally while the grave-diggers widened the hole. But they don't cut contracts so fine in the West. Our grave-digger was not altogether bowelless, and, out of respect for that human quality described as "feelin's," he scraped up some light and dusty soil and threw it down to deaden the fall of the clay lumps on the coffin. He also tried to steer the first few shovelsful gently down against the end of the grave with the back of the shovel turned outwards, but the hard dry Darling River clods rebounded and knocked all the same. It didn't matter much—nothing does. The fall of lumps of clay on a stranger's coffin doesn't sound any different from the fall of the same things on an ordinary wooden box—at least I didn't notice anything awesome or unusual in the sound; but, perhaps, one of us—the most sensitive—might have been impressed by being reminded of a burial of long ago, when the thump of every sod jolted his heart.

I have left out the wattle—because it wasn't there. I have also neglected to mention the heart-broken old mate, with his grizzled head bowed and great pearly drops streaming down his rugged cheeks. He was absent—he was probably "Out Back." For similar reasons I have omitted reference to the suspicious moisture in the eyes of a bearded bush ruffian named Bill. Bill failed to turn up, and the only moisture was that which was induced by the heat. I left out the "sad Australian sunset" because the sun was not going down at the time. The burial took place exactly at mid-day.

The dead bushman's name was Jim, apparently; but they found no portraits, nor locks of hair, nor any love letters, nor anything of that kind in his swag—not even a reference to his mother; only some papers relating to union matters. Most of us didn't know the name till we saw it on the coffin; we knew him as "that poor chap that got drowned yesterday."

"So his name's James Tyson," said my drover acquaintance, looking at the plate.

"Why! Didn't you know that before?" I asked.

---

4 **wattlebark:** Astringent, hard bark from the wattle tree.

"No; but I knew he was a union man."

It turned out, afterwards, that J.T. wasn't his real name—only "the name he went by."

Anyhow he was buried by it, and most of the "Great Australian Dailies" have mentioned in their brevity columns that a young man named James John Tyson was drowned in a billabong of the Darling last Sunday.

We did hear, later on, what his real name was; but if we ever chance to read it in the "Missing Friends Column," we shall not be able to give any information to heart-broken Mother or Sister or Wife, nor to anyone who could let him hear something to his advantage—for we have already forgotten the name.

QUESTIONS

1. What is the nature of Australian bush life in this tale?

2. Describe the narrative voice in this story.

3. Comment on the symbolic significance of the relationship between the priest and the publican.

4. How important is the element of mateship in this story?

5. How does the comment that everyone has forgotten the dead drover's name reinforce the theme of Lawson's story?

The Drover's[1] *Wife*   *1896*

The two-roomed house is built of round timber, slabs, and stringy-bark, and floored with split slabs. A big bark kitchen standing at one end is larger than the house itself, veranda included.

Bush all round—bush with no horizons, for the country is flat. No ranges in the distance. The bush consists of stunted, rotten, native apple-trees. No undergrowth. Nothing to relieve the eye save the darker green of a few she-oaks which are sighing above the narrow, almost waterless creek. Nineteen miles to the nearest sign of civilization—a shanty on the main road.

The drover, an ex-squatter, is away with sheep. His wife and children are left here alone.

Four ragged, dried-up-looking children are playing about the house. Suddenly one of them yells: "Snake! Mother, here's a snake!"

The gaunt, sun-browned bushwoman dashes from the kitchen, snatches her baby from the ground, holds it on her left hip, and reaches for a stick.

---

1 **drover:** Someone who herds cattle or sheep from one place to another.

"Where is it?"

"Here! gone into the woodheap!" yells the eldest boy—a sharp-faced urchin of eleven. "Stop there, mother! I'll have him. Stand back! I'll have the beggar!"

"Tommy, come here, or you'll be bit. Come here at once when I tell you, you little wretch!"

The youngster comes reluctantly, carrying a stick bigger than himself. Then he yells, triumphantly:

"There it goes—under the house!" and darts away with club uplifted. At the same time the big, black, yellow-eyed dog-of-all-breeds, who has shown the wildest interest in the proceedings, breaks his chain and rushes after that snake. He is a moment late, however, and his nose reaches the crack in the slabs just as the end of its tail disappears. Almost at the same moment the boy's club comes down and skins the aforesaid nose. Alligator takes small notice of this, and proceeds to undermine the building; but he is subdued after a struggle and chained up. They cannot afford to lose him.

The drover's wife makes the children stand together near the dog-house while she watches for the snake. She gets two small dishes of milk and sets them down near the wall to tempt it to come out; but an hour goes by and it does not show itself.

It is near sunset, and a thunderstorm is coming. The children must be brought inside. She will not take them into the house, for she knows the snake is there, and may at any moment come up through a crack in the rough slab floor: so she carries several armfuls of firewood into the kitchen, and then takes the children there. The kitchen has no floor—or, rather, an earthen one—called a "ground floor" in this part of the bush. There is a large, roughly-made table in the centre of the place. She brings the children in, and makes them get on this table. They are two boys and two girls—mere babies. She gives them some supper, and then, before it gets dark, she goes into the house, and snatches up some pillows and bedclothes—expecting to see or lay her hand on the snake any minute. She makes a bed on the kitchen table for the children, and sits down beside it to watch all night.

She has an eye on the corner, and a green sapling club laid in readiness on the dresser by her side; also her sewing basket and a copy of the *Young Ladies' Journal*. She has brought the dog into the room.

Tommy turns in, under protest, but says he'll lie awake all night and smash that blinded snake.

His mother asks him how many times she has told him not to swear.

He has his club with him under the bedclothes, and Jacky protests:

"Mummy! Tommy's skinnin' me alive wif his club. Make him take it out."

Tommy: "Shet up, you little ——! D'yer want to be bit with the snake?"

Jacky shuts up.

"If yer bit," says Tommy, after a pause, "you'll swell up, an' smell, an' turn red an' green an' blue all over till yer bust. Won't he, mother?"

"Now then, don't frighten the child. Go to sleep," she says.

She thinks how she fought a flood during her husband's absence. She stood for hours in the drenching downpour, and dug an overflow gutter to save the dam across the creek. But she could not save it. There are things that a bushwoman cannot do. Next morning the dam was broken, and her heart was nearly broken too, for she thought how her husband would feel when he came home and saw the result of years of labour swept away. She cried then.

She also fought the pleuro-pneumonia—dosed and bled the few remaining cattle, and wept again when her two best cows died.

Again, she fought a mad bullock that besieged the house for a day. She made bullets and fired at him through cracks in the slabs with an old shotgun. He was dead in the morning. She skinned him and got seventeen-and-sixpence for the hide.

She also fights the crows and eagles that have designs on her chickens. Her plan of campaign is very original. The children cry, "Crows, mother!" and she rushes out and aims a broomstick at the birds as though it were a gun, and says, "Bung!" The crows leave in a hurry; they are cunning, but a woman's cunning is greater.

Occasionally a bushman in the horrors, or a villainous-looking sundowner,[6] comes and nearly scares the life out of her. She generally tells the suspicious-looking stranger that her husband and two sons are at work below the dam, or over at the yard, for he always cunningly inquires for the boss.

Only last week a gallows-faced swagman[7]—having satisfied himself that there were no men on the place—threw his swag[8] down on the veranda, and demanded tucker.[9] She gave him something to eat; then he expressed his intention of staying for the night. It was sundown then. She got a batten from the sofa, loosened the dog, and confronted the stranger, holding the batten in one hand and the dog's collar with the other. "Now you go!" she said. He looked at her and at the dog, said "All right, mum," in a cringing tone, and left. She was a determined-looking woman, and Alligator's yellow eyes glared unpleasantly—besides, the dog's chawing-up apparatus greatly resembled that of the reptile he was named after.

She has few pleasures to think of as she sits here alone by the fire, on guard against the snake. All days are much the same to her; but on Sunday afternoon she dresses herself, tidies the children, smartens up baby, and goes for a lonely walk along the bush-track, pushing an old perambulator in front of her. She does this every Sunday. She takes as much care to make herself and the children look smart as she would if she were going to do the block in the city. There is nothing to see, however, and not a soul to meet. You might walk twenty miles along this track without being able to fix a point in your mind, unless you are a bushman. This is because of the everlasting, maddening sameness of the stunted trees—that monotony which makes a man long to break away and travel as far as trains can go, and sail as far as ship can sail—and further.

6 **sundowner:** A vagrant; a tramp.
7 **swagman:** A man who seeks casual work while traveling around carrying his swag.
8 **swag:** Possessions.
9 **tucker:** Daily food; meals.

But this bushwoman is used to the loneliness of it. As a girl-wife she hated it, and now she would feel strange away from it.

She is glad when her husband returns, but she does not gush or make a fuss about it. She gets him something good to eat, and tidies up the children.

She seems contented with her lot. She loves her children, but has no time to show it. She seems harsh to them. Her surroundings are not favourable to the development of the "womanly" or sentimental side of nature.

It must be near morning now; but the clock is in the dwelling-house. Her candle is nearly done; she forgot that she was out of candles. Some more wood must be got to keep the fire up, and so she shuts the dog inside and hurries round to the wood-heap. The rain has cleared off. She seizes a stick, pulls it out, and—crash! the whole pile collapses.

Yesterday she bargained with a stray blackfellow to bring her some wood, and while he was at work she went in search of a missing cow. She was absent an hour or so, and the native black made good use of his time. On her return she was so astonished to see a good heap of wood by the chimney that she gave him an extra fig of tobacco, and praised him for not being lazy. He thanked her, and left with head erect and chest well out. He was the last of his tribe and a king; but he had built that woodheap hollow.

She is hurt now, and tears spring to her eyes as she sits down again by the table. She takes up a handkerchief to wipe the tears away, but pokes her eyes with her bare fingers instead. The handkerchief is full of holes, and she finds that she has put her thumb through one, and her forefinger through another.

This makes her laugh, to the surprise of the dog. She has a keen, very keen, sense of the ridiculous; and some time or other she will amuse bushmen with the story.

She had been amused before like that. One day she sat down "to have a good cry," as she said—and the old cat rubbed against her dress and "cried too." Then she had to laugh.

It must be near daylight now. The room is very close and hot because of the fire. Alligator still watches the wall from time to time. Suddenly he becomes greatly interested; he draws himself a few inches nearer the partition, and a thrill runs through his body. The hair on the back of his neck begins to bristle, and the battle-light is in his yellow eyes. She knows what this means, and lays her hand on the stick. The lower end of one of the partition slabs has a large crack on both sides. An evil pair of small bright bead-like eyes glisten at one of these holes. The snake—a black one— comes slowly out, about a foot, and moves its head up and down. The dog lies still, and the woman sits as one fascinated. The snake comes out a foot further. She lifts her stick, and the reptile, as though suddenly aware of danger, sticks his head in through the crack on the other side of the slab, and hurries to get his tail round after him. Alligator springs, and his jaws come together with a snap. He misses, for his nose is large, and the snake's body close down in the angle formed by the slabs and the floor. He snaps again as the tail comes round. He has the snake now, and tugs it out eighteen inches. Thud, thud, comes the woman's club on the ground. Alligator pulls again. Thud, thud. Alligator gives another pull and he has the snake out—a black brute, five feet long. The head rises to dart about, but the dog has the enemy close to the neck. He is a big heavy dog, but quick as a terrier. He shakes the snake as though he felt the original curse in common with mankind. The eldest boy wakes up, seizes his stick, and tries to get out of bed, but his mother forces him back with a grip of iron. Thud, thud—the snake's back is broken in several places. Thud, thud—its head is crushed, and Alligator's nose skinned again.

She lifts the mangled reptile on the point of her stick, carries it to the fire, and throws it in; then piles on the wood and watches the snake burn. The boy and dog watch too. She lays her hand on the dog's head, and all the fierce, angry light dies out of his yellow eyes. The younger children are quieted, and presently go to sleep. The dirty-legged boy stands for a moment in his shirt, watching the fire. Presently he looks up at her, sees the tears in her eyes, and, throwing his arms round her neck, exclaims:

"Mother, I won't never go drovin'; blast me if I do!"

And she hugs him to her worn-out breast and kisses him; and they sit thus together while the sickly daylight breaks over the bush.

QUESTIONS

1. What makes the perspective of this story different from most bush adventure stories?

2. From reading this story, can you discover why the life in the bush caught the attention of so many readers at the beginning of the twentieth century?

3. Discuss the character of the drover's wife.

4. Compare this story with Murray Bail's story of the same title later in this section. How are the stories different?

Katharine Susannah Prichard

(1884–1969)

Katharine Prichard was born in Levuka, Fiji, where her father was the editor of the local newspaper, but she spent most of her childhood in Tasmania and Victoria states. She attended South Melbourne College in Melbourne before she moved to Perth in Western Australia, where she worked as a governess. She returned to Melbourne and by 1908 was a staff journalist for the *Melbourne Herald*. Sent to London and Paris, Prichard was shocked by the poverty and squalor in these cities. She quickly championed the cause of a more equitable distribution of wealth. Her socialist tendencies stayed with her throughout her life (she became a Communist in 1920) and often informed her stories. During World War I, her first novel, *The Pioneers* (1915), won international recognition, and her literary career was launched.

After the war, she met an Australian Victoria Cross recipient, Hugh Throssell, and the two were married in 1919; this led to the most creative and productive period of Prichard's life. She decided to write plays and fiction about her fellow Australian working people. Her novels *The Black Opal* (1921), *Working Bullocks* (1926), and *Haxby's Circus* (1930) all celebrate the working classes and their struggles to make ends meet. Her most controversial novel is *Coonardoo* (1928), a story dealing with the delicate situation of a white cattle station owner and his housekeeper, Coonardoo, an Aboriginal woman. The lovers' inability to voice their socially unacceptable love turns the entire community upside down.

Prichard's own world was torn apart by the economic effects of the Great Depression. Her husband, unable to cope with the debts he had incurred, committed suicide. Part of the healing process included the writing of a novel depicting the Great Depression, *Intimate Strangers* (1937). She finished her writing career after World War II writing about the discovery of gold in Western Australia and its effects on three generations of Australians. Until the end of her life, Prichard was dedicated to social reform and civil liberties. Her *Happiness* (1967), a collection of short stories, contains the short story reprinted below. It tells of the relationship between a white man and Aborigine woman and the complexities of a cross-cultural relationship.

Happiness   *1915*

Nardadu, grandmother of Munga, was singing as she gazed before her over the red plains under blue sky. Singing, in a low wandering undertone, like wind coming from far over the plains at night:

> *Be-be coon-doo-loo*
> *Multha-lala coorin-coorin . . .*[1]

She was sitting beside the stockyard fence in the offal of a dead beast. There had been a kill the night before. A stench of blood and filth flowed through the air about her. On an old hide rotting in the sun, a little lizard lay quite still. Nardadu plucked over a length of entrail and set it aside. She reached for another, grey-green, and dark with blood.

A small squat woman, with broad square features, wide jawbone, short hair in greasy strands packed with mud and bound by a dirty white rag, she sat there singing, and picking over all that was left of the dead bullock.[2] A gina-gina,[3] blue for a length, almost black with dust and grease, showed her bony legs and feet. Her face all placid satisfaction, the black sticks of her arms and fingers swung backwards and

---

1 **Be-be . . . coorin:** "Cuddle your nose into my breast / And know happiness."
2 **bullock:** A young bull.
3 **gina-gina:** A type of female dress.

forwards, disturbing flies. Flies clung at the sunken wells of her eyes; but she plucked on over the mess of blood and dung, singing:

> *Be-be coon-doo-loo, coon-doo-loo,*
> *Be-be, be-be coon-doo-loo,*
> *Multhalala, la-la, lala, lala,*
> *Coorin-coorin, coorin-coorin.*

Across a stretch of ironstone pebbles the buildings of Nyedee homestead were clear in the high light of early morning. There were trees round the long white house with verandahs where John Gray slept and ate with his women and children. Megga had planted the trees long ago, the tall dark ones, those bushes with curds of blossom, and the kurrajongs whose leaves were light green and fluttering just now.

Megga had ridden and worked with John when he first camped by Nyedee well. Tall and gaunt and hard, she had cooked in the mustering and droving camps, driven men and beasts through long dry seasons. Eh-erm, she drove John. He was still her little brother.

Half a mile away, Nardadu could see every plank and post of the verandah; white hens stalking across it; harsh green of cabbages, onions, turnips surging beside the big windmill; the mill, its wheel and long fine lines ruled against the sky; and the little mill on mulga[4] posts with gauge stuck out like the tail of a bird. Kinerra and Minyi came out from the house for water. Slight, straight figures in dungaree gina-ginas, they moved slowly to the little mill. But it was out of order: would not give water except in a high wind.

White hens scattered and flew before Megga as she came along the verandah, Meetchie behind her, John after them both. A shrill screaming and flow of women's voices reached Nardadu; the throb and deeper reverberation of John's voice, as he came between the women, throwing a word or two before him. Small and stiff as chalk drawings her people had made on rocks in the hills, John and the two women rocked and moved with sharp little gestures before the house.

Nardadu knew what it was all about. She had heard that screaming and quarrelling of women and the anger of John's voice so often before. She smiled to herself and went on with her singing. Winding and rumbling through her, on and on it went, the eerie remote melody. Nardadu remembered her mother singing that song. It did not belong to Nyedee people. Nardadu had brought it with her to Nyedee from beyond those wild tumbled hills which stood on the edge of the plain, northeast. Her mother had sung the little song to Nardadu when she was a cooboo.[5] Nardadu had sung it to Beilba and Munga. Always it came fluttering out of her when she was pleased or afraid.

She was pleased this morning to have found something she could cook in the ashes of her fire to satisfy the hunger of Munga when he came in from the dogging.

---

4 **mulga:** Wooden posts found in dry regions of Australia.
5 **cooboo:** An Aborigine child.

All the men of the uloo[6] had been out trapping dingoes while John was away. But John was home again, the men would be in soon. The old, high, four-wheeled, single-seated buggy in which John had come from Karara station, with Chitali and old Tommy, still stood red with dust, out before the shed. Horses which had drawn the buggy, rough hair streaked and matted with dust and sweat, were feeding beneath the acacias and mulga, beyond the stockyards.

The little windmill would be mended. There would be the good smell of meat roasted on ashes, in the evening air, down by the uloo. When the men had eaten, talk would be made of dingoes: of wild dogs caught, or too cunning for any trap. Wongana would make a song about a dingo, clicking kylies[7] beside his camp-fire. There would be singing: singing and sleeping in the warm, starlit darkness.

On other stations Nardadu knew, men of the camp would not have gone dogging and left their women at the uloo. Wiah! A curse threaded the words of her song. But Nyedee was not like other places. John Gray left the uloo to the ways of the uloo. Megga? Eh-erm—Nardadu guessed Megga was responsible for that. By her will it was, John did not drink whisky until his legs would not carry him; or take a gin even when old men of the camp sent her to him.

Nardadu did not understand how a woman came to have such power with a man that her will should be stronger than his. But Megga—Nardadu understood something of her and her will, having lived so long with her. Had she not made men of the uloo even wear wandy-warra,[8] and the women grass and leaves from a string round their waists, before there were gina-ginas or trousers and boots on Nyedee? But that John should come under her will so, John who was a man of men! Nardadu clucked and threw out her hands in the native gesture of surprise.

Master he might be of all the country which lay before her old brown eyes, from the wedge of red and yellow purple-riven hills along the west, to those wild and tumbled timbered ridges north and east, beyond which stretched the country of her people and the buck spinifex flats, away and away inland. Yet John he was to her: John the all-powerful to be sure, giver of food and clothing, whose anger and boot you avoided; but who laughed and made fun with you, good-humouredly, when all went well with him.

She had come through the gorge of Nyedee hills with him, how long ago? Nardadu could not count beyond three. "Plenty years," she would say it was since John Gray had first brought cattle through the gorge of Nyedee hills, over there where the great koodgeeda's[9] eyes made a pool of fresh drinking-water. Trembling, she remembered the great silver lidless eye in the shadow of dark rocks. How it had flashed at her, glimmered from beneath the water when she went down with her jindie![10] They had camped quite near, and Wagola, her man, had sent her down to the pool for

---

6 **uloo:** Native camp.
7 **kylies:** Australian boomerang.
8 **wandy-warra:** Underwear.
9 **koodgeeda:** A demon, spirit, or monster.
10 **jindie:** A container or vessel.

water because he said the koodgeeda would not hurt a gin. He had made her sleep on the side nearest the pool, too. How terrified she had been, plenty years ago, when she first came to Nyedee with John Gray!

Wagola, her man, had been speared over there on the range by one of her own people. Wagola's brother claimed her. She had grown Beilba then; and Munga was Beilba's son. Her eyes wavered to the creek gums and burying-ground of the uloo, railed places and mounds covered with bark and branches. Her voice had the shrill anguish of wailing for her daughter.

Now she was an old woman, had bulyas[11] on her hands, and led the women's singing in the corroborees. She had no husband to concern herself about, only Munga, her grandson, who put up her low humpy of boughs and hide. And the cows. Nardadu was cow-woman on Nyedee, drove the milkers from their night wandering on wide plains where the windgrass was yellow, and acacias, in their young green, stood against hills blue as the dungaree of a new gina-gina.

While a coolwenda was putting his slow melodious notes across the vast spaces of hill and plain, and stars were still in the sky, she went scurrying after the cows, and brought them through the Two-mile gate to the yards, red heifers and calves, a huge white cow who charged whenever she got a chance, and the old red bull, lumbering and sulky. Nardadu ruled the cows. A drab gnomish figure in dirty gina-gina and the old felt hat which had been Wagola's, she shambled swiftly over the stones, banging two tins to make the cows hurry: proud of herself, of being on the strength of the station, old woman though she was, cow-tailer.

She had not been away since first she came to Nyedee. She had never been pink-eye; but then none of the Nyedee people went pink-eye. Other tribes came to pink-eye on Nyedee every year. There were corroborees, and youths for hundreds of miles about were made men in the wide-spreading scrub of mulga and minnerichi[12] which stretched to the foot of the dog-toothed range.

The hut of mud-bricks, baked in the sun, on the place where Nyedee homestead now stood—Nardadu had helped to build that. After its walls were up Megga had not ridden out with the men. She had stayed at the hut to watch the sinking of wells, raising of windmills and stockyards. Every plank was set under her eyes: the windmills with their great wheels and wedge tails of blue-grey iron, stretched taut against the sky.

Then camels bringing stores and sheets of ribbed iron had come over the creek! Again and again they had come, the great beasts, so savage and evil-smelling, yet led by a little stick through the nose and rope reins, bringing more and more sheets of iron and painted wood, flour, sugar, tea, gina-ginas; trousers, boots and hats for the men who went riding with John, pipes, tobacco and boiled lollies. Such days they were, great days of bustle and excitement, from the first fluting of the butcher-bird before stars paled in the eastern sky, until the sun went away behind the back of the hills.

---

11 **bulyas:** Skin blemishes; signs of old age.
12 **minnerichi:** A shrub plant.

The first room of mud-bricks was kept for a kitchen and the new house grew out from it, with verandahs, doors, wire cages for rooms. Megga had sent old men, women and children from the uloo to gather white clay in a creek bed, miles away, and had showed them how to paint the house. But to Nardadu, it still seemed, that the long white house among trees had reared itself by magic on the floor of the dead sea. Far out across the plains she had seen a mirage lying across it, reflections of a house in the sky, and had sung her song as a movin against evil, any evil magic could do an old woman by stealing her wits, when she was minding cows by herself, far away from her kin and the uloo of her people.

Megga herself had worn white clothes when the house was finished. The gins washed them, hung them out to dry and pressed them smooth with irons made hot in the fire. She had gathered about herself, too, china dishes and pots which broke when you dropped them, bringing down Megga's wrath as nothing had ever done.

Then the chickens came. Small fluffy creatures Megga had loved and tended until they were neat white hens, which if a dog killed—eh-erm, there was hell to pay.

Nardadu remembered the killing of one of those hens by Midgelerrie, her own dog, a brindle kangaroo hound, as dear to her almost as Munga. There was no better hunter on Nyedee; but he had pounced on and devoured one of those hens. Lowering, Megga, she remembered, had sent John out with his gun and he had shot the dog. John had told everybody in the uloo he would shoot any dog if it ate Megga's hens; but Nardadu had never forgiven Megga for the shooting. She did not blame John. He did as he was told.

Nothing had been the same on Nyedee since the chickens came. Nardadu believed that Megga's hens were the cause of all that went awry on Nyedee afterwards. Nardadu's was not the only dog John shot because he had eaten one of Megga's hens. The uloo bore Megga a grudge because of her hens, and the dogs John had shot for eating them.

It was beyond anything natural to men and women, Nardadu had decided, the way John and Megga lived in their new house among the trees, with an abundance of food and clothing, shade from the sun and shelter from the rain. They looked about them with pride and contentment. John strutted out from the house to the stock-yards and blacksmith's shop, and stretched reading on the verandah when he was not away mustering, or on the road with bullocks for market. Megga cooked, sewed, watched over her china and sat on her chairs, teaching girls from the uloo to scrub, polish, make gina-ginas for themselves. Only two of the youngest gins[13] were allowed into the house, after they had scrubbed their heads and bodies all over with soap and water, every morning, and put on fresh dresses. Other women from the uloo were permitted to sweep round the verandah, in turn, or to help with the washing; but that was all. And always there were new sheds going up, sheds for harness and tools, a butcher miah,[14] shade miah for the hens even.

---

13 **gins:** Native servants.
14 **miah:** Temporary shelters erected by travelers.

The station was growing and prospering. John and Megga were growing with the station; but still, there were no children on Nyedee except children from the uloo who played about the stockyard and woodheap sometimes. Down at the uloo they were concerned about it. The old women suggested that both John and Megga should be advised to take a mate. But Megga, it was agreed, was beyond the age of childbearing.

The men asked John why he did not get a woman. They did not understand his not having a woman except his sister, who was not a wife, to live with him. John laughed and said he had been too busy making the station to think about a wife and family. Men of the uloo believed what he said. They had seen him so often, after a day's hard riding, eat, and sleep as soon as he rolled in a rug beside his campfire. They understood he had thought of nothing but his station and cattle for years.

But the seasons were good. It rained—how it rained that year. It had not rained since on Nyedee as it had rained then. Nardadu herself, and all the other old women in the camp, had gone down to the creek and beaten it back with green branches when the muddy water swirled over its banks towards the uloo. They had been busy patching their huts to keep the rain out. Grass was green on the plains in a day or so; thick and deep in no time. The cows grew fat. Nardadu clucked with pleasure over their milk and calves, thick-set and sturdy. Megga, busy and masterful, directed everybody and everything, looking stouter, more good-humoured, every day. Since the hens and chickens had come, she seemed to have nothing left to wish for.

John went off mustering after the rain, taking all the boys, two or three gins and most of the horses with him. The grass and herbage everywhere made him gay and light-hearted. He talked now and then in easy familiar fashion with Chitali and the boys as he rode along; or when they camped for the night, he by his fire, they by theirs, at a little distance.

They were chasing breakaways in the back hills when the boys came on tracks of wild blacks from the other side of the range. Nyedee boys said these were cousins of theirs. John Gray visited the camp, talked to the old men, and in the evening when Nyedee boys were sitting singing round the camp fire of the strangers, a young gin was sent to John Gray's camp by way of courtesy to an honoured guest.

Nyedee boys marvelled when she did not return, immediately, as others had always done from John Gray's fireside.

And in the morning, John had presented the old men of the camp with pipes, tobacco, and a couple of blankets.

Somehow Megga heard of it. The boys talked when they got back to the uloo. They told their women and the old men, who chuckled, laughing, and smelling what was to follow.

Megga had been angry with Minyi for breaking a cup. Minyi, to make her angrier and to take her mind off the cup, had told Megga of the gin John kept by his camp-fire that night in the Nyedee hills. Megga was furious. The girls heard her talking to John about it. John had been angry, too, angry and sulky. He walked up and down the fence for hours afterwards. For many nights, he walked the fences, morose and restless. Out on the run it was just the same, the boys said. John did not sleep as he used to: threw wood on the fire half the night, and walked about.

The blacks watched him fight out his trouble. They knew well enough what was the matter with him. His mouth took a hard line. Nardadu had seen John striding backwards and forwards at night, sombre and angry as her old bull when he went moaning and bellowing along the fences, separated from the herd. John scowled at everybody who spoke to him during the day. He could not break the habits Megga had imposed on him; would not drink more whisky than he did usually, or have gins about him. But after he had been south with cattle that year he brought back the kurrie.[15]

She was with him in the old high buggy he had driven over from Karara in; and John looked as pleased with himself as Megga had looked when the new house sat, all built-up and whitewashed, on the plains. He had got what he wanted.

And Megga! Nardadu saw Megga's face, as though by lightning so bleached and stiff it was. Megga had not known John would bring this other woman with him to Nyedee. He kissed Megga and said:

"I've got a surprise for you, Meg. This is my wife."

Megga did not speak while the other laughed, saying in a high, singy voice: "My name's Margie!"

John went on, as if he had done something as much for Megga's sake as his own:

"It was getting a bit lonely for you, Meg, with no white woman to talk to. You and Margie'll be company for each other."

Nardadu could see and hear them still as if they were corroboreeing before her. Megga, fat and dumb, in front of the girl on slight, bare-looking legs: Meetchie—which was the uloo's way of saying "Mrs Margie"—in her light frock and hat, holding a red sunshade, John between them, proud and pleased with himself.

They were delighted with the kurrie at the uloo; delighted and excited by her light, brightly coloured dresses, patterned with flowers; her necklaces, high-heeled shoes, the songs she sang, and the tookerdoo[16] she gave them, sweet stuff covered in brown, sticky loam. John himself stepped with a jaunty kick and swing as he walked; his eyes laughed out at you. Nardadu gurgled and chuckled after him, and men of the uloo were very satisfied. Nobody worked very much in those days; and John was easy to get on with. He went about whistling in a queer, tuneless way. Nardadu had even heard him trying to whistle her own little song:

Be-be coon-doo-loo, coon-doo-loo . . .

How the gins laughed, and he with them, though Nardadu blackguarded him furiously when he took her calves off their milk too soon, so that the kurrie should have plenty of cream and milk in her tea! Black tea was all the gins ever tasted. But

15 **kurrie:** Woman.
16 **tookerdoo:** A treat or sweet.

John knew only too well, how he would need her to relieve him of all the little odd jobs he did now round the homestead, in the dry season ahead. He would have to be out on the run, moving cattle from well to well, wherever there was a picking, all through the blazing heat and dust storms.

Nardadu could hear them talking over at the house, Megga, Meetchie and John. Their voices came to her, clashing and clanging against each other.

"Your sister means more to you than I do!"

"What is it you want?" John's voice was surly and menacing. "Meg has left you the house. You want her to clear off of Nyedee, is that it?"

Meetchie made a long wail of grievances. Megga was always interfering, setting the children against their mother, and the gins would only do as she said. Meetchie had told Kinerra to catch and kill a hen for the children's dinner, and Megga had said no more hens were to be killed. It was always the same. If Meetchie told the gins to do one thing and Megga told them to do another, they obeyed Megga. "Either she goes or I go!"

"Turn my sister out for you?" John shouted. "Not on your life! She went to the hut of her own accord. But further she shan't go."

John had left the house and was striding across the red earth and ironstone pebbles towards Nardadu.

Beside the little windmill Kinerra and Minyi, who had been listening to and watching the quarrel, turned to get water. There was no wind; the mill-fans hung motionless; Kinerra, climbing wooden stays of the mill, swung the wheel; Minyi pumped, and filled the fire-blackened kerosene buckets. Two slight, straight figures, buckets on their heads, the girls moved slowly back to the house.

John walked to the shed before which the buggy was still standing. Nardadu had her affections, superstitions. They stirred as she watched John coming from the house towards her. His back was straight: he swung along with as steady, direct steps as when she had first known him, although his body had thickened and swelled in the white moleskin pants and faded blue shirt beneath. But the face under his wide hat-brim, fatter, redder, was sullen and heavy now: the blue of his eyes, burned deeper for the years out there on the plains working cattle under bare skies, held only passion and defeat.

The beat of his heels and spurs, as they clicked on the pebbles with a little silver tinkling, made Nardadu shiver. She remembered she should have been away beyond the gates with her cows: that John would shake his fist and yell angrily, if he saw her. Her song quavered into a queer gurgling laughter.

But John did not see her. He was calling Chitali and old Tommy, who had driven over from Karara with him.

Nardadu listened. John told the boys to put horses in the buggy again.

When the buggy drew up before the house Meetchie hurried forward and climbed into it. John lifted the children in beside her. He took the reins and they drove away; Megga, standing on the verandah, watched them go. Nobody called to her. The buggy whirled off in dust.

"Wiah!" Nardadu muttered, getting to her feet. Her instinct, sure and sensitive, told her Megga had won, and lost, in the fight which had been going on so long in John's house. Megga had got back the place and work which was hers and driven the kurrie off.

But John had brought the kurrie to Nyedee because he wanted a kurrie. And there were the children. Had he not loved and played with his children as men of the uloo loved and played with their children?

More than ever now, he would wander along the fences at night like that sulky old bull from the herd: his face turn to Megga as it did this morning: misery and bitterness crouch under the long white house, with its back to the blue, wild hills.

Against the sky-film, thin, clear blue, soft as the ashes of mulga and minnerichi, dust moved.

A cry rose in Nardadu's throat. She watched that dust grow against the sky and the edge of mulga scratching the sky. The tagged tail of horsemen swept out from it. Men of the uloo were returning from the dogging.

They swerved in a wide curve towards the stockyards, young horses before them. Nardadu could see Munga in charge of the packhorses: Munga on his white horse, ginger with dust, packhorses before him. The bay mare, a bucket lashed to her back, made for the troughs, and Munga, after her. The swing-in of dark, slender legs and flying tails through red mist of dust; bodies of men and horses joined, free-flying, galloping; all wildness and grace! Nardadu exulted. The horseman her Munga would be! And how pleased with the meat she had to feed him from her fire that night, as though he were a man!

The song of her gladness trembled, ranged its high minor notes and went wandering out to Munga:

> Be-be coon-doo-loo, coon-doo-loo,
> Multha-lala coorin-coorin.

QUESTIONS

1. This tale is full of Aboriginal language and observations. Why are these essential to our understanding of the story?

2. How are Aboriginals treated by the white landowners?

3. How does Margie, John's wife, cope with life on the Nyedee homestead? What is the source of her discontent?

4. What does Nardadu's comment that "Megga had won, and lost" suggest at the end of the story?

5. What defines happiness in this story?

Peter Cowan

(1914–2002)

Vale Peter Cowan was born in Western Australia and worked as a laborer throughout most of the 1930s in rural Western Australia. During his youth, he was also a champion motorcycle rough rider, a keen amateur photographer, and a geologist. In 1938, he attended the University of Western Australia and began writing his first short stories. Declared physically unfit for military service, he taught at Geelong Grammar School in Melbourne during the war, where he was involved with the literary arguments over modernist literature and the avant-garde movement in art. By the end of the war, his short story collection *Drift* (1945) was published. Six more published collections included *The Unploughed Land* (1958) and *Voices* (1988).

After the war, caught amidst the intellectual ferment over the importance of realism in modern Australian literature, Cowan began teaching at Scotch College in Melbourne. He taught there until he received a Commonwealth Literary Fellowship that allowed him to write his first novel, *Summer* (1963). Other novels followed, including *Seed* (1966), *The Colour of the Sky* (1986), and *The Hills of Apollo Bay* (1989). In 1987, he was made a Member of the Order of Australia.

Much of Cowan's writing drew on his experiences during the Great Depression. His characters are often challenged by what Cowan called the "impossible task of life," a theme that he presented repeatedly in his stories. He was environmentally conscious in a period when few people stopped to consider the implications of deforestation and pollution. His protagonists are normal men and women who go through life without complication; his writing is realistic and unsentimental; and his eye is always on the way his characters cope with daily situations, successfully or unsuccessfully. The short story that follows is from Cowan's *The Empty Street* (1965) collection. The story pits technological power and progress against the eco-balance beliefs of the native Australians. Only the intervention of a white woman and wife of the antagonist can save the life of who today might be called an eco-warrior.

The Tractor   *1941*

She watched him coming back from the gate, walking towards the slightly ornate suburban-style house she felt to be so incongruous set down on the bare rise, behind it the sheds and yards and the thin belt of shade trees. Yet he and his family were proud of it, grateful for its convenience and modernity, and had so clearly not understood her first quizzical remarks that she had never repeated them.

He stood on the edge of the veranda, and she saw in his face the anger that seemed to deepen because he knew the feeling to be impotent.

She said, "What is it?"

"Mackay's two big tractors—that they were going to use for the scrub-clearing—they've been interfered with. Sand put into the oil. The one they started up will cost a few hundred to repair."

"But no one would do that," she said, as if already it were settled, her temporizing without point.

"We know who did it."

"Surely he didn't come right up to the sheds—as close as that to the house—"

"No. They left the tractors down in the bottom paddock. Where they were going to start clearing."

"And now—they can't?"

"Now they can't. Not till the tractor's repaired."

She looked towards the distant line of the low scrub that was deepening in colour as the evening came. She said, "That is what he wanted."

"What he wants is to make as much trouble as he can. We haven't done anything to him."

"You were going to clear the land along the bottom paddock at the back of Mackay's. Where he lives."

"Where he lives?"

"You told me he lived in the bush there."

"He lives anywhere. And he takes the ball floats off the taps in the sheep tanks and the water runs to waste, and he breaks the fences when he feels like it, and leaves the gates open—"

"You think he does this deliberately?"

"How else?"

"Oh," she said, "yet it is all so ruthless."

"You mean what he does?"

"No. You only ever think of what he does."

"Well, I'll admit he's given us a few things to think about."

"Clearing with those tractors and the chain," she said. "Everything in their path goes—kangaroos—all the small things that live in the scrub—all the trees—"

He looked at her as if her words held some relevance that must come to him. He said, "We clear the land. Yes."

"You clear it," she said. "It seems to be what is happening everywhere today."

"I don't know what you mean, Ann," he said.

She got up from the chair by the steps. "Perhaps he feels something should be left."

"Look," he said, "maybe you teach too much nature study at school. Or you read all this stuff about how we shouldn't shoot the bloody 'roos—so that when some crazy swine wrecks our property you think he's some sort of a—"

"Some sort of a what?"

"I don't know," he said, aware she mocked him. "Better than us."

"No," she said. "Perhaps just different."

"Different all right."

"What are you going to do?"

"Get the police," he said. "They don't take much notice most of the time, but they will of this." He looked at her as if he would provoke the calm he felt to be assumed. "We'll burn him out if we can't get him any other way."

She looked up quickly and for a moment he was afraid.

"You wouldn't do that."

"He's gone too far this time," he said stubbornly.

The long thin streamers of cloud above the darkening line of scrub were becoming deep and hard in colour, scarlet against the dying light. He watched her face that seemed now calm, remote, as if their words were erased. She was small, slight, somehow always neat, contained. Her dark hair was drawn straight back, her brows clearly marked, lifting slightly so that they seemed to give humour sometimes to her serious expression, her firm mouth.

"I'd better go, Ken."

"The family expect you for tea."

"It's Sunday night. I've to work in the morning. I have some things to prepare."

"Look," he said. "If it's this business—"

"No, I'm just tired. And I've assignments to mark."

"All right," he said.

As they drove she watched the long shadows that spread across the road and over the paddocks from the few shade trees, the light now with a clarity denied through the heat of the day. She would have liked to make some gesture to break the tension between them, to explain to him why she had been unwilling to stay and listen to the inevitable talk of what had happened. But to tell him that at such times she became afraid, as if she could never become one of them, certain that the disagreements now easily enough brought to a truce must in the end defeat them, would not lessen their dissension.

He said suddenly, "You're worried about it, aren't you?"

She knew he referred to themselves, as if he had been aware of her own thoughts.

"Yes," she said. "Sometimes."

"It could be all right, Ann. You'd come to like it here."

"In so many ways I do."

"It's nothing like it used to be. This light land has come good now. We've done well. We've got everything—you wouldn't be without anything you'd have in the city."

"I know that, Ken," she said.

"But you're not sure of it."

She thought he perhaps did this deliberately, seeking to provoke an issue on material grounds, these at least being demonstrable of some conclusion, that he was lost, unwilling, in the face of their real uncertainty. He was more perceptive, she knew, than he cared to reveal, but he had a stubbornness she felt it was perhaps impossible to defeat. Before it, she relented a little.

"Not sure of some things. You must give me time. After all, I—hadn't thought to live here. It's different for you."

The few high trees stood out darkly above the low thick scrub, and beyond she could see the roofs of the town.

He said, "This other business will probably be over next week, anyhow."

She supposed he deliberately minimized this which perhaps he did not understand, preferring evasion, the pretence that when it was settled it would not matter. As to him it might not. But he was so clearly afraid that she would escape. She reached out quickly and touched his hand.

He stopped the car before the house near the end of the main street, where she boarded. Farther down, near the club, she could see the cars parked, and people moving without haste along the pavements.

There was no wind, and in the darkness the street was hot, as if the endless heat of summer was never to be dissipated. As he closed the door of the car he said, "I have to go out to the paddock on the way back. It won't take long."

She made no comment and he said, as if to prevent her censure, "I've got to take some stuff from the store out there."

"They haven't found him?"

"No. The police think he's moved out. But we know he hasn't. He makes fools of them in the bush. They've been looking since Sunday, but they've given it up now. Anyhow, you could walk right past him at three feet. And there are no tracks."

"To be able to dodge them like that he must know all this country very well."

"I suppose he does."

"Almost—more than that. He must understand it."

"He doesn't seem to do anything else all day."

She smiled. "Well, do you?"

"I'm not sure what you mean by that. You mean we don't understand it?"

"Perhaps in a different way. You're making it something you can understand."

"Here we go again." He banged his hand against the steering wheel. "We never take a trick. Why don't you go and live with this character?"

She laughed suddenly. "I'm sorry, Ken. But how long has he been here? That's a harmless enough question!"

"He's been around here something like ten years. I remember when I was at school. He's mad."

She said, "All those who oppose us are mad."

"Well," he said, "we're going to get him out this time. We're taking shifts down at the tractors, and we've got a watch on a camp of his we found."

"A camp?"

"Made out of boughs." His voice was grudging. "Pretty well made. You could live in it. We flushed him out, because he left some food, and a radio."

"That's not in keeping—a radio."

not come she went back inside. Idly, rather irritated at his lateness, she took out her paints and began to work on the flower illustration she was making. She had begun to paint the native flowers, their grotesque seeds and leaves, to use for her teaching, but the work had begun to absorb her, and she spent whatever time she could searching for new examples. Many, at first, she could not identify. Now, though she told no one, she had begun to hope the paintings might be publishable if she could complete series of different areas.

It was mid-morning when she heard him outside. In the car as they drove he said, "Some of the fences were broken, out by Hadley's boundary. We've been too busy this week to look down there, and the sheep had gone through into the scrub. We got most of them back."

"You lost some?"

"Some."

"I'm sorry," she said, as if somehow it were her fault.

"He knows we're going to clear that land, and he's out to do as much damage as he can first."

She had no wish to draw him, as if she deliberately sought their disagreement, but it seemed she must form the words, place them before him, his evasion too easy.

"You're sure about it, Ken, aren't you? that he's just getting his own back? That it's as simple as that?"

"It's obvious. He's done pretty well so far."

"And that's the only side there is to it?"

"What else could there be? He can't expect to stop us."

"He might know that."

"Well—that proves it."

"No—perhaps we've all got to make a gesture of some sort. For the things we believe in."

He shook his head. "You put it your way if you like. But what I believe in is using that land."

"Yes, Ken."

"We can't all be dreamers." And then, refusing to be further drawn, he laughed. "It's funny the way I've got caught up with one. Perhaps it will sort out, like you said. You do the dreaming. I'll do the work."

She ran her hands lightly over her arms, smiling at him. "You think we might convert one another?"

"It's a risk we'll have to take."

"Yes. I suppose we're young enough."

"I'll be out a bit this week-end, Ann. We've got to stop this somehow. While we've a few sheep left."

He went out late in the afternoon, and she helped his mother in the kitchen. The older woman had a quietness and a kind of insight that she found attractive, and they had always got on well together, though sometimes Ann was irritated by her acceptance of the men's decisions and views, as if this was something she no longer questioned, or perhaps, Ann thought, she had never questioned.

When Ken came back she heard him talking to his father on the veranda, and then the older man's voice raised in disagreement, though she could distinguish only a few of the words. She went out through the kitchen door and the men stopped talking.

As she came towards them Ken said, "We've found one of his camps. Ted and Don found it, but this time they turned off and kept away. They didn't go near enough for him to realize they'd seen it. We made that mistake last time."

"Where is this?" she said.

"It's new. So he may still be there. It's down in the paddock off the side road to Mackay's. Straight in from the dam. About half a mile north in the scrub."

"There."

"Yes. By the new land. Where we were going to build." He looked at her as if she might have contradicted him. "When we were married."

"What will you do?"

His father said, "I told them to get the police."

"He walked away from the police last time." For a moment his eyes met the girl's. "And us. All right. We were no better. And the reporters came up from town. Photographers all over the place. A seven-day wonder for the suburbanites."

"It's not something that happens every day," she said. "Naturally, it was news."

"They'll make it news again, if we let them. But this time it will be different. We don't do anything until tomorrow night. That way he won't be suspicious if he sees our tracks near the camp. Then Sunday night we'll make a line north of the camp, and if the wind's right we'll burn back towards the firebreak along the paddock. He'll have to break out through the paddock. We'll have a chance that way."

"I think it's too big a risk," his father said. "You'll burn the whole of that country. You can't do it."

"We were going to clear it, anyway."

"You can't start a fire like that."

"If we try to close in on the camp he'll hear us."

"You could still get him. There's enough of you."

"He'd go between us in the bush. No matter how close we were. You know that. No one's been able to get a sight of him in the bush. The police had trackers there last week. They found plenty of tracks. But he kept as far ahead or behind them as he liked. No," he said, "he's made fools of us long enough. I think we've got a chance now."

He turned suddenly towards the girl, and she stood beside him, not moving. His words seemed to her to hold a kind of defiance as if he did not himself believe in them, and she thought that it was not simply that he doubted their ability to carry out the plan, but that he did not really believe in the idea of the fire himself. That if she or his father did not further pursue it he might be glad to drop it. But she could not be certain, and before she could speak, as if he intended to prevent her words, he said, "Let's forget this now, Ann. We'll go over to Harris's after tea. They've got a bit of a show on there for May's birthday."

Almost all those she had come to know seemed to have found their way to the party. And all of them discussed the hermit, as they called him; she realized it was general knowledge that he was expected to be caught soon. She listened to the undercurrent of derision that the police with all their resources had been mocked by this man it seemed none of them had seen, as if in this they were on his side. Some of the older people she spoke to claimed to have caught glimpses of him when, some years earlier, he had taken food quite freely for a time from the farmhouses. Some claimed to know his name. But it seemed to her, as she mixed with them and listened to them, that none of them really cared. She felt they simply accepted the idea that he must be denied, driven from cover and killed if necessary, as they might have accepted the killing of a dingo or a fox, a creature for them without motive or reason. When she tried to turn their words, to question them, they looked at her with a kind of surprise, or the beginning of suspicion, perhaps in doubt of her as a teacher of their children. And she saw that quite quickly they exhausted the topic, turning to the enjoyment of the evening, as if already the whole thing was disposed of. In the end she thought it was their lack of involvement, their bland rejection of responsibility, that irritated her to the point of anger, so that she was forced to hold herself from rudeness.

It was late when they returned, and in her room, after she had changed, she stood for a time by the window in the darkness. There was a small moon that seemed scarcely to break the dark ground shadow, and beyond the paddocks she could not see where the scrub began. Her sense of anger had given place to dejection and a kind of fear. She tried to imagine the man who in the darkness slept in what they had described as his camp, something she could picture only as a kind of child's cubby house in the thick scrub. But she could form no picture of him as a physical being, only that it seemed to her he must possess imagination and sensibility beyond that of his pursuers, that he must be someone not difficult to talk to, someone who would understand her own feeling about these things for which he was persecuted. And who might even, she thought, be glad to know, however briefly, that they were shared. She was aware of a sense of disloyalty, but the image persisted, and it was suddenly monstrous that the darkness of the scrub should be swept by the glare of fire, as she would see it from the window where she stood now, the man stumbling from it in some unimaginable indignity. And though she had doubted the men's intention to carry out their plan, it seemed now in the darkness only too probable that in anger they might do what she, and perhaps they, feared. And it was impossible. Her hands felt the cold of the sill, she was aware of the faint wind that blew in through the window, cool upon her skin, and she could hear it in the boughs of the few shade trees behind the house.

On Sunday, in the afternoon, Ken left to make arrangements with the other men. His parents were resting, but she knew they would not question her going out, they were used to her wandering about the farm, looking for the plants she wished to paint. She went down through the yard gate, across the paddock towards the track that led out to the belt of scrub and timber. It seemed, in the heat, farther than she had expected.

She walked along the side fence, where the brush began, feeling that it would hide her if any of the men were watching. If she met them she would say she had come to look for Ken. She could see the dam ahead, the smooth red banks rising steeply, to one side a few thin trees, motionless in the heat.

At the dam she paused. The side track to Mackay's had turned some distance back to the left. In front of her, facing north, the scrub was thick, untouched, she was suddenly reluctant to go beyond the fence on the far side of the dam.

She pushed the wires down and stepped through. She began to pick her way through the scrub, choosing the small, almost imperceptible pockets where the bushes were thinner. It was only after a time, when she could no longer see the dam or the trees beside it, that she realized her method of walking had led her away from a straight line. She had no clear idea how far she had come. She went on until she was certain she had covered half a mile, but as she stopped it was suddenly clear she could have deviated in any direction.

The bushes grew upward on their thin sparse stems to a rounded umbrella-like top, the leaves tough, elongated and spindly. They stretched away like endless replicas, rising head-high, become too thick for her to go farther. As she looked about it seemed improbable she had come so far. In the heat the scrub was silent. Along the reddish ground, over the thin stalks, the ants moved, in places she had walked round their mud-coloured mounds. She looked down at the ground, at the hard brittle twigs and fallen leaves, some of them already cemented by the ants. In a kind of fear she began to walk.

A short distance to the right a thin patch of trees lifted above the bushes, and though she thought it was the wrong direction she began to push her way towards it. The trees were like some sharp variation in the endless grey pattern of the brush that rose about her.

Beneath them the bark and leaves were thick upon the ground. She stood in the patch of shade, and she tried to reason that she could not have come far, that she could find her way back if she was careful. And in the silence she thought again, as she had the night before, of the man she had come to warn. It had seemed that if she could explain to him, he must understand, and that perhaps he would go. She had relied on there being understanding between them, that at least in these things they must feel alike. So that it had seemed her words would have effect. Now, in the heat and the silence, it was a dream, holding in this place no reality. She could never have thought to do it. And it was here he had spent ten years. It was like nothing she could encompass. She felt a sharp, childish misery, as if she might have allowed herself tears.

It occurred to her that if she could climb one of the trees she might gain an idea of direction. But the trunks were slippery, without foothold, and at the second attempt she fell, twisting her leg. She leant against the trunk, afraid of the pain, trying to deny it, as if she would will herself to be without injury that might imprison her.

She was not aware of any movement or sound, but she looked up, and turned slightly, still holding to the smooth trunk. He was standing just at the edge of the clump of trees. He might have been there all the time. Or been attracted by the noise she had made.

She said weakly, "I—didn't see you—"

His face held no expression she could read. His hair was grey and short, and she was vaguely surprised, as if she had imagined something different, but cut crudely, and streaked across his head by sweat. He was very thin, all the redundant flesh might long ago have been burnt from him, his arms stick-like, knotted and black. His hands held a rifle, and she knew a sudden fear that he would kill her, that somehow she must place words between them before he took her simply as one of his persecutors.

She said quickly, "I came to warn you—they have found your camp—tonight they mean to drive you out towards the paddocks—"

But they were not the words she had planned. His eyes gave her no sign. They were very dark, sharp somehow, and she knew suddenly they were like the eyes of an animal or a bird, watchful, with their own recognition and knowledge which was not hers. The stubble of beard across his face was whitish, his skin dark from the sun.

"I—if only you would go from here," she said. "They only want you to go—they don't understand—"

The words were dead in the heat and the silence. She saw the flies that crawled across his face.

"I wanted to help you," she said, and she despised herself in her terror. Only his hands seemed to move faintly about the rifle. His stillness was insupportable. Abruptly she began to sob, the sound loud, gulping, ridiculous, her hands lifting to her face.

He seemed to step backwards. His movement was somehow liquid, unhuman, and then she thought of the natives she had once seen in the north, not the town natives whose movements had grown like her own. But with a strange inevitability he moved like an animal or the vibration of the thin sparse trees before the wind. She did not see him go. She looked at the boles of the trees where he had stood, and she could hear her own sobbing.

Some time in the afternoon she heard the sudden sound of shots, flat, unreal, soon lost in the silence. But she walked towards where the sound had seemed to be, and after a time, without warning she came on the track that ran towards Mackay's place. She had gone only a short distance when she heard the voices, and called out. The men came through the scrub and she saw them on the track. She began to run towards them but checked herself. Farther down she saw a Landrover and one of the police. Ken said, "We missed you—we've been searching—it was only that Ted saw where you'd walked down the fence—"

She said, "The shots—I heard them—"

"We were looking for you. We didn't see him. He tried to get past us, then shot at Don—we had to shoot."

She did not speak and he said, "We had to do it, Ann. We sent for the police. But where were you? How did you get out here?"

There was nothing she could tell him. She said, "I was looking for you, I think."

The Landrover had drawn up beside them, and the driver opened the door for her. They moved back down the dry rutted track where the thin shade had begun to stretch in from the broken scrub.

QUESTIONS

1. Is this a story about two distinct approaches to life? Elaborate.

2. Describe the social dynamics in the relationship between Ken and Ann.

3. Are the bushman's sabotage actions justified in any way? What motivates the bushman to perform these clandestine acts of destruction?

4. Why can't Ann speak to the bushman when she finally confronts him? Is this inability to communicate symbolic in any way?

5. What is the attitude toward race in this story?

Elizabeth Jolley

(b. 1923)

Elizabeth Jolley was born in Birmingham, England, and educated at home until she was eleven, when she attended a Quaker school. She trained as a nurse during World War II, and her experiences are evident in *My Father's Moon* (1989) and *Cabin Fever* (1990). In 1959, she and her husband, Leonard Jolley, immigrated to Australia, where Jolley began to write short stories and novels.

She published her first short story, "The Talking Bricks," in 1965, and won the State of Victoria Short Story Award for "A Hedge of Rosemary" in the same year. Her output since then has been prolific. In 1974, Jolley began teaching creative writing classes at the Fremantle Arts Centre and began teaching part time at Curtin University, becoming Writer in Residence. When her first short story collection, *Five Acre Virgin* (1976), was published, Jolley's work began to receive critical acclaim. She has also written a number of radio plays. Her first novel, *Palomino* (1980), showed her growing concerns with the role of women in a repressive male-dominated society; nevertheless, her sense of humor and ear for dialogue offer the reader a sardonic perspective that helps to mitigate the more strident attacks on male chauvinism that were prominent in the late 1970s and into the 1980s.

The story that follows is about the marginalization of the elderly in modern society. The "old man" in the story is not in any way ill treated by his children; he simply does not have a role to play in their daily lives. Jolley's delicate handling of the man's wanderings and reflections on his childhood near Birmingham gives the story a melancholy aura that is difficult to escape.

A Hedge of Rosemary

No one knew where the old man went every night at dusk. He sat to his tea in his daughter-in-law's kitchen and ate up obediently everything she put before him. She was a sharp woman but quite kind, she called him Dad and stirred his tea for him as she put the cup beside him. She put it a bit towards the middle of the table so he would not knock it over.

"Mind your tea now Dad," she always said, and without looking up from his plate he answered, "Thank you kindly, much obliged." After the meal he would sit for a while with his boots off: he held them in both hands and studied the soles intently sometimes shaking his head over them, and Sarah would get his dishes done out of the way.

Just about this time, as on other nights, his son John, who had a business in town, came in and he and Sarah had their dinner. When that and the necessary bits of conversation were over they all went into the lounge room and sat in comfortable chairs to watch the television. The house was very quiet with John's three boys all grown up and gone their ways, two to Sydney and one overseas. When the old man had sat a short while with John and Sarah in the lounge he put on his boots slowly and carefully and then getting up carefully from his comfortable chair he went out through the back verandah.

"Mind how you go Dad!" Sarah called after him and he replied, "That's right, that's right!" and went off into the dusk round the side of the house and through a door in a vine-covered trellis and down into the street. After he had gone Sarah wondered where he was going. On other evenings she had peered out into the dark fragrance to see if he had gone up to the end of the garden. She thought he might have gone up to the shed for something. Sometimes she had looked in there and had even pushed open the door of the whitewashed place next to the shed thinking he might be ill in there. He never would use the one in the bathroom which was so much nicer. But he was never in either place. If she went out of the front door she could never see him: by the time she had picked her way across her neatly laid out suburban garden he was always gone from sight and all she could do was to peer up the street and down the street into the gathering darkness and go back into the house where John was absorbed into the television.

"I wonder where Dad's off to again," she said, but on this night, as on all other nights, John was not listening to her.

"The Queen's not looking so well," Sarah remarked as some activities of the Royal Family came on in the news. John grunted some sort of reply and they both sank into the next programme and did not think too much about the old man walking off on his own into the night.

During the day the old man did practically nothing, he tidied the garden a bit and stacked wood slowly and neatly outside the verandah so Sarah had only to reach out an arm for it. Mostly he sat in the barber's shop. He went shopping, too, with his battered attaché case. He laid it on the counter in the Post Office and opened it with his trembling old hands. Glossy magazines lay in neat rows over the counter.

"Mind my magazines now Dad!" the postmistress said, and he replied, "That's right, that's right!" and when he had drawn his money he said, "thank you kindly, much obliged," and back to the barber's shop where the paint was peeling from the ceiling and the shelves were littered with old-fashioned hair nets and curlers and other toilet requisites long out of date and covered in dust. Faded advertisements hung on the walls but no one ever read them.

Towards the end of the afternoon the shop filled with little boys from school and sometimes little girls came in and would take their turn in the chair unnoticed by the barber who did not do girls. The children ignored the old man and brushed past him to reach for old magazines and tattered comics which they read greedily sprawled on the linoleum. The barber greeted every customer in a nasal drawling voice. He spoke to the old man.

"And how are they treating you eh? Pretty good eh?" He said the same thing to everybody, and the old man replied, "That's right, that's right." If the children had asked him he could have thought up stories about the Great Red Fox and Brother Wolf, but the children never asked him anything, not even the time.

Some days he wandered by the river watching the weaving pattern of children playing on the shore. They never took any notice of him and he sat half-asleep in the shade of one of the peppermint trees that grew at intervals along the bank. He sat just a bit back from the sandy edges where the kind-hearted water rippled gentle and lazy and shallow. He was always sleepy at noon after his midday meal which Sarah gave him early at half-past eleven so that she could get cleared up in the kitchen. The children never came to him to ask his advice or to show him things. He supposed he was too old. Yet he knew a good many things about the foreshore[1] and about playing in the sand. Back at home he had three things better than plastic spades; he had an iron gravy spoon and an ash scoop and an old iron trowel. These had been for his grandchildren years ago when he had brought them down to the shore to play, minding them for Sarah so she could get on and do the house and the cooking and the washing. He never thought about these three things now, they lay somewhere at home behind the stove, he never thought about the Great Red Fox and Brother Wolf either. But if someone had asked him, he could have thought about them.

There was a little merry-go-round there, a corner of jangling music and laughter, a corner of enchantment. When the children went round and round on the little painted horses the old man forgot everything as he sat on a bench and watched them. They smiled and waved and he would nod and smile and wave and then shake his head because the children were nothing of his and were not waving to him. Once a child was crying on the path and he fished a penny out of his pocket and held it out but she would not take it and hid her face in the uneven hem of her mother's dress.

---

1 **foreshore:** The ground between the water's edge and cultivated land.

"You can't get anything for a penny now Gran'pa," the mother said and laughing quite kindly walked on along the path.

When he went out in the evening he walked straight down the middle of the road, down towards the river. The evening was oriental, with dark verandahs and curving ornamental roof tops, palm fronds and the long weeping hair of peppermint trailing, a mysterious profile sketched temporarily purple on a green and grey sky. Fingers of darkness crept across the moon, thinly crescent and frail, hung in the gum-leaf lace. Dampness and fragrance brushed his old face and he made his way to the river where the shores were deserted. The magpies caressed him with their cascade of watery music. This was their time for singing at dusk and all night if they wanted to. Down by the water's edge the old man crouched to rest and his voice sighed into a whisper sliding into the great plate of smooth water before him.

"No one should be alone when they are old." His thought and his word and his voice were like dry reeds rustling at the edge of the gentle water.

When he had rested a few moments he walked on through the stranded ghosts of the swings and the merry-go-round. The little wooden horses, their heads bent and devout, were dignified in their silence. The old man walked by unnoticed, for why should the little horses notice him, he walked this way so often. A little farther on he turned up the grass bank away from the river. The slope was hardly a slope at all but he had to pause more than once for breath. Soon his hand brushed the roughness and fragrance of rosemary and his nostrils filled with the sharper scent of geranium, and he fumbled the wooden latch of a gate and went in and along the overgrown path of a neglected garden. The hedge of rosemary was nearly three feet thick and sang with bees in the heat of a summer day. Geraniums like pale pink sugar roses climbed and hung and trailed at the gate-posts, and again on either side of the crumbling woodwork of the verandah trellis. Later on the air would be heavy with the sweetness of honeysuckle but the old man was not thinking of this. He fumbled again at the latch of the door and made his way into the darkness inside the familiar place which had been his home and his wife's home and his children's home for more years than he ever thought about now. In the kitchen he felt about with his old hands till he had candle and matches.

Three years back he had been ill with pneumonia and fever and Sarah declared the place unhealthy and smelling of the river and drains, or lack of them; and herself finding it too much to come there every day to see to him and his house as well as her own house which took a deal of doing on her own. So she and John had come one Sunday afternoon in the car and fetched him to their place and had nursed him well and comfortable. And later, had sold his place to the owner of some tea-rooms further along the river, the other side of the swings and the merry-go-round. So far the man who had bought it had done nothing except sell the furniture and even some of that, the shabby good-for-nothing stuff, was still there. As soon as the old man was better enough from his illness he had started to walk back to his place. At first he had only got as far as the barber's shop on the corner, and then to the post-mistress where the road widened before turning down to the sandy wastes by the river. And then one day he managed to get to a bench at the merry-go-round, and after that strength was his to walk right to his place. And he went inside and sat in the kitchen and looked about him thinking and remembering. But he did not think and remember too much, mostly he rested and was pleased to be there. He laid his attaché case on the kitchen table and opened it with his trembling old hands, he unpacked his shopping into the cupboard by the stove. He had little packages of tea, sugar and matches. Then he took out his pipe and tobacco and he sat and smoked his pipe. Sarah objected to the smell of his cheap tobacco in her home, even if he smoked out on the verandah. She complained all the time afterwards, and went from room to room opening windows, shaking curtains and spraying the air with something pine-scented to freshen the place up, as she called it. So every night he walked down home and had his pipe there. He did not say where he was going because Sarah would insist that he stayed in her place to smoke and then all that airing and freshing up afterwards.

During the day he sometimes spent an hour tidying up the old tangled garden as much as an old man can. He stacked up some wood and split a few chips for the stove. People passing the rosemary hedge would wish him "good day" if they saw him in the garden, but mostly people took no notice of him. They were busy with their children or with their thoughts or with each other. The old man came and went in peace and every night he came home to his place and smoked his pipe and sat and rested. He did not think very much because there is no use thinking over things when you can do nothing about them any more. His children were gone their ways, they mostly were like her. She had been a great reader and had sat reading her life away. She read everything the old postmistress could get for her, novelettes they were called years ago. Bundles of them had come to the house. The children had mostly been like her and she had taken them with her into the kind of world she lived in.

He had come, as a very young man, from the Black Country in England, from the noise and dirt of the chain-making industrial area where people lived crowded and jostled together in indescribable poverty. The women there had muscles like men and they worked side by side with their men in the chainshops pausing only at intervals to suckle their babies. He had carried his younger sisters daily to his mother and had later cared for them in other intimate ways as he minded them in the blue-brick backyards and alleys which were the only playgrounds. When he had come to Australia he had gone straight to the country where he had been terrified by the silence and loneliness. He was afraid of the heat and the drought too, but more than that he could not stand the still quiet nights in the bush when he was alone with the silence. And the white trunks of the gum-trees were like ghosts in the white light of the moon. He had longed to hear the chiming of city clocks through the comforting roar of the city and the friendly screech of the trams as they turned out of the High Street into Hill Street. He missed the heave and roar of the blast furnace and the nightly glow on the sky when the furnace was opened. All his life these had been his night light and his cradle song. So he went from the country to the town and found work in one place and then in another and later was employed to look after the foreshore, there was the house there for him too, and though it was quiet, the city and the suburbs were spreading towards him reassuringly.

If any one had said, "Tell me about the chainshop," he could have told them about it and about a place he once visited as a boy where, in the late afternoon sunshine, he had walked with his father down a village street. Standing on the village green were twelve geese. They were so still and clean and white. Beautiful birds, his father had said so. It was the stillness of the geese in his brief memory of the countryside that had made him leave the jostled crowded life among the chainmakers and come to Australia. But no one ever asked him about it so he never really thought about it any more except perhaps for a moment while he sat smoking, but only for a moment.

So on this night as on all the other nights he sat and rested and smoked his pipe in the neglected old house which had once been his place. He was so comfortable there he forgot it had been sold. Though Mr Hickman, the man who had bought it, had called once when the old man was doing the garden. Mr Hickman had said he was having the place demolished in a week or two because he wanted to start building.

"You've got some fine roses there," Mr Hickman had said after the pause which had followed his previous statement.

"That's right, that's right," the old man had replied and they had stared at the roses together while the bees hummed and sang in the hedge of rosemary.

But this had been nearly a year ago and the old man did not think about it because there was nothing he could do about it. So just now he sat and rested and enjoyed his pipe and was pleased to be there. When his pipe was finished he remembered he must walk back. He got back to his son's place just after nine and Sarah said, "how about a nice cup of tea before bed Dad," and he replied, "Thank you kindly, much obliged." And he sat down in the kitchen and took his boots off carefully and stared at the soles of his boots. He shook his head a bit very slowly and set the boots down beside his chair. Sarah stirred his tea and put the cup down towards the middle of the table.

"Mind your tea now Dad," she said.

"Thank you kindly, much obliged," he replied.

"Have a good walk Dad?" John asked him.

"That's right, that's right," the old man said and he drank up his tea.

"Good night Dad," Sarah said.

"Good night Dad," John said.

"Good night, good night," the old man said and he took up his boots and he went off to his bed.

QUESTIONS

1. What does this story demonstrate about the nature of Australian suburban life?

2. How are the elderly treated in suburban Australia from the perspective of this tale?

3. How does contemporary Australian life deaden its participants to the significance of marginalized people?

4. What does the man miss about his early life in the Black Country?

5. How are the main contrasts presented in this story, and in what ways are they developed?

Frank Moorhouse

(b. 1938)

Frank Moorhouse was born in Nowra, New South Wales. His writing career began as a cadet journalist on the *Daily Telegraph* in Sydney; after his apprenticeship was completed, he wrote for a variety of newspapers throughout Australia. His first published short story appeared in the influential literary journal *Southerly* while he was working in Wagga. He soon returned to Sydney in 1963 to edit the *Australian Worker* and later became the editor of *City Voices*, a trendy popular entertainment paper not unlike New York City's *Village Voice*. After the modest success of his first short story collection, *Futility and Other Animals* (1969), he dedicated himself exclusively to a writing career.

Moorhouse was considered in the early 1970s to be somewhat of a revolutionary fiction writer because of the controversial nature of his subject matter: He was not afraid to explore the importance of sexuality in modern life or to satirize the political ineptitude of the period. And while Moorhouse felt a great deal of kinship with the underground and counterculture writings emerging from the United States, he also felt that the Americanization of Australian society produced a negative impact on the Australian way of life. In 1972, he completed a collection of short stories entitled *The Americans, Baby*, in which the selection that follows was published. Although the story contains a good deal of humor, it is a warning about the sterility of U.S. values and lifestyles. In this collection, Moorhouse began experimenting with "discontinuous narratives," that is, collections of short stories revolving around a group of core characters. He has used this method throughout his writing career.

Throughout the 1970s and into the mid-1980s, Moorhouse published five more volumes of short stories. In 1988, his first novel, *Forty-Seventeen*, was published. Although primarily a series of sketches, the novel follows a hard-drinking, forty-something Australian everyman named Sean as he faces growing old and a complex double relationship with a perky schoolgirl and his cancer-stricken ex-wife Robyn. The novel brought Moorhouse international success, and he was awarded the Australian Literature Society Gold Medal in 1989. His novel *Grand Days* (1993) traces Australia's role in the development of the League of Nations between the two world wars. He uses the character of Edith, an innocent from a new country, as a symbol for Australia. A sequel entitled *Dark Palace* (2000) won him the Miles Franklin Award. He is currently editor for *Best Australian Stories*, and one of his aims is to revitalize the short story form in Australia.

A Person of Accomplishment   1972

The invitation to go home with him to his place was absolutely unexpected. There they were writing up test analyses in his office, her mind running a fantasy about going to MIT[1] for a PhD and finding a big buck Negro in a white lab coat, when she'd felt a hand on her knee and heard him say, "Why don't we stop at this point and go back to my place for a drink?" The pressure of his hand on her knee said drinks and sex.

Her second thoughts were whether she'd stay overnight with him. Whether she'd need a change of clothes for tomorrow and other things. She was also faintly blushing.

She felt like saying "But we hardly know each other," but that was not a particularly liberated thing to say, and checked it. Nor particularly honest because she'd never made this a real requirement with other men. Unexpected, that was what it was, unexpected. Over the months there hadn't been a sexual breath to stir the clinical atmosphere between them.

"I guess you must have sensed I was going to invite you home one of these fine nights," he said.

She looked at his smile. "Well, not exactly . . ."

"You will come, though?"

"Well, yes," she said. There was the slight obligation of an invitation which comes from an associate professor to a humble research assistant—and then the difference in their ages—twenty-eight and forty, gave him some sort of command. She also felt gently encircled by his clean, serious, American gregariousness. His American geniality.

At his place he took her in his arms in the clean kitchen and with her backside against the stainless steel sink, kissed her very seriously.

"I've been wanting to do that for some days," he said, with some satisfaction, and having got that out of the way, went about getting her a drink and putting out black bread and cheese—two types—on a cheese board.

He showed her around. Showed her his study with its carved pipe rack, Steelbilt filing cabinets and Tensor reading lamp.

Besides his doctorate from MIT and his pharmacy degree from the University of Nebraska, Lincoln, framed on the wall, she saw a cup for canoeing and a silver chess piece from some American competition.

"Spacious," she commented.

"I prefer it to my office at the university," he said. She mentally corrected it to "room at the university."

Back in the living room she ran her fingers along the keyboard of his piano.

"Do you play?" she asked.

---

1 **MIT:** Massachusetts Institute of Technology.

"Yes. A little." Sitting down, he played.

"Schoenberg[2]—discordant? You find it discordant? Twelve-tone system—a rigid intellectual exercise—say, like a sonnet."

"You seem to have a wide range of interests—chess, canoeing, piano . . ."

"There's a reason," he said quietly, stopping playing. "I had a marriage break up on me—years ago—when I was young." He shrugged, looked at her, and then seemed to decide not to go on.

She felt unable to inquire further.

He swivelled on the piano stool, looking fit and spruce.

She was frightened then for a second that the conversation had lapsed and the situation would become physical. She wasn't ready.

"Do you cook?" she said, looking through at the shadow board and the shelves holding the kitchen utensils—the natural colourings of the handmade wood and pottery and the machined brightness of the duralumin and stainless steel. She could see a cutlet bat, a red casserole dish, brownware dishes, wooden cutting board with inset blades, a crescent-shaped double-handed chopping knife, and a mortar and pestle.

"A playboy cook." He chuckled. "Get the woman to do the vegetables and set the table." He chuckled some more. "Yes, I cook, I cook a passable *coq au vin*[3]—provincial style—actually I'm a peasant cook—love the primitive. You must let me cook dinner for you one night."

Whatever sort of cook you are, she thought, you're not a playboy.

"Oh," she said, "here I am at twenty-eight and have never cooked *coq au vin* in my life."

They sat there, he talked about cooking. She heard Bearnaise, Bordelaise, and vaguely listened while thinking about him, trying to get a feel for him. She was brought back to the conversation by him showing her a hand-written recipe book which she riffled through but could not concentrate on. A book, he told her, begun by his pioneer grandmother, which he had continued. It was in his handwriting, with great clarity—like one of his experiment reports. She saw the headings, Corn Fritter, Rye Bread, Wheat Cake.

"Another drink?"

"Oh yes," she said, looking at her glass, wanting another drink all right, "yes please."

Coming back from the kitchen, smiling, the host [said], "Would you like to hear a record or tape?"

He opened a large cabinet containing records and tapes.

"I'm a hi-fi fanatic," he said. "Constructed this set-up myself." And burbled on about sound reproduction as though switched on by the opening of the cabinet.

---

2 **Schoenberg:** Arnold Schoenberg, American composer and music theorist born in Austria who developed atonal composition.

3 *coq au vin:* A dish of chicken cooked in red wine.

She went over and knelt beside him in front of the cabinet. "About five hundred records and as many tapes." He handed her a catalogue.

"Done by your last research assistant?" she said playfully—it was indexed under title, composer, and musician.

"Oh no," he said, "myself—all my own work."

"How impressive."

"Not really—clerical, simply clerical."

She couldn't think of a record—the choice was too great. "I can't think," she said. "You select something."

"A tape?" he said. "Let's see—aboriginal music—actual field recording, how's that?"

"Field recording?"

"I was cook on a dig once."

"Dig? Cook?"

Her queries seemed imbecilic.

"Cook—sound recordist—pharmacist." He smiled at her. "I went with some of the Anthrop people—up North—fascinating—actually managed to get a superb collection."

He put on a tape.

They settled back in their chairs. She didn't know whether one talked during the field recordings. "May I talk?" she whispered, childlike, above the scrape and clack of the music.

Although there seemed plenty to talk about she had nothing to say.

"When's your book coming out?" she said after a longish pause.

"Which one?" he asked.

"I thought there was only one—*Drugs and Body Chemistry*."

"Oh, August," he said, "but I have another book—poems—a slim volume."

"You write poems?" she said, almost disbelieving.

"Yes, I'm no Holub,[4] but I have two slim volumes."

He went to the bookcase and pulled out a couple of books. He handed them to her, *Neutrons and Neurones—Poetic Explorations I-XII*, and *In Praise of the Epigamic—Collected Poems*. She opened them but her mind was still preoccupied with him and his atmosphere and she found she couldn't read. "I can't concentrate now," she said. "May I borrow them?"

"By all means," he said. "Better still," he jumped up, "let me present you with a copy of *Praise of Epigamic*."

"I love the title," she said, as he left the room.

He came back with a copy, autographed. He must have a stock of autographed copies for his lady visitors.

"But this one is different," she said, comparing it with the other, "it's a thicker and richer kind of paper."

---

4 **Holub:** Miroslav Holub, a Czech poet and writer, but also a practicing immunologist.

"Yes, if you look closely you'll see the binding's different too."

She examined it.

"I hand-printed it, hand-cut the paper, and hand-bound it."

"You did it yourself?"

"Yes," he said without boast, "I have a friend who has a printery—he taught me the rudiments."

"But it's beautifully done," she said.

"Thank you," he said.

"Fancy writing your own poems and then setting about printing and binding the book!"

He laughed. "This will amuse you too," he said. "I mix my own inks."

"No!" she said, marvelling. She looked again at the ink and saw that it was a delicate strange brown. "Well," she said, "too much," and then felt that not enough and added, "I'm impressed once again."

"You shouldn't be," he said. "It's simply a matter of following a recipe—as it happens a fifteenth-century recipe."

"Fifteenth century!"

"Little more than lampblack, iron, manganese oxides, linseed oil—the early inks are fairly stable—although modern inks probably have greater longevity—we don't know of course," he grinned, "superior compounding. I had most of the copies done with modern inks."

"Oh."

"Want another little surprise?" he said, boyishly.

"I don't know whether I can stand it."

"The paper—I made it—even pulped my own wood—sulphite—although it's mainly macerated old rags."

"I'm flabbergasted."

They sat there for a few seconds in silence. She could think of a hundred banal questions about how and why but stubbornly resisted asking them, perversely—she didn't want to be an interviewer. To further compliment him would be embarrassing for both of them. For one thing she was running out of natural compliments.

He mended the conversation by saying, "Have some cheese." She took a piece.

"I suppose you made the cheese too," she said, chomping hard as she caught the sound of it—worried that it carried the implication he was a tiresome boaster or that she resented his accomplishments. She willed that it didn't sound that way. He didn't show any offence.

"I didn't," he said; hesitated and smiled and said, "I do make cheese—it just so happens that it isn't mine."

Under her breath she said, oh no. She thought he might be joking and looked again at his face. He wasn't joking. He went to a board in his study containing carefully labelled keys and took down a key. "Come with me—I have some cheeses ripening."

He opened a three-quarter door under the stairway, switched on a light and, taking her hand, led her down the stone steps to the cellar.

"I hope I didn't sound offensive just then," she said, "about the cheese."

"About the cheese?" he said, puzzled.

"It doesn't matter," she said.

She loved the cellar. "This is a really authentic cellar—just how a cellar should be—stone steps, stone walls, cheeses ripening—oh, and racks of wine."

She didn't have to ask about the wine because she could see the bottling equipment and the wine press and stainless steel vats in a section at the far end.

"They're not cheeses," she said hesitantly, pointing at cylindrical moulds hanging from a frame.

"No, they're candles," he said, "I turn out my own—God knows why—both paraffin—stearic acid and tallow—I suppose it makes dinner party conversation."

"Here are my cheeses," he said, taking her to another part of the cellar, "still fairly green—that's Brick, sweetish type of cheese—and the rest are dull cheddars."

She didn't hear his description of the manufacture of cheese—she kept looking around and thinking, my God, he's buried his wife down here.

"I worry about tyrotoxicon—aptomaine—so far I'm still alive."

"It's rather cool down here," she said, moving towards the stairs. "Could we go up?" She didn't want to hear about the candles or the tyrotoxicon—she didn't want to be buried with his wife either. But she wasn't really scared; it was simply a game of nerves.

They went up the steps. He closed the cellar door, locked it, and switched off the light.

He still held her hand. How sweet, he liked it.

"I'd love a drink."

"Of course."

"Any other hobbies?" She wondered if "hobbies" was the correct word.

"Oh, I do a few other things to fill in the time," he said humorously.

Like strangling women. She laughed at herself.

He didn't offer to tell her what they were. But she knew she was obliged to ask although she felt she didn't really want to know. She might even enjoy saying something about herself—but there didn't seem anything to say—he was a hard act to follow. What else could she do?

She asked.

"For instance," he said, "I make my own furniture." She looked around and could see now that it was not factory furniture.

"How unobservant of me. Do you design it?"

"I design it—and also make the glues and the nails—I take the fact you didn't notice it as a compliment."

She looked at him.

"Did you say 'nails'?"

"The nails I make from iron ore—at a small foundry not far from here—a very low grade steel—but my own."

She must have had a why-for-Godsake look on her face.

He seemed to rush to tell her, "You see I like to follow a process right the way through—if it's a thing I eat, I want to grow it, harvest it, cure it or whatever. Usually it's not possible," he said disappointedly. "I have actually cut the timber for furniture—not this furniture—other pieces I've made . . ." He was scrutinising her and his voice was trailing as though he needed to be reassured that he didn't sound nutty.

"You don't think I'm . . ." he tapped his head.

She shook her head. "You made the mat then," she said, looking down at the coarse weave.

"Yes—that's a good case in point." He gathered new impetus. "I actually shore the sheep, spun the wool, dyed the wool, made the dyes."

"What about the machines—the tools—and so on that you use to make things—do you make those too?" It sounded as though she were trying to catch him out.

"Ha! now you've got me—but I have made some simple tools—and I made a spinning wheel—but lathes, no, electric drills, no, saws, no."

"You didn't build the house," she said looking around, laughing, almost out of control, almost rudely.

"No, I didn't build the house, but . . ."

She interrupted him, "Let me guess—you could if you wanted to—you know how."

Modestly, quietly, as though he'd gone too far, he said, "Back in the States I built a four-room sod cabin using the techniques of the pioneers—up in the Pine Cat Range. It leaked."

His first joke. She laughed and let herself fall back on the settee. "Another drink, please," she said, holding out her glass—noting that she was drinking quickly.

"I didn't make the whisky," he said, grinning.

"But you did back in the States—in the sod cabin."

"No," he chuckled, obviously pleased with his humour, "it's illegal—all the same I do have a corn mash still under construction—out the back in the workshop."

She giggled and giggled, shaking her head. "No—please—excuse me," she said, choking, "I can't help laughing—with admiration."

He knelt in front of her in quick unexpected movement. She stopped laughing instantly. Holding their empty glasses still in his hands he put his head on her lap. She had stiffened. "You're a very attractive woman," he said. "I want very much to impress you."

"You have," she said, embarrassed, wanting him to get up, unsettled by his sudden seriousness, "you have impressed me—and you're a very attractive man," she said, wondering if in fact he was, and sorry she couldn't do better than directly return his compliment, "a very attractive man."

She sensed he felt it time to make advances and to move towards sex.

"Will we take our drinks into the bedroom?" she said softly, trying to make it smooth—and in a way, to get it over with. She was as ready as she'd ever be.

He looked into her eyes, "I want to make a request."

She readied herself.

"I hope you have no objections," he said, perhaps fearfully but certainly determined to ask it, "and I hope you don't find it insulting."

"What is it?" she almost shouted.

Still staring into her eyes he said, "Would you take a bath with me?"

The request wasn't as odd as she'd feared. It was his possible motive which perturbed her—he was going to drown her and bury her with his wife.

"I don't mind," she answered, a little unsteadily. "Why?"

"I'm glad you will," he said, relieved, "I know it sounds a queer deal—but—I like to begin from the beginning."

"Oh."

"Are you with me?"

"More or less." Less than more.

He began to talk very quickly, trying to convince, "A bath is a symbolic beginning—a rebirth, so as to speak—we remove all connection with the everyday world—our clothes—and we wash away the traces."

He looked intently at her. "Odd?"

"I can follow you," she said, noncommittally.

He coloured. "I know it sounds odd."

"Oh no," she said, lying, but emotionally spellbound by the gregarious pipe-smoking associate professor from MIT on his knees struggling to gain her approval, captured briefly by his mesh of theories and practices. "It's just different," she added, for honesty.

"Good," he said, rising to his feet and guiding her up. "First, a taste of my wine—light red."

"Yes, I saw the equipment down in the cellar."

"I don't grow my own grapes—I buy them." They went to the kitchen. "I like to finish the evening with something of my own. Simple vanity."

In the kitchen he took down two wine glasses and took a bottle of red wine from a rack.

"The glasses!" she exclaimed, "of course—the glasses—they're home made—you made them."

"Yes, I blew them," he said.

He led her then into the bathroom. It was large with a large, almost square, almost Roman, bath—which could hold at least two people. "Why, this bathroom is fantastic," she said.

"I didn't make the tiles but I did design it," he said. "I very much wanted to build it—but really the only thing of mine is the towels."

He turned on the taps.

He coughed. "Could I take your clothes?"

"Oh yes," she said, swallowing the unnaturalness. She stripped. He stripped along with her.

He took her clothes and his and went out. He was going to burn them and keep her prisoner, she thought—or more likely he was going to fumigate them. Or do something kinky with her underwear.

He came back. "I use the tallow for both candles and soap," he said handing her a cake of yellow-brown soap, almost larger than her hand, "coconut oil—resin—the usual phosphates—and the rest—common household formula. I faintly odourised it with lavender and cassia."

She smelt it. "It smells positively caustic," she said, the cavernous bathroom making her sound like a small girl.

She felt bizarre standing beside the nude forty-year-old American professor, his hand on her arse, holding a cake of handmade soap. It made her think of Nazi prison camps.

"Shall we bathe?" He tried the water. "It's OK." They both went into the bath. He began to scrub her with the soap, quite hard. She simply sat there in a half slump. She did as she was told. He washed her as though she were a little girl—between the legs and under the armpits.

"Your hair, too," he said.

"My hair?"

"Just put it under the water, the soap makes an excellent shampoo." She wasn't so sure. She wasn't so sure about putting her head under the water with his hand on her neck.

She braced herself for a life or death struggle.

But he was gentle—and practised.

He complimented her on her body.

"Thank you," she said, aroused in a way by his scrubbing touch and his strong intention—aware that he knew precisely what he wanted to do with her and intended doing it.

After drying her with a coarse handwoven towel he took her upstairs to the bedroom where they lay down on the wide bed which she could see was hewn from logs. He lit a small oil lamp beside the bed. Her damp hair made her slightly uncomfortable.

She was relieved to see her clothes in the room—carefully folded and hung.

"Do you have trouble with orgasm?" he asked, softly.

God. She lay there irritated, without answering, disliking the question.

"I suppose not," she said, thinking that she'd never had to worry much about it.

"I mean do you take long? Should I wait for you?"

Not only was she embarrassed, she was affronted—did he have a questionnaire?—"I really don't know," she said, "I haven't timed myself." A little nastily.

"I don't mean to be embarrassing," he said, apologetically, "but I always think it's best to get these things out—out of the way."

He was stroking her legs with his hand and feeling her breast.

"You tell me when you're ready to climax," he said, "I'll wait for you."

She didn't speak. His strong sense of intention had frayed into a desperate effort to please. She was turned off.

"All right?" he asked.

"Yes," she said, closing her eyes, resigned to enduring it.

"Do you like breast stimulation?"

She didn't answer.

They fucked, she didn't relax and faked climax, telling him by sounds, she hoped, that she'd finished, although he kept saying, "You right? you right? you finished?," and to stop him she nodded and then he whispered, "That was great—was it great for you?"

She again nodded, keeping her eyes shut, and reaching blindly for cigarettes she'd put beside the bed.

He chattered for a while about the nature of orgasm; sexual difficulty; being candid about sex; and how few men and women knew women had orgasms. She didn't comment. She wondered how many women had lied to him about himself and about their reaction to him. What could you do?

She stubbed out her cigarette, feeling bad, and feigned sleep.

She was awoken in the morning by him doing his exercises on parallel bars at the far end of the room. He didn't say a word or smile or wink but kept solidly on. She watched him from the bed, dying for a cup of coffee.

When he finished he came over panting and sat on the edge of the bed. "Started," he panted, "on the 5BX—Canadian Air Force—have developed—my own—programme—a hybrid of yoga and Scandinavian gymnastics."

From a drawer beside the bed he took a book containing hand drawings of various exercise positions and tables—all lettered in his handwriting. "That's my programme," he said.

She could think only of coffee. "I don't even exercise—let alone have my own programme," she said. "I'm basically unhealthy," she said with barely concealed hostility.

He went to the kitchen and returned with herbal tea and meal porridge, hand ground—"See if you like these," he said.

She left half of both.

And as she smoked her second cigarette he said, "Well, how do you feel," anxiously, and she saw that the question was directed at her psyche, health, and mood all at once. As though he was saying, "How was I?"

"Oh, great," she said, not wanting to give any sort of analysis of the evening, not wanting to deceive him any more than she had to.

She washed with the home-made soap she now found repugnant, and dressed. They walked through the garden of the house.

"Would you have time to look at my observatory?" He pointed to a dome structure at the back.

"No, must rush, really, some other time," she said.

"Then there will be another time?" he said.

She'd trapped herself, "I do have a regular sort of thing with a boy," she said, as a way out, smiling.

"Then there won't be another time," he said, logically.

"Let's leave it to chance."

They walked for a distance without speaking.

"Do you find me a bore?" he asked.

She went on guard. She did. But what could you say? "But you're a very interesting man," she said, "a very accomplished man."

"My wife—just after we separated—said to me, 'The trouble with you, Hugo—you're a damn bore!'"

"That was a fairly destructive thing to say."

"It gave me a devastating insight—I was a damn bore."

She went to her bag for a cigarette.

"Her words are forever inscribed on my mind as a warning—and it permitted me to correct the fault—in your words I made myself, 'an interesting man.'"

They reached the gate.

The first personal statement made during the whole overnight visit or the months, in fact, that she'd worked with him. She had to get out before she felt she had to be honest with him. She had her own problems.

She kissed him on the cheek and said, "You are—you are a very interesting man—you must be a very fulfilled man." It sounded so formal. Too bad.

"But one needs more than that, one needs more, one needs a woman—about the place," he said, hopelessly, pleadingly, not only to her, perhaps not to her at all, but to all damn womanhood.

She nodded sympathetically. "I really must rush," she said, "I must be off. I must rush."

QUESTIONS

1. What is the nature of the relationship between the researcher and the professor at the beginning of the story? Give details from the story to support your answer.

2. How does the nature of the relationship change as the story progresses? Why does this happen?

3. How does the language and pace of the story reflect the moral milieu in which the story is told?

4. What is it about the American professor that puts women off him?

5. Can this tale be read as an allegory of American cultural hegemony? In what ways?

Of course, I want to know all about him. I don't even know his name. In Drysdale's picture he is a silhouette. A completely black figure. He could have been an Aborigine; by the late forties I understand some were employed as drovers.

But I rejected that.

I took a magnifying glass. I wanted to see the expression on his face. What colour is his hair? Magnified, he is nothing but brush strokes. A real mystery man.

It is my opinion, however, that he is a small character. See his size in relation to the horse, to the wheels of the cart. Either that, or it is a ruddy big horse.

It begins to fall into place.

I had an argument with our youngest, Kay, the other day. Both she and Trevor sometimes visit me. I might add, she hasn't married and has her mother's general build. She was blaming me, said people said mum was a good sort.

Right. I nodded.

"Then why did she scoot?"

"Your mother," I said thinking quickly, "had a silly streak."

If looks could kill!

I searched around—"She liked to paddle in water!"

Kay gave a nasty laugh, "What? You're the limit. You really are."

Of course, I hadn't explained properly. And I didn't even know then she had gone off with a drover.

Hazel was basically shy, even with me: quiet, generally noncommittal. At the same time, I can imagine her allowing herself to be painted so soon after running off without leaving even a phone number or forwarding address. It fits. It sounds funny, but it does.

This silly streak. Heavy snow covered Mt. Barker for the first time and we took the Austin up on the Sunday. From a visual point of view it was certainly remarkable. Our gum trees and stringy barks somehow do not go with the white stuff, not even the old Ghost Gum. I mentioned this to Hazel but she just ran into it and began chucking snowballs at me. People were laughing. Then she fell in up to her knees, squawking like a schoolgirl. I didn't mean to speak harshly, but I went up to her, "Come on, don't be stupid. Get up." She went very quiet. She didn't speak for hours.

Kay of course wouldn't remember that.

With the benefit of hindsight, and looking at this portrait by Drysdale, I can see Hazel had a soft side. I think I let her clumsiness get me down. The sight of sweat patches under her arms, for example, somehow put me in a bad mood. It irritated me the way she chopped wood. I think she enjoyed chopping wood. There was the time I caught her lugging into the house the ice for the ice chest—this is just after the war. The ice man didn't seem to notice; he was following, working out his change. It somehow made her less attractive in my eyes, I don't know why. And then of course she killed that snake down at the beach shack we took one Christmas. I happened to lift the lid of the incinerator—a black brute, its head bashed in. "It was under the house," she explained.

It was a two-roomed shack, bare floorboards. It had a primus stove, and an asbestos toilet down the back. Hazel didn't mind. Quite the contrary; when it came time to leave she was downcast. I had to be at town for work.

The picture reminds me. It was around then Hazel took to wearing just a slip around the house. And bare feet. The dress in the picture looks like a slip. She even used to burn rubbish in it down the back.

I don't know.

"Hello, missus!" I used to say, entering the kitchen. Not perfect perhaps, especially by today's standards, but that is my way of showing affection. I think Hazel understood. Sometimes I could see she was touched.

I mention that to illustrate our marriage was not all nit-picking and argument. When I realized she had gone I sat for nights in the lounge with the lights out. I am a dentist. You can't have shaking hands and be a dentist. The word passed around. Only now, touch wood, has the practice picked up to any extent.

Does this explain at all why she left?

Not really.

To return to the picture. Drysdale has left out the flies. No doubt he didn't want Hazel waving her hand, or them crawling over her face. Nevertheless, this is a serious omission. It is altering the truth for the sake of a pretty picture, or "composition." I've been up around there—and there are hundreds of flies. Not necessarily germ carriers, "bush flies" I think these are called; and they drive you mad. Hazel of course accepted everything without a song and dance. She didn't mind the heat, or the flies.

It was a camping holiday. We had one of those striped beach tents shaped like a bell. I thought at the time it would prove handy—visible from the air—if we got lost. Now that is a point. Although I will never forget the colours and the assortment of rocks I saw up there I have no desire to return, none. I realized one night. Standing a few yards from the tent, the cavernous sky and the silence all round suddenly made me shudder. I felt lost. It defied logic. And during the day the bush, which is small and prickly, offered no help (I was going to say "sympathy"). It was stinking hot.

Yet Hazel was in her element, so much so she seemed to take no interest in the surroundings. She acted as if she were part of it. I felt ourselves moving apart, as if I didn't belong there, especially with her. I felt left out. My mistake was to believe it was a passing phase, almost a form of indolence on her part.

An unfortunate incident didn't help. We were looking for a camp site. "Not yet. No, not there," I kept saying—mainly to myself, for Hazel let me go on, barely saying a word. At last I found a spot. A tree showed in the dark. We bedded down. Past midnight we were woken by a terrifying noise and lights. The children all began to cry. I had pitched camp alongside the Adelaide-Port Augusta railway line.

Twenty or thirty miles north of Port Augusta I turned back. I had to. We seemed to be losing our senses. We actually met a drover somewhere around there. He was off on the side making tea. When I asked where were his sheep, or the cattle, he gave a wave of his hand. For some reason this amused Hazel. She squatted down. I can still see her expression, silly girl.

The man didn't say much. He did offer tea though. "Come on," said Hazel, smiling up at me.

Hazel and her silly streak—she knew I wanted to get back. The drover, a diplomat, poked at the fire with a stick.

I said:

"You can if you want. I'll be in the car."

That is all.

I recall the drover as a thin head in a khaki hat, not talkative, with dusty boots. He is indistinct. Is it him? I don't know. Hazel—it is Hazel and the rotten landscape that dominate everything.

QUESTIONS

1. This story is based on a Henry Lawson short story written in the 1890s as well as a 1945 painting by Russell Drysdale. Why do you think there has been this continual fascination with this figure of the wife in Australian literature and art?

2. Is this a story that rejects the traditional Australian stereotypical values of the rugged Australian man and woman and manages to reassess the contemporary Australian woman? Explain your answer.

3. Why is the character of the drover neglected in this rendering of the story?

4. Bail is writing back to Lawson's story and Drysdale's painting. What are his intentions? Comment on the character of the narrator and his relationship with the family.

Peter Carey

(b. 1943)

Peter Carey is the son of a successful car dealer from Bacchus Marsh, Victoria; his birthplace provides the background for one of his most popular short stories, "American Dreams," as well as two of his more successful novels, *Illywhacker* (1985) and *The Tax Inspector* (1991). He was educated at both state and private schools, and the mixed expectations of the two distinct establishments made Carey's childhood difficult at times. In 1961, he began a degree in chemistry and zoology at Monash University in Melbourne, but lack of application and injuries from a car accident contributed to his dropping out during his first year. While working in an advertising agency, Carey met two Australian writers, Maurice Laurie and Barry Oakley, who introduced him to writings of William Faulkner, whose experimentation with language and novel form fascinated Carey.

He wrote several unpublished novels before leaving Australia in 1967 because of what he saw as a reactionary political and barren cultural landscape. From 1968 to 1970 he lived in London, where he was active in the literary counterculture. Back in Australia, he began working on his first published collection of short stories, *The Fat Man in History* (1974). This work contains his story "American Dreams," which demonstrates the corrupting influence of the capitalist ethic on a small Australian town, an ongoing concern in Carey's subsequent fiction. Carey, tired of his conventional lifestyle, moved to the bohemian Balmain section of Sydney, where he was soon involved with artists and intellectuals who were determined to change the conservative aspects of Australian cultural life.

By late 1977, Carey was living part time in a hippie community in the rain forest north of Brisbane, but keeping himself financially solvent working in advertising in Sydney. During this period, he published his second collection of stories, *War Crimes* (1979). The story of the same name that follows deals with gun-toting capitalist hippies who are sent out to make sure that the business runs smoothly and at maximum profit. There is no human consideration in this tale of lust and power.

Carey's first published novel, *Bliss* (1982), won several prestigious national awards; here again Carey chooses to satirize the business world and the cancer of a corrupt society whose values are based largely on those mirrored in capitalist ethics. *Illywhacker*, an epic novel of the last century of Australian history, was followed by perhaps Carey's most popular novel, *Oscar and Lucinda* (1988). His harshest criticism of contemporary society appears in *The Tax Inspector*, which tackles child abuse, capitalistic corruption, and the degeneration of social mores. He followed this with *The Unusual Life of Tristan Smith* (1994), a psychological study of an individual who struggles to cope with what Carey calls the "monsters within us." His novel *True History of the Kelly Gang* (2000) shows a writer at the apex of his career still willing to experiment with his fiction and able to excite the reader with imaginative recreations and new ways of seeing the expected and commonplace. His most recent novel is *My Life as a Fake* (2003).

War Crimes   *1979*

1.

In the end I shall be judged.

They will write about me in books and take care to explain me so badly that it is better that I do it myself. They will write with the stupid smugness of middle-class intellectuals, people of moral rectitude who have never seriously placed themselves at risk. They have supported wars they have not fought in, and damned companies they have not had the courage to destroy. Their skins are fair and pampered and their bellies are corseted by expensively made jeans.

They will write about me as a tyrant, a psychopath, an aberrant accountant, and many other things but it would never once occur to them that I might know exactly what I am doing. Neither would they imagine that I might have feelings other than those of a mad dog.

But they do not have a monopoly on finer feelings, as you shall soon see.

I cannot begin to tell you how I loathe them, how I have, in weaker moments, envied them, how I longed to be accepted by them and how at the first hint of serious threat from them I would not have the faintest qualms about incarcerating them all.

The vermin, may they feast on this and cover it with their idiot foot notes.

2.

The most elegant Barto was driving the car, a Cadillac Eldorado with leaking airconditioning. In a purple T-shirt and waist-length fur coat, he looked the very embodiment of sexual decadence; his shoulder-length raven hair, his large nose and chin made him as severely handsome as an Indian on a postage stamp.

Beside him, I felt graceless and boring. My trousers were shapeless and baggy. My hair was tangled and knotted, my glasses filthy, and my unshaven face looked pasty, patchy and particularly unhealthy. It was a face made to appear in the dock, a poor man's face, squinting nervously into the future.

I had filled the trunk of the Eldorado with an armory of modern weapons but I carried a small .22 under my arm. The .22 is a punk's weapon. It was my secret and I shared it with no one.

Barto kept a Colt .45 in the glove box. It was big and heavy and perfectly melodramatic. "If it doesn't scare the cunts to death we can always shoot them."

It was a hard time and only the most unconventional methods were succeeding in business. Certainly we didn't look like the popular image of businessmen. We were special. Once you appreciated the power we held, you could only be astonished at our cleverness. For me, my grubbiness had become a habit so long ingrained that it is difficult to think back to how it started or why it continued. But it was, finally, a perverse identification with the poor people I was raised amongst. Excepting the years when I was a young accountant, I have continued to wear the marks of my caste for they are stamped, not only on my face, but also on my poorly fed bones. No matter what rich clothes I wore, I would deceive no one. So I wear them proudly. They stink. The most casual observer will know that I am someone of great note: to dress like a beggar and be given the accord due to a prince. It was a costume fit for an age which had begun by proudly proclaiming its lack of regimentation and ended railing at its own disarray.

Unemployment had become a way of life and the vagabonds had formed into bands with leaders, organizations and even, in some cases, apocalyptic religions whose leaders preached the coming of the millennium. These last were as rare as threatened species, cosseted, protected and filmed by bored journalists eager for symbols of the times. The rest of the bands roamed the country, godless, hungry and unpublicized.

We saw only one group on the six-hundred-mile journey north. They were camped by a bridge at the Thirty-Two Mile Creek. As we approached they attempted to drag a dead tree across the road.

I felt Bart hesitate. The cowboy boot came back off the accelerator, making a stoned decision at eighty miles an hour.

"Plant it," I said. I said it fast and hard.

He planted it. The Cadillac responded perfectly. I heard the crunch of breaking wood. Tearing noises. Looking back I saw two bundles of rags lying on the road.

"Shit." The word was very quiet. I looked at Bart. He looked a little pale.

"How did it feel?"

He considered my question. "I don't know," he drawled out the words, beginning to luxuriate in the puzzle they contained, "just sort of *soft*. Sort of . . ." he furrowed his brow, "sort of did-it-happen, didn't-it-happen type of thing."

I leant into the back seat and pulled up a bag of dope and rolled an exceedingly large trumpet-shaped joint. The Cadillac devoured the miles while the faulty airconditioner dripped cold water onto Bart's cowboy boots, and I thought once again how genuinely strange our lives had become. I often stepped back and looked at myself from the outside. I was unthinkable to myself. Now I found it amazing to consider that only a week ago I had been making a most unconventional presentation to a highly conservative board of directors. The success of the presentation was the reason we were now heading north in this elegant motor car.

The board, of course, knew a great deal about us before we made the presentation. They were prepared for, and wanted, the unconventional. They expected to be frightened. They also expected to be given hope. Given their desire to believe in us, it would have been exceedingly difficult to do the presentation badly.

I dressed as badly as they would have expected me to, and spoke as arrogantly as they had been led to expect I would. There was nothing terribly original in the way we analysed the ills of the frozen meals subsidiary. It was simply professional, a quality that was lacking in the subsidiary's present management. We presented a market analysis, and pointed out that their company was in a unique position to take advantage of the present economic conditions. We presented a profit projection for the next twelve months and claimed a fee of half this figure, or whatever profit was finally delivered. If there was no profit we would ask for no fee. This money was to be delivered to us, in whatever way their lawyers could discover, tax free.

We demanded complete autonomy during those twelve months and asked the board's guarantee that they would not interfere.

It was not difficult to imagine that they would buy it. They were making heavy losses and we were obviously confident of making considerable profits. In addition I had two successes behind me: a pharmaceutical company and a supermarket chain, both of which had been rescued from the hands of the receivers and turned into profitable businesses.

When you kill flathead you put a knife in their foreheads. Their eyes roll and sometimes pop out. The marketing manager reacted in a similar manner when it occurred to him that he was being fired. His mouth opened wide with shock and I was reminded of a flathead when I looked at his eyes.

As with the fish, I found it necessary not to think too much about what I was doing. I consoled myself with the knowledge that there would have been no job for him if we had not arrived. He had been thorough enough to have destroyed any hope of his own survival. He had covered it from every angle.

With the marketing manager's departure I discovered a whole filing cabinet full of documents that he had withheld from me. As I examined them I felt like a surgeon who comes to remove a small growth and finds a body riddled with secondary cancers. I had promised the board of directors things which, given all the available information, had seemed reasonable at the time. But here the gap between the diseased body and my promises of glowing health seemed an inseparable gulf.

I began to feel that I might be less remarkable than the glorious picture the board had of me. When I had presented my credentials and broad methods to them I had felt myself to be quite glamorous, a superior being who could succeed where they and their underlings had failed. It was a good picture. I preened myself before it as if it were a mirror.

I claimed to despise the board but I didn't want that mirror taken away from me. It was very important that they hold me in high esteem.

Incensed by the appalling news we found in marketing, we recalled the sales force and threatened them with violence and torture if they did not succeed. I am thin and not particularly strong but I had a gun and I had the genuine craziness of a man who will do anything to get what he wants. Anger filled me like electricity. My fingertips were full of it. They felt so tight and tense I couldn't keep them still. Bart stood smoking a joint and waving the Colt around the office with the most carefree abandon, sighting down the barrel at first one head and then another. We spoke to them quietly and politely about the sales targets we expected them to meet in the coming year.

Whether through accident or design Bart let off a shot into the ceiling and the sales manager involuntarily wet his pants. His staff laughed out loud at his misfortune. I thought how ugly they looked with their big cufflinks and silly grins.

It was not the ideal way to do business, but the times were hard, other job opportunities non-existent, and the competition in the trade intense. Our products had been de-listed by five major chains and were in danger of being kicked out of another three. Only our cheapest lines survived, and these—frozen dinners of exceptionally low quality and price—would have to spearhead our return to the market. They were cheap and filling and there were a lot of people who needed cheap filling meals.

I gave Bart control of the marketing function and watched him nervously like a driver who takes his hands from the wheel but is ready to take it back at any serious deviation. Apart from twelve months as a trainee product manager with Procter and Gamble, Bart's previous experience had been totally in advertising agencies. There was really nothing but my intuitive judgement to say that he'd be a success in this new role.

I needn't have worried. He had a business brain the like of which is rarely seen, as cool and clean as stainless steel and totally without compassion. It was Bart who dumped two warehouses full of frozen food straight into the river, thus clearing a serious bottleneck in the system and creating space for products that could actually be sold. He budgeted for the $200 fine and spent another $200 on the finest cocaine to celebrate with. I approved these expenses without question. The goods had been sitting in the warehouse for two years and had been written down in value by a thoughtful accountant who seemed the only person to have anticipated the company's present plight.

Bart doubled the advertising budget, a move which terrified me but which I approved. He planned to drop advertising altogether in the second half and plough an equivalent amount into promotions. It was pressure-cooked marketing. It was unorthodox and expensive but it was the sort of brutal tactic that could be necessary for our success.

Bart pursued the practice of business with the logic of an abstract artist. Things were, for him, problems of form, colour and design. He pursued cool acts with relentless enthusiasm.

From my office I watched him walk across the wide bitumen apron to fire the production manager. His hair was now dyed a henna red, and his cowboy boots made his out-turned toes look curiously elegant. He walked as casually as a man who has run out of cigarette papers taking a stroll to a corner shop.

6.

The typists had stopped staring at us and were actually managing to get some work done. However I still continued to have trouble with my secretary. She was nearly forty-five, matronly in style, and as the secretary to the most senior executive, she was the leader of the others. She was pursuing some guerrilla war of her own, expressing her distaste for me in a hundred little ways which were almost impossible to confront directly.

On this occasion she found me alone in my office. I was sitting on the floor going through the computer print-outs from the Nielsen survey when she crept up behind me and hissed in my ear.

"May I have a word."

The bitch. She made me jump. I turned in time to catch the last sign of a smirk disappearing from her face.

I stood up. The idea of looking up her dress was beyond contemplation. I thought, as I stumbled to my feet, that I should fire her or at least exchange her with someone who could handle her. As she continued to disapprove of me she was making me more and more irritable. Yet she seemed able to bully me. I felt awkward and embarrassed every time I talked to her.

"I think," she declared, "there is something you should know."

"Yes." I put the Nielsen survey carefully on the desk. Her face was pinched and her lips had become tightly pursed. If there had been a smirk it had well and truly been superseded by this angry, self-righteous expression.

"I have come to tell you that I can't work for you." I felt enormously relieved. "I'm sorry to hear that," I said.

"I don't suppose you'd be interested in why."

"Yes, of course I would."

This would be her moment and I would pay attention. I did as she wished.

"I cannot respect you." Her sanctimonious little face gave me the shits.

"Oh," I said, "and why not?"

"Because you are not worthy of respect." She stood stiffly upright, tapping her lolly-pink suit with a ballpoint pen which was putting little blue flecks all over it.

"You don't respect yourself." She cast a derisive glance over me as if I were someone at the back door begging for sandwiches. So she didn't like the way I dressed. "You don't respect yourself, how can I respect you."

"Oh," I laughed, "I respect myself, please don't concern yourself on that one."

"You've obviously had a good education. Why don't you use it?"

She was beginning to push it a bit far. Her complete ridiculousness didn't stop her from upsetting me. I should have been beyond all this. "I'm your general manager," I said, "surely that's using my education."

She tossed her head. "Ah, but you're not the *real* general manager."

She shouldn't have upset me at all. Her values were nothing like mine. She was trapped and helpless and had to work for me. She had no education, no chance of change. All she had was the conviction that I was worthless. It shouldn't have upset me, but it is exactly the sort of thing that upsets me. The thing she wouldn't give me was the only thing I wanted from her. I felt my temper welling up.

"Do you realize the power I have over you?" I asked her.

"You have no power over me, young man."

She didn't understand me. She thought I was just a scruffy punk who had come to make a mess in her old boss's office. She couldn't know that I have a terrible character weakness, a temper that comes from nowhere and stuns even me with its ferocity and total unreasonableness.

She shouldn't have spoken to me like that, but she wouldn't stop. She wouldn't leave when I asked her to. I stood in my office and I asked the old bitch to leave. I asked her coolly and nicely and politely, but she continued to berate me.

I watched her mouth move. It became unreal. I had the .22 under my arm, and my feelings were not like the real world, they were hot and pleasurable and electrically intense.

It was rage.

She had just repeated herself. She had just said something about respect when I drew the pistol and shot her in the foot.

She stopped talking. I watched the red mark on her stockinged foot and thought how amazingly accurate I had been.

She sat on the floor with surprise and a slight grunt.

Barto came running through the door and I stood there with the gun in my hand feeling stupid.

Later the incident made me think about myself and what I wanted from life.

7.

The provincial city nearest the plant was a most unappealing place, catering to the tastes of farmers and factory hands. We devised, therefore, quarters of our own at the plant itself and managed to create a very pleasant island within the administration block.

Here a quite unique little society began to evolve, hidden from a hostile environment by dull red brick walls. Here we devoted ourselves to the pursuit of good talk, fanciful ideas and the appreciation of good music.

We introduced fine old Belouch rugs, rich in colour, others from Shiraz, Luristan, old Khelims, mellow and pleasant, glowing like jewels. Here we had huge couches and leather armchairs, soft and old and vibrating with the dying snores of retired soldiers, the suppleness of ancient leathers a delight to the senses. We had low, slow, yellow lights, as gentle as moonlight, and stereo equipment, its fidelity best evoked by considering the sound of Tibetan temple bells. The food, at first, was largely indifferent but the drugs and wine were always plentiful, of extraordinary variety and excellent quality.

In these conditions we marvelled at ourselves, that we, the sons of process workers and hotelkeepers, should live like this. We were still young enough to be so entranced by our success and Barto, whose father sold stolen goods in a series of hotels, was eager that a photograph be taken.

Barto seemed the most innocent of men. He approached life languidly, rarely rising before ten and never retiring before three. Ideas came from him in vast numbers and hardly ever appeared to be anything but wisps of smoke.

Lying on the great Belouch saddle bag, graceful as a cat in repose, he would begin by saying, "What if . . ." It was normally Bart who said "What if . . ." and normally me who said "yes" or "no." His mind was relentless in its logic, yet fanciful in style, so the most circuitous and fanciful plans would always, on examination, be found to have cold hard bones within their diaphanous folds.

We were all-powerful. We only had to dream and the dream could be made real. We planned the most unlikely strategies and carried them out, whole plots as involved and chancy as movie scenarios. It was our most remarkable talent. For instance, we evolved a plan for keeping a defecting product manager faithful by getting him a three-bag smack habit and then supplying it.

Our character judgment was perfect. We were delighted by our astuteness.

The product manager stayed but unfortunately killed himself a few months later, so not everything worked out as perfectly as we would have hoped.

We saw ourselves anew, mirrored in the eyes of each new arrival and we preened ourselves before their gaze.

Thelma was the first to arrive. She came to be with Bart and was astounded, firstly by the ugliness of the plant, secondly by the beauty of our private world, and thirdly by the change she claimed had occurred in Bart. She found him obsessed with the business enterprise and unbearably arrogant about his part in it. This she blamed me for. She sat in a corner whispering with Bart and I fretted lest she persuade him to go away with her. She was slender and elegant and dark as a gypsy. She had little needle tracks on her arms, so later on I was able to do a deal with her whereby she agreed to go away for a while.

Ian arrived to take over the sales force and we delighted in his company. He thought our methods of enthusing the salesmen historically necessary but not the most productive in the long term. He took them fifteen miles into town and got drunk with them for two days. He had two fist fights and, somewhere along the line, lost the representative for southern country districts, a point he continued to remain vague about.

He was the perfect chameleon and won them over by becoming vulgar and loud-mouthed. He affected big cufflinks and changed his shirt twice a day. He had his hair cut perfectly and he looked handsome and macho with his smiling dark eyes.

The sales force loved him, having the mistaken idea that he was normal. Naturally he didn't discuss his enthusiastic appetite for a substance called ACP, a veterinary tranquillizer normally administered to nervous horses which he took, rather ostentatiously, from a teaspoon marked "Souvenir of Anglesea."

It was Ian who persuaded me to fly in Sergei from Hong Kong. With his arrival, a huge weight was lifted from my shoulders and I had more time to relax and enjoy the music and talk. Sergei was unknown to me and I found him, in some respects, alarming. It was as if he found nothing remarkable in our situation. He made no comment on the decor of our private quarters, our penchant for drugs, or the brilliance of our strategies. It was as if we stood before a mirror which reflected everything but ourselves. He made me nervous. I didn't know how I stood with him.

Yet he was the most ordinary of men: short, slim, and dark, moving with a preciseness which I found comforting in such a skilled accountant. He was eccentric in his dress, choosing neatly pressed grey flannel trousers, very expensive knitted shirts, and slip-on shoes of the softest leather. Only the small silver earring on his left earlobe gave an indication that he was not totally straight.

Sergei talked little but went quietly about the business of wrestling with our cash flow. In the first week he completely reprogrammed our computer to give us a simpler and faster idea of our situation. Each week's figures would be available on the Monday of the next week, which made life easier for all of us.

After three weeks I gave over the financial function almost completely to his care and tried to spend some time evolving a sensible long-term strategy suited to the economic climate.

Whilst the unemployed continued to receive government assistance there would be a multi-million dollar business in satisfying their needs. Companies which should have had the sense to see this continued to ignore it. Obviously they viewed the present circumstances as some temporary aberration and were planning their long-term strategies in the belief that we would shortly be returning to normal market conditions.

My view was that we were experiencing "normal" market conditions.

I instructed our new product development team to investigate the possibility of producing a range of very simple frozen meals which would be extremely filling, could be eaten cold when cooking facilities were not available, and would be lower in cost than anything comparable. I had a series of pie-like dishes in mind but I left the brief open. It seemed like a golden opportunity.

Whilst I was engaged in this, word came from Ian that they had had a highly successful sell-in of our existing lines of frozen meals. He had given the trade substantial discounts and we were operating on very low profit margins, hoping to achieve a very high volume turnover and, more importantly, get our relationship with the trade back to a healthier state.

The telex from Ian was very short: "They love us till their balls ache. Sell-in is 180 per cent of forecast."

I looked out my window as Barto and Sergei walked towards the storeroom which hid the plant itself from my view. Bart's Colt now sat snugly in a hand-tooled leather holster he had spent the last few nights making.

Beside Bart's pointy-toed languid walk, Sergei looked as strict as a wound-up toy.

I watched them thoughtfully, thinking that they had the comic appearance of truly lethal things.

8.

My father lost his hand in a factory. He carried the stump with him as a badge of his oppression by factories. When I was very small I saw that my father had no hand and concluded that my hand would also be cut off when the time came. I carried this belief quietly in the dark part of the mind reserved for dreadful truths. Thus it was with a most peculiar and personal interest that I watched the beheading of chickens, the amputation of fox-terriers' tails, and even the tarring of young lambs. My fear was so intense that all communication on the subject was unthinkable. It would be done just as they had mutilated my cock by cutting off the skin on its head.

I envied my two sisters, who, I was sure, would be allowed to have two hands like my mother.

The factories my father worked in were many and various. I remember only their dark cavernous doors, their dull, hot metal exteriors, the various stinks they left

I got my arse out of the factory as fast as I could.

Bart met me at the door of the No. 2. "How's your nightmare?"

I was still in its grip. I was shaking and angry. "It's really shitty in there. It is *really* shitty."

Bart polished his cowboy boot, rubbing the right toe on the back of his left leg. "What are you going to do about it?" he asked, innocently enough.

A confession is a fart. You should never make a confession, no matter what dope you're on. "I'm not going to do anything, pig face. There's not a fucking thing to do, if I wanted to. That's what factories are like." My suede boots were soaked in muck. I flicked a pea off and watched it bounce across the bitumen.

"Listen," the word drawled out of Bart as slow and lazy as the kicking pointy-toed walk he was walking. The word was inquisitive, tentative, curious and also politely helpful. "Listen, do you think they hate you?"

"Yes." I said it before I had time to think.

"Well," the word came out as lazily as the "listen," "I'll tell you what I'll do in the next two months."

I grinned at him. "What'll you do, smart-arse?"

"I'll fucking make them love you, smart-arse, if that's what you want."

He was grinning delightedly, his hands in his back pockets, his great Indian face turned up towards the screaming sun as if he was drinking power from it.

"And how will you do that?"

"Delegate, delegate," he drawled, "you've got to learn to delegate. Just leave it to me and I'll fix it for you." He finished the conversation in my office. "Easy," he said, "easy-peasy."

9.

Almost without noticing it, we became quite famous. This gave me a lot of pleasure, but also disappointed me. You imagine it will amount to more, that it will feel more substantial than it is. This, after all, is the bit you've dreamed of in all the grubby corners of your life. It is almost the reason you've done what you've done. This is where the world is forced to accept you no matter what you wear, no matter what you look like, no matter what your accent is. You re-define what is acceptable. This is when they ask you for your comments on the economy and war and peace, and beautiful girls want to fuck you because you are emanating power which has been the secret of all those strong physiques which you lack, which you needlessly envied. This is what you dreamed about jerking off in your stinking hot bungalow, treasuring your two hands. It is what you told the red-mouthed naked girl in the *Playboy* pin-up when you came all over the glossy page, and what you wished while you wiped the come off the printed image, so as to keep it in good condition for next time.

The middle-class intellectuals were the first to discover us and we were happy enough to have them around. They came up from the south pretending they weren't middle class. They drank our wine and smoked our dope and drove around in our

Cadillac and did tours of the factory. They were most surprised to find that we dressed just like they did. We were flattered that they found us so fascinating and delighted when they were scandalized. In truth we despised them. They were comfortable and had fat-arsed ideas. They went to bed early to read books about people they would try to copy. They didn't know whether to love us or hate us.

We bought a French chef and we had long dinners with bottles of Chateau Latour, Corton, Chambertin, and old luscious vintages of Chateau d'Yquem. They couldn't get over the wine.

We discussed Dada, ecology, Virginia Woolf, Jean Paul Sartre, and the whole principle of making stacks of money and going to live in Penang or the south of France.

Occasionally we had rows on important issues and we normally resolved these by the use of violence.

The simplicity of this ploy struck me as obvious and delightful, yet they were too stupid to learn the lessons we could have taught them. They couldn't get past the style. They'd seen too many movies and hung around with too many wardrobe mistresses. They couldn't see or understand that we were no different from Henry Ford or any of the other punks.

We were true artists. We showed them the bones of business and power. We instructed them in the uses of violence. Metaphorically, we shat with the door open.

They learned nothing, but were attracted to the power with the dumb misunderstanding of lost moths. They criticized us and asked us for jobs.

Finally, of course, the media arrived and allowed themselves to be publicly scandalized by the contradiction in our lives.

The "Late Night" man couldn't understand why we kept playing "Burning and a-Looting" by Bob Marley and the Wailers. I can still see his stupid good-looking face peering at me while he said: "But how can you listen to that type of material? They're singing about *you*. They want to burn and loot *you*."

The television audience was then treated to the sight of Ian, stoned out of his head on horse tranquillizer, smiling blissfully without even the politeness to act uncomfortable.

"We are," he said, "the Andy Warhols of business."

In the first six months we had achieved almost 100 per cent distribution, increased sales by 228 per cent, introduced a new line of low-price dinners, and, as the seventh month finished, we began to look as if we might meet the profit forecast we had made.

We entertained the board of directors at a special luncheon. They were delighted with us.

10.

The camp fires of the unemployed flicker around the perimeter. Tonight, once more, their numbers have increased. They grew from three to six, to twenty. Now I choose not to count them. The unemployed have assumed the nature of a distinct and real threat. Yet they have done nothing. During grey days they have been nothing but poorly defined figures in a drab landscape, sitting, standing, concerned with matters I cannot imagine. They have done nothing to hamper trucks full of raw materials. Neither have they tried to intercept the freezer vans. Their inactivity sits most uneasily with their cancerous multiplication.

I can hear some of them singing. They sound like men on a bus coming home from a picnic.

The night buzzes with insects and great grey clouds roll across the sky, whipped across by a high, warm wind. Occasionally lightning flickers around the edge of the sky. Out in the scrub the mosquitoes must be fierce and relentless. It must be a poor feast for them.

Although the gate is guarded and the perimeter patrolled I have chosen to set up my own guard in this darkened window. It was not a popular decision. An open window makes the airconditioning behave badly. Sergei thinks that I am being an alarmist but I have always been an alarmist.

I have spent my life in a state of constant fear that could be understood by very few. I have anticipated disaster at every turn, physical attack at every instant. To be born small and thin and poor, one learns, very quickly, of one's vulnerability. My fear kept me in constant readiness and it also gave me fuel for my most incredible defence. My strength has been my preparedness to do anything, to be totally crazy, to go past the limits that even the strongest will dare to contemplate. The extent of my terrible quaking fear was in exact correspondence with the degree of my craziness. For I performed unthinkable acts of cruelty to others, total bluffs that would prevent all thought of retaliation.

I learnt this early, as a child, when I got my nose busted up by a boy four years older and much, much bigger. I can still remember the bastard. He had wire-framed glasses and must have been blind in one eye because he had white tape obscuring one lens. I can remember the day after he bashed me. I can remember as if it were yesterday. I waited for him just around the side of the Catholic Church. There was a lane there which he always walked down and beside the lane was a big pile of house bricks, neatly stacked. I was eight years old. I waited for the bastard as he came down the lane kicking a small stone. He looked arrogant and self-confident and I knew I couldn't afford to fail. As he passed me I stood up and threw the first brick. It sounded soft and quiet as it hit his shoulder, but I'd thrown it so hard it knocked him over. He looked round with astonishment but I already had the second brick in the air. It gashed his arm. He started crying. His glasses had gone. They were on the ground. I stood on them. Then I kicked him for good measure.

The effectiveness of this action was greatly enhanced by the fact that I had been seen by others. It helped me get a reputation. I built on this with other bricks and great lumps of wood. I cut and burned and slashed. I pursued unthinkable actions with the fearful skill and sensitivity of someone who can't afford to have his bluff called. I developed the art of rages and found a way to let my eyes go slightly mad and, on occasions, to dribble a little. It was peculiar that these theatrical effects often became real. I forgot I was acting.

But there was no real defence against the fires of the unemployed. They were nothing more than threatening phantoms licking at the darkness. My mind drifted in and out of fantasies about them and ended, inevitably, with the trap corridors of a maze, at the place where they killed or tortured me.

Below me Bart was sitting on the steps. I could hear him fiddling with his weapon. All week he has been working on a new, better, hand-tooled leather holster. Now it is finished he wears it everywhere. He looks good enough for the cover of *Rolling Stone.*

The unemployed are singing "Blowing in the Wind." Bart starts to hum the tune along with them, then decides not to. I can hear him shifting around uncomfortably, but there is nothing I can say to him that would make his mind any more at ease.

The unemployed will have the benefit of their own holy rage.

It is difficult to see across the plant. The spotlights we rigged up seem to create more darkness than light. I stare into the darkness, imagining movements, and thinking about my day's work. Today I went through the last three months' cost reports and discovered that our raw material costs are up over 10 per cent on eight of our lines. This is making me edgy. Something nags at me about it. I feel irritable that no one has told me. But there is nothing that can be done until tomorrow.

The movement across the face of the No. 1 store is vague and uncertain. I rub my eyes and squint. Below me I can hear Bart shift. He has taken off his boots and now he moves out towards the No. 1, sleek as a night cat, his gun hand out from his side like a man in a movie. I hold my breath. He fades into almost-dark. The figure near the No. 1 stops and becomes invisible to me. At that moment there is a shot. The figure flows out of the dark, dropping quietly like a shadow to the ground.

I am running down the stairs and am halfway across the apron before Bart has reached the No. 1. I pray to god he hasn't shot a guard.

"Not bad, eh? That's about fifty yards."

I don't say anything. He is fussing over his gun, replacing the dead shell with a live bullet. I let him walk ahead. I'm not going to get any fun out of this. He walks forward, as nonchalant as if he were going to change a record or go and get another drink.

I see his flashlight turn on and then a pause as he kneels to look at the body. And then the light goes out and he is running around and around in circles. He is yelping and running like a dog whose foot has been run over. As he circles he says, "Shit, Shit, Shit, oh fucking Christ." He looks comical and terrible dancing in his bare feet. He can't stay still. He runs around saying shit.

Then I am looking at the body. In the yellow light of my flashlight I see the face of a sixteen-year-old boy. I notice strange things, small details: golden down on the cheeks, bad pimples, and something else. At first, in dumb shock, I think it's his guts coming up. And a pea rolls out. In his mouth is a chunk of TV dinner, slowly thawing.

11.

When I was six years old I threw a cat into an incinerator. It wasn't until the cat came running out the grate at the bottom, burning, screaming, that I had any comprehension of what I had done.

The burning cat still runs through my dreams searing me with its dreadful knowledge.

When I saw the dead boy I knew it was Bart's burning cat.

He is like the girls in *Vogue,* wearing combat clothes and carrying guns and smoking pink cigarettes. He is like the intellectuals: he lives on the wrong side of the chasm between ideas and action. The gap is exactly equal to the portion of time that separates the live cat from the burning cat.

That is the difference between us.

It should be said to him: "If you wear guns on your hip you will need to see young boys lying dead at your feet and confront what 'dead' is. That is what it takes to live that fantasy. If you cannot do this, you should take off your uniform. Others will perform the unpleasant acts for you. It is the nature of business that as a result of your decisions some people will starve and others be killed. It is simply a matter of confronting the effects of your actions. If you can grasp this nettle you will be strong. If you cannot, you are a fool and are deluding yourself."

12.

Our burning cats are loose.

Bart's is sedated, slowed down, held tightly on a fearful leash by Mandies or some other downer. Perhaps he has been shooting up with morphine. His eyes are dull and his movements clumsy but his cat stirs threateningly within him, intimidating him with its most obvious horror.

My cat is loose and raging and my eyes are wide. Black smoke curls like friendly poison through my veins and bubbles of rage course through my brain. My cat is clawing and killing, victim and killer. I am in an ecstasy. I can't say. My eyes stretch wide and nostrils, also, are flaring.

Oh, the electricity. The batteries of torches firing little hits of electricity behind the eyes. To stretch my fingers and feel the tautness behind the knuckles like full sails under heavy wind.

For I have found out.

I have discovered a most simple thing. The little bastard Sergei has been cheating me in such a foolish and simple way that I cannot contain my rage at the insult to my intelligence. He has been siphoning funds like a punk. A dull stupid punk without inventiveness. He is someone trying to club a knife-fighter to death. He is so stupid I cannot believe it.

Ah, the rage. The rage, the fucking rage. He has no sense. He hasn't even the sense to be afraid. He stands before me, Bart by his side. Bart does not live here. He is away on soft beds of morphine which cannot ease his pain. Sergei is threatening. He is being smart. He thinks I'm a fool. He casts collusive glances towards Bart who is like a man lobotomized. Smiling vaguely, insulated by blankets of morphine from my rage, like a man in an asbestos suit in the middle of a terrible fire.

Oh, and fire it is.

For the cost of raw materials has not risen by 10 per cent. The cost of raw materials has not risen at all. Sergei, the fool, has been paying a fictitious company on his cheque butts and using the actual cheques to both pay the real suppliers and himself.

I only do this for the profit, for the safety, for the armour and strength that money gives. That I may be insulated from disaster and danger and threats and little bastards who are trying to subvert my friends and take my money.

And now there will be an example.

For he is trying to place me in a factory. He is trying to take my power. He shall be fucking well cut, and slashed, and shall not breathe to spread his hurt.

He is smart and self-contained. He speaks with the voice of the well-educated and powerful. His eyebrows meet across his forehead.

It took me three hours to trace his schoolboy fiddle. And it only took that long because the bastards who were doing the company's search took so long to confirm that the company he's been writing on his cheque butts doesn't exist. It took me five minutes to check that his prices were inflated. Five minutes to guess what he was up to.

The body of Bart's victim has been tied to the top of the perimeter fence. Let that warn the bastards. Even the wind will not keep down the flies. The unemployed shall buzz with powerless rage.

And now Sergei. An example will be made. I have called for his suit and his white business shirt and black shoes. The suit is being pressed. The shoes are being polished. It will be a most inventive execution, far more interesting than his dull childish cheating.

Under my surveillance his hair is being cut. Very neat. He is shaved cleanly. He is shaved twice. The poor idiot does not know what is happening. Bart watches with dumb incomprehension, helping the girl who is cutting the hair. He holds the bowl of hot water. He brings a towel. He points out a little bit of side-burn that needs trimming better. He is stumbling and dazed. Only I know. I have Bart's gun, just in case.

The suit is pressed. Bart helps with the tie. He fusses, tying and re-tying. Sergei's eyes have started to show fear. He tries to talk casually to me, to Bart. He is asking what is happening but Bart is so far away that his mind is totally filled with the simple problem of tying the tie, its loops and folds provide intricate problems of engineering and aesthetics.

I never liked Sergei. He never treated me with respect. He showed disdain.

I will donate him a briefcase. I have a beautiful one left me by the old general manager. It is slim and black with smart snappy little chrome clips on it. In it I place Sergei's excellent references and about five hundred dollars worth of cash. It is a shame about the money, but no one must ever think him poor or helpless.

I order him to hold the briefcase. He looks so dapper. Who could not believe he was a senior executive? Who indeed!

It is time now for the little procession to the gate. The knowledge of what is happening hits Sergei on this, his walk to the scaffold. He handles it well enough, saying nothing I remember.

High on the wire the dead boy stands like a casualty of an awkward levitation trick.

I have the main gate opened and Sergei walks out of it. The guards stand dumbly like horses in a paddock swishing flies away. I am watching Bart's eyes but they are clouded from me. He has become a foreign world veiled in mists. I know now that we will not discuss Kandinsky again or get stoned together. But he will do what I want because he knows I am crazy and cannot be deceived.

He seems to see nothing as the great wire mesh gate is rolled back into place and locked with chains. Sergei walks slowly down the gravel road away from us.

A grey figure slides out from the scrub a mile or so away. They will welcome him soon, this representative of management with his references in his briefcase.

The fact of Sergei's execution could not possibly be nearly as elegant as my plan. I return to my office, leaving the grisly reality of it to the watchers at the gate.

13.

In the night they put Sergei's head on the wire. It stares towards my office in fear and horror, a reminder of my foolishness.

For now it appears that I misunderstood the situation. It appears that he was acting on Bart's instructions, that the siphoned funds were being used to rebuild the inside of the factory.

To please me, dear god.

How could I have guarded against Bart's "What if . . ." or protected us all from his laconic "easy-peasy"? If one lives with dreamers and encourages their aberrations something is bound to go wrong. Now I understand what it is to be the parent of brilliant children, children reared with no discipline, their every fantasy pandered to. Thus one creates one's own assassins.

The factory tour is over now and Bart sits in my office eyeing me with the cunning of a dog, pretending servility, but with confused plans and strategies showing in his dog-wet eyes.

He understood nothing of factories nor my fear of them. His model factory is a nightmare far more obscene than anything my simple mind could have created.

For they have made a factory that is quiet. They have worried about aesthetics.

Areas of peaceful blue and whole fields of the most lyrical green. In these ideal conditions people perform insulting functions, successfully imitating the functions of midtwentieth century machinery.

This is Bart and Sergei's masterpiece, their gift to me. They have the mentality of art students who think they can change the world by spraying their hair silver.

They make me think of other obscenities. For instance: a Georg Jensen guillotine made from the finest silver and shaped with due concern for function and aesthetic appeal. Alternatively: condemned cells decorated with pretty blue bunny patterns from children's nurseries.

In order to achieve these effects they have reduced profit by 6.5 per cent.

In here it is very quiet. No noise comes from the staff outside. I have seen them, huddled together in little groups at the windows staring at Sergei. They seem anesthetized. They have the glazed eyes of people too frightened to see anything that might get them into trouble. Thus they avoided Bart's eyes. He pranced through like a spider, his hand on his gun, the fury in his veins bursting to fill the room like black ink in water.

Now in the silence of my office I see the extent to which he is afflicted by hurt and misunderstanding. Trying to talk to him, I put my hand on his arm. He flinches from me. In that terrible instant I am alone on the pack ice, the string inside me taut and all that lonely ice going in front of me no matter which way I turn. And he, Bart, looking at me guilty and afraid and angry and does he want to kill me?

Yes, he does.

He will learn to use his burning cat. He hates me because I killed his friend. It was a misunderstanding. It was his fault, not mine. If they hadn't cheated I would never have made the mistake. His friend Sergei, the little turd, he thought he was clever but he was a fool. Sergei, his stupid mouth dribbling black blood on the top of the wire fence. If only his siphoning of funds had been more subtle. There were two other ways to do it, but he did it like a petty-cash clerk. It was this which upset me the most. It was this which put me over the line and left me here, alone, threatened by the one person I thought my friend.

He may wish to kill me.

But I, alone on the ice, have eyes like the headlights of a truck. I have power. I will do anything. And I have made enough bad dreams that one more dying face will make not the slightest scrap of difference. Anyone who wants to cling onto their life won't fuck around with me too willingly, though their hand might easily encircle my wrist, though they have the strength to crush me with their bare arms, for I am fearful and my fear makes me mighty.

And I am not mad, but rather I have opened the door you all keep locked with frightened bolts and little prayers. I am more like you than you know. You have not inspected the halls and attics. You haven't got yourself grubby in the cellars. Instead you sit in the front room in worn blue jeans, reading about atrocities in the Sunday papers.

Now Bart will do as I wish for he wishes to live and is weak because of it. I am a freight train, black smoke curling back, thundering down the steel lines of terrible logic.

So now I speak to him so quietly that I am forcing him to strain towards me. Trucks have been destroyed attempting to enter the plant. It is time, I tell him, that the scrub be cleared of unemployed.

It will give him something to do. It will give him a use for his rage. He can think about his friend, whom I didn't kill. He was killed by the people in the scrub, whoever they are. They are the ones holding up trucks and stopping business, and business must go on. BUSINESS MUST GO ON. That is what the hell we are here for. There is no other reason for this. This is the time that is sold to the devil. It is time lost, never to be re-lived, time stolen so it can be OK later and I can live in white sheets and ironed shirts and drink gin and tonic in long glasses, well away from all this.

Then I can have the luxury of nightmares, and pay the price gladly, for it will only be my sleep which will be taken and not my waking hours as well.

14.

All around the plant seemed very, very still. The sun had gone down, leaving behind a sky of the clearest blue I had ever seen. But even as I watched, this moment passed and darkness claimed it.

I watched Bart lead his contingent of workers through the dusk in the direction of the front gate. Each man had a flamethrower strapped to his back and I smiled to think that these men had been producing food to feed those whom they would now destroy.

I watched the operation from the roof of the canteen, using binoculars Sergei had left behind.

As I watched men run through the heat burning other men alive, I knew that thousands of men had stood on hills or roofs and watched such scenes of terrible destruction, the result of nothing more than their fear and their intelligence.

In the scrub the bodies of those who hated me were charred and smouldering.

I touched my arm, marvelling at the fineness of hairs and skin, the pretty pinkness glowing through the fingernails, the web-like mystery of the palm, the whiteness underneath the fore-arm and the curious sensitivity where the arm bends.

I wished I had been born a great painter. I would have worn fine clothes and celebrated the glories of man. I would have stood aloft, a judge, rather than wearily kept vigil on this hill, hunchbacked, crippled, one more guilty fool with blood on his hands.

QUESTIONS

1. What is this story allegorizing?

2. What are the roles of the employed and unemployed in this story?

3. What is the story's attitude toward capitalism and capitalistic ethics?

4. How do Barto and the narrator manage to succeed in this postapocalyptic industrial madness?

5. How reliable is the narrator in this story? Examine the opening and closing in particular.

Barry Hill

(b. 1943)

Barry Hill was born in Melbourne and educated at the University of Melbourne. Like many Australian writers, he moved to London in his twenties, where he worked as an educational psychologist, earned an MA in philosophy, and worked on the *Times Educational Supplement*. In 1972, he returned to Melbourne as founding education editor at *The Age*. He left the paper in 1975 to write full time, but continued as the paper's radio critic for fifteen years. His first book was *The Schools* (1977); his first fiction, *A Rim of Blue*, appeared in 1978. He has written two novels along with two collections of short stories, and his short fiction has been widely anthologized. In recent years, he has focused on writing poetry (his three poetry collections include his prize-winning *Ghosting William Buckley* [1993]). Most recently, his *Broken Song: T. G. H. Strehlow and Aboriginal Possession* (2002), a study concerning the poetics of translation and social history, won many of the major literary awards in Australia. Described as "a landmark event in Australian High Culture," the book's appearance brought to a close Hill's preoccupation with central Australia and its strong postcolonial themes.

He is poetry editor of *The Australian* as well as a postdoctoral fellow at the University of Melbourne, where he has taught part time. He is still a full-time writer, lives in Queenscliff on the south coast, and is currently working on *Naked Clay*, a book of poems in response to the work of Lucian Freud.

Sitting In (1992), which won the 1992 N.S.W. Premier's Award for Nonfiction, deals with one of Australia's major industrial disputes at a petrochemical works during 1979 and 1980. It is perhaps Hill's most powerful work. He uses a mixture of autobiography, fictionalization, political essay, and history to track the implications of the sit-in on people, like his father, who were directly involved. *Sitting In* is set in a working-class community and describes the dispute between labor and management in the factory, which was mostly over working conditions. In Hill's hand, however, the study emphasizes that the dispute was not simply a local issue, but a commentary on the different priorities between industry and communities over environmental and economic welfare.

The short story that follows, "Lizards," is an early inquiry into environmental issues and their political implications. The first version of the story was published in *London Magazine* and then appeared in Hill's *Headlocks and Other Stories* (1983). Later, it was reworked for the first chapter of *Sitting In*. It is clearly one of the most probing accounts of the way in which partisan politics impose themselves on individual families in the industrial suburbs of most Western nations. Idiomatically, the story is fully within the Australian realistic tradition, but philosophically, with its use of Gramsci's *Prison Letters*, it gestures toward European political theory and gender issues of confinement.

Lizards

They were easy enough to find. You only had to lift a rock in the stone wall and there they were: or there was one at least—flat as a tack, an eye watching, legs in that dancing position, like a frog about to leap, except that lizards seldom leap, they dart, sliding off and out and under. You have to be really quick; I had no trouble catching half a dozen in a Saturday afternoon.

Most of the kids chucked them away before we got home; or they let them go on the spot, since catching lizards wasn't much compared to catching snakes, which we were also after, moving around the stone walls as far as the coal dump, then out behind it onto the swampy part of the flats. Our house, in those days, was on the edge of the flats. I kept lizards because I liked them; I was not that keen on the big ones that reminded you of goannas,[1] their pale bellies pulsing and swollen as if they'd been drinking too much beer as they lay in the sun, but the slim quick ones as long as your finger, I tucked into my pocket, or carried home in a brown paper bag. They seemed quite happy travelling there, in the folds of things, and when I showed them to mum and dad I had that nice feeling which comes from being proprietorial and kind.

I especially liked taking them into our front room when people were there. On Saturdays dad was usually talking with his union mates and members of the party. They were big blokes mostly (or they seemed to be at the time)—boilermakers, blacksmiths, welders, filling up our armchairs. They could talk those men, and to listen to some of them there you might have thought they were standing on boxes in the back yard: but when I came in with the lizards they went quiet, and grinned, and asked if they could have a look.

I held up my favourite. The best way to hold a lizard is just below the skull, towards the back of its head rather than low down near the throat. When you're not squeezing its gizzard it can look at its audience quite comfortably.

Give it a run, someone said, as if he was unhappy with the idea of anything being held in captivity.

No, I'd say, it's not ready yet. What I meant was that it would run under his chair and try to get into the fringe of the mat. It would be hard to get out again, and mum would go crook.

Let's have a go, he said, reaching towards the lizard.

I backed off a bit. I don't want it to drop a tail, I explained.

Fair enough, mate.

They were all pretty pleased with this and went on talking. I could hear mum in the kitchen, coughing, and moving about getting the cups and saucers. I sat down on the floor, slipping the lizard up under my collar. I felt it wriggle to the back of my neck, and settle down to doze, apparently soothed by the growling tones of the conversation.

---

1 **goannas:** A type of lizard.

There was a war on, I knew that much. The newsagent was selling a beaut new comic called "Marines," and one copy my dad had held up to his mates, saying, "propaganda." They had shaken their heads and the comic was passed back to me. I remember reading it in a fresh light then; I could see that the Yanks couldn't be as good as all that, even though the drawings were the best I'd seen. Yet each week the comic seemed to have more rather than less pages for the same price.

I listened to them talk about the war, and I heard them speculate on the possibilities of the General getting permission to drop the bomb. There were no comics, as yet, about the bomb; or, if it came to that, about the banning of the party. As I understood it, the Government wanted to lock up people like my dad and his mates, and if they didn't watch out it would happen soon, while no one else gave a damn.

Most people don't care, one way or the other, someone said. Capitalism has it in the bag.

Oh yes they do, it's a matter of people being brought into the picture, becoming part of the struggle.

Let's hope so, I heard my father say, as the tea was served.

As much as a boy of that age could, I worried too. A disciple, I entered into their disgruntlements, and the tension and determination that went into their conversation made me feel satisfied rather than unhappy; it gave me a sense of self-assurance, as if an important part of me could afford to stretch out and be comfortable against the body of their opinion. Even today, I think that I owe a good deal of myself to the strength and warmth that inhabited the room, though the odd thing was that there was an undercurrent to their conversation which made me think of crabs rather than lizards.

The crabs we used to hunt at the back beach. We tied cat's meat to a length of string and when the tide was out fished the crabs out from beneath the rock ledges. As soon as a claw took hold of the meat you pulled it up, flicking the crab onto the dry rock. Then with the knife you stabbed the crab through the back; there was an explosion of sea water and flesh, and the crab was grounded. Some of us had spears—bamboo with scrap metal as tips, which we used as well, crushing through the shells as near to dead centre as possible, swearing and screaming at the crab as we did.

It was interesting the way we carried on like that. I remember using words that I was not going to use freely again until I'd grown up, but somehow, leaping and dancing about the broken shells, it seemed the right thing to do, a way of making up for the creatures being so well defended, and otherwise so inaccessible. Since so much that worried my dad and his mates was invisible and intractable, I suppose I felt that some purpose might be served by yelling a lot, and tearing into things, though at the time, I was incapable of making this connection clear to myself, or to anybody else.

In any case I had come to prefer lizards. I liked their silkiness, their liquid movements and their apparent adaptability, and I had been pleased to leave the crabs rotting in the sun, despite the fact that if I'd brought them home alive dad would have cooked them in a pot and eaten them as a treat—as chicken was then a treat, and pork. Lamb was not a treat as we had it hot every Sunday and for the following two nights ate it cold with plenty of pickles. The point is, I didn't care for delicacies so much as keeping things that seemed to invite a secure alternative to what they had known, and which seemed able to survive in the conditions I was able to provide myself.

The box I built for the lizards was about three feet long with wire netting on top. Beneath the wire were rocks, weeds, sand, clay soil—an attractive and varied landscape, with a lake as its centre. This was the top of a jam jar filled with water from the gully trap. From the army of ants at the base of the gully trap it was a simple matter to ambush provisions for the lizards; flies were harder to get, but you could raid the cobwebs in the back of the tool shed. All food was placed into the nooks and crannies of the lizard's garden, and for ages it puzzled me as to why they seemed to have very little appetite.

At school, my lizard for the day was transferred from pocket or collar to another box: the pencil case which sat on the edge of my desk. It seemed happy enough in there. Occasionally, when we were not flat out putting our hands up to answer questions, I gave it a run on top. It would make a dart for the aisle and was checked with a ruler when it dipped its tongue into the inkwell, I would, for its own good pull it back then before it got too frisky, I put it back in the case—though never, never, before showing it to Mary, the girl who sat right in front of me.

Mary had long blonde hair that hung down her back as far as my pencil case, and when I chose to fiddle about in that area the tips of her hair touched my knuckles.

Look, I'd say. She was the first girl I ever wanted to show anything to.

I can see, she replied. She was not frightened. I was not trying to scare her as some kids would.

Does it have a name?

Nup.

It looks sick, she said.

It did too, now that she came to mention it. At recess time I let it run along the wet bottom of the tap troughs. Afterwards I gave her another look.

You're torturing it, she said. The comment hurt me deeply, and made me realize, much later, how much I'd been in love with her. She had given me my first experience of hopes dashed. At the time it struck me that the word torture was vicious and unjust, entirely unsuited to my best intentions, and I had as much trouble getting to grips with it as my dad and his mates were having with terms like purge, and slave labour camp. It was a word that I found impossible to accept, until, one by one, my lizards began to die. I'd open the garden box, lift a stone, and there another would be—dead, and wizzened looking. I imported new batches but they went as well. Then Stalin died too, and I could see that my dad was having to do a lot of thinking about that. My box had become pungent and rank, as if disappointment, or folly, had developed a special smell of its own. Mum helped me clean the box out: in the end I gave lizards away, and threw myself into that enterprising schoolground sport of marbles.

We give up one thing, we take up another, something is cleared away, something else takes its place: life seems to be like that. In the years I was going through school, from primary school into high school, moving past the Merit Certificate that had been the stopping post for my father and his mates, the stone walls out on the flats were being taken down, thistles cleared away, the swamps drained and cranes and wild duck driven off. Lizards and snakes moved west as the great paddocks were bought up and sold for factory allotments. One day a leaflet appeared in our letter box saying that the sky at night would take on an orange glow: we were not to be alarmed at this, the leaflet said, as the new cloud was harmless. A refinery was to be built, and a refinery had to burn off its waste.

The construction of the refinery was followed by a plant to produce carbon black: then another which turned out polyethylene and styrene; and another which extracted chemicals from the by-products of its neighbours. A petrochemical complex as big as any in the world had grown up, the affairs of which were directed from boardrooms as far as Kansas City and London, places I had read about in books. There was something remote and grand about the gleaming assembly of pipes and tanks that roared and hissed all day and all night, ejecting their flames, invisible heat, and unnameable gases into the sky.

The landscape was becoming, now that I think of it, more political, but the strange thing was that in so many other ways our life was not. Over many weekends dad spent his time building a garage to house and protect our first car. We already had a refrigerator, and mum had enough money left out of housekeeping to layby a washing machine. In the old days, when I left my towel at the beach, I got into trouble: there were now plenty of towels to go round which meant that, my anxiety lowered, I seldom left a towel or anything else behind. In fact in most respects this was an orderly, forward-looking period, where talk about the days when people had to battle for a decent living, while it was interesting in a way (and was written up in some of our history books), was not the sort of information you needed to base a decision on. We were eating chicken once a week, I was getting on well at school and mum and dad were going to keep me there until I had gone as far as I could go—so while none of these things were planned, they kept happening, they evolved, enemy or no enemy.

Oh, there *was* an enemy all right, I still felt that. At school I spent a lot of time defending, or being seen to defend, moves to oust the agents provocateurs in Hungary, the liberation of Tibet from feudalism, and the assaults from all fronts upon our unions, the unions which some of dad's mates were now working for full time, having responded to suggestions that organization at levels other than the shop floor was necessary. The enemy was the mis-representer of the truths I had carried within me for so long, and I saw no reason why people should get away with mutilating them. I was an energetic protagonist, sometimes lying low and making quick, attacking runs on an argument; sometimes using crab hunting strategies. These habits I carried from school to university, through election campaigns and into the movement against the next war in Asia, the war that never ceased to remind me of the one dad and his mates had worried about when I was a boy. Now we—two or three

She has been going down for a number of years. Her lungs, her heart, the circulation of her blood, are cracking up. Most of all her lungs are failing her, and it is all she can do, some days to prepare a meal. The most ego-less person I know, self-denying to a fault, has difficulty walking from the oven to the kitchen table, and when she gets as far as the garden she inhales, as best she can, the air of our neighbourhood: with what she has working of the wretched sacks in her chest, she takes in the output from our petrochemical complex.

Her throat and neck have become swollen from the exertion of breathing. Her face is ruddy, blotched and puffy, and even describing her like this makes me wince on her behalf, for her despair at the disintegration of her looks. She would prefer to have no face at all. Already she has known degrees of self-loathing that would send most men to their graves in a month. Yet there is nothing direct, is there, that the men, my dad and his mates, I—can do? We live where we live. It must be conceded that the drugs which have helped wreck my mother's appearance have also given her great relief, and that no doubt many of them have their origins in some of the plants nearby. You have to retain a degree of rationality about such matters.

Going away, then coming back, makes any steady change, or no change, much more conspicuous, and the other thing I struggle to be rational about is the fact that I have seldom, as an adult, found it easy to talk with my mother. She remembers my lizards all right, but I have spent so much time, over the years, in a spoken or silent dialogue with my dad and his mates, a dialogue that she has removed herself from or was in other ways discouraged from joining, that I find it difficult to get a bearing on her being.

There are long silences between us: one of us seems always to be waiting for my father to come in. I fear that I lack generosity. As I sit with her I often think of Brecht's song about his mother. *Oh, why do we not say the important things, it would be so easy, and we are damned because we do not,* and at night when I leave to go home, I drive out and around the complex, circling and circling.

QUESTIONS

1. What political insights can be gained from this story?

2. What or who do the lizards symbolize in this story?

3. How does Hill describe the changing circumstances of family life in the Australian industrial suburbs?

4. Why do the narrator's father's union friends feel uncomfortable being around the narrator when he comes back from London?

5. Discuss the roles and representations of Mary and the narrator's mother.

New Zealand

The earliest human settlers of what is today New Zealand are thought to have come from eastern Polynesia in about 600 C.E. These voyagers, who settled in tribal groups around the country, were known as Maori. Their culture was distinguished by the curvilinear, decorative patterns carved on the wooden panel decorations in their meetinghouses and on their stone tools, such as quadrangular adzes, and used in the facial decoration of tattoos and mokos; these shapes also appear in the characteristic formation of the paas (hilltop fortresses) of the different tribes. The Maori people had a very strong oral tradition but no written alphabet. In spite of this, they had an abundant poetic ritual that they used for ceremonial and social occasions. Unfortunately, much of this cultural heritage was lost when European settlers inflicted their European values on the Maori civilization.

Probably the first Europeans to set eyes on New Zealand were Abel Tasman and his Dutch crew in 1642. There followed visits from other Dutch, French, and British navigators, but Tasman's surgeon, Henrick Haelbos, was the first European to write about New Zealand. His recollections of wild men and unlandable shorelines in his 1671 memoirs became the food of conjecture for several decades. Just over a century later, James Cook arrived in New Zealand; the adventures of the captain and his crew were transcribed by John Hawkesworth in 1773. The excitement generated in Europe from this book of memoirs was surprising considering its rather tedious style and laborious descriptions. Fortunately, the ship's surgeon, John Savage, wrote a lively account of Cook's voyage in 1807 entitled *Some Account of New Zealand*. This effort was soon followed by French diarists who vividly described the expeditions of French explorers Jean François Marie de Surville (1769) and Marc Joseph Marion du Fresne (1772). These accounts are crucial because they are based on firsthand observation of the New Zealand landscape as well as the native peoples, albeit a rather cursory description of both. In 1815, Thomas Kendall made a valiant attempt to convert Maori into written form, publishing *A Korao No New Zealand* in Australia.

In the early decades of the nineteenth century, a considerable number of books were written by travelers and missionaries to the country. One of the most readable memoirs of contemporary New Zealand life was J. L. Nicholas's *Narrative of a Voyage to New Zealand* (1817). The book describes the introduction of Christianity to the Maori people by the English missionary Samuel Marsden. Marsden was a dedicated follower of Jean Jacques Rousseau and believed not only in the perfectibility of humankind but also in the intrinsic goodness of the natives. August Earle did not share Nicholas's enthusiasm for the clergy, and in his memoirs, *Nine Months' Residence in New Zealand in 1827* (1832), and in *Sketches Illustrative of the Native Inhabitants and the Islands of New Zealand* (1838), he castigates the missionaries for corrupting a natural way of life. Earle had an artist's sensibility, and his work is anything but a Christian tract; instead, it could be better described as a detached observance of this untamed wilderness.

Until 1840, New Zealand was little more than a few small settlements in the north of the country where sealers, whalers, boat builders, missionaries, and convicts from Australia eked out a living. The following year, the New Zealand Company was incorporated with the purpose of testing the social theories of Edward Gibbon Wakefield, who was convinced that many of the problems inherent in capitalist Britain centered on the solidification of middle-class values into a rigid class structure. He felt if one modified capitalism by destroying privilege, by expanding educational opportunities, by offering secure and steady employment, by providing free medical care and inexpensive housing, then a healthy society could survive. Wakefield further realized that a successful export base would augment a firm economic base and allow the society to flourish.

In 1840, a group of settlers was sent by the New Zealand Company in an attempt to promote a systematic colonization. New Zealand was promoted as a utopian ideal of a "better Britain" with opportunities of land ownership and meaningful employment. At the same time, this group was meant to establish some sort of legal and political hegemony in the new land. The proposed settlement coincided with a veritable invasion by Australian settlers eager to obtain available land; unfortunately, increasing lawlessness was a consequence of the colonization of New Zealand. As a result, the British government, in response to the concerns of an active evangelical movement in the United Kingdom, sent James Busby to enforce law and order. Despite very little political control, Busby attempted to restrict the purchase of Maori land and to prevent unrestricted settlement by the New Zealand Company. Eventually, the Maori signed the Treaty of Waitangi (1840) in which over 500 Maori chiefs ceded their governing power to Queen Victoria. In return, the British consul, William Hobson, ensured that the native people were guaranteed the right to hold their own property as well as the rights and privileges enjoyed by British subjects.

The ramifications of this foundational document are still discussed vociferously in New Zealand. The predominant view today is that successive governments dishonored the agreements implicit in the ceding of crown control over purchase of Maori land. In fact, as early as 1843, Anglo-Maori conflict had begun. The continuing influx of Europeans into New Zealand meant that more land was required for settlement, and the Maori were continually being pushed off their own land, their land-holding rights ignored. Eventually, under Governor Grey, the continuing warfare was brought under control, but not before many native people and Europeans had been killed in battles that raged off and on for ten years. By 1858, the population of the Maori had been halved to a mere 56,000 people.

Wakefield wrote a book of contemporary memoirs entitled *Adventures in New Zealand* (1845), which favorably presented the colony founded by the New Zealand Company in order to help avoid censure in the House of Commons. Despite its overtly propagandistic purpose, the memoir offered the reader a glimpse of local customs and manners. In 1859, Arthur S. Thomson attempted to write the first comprehensive history of the new country. A military surgeon, Thomson spent eleven years in the country and believed that an objective social and historical rendering of New Zealand would be a valuable asset. Despite the purposeful omission of how the troubling issue of race relations had been flamed by the inequalities over land rights following the signing of the Treaty of Waitangi, the study proved valuable. The New Zealand economy, based on sheep farming and timber products, continued to prosper. When in 1861, gold was discovered on the South Island, European prospectors filled towns like Dunedin overnight. In two years, this South Island city's population jumped from 12,000 to 60,000. This national growth spurt gave rise to a sense of political unity, which resulted in a constitution being written in 1862.

Perhaps with a growing sense of unity in the country, it is not surprising that the first novel written with a New Zealand background was published a year before the constitution appeared. *Taranaki* (1861) was written by Major Henry Butler Stoney and is primarily a love story that takes place against the backdrop of the ongoing land wars. The hero, a newly arrived British soldier from India, falls in love with the daughter of a New Zealand settler. The romantic tale is interrupted by the capture and escape of the hero from the Maori, and in the predictable climax, the couple escapes to England to ensure the happy ending. The story is trite and full of cliché; however, the depiction of the war between Maori and the Europeans gives the tale some historical credence.

Even in the 1860s, the British government controlled New Zealand land sales and profited quite well. But the unashamed expropriation of Maori land for national profit was bound to cause difficulties; the spark that ignited the flame occurred in 1860 when a minor chief sold land to the crown without the consent of his tribe. The British governor endorsed the sale, but when the Maori refused to leave their land, battles were fought and temporary truces were signed. Then, the government attempted to purchase Maori land near Taranaki. When the Maori refused to sell, the British troops invaded the lands of Maori king Potatau. This particular land war raged for over a decade; when the wars died out in 1872, over 2,000 Maori had been killed. Further, the government seized over 3 million acres of "rebel" land, land that to this day the Maori claim was forceably stolen from them. The victory over the Maori opened up the North Island for development.

In the early 1870s, the colonial treasurer, Julius Vogel, proposed borrowing $20 million to invest in roads and railways, but the shortsighted provincial governments vetoed the plans, and the country became largely a sleepy agrarian nation dealing mostly in farm and dairy products.

During this period of gradual domesticity, fiction writers began to exploit the country's charms and manners. Isabella Aylmer wrote *Distant Homes: Or The Graham Family in New Zealand* (1862). The short novel concerns the positive influences of women on the refinement and cultural development of the new colony. Lady Campbell's *Martin Tobin* (1864) and Benjamin Farjeon's *Shadows on the Snow* (1865) and *Grif* (1866) demonstrate the maturation process of literary responses in the country. Farjeon was a newspaper journalist in Dunedin whose literary reputation soared when Charles Dickens commented favorably on his sentimental tale of miners during the heady days of the gold rush. In fact, *Grif* was probably the first international best seller in New Zealand's literary history.

When English writer Samuel Butler arrived in Canterbury in 1860, he observed that New Zealand life prioritized the physical attributes of life over the mental. This pioneering physicality is obvious in many of the fiction works of the 1870s and 1880s. Lady Barker's *Station Life in New Zealand* (1870) concerns the inevitable transformation of a young English woman confronted by a new order of societal values and mores as well as the hardships required in being a squatter's wife in the outposts of the Canterbury foothills. *Poenamo* (1881), written by Auckland civic leader John Logan Campbell, is another tale of pioneering, as is William Reeves's *The Long White Cloud* (1898), which emphasizes the importance of physicality in New Zealand life.

During the last three decades of the nineteenth century, small, independent landowners worked to gain an economic foothold in the country. Until then, the great estates and socially upward cliques ruled New Zealand. The long economic depression of the 1880s forced small farmers to demand land of their own from the landowner class; changes, then, occurred rapidly. The Liberal Party, under the leadership of John Balance and Richard John Seddon, passed radical legislation: Land taxes were levied on the landowning class, huge estates were replaced with crown leases, compulsory arbitration for industrial disputes was mandatory, women were granted the right to vote, and old-age pensions were established. By 1900, New Zealanders had the highest standard of living in the world and were proud of their association with Great Britain. Sixty-five hundred New Zealanders fought with the British in the Boer War, and 58,000 combatants were killed or wounded during World War I.

Just after the Boer War in South Africa, William Satchell arrived from England and proceeded to write quality fiction from his base in North Auckland. His early novels, *The Land of the Lost* (1902) and *The Toll of the Bush* (1905), are overly sentimental, and his depictions of Maori characters are often described as inauthentic. Part of this critical harshness resides in Satchell's choice to write in a naturalistic mode, a literary movement that was never popular in New Zealand. In his *The Greenstone Door* (1914), echoes of Thomas Hardy's deterministic philosophy and pessimism are apparent. Satchell's literary strength, however, is observed in his creation of a dark, forbidding atmosphere. While critics consider Satchell's short stories too commercial to be reprinted, he was one of the first New Zealand practitioners to experiment with the genre successfully.

New Zealand involvement in World War I did not result in any memorable fiction either during or immediately after the armistice. However, the emotional and psychological impact of the war resulted in a drastic change in the most famous of all New Zealand literary figures and its greatest short story writer: Katherine Mansfield. Mansfield was brought up in provincial Wellington, but was sent to England during World War I to complete her formal education. While in England, the tragic death of her brother Leslie on the battlefield in Belgium affected her deeply and made her return imaginatively to her New Zealand childhood, prompting some of her most powerful stories. Upon her return, she found the social and cultural life in Wellington stifling and returned to London, where she died in 1922. Mansfield's talent was her ability to find significance in the minutiae of life and to create portraits of memorable characters with which readers identify.

The search for an authentic New Zealand voice was a major concern between the two world wars with various fictional voices vying for attention. Jane Mander's two major novels, *The Story of a New Zealand River* (1920) and *Allen Adair* (1925), returned to the plight of the pioneer woman. In *Allen Adair*, the struggle to hold on to middle-class values amidst the grim veracity of a crude existence in the isolated gum fields and timber settlements of the Kaipara district are acted out. In the novel, an English woman's cultural baggage is stripped away as she confronts life in the rural backwaters. The novel is reminiscent of Olive Schreiner's *The Story of an African Farm* (1887), and any comparison between the two fictional works demonstrates the commonality of the experience across national borders.

The plight of women became a dominant theme in New Zealand fiction through the interwar period. Jean Devanny wrote socially progressive fiction as early as 1926, and her *The Butcher Shop* (1926) became the first feminist novel to be banned in New Zealand. Robin Hyde, whose short stories lacked the power of her full-length works, was a truly tragic figure. She was a childhood prodigy; her *Check to Your King* (1936) and *The Godwits Fly* (1938) suggested great promise. *Godwits* is a brilliant work that is full of a New Zealand flavor as well as a powerful feminist message; however, Hyde committed suicide in 1939.

When the economic depression struck New Zealand in the 1930s, the standard of living dropped significantly. New Zealand had become politically conservative, and a strong desire for uniformity became part of the cultural expectations. Frank S. Anthony's humorous sketches of his experiences on a derelict Taranaki farm offer the essence of this consciously constructed identity. The tales in *Me and Gus* (1938) reinforce the pioneering values where masculine standards are dominant and women are the domesticators. The tone is playful, but the sketches are filled with New Zealand speech patterns and colorful language that give the work an energy and verve completely original in the nation's literature. Anthony's sketches reveal a more homespun popular side of New Zealand culture and are markedly different from the high culture associated with literary forms emerging from the universities. These New Zealand homespun themes predominated for a quarter of a century (1940–1965), and writers as varied as Roderick Finlayson, Dan Davin, and Frank Sargeson all contributed their own literary flourishes to the form.

Frank Sargeson was born and raised in New Zealand; his profession was the law, but his passion was writing. His short fiction is unique, and while the influence of Mansfield and the U.S. writer Sherwood Anderson can be detected, Sargeson evolved a style and form that are original. His limited, inarticulate narrators represent the puritanical, emotionally sterile world of the New Zealand male, including the mateship ethos, and express the authentic New Zealand society of the period. Sargeson wrote about New Zealand between the world wars and focused on itinerant laborers and unemployed men, outsiders in society. He often used rural farmland settings and was adept at reproducing the vernacular of its inhabitants.

Like Sargeson, Roderick Finlayson used simple language and quiet cadences that were no doubt influenced by Anderson's *Winesburg, Ohio* (1919). Unlike Anderson, however, Finlayson loathed technological progress and scientific explanations; his short fiction is often a lament for the lost harmony that he believed had been eroded away in the modern world. As a result of this philosophical stance, his short stories are often concerned with the negative Western influences picked up by the Maori peoples he observed while working in rural New Zealand as a mechanical draftsman and assistant architect. His sketches about farming life in Northland, originally published in the *Bulletin* in Sydney, combine to form his first novel, *Tidal Creek* (1948).

New Zealander Dan Davin spent a good portion of his life in England. His fiction focuses on the South Island and the Irish Catholic families who populate the area. Davin's stories are socio-documentaries of this particularized religious group with a particular moral code as well as strict family loyalties. His style and use of the vernacular influenced the fictional works of Barry Crump and Ronald Hugh Morrieson in the latter half of the century.

Of course, the ramifications of the Great Depression influenced many New Zealand writers and intellectuals to embrace socialist and communist alternatives. For example, the Literary Society of Auckland University College founded the literary and left-wing journal *Phoenix* (1930), edited by James Bertram and the poet R. A. K. Mason, and at Canterbury College in Christchurch, *Oriflamme* (1933) was edited by Denis Glover and Ian Milner.

Admittedly, there was a tradition of light romantic fiction between the wars in New Zealand, but the genre was not particularly popular with short story writers. On the other hand, the shorn-down-to-essential style of Maurice Duggan's exquisite short stories offers a stark antithesis to the romantic style popular in the novel. His thirty or so published short stories are stylistically rich and beautifully crafted. A number of his stories spotlight a Catholic boarding school and examine this microcosm of New Zealand life. John A. Lee was a socialist with a sense of irony. Many of his stories revolve around children and youth, but he wrote comfortably about tramps and vagabonds, as in *Shining with the Shiner* (1944). This New Zealand tradition of writing about outsiders, a theme developed in the 1930s, reached its climax in John Mulgan's classic novel, *Man Alone* (1939). The novel tells the story of an English survivor of World War I who is caught up in the Auckland riots during the Depression, takes up farming, and then, after accidentally killing his boss, undergoes an epic journey through the bush and finally leaves New Zealand for the Spanish civil war. Johnson, the antihero, is characterized as a drifter, a loner who comes to depend for his survival on his wits and native intelligence, but who values his freedom in contrast to the ownership ethic of his society. Mulgan's fictional creation of the "man alone" topos, a familiar element in even the earliest New Zealand fiction, became the model for other constructions of the New Zealand outsider—whether disenfranchised, alienated, rebellious, lawless, social victim, or existential agent—for the rest of the century.

In 1935, the Labour Party was elected with the hope that the help of the national government would ease the worst results of the economic depression. Under the leadership of Michael Savage, New Zealand introduced a comprehensive welfare program whereby the federal government controlled credit; social security was introduced as well. While these progressive policies were developing, New Zealand found itself involved in another global war. The country suffered nearly 30,000 casualties in World War II; with these losses and sacrifices, the nationalist ethos was reborn. In fact, from 1949 to 1957, a national government ruled the country and implemented a "New Zealand First" policy, but the economic realities of the period made it difficult for New Zealand to remain self-contained. New ties were forged with the United States and its causes; New Zealand joined Australia in signing defense pacts with the Americans and supported its intervention in Korea and Vietnam.

Many war books and stories were written during the postwar period, and generally, the realist tradition continued to flourish. Many of the writers mentioned above began to publish short stories in the literary periodicals that began to appear regularly; the two most important were Charles Brasch's *Landfall* (1947) and Robin Dudding's *Islands* (1972). These journals gave short story writers a forum, and some of the most effective fiction of the postwar era appeared in these periodicals.

Some major literary developments occurred during the last half of the twentieth century. The base of the literary culture has expanded, and as a result previously marginal or invisible groups such as women and Maori have become increasingly articulate and influential. Women writers have explored different themes than writers from the male tradition and have critiqued the masculine realist style and preoccupations of the early twentieth century. Among the women short story writers to emerge in the last three decades are Shonagh Koea, Elizabeth Smither, Stephanie Johnson, Fiona Kidman, and Barbara Anderson. Further, since the early 1970s, there has been an explosion of Maori writing, known as the Maori Renaissance.

Janet Frame, whom many critics judge as the most important writer to emerge from New Zealand since Katherine Mansfield, wrote incredible stories about escaping the emerging postmodern madness. Her literary vision is comprehensive in its implications. Her fiction lays bare the human condition of vulnerability that pervades the postmodern world. Raised in rural isolation on the South Island, surrounded by poverty and tragedy in her personal life, Frame had difficulty adjusting to modern life as an adult. She spent many years under psychiatric care and was saved from a leukotomy only when reports of her being awarded the Hubert Church Award for her first short story collection, *The Lagoon* (1951), were published in a local paper. She continued her career in London, where despite periodic psychiatric treatment, she learned to survive. All these negative experiences filled her vivid imagination, and by 1964, when she returned to New Zealand, she was ready to embark on a very productive literary career.

Noel Hilliard's 1960 novel *Maori Girl,* the first of a tetralogy of novels concerning the Maori, although criticized by some as sentimental, attempted to deal seriously with the issue of prejudice and poverty in Maori life at a time when land marches and demonstrations against the government for holding onto Maori land, as at Bastion Point (1978), were energizing the Maori Renaissance. But it was not until the Maori writer Witi Ihimaera's collection of short stories appeared in

Pounamu Pounamu (1972) that the authentic voice of the indigenous people was heard. His second collection, *The New Net Goes Fishing* (1977), contrasted the rural life of the Maori in his first volume with the new urban reality in the 1970s. The stories in this volume are much more politically charged as well.

New Zealand's economy was rocked by the global depression in the 1970s; the standard of living dropped considerably as the oil crisis developed. This problem was exacerbated by high import costs for most products as well as high inflation rates. Because of the financial crises, many social problems developed, and they impacted most directly on Maori and new immigrants. By the mid-1980s, racial problems became more a cause for concern as the cities filled with unemployed Maori and newly arrived Pacific Islanders trying to find ways to survive the economic disaster.

Two successful Maori writers of the Maori Renaissance are Keri Hulme and Patricia Grace. Hulme's sprawling novel *The Bone People* (1985) won the Booker Prize and brought New Zealand letters to international attention. The novel is difficult to summarize, but concerns Kerewin Holmes, an artistic part-Maori woman who attempts to discover her authentic self amidst all the diversions of the postmodern world. The heroine and her Maori friend, Joe Gillaley, are both guided through the pressures of self-discovery by Maori teachings and philosophy. Through their mutual guardianship of a child who does not speak, the three characters celebrate an unusual union based on aroha (love) and emerge more authentic for their efforts. Patricia Grace in her three collections of short stories (the first one published in 1975) is essentially a moralist without judgment. Her stories force the reader to look at divergent cultural values and then to reflect on the reason for their disparity. Grace traces the Maori's struggle to find an identity amidst the dominating Western culture, reveals the inadequacy of the English language to transmit the authentic Maori experience, and acts on the need to unsettle the reader in order to shake him or her out of complacency.

New Zealand short fiction in the twenty-first century reflects the broadening of a reading public as well as the diverse population that it serves. This new literary awareness is evident in the renovation of literary realism and the exploration of genres such as myth, magic realism, fantasy, and even postmodernism. All of these are testimonies to the renewed energy emanating from previously marginalized groups and to a predominately bicultural, often multicultural view in contrast to the monolingual, monocultural, masculine-dominated fiction of an earlier period.

Lady Barker

(1831–1911)

There is a great deal of truth in the claim that Mary Anne Stewart, later Lady Barker, deserves the label of a "colonial writer" as opposed to a New Zealand writer, for she resided in New Zealand for only three years. But her two seminal works, *Station Life in New Zealand* (1870) and *Station Amusements in New Zealand* (1873), are essential depictions of sheep station life in the early days of the Canterbury settlement. Criticized in the past as stylized portraits of early New Zealand life and further demeaned as simply comedies of manners, the two volumes deserve a great deal more recognition in terms of their stylistic and artistic accomplishments. Barker has a wonderful approach to the rural customs and traditions of early New Zealand life as well as the difficulties of making a living off the land in a harsh climate such as that near Christchurch.

Mary Anne Stewart was born in Spanish Town, Jamaica; her father was the island secretary. He sent his daughter to England at age two to be brought up. At twenty, she married Captain George Barker, who was knighted in 1859 for services in the Indian Mutiny. Lady Barker went to Bengal with her husband in 1860, but in July 1861, he died. She returned to England and married Canadian-born Frederick Napier Broome in June 1865. Broome was a product of his class and era; he was a sportsman, poet, journalist, and diplomat, but not, unfortunately, a very productive sheep farmer. The couple went out to Steventon, a sheep run of 9,700 acres on the Selwyn River in the Malvern Hills (near Canterbury), to give sheep farming a try, but the great snowstorm of 1867 forced them to sell their share of the farm to their partner, leave New Zealand, and rethink their future. It is while she was in England that she decided to write up her experiences based on letters sent home to her younger sister Jesse in the two volumes of connected anecdotes mentioned above. Lady Barker continued to travel and write for the next twenty years; she lived in South Africa, Mauritius, Western Australia (where her husband Frederick was governor), and Trinidad, and continually wrote about what she saw and did on her travels. When her husband was knighted in 1884, she became Lady Broome. After her husband's death in 1896, she settled in England, where she died.

"Christmas Day in New Zealand" is a record of what New Zealand life was like for the colonial settlers. It is a story of hunting, of ceremony, of religion, of telling tales, of games; however, the heart of the story occurs when the old shepherd Bob muses about life in the colony before refined people like Lady Barker arrived. It is the classic man against nature theme: the hard life of shepherds struggling to survive in a harsh and unforgiving environment.

Christmas Day in New Zealand   *1870*

A great deal of the success of mustering depends on the clearness of the weather, as it is of no use going on the hills if a mist is hanging about. Very often, in the early summer, the hills are covered during the night by filmy clouds, which do not always disperse until the sun has risen and shrivelled them into light, upward-floating wreaths by one touch of his lance-like beams. But it is a great disadvantage in a day's mustering to make a late start; the sheep have dispersed from their high camping

sharp ears. It seemed ages to me before the loud crack of his rifle rang through the clear mountain air, and the boar gave a bound into the air—only to fall flat on his great side, shot through the heart.

F—— and I were over the hedge and wading through the flax swamp before we saw that our game was bagged; indeed, we did not know he was dead and approached him with the greatest caution, for a wounded boar is about the most dangerous animal to attack. When we were able to perceive his huge black side upheaving through the flax bushes we fell into our usual line of march when on sporting expeditions. F—— first, with his finger on the trigger of his revolver, and I as far behind as was compatible with my own safety, carrying the hunting-knife in a very shaky hand.

Our precautions were useless on this occasion, for poor piggy (I am always sorry for them as soon as they are hit) was quite stone dead. He must have been a great age: his gigantic tusks were notched and broken, and his thick hide bore traces of old scars, received in former battles with his enemies; for boars are very pugnacious and will not brook "a rival near the throne."

The report of the rifle had aroused the whole establishment. The dogs barked and bayed furiously, the inmates of the poultry-yard seemed to become distracted, to judge by their clamour, and from every window in the house and its outbuildings a bearded head was popped, whilst cries of "What's up?" "Wait till I come," etc. etc., were heard amid the noise of the animals. High and clear, piercing through the Babel of sounds, my maids' shrieks came at intervals like minute-guns at sea. Whenever anything was the matter, from a cut finger to the chimney on fire, the two girls screamed at the pitch of their exceedingly shrill voices. So this Christmas Day was ushered very noisily into existence; but you will be glad to hear that I got back into my own room very cleverly before anyone could array themselves sufficiently to sally forth, so I was spared the disgrace of being seen by my small household with bare feet and muddy skirts.

F—— could not tear himself away from his victim quite so soon, and when next I peeped round the corner of the verandah, I saw him, looking more ridiculous than ever in his short white garment, the centre figure of an admiring and excited group of shepherds and shearers. Pepper, our head shepherd, recognized an old enemy in the dead boar, and declared that he and his dogs had bailed him up unsuccessfully "many a time and oft."

I was not sorry, as it happened, that the episode of the boar had aroused the whole household at so early an hour, for it enabled me to get a great deal done before breakfast towards the reception of our Christmas guests. As soon as I had dressed myself, I sallied forth with F——, following the windings of the creek until it led us far back into the hills, to a little wooded gully which nestled between two steep ascents. If only we could have seen that strip of green anywhere from the house! but alas! it was too securely hidden to be visible, and I lighted upon the lonely spot quite by accident in one of my many rambles. At this part the creek was quite as noisy as a Scotch burn, and, like it, rippled and chattered noisily over a stony bed, as it wound for a few hundred yards under the shadow of the trees. Its banks were beautifully fringed with many varieties of ferns, which even in winter were kept green and fresh by the sheltering bushes above. It was upon these lovely feathery ferns my raid was directed; and if F—— and I could have only come across a magical carpet, or that delightful horse in the fairy tale who was set in motion by a peg, either of which would have borne us swiftly across land and sea, we might perhaps have realized a handsome fortune in a few minutes by selling our enormous green bundles in Covent Garden that Christmas morning.

But what a cruel change it would have been for the beautiful ferns from their enchanted mountain nook with the wood-pigeons cooing in the trees above them and the little green paroquets flashing past their waving plume-like tufts, to a cold, raw Christmas morning in smoky London! . . .

When the little homestead was once more reached we deposited our huge armfuls of ferns in a shady hole in the creek, and went in to breakfast with splendid appetites. I am afraid there were no presents exchanged that morning, for we were fifty miles away from the nearest shop, and had not been down to Christchurch for months. However, we received and returned many hearty good wishes; and in that foreign land it is something to be among friends on Christmas Day, even if there are no presents going about.

After breakfast I filled all the vases, and decorated the hall, and covered up the stand of Indian arms with my beautiful ferns, each spray of which was a marvel of grace and loveliness, and then it was time to arrange the verandah for service, which was soon done by the aid of boxes and red blankets. But it was fated that our gravity was to be sorely tried long before the short sermon which F—— read us was ended.

I think I have told you before, that the shepherds who formed the principal portion of our congregation always brought their dogs with them, and these dear sensible animals behaved in the most exemplary manner, lying down by their masters' saddles and never moving aught but their intelligent eyes until church was over, when they greeted their owners with rapture, as if to congratulate them on escaping from some dangerous ceremony. Amongst our most constant guests were the Scotch shepherds of a neighbouring "squatter." These men, M'Nab and M'Pherson by name, were excellent specimens of their class. Sober and industrious, they were also exceedingly intelligent, and thoroughly enjoyed the privilege of an invitation to attend our Sunday services. I observed that they invariably took it in turn to come to us; and when I asked M'Nab to come over on Christmas Day, I added, "Don't you think you could manage to put the sheep in some place from which they would be safe not to stray, and *both* of you come to us at Christmas?"

"It is na the sheep, mem," replied M'Nab bashfully; "it's the claes."

"But your clothes are very nice," I said, looking at the neat little figure before me, clad in a suit of Lowland plaid, which was somewhat baggy, but clean and whole.

"Yes, mem, but we've naight but the one suit between us. So we can only come one at a time, like," said M'Nab turning red through his sunbrown.

"Dear me, how can you both wear the same clothes?" I inquired. "M'Pherson is such a giant, and you are not very tall, M'Nab."

"Well, mem, we made them our ainsells, and we cut them on a *between* size, you see, so they fit baith, fine. The trews were hard to manage, but 'Phairson wears 'em with gaiters, and I rolls 'em up; so though they're a deal too short for him and too lang for me, we manage first class," said M'Nab, relapsing into colonial phraseology.

On this Christmas Day it was Long 'Phairson's (as he was generally called) turn to wear the Lowland suit, and he had appeared in due season, accompanied not only by his colleys, but by a small white bull-terrier, with a knowing patch of yellowish-brown over one eye, a most vicious turned-up nose, and a short upper lip.

Fortunately, 'Phairson's arrival had been early, so I contrived to collect my hens and chickens, and decoy them into the fowl-house, out of the reach of this ferocious-looking animal. At church time, therefore, I took my place in the verandah with no domestic anxieties to distract my attention from the beautiful service which had never seemed more beautiful to me than when held in that distant hidden valley with nothing but hills and mountains around us, and a New Zealand summer sky overhead. The great tidings of "To us a Child is born," rang as sweet and clear and welcome in my ears, amid that profound unbroken silence, as they have done when pealed from organs or proclaimed to hundreds of gathered worshippers with all the pomp and ceremony of the most gorgeous cathedral.

We had even managed to get through a hymn with tolerable correctness, and the last page of the sermon had been reached, when we were "ware" of an extraordinary scuffling and rustling beneath our feet, accompanied by violent thumps against the wooden flooring of the verandah. It was evidently a battle; but who could the combatants be? Our own dogs were securely fastened up in their kennels, our cat had prudently retreated to a loft as soon as 'Phairson and his dog Nip appeared, and the other colleys, though bristling with excitement at the strange sounds, lay motionless as statues in obedience to their masters' warning glances. I am sorry to own that, as the noise increased, our repressed curiosity and wonder became too much for us, and it was fortunate for the decorum of the congregation that F——'s discourse (borrowed from one of Canon Kingsley's volumes of Cottage Sermons)[2] came to an end, for hardly was the service over before we were perfectly deafened by the thumps. What could they mean? Nip was concerned, no doubt, for M'Pherson looked guilty and nervous; but what unhappy object was he dragging from end to end beneath the verandah? No dog but himself could get beneath the flooring,—the cat we knew was safe. "Oh! it's Betty, poor Betty!" I shrieked in dismay, as I remembered that a favourite white Aylesbury duck was sitting on her first nest beneath the flooring of the verandah. In vain I had tried to coax her into arranging her nursery elsewhere; she insisted on taking up her abode in a hole scratched by a tame rabbit which had met with an untimely fate some months before.

2 **Canon . . . Sermons:** Likely a reference to Charles Kingsley, the Rector of Eversley in England and Canon of Westminster.

And so it was Betty, who soon appeared before us, dragged to M'Pherson's feet by Nip, in answer to his summons of "Nip, ye scamp, come here, sir!" Not a vestige of tail was left to her, but still Nip held firmly on to her poor stump feathers. She had flapped against the boards with her wings as he ruthlessly dragged her up and down beneath our feet; but she must have been too terrified to cry out, for no "quack" or sound did she utter under this ignominious treatment. In addition to her bodily suffering during the process of parting from her tail, she must have gone through much mental anguish at beholding her cherished eggs scattered and broken. When Nip released her at last with great reluctance, she lay at M'Pherson's feet too utterly exhausted to stir; her snowy plumage, of which she was so daintily careful, all draggled and dusty, her wings extended, and only her bright terrified eyes giving evidence that Nip had not succeeded in killing her. Poor Betty! I took her up in my arms, though she was an immense and very heavy bird, and carried her tenderly into the house, soothing her as well as I could; but still she remained gasping and unable to move. At last I remembered my medicine-bottle full of brandy, and I administered such a tremendous dose of the stimulant, that Betty choked and struggled back into life and movement. In fact, I believe she spent the remainder of Christmas Day in a box full of hay in the stable—very tipsy, but safe, and, I hope, happy. For many weeks no one could look at Betty's ridiculous tail, or rather no-tail, without laughing, but in my eyes it was a very sad sight and I asked M'Pherson never to bring Nip to church again.

As soon as we had restored some sort of gravity, and after Nip had been well scolded and Betty soothed, the men (for alas! there were no women, except my servants, who were busy cooking) adjourned to the washhouse, where F—— presided over a substantial dinner of beef and poultry, for the great point is to have no mutton at a party in New Zealand. We happened to possess a big musical box, which was wound up and set playing, and the dinner proceeded to the sound of a succession of old-fashioned waltz tunes. It was much too hot to remain indoors; so directly the huge dishes of cherries and strawberries (presents from my neighbours' gardens on either side of the ranges) had been duly emptied, the company adjourned to the only spot of shade out-of-doors, the south-eastern side of the stables. We could contemplate little plantations of tiny trees about three feet high, dotted over the low downs, and carefully fenced in from investigating animals. We could contemplate them, I say, and speculate as to how many of us would be in that valley on a Christmas Day in the far future, when these trees would have struggled up against their enemy the Nor'-wester, and attained sufficient stature to afford shelter from the afternoon sun.

Probably not one of the party then assembled will ever sit under those imaginary branches; but at the date I am telling you of, Tom Thumb could not have found shade enough to shield himself from the bath of golden sunbeams anywhere on the run, unless he had joined our party, seated on hen-coops, in the lee of the stable.

The question then seriously presented itself to my mind, of how to amuse my twenty stalwart guests from 3 o'clock until 7. I intended them to have tea again about 5, and quantities of plum cake if they could possibly eat it; but there were two hours of broiling heat to be got through, socially speaking, before they could be invited to eat again. After tea I knew there would be athletic games, so soon as Flagpole's mighty shadow had laid a cool patch over the valley. My guests would be affronted if I went away, and yet my presence evidently made them miserable. They all sat in rigid and uncomfortable attitudes, and blushed furiously if I spoke to them, trying hard all the time to persuade themselves and me that they were enjoying themselves. Even the unfailing pipes, which I had insisted on being produced, failed to create an element of contentment, for the smokers suffered incessant anxiety lest the light shifting summer air should send a puff of tobacco-smoke towards me. We were all very polite, but wretched; and I shall never forgive F——'s unkind enjoyment of the horrible dullness of this stage of my party. "Dear me, this is too exciting," he would whisper; "don't let them all talk at once"; or else he would ask me if it was not "going off" very brilliantly, when all the time it was not going off at all.

I began to grow desperate; my company would not talk or do anything, but sit steadily staring at each other and me. In vain I asked questions about subjects which I thought might interest them. Conversation seemed impossible, and I had firmly resolved to go away in five minutes, and see if they would be more lively without me, when some bold individual started the subject of gold-digging. Everybody's tongue was unloosed as if by magic, and all had some really interesting story to tell about either their own or their "mate's" experiences at the West Coast gold-diggings. One man described with much humour how he had been in the very first "rush," and how amazed a lonely settler in the Bush had been at the sudden appearance of a thousand men in the silence and solitude of his hut, which was built up a gully. When the eager gold-seekers questioned him as to whether he had found the "colour" in the creek which they were bent on tracing to its rich source, he lazily shook his head and said, coolly, pointing over his shoulder, "Me and the boys" (his equally lazy sons) "have never earned no wages, no, nor had any money of our own. Whenever we wanted to go to the store"—about twenty miles off, and a wretched track between— "we jest took and we washed a bit among that 'ere dirt, and we allers found as much dust as we wanted." The bed of that creek contained nearly as many particles of fine flake-gold as of sand; and that lazy old man could have made a fabulous fortune years and years before, if he had taken the trouble to see it, as it rippled past his log hut. He never found a speck of gold in all his life afterwards, for no sooner had he finished his dawdling speech than the diggers had flung themselves into the wealth-bearing streamlet and fought and scrambled for its golden sands, which glided away during the night like a fairy vision. Great boulders were upheaved by the gold-seekers in their first eager rush, so the natural dams being thus removed, when the next morning dawned the water had rushed away into a new channel, bearing its precious freight with it.

The spokesman took from his neck a little wash-leather bag as he finished his story, with the words, "All gone—clean gone"; and opening it shook a few pinches of the sparkling flaky dust into my lap, saying, "That's some o' wot I got evenin' before. It's beautiful, ain't it, mum?" I duly admired the shining treasure, and he bade me keep it "for my Christmas box," and I have it safely put away to this day. But I very nearly lost it, and this is how it happened. A discussion arose as to the most successful method of washing sand for gold, and some new inventions were freely discussed. "Well, I reckon I got them there nuggets"—the largest no bigger than a small pin's head—"by washin' with a milk dish." "How?" I asked. "I'll show you, mum, if I may get a dish from the gals"; and he strode off towards the house, returning with a large milk-tin in his hands. He then proceeded to the side of the duck-pond, and, in spite of the "agony of dress" in which he was arrayed, filled the shallow dish with mud and stones and grit of all sorts. At this stage of the proceedings he appeared intent on making a huge dirt-pie. Imagine my dismay when he pounced on the paper packet into which I had just carefully collected my gold-dust, counted the tiny flakes rapidly up to fifteen, and then scattered them ruthlessly over the surface of this abominable mess. He next proceeded to stir it all up with a piece of wooden shingle, and regardless of my face of dismay, said calmly, "Now we'll wash 'em out." I should have had no objection to seeing the experiment tried with anybody else's gold dust, but I must say I was very sorry to find that my newly acquired treasure was thus lightly disposed of. "Lightly won, lightly lost," I thought to myself, "for I shall never see it again."

Pratchard (that was the name of the quondam[3] digger) now marched off to the creek close by, and in spite of the blazing sunshine we all followed him. He stooped down, and, scooping up some water, began shaking his great heavy tin backwards and forwards. By degrees he got rid of the surface mud, then he added more water, until in half an hour or so he had washed and shaken all the materials for his dirt-pie out of the dish, and disclosed my fifteen wee nuggets shining like so many flecks of sunlight at the bottom of the tin vessel. "Count 'em, mum, if *you* please," said Pratchard, hot, but triumphant; and so I did, to find not one missing. To me it seemed like a conjuror's trick, but Pratchard and the rest of my company hastened to assure me that it was not possible to wash away gold. It sank and sank, being so much heavier than anything else, until it could be perceived at the bottom of whatever dish or even plate was used to scoop up the dirt among which it was to be found.

We were more sociable now, but hotter than ever, and we returned gladly to the shade of the stable. As things looked more promising at this stage of my party, I suggested that everybody should, in turn, tell a story. Of course they all declared "they didn't know nothing," but finally I coaxed old Bob, a shepherd, to tell me about one of his early Christmas Days in the colony, and this is his narrative, but not in his own phraseology. I wish I could spell it as he pronounced it.

"Things are very different now," said Bob, "all over the country, though it is not so many years ago, not more than six or seven perhaps. We did not think much of Sunday in the early days; we didn't exactly work, such as digging or such-like on that day, but we did other jobs which had been waiting for a spare moment all the week. We used not to think any harm of breaking a young colt on Sunday, or of riding over to the next run with a draughting notice[4]; or if it was wet we lay in our bunks and

---

3 **quondam:** Former.
4 **a draughting notice:** Notification to separate a group of sheep from the main mob.

smoked, or p'raps we got up and sat on a bucket turned wrong side up, and mended our clothes. As for Christmas Day, we never thought of it beyond wondering what sort of 'duff' we were going to have. That's colonial for a pudding, ma'am, you know, don't you? If we had a couple of handfuls of currants and raisins, we shoved them into a lot of flour and sugar, and we put a bit of mutton fat into the middle, and tied it all up together in the sleeve of an old flannel shirt and boiled it, and it used to come out a first-rate plum duff and we thought we had no end of a Christmas if we could manage such a pudding as that.

"But we could not always get even a holiday on Christmas Day, because of the shearing. Shearers were too scarce in those days, and wages too high to miss a day's work, so it often happened that we had to work just as hard, or harder on Christmas than on any other day of the year. I was working then up at Mr Vansittart's ('Vans-start's,' Bob called his master), and we had hopes of getting finished by Christmas Eve, and having at all events a good lie-in-bed on Christmas Day; but as ill-luck would have it, a mob of wethers[5] bolted from the flat where Tom Duckworth was watching them, and got right away into the hills at the back of the run. *He* said it was because his dogs were new and wouldn't work properly for him, but I knew better—he done it a-purpose. Tom's sheep were always coming to grief. He couldn't cross 'em over a river without losing half the mob, and never a week passed without his getting boxed. That's mixed-up, ma'am," explained Bob politely, observing a puzzled expression in my eyes. "We calls it boxing when your sheep go and join another mob feeding close by, and you can't tell one from another except by the brand or the ear-mark. It's a nasty business is boxing, and *werry* trying to the temper. Even the dogs get out of patience like, and nip the stupid sheep harder than they do at any other time.

"Well, ma'am, as I was saying, Tom Duckworth let a fine mob of young wethers get away the day before Christmas Day, and started to look for them with his precious dogs. They were the very last mob which had to come up to be shorn, so, as he couldn't find 'em—I never expected he could,—there was the skillions[6] standing empty, and the shearers lounging about idling when Christmas Day came; and a werry beautiful day it was, just like this one. The boss, that's Master Vans-start, he was at his wits' ends what to do. He knew right well that if the wethers wasn't in the yards that night, the shearers would be off across the hills to Brown and Wetherby's next morning first thing. You couldn't expect men who had their two pounds a day waiting for them to lose many days, especially as Brown and Wetherby's was an 'open shed,' where any shearers that came were taken on until there were hands enough, so they knew they might lose the job if they didn't look sharp. The boss managed to keep them quiet on Christmas Day, by pretending he always meant to take a spell on that day. He got the cook to make a stunning duff, and he sent a boy on horseback across the river to Mulready's for some beef; he knew Mulready always killed a bullock about Christmas and he served out some grog, so in that way he kept the shear-

---

5 **a mob of wethers:** Drove or flock of castrated rams.
6 **skillions:** Shearing sheds for sheep.

ers well fed and rested all Christmas Day. He never let them out of his sight, not even down to the creek to wash their shirts, lest any of them should slip away.

"I didn't come in for any of these good things: so far from it, quite the contra-*ry*"; and here Bob paused and took a pull at his pipe, resting his hands on his knees and gazing straight before him with regretful eyes, as the memory of his wrongs rose freshly to his mind. "Tom Duckworth did, though, the stupid fool! He laid in his bunk on Christmas morning and had his snooze out, and then he got up and eat the best part of a cold leg of mutton for his breakfast, and he came in for the duff, and the grog, and all the rest of it afterwards. But I'll tell you how I spent my Christmas Day, ma'am, and I hope I'll never have to spend another like it.

"As soon as ever it was light, the boss, leastways Master Vans-start, he came into the kitchen where I was sleeping, and he says, 'Bob, I must have that mob of wethers by tonight, and that's all about it. They're quite likely to have gone up into the back ranges, but unless they're gone up into the sky I'm bound to have 'em in the skillions tonight.' You see, ma'am, when Master Vans-start put it in that way, I knew that mob had got to be found before nightfall, and that he was going to tell me off to find 'em. So I lay there and listened, as was my dooty to. 'Bob,' says Master Vans-start, 'I'll tell you what it is, I'll give you a fiver,'—that's a five-pound note, ma'am, you'll understand,—'yes, Bob, a fiver, over and above your year's pay when I draws a cheque for your wages next week, and you can go down to town and spend it, Bob, if you bring me in the whole of that mob of wethers by sundown. Take any body you like with you and the best of the dogs, only you bring them in; for if you don't, I shall be three hundred pounds short in my wool-money this year, and I've got too heavy a mortgage on this run, Bob, to be able to afford to lose that much, and all through Tom Duckworth's sleepy-headedness.'

"Well, ma'am, when the boss spoke so feelingly, and put it to me in that way, I knew it had to be done, so I said, 'Right you are, sir,' and then he only said, 'I looks to you, Bob, for them sheep,' and he went away. It was barely light enough to see your hand, and I knew that the *mistesses* (that was the way Bob pronounced mists) would be hanging about the hills for a good time yet, so I reached out my hand and I got my pipe and a match and I smoked a bit, whilst I considered which way I should go and who I should take with me. Men, I mean; I didn't want to know what dogs I should take, for if Sharp and Sally couldn't find 'em, all I could say was, they wasn't to be found. I'd a good mind to name Tom Duckworth to come, but I meant to give whoever went with me a pound a-piece, and I didn't want to tip him for giving all this bother; besides, he was just as likely as not to sit down under the lea of a rock and smoke the moment he got out of my sight. No, I wouldn't take Tom, but I'd take little Joe Smelt, who was as active as a kid on the hills, and Munro, who, although he belonged to the next station, knew every yard of country round, and who had the best head on his shoulders of any man I knew. Besides, Munro had always been a chum of mine, and was such a decent well-spoken fellow, it was a pleasure to have any dealin's with him.

"By the time I had settled all this in my own mind, I thought it was about time to get up, so up I got and I lighted the stove and put the kettle on to boil, and a whole lot of chops on to fry, and I got the pannikins out and the tin plates. I remember well I was so anxious to have a good comfortable breakfast ready before I called Joe and Munro, that I even cleaned up the knives and forks for 'em. How did I do that, is it you want to know, ma'am? Oh, very easy: I just stuck 'em into the soft ground outside the back door, and worked 'em up and down a bit, and they came out fine and clean. Well, as soon as I had got everything ready, I went into the men's hut, and I got out Munro and little Joe Smelt without waking up any of the others; and when they got on their boots and moleskins, saving your presence, ma'am, they come into the kitchen, and I showed 'em the breakfast all ready and smelling uncommon good, and I told 'em what the boss had said, and I lays it before 'em whether they likes to come up the hills with me and earn their pound a-piece, or whether they'd *pre*-fer to loaf about the station all day, whiles I goes out by myself and sticks to the whole of the fiver.

"Munro, he goes on eating his breakfast quite quiet-like—for that matter we was all pegging away pretty tidily—and then, after a bit, he says in his pretty peaceable way—I've told you he was a very well spoken man, ma'am, haven't I?—he says, 'Well, Bob, I don't mind if I do come'; and then Joe Smelt says, as well as he can speak for a mouthful of damper, 'The same here'; so then I knew it was settled, and I enjoyed my breakfast with the rest. We didn't dawdle too long, though, for it was getting light enough to see, though them mistesses was still too low to please me, but I thought we might be making our way up the river-gorge and smoke our pipes as we went. The sheep had gone up that way, I knew, and there was no way out. Besides, sheep don't like crossing the water oftener than they can help. Nine times we had to cross that there river on that there blessed Christmas morning. Get wet! I should just think we did: leastways I took off my Cookhams and worsted[7] socks at each ford, because I knew right well that if I went up the hills and walked all day in wet things my feet would get that blistered I'd feel like a cat in walnut-shells. Joe Smelt found that out to his cost before the day was over. He started werry cocky and turned up his trouser-legs and walked right through the water, saying he couldn't be bothered to stop and take his boots off and on at each crossing. Munro, he walked through all nine fords in his boots; and then, when we had done with them for that day, he sat down on a big stone and took off his socks and his boots and drew out a nice dry pair of worsted socks, and put 'em on; then he poured the water out of his boots and shook 'em up and down a bit and put 'em on again, and laced 'em up werry tight. But still, long before the day was done, his feet was smartin' and his boots was all out o' shape, and wringing him awful. Joe and I couldn't have managed that way if it had been ever so, for socks wasn't plenty with us in those days. We just used to get one pair at a time from the nighest store, and wear 'em until they got into one big hole all over, and then we chucked 'em away and got another pair. Now, Munro, he had a nice little Scotch wife up at his place, and she was always a-spinning and a-knitting for him, and kept him as comfortable as could be. But Joe and me, we

---

7 **worsted:** Woolen.

hadn't neither wives, nor socks, nor anything nice about us, but we just pulled through as well as we could.

"Well, ma'am, to come back to that Christmas Day. It was as beautiful a morning as you would wish to see, and not too hot, neither; the sun just beginning to shine, and drinking up them mistesses as if they was grog, till there wasn't one to be seen, and Munro's glass showed him every sheep on every hill within sight as plain as you see your hand now. Lots of sheep there were too, and werry cheerful it sounded their calling to each other, and werry good feed there was for 'em on those hills. But they was all too white for what we wanted. They'd all been *shored*, 'twas easy to see that, and the mob we wanted was still in their wool, and would have looked dirty and much larger among the fresh-shored ones. We could track 'em easy enough by their footmarks up to the head of the gorge, but there we lost all trace, and though we spent a good hour hunting. We felt sure they'd all keep together, for they'd be frightened at the sight of all their fellows so white and so bare, and likely as not travel away from 'em. They wasn't anywhere on the low hills, that was certain; there was no use funking[8] it, we had got to separate and go carefully over the back ranges, and a long hot climb we had before us that Christmas morning; and, not to be too long about it, ma'am, a long hot climb we had if ever there was one in this world. I sent the dogs many and many a time after what I thought might be a part of the mob; but though I hunted as close as ever I could, never a sheep did I see, no, nor a sign of one. Well, ma'am, it was very disheartening, you'll allow that, and I was so vexed I couldn't feel properly hungry even long after dinner-time came, and I kept thinking whatever I should do if they wasn't to be found. You see, I had chosen the most likely place to search in myself, as was but nat'ral, so I never thought that if *I* couldn't find 'em anybody else could. There's where I deceived myself; because when I had worked all round that blessed range and come upon Davis's hut—that was the out-station where we had settled to meet some time in the afternoon—what should I see but Munro and Joe Smelt a-lying on the shady side of the hut as cool and comfortable as you please smoking their pipes, and the whole mob of sheep lying quiet and peaceable on the little flat, with Munro's dog watching 'em. Not that they wanted any watching just then, for sheep always take a good spell in the afternoon of a hot day, and lie down and go to sleep, maybe, until it gets cool enough to make it pleasant to wander about and feed before dark.

"As soon as ever I see that sight I flung up my hat and danced for joy, and I felt desperate hungry all of a minute. I can tell you, my mates, I didn't lose much time getting down that hill, though I come pretty quiet for fear of scaring the sheep.

"When I comes up to the men, before I could speak, Joe Smelt says, first thing, 'Munro found 'em; I haven't been long here.' And Munro smiles quiet and pleased-like, and says, 'I had a mob once served me the same trick, and I thought I knew where to look for 'em, and sure enough they was there, reg'larly hiding; I had to

---

8 **funking:** Shrinking from; copping out.

bring 'em down uncommon easy, for it was a nasty place, and I didn't want half of 'em to be smothered in the creek.'

"Well, of course I meant to ask and to hear all about it, but I thought it would keep until we had had a bit of dinner, for it was about two o'clock, and you must please to remember, ma'am, that we had breakfasted somewhere about five, and likewise that walking up and down them back ranges is hungry work at the best of times, besides being wearing to the boots. 'Where's Davis?' was my first words. 'Davis must have gone away altogether for a bit' they said, 'for the hut is locked and fastened up until it can't be fastened no more, and unless we reg'larly break into it, we shall never get in it.'

" 'Drat the fellow!' I cried, 'there ain't no bush-rangers about. Why doesn't he just lock his door and hang the key on a nail outside where anybody can see it, as I used to do when I was a back-country shepherd, and wanted to go away for a bit.' But it was no manner of use pitching into Davis, not then, because you see, ma'am, he wasn't there to hear himself abused, though we did that same and no mistake. It *was* aggravating—now, ma'am, wasn't it? There was we three, and the dogs, poor things! as hungry as hungry could be; and we knew there'd be flour and tea and sugar, and likely a bit of bacon (for Davis was a good hand at curing a ham of a wild pig), inside the door, if we could only open it. Not a bit of it would stir, though, for all our kicks, and Joe Smelt ran at it with his shoulders until I thought he must burst it open; but no, the lock didn't give one bit. 'Tell you what,' said Joe, rubbing his shoulder after his last attempt, 'Davis has gone and barred this 'ere door up on the inside, and then got out of the window and fastened it up outside afterwards.' When we came to look, it seemed quite likely, for the shutter was driven home and kept in its place by good-sized nails; but we got a big stone, and we used our knives, and Munro worked away that patiently that at last down came the shutter, and we had the little bit of a window open in no time after that. We made little Joe get through first, and we laughed and said we felt just like real house-breakers, but we thought we'd keep our jokes until we had had something to eat. Before Joe had well unbarred the door—for it was fastened up as if it was never meant to be opened again— Munro and me had settled that he should make some flap-jacks as soon as ever we could get the fire to burn; that is, supposing there wasn't any bacon or mutton lying about.

"The minute Joe opened the door with a cheery, 'Here you are,' we looked round us like so many hungry wolves, and the first thing we see is a fine big shoulder of mutton on the floor. Well, it was easy to see how it had got there, for there were marks of rats' teeth and feet too, all over it. Davis hadn't been long gone that was easy to see—not more than a few hours likely, though he plainly intended to be away for some time by the way he'd fastened up everything; but still it was very neglectful of him not to have flung that shoulder of mutton outside before he went because you see, ma'am, in a day or two it would surely be very unpleasant. A neat man was Davis—a very neat man—and when we'd prized open his cupboard made out of old gin-cases, we found his couple of tin-plates and pannikins, and his tea and sugar, and his flour and his matches, and his salt, all as tidy as tidy could be, and there was a big packet of 'Vermin Destroyer' too, open and half used. We gave that a wide berth, however, as you may fancy; but we had some sticks in the fire-place and the kettle on to boil before you could say 'Jack Robinson.' We found half a loaf of bread also in the cupboard, which we concluded to eat, lest it should get stale by the time Davis came back, and we told Munro we'd have his flap-jacks for second course. 'Here's a capital Christmas dinner after all,' said Joe; and he picked up the meat carefully off the floor, and blew the dust off, and we sat down to the table with that shoulder of mutton before us; and all I can tell you, ma'am, is, that long before the kettle boiled—and it had a good fire under it too—there wasn't a scrap left on the bone. Cooked! in course it was cooked; you don't think we was going to eat raw wittles on Christmas Day. No, no, ma'am, we weren't such cannibals as that! Davis had baked it as nice as could be, but it seemed uncommon funny that he should have taken so much trouble for nothing. However, there it was, or, I *should* say, there it wasn't, for we had eaten it up, every bite; and we told Joe Smelt to get the tea out of the cupboard, and throw a couple of handfuls into the kettle, which was beginning to boil. Joe got up, saying, 'I haven't half done yet; I'm just as hungry as ever I can be'; and he went to the cupboard and began to rummage among the things in it. 'Don't give us any pison by mistake, Joe,' said Munro, joking. Just as he said the words, Joe turned short round, his face looking as white as death underneath all the sunburn and freckles, his very lips white, and his eyes open wider than I thought mortal eyes could open; and he said in a dreadful voice—a sort of whisper, and yet you might have heard it all over the place—'That's where it is, we're pisoned!' With that Munro and I jumped up from the table, and we gasped out, 'Pisoned, Joe!' but we needn't to ask—we couldn't speak if we wished. Joe pointed to the bare mutton bone, and held out the half-used paper of the poison in the other, and never a word did he say but, 'Rats.'

"We guessed it all then. Davis must have been fairly bullied by the impudent hungry critturs, and he had taken the trouble to cook for 'em, as if they had been Christians, and then he'd quite likely as not rubbed an ounce or two of strychnine into that shoulder of mutton, and left it where the rats could get at it, and we'd been and eaten it all up instead o' they. Yes, ma'am, it's all very well to laugh," said Bob, taking his hat off, and wiping his head with the handkerchief stowed away in its crown, looking into the hat afterwards as if he saw the scene he was describing pictured there—"It was the werry roughest moment of all *my* life. To be pisoned like a rat, and in a lonely gully, where no one would ever pass. Most likely we shouldn't even be found before Davis came back. It was lucky Davis didn't come back, though—not at that moment, I mean—for I'm certain that if he stood in his own doorway just then we'd 'a set on him and killed him without so much as saying 'with your leave or by your leave.' We couldn't have been whiter than Joe, not if we'd tried; but we was white enough no doubt. Munro was a good man, so he was the bravest of the lot, and he said, or he tried to say, for he couldn't speak very clear, 'The will of God be done, my poor Jeanie!' and with that he threw himself down on Davis's bed and hid his face.

"I don't rightly know what poor little Joe did, for I felt desperate mad. I caught sight of half a bar of soap stowed away at the back of the cupboard, and I seized it as if it had been a life-buouy, and I'd been a drowning man. I couldn't have gripped it harder or held it tighter if it *had* been a buouy," said Bob, shaking his head meditatively. "And I runs down to the creek with it. I don't know why I went there, unless it was to be handy to the water to gulp it down with. Well, ma'am, I had picked up my knife off the table as I passed, and I cut great junks of that bar of soap, and bolted 'em, whole. I seemed to remember having heard some one say that soap was good as a hemetick; and so I found it; for by the time I had swallowed half the bar I felt desperate sick, and joyful I was to feel it, I can tell you; but still I wasn't bad enough to please myself, so I drank some water and had three or four slices more, and that about finished me, and I lay down among the tussocks by the water side; and what with the fright, and the early rising, and the long walk, and the heat of the sun, joined to the murmur-like of the creek, I went off into the comfortablest sleep as I ever had, and it wasn't till the sun had got right behind the high hills to the westward that I woke up. I reckon it was the barking of Munro's dog that woke me, for the poor beast found he had more than he could do to manage the mob of sheep. They must have been feeding some time, and now wanted to be off up the hill to their camping ground; for you must know, ma'am, that sheep never settle for the night on low ground. They always travel up as high as they can conveniently get, and camp on the top of a hill.

"The poor beast seemed quite joyful to see it was me coming to help him, as he thought, but I couldn't give my mind to the sheep, not just yet. I was rather empty and a bit weak, but as well as ever I felt in my life. I remember I took off my hat, and looked up to the sky and I thanked God in my own rough fashion for saving my life all along of that bar of soap, and I give you my word, ma'am, I meant it, even when I found out my mistake. I thought I'd look up Munro and the other little chap, but I was more than half frightened to go and see about 'em, for at that time you see, I thought I was wot you may call the sole surwivor. However, the others were surwivors too, and a very good job for 'em *that* was. Munro had pegged away into a bag of salt until he must have reg'larly *cured* his inside in more senses than one, whilst Joe had hemeticked himself by shoving his fingers down his throat. Poor Joe! he must have been desperate bad too. Well, they'd been to sleep as well as me, and there we stood staring at each other, awful pale and haggard-looking, but still safe and well so far.

"Munro was the first to recover himself, and he said, 'Them sheep'll be off before we can count ten,' so with that we went to help the dog, who was barking hisself off his legs. Joe Smelt hung back a bit at first, for he said he'd heard as how exercise caused pison to work, but Munro called out, 'Do your duty Joe, and never mind the pison.'

"So we got the sheep together, and we brought 'em down to the homestead, and right glad the boss was to see 'em. When I told him the story of the shoulder of mutton, he went nearly as white as we did, and he said he'd send for the doctor and tell him to bring proper hemeticks along, but we felt we couldn't stand no more not just then, and Joe says, says he, 'It wouldn't be no manner of use, sir, not till we'd had some supper.' With that the boss laughs and tells the manager to give us each a glass of hot grog; and very comfortin' it was. That's all, ma'am," concluded Bob, getting up from his hencoop and making me a bow.

"No, no, Bob," I cried, "that isn't all; I must know the end."

"There wasn't no more end than that, ma'am; leastways when Davis turned up, which he did by chance next day, at the home station, we werry nearly made an end to him when he lets out that there never had been no pison on the shoulder of mutton at all. He said he'd cooked it, meaning to take it in his swag for his supper that night, and was fine and mad when he found he'd forgotten it. Mr Vans-start, he said we ought to be downright thankful to Davis when we found he hadn't let us in for his pison, but we couldn't see it in that light no how, and we give Davis, one and all of us, a bit of our minds, and Joe Smelt offered to fight him the very next Sunday for five pounds a side. Poor Davis! he made us mad by the way he laughed and he tried to comfort us by telling us that if the 'Vermin Destroyer' did us as little harm as it did the rats, we needn't to have cried out. 'Why, they thrive on it,' he said. 'I lets 'em have it pretty often, and they comes about more than ever arter a dose on it.'"

Bob's story took a long time in the telling, for he told it very deliberately, and enjoyed a long word, or any pet expression, such as his life-buouy, so intensely that he repeated it over and over again, rolling the words in his mouth as if they were good to taste. By the time he had finished, the valley was in deep shadow, and the delicious crisp feeling in the air, which always follows a summer's day in our New Zealand hills, made us feel inclined for a change of occupation. The quoits were got out, and the iron pegs stuck in the ground, and some of the shearers were soon hard at work pitching the heavy circlets through the air. Another group were putting the stone or the hammer, whilst a few made themselves very hot by running races or having hopping matches. The constant open-air exercise, keeps men of all grades in New Zealand in such good condition that, even in such rough primitive sports as these were, I have seen far more surprising feats of strength performed by athletes who had had no other training than their daily hill-walks and frugal, wholesome fare, than in the *champ-clos* of a fashionable arena in the old country.

But to-morrow's work must begin with the dawn so whilst there was yet light to see their way home across the rolling downs which stretched like a green sea before us, the good-nights were said. I stood in the porch and shook hands with each guest as he passed, though the performance of this ceremony entailed deep blushes on the part of my stalwart company. "Here's wishin' you the best o' luck, mum," was the general adieu; but when they all got to the bottom of the paddock, they consulted together and gave a ringing hearty cheer, which woke up the valley's quiet echoes, may be for the first time since it emerged from the water-world. "One more for Old Father Christmas," were the last words I heard, as I turned indoors, leaving the joyous sounds to die gradually away into the deep perfumy silence which hung over that lonely valley of the Malvern Hills.

QUESTIONS

1. What does the story of the boar hunt and the Christmas celebrations tell the reader about gender and class restrictions of the period?

2. Why do the men at the Christmas party feel so uncomfortable in the presence of the narrator?

3. What can we discern about the nature of the early settlers' lives from Bob's tale?

4. There is only one mention of the Maori people in the story. How does the narrator view them from this reference, and what events in New Zealand at this time would have influenced her?

Alfred A. Grace

(1867–1942)

Son of a Christian missionary and one of a dozen children, Alfred Grace was born in Auckland. His family had brought Christianity to the Maori people, so the growing boy was familiar with Maori customs and stories. Grace was sent to England to be educated when he was eight, and when a teenager in Sussex, his family was visited by the Maori king, Tawhiao, which demonstrates the family's close ties with the Maori people.

When he finished his English high school education at St. John's College, Grace returned to New Zealand to teach and write in Nelson. He married and took a predominant role in local government and the militia. Amidst these activities and raising a family, Grace began writing short stories and articles for the *Bulletin*, probably the most prestigious journal in Australasia at the time. He published three collections of stories during his lifetime: *Maoriland Stories* (1895), *Tales of a Dying Race* (1901), and *Hone Tiki Dialogues* (1910). Not surprisingly, these collections are all concerned with his experiences with the Maori. "The Ngarara" is from his 1901 collection *Tales of a Dying Race*. Although Grace had an extensive knowledge of the Maori, throughout his writings his imperialistic representation of them is somewhat problematic from a postcolonial perspective. It is difficult to escape the feeling that Grace displays a rather paternalistic attitude toward the Maori and that he never quite takes them seriously. This is not to suggest that he demeans them, but rather that he treats them a bit like precocious children.

Further, especially in the last two short story collections, Grace writes with an aura of sentimentality about the passing of the Maori civilization. Clearly, Grace observes much in the Maori attitude toward life that deserves mention, but these values and lifestyles are regretfully an impediment to British imperialism and must be cast aside. "The Ngarara" is an example of this attitude. The story is clearly a traditional Maori folktale retold by a person without much empathy for the values and underlying cultural mores being emphasized. If one "unpacks" the story, the values of communal effort, bravery against impossible odds, originality, and romance are seen at its core. In Grace's rendering, the fairy tale element and the sentimental happy ending seem somehow at odds with the purport of the tale. The story is not critical of the Maori; it simply fails to do justice to their values.

Grace's work met with interest in the United Kingdom, and he wrote several novels about the Maori: *Atareta* (1908) and *The Tale of Timber Town* (1914). He wrote a history of Maori folktales and a number of historical studies of his district. Grace was able to bring Europeans a good deal of the local color and adventure of New Zealand life with his writings.

The Ngarara 1901

The canoe, carried helpless on the top of a big roller, grounded on the beach with a bump which shook the thwarts out of her and threw Kahu-ki-te-rangi and his companions sprawling on the sand.

Kahu' 's companions were Popoia and Kareao: they three were the sole survivors of a large fishing-party which had left Mamaku, a hundred miles and more down the coast, and had been blown out to sea.

Kahu', Popoia, and Kareao were almost dead with cold and hunger, and for a while lay stiff and motionless, till Kahu' rose and began to stamp his feet and chafe himself.

"Then, you are not dead, Kahu'?" said Kareao. "I, too, have some life left in me"; and he rose, and began to run to and fro to restore his circulation.

Popoia got up last.

"I, too, am here," he said; "but my limbs are stiff like the branches of a tree."

The sun just then broke out brightly, and the three men soon got warm, though they were hungrier than ever.

First they hauled the canoe high and dry; then they took their wet *korowai* cloaks and hung them in the sun. "Now," said Kahu', "we will see what sort of food we can find in this place." And he led the others up the beach.

They closely examined the vegetation which grew thickly along the shore, but could find nothing to eat—not so much as a berry. They had almost given up in despair, when Kahu', who was ahead of Popoia and Kareao, cried out:

"Come here! These look like wild *kumara*."[1]

"This is an old plantation which has been overgrown," said Kareao.

---

1 *kumara:* New Zealand sweet potato.

"Anyhow," said Popoia, "we have found food."

Some of the sweet tubers they ate raw, others they took to the place where they had come ashore.

"Now," said Kahu', "we will make a fire." With a heavy stone he broke one of the canoe thwarts,[2] from which he split a piece about an inch thick. This last he handed to Kareao. "There," he said, "you take the *kaureure*[3]; I and Popoia will hold the *kauati*," which was what he called the rest of the thwart.

Kareao put the point of the *kaureure* upon the middle of the *kauati*, and worked it backwards and forwards with sharp, strong strokes.

"Ah," he said, "you two have the easy part, holding the *kauati*. You know that part; you have done it before. But I am the strong man—I have the *kaureure*. I make the *kauati* hot, I make the fire come. I am the man."

The other two laughed.

But, all the same, Kareao grew tired, and was glad when Popoia rose to help him with the *kaureure*. When Popoia had got a good hold of the implement. Kareao let go, and helped to hold the *kauati*.

"Hah!" said Popoia. "You are not the man, Kareao. With you the *kaureure* had no strength, no heat; but the *kumara* I have eaten give me power; I give the power to the *kaureure*, and the *kaureure* gives it to the *kauati*. But I have done that before, many times. I am the man with the burning *kaureure*!"

And the others laughed.

But at last Popoia grew tired, and his rubbing flagged. Kahu' rose and relieved him.

"Now," said Kahu', "you will see what I can do. So far I have been silent, but that was because I waited to see how you two would succeed. One, two, three, four! Hoo! ha! hoo! ha! Now watch. In my hands the *kaureure* is the begetter of fire. One, two; one, two. I do with the *kauati* what I please. See, it smokes! Hoo! ha! hoo! ha! It burns! Quick, Popoia! the dry grass!"

The *kauati* was now smouldering, and the charred wood and tinder were soon fanned into a flame: the men had made a fire, blazing and hot.

"Now," said Kahu', when they had eaten as many roasted *kumara* as they could, "we will look for water and explore the island. We will see what people live here."

They walked along the beach till they came to high, beetling cliffs, where there was a big cave, and half a mile beyond this they found ruined huts and the remains of a *pa,* which was overgrown with fern and bushes.

"How is this?" said Kareao. "Where are the people?"

"They have gone away," said Kahu'. "They have found a better fishing-ground."

"You two are clever," said Popoia; "you answer a question before it is asked. But what is that at the edge of the clearing?"

A figure was moving from bush to bush, as though watching them.

---

2 **thwarts:** Crosspiece forming a seat for a rower in a boat.

3 *kaureure:* Heavy rock.

"We see you hiding there!" cried Kareao. "Come into the open."

"We won't hurt you," cried Popoia. "Come and tell us who you are."

"Why are you so frightened of us?" asked Kahu', as a bent and skinny old woman approached them.

"Aaaaah! *tena koutou*," wailed she, seizing them by the hands. "*Tena koe! tena koe! Katahi te koa!*" she cried, as she rubbed noses with them one by one. "You are strong handsome men, and I thought you were the Ngarara."

"The Ngarara?" said Popoia.

"Who's he?" said Kareao. "We don't know him."

"What tribe does he belong to?" said Kahu'.

"The Ngarara—you never heard of *him*?" said the old woman. "He is *the* Ngarara—the real one. Big body, eight feet long; big webbed foot; big wings like a bat's, with which he flies and catches fish; long tail like a *tuatara*[4] lizard's, but bigger; skin like the bark of the red pine."

"This is very strange," said Kareao.

"You astonish us," said Popoia.

"Is it really possible?" said Kahu'.

"He came to the island nearly four years ago," said the old woman, "and made his home in a cave which winds far into the cliff. No one but the Ngarara knows all the windings of the cave. When the people were on the beach launching a canoe or looking for *pipi*,[5] out of his cave would rush the Ngarara and catch two or three with his claws, and carry them into his cave, where he would eat them up. Sometimes he would lie in the 'bush' and catch them when they went to snare birds; he would seize the women as they were digging *kumara* in the plantation, and the men as they were fishing from canoes. He was fond of the Maori; he made *kai*[6] of my tribe, of all but me—I am too old, too skinny—and my daughter Hinana."

"Your daughter—why did he spare her?" asked Kareao.

"She is his wife. He keeps her in his cave."

The men's faces were filled with horror.

"Your daughter is the Ngarara's wife!" exclaimed Popoia.

"We must take her from him," said Kahu'.

"She was the prettiest girl on the island," said the old woman. "The Ngarara saw that—he keeps her for himself. But if you stay here inactive he will catch you, too, and eat *you* up! Yet, if you are brave, very brave, I will show you a way to kill him. We shall see—we shall see. Come down with me to the beach."

The old woman led them through the "bush" to a distant part of the island, where the smooth sand stretched half a mile.

"Now," she said, as they stood in a group round her, "you see that pile of drift-wood lying just below high-water mark? You shall run a race to that and back again,

---

4 **tuatara:** Type of lizard.
5 **pipi:** Clams and cockles.
6 **kai:** Food.

and the man who wins shall have my daughter when we have rescued her from the Ngarara. One, two, three—go!"

Away raced the men across the soft, smooth sand, their feet leaving long tracks behind them, till the old woman's weak sight could no longer distinguish one runner from another.

When they rounded the driftwood they came back, each straining every muscle to reach the old woman first. But one man was far ahead of the others. It was Kahu-ki-te-rangi; he won easily.

"Very good," said the old woman; "you are a quick runner; you are rightly called Kahu-ki-te-rangi—'the Hawk in the Heavens.' I will now show you the Ngarara."

So they all went through the "bush" to the other side of the island, and lay concealed on the top of a high cliff.

"The tide has turned," said the old woman. "When it is nearly full the Ngarara comes out to catch fish. His cave is underneath the spot where we are lying."

What she said was quite true, for before very long they heard a terrific noise in the earth beneath them, and the Ngarara appeared on the sands below.

He was black all over. His great head was like a bird's, but featherless and bare, and ended in a huge tapering muzzle, which was armed with numberless sharp teeth. His body was like a great bat's, and his wings, which at first he held close to his sides, ended at the top in bunches of sharp claws. He ran down to the water's edge after the manner of a great sea-fowl, snapping his horrible teeth this way and that in his eagerness to catch his prey.

When he had waded into the water up to his middle, he stretched out his wings, which extended twenty feet from tip to tip, and scooped the fish first with one wing and then with the other into his open mouth. But when the fish fled in fear into deep water, the Ngarara flew after them like a bird, dived, and caught them with his immense jaws, which he snapped together so loudly that the sound reached Kahu', Kareao, and Popoia, as they stood on the cliff.

"It is time we went," said the old woman. "If we stay here any longer he will see us, and then he will certainly eat you up. Let us go and make the *taiepa-whare*[7] in which to catch him."

"Urrrgh!" exclaimed Kahu', shuddering, "it would be better to be eaten than to be the wife of such a monster."

So they went into the heart of the "bush," and there the old woman gave them heavy stone axes with which they cut down thick branches of the trees. These they placed firmly side by side, in two rows each, a chain long and six feet apart, and the roof, which was ten feet from the ground, they made of lighter boughs and *toé-toé*. Then they drove a strong stake into the ground so as to block one entrance, and heaped dry fern and *toé-toé* on each side of the *taiepa-whare*, and all the preparations were made for the reception of the Ngarara.

---

7 **taiepa-whare:** Type of trap.

"Now," said the old woman, "there remains but one thing. Here is a *pouwhenua*,[8] stout and strong, for each of you. You, Kareao, stand with this big spear on one side of the *taiepa-whare*, and you, Popoia, take this and stand on the other. Kahu', take yours and place it in the *taiepa-whare*, about the middle, and then go and do as I have directed. You are a good runner; now is the time to prove that you are indeed Kahu-ki-te-rangi, that you can run as fast as a hawk flies in the heavens. See if you can race the Ngarara."

So Kahu' departed, alone and unarmed. He passed through the forest till he came to the beetling cliff above the Ngarara's cave, and there he called out:

"Cooooeeeeee! Cooooooooooooeeee! Cooooooooooooeeee!"

Soon there was a noise like rumbling thunder in the bowels of the earth, and out of his cave came the Ngarara.

First he ran this way along the beach, then he ran that, but could see nothing.

"Cooooooooooooeeeee!" called Kahu' from the top of the cliff, and in a moment the Ngarara caught sight of him.

Kahu' saw the great jaws open and display their lines of teeth, and he retreated to the shelter of the "bush."

There was a great flapping and the sound of falling rocks, and right over the face of the cliff came the Ngarara, with open mouth and scrambling feet and flapping wings.

Kahu' turned and ran.

The Ngarara pursued. First he stretched out one wing to scoop the Maori into his mouth, then he stretched out the other; but each wing caught in a tree, and Kahu' ran uninjured through the forest. But now the Ngarara folded his wings and ran, too. Kahu' could hear his heavy breathing, and smelt the horrible odour of his body. Again and again the Ngarara had almost caught his prey in his teeth, but Kahu-ki-te-rangi had not received his name for nothing, and he ran fast to the mouth of the *taiepa-whare*—on either side of which his comrades lay concealed— and disappeared inside of the trap.

The Ngarara, in his eagerness to catch his prey never noticed that the leaves on the boughs of the *taiepa-whare* were beginning to wither. He did not see Popoia and Kareao hiding behind the heaps of *toé-toé* and fern. He plunged straight into the *taiepa-whare* after Kahu'.

Kareao and Popoia immediately arose, each grasping his *pouwhenua*, and stood ready. Kahu' ran to the middle of the trap, where he found his weapon, and seizing this he turned and faced the Ngarara.

And now the great reptile was caught at a disadvantage. The constricted space of the *taiepa-whare* pressed his formidable wings close to his sides, and rendered his claws almost useless. His teeth were the only weapons he had left; but they were many, and sharp, and long.

---

8 **pouwhenua:** Sharp spear.

With these he snapped menacingly at Kahu', but Kahu' never flinched, and bravely awaited the onslaught of the Ngarara.

Plunge! He had driven his big spear into the reptile's eye, and pinned the monster's great head to the earth.

The Ngarara lashed with his tail, and in his agony tried to burst the walls of the trap with the weight of his huge body; but his endeavours only made matters worse for him, for Popoia and Kareao could now see in what part of the *taiepa-whare* Karu' held him pinned by his head to the ground. From either side they plunged their stout spears into his belly, and transfixed him to the earth.

Thus they held him, calling to and encouraging each other, till the Ngarara was exhausted and could struggle no more.

Then Kahu' came out of the *taiepa-whare* and set fire to the fern and *toé-toé*.

The Ngarara was burned to ashes.

Throughout this exciting scene the old woman had stood behind a tree, praising the men and cheering them on; but when the Ngarara was dead and burnt she led them down to the mouth of the cave, and called:

"Hinana, come to us. The Ngarara is dead; nothing remains of him. Come to your mother and the brave men who have saved you."

Softly and full of fear the girl crept to the cave's entrance till she caught sight of Kahu', Popoia, Kareao, and her mother.

"But I dare not come," she said, crying. "If the Ngarara were to know that I came out of the cave, he would kill and eat me as he did all my relations."

"But the Ngarara is dead," said Kareao. "I plunged my spear into his body."

"There is nothing left of him but a few charred bones," said Popoia.

"You need not fear," said Kahu'. "If the Ngarara were alive we should not dare to come openly to his cave. When he last left you he pursued me into the *taiepa-whare*, and there I transfixed him with my *pouwhenua*. He is dead, and you are now *my* wife."

"That is all true," said the old woman. "Come, Hinana, and greet your mother and your husband, and then we will show you the place where the Ngarara died."

Convinced, Hinana came out of the cave and *tangi'd*[9] with her deliverers.

"*This* is your husband, Kahu-ki-te-rangi, the man who raced the Ngarara," said her mother. "He will soon make you happy."

"I am quite light-hearted already," said Hinana, "for you can imagine what joy it is to become the wife of such a brave *toa* after having been married to the Ngarara for nearly three years."

QUESTIONS

1. The author is retelling Maori stories from his perspective. What do you sense is his attitude toward the Maori from his tone and description?

---

9 *tangi'd:* Cried.

2. Some critics have condemned Grace's depiction of the Maori as a light-hearted people living in harmony with nature as being a worn-out literary convention. Are the Maori adventurers in this story simply stereotyped creatures in tune with nature, or is there more to them?

3. What exactly is the nature of the quest in this story?

4. Does this tale remind you of similar quests in English or U.S. fiction or cinema? Which ones? In what ways are they alike?

Katherine Mansfield

(1888–1923)

Katherine Mansfield Beauchamp was brought up in provincial Wellington, but at fifteen was sent to London to complete her education at Queen's College. She spent three years there and returned to New Zealand, where she experimented with writing poetry and prose. With limited success, she decided on a literary career in England, and in 1908 she moved to London. She married George C. Bowden in 1909, and ran away from him on the day of her marriage. Eventually, she came back to live with him in London, and it was Bowden who encouraged her to submit some of her short fiction to A. R. Orage, editor of the lively journal *New Age*, which she did with some success.

Her writing career continued to flourish after she met the publisher and critic John Middleton Murry, whom she married in 1918. Mansfield suffered from poor health, and this was exacerbated by the death of her only brother on the battlefield in World War I. By the end of the war, Mansfield's tuberculosis was growing more acute, and she died in France in 1923.

Mansfield's particular talent was her knack of finding significance in the minutiae of life; she was able to create portraits of memorable characters with whom her readers easily identify. Her three collections of short stories are among the finest in any literature. *In a German Pension* (1911) consists of stories set in Bavaria, where Mansfield's foreign scenes are carefully orchestrated and delicately observed. In "A Birthday," the reader observes the bullying of a dominating husband and the travails of a sensitive wife. "At the Bay" deals with the difficulties of pioneering life, and "The Child-Who-Was-Tired," with its well-observed influence of Anton Chekhov, offers democratic sympathy with the underdog. The wide-ranging nature of Mansfield's subject matter and keen scrutiny continued to develop in her last two collections of short stories, *Bliss* (1920) and *The Garden Party* (1922). It is evident that the shock of the Great War permeated Mansfield's fiction; no longer was she only the spectator of life's minutiae, but she developed an agenda that raged against the mechanized postwar world. Her later stories harken back to the idealized New

Zealand of her youth where the past was viewed through rose-tinted nostalgia. Mansfield left a legacy of short fiction, which was continued by Frank Sargeson and countless other New Zealand writers.

The story that follows, "How Pearl Button Was Kidnapped," is perhaps based on a camping excursion to the Urewera district that Mansfield took in 1907. She kept a diary and carefully recorded her reflections of this Maori-populated region. She was deeply impressed with the attitudes and lifestyles of the Maori she encountered and could not help comparing their idealized lifestyles to the restrictive colonial bourgeois world she inhabited. In her short story, much of her depiction of the kidnappers (who probably are Maori) reflects the romantic musings of a writer who is dissastisfied with the limitations and expectations of her own society and craves the spontaneity of what she perceives to be the freedom of the native peoples. But reality, in the form of the "Little men in blue coats," will not allow her to escape her proscribed world easily.

How Pearl Button Was Kidnapped   *1910*

Pearl Button swung on the little gate in front of the House of Boxes. It was the early afternoon of a sunshiny day with little winds playing hide-and-seek in it. They blew Pearl Button's pinafore frill into her mouth, and they blew the street dust all over the House of Boxes. Pearl watched it—like a cloud—like when mother peppered her fish and the top of the pepper-pot came off. She swung on the little gate, all alone, and she sang a small song. Two big women came walking down the street. One was dressed in red and the other was dressed in yellow and green. They had pink handkerchiefs over their heads, and both of them carried a big flax basket of ferns. They had no shoes and stockings on, and they came walking along, slowly, because they were so fat, and talking to each other and always smiling. Pearl stopped swinging, and when they saw her they stopped walking. They looked and looked at her and then they talked to each other, waving their arms and clapping their hands together. Pearl began to laugh.

The two women came up to her, keeping close to the hedge and looking in a frightened way towards the House of Boxes.

"Hallo, little girl!" said one.

Pearl said, "Hallo!"

"You all alone by yourself?"

Pearl nodded.

"Where's your mother?"

"In the kitching, ironing-because-its-Tuesday."

The women smiled at her and Pearl smiled back. "Oh," she said, "haven't you got very white teeth indeed! Do it again."

The dark women laughed, and again they talked to each other with funny words and wavings of the hands. "What's your name?" they asked her.

"Pearl Button."

"You coming with us, Pearl Button? We got beautiful things to show you," whispered one of the women. So Pearl got down from the gate and she slipped out into the road. And she walked between the two dark women down the windy road, taking little running steps to keep up, and wondering what they had in their House of Boxes.

They walked a long way. "You tired?" asked one of the women, bending down to Pearl. Pearl shook her head. They walked much further. "You not tired?" asked the other woman. And Pearl shook her head again, but tears shook from her eyes at the same time and her lips trembled. One of the women gave over her flax basket of ferns and caught Pearl Button up in her arms, and walked with Pearl Button's head against her shoulder and her dusty little legs dangling. She was softer than a bed and she had a nice smell—a smell that made you bury your head and breathe and breathe it. . . .

They set Pearl Button down in a log room full of other people the same colour as they were—and all these people came close to her and looked at her, nodding and laughing and throwing up their eyes. The woman who had carried Pearl took off her hair ribbon and shook her curls loose. There was a cry from the other women, and they crowded close and some of them ran a finger through Pearl's yellow curls, very gently, and one of them, a young one, lifted all Pearl's hair and kissed the back of her little white neck. Pearl felt shy but happy at the same time. There were some men on the floor, smoking, with rugs and feather mats round their shoulders. One of them made a funny face at her and he pulled a great big peach out of his pocket and set it on the floor, and flicked it with his finger as though it were a marble. It rolled right over to her. Pearl picked it up. "Please can I eat it?" she asked. At that they all laughed and clapped their hands, and the man with the funny face made another at her and pulled a pear out of his pocket and sent it bobbling over the floor. Pearl laughed. The women sat on the floor and Pearl sat down too. The floor was very dusty. She carefully pulled up her pinafore and dress and sat on her petticoat as she had been taught to sit in dusty places, and she ate the fruit, the juice running all down her front.

"Oh!" she said in a very frightened voice to one of the women, "I've spilt all the juice!"

"That doesn't matter at all," said the woman, patting her cheek. A man came into the room with a long whip in his hand. He shouted something. They all got up, shouting, laughing, wrapping themselves up in rugs and blankets and feather mats. Pearl was carried again, this time into a great cart, and she sat on the lap of one of her women with the driver beside her. It was a green cart with a red pony and a black pony. It went very fast out of the town. The driver stood up and waved the whip round his head. Pearl peered over the shoulder of her woman. Other carts were behind like a procession. She waved at them. Then the country came. First fields of short grass with sheep on them and little bushes of white flowers and pink briar rose baskets—then big trees on both sides of the road—and nothing to be seen except big trees. Pearl tried to look through them but it was quite dark. Birds were singing. She nestled closer in the big lap. The woman was warm as a cat, and she moved up and down when she breathed, just like purring. Pearl played with a green ornament round her neck, and the woman took the little hand and kissed each of her fingers and then turned it over and kissed the dimples. Pearl had never been happy like this before. On the top of a big hill they stopped. The driving man turned to Pearl and said, "Look, look!" and pointed with his whip.

And down at the bottom of the hill was something perfectly different—a great big piece of blue water was creeping over the land. She screamed and clutched at the big woman. "What is it, what is it?"

"Why," said the woman, "it's the sea."

"Will it hurt us—is it coming?"

"Ai-e, no, it doesn't come to us. It's very beautiful. You look again."

Pearl looked. "You're sure it can't come," she said.

"Ai-e, no. It stays in its place," said the big woman. Waves with white tops came leaping over the blue. Pearl watched them break on a long piece of land covered with garden-path shells. They drove round a corner.

There were some little houses down close to the sea, with wood fences round them and gardens inside. They comforted her. Pink and red and blue washing hung over the fences, and as they came near more people came out, and five yellow dogs with long thin tails. All the people were fat and laughing, with little naked babies holding on to them or rolling about in the gardens like puppies. Pearl was lifted down and taken into a tiny house with only one room and a veranda. There was a girl there with two pieces of black hair down to her feet. She was setting the dinner on the floor. "It *is* a funny place," said Pearl, watching the pretty girl while the woman unbuttoned her little drawers for her. She was very hungry. She ate meat and vegetables and fruit and the woman gave her milk out of a green cup. And it was quite silent except for the sea outside and the laughs of the two women watching her. "Haven't you got any Houses of Boxes?" she said. "Don't you all live in a row? Don't the men go to offices? Aren't there any nasty things?"

They took off her shoes and stockings, her pinafore and dress. She walked about in her petticoat and then she walked outside with the grass pushing between her toes. The two women came out with different sorts of baskets. They took her hands. Over a little paddock, through a fence, and then on warm sand with brown grass in it they went down to the sea. Pearl held back when the sand grew wet, but the women coaxed, "Nothing to hurt, very beautiful. You come." They dug in the sand and found some shells which they threw into the baskets. The sand was wet as mud pies. Pearl forgot her fright and began digging too. She got hot and wet, and suddenly over her feet broke a little line of foam. "Oo, oo!" she shrieked, dabbling with her feet. "Lovely, lovely!" She paddled in the shallow water. It was warm. She made a cup of her hands and caught some of it. But it stopped being blue in her hands. She was so excited that she rushed over to her woman and flung her little thin arms round the woman's neck, hugging her, kissing. . . .

Suddenly the girl gave a frightful scream. The woman raised herself and Pearl slipped down on the sand and looked towards the land. Little men in blue coats—

little blue men came running, running towards her with shouts and whistlings—a crowd of little blue men to carry her back to the House of Boxes.

QUESTIONS

1. Despite the frightening aspects of Pearl's kidnapping, why does the reader feel unthreatened by her abduction?

2. What is the reader's reaction when the "little blue men" come to rescue Pearl?

3. How is colonial bourgeois life compared to the romantic lives of the kidnappers?

4. What are the main contrasts in this story? Is there any reconciliation between them?

5. How does color symbolism function in this story?

Frank Sargeson

(1903–1982)

Frank Sargeson (Norris Frank Davey) was born and raised on the North Island of New Zealand in the town of Hamilton; his profession was the law, but his passion was writing. He was the kind of man who mixed with all levels of society, but found particular difficulties with people who held bourgeois values. Like many writers of his age, the effects of the Great Depression colored his writing experience, and he was concerned with depicting the way in which the poor were exploited by the vicissitudes of the economy and those in power. During the 1920s, he traveled throughout Europe, but he decided to return to New Zealand and raise sheep and grow vegetables in the area around Takapuna. Many of his early stories were published in the 1930s in *Tomorrow*, a Christchurch literary journal.

His short fiction is unique, and while the influence of the Americans Sherwood Anderson and Ernest Hemingway can be detected, he evolved a style and form that are original. Like Mansfield, the span of his literary concerns is very broad. In his first collection of short stories, *Conversations with My Uncle and Other Sketches* (1936), Sargeson was content to question the values taken for granted in a bourgeois society—such as the acceptance of economic monopoly or the importance of property. In his 1940 collection, *A Man and His Wife*, a number of the sketches focus on the vulnerability of childhood or the world of inarticulate or marginalized people who strive in vain to articulate their secret needs and desires. With the publication of *That Summer and Other Stories* (1946), Sargeson continued his investigations into the sterility of

The next day one of the Dallies brought the billy over but I didn't see him. When we were milking Mrs Crump told me. He was the one called Nick, and the evening before he'd had to take his mate into hospital. He'd had a spill off his bike and broken some ribs and his collar-bone. Mrs Crump thought perhaps there'd been some drinking, she said they made wine. Anyhow Nick was upset. If his mate died, he said, he would die too. He'd have nothing left, nothing. And how could he work and live there by himself when his mate was lying all broken up in the hospital? Every afternoon he would leave off working and ride into town to see his mate.

There's a pal for you, Mrs Crump said.

Well, up at the fence the billy would always be on the hook, but if Nick was in town seeing his cobber[5] I'd think it would be no use going over. Then one evening he was just coming across with the billy so I went over to meet him. We greeted each other, and I think we both felt a bit shy. He was small and dark, almost black, and his flannel and denims were pretty far gone the same as mine were. I gave him my tin and told him to roll a cigarette, and when he lit up he went cross-eyed. I noticed that, and I saw too that there was a sort of sadness on his face.

I asked him how his cobber was, and he said he was good.

In two days he will be here, he said. You could see he was excited about it and his face didn't look so sad. In two weeks, he said, it will be just as if it never happened.

That's great, I said, and we sat down and smoked.

How's the dog? I said.

He is getting better too, Nick said.

He whistled, and the dog pulled himself over to us by his front paws and put his chin on Nick's leg, and somehow with the dog there it was easier to talk.

I asked Nick about his trees and he said they were all right, but there were too many diseases.

Too much quick manure, I said.

He said yes, but what could they do? It would take a long time to make the soil deep and sweet like it was in the part of Dalmatia he came from. Out here everybody wanted money quick, so they put on the manure. It was money, money, all the time. But he and his mate never had any. Everything they got they had to pay out, and if the black-spot got among the apples they had to pay out more than they got. Then one of them had to go out and try for a job.

It's the manure that gives you the black-spot, I said.

Sometimes I think it is God, Nick said.

Well, maybe you're right, I said, but what about the grapes?

Oh, Nick said, they grow, yes. But they are not sweet. To make wine we must put in sugar. In Dalmatia it is not done. Never.

Yes, I said, but you don't go back to Dalmatia.

Oh no, he said, now I am a New Zealander.

No, I said, but your children will be.

I have no children and I will never marry, Nick said.

5 **cobber:** Buddy; pal.

No? I said, then your cobber will.

He will never marry either, Nick said.

Why? I said, there are plenty of Dalmatian girls out here. I bet you could get New Zealand girls too.

But Nick only said no, no, no, no, no.

If you were in Dalmatia I bet you'd be married, I said.

But I am not in Dalmatia, Nick said, now I am a New Zealander. In New Zealand everybody says they cannot afford to get married.

Yes, I said, that's what they say. But it's all wrong.

Yes, Nick said, it is all wrong. Because it is all wrong I am a Communist.

Good, I said. Well, I thought, spoil a good peasant and you might as well go the whole hog.

I bet you don't tell Mrs Crump you're a Communist, I said.

Oh no, Nick said, she would never be a Communist.

No fear, I said.

I will tell you about Mrs Crump, Nick said. She should go to Dalmatia. In Dalmatia our women wear bags on their heads just like her, and she would be happy there.

Yes, I said, I believe you're right. But Nick, I said, I thought you'd be a Catholic.

No, Nick said. It is all lies. In Dalmatia they say that Christ was born when there was snow on the ground in Palestine. But now I have read in a book there is no snow in Palestine. So now I know that they tell lies.

So you're a Communist instead, I said.

Yes, I am a Communist, Nick said. But what is the good of that? I am born too soon, eh? What do you think?

Maybe, I said.

You too, Nick said. You think that you and me are born too soon? What do you think?

He said it over and over, and I couldn't look him in the face. It had too much of that sadness . . . I mightn't have put it the way Nick had, I mightn't have said I was born too soon, but Nick knew what he was talking about. Nick and I were sitting on the hillside and Nick was saying he was a New Zealander, but he knew he wasn't a New Zealander. And he knew he wasn't a Dalmatian any more.

He knew he wasn't anything any more.

Listen, Nick said, do you drink wine?

Yes, I said.

Then to-morrow night you come up here and we will drink wine, Nick said.

Yes, I said, that's O.K. with me.

There is only to-morrow night, Nick said, then my mate will be here. We will drink a lot of wine, I have plenty and we will get very, very drunk. Oh, heaps drunk.

Yes, I said. Sure thing.

To-morrow night, he said.

He got up and I got up, he just waved his hand at me and walked off. He picked the dog up under his arm and walked off, and I just stood there and watched him go.

But it turned out I never went up to Nick's place. When I was having my tea that evening Mrs Crump told me about how a woman she knew had worked too hard and dropped dead with heart failure. But there's nothing wrong with my heart, she said.

No, I said, except that maybe it's not in the right place.

Of course it must have sounded like one of my wisecracks, but I was thinking of Dalmatia.

Anyhow Mrs Crump said she's stood enough from me, so when I'd finished my tea I could go.

I wasn't sorry. I stood on the road and wondered if I'd go up to Nick's place, but instead I walked into town, and for a good few days I never left off drinking.

I wanted to get Nick out of my mind. He knew what he was talking about, but maybe it's best for a man to hang on.

QUESTIONS

1. Sargeson's characters are delineated very economically with very little narration and idiomatic vocabulary. How do these qualities add to the story's veracity?

2. What is the economic situation in this story? How does it affect the unfolding of the story?

3. What is the nature of "mateship" in this story? Why are the two Dalmatians so dependent on each other?

4. In what ways does the narrator's relationship with Mrs. Crump function as a frame for the story about Nick?

5. What disconcerting truth does the narrator discover from his experience with Nick at the conclusion of the story?

Douglas Stewart

(1913–1985)

Douglas Alexander Stewart was born in Eltham, Taranaki, New Zealand. His father was an Australian-born lawyer who educated his son at New Plymouth Boys' High School. Stewart studied law at Wellington University College, but he never finished the degree. Instead, he decided to try his hand at journalism, but he moved to Sydney without any results. In 1938, he returned to Sydney and, by 1940, had become the literary editor of the very prestigious *Bulletin*, a job he held until 1961. After this, he became a very influential literary critic in Australia.

Stewart's creative career was stimulated by a series of successful theater and radio plays that he wrote during World War II. His radio plays included *The Fire on the Snow* (1941) and *The Golden Lover* (1944), while his most successful stage plays include *Shipwreck* (1941) and *Ned Kelly* (1943). He was also a successful poet, and his poems were collected into one volume in 1967. He published only one volume of short stories, entitled *A Girl with Red Hair and Other Stories* (1944). He wrote a number of critical studies of Australian literature, including *Short Stories of Australia, the Lawson Tradition* (1967), and his autobiography, *Springtime in Taranaki,* was published just before his death in 1985. In the majority of his works, Stewart was concerned with the spirit of place and man's continual struggle with the environment.

"The Whare" first appeared in *The Girl with Red Hair and Other Stories* and is full of the detailed description for which Stewart is rightly commended. The depiction of the meeting between the narrator and the Maori family is detailed with deft artistic images. The whare and its surroundings come vividly alive under the lush, sensitive writing. But the story is about the legendary Maori hospitality and generosity that the narrator receives from the old Maori couple and his "repayment" by leaving stealthily at night in order to escape being made part of the family. One of his fears is that the honest communal life of the Maori will somehow seduce him from the free but solitary life of the road.

The Whare[1]

1944

It was six months since those fleas had tasted anything but Maori. They leaped at a white skin like a shoal of herrings at a loaf of bread. They came from the dust under the raupo[2] mats and they were there in millions. Every ten minutes or so, when the irritation became unendurable, you could roll up your trousers and scrape them off like sand or bid-a-bid seeds. But attacking them was a waste of time, and unless a particularly savage pang forced you into action, you just sat and let yourself be devoured.

The old chief and his wife, with their hard, leathery skins, hardly seemed to notice them. Sometimes when the woman saw that I was in trouble she would say, "Ah! You got te flea, eh?" and she would promise to boil a kerosene tin of water, shift the mats and scald the brutes to death. "T'ose flea! We boil 'em, t'at te way to fix 'em." If the chief on some rare occasion, sitting by the open fire in the whare at night, felt a pinprick through his hide, he said "Flea! Bitem!" in a tone of pleased discovery. He took a pride in his fleas. Their presence cheered him, their habits interested him, and

---

1 **whare:** A Maori hut or house.
2 **raupo:** Like a bullrush, a wetland plant.

their prowess delighted him. They were his *lares et penates*,[3] or the flocks and herds of a patriarch.

Maybe I exaggerate the importance of the fleas. In the long run, for there were processes of the mind more powerful than those ridiculous irritations of the flesh, I should probably have come to the same decision without their prompting. But I don't want memory, always a romantic, to sentimentalize them out of existence. They did force a decision.

I drifted into the Maori settlement with the greatest simplicity. I was trudging along the road in the sunny midday, heading north, when a tall native, riding bareback on an old grey mare, came cantering up the road behind me. He stopped short beside me, the mare grunting with relief and indignation, and said, "You've got a heavy swag,[4] Jack. Carry it for you?"

The morning seemed sunnier after that. It was good to be able to walk freely. The road wound along a ridge from which the ragged country, broken into gullies and patchworked with leaden tea-tree and an occasional acre of ploughed land or yellowish grass, fell with the slow sweep of a glacier into the shallow harbour of Kaipara. The water, so far away, had lost its quick sparkle and become some new element more like metal, a sheet of silvery tinfoil among the gigantic hills. It was hard desolate country, but it couldn't depress you when the sun was shining on the red clay cuttings and the mare's hooves were clip-clopping on the stones, and you had nothing to do but walk along the road and look at things.

The Maori, who seemed to be about thirty-five years old, was slim and sombre. He spoke little, and appeared to be turning something over in his mind. At last he said, "My father will give you some lunch."

I said "Good!" and then wished I hadn't, for the monosyllable might have sounded like pidgin-English, and his own was perfect. He had probably been to one of the Maori colleges and then, as most of his people do, come back to the pa.

We plodded on until we caught sight of a tumble-down whare standing among the rushes of an upland swamp on a plateau above the harbour. "That's my place," said the horseman. "You can sleep there if you like, have a rest for a day or two. I don't live there now. It's pretty rough," he added.

He wasn't very enthusiastic. Afterwards I found out that various swaggies in the past had abused the hospitality of the little tribe, and I came to the conclusion that the young Maori resented it and that, although the tradition of welcome to the stranger was too strong for him to break, maybe his children would rebel against it.

The whare, like all deserted homes, was dirty and forlorn. The broken iron bedstead, the torn mats, the cook-pot lying on its side in the dust, the rain-sodden, long-dead ashes, the cobwebs and the rat-droppings—they were the apparatus of ghosts. Behind the building was the Maori's inevitable totem—a broken-down limousine,

---

3 ***lares et penates:*** Household gods.
4 **swag:** Load of personal belongings.

rusting into the grass. The Maori dropped my swag and we went back to the road and up to the settlement on the hill-side.

Half a dozen Maoris, squatting on the grass outside one of the whares, stared at us in good-humoured curiosity. They were all eating and drinking. One of the young fellows said something in Maori to a squat, dumpy girl, and she laughed. They went on eating.

The Maori took me to the whare door and introduced me to his father and mother, chief and chieftainess of the settlement. The woman, bent and skinny and weather-beaten like a twist of a withered grass, smiled a welcome. From her beaked nose her face fell away in a landslide of wrinkles to a toothless mouth, achieving some dignity again in a firm, tattooed chin. The old man had the stamp of aristocracy both in manners and features. His hair and moustache were grey, his brown eyes clear, his cheeks smooth. But for his colouring and his thick lower lip he could have passed for a European.

"Eh, Jack," he said, "you come a long way?"

"From Taranaki," I told him.

"Eh, Tara-naki," he drawled in soft amazement, as if I had come from the moon. His geography was vague. He had been to Auckland, though. He and the old woman had stayed with relations in the city—probably at that squalid settlement by the blue harbour—for several months, and then come back to the kumara[5] patch and the whare. I imagined them labouring along Queen Street, staring in wonder and delight at the shops and the traffic. It would be like a visit to a foreign country.

The woman came out of the darkness of the whare with a mug of tea and a plate piled with pipis[6] and something which looked like green string and which I was told was boiled watercress.

"You like te pipi?"

"Kapai!"[7]

"Kapai!" She laughed. There was no fear of insulting her by using pidgin-English. Her pakeha[8] vocabulary was small, and you had to speak simply and slowly to make her understand. She treated the barrier of tongues as a joke laughing with pleasure when she could comprehend and with amusement when she couldn't. Her conversation was full of expressive "what-you-callums."

Some sort of council-of-war, which I sensed concerned me, went on while I was negotiating the shell-fish and the boiled watercress (which tasted like barbed wire), and when it was over the young Maori went off on the mare and the old man said, "You stay wit' me, eh, Jack? T'at other place no good. You stay here wit' me. The missus make you a bed in te whare-puni.[9]"

---

5 **kumara:** New Zealand sweet potato.
6 **pipis:** Clams and cockles.
7 **Kapai!:** Good! Excellent!
8 **pakeha:** White European.
9 **te whare-puni:** Guest house.

meaning but as a token of friendship. You said something to the old woman, or she said something to you, in the comradely way you'd talk to a dog you were fond of. The response was the same—a tail wagged in the mind.

On the second day I helped the tribe to store the kumaras for the winter. They gave me a black stallion to ride—not, unfortunately, a great proud snorting beast with a fiery eye and a flowing mane, but a typical product of Maori horse-breeding, a dusty, ragged, somnambulistic runt—and I made repeated trips from the whare to the field across the road where the women were digging the earthy red-purple sweet-potatoes. Taking their time about it, grubbing in the earth with their hands, they'd fill a sack and lift it up to me while I sat on the stallion. They cracked jokes to each other in Maori and laughed a lot.

The men had a pit dug at the back of the whare, lined with fern leaves. They tipped the kumaras into the pit and, when there was a fair-sized mound, laid more fern leaves around the sides and on top, then covered the pile with clay. It was easy work, very pleasant in the light May sunshine. The men smoked and lazed between trips. Nobody hurried. The little stallion was the only one tired enough to feel relieved when I brought the last load home in the dark and sent him off into the tea-tree with a smack on the rump.

Both the Maoris were sympathetic about the fleas that night. They would "get te boiling water and kill 'em all for sure" one day—tomorrow. It wouldn't be long till the frosts came, and they weren't so bad then.

The futile promises were a bit irritating; the fleas were maddening. I'd get up and stamp about the room for relief, then sit down beside the old man and stare at the fire again. When the fleas had drunk their fill and were sleeping it off, there was something curiously attractive about the whare, especially one night when it rained and the big drops fell hissing into the fire. You thought of those miles of lonely wet hills, and it was good to be indoors. We sat for hours, it seemed, without talking, listening to the rain hammering on the iron roof. It drove us closer together, wove us into a primitive human companionship—three against the storm. I imagined the old couple sitting together by the fire year after year, and saw myself with them, staring at the flames interminably, not talking and not thinking, sunk in a dark tide of physical sympathy, with somewhere in the chasms of the mind a vague sadness. There was a touch of nightmare about the vision and afterwards it haunted me.

That wet night the woman, grinning, asked me, "You got a girl, eh? You sad. You got a girl somewhere, a long way away? You leave te girl behind and forget her now?"

"Yes," I told her. "I've got a girl. She's a long way away."

"Maybe you get te Maori girl, eh? How you like te Maori wife?"

Then she told me there was to be a dance at the meeting-house on the Saturday. "You meet te nice girl at te dance. Plenty wahine!"[11]

When I was alone with the rats and the sparrows, with the feeble light of the candle emphasizing the cavernous gloom of the whare-puni, I began to see that the

---

11 **wahine:** Women.

woman had been testing me out. The old man that day had bought me another tin of tobacco and broached a great scheme whereby we were going to earn twelve pounds between us cutting rushes for a pakeha farmer down the road. Before the job started, we were to go down to the harbour and get in a store of pipis from the mud-flats. He was including me in all his plans as a matter of course. I had come to stay.

"You not want to go, eh? You stay here as long as you like. You stay wit' us. You not want to go away."

I didn't work the next day. I felt restless and went for a walk along the road. A farmer—perhaps the one for whom we were to cut the rushes—saw me leaning over a bridge and had a yarn. He said if I registered on the unemployed he'd give me a job, with five bob a week added to the Government subsidy. I told him I'd think it over.

I was thinking everything over, and thinking with a queer urgency, almost panic, in the whare that night.

"Tomorrow we get te pipi."

"We cut te rushes, contrac' for a fortnight; make twelve poun'."

"Plenty nice Maori girl come on Saturday."

"You not want to go away."

Well, it would be interesting getting the pipis. I'd often watched the Maoris wading in shallow waters and reaching into the blue mud for the shell-fish, and it would be good to help them. I wouldn't mind rush-cutting, either. That would be something new and it ought to be as pleasant as scything the ragwort at Whangamomona. As for a Maori girl, the ukuleles and steel guitars and the rattle-trap piano all going like mad and the young bucks shouting the choruses—the way I'd often seen them—good!

Or would it be? Wouldn't you be isolated, mooching about on your own between dances, a stranger at the party? Maybe they'd be a bit antagonistic; certainly they'd be curious. Even if they gave you a good time and you joined in the singing, you'd be acting a part. You wouldn't belong.

"How you like te Maori wife, eh, Jack?"

I looked at the old couple nodding by the fire, the light on their dark faces. What did I really know about them? What went on in those secretive Maori minds? They weren't animals. They had their own thoughts, based on a conception of life beyond my understanding. What possible communion could there be between the white man and the native? The memory of that deep, mindless sympathy when we sat quietly by the fire on the wet night was uncannily disturbing, horrible. The friendly little whare was a prison.

"T'at flea! Tomorrow I kill te lot of 'em."

When I went to bed they bit like devils. It was going to be a long, restless night. I thought of the Maoris' incredible kindliness. What lovable people they were! But I saw how their generosity was binding me to them. "Tomorrow we get te pipis." "Next week we cut te rushes." Next month, next year——

After a while I climbed out of bed and wrote a note.

Thank you to being so good to me. I hope I can repay you some day. I'm
sorry to go away like this without saying good-bye. I hope you'll understand; it's just that I have to be moving on. Don't think I'm not grateful.

JACK.

Feeling as guilty as if I'd been the swaggie who stole the blankets, I packed my
swag and crept out of the whare. There was a full moon, and the old mysterious enchantment in the vast hills and the tea-tree. Along the ridge above the glitter of the
harbour, the road was white. I could have shouted for joy at the way it ran over the
rise and disappeared into the country I'd never seen.

I walked hard all night, half expecting to see the young Maori come galloping
after me on the indignant grey mare and force me to go back to the pa for fear of
hurting his feelings.

QUESTIONS

1. Discuss the nature of Maori hospitality as portrayed in this story.

2. What "processes of the mind" are at work on Jack as he stays at the whare?
   What is he learning about?

3. Is this a sentimental or realistic depiction of Maori life?

4. Ultimately, what causes Jack to leave the whare secretly and guiltily during the
   night?

A. P. Gaskell

(1913–?)

A. P. Gaskell (born Alexander Gaskell Pickard) was born in Kurow, North
Otago, New Zealand. His father worked for the railway, so much of his early life
consisted of moving around New Zealand. He attended eight different schools
before graduating from high school. He was educated at Dunedin Teacher's
College and gained an MA in English and French at the University of Otago.
Most of his adult life he worked as a schoolteacher, and he retired in 1974. He
began publishing stories in New Zealand and Australian periodicals in the early
1940s, and several of his more impressive ones appeared in Frank Sargeson's influential short story anthology *Speaking for Ourselves* (1945).

Gaskell was deeply influenced by Frank Sargeson and was considered one of
his literary protégés. It was Sargeson who prompted Gaskell to look carefully at
the writings of the U.S. short story writer Sherwood Anderson instead of concentrating on the more stylized work of Ernest Hemingway. In fact, *The Big*

Game (1947), the collection from which the following story comes, is filled with stories that use the sparse style of Hemingway's prose stories.

"School Picnic" is an indictment of the mean-spirited substitute school-teacher Miss Brown, who is asked to attend a Saturday picnic at a backwater Maori school. She resents that she has to attend the function; she dislikes the children and their elders, their customs and their poverty. Miss Brown is a snob, with little reason to be so. But the story is written to contrast the generosity of spirit of the Maori with the self-contentment and false assurance that Miss Brown feels about her values and worth. By the end of the tale, Miss Brown ironically labels the Maoris as "bloody savages" when, in truth, her rude and thoughtless behavior is manifestly insulting to her gracious and forgiving hosts.

School Picnic   *1947*

Miss Brown dismounted at the school gate. She hoped the bicycle saddle was not making the seat of her tweed skirt shiny. It was damn good tweed and black-market prices were terribly high. She pushed her bike into the wood-shed and took her case off the carrier. Oh hell . . . Joggling across those blasted sleepers[1] had shaken open the powder-compact in her handbag. She shook it out and glanced at her watch. A quarter past and those damned Maoris had said they would be here at ten. Now after all her bustle she had to wait. As she lit a cigarette she noticed that she had chipped the varnish off one nail. Talk about roughing it.

She went round the front into the sunshine, unlocked the school door and entered. The sunlight was flooding the room through the windows and doorway, showing up the roughness of the match-lined walls and low ceiling. Little heaps of borer-dust lay on the desks, and as she entered a tiny stream of it filtered delicately down from the ceiling, through the slab of sunlight. The place some 30 years ago had been built as a cookhouse for the old sawmill, and no quantity of desks and blackboards, of "Rules for Writing" or lists of "Joining Words" could make it look like the city schools she was used to. It wasn't even painted inside.

She dusted her chair and sat down, pulling impatiently at the now pink-tipped cigarette. Me of all people, she thought, stuck away out here in this god-forsaken hole, and two weeks to go yet. I'm just halfway.

She had been sent to relieve for a month at this small King Country school, four miles "by cycle track" from a station she had never even heard of. She had to board with the railway porter and bike it each day. The cycle track was simply a mark in the pumice that wound through the tea-tree and led to a crazy swing-bridge over the river. If she watched the boards as she bounced across, the water sliding beneath

---

1 **sleepers:** Wooden or steel beams forming part of tramway track.

them made her feel dizzy as though she were falling sideways. The other half of the track was along the sleepers of an old bush tramway which wound through the scrub and blackberry above the river until it finally reached the clearing where the charred wreckage of the sawmill stood near the school. Beyond that, another swing-bridge led across the river to a flat wilderness of grey scaly tea-tree, fire-blackened in places. Somewhere in that mess of second growth the pupils lived. She often saw wisps of smoke rising against the bush on the hills at the back. Somewhere in there too the men were working. Sometimes she heard a lokey[2] puffing, but where it was or what it was doing she neither knew nor cared. It was quite enough being expected to teach their snotty-nosed little Maori brats. She couldn't bear to touch them. One of them smelled smoky, just like an old roll of bacon. Jabbering at her in their excited pidgin English.

And to crown it all the damned School Committee had to pick on this Saturday for their school picnic. The first time she had seen old Araroa and big fat Terari was the day she arrived. She had thought they were rather cute then. The two of them met her at the gate. Old Araroa was still very erect, white-haired, his face wrinkled like a dried apple, blue markings on his chin, his eyes looking so very old and brown and tired. He spoke softly to her in Maori, leaning on his stick and gesturing with his free hand. The skin was very dry and shiny and stretched tight over the bones. After the old man finished, Fatty rolled his eyes at her and said, "Hello, Miss Brown. The old man he say you be very happy here while the mahita[3] away." Fatty wore an old hat, disgraceful pants that folded back under his belly, showing a filthy lining, and a thick black woollen jersey with short sleeves. His arms were bigger than her legs. He had long yellow teeth like a horse. He was so much like the comic Maori of the illustrated papers that she felt safe and reassured at once. But she wasn't so pleased when they visited her again to tell her about the picnic. Fatty was rather excited himself at the idea. "We give the kids the jolly good picnic eh?" he said. "The old man here he say pretty near time we give the kids the picnic. Have the feed eh, and the races. You don't worry Miss Brown, we fix him all up. These jolly good worker these committee. We have him on Saturday."

"On Saturday?" Of all days. Her voice was shrill.

"Saturday," the old man whispered, and apparently satisfied, turned and walked off. Fatty stayed to reassure her. "You don't worry Miss Brown. These committee fix him. You be here ten o'clock."

And of course Saturday was the worst possible day. She had intended to have the day in Taumarunui, to go to the matinee and see Joan Crawford who always wore such stunning dresses and really did look wizard when she sat round sipping cocktails. She had really been looking forward to that. It was a pity Taumarunui was dry. She could do with a few spots herself to take away the taste of these last two weeks.

2 **lokey:** Small locomotive engine for hauling logs.
3 **mahita:** Teacher.

Besides, she needed to have her hair set again, some of the rolls were coming out of place. At any rate she would feel a bit civilized again for a day at least.

She threw her butt in the empty fireplace. One of the schoolgirls usually cleaned the place. The sunlight outside was just pouring down and glinting off the pumice[4] bank. She had to squint to see properly. Damn it, she should have brought her sunglasses. George didn't like wrinkles.

How the gang at home would laugh if they could see me now, she thought, awaiting the pleasure of a tribe of Maoris. I wonder if George has thought of me at all. Lucky devils, I suppose they'll all be going out on George's launch again. They'll probably have a few in by this time too, and boy, would I like to be the same. If it's fine George will be taking them up to his crib. George was a nice job, beautifully muscled. He had dark wavy hair, white teeth, and he oiled his body before he lay in the sun. Sometimes he would let her do it for him. His swimming shorts were always tight around his small hips and flat stomach. He knew what he wanted and had a lot of fun. She was trying to do a line with George but the competition was so keen. Still, just before she left she had thrown a spanner in Vonnie's works. She told George there was a rumour that Vonnie had a dose. George would keep well clear of her. Anything like that, even people with skin trouble, made him feel sick.

A shadow darkened the doorway. "Hello, Miss Brown," cried Terari, his big belly bulging out above his pants. "You the first one here? Look nobody else here. You pretty keen on these picnic eh?"

"You said ten o'clock, and look at it, nearly eleven." Her eyes focussed, hardened.

"Crikey, that late? By golly I ring the bell. Wake them up. Those lazy Maori must sleep in eh? You can't trust those Maori. Always late." A dark smell of sweat preceded him into the room. "You didn't light the fire?"

"I certainly didn't light the fire."

"Nemind. We put him outside. If those fellow come you tell him off eh? They shouldn't be late." He lumbered out and began striking the length of iron railing that hung from a tree near the door. The strong sound dinned and vibrated around her and rolled back off the hills. He was grinning in at her again. "Just like school eh? You give them the strap for late."

She heard the sound of his axe at the back.

A small head was thrust round the doorpost. "Please Miss Brown."

"Hello Lena. Are you the first one? Have you got a clean nose this morning?"

Lena sniffed and licked her upper lip. She came shyly into the room, barefoot but clean, with her hair drawn back and plaited tightly. Two even smaller children stayed at the door looking in at the teacher.

"Please Miss Brown, we gotta hundred pies."

"My word that's a lot. You'll all have the bellyache. It's a pity they don't get you some decent food." The poor kid had hardly a sound tooth in her head.

---

4 **pumice:** Porous or spongy form of volcanic glass.

somewhere to a Maori High School and then come back to the mat. Another baby hung on to her skirt and a third stared over her shoulder.

"I don't want Micky to run round," said the young woman. "He must keep quiet. He going to die soon."

"To die!" Good Lord. And so matter-of-fact about it too. In school Micky was always full of beans.

"Yes." The young woman fixed serious eyes on her. "You know that Chinese doctor who come around with all the medicine?"

Miss Brown nodded. Some peddling herbalist had been around just before she came, she had heard the kids talking about him.

"I took Micky to see him. Micky not well, he so thin."

"And what did he say?"

"When I go in the room he just look at me. He don't speak, he just look for long time. He got sharp eyes too. Then he say 'You Mrs Pine?' I say 'Yes.' He say 'Your husband name Joe?' I say 'Yes.' He say 'I can tell all about you. Your husband fall off his horse and break his shoulder. He can't chop the trees now.' He say 'Your second baby die and this one Micky not Joe's baby. This Micky very sick.' He keep looking at me all the time and I get frightened and think I go out but he say 'Don't go out. I tell you about Micky.' So he say Micky all twisted up inside and pretty soon he die. He give me some medicine in the little bottle." She showed the size with her finger and thumb. "Seven and six. But I don't get many bottle. Too dear. So I suppose Micky going to die." She rubbed Micky's head gently with her hand. "That doctor right about those other things. You think he right about Micky too?"

"Good Heavens no," said Miss Brown. "That's terrible. Why don't you tell the police?"

"He make me frightened. Those sharp eyes they go right in me."

"But, but really you mustn't take any notice of all that nonsense. You get the nurse to look at Micky next time she's round. I don't think there's much the matter with him." Poor thing, how terrible. She must have believed it all too, the way she was looking. They were all so damnably ignorant of civilized procedure. "I'll tell the nurse about it."

The clang of the iron railing was reverberating through the room. "Come and get it," yelled Mrs Terari. "Heigh-oh Silver," called one of the men, and they all came trooping in. The smell got stronger. They moved about, pushing, laughing, calling, helping themselves. Each child was sucking fizz through a straw, even the tiny ones. Miss Brown worked her way through them to the table, and from her case took her small lunch wrapped in a clean white serviette.

"Here Miss Brown, you sit down." Fatty was offering her a chair. "Wah, the poetry eh? By golly I say the poetry. Here Miss Brown, you sit down. Here Miss Brown, you sit down." He roared with laughter. Fragments of half-chewed food lay on his tongue. She shuddered and looked away.

"Miss Brown, you have this nice pie." Old Mrs Te Ahuru held out a clean plate with a pie on it. "I keep him for you. And these sandwich."

"But I have my own lunch here."

"That leetle bit. You eat more, that's why you so thin eh? You have this nice pie."

"Oh no really I. . . ."

"Oh but you must. You shouldn't brought your dinner. You come to our picnic you eat our dinner." She turned to her son-in-law. "You get Miss Brown the nice cup of tea. In the clean cup."

Somehow she got them down. There were so many things she couldn't bear to watch—the old women mumbling soft sandwiches, Fatty eating pies enormously, the children with the wet under their noses mingling with the sticky wet round their mouths and chins from the fizz. Somehow the lunch ended and they went outside. Half-way, she thought. I've got the worst half over.

The sky was clouding, and a cool breeze came rustling across the tops of the tea-tree.

"By golly we better hurry before the rain," shouted Fatty, and they ran the races in a frenzy of haste and shouting. The cheering was deafening for the grown-ups' races. Some of the men were going out into the bushes just outside the gate and coming back wiping their mouths. When the unmarried women ran with their skirts tucked up above their knees the men whistled and cat-called.

Miss Brown sneaked away to the girls' lavatory but when she tried to open the door there was a whiff of cigarette smoke and a guttural voice muttered something. She paused in indecision and an old crone came out and held the door for her, smiling gummily. She went in but could not bear to sit on that seat. After a decent interval she went back to the sports. Large isolated drops of rain were falling and rolling, still globular, in the dust. There was a sighing in the tea-tree as a grey curtain of rain moved towards them.

Soon they were all inside again. It's beer they've got out there, thought Miss Brown, sniffing. Fatty lit the fire inside and carried in kerosene tins of water for another cup of tea. The tins looked small when he held them. Old Araroa had arrived and was standing there leaning firmly on his stick, white-haired, full of gentleness and dignity, handing out the cheap toys for prizes. The children were rather in awe of him. He spoke softly, knowing most of the names. When all the prizes were gone and Micky was left standing beside his mother, the old man beckoned him over and gave him some money out of his pocket. The other kids crowded round. "How much you got, Micky?" but he wouldn't show them. He couldn't count it.

No one knew what to do next. The rain was rattling on the roof and splashing against the windows. One young woman opened her blouse and began feeding her baby.

Fatty was approaching. "The old man like to hear the kids sing." Even he spoke quietly. "You make them sing something?" Miss Brown finally had them in their desks, all self-conscious, pushing and showing off a little, looking to the sides to see who was watching.

The singing started, school songs for a while with Miss Brown beating time, then requests for popular songs and Maori tunes. Some of the men and women joined in. They began to warm up. The girls went in front and sang an action song. Even Lena went with them. The small girls moved stiffly, but the bigger ones were relaxed, their hands fluttered delicately, moving easily and clapping exactly in time. They finished and blushed at the applause. Some young women came out. More familiar cheering and whistling followed their number. Then the men lined up and started a vigorous song. The old ladies round the wall were nodding and smiling and moving their hands. Fatty was out in front leading the men with actions. Miss Brown was feeling out of things, when she noticed Fatty's eye upon her. Oh hell, here he was, coming over, showing the whites of his eyes, his tongue, jerking and posturing about, wobbling his big belly, quivering his hands. She shrank back against the wall while he performed in front of her. She could smell beer. The crowd was shrieking with laughter. She felt her throat and cheeks burning. The big fat bastard, making a laughing-stock of her. Suddenly and savagely she smacked his face. There was a sudden silence, then a scream of laughter. His face was hanging there before her, utterly astonished, his mouth hung open, his hands slowly sank. She was amazed at what she had done and very frightened, but he turned and saw the mirth, then clowning, clapped his hand over one eye and staggered back shouting with laughter. Old Mrs Te Ahuru was beside her. "You serve him right," she was shouting. "You serve him damn well right." She shooed some children out of a desk. "We sit here."

The show went on, there was no stopping them now. A new man was out in front leading a haka.[8] The men shouted, smacked, jumped, stamped, the beat thundered round the room. The veins stood out on their throats and foreheads. The old women around the walls were mouthing, twitching, jerking their hands, grimacing. First one then another got up and moved jerkily across the floor, keeping in time with the beat, to join the line. Everybody was doing it, the kids too. The din was immense, the building shook, borer-dust showered down, dust rose from the floor. Crash! The climax. Sweaty faces smiling, all coughing in the dust.

"Tea, tea," called old Mrs Te Ahuru beside her. "Water boiling. We make tea."

Miss Brown felt overpowered, helpless. These people were of another kind altogether. She was utterly alone among them. She felt suffocated. She couldn't stand it. She got her case and made for the door. A hand on her arm. Old Mrs Te Ahuru. And Fatty too.

"You can't go. Look. It's still raining."

"I must. I've got to be back early."

"But raining. You get wet through."

"I can't help it. I can't stay any longer."

"You got no coat?"

"No."

"You take my rug." Old Mrs Te Ahuru was unwrapping it. "Look, I show you how to wear it."

"No, no, please."

"You want some coat?" Fatty turned and called to the crowd. A girl came forward with a raincoat. "Here. You bring him back on Monday eh?"

---

8 **haka:** Vigorous dance.

They helped her into the coat. "You come and see us some more," said Mrs Te Ahuru. Old Araroa was approaching but she picked up her bag, got her bike. The rain was cold on her face and neck but oh, the air was clean and sweet, and she was away from them. Oh Christ, she thought, I must get out of it. I must get George somehow, get him drunk, have a baby even. Anything.

After all, she thought, they're nothing but a pack of savages. Not even civilized.

The rain was very steady, and by the time she reached the porter's house she was wet through. All the rolls were washed out of her hair and her make-up was streaky.

All this for a pack of bloody savages, she thought.

QUESTIONS

1. How does this story reflect the inability of Miss Brown to appreciate or even tolerate the Maori culture?

2. Point out examples of Miss Brown's prejudices and evidence that the Maori are savages.

3. What are the attitudes of Miss Brown and the Maori woman to the Chinese herbalist?

4. How do the Maori react to Miss Brown? Are they aware of her loathing of them?

5. Why does Miss Brown slap Fatty? What are his and her reactions after the incident?

Witi Ihimaera

(b. 1944)

Witi Ihimaera was born in Gisborne of Maori descent. He spent three years at a district high school, attended a year at the Mormon Church College near Hamilton, and graduated from high school at Gisborne Boys' High School. From 1963 to 1966, he attended Auckland University, but he never completed his degree, choosing instead to try his hand at journalism with the *Gisborne Herald.*

After a brief period, Ihimaera took a job as a postman, moved to Wellington, the capital, and then moved back into journalism. While working, he began a part-time degree in Maori studies and graduated with a BA from Victoria University of Wellington in 1971. While working on the degree, Ihimaera spent six months in London writing short stories. The distance from New Zealand seemed to open a seam of literary experiences, and the result was *Pounamu Pounamu* (1972), a collection of stories in which he was able to express his experience of Maori life through the creation of a fictional people called the Waituhi. The impact of the book was such that upon reading it, Prime Minister Norman Kirk asked Ihimaera to join the Ministry of Foreign Affairs, which he did. He remained with the Ministry until 1989, but the nature of the position gave him enough free time to write two novels, *Tangi* (1973) and *Whanau* (1974). He took leave from the Ministry post to accept fellowships at the University of Otago (1975) and Victoria University of Wellington (1982). His position with the New Zealand government took him to Canberra, New York, and Washington. Since 1990, he has been on the staff of Auckland University as the Distinguished Creative Fellow in Maori Literature.

In his early writings, Ihimaera captured very poignantly the emotional aspects of the Maori's character. In "The Whale," which is from *Pounamu Pounamu,* he does precisely that. The story is a lament for the changes that have been wrought on traditional Maori life as the land is deserted for lucrative work in the cities. The symbol of the empty village becomes a trope for the loss of vitality, of joy. Redolent of T. S. Eliot's *Waste Land,* Ihimaera describes the deserted houses and the empty fields, the untended gravesites and the lack of children's laughter. This nostalgia is a far cry from the more hard-hitting depictions of the Maori's loss of their traditional way of life in the fiction of his contemporary Patricia Grace, but by the 1980s, Ihimaera's fiction became more politically and socially potent as well.

In 1986, after a writing hiatus of ten years, Ihimaera wrote *The Matriarch,* which examines the cultural history of his imaginary tribe. The sequel, *The Dream Swimmer* (1997), continues the voyage of his hero Tama Mahana and leads him to the recognition that his role is to lead his people to Parliament and demand the return of Maori land taken during the unjust land wars in the nineteenth century.

Ihimaera's *The Whale Rider* (1987), a wonderful fairy tale about a Maori girl's relationship with a whale that saves her village, has now become the internationally successful film *Whale Rider,* directed by Niki Caro. His *Dear Miss Mansfield* (1989) is a rewriting of a number of Katherine Mansfield's short stories from a Maori point of view, while *Nights in the Gardens of Spain* (1995), a novel about a married man with children confronting his homosexuality, indicates Ihimaera's willingness to deal with politically charged topics. The question of sexuality in a Maori context has informed *The Uncle's Story* (2000), while his most recent novel, the spectacular *Sky Dancer* (2003), inspired by the success of the film *Whale Rider,* is a remake of Maori bird myth, a Pacific version of Daphne du Maurier's *The Birds.* Its mix of mythological narrative with the special effects of magic realism confirms Ihimaera's facility in mastering both fictional and filmic genres.

The Whale   *1972*

He sits, this old kaumatua,[1] in the darkness of the meeting house. He has come to this place because it is the only thing remaining in his dying world.

In this whanau,[2] this old one is the last of his generation. All his family, they have died: parents, brothers, sisters, relations of his generation, all gone. Ruia, his wife, she's been dead many years. His friends, there are none. Children, mokopuna,[3] yes, there are many of those. But of his time, only he and this meeting house remain.

The meeting house. . . .

This old one, he sighs, and the sound fills the darkness. He looks upon the carved panels, the tukutuku[4] reed work, the swirling red and black and white kowhaiwhai[5] designs, and he remembers he awoke to life here. That was long ago, another world ago, when this meeting house and whanau, this village, brimmed over with happiness and aroha.[6] Always he has lived here. This meeting house has been his heart, his strength. He has never wished to leave it. In this place lie his family and memories. Some are happy, others are sad. Some are like dreams, so beautiful that they seem never to have existed. But his dreams died long ago. With each tangi, each funeral, they have died. And he is the last of the dreamers.

This kaumatua, his eyes dim. In this falling afternoon he has come to visit the meeting house for the last time. He knows it is the last time. Just as the sun falls and the shadows lengthen within the meeting house, so too is his life closing. Soon his photograph will be placed along the wall with those of his other friends, relations and tipuna[7]—his ancestors. He will be glad to join them there. The world has changed too much and it is sad to see his world decaying.

This village was once a proud place, ringing with joy. Its people were a proud people, a family. One great family, clustered around this meeting house. Ae, they quarrelled sometimes, but it is only the happiness that this old one remembers.

But now many of the houses lie deserted. The fields are choked with weeds. The gorse creeps over the graveyard. And the sound of children laughing grows smaller each year.

Even the aroha, it is disappearing from this place. That is the most heartbreaking thing of all. Once the manawa, the heart, throbbed with life and the whanau gave it life. But over the years more and more of its children left and the family began to break apart. Of those that went few returned. And the heart-beat is weaker now.

1 **kaumatua:** Old man.
2 **whanau:** Family.
3 **mokopuna:** Grandchild.
4 **tukutuku:** Panel work.
5 **kowhaiwhai:** Cobweb-like.
6 **aroha:** Love.
7 **tipuna:** Ancestors.

He sighs again, this kaumatua. He will be glad to die, yet sad to leave. His people they will weep for him. Hera, his niece, she will cry very much. But in the end, she will remember. . . .

—Hera, don't you be too sad when I'm gone. If you are, you come to this meeting house. I'll be here, Hera. You come and share your aroha with me. You talk to me; I will listen.

He'd told her that when she was a little girl. Even then the world had been changing. Hera, she'd been one of the few of his mokopuna who'd been interested in the Maori of the past. The rest, they'd felt the pull of the Pakeha[8] world, like fish too eager to grab at a dangling hook. Only in Hera had he seen the spark, the hope that she might retain her Maoritanga.[9] And he had taught her all he knew.

—Hera, this is not only a meeting house; it is also the body of a tipuna, an ancestor. The head is at the top of the meeting house, above the entrance. That is called the koruru. His arms are the maihi, the boards sloping down from the koruru to form the roof. See the tahuhu, ridgepole? That long beam running from the front to the back along the roof? That is the backbone. The rafters, the heke, they are the ribs. And where we are standing, this is the heart of the house. Can you hear it beating?

And Hera, she had listened and heard. She had clutched him, afraid.

—Nanny! The meeting house, it lives!

—The meeting house, it won't hurt you, Hera, he had told her. You are one of its children. Turi turi now.

And he had lifted the veils from the photographs of all her family dead and told her about them.

—That's your Nanny Whiti. He was a brave man. This is my Auntie Hiria, she was very beautiful, ay? She's your auntie too. This man, he was a great rangatira[10]. . . .

Later, they had sat in the middle of the meeting house, he on a chair, she sitting on the floor next to him, and he had told her its history.

—This meeting house, it is like a book, Hera. All the carvings, they are the pages telling the story of this whanau. The Pakeha, he says they're legends. But for me they are history.

And page by page, panel by panel, he had recounted the history.

—That is Pou, coming from Hawaiki on the back of a giant bird. He brought the kumara to Aotearoa. This is Paikea, riding a whale across the sea to Aotearoa. He was told not to let the whale touch the land. But he was tired after the long journey, and he made the whale come to shore. It touched the sand, and became an island. You can still see it, near Whangara . . . See the tukutuku work on the walls? All those weavings, they represent the stars and the sky. . . .

And Hera, her eyes had glistened with excitement.

—Really, Nanny, really?

—Ae, Hera. You remember. . . .

---

8 **Pakeha:** White man.
9 **Maoritanga:** Maori beliefs and culture.
10 **rangatira:** Chief.

*   *   *

This old one, he closes his eyes to try to keep the sadness away. But closed eyes cannot hide the memory that even Hera had changed as she grew older. She too, like many of the other young people, had gone away to the city. And when she had returned for a visit, this old one could see that the Pakeha life had proved too strong for her. He had tried to lead her back to his world, and she had quarrelled with him.

—Don't, Nanny! The world isn't Maori any more. But it's the world I have to live in. You dream too much. Your world is gone. I can't live it for you. Can't you see?

But he had been stubborn, this kaumatua. He'd always been stubborn. If she would not come back to his world, then she would take it to the city with her.

—Come, Hera, I want to show you something.

—No, Nanny. . . .

—These books, in them is your whakapapa, your ancestry. All these names, they are your family who lived long ago, traced back to the Takitimu canoe. You take them with you when you go back.

—Nanny. . . .

—No, you take them. And see this space? You put my name there when I die. You do that for me. You keep this whakapapa safe. And don't you ever forget who you are. You're Maori, understand? You are Maori. . . .

His voice had broken with grief then. And Hera had embraced him to comfort him.

—Nanny, you gave me too much love, she had whispered. You taught me too well to be Maori. But you didn't teach me about the Pakeha world. . . .

He opens his eyes, this old one, but he still hears his Hera's whisper. Ae, he had taught her well. And one day her confusion would pass and she would understand why. He'd known his world had died. But the spirit of his people, he didn't want that to die too. That's why he had taught her well. That's why.

For a moment he mourns to himself, this old one. Sadly he recalls an ancient saying. How old it is he does not know. Perhaps it had come with the Maori when he journeyed across the sea to Aotearoa. From Hawaiki. From Tawhiti-roa, Tawhiti-nui, Tawhiti-pamamao, the magical names for the first home of the Maori. No matter. . . . Even before the Pakeha had come to this land, his coming had been foretold.

> *Kei muri i te awe kapara he tangata ke,*
> *mana te ao, he ma.*
> Shadowed behind the tattooed face a stranger stands,
> he who owns the earth, and he is white.

And with his coming, the tattooed face had changed. That was the way of things, relentless and unalterable. But the spirit of the Maori, did that need to change as well? Ae, even in his own day, Maoritanga had been dying. But not the spirit, not the joy or aroha. Now. . . .

He cannot help it, this kaumatua, but the tears fall.

The Maori language has almost gone from this whanau. The respect for Maori customs and Maori tapu, that too was disappearing. No more did people take their shoes off before coming into this meeting house. The floor is scuffed with shoe-marks. The tukutuku work is pitted with cigarette burns. And even the gods and tipuna, they have been defaced. A name has been chipped into a carved panel. Another panel bears a deep scratch. And a paua eye has been prised from a carved figure, a wheku.[11]

This meeting house, it had once been noble. Now, the red ochre is peeling from the carvings. The reed work is falling apart. The paint is flaking from the swirling kowhaiwhai designs. And the floor is stained with the pirau, the beer, for even that has been brought into this meeting house.

So too have the Maori fallen from nobility. They do not come to this meeting house with respect, nor with aroha. They look with blind eyes at the carvings and do not see the beauty and strength of spirit which is etched in every whorl, every bold and sweeping spiral. They too are the strangers behind the tattooed face.

This old one, he has seen too many of his people come as strangers. The Maori of this time is different from the Maori of his own time. The whanau, the family, and the aroha which binds them together as one heart, is breaking, slowly loosening. The children of the whanau seek different ways to walk in this world. Before, there was a sharing of aroha with one another. No matter how far away some of the children went there was still the aroha which bound them closely to this meeting house and village. But the links are breaking. The young grow apart from each other. They look with shame at their meeting house and this village because it is decaying. They walk away and do not come back. That is why the manawa[12] beats so loud with agony, that is why this meeting house is dying. When Maori aroha dies, when the Maori walks away into another life, the meeting house weeps....
—Aue! Aue!

This kaumatua, he fills the meeting house with the sound of his grief.
—Aue! Aue!

And from his grief springs a memory which adds to his despair. Of a time not long ago, when people from all Aotearoa gathered at this meeting house to celebrate the wedding of a child of this whanau.

The visitors, they had come from the Taranaki, from the Waikato, from the many parts of Te Ika a Maui, even from Te Waipounamu—the South Island. They had arrived for the hui[13] throughout the day. By car, by bus, by train they had come, and the manawa of this whanau had beaten with joy at their gathering together.

It had been like his own time, this old one remembers. The children laughing and playing around the meeting house. The men and women renewing their friendships. The laughing and the weeping. The sweet smell of the hangi, and the sudden clouds of steam as the kai[14] was taken from the earth. The girls swaying past the young men, eyeing the ones they wanted. The boys standing together, both bold and

11 **wheku:** A body.
12 **manawa:** Heart.
13 **hui:** Gathering.
14 **kai:** Nourishment.

shy, but hiding their shyness beneath their jokes and bantering. The kuias[15] gossiping in the cookhouse. The big wedding kai, and the bride and groom pretending not to hear the jokes about their first night to be spent together. The singing of the old songs . . . the cooks coming into the hall in their gumboots and old clothes to sing with the guests . . .

> *Karangatia ra! Karangatia ra!*
> *Pohiritia ra, nga iwi o te motu*
> *Ki runga o Turanga. Haere mai!*
> Call them! Call them!
> Welcome them, the people of the land
> Coming onto this marae, Turanga. Welcome!

Ae, it had indeed been like the old times. The laughter and the joy had sung through the afternoon into the night. And he had sat with the other old men, watching the young people dancing in the hall.

Then it had happened. Late in the night. Raised voices. The sound of quarrelling.

—Nanny! Come quick!

A mokopuna had grabbed his hand and pulled him outside, along the path to the dining room. More visitors had arrived. They had come from the Whangarei, and they were tired and hungry. He saw their faces in the light. But people of his whanau, they were quarrelling with the visitors. They would not open the door to the storeroom. It was locked now. There would be no kai for these visitors. They had come too late. Heart was locking out heart.

He had been stunned, this old one. Always there was food, always aroha, always open heart. That was the Maori way. Aroha.

And he had said to his mokopuna:

—Te toki. Homai te toki . . . the axe. Bring me the axe. . . .

The crowd had heard his whispered fury. They parted for him. His tokotoko, his walking stick, it supported him as he approached the door. The music stopped in the hall. The kanikani, the dancing, stopped. People gathered. His fury gathered. The axe in his hand. He lifted it and. . . .

—Aue. . . .

The first blow upon the locked door.

—Aue. . . .

His tears streaming from his face.

—Aue. . . .

The wood splintering beneath the blade.

—Aue. . . .

His heart splintering too.

15 **kuias:** Old women.

He gave his anger to the axe. He gave his sorrow to the blows upon the door. The axe rose and fell, rose and fell, and it flashed silver from the light. And people began to weep with him.

Then it was done. The door gave way. Silence fell. Weeping, he turned to the visitors. His voice was strained with agony.

—Haere mai, e te manuhiri. Haere mai. Haere mai. Come, visitors, Come. Enter.

He had opened his arms to them. Then, trembling, he had pointed at the splintered door.

—Ka nui te whakama o toku iwi ki a au. Anei ra toku whakama. . . . My people shame me. See? This is my shame. . . .

Then he had walked away, not looking back. Away from the light into the darkness. His heart, it was breaking. And he wished only to die and not see the shame.

This kaumatua, the memory falls away from him. He sees the darkness gathering quickly in the meeting house. How long has he been here, mourning? A long time. He sighs. Better to die than to see this changing world. He is too old for it. He is stranded here.

This old one, he grips his tokotoko[16] and stands. Aue, he has lingered too long. One last look at this meeting house. The carved panels glint in the darkness. The kowhaiwhai designs flash with the falling sun. The evening wind flutters the black veils which hang upon the photographs of his dead. Soon he will join them. Soon his name will fill a space in the whakapapa of this whanau. Soon. . . .

So still he stands, this kaumatua, that he seems to merge into the meeting house and become a carved figure himself. Then his lips move. One last whisper to this meeting house, and he turns and walks away.

—No wai te he?

He walks along the dusty road, through the village. The houses are clustered close together, but closed to one another. Some are deserted, lifeless. A truck speeds past him, and he coughs with the choking dust.

—No wai te he?

He hears a gramophone blaring loudly from one of the houses. He sees into a lighted window, where the walls are covered with glossy pictures that have been carefully cut out of magazines. A group of young people are gathered around another house, laughing and singing party songs. They wave the pirau at him, and beckon him to come and join them. He turns away.

—No wai te he?

Down the path from the village he goes, to where his own house lies on the beach, apart from the village. Through the manuka, down the cliff to the sand he walks. The sea is calm, the waves softly rippling. And far away the sun is setting, slowly drowning in the water.

—No wai te he?

16 **tokotoko:** Walking stick.

Then he sees a cloud of gulls blackening the sky. Their guttural screams fill the air. They dive and swoop and cluster upon a dark mound, moving feebly in the eddying water.

And as the old one approaches, he sees that it is a whale, stranded in the breakwater, threshing in the sand, already stripped of flesh by the falling gulls. The water is washed with red, the foam flecked with blood.

He cries out then, this kaumatua.

The gulls shriek and wheel away from him. And in their claws they clasp his shouted words, battling and circling against one another with a flurry of black wings.

—No wai te he . . . Where lies the blame . . . the blame.

Where lies the blame, the blame. . . .

And the whale lifts a fluke of its giant tail to beat the air with its dying agony.

QUESTIONS

1. What exactly is the "old one's" lament for in the story?

2. What is causing the mass exodus from the village and the Maori way of life?

3. What is the startling realization that the old one has at the wedding celebration?

4. What aspects of the Maori way of life are reinforced by the choice of language and the particular style of this story?

5. How is the conclusion of this story a challenge to the dominant Pakeha's discourse?

Keri Hulme

(b. 1947)

Born in March 1947 of mixed heritage—part Scot, English, and Maori—Keri Hulme was raised in Christchurch, New Zealand, by a carpenter and businessman father and half Maori and half Orkney Scot mother, who worked as a credit manager. The eldest of six children, Hulme was educated at North Brighton Primary and Aranui High School, where she strongly identified with her Maori blood. At eighteen, she began working part-time jobs, including on a tobacco plantation at Montucka. She studied at the University of Canterbury in 1967–1968 and then worked as a fish-and-chip cook, a letter carrier, and a television director. It was not until 1972 that she took up writing full time. She settled in Okarito, a small isolated settlement on the west coast of the South

Island, where she built her own house. Hulme was awarded the 1975 Katherine Mansfield Memorial Award for her short story "Hooks and Feelers," which led her to be offered the post of writer in residence at Otago University. While resident there, she published her first collection of short stories, *The Windeater/Te Kaihau* (1982), as well as her first book of poetry, *The Silences Between* (1982).

The following year, her most important book to date appeared. Based on an idea from a short story, Hulme struggled over a decade to expand the story into a novel, and when *The Bone People* was eventually published by a feminist collective in Wellington, it was an immediate success. In 1985, this book about three wounded people who are brought back from the brink of disaster through an evocation of Maori spiritualism won the prestigious Booker Prize. Hulme has continued to publish poetry and fiction over the last two decades, including her second collection of poetry, *Strands* (1992). Currently, she is completing work on two twinned novels, *Bait* and *On the Shadow Side*. Her most recently published work is *Stonefish* (2004).

The story that follows, "One Whale, Singing," is more than just a primal story of pregnancy and birth. It examines the difference in thought patterns between the pompous and assured intellectual in the guise of a scientist and the poetic and dreamy vision of his pregnant wife. The husband's casual dismissal of the wife's sympathy with the whale, and by extension all the lives on this planet with us, represents the height of arrogant insensitivity. Hulme still lives, works, and paints in the tiny settlement of Okarito.

One Whale, Singing   1975

The ship drifted on the summer night sea.

"It is a pity," she thought, "that one must come on deck to see the stars. Perhaps a boat of glass, to see the sea streaming past, to watch the nightly splendour of stars." Something small jumped from the water, away to the left. A flash of phosphorescence after the sound, and then all was quiet and starlit again.

They had passed through krillswarms[1] all day. Large areas of the sea were reddish-brown, as though an enormous creature had wallowed ahead of the boat, streaming blood.

"Whale-feed," she had said, laughing and hugging herself at the thought of seeing whales again.

"Lobster-krill," he had corrected, pedantically.

The crustaceans had swum in their frightened jerking shoals, mile upon mile of them, harried by fish that were in turn pursued and torn by larger fish.

---

1 **krillswarms:** A school of shrimp-like planktonic crustaceans; major source of food for baleen whales.

She thought, it was probably a fish after krill that had leaped then. She sighed, stroking her belly. It was the lesser of the two evils to go below now, so he didn't have an opportunity to come on deck and suggest it was better for the coming baby's health, and hers, of course, that she came down. The cramped cabin held no attraction: all that was there was boneless talk, and one couldn't see stars, or really hear the waters moving.

Far below, deep under the keel of the ship, a humpback whale sported and fed. Occasionally, she yodelled to herself, a long undulating call of content. When she found a series of sounds that pleased, she repeated them, wove them into a band of harmonious pulses.

Periodically she reared to the surface, blew, and slid smoothly back under the sea in a wheel-like motion. Because she was pregnant, and at the tailend of the southward migration, she had no reason now to leap and display on the surface.

She was not feeding seriously; the krill was there, and she swam amongst them, forcing water through her lips with her large tongue, stranding food amongst the baleen.[2] When her mouth was full, she swallowed. It was leisurely, lazy eating. Time enough for recovering her full weight when she reached the cold seas, and she could gorge on a ton and a half of plankton daily.

Along this coast, there was life and noise in plenty. Shallow grunting from a herd of fish, gingerly feeding on the fringes of the krill shoal. The krill themselves, a thin hiss and crackle through the water. The interminable background clicking of shrimps. At times, a wayward band of sound like bass organ-notes sang through the chatter, and to this the whale listened attentively, and sometimes replied.

The krill thinned; she tested, tasted the water. Dolphins had passed recently. She heard their brief commenting chatter, but did not spend time on it. The school swept round ahead of her, and vanished into the vibrant dark.

He had the annoying habit of reading what he'd written out loud. "We can conclusively demonstrate that to man alone belongs true intelligence and self-knowledge."

He coughs.

Taps his pen against his lips. He has soft, wet lips, and the sound is a fleshy slop! slop!

She thinks:

> Man indeed! How arrogant! How ignorant! Woman would be as correct,
> but I'll settle for humanity. And it strikes me that the quality humanity
> stands in need of most is true intelligence and self-knowledge.

"For instance, Man alone as a species, makes significant artefacts, and transmits knowledge in permanent and durable form."

---

2 **baleen:** Horny material from the upper jaws of certain whales.

He grunts happily.

"In this lecture, I propose to. . . ."

> But how do they know? she asks herself. About the passing on of knowl-
> edge among other species? They may do it in ways beyond our capacity to
> understand . . . that we are the only ones to make artefacts I'll grant you,
> but that's because us needy little adapts have such pathetic bodies, and no
> especial ecological niche. So hooks and hoes, and steel things that gouge
> and slay, we produce in plenty. And build a wasteland of drear ungainly
> hovels to shelter our vulnerable hides.

She remembers her glass boat, and sighs. The things one could create if one
made technology servant to a humble and creative imagination. . . . He's booming
on, getting into full lecture room style and stride.

". . . thus we will show that no other species, lacking as they do artefacts, an organized society, or even semblances of culture. . . ."

> What would a whale do with an artefact, who is so perfectly adapted to
> the sea? Their conception of culture, of civilization, must be so alien that
> we'd never recognize it, even if we were to stumble on its traces daily.

She snorts.

He looks at her, eyes unglazing, and smiles.

"Criticism, my dear? Or you like that bit?"

"I was just thinking. . . ."

> Thinking, as for us passing on our knowledge, hah! We rarely learn from
> the past or the present, and what we pass on for future humanity is a
> mere jumble of momentarily true facts, and odd snippets of surprised
> self-discoveries. That's not knowledge. . . .

She folds her hands over her belly. You in there, you won't learn much. What I
can teach you is limited by what we are. Splotch goes the pen against his lips.

"You had better heat up that fortified drink, dear. We can't have either of you
wasting from lack of proper nourishment."

Unspoken haw haw haw.

> Don't refer to it as a person! It is a canker in me, a parasite. It is nothing to
> me. I feel it squirm and kick, and sicken at the movement.

He says he's worried by her pale face.

"You shouldn't have gone up on deck so late. You could have slipped, or something, and climbing tires you now, you know."

She doesn't argue any longer. The arguments follow well-worn tracks and go in
circles.

"Yes," she answers.

> but I should wither without that release, that solitude, that keep away
> from you.

She stirs the powder into the milk and begins to mix it rhythmically.

> I wonder what a whale thinks of its calf? So large a creature, so proven peaceful a beast, must be motherly, protective, a shielding benevolence against all wildness. It would be a sweet and milky love, magnified and sustained by the encompassing purity of water. . . .

A swarm of insect-like creatures, sparkling like a galaxy, each a pulsing light-form in blue and silver and gold. The whale sang for them, a ripple of delicate notes, spaced in a timeless curve. It stole through the lightswarm, and the luminescence increased brilliantly.

Deep within her, the other spark of light also grew. It was the third calf she had borne; it delighted her still, that the swift airy copulation should spring so opportunely to this new life. She feeds it love and music and her body's bounty. Already it responds to her crooning tenderness and the dark pictures she sends it. It absorbs both, as part of the life to come, as it nests securely in the waters within.

She remembers the nautilids[3] in the warm oceans to the north snapping at one another in a cannibalistic frenzy.

She remembers the oil-bedraggled albatross,[4] resting with patient finality on the water-top, waiting for death.

She remembers her flight, not long past, from killer whales, and the terrible end of the other female who had companied her south, tongue eaten from her mouth, flukes and genitals ripped, bleeding to a slow fought-against end.

And all the memories are part of the growing calf.

More krill appeared. She opened her mouth, and glided through the shoal. Sudden darkness for the krill. The whale hummed meanwhile.

He folded his papers contentedly.

"Sam was going on about his blasted dolphins the other night dear."

"Yes?"

He laughed deprecatingly. "But it wouldn't interest you. All dull scientific chatter, eh?"

"What was he saying about, umm, his dolphins?"

"O, insisted that his latest series of tests demonstrated their high intelligence. No, that's misquoting him, potentially high intelligence. Of course, I brought him down to earth smartly. Results are as you make them, I said. Nobody has proved that the animals have intelligence to a degree above that of a dog. But it made me think of the rot that's setting in lately. Inspiration for this lecture indeed."

"Lilley?"[5] she asked, still thinking of the dolphins,

"Lilley demonstrated evidence of dolphinese."

---

3 **nautilids:** A type of mollusk.

4 **albatross:** Any of several large web-footed birds constituting the family *Diomedeidae*, chiefly of the oceans of the Southern Hemisphere and having a hooked beak and long narrow wings.

5 **Lilley:** Dr. John Lilley, researcher who investigated the intelligence and communicative abilities of dolphins (particularly the Bottlenose dolphin).

"Lilley? That mystical crackpot? Can you imagine anyone ever duplicating his work? Hah! Nobody has, of course. It was all in the man's mind."

"Dolphins and whales are still largely unknown entities," she murmured, more to herself than to him.

"Nonsense, my sweet. They've been thoroughly studied and dissected for the last century and more." She shuddered. "Rather dumb animals, all told, and probably of bovine origin. Look at the incredibly stupid way they persist in migrating straight into the hands of whalers year after year. If they were smart, they'd have organized an attacking force and protected themselves!"

He chuckled at the thought, and lit his pipe.

"It would be nice to communicate with another species," she said, more softly still.

"That's the trouble with you poets," he said fondly. "Dream marvels are to be found from every half-baked piece of pseudo-science that drifts around. That's not seeing the world as it is. We scientists rely on reliably ascertained facts for a true picture of the world."

She sat silently by the pot on the galley stove.

An echo from the world around, a deep throbbing from miles away. It was both message and invitation to contribute. She mused on it for minutes, absorbing, storing, correlating, winding her song meanwhile experimentally through its interstices—then dropped her voice to the lowest frequencies. She sent the message along first, and then added another strength to the cold wave that travelled after the message. An ocean away, someone would collect the cold wave, and store it, while it coiled and built to uncontrollable strength. Then, just enough would be released to generate a superwave, a gigantic wall of water on the surface of the sea. It was a new thing the sea-people were experimenting with. A protection. In case.

She began to swim further out from the coast. The water flowed like warm silk over her flanks, an occasional interjectory current swept her, cold and bracing, a touch from the sea to the south. It became quieter, a calm freed from the fights of crabs and the bickerings of small fish. There was less noise too, from the strange turgid craft that buzzed and clattered across the ocean-ceiling, dropping down wastes that stank and sickened.

A great ocean-going shark prudently shifted course and flicked away to the side of her. It measured twenty feet from shovel-nose to crescentic tailfin, but she was twice as long and would grow a little yet. Her broad deep body was still well fleshed and strong, in spite of the vicissitudes of the northwind breeding trek: there were barnacles encrusting her fins and lips and head, but she was unhampered by other parasites. She blew a raspberry at the fleeing shark and beat her flukes against the ocean's pull in an ecstasy of strength.

"This lecture," he says, sipping his drink, "this lecture should cause quite a stir. They'll probably label it conservative, or even reactionary, but of course it isn't. It merely urges us to keep our feet on the ground, not go hunting off down worthless blind sidetrails. To consolidate data we already have, not, for example, to speculate about so-called ESP phenomena. There is far too much mysticism and airy-fairy folderol in science these days. I don't wholly agree with the Victorians' attitude, that science could explain all, and very shortly would, but it's high time we got things back to a solid factual basis."

"The Russians," she says, after a long moment of non-committal silence, "the Russians have discovered a form of photography that shows all living things to be sources of a strange and beautiful energy. Lights flare from fingertips. Leaves coruscate. All is living effulgence."

He chuckles again.

"I can always tell when you're waxing poetic." Then he taps out the bowl of his pipe against the side of the bunk, and leans forward in a fatherly way.

"My dear, if they have, and that's a big if, what difference could that possibly make. Another form of energy? So what?"

"Not just another form of energy," she says sombrely. "It makes for a whole new view of the world. If all things are repositories of related energy, then humanity is not alone. . . ."

"Why this of solitariness, of being alone. Communication with other species, man is not alone, for God's sake! One would think you're becoming tired of us all!"

He's joking.

She is getting very tired. She speaks tiredly.

"It would mean that the things you think you are demonstrating in your paper. . . ."

"Lecture."

"Work . . . those things are totally irrelevant. That we may be on the bottom of the pile, not the top. It may be that other creatures are aware of their place and purpose in the world, have no need to delve and paw a meaning out. Justify themselves. That they accept all that happens, the beautiful, the terrible, the sickening, as part of the dance, as the joy or pain of the joke. Other species may somehow be equipped to know fully and consciously what truth is, whereas we humans must struggle, must struggle blindly to the end."

He frowns, a concerned benevolent frown.

"Listen dear, has this trip been too much. Are you feeling at the end of your tether, tell us truly? I know the boat is old, and not much of a sailer, but it's the best I could do for the weekend. And I thought it would be a nice break for us, to get away from the university and home. Has there been too much work involved? The boat's got an engine after all . . . would you like me to start it and head back for the coast?"

She is shaking her head numbly.

He stands up and swallows what is left of his drink in one gulp.

"It won't take a minute to start the engine, and then I'll set that pilot thing, and we'll be back in sight of land before the morning. You'll feel happier then."

She grips the small table.

Don't scream, she tells herself, don't scream.

* * *

Diatoms of phantom light, stray single brilliances. A high burst of dolphin sonics. The school was returning. A muted rasp from shoalfish hurrying past. A thing that curled and coiled in a drifting aureole of green light.

She slows, buoyant in the water.

Green light: it brings up the memories that are bone deep in her, written in her very cells. Green light of land.

She had once gone within yards of shore, without stranding. Curiosity had impelled her up a long narrow bay. She had edged carefully along, until her long flippers touched the rocky bottom. Sculling with her tail, she had slid forward a little further, and then lifted her head out of the water. The light was bent, the sounds that came to her were thin and distorted, but she could see colours known only from dreams and hear a music that was both alien and familiar.

(Christlookitthat!)

(Fuckinghellgetoutahereitscomingin)

The sound waves pooped and spattered through the air, and things scrambled away, as she moved herself back smoothly into deeper water.

A strange visit, but it enabled her to put images of her own to the calling dream.

Follow the line to the hard and aching airswept land, lie upon solidity never before known until strained ribs collapse from weight of body never before felt. And then, the second beginning of joy. . . .

She dreams a moment, recalling other ends, other beginnings. And because of the web that streamed between all members of her kind, she was ready for the softly insistent pulsation that wound itself into her dreaming. Mourning for a male of the species, up in the cold southern seas where the greenbellied krill swarm in unending abundance. Where the killing ships of the harpooners lurk. A barb sliced through the air in an arc and embedded itself in the lungs, so the whale blew red in his threshing agony. Another that sunk into his flesh by the heart. Long minutes later, his slow exhalation of death. Then the gathering of light from all parts of the drifting corpse. It condensed, vanished . . . streamers of sound from the dolphins who shoot past her, somersaulting in their strange joy.

The long siren call urges her south. She begins to surge upward to the sweet night air.

She says, "I must go on deck for a minute."

They had finished the quarrel, but still had not come together. He grunts, fondles his notes a last time, and rolls over in his sleeping bag, drawing the neck of it tightly close.

She says wistfully, "Goodnight then," and climbs the stairs heavily up to the hatchway.

"You're slightly offskew," she says to the Southern Cross, and feels the repressed tears begin to flow down her cheeks. The stars blur.

Have I changed so much?
Or is it this interminable deadening pregnancy?

But his stolid, sullen, stupidity!

He won't see, he won't see, he won't see anything.

She walks to the bow, and settles herself down, uncomfortably aware of her protuberant belly, and begins to croon a song of comfort to herself.

And at that moment the humpback hit the ship, smashing through her old and weakened hull, collapsing the cabin, rending timbers. A mighty chaos. . . .

Somehow she found herself in the water, crying for him, swimming in a circle as though among the small debris she might find a floating sleeping bag. The stern of the ship is sinking, poised a moment a moment dark against the stars, and then it slides silently under.

She strikes out for a shape in the water, the liferaft? the dinghy?

And the shape moves.

The humpback, full of her dreams and her song, had beat blindly upward, and was shocked by the unexpected fouling. She lies, waiting on the water-top.

The woman stays where she is, motionless except for her paddling hands. She has no fear of the whale, but thinks, "It may not know I am here, may hit me accidentally as it goes down."

She can see the whale more clearly now, an immense zeppelin shape, bigger by far than their flimsy craft had been, but it lies there, very still. . . .

She hopes it hasn't been hurt by the impact, and chokes on the hope.

There is a long moaning call then, that reverberated through her. She is physically swept, shaken by an intensity of feeling, as though the whale has sensed her being and predicament, and has offered all it can, a sorrowing compassion.

Again the whale makes the moaning noise, and the woman calls, as loudly as she can, "Thank you, thank you," knowing that it is meaningless, and probably unheard. Tears stream down her face once more.

The whale sounded so gently she didn't realize it was going at all.

"I am now alone in the dark," she thinks, and the salt water laps round her mouth. "How strange, if this is to be the summation of my life."

In her womb the child kicked. Buoyed by the sea, she feels the movement as something gentle and familiar, dear to her for the first time.

But she begins to laugh.

The sea is warm and confiding, and it is a long long way to shore.

QUESTIONS

1. What comment is Hulme making about the nature of pregnancy and birth in this tale?

2. What is the nature of the relationship between the woman poet and the female humpback whale in the story?

3. What does the husband's occupation tell you about him and his attitude toward his wife and her vocation?

4. In what way is this story commenting on the scientific and nonscientific approaches to life?

5. In what ways is this story about more than "animal rights"?

Patricia Grace

(b. 1937)

Patricia Grace is a Maori writer whose versatility is evident in her emergence as a novelist, short story writer, and children's fiction writer since the 1970s. Her work celebrates the wide variety of Maori experience, for she aims to show the world "who we are"; her approach to the issues of colonialization (such as Maori land rights, the loss of their language, and the threat to Maoritanga) is often overtly political. Her novels and stories, commended for their originality of style, are realistic rather than sentimental or nostalgic and anchored in human experience; her descriptions of countryside and economic use of detail demonstrate a poetic eye for evoking a sense of place.

Grace was born and educated in Wellington and was awarded a diploma in Teaching English as a Second Language from Victoria University of Wellington. While studying for her diploma, she began to read other New Zealand writers and began publishing her own fiction while raising her own family and teaching in North Auckland. Eventually, she moved near to Wellington, where her first book, *Waiariki*, was published in 1975.

Waiariki, where the story that follows is found, is a very powerful first work. Almost single-handedly, this collection brought the female Maori voice to the ears of the New Zealand people. Not surprisingly, considering the quality and intensity of this collection, it was awarded the PEN/Hubert Church Award for the Best First Book of Fiction. The collection is a voyage for the reader in the discovery of a marginalized people. The opening story, "A Way of Talking," could easily have been chosen for this anthology as well, for it depicts the isolation and inarticulateness of the Maori schoolgirl Hera. As the interconnected stories progress, the voice of the Maori is heard more and more clearly, until by the time we reach the final story, "Parade," the canoe chanting affirms the strength and the vitality of the Maori people in their struggle to be made autonomous and to reinforce their claim for power sharing in their own nation.

In *Mutuwhenua: The Moon Sleeps* (1978), her first novel, Grace provokingly plots the story around the delicate issue of interracial marriage—here between a Maori woman and Pakeha (white) man. She meticulously explores the cultural issues implicit in the marriage and depicts the challenges the couple must endure. Throughout the 1980s, Grace's fiction examined the perceptions of Maori children in New Zealand society as well as the values of multiculturalism in the modern age. With the publication of her second novel, *Potiki* (1986), one feels Grace's political frustration with the New Zealand government's inability to address the injustices inherent in the system that continued to discriminate against full Maori participation in the decision-making process. In the 1990s, Grace's vision continued to turn predictably dark and introspective; this pessimism culminates in her fourth collection of stories, *The Sky People* (1994). Here, the plight of the Maori people is dissected with a realistic scalpel; the suicides, madness, and poverty of the marginalized people are foregrounded in nearly all the stories. Her two latest novels deal with issues concerning Maori survival. In *Baby No-Eyes* (1998), it is the Pakeha use of body parts for genetic experimentation with ethnicity. In *Dogside Story* (2001), the shameful and deviant behavior of the whanau (extended family)—drug abuse, child neglect, and incest—is exposed in order to forge greater community leadership.

Parade   1975

Yesterday I went with Hoani, Lena, and the little ones up along the creek where the bush begins, to cut fern and flax. Back there at the quiet edge of the bush with the hills rolling skyward and the sound of the sea behind me I was glad I had come home in response to Auntie's letter. It was easy, there, to put aside the heaviness of spirit which had come upon me during the week of carnival. It was soothing to follow with my eyes the spreading circles of fern patterning the hills' sides, and good to feel the coolness of flax and to realise again the quiet strength of each speared leaf. It was good to look into the open-throated flax blooms with their lit-coal colours, and to put a hand over the swollen black splitting pods with the seed heavy in them.

And I thought of how each pod would soon cast aside its heaviness and become a mere shell, warped and empty, while that which had been its own heaviness would become new life. New growth and strength.

As we carried the bundles of fern and flax that we had collected and put them into the creek to keep fresh for the morning I was able to feel that tomorrow, the final day of the carnival, would be different from the ones recently passed when realisation had come to me, resting in me like stone.

"Please come for the carnival," Auntie's letter had said. And the letter from my little cousin Ruby: "Please come, Matewai. We haven't seen you for two years." I had felt excitement in me at the thought of returning, being back with them. And I came for the carnival as they had asked.

It was easy this morning to feel a lightness of spirit, waking to a morning so warm and full-scented, with odours rising to the nostrils as though every morning comes from inside the earth. Rich damp smells drenched every grass blade, every seeded stalk, and every cluster of ragwort, thistle and blackberry. Steaming up through the warming rosettes of cow dung. Stealing up the stems of lupin and along the lupin arms, out on to the little spread hands of lupin leaves.

And a sweet wood smell coming from the strewn chips and wood stack by the shed. A tangle of damp stinks from the fowl-yard and orchard, and from the cold rustiness of the cow-holed swamp. Some of the earth morning smells had become trapped under the hot bodies of cows, and were being dispensed, along with the cows' own milk and saliva smells, from the swinging bellies and milk-filled udders as the animals made their way poke-legged to the milking sheds. That was what it was like this morning.

And there was a breath of sea. Somewhere—barely discernible since evening had been long forgotten and the night had been shrugged aside—somewhere the sea was casting its breath at the land. It was as though it were calling to the land, and to us as we woke and walked into the day, "I'm here, I'm here. Don't forget about me."

The sun fingered the ridges of hills as we pulled the flax and fern from the creek and began to decorate the truck for the parade. We worked quickly, tying and nailing the fronds and leaves into place. And when we had finished, Uncle Hirini drove the truck in under some trees where the sun could not reach it, while we went inside to change into our costumes.

Auntie had sent all the children to wash in the creek, and as I watched them from the window it was like seeing myself as I had been not very long ago. As if it were my own innocence that they cast on to the willow branches with their clothes. Light had filtered through the willow branches on to the creek's surface, spreading in small pools to the creek banks and on to the patches of watercress and shafts of reed.

The sun had put a finger on almost everything by now. It had touched our houses and the paddocks and tree tops, and stroked its silver over the sea. The beach stones were warming from the sun's touching, and black weed, thrown up by the sea, lay in heaps on the shore drying and helpless in the sun's relentless stroking.

I watched the bodies falling into water warmed from the sun's touching, and fingers, not his, squeezing at large bars of yellow soap. Fingers spreading blistery trails of suds up and over legs and arms. Bodies, heads, ears. "Wash your taringas."[1] Auntie from the creek bank. Backsides, frontsides, fingers, toes. Then splashing, diving, puffing and blowing in this pool of light. Out on to the banks, rubbing with towels, wrapping the towels around, scrambling back through the willows, across the yard where the sun caught them for a moment before they ran inside to dress. It was like seeing myself as I had been such a short time ago.

Auntie stood back on the heels of her bare feet, puffing at a cigarette, and looking at me through half shut eyes. Her round head was nodding at me, her long hair which she had brushed out of the two thick plaits which usually circled her head fell about her shoulders, and two more hanks of hair glistened under her armpits. The skin on her shoulders and back was pale in its unaccustomed bareness, cream coloured and cool looking. And there was Granny Rita stretching lips over bare gums to smile at me.

---

1 **taringas:** Ears.

"Very pretty, dia. Very pretty, dia," she kept saying, stroking the cloak that they had put on me, her old hands aged and grey like burnt paper. The little ones admiring, staring.

Setting me apart.

And I stood before them in the precious cloak, trying to smile.

"I knew our girl would come," Auntie was saying again. "I knew our girl would come if we sent for her."

We could hear the truck wheezing out in the yard, and Grandpa Hohepa who is bent and crabby was hurrying everyone along, banging his stick on the floor. "Kia tere," he kept on saying. "Kia tere."

The men helped Granny Rita and Grandpa Hohepa on to the truck and sat them where they could see, then I stepped on to the platform which had been erected for me and sat down for the journey into town. The others formed their lines along each side of the tray and sat down too.

In town, in the heat of late morning, we moved slowly with the other parade floats along the streets lined with people. Past the railway station and shops, and over bridges and crossings, singing one action song after another. Hakas[2] and pois.

And as I watched I noted again, as I had on the other carnival days of concerts and socials, the crowd reaction. I tried not to think. Tried not to let my early morning feelings leave me. Tried not to know that there was something different and strange in the people's reaction to us. And yet I knew this was not something new and strange, but only that during my time away from here my vision and understanding had expanded. I was able now to see myself and other members of my race as others see us. And this new understanding left me as abandoned and dry as an emptied pod of flax that rattles and rattles into the wind.

Everyone was clapping and cheering for Uncle Hirini and my cousin Hoani who kept jumping from the truck to the road, patterning with their taiaha,[3] springing on their toes and doing the pukana,[4] making high pipping noises with their voices. Their tongues lolled and their eyes popped.

But it was as though my uncle and Hoani were a pair of clowns. As though they wore frilled collars and had paint on their noses, and kept dropping baggy pants to display spotted underwear and sock suspenders. As though they turned cartwheels and hit each other on the head, while someone else banged on a tin to show everyone that clowns have tin heads.

And the people's reaction to the rest of us? The singing, the pois? I could see enjoyment on the upturned faces and yet it occurred to me again and again that many people enjoyed zoos. That's how I felt. Animals in cages to be stared at. This one with stripes, this one with spots—or a trunk, or bad breath, the remains of a third eye. Talking, swinging by the tail, walking in circles, laughing, crying, having babies.

---

2 **hakas:** Fierce dances with chants.
3 **taiaha:** Long club.
4 **pukana:** Wild stares.

Or museums. Stuffed birds, rows of shells under glass, the wing span of an albatross, preserved bodies, shrunken heads. Empty gourds, and meeting houses where no one met any more.

I kept thinking and trying not to think, "Is that what we are to them?" Museum pieces, curios, antiques, shells under glass. A travelling circus, a floating zoo. People clapping and cheering to show that they know about such things.

The sun was hot. Auntie at the end of the row was beaming, shining, as though she were the sun. A happy sun, smiling and singing to fill the whole world with song. And with her were all the little sunlets singing too, and stamping. Arms out, fingers to the heart, fists clenched, hands open, head to one side, face the front. Piupius[5] swinging, making their own music, pois bobbing. And voices calling the names of the canoes—Tainui, Takitimu, Kurahaupo, Te Arawa . . . the little ones in the front bursting with the fullness of their own high voices and their dancing hands and stamping feet, unaware that the crowd had put us under glass and that our uncle and cousin with their rolling eyes and prancing feet wore frilled collars and size nineteen shoes and had had pointed hats clapped down upon their heads.

Suddenly I felt a need to reach out to my auntie and uncle, to Hoani and the little ones, to old Rita and Hohepa.

We entered the sports ground, and when the truck stopped the little ones scrambled down and ran off to look for their mates from school. Auntie and Hoani helped Granny Rita and Grandpa Hohepa down. I felt older than any of them.

And it was hot. The sun threw down his spinnings of heat and weavings of light on to the cracked summer earth as we walked towards the pavilion.

"Do you ever feel as though you're in a circus?" I said to Hoani who is the same age as I am. He flipped onto his hands and walked the rest of the way upside down. I had a feeling Hoani knew what I was talking about.

Tea. Tea and curling sandwiches. Slabs of crumbling fruit cake, bottles of blood-warm fizz, and someone saying, "What're you doing in that outfit?" Boys from cousin Lena's school.

"Didn't you see us on the truck?" Lena was saying.

"Yeh, we saw." One of the boys had Lena's poi[6] and was swinging it round and round and making aeroplane noises.

Mr Goodwin, town councillor, town butcher, touching Uncle Hirini's shoulder and saying, "Great, great," to show what a great person he himself was, being one of the carnival organisers and having lived in the township all his life amongst dangling sausages, crescents of black pudding, leg roasts, rib roasts, flannelled tripe, silverside, rolled beef, cutlets, dripping. "Great." He was Great. You could tell by the prime steak hand on Uncle's shoulder.

Uncle Hirini believed the hand. Everyone who saw the hand believed it too, or so it seemed to me. They were all believers on days such as these.

5 **Piupius:** Flax shirts.
6 **poi:** Ball.

And the woman president of the CWI shouting at Granny Rita as though Granny were deaf or simple. Granny Rita nodding her head, waiting for the woman to go away so she could eat her cake.

It was stuffy and hot in the hall with the stale beer and smoke smell clinging to its walls and floor, and to the old chipped forms and sagging trestle tables. Bird dirt, spider webs, mice droppings. The little ones had had enough to eat and were running up and down with their mates from school, their piupius swinging and clacking about their legs. Auntie rounding them all up and whispering to go outside. Auntie on her best behaviour wishing those kids would get out and stop shaming her. Wanting to yell, "Get out you kids. Get outside and play. You spoil those piupius and I'll whack your bums." Auntie sipping tea and nibbling at a sandwich.

We began to collect the dishes. Squashed raisins, tea dregs. The men were stacking the trestles and shifting forms. Mrs President put her hands into the soapy water and smiled at the ceiling, smiled to show what sort of day it was. "Many hands make light work," she sang out. We reached for towels, we reached for wet plates to prove how right she was.

Outside, people were buying and selling, guessing weights and stepping chains, but I went to where Granny Rita and Grandpa Hohepa were sitting in the shade of a tree, guarding the cloak between them.

More entertainment. The lines were forming again but I sat down by old Rita and Hohepa out of the sun's heat.

"Go," Granny Rita was saying to me. "Take your place."

"I think I'll watch this time, Nanny."

"You're very sad today, dia. Very sad."

Granny Rita's eyes pricking at my skin. Old Hohepa's too.

"It's hot, Nanny."

A crowd had gathered to watch the group and the singing had begun, but those two put their eyes on me, waiting for me to speak.

"They think that's all we're good for," I said. "A laugh and that's all. Amusement. In any other week of the year we don't exist. Once a year we're taken out and put on show, like relics." And silence.

Silence with people laughing and talking.

Silence with the singing lifting skyward, and children playing.

Silence. Waiting for them to say something to me. Wondering what they would say.

"You grow older, you understand more," Granny Rita said to me.

Silence and waiting.

"No one can take your eyes from you," she said. Which is true.

Then old Hohepa, who is bent and sometimes crabby, said, "It is your job, this. To show others who we are."

And I sat there with them for a long time. Quiet. Realising what had been put upon me. Then I went towards the group and took my place, and began to stamp my feet on to the cracked earth, and to lift my voice to the sun who holds the earth's strength within himself.

And gradually the sun withdrew his touch and the grounds began to empty, leaving a flutter of paper, trampled heads of dandelion and clover, and insects finding a way into the sticky sweet necks of empty bottles.

The truck had been in the sun all afternoon. The withered curling fern and drooping flax gave it the appearance of a scaly monster, asleep and forgotten, left in a corner to die. I helped Granny Rita into the cab beside Grandpa Hohepa.

"This old bum gets too sore on those hard boards. This old bum wants a soft chair for going home. Ah lovely, dia. Move your fat bum ova, Hepa." The old parched hand on my cheek. "Not to worry, dia, not to worry."

And on the back of the truck we all moved close together against the small chill that evening had brought in. Through the town's centre then along the blackening roads. On into the night until the road ended. Opening gates, closing them. Crossing the dark paddocks with the hills dense on one hand, the black patch of sea on the other. And the only visible thing the narrow rind of foam curling shoreward under a sky emptied of light. Listening, I could hear the shuffle of water on stone, and rising above this were the groans and sighs of a derelict monster with his scales withered and dropping, making his short-sighted way through prickles and fern, over cow pats and stinging nettle, along fence lines, past the lupin bushes, their fingers crimped against the withdrawal of the day.

I took in a big breath, filling my lungs with sea and air and land and people. And with past and present and future, and felt a new strength course through me. I lifted my voice to sing and heard and felt the others join with me. Singing loudly into the darkest of nights. Calling on the strength of the people. Calling them to paddle the canoes and to paddle on and on. To haul the canoes down and paddle. On and on—

> Hoea ra nga waka
> E te iwi e,
> Hoea hoea ra,
> Aotea, Tainui, Kurahaupo,
> Hoea hoea ra.
>
> Toia mai nga waka
> E te iwi e,
> Hoea hoea ra,
> Mataatua, Te Arawa,
> Takitimu, Tokomaru,
> Hoea hoea ra.[7]

7 **Final song:** "The Coming of the Maori": Haul the canoes, all / Paddle, paddle back / Aotea, Tainui, Kurahaupo, / Paddle, paddle back. Haul canoes, all / Paddle back / Mataatua, Te Arawa, Takitimu, Tokomaru / Paddle, paddle back.

QUESTIONS

1. Grace seems to desire to reintegrate the present with elements of the Maori past. How is this story an attempt to recover Maoritanga (Maori cultural values)?

2. Why has Matewai come back to the village from the city?

3. Why does Matewai's experience of the carnival depress her and make her unhappy?

4. What affirmation can be read into the final poetic lines of the tale?

Shonagh Koea

(b. 1939)

Shonagh Koea was born in Taranaki and spent her childhood in Hawkes Bay. She appears to have been born a writer: At eight years old, she won a writing prize in a *Women's Weekly* competition. In her teens, she began a journalism career and married a fellow journalist, who later became the editor of the Taranaki *Herald*. Eventually, she tried her hand at creative writing, and her first published fiction appeared in the early 1970s. By 1981, she had won the Air New Zealand Short Story Competition, and her writing career was under way. The short story in this anthology, "Meat," was included in her first published volume of collected short stories, entitled *The Woman Who Never Went Home and Other Stories* (1987).

Many stories in this anthology describe the desperate everyday worlds of women who are ground down by daily cruelties in their existence. Some of the characters escape their fates by heading off to romantic locations, but the protagonist in "Meat," Marigold, a beautiful semi-autistic child, eventually reacts with unbridled violence to her domestic conditions. Koea's second collection of short fiction, *Fifteen Rubies by Candlelight* (1993), continues her investigation on the theme of domestic cruelty, but it also acknowledges a growing awareness of the ironic situations engendered in the human condition.

Koea's husband died suddenly in 1987, an event that is revisited fictionally in her first novel, *The Grandiflora Tree* (1989). The novel turns on the protagonist's discovery that Charlie, her husband, kept diaries in which their marriage is viewed far differently than she had imagined. Through the process of grieving, Bernadette learns to reevaluate her vision of their life together and rejects the conventional platitudes of condolence by her acquaintances. She escapes into anonymous isolation. Not long after the publication of the novel, Koea moved to Auckland, where she still lives. Her second novel, *Staying Home and*

Being Rotten (1992), continues her exploration of a woman's life after the death of a husband. Having been seduced by a conniving lover, Rosalind, the protagonist, returns to New Zealand from a disastrous relationship in London to achieve a modicum of self-respect and autonomy as an art dealer.

In 1993, Koea became writing fellow at Auckland University, where she completed her third novel, *Sing to Me, Dreamer* (1994). Her fourth novel, *The Wedding at Bueno-Vista,* was published in 1996. *Sing to Me, Dreamer* continues a common concern in Koea's fiction, that of the oppression of helpless women by bullying men. However, by keeping their composure and developing stoical attitudes against the adversities in patriarchal societies, her women prevail.

Koea's latest novels include *The Lonely Margins of the Sea* (1998), *Time for Killing* (2001), and *Yet Another Ghastly Christmas* (2003). These works suggest a lighter vision of despair and patriarchy. Her style appears to be growing more satiric, and her critique has broadened to include all the players in twenty-first-century society.

Meat

1982

After the murder I always said the seeds of that carve-up were sown right back when the council decided to build a new gymnasium.

When I say the council decided I really mean that a few bright boys decided and they out-voted the older ones. One thing about age is that it teaches you that this year's new doesn't stay new. The bright boys weren't that bright.

In a town like this there isn't much besides the main street, Carter's Wholesalers, the pub and the picture theatre. The old gym was where everybody went, even people who never climbed a rope in their lives. It was like a club.

Bill Arthur was the caretaker and he kept the place going right through the war, and afterwards when there were all the shortages.

In those days people lived with their in-laws, or they knocked themselves up a garage to live in if they could afford a section. The housing shortage got everyone. A lot of people lived in the transit camp down by the railway-line.

For a lot of them the old gym was the only place they could go at a weekend to talk without the relatives hearing. There was always a big crowd but you can be very private in the middle of a lot of people.

Bill lived at the back in a big flat that ran right along the building behind the kitchen where the ladies' committee used to make cups of tea on a Saturday night. Everyone knew it was Bring a Plate, Please, and it used to be quite a spread.

There were the changing-rooms, the showers, the kitchen and then there was Bill's flat, as big as a house, right along the back. He needed the room. His wife was what my wife called a messer and she always said a messer needs more space than a tidy person. Bill's two boys were at high school when the war broke out. They used to make those aeroplane models, I remember, with size and tissue-paper and bits of balsa wood all over the place.

They were both nearly grown up when Marigold was born towards the end of 1944. My wife said that you could just bet on a messer like Mavis Arthur, to have another baby at her age. She said it was just plain undiluted untidiness, and she could have been right.

Right from the start Marigold was a beautiful child, but there was something wrong. You lifted her little arm up, it stayed up. She was no bother, they said, and everyone thought that was a bad sign. Nobody said Marigold wasn't quite right. After a while there was no need to. Even old Dr Hellaby only said, "So you've noticed," when Bill asked him. Sometimes you could swear she was all there, and then she'd get that blank look. She was a beautiful child, though, and my wife was very fond of her.

We lived next door to the gym and when we worked in the garden Marigold used to come to the hedge and call through to my wife. She was a child that was very fond of flowers and any little living creature. I've known the time when we'd have ten or twelve jars in a row on the veranda, and each one would have a spider with a broken leg or a fly with one wing.

Marigold used to get very upset over those broken creatures and often after dark we would be out with the torch trying to find another one the same. We used to let the damaged one go and replace it with a good one ready for the morning when she came over. You couldn't have the heart to disappoint her.

I've tried telling them how she likes insects and little creatures and they were quite nice about it but they said the problem is the jars. Even plastic can get quite an edge on it, they said, and they couldn't take the responsibility.

In the beginning, years before all the trouble, when Marigold was just a little thing she used to sing out to us over the hedge. Then there was the day I got home from the shop and there was my wife waiting for me with the clippers. She wanted me to cut through the phenalbium towards the back of the section, where it always grew thinner than the rest. I could tell she was set on it, otherwise she'd never have bothered me on a Thursday. She knew Thursday was my busy day getting all the mince and sausages done ready for the Friday.

I cut through the hedge and at the weekend I put in a couple of old fence posts and swung a little gate in the gap so it looked neat and tidy. The trouble about having no children is that you get too tidy. Everything has to be just so.

Marigold liked flowers. My wife had a lovely garden in those days—all lilies round the back, and roses too. If I got home from the shop and found the house empty I always knew I'd find the pair of them out in the garden. My wife bought Marigold a little set of garden tools and made her a frilly pinafore all patterned with pansies so she kept clean. Not that her mother bothered but my wife liked everything proper and in its place. Nothing must do but Marigold must wear her pinafore in the garden.

My wife loved lilies. She used to take all the prizes in the show every year—Best Lily, Best Arum, Open Lily, Best in Show. I've got all her cups in the china cabinet.

Lilies multiply wonderfully but I've let them spread too far. There are even some coming up through the front lawn but I don't like to dig them up. They remind me of my wife and the old times, before all the troubles next door, and before she got too sick to look after them. Even right at the end when she could only take diluted orange juice and the doctor said it could be a day or a week, she used to like me to lift her up so she could see the flowers.

I was home all the time then, retired. The boy I had in the shop turned out quite a good lad and he bought me out later on. Mind you, the shop's not what it was. It's gone very modern now. They have smoked duck and schnitzel and slices of pork done so thin you could see through them if you held them up. It's not like when I started off in the business and you had your sausages and your roasts and a nice bit of lamb, the cheaper cuts for stews all trimmed up, and something a bit different for a Friday like Spanish roll. I did a very nice window too with a parsley trim round the edge like a miniature hedge, but you don't want me to be telling you about the shop. I was telling you about the lilies and the garden and the old days, before the murder.

I take Marigold a bunch of lilies every Christmas when I go to see her. It's a long drive and I'm not getting any younger but I make it my holiday for the year. I stay a few days near where she is. She doesn't take the interest in things that she used to. It's being kept like that.

Every day I go to see her and she always asks me about my wife. Aunty Muriel, she calls her. I'm Uncle Athol. I haven't the heart to tell her so I always say Aunty Muriel's gone shopping and she'll be coming tomorrow. Then she forgets. She's much blanker than she used to be but, like I said, she doesn't feel the interest.

Her father was a marvellous handyman and in the old days at the gym we used to hear him belting up new sheets of iron on the roof or mixing up a barrowload of concrete to patch the walls. He was a great chap for getting what he wanted, even with all the shortages. If that place needed a sleeve put in the roof to cure a leak or a bit of mortar over a crack in a wall he'd be out round the town begging a bit here and there. He had a real nose for smelling out who had a bag of cement hidden away or a few four-by-twos.

The place looked like a piebald[1] horse after the war, with all the patches here and there and no paint to cover them up. But he'd kept the place going. The town had kept going and a lot of things that kept it going were started off right there, at the gym. I remember the night we introduced Neville Bailey who had the men's out-fitters down at the corner to Pam Stacey whose husband was killed in the Western Desert the year before. It stopped her crying over spilt milk and it stopped him making such a mess of bringing up that little boy of his after his wife drowned in the dam. A lot of things were settled at the gym, one way and another.

Bill never thought of any other job. That was why when the bright boys decided to build a new gym he hadn't an idea in the world he'd be passed over. It turned out they wanted someone who knew about gymnastics so he could train a team, something to make a splash for the town.

---

1 **piebald:** Spotted or patched, especially in black and white.

The next thing was they gave Bill a golden handshake to make up for the three years' work he'd miss retiring early and they advertised in the cities for a replacement.

He used to sit in his chair in the house he bought behind us holding the letter he got from the council when the new gymnasium was first mentioned. The letter said in all probability his employment would continue. He read that letter every day and he showed it to anyone who would look. About a year later he nodded off in that very chair and he didn't wake up. My wife said he died of a broken heart.

I had made a gateway for Marigold in the back hedge by that time. The old posts had rotted but I could use the gate again. It didn't seem any more than a year or two since I'd swung it on its hinges the first time though by now Marigold was coming up to fifteen. She could read a bit—just simple things like *The Everyday and Nowaday Fairy Book*—and she could write a few things like her name and address.

I told you before that Mavis Arthur was a messer. Bill used to keep her at things, "What about cooking a nice pie with these windfalls," he'd say. Or, "What about finishing cleaning the windows, May?" He used to do all the shopping, managed the money. She couldn't even get the hang of driving a car so Bill drove her everywhere.

We all thought when Bill died she'd do all the things widows do but we were in for a shock. My wife tried to get her interested in the Women's Institute and the Ladies' Guild but she just laughed. She was out here, there and everywhere. Three nights after Bill's funeral she was out dancing at the timberyard fancy-dress ball dressed as a panda. She even used to go down to the lounge bar of the pub on a Saturday night, and that's where she met Wally Carmichael.

Six months to the day that we buried poor old Bill she upped and married him. He wasn't a bad workman if you could keep him off the booze, but he could be nasty-tempered. His first wife ran off with an American during the war and everyone said that all the free nylons would be a change from Wally's black eyes.

He won a prize once at the winter show for wood-chopping. The only thing he took a pride in was his axe and if you asked him to show you how sharp it was he used to shave the hairs off his arm. . . .

You could tell when Wally got home from the pub by the noise. When he first went to live over the back you'd hear crashes as he hit the fence or the gate posts with his old truck but he knocked them right down after a while. Then it was a straight, clear run into Bill's shed. The posts and part of the fence stayed where they lay on the lawn and after a while the long grass grew over them. Bill would have had a fit at the condition that place was in, and if he hadn't already died it would have killed him to hear what went on.

We used to ring young Barney Marks when it got too bad. He was old Barney Marks's youngest boy, the big one that went into the Police and married the redheaded girl from the Tip-Top. But, as he said, if you go into a place and they tell you to bugger off you've got to go, even the police.

It all happened just before Marigold's seventeenth birthday. I remember the moon was on the wane because it looked just like a lamb chop thrown up into the sky. I was out late that night digging the garden ready for the spring sowing and the turfs were curling off the shovel a treat, just like the best slices of sirloin. The ground was in such good heart that I stayed and stayed digging till in the end I had to go and open the kitchen door so the light shone out across the garden.

That was when I saw her standing in her little gateway in a splashy print dress. She didn't speak or move so I walked right up to her, to see what the matter was, and after that I called my wife.

"What's been going on, my darling?" my wife said, and took her hand. Without a word Marigold walked back through the hedge with us after her.

We found them inside. I wasn't upset, really. You get used to making the brawn and sausage meat out of all the bits, but if anyone had to find it I'm glad it was me.

I often put one in the window on a Friday when I had the shop. It used to amuse the kids, with a hat on and a pipe in its mouth. If you think of it just as the top end of something, a pig's head or a man's head are just top ends. In my trade you get used to meat.

My wife took Marigold outside and they went down through the gap in the hedge again, where the lilies were coming through the ground.

She said later she was sorry there was nothing in the garden for Marigold but daisies. Marigold just stood there, in the light from the kitchen, holding the flowers till they took her away. My wife always said the only things that make misery and heartbreak bearable are the flowers and the singing of the birds.

I remember standing there with them and thinking so many things all at once that it seemed I was thinking about the whole world. I remembered when she was born and when Bill and I were at school in old Miss Tucker's class and she gave us six of the best for writing on the desk with a pin and I couldn't help thinking, over and over again, that in all my years in the trade I'd never seen a better set of neck chops. He'd always been such a bull-necked fellow.

QUESTIONS

1. Describe how the narrative voice influences the reader's perception of the story.

2. Describe the nature of Mavis Arthur's personality. Describe her life with her two husbands.

3. What can we learn about Marigold from the narrator and from Marigold's actions at the conclusion of the story?

4. How do flowers and music function as symbols in the story?

Text Credits

Achebe, Chinua "Girls at War" from *Girls at War and Other Stories* by Chinua Achebe, copyright © 1972, 1973 by Chinua Achebe. Used by permission of Doubleday, a division of Random House, Inc., and Harold Ober Associates Incorporated.

Aidoo, Ama Ata "Two Sisters" by Ama Ata Aidoo from *No Sweetness Here,* pp. 87–102. Copyright © 1995. Reprinted by permission of The Feminist Press.

Anand, Mulk Raj "The Cobbler and the Machine" by Mulk Raj Anand from *Selected Short Stories of Mulk Raj Anand,* edited by M.K. Naik, 1977, pp. 138–153. Reprinted by permission of Lokayata: Mulk Raj Anand Centre.

Atwood, Margaret "The Age of Lead" from *Wilderness Tips* by Margaret Atwood, copyright © 1991 by O. W. Toad Limited. Used by permission of Doubleday, a division of Random House, Inc.

Bail, Murray "The Drover's Wife" by Murray Bail, 1975. Reprinted by permission of PFD on behalf of Murray Bail.

Beckett, Mary "A Belfast Woman" from *A Belfast Woman* by Mary Beckett, 1980, pp. 84–99. Reprinted by permission of Christine Green, agent for Mary Beckett.

Bissoondath, Neil "Digging Up the Mountains" from *Digging up the Mountains* by Neil Bissoondath, copyright © 1986 by Neil Bissoondath. Used by permission of Viking Penguin, a division of Penguin Group (USA) Inc.

Blaise, Clark "A Class of New Canadians" by Clark Blaise from *A North American Education.* Copyright © 1973. Reprinted by permission of the author.

Bowering, George "Bring Forth a Wonder" copyright © 1980 by George Bowering. Published in Canada in the novel *Burning Water* (Penguin Books). Reprinted by permission of The Bukowski Agency.

Brand, Dionne "Sans Souci" from Dionne Brand, *Sans Souci,* Firebrand Books, Ann Arbor, Mich., © 1989 by Dionne Brand. Reprinted by permission of Firebrand Books.

Carey, Peter From Peter Carey, *War Crimes.* Reprinted by permission of International Creative Management, Inc. Copyright © 1979 by Peter Carey.

Chander, Krishan "Peshawar Express" by Krishan Chander, translated by K. S. Duggal, from *Orphans of the Storm,* edited by Saros Cowasjee and K. S. Duggal, 1995, pp. 79–88, 348–354. Reprinted by permission of K. S. Duggal.

Clarke, Austin "Griff" by Austin Clarke. Copyright © 2003 by Austin Clarke. Published in Canada in *Choosing His Coffin: The Best Stories of Austin Clarke* by Thomas Allen Publishers, 2003. Reprinted by permission of The Bukowski Agency.

Cowan, Peter "The Tractor" by Peter Cowan from *The Empty Street: Stories.* Copyright © 1965. Reprinted by permission of HarperCollins Publishers Australia.

911

Desai, Anita "Studies in the Park" from *Games at Twilight and Other Stories* (pp. 20–33) by Anita Desai. Copyright © 1978 by Anita Desai. Reprinted by permission of HarperCollins Publishers Inc.

Divakaruni, Chitra Banerjee "Clothes" from *Arranged Marriage* by Chitra Divakaruni, copyright © 1995 by Chitra Divakaruni. Used by permission of Doubleday, a division of Random House, Inc.

Garner, Hugh "One-Two-Three Little Indians" from *Hugh Garner's Best Short Stories.* Copyright © 1963. Reproduced with permission of the publisher, McGraw-Hill Ryerson Ltd.

Gaskell, A. P. "School Picnic" by A.P. Gaskell from *The Big Game,* 1947. Reprinted by permission of the author.

Gordimer, Nadine "Amnesty" from *Jump and Other Stories* by Nadine Gordimer. Copyright © 1991 by Felix Licensing, B.V. Reprinted by permission of Farrar, Straus and Giroux LLC.

Grace, Patricia "Parade" by Patricia Grace from *Collected Stories,* 1975. Reprinted by permission of Pearson Education New Zealand.

Head, Bessie "The Wind and a Boy," copyright © Bessie Head, *The Collector of Treasures,* Heinemann 1977. Reprinted by permission of Johnson & Alcock, Literary Agents.

Hill, Barry "Lizards" reprinted by permission of the author.

Hosain, Attia "The First Party" from *Phoenix Fled* by Attia Hosain, copyright 1953 by Attia Hosain. Used by permission of Viking Penguin, a division of Penguin Group (USA) Inc.

Hulme, Keri "One Whale, Singing" from *The Wind Eater,* 1986. Originally published in the "NZ Listener," 1975. Reprinted by permission of the author.

Ihimaera, Witi "The Whale" by Witi Ihimaera from *Pounamu Pounamu.* Copyright © 1972. Reprinted by permission of Reed Publishing (NZ) Ltd.

James, C. L. R. "Triumph" by C. L. R. James, 1965. Reprinted by permission of the C. L. R. James Literary Estate.

Jhabvala, Ruth Prawer "Miss Sahib," from *A Stronger Climate,* pp. 169–190. Copyright © 1968. Reprinted by permission of the author.

Jolley, Elizabeth "A Hedge of Rosemary" by Elizabeth Jolley from *Five Acre Virgin: The Travelling Entertainment,* 1976. Reprinted by permission of Jenny Darling & Associates.

Joyce, James "Eveline" by James Joyce from *Dubliners.* Published by Random House, Inc.

Kanengoni, Alexander "Effortless Tears" by Alexander Kanengoni. Copyright © 1993. Reprinted by permission of Michigan State University Press.

Kincaid, Jamaica "Blackness" from *At the Bottom of the River* by Jamaica Kincaid. Copyright © 1983 by Jamaica Kincaid. Reprinted by permission of Farrar, Straus and Giroux, LLC.

Kipling, Rudyard "The Man Who Would Be King" from *Kipling: A Selection of His Short Stories and Poems* by John Beecroft, pp. 117–141. Copyright © 1956.

Koea, Shonagh "Meat" from Shonagh Koea, *The Woman Who Never Went Home and Other Stories,* 1982. Reprinted by permission of Penguin Group (NZ).

Lessing, Doris "The Old Chief Mshlanga." Copyright © 1951 Doris Lessing. Reprinted by kind permission of Jonathan Clowes Ltd., London, on behalf of Doris Lessing.

Levine, Norman "Something Happened Here" from Norman Levine, *Something Happened Here.* Copyright © 1991. Reprinted by permission of Leipman AG.

Magona, Sindiwe "I'm Not Talking About That, Now" by Sindiwe Magona from *Push-Push and Other Stories,* pp. 272–287. Copyright © 1996. Reprinted by permission of New Africa Books.

Marchall, Paule "To Da-duh, in Memoriam" from *Reena and Other Stories*. Copyright © 1983 by The Feminist Press. Reprinted with the permission of The Feminist Press at the City University of New York, www.feministpress.org.

McCann, Colum "Everything in This Country Must" from *Everything in This Country Must* by Colum McCann, © 2000 by Colum McCann. Reprinted by permission of Henry Holt and Company, LLC.

Moorhouse, Frank "A Person of Accomplishment" by Frank Moorhouse. First published in *The Americans, Baby* by Angus & Robertson Publishers, Australia, 1972. Reprinted by permission.

Mungoshi, Charles "Shadows on the Wall" from *The Setting Sun and the Rolling World* by Charles Mungoshi. Copyright © 1972, 1980 by Charles Mungoshi. Reprinted by permission of Beacon Press, Boston.

Naipaul, V. S. "The Night Watchman's Occurrence Book" from *A Flag on the Island*, copyright © 1967, copyright renewed 1995 by V. S. Naipaul.

Narayan, R. K. "A Horse and Two Goats" from *Under the Banyan Tree and Other Stories* by R. K. Narayan. Copyright © 1970 by R. K. Narayan. Used by permission of the Wallace Literary Agency, Inc.

O'Connor, Frank "Guests of the Nation" from *The Collected Stories of Frank O'Connor* by Frank O'Connor, copyright © 1981 by Harriet O'Donovan Sheehy, Executrix of the Estate of Frank O'Connor. Used by permission of Alfred A. Knopf, a division of Random House, Inc., and Writer's House, LLC.

O'Flaherty, Liam "Going into Exile" from Liam O'Flaherty, *The Collected Stories*, Volume 1, 1999, St. Martin's Press. Reproduced with permission of Palgrave Macmillan.

Ogot, Grace "Green Leaves" by Grace Ogot from *Land Without Thunder*, 1968, pp. 89–99. Reprinted by permission of East African Educational Publishers.

Orwell, George "A Hanging" from *Shooting an Elephant and Other Essays* by George Orwell, copyright 1950 by Sonia Brownell Orwell and renewed 1978 by Sonia Pitt-Rivers, reprinted by permission of Harcourt, Inc.

Persaud, Sasenarine "Canada Geese and Apple Chatney" by Sasenarine Persaud, 1997. Reprinted by permission.

Plomer, William "A Child of Queen Victoria" by William Plomer from *Four Countries*, 1949, pp. 65–107. Reprinted by permission of the William Plomer Trust.

Prichard, Katharine Susannah "Happiness" by Katharine S. Prichard, © 1915.

Rao, Raja "The Cow of the Barricades" printed with permission from New Age International (P) Ltd, New Delhi, India.

Rhys, Jean "The Day They Burnt the Books" by Jean Rhys (copyright © Jean Rhys, 1960) is reproduced by permission of Sheil Land Associates Ltd on behalf of Jean Rhys Ltd.

Ross, Sinclair "The Painted Door" taken from *The Lamp at Noon and Other Stories* by Sinclair Ross. Used by permission of McClelland & Stewart Ltd.

Rule, Jane "The End of Summer" from *Inland Passage and Other Stories* by Jane Rule. Copyright © 1985 by Jane Rule. Reprinted by permission of Georges Borchardt, Inc., for the author.

Rushdie, Salman "The Courter" from *East, West: Stories* by Salman Rushdie, copyright © 1994 by Salman Rushdie. Used by permission of Pantheon Books, a division of Random House, Inc.

Sargeson, Frank "The Making of a New Zealander" reprinted by permission of The Frank Sargeson Trust.

Saro-Wiwa, Ken "Africa Kills Her Sun" by Ken Saro-Wiwa from *Adaku and Other Stories,* 1989. Reprinted by permission of Becky Ayebia Clarke, Agent for the Ken Saro-Wiwa Estate.

Scott, Lawrence "Ballad for the New World" by Lawrence Scott. Reprinted by permission of the author. © Lawrence Scott, 2005.

Sealy, Karl "My Fathers Before Me." Reprinted by permission of Beryl Sealy, wife of the late Karl Sealy, for *My Fathers Before Me.*

Selvon, Sam "The Cricket Match" by Sam Selvon, © 1951. Reprinted by permission of the Estate of Sam Selvon.

Senior, Olive "Do Angels Wear Brassieres?" by Olive Senior from *Summer Lightning and Other Stories,* 1994. Reprinted by permission of Pearson Education Limited.

Sidhwa, Bapsi "Serahbai's Story" reprinted by permission of the author.

Stewart, Douglas "The Whare" by Douglas Stewart from *A Girl with Red Hair.* Copyright © 1944. Reprinted by permission of HarperCollins Publishers Australia.

Stewart, John "The Old Men Used to Dance" reprinted with permission from *Looking for Josephine,* TSAR Publications, 1998.

Subject Index

Index of Authors and Titles

Selected Former British Colonies (Today)

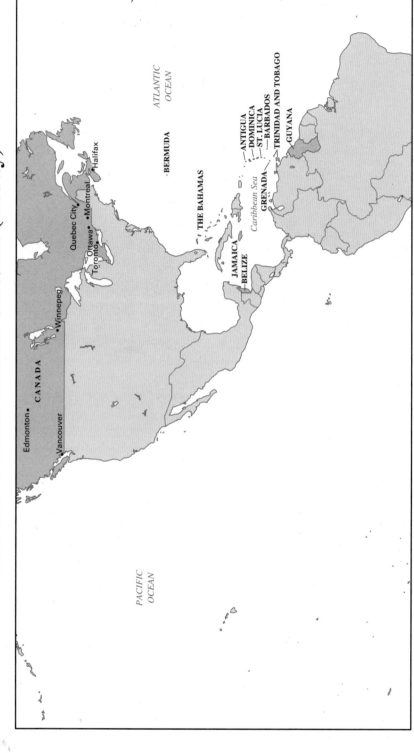